D0605666

MARK MY WORDS

Mark My Words

Great Quotations and the Stories Behind Them

Nigel Rees

Barnes & Noble Books
New York

Originally published as *Cassell Companion to Quotations*

This edition published by Barnes & Noble, Inc.,
by arrangement with Orion Publishing Group

2002 Barnes & Noble Books

ISBN 0-7607-3532-8

Printed and bound in the United States of America

02 03 04 05 06 M 9 8 7 6 5 4 3 2 1

FG

Contents

Introduction

Traditionally, there have been two ways to go about compiling a dictionary of quotations. One has been to anticipate the kind of quotations that readers would be interested in and then to provide accurate wording and source material for them. The second has been to put forward quotations that the compiler has gathered together – possibly on a theme or themes – and that the reader may in time find useful or simply enjoyable.

The *Cassell Companion to Quotations* is, as its title may suggest, not quite either of these things. What it seeks to provide is the context for, and ancillary information about, quotations that already exist – that is to say, written or spoken words that have already been quoted, but about which there is something to be said for their meaning to be properly appreciated. A complaint that can often be made about dictionaries of quotations – however substantial and 'comprehensive' they may be – is that they lack contextual commentary or, indeed, any commentary at all. There is a tendency for such books simply to deposit the minimum of information upon the page and then hurry on, however misleading (or inaccurate) this might be.

Accordingly, this *Companion* is, if you like, composed largely of footnotes. It provides information about the quotations that have been selected for inclusion and relates tales about their provenance, their ascriptions – and any other thing that may be relevant.

It stands to reason that if this technique were to be applied to the number of quotations in, say, *The Oxford Dictionary of Quotations* or *Bartlett's Familiar Quotations*, a very unwieldy and impractical volume would result. So a selection process has been invoked. In order to make room for a good number of quotations that have been so far ignored by the major dictionaries (but that are known to be of interest to readers), a sizeable proportion of standard quotations has been jettisoned. Broadly, these are the quotations that are self-explanatory or about which there is nothing much to say. I have also tended not to include lines from songs and hymns that, although they may be familiar, are so more because of repeated performance than from actual quotation.

Alongside this process has been a parallel one of rejecting quotations that no one might think of using these days. Whereas most dictionary compilers have to rely on hunch, this *Companion* benefits from the knowledge of its compiler about what sort of quotations are of interest to readers or that have provoked debate or inquiry in the past. I am lucky to be able to speak with some confidence on this matter. More than twenty years of work as deviser and presenter of the BBC Radio programme *Quote ... Unquote* has given me a good idea of the problem quotations. Since 1992 my editing of the quarterly *'Quote ... Unquote' Newsletter* has given me further working knowledge of these matters.

Accordingly, it is my hope, that there will be very little dead wood in this book – the sort of quotation that is included by an editor just because it takes his or her fancy, or to meet the demands of political correctness, or that one can never imagine anyone in their right minds actually using. Foreign language quotations are given in their original form only if they still tend to be quoted in that rather than in English.

Inevitably, there will be one or two quotations in this *Companion* that do not meet these criteria. Some have been included when there is nothing much to say about them, because to exclude them would significantly reduce the work's usefulness as a reference work. Additionally, some quotations about which there is a problem have been set baldly down with the labels 'untraced' or 'unverified' attached in the hope that this will attract any further information that may be forthcoming about them. Some also have been included (when they might have been excluded by another editor) simply because they have formed the basis of questions or talking-points on *Quote ... Unquote*. But at least there is no doubt in these instances that the sayings *have* certainly been quoted before by somebody – if only on the radio show. Again, a special category of quotations has been given prominence that might not be justified anywhere else and that requires little in the way of annotation – observations on the art of quotation itself.

The *Companion* aspect also comes to the fore in the way I have tried to reflect not just the origin, context and background of a quotation but the way in which it has been used. Accordingly, where appropriate, I record instances of a quotation being used in a significant way. In addition, I give numerous indications of the way quotations have been borrowed or put to work, especially as the titles of books, films, plays and broadcast programmes.

If there is one word that I hope the reader will not find too often in these pages, it is 'attributed'. On other occasions, I have felt that this word was better than nothing when no origin could be traced for a quotation. In this book, however, where so much effort has gone into source-finding, I thought it was justified to put the earliest secondary source when the actual origin of a saying proved impossible to find.

A slight change to the method used in this book's two predecessors – *Why Do We Quote ...?* (Blandford Press, 1989) and *Brewer's Quotations* (Cassell, 1995) – is that I have eschewed very much investigation of catchphrases and other forms of popular phraseology, which modern custom has been to include in dictionaries of quotations. These have been dealt with more than adequately in some other of my books, such as the *Dictionary of Catchphrases* (Cassell, 1995), the *Dictionary of Clichés* (Cassell, 1996) and the *Dictionary of Word and Phrase Origins* (Cassell, revised edition, 1996).

Many, many people have helped me in making this *Companion*. They have either written to point out errors and to discuss points in my earlier books; or they have written to me seeking a 'lost' quotation, hence alerting me to it; or they have been simply supportive in a general way to my (I hope) benign pedantry in this field.

I am indebted in particular, for these different reasons, to: Dr Eric Anderson; Dr J.K. Aronson; Frank Atkinson; Paul Beale; H.E. Bell; the late Peter Black; Dr David Butler; Professor Denis J. Conlon; David Cottis; Barry Day; T.A. Dyer; Susan Eden; David Elias; Jaap Engelsman; Jean English; Mark English; P.S. Falla; John Fletcher; Charles G. Francis; Mike Fraser; Ian Gillies; David Gillman; W. Eric Gustafson; Celia Haddon; Raymond Harris; Donald Hickling; Michael Holroyd; Sir David Hunt; W.W. Keen James; Sir Antony Jay; Martin Knapp; Elizabeth Knowles; Oonagh Lahr; Michael R. Lewis; R.P.W. Lewis; Frank Loxley; Henry B. McNulty; Leonard Miall; Professor Wolfgang Mieder; Jan Morris; the late John G. Murray; Michael and Valerie Grosvenor Myer; the late Vernon Noble; John Julius Norwich; Charles

Osborne; Derek Parker; Colonel Geoffrey S. Powell; Philip Purser; Steve Race; Claire Rayner; Derek Robinson; Adrian Room; William Shawcross; Anthony W. Shipps; Godfrey Smith; Michael Swan; the late William J. Weatherby; Barbara Wild; and many others.

A final word may be necessary about where I have chosen to place quotations in the *Companion* – quotations which are not obviously the result of something said or spoken by an identifiable person. I may not have been entirely consistent on this point. Rather than provide an entry for a song lyricist who may have contributed only one line to the language (and what's more he may have worked with a composer and any number of other lyricists), I have sometimes put such a quote in ANONYMOUS. Where the true originator of a line or joke or film title (for example) may be in doubt – and may most safely be attributed to some sort of group effort – I have sometimes opened an entry under a film title. Just consider who should really be credited with Groucho's lines from the Marx Brothers films or some of Bogart's misquoted lines from *Casablanca*.

Where a line is frequently misattributed, should it appear in the entry for the correct source or the incorrect one? These are not matters that I have agonized over very greatly. It seems to me that as long as the quotation is discussed *somewhere* in the book it really does not matter where it is positioned. Although there is a good deal of cross-referencing, the only sure way of finding a line is by consulting the index. This should always be your route into the book.

Abbreviations

Bartlett: *Bartlett's Familiar Quotations* (15th ed.), 1980, (16th ed.), 1992

Benham: *Benham's Book of Quotations*, 1907, 1948, 1960

Bible: The Authorized Version, 1611 (except where stated otherwise)

Brewer: *Brewer's Dictionary of Phrase and Fable*, (13th ed.), 1975, (14th ed.), 1989, (15th ed.), 1995

CODP: *The Concise Oxford Dictionary of Proverbs*, 1982

DNB: *The Dictionary of National Biography* (and its supplements)

Flexner: Stuart Berg Flexner, *I Hear America Talking*, 1976; *Listening to America*, 1982

Mencken: *H.L. Mencken's Dictionary of Quotations*, 1942

ODMQ: *The Oxford Dictionary of Modern Quotations*, 1991

ODP: *The Oxford Dictionary of Proverbs* (3rd ed.), 1970

ODQ: *The Oxford Dictionary of Quotations* (2nd ed.), 1953, (3rd ed.), 1979, (4th ed.), 1992

OED2: *The Oxford English Dictionary* (2nd ed.), 1989, (CD-ROM version), 1992

Partridge/*Catch Phrases*: Eric Partridge, *A Dictionary of Catch Phrases* (2nd ed., edited by Paul Beale), 1985

Partridge/*Slang*: Eric Partridge, *A Dictionary of Slang and Unconventional English* (8th ed., edited by Paul Beale), 1984

PDQ: *The Penguin Dictionary of Quotations* (edited by J.M. & M.J. Cohen), 1960, 1992

PDMQ: *The Penguin Dictionary of Modern Quotations* (edited by J.M. & M.J. Cohen), 1971, 1980

PD20: *The Penguin Dictionary of Twentieth-Century Quotations* (edited by J.M. & M.J. Cohen), 1993, 1995

Pearson: Hesketh Pearson, *Common Misquotations*, 1937

RQ: *Respectfully Quoted* (edited by Suzy Platt, Congressional Reference Division), 1989

Safire: William Safire, *Safire's Political Dictionary*, 1978

Shakespeare: The Arden Shakespeare (2nd ed.)

A

ABBOTT, Bud

American comedian (1895–1974)

1 Now, on the St Louis team we have Who's on first, What's on second, I Don't Know is on third.

From a classic routine based on misunderstanding and performed by Abbott and his partner Lou Costello (1906–59) included in the film *Naughty Nineties* (US, 1945). Accordingly, Richard J. Anobile's celebration of their act was entitled *Who's On First?* (1973).

ABBOTT, Diane

British Labour politician (1953–)

2 Being an MP is a good job, the sort of job all working-class parents want for their children – clean, indoors and no heavy lifting. What could be nicer?

In an interview with Hunter Davies in *The Independent* (18 January 1994). Much the same claim had earlier been made by Senator Robert Dole about the US vice-presidency (ABC TV broadcast, 24 July 1988): 'It is inside work with no heavy lifting.'

ACE, Goodman

American writer (1899–1982)

3 TV ... is our latest medium – we call it a medium because nothing's well done.

Letter (1954) to Groucho Marx, quoted in *The Groucho Letters* (1967). However, Leslie Halliwell, *The Filmgoer's Book of Quotes* (1973) ascribes, 'A medium, so called because it is neither rare nor well done' to Ernie Kovacs, the American entertainer (1919–62).

ACHESON, Dean

American Democratic politician (1893–1971)

4 Great Britain ... has lost an Empire and not yet found a role.

Speech at the Military Academy, West Point (5 December 1962). Acheson was a former Secretary of State (under President Truman) and the son of a British army officer who went to Canada, so the home truth was thus all the more painful when he went on to say: '[Britain's] attempt to play a separate power role – that is, a role apart from Europe, a role based on a "special relationship" with the United States, a role based on being the head of a "Commonwealth"... this role is about to be played out ... Her Majesty's Government is now attempting, wisely in my opinion, to re-enter Europe.'

Lord Chandos, President of the Institute of Directors, protested that such words coming from one of President Kennedy's advisers were 'a calculated insult'. Prime Minister Harold Macmillan quietly observed that, in any case, the general drift of world affairs was against Britain or any other country trying to play 'a separate power role'. More than thirty years later, one can say that Britain's European 're-entry' is to some extent accomplished.

5 Present at the Creation.

Title of memoirs (1969). From a remark by Alfonso X, the Wise (1221–84), King of Castile, on studying the Ptolemaic system: 'Had I been present at the Creation, I would have given some useful hints for the better ordering of the universe.'

Thomas Carlyle had earlier quoted the remark in his *Life of Frederick the Great* (1858–65). In Bishop Berkeley's *Three Dialogues Between Hylas and Philonus* (1713), Philonus says: 'Why, I imagine that if I had been present at the Creation, I should have seen things produced into being; that is, become perceptible, in the order described by the sacred historian.'

ACKERLEY, J.R.

English writer (1896–1967)

1 I was born in 1896, and my parents were married in 1919.

My Father and Myself (1968), opening words. Compare the opening words of *Lady Sings the Blues* (1958), the autobiography of the American blues singer Billie Holiday (1915–59): 'Mom and Pop were just a couple of kids when they got married. He was eighteen, she was sixteen, and I was three.'

ACTON, Lord

English historian (1834–1902)

2 Power tends to corrupt and absolute power corrupts absolutely.

Letter to Bishop Mandell Creighton, dated 3 April 1887 (published 1904). It is often quoted as 'all power corrupts' – i.e., without the 'tends'. Acton had been anticipated by William Pitt, Earl of Chatham, speaking in the House of Lords (9 January 1770): 'Unlimited power is apt to corrupt the minds of those who possess it.' William Wordsworth's political tract *The Convention of Centra* (1809) stated: 'There is an unconquerable tendency in all power ... to injure the mind of him who exercises that power.' In 1839 Lord Brougham had written in *Historical Sketches of Statesmen of the Time of George III*: 'Unlimited power corrupts the possessor.' A.J.P. Taylor questioned the accuracy of the remark in a *New Statesman* article, *c.*1955, calling it, 'Windy rot ... many an engine-driver is not corrupted' (which misses the point, surely?)

ADAMS, Douglas

English novelist (1952–)

3 Don't panic!

Words written on the cover of the eponymous fictional guide featured in *The Hitch-Hiker's Guide to the Galaxy* (BBC Radio programme, 1978; novel, 1979).

4 Life the Universe and Everything.

Title of novel (1982), though the phrase had first appeared in *The Hitch-Hiker's Guide to the Galaxy* in which an alien race programs a computer called Deep Thought to provide the ultimate answer to 'Life, the Universe and Everything'. The answer is 42. In 1996 it was reported that Cambridge astronomers had found that 42 was the value of an essential scientific constant, the Hubble Constant – one that determines the age of the universe (source: *The Independent*, 8 November 1996).

The phrase was adapted to form an advertising slogan for *The Daily Telegraph* (current 1988): 'The Earth Dweller's Guide to Life the Universe and Everything'. The format, from an untraced source, is now used to signify 'absolutely everything'. Compare the all-embracing title of *The Quote ... Unquote Book of Love, Death and the Universe* (1980).

ADAMS, John

American Federalist 2nd President (1735–1826)

5 I agree with you that in politics the middle way is none at all.

Letter to Horatio Gates (23 March 1776). *Compare* MACMILLAN 372:6.

6 All great nations inevitably end up committing suicide.

What Adams wrote, precisely, in a letter to John Taylor (15 April 1814) was: 'Remember, democracy never lasts long. It soon wastes, exhausts, and murders itself. There never was a democracy that did not commit suicide.'

7 Thomas Jefferson still survives.

Dying words and, by a remarkable accident, untrue: Jefferson had died a few hours earlier. Both former presidents died on 4 July 1826, exactly fifty years since the founding of the republic. Brewer (1975) has it that his dying words were 'Independence for ever'.

ADAMS, Samuel

American revolutionary politician (1722–1803)

8 What a glorious morning for America!

Thus is it usually quoted, but what Adams most likely said on hearing the sound of gunfire at Lexington (the opening battle of the War of American Independence) on 19 April 1775 was, 'What a glorious morning is this'.

ADAMS, Mrs Sarah Flower

English hymnwriter (1805–48)

9 Nearer, My God, to Thee.

Title of hymn first published in 1841. This is often said to have been what the ship's band was playing when the *Titanic* sank in 1912. In the song 'Be British', written and composed by Paul Pelham and Lawrence Wright in the year the ship sank, there is a tear-jerking 'recitation after 2nd verse' enshrining the belief that the band played the hymn 'Nearer My God To Thee' as the ship went down. According to Tom Burnam, *More Misinformation* (1980), however, the band played ragtime until the ship's bridge dipped underwater, and then the bandmaster led his men in the Episcopal hymn, 'Autumn'. This version of events was based on a reported remark of the surviving wireless operator in *The New York Times* (19 April 1912). According to Walter Lord, *A Night to Remember* (1955), the 'Nearer My God To Thee' version was one of many rumours circulating within a few days of the ship sinking.

ADAMSON, Harold

American songwriter (1906–80)

1 Coming in on a Wing and a Prayer.

Title of song popular in the Second World War (published in 1943), and which derived from an alleged remark by a real pilot who was coming in to land with a badly damaged plane. Adamson's lyric (to music by Jimmy McHugh) includes the lines:

> Tho' there's one motor gone, we can still carry on
> Comin' in on a wing and a pray'r.

A film (US, 1944) about life on an aircraft carrier was called simply *Wing and a Prayer.*

ADDISON, Joseph

English essayist and politician (1672–1719)

2 And pleas'd th' Almighty's orders to perform,
Rides in the whirlwind, and directs the storm.

Of the 1st Duke of Marlborough. *The Campaign* (1705), a celebration of the Battle of Blenheim (1704). Addison's second line has become a figure of speech. Alexander Pope repeated it with comic effect in *The Dunciad* (1728). Henry Buckle in his *History of Civilisation in England* (1857) had: 'To see whether they who had raised the storm could ride the whirlwind.' Nowadays it simply means to deal with an extremely difficult situation: 'With his overall Commons majority already down to 18 and his Government fighting on several other damaging policy fronts, Mr Major is riding a whirlwind' (*Daily Mail*, 21 May 1993).

3 'That nothing is capable of being well set to music that is not nonsense.'

In *The Spectator*, No. 18 (21 March 1711). Quoting a supposed maxim concerning Italian opera – i.e., not necessarily his own view.

4 When I look upon the tombs of the great, every emotion of envy dies in me; when I read the epitaphs of the beautiful, every inordinate desire goes out; when I meet with the grief of parents, upon a tombstone, my heart melts with compassion; when I see the tomb of the parents themselves, I consider the vanity of grieving for those, whom they must quickly follow. When I see kings lying by those who deposed them; when I consider rival wits placed side by side; or the holy men, that divided the world with their contests and disputes; I reflect, with sorrow and astonishment, on the little competitions, factions, and debates of mankind. When I read the several dates of the tombs, of some that died yesterday, and some six hundred years ago, I consider that great day, when we shall all of us be contemporaries, and make our appearance together.

Ib., No. 26 (30 March 1711). Concerning the tombs in Westminster Abbey specifically.

5 The woman that deliberates is lost.

Cato, IV.i.31 (1713). Most early uses of the phrase were about women, but the proverbial form is now mostly 'He who hesitates is lost.' The *CODP* has not found an earlier citation.

6 'We are always doing,' says he, 'something for Posterity, but I would fain see Posterity do something for us.'

The Spectator, No. 583 (20 August 1714). *See also* ROCHE 457:5.

7 I have but ninepence in ready money, but I can draw for a thousand pounds.

On the difference between his conversational and writing abilities. Remark recorded in James Boswell, *The Life of Samuel Johnson* (1791), as recalled on 7 May 1773.

ADLER, Alfred

Austrian psychoanalyst (1870–1937)

8 Individual psychology holds that the most important key to the understanding of both personal and mass problems is the so-called

sense of inferiority, or inferiority complex, and its consequences.

Quoted in *The New York Times* (20 September 1925). Adler had presented his theory which gave rise to the phrase 'inferiority complex' (repressed fear and resentment at being inferior) somewhat earlier: 'To be a human being means to possess a feeling of inferiority which constantly presses towards its own conquest ... The greater the feeling of inferiority that has been experienced, the more powerful is the urge for contest and the more violent the emotional agitation.'

ADLER, Polly

American brothel keeper (1900–62)

1 A House is Not a Home.

Title of memoirs (1954). Adler was a notable New York madam in the 1920s and 1930s. She finally closed her bordello in 1945 and spent part of her twilight years writing memoirs. Then:

> 'One day I happened to be spraying a rose-bush in my back yard, and Dora [Maugham] ... was profoundly impressed by this spectacle of suburban domesticity.
> '"I wonder what the cops would say," she mused, "if they could see you now".
> '"Oh," said I, "probably they'd be disappointed that my home is not a house." Dora's reaction to this remark was so unusual ... "Eyeow!" she squealed. "Hold everything! ... Turn that around and you've got it!"
> '"What on earth are you talking about?"
> '"The perfect title for your book ..."
> 'So far as I was concerned, I told her, it was the most inspired piece of thinking anyone had done in a garden since the day Isaac Newton got conked by an apple.'

Of course, 'house' here means 'brothel'. When the book was filmed (US, 1964), there had to be a theme song incorporating the title, which managed coyly to avoid any suggestion as to what sort of 'house' was being talked about.

AGATE, James

English drama critic (1877–1947)

2 A professional is a man who can do his job when he doesn't feel like it; an amateur is one who can't [do his job] when he does feel like it.

From *Ego* (1935, entry for 17 September 1933). The context was a lunch with the actor Cedric Hardwicke, who said: 'My theory of acting is that it is so minor an art that the only self-respect attaching to it is to be able to reproduce one's performance with mathematical accuracy.' The above was Agate's concurrence. Hardwicke added: 'It shouldn't make a hair's breadth of difference to an actor if he has a dead baby at home and a wife dying.'

There have been several other attempts to define the difference between amateurs and professionals, beyond the acting profession: 'Amateurs [musicians] practice until they can get it right; professionals practice until they can't get it wrong' (quoted by Harold Craxton, one-time professor at the Royal Academy of Music); 'Professionals built the *Titanic*; amateurs built the Ark' (Anon.)

AGNEW, Spiro T.

American Republican Vice-President (1918–96)

3 I agree with you that the name of Spiro Agnew is not a household name. I certainly hope that it will become one within the next couple of months.

In interview with Mike Wallace of ABC TV, on becoming US vice-presidential candidate (8–9 August 1968).

4 To some extent, if you've seen one city slum you've seen them all.

Speech, Detroit (18 October 1968). A less than gracious observation which, nevertheless, did not impede his assuming the vice-presidency.

5 A spirit of national masochism prevails, encouraged by an effete corps of impudent snobs who characterize themselves as intellectuals.

Speech attacking media pundits, New Orleans (19 October 1969). For a further example of his alliterative style, see next:

6 In the United States today we have more than our share of the nattering nabobs of negativism. They have formed their own 4-H Club – the 'hopeless, hysterical hypochondriacs of history'.

Speech attacking media pundits, San Diego (11 September 1970). Written for him by William Safire.

AKINS, Zoë

American playwright (1886–1958)

1 The Greeks Had a Word for It.

Title of play (1929). For seemingly so venerable a phrase, it may come as a surprise to learn that this dates back no further than 1929. Although, as Akins said, 'the phrase is original and grew out of the dialogue', it does not appear anywhere in the text. Akins told Burton Stevenson's *Dictionary of Quotations* (1946 ed.) that in dialogue cut from her play the 'word' was used to describe a type of woman. One character thinks that 'tart' is meant but another corrects this and says that 'free soul' is more to the point. Nowadays the phrase is used a trifle archly, as when one wishes to express disapproval and say, 'There's a name for that sort of behaviour'.

ALBEE, Edward

American playwright (1928–)

2 Who's Afraid of Virginia Woolf?

Title of play (1962), from a graffito seen in Greenwich Village. The character Martha sings it in the play to the tune of 'Who's Afraid of the Big Bad Wolf?' – that is her little joke.

See also DAVIS 197:2.

ALBERT

German-born British Prince, Consort of Queen Victoria (1819–61)

3 Old mismanagement is no excuse for the continuance of it.

Letter to Lord Seymour (19 March 1851). Possibly not original and a statement used, with some rephrasing, by everyone who has ever spoken in favour of reform. Another version is: 'The antiquity of an abuse is no justification for its continuance.' *See* VOLTAIRE 552:3.

ALCOTT, Amos Bronson

American teacher (1799–1888)

4 One must be a wise reader to quote wisely and well.

'Quotation', *Table Talk* (1877). Amos was the father of Louisa May Alcott, author of *Little Women* (1868).

ALDEN, Robert

American theologian (1937–)

5 There is not enough darkness in all the world to put out the light of even one small candle.

So attributed by *The David & Charles Book of Quotations* (1986). On the other hand, Bernard Levin describes this in *Conducted Tour* (1981) as 'an ancient proverb'. On yet another hand, in her *Magnificent Menagerie* (1992), Lucinda Lambton casts further doubt on the Alden provenance by quoting a 'gravestone on the Oxford Road, Henley-on-Thames': 'JIMMY/A TINY MARMOSET/ AUGUST 16TH 1937/There isn't enough/ Darkness in the world/To quench the light/Of one small candle.' If this epitaph was applied near to the date of death it would also preclude Alden's claim to authorship.

ALEXANDER, Mrs Cecil Frances

Irish poet and hymnwriter (1818–95)

6 All things bright and beautiful,
All creatures great and small,
All things wise and wonderful,
The Lord God made them all.

Hymn, 'All Things Bright and Beautiful' (1848). The English author James Herriot originally gave his books about life as a vet titles such as *It Shouldn't Happen To a Vet*, *Let Sleeping Vets Lie*, *Vets Might Fly*, etc. When these titles were coupled together in three omnibus editions especially for the US market, Mrs Alexander's hymn was plundered for titles and they became *All Creatures Great and Small* (1972), *All Things Bright and Beautiful* (1973) and *All Things Wise and Wonderful* (1978). *The Lord God Made Them All* was given to a further original volume (1981).

7 The rich man in his castle,
The poor man at his gate.
God made them, high or lowly,
And ordered their estate.

Ib. An omission rather than a misquotation. Mrs Alexander's hymn is in danger of becoming known as the one from which a verse – the third – had to be dropped because of its apparent acceptance of an unacceptable *status quo*.

From Barbara Pym's novel *No Fond Return of Love* (1961): 'Dulcie sang in a loud indignant voice, waiting for the lines

> 'The rich man in his castle, the poor man at his gate, God made them, high or lowly, and ordered their estate.

'but they never came. Then she saw that the verse had been left out. She sat down, feeling cheated of her indignation.'

Most modern hymnbook compilers omit the verse and they started doing so about 1930. *Songs of Praise Discussed* (1933) calls it an 'appalling verse ... She must have forgotten Dives, and how Lazarus lay "at his gate"; but then she had been brought up in the atmosphere of a land-agent on an Irish estate. The *English Hymnal* led the way in obliterating this verse from the Anglican mind.' It remains in *Hymns Ancient and Modern* (Standard Edition, reprinted 1986), but it has disappeared from the *Irish Hymnal*. The authors of *The Houses of Ireland* (1975) note that by the present century 'the ecclesiastical authorities had decided that God's intentions are not to preclude movement within the social system. However, few of her contemporaries doubted that Mrs Alexander's interpretation was correct.'

Born in County Wicklow, Mrs Alexander was the wife of the Bishop of Derry and Archbishop of Armagh. The hymn was written while she was staying at Markree Castle, near Sligo. The 'purple-headed mountain' is thought to be a reference to Ben Bulben.

ALGREN, Nelson

American novelist and short-story writer (1909–81)

1 Never eat at a place called Mom's. Never play cards with a man called Doc. Never go to bed with a woman whose troubles are greater than your own.

A Walk on the Wild Side (1956), but Bartlett (1992) finds it only in H.E.F. Donahue, *Conversations with Nelson Algren* (1964) where Algren says he was taught it by 'a nice old Negro lady'. *ODQ* (1992) and *ODMQ* (1991) both cite a *Newsweek* report (1956) rather than Algren's book itself.

ALI, Muhammad (formerly Cassius Clay)

American heavyweight boxing champion (1942–)

2 You don't want no pie in the sky when you
die,
You want something here on the ground
while you're still around.

Quoted in 1978 and typical of the little rhymes he resorted to at the height of his fame. Based on HILL 294:3.

ALLAIS, Alphonse

French humorist (1854–1905)

3 The most striking thing about the City of Venice is the complete absence of the smell of horse dung.

Quoted in *The World of Alphonse Allais*, selected, translated and introduced by Miles Kington (1976).

ALLEN, Fred

American comedian (1894–1956)

4 Hollywood is a place where people from Iowa mistake themselves for movie stars.

Attributed by Maurice Zolotow in *No People Like Show People* (1951). Said in about 1941.

5 A celebrity is one who works hard all his life to become well-known and then goes through back streets wearing dark glasses so he won't be recognized.

Unconfirmed as coming from *Treadmill to Oblivion* (1956). Has also been attributed to Jane Powell, the American film actress (1929–).

6 Hanging is too good for a man who makes puns. He should be drawn and quoted.

Quoted in Laurence J. Peter, *Quotations for Our Time* (1977).

7 A conference is a gathering of important people who singly can do nothing, but together can decide that nothing can be done.

Quoted in *The Treasury of Humorous Quotations*, ed. by Evan Esar & Nicolas Bentley (1951). Compare 'A committee is a group of men who, individually, can do nothing, but collectively can meet and decide that nothing can be done', ascribed to 'Anonymous' in Prochnow & Prochnow, *Treasury of Humorous Quotations* (1969). *See* COCKS 176:5; TREE 542:4.

ALLEN, Woody

American film actor, writer and director (1937–)

8 Sex between a man and a woman can be wonderful – provided you get between the right man and the right woman.

Attributed. Compare 'I believe that sex is a beautiful thing between two people. Between *five*, it's fantastic ...'

on Allen's record album *The Nightclub Years 1964–1968* (1972).

1 The psychiatrist asked me if I thought sex was dirty and I said, 'It is if you're doing it right'.

Film, *Take the Money and Run* (US, 1969). Compare: 'Is sex dirty? Only if it's done right' – film, *Everything You Always Wanted to Know About Sex* (1972).

2 The lion and the calf shall lie down together, but the calf won't get much sleep.

In *The New Republic* (31 August 1974). *See* BIBLE 97:12

3 Love and Death.

Title of film (US 1975), a parody of *War and Peace* (*see* TOLSTOY 541:1). Compare Oscar Wilde, *The Picture of Dorian Gray* (1891): 'There was something fascinating in this son of Love and Death.'

4 Fun? That was the most fun I've ever had without laughing.

On sex. Film *Annie Hall* (US, 1977), written with Marshall Brickman. Alvy speaking. Also attributed to Humphrey Bogart in the form 'It was the most fun I ever had without laughing'.

ALLINGHAM, Margery

English detective novelist (1904–66)

5 Once sex rears its ugly 'ead it's time to steer clear.

Flowers for the Judge (1936). The *ODMQ* (1991) by giving this quotation might appear to be suggesting that Allingham coined the expression 'sex rears its ugly head'. But the expression had been current since at least 1930, when James R. Quirk used it in a *Photoplay* editorial about the film *Hell's Angels*. It is used both as an explanation for people's behaviour (like '*cherchez la femme*') and as a complaint of the intrusion of sex into books, TV programmes and so on, where the speaker would rather not find it. And how curious. Why? Because the penis rises? If so, then why ugly? A very odd usage, except that the construction 'to raise/rear its ugly head' was used about other matters before sex. Anthony Trollope in *Barchester Towers* (1857) has: 'Rebellion had already raised her hideous head within the [bishop's] palace.' The image is presumably of a Loch Ness-type monster, emerging from the deep.

ALTRINCHAM, Lord (later disclaimed peerage and known as John Grigg)

English writer (1924–)

6 Frankly a pain in the neck.

On Queen Elizabeth II's style of public speaking, in the *National and English Review* (August 1958). In the next issue, following the furore caused by this article, he insisted, 'I never mentioned her voice'. The 'straightforward English idiom' was applied merely 'to her style of speaking.' He went on: 'The personality conveyed by the utterances which are put into her mouth is that of a priggish schoolgirl, captain of the hockey team, a prefect, and a recent candidate for confirmation. It is not thus that she will be able to come into her own as an independent and distinctive character.'

AMERY, Leo S.

English Conservative politician (1873–1955)

7 Speak for England, Arthur!

Interjection, House of Commons (2 September 1939). On the eve of war, Prime Minister Neville Chamberlain appeared in the Commons and held out the prospect of a further Munich-type peace conference and did not announce any ultimatum to Germany. When the acting Labour leader, Arthur Greenwood, rose to respond, a Conservative MP shouted, 'Speak for England, Arthur!' For many years, it was generally accepted that the MP was Amery and, indeed, he wrote in *My Political Life* (Vol. 3, 1955): 'It was essential that someone should ... voice the feelings of the House and of the whole country. Arthur Greenwood rose ... I dreaded a purely partisan speech, and called out to him across the floor of the House, Speak for England.' (Note, no 'Arthur'.) By 30 October James Agate was writing in his diary (published in *Ego 4*) of the anthology for the forces he had been busy compiling called *Speak for England*: 'Clemence Dane gave me the title; it is the phrase shouted in the House the other day when Arthur Greenwood got up to speak on the declaration of the war.'

However, writing up an account of the session in *his* diary, Harold Nicolson (whose usual habit was to make his record first thing the following morning) wrote: 'Bob Boothby cried out, "*You* speak for Britain".' Boothby confirmed that he had said this when shown the diary passage in 1964.

The explanation would seem to be that after Amery spoke, his cry was taken up not only by Boothby but by others on the Tory benches. From the Labour benches came cries of 'What about Britain?' and 'Speak for the working classes!' Interestingly, nobody claims to have said the exact words as popularly remembered. The intervention went unrecorded in *Hansard*.

1 This is what Cromwell said to the Long Parliament when he thought it was no longer fit to conduct the affairs of the nation: 'You have sat too long here for any good you have been doing. Depart, I say, and let us have done with you. In the name of God, go!'

Speech, House of Commons (7 May 1940). By this date, criticism was growing of the British government's handling of the war. Norway and most of Scandinavia had been lost to the Germans and yet a War Cabinet had not yet been formed. It was obvious that things were getting very bad indeed. In a dramatic speech, Amery said, 'Somehow or other we must get into the Government men who can match our enemies in fighting spirit' and he quoted something that Oliver Cromwell had said to John Hampden 'some three hundred years ago, when this House found that its troops were being beaten again and again by the dash and daring of the Cavaliers', namely, 'We cannot go on being led as we are'.

In his autobiography, Amery said: 'I was not out for a dramatic finish, but for a practical purpose; to bring down the Government if I could.' And so he quoted Cromwell's words when dismissing the Rump of the Long Parliament in 1653. Chamberlain's government did indeed go. Churchill became Prime Minister and formed a National government three days later.

AMIS, Kingsley (later Sir Kingsley)

English novelist, poet and critic (1922–95)

2 Lucky Jim.

Amis's comic novel (1953) about a hapless university lecturer, Jim Dixon, takes its title from a not very relevant American song by Frederick Bowers (1874–1961) and his vaudeville partner Charles Horwitz (though it is usually ascribed to Anon.). It tells of a man who has to wait for his childhood friend Jim to die before he can marry the girl they were once both after. Then, married to the woman and not enjoying it, he would rather he was dead like his friend: 'Oh, lucky Jim, how I envy him.'

3 More will mean worse.

In *Encounter* (July 1960) Amis wrote about the expansion of higher education, especially on 'the delusion that there are thousands of young people who are capable of benefiting from university training but have somehow failed to find their way there'. He added: 'I wish I could have a little tape-and-loudspeaker arrangement sewn into the binding of this magazine, to be triggered off by the light reflected from the reader's eyes on to this part of the page, and set to bawl out at several bels: MORE WILL MEAN WORSE.'

When *The Times* misquoted this as 'more means worse' on one occasion, Amis fired off a broadside (22 February 1983):

> I think the difference is substantial, but let that go for now. You show by your misquotation that you couldn't be bothered to look up the reference, thereby ignoring the context, any arguments or evidence put forward, etc.
>
> Having garbled my remark you say roundly that in the event I was wrong. Not altogether perhaps. Laziness and incuriosity about sources are familiar symptoms of academic decline.

4 Outside every fat man there was an even fatter man trying to close in.

One Fat Englishman (1963). *Compare* CONNOLLY 181:4.

5 The Folk That Live On the Hill.

Title of novel (1990). It would be interesting to know on what linguistic grounds Amis chose 'that' instead of 'who'. The song is actually called 'The Folks *Who* Live on the Hill' and was written by Jerome Kern and Oscar Hammerstein II for the 1937 US film *High, Wide and Handsome*.

6 A bad review may spoil your breakfast but you shouldn't allow it to spoil your lunch.

Quoted in the *Independent on Sunday* (6 September 1992) and widely elsewhere. Unverified.

ANDERSEN, Hans Christian

Danish story-teller (1805–75)

7 'But the Emperor has nothing on at all,' cried a little child.

The Emperor's New Clothes (*c.*1843). Hence, the phrase 'the emperor's (new) clothes', describing a person's imaginary qualities whose fictitiousness other people forbear to point out. In the story, tailors gull an emperor into wearing a new suit of clothes, invisible to unworthy people, that does not, in fact, exist at all. None of the emperor's subjects dares point out that this renders him naked – until an innocent boy does just that.

ANDERSON, Maxwell

American playwright (1888–1959)

1 But it's a long, long while
From May to December;
And the days grow short
When you reach September.

'September Song' (1938). Music by Kurt Weill. *Compare* WALKER 554:2.

ANDERSON, Robert

American playwright (1917–)

2 Tea and Sympathy.

Title of play (1953; film US, 1956). Brewer (1995) defines the phrase as 'A caring attitude, especially towards someone in trouble.' Popularized though probably not coined by Anderson.

ANDREWES, Lancelot

English bishop and scholar (1555–1626)

3 It was no summer progress. A cold coming they had of it, at this time of the year; just, the worst time of the year, to take a journey, and specially a long journey, in. The ways deep, the weather sharp, the days short, the sun farthest off *in solstitio brumali*, the very dead of winter.

Sermon 15, 'Of the Nativity' (1629). Paraphrased in T.S. Eliot's 'The Journey of the Magi' (1927); *see* ELIOT 226:6.

4 The nearer the Church, the further from God.

Ib. Compare DÍAZ 203:5.

ANGELL, Sir Norman

English pacifist (1872–1967)

5 The Great Illusion.

Angell's anti-war book was first published in 1909 with the title *Europe's Optical Illusion*. A year later it was republished as *The Great Illusion*. Angell was awarded the Nobel Peace Prize in 1933. Use of the phrase was further encouraged by its choice by Jean Renoir for his 1937 film *La Grande Illusion*, about French pilots captured by the Germans in the First World War.

ANGELOU, Maya

American novelist and poet (1928–)

6 I Know Why the Caged Bird Sings.

Title of book (1969), taken from last line of 'Sympathy' by Paul Laurence Dunbar in *Lyrics of Hearthside* (1899).

ANGLESEY, 1st Marquess of

English cavalry officer (1768–1854)

7 By God! I've lost my leg!

At the Battle of Waterloo (1815), Lord Uxbridge (later to become Marquess of Anglesey) said this to the Duke of Wellington who replied, 'Have you, by God?' and rode on. The partly severed leg was amputated and buried in a garden in the village of Waterloo. He consequently acquired the nickname 'One-Leg'. Discussed in Elizabeth Longford, *Wellington: The Years of the Sword*, Chap. 23 (1969).

ANIMAL CRACKERS

American film 1930. Script by Morrie Ryskind, from a musical by himself and George S. Kaufman. With the Marx Brothers.

8 Hello, I must be going.

From the song, 'Hooray for Captain Spaulding', written by Harry Ruby and Bert Kalmar, and sung by Groucho. Hence, 'Hello I Must be Going!', title of a record album (1982) by Phil Collins.

9 *Groucho*: Quotes, unquotes and quotes. That's three quotes. And another quote'll make it a gallon.

Soundtrack. The use of the words 'quote' and 'unquote' to act as audible quotation marks in speech (perhaps originally in dictation) appears to be of American origin. The *OED2*'s earliest citation is from a letter by e.e. cummings in 1935, but Groucho's 1930 allusion suggests that the formula is older.

ANKA, Paul

Canadian singer and songwriter (1941–)

10 And now the end is near
And so I face the final curtain,
My friend, I'll say it clear,
I'll state my case of which I'm certain.

I've lived a life that's full, I've travelled each
and evr'y high-way
And more, much more than this, I did it my
way.

Song, 'My Way' (1965). Anka's English lyrics (1969) were set to the music of a French song *Comme d'habitude* by Claude François and Jacques Revaux. A clear-eyed look at the lyrics reveals that they are at best not entirely literate, nor is their meaning clear. But that is the song's apparent strength – people can (and have) read into it whatever they like, above all, a feeling of triumphant individualism – that 'I' counts most of all. It gives them a feeling of self-justification, even if with no real basis. Lord George-Brown made an odd use of this song when he entitled his 1971 autobiography *In My Way*, but referring to 'My Way' he undoubtedly was.

ANNAN, Noël (later Lord Annan)

English academic and writer (1916–)

1 The day of the jewelled epigram is past and, whether one likes it or not, one is moving into the stern puritanical era of the four-letter word.

Quoted in *The Observer* (20 February 1966). Compare Curzon on Disraeli: 'Men were on the look out for the jewelled phrase, the exquisite epigram, the stinging sneer'; quoted in Kenneth Rose, *Superior Person* (1969).

2 The BBC does itself untold harm by its excessive sensitivity. At the first breath of criticism the Corporation adopts a posture of a hedgehog at bay.

Report of the Committee on the Future of Broadcasting (1977). This British official inquiry was chaired by Annan who, although he may not have written this passage, was certainly responsible for the overall tone of the piece and its unusual readability.

ANNENBERG, Walter

American publisher and diplomat (1908–)

3 We're in the Embassy residence, subject, of course, to some of the discomfiture as a result of a need for, uh, elements of refurbishment and rehabilitation.

To Queen Elizabeth II, when she asked him about his accommodation as Ambassador to the Court of St James's (1969). Unfortunately, when he went to present his credentials to her, a TV crew was hovering at his elbow making the film *Royal Family*. So millions were able to hear the peculiarly orotund remarks he thought appropriate for the occasion.

ANONYMOUS

4 Absinthe makes the tart grow fonder.

In Sir Seymour Hicks's *Vintage Years* (1943) this is given as a toast proposed by one Hugh Drummond. It rides on the back of 'absinthe makes the heart grow fonder', the original pun, which has been ascribed (inevitably perhaps) to Oscar Wilde, but also to Addison Mizner, the American architect (1872–1933) and so quoted in *The Treasury of Humorous Quotations*, ed. by Evan Esar & Nicolas Bentley (1951). The proverb 'absence makes the heart grow fonder' was first recorded *c.*1850.

5 *Ah! Ah! ça ira, ça ira*
Les aristocrates à la lanterne.

Refrain of French revolutionary song, first heard when the Parisians marched on Versailles (5–6 October 1789). *Ça ira*, though almost impossible to translate, means something like 'That will certainly happen', 'Things will work out.' *À la lanterne* is the equivalent of the modern 'string 'em up' (*lanterne* being a street lamp in Paris useful for hanging aristocrats). The inspiration for the first line of refrain may have been Benjamin Franklin's recent use of the phrase in connection with the American Revolution of 1776.

6 All in the family.

All In the Family was the title of the American TV version (from 1971) of the BBC's sitcom *Till Death Us Do Part*. The respective main characters were Archie Bunker and Alf Garnett, racists and bigots both. But the American title is not a phrase particularly well known elsewhere. The implication would seem to be '... so there's no need to be over-punctilious, stand on ceremony, or fuss too much about obligations'. Compare 'we are all friends here!' Not a trace of the phrase in the *OED2*, though there is an 1874 citation 'all outside the family, tribe or nation were usually held as enemies', which may hint at the possible existence of an opposite construction.

The phrase occurs in Chap. 21, 'Going Aboard', of Herman Melville's *Moby-Dick* (1851), emphasizing a likely American origin. Elijah is trying to warn Ishmael and Queequeg against the *Pequod* and its captain: '"Morning to ye! morning to ye!" he rejoined, again moving off. "Oh! I was going to warn ye against

– but never mind, never mind – it's all one, all in the family too; – sharp frost this morning, ain't it? Good bye to ye. Shan't see ye again very soon, I guess; unless it's before the Grand Jury."'

1 All publicity is good publicity.

An almost proverbial saying, certainly around in the 1960s but itself probably as old as the public relations industry. Alternative forms include: 'There's no such thing as bad publicity' (*see* BEHAN 81:3), 'There's no such thing as over-exposure – only bad exposure', 'Don't read it – measure it' and 'I don't care what the papers say about me as long as they spell my name right'. The latter saying has been attributed to the American Tammany leader 'Big Tim' Sullivan.

CODP includes it in the form 'Any publicity is good publicity' but finds no example before 1974. James Agate in *Ego 7* (for 19 February 1944) quotes Arnold Bennett, 'All praise is good', and adds: 'I suppose the same could be said about publicity.'

2 The almighty dollar is the only object of worship.

Philadelphia Public Ledger (2 December 1836). In fact, this possible first use of the term 'almighty dollar' to describe the currency's all-powerful role in American life had just been preceded by Washington Irving's statement in *The New Yorker* (12 November 1836): 'The almighty dollar, that great object of universal devotion throughout our land.' *See also* 309:1.

3 And I, too, my lord, have not been idle.

According to G.W.E. Russell, *Collections and Recollections* (1898), the children of a famous diplomatist [Lord Lytton], 'some twenty years ago', organized a charade. 'The scene displayed a Crusader knight returning from the wars to his ancestral castle. At the castle-gate he was welcomed by his beautiful and rejoicing wife, to whom, after tender salutations, he recounted his triumphs on the tented fields and the number of paynim whom he had slain. "And I too, my lord," replied his wife, pointing with conscious pride to a long row of dolls of various sizes – "and I too, my lord, have not been idle".'

4 And this too shall pass away.

Chuck Berry spoke the words of a 'song' called 'Pass Away' (1979), which told of a Persian king who had had carved the words 'Even this shall pass away'. George Harrison earlier called his first (mostly solo) record album 'All Things Must Pass' (1970). These musicians were by no means the first people to be drawn to this saying. As Abraham Lincoln explained in an address to the Wisconsin State Agricultural Society (1859): 'An Eastern monarch once charged his wise men to invent him a sentence to be ever in view, and which should be true and appropriate in all times and situations. They presented him with the words, "And this, too, shall pass away". How much it expresses! How chastening in the hour of pride! How consoling in the depths of affliction!'

But who was the oriental monarch? Benham (1948) says the phrase was an inscription on a ring – 'according to an oriental tale' – and the phrase was given by Solomon to a Sultan who 'desired that the words should be appropriate at all time'. In 1860 Nathaniel Hawthorne wrote in *The Marble Faun* of the 'greatest mortal consolation, which we derive from the transitoriness of all things – from the right of saying, in every conjuncture, "This, too, will pass away".'

5 And what they could not eat that night,
The queen next morning fried.

Referring to a bag pudding, well-stuffed with plums, this tantalizing couplet comes from a nursery rhyme, 'When good King Arthur ruled this land,/He was a goodly king'. *The Oxford Dictionary of Nursery Rhymes* (1951) finds a version *c.*1799.

6 The angel's trumpet sounded,
St Peter called out 'Come',
The pearly gates swung open,
And in walked Mum.

'This must have appeared at least 30 years ago ... I remember a correspondence about it in the Live Letters column of the Daily Mirror, where some readers condemned its tastelessness, and others praised its simple sentiment'; letter from Margaret Holt, Manchester (1981). In *Ego 7* (for 6 March 1944), James Agate stakes an earlier claim: 'The members [of the Column Club] were delighted with something I bagged out of the obituary notices in an august paper a few days ago:

The silver trumpets sounded loud,
The angels shouted "Come!"
Opened wide the Golden Gate,
And in walked Mum!'

7 Anyone who isn't confused here doesn't really understand what's going on.

Ascribed to a 'Belfast citizen, 1970' in the book *Quote ... Unquote* (1978). However, Walter Bryan, *The Improbable Irish* (1969), has: 'As Ed Murrow once said about Vietnam, anyone who isn't confused doesn't really understand the situation.' *See also* 404:3.

1 Any reform that does not result in the exact opposite of what it was intended to do must be considered a success.

Quoted by Katharine Whitehorn in *The Observer* (1992), but untraced. However, Samuel Taylor Coleridge wrote in *Biographia Literaria* (1815–16): 'Every reform, however necessary, will by weak minds be carried to an excess which will itself need reforming.' Peter F. Drucker (1909–), the American management consultant and author, has written: 'Look at governmental programs for the past fifty years. Every single one – except for warfare – achieved the exact opposite of its announced goal.'

Compare also what Garrett Hardin (1915–), an American biologist, wrote in the February 1974 issue of *Fortune*: 'You can never do merely one thing. The law applies to any action that changes something in a complex system. The point is that an action taken to alleviate a problem will trigger several effects, some of which may offset or even negate the one intended.'

2 At Play in the Fields of the Lord.

Title of novel by Peter Matthiessen (1965; film US, 1992). Set among the Amazonian Indians, it describes the desecration of an Arcadia – the rain forests – in the rival accounts of missionaries and mercenaries. Compare *Beyond the Fields of Play*, title of a memoir (1996) by the former rugby union player, Cliff Morgan.

3 Attempt great things for God.

Written on a lectern in Westminster Abbey, but untraced as a quotation. In the Bible it is God who is frequently credited with having done the great things, but 2 Kings 5:13 has: 'My father, if the prophet had bid thee do some great thing, wouldest thou not have done it?' Compare the exhortation to the young: 'Do great things.'

4 The audience came out whistling the set.

Supposedly said by a critic about Irving Berlin's musical *Miss Liberty* (1949) – the paradigm of criticisms made when the incidentals are more impressive than the songs in a musical.

5 Back to square one.

Meaning 'back to the beginning'. This is sometimes said to have gained currency in the 1930s onwards through its use by British radio football commentators. *Radio Times* used to print a map of the football field divided into numbered squares, to which commentators would refer thus: 'Cresswell's going to make it – FIVE. There it goes, slap into the middle of the goal – SEVEN. Cann's header there – EIGHT. The ball comes out to Britton. Britton manoeuvres. The centre goes right in – BACK TO EIGHT. Comes on to Marshall – SIX' (an extract from the BBC commentary on the 1933 Cup Final between Everton and Manchester City). The idea had largely been abandoned by 1940. Against this proposition is the fact that square 'one' was nowhere near the beginning. The game began at the centre spot, which was at the meeting point of squares 3, 4, 5 and 6. In fact, Partridge/*Catch Phrases* prefers an earlier origin in the children's game of hopscotch or in the board game Snakes and Ladders. If a player was unlucky and his or her counter landed on the snake's head in square 97 or thereabouts, it had to make the long journey 'back to square one'.

6 A beast but a just beast.

Said of Dr Frederick Temple (1821–1902), Headmaster of Rugby School and later Archbishop of Canterbury. Quoted in *The Rugby Memoir of Archbishop Temple 1857–69* (1907).

7 Beautiful girls, walk a little slower when you walk by me.

Graffito seen in New York City by Gordon Jenkins (1910–) who included the line in his song 'This Is All I Ask' (1960s).

8 Because the pictures are/the scenery is/better.

A view promoting the superior imagination-stirring qualities of radio as a creative medium. Sometimes said to have originated in a letter to *Radio Times* in the 1920s, quoting a child who had said, 'The pictures are better' when comparing the radio version of a story with that seen on the stage. But it was the early 1960s rather than the 1920s that were evoked when Trevor Hill, former North of England head of BBC Radio's Children's Hour, was invited to comment on the origin of the phrase in 1996. He wrote: 'What I do know is that in January 1960, Dorothea Brooking produced a splendid visual adaptation of Frances Hodgson Burnett's *The Secret Garden* for BBC Children's Television; and then, in the spring of 1962, radio also did a version as the Sunday serial and I most definitely received a letter from a young listener who came either from Bolton or Bingley telling me how much she was enjoying David Davis's production. She thought the television was good – but liked the radio version, "because the scenery is better". Now she may have got that phrase from a parent; there is no knowing.' Consider these citations: 'By way of illustration a young lad was quoted as saying he preferred radio to television – because the scenery is better. A proof of the power of imagination!' – Prayer Book Society Newsletter (August 1995). '"I like the wireless better than the theatre," one London child wrote in a now legendary letter, "because the scenery is better"' – Derek Parker, *Radio: The Great Years* (1977). In a Joyce Grenfell letter of 22 September 1962 which is included in the book *An Invisible Friendship* (1981): 'Do you ever listen [to the radio]? I do. I like it best. As a child I know says: "I see it much better on radio than on TV."' Note how Grenfell personalizes the anecdote. She had been on the Pilkington Committee, which presented its report on broadcasting a month or two before that letter was written – perhaps she had collected the story in the course of her duties.

1 Because you're in Chatham.

Heckler's reply when Harold Wilson asked rhetorically, 'Why do I emphasize the importance of the Royal Navy?' (1964). Quoted in A. Andrews, *Quotations for Speakers and Writers* (1969).

2 Bed is the poor man's opera.

(Sometimes 'sex is ...') Aldous Huxley gives the 'bed' version 'as the Italian proverb succinctly puts it' in *Heaven and Hell* (1956). Compare Charles Baudelaire, *Journaux intimes*, (1887): 'Sexuality is the lyricism of the masses.'

3 Behind every great man stands a woman.

An unascribed saying that takes a number of forms and is probably most often encountered nowadays in parodied versions. Working backwards, here are some of the parodies: 'Behind every good man is a good woman – I mean an exhausted one' – the Duchess of York, speech, September 1987. 'As usual there's a great woman behind every idiot' – John Lennon (quoted 1979). 'Behind every successful man you'll find a woman who has nothing to wear' – L. Grant Glickman (quoted 1977) or James Stewart (quoted 1979). 'We in the industry know that behind every successful screenwriter stands a woman. And behind her stands his wife' – Groucho Marx (quoted 1977). 'The road to success is filled with women pushing their husbands along' – Lord (Thomas R.) Dewar, quoted in Stevenson, *The Home Book of Quotations* (1967). 'And behind every man who is a failure there's a woman, too!' – John Ruge, cartoon caption, *Playboy* (March 1967). 'Behind every successful man stands a surprised mother-in-law' – Hubert Humphrey, speech (1964).

An early example of the basic expression occurs in an interview with Lady Dorothy Macmillan, wife of the then just retired British Prime Minister (7 December 1963). In the *Daily Sketch*, Godfrey Winn concluded his piece with the typical sentiment (his capitals): 'NO MAN SUCCEEDS WITHOUT A GOOD WOMAN BEHIND HIM. WIFE OR MOTHER. IF IT IS BOTH, HE IS TWICE BLESSED INDEED.'

In *Love All*, a little known play by Dorothy L. Sayers, which opened at the Torch Theatre, Knightsbridge, London, on 9 April 1940 and closed before the end of the month, was this: 'Every great man has a woman behind him ... And every great woman has some man or other in front of her, tripping her up.'

4 Believe only half of what you see and nothing that you hear.

This appears in *A Woman's Thoughts* (1858) by Mrs Craik where it is described as a 'cynical saying, and yet less bitter than at first appears'. As such, it builds upon the simpler 'Don't believe all you hear' which *CODP* finds in some form before 1300, perhaps even as a proverb of King Alfred the Great's.

The thought also appears in the song 'I Heard It Through the Grapevine' (by Norman Whitfield and Barrett Strong, *c.*1967), recorded notably by Marvin Gaye. One verse begins:

> People say believe half of what you see,
> Son, and none of what you hear.

5 Bell, book and candle.

As in the title of John Van Druten's play (1950; film US, 1958) about a publisher who discovers his girlfriend is a witch, this refers to a solemn form of excommunication from the Roman Catholic Church. Bartlett (1980) says the ceremony has been current since the eighth century AD. There is a version dating from AD1200, which goes: 'Do to the book [meaning, close it], quench the candle, ring the bell.' These actions symbolize the spiritual darkness the person is condemned to when denied further participation in the sacraments of the church.

Sir Thomas Malory in *Le Morte d'Arthur* (1485) has, 'I shall curse you with book and bell and candle'. Shakespeare has the modern configuration in *King John*, III.ii.22 (1596): 'Bell, book and candle shall not drive me back.'

6 The best contraceptive is a glass of cold water: not before or after, but instead.

Anonymous Pakistani delegate at International Planned Parenthood Federation Conference. Quoted in *PDMQ* (1971). The earliest source found for this frequently attributed remark.

1 The best [*sometimes* finest] swordsman in all France.

A cliché of swashbuckling epics. 'Don't worry ... my father was the best swordsman in France' is said to be spoken in the film *Son of Monte Cristo* (1940), though this is unverified. In 1984 a book by Keith Miles on the subject of clichés in general was given the title *The Finest Swordsman in All France.* A relatively unselfconscious use occurs in Charles Dickens, *Barnaby Rudge*, Chap. 27 (1841): 'I have been tempted in these two short interviews, to draw upon that fellow, fifty times. Five men in six would have yielded to the impulse. By suppressing mine, I wound him deeper and more keenly than if I were the best swordsman in all Europe.' Completely straightforward is John Aubrey's use in his *Lives* (*c.*1697): 'Sir John Digby yielded to be the best swordsman of his time.'

2 The best things in life are free.

Title of a song (1927) by Buddy De Sylva and Lew Brown, to music by Ray Henderson. The origin of a modern proverb.

3 Better the chill blast of winter than the hot breath of a pursuing elephant.

Said to be a 'Chinese saying' and included in *Livres Sans Nom*, five anonymous pamphlets (1929–33) by Geoffrey Madan (though not to be found in all the versions). As with most such sayings, authenticity is in doubt (*compare* CONFUCIUS 180:1). In any case, might not Madan have invented it himself? The matter is discussed in *The Lyttelton Hart-Davis Letters*, Vol. 4 (1982).

4 The bloody deed is/was done.

The provenance of this phrase is elusive. All that the *OED2* has to offer is from L.A.G. Strong's *Swift Shadow* (1937): 'Standing by like gawps to see bloody murder done'. In Shakespeare, of course, the phrase 'bloody deed' occurs several times and what with Macbeth's 'I have done the deed' and the almost immediate references to 'blood', not to mention Rosse's 'Is't known who did this more than bloody deed?' (II.iv.22), might have produced this conflation. The nearest one gets is *Richard III* (IV.iii.1): 'The tyrannous and bloody act is done', which is what Tyrrel says about the murder of the Princes in the Tower. As with 'the bloody dog is dead' from the end of the same play (V.v.2), we are almost there, but the exact words remain untraced, except in the works of obscure poets of the early nineteenth century:

Pallid grew every face; and man on man,
Speechless with horror, looked; for well they knew
The bloody deed was done.

– from *The Fall of Nineveh*, the chief poem by Edwin Atherstone (1788–1875), who was born in Nottingham.

'Tis past! – the bloody deed is done,
A father's hand hath sealed the slaughter!
Yet in Grenada's many a one
Bewails the fate of Selim's daughter.

– from 'Zara' by William Motherwell (1797–1835), a Scottish balladeer and editor of Robert Burns's poems.

These two quotations encourage one to think that the original coinage will not be found: it is simply a proverbial expression.

5 Box-office poison.

This is said to be the verdict of the US Independent Motion Picture Theatre Proprietors on the actress Katharine Hepburn in 1938. The phrase is also said to have been used about her by a cinema-owner in a famous advertisement. However, in the same year, the *Independent Film Journal* also put Mae West, Greta Garbo, Joan Crawford, Marlene Dietrich and Fred Astaire in the same category.

6 Bring out your dead.

Cry of the carters who went about at night collecting corpses during the Great Plague of London (1665) and in other plagues, too.

7 The butler did it.

The origins of this phrase – an (often ironic) suggested solution to detective stories in their 1920s and 1930s heyday – remain untraced. A review of Edgar Wallace's play *The Man Who Changed His Name* in *Punch* (28 March 1928) appears to be alluding to the idea: 'For a long time, I must say, I thought the butler had something to do with it ... I think the play would have been subtler if the unravelling of the mystery had included the butler.' So maybe the phrase was current by the 1910s to 1920s – but why did it enter common parlance? One of the conventions of whodunit writing of the period in question is that the butler or servants seldom, if ever, did 'do it'. Father Ronald Knox, compiling a list of rules for this kind of fiction in his introductions to *The Best Detective Stories of the Year*, 1928, noted: 'The only person who is really scratch on morals is the aged butler. I cannot off-hand recall any lapse of virtue on the part of a man who has been with the family for sixteen years. But I may be wrong; I have not read all the detective stories.' The earliest use of the phrase it is possible to give chapter and verse for is the caption to a *Punch* cartoon by Norman Mansbridge in the issue of 14 September 1938. Two policemen are standing outside a cinema which is showing *The Mansion Murder* and on the posters it asks 'Who killed the duke?' One policeman is saying to the other: 'I guessed the butler did it.' In 1956, Robert Robinson made an allusion in his Oxford thriller *Landscape With Dead Dons*: '"Well, well," said the Inspector, handing his coffee cup to Dimbleby, who was passing with a tray, "it always turns out to be the butler in the end."' In the film *My Man Godfrey* (1957, not the 1936 original), which is not even a whodunit, there is the line: 'The butler did it! He made every lady in the house, oh, so very happy!'

1 By/my God, how the money rolls in.

This is the last line of each verse in an anonymous song included in *Rugby Songs* (1967). It tells of the various fund-raising activities of a family. A typical verse:

My brother's a poor missionary,
He saves fallen women from sin,
He'll save you a blonde for a guinea,
My God how the money rolls in.

Sometimes 'By God' is sung in the last line.

2 Can't act, can't sing, slightly bald. Can dance a little.

Hollywood executive, allegedly, on Fred Astaire's first screen test. Quoted in Leslie Halliwell, *The Filmgoer's Book of Quotes* (1973).

3 Channel storms. Continent isolated.

The original of this English newspaper headline remains untraced (if, indeed, it ever existed). In Maurice Bowra's *Memories 1898–1939* (1966) he recalled Ernst Kantorowicz, a refugee from Germany in the 1930s: 'He liked the insularity of England and was much pleased by the newspaper headline, "Channel storms. Continent isolated", just as he liked the imagery in, "Shepherd's Bush combed for dead girl's body".'

As an indicator of English isolationism, the phrase does indeed seem to have surfaced in the 1930s. John Gunther in his *Inside Europe* (1938 edition) had: 'Two or three winters ago a heavy storm completely blocked traffic across the Channel. "CONTINENT ISOLATED", the newspapers couldn't help saying.' The cartoonist Russell Brockbank drew a newspaper placard stating 'FOG IN CHANNEL – CONTINENT ISOLATED' (as shown in his book *Round the Bend with Brockbank*, published by Temple Press, 1948). By the 1960s and 1970s, and by the time of Britain's attempts to join the European Community, the headline was more often invoked as: 'FOG IN CHANNEL. EUROPE ISOLATED.'

4 *Che sera sera.*

In 1956 Doris Day had a hit with the song 'Whatever Will Be Will Be', the title being a translation of this foreign phrase which was also used in the choruses. She had sung it in the re-make of Alfred Hitchcock's *The Man Who Knew Too Much* in that year. Ten years later Geno Washington and the Ram Jam Band had a hit with a song entitled 'Que Sera Sera'. So is it *che* or *que*? There is no such phrase as *che sera sera* in modern Spanish or Italian, though *che* is an Italian word and *sera* is a Spanish one. *Que sera? sera?* in Spanish translates as 'what will be? will be?' which is not quite right; *lo que sera, sera* makes sense but is not the wording of the song. However, in Christopher Marlowe's *Dr Faustus* (published 1604) Faustus's first soliloquy has:

What doctrine call you this? Che sera, sera,
What will be, shall be.

This is an old spelling of what would be, in modern Italian *che sara, sara*. In *Faustus*, however, it is probably Old French.

The idea behind the proverbial saying is simpler to trace. 'What must be, must be' can be found as far back as Chaucer's 'Knight's Tale' (*c.*1390): 'When a thyng is shapen, it shal be.' However, *che sera sera* is the form in which the Duke of Bedford's motto has always been written and so presumably that, too, is Old French or Old Italian.

5 *Chevalier sans peur et sans reproche.*
Knight without fear and without blame.

Description of the Chevalier Pierre Bayard (1476–1524). Mark Twain once proposed 'sans peur et sans culottes' (knee britches) as the motto of a gentlemen's dining club and Harry Graham of *Punch* had 'sans beurre et sans brioche' (butter ... brioches).

6 Cometh the hour, cometh the man.

John 4:23 has 'But the hour cometh, and now is' and there is an English proverb 'Opportunity makes the man' (though originally, in the fourteenth century, it was 'makes the thief'), but when did the phrases come together? Harriet Martineau entitled her biography of Toussaint L'Ouverture (1840), *The Hour and the Man.* An American, William Yancey, said about Jefferson Davis, President-elect of the Confederacy in 1861: 'The man and the hour have met', which says the same thing in a different way. P.G. Wodehouse in *Aunts*

Aren't Gentlemen (1974) has: 'And the hour ... produced the man.'

Earlier, at the climax of Sir Walter Scott's novel *Guy Mannering*, Chap. 54 (1815), Meg Merrilies says, 'Because the Hour's come, and the Man'. In the first edition and in the *magnum opus* edition that Scott supervised in his last years the phrase is emphasized by being put in italics.

Then, in 1818, Scott used 'The hour's come, but not [*sic*] the man' as the fourth chapter heading in *The Heart of Midlothian*, adding in a footnote: 'There is a tradition, that while a little stream was swollen into a torrent by recent showers, the discontented voice of the Water Spirit [or Kelpie] was heard to pronounce these words. At the same moment a man, urged on by his fate, or, in Scottish language, fey, arrived at a gallop, and prepared to cross the water. No remonstrance from the bystanders was of power to stop him – he plunged into the stream, and perished.' Both these examples appear to be hinting at some earlier core saying which is still untraced.

It appears from a survey of ten British newspapers in recent years that the saying is especially a weapon (or cliché) in the sportswriter's armoury. From *Today* (22 June 1986): 'Beating England may not be winning the World Cup, but, for obvious reasons, it would come a pretty close second back in Buenos Aires. Cometh the hour, cometh the man? Destiny beckons. England beware.' From *The Times* (13 August 1991): '"Graham [Gooch] is a very special guy," [Ted] Dexter said. "It has been a case of 'Cometh the hour, cometh the man.' I do not know anyone who would have taken the tough times in Australia harder than he did".' From *The Scotsman* (29 February 1992): 'In the maxim of "Cometh the hour, cometh the man," both the Scotland [Rugby Union] manager, Duncan Paterson, and forwards coach, Richie Dixon, indicated yesterday the need to look to the future.'

1 Comfort the afflicted, and afflict the comfortable.

This is a good example of a quotation formula that can be applied to more than one subject, to the extent that it is difficult to say what it was originally directed at. However, Mencken (1942) has 'Anon.' saying, 'The duty of a newspaper is to comfort the afflicted and afflict the comfortable', and newspapers seem likely to have been the original subject of the remark. In the film *Inherit the Wind* (1960), Gene Kelly gets to say to Fredric March: 'Mr Brady, it's the duty of a newspaper to comfort the afflicted and to flick the comfortable.'

To Michael Ramsey, the former Archbishop of Canterbury (1904–88), has been attributed this version: 'The duty of the church is to comfort the disturbed and to disturb the comfortable.' Clare Booth Luce introduced Eleanor Roosevelt at a 1950 dinner, saying: 'No woman has ever so comforted the distressed – or so distressed the comfortable.'

2 The condemned man ate a hearty breakfast.

The tradition seems to have been established that a condemned man can have anything he desires for a last meal. Boswell in his *Life of Johnson* (for 27 June 1784) has General Paoli saying: 'There is a humane custom in Italy, by which persons [sentenced to death] are indulged with having whatever they like best to eat and drink, even with expensive delicacies'. This, presumably, was not then an English custom or Paoli would not have bothered to mention it, nor Boswell to repeat it.

Since then, several such people have taken the opportunity to have something of a blow-out. Nothing changes: in April 1992, when Robert Alton Harris, a double murderer, was executed at dawn in San Quentin prison, California, the authorities gave the media a description of his last meal – a huge bucket of Kentucky Fried Chicken, pizza and jellybeans.

As to the origin of the cliché, it presumably lies in ghoulish newspaper reports of the events surrounding executions in the days of capital punishment in Britain. There was a vast amount of popular literature concerning prominent criminals and public executions, especially in the late eighteenth and early nineteenth century, but so far citations date only from the twentieth century and tend to be of a metaphorical nature.

Working backwards: in *No Chip on My Shoulder* (1957), Eric Maschwitz wrote: 'Far from closing for ever, Balalaika [was merely to be] withdrawn for a fortnight during which time a revolving stage was to be installed at Her Majesty's! It was almost ridiculously like an episode from fiction, the condemned man, in the midst of eating that famous "hearty breakfast", suddenly restored to life and liberty.' In the film *Kind Hearts and Coronets* (1949), Louis Mazzini, on the morning of his supposed execution, disavows his intention of eating 'the traditional hearty breakfast'. *The Prisoner Ate a Hearty Breakfast* was the title of a novel (1940) written by Jerome Ellison. In 1914, a book of short stories about the Royal Navy called *Naval Occasions and Some Traits of the Sailor* by 'Bartimeus', had: 'The Indiarubber Man opposite feigned breathless interest in his actions, and murmured something into his cup about condemned men partaking of hearty breakfasts.' The tone of this suggests it was, indeed, getting on for a cliché even then.

3 *Con la patciencia et la saliva l'elephante la metio a la formiga.*

With patience and saliva, the elephant screws the ant.

A saying quoted by Valerie Bornstein in *Proverbium Yearbook of International Proverb Scholarship* (1991). The original language may have been Mexican Spanish or Catalan: it does not appear to be regular Spanish or Italian.

1 Crime doesn't pay.

A slogan used variously both by the FBI and the cartoon character Dick Tracy. Of American origin and known since 1927. 'Crime never pays, not even life insurance benefits' – Zelda Popkin, *No Crime For a Lady* (1942).

2 Dance to your daddy.
My little babby ...
In a little dishy,
You shall have a fishy when the boat comes in.

Nursery rhyme (first recorded *c.*1806). Hence, *When the Boat Comes In*, title of a BBC TV drama series (1975–7).

3 Death is nature's way of telling you to slow down.

A joke current in the US by 1960 (as in *Newsweek* Magazine, 25 April). It has been specifically attributed to Severn Darden (1937–), the American film character actor. It is capable of infinite variation: from *Punch* (3 January 1962): 'Some neo-Malthusians have been heard to suggest that the bomb is Nature's way ... of checking ... the over-spawning of our species.' In 1978, the American cartoonist Garfield produced a bumper-sticker with the slogan: 'My car is God's way of telling you to slow down.'

4 Der spring is sprung
Der grass is riz
I wonder where dem boidies is?

Der little boids is on der wing,
Ain't dat absoid?
Der little wings is on der boid!

Entitled 'The Budding Bronx', this is described as by 'Anon (New York)' in Arnold Silcock's *Verse and Worse* (1952). Beyond that, no source has been found.

5 Do not remove a fly from your friend's forehead with a hatchet.

Supposedly Chinese proverb, quoted in A. Andrews, *Quotations for Speakers and Writers* (1969). As with all such 'Chinese' sayings, there is no source or certainty of origin.

6 Do not stand at my grave and weep.
I am not there, I do not sleep.
I am the thousand winds that blow.
I am diamond glints on snow.
I am the sunlight on ripened grain.
I am gentle autumnal rain.
When you waken in the morning hush.
I am the soft uplifting rush
Of quiet birds in circled flight.
I am the soft stars that shine at night.
Do not stand at my grave and cry –
I am not there. I did not die.

A poem that the British soldier Stephen Cummins left behind him when he was killed by an IRA landmine in Londonderry in 1989. In November 1995 when these words were reprised on the BBC TV programme *Bookworm* – read by the dead soldier's father – there were apparently 10,000 requests from viewers for the text of the poem. What is not clear is who wrote it, though it could have been Cummins himself. Debbie Turley, his fiancée, was quoted in 1989 as saying, 'He used to write every day and he was always writing poems.'

Barbara King, calligrapher of Llandeilo, stated (1996) that she had looked into the copyright position. It transpired that before Cummins used it in his farewell note, an American called Marilyn Rhinehart had sent the poem to Terry Boyle, a Republican prisoner of Strabane (with the last line reading, 'While Ireland lives I will not die'.) Another very similar poem with just a few divergencies in the text has been found as written by an Englishwoman, Mary E. Frye, in 1932.

7 The dove says, Coo, coo, what shall I do?
I can scarce maintain two.
Pooh, pooh, says the wren, I have ten,
And keep them all like gentlemen.

Nursery rhyme (recorded by 1853), of which there is more than one version. *The Oxford Dictionary of Nursery Rhymes* (1951) suggests that 'What shall I do? I can scarce maintain two' is how country folk interpret a dove's (or pigeon's) cooing, 'referring to the fact she seldom has more than two eggs in each brood. This is in contrast to the wren who rears a family of fourteen, fifteen, or sixteen.'

8 Down the lanes of memory
The lights are never dim
Until the stars forget to shine
We shall remember her.

Quoted by Alan Bennett from 'a Lancashire newspaper' on *Quote ... Unquote*, BBC Radio (26 January 1982).

He had earlier included the lines in 'The English Way of Death' in *Beyond the Fringe* (Broadway version, 1964). In their Classified Ads offices, many provincial newspapers keep a volume of standard tributes for the bereaved to consult. Presumably it was one such stock verse that gave rise to this interesting rhyme.

1 The eleventh commandment.

Mencken (1942) has it that the so-called 'eleventh commandment' is 'mind your own business' as 'borrowed from Cervantes, *Don Quixote*, 1605'. Indeed, it is to be found there (in Pt I, Bk 3, Chap. 8), although it is not described as the 'eleventh commandment'. But Mencken also records, 'The Eleventh Commandment: Thou shalt not be found out – George Whyte-Melville, *Holmby House*, 1860', and this is certainly the more usual meaning. The *OED2* adds from the *Pall Mall Gazette* (10 September 1884): 'The new and great commandment that nothing succeeds like success'; and from *Paston Carew* (1886) by Mrs Lynn Lynton that the eleventh commandment was 'do not tell tales out of school'. Unverified is Charles Kingsley's 1850 observation that it is, 'Buy cheap, sell dear'.

It could be argued that the eleventh commandment ought to be what Christ suggests in John 13:34: 'A new commandment I give unto you, That ye love one another; as I have loved you, that ye also love one another.' Safire (1978) reports that 'Thou Shalt Not Speak Ill of Fellow Republicans' was the eleventh commandment advanced by Dr Gaylord E. Parkinson, California State Republican Chairman, in the run-up to the 1966 governorship elections. The 1981 re-make of the film *The Postman Always Rings Twice* was promoted with the slogan: 'If there was an 11th Commandment, they would have broken that too.'

2 English as she is spoke.

This way of referring to the language as it might be spoken by foreigners or the illiterate comes from an actual 'guide of the conversation in Portuguese and English' published in the nineteenth century. The guilty author, according to Mencken (1942), was 'P. Carolino'. According to the *PDQ* (1960) it was 'A.W. Tuer (1838–1900)'.

In *Baldness Be My Friend* (1977) Richard Boston explored the facts. Originally, there was a French-Portuguese phrase-book, *O Novo Guia da Conversacão em frances e portuguez* by José da Fonseca, published in Paris in 1836. The text was in parallel columns. Then in 1865 a third column, carrying English translations, was added by one Pedro Carolino. His excellence as a translator can be shown by quoting from a section he cleverly but unwittingly called 'Idiotisms and Proverbs'. It included:

In the country of blinds, the one-eyed men are kings.
To do a wink to some body.
The stone as roll not, heap up not foam.
After the paunch comes the dance.
To craunch the marmoset.
To come back to their muttons.
He sin in trouble water.

By 1883, the awfulness of this non-joke was known in London. Publishers Field and Tuer brought out a selection under the title *English as She is Spoke* (a phrase taken from the chapter on 'Familiar Dialogues'). The same year, Mark Twain introduced an edition of the complete work in the US.

3 An English summer – three fine days and a thunderstorm.

The observation has been attributed to King Henry VIII, but John Aiton's *Manual of Domestic Economy for Clergymen* (1842) has: 'Our [Scotch] summers are said to consist of 3 hot days and a thunder-storm', which would seem to suggest it is an old Scottish saying.

4 *Et in Arcadia ego.*

One finds these words associated with tombs, skulls and Arcadian shepherds in classical paintings, but not before the seventeenth century. Most notably the phrase occurs in two paintings by the French artist Nicolas Poussin, both of which depict shepherds reading the words carved on a tomb. One, painted 1626–8, hangs in Chatsworth House, Derbyshire; the other, 'The Shepherds of Arcady', 1630–5, in the Louvre. Just before this, however, the Italian artist Guercino had painted a painting known as 'Et in Arcadia ego' which hangs in the Galleria Corsino, Rome. This was painted no later than 1623.

Is the inscription meant to suggest that, in death, the speaker is in Arcadia, the Greek name for a place of rural peace and calm taken from an actual area in the Peloponnese? Or is he saying he was formerly there? '*Et in Arcadia ego vixi*' ('I lived') or '*Et in Arcadia fui pastor*' ('I was a shepherd') are variants. Or is it Death speaking – 'Even in Arcadia, I, Death, cannot be avoided'?

L.A. Moritz of University College, Cardiff, wrote in a letter to *The Times* (27 January 1982), 'The Latin cannot mean what Goethe and many others ... took it to mean: "I too was in Arcadia." Its only possible meaning is "Even in Arcadia am I" ... this association of the pastoral Arcadia with death goes back to Virgil's tenth Eclogue, which first placed idyllic shepherds in an Arcadian landscape.'

Erwin Panofsky pointed this out first in *Philosophy and History, Essays presented to E. Casstrer* (1936) in which he claimed that since the eighteenth century the English had had an instinct not shared by Continentals for making a special kind of sense out of the classical tag. '"Even in Arcadia I, Death, hold sway" ... while long forgotten on the Continent remained familiar', he asserted, in England, and ultimately 'became part of what may be termed a specifically English or "insular" tradition – a tradition which tended to retain the idea of a memento mori'. Skulls juxtaposed with roses could be conventionally employed as an emblem of the omnipotence of Death, whose power is not finally to be excluded even from the sequestered "safe" world of pastoral.'

In German literature, the phrase first appeared in *Winterreise* (1769) by Johann Georg Jacobi: 'Whenever, in a beautiful landscape, I encounter a tomb with the inscription: "I too was in Arcadia", I point it out to my friends, we stop a moment, press each other's hands, and proceed.' The phrase was later used by Goethe as the motto of his *Travels in Italy* (1816).

In England, Sir Joshua Reynolds painted a picture in 1769 on which a tomb can be seen with the words inscribed. In Evelyn Waugh's *Brideshead Revisited* (1945), the narrator, while an undergraduate at Oxford, adorns his rooms with a 'human skull lately purchased from the School of Medicine which, resting in a bowl of roses, formed, at the moment, the chief decoration of my table. It bore the motto "Et in Arcadia ego" inscribed on its forehead.' (Book One of the novel is entitled 'Et in Arcadia Ego'.)

1 Even your best friends won't tell you.

A line that comes from the famous Listerine mouthwash advertisement headed 'Often a bridesmaid but never a bride', in the US in the 1920s. Originally, the line was 'and even your closest friends won't tell you'. Partridge/*Catch Phrases* suggests that it became a catchphrase in the form 'your best friend(s) won't tell you (= "you stink!")'. In the film *Dangerous Moonlight* (UK, 1941), the Anton Walbrook character says to a man putting on hair oil (in New York), 'Even your best friend won't smell you'.

2 Everyman, I will go with thee and be thy guide,
In thy most need to go by thy side.

From the Everyman morality play of *c.*1509–91. These legendary lines are spoken by Knowledge and thus have been an appropriate choice as a slogan to promote the Everyman's Library series of book reprints of the classics. These have been published by J.M. Dent in Britain since the 1900s (and by E.P. Dutton in the US). *Compare* MILTON 393:4 and SIDNEY 504:3.

3 Every man likes the smell of his own farts.

Quoted in *Viking Book of Aphorisms* (ed. Auden & Kronenberger, 1962) and described as of Icelandic origin. Might it have been the editors' invention? *See also* AUDEN 66:2.

4 Every time a sheep bleats it misses a nibble.

Quoted on BBC Radio *Quote ... Unquote* (25 August 1984). Sometimes rendered as 'Every time a sheep ba's it loses a bite'. Mencken (1942) has 'Every time the sheep bleats it loses a mouthful' as an English proverb 'apparently borrowed from the Italian and familiar since the 17th century'. In this form it certainly appears in Thomas Fuller's *Gnomologia* (1732). *CODP* finds a version in 1599 and seems to prefer the form, 'A bleating sheep loses a bite', explaining it as, 'Opportunities are missed through too much chatter.'

5 The Father, the Son and the Pigeon.

A French rhyme appeared in the introduction to *Some Limericks* (1928), privately printed by Norman Douglas (published 1969 as *The Norman Douglas Limerick Book*):

Il y avait un jeune homme de Dijon
Qui n'avait que peu de religion.
Il dit: 'Quant à moi,
Je déteste tous les trois,
Le Père, et le Fils, et le Pigeon.'

Which may be translated:

There was young man of Dijon
Who had only a little religion,
He said, 'As for me,
'I detest all the three,
'The Father, the Son and the Pigeon.'

To talk of the Holy Ghost in these terms seems to have been nothing new, even in the 1920s. Lord Berners describing his time at Eton in the 1890s in *A Distant Prospect* (1945) tells of a friend called Manston: 'At first I was inclined to be shocked by his irreverence – for instance, when he had said that the Trinity put him in mind of a music-hall turn – the Father, the Son and the Performing Pigeon.'

6 A few days on your feet and we'll soon have you back in bed.

Anonymous doctor to Christine Keeler, the 'good time girl' in the British political Profumo scandal of 1963, quoted in H. Montgomery Hyde, *A Tangled Web* (1986).

7 Forget-Me-Not Lane.

Title of a play (1971) by Peter Nichols. Derived from the Flanagan and Allen song 'Down Forget-Me-Not

Lane' (1941) written by Horatio Nicholls, Charlie Chester and Reg Morgan.

1 For want of a nail, the shoe is lost; for want of a shoe, the horse is lost; for want of a horse, the rider is lost.

Proverbial expression (known by the seventeenth century) about the perils of penny-pinching or lack of attention to detail. Hence, the title of a novel, *For Want of a Nail* (1965), by Melvyn Bragg.

2 Friday night too tired, Saturday night too drunk, Sunday night too far away.

The lament of an anonymous (Australian) sheep-shearer's wife. Hence, *Sunday Too Far Away*, the title of a film (Australia, 1977).

3 From a grateful country/nation.

A memorial phrase especially popular in the nineteenth century. At St Deiniol's, W.E. Gladstone's library in the village of Hawarden, Wales, where the British Prime Minister (1809–98) had his family home for almost fifty years, there is a plaque saying it was 'erected to his memory by a grateful nation'. W.M. Thackeray, writing in *The Virginians*, Chap. 35 (1859), has: 'The late lamented O'Connell ... over whom a grateful country has raised such a magnificent testimonial.' On the statue to General Havelock (1795–1857) in Trafalgar Square, London, is written: 'Soldiers! Your valour will not be forgotten by a grateful country.' The notable Alexander Column in the square outside the Winter Palace at St Petersburg was completed in 1834. On the base was the inscription (in Russian): 'To Alexander the First from a Grateful Russia.'

Nowadays, the phrase is invariably used with irony. From *The Independent* (23 July 1992): 'There have been loads of Roy Orbisons and Neil Diamonds and Gene Pitneys, and, after Elvis, the man most often impersonated by a grateful nation ... Cliff Richard.'

4 Georgie Porgie, pudding and pie,
Kissed the girls and made them cry;
When the girls came out to play,
Georgie Porgie ran away.

Nursery rhyme (first recorded 1844). Hence, *Kiss the Girls and Make Them Cry*, title of a BBC TV drama series (1979).

5 Ginger, you're barmy!

Addressed to any male, this street cry merely means he is stupid or crazy. It most probably originated in the British music-hall song with the title 'Ginger, You're Balmy [the alternative spelling]!' written by Fred Murray and published in 1912. This was sung by Harry Champion (1866–1942). In the song the following phrase is 'GET YOUR HAIR CUT!' Also in the chorus there occurs another line sometimes coupled with 'Ginger, you're barmy!' – 'Why don't you join the army'. *Ginger, You're Barmy* was the title of a novel (1962) by David Lodge.

Separately, the word 'ginger' has been applied in the UK to male homosexuals (since the 1930s, at least) on account of the rhyming slang, 'ginger beer = queer'. 'Ginger' is also the name given to a red-headed man. But neither of these appears relevant to the song. Ian Gillies commented (1995): 'The plot of "Ginger" is very similar [to another Champion song] "Any Old Iron" – someone who fancies himself well-dressed, being shouted at in the one case because of his "old iron" watch-chain, and in the other because he isn't wearing a hat and not, apparently, because he is ginger. Indeed, there is no specific reference to his being ginger.' Here are the lines:

'Don't walk a-bout without your cady [= hat] on;
Ginger, you're balmy!
Get your hair cut!', they all be-gin to cry.
'With nothing on your nap-per, oh, you are a pie!

'Pies must have a lit-tle bit of crust,
Why don't you join the army?
If you want to look a don you want a bit of some thing on –
Ginger, you're balmy!'

6 God Protect Me from My Friends.

Title of a book (1956) by Gavin Maxwell about Salvatore Giuliano, the Sicilian bandit. From the proverbial expression: 'I can look after my enemies, but God protect me from my friends.' *CODP* traces this to 1477 in the forms 'God keep/save/defend us from our friends' and says it now often appears simply as, 'Save us from our friends'. It is common to many languages. 'With friends like these/with a Hungarian for a friend, who needs enemies?' are but two versions.

The diarist Chips Channon (21 February 1938) has: 'This evening a group of excited Communists even invaded the Lobby, demanding Anthony [Eden]'s reinstatement. God preserve us from our friends, they did him harm.' *The Morris Dictionary of Word and Phrase Origins* (1977) finds a quotation from Maréchal Villars who, on leaving Louis XIV, said: 'Defend me from my friends; I can defend myself from my enemies.' In 1821, George Canning rhymed: 'Give me the avowed, the erect, the manly foe,/Bold I can meet – perhaps may turn his blow!/But of all plagues, Good Heaven, thy wrath can send,/Save, save, Oh, save me from the candid friend!' Charlotte Brontë also used the idea in a letter (untraced) in response to a patronizing review of one of her books.

1 The Gods do not deduct from man's allotted span the hours spent in fishing.

Described as a 'Babylonian proverb' in *The International Thesaurus of Quotations* (1970), this was apparently a favourite saying of President Hoover.

2 God will be too busy unpacking King Edward.

Said to have been given by the little daughter of Lord Kinnoull as the reason for her refusal to say prayers. She had been the 'awed witness' of the funeral of King Edward VII (1910). Quoted in Lord Riddell, *More Pages from My Diary 1908–14* (1934).

3 God writes straight with crooked lines.

Paul Claudel's play *Le Soulier de Satin* (1921) has for its epigraph a 'Portuguese proverb': '*Deus escreve direito por linhas tortas.*'

4 Gone but not forgotten.

A sentiment frequently displayed on tombstones, memorial notices and such, and (reportedly) used as the title of a Victorian print showing children at a grave. The earliest example of its use (in a far from exhaustive search) is on the headstone to John Worth (died 7 June 1879, aged 71) in Princetown churchyard, Devon. On the headstone of Jane Damerell (died 26 March 1883 aged 70) at Shaugh Prior in Devon, there is:

Gone from us but not forgotten
Never shall thy memory fade
Sweetest thoughts shall ever linger
Round the spot where thou art laid.

Ludovic Kennedy in his autobiography *On My Way to the Club* (1989) suggests that it is an epitaph much found in the English graveyard at Poona, India.

5 The Good, the Bad and the Ugly.

English title of the Italian 'spaghetti Western' *Il Buono, il Bruto, il Cattivo* (1966), co-written and directed by Sergio Leone. Colonel Oliver North giving evidence to the Washington hearings on the Irangate scandal in the summer of 1987, said: 'I came here to tell you the truth – the good, the bad, and the ugly'. Two headlines, both from *The Independent* (16 September 1996): 'The Good ... the Bad ... and the Ugly: The Premiership's Leading Scorers'; 'The Good, the Bad and the Spoilt: How Children React'.

6 The grass is always greener on the other side of the fence.

ODP (1970) ignored the proverb in this form, preferring to cite a sixteenth-century translation of a Latin proverb, 'The corn in another man's ground seemeth ever more fertile than doth our own'. By 1956, the time of the Hugh and Margaret Williams play *The Grass is Greener*, the modern form was well established. Wolfgang Mieder in *Proverbium* (1993) questions whether the two proverbs are in fact related but finds an earlier citation of the modern one: an American song with words by Raymond B. Egan and music by Richard A. Whiting entitled 'The Grass is Always Greener (In the Other Fellow's Yard)', published in 1924.

7 A great man! Why, I doubt if there are six his equal in the whole of Boston.

On Shakespeare. Said to W.E. Gladstone by an unnamed Bostonian. Quoted in the book *Quote ... Unquote* (1978). Mencken (1942) has it that Gladstone got it from Lionel A. Tollemache (23 December 1897) as, 'There are not ten men in Boston equal to Shakespeare.'

8 Hallelujah, I'm a Bum.

Title of song (1928) by Harry Kirby McClintock, later popularized by Burl Ives. In 1933, the song was used as the basis of the US film *Hallelujah, I'm a Bum*, which starred Al Jolson as a tramp. In Britain, a change of title to *Hallelujah, I'm a Tramp* was forced upon the distributors. For the film, a new song with the title was written by Lorenz Hart (music by Richard Rodgers) which, in fact, included only the line 'Hallelujah, I'm a bum again!' Even so, a separate version had to be made for the sensitive British censor.

9 Hark the herald angels sing
Mrs Simpson's pinched our king.

Within days of the abdication of King Edward VIII in December 1936 schoolchildren were singing this. A letter from Clement Attlee on 26 December included the information that his daughter Felicity had produced the 'ribald verse which was new to me' (quoted in Kenneth Harris, *Attlee*, 1982). Iona and Peter Opie in *The Lore and Language of Schoolchildren* (1959) comment on the rapidity with which the rhyme spread across the country. The constitutional crisis did not become public until 25 November, the King abdicated on 10 December, 'yet at a school party in Swansea given before the end of term ... when the tune played happened to be "Hark the Herald Angels Sing", a mistress found herself having to restrain her small children from singing this lyric, known to all of them, which cannot have been composed more than three weeks previously'.

1 Has anyone here been raped and speaks English?

The absurdity of the war correspondent's job was neatly encapsulated by a question heard during the war in the Congo (1960). Thousands of frightened Belgian civilians were waiting for a plane to take them to safety from the newly independent ex-Belgian colony when a BBC television reporter walked among them with his camera team and posed this question. The incident was reported – and used as the title of a book *Anyone Here Been Raped and Speaks English* (1981) – by the American journalist Edward Behr, who went on to comment: 'The callous cry summed up for me the tragic, yet wildly surrealist nature of the country itself.'

2 Hear no evil, see no evil, speak no evil.

Bartlett (1980) describes this as a legend related to the Three Wise Monkeys and carved over the door of the Sacred Stable, Nikko, Japan, in the seventeenth century. The three monkeys are shown with their paws over, respectively, their ears, eyes and mouth. This is referred to in a poem 'The Three Wise Monkeys' by Pauline Carrington Rust Bouv (1860–1928): 'The three wise monkeys of Nikko,/Who see, speak, hear but the good!' 'Hear, see, keep silence' (often accompanied by a sketch of the Three Wise Monkeys) is the motto of the United Grand Lodge of Freemasons in the form *Audi, Vide, Tace*.

> The motto of Yorkshiremen is said to be:
> Hear all, see all, say nowt,
> Aight all, sup all, pay nowt,
> And if ever tha does owt for nowt
> Do it for thisen.

A Noel Gay song written in 1938 for Sandy Powell, the Yorkshire comedian, had the title 'Hear all, see all, say nowt'. *See No Evil* was the American title of the film *Blind Terror* (UK, 1971); *See No Evil, Hear No Evil* was the title of a film (US, 1989).

3 A heart the size of Waterloo station.

From James Agate, *Ego 4* (1940, entry for 19 April 1939): 'As the bookmaker said of Marie Lloyd, she had ...'

4 He didn't love God, he just fancied him.

On W.H. Auden. Quoted in the book, *Quote ... Unquote* (1983), otherwise unverified.

5 He died as he lived – at sea.

On Ramsay MacDonald, the British Labour Prime Minister, who died during a cruise (1937). Quoted in Atyeo & Green, *Don't Quote Me* (1981).

6 Here lies a poor woman who always was tired,
For she lived in a place where help wasn't hired,
Her last words on earth were, 'Dear friends, I am going,
Where washing ain't done nor cooking nor sewing,
And everything there is exact to my wishes,
For there they don't eat, there's no washing of dishes,
I'll be where loud anthems will always be ringing
(But having no voice, I'll be out of the singing).
Don't mourn for me now, don't grieve for me never,
For I'm going to do nothing for ever and ever'.

Sometimes referred to as 'The Maid-of-all-Works' Epitaph' or 'The Tired Woman's Epitaph', this has two possible sources. As 'an epitaph for Catherine Alsopp, a Sheffield washerwoman, who hanged herself, 7 August 1905', it was composed by herself and included in E. Jameson, *1000 Curiosities of Britain* (1937). But a letter in *The Spectator* (2 December 1922) from a correspondent at the British Museum asserted that the inscription was once to be found in a churchyard in Bushey, Hertfordshire. A copy of the text was made before 1860, but the actual stone had been destroyed by 1916. It was also discussed in *Notes and Queries* for March 1889 and *Longman's Magazine* for January 1884. Benham (1907) states that it had been quoted 'before 1850'.

7 Here lies Fred,
Who was alive and is dead:
Had it been his father,
I had much rather;
Had it been his brother,
Still better than another;
Had it been his sister
No one would have missed her;
Had it been the whole generation,
Still better for the nation:
But since 'tis only Fred,
Who was alive and is dead, –
There's no more to be said.

Epitaph on Frederick Louis, Prince of Wales (1707–51), eldest son of George II and father of George III, quoted by Horace Walpole in an appendix to his *Memoirs of George II* (1847). Frederick quarrelled with his father and was banished from court. Compare from Frobisher's *New Select Collection of Epitaphs* ... (?1790), 'On a tombstone in Cornwall: Here lies honest Ned, / Because he is dead. / Had it been his father ...' *A Collection of Epitaphs* ... (1806) has from 'a headstone in the church-yard of Storrington in the County of Sussex: Here lies the body of Edward Hide;/We laid him here because he died./We had rather it had been his father./If it had been his sister,/We should not have miss'd her./But since 'tis honest Ned/No more shall be said ...' Peter Haining, *Graveyard Wit* (1973), has a version beginning 'Here lies HONEST NED ...' from 'Kirkby Stephen parish church, Westmorland'.

1 Here lies the body of
LADY O'LOONEY
Great niece of BURKE
Commonly called the Sublime
She was Bland, Passionate
and deeply Religious, also
she painted in water colours
and sent several pictures
to the Exhibition
She was first Cousin to
LADY JONES
and of such is the
Kingdom of Heaven.

This most delightful of epitaphs can no longer be found. W. Fairley, *Epitaphiana: or the Curiosities of Churchyard Literature* (1875) placed it in 'Pewsey churchyard'. Others have placed it in 'Pewsey, Bedfordshire' (which does not exist), in Dorsetshire, in Devon, in Bridgwater Cemetery, Somerset. Compare Philip Reder, *Epitaphs* (1969), in Bandon, Ireland: 'Sacred to the memory of Mrs Maria Boyle/Who was a good wife, a devoted Mother/And a kind and charitable neighbour./She painted in water colours,/And was the first cousin to the Earl of Cork,/And of such is the Kingdom of Heaven.' At which point one wonders whether what G.W.E. Russell in *Collections and Recollections* (1898) calls 'the best-known of all epitaphs' ever existed anywhere at all. The name O'Looney does not occur in the DNB or Debrett, though it was in the 1991 London telephone directory.

2 Here lies the loyal Duke of Newcastle and his Duchess his second wife by whom he had no issue her name was Margaret Lucas youngest sister to the Lord Lucas of Colchester a noble family for all the brothers were valiant and all the sisters virtuous.

Inscription on the monument of the 1st Duke and Duchess of Newcastle in the North Transept of Westminster Abbey. The monument was erected during the lifetime of William (Cavendish), 1st Duke (1592–1676), his second wife, Margaret (1623–73), having predeceased him. His duchess was quite a figure in her own right. She wrote plays, letters, verses, a biography of her husband, and an autobiography.

3 Here on 11 November 1918 succumbed the criminal pride of the German Reich, vanquished by the free peoples which it tried to enslave.

Inscription in the forest of Compiègne, France, where the Armistice was signed at the end of the First World War. No wonder the Germans felt like starting the Second.

4 Here's one I made/prepared earlier.

Or 'This is one I prepared earlier ...' A curiously popular catchphrase in Britain. It originated with 'live' TV cookery demonstrations in the 1950s in which it was important that the showing of the finished product was not left to chance. But the phrase was also borrowed by presenters of BBC TV's children's programme *Blue Peter* (from 1963 onwards), who had to explain how to make models of the Taj Mahal out of milk-bottle tops, for example, but wouldn't actually be seen doing so there and then.

5 Here's to our next Merrie Meeting.

As a catchphrase, this seemed at first to be linked to Henry Hall's signature theme for the BBC Dance Orchestra (which Hall took over in March 1932):

> Here's to the next time and a merry meeting,
> Here's to the next time, we send you all our greeting,
> Set it to music, sing it in rhyme,
> Now, all together, Here's to the next time!

Then it was remembered that BBC Radio's popular organist, Robin Richmond, was for many years presenter of *The Organist Entertains* and the phrase was his weekly signing off. But the alliterative lure of 'merry meeting(s)' has been around a good deal longer. In Sir Walter Scott's *Ivanhoe*, Chap. 35 (1819), Aymer signs off with: 'Till which merry meeting, we wish you farewell.' In Shakespeare's *Richard III*, I.i.7 (1592–3): 'Our stern alarums chang'd to merry meetings,/Our dreadful marches to delightful measures.' *Punch* for 27 July 1904 has in the caption to a cartoon accompanying 'Operatic Notes' 'TO OUR NEXT MERRY MEETING!'

Even more significantly, the *Punch Almanack* for 1902 has a cartoon of two foxes drinking in a club, celebrating the fact that all the best hunting horses are away in the Boer War. One fox is saying, 'To our next merry meeting!' Does this indicate that this was an established toast? Does it also suggest that the original 'meeting' referred to in the phrase was the kind you have in fox-hunting?

1 Here's to pure scholarship. May it never be of any use to anyone!

A bravura toast, given at the centenary of a college. John Julius Norwich commented that his father, Duff Cooper (1890–1954), used to quote this as a toast specifically to higher mathematics.

2 Here we go round the mulberry bush.

Derives from the refrain sung in the children's game (first recorded in the mid-nineteenth century, though probably earlier) in which the participants hold hands and dance in a ring. There are numerous variations, using various fruits. Hence, however, the title of the novel (1965; film UK, 1967) by Hunter Davies.

One theory of the rhyme's origin is that a mulberry tree stood in the middle of the exercise yard at Wakefield Prison in Yorkshire. The prisoners would have to go round and round it on a 'cold and frosty morning'. This may be, however, no more than a coincidence.

3 He was my man, but I done him wrong.

From the famous anonymous American ballad 'Frankie and Johnny' (which Mencken dates *c.*1875). There are numerous versions (two hundred is one estimate) and it may be of Negro origin. 'Frankie and Johnnie were lovers' (or husband and wife) but he (Johnnie) went off with other women – 'He was her man, but he done her wrong.' So, to equal the score, Frankie shoots him and has to be punished for it (in some versions in the electric chair):

Frankie walked up to the scaffold, as
  Calm as a girl could be,
She turned her eyes to Heaven and said
  'Good Lord, I'm coming to Thee;
He was my man, but I done him wrong'.

Bartlett (1980) draws a comparison with Shakespeare, *The Rape of Lucrece* (l. 1462): 'Lucrece swears he did her wrong' and *King Lear* (I.ii.161): 'Some villain hath done me wrong.'

When Mae West's play *Diamond Lil* was transferred to the cinema screen in 1933, it was renamed *She Done Him Wrong* – surely an allusion.

4 He who has the sea has the shore,
And the castle is his who has the plain;
But freedom dwells upon the mountain
  peaks.

Untraced words quoted (1981) by a Colonel Harcourt, Commanding Officer of the Sultan of Oman's Royal Guard. The connection between freedom and mountain top also occurs in Joseph Rodman Drake's 'The American Flag' (1819) which begins: 'When Freedom from her mountain height.' In Schiller's play *The Bride of Messina* (1803) there is, 'Auf den Bergen ist Freiheit' [Freedom is on the mountains]. In a speech to the Conservative Party Conference at Llandudno on 9 October 1948, Winston Churchill brandished the saying (appropriate in a Welsh context), 'Freedom dwells among the mountains.' Clearly, all these people are referring to some core quotation, so far not found.

5 Hickory, dickory, dock,
The mouse ran up the clock.
The clock struck one,
The mouse ran down,
Hickory, dickory, dock.

Children's counting rhyme, first recorded *c.*1744, possibly derived from the sheep-counting method, 'hevera, devera, dick' (*see under* Yan Tan Tethera at HARRISON 283:4). Hence, *Hickory Dickory Dock*, British title of a Hercule Poirot novel (1955) by Agatha Christie. In the US, the book is known as *Hickory Dickory Death*.

6 The higher the monkey climbs, the more he shows his tail.

'The egotistical surgeon is like a monkey; the higher he climbs the more you see of his less attractive features' is an anonymous saying applied to anyone in any profession who has achieved high rank. On BBC Radio *Quote ... Unquote* (29 March 1994), John Oaksey recalled that his father, Geoffrey Lawrence (Lord Oaksey) (1880–1971) had said the same sort of thing about judges and other high-ups in the legal profession, drawing a parallel rather with orang-utans. The basic proverbial saying (as above) was discussed in *Notes and Queries* (1887).

7 Hitler
Has only got one ball!
Goering
Has two, but very small!
Himmler
Has something similar,
But poor old Goebbels
Has no balls at all!

This was the title of an anonymous song (sung to the tune of 'Colonel Bogey') that was in existence by 1940. As with 'Not tonight Josephine' (406:5), the basis for this assertion about the sexuality of a political figure is obscure. The rumour had been widespread in Central Europe in the 1930s, and Martin Page in *Kiss Me Goodnight, Sergeant Major* (1973) wrote of a Czech refugee who had referred in 1938 to the fact that Hitler had been wounded in the First World War, since when '*ihm fehlt einer* [he lacks one]'. Perhaps it was no more than a generalized slight against the Nazi leader's virility, which conveniently fitted the tune and also permitted a 'Goebbels/no balls' rhyme. There had earlier been a nineteenth-century American ballad about a trade union leader which began: 'Arthur Hall/Has only got one ball.'

1 Home is where the heart is.

The first appearance of this proverbial expression may well have been in an 1870 American play by J.J. McCloskey, but even then it was 'Home, they say, is where the heart is', so it was obviously an established saying by then. Mencken (1942) has it as an 'American saying, author unidentified'. Hence, *Where the Heart Is*, title of a film (US, 1990), directed by John Boorman.

2 Hooray, Hooray, the first of May,
Outdoor fucking begins today.

This 'Old Thurlestone saying' (whatever that may be – from the place in Devon?) was included in *Vice: An Anthology*, ed. Richard Davenport-Hines (1993). As 'Horray, horray, It is the first of May,/Outdoor f—-ing starts today,' it appears in Reisner & Wechsler, *Encyclopedia of Graffiti* (1974) from 'Ladies' room, New York City'. But the rhyme was certainly current by the 1960s at least. In May *c.*1965, a version with 'outdoor sex' was published in the Oxford undergraduate magazine, *Isis*.

3 How different – how very different from the home life of our own dear Queen!

One night Sarah Bernhardt (1844–1923) essayed the role of Cleopatra in Shakespeare's *Antony and Cleopatra* during a London season sometime in the reign of Queen Victoria. In the scene where Cleopatra receives the news of Mark Antony's defeat at the battle of Actium, she stabbed the messenger who brought her the news, 'stormed, raved, frothed at the mouth, wrecked some of the scenery in her frenzy and finally, as the curtain fell, dropped in a shuddering convulsive heap.' As the applause died down, an American visitor overhead a middle-aged British matron speaking to her friend in the next seat, saying the above. So attributed by Irvin S. Cobb in *A Laugh a Day Keeps the Doctor Away* ... (1921).

4 If God had intended us to —— he wouldn't have ——.

This format phrase is used as an argument against doing or using something, especially some new invention. From Lord Berners, *First Childhood* (1934): 'My [model flying machine] elicited a reproof from the Headmaster, who happened to see it [in *c.*1893]. '"Men," he said, "were never meant to fly; otherwise God would have given them wings".' From J.E. Morpurgo, *The Road to Athens* (1963): 'God would not have invented the automobile if he had intended me to walk.' 'I always said, if God had meant us to fly, he'd have given me guts' – in the final chapter of David Lodge's novel, *Changing Places* (1975), Morris Zapp comments thus, after a close air miss. 'If God had meant us to travel tourist class He would have made us narrower' – Martha Zimmerman, American air hostess, quoted in *The Wall Street Journal* (1977). 'If God had not meant us to write on walls, he would never have given us the example' – included in the book *Graffiti 2* (1980). 'If God had intended Jewish women to exercise, he'd have put diamonds on the floor' – attributed to Joan Rivers. 'If God had not meant everyone to be in bed by ten-thirty, He would never have provided the ten o'clock newscast' – Garrison Keillor, *Lake Wobegon Days* (1985). 'If God had intended us to fly, He would have sent us tickets' – attributed to Mel Brooks by Frederic Raphael in 1994. *See also* FLANDERS 238:7; PRIESTLEY 438:4.

5 If the soup had been as warm as the wine, and the wine as old as the fish, and the fish as young as the maid, and the maid as willing as the hostess, it would have been a very good meal.

Untraced restaurant criticism dating from the Austro-Hungarian Empire – at least, according to Clement Freud who quoted it on BBC Radio *Quote ... Unquote* (1979).

6 If you can remember the sixties you weren't really there.

'Who said "If you can remember the sixties you weren't really there"? I can't remember.' In *The Guardian* (2 June 1987), Nancy Banks-Smith made it clear that this was an established saying by that date, but it was oddly popular at that time: '"If you can remember the sixties, you weren't really there," said a guy from Jefferson Airplane' – *Today* (2 June 1987); 'The best quote about the period came from a leading

American hippie – now, I think, something huge on Wall Street – who said: "If you can remember the sixties, you weren't there." There's a lot of truth in that, though I think he's pointing at certain kinds of substance' – *The Independent* (11 March 1989). This hippie might well have been Jerry Rubin (*q.v.*).

1 If you want to be happy for a day, go fishing. If you want to be happy for a week, get married. If you want to be happy for a month, kill a pig. If you want to be happy and contented for all time, smoke a pipe.

Quoted by Lord Mason, convenor of the Lords and Commons Pipesmokers' Club in March 1995, but untraced. On the other hand, this version described as a 'Chinese proverb' was heard in 1993: 'If you wish to be happy for an hour, drink wine; if you wish to be happy for three days, get married; if you wish to be happy for eight days, kill your pig and eat it; but if you wish to be happy for ever, become a gardener.'

2 I know two things about the horse
And one of them is rather coarse.

Anonymous rhyme. However, in *The Weekend Book* (1928), it is attributed to Naomi Royde-Smith (*c.*1875–1964).

3 I know where I'm going
And I know who goes with me
I know whom I love
But the dear devil [de'il/Lord] knows whom
I'll marry.

The film *I Know Where I'm Going!* (UK, 1945) about a headstrong girl and set in Scotland, takes its title from an Irish song which also provides the theme song. Co-writer and director, Michael Powell, explains in *A Life in Movies* (1986) that his wife suggested the title to him while travelling on 'the Number 9 bus to Piccadilly Circus ... And standing there in the swaying bus, she sang it ...' By which time, 'we were opposite Fortnum and Masons'.

4 I know why the sun never sets on the British Empire: God wouldn't trust an Englishman in the dark.

In Nancy McPhee, *The Book of Insults* (1978), this is ascribed to 'Duncan Spaeth' (is this John Duncan Spaeth, the US educator?) Clearly it plays upon NORTH 414:9. An Irish Republican placard held up during Prince Charles's visit to New York in June 1981 had the slogan: 'The sun never sets on the British Empire because God doesn't trust the Brits in the dark.'

5 I'll tell you a story
About Jack a Nory,
And now the story's begun;
I'll tell you another
Of Jack and his brother,
And now my story is done.

Nursery rhyme first recorded in 1760. Hence, *Jackanory*, the title of the BBC TV story-telling series for children (from the 1960s onwards).

6 I'm sixty-one today,
A year beyond the barrier,
And what was once a Magic Flute
Is now a Water Carrier.

Quoted in *PDMQ* (1971). Traditionally quoted by men who have undergone a prostate operation.

7 In God we trust, all others pay cash.

Mencken (1942) listed 'In God we trust; all others must pay cash' as an 'American saying'. 'In God we trust' has been the official national motto of the United States since 1956, when it superseded *E Pluribus Unum*, but had been known since 1864 when it was first put on a 2-cent bronze coin.

There is a similar joke in Britain, of the type printed on small cards and sold for display in pubs and shops. It made an appearance as a quote in the early 1940s in Flann O'Brien's column for the *Irish Times*: 'We have come to an arrangement with our bankers. They have agreed not to sell drink. We, on our part, have agreed not to cash cheques.' *See also* LEE 348:3.

8 In good King Charles's golden days,
When loyalty no harm meant;
A furious High-Churchman I was,
And so I gained preferment.

Song 'The Vicar of Bray' in *The British Musical Miscellany* (1734), referring to a person who changes allegiance according to the way the wind blows. The original was a vicar of Bray, Berkshire, in the sixteenth century who is supposed to have changed his religious affiliation from Roman Catholic to Protestant more than once during the reigns of Henry VIII to Elizabeth I. However, there were, in fact, several vicars at Bray in this period. Whatever the case, by the time of Thomas Fuller's *Worthies* (1662) there was a proverb: 'The Vicar of Bray will be Vicar of Bray still.' As for the song, it was probably written at the beginning of the eighteenth century and describes a different (perhaps completely fictional) vicar of Bray who changed his religion to suit the different faiths of monarchs from Charles II to George I. Can there have been two such turncoat vicars – or was the song merely an updating of the circumstances of the actual first vicar?

Hence, the play *In Good King Charles's Golden Days* (1939) by George Bernard Shaw, about a visit of Charles II to Isaac Newton in 1680 (and introducing other well-known names from that time).

1 In his chamber, weak and dying,
While the Norman Baron lay,
Loud, without, his men were crying,
'Shorter hours and better pay' ...

Lives of great men all remind us
We can make as much as they,
Work no more, until they find us
Shorter hours and better pay.

'A Strike Among the Poets' – included in *The Faber Book of Comic Verse* (1974 ed.) Probably from the late nineteenth century. For the original of the second verse, *see* LONGFELLOW 360:4.

2 I picked a lemon in the garden of love
Where I thought only roses bloom.

Said in reference to an unloved wife. From the song 'A Lemon in the Garden of Love', words by M.E. Rourke, music by Richard Carle. Dates from 1906 when it was sung in the New York production of *The Spring Chicken*. This comic number of romantic misjudgement was reprised in the 1940 film *Ma! He's Making Eyes at Me*, which starred Constance Moore and Tom Brown. There may also have been a parody entitled 'I Picked a Pansy in the Garden of Love' which Sophie Tucker sang in London around 1925.

3 Is it kind? Is it true? Is it necessary?

In George Seaver's *Edward Wilson of the Antarctic* (1963), it is stated that Wilson's widow had this motto printed on her mantelshelf to remind herself to curb her sharp tongue. In the Dorothy L. Sayers novel *Gaudy Night* (1935) it is said (with the first two queries reversed) by that arch-quoter, Lord Peter Wimsey. As such it bears a certain resemblance to part of the Four Way Test 'of the things we think, say or do' that Rotarians in the US devised in 1931: 'Is it the truth? Is it fair? Will it be beneficial to all concerned?' The most likely origin, however, is a poem called 'Three Gates' written in 1855 by Beth Day and said to be 'after the Arabian':

If you are tempted to reveal
A tale to you someone has told
About another, make it pass
Before you speak, three gates of gold.
These narrow gates: First, 'Is it true?'
Then, 'Is it needful?' In your mind
Give truthful answer. And the next
Is last and narrowest, 'Is it kind?'
And if to reach your lips at last
It passes through these gateways three,
Then you may tell the tale, nor fear
What the result of speech may be.

4 Is there a life before death?

This graffito was reported from Ballymurphy in Ireland, *c.*1971, and is confirmed by Seamus Heaney's poem 'Whatever You Say Say Nothing' from *North* (1975), which has:

Is there a life before death? That's chalked up
In Ballymurphy ...

But as if this underlines the saying's Irish origins too well, bear in mind that 'Is there life before death?' is the epigraph to Chap. 9 of Stephen Vizinczey's novel *In Praise of Older Women* (1966). There, it is credited to 'Anon. Hungarian'.

5 It is a good thing not to put confidence in observations until they have been checked against theory.

Unsourced. Also known in a French form, sarcastically applied by graduates of the Napoleonic Grandes Écoles to the graduates of the post-war, Gaullist École Nationale d'Administration (ENA): '*Ça marche en pratique, mais en théorie ...?* [Well, it works in practice, but will it work in theory?]'

6 It is now proved beyond doubt that cigarettes are the biggest single cause of statistics.

Graffito contributed to BBC Radio *Quote ... Unquote* (19 June 1980). In *Reader's Digest* (December 1961), a similar observation was attributed to Fletcher Knebel (1911–).

7 I told you I was sick.

Epitaph on a hypochondriac – from the southern US – remembered on BBC Radio *Quote ... Unquote* (22 December 1981). In January 1994 it was reported that the dying wish of Keith Woodward of Shrivenham, Wiltshire, had been to have a tombstone bearing the joke 'I told them I was ill'. However, parish councillors ordered the message to be removed.

8 It pays to advertise.

We are probably looking for an origin in the 1870s to 1890s when advertising really took off in America (as in Britain). Indeed, Benham (1960) lists an 'American saying *c.*1870' – 'The man who on his trade relies must either bust or advertise' – and notes that 'Sir Thomas Lipton [d.1931] is said to have derived inspiration and success through seeing this couplet in New York about 1875'. Ezra Pound wrote in a letter to his father in 1908 about the launch of his poems: 'Sound trumpet. Let rip the drum & swatt the big bassoon. It pays to advertise.' Cole Porter entitled one of his earliest songs 'It Pays To Advertise', in which he alluded to a number of advertising lines that were current when he was a student at Yale (*c.*1912).

1 It's not the heat, it's the humidity.

One of S.J. Perelman's prose pieces had the punning title 'It's Not the Heat, It's the Cupidity'. What was the allusion there? Presumably the same as contained in the title of a revue put on by Combined Services Entertainment in the Far East (*c.*1947) and featuring the young actor Kenneth Williams. It was called *It's Not So Much the Heat, It's the Humidity*, though in his memoirs he simply calls it *Not So Much the Heat*. Whatever the form, it was a common expression in the Second World War.

There is a case, however, for supporting an earlier Anglo-American origin. In the first paragraph of *Sam the Sudden* (1925), P.G. Wodehouse describes the inhabitants of New York on a late August afternoon: '[one half] crawling about and asking those they met if this was hot enough for them, the other maintaining that what they minded was not so much the heat as the humidity.' In *Are You a Bromide?* (1906) by Gelett Burgess, the remark is given as the sort of thing a bromide (someone addicted to clichés) would say.

2 It's not the wild, ecstatic leap across that I deplore. It is the weary trudge home.

From something called 'Double Beds versus Single Beds', quoted in *PDMQ* (1971). Derek Parker recalls the comedian Derek Roy saying something similar in his act at the Palace Theatre, Plymouth, in 1957: 'It's not the quick dash over – it's the slow drag back.'

3 It's worse than a crime, it's a blunder!

There is no doubting that this was said about the execution of the Duc d'Enghien in 1804. Napoleon, suspecting the Duc of being involved in royalist conspiracies against him, had him found and executed, an act that hardened opinion against the French Emperor. But who said it? Comte Boulay de la Meurthe (1761–1840) was credited with the remark in C.-A. Sainte-Beuve's *Nouveaux Lundis* (1870), but among other names sometimes linked to it are Talleyrand, Joseph Fouch and Napoleon himself.

In French, the remark is usually rendered as: '*C'est pire qu'un crime; c'est une faute!*' Pearson (1937) has what he seems to think is the more correct translation: 'It is more than a crime; it is a political fault', from the *Memoirs of Fouché*.

4 It takes seventy-two muscles to frown, but only thirteen to smile.

A saying included in Celia Haddon, *The Yearbook of Comfort and Joy* (1991). 'This reminder,' she says, 'came from a newsletter sent to traffic wardens.' But it is quite old and probably of American origin. Keith Waterhouse, *Billy Liar* (1959) has it as a quotation on a calendar: 'It takes sixty muscles to frown, but only thirteen to smile. Why waste energy?'

5 It takes two to tango.

From the song with the title 'Takes Two to Tango' by Al Hoffman and Dick Manning (1952). The origin of a modern proverbial expression.

6 It was the wrong kind of snow.

The archetypal limp excuse, now a part of British folklore. In *The Independent* (16 February 1991), it was ascribed to Terry Worrall, British Rail's director of operations. He had been attempting to explain why snow had disrupted services, even though a 'big chill' had been correctly forecast.

The other most often quoted excuse for disruption on British railways is '[there were] leaves on the line'. In the autumn damp falling leaves have been known to form a layer on the rails and thus hinder the safe passage of wheels over them. The excuse was cited as though it was already an established one in *The Guardian* (22 December 1984).

7 I was much younger in those days.

The distinguished actress had been so impressed by the flattering work of this particular photographer that she engaged him again to take her picture. 'Oh dear,' she remarked, looking at the new prints when they were finished, 'you make me look older than last time.' The photographer was the quintessence of tact: 'Ah yes,' said he, 'but I was much younger in those days.' Heard in April 1994. But who were the original participants? Possibly Marlene Dietrich and the cinematographer Hal Mohr. When they were working together on the film *Rancho Notorious* (1952), Dietrich asked why she wasn't looking as good on the film as when the same cinematographer had shot her in *Destry Rides Again* thirteen years before. Mohr replied that he was, of course, thirteen years older.

1 I was only obeying orders.

The Charter of the International Military Tribunal at Nuremberg (1945–6) specifically excluded the traditional German defence of 'superior orders'. But the plea was, nevertheless, much advanced. This approach was summed up in the catchphrase 'I was only obeying orders', often used grotesquely in parody of such buck-passing. As early as 1940, Rex Harrison was saying in the British film *Night Train to Munich*: 'Captain Marsen was only obeying orders.' Kenneth Mars as a mad, Nazi-fixated playwright in *The Producers* (US, 1967) says, 'I only followed orders!'

Not that everyone seemed aware of the parodying. From *The New York Times* (6 July 1983): 'Herbert Bechtold, a German-born officer in the [US] counter-intelligence who became [the "handler" of Klaus Barbie, the Nazi war criminal] was asked if he questioned the morality of hiring a man like Barbie by the United States. "I am not in a position to pass judgement on that," Mr Bechtold replied, "I was just following orders".'

2 I went to New Zealand but it was closed.

This is a joke that gets rediscovered every so often. The Beatles found it in the 1960s; slightly before then, Anna Russell, the musical comedienne, said it on one of her records. It has also been attributed to Clement Freud. But William Franklyn, son of the Antipodean actor, Leo Franklyn, says that his father was saying it in the 1920s. Perhaps W.C. Fields began it all by saying 'Last week, I went to Philadelphia, but it was closed' about the same time (if indeed he did). This last attribution comes from Richard J. Anobile, *Godfrey Daniels* (1975).

3 I wish I were a fish
In the Aegean Sea
Instead of which, here is my niche
In London, being me.

Verse on a sampler in the Kay-Shuttleworth collection at the National Trust property Gawthorpe Hall in Lancashire. It is signed 'Frances Kay 1961' though whether this is the name of the poet and/or the needleworker is not clear.

4 I write in order to find out what I think.

The kind of thing that any writer might say. The British novelist Ian McEwan in *The Times* (27 June 1987): 'Writers divide between those who simply write to find out exactly what it is that they think, and those who have to think of the sentence first, then put it down, and constantly agonize about the gap between the thought and the language that's going to embody the thought.'

However, there is also this line, which really says the same thing, in E.M. Forster's *Aspects of the Novel* (1927): 'That old lady in the anecdote ... was not so much angry as contemptuous ... "How can I tell what I think till I see what I say?"' Which may be the same as Graham Wallas, *The Art of Thought* (1926): 'The little girl had the making of a poet in her who, being told to be sure of her meaning before she spoke, said, "How can I know what I think till I see what I say?"'

Some near-misses and allusions: Alphonse Daudet has a character in *Numa Roumestan* (1881) say: '*Quand je ne parle pas, je ne pense pas.*' To the poet Louis MacNeice is attributed: 'How do I know what I think till I hear what I say.' And when US journalist James Reston died in 1995 it was recalled what he said when his newspaper did not appear because of a strike: 'How can I know what I think if I can't read what I write?'

5 A Kestrel for a Knave.

The novel with this title by Barry Hines (1968) – filmed simply as *Kes* (UK, 1969) – tells of a boy misfit who learns about life through training his kestrel hawk. The title comes from *The Boke of St Albans* (1486) and it is also in a Harleian manuscript: 'An Eagle for an Emperor, a Gyrfalcon for a King; a Peregrine for a Prince, a Saker for a Knight, a Merlin for a Lady; a Goshawk for a Yeoman, a Sparrowhawk for a Priest, a Musket for a Holy water Clerk, a Kestrel for a Knave.'

6 The Killing Fields.

Title of a film (UK 1984) concerning the mass-murders carried out by the Communist Khmer Rouge, under Pol Pot, in Cambodia between 1975 and 1978, when possibly three million people were killed. The mass graves were discovered in April 1979. In the film the phrase was seen to refer, literally, to paddy fields where prisoners were forced to work and where many of them were callously shot. The film was based on an article 'The Death and Life of Dith Pran' by Sydney Schanberg, published in the *New York Times* Magazine (20 January 1980), which tells of the journalist's quest for a reunion with his former assistant.

The article has the phrase towards the beginning: 'In July of 1975 – two months after Pran and I had been forced apart on April 20 – an American diplomat who had known Pran wrote me a consoling letter. The diplomat, who had served in Phnom Penh, knew the odds of anyone emerging safely from a country that was being transformed into a society of terror and purges and "killing fields".' So it appears that the coinage is due to the unnamed diplomat.

Compare the phrase 'killing ground(s)' which has entered the military vocabulary as a strategic term for an area into which you manoeuvre the enemy before finishing them off and which has been current since the Second World War. In a non-military sense, the phrase was used by Rudyard Kipling in his poem 'The Rhyme of the Three Sealers' (1893) about seal-hunting.

1 The king is dead – long live the king!
Le roi est mort, vive le roi!

This declaration was first used in 1461 on the death of King Charles VII of France. Julia S.H. Pardoe in her *Louis the Fourteenth and the Court of France in the Seventeenth Century* (1847) describes how that king's death (in 1715) was announced by the captain of the bodyguard from a window of the state apartment: 'Raising his truncheon above his head, he broke it in the centre, and throwing the pieces among the crowd exclaimed in a loud voice, "*Le Roi est mort*!" Then seizing another staff, he flourished it in the air as he shouted, "*Vive le Roi*".' The custom ended with the death of Louis XVIII (1824). The expression is now used allusively to denote a smooth transition of power of any sort. From *The Independent* (25 January 1988): 'The cry went up: "The Liberal Party is dead. Long live the Liberal Party." It was hard to distinguish the wake from the marriage feast.'

2 *Laborare est orare.*

In full *Orare est laborare, laborare est orare* [to pray is to work, to work is to pray], this is the ancient motto of the Benedictine order. It has also been used by various families and institutions (the London Borough of Willesden, not least).

3 Labour's Double Whammy.

During the 1992 British general election, the Conservative Party introduced a poster showing a boxer wearing two enormous boxing gloves. One was labelled '1. More tax' and the other '2. Higher prices'. The overall slogan was 'LABOUR'S DOUBLE WHAMMY'. This caused a good deal of puzzlement in Britain, though the concept of the 'double whammy' had been well known in the US since the 1950s. One source suggested that it had come from the Dick Tracy comic strip in which it referred to a death-ray glare emitted by one of the characters. Another stated that cartoonist Al Capp introduced the notion in his 'Li'l Abner' strip – the character Evil-Eye Fleegle boasted a 'double whammy ... which I hopes I never hafta use'. In other words, a double whammy is a powerful blow.

4 The less things change, the more they remain the same.

'Old Sicilian proverb', quoted in Richard Condon, *Prizzi's Honour* (1982). Clearly based on *plus ça change, plus c'est la même chose* [the more it changes, the more it is the same thing] – usually ascribed to the French novelist and journalist, Alphonse Karr (1808–90) in *Les Guêpes* (January 1849). *See* 326:3.

5 Life is just a bowl of cherries.

Title of song (1931), words by Lew Brown, music by Ray Henderson, in the musical *Scandals of 1931*. Origin of the modern proverbial expression.

6 Life's a bitch, and then you die.

This is a popular saying of untraced origin, though probably North American. A development of it, known both in the US and the UK, is 'Life's a bitch, *you marry a bitch*, and then you die'. Citations in print are not very plentiful. Working backwards: during the summer of 1991, the Body Shop chain in the UK was promoting sun-tan products with a window-display under the punning slogan 'Life's a beach – and then you fry'. A caption to an article in the London *Observer* (23 September 1990) about frozen food was the equally punning 'Life's a binge and then you diet'. In Caryl Churchill's play about the City, *Serious Money* (first performed March 1987), we find: 'I thought I'd be extremely rich./You can't be certain what you'll get./I've heard the young say Life's a bitch.' The earliest citation found so far comes from *The Sunday Times* of 21 December 1986: 'Life is a bitch, then you die. So says the pilot of a flying fuel tank who, last week, took off to circumnavigate the globe with his girlfriend.'

Other suggested origins – Woody Allen's film *Love and Death* (1975) and the 1983 re-make of Jean-Luc Godard's *À Bout de Souffle* (in which the Jean-Paul Belmondo character originally died saying, '*La vie – c'est dégeulasse* [Life's a drag])' – have not proved fruitful sources.

'Life's a *beach*' seems to have taken on a life of its own as a slogan, especially in Australia, but probably developed from 'Life's a bitch', rather than the other way round.

Attention might be drawn to *An Essay on Woman* by 'Pego Borewell Esq.' which was published in about 1763 as a bawdy parody of Alexander Pope's *An Essay on Man*. It is thought to have been written by the politician John 'Friend of Liberty' Wilkes and one Thomas Potter, working in some form of collaboration. Wilkes was expelled from parliament on account of it. Interestingly, the poem starts like this:

> Let us (since life can little more supply
> Than just a few good fucks, and then we die)
> Expatiate freely ...

Something of the same spirit comes through here.

1 Little Jack Horner
Sat in the corner,
Eating a Christmas pie.
He put in his thumb,
And pulled out a plum,
And said, What a good boy am I?

A tradition has grown up that in the sixteenth century, at the time of the Dissolution of the Monasteries, the Abbot of Glastonbury sent his steward Jack Horner to London. In an attempt to appease King Henry VIII, Horner was bearing a Christmas pie containing the title deeds of twelve manors. But Horner 'put in his thumb' and pulled out the other kind of 'plum' – the deeds to the Manor of Mells in Somerset – and put them to his own use. A Thomas Horner did take up residence in Mells shortly after the Dissolution and his descendants lived there until late in the twentieth century (source: Iona & Peter Opie, *The Oxford Dictionary of Nursery Rhymes*, 1951).

2 Lonely Are the Brave.

The film (US 1962) with this title was based on a novel by Edward Abbey called *Brave Cowboy*. Not a quotation, apparently.

3 The mail must get/go through.

A slogan of probable North American origin – as indicated by the use of the word 'mail' rather than 'post'. Though 'Royal Mail' is still very much used in the UK, the older term 'post' predominates. There is no citation of the precise slogan being used in Britain. The Longman *Chronicle of America* reports (as for 13 April 1860) the arrival in Sacramento, California, of the first Pony Express delivery – a satchel with 49 letters and three newspapers that had left St Joseph, Missouri, eleven days previously. 'The pace is an astounding improvement over the eight-week wagon convoys. But the brave riders, who vow "the mail must get through" despite all kinds of dangers ranging from hostile Indians on the prairie to storms in the mountains, may only be a temporary link [as the Iron Horse makes progress].'

The *Chronicle* does not provide a solid basis for invoking the slogan at this point but the connection with Pony Express seems very likely. It would be good to have an actual citation from the period. Raymond and Mary Settle in *The Story of the Pony Express* (1955) point out that the organization flourished only about 1860–1, soon being overtaken by telegraph and railroad, and add: 'A schedule, as exacting as that of a railroad timetable, was set up, and each rider was under rigid orders to keep it, day and night, fair weather or foul. Allowance was made for nothing, not even attack by Indians. Their motto was, "The mail must go through", and it did except in a very few, rare cases.'

4 Mairzy doats and dozy doats.

One of the most impenetrable graffiti jokes was (at least on first seeing it), the scribbled addition to a notice in Liverpool proclaiming: 'Mersey Docks and Harbour Board ... and little lambs eat ivy.' This was recorded in 1944. The graffiti-writer had cleverly spotted that a Scouser (Liverpudlian) would pronounce Mersey, 'mairzy' and that the rhythm of 'Mersey Docks and Harbour Board' exactly matched the first line of a nonsense song popular in Britain and America at the time called 'Mairzy Doats and Dozy Doats (Mares Eat Oats and Does Eat Oats)'. It went:

I know a ditty nutty as a fruit cake
Goofy as a goon and silly as a loon ...

Mairzy doats and dozy doats
And liddle lamzy divey.
A kiddley divey too,
Wouldn't you?

The song was 'written' by Milton Drake, Al Hoffman and Jerry Livingston but, as the Opies point out in their *Oxford Dictionary of Nursery Rhymes* (1951), there is a 'catch' which, when said quickly, appears to be in Latin:

In fir tar is,
In oak none is,
In mud eels are,
In clay none are.
Goat eat ivy
Mare eat oats.

Say the Opies: 'The joke may be traced back 500 years to a medical manuscript in Henry VI's time.'

5 A man's gotta do what a man's gotta do.

A statement of obligation, as in film Westerns. Partridge/*Catch Phrases* dates popular use of this saying from *c.*1945, but its origin remains untraced, although an early example occurs in John Steinbeck's novel *The Grapes of Wrath*, Chap. 18 (1939): 'I know this – a man got to do what he got to do'. The film *Shane* (US 1953), based on a novel by Jack Shaeffer, is sometimes said to contain the line, but does not (nor does the book). The John Wayne film *Stagecoach* (1939) does not include it either, as some sources state. By the 1970s, several songs had been recorded with the title.

6 A man who is his own lawyer has a fool for a client.

Proverb first recorded in Philadelphia (1809). Has also

been ascribed to Samuel Johnson, probably inaccurately.

1 Marriage is too important to be treated like a love affair.

Alluded to by Katharine Whitehorn in *The Observer* (1 March 1992). She obtained it from Gillian Tindall, but otherwise the quotation – if it is one – remains untraced.

2 May you live in interesting times.

Robert F. Kennedy, speaking in Cape Town, South Africa, on 7 June 1966, said: 'There is a Chinese curse which says, "May he live in interesting times". Like it or not, we live in interesting times ...' This has since become a very popular observation, almost a cliché, though any Chinese source remains untraced.

3 Miss Buss and Miss Beale
Cupid's darts do not feel.
How different from us,
Miss Beale and Miss Buss.

Of Frances Mary Buss (1827–94), headmistress of the North London Collegiate School, and Dorothea Beale (1831–1906), principal of the Ladies' College, Cheltenham, and original sponsor of what is now St Hilda's College, Oxford. Both were pioneers of women's education. Composed *c.*1884.

4 A more efficient conduct of the war.

A phrase from the First World War, though its precise origin remains untraced. A.J.P. Taylor in his *English History 1914–45* (1965) has: 'The Coalition government, which Asquith announced on 26 May 1915, claimed to demonstrate national unity and to promote a more efficient conduct of the war.' Writing of the following year (1916) in *Clementine Churchill* (1979), Mary Soames has 'more vigorous and efficient prosecution of the war'. Is it also sometimes given as 'more energetic' conduct?

5 *Morituri te salutant.*
We who are about to die salute you.

(Literally, 'those who are ...'). Words addressed to the Emperor by gladiators in ancient Rome on entering the arena. The practice seems to have first been mentioned in Suetonius, *Claudius*. In time, the phrase was extended to anyone facing difficulty, and then ironically so.

6 Most Gracious Queen, we thee implore
To go away and sin no more,
But if that effort be too great,
To go away at any rate.

Epigram on Queen Caroline, quoted in *The Diary and Correspondence of Lord Colchester* (1861, letter from Francis Burton, 15 November 1820). Caroline of Brunswick was the estranged wife and queen of George IV.

7 Mr Gladstone chewed each mouthful of food thirty-two times before swallowing.

William Ewart Gladstone (1809–98) was four times British Liberal Prime Minister and dominated the political scene during the second half of the nineteenth century. Most famously, he was held up as an example to countless generations of children as the man who chewed his food properly, but it is not clear how he became a role model in this regard. In the BBC TV programme *As I Remember* (30 April 1967), Baroness Asquith (Lady Violet Bonham Carter) recalled having had a meal with Gladstone, when she was a little girl, at which he did no such thing. Quite the reverse in fact: he bolted his food.

Confirmation of this deplorable fact also came in a lecture given by George Lyttelton at Hawarden (Gladstone's old home) on 24 June 1955: 'More than one lynx-eyed young spectator [has discovered] that Mr Gladstone did *not* chew every mouthful thirty-two times ... though I am not sure that Mr Gladstone himself might not have made some weighty and useful observations on the common and deplorable gap between principle and practice.'

Presumably, nannies simply chose this towering figure as an example to their charges, simply because he was there, rather as, a little earlier, Napoleon had been selected as the figure of evil who would punish them if they misbehaved. One wonders whether Queen Victoria might not have been a more inspiring person to evoke – or, perhaps, even to contemplate her doing such a physical thing as eating was considered to be indelicate?

8 A mugwump is a sort of bird that sits on a fence with his mug on one side and his wump on the other.

A *mugquomp* in the language of the Algonquin (American Indians) describes a great chief or person of high rank (and was so recorded by 1663). In 1884, however, the word was popularized and used to describe 'the little men attempting to be big chiefs' who felt unable to support James Blaine as the Republican candidate for the US presidency and transferred their allegiance to the Democrat, Grover Cleveland. Hence, in American political parlance, the word mugwump came to describe a 'bolter' or someone who held himself self-importantly aloof. More generally, it has been used to describe a fool.

The above definition of the mugwump as a bird derives from the *Blue Earth* (Minnesota) *Post* in the early 1930s.

1 My eyes are dim
I cannot see
I have not brought my specs with me.

From the traditional British song, 'In the Quartermaster's Stores', known by at least the 1930s. A version 'with words and music adapted by Elton Box, Desmond Cox and Bert Reed' was copyrighted in 1940.

2 My friend's friend is my enemy.

This expression was invoked, for example, at the time of the Suez crisis (1956). It might have been President Nasser of Egypt referring to the United States (the friend) and Israel (the friend's friend). There seem to be many precedents. Mencken (1942) lists a legal maxim, 'The companion of my companion is not my companion (*socii mei socius meus socius non est*)', but compare the French proverb, 'The enemy of my enemy is my friend', and the Flemish proverb, 'The friends of my friends are my friends'.

3 My mother said
That I never should
Play with the gypsies
In the wood
Because she said
That if I did
She'd smack my bottom
With a saucepan lid!

Nursery rhyme recorded *c.*1875. There is more than one version but none from much before the 1860s. Hence, *My Mother Said I Never Should*, the title of a play (1989) by Charlotte Keatley.

4 My name is George Nathaniel Curzon,
I am a most superior person.

Written by an anonymous hand in *The Masque of Balliol* (*c.*1870). Hence, *Superior Person*, the title of Kenneth Rose's biography of Lord Curzon (1969).

5 The Navy's here!

On the night of 16 February 1940, 299 British seamen were freed from captivity aboard the German ship *Altmark* as it lay in a Norwegian fjord. The destroyer *Cossack*, under the command of Captain Philip Vian, had managed to locate the German supply ship and a boarding party discovered that British prisoners were locked in its hold. As Vian described it, Lieut. Bradwell Turner, the leader of the boarding party, called out: 'Any British down there?' 'Yes, we're all British,' came the reply. 'Come on up then,' he said, 'The Navy's here.'

The identity of the speaker is in doubt, however. Correspondence in *The Sunday Telegraph* (February/March 1980) revealed that Turner denied he had said it, that Leading Seaman James Harper was another candidate, and that Lieut. Johnny Parker was the most likely person to have said it (and he had certainly claimed that he did).

The Times (19 February 1940) gave a version from the lips of one of those who had been freed and who had actually heard the exchange: 'John Quigley of London said that the first they knew of their rescue was when they heard a shout of "Any Englishmen here?" They shouted "Yes" and immediately came the cheering words, "Well, the Navy is here." Quigley said – "We were all hoarse with cheering when we heard those words".'

6 Nice legs, shame about her face.

The title of a briefly popular song recorded by The Monks in 1979 gave rise to a format phrase which appeared, for example, in a take-off by BBC TV's *Not the Nine O'Clock News* team – 'Nice video, shame about the song' – and in a slogan for Hofmeister lager – 'Great lager, shame about the ...' (both in 1982). At about the same time, Listerine ran an advertisement with the slogan 'Nice Face, Shame About the Breath'. Other examples include a headline to an *Independent* piece on the hundredth birthday of the 'The Red Flag': 'Good tune, shame about the words' (9 February 1989); a headline from *The Observer* (9 April 1989): 'Nice prints, shame about the books'. It is also used loosely: 'Victoria Wood is almost perfect. Lovely lady, pity about the voice' (*Cosmopolitan*, February 1987); and the headline to an *Observer* report on puny car horns in January 1989 was: 'NICE CAR, BUT WHAT A VOICE!'

7 The noise and the people!

Describing what it was like to be in battle, a certain Captain Strahan exclaimed, 'Oh, my dear fellow, the noise ... and the people!' According to the *ODQ* (1979), quoting the *Hudson Review* (winter 1951), he said it after the Battle of Bastogne in 1944. Various correspondents have suggested it was earlier in the war than this, however. Roy T. Kendall wrote (1986): 'I heard this phrase used, in a humorous manner, during the early part of 1942. It was related to me as having been said by a young Guards officer, newly returned from

Dunkirk, who on being asked what it was like used the expression: the inference being, a blasé attitude to the dangers and a disdain of the common soldiery he was forced to mix with.' Tony Bagnall Smith added that the Guards officer was still properly dressed and equipped when he said it, and that his reply was: 'My dear, the noise and the people – how they smelt!'

The *ODQ* (1992) appears to have come round to the earlier use regarding Dunkirk, in the form 'The noise, my dear! And the people!' It finds it already being quoted in Anthony Rhodes, *Sword of Bone*, Chap. 22 (1942).

1 *Non, je ne regrette rien.*
No, I regret nothing.

Title of song (1960), words by Michael Vaucaire, music by Charles Dumont, popularized by Edith Piaf (1915–63). A favourite song of many people because, like 'My Way', it seems to assert one's individuality. Broadcaster – and at that time satirist – David Frost chose it as his favourite record on BBC Radio's *Desert Island Discs* in 1963. On 23 April 1993 Britain's Chancellor of the Exchequer, Norman Lamont, used the phrase with regard to his handling of the economy, when speaking during the Newbury by-election. The Conservatives lost the seat and he was sacked on 27 May.

2 No one likes us – we don't care.

From the new lyrics sung by fans of Millwall football club to the tune of Rod Stewart's song 'Sailing'. Millwall fans are famous in London for their vocal and physical forcefulness. *No One Likes Us, We Don't Care* was, consequently, the title given to a Channel 4 TV documentary about them in January 1990.

3 Not As a Stranger.

The title of a novel (1954) by Morton Thompson and the film (US, 1955) appear not to be quoting anything. The song which came out of the film goes, 'Not as a stranger, dear, but my own true love ...'.

4 Oh, wash me in the water
That you washed the colonel's daughter in
And I shall be whiter
Than the whitewash on the wall.

Song popular among British troops in France during the First World War. This would appear to be a parody of (or at least inspired by) one of the Sankey and Moody hymns, 'The Blood of the Lamb', which has the chorus:

Wash me in the Blood of the Lamb
And I shall be whiter than snow!
(Whiter than the snow!
Whiter than the snow!)
Wash me in the Blood of the Lamb
And I shall be whiter than snow, (the snow!)

5 Old Noah once he built the Ark
There's one more river to cross.
And patched it up with hick'ry bark
There's one more river to cross.
One more river, and that's the river of Jordan,
One more river
There's one more river to cross.

From the traditional song 'One More River to Cross' (also known as 'Noah's Ark'), which refers to the Jordan. Hence, *One More River*, the title of a film (US, 1934) based on John Galsworthy's 1933 novel *Over the River* (which was how the film was known in the UK).

6 Once aboard the lugger and the girl is mine.

In 1908, A.S.M. Hutchinson (1879–1971) called a novel *Once Aboard the Lugger – the History of George and Mary*, but he was merely alluding to an established 'male catchphrase either joyously or derisively jocular', as Partridge/*Catch Phrases* notes. It may have come originally from a late Victorian melodrama – either *My Jack and Dorothy* by Ben Landeck (*c.*1890) or from a passage in *The Gypsy Farmer* by John Benn Johnstone (d.1891): 'I want you to assist me in forcing her on board the lugger; once there, I'll frighten her into marriage.' The phrase also occurred later in the music-hall song 'On the Good Ship Yacki-Hicki-Doo-La', written and composed by Billy Merson in 1918. Benham (1948) has a different version, as often. According to him 'Once aboard the lugger and all is well' was said to have been an actor's gag in *Black Eyed Susan*, a nautical melodrama (*c.*1830).

7 One flew east, one flew west
One flew over the cuckoo's nest.

Nursery rhyme (chiefly known in this version and in the US). Hence, *One Flew Over the Cuckoo's Nest*, title of the novel (1962) by Ken Kesey (film US, 1975).

8 One, two,
Buckle my shoe;
Three, four,
Knock at the door.

Children's counting rhyme, first recorded *c.*1821 in this form. Hence, *One Two Buckle My Shoe*, title of a novel (1940) by Agatha Christie.

1 **On Ilkla Moor Bah t'at.**

The most famous – and impenetrable – of Yorkshire songs comes in two versions. The older, said to have been written by Thomas Clark to the hymn tune 'Cranbrook' in 1805, was sung in a spirited way:

1 Wheear baht thee bahn when I been gone?
[repeated three times]
Wheear baht?
On Ilkla Moor bah t'at *[repeated twice]*
Bah t'at, bah t'at.

2 Then thou wilt catch a cold and dee
In Lonnenfuit bah t'buit *[repeated twice]*
Bah t'buit, bah t'buit.

3 Then we shall cum and bury thee
Inn Saltruble Docks bah t'socks *[repeated twice]*
Bah t'socks, bah t'socks.

4 Then worms'll cum and eat up thee
On Ikla Moor bah t'at *[etc.]*

5 Then doocks'll cum and eat them worms
In Lonnenfuit bah t'buit *[etc.]*

6 Then we shall cum and eat them doocks
In Saltruble Docks bah t'socks *[etc.]*

7 Then we shall catch th'auld cold and dee
On Ilka Moor bah t'at *[etc.]*

(Salter Hebble Docks and Luddenden Foot are canal points on the Hebble and Calder rivers near Halifax.)

A later (and now more popular) version, is sung more dolefully. It has a second verse, beginning 'I've been a courting Mary Jane', and a final verse sung thus:

Then we shall all 'av 'etten thee
That's how we get our owen back
This is the moral of this tale
Doan't go a-courtin Mary Jane.

This version was reputedly composed on an outing to Ilkley Moor by the choir of Ebenezer Chapel, Halifax, in 1886. The meaning of the old saga is roughly this: 'You've been on Ilkley Moor without a hat, courting Mary Jane. You'll catch your death of cold, and we shall have to bury you. The worms will eat you up, and the ducks will eat up the worms. Then we shall eat the ducks, so we shall have eaten you.'

2 **The only difference between men and boys is the price of their toys.**

This modern proverbial expression has been credited both to Liberace and to Joyce Brothers in the US. A different version has been reported in the UK: writer Derek Robinson talking in 1990 about the making of a TV version of his novel *Piece of Cake* said he noticed that everyone was fascinated by the Spitfire aircraft. All work would come to a stop whenever they were being used. A technician standing by remarked: 'You can tell the men from the boys by the size of their toys.'

3 **The opera ain't/isn't over till the fat lady sings.**

Relatively few modern proverbs have caught on in a big way but, of those that have, this one has produced sharp division over its origin. It is also used with surprising vagueness and lack of perception. If it is a warning 'not to count your chickens before they are hatched', it is too often simply employed to express a generalized view that 'it isn't over till it's over'.

So how did the saying come about? A report in the *Washington Post* (13 June 1978) had this version: 'One day three years ago [i.e., 1975], Ralph Carpenter, who was then Texas Tech's sports information director, declared to the press box contingent in Austin, "The rodeo ain't over till the bull riders ride." Stirred to that deep insight, San Antonio sports editor Dan Cook countered with, "The opera ain't over till the fat lady sings".'

However, proof that this 'opera' version is merely a derivative of some earlier American expression appears to be provided by *A Dictionary of American Proverbs* (1992), which lists both 'The game's not over until the last man strikes out' and 'Church is not out 'til they sing'. Bartlett (1992) finds in *Southern Words and Sayings* (1976) by F.R. and C.R. Smith, the expression 'Church ain't out till the fat lady sings'.

4 **Our Farnham which art in Hendon, Harrow be thy Name. Thy Kingston come. Thy Wimbledon, in Erith as it is in Heston. Give us this day our Leatherhead. And forgive us our Westminsters. As we forgive them that Westminster against us. And lead us not into Thames Ditton; But deliver us from Ealing: For thine is the Kingston, the Purley, and the Crawley, For Iver and Iver. Crouch End.**

This 'Home Counties' version of the Lord's Prayer was quoted in my book *Say No More!* (1987). Correspondence in the magazine *Oxford Today* (Hilary/Trinity terms 1990) produced a number of variations and a date of composition somewhere in the 1930s, but no author. Peter Hay in *Business Anecdotes* (1988) includes a faintly similar parody written in 1930s America by a Ford motors worker before unionization. It begins:

Our Father, who art in Dearborn, Henry be thine name.
Let payday come. Thy will be done in Fordson as it is in Highland Park ...

1 [An] outright romp in which the couples not only embrace throughout the dance but, flushed and palpitating, whirl about in the posture of copulation.

On the waltz, when it was introduced to England from Germany in 1812. Quoted in *The Frank Muir Book* (1976). Unverified.

2 A picture is worth a thousand words.

This famous saying, which occurs, for example, in the song 'If', popularized by Bread in 1971, is sometimes said to be a Chinese proverb. Bartlett (1980) listed it as such in the form 'One picture is worth more than ten thousand words' and compared this with what Turgenev says in *Fathers and Sons* (1862): 'A picture shows me at a glance what it takes dozens of pages of a book to expound.'

But *CODP* points out that it originated in an American paper *Printers' Ink* (8 December 1921) in the form 'One look is worth a thousand words'. It was later reprinted in the better known form in the same paper (10 March 1927) and there ascribed by its actual author, Frederick R. Barnard, to a Chinese source ('so that people would take it seriously', as he told Burton Stevenson in 1948).

3 A place within the meaning of the act.

The *ODQ* (1979) merely stated that this was from 'the Betting Act', ignoring the fact that there was more than one such. In fact, the phrase comes from Section 2 of the 1853 Betting Act (which banned off-course betting on race horses).

4 A politician is an animal who can sit on a fence and yet keep both ears to the ground.

Quoted in Mencken (1942). A commonly evoked criticism – from *The Observer* (8 September 1996): '[Archbishop Robert Runcie] was once described in a speech in the General Synod by the then Bishop of Leicester as a man who enjoyed "sitting on the fence with both ears to the ground". It helped him to accommodate both sides in every argument, but in the long term had the effect of destroying trust in his own statements.'

5 A politician is a person who approaches every subject with an open mouth.

Another of those quotations that floats continually in search of a definite source and could have been said by anyone and everybody. Was it Oscar Wilde? Or Adlai Stevenson? Or Arthur Goldberg? The first two sources are given by different contributors to *Kindly Sit Down*, a compilation of after-dinner speech jokes by politicians (1983) collected by Jack Aspinwall. Writing the foreword, Margaret Thatcher put this: 'It was after all, the late Governor Adlai Stevenson who defined a politician as one who approached every question with an open mouth.' Unfortunately, another of the book's contributors, Roger Moate, ascribed it rather to Oscar Wilde.

PDMQ (1971) gives Stevenson as the source, adding Goldberg (on diplomats) in 1980. Earlier Leon A. Harris in *The Fine Art of Political Wit* (1966) had plumped for Stevenson. In the absence of any hard evidence, one feels inclined to award the palm to Stevenson.

6 *Post coitum omne animal triste est.*
Every creature is sad after sexual intercourse.

A post-classical Latin proverb, according to *ODQ* (1979) – on the grounds that it does not appear in classical texts. However, Laurence Sterne in *Tristram Shandy* (1662) ascribes it to Aristotle, presumably because Aristotle did write: 'Why do young men, on first having sexual intercourse, afterwards hate those with whom they have just been associated?' The Roman author Pliny also wrote: 'Man alone experiences regret after first having intercourse.'

7 The postillion has been struck by lightning.

Said to be a useful expression from an old phrase book. Hence, *A Postillion Struck by Lightning*, title of the first volume of Dirk Bogarde's autobiography (1977). Describing a holiday in early childhood (the 1920s presumably), he mentions an old phrase book (seemingly dated 1898), which contained lines like: 'This muslin is too thin, have you something thicker?'; 'My leg, arm, foot, elbow, nose, finger is broken'; and 'The postillion has been struck by lightning'. Which phrase book is this? Not *English as She is Spoke* (*see* 28:2), in which the 'postillion' line does not occur.

A writer in *The Times* (30 July 1983) noted: '"Look, the front postillion has been struck by lightning" ... supposed to feature in a Scandinavian phrase book: but it may well be apocryphal.' In the third volume of Bogarde's autobiography, *An Orderly Man* (1983), describing the writing of the first, he says: 'My sister-in-law, Cilla, on a wet camping holiday somewhere in northern France ... once sent me a postcard on which she said ... she had been forced to learn a little more French than the phrase "Help! My postillion has been struck by lightning!" I took the old phrase for the title of my book.'

A similarly untraced Russian/English phrasebook is said to have included: 'Don't bother to unsaddle the horses, lightning has struck the innkeeper.'

1 A pound of tea at one and three
And a pot of raspberry jam,
Two new-laid eggs, a dozen pegs,
And a pound of rashers of ham.

Eleanor Farjeon in her childhood autobiography *A Nursery in the Nineties* (1935) relates how she had to learn a 'rather silly poem' about a girl who tries to remember her shopping list and grows steadily more muddled. In those days children were expected to perform at parties. Farjeon had to recite 'A pound of tea', but soon got mixed up, gave up in despair and ran to her mother in tears. In fact, the sex of the child is not apparent. The author of 'Going on an Errand', as it is usually called, has not been traced. The full text may be found in *This England's Book of Parlour Poetry* (1989).

2 Power to the people.

A slogan of the Black Panther movement in the US. Shouted, and with clenched fist raised, this cry was publicized by the Black Panthers' leader, Bobby Seale, in Oakland, California, July 1969. Also used by other dissident groups, as illustrated by Eldridge Cleaver: 'We say "All Power to the People" – Black Power for Black People, White Power for White People, Brown Power for Brown People, Red Power for Red People, and X Power for any group we've left out.' It was this somewhat generalized view of 'People Power' that John Lennon appeared to promote in the 1971 song 'Power to the People (Right on!)'

3 Pray, Mrs Mouse, are you within?
Heigh ho! says Rowley.

From the nursery rhyme 'A Frog He Would A-wooing Go' (first recorded 1611). Hence, *Mrs Mouse Are You Within?*, the title of a play (1968) by Frank Marcus. *Private Eye* (No. 299, June 1973) quoted what the elderly 10th Duke of Marlborough had said on returning from one of his honeymoons: 'I'm afraid Mr Mouse didn't come out to play'.

4 A priest is a man who is called Father by everyone except his own children who are obliged to call him Uncle.

Rupert Hart-Davis says he came across this 'Italian saying' in 'a French novel, read in the train', but gives no further information. From *The Lyttelton Hart-Davis Letters*, Vol. 1 (1978).

5 Pure water is the best of gifts that man to man can bring,
But who am I that I should have the best of anything?
Let princes revel at the pump, let peers with ponds make free;
Brandy or wine or even beer is good enough for me.

Ascribed to G.W.E. Russell and also to Lord Neaves, but neither ascription has been verified (*Notes and Queries*, March 1925).

6 *Les Quatre Cents Coups*.
The Four Hundred Blows.

Title of film (France, 1958) by François Truffaut. It comes from the French slang expression *faire les quatre cents coups* (meaning, 'to paint the town red' or 'to be up to all sorts of tricks').

7 Reader!
If thou hast a heart fam'd for
Tenderness and Pity, Contemplate this Spot.
In which are deposited the Remains
of a Young Lady, whose artless Beauty,
innocence of Mind and gentle Manners,
once obtained her the Love and
Esteem of all who knew her, But when
Nerves were too delicately spun to
bear the rude Shakes and Jostlings
which we meet with in this transitory
World, Nature gave way; She sunk
and died a Martyr to Excessive Sensibility.

One of the most touching epitaphs of all – to be found on a floor slab in Dorchester Abbey, Oxfordshire. It is to Mrs Sarah Fletcher, wife of Captain Fletcher, who 'departed this Life at the Village of Clifton, on the 7 of June 1799, in the 29th Year of her Age. May her Soul meet that Peace in Heaven which this Earth denied her.' The 'Clifton' presumably refers to the nearby village of Clifton Hampden.

8 Real pain for your sham friends, champagne for your real friends.

An Edwardian toast that the painter Francis Bacon (1909–92) acquired from his father, according to Daniel Farson, *The Gilded Gutter Life of Francis Bacon* (1993).

9 *Revenons à ces moutons*.
Let's get back to these sheep.

Sometimes quoted as '*retournons à nos moutons*', as by Rabelais in *Pantagruel* (1545). The meaning is, 'let us get back to the subject'. From an anonymous fifteenth-century play entitled *La Farce de Maître Pierre Pathelin*. A woollen draper charges a shepherd with maltreating his sheep but continually wanders from the point in court. The judge attempts to bring him back with this phrase. Alluding perhaps to Martial: '*Jam dic, Postume, de tribus capellis*'?

1 Rings on her fingers and bells on her toes.

From the nursery rhyme 'Ride a cock-horse to Banbury Cross' (first recorded 1784). Hence, *Rings On Their Fingers*, the title of a BBC TV comedy series (from 1979) about live-in lovers who decide to get married.

2 The rose is red, the violet's blue,
The honey's sweet, and so are you.

Nursery rhyme – and Valentine rhyme – recorded by 1784. There is more than one version and 'Roses are red, violets are blue' occurs at the start of numerous parodies.

3 Rough seas make tough sailors.

A search for a proverb to this effect in 1993 produced no result. However, *The Dictionary of American Proverbs* (1992) contains 'A good sailor likes a rough sea' (collected in Ontario, Canada) and Benham (1948) has an Italian proverb, 'The good seaman is known in bad weather'.

4 Russians with snow on their boots.

Within a month of war being declared in August 1914, there was an unfounded rumour that a million Russian troops had landed at Aberdeen in Scotland and passed through England on their way to the Western Front. The detail that they were seen to have had 'snow on their boots' was supposed to add credence to the report. Arnold Bennett was one of several people who noted the rumour at the time. In his Journals (for 31 August 1914), he wrote: 'The girls came home with a positive statement from the camp that 160,000 Russians were being landed in Britain, to be taken to France ... The statement was so positive that at first I almost believed it ... In the end I dismissed it, and yet could not help hoping ... The most curious embroidery on this rumour was from Mrs A. W., who told Mrs W. that the Russians were coming via us to France, where they would turn treacherous to France and join Germans in taking Paris ... This rumour I think took the cake.'

In Osbert Sitwell's *Great Morning* (1951), he records how his 'unusually wise and cautious' sixteen-year-old brother Sacheverell had written to tell him: 'They saw the Russians pass through the station last night ... and Miss Vasalt telephoned to Mother this afternoon and said trains in great number had passed through Grantham Station all day with the blinds down. So there must, I think, be some truth in it, don't you?'

In *Falsehood in War-time* (1928), Arthur Ponsonby said of 'Russians with snow on their boots', that 'nothing illustrates better the credulity of the public mind in wartime and what favourable soil it becomes for the cultivation of falsehood.' Several suggestions have been made as to how this false information caught hold: that the Secret Service had intercepted a telegram to the effect that '100,000 Russians are on their way from Aberdeen to London' (without realizing that this referred to a consignment of Russian eggs); that a tall, bearded fellow had declared in a train that he came from 'Ross-shire', and so on.

In fact, the British ambassador to Russia had requested the dispatch of a complete army corps but the request was never acceded to. Ponsonby commented: 'As the rumour had undoubted military value, the authorities took no steps to deny it ... [but] an official War Office denial of the rumour was noted by the *Daily News* on September 16, 1914.'

5 Sarcasm is the lowest form of wit.

There is no doubt that this proverbial expression exists: 'Sarcasm is supposed to be the lowest form of wit. Never mind. It has its moments' – Greville Janner, *Janner's Complete Letterwriter* (1989). But it is hard to say where it came from. Thomas Carlyle remarked in *Sartor Resartus*, II.iv (1834) that, 'Sarcasm is the language of the devil'. The more usual observation is that 'Punning is the lowest form of wit', which probably derives from Dryden's comment on Ben Jonson's 'clenches' – 'the lowest and most grovelling kind of wit'. At some stage the comment on the one has been applied to the other. The saying is definitely not Dr Johnson's definition of wit in his *Dictionary*.

6 Say it ain't so, Joe!

A small boy is reputed to have said this to the American baseball player 'Shoeless Joe' Jackson as he came out of a grand jury session in 1920 about corruption in the 1919 World Series. Jackson, of the Chicago White Sox, had been accused with others of deliberately losing the Series at the behest of gamblers. A journalist called Hugh Fullerton reported a boy asking, 'It ain't so, Joe, is it?' and him replying, 'Yes, kid, I'm afraid it is'. Over the years, the words re-arranged themselves into the more euphonious order. Ironically, Jackson denied that the exchange had ever taken place – using any set of words.

7 Say not in grief that he/she is no more
But in thankfulness that he/she was.

These words, spoken at many a memorial or thanksgiving service, have been variously described as a Jewish prayer and/or from the Talmud. The underlying thought is almost a commonplace, however. General George S. Patton said in a speech in 1945: 'It is foolish and wrong to mourn the men who died. Rather we should thank God that such men lived.' In 1992 *The Times* quoted the Queen Mother as having said of her husband King George VI's death in 1952: 'One must feel gratitude for what has been, rather than distress for what is lost.' Another suggestion is that the lines may have been said by or about Pushkin.

And, although it is not quite the same thing, that well-known quotation-scruncher, Margaret Thatcher, incorporated this in a VE-Day message to the Kremlin in May 1985: 'It is right that we should look back and pay tribute with pride and thankfulness for the heroism of those in both our countries who fought in a common cause, and with grief for the terrible sufferings involved.'

1 A scheme so prodigal of expenditure might be dealing a mortal blow at the Empire.

A member of the House of Lords during a debate on the 1908 Welfare Act. Another feared that state pensions of five shillings at the age of 70, 'would weaken the moral fibre of the nation ... and diminish the self-respect of our people.' Quoted by J.H. (Jim) Griffiths in his speech to the House of Commons introducing the National Insurance Bill (6 February 1946).

2 Seems Like Old Times.

Title of a song (*c.*1946) by John Jacob Loeb and Carmen Lombardo. It had been preceded by 'It seems like old times' (1939) by Sammy Stept and Charles Tobias. Hence, however, *Seems Like Old Times*, the title of a film (US, 1980) and of a book (1989) by Alan Coren (made up of his old pieces from *The Times*).

3 Serendipity means searching for a needle in a haystack and instead finding a farmer's daughter.

Definition quoted by the scientist Sir Herman Bondi. Serendipity – a word meaning 'the making of happy and unexpected discoveries by accident' – was coined by Horace Walpole in 1754 after 'Serendip', a former name for Sri Lanka.

4 Set a thief to catch a thief.

Quoted as an old saying already in Richard Howard's *The Committee* (1665). Hence, *To Catch a Thief*, title of a film (US, 1955). *Compare* SHAKESPEARE 490:5.

5 Set the people free.

Slogan used by the British Conservative Party, which helped it regain power, with Winston Churchill as Prime Minister, in the 1951 General Election. In a radio broadcast (3 May 1952) Churchill returned to the theme: 'We think it is a good idea to set the people free as much as it is possible in our complicated modern society, from the trammels of state control and bureaucratic management.' Many years later, in a House of Commons debate on the Rates Bill, Edward Heath recalled how he had entered the House having fought an election on Mr Churchill's theme that Conservatives were to set the people free. 'It was not a theme,' he said, 'that we were to set the people free to do what we tell them' (17 January 1984).

The slogan was taken from the lyrics of a patriotic song of the Second World War. In 'Song of Liberty' (1940), A.P. Herbert put words to the *nobilmente* theme from Edward Elgar's 'Pomp and Circumstance March No. 4':

All men must be free
March for liberty with me
Brutes and braggarts may have their little day,
We shall never bow the knee.

God is drawing His sword
We are marching with the Lord
Sing, then, brother, sing, giving ev'ry thing,
All you are and hope to be,
To set the peoples free.

6 She had remarkably lively eyes, but so small they were almost invisible when she laughed; and a foot, the least of any woman in England.

Of Nell Gwyn (1650–87), actress and mistress of Charles II. From *The Manager's Note-Book*, quoted in *The Dictionary of Biographical Quotation* (1978).

7 She was poor but she was honest
Victim of a rich man's game.
First he loved her, then he left her,
And she lost her maiden name ...
It's the same the whole world over,
It's the poor wot gets the blame,
It's the rich wot gets the gravy.
Ain't it all a bleedin' shame?

Song, 'She Was Poor But She Was Honest', which was popular with British soldiers in the First World War. The fifth and sixth lines here have achieved near proverbial status.

1 Sing a song of sixpence,
A pocket full of rye;
Four and twenty blackbirds,
Baked in a pie.

From the nursery rhyme, first recorded *c.*1744, and capable of any number of allegorical interpretations. The belief that it sprang from the occasion when Henry James Pye was appointed Poet Laureate in 1790 is clearly erroneous, given that the rhyme had appeared fifty years previously. Hence, however, *A Pocket Full of Rye*, title of a Miss Marple novel (1953) by Agatha Christie who also used 'Sing a Song of Sixpence' (1934) and 'Four and Twenty Blackbirds' (1960) from the same source for the titles of short stories.

2 The Singer Not the Song.

Title of novel (1959) by Audrey Erskine Lindop (film UK, 1960). She took it from a West Indian calypso.

3 The situation in Germany is serious but not hopeless; the situation in Austria is hopeless but not serious.

Described as 'an Austrian proverb collected by Franklin Pierce Adams' in A. Andrews, *Quotations for Speakers and Writers* (1969). Hence, *Situation Hopeless But Not Serious*, the title of a film (US 1965).

4 Socialism is no more than the family writ large.

Quoted by the sociologist Michael Young (*q.v.*) in 1995, who commented: 'My memory was that it was part of an election broadcast that Clement Attlee made in 1945 or 1950 or 1951. I was employed myself then as Head of the Research Department of the Labour Party and was responsible for the broadcasts ... but someone has checked this for me and it looks as though it's not the case.'

5 So Deep Is the Night.

Title of song (1939) by Sonny Miller, first featured in the 1940 film *Hear My Song*, though originally Mario Melfi's setting of Chopin's Étude in E Major, Op. 10, No. 3 appears to have had French words under the title 'Tristesse'. Compare the film title (US, 1946), *So Dark the Night*.

6 Somebody's Husband, Somebody's Son.

The title of Gordon Burn's (1984) book about the 'Yorkshire Ripper' murder investigation is taken from something said during the prolonged police hunt for the killer. George Oldfield, leading the police hunt, appeared on the Jimmy Young radio show on 9 February 1978 and 'urged the predominantly female audience to search their collective conscience and report any man of their acquaintance who they suspected of behaving oddly. Husband, father, brother, son – it shouldn't matter.' After another killing, a Yorkshire clergyman, the Rev. Michael Walker, told his congregation on Palm Sunday, 1979, 'He [the Ripper] needs help, he is somebody's child, husband or father.'

7 The son of a duck is a floater.

Arab saying. Dr Rosalind Miles commented (1995): '"Son of a duck" means far more than the literal "like father like son". It means more like the US Western proverb "There is no education in the second kick of a mule." It also applies to projects and suggestions – i.e., a second or subsequent idea from someone whose ideas or efforts have bombed before will bomb again.'

The Son of a Duck Is a Floater is the title of a collection of Arab sayings with English equivalents published in 1985 by Primrose Arnander and Ashkhain Skipwith. The 1992 sequel was *Apricots Tomorrow*, a title taken from the Arab saying, 'tomorrow [there] will be apricots' which means 'never do today what you can possibly put off till tomorrow'. This comes from the story in the *Arabian Nights* about the princess's servant who was instructed to pick the ripening fruit every evening and so preserve her mistress's life and honour. Arnander and Skipwith give the Western equivalents 'Tomorrow never comes' and 'Jam tomorrow ...'

8 Spake as he champed the unaccustomed food,
This may be wholesome but it is not good.

'Anon. 1852' is the only hint given in *The Making of Verse: A Guide to English Metres* (1934) by Robert Swan and Frank Sidgwick, where this appears among examples of heroic couplets. In *The Dublin Review* (July 1937), J. Lewis May, while discussing 'Flashed from his bed the electric tidings came' (*see* AUSTIN 67:5), says: 'The name of the inventor of these immortal lines has not been handed down, but one may hazard a guess that they proceeded from the same source as those on another prince, also a subject for the Newdigate [prize poem at Oxford] – to wit, Nebuchadnezzar, "Who murmured – as he ate the unaccustomed food –/It may be wholesome, but it is not good".'

9 Starkle, starkle, little twink,
Who the hell you are, I think.
I'm not under the affluence of incohol,
Like some tinkle peep I are.

Drunken parody of 'Twinkle, twinkle, little star', current in the 1960s, if not earlier. *Compare* CARROLL 147:4.

1 Stop the World, I Want To Get Off.

Title of musical by Anthony Newley and Leslie Bricusse (1961; film UK 1966). Said to have been found as a graffito.

2 Ten little nigger boys went out to dine;
One choked his little self, and then there were nine.

'Ten Little Niggers' – Frank Green's British version (1869) of the American rhyme. Actually 'Ten Little Injuns' was the title of the original piece, written by the US songwriter Septimus Winner (*c.*1868). Hence, however, *Ten Little Niggers*, title of a novel (1939) by Agatha Christie, which has been dramatized and thrice filmed. Understandably, the US title of the book became *Ten Little Indians*, and the UK 1966 film also had this more acceptable title. *And Then There Were None* was the title of the US 1945 film (UK, *Ten Little Niggers*) and also of the UK 1974 film.

3 [Texas is] the place where there are the most cows and the least milk and the most rivers and the least water in them, and where you can look the furthest and see the least.

Mencken (1942) had this from an 'Author unidentified'. In 1993 it provoked a discussion whether there had ever been anything said that was quotable and complimentary about Texas? Possibly coming into this category is the passage from John Gunther, *Inside U.S.A.* (1947): 'I like the story, doubtless antique, that I heard near San Antonio. A child asks a stranger where he comes from, whereupon his father rebukes him gently, "Never do that, son. If a man's from Texas, he'll tell you. If he's not, why embarrass him by asking".' Roy Hattersley reworked this on BBC Radio *Quote ... Unquote* (27 October 1984) as though said by Sydney Smith to the French Ambassador. 'Never ask a man if he comes from Yorkshire. If he does, he'll already have told you. If he does not, why humiliate him?'

Then there is this from *LBJ: Images of a Vibrant Life* (published by Friends of the LBJ Library, 1973): 'The President [Lyndon Johnson] will rest in his beloved Hill Country [in Texas], where he has told us his father before him said he wanted to be – "Where folks know when you're sick and care when you die".' In addition, there is the song (author untraced):

O beautiful, beautiful Texas,
Where the beautiful bluebonnets grow,
We're proud of our forefathers
Who died at the Alamo.
You can live in the plains or the mountains
Or down where the sea breezes blow,
But you'll still be in beautiful Texas –
The most beautiful State that I know.

(The bluebonnet is the state flower of Texas.)

4 There are three sides to every argument: my side, your side and the truth.

Modern proverbial saying, variously ascribed: '... to every case' is said to be 'an old lawyer' advising his pupil; '... to every argument' was 'a quote from a bloke in the pub'; from the *Financial Times* (25 October 1986): 'As everyone knows there are always three sides to the story of any marriage: His, Hers and the Truth. Here we have Hers [Dylan Thomas's widow's] with nothing kept back this time.'

5 The things that will destroy us are ...
politics without principle;
pleasure without conscience;
wealth without work;
knowledge without character;
business without morality;
science without humanity; and
worship without sacrifice.

Probably American in origin, this was current in 1992 but the source remains untraced.

6 This is not a dress rehearsal, this is real life.

In December 1980, this line was spotted in the Eight-O Club, Dallas, Texas, and included in the book *Graffiti 3* (1981). It has since become a popular modern proverb. For example, from Billy Connolly's *Gullible's Travels*, 'Scotland' (1983): 'Still you can't worry too much about the future. Life is not a rehearsal.' Sybille Bedford was quoted in John Julius Norwich's *A Christmas Cracker* (1995) as having written: 'You see, when one's young one doesn't feel part of it yet, the human condition; one does things because they are not for good; everything is a rehearsal. To be repeated ad lib, to be put right when the curtain goes up in earnest. One day you know that the curtain was up all the time. That was the performance.'

7 This must be the first time a rat has come to the aid of a sinking ship.

A BBC spokesman on puppet Roland Rat's success in reversing the fortunes of TV-am, a rival breakfast television station (1983). Not entirely original, however: *see* CHURCHILL 167:8.

8 The tie that binds.

This proverbial expression (sometimes 'the ties that bind') may possibly have originated in a hymn written by John Fawcett, an English Baptist minister, in 1782:

Blest be the tie that binds
Our hearts in Christian love:
The fellowship of kindred minds
I like to that above.

The story goes that Fawcett had already set out on the road leaving a chapel where he had been minister, but his congregation prevailed on him to return. When he got back to his manse he sat down right away and wrote the hymn. It is used prominently in Thornton Wilder's play *Our Town* (1938) and occasioned a parody (probably American):

Blest be the tie that binds
Our collar to our shirt,
For it is the only things that hides
A little rim of dirt.

Later references: in *Lux Mundi* (a journal) (1889): 'The ties which bind men in the relation of brotherhood and sonhood are the noblest.' A film (US, 1996) about adoption, with Keith Carradine and Daryl Hannah, had the title *The Tie That Binds.*

1 The time is now.

A slogan that has been used variously over the years. It was one of the promotional lines in the Ronald Reagan presidential campaign of 1980. In a speech at Wheeling, West Virginia on 20 February 1950, Senator Joseph McCarthy, began his career as America's leading Red hunter by asking: 'Can there be anyone who fails to realize that the Communist world has said, "The time is now" – that this is the time for the showdown between a democratic Christian world and the Communist atheistic world?'

2 *The Times* is a tribal noticeboard.

It was said (in *The Times*, 21 January 1984) that a candidate for the editorship of the paper's Woman's Page in the 1960s had described the newspaper thus. The then editor, Sir William Haley, was so tickled that he gave her the job, though he usually reacted against any suggestion that the paper was exclusive (and had opposed the advertising slogan 'Top People Take The Times', for example). According to Godfrey Smith in *The Sunday Times* (31 May 1987), the successful candidate in question was Suzanne Puddefoot.

3 Tinker, tailor, soldier, sailor, rich man, poor man, beggarman, thief.

From the children's fortune-telling rhyme, first recorded in something like this form, 1883. Hence, *Tinker Tailor Soldier Spy*, the title of a spy novel (1974) by John Le Carré. *Rich Man, Poor Man* was the title of a novel (1970) by Irwin Shaw, to which the sequel was *Beggarman, Thief* (1977).

4 TITANIC SINKS – HECKMONDWIKE MAN ABOARD.

A probably apocryphal headline from a Yorkshire newspaper in 1912. Even if it never actually appeared, it has become the paradigm of 'finding the local angle' in any story by the provincial press. (One headline that really did appear – in the *Weekly Dispatch* (London) – was 'MANY MILLIONAIRES MISSING'.)

In 1994 Mark English of Bradford – i.e., not a million miles from Heckmondwike – tried to find out whether the headline ever did appear: 'This story struck me as being inherently unlikely, since Yorkshiremen don't have the narrow local chauvinism implied by this story; rather, they are citizens of the world. At all events, I took a look at some local newspapers [dated 17 April 1912] at Bradford Library. The Bradford *Daily Argus*, the *Yorkshire Evening Post* and the *Yorkshire Daily Observer* yielded nothing very close to your quote. The *Yorkshire Post* was conventional enough in its main headlines, but the sub-heads included "A Hessle Magistrate Among the Saved", "A Hull Officer On Board" and "A Dewsbury Man On Board". Now, Heckmondwike is an outlying district of Dewsbury, so perhaps more research will turn up the headline ... Incidentally, I have always quoted this story as "Scotsman Dies At Sea".'

5 Today Germany, tomorrow the world!

The slogan for the National Socialist Press in Germany of the early 1930s, '*Heute Presse der Nationalsozialisten, Morgen Presse der Nation*' [Today the press of the Nazis, tomorrow the nation's press], reached its final form in '*Heute gehört uns Deutschland – morgen die ganze Welt*' [Today Germany belongs to us – tomorrow the whole world.] Although John Colville in *The Fringes of Power* states that by 3 September 1939, Hitler 'had already ... proclaimed that "Today Germany is ours; tomorrow the whole world",' an example of Hitler actually saying it has yet to be found. However, in *Mein Kampf* (1925) he had said: 'If the German people, in their historic development, had possessed tribal unity like other nations, the German Reich today would be the master of the entire world.'

The phrase seems to have come from the chorus of a song in the Hitler Youth 'songbook':

Wir werden weiter marschieren
Wenn alles in Scherben fällt
Denn heute gehört uns Deutschland
Und morgen die ganze Welt.

which may be roughly translated as:

We shall keep marching on
Even if everything breaks into fragments,
For today Germany belongs to us
And tomorrow the whole world.

Another version replaces the second line with '*Wenn Scheiße vom Himmel fällt* [When shit from Heaven falls]'. Sir David Hunt recalled hearing the song in 1933 or possibly 1934.

1 Tomorrow will be Friday,
But we've caught no fish today.

Lines from the song 'Tomorrow Will Be Friday' popular around 1900 about a group of monks on a Thursday who are finding it difficult to cater for the morrow. Words by F.E. Weatherley, music by J.L. Molloy (and sung originally by Mr F. Barrington Foote). There may also be a painting with the same title by Walter Dendy Sadler (though perhaps this is just called 'Thursday').

2 Too small to live in and too large to hang on a watch-chain.

Of Chiswick House, London – a Palladian villa built by the 3rd Earl of Burlington in 1725–9. Quoted in Cecil Roberts, *And So to Bath* (1940). In Richard Hewlings, *Chiswick House and Gardens* (1989), 'too little to live in and too large to hang to one's watch' is ascribed to Lord Hervey.

3 To save the town, it became necessary to destroy it.

An unnamed American major on the town of Ben Tre, Vietnam, during the Tet offensive, according to an AP dispatch published in *The New York Times* (8 February 1968). A token of the futility of American activities in Vietnam.

4 To The Perpetual Disgrace
of PUBLICK JUSTICE
The Honble JOHN BYNG Esqr
Admiral of the Blue
Fell a MARTYR to
POLITICAL PERSECUTION
March 14th in the Year 1757 when
BRAVERY and LOYALTY
Were Insufficient Securities
For the
Life and Honour
of a
NAVAL OFFICER

Inscription in Southill Church, Bedfordshire. Admiral Byng (1704–57) was executed at Portsmouth after failing to relieve Minorca, giving rise to Voltaire's comment 552:6. Dr Samuel Johnson, who visited Southill, has been credited with the inscription but Boswell, while quoting it in his *Life of Johnson*, makes no such assertion.

5 To the world he was a soldier
To me he was the world.

Said to be on a Second World War grave in the Western Desert (as reported by Colin Smith in *The Observer*, 8 November 1981), but also found elsewhere. On the grave in Brookwood Military Cemetery, Surrey, of Wing Commander H.J. Fish, RAF, who died on 19 October 1945, age 30, there is: 'TO THE WORLD/HE WAS JUST A PART/TO ME HE WAS THE WORLD.'

6 The twelfth day of Christmas,
My true love sent to me
Twelve lords a-leaping,
Eleven ladies dancing,
Ten pipers piping,
Nine drummers drumming,
Eight maids a-milking,
Seven swans a-swimming,
Six geese a-laying,
Five gold rings,
Four calling birds,
Three French hens,
Two turtle doves, and
A partridge in a pear tree.

A rhyme, also known in French, first recorded in English *c.*1780. The numbering of the gifts varies from version to version. Hence, for example, *Ten Lords A-Leaping*, title of a crime novel (1995) by Ruth Dudley Edwards. Most discussion has been about the last line, chiefly because the game bird is a famously low flyer and is never seen in trees. A popular suggestion (which also explains some of the other gifts listed in the song) is that a 'partridge in a pear tree' is a corruption of the Latin *parturit in aperto* [she gave birth in the open], referring to Mary's delivery of Christ in a stable. Similarly, the shepherds coming down from the hills [*descendens de collibus*] could explain the phrases 'three French hens' and 'four colly/calling birds'. Another ingenious explanation for 'partridge in a pear tree' is that it is a mixture of the English and French words for 'partridge' – 'a partridge, *une perdrix*'.

7 Until we meet again.

A staple thought of the bereaved, to be found on many gravestones. One can't help wondering, however, whether its popularity, particularly on war graves, has anything to do with the enormous success of Vera Lynn's song 'We'll meet again, don't know where,/ Don't know when,/But I know we'll meet again some sunny day' (1939), written by Ross Parker and Hugh Charles. However, in 1918, there had been a song with the title 'Till We Meet Again' which was a great success for its writers Richard Whiting and Ray Egar.

From the grave in Brookwood Military Cemetery, Surrey, of Sergeant D.J. Ansell, 'wireless operator/air gunner, Royal Air Force' who died on 23 September 1944, aged 34 years: 'HE IS ALWAYS IN OUR HEARTS/UNTIL WE MEET AGAIN.' 'Always In My Heart' was, incidentally, the title of a song (1942) by Kim Gannon and Ernesto Lecuona, popularized by Deanna Durbin.

1 Uprose the Monarch of the Glen
Majestic from his lair,
Surveyed the scene with piercing ken,
And snuffed the fragrant air.

Hence, 'The Monarch of the Glen', title of a much-reproduced painting (1851) by Sir Edwin Landseer, showing a stag rampant on a small rock (and now in the possession of John Dewar & Sons Ltd, the whisky firm). When the painting was first exhibited at the Royal Academy, the catalogue entry contained a poem identified only as 'Legends of Glenorchay', which ended thus.

2 A walk in the woods.

Name given to a negotiating tactic employed by high officials in SALT (Strategic Arms Limitation Talks) between the United States and the USSR. A play inspired by the compromise achieved on a specific occasion by negotiators in 1982 and showing how they might have talked through their personal and political differences was accordingly entitled *A Walk in the Woods*. Written by Lee Blessing, it was first performed on Broadway in 1988.

From the *Financial Times* (9 March 1983): 'The package that Mr Nitze and Mr Kvitsinsky worked out in their now famous "walk in the woods" near Geneva last July involved equal ceilings for both sides' medium-range nuclear weapons in Europe.' From Denis Healey, *The Time of My Life* (1989): 'In the summer of 1982 Perle sabotaged the formula agreed between Nitze and the Soviet negotiator, Kvitsinsky, during their famous "walk in the woods".'

3 We are the unwilling, led by the unqualified, doing the unnecessary for the ungrateful.

Slogan said to have been seen written on GI helmets in Vietnam. In the June 1980 issue of *Playboy* was a slightly different version from 'the Ninth Precinct': 'We the willing, led by the unknowing, are doing the impossible for the ungrateful. We have done so much for so long with so little, we are now qualified to do anything with nothing.' Somebody bitter about police salaries had amended the last line to read, 'To do anything for nothing'.

Compare: 'What is a committee? A group of the unwilling, picked from the unfit, to do the unnecessary' – Richard Harkness, *New York Herald Tribune* (15 June 1960).

4 We have ways of making you talk.

The threat by an evil inquisitor to his victim appears to have come originally from 1930s Hollywood villains and was then handed on to Nazi characters from the 1940s onwards. In the film *Lives of a Bengal Lancer* (1935) Douglas Dumbrille, as the evil Mohammed Khan, said, 'We have ways of making men talk'. A typical 'Nazi' use can be found in the British film *Odette* (1950) when the eponymous French Resistance worker (Anna Neagle) is threatened with unmentioned nastiness by one of her captors. Says he: 'We have ways and means of making you talk.' Then, after a little stoking of the fire with a poker, he urges her on with: 'We have ways and means of making a woman talk.'

Later, used in caricature, the phrase saw further action in TV programmes like *Rowan and Martin's Laugh-In* (*c.*1968) when it was invariably pronounced with a strong German accent. Frank Muir presented a comedy series for London Weekend Television with the title *We Have Ways of Making You Laugh* (1968).

5 The Welsh are the Italians in the rain.

Quoted by the writer Elaine Morgan on BBC Radio *Quote ... Unquote* (1983). An earlier version spoken, though probably not coined, by the journalist René Cutforth was: 'The Welsh are the Mediterraneans in the rain', which was quoted by Nancy Banks-Smith in *The Guardian* (17 October 1979).

6 What a difference a day makes.

Almost proverbial, yet not listed in any proverb books. The phrase either expresses surprise at someone's rapid recovery from a mood that has laid them low or the old thought that time is a great healer. Did it begin in a song? 'What a Difference a Day Made' was a hit for Esther Phillips in 1975 (though translated in 1934 by Stanley Adams from the Spanish lyric '*Cuando Vuelva a Tu Lado*' by Maria Grever.)

1 What a wonderful bird the frog are!
When he walk, he fly almost;
When he sing, he cry almost.
He ain't got no tail hardly, either.
He sit on what he ain't got almost.

A leading article in *The Times* (20 May 1948) ascribed these lines to the pen of an African schoolgirl, causing one reader to write in and say he had always believed they had come from the mouth of a French Canadian. He also said he had an idea that he had first seen them in the *Manchester Guardian* 'about twenty years ago'.

The version that appears in Arnold Silcock's *Verse and Worse* (1952) is also ascribed to 'Anon (French Canadian)' and is fractionally different:

> What a wonderful bird the frog are –
> When he stand he sit almost;
> When he hop, he fly almost.
> He ain't got no sense hardly;
> He ain't got no tail hardly either.
> When he sit, he sit on what he ain't got almost.

2 When captains courageous whom death could not daunt,
Did march to the siege of the city of Gaunt,
They mustered their soldiers by two and by three,
And the foremost in battle was Mary Ambree.

Ballad, 'Mary Ambree' (undated). Hence, *Captains Courageous*, title of a novel (1897) by Rudyard Kipling.

3 When I am dead
Cry for me a little
Think of me sometimes
But not too much.
Think of me now and again
As I was in life
At some moments it's pleasant to recall
But not for long.
Leave me in peace
And I shall leave you in peace
And while you live
Let your thoughts be with the living.

Poem read, for example, at the funeral of the actress Hattie Jacques (in 1980). Described as 'anonymous traditional Indian' in *Who Do You Think You Are?* (ed. David Woolger, 1990).

4 When it's night-time in Italy it's Wednesday over here.

Title of nonsense song (1923) with words and music by James Kendis and Lew Brown. Recorded by Billy Jones with orchestra in New York (1922).

5 When Pictures Look Alive With Movement Free
When Ships Like Fishes Swim Beneath the Sea
When Men Outstripping Birds Can Scan the Sky
Then Half the World Deep Trenched in Blood Will Lie.

It has been said that this prophecy was 'carved on an Essex tombstone five hundred years ago'. It sounds more like a prediction by Mother Shipton, the sixteenth-century Yorkshire 'witch' or one of the nineteenth-century fakers of her works. Described as 'A Prophecy ... Anonymous, Written about AD 1400' it appears in *Junior Voices: The Fourth Book* (Penguin Education, 1970).

6 When rape is inevitable, lie back and enjoy it.

This is best described – as it is in Paul Scott's novel *The Jewel in the Crown* (1966) – as 'that old, disreputable saying'. Daphne Manners, upon whose 'rape' the story hinges, adds: 'I can't say, Auntie, that I lay back and enjoyed mine.' It is no more than a saying – a 'mock-Confucianism' is how Partridge/Slang describes it (giving a date *c.*1950) – and one is unlikely ever to learn when, or from whom, it first arose. A word of caution to anyone thinking of using it. An American broadcaster, Tex Antoine, said in 1975: 'With rape so predominant in the news lately, it is well to remember the words of Confucius: "If rape is inevitable, lie back and enjoy it".' ABC News suspended Antoine for this remark, then demoted him to working in the weather department and prohibited him from appearing on the air.

7 When the Fields Are White With Daisies (I'll Return).

Title of a song (1904) with words and music by the Americans C.M. Denison and W.A. Pratt. In fact, there is more than one song with this title, but this one goes:

> I stood once in a harbor as a ship was going out
> On a voyage to a port beyond the sea ...
> And I heard the sailor promise to a lassie now in tears,
> 'When the fields are white with daisies I'll return.'
> (*Chorus*) When the fields are white with daisies, and the roses bloom again,
> Let the love flame in your heart more brightly burn;
> For I love you sweetheart only, so remember when you're lonely,

When the fields are white with daisies I'll return.

Alluded to, for example, in P.G. Wodehouse, *Psmith in the City*, Chap. 6 (1910): 'No, he has not gone permanently. Psmith will return. When the fields are white with daisies he'll return.'

1 Where the elite meet to eat.

A fictional advertising slogan from the American radio series *Duffy's Tavern* starring Ed Gardner (also on UK radio, 1944 and in a film, US 1945). Later, it was spoken by Bette Davis in the film *All About Eve* (US, 1950). On British radio, Duffy's Tavern made a further appearance as *Finkel's Café*, starring Peter Sellers (1956). Hence, the headline from *The Wall Street Journal* (8 October 1981): 'FOR THE DEMOCRATS PAM'S [Pamela Harriman's] IS THE PLACE FOR THE ELITE TO MEET.'

2 Where Were You When the Lights Went Out?

Title of film (US, 1968) inspired by the great New York blackout of 1965 when the electricity supply failed and, it was popularly believed, the birth-rate shot up nine months later. The phrase echoes an old music-hall song and/or the (American?) nonsense rhyme 'Where was Moses when the light went out?/Down in the cellar eating sauerkraut'. This last appears to have developed from the 'almost proverbial' riddle (as the Opies call it in *The Lore and Language of Schoolchildren*, 1959):

Q. Where was Moses when the light went out?
A. In the dark.

The Opies find this in *The Riddler's Oracle*, *c.*1821.

3 Who Pays the Ferryman?

Title of a BBC TV drama series (1977) by Michael J. Bird, about a former Greek Resistance fighter in Crete. Not a quotation but an allusion to the Greek legend of Charon, who demanded a fee to ferry the dead across the River Styx.

4 Who were you with last night?
Out in the pale moonlight.

Song, 'Who Were You With Last Night?' (1912). In fact, this was written by the British composer of music-hall songs, Fred Godfrey (1889–1953) with Mark Sheridan. Compare the line from the much later film *Batman* (US, 1989): 'Have you ever danced with the devil in the pale moonlight?' The phrase 'in the pale moonlight' occurs earlier in Charles Dickens, *The Old Curiosity Shop*, Chap. 43 (1840). *See also* GILBERT 261:6 and SCOTT 471:6.

5 Willie, Willie, Harry, Stee,
Harry, Dick, John, Harry Three.
One, Two, Three Neds, Richard Two.
Henries Four, Five, Six ... then who?
Edward Four, Five, Dick the Bad.
Harries twain and Ned the Lad.
Mary, Bessie, James the Vain.
Charlie, Charlie, James Again.
William and Mary, Anna Gloria,
Four Georges, William and Victoria.

The mnemonic for remembering the order of the reigns of the Kings and Queens of England was probably in existence by 1900. A correspondent recalls learning it in 1933 with the additional couplet:

Edward Seventh next, and then
George the Fifth in 1910.

Further amendments were made in due course:

In '36 came Edward Eight
Who, in that year, did abdicate.

George Six followed. At his death
In '52, Elizabeth.

An American update for the reigns of Edward VIII and George VI was:

Eddie Eight went helter-skelter
Georgie reigned from a bomb-proof shelter.

Another version of the post-Victoria reigns is:

Edward Seven, George again
Edward Eight gave up his reign.
George Six, he of gentle mien
Elizabeth Two, God Save the Queen.

6 With drums and guns, and guns and drums
The enemy nearly slew ye.
My darling dear, you look so queer,
Oh, Johnny, I hardly knew ye.

'Johnny, I hardly knew Ye', an Irish folk song. Hence: *Johnnie I Hardly Knew You*, the title of a novel (1977) by Edna O'Brien; *Johnny, We Hardly Knew Ye*, the title given to a volume (1972) by Ken O'Donnell and Dave Powers commemorating the death of President Kennedy (who was of Irish descent); *Daddy, We Hardly Knew You*, title of a memoir of her father (1989) by Germaine Greer.

7 With one bound Jack was free.

Said now of anyone who escapes from a tricky situation or tight corner, the phrase underlines the preposterousness of the adventures in which such lines could be 'spoken' – in cartoon strips, subtitles to silent films, or from Boy's Own Paper-type serials of the early twentieth century in which the hero would frequently escape from seemingly impossible situations, most usually after he had been condemned to them in a 'cliff-hanger' situation. Possibly it all stems from a joke re-told in E.S. Turner, *Boys Will Be Boys* (1948): 'There is a delightful story, attributed to more than one publishing house, of the serial writer who disappears in the middle of a story. As he shows no sign of turning up, it is decided to carry on without him. Unfortunately he has left his hero bound to a stake, with lions circling him, and an avalanche about to fall for good measure (or some such situation). Relays of writers try to think of a way out, and give it up. Then at the eleventh hour the missing author returns. He takes the briefest look at the previous instalment and then, without a moment's hesitation, writes: "With one bound Jack was free".'

1 With twenty-six soldiers of lead, I can conquer the world.

The typographer F.W. Goudy (1865–1947) wrote in *The Type Speaks*, 'I am the leaden army that conquers the world – I am TYPE' – but he was probably reworking an old riddle. The *ODQ* (1979) finds in Hugh Rowley's *Puniana* (1867) the saying, 'With twenty-six lead soldiers [the characters of the alphabet set up for printing] I can conquer the world', and points to the (probably independently arrived at) French riddle: '*Je suis le capitaine de vingt-quatre soldats, et sans moi Paris serait pris*,' to which the answer is 'A'. ('I am the captain of twenty-four [*sic*] soldiers and without me Paris would be taken' – remove the 'a' from '*Paris*' and it becomes '*pris*' or 'taken'.) But is the French alphabet at this time presumed to have had only 25 letters? If so, which was the missing letter – K perhaps?

The phrase has been used as the title of a spiritual quest book, *Twenty-Six Lead Soldiers*, by Dan Wooding (1987): 'A top Fleet Street journalist and his search for the truth ...' Wooding attributes the saying to 'Karl Marx or Benjamin Franklin'.

2 Women's faults are many
Men have only two:
Everything they say
And everything they do.

The observation regarding quotations or jokes that there is always an earlier example if only you can find it, is particularly true of graffiti. The rash of feminist graffiti of the 1970s (spreading in time to T-shirts, buttons and so on) produced this popular verse. How ironic, therefore, that Mencken (1942) has this well-documented rhyme from the eighteenth century – and note the change of gender:

We men have many faults:
Poor women have but two –
There's nothing good they say,
There's nothing good they do.

Anon.: 'On Women's Faults' (1727)

3 Work hard, play hard, Xenophon was a Greek, use your toothbrush daily, hack no furniture.

Said to have been embroidered on a cushion cover in the house of the publisher, Sir Rupert Hart-Davis. In 1992 a number of correspondents recognized the phrases as coming from the 'copy books' that schoolchildren once used to practise their handwriting. These consisted of lines of printed copperplate writing interspersed with blank lines for the child to write on. One correspondent said she remembered these from her own schooldays *c.*1925 and said the books were still in print in 1948. Another noted, 'The phrases were quite random – chosen, I imagine, to fit the space available and/or to give the child the opportunity of practising different combinations of letters ... The compiler must have had quite a sense of humour to juxtapose such phrases – it certainly amused my husband (who was born in 1917) or he would hardly have remembered it from his early childhood.'

4 The Years Between.

Title of play by Daphne du Maurier (1944; film UK, 1946). Also, at this time, in 'I'm gonna love that guy, like he's never been loved before' – a British song (1945) by Frances Ash – there occur the lines, 'The years between/Might never have been./We'll be starting our life anew.' Recorded by Adelaide Hall and Paula Green.

5 Yield To the Night.

The title of a film (UK, 1956), from a novel by Joan Henry about a convicted murderess. The source is untraced – except that it occurs in a translation of a passage in Bk 7 of Homer's *Iliad*: 'But night is already at hand; it is well to yield to the night'.

6 You're phoney. Everything about you is phoney. Even your hair – which looks false – is real.

American diplomat to Brendan Bracken (Churchill's Minister of Information 1941–5) during the Second World War. Charles Edward Lysaght, in *Brendan Bracken* (1979), attributes it to a 'journalist', in the form: 'I don't believe a word you say, Brendan. Everything about you is phoney. Even your hair, which looks like a wig, isn't.'

ANOUILH, Jean

French playwright (1910–87)

1 Ring Round the Moon.

Christopher Fry's adaptation of Anouilh's play *L'Invitation au château* [*The Invitation to the Castle/Château*] was first performed in 1950 (following the Paris production of 1947). The English title alludes to the proverb 'Ring around the moon, brings a storm soon' (sometimes, '... rain comes soon'). This is a modern version of 'When round the moon there is a brugh [halo], the weather will be cold and rough' (*ODP* has it by 1631).

ARCHELAUS

Macedonian King (reigned 413–399BC)

2 In silence.

His reply when asked by a barber how he would like his hair cut. Quoted by W. & A. Durant in *The Story of Civilization* (1935–64) Possibly said, rather, by a successor, Philip II. Plutarch, however, in his *Moralia* attributes it to Archelaus.

ARCHILOCHUS

Greek poet (seventh century BC)

3 The fox knows many things – the hedgehog one *big* thing.

A somewhat obscure opinion, but note how it is used by Isaiah Berlin in *The Hedgehog and the Fox: An Essay on Tolstoy's View of History* (1953): 'There exists a great chasm between those, on one side, who relate everything to a single central vision ... and, on the other side, those who pursue many ends, often unrelated and even contradictory ... The first kind of intellectual and artistic personality belongs to the hedgehogs, the second to the foxes.' Benham (1948) gives it as an anonymous proverb: *Ars varia vulpis, ast una echino maxima* (The fox is versatile in its resources, but the hedgehog has one, and that chief of all). Note how Erasmus renders the idea in *Adagia* (1500): 'The fox has many tricks, and the hedgehog has only one [i.e., it can roll itself up into a ball for protection], but that is the best of all.' Apparently Archilochus is so quoted in Plutarch, *Moralia*, 'The Cleverness of Animals'.

ARCHIMEDES

Greek mathematician and inventor (c.287–212BC)

4 Give me but one firm spot on which to stand, and I will move the earth.

On the action of a lever. Quoted in Pappus of Alexandria, *Synagoge*.

5 *Eureka*!
I've got it!

Leaping out of his bath having discovered the principle of water displacement. Quoted in Vitruvius Pollio, *De Architectura* (first century BC). The Archimedes Principle is: 'When a body is immersed in water (or a fluid), its apparent loss of weight is equal to the weight of the water (or fluid) displaced.'

6 Wait till I have finished my problem.

Or, 'Stand away, fellow, from my diagram.' Last words. When the city of Syracuse was taken by the Romans, Archimedes was ordered by a soldier to follow him. Engaged as he was on a mathematical problem by drawing figures in the sand, he gave one or both of these responses. The soldier killed him. Quoted in Barnaby Conrad, *Famous Last Words* (1961).

ARENDT, Hannah

German-born American philosopher (1906–75)

7 It was as though in those last minutes he was summing up the lessons that this long course in human wickedness had taught us – the lesson of the fearsome, word-and-thought-defying banality of evil.

The final phrase was Arendt's key observation when writing about the trial of Adolf Eichmann, the Nazi official who was executed as a war criminal by Israel in 1962. Her book *Eichmann in Jerusalem* (1963) was subtitled 'A Report on the Banality of Evil'. Her essay was controversial in arguing that Europe's Jews might have been complicit in their own destruction and that Eichmann was not an abnormal monster but a mechanical one, unable to pit a personal morality against the Nazi system.

ARENS, Richard

American lawyer (1913–69)

8 Are you now or have you ever been a member of a godless conspiracy controlled by a foreign power?

Quoted in Peter Lewis, *The Fifties* (1978), this is Arens's version of the more usual question, 'Are you now or have you ever been a member of the Communist Party?', put to those appearing at hearings of the House of Representatives Committee on un-American Activities (1947–*c.*1957), especially by J. Parnell Thomas. It was the stock phrase of McCarthyism, the pursuit and public ostracism of suspected US Communist sympathizers at the time of the war with Korea in the early 1950s. Senator Joseph McCarthy was the instigator of the 'witch hunts', which led to the blacklisting of people in various walks of life, notably the film business. *Are You Now Or Have You Ever Been?* was the title of a radio/stage play (1978) by Eric Bentley.

ARISTOPHANES

Greek comic playwright (c.450–c.385BC)

1 How about 'Cloudcuckooland [*Nepheloco-ccygia*]'?

The Birds. This suggested name for the capital city of the birds (in the air) came to be included in the expression 'to live in cloud-cuckoo land', meaning 'to have impractical ideas'.

ARISTOTLE

Greek philosopher (384–322BC)

2 Tragedy is thus a representation of an action that is worth serious attention, complete in itself and of some amplitude ... by means of pity and fear bringing about the purgation of such emotions.

Poetics, Chap. 6. Hence, the word *catharsis* (Greek for cleansing, purging), which Aristotle used and is now applied to the purification of the emotions, especially through drama.

3 A gentleman should be able to play the flute, but not too expertly.

Attributed to Aristotle – possibly an encapsulation of the point he makes in Bk 8 of his *Politics* where he says that children of free men should learn and practise music only until they are able to feel delight in it and should not become professional musicians because this would make them vulgar.

ARKELL, Reginald

English poet (1882–1959)

4 There is a lady, sweet and kind
As any lady you will find.
I've known her nearly all my life;
She is, in fact, my present wife.

In daylight, she is kind to all,
But, as the evening shadows fall,
With jam-pot, salt and sugar-tongs
She starts to right her garden's wrongs.

An extract from Arkell's poem 'The Lady with the Lamp', which appeared in his *Green Fingers* (1934). 'There is a lady sweet and kind' is also the first line of a poem attributed to Thomas Ford (d.1648).

ARKWRIGHT, Sir John S.

English lawyer and poet (1872–1954)

5 O valiant hearts, who to your glory came
Through dust of conflict and through battle flame;
Tranquil you lie, your knightly virtue proved,
Your memory hallowed in the land you loved.

Proudly you gathered, rank on rank, to war,
As who had heard God's message from afar;
All you had hoped for, all you had, you gave
To save mankind – yourselves you scorned to save.

'The Supreme Sacrifice and Other Poems in Time of War' (1919). In the 1950s this moving hymn suffered a backlash and was dropped from Remembrance Day services by those who believed it was insufficiently critical of militarism. The *OED2*'s earliest citation for the phrase 'supreme sacrifice' which, alas, became a cliché for death, is 1916.

ARMSTRONG, Neil

American astronaut (1930–)

6 Tranquillity Base here – the Eagle has landed.

The Apollo 11 space mission that first put a man on the surface of the moon in July 1969 provided another phrase in addition to – and before – Armstrong's famous first words (below). As the lunar module touched down, this was what he announced. Nobody at Mission Control had known that Armstrong would call it that, although the name was logical enough: the landing area was in the Sea of Tranquillity; 'Eagle' was the name of the craft (referring to the American national symbol). The *ODQ* (1992), basing itself on an inaccurate report in *The Times*, has the words spoken by Buzz Aldrin. Confusingly, the writer Jack Higgins later used the phrase *The Eagle Has Landed* as the title of a 1975 thriller about a German kidnap attempt on Winston Churchill during the Second World War.

1 That's one small step for a man, one giant leap for mankind.

Armstrong claimed that this was what he actually said when stepping on to the moon's surface for the first time at 10.56 p.m. (EDT) on 20 July 1969. Six hundred million television viewers round the world watched, but what were his first words going to be? It seemed to him that every person he had met in the previous three months had asked him what he was going to say or had made suggestions. Among the hundreds of sayings he was offered were passages from Shakespeare and whole chapters from the Bible.

'I had thought about what I was going to say, largely because so many people had asked me to think about it,' Armstrong reflected afterwards in *First on the Moon* (1970). 'I thought about [it] a little bit on the way to the moon, and it wasn't really decided until after we got to the lunar surface. I guess I hadn't actually decided what I wanted to say until just before we went out.'

What the six hundred million *heard* was another matter. The indefinite article before 'man' was completely inaudible, thus ruining the nice contrast between 'a man' (one individual) and 'mankind' (all of us). However, this was how the line was first reported and, indeed, exactly how it sounds on recordings. There is no perceptible gap between 'for' and 'man'.

It is probably the most misheard remark ever. *The Times* of 21 July had it as: 'That's one small step for man but [*sic*] one giant leap for mankind.' The *Observer* 'Sayings of the Week' column on the Sunday following the landing had: 'That's one small step for man, one giant leap for all [*sic*] mankind'. And reference books have continued the confusion ever since. Several follow the version – 'One small step for [...] man, one big step [*sic*] for mankind' – which appeared in the magazine *Nature* in 1974.

When he returned to earth, the astronaut spotted the near-tautology in a transcript of the mission and tried to put over a correct version. It was explained that the indefinite article 'a' had not been heard because of static on the radio link or because 'tape recorders are fallible'. But it is just as possible that Armstrong fluffed his mighty line. If the twentieth-century's most *audible* saying could result in such confusion, what hope is there for the rest?

ARMSTRONG, Sir Robert (later Lord Armstrong)

English civil servant (1927–)

2 It is perhaps being economical with the truth.

On 18 November 1986 Armstrong, then the British Cabinet Secretary, was being cross-examined in the Supreme Court of New South Wales. The British government was attempting to prevent publication in Australia of a book about MI5, the British secret service. Defence counsel Malcolm Turnbull asked Sir Robert about the contents of a letter he had written which had been intended to convey a misleading impression. 'What's a "misleading impression"?' inquired Turnbull. 'A sort of bent untruth?'

Sir Robert replied: 'It is perhaps being economical with the truth.' This explanation was greeted with derision not only in the court but in the world beyond, and it looked as if a new euphemism for lying had been coined. In fact, Sir Robert had prefaced his remark with: 'As one person said ...' and, when the court apparently found cause for laughter in what he said, added: 'It is not very original, I'm afraid.'

Indeed not. Dr E.H.H. Green, writing to *The Guardian* on 4 February 1987, said he had found a note penned by Sir William Strang, later to become head of the Foreign Office, in February 1942. Describing the character of the exiled Czech President Benes, Strang had written: 'Dr Benes's methods are exasperating; he is a master of representation and ... he is apt to be economical with the truth.'

The notion thus appears to have been a familiar one in the British Civil Service for a very long time. Samuel Pepys apparently used the precise phrase in his evidence before the Brooke House Committee in its examination of the Navy Board in 1669–70.

In March 1988 Armstrong said in a TV interview that he had no regrets about having used the phrase. And he said again, it was not his own, indeed, but Edmund Burke's. The reference was to Burke's *Two Letters on Proposals for Peace* (1796): 'Falsehood and delusion are allowed in no case whatsoever. But, as in the exercise of all the virtues, there is an economy of truth.'

ARNO, Peter

American cartoonist (1904–68)

3 Well, back to the old drawing board.

In the form 'back to the drawing board' this means 'we've got to start again from scratch' and is usually said after an earlier plan has ended in failure. It is just possible that this began life in the caption to Arno's cartoon that appeared in *The New Yorker* during the early 1940s (exact date unknown). An official, with a rolled-up engineering plan under his arm, is walking away from a recently crashed plane and saying this.

ARNOLD, Matthew

English poet and essayist (1822–88)

1 A God, a God their severance ruled!
And bade betwixt their shores to be
The unplumb'd, salt, estranging sea.

'To Marguerite – Continued' (1852). The last sentence of *The French Lieutenant's Woman* (1969) by John Fowles (unattributed at that point, though it has been earlier) is: 'And out again, upon the unplumb'd, salt, estranging sea.'

2 Beautiful city! so venerable, so lovely, so unravaged by the fierce intellectual life of our century, so serene! ...whispering from her towers the last enchantments of the Middle Age ... home of lost causes, and forsaken beliefs, and unpopular names, and impossible loyalties!

Preface, *Essays in Criticism*, First Series (1865). On Oxford. James Morris, *Oxford* (1965), comments: 'Matthew Arnold said it was still "whispering the last enchantments of the Middle Ages", but Max Beerbohm thought he must have been referring to the railway station.' And adds: 'It is no such Arcady now, and its University no longer whispers those last enchantments. It is a turmoil, always dissatisfied, always in disagreement.'

3 And that sweet city with her dreaming spires,
She needs not June for beauty's heightening.

'Thyrsis' (1866). On Oxford. Morris (in *op. cit.*) comments: 'Nor does she. The particular magic of Oxford rides out the seasons ... all four seasons suit Oxford, and each enhances the look of her in a different way.' For appalling word-play on this, *see* RAPHAEL 446:6.

4 The sea is calm to-night,
The tide is full, the moon lies fair
Upon the straits ...
For the world, which seems
To lie before us like a land of dreams.

'Dover Beach' (1867). The last two lines here were famously misquoted by Lyndon Johnson in a speech in the summer of 1965. He (or his speechwriter) put 'lie out' and attributed the poem to Robert Lowell (who had merely used the lines as epigraph to his book *The Mills of the Kavanaughs*).

5 And we are here as on a darkling plain
Swept with confused alarms of struggle and flight,
Where ignorant armies clash by night.

Ib. Hence, possibly, the title of Norman Mailer's non-fiction work *Armies of the Night* (1968).

6 Let the long contention cease!
Geese are swans, and swans are geese.

'The Last Word' (1867). The 'geese/swans' comparison is in a long tradition. Three years before this, Cardinal Newman had written in his *Apologia*: 'He was particularly loyal to his friends, and, to use the common phrase, "all his geese were swans."' Horace Walpole said of Sir Joshua Reynolds, 'All his own geese are swans, as the swans of others are geese' (letter to the Countess of Upper Ossory, 1 December 1786). 'All their geese are swans' occurs in 'Democritus to the Reader' in Robert Burton, *The Anatomy of Melancholy* (1621). 'All his geese are swans' was a proverbial expression by 1529.

7 The pursuit of perfection, then, is the pursuit of sweetness and light. He who works for sweetness and light, works to make reason and the will of God prevail.

Culture and Anarchy, Chap. 1 (1869). *The Lyttelton Hart-Davis Letters* (for 25 January 1956) affirms that Arnold believed this conjunction of sweetness and light was the *sine qua non* of all real civilization. *Compare* SWIFT 524:8.

ASHFORD, Daisy

English child author (1881–1972)

8 Mr Salteena was an elderly man of 42 and was fond of asking peaple to stay with him.

The Young Visiters, Chap. 1 (1919). This story of romance and high society was written when Daisy was nine. It was published, complete with crude spellings and interesting punctuation, when she was thirty-eight. Because there was an introduction by J.M. Barrie, it has sometimes been wrongly believed that he was the actual author. Other choice extracts: 'I do hope I shall enjoy myself with you ... I am parshial to ladies if they are nice I suppose it is my nature. I am not quite a gentleman but you would hardly notice it' (Chap. 1); 'I am very fond of fresh air and royalties' (Chap. 5).

ASQUITH, H.H. (later 1st Earl of Oxford and Asquith)

British Liberal Prime Minister (1852–1928)

1 You had better wait and see.

To a persistent inquirer about the Parliament Act Procedure Bill, in the House of Commons (4 April 1910). In fact, this was the fourth occasion on which Asquith had said 'Wait and see'. On 3 March he had replied 'We had better wait and see' to Lord Helmsey concerning the government's intentions over the Budget and whether the House of Lords would be flooded with Liberal peers to ensure the passage of the Finance Bill. So he was clearly deliberate in his use of the words. His intention was not to delay making an answer but to warn people off. Roy Jenkins commented in *Asquith* (1964): 'It was a use for which he was to pay dearly in the last years of his premiership when the phrase came to be erected by his enemies as a symbol of his alleged inactivity.'

In consequence, Asquith acquired the nickname 'Old Wait and See', and during the First World War French matches that failed to ignite were known either as 'Asquiths' or 'Wait and sees'.

It was, of course, an old phrase: Daniel Defoe has it in *Robinson Crusoe* (1719): 'However, we had no remedy, but to wait and see what the issue of things might present.'

2 [Balliol men are distinguished from lesser souls by their] tranquil consciousness of effortless superiority.

This is the version of Asquith's remark given by John Jones in his *Balliol College: A History 1263–1939*. Frances Bennion wrote to *Oxford Today* (Hilary Term 1992) to point out that the British Labour politician Denis Healey – an old member of the college – had misquoted this in his memoirs, *The Time of My Life* (1989), as, 'the conscious tranquillity of effortless superiority'. Which is not quite the same thing.

3 Another little drink wouldn't do us any harm.

The boozer's jocular justification for another snort is, in fact, rather more than a catchphrase. It is alluded to in Edith Sitwell's bizarre lyrics for 'Scotch Rhapsody' in *Façade* (1922):

> There is a hotel at Ostend
> Cold as the wind, without an end,
> Haunted by ghostly poor relations ...
> And 'Another little drink wouldn't do us any harm,'
> Pierces through the sabbatical calm.

The actual origin is in a song with the phrase as title, written by Clifford Grey to music by Nat D. Ayer, and sung by the comedian George Robey in *The Bing Boys Are Here* (1916). The song includes a reference to the well known fact that Prime Minister Asquith was at times the worse for drink when on the Treasury Bench:

> Mr Asquith says in a manner sweet and calm:
> And another little drink wouldn't do us any harm.

4 It is fitting that we should have buried the Unknown Prime Minister by the side of the Unknown Soldier.

At the Westminster Abbey funeral of Andrew Bonar Law (5 November 1923). Hence, *The Unknown Prime Minister*, the title of Law's biography (1955) by Robert Blake.

ASQUITH, Margot (later Countess of Oxford and Asquith)

Wife of H.H. Asquith (1864–1945)

5 Kitchener is a great poster.

A remark often attributed to Margot, but in *More Memories*, Chap. 6 (1933) she ascribed it to her daughter Elizabeth (1897–1945).

6 He has a brilliant mind until he makes it up.

On Sir Stafford Cripps. *The Autobiography of Margot Asquith* (1936 ed.).

7 He couldn't see a belt without hitting below it.

On David Lloyd George. Quoted in Mark Bonham Carter's Introduction to *The Autobiography of Margot Asquith* (1962 ed.)

8 My dear old friend King George V told me he would never have died but for that vile doctor, Lord Dawson of Penn.

An observation that Lady Asquith made several times in her old age, but especially to Lord David Cecil (and recorded first by Mark Bonham Carter in his introduction to *The Autobiography of Margot Asquith*, 1962 ed.). It turns out to be not so preposterous as might appear. On 20 January 1936, King George V lay dying at Sandringham. At 9.25 p.m., Lord Dawson of Penn, the King's doctor, issued a bulletin 'The King's life is moving peacefully towards its close' (*see* DAWSON 197:5). This was taken up by the BBC and repeated until the King died at 11.55 p.m. In December 1986, Dawson's biographer suggested in *History Today* that the doctor had in fact hastened the King's departure with lethal injections of morphine and cocaine at the request of the Queen and the future Edward VIII. Dawson's notes reveal that the death was induced at 11 p.m. not only to ease the King's pain but to enable the news to make the morning papers, 'rather than the less appropriate evening journals'. *The Times* was advised that important news was coming and to hold back publication. So Dawson of Penn *might* have had a hand in the King's death, though quite how George V communicated his view of the matter to Margot Asquith is not known.

1 His modesty amounts to deformity.

On her husband. Quoted by her stepdaughter Baroness Asquith in BBC TV programme *As I Remember* (30 April 1967).

2 He's very clever, but sometimes his brains go to his head.

On F.E. Smith in *ib.* But also given earlier by Lady Violet Bonham Carter (as she then was) in 'Margot Oxford' in *The Listener* (11 June 1953).

3 The 't' is silent – as in 'Harlow'.

Margot Asquith was noted for the sharp remarks she made about people, but her most famous shaft was probably said by someone else. The story goes that Margot visited the United States (*that* is not in dispute) where she met Jean Harlow. The film actress inquired whether the name of the Countess (which she was by this time, the 1930s) was pronounced 'Margo' or 'Margott'. '"Margo",' replied the Countess, 'the "T" is silent – as in "Harlow".' The story did not appear in print until T.S. Matthews's *Great Tom* in 1973. Then, in about 1983, a much more convincing version of its origin was given. Margot *Grahame* (1911–82) was an English actress who, after stage appearances in Johannesburg and London, went to Hollywood in 1934. Her comparatively brief career as a film star included appearances in *The Informer*, *The Buccaneer* and *The Three Musketeers* in the mid-1930s.

It was when she was being built up as a rival to the likes of Harlow (who died in 1937) that Grahame herself claimed the celebrated exchange had occurred. She added that it was not intended as a put down. She did not realize what she had said until afterwards.

Grahame seems a convincing candidate for speaker of the famous line. When her star waned people attributed the remark to the other, better known and more quotable source.

See also KEYNES 333:6.

ASQUITH, Violet See BONHAM CARTER

ASTLEY, Sir Jacob

English soldier (1579–1652)

4 O Lord! Thou knowest how busy I must be this day: if I forget thee, do not Thou forget me.

Astley was a Royalist in the English Civil War and was hurt at the Battle of Edgehill (13 October 1642), the indecisive first engagement of the Civil War. His prayer before the battle was quoted in Sir Philip Warwick's *Memoirs* (1701).

ASTOR, Viscountess Nancy

American-born British politician (1879–1964)

5 I married beneath me. All women do.

Speech, Oldham (1951), quoted in the *Dictionary of National Biography 1961–70* (1981). She was the first British woman MP to take her seat in the House of Commons and, in fact, was wealthy in her own right. She married Waldorf Astor who later succeeded his father as Viscount Astor.

6 You'll never get on in politics, my dear, with *that* hair.

On the young Shirley Williams. Confirmed as having been made, by the remark's recipient on BBC Radio *Quote ... Unquote* (9 November 1982).

7 Jakie, is it my birthday or am I dying?

To her son, on her death bed. He replied: 'A bit of both, Mum.' Her last word was 'Waldorf' (the name of her husband). Quoted in John Grigg, *Nancy Astor: Portrait of a Pioneer* (1980).

ATTLEE, Clement (later 1st Earl Attlee)

British Labour Prime Minister (1883–1967)

8 You have no right whatever to speak on behalf of the Government. Foreign Affairs are in the capable hands of Ernest Bevin. His task is quite sufficiently difficult without the embarrassment of irresponsible statements of the kind which you are making ... a period of silence on your part would be welcome.

Quoted in *British Political Facts 1900–75*. From a letter to Harold Laski, Chairman of the Labour Party NEC (20

August 1945). Just after the Labour government had come to power, Laski had been giving a constant flow of speeches and interviews, not always in accord with party policy. The put-down was typical of Attlee's clipped way and also reflected his own more reticent way with words.

1 Few thought he was even a starter
There were many who thought themselves smarter
But he ended PM, CH and OM
An Earl and a Knight of the Garter.

Of himself. Lines written on 8 April 1956, quoted in Kenneth Harris, *Attlee* (1982). Of modest demeanour (hence CHURCHILL 168:2), Attlee was a man of considerable achievement, as he gently points out here.

AUBREY, John

English antiquary (1626–97)

2 How these curiosities would be quite forgot, did not such idle fellows as I am put them down.

'Venetia Digby', *Brief Lives*, (*c.*1693) – as in Oliver Lawson Dick, *Aubrey's Brief Lives* (1958).

3 He was a learned man, of immense reading, but is much blamed for his unfaithful quotations.

In *ib.* Of the Puritan pamphleteer William Prynne (1600–69) who was branded for seditious libel.

4 Grubbing in churchyards.

His method of historical research. Quoted in Fritz Spiegl, *A Small Book of Grave Humour* (1971). Unverified.

See also ELIZABETH I 228:1.

AUDEN, W.H.

Anglo-American poet (1907–73)

5 Private faces in public places
Are wiser and nicer
Than public faces in private places.

Dedication, *Orators* (1932). Hence, possibly, *Public Faces*, title of a book (1932) by Harold Nicolson.

6 The Dog Beneath the Skin.

Title of play (1935), written with Christopher Isherwood. According to Humphrey Carpenter's biography of Auden (1981), the title was suggested by Rupert Doone and probable alludes to ELIOT 225:5.

7 August for the people and their favourite islands.

'Birthday Poem' (1935). Hence, *August for the People*, title of a play (1961) by Nigel Dennis.

8 This is the Night Mail crossing the Border
Bringing the cheque and the postal order,
Letters for the rich, letters for the poor,
The shop at the corner, the girl next door.

'Night Mail' (1935). Commentary for Post Office Film Unit documentary film. 'We were experimenting,' Auden said, 'to see whether poetry could be used in films, and I think we showed it could.' The first draft contained lines that Harry Watt, the director, felt 'could not be matched with adequate images on the screen – lines such as "Uplands heaped like slaughtered horses" ... Watt observed: "No picture we put on the screen could be as strong as that"' (source: Humphrey Carpenter, *W.H. Auden*, 1981). Nevertheless, the cut line has not been forgotten and is still quoted.

9 And make us as Newton was, who in his garden watching
The apple falling towards England, became aware
Between himself and her of an eternal tie.

'O Love, the interest itself' (1936). Hence, probably, *Falling Towards England*, title of a volume of memoirs (1985) by the Australian-born writer, Clive James. Julian Mitchell's 1994 play about a family in the early part of the twentieth century has the similar title, *Falling Over England.*

10 Look, stranger, at this island now.

'Look, Stranger' (1936). Hence, *Look, Stranger!* – the use of Auden's phrase as the title of a BBC TV documentary series (1976) revealed an interesting state of affairs. Auden's famous poem has two versions of its first line: 'Look, stranger, at this island now' and '... on this island now'. 'At' is the original reading in the title poem of the collection *Look, Stranger!* published in the UK (1936). But the US title of the collection was *On This Island.* The text of the poem was changed to 'on' for the 1945 *Collected Poems*, published in the US. Just to complicate matters, the poem's title was changed variously to 'Seascape' and 'Seaside'.

The reason for all this is that when he was inaccessible in Iceland, his publishers Faber & Faber (in the person of T.S. Eliot) applied the title *Look, Stranger!* to the collection that Auden wanted called 'Poems 1936'. He said the Faber title sounded 'like the work of a vegetarian lady novelist' and made sure that it was subsequently dropped.

1 Stop all the clocks, cut off the telephone,
Prevent the dog from barking with a juicy bone,
Silence the pianos and with muffled drum
Bring out the coffin, let the mourners come.

... He was my North, my South, my East and West,
My working week and my Sunday rest,
My noon, my midnight, my talk, my song;
I thought that love would last for ever. I was wrong.

From 'Funeral Blues', originally in *The Ascent of F6* (1937), a play jointly written with Christopher Isherwood. Set to music, a pastiche blues, by Benjamin Britten for the original production, the original words mocked the death of a political leader. Auden then rewrote the poem as more of a love-song and it had a separate existence for many years as one of Britten's 'Cabaret Songs'. Then, in 1994, the text was spoken at the funeral 'of another bugger' in the UK film *Four Weddings and a Funeral.* Seldom can a poem have become so immediately known and made popular.

2 He disappeared in the dead of winter:
The brooks were frozen, the airports almost deserted,
And snow disfigured the public statues;
The mercury sank in the mouth of the dying day.
What instruments we have agree
The day of his death was a dark cold day ...
Mad Ireland hurt you into poetry.
Now Ireland has her madness and her weather still,
For poetry makes nothing happen ...
Earth, receive an honoured guest:
William Yeats is laid to rest.
Let the Irish vessel lie
Emptied of its poetry.

'In Memory of W.B. Yeats' (1939). Carpenter (*op. cit.*) comments: 'Yeats had been an important influence on Auden's poetic style during the 1930s, but Auden did not have an unmitigated admiration for him ... By contrast the poem was scarcely critical of Yeats; in fact it was not really about him, but about the nature and function of poetry – and thus really about Auden himself.'

3 In the deserts of the heart
Let the healing fountain start,
In the prison of his days
Teach the free man how to praise.

Ib. The last two lines are quoted on the memorial slab to Auden in Poets' Corner, Westminster Abbey. The memorial was unveiled on 2 October 1974. Auden is actually buried at Kirchstetten, Austria.

4 There is no such thing as the State
And no one exists alone;
Hunger allows no choice
To the citizen or the police;
We must love one another or die.

Auden became embarrassed by the last line of his poem 'September 1, 1939' ('the most dishonest poem I have ever written') because it was 'a damned lie' – we must die in any case. When the editor of a 1955 anthology pleaded with Auden to include the entire text of the poem, Auden agreed provided that 'We must love one another *and* die' was substituted.

5 Perfection, of a kind, was what he was after,
And the poetry he invented was easy to understand;
He knew human folly like the back of his hand,
And was greatly interested in armies and fleets;
When he laughed, respectable senators burst with laughter,
And when he cried the little children died in the streets.

'Epitaph on a Tyrant' (1940). The last line echoes J.L. Motley's description of William of Orange in *The Rise of the Dutch Republic* (1856): 'As long as he lived, he was the guiding-star of a whole brave nation, and when he died the little children cried in the streets.'

6 Lay your sleeping head, my love,
Human on my faithless arm.

'Lullaby' (1940). Carpenter (*op. cit.*) comments: '[This poem] became, in the years that followed, the most famous of all his short lyrics ... [this and other poems] are not usually even explicitly homosexual: their subject is the impermanence of all love, whatever sex the loved may be.'

7 To the man-in-the-street, who, I'm sorry to say
Is a keen observer of life,
The word Intellectual suggests straight away
A man who's untrue to his wife.

New Year Letter (1941), also published as 'Note on Intellectuals' (1947).

1 A professor is one who talks in someone else's sleep.

Quoted in *The Treasury of Humorous Quotations*, ed. by Evan Esar & Nicolas Bentley (1951). The earliest source found for this frequently attributed remark.

2 Most people enjoy the sight of their own handwriting as they enjoy the smell of their own farts.

'Writing', *The Dyer's Hand* (1962). *See also* ANONYMOUS 29:3.

3 My face looks like a wedding-cake left out in the rain.

No, it was not said *about* Auden (as stated, for example, in L. Levinson, *Bartlett's Unfamiliar Quotations*, 1972). The poet himself said to a reporter: 'Your cameraman might enjoy himself, because my face looks like a wedding-cake left out in the rain' (cited in Humphrey Carpenter, *W.H. Auden*, 1981). However, according to Noël Annan in *Maurice Bowra: a celebration* (1974), Bowra once referred to E.M. Forster's *work* as a wedding-cake left out in the rain.

Someone once said of Auden's face: 'If a fly walked over it, it would break its leg.' Quoted on BBC Radio *Quote ... Unquote* (5 June 1980).

AUGIER, Émile

French poet and playwright (1820–89)

4 *La nostalgie de la boue.*
Longing to be back in the mud.

In the play *Le Mariage d'Olympe* (1855), Augier gave this as an explanation of what happens when you put a duck on a lake with swans. He will miss his own pond and eventually return to it. Taken up in many situations where there is a desire for degradation. At the very end of D.H. Lawrence's *Lady Chatterley's Lover* (1928), Sir Clifford says to Lady Connie: 'You're one of those half-insane, perverted women who must run after depravity, the *nostalgie de la boue*.'

AUGUSTINE OF HIPPO

North African Christian theologian and saint (AD354–430)

5 A stiff prick hath no conscience.

Ascribed confidently by John Osborne in *Almost a Gentleman* (1991), this remark remains unverified, though, in one sense, it would not be surprising given Augustine's interesting activities prior to conversion. After all, he did write '*Da mihi castitatem et continentiam, sed noli modo* [give me chastity and continence – but not yet]' in his *Confessions* (AD397–398). The proverbial status of the remark was, however, evident by the 1880s when 'Walter' in *My Secret Life* (Vol. 1, Chap. 12) wrote: 'I thought how unfair it was to her sister, who was in the family way by me ... but a standing prick stifles all conscience.' Indeed, 'a *standing* prick has no conscience' is an equally well-known variant. Partridge/ *Catch Phrases* adds that this proverbial view is sometimes completed with, '... and an itching c*** feels no shame', just to even out the matter.

Compare: 'Another writer whom [Wilde] did not spare was his old teacher J.P. Mahaffy, two of whose books Wilde reviewed ... [he] might have treated Mahaffy nostalgically, but the erect pen has no conscience' – Richard Ellman, *Oscar Wilde* (1987).

AUSTEN, Jane

English novelist (1775–1817)

6 Pride and Prejudice.

The title of Austen's novel (written as *First Impressions*, 1797, published 1813) has been said to derive from the second chapter of Edward Gibbon's *The Decline and Fall of the Roman Empire* (published 1776). Writing of the enfranchisement of the slaves, Gibbon writes: 'Without destroying the distinction of ranks a distant prospect of freedom and honours was presented, even to those whom pride and prejudice almost disdained to number among the human species.'

More to the point, the phrase occurs no fewer than three times, in bold print, towards the end of Fanny Burney's *Cecilia* (1787): '"The whole of this unfortunate business," said Dr Lyster, "has been the result of Pride and Prejudice ... Yet this, however, remember; if to Pride and Prejudice you owe your miseries, so wonderfully is good and evil balanced, that to Pride and Prejudice you will also owe their termination".' This seems the most likely cue to Jane Austen. On the other hand, *OED2* provides six citations of the phrase 'pride and prejudice' before Burney, one of which has capital Ps.

7 It is a truth universally acknowledged, that a single man in possession of a good fortune, must be in want of a wife.

Pride and Prejudice (1813), opening words – probably the most imitated and parodied of all such.

1 It is happy for you that you possess the talent of flattering with delicacy. May I ask whether these pleasing attentions proceed from the impulse of the moment, or are the result of previous study?

Ib., Chap.14. Said by Mr Bennet to Mr Collins who has been describing his flattery of Lady Catherine de Bourgh.

2 You have delighted us long enough.

Ib., Chap. 18. Said by Mr Bennet to his daughter Mary who has been singing.

3 An egg boiled very soft is not unwholesome.

Emma, Chap. 3 (1816). Emma's father, the rather tiresome Mr Woodhouse, says it – convinced that suppers are unwholesome. His care for his guests' health consequently means that they are given little to eat.

4 Do you know, I get so immoderately sick of Bath! Your brother and I were agreeing this morning that, though it is vastly well to be here for a few weeks, we would not *live* here for millions.

Northanger Abbey, Chap. 10 (1818) – published the year after Austen's death. Balancing Isabella Thorpe's view, in the same chapter, is her friend Catherine Morland's remark: 'Oh! who can ever be tired of Bath!'

AUSTIN, Alfred

English Poet Laureate (1835–1913)

5 Flash'd from his bed the electric tidings came, 'He is no better, he is much the same.'

Lines often ascribed to Austin, as in A.& V. Palmer, *Quotations in History* (1976), and sometimes remembered as 'Across/along the electric wire the message came ...' The couplet is quoted as an example of bathos and of a Poet Laureate writing to order at his worst. As such, it needs some qualification, if not an actual apology to the poet's shade. D.B. Wyndham Lewis and Charles Lee in their noted selection of bad verse, *The Stuffed Owl* (1930), interestingly included a similar couplet, but ascribed it to a 'university poet unknown', and quite right, too. F.H. Gribble had included the slightly different version, 'Along the electric wire ...', in his *Romance of the Cambridge Colleges* (1913).

What is not in dispute is that the lines were written to mark the Prince of Wales's illness in 1871. Unfortunately, to spoil a good story, it has to be pointed out that Austin never wrote them (though he *did* match them in awfulness on other occasions) and he did not become Poet Laureate until 1896, following in the illustrious footsteps of Tennyson. As J. Lewis May observed in *The Dublin Review* (July 1937), in an article about Austin as 'a neglected poet', the couplet was written 'when the then Prince of Wales (he who afterwards became King Edward VII) had recovered from the attack of typhoid fever which had caused the gravest anxiety throughout the country, [and] the subject set for the Newdigate Prize Poem at Oxford was "The Prince of Wales's illness"; whereupon some wag, with consequences of which he never dreamed, produced the following couplet, as a specimen of the sort of thing that might be sent in by competitors for the coveted guerdon ... The name of the inventor of those immortal lines has not been handed down.'

The Editor of *The Author* (spring 1993) questioned whether Austin had really attracted 'universal derision' (my phrase) because of his supposed authorship of the lines. To which I replied that, almost invariably, Austin was linked to them, with or without an 'attributed to' or other qualification, in such dictionaries of quotations as the *PDQ* (1960), the *Bloomsbury* (1987) and Robin Hyman's *Dictionary of Famous Quotations* (1962). Even the *ODQ* (1992) *mentions* Austin, although it places the couplet under 'Anonymous'.

As for Austin generally, Mrs Claude Bettington recalled in *All That I Have Met* (1929) that he had said to her in all seriousness one day, 'My child, have you ever noticed how many great men are called *Alfred* – Alfred the Great, Alfred Tennyson?' As a dutiful niece, she added, 'And *you*, Uncle Alf.' Mrs Bettington goes on: 'No one could fathom why he was made Poet Laureate, since his only claim to fame was his exquisite prose. I therefore asked a niece of Lord Salisbury point blank, "Why on earth did your uncle give the laureateship to Uncle Alfred?" She answered, "Because it was absolutely the only honour Mr Austin would accept from the Government for his long years of service to the Conservative cause".'

AWDRY, Rev. W(ilbert)

English clergyman and author (1911–97)

6 After pushing [trucks] about here for a few weeks you'll know almost as much about them as Edward. Then you'll be a Really Useful Engine.

Thomas the Tank Engine (1946). Accordingly, since the 1980s, the composer Andrew Lloyd Webber has presided over a business empire called the Really Useful Group.

1 We are nationalised now, but the same engines still work the Region. I am glad, too, to tell you that the Fat Director, who understands our friends' ways, is still in charge, but is now the Fat Controller.

Introduction, *James the Red Engine* (1948). In fact, he has twice undergone a name change. Initially, indeed, he was shown very much as a director of a private railway company, wearing striped pants, tail coat and top hat, but the nationalization of Britain's railways in the late 1940s did necessitate the change from 'director' to 'controller'. Then again, in the 1990s, when a hugely successful TV film version was made of the stories, sales to the politically correct US market necessitated that the character be referred to not by the fat-ist 'Fat Controller' but by Awdry's actual name for the character, Sir Topham Hat.

AXELROD, George

American screenwriter (1922–)

2 The seven year itch.

Title of play *The Seven Year Itch* (1952; film US, 1955) – a term for the urge to be unfaithful to a spouse after a certain period of matrimony. The *OED2* provides various examples of this phrase going back from the mid-twentieth to the mid-nineteenth century, but without the specific matrimonial context. For example, the 'seven year itch' describes a rash from poison ivy that was believed to recur every year for a seven-year period. Then one has to recall that since biblical days seven-year periods (of lean or fat) have had especial significance, and there has also been the army saying, 'Cheer up – the first seven years are the worst!'

But the specific matrimonial application was not popularized until Axelrod's play. 'Itch' had long been used for the sexual urge but, as Axelrod commented on BBC Radio *Quote ... Unquote* (1979): 'There was a phrase which referred to a somewhat unpleasant disease but nobody had used it in a sexual [he meant 'matrimonial'] context before. I do believe I invented it in that sense.'

Oddly, there is no mention in reference books of 'itch' being used in connection with venereal diseases. Nonetheless, the following remark occurs in Robert Lewis Taylor, *W.C. Fields: His Follies and Fortunes* (published as early as 1950): 'Bill exchanged women every seven years, as some people get rid of the itch.'

B

BABA, Meher

Indian guru and avatar (1894–1969)

1 Don't worry, be happy.

A saying of Baba, the so-called Indian God-Man, had a new lease of life in 1988 when it became the title of a song by the American singer Bobby McFerrin and won the Grammy award for the year's best song. 'The landlord says the rent is late, he might have to litigate, but don't worry, be happy,' McFerrin sang, in a song which became a minor national anthem, reflecting a feeling in the US at the time. *The Times* (8 March 1989) noted: 'The song has spawned a whole "happy" industry and re-launched the Smiley face emblem that emerged in America in the late 1960s and was taken up in Britain by the acid-house scene last year. Bloomingdales, the Manhattan department store, now features a "Don't worry, be happy shop".' The song even became George Bush's unofficial campaign theme in the presidential election of 1988.

BACON, Francis (1st Baron Verulam and Viscount St Albans)

English philosopher and politician (1561–1626)

2 I have taken all knowledge to be my province.

Letter to Lord Burghley (1592). Bacon also wrote: '*Nam et ipsa scientia postestas est* [knowledge is itself power]' in *De Haeresibus* (1597). Sir James Murray (*q.v.*), first editor of what became *The Oxford English Dictionary*, wrote 'Knowledge is power' (in English) on the flyleaf of his copy of Cassell's *Popular Educator* – quoted in Elizabeth Murray, *Caught in the Web of Words* (1977).

3 My essays, which of all my other works have been most current; for that, as it seems, they come home, to men's business, and bosoms.

Dedication of the 1625 edition of his *Essays*. Business = concerns; bosoms = emotions.

4 If the mountain won't come to Mahomet, Mahomet must go to the mountain.

What Bacon actually wrote in 'Of Boldness' in *ib.*, where the proverb made its first appearance, was: 'If the hill will not come to Mahomet, Mahomet will go to the hill.'

5 Men fear death as children fear to go into the dark; and as that natural fear in children is increased with tales, so is the other.

'Of Death' in *ib.* Also: 'I do not believe that any man fears to be dead, but only the stroke of death.' *See also* FIELDING 235:2.

6 It is the wisdom of the crocodiles, that shed tears when they would devour.

'Of Wisdom for a Man's Self' in *ib.* The legend that crocodiles shed tears in order to lure victims to their deaths was established by the year 1400. In an account of a 1565 voyage by Sir John Hawkins (published by Richard Hakluyt, 1600), there is: 'In this river we saw many crocodiles ... His nature is ever when he would have his prey, to cry and sob like a Christian body, to provoke them to come to him, and then he snatcheth at them.' Shakespeare makes reference to crocodile tears in *Antony and Cleopatra*, *Othello* and *Henry VI*. Hence, the modern use of 'crocodile tears' to denote a false display of sorrow.

7 If a man be gracious and courteous to strangers, it shows he is a citizen of the world.

'Of Goodness, and Goodness of Nature' in *ib.* Cicero had the phrase 'citizen of the world' as '*civem totius mundi*', meaning 'one who is cosmopolitan, at home anywhere'. Similarly, Socrates said, 'I am citizen, not of Athens or Greece, but of the world.' The *OED2* finds the English phrase in Caxton (1474). Later *The Citizen of the World* was the title of a collection of letters by Oliver Goldsmith purporting to be those of Lien Chi Altangi, a philosophic Chinaman living in London and commenting on English life and characters. They were first published as 'Chinese Letters' in the *Public Ledger* (1760–1), and then again under this title in 1762.

James Boswell, not unexpectedly, in his *Journal of a Tour to the Hebrides* (1786) reflects: 'I am, I flatter myself, completely a citizen of the world ... In my travels through Holland, Germany, Switzerland, Italy, Corsica, France, I never felt myself from home; and I sincerely love "every kindred and tongue and people and nation".'

1 He that hath wife and children, hath given hostages to fortune; for they are impediments to great enterprises, either of virtue or mischief.

'Of Marriage and Single Life' in *ib.* This is probably the origin of the expression 'hostage to fortune', for what one establishes by delivering one's future into the hands of fate, usually by making some specific move or decision.

2 What is Truth? said jesting Pilate; and would not stay for an answer.

'Of Truth' in *ib.* The allusion is to Pilate's question to Jesus Christ, as reported in John 18:38. Hence, *Jesting Pilate*, title of a travel book (1926) by Aldous Huxley.

See also ELIZABETH I 227:5.

BACON, Francis

Irish-born painter (1909–92)

3 Three Screaming Popes.

This is not the title of any painting by Bacon but of a musical work inspired by his three paintings of Popes which, in turn, were based on the Velázquez portrait 'Pope Innocent X'. The English composer Mark-Anthony Turnage (1960–), whose orchestral work with the title was first performed in 1989, says his initial idea was 'to write a piece which distorted a set of Spanish dances as Bacon had distorted and restated the Velázquez'. Bacon's paintings tend to be referred to drily along the lines of 'Study after Velázquez's Portrait of Pope Innocent X' (1953).

See also WERTENBAKER 562:2.

BADEN-POWELL, Sir Robert (later 1st Baron Baden-Powell)

English soldier (1857–1941)

4 Be Prepared ... the meaning of the motto is that a scout must prepare himself by previous thinking out and practising how to act on any accident or emergency so that he is never taken by surprise; he knows exactly what to do when anything unexpected happens.

Scouting for Boys (1908). 'Be prepared' is the motto of the Boy Scout movement and shares its initials with those of its founder (who was often referred to by its members as 'B-P'). The words first appeared in a handbook and mean that Scouts should always be 'in a state of readiness in mind and body' to do their duty. Winston Churchill wrote in *Great Contemporaries* (1937): 'It is difficult to exaggerate the moral and mental health which our nation had derived from this profound and simple conception. In those bygone days the motto Be Prepared had a special meaning for our country. Those who looked to the coming of a great war welcomed the awakening of British boyhood.'

With permission, the words were subsequently used as an advertising slogan for Pears' soap.

5 It is called in our schools 'beastliness', and this is about the best name for it ... should it become a habit it quickly destroys both health and spirits; he becomes feeble in body and mind, and often ends in a lunatic asylum.

On masturbation in *ib.*, though 'beastliness' has also been taken to refer to homosexuality.

BAER, Arthur ('Bugs')

American columnist and writer (1897?–1969)

6 Alimony is like buying oats for a dead horse.

Quoted in *The Treasury of Humorous Quotations*, ed. by Evan Esar & Nicolas Bentley (1951). The earliest source found for this frequently attributed remark.

BAGEHOT, Walter

English constitutional historian (1826–77)

7 The soldier ... of today is ... a quiet, grave man ... perhaps like Count Moltke, 'silent in seven languages'.

'Checks and Balances', *The English Constitution* (1867). The source of Bagehot's quotation is unknown, but it is yet another interesting description of the taciturn German, Helmuth Graf von Moltke (1800–91). 'Moltke' is, in consequence, a nickname given to any taciturn, unsmiling person. Michael Wharton ('Peter Simple' columnist in *The Daily Telegraph*) described in *The Missing Will* (1984) how he was so nicknamed, as a child, by his German grandfather after the famous general, 'who seldom spoke and was said to have smiled only twice in his life'. Geoffrey Madan's *Notebooks* (1981) recorded that these two occasions were 'once when his mother-in-law died and once when a certain fortress was declared to be impregnable'.

1 A severe though not unfriendly critic of our institutions said that 'the *cure* for admiring the House of Lords was to go and look at it.'

'The House of Lords' in *ib.* Note that this was not necessarily Bagehot's own view, as is sometimes asserted.

2 Nations touch at their summits.

Ib. Possibly the origin of the modern concept of summit conferences – meetings of the chief representatives of anything, usually political leaders of major world powers. In which case, the usage was revived by Winston Churchill: 'It is not easy to see how things could be worsened by a parley at the summit, if such a thing were possible' – quoted in *The Times* (15 February 1950).

3 The best reason why Monarchy is a strong government is, that it is an intelligible government. The mass of mankind understand it, and they hardly anywhere in the world understand any other.

'The Monarchy' in *ib.* Much quoted in the debates over the continuation of the British monarchy in the 1980s and 1990s.

4 A princely marriage is the brilliant edition of a universal fact, and as such, it rivets mankind.

Ib. Much quoted at the time of the marriage of the Prince of Wales to Lady Diana Spencer in 1981.

5 Our royalty is to be reverenced, and if you begin to poke about it you cannot reverence it ... Its mystery is its life. We must not let in daylight upon magic.

Ib. Compare DE GAULLE 200:6.

6 The sovereign has, under a constitutional monarchy such as ours, three rights – the right to be consulted, the right to encourage, the right to warn.

Ib. Referring specifically to the British sovereign.

BAILEY, Sydney D.

English writer (1916–)

7 It has been said that this minister [the Lord Privy Seal] is neither a Lord, nor a privy, nor a seal.

British Parliamentary Democracy (3rd ed., 1971). The *ODMQ* (1991) curiously elevates Bailey to the status of originator for this joke when it is obvious that even he is not claiming it. The observation was already widely known by the time of Bailey's book, not least from its use on BBC TV's *The Frost Report* (1966–7). It was possibly inspired by Voltaire's joke that the Holy Roman Empire was neither holy, nor Roman, nor an empire (*Essai sur l'histoire générale et sur les moeurs et l'esprit des nations*, 1756). The Lord Privy Seal is now the title of a Cabinet Minister, sometimes one without portfolio. His job was formerly to keep the Great Seal of England, which was put on official documents.

BAIRNSFATHER, Bruce

British cartoonist (1888–1959)

8 Well, if you knows of a better 'ole, go to it.

Caption to cartoon published in *Fragments from France* (1915) depicting the gloomy soldier 'Old Bill', sitting on a shell crater in the mud on the Somme during the First World War. The cartoon series was enormously popular. A musical (London, 1917; New York, 1918) and two films (UK, 1918; US, 1926), based on the strip, all had the title *The Better 'Ole.*

BAKER, Howard

American Republican politician (1925–)

9 What did the President know, and when did he know it?

At the US Senate Watergate Committee hearings during the summer of 1973, Baker, the vice-chairman – an earnest lawmaker from Tennessee – became famous when he framed this essential question about Richard Nixon. He repeated it several times, and the answer led to Nixon's downfall. Later, during the investigations into the Iran-Contra affair and when President Reagan repeatedly said he knew nothing of the matter (1987), Washingtonians joked: 'What did Reagan know, and when did he forget it?'

BALDWIN, James

American novelist (1924–87)

1 The Fire Next Time.

Title of novel (1963). It is explained in the concluding sentence: 'If we do not now dare everything, the fulfilment of that prophecy, re-created from the Bible in song by a slave, is upon us: *God gave Noah the rainbow sign, No more water, the fire next time!*' As a warning of the use of fire in racial clashes it anticipated 'Burn, baby, burn!', the Black extremist slogan used following the August 1965 riots in the Watts district of Los Angeles, when entire blocks were burned down and thirty-four people killed.

BALDWIN, Monica

English writer (c.1896–1975)

2 I Leap Over the Wall.

Title of book (1949) that described 'a return to the world after twenty-eight years in a convent'. The author traced the title to a Baldwin family motto, '*Per Deum Meum Transilio Murum* [By the help of my God I leap over the wall]', which derived from the escape of an earlier Baldwin: 'Nearly 400 years ago, my ancestor Thomas Baldwin of Diddlesbury leaped to freedom from behind the walls of the Tower of London ... His name with an inscription and the date "July 1585" can still be seen where he carved it on the wall of his cell in the Beauchamp Tower.' He added the motto to his arms and it was taken up again by Stanley Baldwin when he took his Earldom. There may be an echo in it, too, of 2 Samuel 22:30, 'By my God have I leaped over a wall.'

Noël Coward in his published diary mentions having read Monica Baldwin's book and gives this critical comment: 'Very interesting, I must say. It has strengthened my decision not to become a nun.'

BALDWIN, Stanley (later 1st Earl Baldwin of Bewdley)

British Conservative Prime Minister (1867–1947)

3 They are a lot of hard-faced men ... who look as if they had done well out of the war.

The members of the House of Commons who had been returned in the 1918 General Election were so described by a 'Conservative politician', according to John Maynard Keynes, the economist, in *The Economic Consequences of Peace* (1919). Baldwin is taken to be the man who said it. In his biography (1969) by Keith Middlemas and John Barnes, Baldwin is also quoted as having noted privately on 12 February 1918: 'We have started with the new House of Commons. They look much as usual – not so young as I had expected. The prevailing type is a rather successful-looking business kind which is not very attractive.'

The playwright Julian Mitchell, surveying the members of Mrs Thatcher's government in 1987, remarked that they looked like 'hard-faced men who had done well out of the peace.'

4 The papers conducted by Lord Rothermere and Lord Beaverbrook are not newspapers in the ordinary acceptance of the term. They are engines of propaganda, for the constantly changing policies, desires, personal wishes, personal likes and dislikes of two men ... What the proprietorship of these papers is aiming at is power, and power without responsibility – the prerogative of the harlot throughout the ages.

Attacking the press lords during a by-election campaign in London (18 March 1931). Baldwin's cousin, Rudyard Kipling, had originated the remark many years previously. He had also already used them in argument with Beaverbrook. It is often misquoted: in Frank S. Pepper, *Handbook of 20th Century Quotations* (1984), it is given as 'the *privilege* of the harlot'. There are also those who would say that it is not actually the harlot who has the power without the responsibility – it is the harlot's customer. Hence, however, *The Prerogative of the Harlot*, title of a book (1980) by Hugh (Lord) Cudlipp, about Fleet Street.

Harold Macmillan recalled that his father-in-law, the Duke of Devonshire, exclaimed at this point in Baldwin's speech: 'Good God, that's done it, he's lost us the tarts' vote.'

5 The bomber will always get through.

Speech, House of Commons (10 November 1932). This remark has to be seen in the context of the times – the First World War had introduced the completely new concept of airborne bombardment. Said Baldwin in full: 'I think it is well for the man in the street to realize that there is no power on earth that can protect him from being bombed. Whatever people may tell him, the bomber will always get through. The only defence is in offence, which means that you have to kill more women and children more quickly than the enemy if you want to save yourselves.' In a speech to the House of Commons (30 July 1934) Baldwin provided a corollary: 'Since the day of the air, the old frontiers are gone. When you think of the chalk cliffs of Dover, you think of the Rhine. That is where our frontier lies.'

1 I met Curzon in Downing Street, from whom I got the sort of greeting a corpse would give to an undertaker.

On becoming Prime Minister – a job Curzon had always wanted – in 1933. Quoted in A. & V. Palmer, *Quotations from History* (1976).

2 There is a wind of nationalism and freedom blowing round the world, and blowing as strongly in Asia as elsewhere.

Speech, London (4 December 1934). *Compare* MACMILLAN 374:2.

3 I shall be but a short time tonight. I have seldom spoken with greater regret, for my lips are not yet unsealed.

Speech in the House of Commons on the Abyssinia crisis (10 December 1935). He was playing for time with what, he admitted, was one of the stupidest things he had ever said. Popularly quoted as 'My lips are sealed'. The cartoonist Low portrayed him for weeks afterwards with sticking plaster over his lips. Meaning 'I am not giving anything away', and deriving originally perhaps, from the expression to seal up *another* person's lips or mouth, to prevent betrayal of a secret, the *OED2* has the expression by 1782.

4 I put before the whole House my own view with appalling frankness ... supposing I had gone to the country and said ... that we must rearm, does anybody think that this pacific democracy would have rallied to that cry at that moment? I cannot think of anything that would have made the loss of the election from my point of view more certain.

Speech in the House of Commons (12 November 1936). Winston Churchill had reproached him for failing to keep his pledge that parity should be maintained against air forces within striking distance of British soil. Why had this happened? Churchill commented on the reply in *The Second World War*, Vol. 1 (1948): 'This was indeed appalling frankness. It carried naked truth about his motives into indecency. That a prime minister should avow that he had not done his duty in regard to national safety because he was afraid of losing the election was an incident without parallel in our Parliamentary history.' G.M. Young wrote: 'Never I suppose in our history has a statesman used a phrase so fatal to his own good name and at the same time, so wholly unnecessary, so incomprehensible.'

In *Baldwin* (1969), Keith Middlemas and John Barnes are at pains to assert that these judgements were made very much after the event and that the speech did not set off a horrified reaction at the time.

5 Once I leave, I leave. I am not going to speak to the man on the bridge, and I am not going to spit on the deck.

Statement to the Cabinet (28 May 1937) later released to the press, when Baldwin stepped down, flushed with success over his handling of the Abdication crisis. Earlier, on his inauguration as Rector of Edinburgh University in 1925, Baldwin had expressed a view of the limitations on the freedom of a former Prime Minister in similar terms: 'A sailor does not spit on the deck, thereby strengthening his control and saving unnecessary work for someone else; nor does he speak to the man at the wheel, thereby leaving him to devote his whole time to his task and increasing the probability of the ship arriving at or near her destination.'

When Harold Wilson resigned as Prime Minister, he quoted Baldwin's 'Once I leave ...' words in his own statement to the Cabinet (16 March 1976), also later released to the press.

6 Do not run up your nose against the Pope or the NUM [National Union of Mineworkers]!

Quoted by Lord Butler in *The Art of Memory* (1982). *Compare* MACMILLAN 375:1.

7 You will find in politics that you are much exposed to the attribution of false motive. Never complain and never explain.

To Harold Nicolson (21 July 1943), alluding to DISRAELI 210:9.

BALFOUR, Arthur (later 1st Earl of Balfour)

British Conservative Prime Minister (1848–1930)

8 Christianity, yes, but why journalism?

To Frank Harris who had claimed that Christianity and journalism were the two main curses of civilization. Quoted in *The Autobiography of Margot Asquith*, Chap. 10 (1920–2).

9 I rather think of having a career of my own.

On being asked whether he was going to marry Margot Tennant (later Asquith). In *ib.*

10 His Majesty's Government looks with favour upon the establishment in Palestine of a national home for the Jewish people.

Although Balfour had been Prime Minister (1902–5), he became Foreign Secretary in Lloyd George's wartime cabinet. Just before the British army in Palestine took Jerusalem in 1917, Balfour sought to curry favour with Jews in the United States and Central Europe by promising that Palestine should become a national home for the Jews and issued what has become known as the Balfour Declaration on 2 November 1917. This acted as a spur to Zionism and paved the way for the founding of the modern state of Israel in 1948. The declaration was contained in a letter addressed to the 2nd Lord Rothschild, a leader of British Jewry. The ambiguous rider was: 'Nothing shall be done which may prejudice the civil and religious rights of existing non-Jewish communities in Palestine.'

Hence, *Dear Lord Rothschild*, title of Miriam Rothschild's biography (1983) of her uncle, taken from the first words of Balfour's letter.

1 Nothing matters very much and very few things matter at all.

Quoted in *PDMQ* (1971). Compare what Bishop Creighton (1843–1901) said when reassuring an anxious seeker after truth, that it was 'almost impossible to exaggerate the complete unimportance of everything' – quoted in *The Lyttelton Hart-Davis Letters* (for 2 May 1956).

BALZAC, Honoré de

French novelist (1799–1850)

2 The county where women die of love.

Of Lancashire. This extraordinary statement was quoted once by A.J.P. Taylor (who might have had an interest: he was born there). One of Balzac's biographers, Graham Robb, traced it to the novel *Le Lys dans La Vallée* (1836) where it is uttered by the Lancastrian Lady Arabella Dudley to her lover, Felix de Vandenesse. It is thought that Balzac's authority was his English lover, Sarah Lovell. But she came from Bath, Wiltshire.

BANKHEAD, Tallulah

American actress (1903–68)

3 There's less in this than meets the eye.

A frequently employed critical witticism derives its modern popularity from the use made of the words by Bankhead to Alexander Woollcott about the play *Aglavaine and Selysette* by Maurice Maeterlinck on 3 January 1922. However, in his journal, James Boswell attributed a version to Richard Burke, son of Edmund (1 May 1783): 'I suppose here *less* is meant than meets the ear.'

4 I thought I told you to wait in the car.

To a man who came up to her at a party and exclaimed, effusively, 'Tallulah! I haven't seen you for 41 years!' Told by Clement Freud on BBC Radio *Quote ... Unquote* (1979).

5 I'll come and make love to you at five o'clock. If I'm late start without me.

To an admirer. Quoted in Ted Morgan, *Somerset Maugham* (1980).

6 Don't bother to thank me. I know what a perfectly ghastly season it's been for you Spanish dancers.

Outside the theatre one night she encountered a group from the Salvation Army, tambourines as always well to the fore. She promptly dropped a $50 dollar bill into one of the tambourines, saying this. Recounted in Dorothy Herrmann, *With Malice Towards All* (1980).

7 Cocaine habit-forming? Of course not. I ought to know. I've been using it for years.

Tallulah (1952). Compare: 'Typhoid is a terrible disease; it can kill you or damage your brain. I know what I'm talking about, I've had typhoid.' – Comte Maurice de MacMahon, quoted by Walter Redfern in *Clichés* (1989).

See also DIETZ 208:2.

BARBELLION, W.N.P.

English essayist and diarist (1889–1919)

8 On the bus the other day a woman with a baby sat opposite, the baby bawled, and the woman at once began to unlace herself, exposing a large red udder, which she swung into the baby's face. The infant, however, continued to cry and the woman said, 'Come on, there's a good boy – if you don't, I shall give it to the gentleman opposite.'

The Journal of a Disappointed Man (1919). This was included in the book *Eavesdroppings* (1981) as an early example of an 'overheard' but it was subsequently discovered that – like so much else – it probably began life as a *Punch* cartoon caption. In the edition of 11 May 1904 (Vol. 126), 'THE UNPROTECTED MALE' shows a man in an omnibus being addressed thus: '*Mother (after vainly offering a bottle to refractory infant)* "'ERE, TIKE IT, WILL YER! IF YER DON'T 'URRY UP, I'LL GIVE IT TO THE GENTLEMAN OPPOSITE!"'

BARING, Maurice

English writer (1874–1945)

1 If you would know what the Lord God thinks of money, you have only to look at those to whom He gave it.

Attributed by Dorothy Parker, according to Malcolm Cowley (ed.), *Writers at Work*, First Series (1958).

2 Puppet Show of Memory.

Title of reminiscences (1922) and the origin of the phrase.

3 We see the contrast between the genius which does what it must and the talent which does what it can.

An Outline of Russian Literature, Chap. 3 (1914). Contrasting Mozart and Salieri in Pushkin's play *Mozart and Salieri*.

See also PUSHKIN 442:4.

BARNUM, P(hineas) T.

American showman (1810–91)

4 There's a sucker born every minute.

No evidence exists that Barnum ever used this expression – not least, it is said, because 'sucker' was not a common term in his day. He did, however, express the view that, 'The people like to be humbugged', which conveys the same idea. There was also a song of the period, 'There's a New Jay Born Every Day' (jay = gullible hick). By whatever route, Barnum took the attribution.

Going further back, '*Populus vult decipi* [people wish to be deceived]' is attributed to Cardinal Carafa (d.1591), Legate of Pope Paul IV.

BARRIE, Sir James

Scottish playwright (1860–1937)

5 Greatest horror – dream I am married – wake up shrieking.

Entry in notebook, as a student. Quoted in Andrew Birkin, *J.M. Barrie and the Lost Boys* (1979).

6 Second to the right, and straight on till morning

Peter Pan, Act 1 (1904). Peter Pan responds to Wendy's question, 'Where do you live?' Second 'star', understood. The way to the Neverland. Hence, *Straight On Till Morning*, title of film (UK, 1972).

7 To die will be an awfully big adventure.

Ib., Act 3. Peter Llewellyn Davies, the original of Peter Pan, supposedly said this first, though Andrew Birkin, *J.M. Barrie and the Lost Boys* (1979) credits it to his brother George. Hence, however, *An Awfully Big Adventure*, the title of a novel by Beryl Bainbridge (1989; film UK, 1995) – about a small repertory company in Liverpool which is putting on a seasonal production of *Peter Pan*. *See also* FROHMAN 247:1.

8 *Floreat Etona*
May Eton flourish.

Ib., Act 5, Sc. 1. Spoken by the villain Captain Hook (presumably an Old Etonian), just before he is eaten by a crocodile. It is the motto of Eton College (founded 1440) in Berkshire. In the novel version, *Peter Pan and Wendy* (1911), Hook merely cries, 'Bad form'. It was earlier used as the title of a painting (1882) by Elizabeth, Lady Butler depicting an attack on Laing's Neck (against the Boers in South Africa, 1881), after this eye-witness account: 'Poor Elwes fell among the 58th. He shouted to another Eton boy (adjutant of the 58th, whose horse had been shot) "Come along, Monck! Floreat Etona! we must be in the front rank!" and he was shot immediately.'

9 There are few more impressive sights in the world than a Scotsman on the make.

What Every Woman Knows, Act 2 (1908). David.

10 Without Drums or Trumpets.

There is a story told about Barrie's advice to a young writer who did not know what title to give his work. 'Are there any trumpets in it?' Barrie asked, and got the answer 'No'. 'Are there any drums in it?' he asked. 'No.' 'Then why not call it *Without Drums or Trumpets*?' Untraced. A similar story is told about the French playwright, Tristan Bernard (1866–1947) in Cornelia Otis Skinner's *Elegant Wits and Grand Horizontals* (1962). Somebody did take the advice: the Dutch author Jeroen Brouwers published a novel entitled *Zonder trommels en trompetten* [Without Drums and Trumpets] (1973); the English translation of Alec Le Vernoy's Second World War memoirs was entitled *No Drums – No Trumpets* (1983).

BARRYMORE, John

American actor (1882–1942)

1 Busy yourselves with *this*, you damned walruses, while the rest of us proceed with the libretto.

Throwing a sea-bass to a noisily coughing audience. Quoted in Bennett Cerf, *Try and Stop Me* (1944). Cerf has it that the incident occurred when Barrymore was playing Fedor in *The Living Corpse*, a version of Tolstoy's *Redemption*, in 1918.

2 Love – the delightful interval between meeting a beautiful girl and discovering that she looks like a haddock.

Quoted in *The Treasury of Humorous Quotations*, ed. by Evan Esar & Nicolas Bentley (1951). The earliest source found for this frequently attributed remark.

BARTH, Karl

Swiss theologian (1886–1942)

3 It may be that when the angels go about their task of praising God, they play only Bach. I am sure, however, that when they are together *en famille*, they play Mozart and that then too our dear Lord listens with special pleasure.

Wolfgang Amadeus Mozart (1956) – here in a translation by Clarence K. Pott (1986). Usually, the quotation is given as a remark taken from Barth's obituaries, but this is the true source.

BARUCH, Bernard

American financier (1870–1965)

4 Let us not be deceived – we are today in the midst of a cold war.

The final phrase describes any tension between powers, short of all-out war, but specifically that between the Soviet Union and the West following the Second World War. In this latter sense it was popularized by Baruch, the American financier and Presidential adviser in a speech in South Carolina (16 April 1947). A year later he was able to note a worsening of the situation to the extent that he could tell the Senate War Investigating Committee: 'We are in the midst of a cold war which is getting warmer.'

The phrase was suggested to Baruch in June 1946 by his speechwriter Herbert Bayard Swope, former editor of the New York *World*, who had been using it privately since 1940. The columnist Walter Lippmann gave the term wide currency and is sometimes mistakenly credited with coining it. Swope clearly coined it; Baruch gave it currency.

BATEMAN, C.H(enry)

English hymnwriter (1802–72)

5 There is a Happy Land.

Title of children's hymn. Sometimes misascribed to Bateman. *See* YOUNG 558:4.

BATEMAN, Edgar

English songwriter (fl.1900)

6 Oh it really is a wery pretty garden, and
Chingford to the eastward can be seen;
Wiv a ladder and some glasses
You could see to 'Ackney Marshes,
If it wasn't for the 'ouses in between.

Song (1894), popularized by Gus Elen (d.1940), which had lyrics by Bateman and music by George Le Brunn (1862–1905). Hence, *The Houses in Between*, title of a novel (1951) by Howard Spring who mentions in a foreword a music-hall song containing the words, 'You could see the Crystal Palace – if it wasn't for the houses in between'. The full lyrics given in *The Last Empires* (ed. Benny Green, 1986) do not include mention of the Crystal Palace, but no doubt extra verses were added over the years.

BATEMAN, H.M.

British cartoonist (1887–1970)

7 The Man Who ...

... committed some solecism or other. Caption of cartoons in the 1920s and 1930s. For example, 'The Man Who Missed the Ball on the First Tee at St Andrews', 'The Man Who Lit His Cigar Before the Royal Toast', 'The Girl Who Ordered a Glass of Milk at the Café Royal' and 'The Man Who Asked for "A Double Scotch" in the Grand Pump Room at Bath'.

BATES, H.E.

English writer (1905–74)

8 Perfick wevver.

The Darling Buds of May, Chap.1 (1958). Pa Larkin's

use of 'perfick' (a Kentish pronunciation of 'perfect') extends through all the novels about the Larkin family. Hence, perfick wevver = perfect weather. The expression 'perfick!' again had a vogue in the spring of 1991 when the stories were dramatized for British TV with huge success. At that time, 'Perfick' was the *Sun*'s headline over a front-page story about the new council tax (Pa Larkin is a notable income tax dodger); the Family Assurance Society promoted a tax-free investment with the word as headline in newspaper adverts in May 1991 (revealing, at the same time, that the word had been registered as a trade mark by Yorkshire Television, the programme's producer).

BAUDELAIRE, Charles

French poet (1821–67)

1 *Hypocrite lecteur, – mon semblable, – mon frère!*
Hypocrite reader, my likeness, my brother!

'Au Lecteur', *Les Fleurs du mal* (1857). T.S. Eliot quotes the original French in 'The Burial of the Dead', *The Waste Land* (1922).

2 *Il faut épater les bourgeois.*
One must shock the bourgeois.

Attributed remark. To Baudelaire's contemporary, Alexandre Privat d'Anglemont (*c.*1820–59) is attributed the similar, '*Je les épatés, les bourgeois* [I shocked them, the *bourgeois*]'.

BAUM, L. Frank

American author (1856–1919)

3 The Wizard of Oz.

Actually the title of Baum's children's classic is *The Wonderful Wizard of Oz*. It was shortened for the 1939 film and also for some later editions of the book. Baum wrote another thirteen volumes about Oz and twenty-six further titles were added after his death. Legend has it that Baum took the name 'Oz' from the label 'O-Z' on a filing cabinet. It has been observed how similar are Dorothy's adventures to those of *Alice in Wonderland* (1865). In each case, the heroine endures a succession of (mostly) unpleasant encounters and finally escapes back home – Dorothy to Kansas after a cyclone has blown her to Oz, Alice to her sister after she has fallen down a rabbit hole.

Note these other alterations between book and film:

4 The road to the City of Emeralds is paved with yellow brick.

That is what Baum put. He also wrote of 'the road of yellow brick'. The phrase 'Yellow Brick Road' comes only from the song 'Follow the Yellow Brick Road' in the film. 'Goodbye Yellow Brick Road' was the title of a song (1973) by Bernie Taupin and Elton John. The song 'Over the rainbow' (by E.Y. Harburg, *q.v.*, with music by Harold Arlen) does not derive from anything in the book.

5 Toto, I have a feeling we're not in Kansas any more.

Again, this is a line from the film, not the book, but one that has achieved catchphrase status. Judy Garland as Dorothy says it on arrival in the Land of Oz, concluding, 'We must be over the rainbow'.

6 The Wicked Witch of the West.

This *was* the name of a character in *The Wonderful Wizard of Oz* (there was also one of the East; North and South were good witches). It produced a wonderfully alliterative way of describing women not liked. Allan Massie wrote of Margaret Thatcher : 'It would not convert those for whom she is She Who Must Be Obeyed and the Wicked Witch of the West rolled into one' (quoted in Michael Cockerell, *Live From Number 10*, 1989).

7 Close your eyes and tap your heels together three times. And think to yourself, 'There's no place like home'.

On how to get from the Land of Oz back to Kansas. Said at the end of the film by Glinda, The (Good) Witch of the South. In the book she says: 'All you have to do is to knock the heels together three times and command the shoes to carry you wherever you wish to go.'

BAX, Sir Arnold

English composer (1883–1953)

8 You should make a point of trying every experience once, excepting incest and folk-dancing.

Often wrongly ascribed to Sir Thomas Beecham and others – also to Bax himself. In fact, it was said by 'a sympathetic Scotsman' and quoted *by* Bax in his book *Farewell, My Youth* (1943).

9 You know you are getting old when the policemen start looking younger.

Not said *by* Bax. What he said of *Arnold Bennett* in *ib.* was: '[He] once remarked that his earliest recognition of his own middle age came at a certain appalling moment when he realized for the first time that the policeman at the corner was a mere youth.' This realization has also been attributed to Sir Seymour Hicks (1871–1949), the actor, in connection with *old* age (in C.R.D. Pulling, *They Were Singing*, 1952, for example). The source for this may be Hicks's own *Between Ourselves* (1930).

BAYLY, Thomas Haynes

English poet and playwright (1797–1839)

1 Oh! no! we never mention her,
Her name is never heard;
My lips are now forbid to speak
That once familiar word ...

From sport to sport they hurry me
To banish my regret,
And when they win a smile from me,
They think that I forget.

Song, 'Oh! No! We Never Mention Her' (1844). A 'lost' quotation until traced to its source (1997) using the Chadwyck–Healey Poetry Full-Text Database (600–1900) on CD-ROM. The second of these verses is alluded to, anonymously, in P.G. Wodehouse, *Psmith in the City*, Chap. 14 (1910): 'From ledger to ledger they hurry me to stifle my regret. And when they win a smile from me they think that I forget.'

BEACHCOMBER *See* MORTON, J.B.

BEATTY, Sir David (later 1st Earl Beatty)

English admiral (1871–1936)

2 There seems to be something wrong with our bloody ships today, Chatfield.

The Battle of Jutland on 31 May – 1 June 1916 was not only the first naval engagement of the twentieth century but also the only major sea battle of the First World War. It was, on the face of it, an indecisive affair. The British grand fleet under its Commander-in-Chief, Sir John Jellicoe, failed to secure an outright victory. Admiral Beatty, commanding a battle cruiser squadron, saw one ship after another sunk by the Germans. At 4.26 on the afternoon of 31 May, the *Queen Mary* was sunk with the loss of 1,266 officers and men. This was what led Beatty to make the above comment to his Flag Captain, Ernle Chatfield. Sometimes the words 'and with our system' have been added to the remark, as also 'Turn two points to port' (i.e., nearer the enemy) and 'Steer two points nearer the enemy', but Chatfield denied that anything more was said (source: *ODQ*, 1953 and 1979).

Ultimately, the battle marked the end of any German claim to have naval control of the North Sea and, in that light, was a British victory, but Jutland was a disappointment at the time and has been chewed over ever since as a controversial episode in British naval history.

BEAVERBROOK, 1st Baron (Maxwell Aitken)

Canadian-born British politician and newspaper proprietor (1879–1964)

3 Our cock won't fight.

To Winston Churchill, of Edward VIII during the abdication crisis. Quoted in Frances Donaldson, *Edward VIII* (1974).

4 Let me say that the credit belongs to the boys in the back-rooms. It isn't the man who sits in the limelight like me who should have the praise. It is not the men who sit in prominent places. It is the men in the back-rooms.

As Minister of Aircraft Production, Beaverbrook paid tribute to the Ministry's research department in a broadcast on 19 March 1941. This version of the text has been taken direct from a recording and differs from that usually given (as for example in the *ODQ*, 1992).

In North America the phrase 'back-room boys' can be traced back to the 1870s at least, but Beaverbrook may be credited with the modern application to scientific and technical boffins. His inspiration for the phrase was quite obviously Marlene Dietrich singing his favourite song 'The Boys in the Back Room' in the film *Destry Rides Again* (1939). Written by Frank Loesser/Frederick Hollander, this is more properly called 'See What the Boys in the Back Room Will Have'. According to A.J.P. Taylor, Beaverbrook believed that 'Dietrich singing the Boys in the Backroom is a greater work of art than the Mona Lisa'. Also in 1941, Edmund Wilson entitled a book, *The Boys in the Back Room: Notes on California Novelists*. A British film with Arthur Askey was entitled *Back Room Boy* (1942).

An even earlier appearance of the bar phrase occurs in the Marx Brothers film *Animal Crackers* (1930): 'Let's go and see what the boys in the backroom will have.'

5 Who's in charge of the clattering train?

Beaverbrook was notorious for interfering with the running of his newspapers. His favourite inquiry as his mighty media machine rumbled on was: 'Who is in charge of the clattering train?' Ominously, this quotation was based on a remembering of the anonymous poem 'Death and His Brother Sleep', which includes the lines:

Who is in charge of the clattering train?
The axles creak, and the couplings strain ...
For the pace is hot, and the points are near,
And Sleep hath deadened the driver's ear;
And signals flash through the night in vain.
Death is in charge of the clattering train!

It is possible that Beaverbrook borrowed the expression from Winston Churchill, who also quoted the poem in the first volume of his *The Second World War* (1948) saying: 'I had learnt them from a volume of *Punch* cartoons which I used to pore over when I was eight or nine years old at school in Brighton.' That would have been in 1882–3. In fact, the poem did not appear in *Punch* until 4 October 1890. It concerns a railway collision at Eastleigh. Due to fatigue, the driver and stoker had failed to keep a proper look-out.

A.J.P. Taylor in *Beaverbrook* (1972) states that Beaverbook's quotation was not quite accurate, but then proceeds to print an inaccurate version himself, beginning 'Who is in charge of the *rattling* train ...'.

1 The British electors will not vote for a man who doesn't wear a hat.

Advice to Tom Driberg in 1942. Quoted in Alan Watkins, *Brief Lives* (1982).

2 Go out and speak for the inarticulate and the submerged.

To Godfrey Winn. Quoted in Ted Morgan, *Somerset Maugham* (1980).

3 Because he shakes hands with people's hearts.

When asked why Winn was paid more than the rest of the staff. Quoted in *ib.*

4 With the publication of his Private Papers in 1952, he committed suicide twenty-five years after his death.

On Earl Haig. *Men and Power* (1956).

5 He did not care which direction the car was travelling, so long as he was in the driver's seat.

On David Lloyd George. *The Decline and Fall of Lloyd George* (1963).

See also DAILY EXPRESS 194:1; KIPLING 339:3.

BEECHAM, Sir Thomas

English conductor (1879–1961)

6 Sounds like two skeletons copulating on a corrugated tin roof.

On a harpsichord. Quoted in *Beecham Stories* by Harold Atkins and Archie Newman (1978). Sometimes quoted as 'resembles a bird-cage played with toasting-forks.'

7 Madam, you have between your legs an instrument capable of giving pleasure to thousands – and all you can do is scratch it.

To a lady cellist. Quoted by Fred Metcalf in *The Penguin Dictionary of Modern Humorous Quotations* (1986), without source. Also attributed to Arturo Toscanini.

BEECHING, H.C.

English clergyman and writer (1859–1919)

8 First come I; my name is Jowett.
There's no knowledge but I know it.
I am the Master of this College:
What I don't know isn't knowledge.

A contribution to the mostly anonymous 'The Masque of Balliol', which was current at Balliol College, Oxford, in the 1870s. Jowett was Master of Balliol from 1870.

BEERBOHM, Sir Max

English writer and caricaturist (1872–1956)

9 It is a pity that critics should show so little sympathy with writers, and curious when we consider that most of them tried to be writers themselves, once.

A delightful insult which contains, so it has been said, 'the second most effective comma I know in literature.' *The Yellow Book*, Vol. 2 (1894–7), answering serious abuse poured upon his essay in Vol. 1.

10 Often, even in his heyday, his acting and his waggishness did not carry him very far. Only mediocrity can be trusted to be always at its best. Genius must always have lapses proportionate to its triumphs.

Obituary of the British music-hall comic Dan Leno in the *Saturday Review* (5 November 1904) – the earliest found formulation of the thought that 'only the mediocre are always at their best'. Among those also credited with it have been Jean Giraudoux and W. Somerset Maugham. The Giraudoux attribution appears without source in Robert Byrne's *The 637 Best Things Anybody Ever Said* (1982). In his introduction to *The Portable Dorothy Parker* (1944), Maugham chooses his words carefully (Parker was, of course, still alive) in discussing the uneven quality of her output. With (for him), unusual tact, Maugham wrote: 'Only a very mediocre writer is always at his best, and Dorothy Parker is not a mediocre writer.' Compare what the film director Ernst Lubitsch (1892–1947) is quoted as having said: 'I sometimes make pictures which are not up to my standard, but then it can only be said of a mediocrity that all his work is up to his standard' – quoted in Leslie Halliwell, *The Filmgoer's Book of Quotes* (1973).

1 'I don't,' she added, 'know anything about music, really. But I know what I like.'

Zuleika Dobson, Chap. 16 (1911). In Chap. 9, Beerbohm had already commented of his heroine at a college concert: 'She was one of the people who say, "I don't know anything about music really, but I know what I like".' In the same year (1911), Gelett Burgess identified this philistine's slogan (also applied to art and literature) as a platitude in *Are You a Bromide?*

See also BENSON 85:8; LINCOLN 355:5.

BEETHOVEN, Ludwig van

German composer (1770–1827)

2 *Muss es sein? Es muss sein.*
Must it be? It must be.

Epigraph to the final movement of his String Quartet in F Major, Op. 135 (1826), which was more or less his last completed composition. Accordingly, some deep philosophical significance has been read into the words, or at least a parallel with the musical resolution at this point, but Robert Simpson in *The Beethoven Companion* (1973) quotes Joseph Kerman as treating it as a 'not very good joke': when someone who owed Beethoven money asked, '*Muss es sein?*', Beethoven, 'with some lack of originality', replied, '*Es muss sein!*'

3 I like your opera – I think I will set it to music.

Having listened to a performance of an opera by a somewhat lesser composer. Contributed to BBC Radio *Quote ... Unquote* (6 July 1977). Also attributed to Richard Wagner.

4 England is a land without music.

It seems he never said it. *Das Land ohne Musik* was, however, the title of a British-bashing book by Oscar A. Schmitz, published at the start of the First World War. The book had nothing to do with music but depicted England as a country 'without a soul'. The criticism has also been ascribed to Felix Mendelssohn, a frequent visitor to Britain, with even less reason (source: letter from Arthur Jacobs in *The Independent* Magazine, 1 February 1992.)

Land Without Music was, coincidentally, the title of a film operetta (UK, 1936; US title *Forbidden Music*) about a Ruritanian ruler who bans music because her subjects are too busy singing to make money. Richard Tauber, Jimmy Durante and Diana Napier were in it.

5 *Plaudite, amici, comedia finita est.*
Applaud, my friends, the comedy is over.

Words on his deathbed, quoted in 'Bega', *Last Words of Famous Men* (1930). *Compare* RABELAIS 445:4. However, 'I shall hear in heaven' are the last words attributed in Barnaby Conrad, *Famous Last Words* (1961).

BEETON, Mrs (Isabella)

English writer (1836–65)

6 First catch your hare.

In the proverbial sense this means, 'You can't begin to do something until you have acquired a necessary basic something (which may be difficult to acquire)'. *CODP* finds the equivalent thought *c.*1300 in Latin: 'It is commonly said that one must first catch the deer, and afterwards, when he has been caught, skin him.'

For a long time the saying was taken to be a piece of practical, blunt good sense to be found in Mrs Beeton's *Book of Household Management* (1851), but it does not appear there. In Mrs Hannah Glasse's *The Art of Cookery made plain and easy* (1747), however, there is the practical advice, 'Take your hare when it is cased' (skinned).

It was known in the familiar form by 1855 when it appeared in Thackeray's *The Rose and the Ring*. Similar proverbs include: 'Catch your bear before you sell its skin', 'Never spend your money before you have it' and 'Don't count your chickens before they are hatched.'

7 A place for everything and everything in its place.

The Book of Household Management, Chap. 2 (1861). A prescription for orderly domestic arrangements. One feels that Mrs Beeton was probably more interested in domestic order than in making delicious food. This saying was not, however, original to her – the idea goes back in proverbial form to 1640 at least.

BEGIN, Menachem

Israeli Prime Minister (1913–92)

1 BLOOD LIBEL. On the New Year (Rosh Hashana), a blood libel was levelled against the Jewish state, its government and the Israel Defense Forces ...

In September 1982, following allegations that Israeli forces in Lebanon had allowed massacres to take place in refugee camps, the Israeli government (headed by Begin) invoked the phrase 'blood libel' in a statement. Traditionally, this was the name given to accusations by medieval anti-Semites that Jews had crucified Christian children and drunk their blood at Passover.

BEHAN, Brendan

Irish playwright (1923–64)

2 O, Death where is thy sting-a-ling-a-ling,
O, grave, thy victoree?
The Bells of Hell go ting-a-ling-a-ling
For you but not for me.

Behan made notable use of this in his play *The Hostage* (1958) but he was, in fact, merely adopting a song popular in the British Army in 1914–18. Even before that, though, it was sung – just like this – as a Sunday School chorus. It may have been in a Sankey and Moody hymnal, though it has not been traced. The basic element is from 1 Corinthians 15:55: 'O death, where is thy sting? O grave, where is thy victory?'

3 There's no such thing as bad publicity except your own obituary.

Quoted in Dominic Behan, *My Brother Brendan* (1965). *See also* ANONYMOUS 21:1.

4 I saw a notice which said 'Drink Canada Dry' and I've just started.

Attributed remark. Quoted in *The 'Quote ... Unquote' Book of Love, Death and the Universe* (1980), but probably a joke ascribed to any famous drinker. The following version was used in his act by the American comedian Pat Henning (*fl.*1950s): 'He was a drinkin' man, my fadder. One day he's standin' onna banks of the river, wonderin' what the hell folks can do with all that water, when suddenly he sees a great sign on the other side DRINK CANADA DRY. [Pause] So he went up there.'

5 Critics are like eunuchs in a harem: they know how it's done, they've seen it done every day, but they're unable to do it themselves.

Quoted in Laurence J. Peter, *Quotations for Our Time* (1977). Compare Kenneth Tynan in *The New York Times* Magazine (9 January 1966): 'A critic is a man who knows the way but can't drive the car.'

BELL, Alexander Graham

Scottish-born American inventor (1847–1922)

6 Mr Watson, come here: I want you.

First intelligible words transmitted by telephone (10 March 1876). Bell said them three days after receiving his patent on his invention. He had just spilled acid on his clothes and was calling to his assistant, Thomas A. Watson, for help. Interesting how, from the word go, the telephone was used in a peremptory manner (source: Flexner, 1982).

BELL, Daniel

American sociologist (1919–)

7 Capitalism, it is said, is a system wherein man exploits man. And communism – is vice versa.

The End of Ideology (1960). Note the 'it is said'. Laurence J. Peter in *Quotations for Our Time* (1977) describes it as a 'Polish proverb' and another source has it 'reported from Warsaw'.

8 The Coming of Post-Industrial Society.

Title of book (1973). 'Post-industrial society' was Bell's term for changed social structures in the latter part of the twentieth century. The predominant features, he observed, would include a switch from goods-producing to service economies, the pre-eminence of the professional and technical classes, and a new 'intellectual technology' in decision making.

BELL, H.E.

English university administrator (1925–)

9 Parents are the very last people who ought to be allowed to have children.

Ted Bell has an unusual problem – a remark has been fathered on him and he does not know whether he is entitled to claim paternity. In March 1977, as Senior Assistant Registrar in charge of undergraduate admissions at the University of Reading, he was speaking to a mixed group of people about the increasing complexity of the selection procedures and the variety of guidance available to prospective students. 'In this respect, being a parent of three children myself,' he noted (1992), 'I happened to say that in my view, "Parents are the very last people who ought to be allowed to have children". Reporters were present (I had invited them), the words appeared in *The Guardian*, and they were repeated in "Sayings of the Week" in *The Observer*. Later, in 1980, they appeared under my name in the second edition of *The Penguin Dictionary of Modern Quotations*.'

In truth, Bell was merely saying what oft had been thought but ne'er so pithily expressed. According to *The Treasury of Humorous Quotations* (1951), Bernard Shaw (inevitably) was credited with making the same point in rather more words: 'There may be some doubt as to who are the best people to have charge of children, but there can be no doubt that parents are the worst.' In fact, that was a misattribution. In Shaw's *Everybody's Political What's What?*, Chap. 19 (1944), he quotes *William Morris* ('great among the greatest Victorians as poet, craftsman, and practical man of business, and one of the few who remained uncorrupted by Victorian false prosperity to the end'). Speaking 'as a parent and as a Communist', Morris had said: 'The question of who are the best people to take charge of children is a very difficult one; but it is quite certain that the parents are the very worst.'

An unverified suggestion is that 'Parents are the last people on earth who ought to have children' appears in Samuel Butler's *Notebooks*. This is according to *Medical Quotations* (1989).

BELL, Mary Hayley

English novelist (1911–)

1 Whistle Down the Wind.

Title of novel (1958; film UK, 1961). It comes from an expression meaning either (1): to abandon or to cast off lightly (after the releasing of a hawk down wind, from the fist, by whistling), as in Shakespeare's *Othello* (III.iii.266): 'I'ld whistle her off, and let her down the wind'. This is what you do in falconry when you are turning a hawk loose. You send it into or against the wind when it is pursuing prey. Or (2): To vanish. From J.M. Barrie, *What Every Woman Knows*, Act 3 (1908): 'Where's your marrying now? ... all gone whistling down the wind'. Noël Coward was quoted in *Panorama* Magazine (Spring 1952), as saying: 'I marched down to the footlights and screamed: "I gave you my youth! Where is it now? Whistling down the wind! *où song les neiges d'antan*?" ... And I went madly on in French and Italian.' Or (3): Something to be avoided on board ship. The superstition is that whistling, because it sounds like the wind, can raise the wind, as if by magic – though this may more properly be 'whistle up the wind', as in 'to whistle for something'. (Whistling backstage at the theatre is also said to bring bad luck.) Nevertheless, in the seafaring novels (1970–) of Patrick O'Brian, the hero 'Lucky' Jack Aubrey is sometimes said to 'whistle down the wind' in order to raise wind to fills his sails.

Mary Hayley Bell said in 1980 that she had not been aware of the Shakespeare use until Len Deighton pointed it out to her. The relevance of the title to a story of children who believe that a murderer on the run is Jesus Christ may not be immediately apparent.

BELLAMY, Francis

American clergyman and editor (1856–1931)

2 I pledge allegiance to the flag of the United States of America and to the republic for which it stands, one nation under God, indivisible, with liberty and justice for all.

The Pledge of Allegiance to the Flag was put into its final form by Bellamy in 1892. A dispute as to who wrote it – he or James Upham – was decided in Bellamy's favour, after his death, in 1939.

Hence, the title of a 1979 film about the US legal system, *And Justice for All*. The idea of 'justice for all' is, however, one that goes back to the Greeks. It also gave rise to MATHEW 386:4.

BELLOC, Hilaire

French-born British poet and writer (1870–1953)

3 When I am dead, I hope it may be said:
'His sins were scarlet, but his books were read'.

Belloc wrote this jocular epitaph for himself in 'On his Books', *Sonnets and Verse* (1923). He is actually buried in a family grave at the Church of Our Lady of Consolation, West Grinstead, Sussex, but, understandably, without this inscription. A few yards away, a plaque on the tower commemorates him, noting that he had been a member of the congregation for forty-eight years. The tower and spire were completed in 1964, 'in grateful recognition of his zealous and unwavering profession of our Holy Faith which he defended in his writings and noble verse'. Then follow these lines:

4 This is the Faith that I have held and hold
and This is That in which I mean to die.

'The Ballade to Our Lady of Czestochowa' in *ib.*

1 Like many of the Upper Class
He liked the Sound of Broken Glass.

'About John who Lost a Fortune Throwing Stones', *New Cautionary Tales* (1930). *Compare* WAUGH 556:5.

BELLOW, Saul

Canadian-born novelist (1915–)

2 All a writer has to do to get a woman is to say he's a writer. It's an aphrodisiac.

Believed to have come from a BBC TV interview in the 1970s. Compare GREENE 272:6, KISSINGER 340:3 and NAPOLEON 406:6.

3 The Papuans have had no Proust and the Zulus have not yet produced a Tolstoy.

Unverified statement from an interview given by Bellow in 1988. In *The New Yorker* (7 March 1994), this was found unacceptable by Alfred Kazin, a politically correct writer, who said: 'My heart sank when I heard that Bellow once said, "Who is the Tolstoy of the Zulus? The Proust of the Papuans?"' Apparently, however, Bellow did not say, 'When the Zulus produce *War and Peace* I'll take them seriously' either. When censured for this view, in whatever way expressed, Bellow replied: 'There's no Bulgarian Proust. Have I offended the Bulgarians too?' (source: Keith Botsford in *The Independent*, 31 March 1994).

BENCHLEY, Robert

American humorist (1889–1945)

4 I must get out of these wet clothes and into a dry martini.

This was a line much enjoyed by Benchley and delivered by him to Ginger Rogers in the film *The Major and the Minor* (1942). It was in the form 'Why don't you get out of that wet coat and into a dry Martini?', according to Harry Haun's *The Movie Quote Book* (1980). Sometimes also attributed to Alexander Woollcott, the line may actually have originated with Benchley's press agent in the 1920s or with his friend Charles Butterworth. In any case, apparently, Mae West also adopted the line, as screenwriter, in *Every Day's a Holiday* (1937).

5 See Hebrews 13:8.

A capsule criticism of the play *Abie's Irish Rose*, which ran so long (1922–7) that Benchley was incapable of saying anything new about it in the weekly edition of *Life* Magazine. The text he alluded to read: 'Jesus Christ the same yesterday, and today, and for ever.' Quoted in Diana Rigg, *No Turn Unstoned* (1982).

Between 1975 and 1990, when *A Chorus Line* was running on Broadway, the capsule criticism space for it in *The New Yorker*'s listings was given over to reprinting paragraphs from *War and Peace*.

6 And that, my dears, is how I came to marry your grandfather.

Brief, dismissive line – possibly used in capsule criticism of *Abie's Irish Rose* (1922–7) – and so quoted by Diana Rigg in *No Turn Unstoned* (1982). As though at the end of a long and rambling reminiscence by an old woman.

7 The surest way to make a monkey of a man is to quote him.

My Ten Years in a Quandary (1936). On the downside of the business of quotation.

8 She sleeps alone at last.

Suggested epitaph for actress. Attributed in *The Book of Hollywood Quotes* (*c.*1980).

9 STREETS FLOODED. PLEASE ADVISE.

Telegram to *The New Yorker* on arriving in Venice. Quoted in R.E. Drennan, *Wit's End* (1973).

BENDA, Julien

French writer and philosopher (1867–1956)

10 *La Trahison des clercs.*
The intellectuals' betrayal.

Title of book (1927). The phrase denotes a compromise of intellectual integrity by writers, artists and thinkers.

BENÉT, Stephen Vincent

American poet (1898–1943)

11 I shall not rest quiet in Montparnasse.
I shall not lie easy at Winchelsea.
You may bury my body in Sussex grass,
You may bury my tongue at Champmédy.
I shall not be there, I shall rise and pass.
Bury my heart at Wounded Knee.

In his poem 'American Names' (1927), Benét celebrates the 'sharp names that never get fat' of American places, extraordinary names such as 'Medicine Hat', and 'Lost Mule Flat'. He contrasts them with the names of other possible burial places in Europe – Montparnasse (where there is a famous cemetery) in Paris, Winchelsea (the 'ancient town' of Rye in Sussex and linked to Henry James), and Champmédy (the significance of which escapes one). *Bury My Heart At Wounded Knee* became the title of a book (1970) by Dee Brown, a historical survey of the West.

BENÉT, William Rose

American poet (1886–1950)

1 I like to think of Shakespeare, not as when
In our old London of the spacious time
He took all amorous hearts with honeyed rhyme ...
[But] when, with brow composed and friendly tread,
He sought the little streets of Stratford town,
That knew his dreams and soon must hold him dead,
I like to think how Shakespeare pruned his rose,
And ate his pippin in his orchard close.

Written apparently by Stephen Vincent Benét's brother, this short poem was printed (anonymously) as an epilogue to E.K. Chambers, *Shakespeare: A Survey* (1925) and dated 1916. Some readers concluded that it must have been written by Chambers himself.

BENN, Tony

British Labour politician (1925–)

2 I am on the right wing of the middle of the road and with a strong radical bias.

Remark, from the 1950s. Quoted by Robin Day in a radio interview (1977) when asked about his own political position.

3 Broadcasting is really too important to be left to the broadcasters and somehow we must find some new way of using radio and television to allow us to talk to each other.

Speech, Bristol (18 October 1968). When Minister of Technology. *Compare* CLEMENCEAU 173:4 and DE GAULLE 199:6.

4 If voting changed anything they would make it illegal.

Has been dubiously ascribed to Benn. Whatever else he may be, he is neither anti-democratic nor cynical. Fred Metcalf in *The Penguin Dictionary of Modern Humorous Quotations* (1987) merely places the slogan as on a 'badge, London, 1983'. In Rennie Ellis's *Australian Graffiti Revisited* (1979), there is a photograph of a wall slogan in Carlton, Victoria: 'IF VOTING COULD CHANGE THINGS, IT WOULD BE ILLEGAL.' This may predate the original publication of the book in 1975.

BENNETT, Alan

English playwright and actor (1934–)

5 Life, you know, is rather like opening a tin of sardines. We're all of us looking for the key.

'Take a pew', *Beyond the Fringe* (1961). Bennett's parody of an Anglican church sermon included this banal simile and misattributed quotations (*see* BIBLE 91:4 and RICE 454:6). It was said that a record of the sermon used to be played as a warning to trainee priests, but clearly most of them did not get the message.

6 They are rolling up the maps all over Europe. We shall not see them lit again in our lifetime.

Forty Years On, Act 1 (1969). Alluding to GREY 273:6 and PITT 431:7.

7 All women dress like their mothers, that is their tragedy. No man ever does. That is his.

Ib. Alluding to WILDE 569:11.

8 Two of the nicest people if ever there was one.

Ib., Act 2. On the political thinkers, Sidney and Beatrice Webb. Alternatively, 'Two nice people if there was one'. This line does not appear in the published script of Bennett's play, though it was spoken in the original production. Having quoted the first version in my book *Quote ... Unquote* (1978), I was interested to see it reappear in Kenneth Williams's anthology *Acid Drops* (1980) credited to *Arnold* Bennett.

9 Sapper, Buchan, Dornford Yates, practitioners in that school of Snobbery with Violence that runs like a thread of good-class tweed through twentieth-century literature.

Ib. In its obituary for Colin Watson, the detective story writer (21 January 1983), *The Times* mentioned his book *Snobbery with Violence* (1971) – a survey of the modern crime story – 'from which the phrase comes'. As usual, there is an earlier example of the phrase in use: in Bennett's play. In his preface to the published text of *Forty Years On and Other Plays* (1991), Bennett states that he thought he *had* invented the phrase but was then told it had been used before: it was the title of a pamphlet by the New Zealand eccentric, Count Potocki de Montalk. *Snobbery with Violence. A Poet in Gaol* was published in 1932.

1 He was given the CBE for services to the theatre – which seemed to me at the time like Goering being given the DSO for services to the RAF.

On Clive Barnes. BBC Radio, *Today* (3 March 1977).

2 So boring you fall asleep halfway through her name.

Of Arianna Stassinopoulos, Greek-born writer. Quoted in *The Observer* (18 September 1983). Heavens knows what he would have said when marriage led to her being known as Arianna Stassinopoulos Huffington.

3 You only have to survive in England and all is forgiven you ... if you can eat a boiled egg at ninety in England they think you deserve a Nobel Prize.

On ITV, in the *South Bank Show* (1984). In his TV film *An Englishman Abroad* (1989), this reappears as: 'In England, you see, age wipes the slate clean ... If you live to be ninety in England and can still eat a boiled egg they think you deserve the Nobel Prize.'

4 [That's] a bit like asking a man crawling across the Sahara whether he would prefer Perrier or Malvern Water.

On being asked by Ian McKellen if he was homosexual. Quoted in *The Observer* (12 June 1988).

5 There was a time when I thought my only connection with the literary world would be that I had once delivered meat to T.S. Eliot's mother-in-law.

Quoted in *The Observer* (26 April 1992). Bennett's father was indeed a butcher and T.S. Eliot's second wife, Valerie Fletcher, came from the same town in Yorkshire. Bennett recounted this once more in the Introduction to his *Writing Home* (1994).

BENNETT, Arnold

English novelist (1867–1931)

6 Mrs Laye ... told a good thing of a very old man on his dying bed giving advice to a youngster: 'I've had a long life, and it's been a merry one. Take my advice. Make love to every pretty woman you meet. And remember, if you get 5 per cent on your outlay it's a good return.'

Diary entry for 24 May 1904, published in *The Journals* (1971). *The Treasury of Humorous Quotations*, ed. by Evan Esar & Nicolas Bentley (1951), has this as though said by Bennett himself, in the form: 'Make love to every woman you meet; if you get five per cent on your outlay, it's a good investment.'

See also BAX 77:9.

BENSON, A.C.

English writer (1862–1925)

7 Land of Hope and Glory, Mother of the Free,
How shall we extol thee, who are born of thee?
Wider still and wider shall thy bounds be set;
God who made thee mighty, make thee mightier yet.

'Land of Hope and Glory' is the title popularly given to the Finale of Sir Edward Elgar's *Coronation Ode* (1902), originally written for performance at the time of the Coronation of Edward VII. Elgar, having written the basic *Ode*, invited Benson to fit words to the big tune in the Trio of the 'Pomp and Circumstance March No. 1' which had first been performed the previous year. It is said that the idea for this came from the King himself. In 1914 Benson recast the words as a war song but these have not endured in the way the originals have done. Hence, *Hope and Glory*, the title of a film (UK, 1987).

8 From a College Window.

Title of essay collection (1906). In a book called *A Victorian Boyhood*, L.E. Jones refers to Benson, who taught at Eton and became Master of Magdalene College, Cambridge: 'This was long before the days when sitting at his College window at Magdalene, he was killed dead by the straightest and most lethal arrow ever aimed by the gentle "Max".' This slight allusion is to *A Christmas Garland* (1912) in which Max Beerbohm produced a number of amusing parodies of his contemporaries. What is considered by some to be the book's best parody is that of Benson's windy and waffly essay style. Benson apparently took it amiss – hence, the 'lethal arrow'. And 'sitting at his College window'? – from the title of this book.

BENSON, Stella

English novelist and poet (1892–1933)

1 Call no man foe, but never love a stranger.

To the Unborn, St. 3 (1935). Hence, presumably the title of Harold Robbins's novel *Never Love a Stranger* (1948; film US, 1958).

BENTLEY, E. Clerihew

English novelist, journalist and poet (1875–1956)

2 Sir Christopher Wren
Said, 'I am going to dine with some men.
If anybody calls
Say I am designing St Paul's.'

Biography for Beginners (1905). An example of a 'clerihew', the four-line, amusing biographical verse form he invented at the turn of the century. This volume was published under the name 'E. Clerihew'. There was a second run of these verses in the late 1930s in *Punch* when they were illustrated by his son, Nicolas, (*q.v.*).

BENTLEY, Nicolas

English cartoonist and writer (1907–78)

3 He is remembered chiefly as the man about whom all is forgotten.

An Edwardian Album (1974). Of Sir Henry Campbell-Bannerman (1836–1908), who was the British Liberal Prime Minister from 1905–8. He died seven days after resigning.

BENTSEN, Lloyd

American Senator (1921–)

4 I served with Jack Kennedy. I knew Jack Kennedy. Jack Kennedy was a friend of mine. Senator, you're no Jack Kennedy.

To Dan Quayle who had evoked the name of John F. Kennedy in a vice-presidential TV debate during a presidential election (6 October 1988). Compare: 'Mr Blair, I know Margaret Thatcher. Margaret Thatcher is a friend of mine. When Margaret Thatcher was rebuilding this country, you opposed everything she did. Mr Blair, you're no Margaret Thatcher' – Brian Mawhinney, British Conservative Party chairman at Bournemouth conference (8 October 1996).

BERESFORD, Lord Charles

English politician (1846–1919)

5 VERY SORRY CAN'T COME. LIE FOLLOWS BY POST.

Beresford is supposed to have telegraphed this message to the Prince of Wales (presumably the future Edward VII) after receiving a dinner invitation at short notice. It is reported by Ralph Nevill in *The World of Fashion 1837–1922* (1923). The same joke occurs in Marcel Proust, *Le Temps Retrouvé* (published in 1927 after his death in 1922), in the form: 'One of those telegrams of which M. de Guermantes has wittily fixed the formula: "Can't come, lie follows [*Impossible venir, mensonge suit*]."'

BERKELEY, George

Irish philosopher and Anglican bishop (1685–1753)

6 If a tree falls in a forest, and no one is there to hear it, it makes no sound.

Which philosopher said this? Not Kant, apparently, though it was one of his preoccupations. Berkeley also seems a likely bet. In his writings on 'subjective idealism', he holds that there is no existence of matter independent of perception. But in his three best-known works, *Essays Towards a New Theory of Vision*, *A Treatise Concerning the Principles of Human Knowledge* and *Three Dialogues Between Hylas and Philonous*, the precise example does not occur. However, *Principles*, 1.23, has: 'Surely there is nothing easier to imagine trees, for instance, in a park, or books existing in a closet, and nobody by to perceive them'; in the *Dialogues* there is: 'Can a real thing which is not *audible*, be like a *sound*?' Perhaps these have become linked to the idea expressed by Monsignor Ronald Knox in the limerick attributed to him:

There was once a man who said 'God
Must think it exceedingly odd
If he finds that this tree
Continues to be
When there's no one about in the Quad.'

The editor of *The Book of Cloyne* (1994 ed.) comments: 'Berkeley's philosophy will always be tagged to the lines about the tree that might disappear when there was no one to see it and God's remark that it would not because he was always on the lookout. "To be," said Berkeley, "is to be perceived".'

7 The peasant starves in the midst of plenty.

The Book of Cloyne (1994 ed.), concerning the town in Ireland where Berkeley was bishop, quotes a certain

George Cooper as having written this in 1799 (i.e., after Berkeley's death), while Berkeley, is also credited with being the first to make use of the phrase. Unverified.

See also COWPER 189:8.

BERLIN, Irving

American composer and lyricist (1888–1989)

1 As Thousands Cheer.

Title of show (1933) with words and music by Berlin. Hence, *As Thousands Cheer: The Life of Irving Berlin*, title of book (1990) by Laurence Bugneer. A natural enough phrase found in newspaper reports but somehow still echoic of the Berlin use. From the *Daily Mail* (18 December 1993): 'When Maiden returned to Southampton in 1990, the triumph was enormous. A band played Tina Turner's "You're Simply The Best" as the girls sailed into the marina and thousands cheered and wept.' From *The Mail on Sunday* (27 February 1994): '... So when Paul O'Callaghan laid into an impersonation of Noel Edmonds's brain, thousands cheered.'

2 I'm dreaming of a white Christmas.

'White Christmas', *Holiday Inn* (film US, 1942), in which it is sung by Bing Crosby. His recording of the song is the biggest-selling single record of all time. A re-make of the film called *White Christmas* followed in 1954. The *OED2*'s first recorded use of the term 'white Christmas' (= a snowy one) is from *Two Years Ago* (1857) by Charles Kingsley.

3 Annie Get Your Gun.

Title of musical (1946). Even if it was utterly suitable for the tale of Annie Oakley the gun-toting gal, this title appears to have been an allusion. The song 'Johnny Get Your Gun' with lyrics along the lines of, 'Johnny get your gun, get your gun, get your gun,/Keep them on the run, on the run, on the run' was written by 'F. Belasco' (Monroe H. Rosenfeld), published in New York (1886), and was a popular American song of the First World War. Dalton Trumbo's film *Johnny Got His Gun* (US, 1971) was about a horrendously mutilated soldier in the same war.

4 There's No Business Like Show Business.

Title of song in *Annie Get Your Gun* (1946). Later the title of a musical film (1954) and the origin of a quasi-proverbial modern expression.

5 The Hostess with Mostes' on the Ball.

Title of song, *Call Me Madam* (1950). *Compare* FORREST 242:1.

See also PERKINS 429:2.

BERNARD OF CLAIRVAUX

French theologian and saint (1090–1153)

6 Love me, love my dog.

Meaning 'if you are inclined to take my side in matters generally, you must put up with one or two things you don't like at the same time', this comes from one of St Bernard's sermons: '*Qui me amat, amat et canem meum* [Who loves me, also loves my dog].' A good illustration comes from an article by Valerie Bornstein in *Proverbium* (1991): 'I told my mother that she must love my father a lot because she tolerated his snoring! ... She became aggravated with me and stated the proverb "*Aime moi, aime mon chien*". She told me that when you love someone, you accept all the things that go along with them, their virtues and faults.'

Alas, this was a different St Bernard from the one after whom the breed of Alpine dog is named. It was said (or quoted) by St Bernard of Clairvaux rather than St Bernard of Menthon (d.1008).

BERNARD, Jeffrey

British journalist (1932– 97)

7 Jeffrey Bernard is unwell.

Occasional editorial explanation for the non-appearance of his pieces in *The Spectator*. Used as the title of a London play (1989) by Keith Waterhouse, based on Bernard's writings.

BERNERS, Lord

English writer and composer (1883–1950)

8 He's always backing into the limelight.

On T.E. Lawrence. Quoted in *ODQ* (1979). Winston Churchill said the same thing, according to his secretary, Montague Brown (speech to the International Churchill Society, 25 September 1985): 'He had the art of backing uneasily into the limelight. He was a very remarkable character and very careful of that fact.'

BERRA, Yogi

American baseball player and coach (1925–)

9 The game isn't over till it's over.

It is claimed that *Sports Illustrated* investigated this and found that Berra's actual comment was 'You're not out of it till you're out of it.' Nowadays, the expression is more usually: 'It isn't over until it's over.'

'Berraisms' like Goldwynisms have been put into his mouth more often than they have emerged from it unaided. Some of the more unlikely ones are: 'It's déjà vu all over again', 'We made too many wrong mistakes', 'Baseball is ninety per cent mental, the other half is physical' and 'Always go to other people's funerals, otherwise they won't go to yours'. Of those he has admitted to, 'Nobody ever goes there anymore, it's too crowded' has been said by others before him; 'You can observe a lot by watching' is wisdom through tautology; as is, 'It ain't over till it's over' – his comment on a National League pennant race (1973) when he was managing the New York Mets.

BETJEMAN, John (later Sir John)

English Poet Laureate (1906–84)

1 Ghastly Good Taste.

Title of book (1933), subtitled 'a depressing story of the Rise and Fall of English Architecture', in which Betjeman concludes: 'We have seen in this book how English architecture emerged from the religious unity of Christendom to the reasoned unity of an educated monarchic system, and then to the stranger order of an industrialised community. As soon as it became unsettled, towards the end of the nineteenth century, "architecture" *qua* architecture became self-conscious.' This probably applies equally to design in general.

2 Come, friendly bombs, and fall on Slough.
It isn't fit for humans now.

'Slough' (1937). In a reply to a correspondent (9 January 1967), published in *John Betjeman Letters: Volume Two 1951 to 1984* (1995), the poet explained the precise nature and cause of his aversion: 'The town of Slough was not, when those verses were written, such a congestion as it is now and I was most certainly not thinking of it but of the Trading Estate ... which had originated in a dump that now stretches practically from Reading to London ... The chain stores were only then just beginning to deface the High Street, but already the world of "executives" with little moustaches, smooth cars and smooth manners and ruthless methods was planted in my mind along the fronts of those Trading Estate factories.'

3 Miss J. Hunter Dunn, Miss J. Hunter Dunn
Furnish'd and burnish'd by Aldershot sun.

'A Subaltern's Love-song' (1945). Miss Hunter Dunn was a real person. Betjeman surmised that she came from Aldershot and was a doctor's daughter and was correct on both counts. The title notwithstanding, Betjeman said it was really *his* love song.

4 Phone for the fish knives, Norman,
As Cook is a little unnerved.

'How to Get on in Society' (1954). The poem concerns 'Non-U' language and behaviour – that is to say genteel rather than 'U' language and behaviour of the upper-classes. In that milieu, special knives for eating are frowned upon, the full word 'telephone' is preferred, and so on. *See* ROSS 461:7.

5 Yes, I haven't had enough sex.

When asked if he had any regrets, on BBC TV *Time With Betjeman* (February 1983).

BEVAN, Aneurin

Welsh Labour politician (1897–1960)

6 Listening to a speech by [Neville] Chamberlain is like paying a visit to Woolworths; everything in its place and nothing over sixpence.

In *Tribune* (1937). 'Nothing over sixpence' was the slogan of Woolworth's stores in the UK until the Second World War pushed prices well above this limit.

7 Playing on a fuddled fiddle, somewhere in the muddled middle.

Of J.B. Priestley during the Second World War. From Alan Watkins in *The Observer* (28 September 1987): 'Dr David Owen has a bit of a cheek saying that the new SDP ought not to be "playing on a fuddled fiddle, somewhere in the muddled middle." The words were most recently used by Mr Roy Jenkins of the old SDP. They were first used by Bevan of J.B. Priestley during the last war. Mr Jenkins acknowledges his debt to Bevan. Dr Owen should likewise acknowledge his debt to Mr Jenkins. There is nothing new under the sun.'

8 No amount of cajolery, and no attempts at ethical or social seduction, can eradicate from my heart a deep and burning hatred for the Tory Party that inflicted those experiences on me. So far as I am concerned they are lower than vermin.

The fiery left-winger was on the eve of his most substantial achievement – launching the post-war Labour government's National Health Service – when on 4

July 1948 he spoke at a rally in Belle Vue, Manchester. He contrasted Labour's social programme with the days of his youth between the wars when the Means Test reigned, when he had had to live on the earnings of his sister and when he had been told to emigrate. As abuse goes, it was traditional stuff. In Swift's *Gulliver's Travels* (1726), the King of Brobdingnag considers Gulliver's fellow countrymen to be 'the most pernicious race of little odious vermin that nature ever suffered to crawl upon the face of the earth'. But the Minister was not allowed to forget his remark. Harold Laski estimated that Bevan's use of the word 'vermin' had been worth two million votes lost to the Tories.

1 In Place of Fear.

Title of book about disarmament (1952). *Compare* CASTLE 152:4.

2 We know what happens to people who stay in the middle of the road. They get run over.

Quoted in *The Observer* (9 December 1953). But you can't keep a good line down. According to Kenneth Harris, *Thatcher* (1988), Margaret Thatcher once said to James Prior: 'Standing in the middle of the road is very dangerous, you get knocked down by traffic from both sides.' And a TV play called *A Very British Coup* (1988) had a fictional Prime Minister saying, 'I once tried the middle of the road ... but I was knocked down by traffic in both directions.'

3 I know that the right kind of leader for the Labour Party is a desiccated calculating machine who must not in any way permit himself to be swayed by indignation ... He must speak in calm and objective accents and talk about a dying child in the same way as he would about the pieces inside an internal combustion engine.

During a *Tribune* group meeting held at the Labour Party Conference in Scarborough (29 September 1954), countering Clement Attlee's plea for a non-emotional response to German rearmament. The characterization of a 'desiccated calculating machine' came to be applied to Hugh Gaitskell who beat Bevan for the leadership of the Labour Party the following year. In 1959, however, Bevan told Robin Day in a TV interview: 'I never called him that. I was applying my words to a synthetic figure, but the press took it up and it's never possible to catch up a canard like that, as you know.' After the interview was over, he added: 'Of course I wasn't referring to Hugh Gaitskell. For one thing Hugh is not desiccated – he's highly emotional. And you could hardly call him a calculating machine – because he was three hundred millions out.' (source: Michael Foot, *Aneurin Bevan*, Vol. 2, 1973).

4 I am not going to spend any time whatsoever in attacking the Foreign Secretary. Quite honestly I am beginning to feel extremely sorry for him. If we complain about the tune, there is no reason to attack the monkey when the organ grinder is present.

Wishing to address the Prime Minister (Harold Macmillan) rather than the Foreign Secretary (Selwyn Lloyd) in a post-Suez debate, House of Commons (16 May 1957). The saying has also been attributed to Winston Churchill during the Second World War – replying to a query from the British Ambassador as to whether he should raise a question with Mussolini or with Count Ciano, his Foreign Minister, but this is unverified.

5 If you carry this resolution ... you will send a British Foreign Secretary – whoever he was – naked into the conference chamber.

Speech, Labour Party Conference (3 October 1957) – as Shadow Foreign Secretary – in opposition to a motion proposing unilateral disarmament. By taking this point of view, he shocked those normally on his side.

6 And you call that statesmanship? I call it an emotional spasm.

Ib. On how it would appear if Britain reneged on its international responsibilities, without consultation, and opted for unilateral disarmament.

7 Yesterday, Barbara [Castle] quoted from a speech which I made some years ago, and she said that I believed that Socialism in the context of modern society meant the conquest of the commanding heights of the economy ...

Speech, two-day Labour Conference (November 1959) – referring to the areas of activity which Labour would have to nationalize to bring about fundamental change. Hugh Gaitskell, the party leader, also quoted the phrase 'commanding heights of the economy', apparently, but no one has been able to find Bevan's original coinage, least of all his most recent biographer, John Campbell. Alan Watkins in a throwaway line in his *Observer* column (28 September 1987) said 'the phrase was originally Lenin's'. In his 'white heat of technology' speech in October 1963, Harold Wilson referred to 'the commanding heights of British industry'. At the Labour Party Conference in October 1989 Neil Kinnock also revived the phrase format, saying that education and training were 'the commanding heights of every modern economy'.

1 I read the newspaper avidly. It is my one form of continuous fiction.

Quoted in *The Times* (29 March 1960). *Compare* JEFFERSON 313:6.

BEVIN, Ernest

English Labour politician (1881–1951)

2 Not while I'm alive, he ain't.

On being told that another Labourite was 'his own worst enemy'. Reputedly levelled at Aneurin Bevan, Herbert Morrison, Emanuel Shinwell and others. Quoted by Michael Foot in *Aneurin Bevin*, Vol. 2 (1973), who footnoted: 'Perhaps once he had made it he recited it about all of them. Impossible to determine who was the original victim.' Douglas Jay in *Change and Fortune* (1980) added that it was 'made, I have little doubt, though there is no conclusive proof – about Bevan ... I could never discover direct evidence for this oft-told story.' Earlier, in about 1939, the American Senator Walter George may have said, 'Roosevelt is his own worst enemy' and 'Cotton Ed' Smith may have replied, 'Not so long as I am alive!'

3 My policy is to be able to take a ticket at Victoria Station and go anywhere I damn well please.

On his foreign affairs policy when Labour Foreign Secretary and so quoted in *The Spectator* (20 April 1951). In his biography of Bevin (1952) Francis Williams has a slightly different version, which was said to a diplomat about the most important objective of his foreign policy: 'Just to be able to go down to Victoria station and take a ticket to where the hell I like without a passport.'

4 It was clitch after clitch after clitch.

On the cliché-ridden content of a speech by another politician (possibly Anthony Eden). Quoted in *PDMQ* (1980).

5 The real tragedy of the poor is the poverty of their aspirations.

Attributed to Adam Smith in this form in *c.*1960, but unverified. Since 1987, however, it has frequently been attributed to Bevin, though with no precise source as yet (also to Aneurin Bevan, though with even less backing) and about any number of subjects – the poor, the working class, Britain, the trade unions. 'There was a marvellous remark by Ernest Bevin when he said that what characterized Britain was a poverty of aspiration – and it's true' – *The Times* (19 May 1987). Sometimes the word 'ambition' is substituted: 'John Edmonds, secretary of GMB, the general union, recalled Ernest Bevin's observation 50 years ago that the greatest failing of Britain's trade unions was their poverty of ambition which made them set their sights too low' – *The Guardian* (6 September 1990). 'My family were the same as any other working class family in those days; they suffered from what I shall call the poverty of ambition' – Sir Bernard Ingham, *The Times* (18 May 1991). 'Only the Morgan Motor Company refused to follow his advice to expand – a course of action which Sir John [Harvey Jones] cites as evidence of the poverty of ambition of small and medium-sized British companies' – *Financial Times* (21 April 1993). Perhaps on a balance of probabilities Bevin wins this one over Bevan.

6 Anything you make a mistake about, I will get you out of, and anything you do well, I will take credit for.

Quoted in Alan Bullock, *The Life and Times of Ernest Bevin* (1960–83). Was this addressed to a civil servant?

BIBLE, The

Except where stated these quotations are in the form to be found in the Authorized Version or King James Bible (1611)

7 It was the expectation of many ... upon the setting of that bright Occidental Star, Queen Elizabeth of most happy memory, some thick and palpable clouds of darkness would so have overshadowed this land, that men should have been in doubt which way they were to walk ... The appearance of Your Majesty, as of the Sun in his strength, instantly dispelled those supposed and surmised mists.

Epistle Dedicatory (to King James I). *Compare* DISRAELI 209:10 on the use of a trowel.

Old Testament

GENESIS

8 In the beginning God created the heaven and the earth. And the earth was without form, and void; and darkness was upon the face of the deep. And the Spirit of God moved upon the face of the waters. And God

said, Let there be light: and there was light.

Genesis 1:1. Hence, *fiat lux*, the motto of several institutions, including Moorfields Eye Hospital, London.

1 And the Lord God planted a garden eastward in Eden.

Genesis 2:9. Hence, *East of Eden*, title of a novel (1952; film US, 1955) by John Steinbeck. Or from 4:16.

2 And the Lord God caused a deep sleep to fall upon Adam, and he slept: and he took one of his ribs, and closed up the flesh instead thereof; And the rib, which the Lord God had taken from man, made he a woman, and brought her unto the man. And Adam said, This is now bone of my bones, and flesh of my flesh: she shall be called Woman, because she was taken out of Man.

Genesis 2:21–3, stating that God made woman from one of Adam's ribs. Hence, *Adam's Rib*, the title of a film (US 1949) about husband and wife lawyers opposing each other in court (also of a 1923 Cecil B. de Mille marital film with biblical flashbacks) and *Spare Rib*, the title of a British feminist magazine (founded 1972) – a punning reference to the cuts of meat known as 'spare-ribs'.

3 Esau selleth his birthright for a mess of potage.

The expression 'to sell one's birthright for a mess of potage', meaning to sacrifice something for material comfort, has biblical origins but is not a quotation of a verse in the Bible. It appears as a chapter heading for Genesis 25 in one or two early translations of the Bible, though not in the Authorized Version.

The word 'mess' is used in its sense of 'a portion of liquid or pulpy food'. 'Potage' is thick soup (compare French *potage*).

4 Behold, Esau my brother is a hairy man, and I am a smooth man.

Genesis 27:11. This was the unlikely text preached upon by Alan Bennett's Anglican clergyman in the revue *Beyond the Fringe* (1961), which has become a model for how not to do it. One hopes it was intentional that the clergyman ascribed the text to 2 Kings 14:1. (He also misattributed RICE 454:6 to W.E. Henley.)

EXODUS

5 And I am come to deliver them out of the hand of the Egyptians ... unto a land flowing with milk and honey.

Exodus 3:8, God speaking – hence, the phrase 'land flowing with milk and honey', referring to any idyllic, prosperous situation. *See* GOGARTY 266:2.

6 And thou shalt say unto him, The Lord God of the Hebrews hath sent me unto thee, saying, Let my people go, that they may serve me in the wilderness.

Exodus 7:16. Compare 8:1–2: 'And the Lord spake unto Moses, Go unto Pharaoh, and say unto him, Thus saith the Lord, Let my people go, that they may serve me. And if thou refuse to let them go, behold, I will smite all thy borders with frogs ...' A soft-porn stage revue (1976) had the title *Let My People Come*. *Compare* SAHL 466:4.

7 Would to God we had died by the hand of the Lord in the land of Egypt, when we sat by the flesh pots, and when we did eat bread to the full.

Exodus 16:3, said by the Israelites. Hence, 'the flesh-pots of Egypt', now meaning 'any place of comparative luxury'. Clementine Churchill wrote to Winston on 20 December 1910: 'I do so wish I was at Warter with you enjoying the Flesh Pots of Egypt! It sounds a delightful party ...' (quoted in Mary Soames, *Clementine Churchill*, 1979).

8 Thou shalt have no other gods before me.

Exodus 20:3. How many words are there in the Ten Commandments? The question is neither rhetorical nor uttered because one is too lazy to count them oneself. The test is whether one is talking about Exodus 20:2–17 or Deuteronomy 5:6–21, and then which language you are using and which translation. Raymond Harris declared (1995): 'As the Ten Commandments were written in Hebrew, I thought you would like to know that 120 words were used.' He also points out that the numbering of the commandments varies with different religions and, depending whether one includes 'I am the Lord thy God' as the first commandment, there may or may not be ten in all. But 'ten commandments' are referred to several times in the Old Testament.

Dr J.K. Aronson added (1995): 'By my count the version in Exodus has 172 [Hebrew] words and the version in Deuteronomy 189 words. The corresponding numbers of English words in the Authorized Version are 319 and 372, and in the Revised English Bible 301 and 348.' So, this is a considerably more complicated matter than at first appears. The word count very much depends on whether you restrict it to the actual commandments or whether you include the incidental observations.

1 Honour thy father and thy mother.

Exodus 20:12. Hence, *Honour Thy Father*, the title of a book (1972; film US, 1973) about the Mafia, by Gay Talese.

2 Thou shalt not covet thy neighbour's house, thou shalt not covet thy neighbour's wife.

Exodus 20:17. Hence, the title of Gay Talese's study of sexual *mores* in the US, *Thy Neighbour's Wife* (1980).

3 Thou shalt not commit adultery.

Exodus 20:14. The 1631 'Wicked Bible' through one of the more notable printer's errors advised readers, 'Thou shalt commit adultery'.

NUMBERS

4 What hath God wrought!

Numbers 23:23. Quoted by Samuel F.B. Morse, American inventor (1791–1872), in the first telegraph message he sent to his partner, Alfred Vail, from the Old Supreme Court Chamber in Washington, DC, to Baltimore (24 May 1844). Quoted in Flexner (1982).

DEUTERONOMY

5 He kept him as the apple of his eye.

Deuteronomy 32:10. Hence, 'apple of one's eye' for what one cherishes most. The pupil of the eye has long been known as the 'apple' because of its supposed round, solid shape. To be deprived of the apple is to be blinded and lose something extremely valuable.

JUDGES

6 Out of the eater came forth meat, and out of the strong came forth sweetness.

Judges 14:14. Samson's riddle. Hence, 'Out Of The Strong Came Forth Sweetness', a slogan for Lyle's Golden Syrup in the UK (current from the 1930s). Later, the Tate & Lyle company completely reversed the phrase by saying 'Out Of Sweetness Came Forth Strength' as part of its occasionally necessary campaigns featuring 'Mr Cube' to ward off nationalization of the British sugar industry.

1 SAMUEL

7 God save the king.

1 Samuel 10:24, referring to Saul. The third line of the English National Anthem (possibly written by Henry Carey and sung by him as his own composition, 1740, or James Hogg or taken from an old Jacobite drinking song *c.*1725) occurs several times in the Bible – also in 2 Samuel 16:16, 2 Kings 11:12 and 2 Chronicles 23:11. Benham (1948) comments: 'The words of "God Save the King" appear in the *Gentleman's Magazine* (October 1745). John Bull (1563?–1628), composer, singer, and organist at Antwerp Cathedral in 1617, has been credited with composition of the words and music.'

8 And Saul went in to cover his feet.

1 Samuel 24:3. David was hiding from Samuel in a cave when into the cave came Samuel to evacuate his bowels. Most modern versions of the Bible say, 'to relieve himself.' One American version is reputed to have: 'And Samuel went into the cave to *use the bathroom*.'

9 After whom is the king of Israel come out? after whom dost thou pursue? after a dead dog, after a flea.

1 Samuel 24:14. Yes, fleas are mentioned twice in the Bible, both here and at 26:20.

2 SAMUEL

10 The beauty of Israel is slain upon thy high places: how are the mighty fallen! Tell it not in Gath, publish it not in the streets of Askelon; lest the daughters of the Philistines rejoice.

2 Samuel 1:19–20. This is part of David's lamentation over the deaths of Saul and Jonathan, his son. *Publish It Not* ... was the title of a book (1975) by Christopher Mayhew and Michael Adams and subtitled 'the Middle East cover-up'.

11 Saul and Jonathan were lovely and pleasant in their lives, and in their death they were not divided.

2 Samuel 1:23. Taken from the lament of David for Saul and Jonathan, the line 'in their death they were not divided' has often been used by epitaph writers, though not always with total appropriateness. They are the last words of George Eliot's novel *The Mill on the Floss* (1860), being the epitaph on the tomb of Tom and Maggie Tulliver, brother and sister, who have been drowned. Of course, the original couple, Jonathan and Saul, were of the same sex and died on the battlefield. When Joseph Severn, the friend of John Keats, died in 1879, his son Walter suggest that the text on the grave in the Protestant Cemetery, Rome, should be, 'In their death they were not divided'. He was told that this 'must seem highly inappropriate to anyone who recollects the original application of the phrase ... [and] as

more than sixty years elapsed between Keats's death and your father's.' On the memorial plaque to the British-born actors, Dame May Whitty (1865–1948) and Ben Webster (1864–1947), in St Paul's Church, Covent Garden, London, the full text is used ('They were lovely and pleasant'): they were husband and wife.

The film *They Were Not Divided* (UK, 1950) was about British and American soldiers and friends who died during the advance on Berlin during the Second World War.

1 By my God have I leaped over a wall.

2 Samuel 22:30. *See* BALDWIN 72:2.

1 KINGS

2 I enter into the way of all flesh.

1 Kings 2:2 – in the 1609 Douai Bible translation, repeating an old mistranslation of 'the way of all the earth' (which is what the Authorized Version has) and meaning either 'to die' or 'to experience life'. Hence, *The Way of All Flesh*, title of a novel (1903) by Samuel Butler.

3 To your tents, O Israel: now see to thine own house, David.

1 Kings 12:16. *See* ROSEBERY 461:3.

4 Behold, there ariseth a little cloud out of the sea, like a man's hand.

1 Kings 18:44. In the *New English Bible*, the passage is rendered as, 'I see a cloud no bigger than a man's hand.' When something is described as such, it is not yet very threatening – as though a man could obliterate a cloud in the sky by holding up his hand in front of his face – and the context is usually of trouble ahead perceived while it is still apparently of little consequence.

The Rev. Francis Kilvert, in his diary for 9 August 1871, has: 'Not a cloud was in the sky as big as a man's hand'. In a letter to Winston Churchill on 14 December 1952, Bob Boothby MP wrote of a dinner at Chartwell: 'It took me back to the old carefree days when I was your Parliamentary Private Secretary, and there seemed to be no cloud on the horizon; and on to the fateful days when the cloud was no bigger than a man's hand, and there was still time to save the sum of things.'

2 KINGS

5 Go up, thou bald head; go up, thou bald head.

2 Kings 2:23. One of the more comical effusions in the whole Bible. It is how 'little children out of the city' mocked Elisha – the New English Bible has them saying, 'Get along with you, bald head, get along'. Comical, except that he 'cursed them in the name of the Lord', and two she-bears came out of a wood and mauled forty-two of them ...

2 CHRONICLES

6 And they buried him in the city of David among the kings, because he had done good in Israel, both toward God, and toward his house.

2 Chronicles 24:16, concerning Jehoida, a 130-year-old man. Hence, 'They buried him among the kings, because he had done good toward God and toward his house' – the text placed on the tomb of the Unknown Soldier in Westminster Abbey in 1920.

ESTHER

7 Then said the king unto her, What wilt thou, queen Esther? and what is thy request? it shall be even given thee to the half of the kingdom.

Esther 5:3. The origin of the expression 'Even unto half my kingdom' as much quoted by P.G. Wodehouse. Also at Esther 5:6 and 7:2. The (American) Revised Standard Version (1946–52) has 'even half of my kingdom', which is somewhat nearer to the Wodehouse allusions.

JOB

8 Man is born unto trouble, as the sparks fly upward.

Job 5:7. Hence, *Sparks Fly Upward*, title of the autobiography (1981) of the actor, Stewart Granger. Frank (Lord) Chapple, the former trade union leader called his autobiography (1984), *Sparks Fly*. Chapple had been leader of the Electricians' Union and 'sparks' has been the nickname given to members of that trade since before the First World War.

9 Man that is born of a woman is of few days, and full of trouble.

Job 14:1. *Not* 'Man that is born of woman'. Also Job 15:4 and 25:4.

10 Miserable comforters are ye all.

Job 16:2. Hence, 'Job's comforter' – an expression used to describe one who seeks to give comfort but who, by blaming you for what has happened, makes things worse. Job received rebukes from his friends and, as a result, characterized them thus.

1 My bone cleaveth to my skin and to my flesh, and I am escaped with the skin of my teeth.

Job 19:20. Note that it is '*with* the skin of my teeth'. To escape by the skin of one's teeth now means to do so by a very narrow margin indeed. *The Skin of Our Teeth* was the title of a play (1942) by Thornton Wilder.

2 The price of wisdom is above rubies.

Job 28:18. Compare PROVERBS 31:10.

3 Thus far shalt thou go and no further.

Job 38:11 actually has: 'Hitherto shalt thou come, but no further: and here shall thy proud waves be stayed' Charles Stewart Parnell, the champion of Irish Home Rule, said at Cork in 1885: 'No man has a right to fix the boundary of the march of a nation; no man has a right to say to his country, Thus far shalt thou go and no further.' George Farquhar, the Irish-born playwright has this in *The Beaux' Stratagem*, Act 3, Sc. 3 (1707): 'And thus far I am a captain, and no farther'.

4 He swalloweth the ground with fierceness and rage: neither believeth he that it is the sound of the trumpet. He saith among the trumpets, Ha, ha; and he smelleth the battle afar off, the thunder of the captains, and the shouting.

Job 39:24–5. It is a *horse* that is being talked about.

PSALMS

5 Out of the mouth of babes and sucklings hast thou ordained strength because of thine enemies.

Psalm 8:2. Matthew 21:16 has: 'Out of the mouth of babes and sucklings thou has perfected praise.' Note 'mouth' not 'mouths' in both cases.

6 Deliver my soul from the wicked, which is thy sword: From men which are thy hand, O Lord, from men of the world, which have their portion in this life.

Psalm 17:14. Hence, the expression 'man of the world'. From 'irreligious, worldly', the term has come to mean (less pejoratively) 'one versed in the ways of the world' and has been used as a title of a novel by Henry Mackenzie (1773) and a comedy by Charles Macklin (1871). *See also* GOLDSMITH 266:7.

7 Thou preparest a table before me in the presence of mine enemies: thou anointest my head with oil; my cup runneth over.

Psalm 23:5. Hence, 'my cup runneth over' has come to mean 'I am overjoyed; my blessings are numerous.' In her book *Does She ... Or Doesn't She?* (1975), the advertising agent Shirley Polykoff describes how she once suggested 'Her Cup Runneth Over' as a joke slogan to a corset manufacturer. 'It took an hour to unsell him,' she adds.

8 Weeping may endure for a night, but joy cometh in the morning.

Psalm 30:5. Hence, *Joy in the Morning*, title of a novel (1947) by P.G. Wodehouse.

9 Wash me, and I shall be whiter than snow.

Psalm 51:7. The expression meaning 'of extreme purity, innocence or virtue' is of long standing, as also the similar 'whiter than white'. Shakespeare in *Venus and Adonis*, l. 398 (1592) has: 'Teaching the sheets a whiter hew than white.' Precisely as 'whiter than white', the phrase was known by 1924. Later: 'TOWN THAT'S WHITER THAN WHITE' (*Guardian* headline, 19 March 1992). There is a firm belief in advertising circles that this later phrase has been used as a slogan, possibly in the form 'Washes Whiter Than White' for an unidentified washing powder/detergent in the UK (1950s?) From *Campaign* (3 January 1986): 'How Mrs Thingy discovered that Bloggo could wash her floor whiter than white'; (8 August 1986): 'It could have been something startling and whiter-than-white from Procter and Gamble'; (30 January 1987): 'The classic ad where startled A.N. Other Housewife pulls the whiter-than-white shirt from her machine and gasps with cataclysmic delight when she finds that the baby sick has been washed clean away.'

10 O that I had wings like a dove! for then would I flee away, and be at rest.

Psalm 55:6. 'O for the wings of a dove' is the title of Mendelssohn's famous vocal setting. Compare: 'Oh, had I the wings of a dove,/How soon would I taste you again! [society, friendship and love]' – William Cowper, 'Verses Supposed to be Written by Alexander Selkirk' (1782). Also: 'Alas for the breaking of love/And the lights have died out in the West,/And, oh, for the wings of a dove,/And, oh, for the haven of rest' – quoted by the Rev. Francis Kilvert in his diary (22 April 1872), but untraced.

11 Moab is my washpot; over Edom will I cast out my shoe.

Psalm 60:8. One of the strangest sentences in the Bible. The New English Bible translation may make it clearer: (God speaks from his sanctuary) 'Gilead and

Manasseh are mine; Ephraim is my helmet, Judah my sceptre; Moab is my wash-bowl, I fling my shoes at Edom; Philistia is the target of my anger.' In other words, God is talking about useful objects to throw, in his anger. (Moab was an ancient region of Jordan.)

1 He shall have dominion also from sea to sea.

Psalm 72:8. Perhaps these words led to the line in the poem 'America the Beautiful' (1893) by Katharine Lee Bates (1859–1929):

> America! America!
> God shed his grace on thee
> And crown thy good with brotherhood
> From sea to shining sea!

(The words have also been set to music.) The motto of the Dominion of Canada (adopted 1867) is, however, a direct quote, albeit in Latin: '*A mari usque ad mare* [From sea to sea]'.

2 They that dwell in the wilderness shall bow before him; and his enemies shall lick the dust.

Psalm 72:9. No, the Bible does not have 'to kick the dust' for 'to die'. That usage is nicely illustrated by a passage from Thoreau's *Walden* (1854): 'I was present at the auction of a deacon's effects ... after lying half a century in his garret and other dust holes ... When a man dies he kicks the dust.' Nor does the Bible have 'kiss the dust'. The *OED2* mentions neither of these expressions, though it does find 'bite the dust' in 1856. What Psalm 72 has is '*lick* the dust' – though this is suggesting humiliation rather than death.

3 They that go down to the sea in ships, that do business in great waters.

Psalm 107:23. The Anglican Book of Common Prayer has, rather, '*occupy* their business in the great waters'. The 'go down to the sea' here may have a bearing on MASEFIELD 386:2.

4 My soul fainteth for thy salvation ... for I am become like a bottle in the smoke.

Psalm 119:81–3. Hence, *A Bottle in the Smoke*, title of a novel (1990) by A.N. Wilson.

5 The Lord is thy shade upon thy right hand. The sun shall not smite thee by day, nor the moon by night.

Psalm 121:5–6. Hence, *Nor the Moon by Night*, title of a film (UK, 1958) about a game warden in Africa. In the US, the film was called *Elephant Gun*.

6 If I take the wings of the morning, and dwell in the uttermost parts of the sea; even there shall thy hand lead me, and thy right hand shall hold me.

Psalm 139:9–10. This text is on the tombstone of Charles A. Lindbergh (1902–74), the American aviator, on the island of Maui, Hawaii. Lindbergh made the first non-stop solo flight across the Atlantic in 1927.

See also under BOOK OF COMMON PRAYER 115:7–116:3.

PROVERBS

7 But her end is bitter as wormwood, sharp as a two-edged sword.

Proverbs 5:4. Hence, 'bitter end' in general use, meaning 'the last extremity; the absolute limit' – a common phrase by the mid-nineteenth century. Another explanation given for the phrase hardly allows bitterness to enter into it: the nautical 'bitt' is a bollard on the deck of a ship, on to which cables and ropes are wound. The end of the cable that is wrapped round or otherwise secured to the bollard is the 'bitter end'.

8 Wisdom hath builded a house, she hath hewn out her seven pillars.

Proverbs 9:1. Hence, the title *Seven Pillars of Wisdom* as applied by T.E. Lawrence to his memoir of the Arabian campaign in the First World War (published 1926/35). The relevance of the title is not totally apparent and Lawrence does not explain. However, his brother A.W. Lawrence noted in a preface: 'The title was originally applied by the author to a book of his about seven cities. He decided not to publish this early book because he considered it immature, but he transferred the title as a memento.'

9 Give instruction to a wise man, and he will be yet wiser.

Proverbs 9:9. 'Give counsel unto a wise man, he will be yet wiser' appeared inside the covers of the 'Teach Yourself' series of books for a number of years.

10 He that troubleth his own house shall inherit the wind.

Proverbs 11:29. Hence, *Inherit the Wind*, title of a film (US, 1960) about the 1925 Scopes 'Monkey Trial' (concerning the teaching of evolution in schools), and which is explained *in* the film.

11 A man's heart deviseth his way: but the Lord directeth his steps.

Proverbs 16:9. *See* THOMAS À KEMPIS 536:6.

1 Pride goeth before destruction, and an haughty spirit before a fall.

Proverbs 16:18. The proverb 'Pride goeth before a fall' might seem to be a telescoped version of this but apparently developed on its own. *CODP* cites Alexander Barclay's *The Ship of Fools* (1509), 'First or last foul pride will have a fall', and Samuel Johnson wrote in a letter (2 August 1784), 'Pride must have a fall'. At some stage the biblical wording must have been grafted on to the original proverb. One of Swift's clichés in *Polite Conversation* (1738) is, 'You were afraid that Pride should have a Fall'.

2 As cold waters to a thirsty soul, so is good news from a far country.

Proverbs 25:25. Hence, possibly, *From a Far Country*, title of a TV film (1981) of dramatized episodes from the early life of Pope John Paul II. The source, in fact, could lie in several places in the Old Testament where there are examples of 'from a far land' and 'from a far country' in Deuteronomy 29:22, 2 Kings 20:14, Isaiah 39:3 and so on.

Compare William Caxton in England's first printed book, *Dictes or Sayengis of the Philosophres* (1477), which has: 'Socrates was a Greek born in a far country from here'. Lines 517–8 of Coleridge's 'The Rime of the Ancient Mariner' (1798) are: 'He loves to talk with marineres/That come from a far countree.' H.D. Thoreau, *On the Duty of Civil Disobedience* (1849) has: '[On going to prison] It was like travelling into a far country, such as I had never expected to behold, to lie there for one night.' *Crowned In a Far Country* was the title of a book (1986) by Princess Michael of Kent about people who married into the British Royal Family.

3 As a dog returneth to his vomit, so a fool returneth to his folly.

Proverbs 26:11. *Compare* 2 Peter 2:22. *See* BYRON 138:9.

4 Who can find a virtuous woman? for her price is far above rubies.

Proverbs 31:10. *Compare* Job 28:18.

ECCLESIASTES

5 The sun also riseth, and the sun goeth down, and hasteth to his place where he arose.

Ecclesiastes 1:5. Famous as the title of an Ernest Hemingway novel, *The Sun Also Rises*, about expatriates in Europe (1926; film US, 1957) (also known as *Fiesta* in the UK). It promoted the Hollywood joke, 'The son-in-law also rises', possibly when Louis B. Mayer promoted his daughter's husband William Goetz to a key position at MGM – quoted in Leslie Halliwell, *The Filmgoer's Book of Quotes* (1973). More recently, there has been a book about the Japanese economy called *The Sun Also Sets* (1990) by Bill Emmott.

6 There is no new thing under the sun.

Ecclesiastes 1:9. Often rendered as, 'There is nothing new under the sun.'

7 To everything there is a season, and a time to every purpose under the heaven:
A time to be born, and a time to die; a time to plant, and a time to pluck up that which is planted;
A time to kill, and a time to heal; a time to break down, and a time to build up;
A time to weep, and a time to laugh; a time to mourn, and a time to dance;
A time to cast away stones, and a time to gather stones together; a time to embrace, and a time to refrain from embracing;
A time to get, and a time to lose; a time to keep, and a time to cast away;
A time to rend, and a time to sew; a time to keep silence, and a time to speak;
A time to love, and a time to hate; a time of war, and a time of peace.

Ecclesiastes 3:1–8. Hence, among many borrowings from this passage, *A Time to Love and a Time to Die*, title of a film (US, 1958), from a novel by Erich Maria Remarque (*Zeit zu leben und zeit zu sterben*, 1954). This is a blending of 'a time to love, and a time to hate' from 3:8 and 'a time to be born, and a time to die' (3:2). *A Time to Dance* was the title of a novel (1990) by Melvyn Bragg; *A Time to Kill* (film US, 1996).

8 Evil under the sun.

Used as the title of an Agatha Christie thriller about murder in a holiday hotel (1941; film UK, 1982), it is not explained in the text, though Hercule Poirot, the detective, remarks before any evil has been committed: 'The sun shines. The sea is blue ... but there is evil everywhere under the sun.' Shortly afterwards, another character remarks: 'I was interested, M. Poirot, in something you said just now ... It was almost a quotation from Ecclesiastes ... "Yea, also the heart of the sons of men is full of evil, and madness is in their heart while they live".' But Ecclesiastes (which finds everything 'under the sun') gets nearer than that: 'There is a sore evil which I have seen under the sun, namely, riches kept for the owners thereof to their hurt' (5:13) and: 'There is an evil which I have seen under the sun' (6:1, 10:1). Were it not for the clue about Ecclesiastes, one might be tempted to think that Christie had once more turned to an old English rhyme for one of her titles. In this one, the phrase appears exactly:

For every evil under the sun,
There is a remedy or there is none;
If there be one, try and find it;
If there be none, never mind it.

1 Sorrow is better than laughter: for by the sadness of the countenance the heart is made better. The heart of the wise is in the house of mourning; but the heart of fools is in the house of mirth.

Ecclesiastes 7:3–4. Hence, *The House of Mirth*, title of an Edith Wharton novel (1905) about a failed social climber.

2 The race is not to the swift, nor the battle to the strong ... but time and chance happeneth to them all.

Ecclesiastes 9:11. Hence, *Time and Chance*, title of the autobiographies of Group Capt. Peter Townsend (1978) and James (Lord) Callaghan, the former British Prime Minister (1987).

3 Dead flies cause the ointment of the apothecary to send forth a stinking vapour.

Ecclesiastes 10:1. Hence, probably, the expression 'a fly in the ointment', meaning 'some small factor that spoils the general enjoyment of something'.

4 Cast thy bread upon the waters: for thou shalt find it after many days.

Ecclesiastes 11:1. The origin of the expression 'to cast one's bread upon the waters', meaning 'to reap as you shall sow'. Oddly expressed, the idea is that if you sow seed or corn in a generous fashion now, you will reap the benefits in due course. The New English Bible translates this passage more straightforwardly as 'Send your grain across the seas, and in time you will get a return'.

5 Or ever the silver cord be loosed, or the golden bowl be broken, or the pitcher be broken at the fountain, or the wheel broken at the cistern.

Ecclesiastes 12:6. Hence, *The Golden Bowl*, title of a novel (1904) by Henry James.

6 Of making many books there is no end; and much study is a weariness of the flesh.

Ecclesiastes 12:12. Does the first half of this verse mean that (as is certainly the case nowadays) too many titles are published, or does it mean that the production of a lot of books is a never-ending task? Discuss.

SONG OF SOLOMON

7 The flowers appear on the earth; the time of the singing of birds is come, and the voice of the turtle is heard in our land.

Song of Solomon 2:12 – referring to spring. The turtle here is not the thing with a shell that ends up in soup, but the turtle dove, a more poetic image.

8 Take us the foxes, the little foxes, that spoil the vines.

Song of Solomon 2:15. Hence, *The Little Foxes*, title of a play (1939; film US, 1941) by Lillian Hellman – in which she writes about a family of schemers.

9 Until the day break, and the shadows flee away, turn, my beloved, and be thou like a roe or a young hart upon the mountains of Bether.

Song of Solomon 2:17. The first nine words are a popular gravestone inscription – e.g., on the grave in Brookwood Military Cemetery, Surrey, of Flying Officer H.G. Holtrop, an RAF pilot who was killed on 10 June 1944, aged thirty-three.

ISAIAH

10 They shall beat their swords into plowshares, and their spears into pruning hooks: nation shall not lift up sword against nation, neither shall they learn war any more.

Isaiah 2:4. Compare Micah 4:3.

11 Then said I, Lord, how long?

Isaiah 6:11. Hence, 'How long, O lord, how long?', now used in mock exasperation. The prophet has a vision in which God tells him to do various things and he reports: 'Then said I, Lord how long?' The more familiar version occurs, for example, in schoolboy verse by G.K. Chesterton (*c.*1890): 'Not from the misery of the weak, the madness of the strong,/Goes upward from our lips the cry, "How long, oh Lord, how long?"'

12 The wolf also shall dwell with the lamb, and the leopard shall lie down with the kid; and

the calf and the young lion and the fatling together. And a little child shall lead them.

Isaiah 11:6. So the simplified version, 'the lion shall lie down with the lamb' is incorrect. *Compare* ALLEN 17:2.

1 Watchman, what of the night?

Not a street cry. In Isaiah 21:11–12 the watchman replies, unhelpfully: 'The morning cometh, and also the night.' Used as the title of a Bernard Partridge cartoon in *Punch* (3 January 1900). Set to music several times, notably by Sir Arthur Sullivan. The line is also in Swinburne's poem 'A Watch in the Night' (part of *Songs Before Sunrise*, 1904).

2 Let us eat and drink; for tomorrow we shall die.

Isaiah 22:13. Ecclesiastes 8:15 has: 'A man hath no better thing under the sun, than to eat, and to drink, and to be merry', and Luke 12:19: 'Take thine ease, eat, drink and be merry.' Luke 15:23 has simply: 'Let us eat, and be merry.' Brewer (1975) calls it, however: 'A traditional saying of the Egyptians who, at their banquets, exhibited a skeleton to the guests to remind them of the brevity of life.'

3 The desert shall rejoice, and blossom as the rose.

Isaiah 35:1. Hence, 'to make the desert bloom' which the modern state of Israel has made come true. Adlai Stevenson also alluded to the phrase in a speech at Hartford, Connecticut (18 September 1952): 'Man has wrested from nature the power to make the world a desert or to make the deserts bloom.' The exact phrase does not appear in the Bible, though Isaiah has the above and, at 51:3: 'For the Lord shall comfort Zion ... and he will make ... her desert like the garden of the Lord.' Cruden's *Concordance* (1737) points out: 'In the Bible this word [desert] means a deserted place, wilderness, not desert in the modern usage of the term.'

4 They shall mount up with wings as eagles; they shall run, and not be weary.

Isaiah 40:31. The words are written in gold on red granite in English and Chinese on the memorial to Eric Liddell (1902–45) in Weifang, Shandong Province, China. Liddell's refusal to race for his country on a Sunday in the 1924 Olympic Games – probably losing himself a second gold medal in the process – was celebrated in the 1981 film *Chariots of Fire*. The son of Scots missionaries, he was born in China and duly returned there after the Olympics to work for the London Missionary Society. He died of a brain tumour in the Japanese internment camp at Weifang. The memorial was not set up until June 1991 (source: report by Andrew Higgins in *The Independent*, 10 June 1991.)

5 There is no peace, saith the Lord, unto the wicked.

Isaiah 48:22. Compare Isaiah 57:21: 'There is no peace, saith my God, to the wicked'. Not simply, 'No peace for the wicked'.

6 They make haste to shed innocent blood.

Isaiah 59:7. Hence, *Innocent Blood*, title of a crime novel (1980) by P.D. James.

JEREMIAH

7 Let us cut him off from the land of the living, that his name may be no more remembered.

Jeremiah 11:19. Hence, the phrase 'land of the living' in general slang use, meaning 'alive'. A cliché by the mid-twentieth century. One might say of a person referred to: 'Oh, is he still in the land of the living?'

8 And it shall be, when thou hast made an end of reading this book, that thou shalt bind a stone to it, and cast it into the midst of Euphrates.

Jeremiah 51:63. An early book review.

DANIEL

9 And whoso falleth not down and worshippeth shall the same hour be cast into the midst of a burning fiery furnace.

Daniel 3:6. 'Burning fiery furnace' also occurs at 3:20, 3:21 and 3:23. Hence, *The Burning Fiery Furnace*, the title of Benjamin Britten/William Plomer's 'parable for church performance' (1966) about the incident.

10 True, O king.

When someone makes an obvious remark, perhaps even a pompous one, other people will sometimes comment, 'True, O King!' In *The Diaries of Kenneth Williams* (1993) – the entry for 5 January 1971 – the comedian recounts being told on TV by an Irishman that he was a bore: 'I smiled acquiescence and said "How true, O King!"' The source for this expression is not absolutely certain but may well derive from the story of Nebuchadnezzar and the gentlemen who were cast into the fiery furnace. 'Did not we cast three men bound into the midst of fire?' Nebuchadnezzar asks

(Daniel 3:24). 'They answered and said unto the king, True, O king.'

The nearest Shakespeare gets is the ironical '"True?" O God!' in *Much Ado About Nothing* (IV.i.68), though he has any number of near misses like 'true, my liege', 'too true, my lord' and 'true, noble prince'.

Another version is 'True, O King! Live for ever'.

1 And this is the writing that was written, MENE MENE, TEKEL, UPHARSIN.

Daniel 5:25. Meaning 'God hath numbered thy kingdom, and finished it ... Thou art weighed in the balances, and art found wanting ... Thy kingdom is divided, and given to the Medes and Persians.' The origin of the phrase 'the writing (is) on the wall'. This way of expressing a hint, sign or portent, often doom-laden, derives – though not the precise phrase – from King Belshazzar's being informed of the forthcoming destruction of the Babylonian Empire through the appearance of 'A handwriting on a wall' (as the Authorized Version's chapter heading has it). *Compare* FITZGERALD 237:8.

The phrase became established in the nineteenth century. Lieutenant-General Sir Ian Hamilton, *A Staff Officer's Scrap Book during the Russo-Japanese War* (1907) has: 'I have today seen the most stupendous spectacle it is possible for the mortal brain to conceive – Asia advancing, Europe falling back, the wall of mist and the writing thereon.' In a BBC broadcast to Resistance workers in Europe (31 July 1941), 'Colonel Britton' (Douglas Ritchie) talked of the 'V for Victory' sign which was being chalked up in occupied countries: 'All over Europe the V sign is seen by the Germans and to the Germans and the Quislings it is indeed the writing on the wall.'

HOSEA

2 They have sown the wind, and they shall reap the whirlwind.

Hosea 8:7. Hence, presumably, *Reap the Wild Wind*, title of a film (US, 1942).

JOEL

3 I will restore to you the years that the locust hath eaten, the cankerworm, and the caterpiller [*sic*], and the palmerworm, my great army which I sent among you.

Joel 2:25. From Winston Churchill, *The Second World War*, Vol. 1, (1948): 'The Locust Years 1931–1935' – heading to Chap. 5; (note) 'Sir Thomas Inskip, Minister for Co-ordination of Defence, who was well versed in the Bible, used the expressive phrase about this dismal period, of which he was the heir: "The years that the locust hath eaten."' In November 1936, Stanley Baldwin had told the House of Commons: 'I want to say a word about the years the locusts have eaten ...'

And hence, presumably, *The Day of the Locust*, title of Nathanael West's novel (1939) about the emptiness of life in Hollywood in the 1930s. The relevance of the title to the book is not totally clear. Locusts are, however, usually associated with times when waste, poverty or hardship are in evidence. They also go about in swarms committing great ravages on crops. The climax of the novel is a scene in which Tod, the hero, gets crushed by a Hollywood mob. In addition to the above, Revelation 9:3 has: 'There came out of the smoke locusts upon the earth: and unto them we give power'; Revelation 9:4: 'locusts give power to hurt only those men which have not the seal of God in their foreheads'.

MICAH

4 Nation shall speak peace unto nation.

The motto of the BBC (decided upon in 1927) echoes Micah 4:3: 'Nation shall not lift up a sword against nation' (compare Isaiah 2:4). In 1932, however, it was decided that the BBC's primary mission was to serve the home audience and not that overseas. Hence, '*Quaecunque*' [whatsoever] was introduced as an alternative reflecting the Latin inscription (composed by Dr Montague Rendall, an ex-headmaster of Winchester College) in the entrance hall of Broadcasting House, London, and based on Philippians 4:8: 'Whatsoever things are beautiful and honest and of good report ...' '*Quaecunque*' was also taken as his own motto by Lord Reith, the BBC's first Director-General, who never liked the Corporation's 'peace' motto. In 1948 the 'peace' motto was nevertheless reintroduced by the BBC.

HABBAKUK

5 He who runs may read.

This expression is an alteration of Habbakuk 2:2, 'That he may run that readeth it', but is no more easily understandable. The New English Bible translates it as 'ready for a herald to carry it with speed' and provides the alternative 'so that a man may read it easily'. The *OED2* has citations from 1672, 1784 and 1821, but possibly the most famous use is in John Keble's hymn 'Septuagesima' from *The Christian Year* (1827):

There is a book, who runs may read,
  Which heavenly truth imparts,
And all the lore its scholars need,
  Pure eyes and Christian hearts.

Given the obscurity, one of the most unlikely uses of the phrase has been as an advertising slogan for *The Golden Book* in the 1920s (according to E.S. Turner in *The Shocking History of Advertising*, 1952).

Apocrypha (Old Testament)

2 ESDRAS

1 For the world hath lost his youth, and the times begin to wax old.

2 Esdras 14:10 might just be the origin of the wistful expression 'When the world was young', a harking back not just to 'long ago' but also to a time more innocent than the present. Precisely as 'When the World Was Young', it was used as the title of a painting (1891) by Sir Edward John Poynter PRA, which shows three young girls in a classical setting, relaxing by a pool. *Compare* KINGSLEY 336:2.

ECCLESIASTICUS

2 Speak, you who are older, for it is
fitting that you should,
but with accurate knowledge, and
do not interrupt the music.

A curious passage from Ecclesiasticus 32:3, in a modern translation. The meaning is made clearer by the New English Bible version of the concluding words in this section concerning 'Counsels upon social behaviour': 'Where entertainment is provided, do not keep up a stream of talk; it is the wrong time to show off your wisdom.'

3 Rich men furnished with ability, living peaceably in their habitations.

Ecclesiasticus 44:6. *See* CHURCHILL 168:10.

4 Their bodies are buried in peace; but their name liveth for evermore.

Ecclesiasticus 44:14. Hence, 'Their name liveth for evermore', the standard epitaph put over lists of the dead in the First World War and chosen by Rudyard Kipling. He was invited by the Imperial War Graves Commission to devise memorial texts for the dead and admitted to 'naked cribs of the Greek anthology'. He also used biblical texts, as here.

Earlier, the diarist Francis Kilvert had written (31 January 1875): 'So Charles Kingsley is dead. "His body is buried in peace, but his name liveth for evermore." We could ill spare him.'

New Testament

MATTHEW

5 I indeed baptize you with water ... but he that cometh after me ... shall baptize you with the Holy Ghost and with fire.

Matthew 3:11. John the Baptist speaking. Hence, the phrase 'baptism of fire' to describe a difficult initial experience, originally a soldier's first time in battle (compare the French *baptême du feu*). 'The first American troops to receive a baptism of fire in Europe in this war were the men of the United States Ranger Battalion who fought in the Dieppe raid today' – *The New York Times* (20 August 1942).

6 Ye are the salt of the earth: but if the salt have lost his savour, wherewith shall it be salted?

Matthew 5:13. From Christ's description of his disciples. Hence, 'salt of the earth', a phrase now meaning 'the best of mankind'. Christ was suggesting, rather, that they should give the world an interesting flavour, be a ginger group, and not that they were simply jolly good chaps. The New English Bible conveys this meaning better as 'you are salt to the world'.

7 Ye are the light of the world. A city that is set on an hill cannot be hid.

Matthew 5:14. *See* REAGAN 448:4.

8 Till heaven and earth pass, one jot or one tittle shall in no wise pass from the law, till all be fulfilled.

Matthew 5:18. Hence, 'every jot and tittle' meaning 'the least item or detail'. 'Jot' is *iota*, the smallest Greek letter (compare 'not one iota'), and 'tittle' is the dot over the letter *i* (Latin *titulus*).

9 And whosoever shall compel thee to go a mile, go with him twain.

Matthew 5:41, which, in the New English Bible, has Jesus Christ advising: 'If a man in authority makes you go one mile, go with him two.' A possible origin of the expression 'to go the extra mile', meaning, 'to make an extra special effort to accomplish something.' President George Bush used this American military/business expression at the time of the Gulf War (1991), referring to his attempts to get a peaceful settlement before resorting to arms. Later that same year, Bush, expressing sorrow for baseball star Magic Johnson who had been found HIV-positive, said: 'If there's more I can do to empathize, to make clear what AIDS is and what it isn't, I want to go the extra mile' (*The Independent*, 9 November 1991). The expression had been around long before that, however. In a revue song by Joyce Grenfell, 'All We Ask Is Kindness' (1957), there is: 'Working like a beaver/Always with a smile/Ready to take the rough and smooth/To go the extra mile.'

1 No man can serve two masters ... Ye cannot serve God and mammon.

Matthew 6:24. *See* GOLDONI 266:4.

2 Consider the lilies of the field, how they grow; they toil not, neither do they spin. And yet I say unto you, That even Solomon in all his glory was not arrayed like one of these.

Matthew 6:28–9. Hence, *Lilies of the Field*, title of a film (US, 1963) from a novel by William E. Barrett.

3 Therefore all things whatsoever ye would that men should do to you, do you even so to them: for this is the law and the prophets.

Matthew 7:12 – from Christ's Sermon on the Mount. *Not* 'Do as you would be done by', or any of the other derivatives. By the seventeenth century this was known as 'The Golden Rule' or 'The Golden Law'. (The 'rule of three' in mathematics was, however, known as the Golden Rule the century before that.)

4 Strait is the gate, and narrow is the way, which leadeth unto life, and few there be that find it.

Matthew 7:14. Hence, 'the straight and narrow' – the idea of a straight and narrow path of law-abiding behaviour or goodness from which it is easy to wander.

5 By their fruits ye shall know them.

Matthew 7:20 in the part of the Sermon on the Mount about being beware of false prophets. Meaning, 'you can judge people by the results they produce'.

6 The foxes have holes, and the birds of the air have nests; but the Son of man hath not where to lay his head.

Matthew 8:20. A variant is 'fowl(s) of the air' (Genesis 1:26), though much more commonly one finds 'fowls of the heavens' in (mostly) the Old Testament. Compare the 'fish(es) of the sea', which occurs at least three times in the Old Testament (e.g., Genesis 1:26). 'All the beasts of the forest' is biblical, too, (Psalm 104:20), though more frequent is 'beasts of the field' (e.g., Psalm 8:7).

The phrase later made a notable appearance in the rhyme 'Who Killed Cock Robin?' (first recorded in the eighteenth century): 'All the birds of the air/Fell a-sighing and a-sobbing,/When they heard the bell toll/For poor Cock Robin.'

7 A prophet is not without honour, save in his own country, and in his own house.

Matthew 13:57. Usually rendered as 'A prophet is without honour in his own country.' Meaning, you tend not to be appreciated where you usually live or are known.

8 They be blind leaders of the blind. And if the blind lead the blind, both shall fall into the ditch.

Matthew 15:14. Hence, 'the blind leading the blind', meaning, the ignorant are incapable of helping anybody similarly incapacitated. A form of words that seemingly demands parody. In 1958 Kenneth Tynan quoted people saying of *The New Yorker* that it was 'the bland leading the bland'. *See* TYNAN 547:2.

9 The sky is red and lowring. O ye hypocrites, ye can discern the face of the sky; but can ye not discern the signs of the times?

Matthew 16:3. Christ speaking. Hence, the expression used by everyone from Thomas Carlyle (as a book title – *Signs of the Times*, 1829) to the pop singer Prince (an album title 'Sign 'o' the Times', 1987) to describe portents or general indications of current trends.

10 Get thee behind me, Satan.

Matthew 16:23. Jesus Christ rebukes Peter with the phrase for something he has said. Nowadays, an exclamation used in answer to the mildest call to temptation.

11 It is easier for a camel to go through the eye of a needle than for a rich man to enter into the kingdom of God.

This is how Christ's words appear in Matthew 19:24 – also in Mark 10:25 and Luke 18:25, though the latter has 'through a needle's eye'. Note that the Koran contains a similar view and in Rabbinical writings there is the expression 'to make an *elephant* pass through the eye of a needle', which also appears in an Arab proverb. But why this camel/elephant confusion? Probably because the word for 'camel' in the older Germanic languages, including Old English, was almost like the modern word for 'elephant' (OE *olfend* 'camel'). In this biblical saying, however, it is possible that neither camel nor elephant was intended. The original Greek word should probably have been read as *kamilos* 'a rope', rather than *kamelos*, 'a camel'. The difficulty of threading a rope through the eye of a needle makes a much neater image.

1 At the eleventh hour.

Meaning 'at the last moment', the origin of this phrase lies in the parable of the labourers, of whom the last 'were hired at the eleventh hour' (Matthew 20:9). The expression was used with a different resonance at the end of the First World War. The Armistice was signed at 5 a.m. on 11 November 1918 and came into force at 11 a.m. that day – 'at the eleventh hour of the eleventh day of the eleventh month'.

2 Woe unto you, scribes and Pharisees, hypocrites! for ye are like unto whited sepulchres, which indeed appear beautiful outward, but which are full of dead men's bones, and of all uncleanness.

Matthew 23:27. Hence, the expression 'whited sepulchre', meaning a person 'coated in white' who pretends to be morally better than he, in fact, is – also 'holier than thou'.

3 The poor are always with us.

That is the phrase as we would most likely say it now, but it is to be found in three different forms in three gospels: in Matthew 26:11 ('For ye have the poor always with you'), Mark 14:7 ('For ye have the poor with you always'), and John 12:8 ('For the poor always ye have with you'). Compare these allusions: *The Rich Are Always With Us* was the title of a film (US, 1932) and *The Rich Are With You Always*, the title of a novel (1976) by Malcolm Macdonald.

MARK

4 If a house be divided against itself, that house cannot stand.

Mark 3:5. *See* JOHNSON 317:6.

5 My name is Legion: for we are many.

Mark 5:9. In other words, 'we are innumerable' – what the untamed 'man with an unclean spirit' tells Jesus who has said, 'Come out of the man, thou unclean spirit' and asked, 'What is thy name?' After Jesus expels the devils from the man, he puts them into a herd of swine which jump into the sea. The man is then referred to as 'him that was possessed with the devil, and had the legion'.

6 Beware of the scribes ... Which devour widows' houses, and for a pretence make long prayers.

Mark 12:38–40. Hence, *Widowers' Houses*, title of a play (1892) by George Bernard Shaw.

LUKE

7 Forbid him not: for he that is not against us is for us.

Luke 9:50. Jesus speaking. *See also* STALIN 515:4.

8 A certain man went down from Jerusalem to Jericho, and fell among thieves.

Luke 10:30. The parable of the good Samaritan. Hence, presumably, the construction 'a good man fallen among ——'. From R.M. Wardle, *Oliver Goldsmith* (1957): 'It was Goldsmith's misfortune that he was a jigger fallen among goons.' John Stonehouse called Edward Heath, 'A good man fallen among bureaucrats' (House of Commons, 13 May 1964). And when former journalist Michael Foot was leader of the British Labour Party, the *Daily Mirror* described him in an editorial (28 February 1983) as 'a good man fallen among politicians'. *See also* LENIN 349:7.

9 He that is not with me is against me.

Luke 11:23. *See also* STALIN 515:4.

10 Go out quickly into the streets and lanes of the city, and bring in hither the poor, and the maimed, and the halt and the blind.

Luke 14:21. From the parable of the great supper. 'Halt' here means 'lame, crippled, limping'.

11 And it came to pass, that the beggar died, and was carried by the angels into Abraham's bosom.

Luke 16:22. Hence, 'Abraham's bosom' as a term for the place where the dead sleep contentedly. This alludes to Abraham, the first of the Hebrew patriarchs.

JOHN

12 Then spake Jesus again unto them, saying, I am the light of the world: he that followeth me shall not walk in darkness, but shall have the light of life.

John 8:12. Hence, 'The Light of the World', title of a painting (1854) by Holman Hunt, showing Jesus Christ with a lantern, knocking on a door in a tree (to represent the soul). This is also the title of an oratorio (1873) by Sir Arthur Sullivan.

1 Jesus wept.

John 11:35 is the shortest verse in the Bible (the shortest sentence would be 'Amen'). It occurs in the story of the raising of Lazarus. Jesus is moved by the plight of Mary and Martha, the sisters of Lazarus, who break down and weep when Lazarus is sick. When Jesus sees the dying man he, too, weeps.

Compare Victor Hugo's centenary oration on Voltaire (1878): 'Jesus wept; Voltaire smiled. Of that divine tear and of that human smile the sweetness of present civilization is composed.'

Like it or not, the phrase has also become an expletive to express exasperation. The most notable uttering was by Richard Dimbleby, the TV commentator, on 27 May 1965. In a broadcast in which everything went wrong during a Royal visit to West Germany, Dimbleby let slip this oath when he thought his words were not being broadcast.

A graffito from the 1970s, from the advertising agency that lost the Schweppes account, was: 'Jesus wepped.'

2 Greater love hath no man than this, that a man lay down his life for his friends.

John 15:13. *See* BUTLER 137:9 and THORPE 539:6.

3 Pilate saith unto him, What is truth?

John 18:38. *See* BACON 70:2.

4 Then cried they all again, saying, Not this man, but Barabbas. Now Barabbas was a robber.

John 18:40 – in which Pilate is asking the crowd whether Jesus should be the prisoner customarily released at Passover. Hence, *Now Barabbas ...*, title of a film (UK, 1949) about prisoners, based on a play by William Douglas-Home, but also known as *Now Barabbas was a Robber*. *See also* BYRON 139:6.

5 The soldiers, when they had crucified Jesus, took ... his coat: now the coat was without seam, woven from the top throughout.

John 19:23. Hence, *The Seamless Robe*, title of a book, subtitled 'Broadcasting Philosophy and Practice' (1979) by Sir Charles Curran, a former Director-General of the BBC. The phrase was meant to describe 'the impossibility of separating out any one strand of the job from another ... It was impossible to disentangle, in the whole pattern, one thread from another'.

ACTS OF THE APOSTLES

6 And he went on his way rejoicing.

This expression used in allusion to Acts 8:39 should be treated with caution. It refers to a eunuch – a high official of the Queen of Ethiopia – who has been baptized by Philip.

7 It is hard for thee to kick against the pricks.

Acts 9:5. Hence, 'kick against the pricks' meaning to resist futilely. Prick here refers to something like a spur used to urge on a horse.

8 These that have turned the world upside down are come hither also.

Acts 17:6. Compare 'Behold, the Lord maketh the earth empty, and maketh it waste, and turneth it upside down' (Isaiah 24:1) as an origin for the phrase 'the world turned upside down'. This is (1) a popular name for English inns; (2) the title of an American tune played when the English surrendered at Yorktown (1781); (3) a figure of speech, as in Robert Burton's *The Anatomy of Melancholy* (1621–51): 'Women wear the breeches ... in a word, the world turned upside downward'; (4) the title of a well-known tract dating from the English Civil War concerning 'ridiculous fashions' (1646). Compare the French expression *la vie à l'envers* [life upside down/the wrong way round], used as the title of a film (1964).

9 And it came to pass, that, as I made my journey, and was come nigh unto Damascus about noon, suddenly there shone from heaven a great light round about me.

Acts 22:6. St Paul's conversion to a fervent belief in Christ – previously he had been a Pharisee persecuting the Christians. This gives us two expressions: 'road to Damascus' meaning 'the occasion of a change of heart, conversion or sudden realization; a turning point'; and 'to see the light'.

ROMANS

10 For the wages of sin is death; but the gift of God is eternal life through Jesus Christ our Lord.

Romans 6:23, St Paul speaking. 'For sin pays a wage, and the wage is death', is the New English Bible's version. The strength of expression derives from the perfectly correct singular verb 'is', where the hearer might be more comfortable with 'are'. There may possibly be an allusion in *The Wages of Fear*, English title of the film *Le Salaire de la Peur* (France/Italy, 1953).

11 If God be for us, who can be against us?

Romans 8:31. Compare Luke 11.23. *See* STALIN 515:4.

1 Vengeance is mine, saith the Lord.

No, he doesn't, nor does Paul the Apostle in his epistle to the Romans (12:19). Paul writes: 'Dearly beloved, avenge not yourselves, but rather give place unto wrath: for it is written, Vengeance is mine; I will repay, saith the Lord. Therefore if thine enemy hunger, feed him; if he thirst, give him drink: for in so doing thou shalt heap coals of fire on his head.'

Paul is quoting 'To me belongeth vengeance, and recompence', which occurs in Deuteronomy 32:35 and is also alluded to in Psalm 94:1 and Hebrews 10:30.

2 Let every soul be subject unto the higher powers. For there is no power but of God: the powers that be are ordained of God.

Romans 13:1. Hence, the term 'powers that be', now used to describe any form of authority exercising social or political control. The New English Bible has: 'the existing authorities are instituted by him.'

1 CORINTHIANS

3 Though I speak with the tongues of men and of angels, and have not charity, I am become as sounding brass, or a tinkling cymbal. And though I have the gift of prophecy, and understand all mysteries, and all knowledge; and though I have all faith; so that I could remove mountains, and have not charity, I am nothing ... Charity vaunteth not itself, is not puffed up.

1 Corinthians 13:1–4.

4 When I was a child, I spake as a child, I understood as a child, I thought as a child: but when I became a man, I put away childish things. For now we see through a glass, darkly; but then face to face ... And now abideth faith, hope, charity, these three; but the greatest of these is charity.

1 Corinthians 13:11–13. Hence, *In a Glass Darkly*, the US title given to *Murder Reflected* (1965) by Janet Caird, and of a novel by Sheridan LeFanu (1872). *Through a Glass Darkly* was the English title of an Ingmar Bergman film (1961).

5 The last enemy that shall be destroyed is death.

1 Corinthians 15:26. Hence, *The Last Enemy*, title of a book (1942) by Richard Hillary, about his experiences as an RAF pilot when he was burned in the Battle of Britain.

6 O death, where is thy sting? O grave, where is thy victory?

1 Corinthians 15:55. *See* BEHAN 81:2.

GALATIANS

7 Be not deceived; God is not mocked: for whatsoever a man soweth, that shall he also reap.

Galatians 6:7. 'God is not mocked' is a favourite text of the super-religious when confronted with any form of blasphemy. The New English Bible chooses rather to say that, 'God is not to be fooled', which does not convey the same element of abusiveness towards the deity.

PHILIPPIANS

8 For I am in a strait betwixt the two, having a desire to depart, and to be with Christ; which is far better.

In St Paul's Epistle to the Philippians 1:23, he compares the folly of living with the wisdom of dying. Hence, 'With Christ, which is far better' is quite a common text on gravestones, though it can seem rather ungenerous to those who survive. 'Better than what?' one is tempted to ask.

9 Who shall change our vile body, that it may be fashioned like unto his glorious body.

Philippians 3:21. Referring to Christ's resurrection. Also part of the interment service in the Anglican Book of Common Prayer. Hence, *Vile Bodies*, title of a novel (1930) by Evelyn Waugh.

10 The peace of God, which passeth all understanding, shall keep your hearts and minds through Christ Jesus.

This 'grace' comes as Paul is signing off his letter (4:7), though the final verse (4:23) is: 'The grace of our Lord Jesus Christ be with you all.' *See also* JAMES I 311:1; LUTYENS 366:2.

1 THESSALONIANS

11 Remembering without ceasing your work of faith, and labour of love.

1 Thessalonians 1:3. Hence, the expression 'labour of love', meaning 'work undertaken through enjoyment of the work itself rather than for any other reward.' Also to be found in Hebrews 6:10.

1 TIMOTHY

1 A bishop then must be blameless, the husband of one wife ... Not given to wine, no striker, not greedy of filthy lucre.

1 Timothy 3:2–3. The New English Bible translates 'no striker' as 'not a brawler'. Filthy lucre is 'money', though the original Greek suggests more 'dishonourable gain'. The phrase is also used by Paul, in the same context, in Titus 1:7 and 1:11, and in 1 Peter 5:2. The word 'lucre' also occurs in the Old Testament (1 Samuel 8:3).

2 The love of money is the root of all evil.

1 Timothy 6:10. Not simply, 'money is the root of all evil'.

HEBREWS

3 He being dead yet speaketh.

Hebrews 11:4. A popular gravestone inscription – as, for example, on the grave of the Rev. Francis Kilvert (1840–79), an Anglican curate at Langley Burrell, Wiltshire, and afterwards at Clyro near the Welsh border. He was then vicar of Saint Harmon and moved to Bredwardine two years before his early death. He died a month or so after marrying. As such, he would now be completely forgotten but for the diary which he kept from 1870 to his death. Having been pruned first by his widow, selections were published in 1938–40. How appropriate therefore that the inscription on the white stone cross over Kilvert's grave at Bredwardine should be this text, chosen, presumably, by his widow, unaware how apt it was to be for a posthumously published diarist.

4 Wherefore seeing we also are compassed about with so great a cloud of witnesses ...

Hebrews 12:1. Hence, *Clouds of Witness*, title of a detective novel (1926) by Dorothy L. Sayers.

5 For here have we no continuing city, but we seek one to come.

Hebrews 13:14. Of heaven. A request from a correspondent in Ireland wanting to know the 'author of the quotation "We have not here a lasting city" and the title of the book or poem, if any, in which it appeared' was instructive. At first glance it was not a very notable saying, but that has never stopped one from appealing to somebody, somewhere. The solution, however, was interesting, if only because it reminds us that there are more translations of the Bible than we may care to realize, and more ways of expressing the simplest thought than we might think possible.

It was soon spotted that the query was probably a version of what is as above in the Authorized Version. The Revised Version says, 'For we have not here an abiding city'; the Good News Bible says, 'For there is no permanent city for us here on earth'; the Jerusalem Bible has, 'For there is no eternal city for us in this life'; the New English Bible, 'For we have no permanent home'; the New International Bible has, 'For here we do not have an enduring city, but we are looking for the city that is to come'.

Relaying this information back to the original questioner, I soon heard from him that he had now found *his* version in the Douai-Rheims Bible (1609): 'For we have not here a lasting city, but we seek one that is to come.' Next day I happened to be reading Chapter 3 of Churchill's *History of the English-Speaking Peoples* (Vol. 1) in which he quotes the verse, in the Authorized Version, of course. In T.S. Eliot's *Murder in the Cathedral* (1937) we find the line: 'Here is no continuing city, here is no abiding stay.'

1 PETER

6 All flesh is as grass, and all the glory of man as the flower of grass. The grass withereth, and the flower thereof falleth away.

1 Peter 1:24. Compare Isaiah 40:6.

7 Wives, be in subjection to your husbands ... husbands ... giving honour unto the wife, as unto the weaker vessel.

1 Peter 3:1–7. Hence, *The Weaker Vessel*, title of a book (1984) by Antonia Fraser about 'woman's lot in seventeenth century England'.

8 The end of all things is at hand.

1 Peter 4:7. Origin of the phrase 'the end is nigh', the traditional slogan of placard-bearing religious fanatics. But, although 'nigh' is a biblical word, this phrase does not occur as such in the Authorized Version. Rather: 'The day of the Lord ... is nigh at hand (Joel 2:1); 'the kingdom of God is nigh at hand' (Luke 21:31); and the above.

2 PETER

9 The dog is turned to his own vomit again.

2 Peter 2:22. Compare 26:11. *See* BYRON 138:9.

REVELATION

10 Be thou faithful unto death, and I will give thee a crown of life.

Revelation 2:10. Hence, 'Faithful Unto Death', title of

a painting by Sir Edward John Poynter PRA, showing a centurion staying at his sentry post during the eruption of Vesuvius that destroyed Pompeii in AD79. In the background, citizens are panicking as molten lava falls upon them. The picture was inspired by the discovery of an actual skeleton of a soldier in full armour excavated at Pompeii in the late eighteenth or early nineteenth century. Many such remains were found of people 'frozen' in the positions they had held as they died. Bulwer-Lytton described what might have happened to the soldier in his *Last Days of Pompeii* (1834). Poynter painted the scene in 1865; it now hangs in the Walker Art Gallery, Liverpool:

1 And I looked, and behold a pale horse: and his name that sat on him was Death.

Revelation 6:8 has given a phrase much used in titles: Katherine Anne Porter's novel *Pale Horse, Pale Rider* (1939), Agatha Christie's novel *Pale Horse* (1961), and Emeric Pressburger's film script *Behold a Pale Horse* (1964).

Hence, *The Four Horsemen of the Apocalypse*, title of a novel (1916, films US, 1921, 1961) by Vicente Blasco Ibánez, referring to the agents of destruction, famine and pestilence, which appear on different coloured horses in Revelation 6. There is a white horse and a red horse; a black horse and a pale horse.

2 And when he had opened the seventh seal, there was silence in heaven about the space of half an hour.

Revelation 8:1. Hence, *The Seventh Seal*, title of a film (1957) by Ingmar Bergman.

3 And I saw an angel come down from heaven, having the key of the bottomless pit.

Revelation 20:1, where 'the bottomless pit' is Hell. The phrase is quoted in Milton *Paradise Lost*, Bk 6, l. 864 (1667):

Headlong themselves they threw
Down from the verge of Heaven, eternal wrath
Burnt after them to the bottomless pit.

William Pitt the Younger, British Prime Minister (1783–1801, 1804–6) was nicknamed 'the Bottomless Pitt', on account of his thinness. A caricature attributed to James Gillray with this title shows Pitt as Chancellor of the Exchequer introducing his 1792 budget. His bottom is non-existent.

4 The street of the city was pure gold.

Revelation 21:21 – a vision of the new Jerusalem. Probable origin of the expression that the streets of some cities are metaphorically 'paved with gold'. In the story of Dick Whittington, he makes his way to London from Gloucestershire because he hears the streets are paved with gold and silver. The actual Dick Whittington was thrice Lord Mayor of London in the late fourteenth and early fifteenth centuries. The popular legend does not appear to have been told before 1605. Benham (1948) comments on the proverbial expression 'London streets are paved with gold' – 'A doubtful story or tradition alleges that this saying was due to the fact that *c.*1470, a number of members of the Goldsmiths' Company, London, joined the Paviors' Company.' George Colman the Younger in *The Heir-at-Law* (1797) wrote:

Oh, London is a fine town,
A very famous city,
Where all the streets are paved with gold,
And all the maidens pretty.

The Percy French song 'The Mountains of Mourne' (1896) mentions 'diggin' for gold in the streets [of London]'. From G.K. Chesterton, *William Cobbett* (1925): 'He had played the traditional part of the country boy who comes up to London where the streets are paved with gold.' In the Marx Brothers film *Go West* (US, 1940), Chico says: 'He's goin' West, and when he gets off the train he's gonna pick up some gold and send it to me. They say that the gold is layin' all over the streets.'

The streets of *heaven* are also sometimes said to be paved with gold – though not specifically as such in the Bible. There is, however, a spiritual where the 'streets in heaven am paved with gold'.

Apocrypha (New Testament)

ACTS OF ST JOHN

5 The heavenly spheres make music for us. All things join in the dance.

This is the unattributed text on the grave of Imogen Holst in the churchyard of St Peter and St Paul's, Aldeburgh, Suffolk. She was a musical educationalist, conductor, composer (especially of songs) and arranger of folk-songs. She collaborated with Benjamin Britten whose grave is but a few feet in front of hers. Her father, the composer Gustav Holst (1874–1934), unwittingly provided his daughter's epitaph. It comes from a text he prepared and translated himself from the Greek of the Apocryphal Acts of St John for his *Hymn of Jesus* (1917). The passage concerns Jesus, 'before he was taken by the lawless Jews', calling on his disciples to 'sing a hymn to the Father', at which they join hands in a ring and dance. Rosamund Strode of the Holst Foundation has commented: 'Since to Imogen dancing was every bit as important as music (and indeed she once hoped to be a dancer), the two lines seemed to us appropriate in every possible way.'

VULGATE

1 *Dominus illuminatio mea, et salus mea, quem timebo.*

The Lord is the source of my light and my safety, so whom shall I fear?

Psalm 26. The first three words, in Latin, are the motto of the University of Oxford.

2 *Non nobis, Domine, non nobis; sed nomini tuo da gloriam.*

Not unto us, Lord, not unto us; but to thy name give glory.

Psalm 113 (second part):1. '*Non Nobis Domine*' is also the title of a vocal canon said to be by William Byrd (1543–1623) and sung at banquets as an after-dinner grace.

3 *De profundis clamavi ad te, Domine; Domine, exaudi vocem meam.*

Out of the depths I have cried to thee, Lord; Lord, hear my voice.

Psalm 129:1. Hence, *De Profundis*, title of Oscar Wilde's letter of self-justification (published posthumously in 1905).

4 *Quo vadis?*

Whither goest thou?

These words come from the Latin translation (the Vulgate) of John 13:36: 'Simon Peter said unto him, Lord, whither goest thou? Jesus answered him, Whither I go, thou canst not follow me now'; and from John 16:5 in which Christ comforts his disciples before the Crucifixion. The words also occur in Genesis 32:17 and in the Acts of St Peter among the New Testament Apocrypha in which, after the Crucifixion, Peter, fleeing Rome, encounters Christ on the Appian Way. He asks Him, '*Domine, quo vadis?* [Lord, whither goest thou?]' and Christ replies, '*Venio Romam, iterum crucifigi* [I am coming to Rome to be crucified again]'.

Quo Vadis? was famously used as the title of a film (US 1951, and of two previous Italian ones) and of an opera (1909) by Jean Nouguès, all of them based on a novel with the title (1896) by the Polish writer, Henryk Sienkiewicz (1846–1916).

5 *Ecce homo.*

Behold the man.

John 19:5. Hence, the title of a sculpture (1934) by Jacob Epstein.

See also: STERNE 519:4; WESLEY 562:6.

BICKERSTAFFE, Isaac

Irish playwright (c.1735–c.1812)

6 I care for nobody, no, not I,
And nobody cares for me.

This should be 'I care for nobody, not I,/If no one cares for me', if one is quoting from Bickerstaffe's comic opera *Love in a Village*, Act 1, Sc. 2 (1762). Is the misquoted version easier to sing?

BICKERSTAFFE, Rodney

British trade union official (1945–)

7 John Major, Norman Lamont – I wouldn't spit in their mouths if their teeth were on fire.

Bickerstaffe, leader of NUPE, the public employees' union [later Unison] was speaking to the Labour Party Conference on 30 September 1992. He added: 'I wasn't going to say "spit" but Willis [TUC General Secretary] made me change it.' He later said it was based on a Scottish insult he had learned in his youth: 'I wouldn't piss down his throat if his chest was on fire.'

BIERCE, Ambrose

American journalist (1842–?1914)

8 He had nothing to say and he said it.

Of Oscar Wilde, but unverified. In Wilde's own *The Picture of Dorian Gray*, there is: 'Women ... never have anything to say, but they say it charmingly.' Similarly, a review in *The Times* (5 May 1937) of a book by A.A. Milne said: 'When there is nothing whatever to say, no one knows better than Mr Milne how to say it.' Compare also: 'Berlioz says nothing in his music but he says it magnificently' – James Gibbons Huneker, *Old Fogy* (1913).

9 Amnesty, *n.* The state's magnanimity towards those offenders whom it would be too expensive to punish.

The Cynic's Word Book (later retitled *The Devil's Dictionary*) (1906). Bierce's definitions also included: 'Bore, *n.* A person who talks when you wish him to listen'; 'Non-combatant, *n.* A dead Quaker'; 'Phonograph, *n.* An irritating toy that restores life to dead noises'; 'Quotation, *n.* The act of repeating erroneously the words of another. The words erroneously repeated.'

BIGG, Nathaniel

Untraced

1 To each generation, that which preceded it must seem in some measure, according to its expectation of a hopeful futurity, the last age of innocence.

A Discourse on the Faculty of Recollection. Quoted in Nicolas Bentley, *An Edwardian Album* (1974), but otherwise not found.

BILLINGS, Josh (Henry Wheeler Shaw)

American humorist (1818–85)

2 Love iz like the meazles.

From the 'Affurisms' in *Josh Billings: His Sayings* (1865). He goes on: 'We kant have it bad but onst, and the later in life we have it the tuffer it goes with us.' *Compare* JEROME 314:3; JERROLD 314:5.

3 'Vote early and vote often' is the Politishun's golden rule.

From *Josh Billings' Wit and Humour* (1874), which seems merely to be recalling an adage. Indeed, earlier, William Porcher Miles had said in a speech to the House of Representatives (31 March 1858): '"Vote early and vote often", the advice openly displayed on the election banners in one of our northern cities.'

Safire (1978) ignores both these sources but mentions that historian James Morgan found 'in his 1926 book of biographies' that the original jokester was John Van Buren (d.1866), a New York lawyer and son of President Martin Van Buren.

BINYON, Laurence

English poet (1869–1943)

4 They shall grow not old, as we that are left
grow old:
Age shall not weary them, nor the years condemn.
At the going down of the sun and in the
morning
We will remember them.

The poem 'For the Fallen' was first printed in *The Times* (21 September 1914) and subsequently in Binyon's *The Four Years.* Spoken at numerous Armistice Day and Remembrance Day services since, the opening phrase is frequently rendered wrongly 'They shall *not grow old* ...' – as, for example, on the war memorial at Staines, Middlesex.

BIRCH, Nigel (later Lord Rhyl)

British Conservative MP (1906–81)

5 My God! They've shot our fox!

On the resignation of the Labour Chancellor Hugh Dalton. Remark (13 November 1947). In other words, the Conservatives had been deprived of their legitimate prey. Shooting the fox is the ultimate type of bad form on the hunting field as it deprives the participants of the thrill of the chase.

6 For the second time the Prime Minister has got rid of a Chancellor of the Exchequer who tried to get expenditure under control. Once is more than enough.

On Harold Macmillan's sacking of Selwyn Lloyd. Letter, *The Times* (14 July 1962).

See also BROWNING 127:2.

BIRD, John

English actor (1936–)

7 That Was the Week That Was.

Title of BBC TV's famous 'satire' series (1962–3), also used in the US. In *A Small Thing – Like an Earthquake* (1983) the producer Ned Sherrin credits the coinage to Bird who was originally going to take part in the programme. It was in conscious imitation of the 'That's Shell – That Was' advertisements of the early 1930s. Often abbreviated to 'TW3'.

BIRKETT, Norman (later Lord Birkett)

English barrister and judge (1883–1962)

8 I do not object to people looking at their watches when I am speaking. But I strongly object when they start shaking them to make sure they are still going.

Quoted in *The Observer* (30 October 1960). However, in *Joyce Grenfell Requests the Pleasure* (1976), Grenfell writes: 'It made me think of my father's story of Edward Marsh, who said he didn't mind if anyone looked at his watch when he was lecturing, but he didn't much like it when they looked at it a second time and shook it to see if it was still going.' As Eddie Marsh died in 1953 and Joyce Grenfell's father died in 1954, there may be grounds for wondering if Birkett really originated the joke. It has also been attributed to the historian G.M. Young.

1 He isn't; I am, and you're not!

To a convicted criminal who had exclaimed, 'As God is my judge – I am innocent.' Attributed to Birkett, but a bit unlikely, surely, except as an after-dinner speech joke. Quoted in Matthew Parris, *Scorn* (1994).

BIRRELL, Augustine

English Liberal politician and writer (1850–1933)

2 That great dust-heap called 'history'.

'Carlyle', *Obiter Dicta* (1884–7). *Compare* TROTSKY 543:3.

3 One whom it was easy to hate but still easier to quote.

'Alexander Pope' in *ib.* Surely, a saving grace.

BIRT, John

English broadcasting executive (1944–)

4 There is a bias in television journalism. It is not against any particular party or point of view – it is a bias against *understanding*.

Birt, who later became Director-General of the BBC and famous for promoting a dry, analytical approach to current affairs broadcasting, was working in the commercial sector when he coined the phrase 'bias against understanding'. In 1986, he told me: 'The problem of authorship that you raise is difficult. The phrase first appeared in the article in *The Times* of 28 February 1975. This article was written by me but was the result of a dialogue of years with Peter Jay. Subsequently we went on to write together a series of articles on the same subject. I don't think it would be wrong of me to claim authorship of the phrase; but it would only be just to acknowledge Peter's role.'

BISHOP, Thomas Brigham

American writer (1835–1905)

5 John Brown's body lies a-mouldering in the grave.

Bishop is but one of several suggested authors of the song 'John Brown's Body'. Brown was hanged in 1859, the song was being sung by 1861. The phrase 'a-mouldering in the grave' was not original to him. In Henry Austen's 'Biographical Notice' of his sister Jane which prefaced the first (posthumous) edition of *Persuasion* and *Northanger Abbey* (1818), he writes of her: 'The hand which guided that pen is now mouldering in the grave.' Earlier, Shelley in *Queen Mab* (1813) had had: 'All around the mouldering relics of my kindred lay.' In a letter to Lady Beaumont (21 May 1807), William Wordsworth had written: 'Long after we ... are mouldered in our graves'. Even earlier connections between 'moulder' and graves occur in Gray's 'Elegy' (1751), 'heaves the turf in many a mouldering heep' (GRAY 271:5) and Hervey's *Meditations* (1746): 'Your grandeur mouldering in an urn.'

BISMARCK, Otto von

Prusso-German statesman (1815–98)

6 Blood and iron.

When Bismarck addressed the Budget Commission of the Prussian House of Delegates on 30 September 1862, what he said was: 'It is desirable and it is necessary that the condition of affairs in Germany and of her constitutional relations should be improved; but this cannot be accomplished by speeches and resolutions of a majority, but only by iron and blood [*Eisen und Blut*].' On 28 January 1886, speaking to the Prussian House of Deputies, he did, however, use the words in the more familiar order: 'This policy cannot succeed through speeches, and shooting-matches and songs; it can only be carried out through blood and iron [*Blut und Eisen*].'

The words may have achieved their more familiar order, at least to English ears, through their use by A.C. Swinburne in his poem 'A Word for the Country' (1884): 'Not with dreams, but with blood and with iron, shall a nation be moulded at last.' (Eric Partridge, while identifying this source correctly in *A Dictionary of Clichés*, 1966 ed., ascribes the authorship to Tennyson.) On the other hand, the Roman orator Quintilian (first century AD) used the exact phrase *sanguinem et ferrum*.

7 I consider [the power of the German empire] ... to be more than that of an honest broker.

Speech, Reichstag (1878). 'Honest broker' is '*eines ehrlichen Maklers*' in German.

8 When a lady says no, she means perhaps ...

In October 1982, Lord Denning, then a senior British

jurist, was quoted as having commented on the difference between a diplomat and a lady, at a meeting of the Magistrates Association, in these words: 'When a diplomat says yes, he means perhaps. When he says perhaps, he means no. When he says no, he is not a diplomat. When a lady says no, she means perhaps. When she says perhaps, she means yes. But when she says yes, she is no lady.'

Whether Denning claimed it as his own is not recorded, but in Hans Severus Ziegler's *Heitere Muse: Anekdoten aus Kultur und Geschichte* (1974), the passage appears in a (possibly apocryphal) anecdote concerning Bismarck at a ball in St Petersburg. His partner, whom he had been flattering, told him, 'One can't believe a word you diplomats say' and provided the first half of the description. Then Bismarck replied with the second half.

1 God protects fools, drunks and the United States of America.

Untraced. But, there is a French proverb that states: 'God helps three sorts of people, fools, children and drunkards'. W. Eric Gustafson commented (1995): 'My history teacher, the great Henry Wilkinson Bragdon, used to ascribe to Bismarck the saying that "There is a special providence that protects idiots, drunkards, children, and the United States of America." I have even quoted it in my own writing, but I can't find it in the standard quotation books.' On 9 January 1995, *US News and World Report* quoted Daniel P. Moynihan as saying of the avoidance of casualties in the Haitian intervention: 'The Lord looks after drunks and Americans.'

2 A Bavarian is half-way between an Austrian and a human being.

Unconfirmed. R.P.W. Lewis recalled this, however, from Edward Teller's obituary of the physicist Werner Heisenberg – a Bavarian – in *Nature* (15 April 1976): 'On the 800th anniversary of the Bavarian state, he appeared on television and said, "The Bavarian unites the discipline of the Austrian with the charm of the Prussian".'

3 If you like laws and sausages, you should never watch either one being made.

Widely attributed to Bismarck, but unverified. A slightly different version, 'Laws are like sausages; you should never watch them being made', has been credited to the French revolutionary statesman Honoré Gabriel de Riqueti, Comte de Mirabeau (1749–91).

4 I have seen three emperors in their nakedness, and the sight was not inspiring.

Quoted in *The Treasury of Humorous Quotations*, ed. by Evan Esar & Nicolas Bentley (1951), but otherwise unverified.

5 You've got to exchange the populations of Holland and Ireland. Then the Dutch will turn Ireland into a beautiful garden and the Irish will forget to mend the dikes and will all be drowned.

On how to resolve the Irish Question. Attributed to Bismarck by Lord Healey on BBC Radio *Quote ... Unquote* (23 May 1995), but unconfirmed.

BLACKSTONE, Sir William

English jurist (1723–80)

6 That the king can do no wrong, is a necessary and fundamental principle of the English constitution.

Commentaries on the Laws of England (1765). The concept was not original, however. John Selden's *Table-Talk* (1689) has, 'The King can do no wrong, that is no Process can be granted against him'; and one is told (unverified) that Judge Orlando Bridgeman said it in the trial of the regicides after the restoration of the monarchy in 1660. But Bridgeman did go on to say that ministers *could* do wrong *in the king's name* and the fault should, therefore, be held against the ministers. In the same year Cunelgus Bonde, in his *Scutum regale; the royal buckler, or vox legis, a lecture to the traytors who most wickedly murthered Charles the I*, wrote: 'The King can do no wrong; Therefore cannot be a disseisor [dispossessor].'

Even earlier, John Milton in *Eikonoklastes* (1649) had written: 'As the King of England can doe no wrong, so neither can he do right but ... by his courts.' In other words, it was a venerable idea, even by the time Blackstone expressed it, as is attested by the legal maxim (of no known date) to the same effect, expressed in Latin: '*Rex non potest peccare*.'

Later, in 1822, giving judgement in the case of 'the goods of King George III, deceased', Mr Justice John Nicholl said: 'The king can do no wrong; he cannot constitutionally be supposed capable of injustice.' And, *mutatis mutandis*, Richard Nixon tried to assert the same principle on behalf of the American Presidency in his TV interviews with David Frost in May 1977, saying: 'When the President does it, that means it is not illegal.'

BLAIR, Tony

British Labour Prime Minister (1953–)

7 The Labour Party is the party of law and order

in Britain today, tough on crime and tough on the causes of crime.

Speech, Labour Party conference (30 September 1993) as Shadow Home Secretary. The 'tough' phrase had been used by Blair for the first time earlier in the year and had been supplied by his colleague, Gordon Brown. When he became the Labour leader in the summer of 1994, there followed any number of 'tough on ——, tough on the causes of ——' imitations and parodies.

1 The Stakeholder Economy.

Title of speech at Derby (18 January 1996). Earlier in the month, in speeches in Tokyo and Singapore, Blair had explored the idea of giving everyone – not just the privileged few – a stake in society. They must be given opportunities to work and improve themselves. In return, they must take more responsibility for themselves. The term 'stakeholder capitalism' had previously been popularized in a book, *The State We're In* (1995) by Will Hutton.

BLAKE, Eubie

American jazz musician (1883–1983)

2 If I'd known I was gonna live this long, I'd have taken better care of myself.

The centenarian boogie-woogie pianist, ragtime composer and lyricist, was so quoted in *The Observer* (13 February 1983). Unfortunately, five days after marking his centennial, Blake died. Even so, his felicitous remark was not original. In *Radio Times* (17 February 1979), Benny Green quoted Adolph Zukor, founder of Paramount Pictures, as having said on the approach to his hundredth birthday: 'If I'd known how old I was going to be I'd have taken better care of myself'. Zukor died in 1976, having been born in 1873.

BLAKE, William

English poet and painter (1757–1827)

3 Tyger Tyger, burning bright
In the forests of the night:
What immortal hand or eye
Could frame thy fearful symmetry?

'The Tyger' in *Songs of Innocence* (1789). Hence, *Forests of the Night*, title of a crime novel (1987) by Margaret Moore and *In the Forests of the Night* by James Riddell (1948).

4 The reason Milton wrote in fetters when he wrote of Angels and God, and at liberty when of Devils and Hell, is because he was a true Poet, and of the Devil's party without knowing it.

'The Voice of the Devil', Plate 6, note, *The Marriage of Heaven and Hell* (*c.*1790–3). Referring to Milton's alleged shortcomings in *Paradise Lost*.

5 If the doors of perception [i.e., the senses] were cleansed, every thing would appear to man as it is, infinite.

'A Memorable Fancy' in *ib.* Aldous Huxley used *The Doors of Perception* as the title of a book (1954) about his experiments with mescaline and LSD. This view was seized upon by proponents of drug culture in the 1960s and from it was also derived the name of the US vocal/instrumental group the Doors.

6 The morning comes, the night decays, the watchmen leave their stations.

'America, a Prophecy' (1793). Blake supported the American Revolution and wrote this in support. Hence, *Watchmen in the Night: Presidential Accountability after Watergate* (1975) by Theodore C. Sorenson. *Compare* BIBLE 98:1.

7 And did those feet in ancient time?
Walk upon England's mountains green?
And was the holy Lamb of God
On England's pleasant pastures seen?

And did the Countenance Divine
Shine forth upon our clouded hills?
And was Jerusalem builded here
Among these dark Satanic mills?

Blake's short preface to his poem *Milton* (1804–10) has come to be called 'Jerusalem' as a result of the immensely popular musical setting (1916) by Sir Hubert Parry, which has become an alternative British National Anthem. It should not be confused with Blake's other poem with the title *Jerusalem: The Emanation of the Giant Albion*. Because of the musical setting's magnificent hymn-like nature, it would not be surprising if most people believed the 'feet' were those of Jesus Christ, but this is not the case. Additionally, because of the poem's date, it might be assumed that the 'dark Satanic mills' had something to do with the Industrial Revolution.

In fact, as F.W. Bateson points out in *English Poetry* (1950), the poem would appear to be an 'anti-clerical paean of free love'. It originally came at the end of a prose preface, Bateson notes, in which Blake attacked the practice of drawing on 'Greek or Roman models'. The phrase 'in ancient time' alludes to the legend that Pythagoras derived his philosophical system from the British Druids. So, Blake is saying, it is foolish to rely on classical models when these originally derived from primitive Britain.

Another interpretation of the piece is that it relates to the legend of Joseph of Arimathea's visit to England with the Holy Grail. Blake might be asking how close the ancient Britons were to the early Christians and, therefore, how close was Blake's generation to God?

As for the significance of the name 'Jerusalem', Blake refers to this in a later Prophetic Book: 'Jerusalem is nam'd Liberty/Among the sons of Albion'. Rather than indicating some Utopian ideal, 'Jerusalem' stands for something much more abstract – sexual liberty, Bateson thinks.

Another passage in *Milton* makes it clear that the 'dark Satanic mills' are nothing industrial but rather the altars of the churches on which the clergy of Blake's time were plying 'their deadly Druidic trade', in Bateson's phrase. They have, however, been interpreted as bearing some rural prejudice against city-dwellers and also as representing the universities of Oxford and Cambridge ...

It is no wonder that the meaning of the poem is so widely misunderstood when it can be perceived only through a thicket of footnotes. As sung, it is a meaningless but joyful assertion of rather vague higher thoughts – a vision of the better world to which the dead have gone and of the nobler society that could be created here on earth if only we could get round to it.

1 Bring me my bow of burning gold,
Bring me my arrow of desire
Bring me my spear! Oh, clouds unfold
Bring me my chariot of fire.

Ib. Hence, *Chariots of Fire*, the title given to a film (UK, 1981) about the inner drives of two athletes (one a future missionary) in the 1924 Olympics. Appropriately for a film whose basic themes included Englishness, Christianity and Judaism, the title comes from Blake's poem which is sung in Parry's setting at the climax of the film. Note the singular 'chariot' in the original. 'Chariots of fire' in the plural occurs in 2 Kings 6:17: 'And the Lord opened the eyes of the young man; and he saw: and, behold, the mountain was full of horses and chariots of fire round about Elisha.'

2 I will not cease from mental fight,
Nor shall my sword sleep in my hand,
Till we have built Jerusalem,
In England's green and pleasant land.

Ib. Unfortunately, 'green and pleasant land' became a cliché by the mid-twentieth century and was included in the parody of sportswriters' clichés in the book *That Was The Week That Was* (1963). 'How is it that, if the New Zealand flatworm's habit of slurping up the good old British earthworm will devastate this green and pleasant land, New Zealand seems a very green and pleasant land, far from an arid wasteland?' – *The Independent* (17 January 1995). 'As the environment is increasingly threatened by developers, the concerned classes are rising up to save our green and pleasant land. Sheila Hale reports from the front line' – by-line, *Harpers & Queen* Magazine (May 1995).

F.R. Leavis, the literary critic, entitled his autobiography *Nor Shall My Sword* (1972).

3 This life's five windows of the soul
Distort the Heavens from pole to pole,
And leads you to believe a lie
When you see with, not thro', the eye.

The Everlasting Gospel (*c.*1818). Here, Blake seems to be saying that the five *senses* (or perhaps two eyes, two ears, and a nose?) are the windows of the soul. In some texts, it is 'life's dim windows of the soul'. In *Zuleika Dobson* (1911) Max Beerbohm wrote: 'It needs no dictionary of quotations to remind me that the eyes are the windows of the soul.' Just in case it does, this is the reference. *Compare* ELIZABETH I 227:5.

4 I give you the end of a golden string;
Only wind it into a ball,
It will lead you in at Heaven's gate,
Built in Jerusalem's wall.

Jerusalem (1820). This use of the phrase 'Heaven's gate' is one of the contenders for the naming of Michael Cimino's 1980 film with the title *Heaven's Gate*, famous for having lost more money than any other film to date – about £34 million. In it, 'Heaven's Gate' is the name of a roller-skating rink used by settlers and immigrants in Wyoming in 1891. Conceivably, the name is meant to be taken as an ironic one for the rough situation many of the characters find themselves in as they arrive to start a new life.

The idea of a 'gate to heaven' goes back to the Bible. For example, Genesis 28:17 has: 'This is none other but the house of God, and this is the gate of heaven.' Psalm 78:23 has: 'He commanded the clouds from above, and opened the doors of heaven.' Shakespeare twice uses the phrase. In *Cymbeline* (II.iii.20) there is the song, 'Hark, hark, the lark at heaven's gate sings' and Sonnet 29 has 'Like to the lark at break of day arising / From sullen earth sings hymns at heaven's gate.'

Browning uses the phrase and Steven Bach in his

book *Final Cut* (1985) about the making of the film cites two more possible sources: the Wallace Stevens poem with the title 'The Worms at Heaven's Gate' and this Blake.

1 Great things are done when men and mountains meet. This is not done by jostling in the street.

MS Note-Book (no date). For his time, an unusual comment in support of communing with nature. For most of the eighteenth century mountains remained things to be feared. The blinds would be drawn down in the carriage so that they could not be seen.

BLANCH, Lesley

English writer (1907–)

2 The Wilder Shores of Love.

Title of a biographical study (1954) in which Blanch describes four nineteenth-century women 'who found fulfilment as women along wilder *Eastern* shores'. Describing Jane Digby (whose fourth husband was an Arab Sheik), Blanch writes: 'She was an Amazon. Her whole life was spent riding at breakneck speed towards the wilder shores of love.' Hence, presumably, such usages as: 'The wilder shores of PC' [political correctness] (*The Independent*, 21 July 1992); 'The consultant, alone in triumph upon the wilder shores of dermatology, raised his eye-glass to me and averred ...' (Duncan Fallowell, *One Hot Summer in St Petersburg*, 1994); 'Gladstone's third major excursion to the wilder shores of political rashness came in May 1864' (Roy Jenkins, *Gladstone*, 1995).

BLEASDALE, Alan

English playwright (1946–)

3 Gi' us a job [*or* gissa job], I could do that.

Stock phrase of unemployed character, Yosser Hughes, in TV play, *The Boys from the Blackstuff* (1982). A rare example of a catchphrase coming out of a TV drama series. Yosser's plea became a nationally repeated phrase, not least because of the political ramifications. It was chanted by football crowds in Liverpool and printed on T-shirts with Yosser confronting Prime Minister Margaret Thatcher. From *The Observer* (30 January 1983): 'At Anfield nowadays whenever the Liverpool goalkeeper makes a save, the Kop affectionately chants at him the catch-phrase of Yosser Hughes: "We could do that." It's a slogan which might usefully rise to the lips of the chairbound viewer just as often.' In fact, there were *two* phrases here, sometimes used independently, and sometimes together in a different form, 'I can do that. Gi'us a job.'

BLUNT, Alfred

English bishop (1879–1957)

4 The benefit of the King's Coronation depends under God upon ... the faith, prayer and self-dedication of the King himself ... We hope that he is aware of this need. Some of us wish that he gave more positive signs of such awareness.

Press comment on the relationship between King Edward VIII and Wallis Simpson finally burst through following these innocuous remarks made on 1 December 1936 by the Bishop of Bradford. Speaking at a diocesan conference, he was dealing with a suggestion that the forthcoming Coronation should be secularized and with criticism that the King was not a regular churchgoer. The *Yorkshire Post* linked the Bishop's words to rumours then in circulation. Dr Blunt claimed subsequently that his address had been written six weeks earlier, without knowledge of the rumours, and added: 'I studiously took care to say nothing of the King's private life, because I know nothing about it.'

BOESKY, Ivan

American financier (1937–)

5 Greed is all right ... Greed is healthy. You can be greedy and still feel good about yourself.

Part of a commencement address when receiving an honorary degree at the University of California at Berkeley on 18 May 1986. Boesky also said, 'Seek wealth, it's good'. In December 1987 he was sentenced to three years imprisonment for insider dealing on the New York Stock Exchange. Bartlett (1992) has: 'Greed is good! Greed is right! Greed works! Greed will save the U.S.A.!' *See also* WALL STREET 555:1.

BOGART, Humphrey

American film actor (1899–1957)

6 Tennis, anyone?

Wrongly said to have been Bogart's sole line in his first appearance in a stage play. A wild-goose chase was launched by Jonah Ruddy and Jonathan Hill in their book *Bogey: The Man, The Actor, The Legend* (1965). Describing Bogart's early career as a stage actor (*c.*1921) they said: 'In those early Broadway days he didn't play menace parts. "I always made my entrance carrying a tennis racquet, baseball bat, or golf club. I was the athletic type, with hair slicked back and wrapped in a blazer. The only line I didn't say was, 'Give me the ball, coach, I'll take it through'. Yes, sir, I was Joe College or Joe Country Club all the time." It was hard to imagine him as the originator of that famous theatrical line – "Tennis anyone?" – but he was.'

It is clear from this extract that the authors were adding their own gloss to what Bogart had said. Bartlett (1968) joined in and said it was his 'sole line in his first play'. But Bogart had denied ever having said it (quoted in Goodman, *Bogey: The Good-Bad Boy*, 1965, and in an ABC TV film of 1974 using old film of him doing so.)

Alistair Cooke in *Six Men* (1977) is more cautious: 'It is said he appeared in an ascot and blue blazer and tossed off the invitation "Tennis, anyone?"' but adds that Bogart probably did not coin the phrase.

See also ALLEN 17:4; CASABLANCA 151:1–2; TO HAVE AND HAVE NOT 540:8.

BOGART, John B.

American journalist (1845–1921)

1 If a man bites a dog, that is news ...

As a definition of news, this has been variously ascribed. Chiefly, in the form, 'When a dog bites a man, that is not news, because it happens so often. But if a man bites a dog, that is news,' to Bogart, city editor of the New York *Sun*, 1873–90. To Charles A. Dana, the editor of the same paper from 1868 to 1897, it has been ascribed in the form: 'If a dog bites a man, it's a story; if a man bites a dog, it's a good story.'

BOLITHO, William

British writer (1890–1930)

2 The shortest way out of Manchester is notoriously a bottle of Gordon's gin.

'Caliogstro and Seraphina', *Twelve Against the Gods* (1930). However, *The Times* (21 June 1921) was writing: 'Certainly if drink, in the proverbial saying, has proved on occasion "the shortest way out of Manchester ..."' – evidence of a much earlier source.

BOLT, Robert

English playwright and screenwriter (1924–95)

3 *Thomas More*: Why not be a teacher? You'd be a fine teacher. Perhaps a great one.
Rich: And if I was, who would know it?
More: You, your pupils, God.

A Man For All Seasons, Act 1 (1960). In *What I Saw At the Revolution* (1990) Peggy Noonan describes her first assignment as a speechwriter for President Reagan – to write something with which he would announce the Teacher of the Year. She was tipped off to use this quotation (albeit in the form, '"You, your students, God ..." Or words to that effect ... Look it up.') She used it. 'The President to my pride and disappointment did not change a word.'

BONE, Sir David

Scottish novelist (1874–1959)

4 It's 'Damn you, Jack – I'm all right!' with you chaps.

From *The Brassbounder* (1910), one of Bone's many novels set on the sea and based on his own experiences (he rose to be Commodore of the Anchor Line). Partridge/*Catch Phrases* suggests this saying (certainly not Bone's coinage) may have arisen *c.*1880 in the form 'Fuck you, Jack, I'm all right'. The bowdlerized versions 'typified concisely the implied and often explicit arrogance of many senior officers towards the ranks', in the *navy*, hence, the use of 'Jack', the traditional name for a sailor since *c.*1700.

BONHAM CARTER, Lady Violet (later Baroness Asquith)

English Liberal politician (1887–1969)

5 I feel amphibious.

Her last words. Quoted in the *Observer* Magazine (24 January 1988) by Lord St John of Fawsley who commented: 'Isn't that wonderful, conveying that feeling of floating off, the *mot juste* to the end.'

THE BOOK OF COMMON PRAYER

1662 version

6 We have erred and strayed from thy ways like lost sheep. We have followed too much the devices and desires of our own hearts.

From the General Confession in Morning Prayer. Hence, *Devices and Desires*, title of a novel (1989) by P.D. James.

7 Our Father, which art in heaven, Hallowed be thy Name. Thy kingdom come. Thy will be

done, in earth as it is in heaven. Give us this day our daily bread. And forgive us our trespasses, As we forgive them that trespass against us. And lead us not into temptation; But deliver us from evil: For thine is the kingdom, The power and the glory, For ever and ever. Amen.

The Lord's Prayer (and so called in the Prayer Book). The translation, as found in the service of Morning Prayer (which differs slightly from that in Matthew 6:9–13) has provided the following titles (among others): *Give Us This Day* (film UK, 1949), *Our Daily Bread* (film US, 1934), *The Power and the Glory* (film US, 1933) and Graham Greene's novel (1940). *World Without End* is the title of a film (US, 1956). *Deliver Us From Evil* is the title of a book (1953) by Hugh Desmond, and *Thine Is The Kingdom* of unrelated books by Heini Arnold, Thomas Dooley and Paul Marshall. *The Power and the Kingdom* is the title of a novel by Michael Williams (1989), while Gay Talese's book (1971) about *The New York Times* with the title *The Kingdom and the Power* is presumably an allusion.

1 From thence he [Christ] shall come to judge the quick and the dead.

In the Apostles' Creed in Morning Prayer. 'Quick' meaning 'alive'. To Lord Dewar (1864–1930), a British industrialist, is credited the joke that there are 'only two classes of pedestrians in these days of reckless motor traffic – the quick, and the dead'. George Robey ascribed it to Dewar in *Looking Back on Life* (1933). A *Times* leader in April that same year merely ventured: 'The saying that there are two sorts of pedestrians, the quick and the dead, is well matured.'

2 In Quires and Places where they sing, here followeth the Anthem.

From the Rubric after the Third Collect in Morning Prayer. Hence, *Places Where They Sing*, title of a novel (1970) by Simon Raven.

3 From fornication, and all other deadly sin; and from all the deceits of the world, the flesh and the devil, Good Lord, deliver us.

The Litany. Hence, the expression 'The world, the flesh, and the devil' with the words in the order given – as used, for example, in a 1959 film title. Again, in the Collect for the Eighteenth Sunday after Trinity, we find: 'Lord, we beseech thee, grant thy people grace to withstand the temptations of the world, the flesh, and the devil.'

The same combination also occurs in the Catechism, where the confirmee is asked what his Godfathers and Godmothers had promised for him at his baptism: 'First, that I should renounce the *devil* and all his works, the pomps and vanity of this wicked *world*, and all the sinful lusts of the *flesh*.'

In the sixteenth and seventeenth centuries, the words were also grouped together in a different order to denote 'our ghostly enemies' – as, for example, 'the devil, the world, and the flesh' (1530).

4 Incline our hearts to keep this law.

From the response to the recital of the Commandments during the service of Holy Communion. Hence, *Incline Our Hearts*, title of a novel (1988) by A.N. Wilson.

5 N or M.

In the Catechism, the guide answer to the first question 'What is your name?' is not intended to indicate where a male or female Christian name should be inserted. 'N' is the first letter of the Latin *nomen* ('name') and 'M' is a contraction of 'NN' standing for the plural *nomina* ('names'). So it just means 'name or names'.

Agatha Christie used the title *N or M?* for a spy story published in 1941.

6 To have and to hold from this day forward, for better for worse, for richer for poorer, in sickness and in health, to love and to cherish, till death us do part, according to God's holy ordinance.

From the marriage vow in the Solemnization of Matrimony, where mistakes are often made in the wording – i.e., it is *not* 'till death do us part'. Originally, the phrase was 'till death us depart' = 'separate completely'.

7 They are as venomous as the poison of a serpent: even like the deaf adder that stoppeth her ears.

Prayer Book version of Psalm 58:4.

8 Whose feet they hurt in the stocks: the iron entered into his soul.

Prayer Book version of Psalm 105:18. In the Bible, it is: 'Whose feet they hurt with fetters: he was laid in iron.' Although 'the iron entered into his soul' is a mistranslation of the Hebrew, it has given us the phrase meaning, 'he has become embittered, anguished'. It was used notably by Lloyd George 258:4. The English title of Jean-Paul Sartre's novel *La Mort dans l'âme* (1949) is *Iron in the Soul*.

1 All good things come to an end.

The proverbial expression meaning 'pleasure cannot go on for ever' would seem to be a corruption of the Prayer Book version of Psalm 119:96: 'I see that all things come to an end: but thy commandment is exceeding broad' (note the lack of 'good'). The original Bible text is: 'I have seen an end of all perfection: but thy commandment is exceeding broad.' But there are versions of the proverb going back to 1440 and as 'Everything has an end', the idea appears in Chaucer's *Troilus and Criseyde* (*c.*1385).

2 By the waters of Babylon we sat down and wept.

The metrical versions of the Psalms in the Prayer Book differ significantly in wording and verse numbering from the Psalms in the Bible. This is the Prayer Book version of Psalm 137:1, of which the original is: 'By the rivers of Babylon, there we sat down, yea, we wept, when we remembered Zion.'

The 'waters' version is the much preferred usage. Horace Walpole (in a letter, 12 June 1775) has: 'By the waters of Babylon we sit down and weep, when we think of thee, O America!'

3 O put not your trust in princes, nor in any child of man: for there is no help in them.

The Prayer Book version of Psalm 146:2 is different from the Bible's 146:3, which is: 'Put not your trust in princes, nor in the son of man, in whom there is no help.'

4 Be pleased to receive into thy Almighty and most gracious protection the persons of us thy servants, and the Fleet in which we serve.

From 'Forms of Prayer to be used at Sea'. Hence, *In Which We Serve*, title of the Noël Coward naval film (UK, 1942).

BOOTH, John Wilkes

American actor and assassin (1838–65)

5 *Sic semper tyrannis!* The South is avenged.

Booth shot President Lincoln in his box at the Ford Theatre, Washington, DC, on 14 April 1865. Then, falling from the box on to the stage, he addressed the audience with the Latin words meaning, 'Thus always to tyrants' (which is the motto of the State of Virginia). The rest of the cry may be apocryphal but was reported in *The New York Times* the following day.

'When Abraham Lincoln was murdered/The one thing that interested Matthew Arnold/Was that the assassin shouted in Latin/As he leapt on the stage./This convinced Matthew/That there was still hope for America' – Christopher Morley, *Points of View* (untraced).

BORGES, Jorge Luis

Argentinian novelist (1899–1986)

6 The Falklands thing was a fight between two bald men over a comb.

The *ODMQ* (1991) and *ODQ* (1992) may have caused readers to think that it was Borges who originated the remark about 'two bald men fighting over a comb'. Not so. Borges was quoted by *Time* Magazine on 14 February 1983 as having characterized the previous year's Falklands conflict between Britain and Argentina in these words. *Time* is unable to say for sure where it acquired this quotation, though it has had a good rummage among its yellowing files. It may have picked it up from the Spanish paper *La Nación* (28 June 1982), which was apparently quoting from an interview with Borges that had appeared in *Le Monde* the previous day.

But the basic expression about bald men fighting over combs had very definitely been around before 1983. Robert Nye wrote in *The Times* (18 June 1981): 'I think it was Christopher Logue who once characterized the drabness of the English Movement poets of the 1950s as being like the antics of two bald men fighting for possession of a comb.'

The saying occurs even earlier in Mencken (1942) as 'Two baldheaded men are fighting over a comb' (listed as a 'Russian saying') and in Champion's *Racial Proverbs* (1938).

BORGIA, Cesare

Italian cardinal, politician and military leader (1476–1507)

7 *Aut Caesar, aut nihil.*
Either Caesar or nothing.

The motto of Borgia, who was the bastard son of Pope Alexander VI and brother to Lucrezia Borgia. Meaning, 'either I'm boss or I'm not interested', it was inscribed on his sword.

BOSQUET, Pierre

French general (1810–61)

8 *C'est magnifique – mais ce n'est pas la guerre.*
It is magnificent, but it is not war.

This remark was made by Maréchal Bosquet about the Charge of the Light Brigade at the Battle of Balaclava (25 October 1854). It is the source of several witticisms: *Punch* during the First World War said of margarine: '*C'est magnifique, mais ce n'est pas le beurre* [butter]', and of the façade of Worcester College, Oxford, which has a splendid clock on it, Anon. said: '*C'est magnifique, mais ce n'est pas la gare* [station]'.

BOSWELL, James

Scottish lawyer, biographer and diarist (1740–95)

1 That favourite subject, Myself.

Letter to William Temple (26 July 1763), quoted in Boswell's *Life of Johnson* (1791). The biographer was, indeed, rather too interested in himself but, without that obsession, his voluminous diaries would not be the extraordinary documents that they are.

2 When I called upon Dr. Johnson next morning, I found him highly satisfied with his colloquial prowess the preceding evening. 'Well, (said he) we had a good talk.' BOSWELL. 'Yes, Sir; you tossed and gored several persons.'

Ib., relating to the summer of 1768. Although Boswell more than admired Johnson, he sharply noted his mode of argument. In the *Life* (concerning 26 October 1769) he noted: 'There is no arguing with Johnson: for if his pistol misses fire, he knocks you down with the butt end of it.'

3 A robust genius, born to grapple with whole libraries.

Of Dr Johnson. In fact, this was said by 'my uncle, Dr Boswell' and was quoted by James in *ib.*, for 3 April 1776.

4 A page of my journal is like a cake of portable soup. A little may be diffused into a considerable portion.

Journal of a Tour to the Hebrides (1785). Boswell had used this simile earlier in one of his articles under the name 'The Hypochondriack' for *The London Magazine* (No. 66, March 1783): 'But it is a labour of very great difficulty to keep a journal of life, occupied in various pursuits, mingled with concomitant speculations and reflections, in so much, that I do not think it possible to do it unless one has a peculiar talent for abridging. I have tried it in that way, when it has been my good fortune to live in a multiplicity of instructive and entertaining scenes, and I have thought my notes like portable soup, of which a little bit by being dissolved in water will make a good large dish; for their substance by being expanded in words would fill a volume.'

5 I have sometimes been obliged to run half over London, in order to fix a date correctly; which, when I had accomplished, I well knew would obtain me no praise, though a failure would have been to my discredit.

This was in the 'advertisement' to the first edition of his *Life of Johnson* (1791).

See also ADDISON 13:7.

BOTTOMLEY, Horatio

British journalist, financier and politician (1860–1933)

6 If it's in *John Bull*, it is so.

Saying, referring to the weekly magazine he edited (from 1906).

7 No, reaping.

When sewing mail-bags in prison and being greeted by a visitor with the words, 'Ah, Bottomley, sewing?' In 1922 Bottomley (an MP) was found guilty of fraudulent conversion and sent to prison. Quoted in S.T. Felstead, *Horatio Bottomley* (1936).

BOUGHTON, Rutland

English composer (1878–1960)

8 They laugh and are glad ... are terrible!

The Immortal Hour (1914). In fact, the libretto of the opera was by Fiona Macleod (William Sharp).

BOURDILLON, F.W.

English poet (1852–1921)

9 The night has a thousand eyes,
And the day but one;
Yet the light of the bright world dies,
With the dying sun.

'Light', *Among the Flowers* (1878). Hence, *The Night Has a Thousand Eyes*, title of a story (1945) by Cornell Woolrich (about a vaudeville entertainer who can predict the future) which was adapted as a film (US, 1948), and gave rise to several songs. The phrase 'Night hath a thousand eyes' had occurred earlier, however, in the play *The Maydes Metamorphosis* (1600) by John Lyly.

BOWEN, Lord

English judge (1835–94)

1 We must ask ourselves what the man on the Clapham omnibus would think.

Apparently this famous man was first evoked in 1903 by Lord Bowen when hearing a case of negligence – i.e., the ordinary or average person, the man in the street, particularly when his/her point of view is instanced by the Courts, newspaper editorials, etc. Quite why he singled out the particular bus route we shall never know. It sounds suitably prosaic, of course, and the present 77A to Clapham Junction does pass though Whitehall and Westminster, thus providing a link between governors and governed. There is evidence to suggest that the 'Clapham omnibus' in itself had already become a figure of speech by the mid-nineteenth century. In 1857 there was talk of the 'occupant of the knife-board of a Clapham omnibus'.

2 The rain, it raineth on the just
And also on the unjust fella:
But chiefly on the just, because
The unjust steals the just's umbrella.

Quoted in Walter Sichel, *The Sands of Time* (1923). Apparently, the true source of this oft-quoted rhyme.

BOWEN, E.E.

English schoolmaster (1836–1901)

3 Forty years on, when afar and asunder
Parted are those who are singing to-day,
When you look back, and forgetfully wonder
What you were like in your work and your
play.

'Forty Years On' (1872) – the Harrow Football Song (which is also the Harrow School Song). Hence, *Forty Years On*, title of Alan Bennett's chronicle play of the twentieth century (1968), set in a boys' public school.

BOWRA, Sir Maurice

English academic (1898–1971)

4 I am a man more dined against than dining.

Attributed in John Betjeman, *Summoned by Bells* (1960).

See also AUDEN 66:3.

BOYER, Charles

French film actor (1899–1978)

5 Come with me to the Casbah.

This is a line forever associated with the film *Algiers* (1938) and Boyer, its star. He is supposed to have said it to Hedy Lamarr. Boyer impersonators used it and the film was laughed at because of it, but nowhere is it said in the film. It was simply a Hollywood legend that grew up. Boyer himself denied he had ever said it and thought it had been invented by a press agent.

BRADBURY, Malcolm

English novelist (1932–)

6 The History Man.

Title of novel (1975). Following the 1981 BBC TV adaptation of this book, the phrase 'history man' was used to describe a particular type of scheming, unidealistic university lecturer. In fact, the title describes a character who does not appear, but was taken to mean the left-wing sociology don 'hero' – and from that, any similar don at a 'new' university.

7 Tony Benn is the Bertie Wooster of Marxism.

Ascribed to Anon. by Matthew Parris in *Scorn* (1995), this was volunteered by Bradbury on BBC Radio *Quote ... Unquote* (11 September 1979) and might well have been of his own manufacture.

See also FLANDERS 238:6.

BRADLEY, Omar

American general (1893–1981)

8 The wrong war, at the wrong place, at the wrong time, and with the wrong enemy.

On General Douglas MacArthur's proposal to carry the Korean war into China. Senate inquiry (May 1951).

BRAHAM, John

English singer and songwriter (1774–1856)

9 England, home and beauty.

'The Death of Nelson', from the opera *The Americans* (1811) by Braham and S.J. Arnold, was one of the most popular songs of the nineteenth century. Here are the lyrics that suggest the phrase 'England, home and beauty', though the words do not appear exactly in this order:

'Twas in Trafalgar bay,
We saw the Frenchmen lay,
Each heart was bounding then,
We scorn'd the foreign yoke
For our ships were British Oak,
And hearts of Oak our men.

Our Nelson mark'd them on the wave,
Three cheers our gallant Seamen gave,
Nor thought of home or beauty (*rpt.*)
Along the line this signal ran,
'England expects that every man
This day will do his duty!' (*rpt.*)

Charles Dickens has Captain Cuttle quote, 'Though lost to sight, to memory dear, and England, Home, and Beauty!' in *Dombey and Son*, Chap. 48 (1844–6), though these words do not appear in the text consulted (there may be other versions).

Braham was not alone in perceiving the rhyming delights of 'duty' and 'beauty'. In Gilbert and Sullivan's *Trial by Jury* (1875), 'Time may do his duty' is rhymed with 'Winter hath a beauty', at which point, Ian Bradley in his annotated edition remarks: 'This is the first of no fewer than fifteen occasions, exclusive of repetitions, when the words "duty" and "beauty" are rhymed in the Savoy Operas ... *HMS Pinafore* holds the record with four separate songs in which the words are rhymed.'

Home and Beauty (simply) was the title of a play (1919) by Somerset Maugham, concerning the complications surrounding a First World War 'widow' who remarries and whose original husband then turns up (in the US the play was known as *Too Many Husbands*).

BRAINE, John

English novelist (1922–86)

1 Room at the Top.

Braine merely re-popularized this phrase as the title of his novel (1957). Much earlier, in reply to advice not to become a lawyer because it was an overcrowded profession, Daniel Webster (1782–1852) had replied, 'There is always room at the top'.

BRAMAH, Ernest

English writer (1868–1942)

2 Although there exist many thousand subjects for elegant conversation, there are persons who cannot meet a cripple without talking about feet.

In *The Wallet of Kai Lung* (1900). Compare: 'I cried because I had no shoes, until I met a man who had no feet' – sometimes described as a Zen saying. *See* CONFUCIUS 180:2.

See also MAO ZEDONG 379:2.

BRANDEIS, Louis D.

American jurist (1856–1941)

3 Publicity is justly commended as a remedy for social and industrial diseases. Sunlight is said to be the best of disinfectants; electric light the most efficient policeman.

In *Harper's Weekly* (20 December 1913). Compare the saying, 'Rain is the best policeman of all', heard from a senior police officer after London's Notting Hill Carnival had been rained off on the Late Summer Bank Holiday in August 1986. Meaning that the incidence of crime falls when the rain does (as it also does in very cold weather).

BRANDO, Marlon

American film actor (1924–)

4 An actor's a guy who, if you ain't talking about him, ain't listening.

Quoted in *The Observer* (January 1956). In fact, Brando appears to have been quoting George Glass (1910–84) (source: Bob Thomas, *Brando*, 1973.)

See also SCHULBERG 470:1.

BRANSON, Richard

English entrepreneur (1950–)

5 I believe in benevolent dictatorships, provided I am the dictator.

His favourite remark. He was quoted as saying it in *The Observer* (25 November 1984) and again in *The Independent* (11 March 1989).

BRECHT, Bertolt

German playwright (1898–1956)

6 The alienation effect.

Brecht's name (*Verfremdungseffekt* in German) for a theory of drama, first promoted in 1937, in which the audience has to be reminded that the play it is watching *is* a play and not real. The effect is to distance the watchers from the players, to prevent too much emotional involvement and to reject the traditional make-believe element in theatre.

Not an entirely new technique. How else to explain this from Shakespeare? In *Twelfth Night*, III.iv.127 (1600): 'If this were played upon a stage now, I could condemn it as an improbable fiction.' Then again, from the Wilkie Collins novel, *No Name* (1862–3): '"Very strange!" he said to himself, vacantly. "It's like a scene in a novel – it's like nothing in real life."'

1 *Der aufhaltsame Aufstieg des Arturo Ui.*
The Resistible Rise of Arturo Ui.

Title of play (1941) and origin of the phrase 'resistible rise' (sometimes misquoted as 'irresistible rise').

BRETON, Nicholas

English poet and writer (c.1545–c.1626)

2 A Mad World, My Masters.

Title of prose dialogue (1603). If not the inspiration for, then a very early forerunner of, the film title *It's a Mad, Mad, Mad, Mad World* (US, 1963).

BRIDSON, D.G.

English radio producer (1910–80)

3 The wriggling ponces of the spoken word.

On disc jockeys. Attributed on BBC Radio *Quote ... Unquote* (10 May 1978), but unconfirmed.

BRIEN, Alan

English writer (1925–)

4 Violence is the repartee of the illiterate.

In *Punch* (7 February 1973). When Brien was asked to source this quotation on BBC Radio *Quote ... Unquote* (10 August 1985) he said: 'I don't think I've heard it before ... modernish? ... it can't be very old. Bernard Shaw would be too good for it ... but it's approaching Bernard Shaw. Perhaps it's Chesterton, is it?'

BRIGGS, Raymond

English children's illustrator and author (1934–)

5 When the Wind Blows.

Title of illustrated book about the aftermath of a nuclear holocaust (1982). From 'When the wind blows the cradle will rock', a line from the nursery rhyme 'Hush-a-bye, baby, on the tree top' (known since 1765), or from 'Grass never grows when the wind blows', a proverb.

BRIGHT, John

English Radical politician (1811–89)

6 The angel of death has been abroad throughout the land; you may almost hear the beating of his wings.

Speech, House of Commons (23 February 1855). He was appealing for an armistice in the Crimean War.

7 He is a self-made man and worships his creator.

Mencken (1942) has, rather, Henry Clapp saying this (*c.*1858) about Horace Greeley, and dates Bright's use of the saying about Benjamin Disraeli ten years later, to *c.*1868. Leon Harris, *The Fine Art of Political Wit* (1965) has *Disraeli* saying it about *Bright*.

8 This regard for the liberties of Europe, this care at one time for the Protestant interest, this excessive love for the balance of power, is neither more nor less than a gigantic system of outdoor relief for the aristocracy of Great Britain.

Speech at Birmingham (12 May 1858). A. & V. Palmer, *Quotations in History* (1976) has the date rather as 29 October. *The Oxford Dictionary of Political Quotations* (1996) prefers: 'A gigantic system of out-relief for the British aristocracy'. A criticism of Britain's foreign policy, though sometimes remembered as 'the foreign service' or 'diplomacy'. In other words, it kept the aristocracy off the streets and in useful employment. Outdoor relief was the name given to charitable relief given in the nineteenth century outside of a charitable institution.

9 England is the mother of parliaments.

That is what Bright said in a speech in Birmingham on 18 January 1865. Frequently misused, even at the highest levels. The phrase is *not* 'Westminster is the mother of parliaments'. Westminster is, rather, one of her children. Icelanders may well object that they have a prior claim to the title anyway, having established the first parliament long in advance, but the point is that Britain's parliamentary system has been copied in so many of her colonies and around the world.

10 My opinion is that the Northern States will manage somehow to muddle through.

On the American Civil War. Quoted in Justin McCarthy, *Reminiscences* (1899).

BRITTAIN, Ronald

English regimental sergeant-major (c.1899–1981)

1 You 'orrible little man.

Reputed to have had the loudest voice in the British Army, Brittain received this accolade in his *Times* obituary (12 January 1981): 'With his stentorian voice and massive parade ground presence [he] came to epitomize the British Army sergeant. Though he himself denied ever using it, he was associated with the celebrated parade ground expression "You 'orrible little man" – in some quarters, indeed, was reputed to have coined it ... His "wake up there!" to the somnolent after a command had in his opinion been inadequately executed was legendary – doubtless the ancestor of all the Wake Up Theres which have succeeded it.'

BRITTON, Colonel (nom de guerre of Douglas Ritchie)

British propagandist (1905–67)

2 The night is your friend. The V is your sign.

During the Second World War the resistance movements in occupied Europe were encouraged from London by broadcasts over the BBC. In an English-language broadcast on 31 July 1941, 'Colonel Britton', as he was known, said: 'It's about the V – the sign of victory – that I want to talk to you now. All over Europe the V sign is seen by the Germans and to the Germans and the Quislings it is indeed the writing on the wall. It is the sign which tells them that one of the unknown soldiers has passed that way. And it's beginning to play on their nerves.

'They see it chalked on pavements, pencilled on posters, scratched on the mudguards of German cars. Flowers come up in the shape of a V; men salute each other with the V sign separating their fingers. The number five is a V and men working in the fields turn to the village clocks as the chimes sound the hour of five.'

In the same broadcast, the 'Colonel' also encouraged the use of the V in Morse code, three short taps and a heavy one: 'When you knock on a door, there's your knock. If you call a waiter in a restaurant, call him like this: "Eh, *garçon!*" [*taps rhythm on wine glass*] ... Tell all your friends about it and teach them the V sound. If you and your friends are in a café and a German comes in, tap out the V sign all together.'

From these broadcasts emerged an evocative slogan: 'You wear no uniforms and your weapons differ from ours – but they are not less deadly. The fact that you wear no uniforms is your strength. The Nazi official and the German soldier don't know you. But they fear you ... The night is your friend. The V is your sign.' (Cole Porter's song 'All Through the Night', 1934, had earlier contained the lines: 'The day is my enemy/The night is my friend.') Hence, presumably, later, *The Night Was Our Friend*, title of a play by Michael Pertwee (1950).

Winston Churchill spoke of the V sign as a symbol of 'the unconquerable will of the people of the occupied territories'. These kinds of broadcasts were also used for sending coded messages to resistance workers in France: '*Le lapin a bu un apéritif*', '*Mademoiselle caresse le nez de son chien*' and '*Jacqueline sait le latin*' are examples of signals used to trigger sabotage operations or to warn of parachute drops.

BRONOWSKI, Jacob

Polish-born British mathematician and scientist (1908–74)

3 The hand is more important than the eye ... The hand is the cutting edge of the mind.

TV series, *The Ascent of Man* (1973). Since this use, the term 'cutting edge' has become a cliché for what is considered to be at the forefront of attention or activity. The term is derived from the ancient notion that the sharp edge is the most important part of a blade, but the *OED2*'s earliest example is from 1966.

BRONTË, Charlotte

English novelist (1816–55)

4 Reader, I married him.

Jane Eyre, Chap. 38 (1847). Of Mr Rochester, who has employed Jane as a governess and is now free to marry her through the death by fire of his mad first wife. These words are not the last in the book, as might be supposed, but the opening words of the final chapter.

BRONTË, Emily

English novelist (1818–48)

5 And I pray one prayer – I repeat it till my tongue stiffens – Catherine Earnshaw, may you not rest as long as I am living! You said I killed you – haunt me, then! The murdered *do* haunt their murderers, I believe. I know that ghosts *have* wandered on earth. Be with me always – take any form – drive me mad – only *do* not leave me in this abyss, where I cannot find you! O God! it is unutterable! I *cannot* live without my life! I *cannot* live without my soul!

Wuthering Heights, Chap. 26 (1847). Heathcliff longs for the death that will reunite him with Catherine. In the film (US, 1939) Laurence Olivier gives the speech almost word for word over Cathy's grave, but it is relocated at the end of the story.

1 I lingered around them, under that benign sky: watched the moths fluttering among the heath and harebells; listened to the soft wind breathing through the grass; and wondered how anyone could ever imagine unquiet slumbers for the sleepers in that quiet earth.

Ib. Last lines, as written by Lockwood, referring to the graves of Heathcliff, Edgar Linton and Catherine Earnshaw.

BROOKE, Rupert

English poet (1887–1915)

2 Unkempt about those hedges blows
An English unofficial rose ...
Stands the Church clock at ten to three?
And is there honey still for tea?

'The Old Vicarage, Grantchester' (1912). Hence, *An Unofficial Rose*, title of a novel (1962) by Iris Murdoch.

3 Incredibly, inordinately, devastatingly, immortally, calamitously, hearteningly, adorably beautiful.

On Cathleen Nesbitt, the actress, with whom he had a mild affair, in a letter to her (*c.* 1913), responding to criticism that he was 'in love with words'. Quoted in Christopher Hassall, *Rupert Brooke* (1964).

4 These I have loved.

'The Great Lover' (1914). This is a 'list' poem in which Brooke mentions some of his 'favourite things' (rather as the song with that title did in the much later musical *The Sound of Music*). Hence, the title of the BBC radio record programme *These You Have Loved* which has a history going back to 1938 when Doris Arnold introduced a selection of favourite middle-of-the-road music. The title was still being used forty years later. Brooke's 'loves' included 'white plates and cups' and 'the cool kindliness of sheets, that soon/Smooth away trouble; and the rough male kiss/Of blankets.'

5 If I should die, think only this of me:
That there's some corner of a foreign field
That is for ever England. There shall be
In that rich earth a richer dust concealed;
A dust whom England bore, shaped, made aware,
Gave, once, her flowers to love, her ways to roam,
A body of England's, breathing English air,
Washed by the rivers, blest by suns of home.
And think, this heart, all evil shed away,
A pulse in the eternal mind, no less
Gives somewhere back the thoughts by England given;
Her sights and sounds; dreams happy as her day;
And laughter, learnt of friends; and gentleness,
In hearts at peace, under an English heaven.

'The Soldier' (1914). This very soon made a perfect epitaph for the poet himself, who died of acute blood poisoning at Lemnos on 23 April 1915, and was buried in a foreign field. He was then a sub-lieutenant in the Royal Naval Division and was on his way by boat to fight in the Dardanelles. According to Edward Marsh's *Memoir*, at Brooke's burial a pencil inscription in Greek was put on a large white cross at the head of his grave, stating: 'Here lies the servant of God, Sub-Lieutenant in the English Navy, who died for the deliverance of Constantinople from the Turks.' Eventually (in 1983), a marble plaque bearing the whole poem was erected on the Greek island of Skyros where the poet is buried and may have replaced an earlier plaque bearing a quotation from the same poem.

Hence, *Forever England*, the UK title given to the reissue of the film version of C.S. Forester's novel *Brown on Resolution* (1929; film UK, 1935). In the US, however, the film was known as *Born for Glory*.

BROOKER, Gary

English musician and songwriter (1945–)

6 We skipped the light fandango
And turned cartwheels cross the floor ...
And so it was that later
As the miller told his tale
That her face just ghostly
Turned a whiter shade of pale ...
One of sixteen vestal virgins
Who were leaving for the coast ...

Song, 'A Whiter Shade of Pale' (1967). In fact, Brooker wrote the music and Keith Reid wrote the lyrics. The song was performed by their group, Procul Harum (sometimes spelled 'Procol Harum'). It *appears* to contain several allusions. 'We skipped the light fandango' echoes the expression 'to trip the light fantastic', for 'to dance', which in turn echoes Milton's

'L'Allegro' ('Come, and trip it as ye go/On the light fantastic toe') or 'Comus' ('Come, knit hands, and beat the ground/In a light fantastic round'). 'Skipped the light fantastic out of town' appears in Tennessee Williams, *The Glass Menagerie* (1944). 'As the miller told his tale' presumably refers to the 'Miller's Tale' in Chaucer's *Canterbury Tales*, though Keith Reid said (1994) that he had never read Chaucer in his life. And 'One of sixteen Vestal Virgins/Were leaving for the coast' presumably refers to 'The Coast', i.e., the eastern/western seaboards of the US.

The song as a whole – and especially the title – is a paradigm of the drug-influenced creativity of the 1960s. The title (according to Reid in *Melody Maker*, 3 June 1967) was overheard at a gathering: 'Some guy looked at a chick and said to her, "You've gone a whiter shade of pale".'

BROOKNER, Anita

British art historian and novelist (1928–)

1 In real life, of course, it is the hare who wins. Every time. Look around you. And in any case it is my contention that Aesop was writing for the tortoise market ... Hares have no time to read. They are too busy winning the game.

Hotel du Lac, Chap. 2 (1984). On the tortoise and hare myth.

2 I am 46, and have been for some time past.

Letter to *The Times* (5 November 1984) when she considered it had drawn too much attention to her actual age. In *Hotel du Lac* (published that same year), she had written: 'She was a handsome woman of forty-five and would remain so for many years.'

BROOKS, Thomas

English Puritan divine (1608–80)

3 Heaven on Earth, or a Serious Discourse touching a well-grounded Assurance of Mens Everlasting Happiness.

Title of book (1654). The phrase 'heaven on earth', meaning 'a perfect, very pleasant, ideal place or state of affairs' is not biblical. This is the only citation for the precise phrase in the *OED2*, but earlier similar occurrences are plentiful: 'For if heaven be on this earth, and ease to any soul,/It is in cloister or in school' – William Langland, *The Vision of Piers Plowman* (B text, *c*.1377–9). 'A heaven on earth I have won by wooing thee' – Shakespeare, *All's Well That Ends Well* (IV.ii.66).

From *The Guardian* (5 June 1986): 'The Prime Minister yesterday promised her party "a little bit of heaven on earth" produced by further tax cuts ... Mrs Thatcher was in lyrical mood at the Conservative Women's Conference in London, talking of her vision of a society of satisfied consumers.' This was a slogan that did not catch on at all.

BROUGHAM, Lord

Scottish jurist and politician (1778–1868)

4 It adds a new terror to death.

Pearson (1937) insists that what Brougham said in a 'speech on an ex-chancellor' was 'Death was now armed with a new terror', but he gives no source for the remark. What was being talked about? Biography, and in particular what Lord Campbell wrote in *Lives of the Lord Chancellors* (1845–7) without the consent of the subjects' heirs or executors. Lord Lyndhurst (three times Lord Chancellor, d.1863) said, 'Campbell has added another terror to death' (quoted 1924).

On the other hand, the lawyer and politician Sir Charles Wetherell (d.1846) is also quoted as having said of Lord Campbell: 'Then there is my noble and biographical friend who has added a new terror to death' – quoted in Lord St Leonards, *Mispresentation in Campbell's Lives of Lyndhurst and Brougham* (1869). So everyone seems to have been saying it.

Pearson adds that before all this, the expression had been used when bookseller Edmund Curll (1683–1747) used to churn out cheap lives of famous people as soon as they were dead. John Arbuthnot had called him, 'One of the new terrors of death' (in a letter to Swift, 13 January 1733).

Later came the remark attributed to Sir Herbert Beerbohm Tree (also by Pearson, as it happens, in his biography of the actor, 1956) on the newly invented gramophone: 'Sir, I have tested your machine. It adds new terror to life and makes death a long-felt want.'

BROWN, 'Capability'

English garden landscaper (1715–83)

5 Nature abhors a straight line.

Quoted in *Broadlands, The Home of Lord Mountbatten* (guide book, *c*.1988). *Compare* RABELAIS 445:1.

BROWN, George (later Lord George-Brown)

English Labour politician (1914–85)

6 Lovely creature in scarlet, dance with me!

When drunk, to a guest at a reception during his time as Foreign Secretary (1966–8). The guest turned and replied, 'I'm the Apostolic Delegate and I don't think you're in any condition to dance with me.' This is the version told by Kenneth Williams on BBC Radio *Quote ... Unquote* (1979), though without naming Brown. Earlier it had appeared in *Pass the Port* (1976), safely consigned to 'a South American country', the politician unnamed, and the put-down: 'First, you are drunk, secondly the music is the National Anthem, and finally, I am the Cardinal Archbishop.' In *The Kenneth Williams Diaries* (1993), it was further revealed that Williams had acquired the story from a friend, the actor Gordon Jackson, in December 1970 in the form of a newspaper cutting detailing some of Brown's eccentricities and taken from *The Sunday Times*.

In Peter Paterson's biography, *Tired and Emotional: The Life of Lord George-Brown* (1993), the story is set in Brazil, Brown is named, the creature is in crimson, and the put-down is administered by the Cardinal Archbishop of Lima (who was on a visit from Peru). Paterson, although hearing from a 'distinguished former member of the Foreign Office' who claimed to have been present at the reception was, unfortunately, unable to prove the veracity of this story. In fact, Brown never seems to have visited Brazil. Another version of the tale has it occurring at a state function in Vienna and the put-down administered by the Cardinal Archbishop thereof.

1 Most British statesman have either drunk too much or womanised too much. I never fell into the second category.

Quoted in *The Observer* (11 November 1974). Famously bibulous, Brown was at least aware of his failings (and eventually became teetotal). *See also* THE TIMES 540:6.

BROWN, Helen Gurley

American journalist (1922–)

2 Sex and the Single Girl.

Title of book (1962; film US, 1964). Hence, 'sex and the (single) ——', a journalistic headline format. Fritz Spiegl, *Keep Taking the Tabloids!* (1983), identified it in the following actual headlines: 'Sex and the single Siberian', 'Sex and the kindly atheist', 'Sex and the girl reporter' and 'Sex and the parish priest'.

3 Good girls go to heaven, bad girls go everywhere.

Promotional line for *Cosmopolitan* Magazine when she relaunched it in 1965.

BROWN, James

American singer and songwriter (1934–)

4 Say It Loud, 'I'm Black and I'm Proud'.

The title of Brown's hit song of 1968 had the force of a slogan. Curiously, it was soon adapted to 'Say it loud, we're gay and we're proud', a slogan of the Gay Liberation Front, *c.*1970.

BROWN, Jerry

American Democratic politician (1938–)

5 We carry in our hearts the true country and that cannot be stolen. We follow in the spirit of our ancestors and that cannot be broken.

In a speech (October 1991), the former Governor of California announced his candidacy for the Democratic nomination for the Presidency (which he did not get – it went to Bill Clinton). Unusually for a politician, Brown had always been associated with rock music and musicians. On this occasion, he quoted from the song 'The Dead Heart' (1988), by the Australian rock group Midnight Oil, which has rather, 'We follow in the *steps* of our *ancestry* ...' Brown did not openly acknowledge the borrowing in his speech though an information sheet given to reporters did (source: *The Guardian*, 26 October 1991.)

BROWN, John Mason

American critic (1900–69)

6 Tallulah Bankhead barged down the Nile last night and sank. As the Serpent of the Nile she proves to be no more dangerous than a garter snake.

On Bankhead as Shakespeare's Cleopatra. In the *New York Post* (11 November 1937). Quoted in *Current Biography* (1941).

7 Some television programmes are so much chewing gum for the eyes.

Interview (28 July 1955). This was not his own remark – he was, in fact, quoting a young friend of his son.

BROWN, Thomas

English satirist (1663–1704)

8 I do not love thee, Dr Fell.
The reason why I cannot tell;
But this I know, and know full well,

I do not love thee, Dr Fell.

On the Dean of Christ Church, Oxford, when Brown was an undergraduate there.

BROWN, T(homas) E(dward)

English poet and schoolmaster (1830–97)

1 A rich man's joke is always funny.

From his poem 'The Doctor' (1887) and preceded by the line, 'Money is honey, my little sonny'.

2 A garden is a lovesome thing, God wot!

'My Garden' (1893). Seldom do any subsequent lines get quoted. But they are, in full:

Rose plot,
Fringed pool,
Fern'd grot –
The veriest school
Of peace; and yet the fool
Contends that God is not –
Not God! in gardens! when the eve is cool?
Nay, but I have a sign;
'Tis very sure God walks in mine.

It was included in *The Oxford Book of English Verse* (1900) and has frequently been parodied. *Yet More Comic and Curious Verse* (ed. J.M. Cohen, 1959) has 'My Garden with a stern look at T.E. Brown' by J.A. Lindon, which begins:

A garden is a lovesome thing? What rot!

'My Garden, New Style' by H.W. Hodges, which appears in *Modern Humour* (ed. Pocock and Bozman, 1940), had:

A garden is a loathsome thing – eh, what?
Blight, snail,
Pea-weevil,
Green-fly such a lot!
My hardest tool
Is powerless, yet the fool
Next door contends that slugs are not –
Not slugs! in gardens? when the eve is cool?
Nay, but I have some lime;
'Tis very sure they shall not walk in mine.

And Gerard Benson (included in *Imitations of Immortality*, ed. E.O. Parrott, 1986) has:

A garden is a loathsome thing, God wot!
... That geezer should be shot
What wrote that lot
Of Palgrave's Golden Tommy-rot ...
I'd rather sun myself on Uncle's yacht.

BROWNE, Sir Thomas

English author and physician (1605–82)

3 That children dream not in the first half year, that men dream not in some countries, are to me sick men's dreams, dreams out of the ivory gate, and visions before midnight.

'On Dreams' (no date). Hence, *Visions Before Midnight*, title of a volume of collected TV criticism (1977) by Clive James.

4 When the living might exceed, and to depart this world could not be properly said to go unto the greater number.

Epistle Dedicatory, *Hydriotaphia* (*Urn-Burial*) (1658). Hence, the expression 'to join the great majority', meaning 'to die'. The *OED2* does not find use of 'to join/pass over to the majority', in this sense, before 1719 (Edward Young, *The Revenge*: 'Death joins us to the great majority'), though it does relate it to the Latin phrase *abiit ad plures* (Petronius, *Satyricon*, 'Cena Tremalchionis', Chap. 42, Sect. 5).

On his way out in 1884, the politician Lord Houghton quipped, 'Yes, I am going to join the Majority and you know I have always preferred Minorities.' *Compare* NIXON 413:4.

5 Man is a noble animal, splendid in ashes, and pompous in the grave.

Ib., Chap. 5. Referring to epitaphic inscriptions on gravestones and memorials.

BROWNE, William

English poet (c.1591–1643)

6 Underneath this sable Herse
Lies the Subject of all Verse:
Sydney's Sister, Pembroke's Mother –
Death! ere thou Kill'st such another
Fair, and good, and learn'd as She,
Time will throw his Dart at thee.

'Epitaph on the Countess Dowager of Pembroke' (1623). John Aubrey (whose transcription this is) states that it was by Browne, who wrote *Britannia's Pastorals* as well as several other epitaphs. Mary Herbert (1561–1621) was sister of the poet Sir Philip Sidney and became a patron of poets and men of letters. The epitaph was probably not actually placed on her grave (no longer visible) in Salisbury Cathedral.

BROWNING, Sir Frederick 'Boy'

English soldier (1896–1965)

1 I think we might be going a bridge too far.

Reported remark to Field Marshal Montgomery on 10 September 1944. Hence, the expression, 'a bridge too far'. Since Cornelius Ryan's 1974 book with the title about the 1944 airborne landings in Holland and the subsequent film (UK/US 1977), the phrase has passed into the language. It is now frequently used allusively when warning of an unwise move. For example: 'A BRIDGE TOO NEAR. A public inquiry opened yesterday into plans to re-span the Ironbridge Gorge in Shropshire' (*The Times*, 20 June 1990); 'Ratners: A bid too far?' (*The Observer*, 8 July 1990).

Operation Market Garden was designed to capture eleven bridges needed for the Allied invasion of Germany – an attempt that came to grief at Arnhem, with the Allies suffering more casualties than in the landings at Normandy. On 10 September 1944, in advance of the action, Lieutenant-General 'Boy' Browning, Corps Commander, is said to have protested to Montgomery, who was in overall command: 'But, sir, we may be going a bridge too far.' This incident was recorded by Major-General Roy Urquhart in his (ghost-written) memoir, *Arnhem* (1958). The remark was hardly noticed when the book was published and remained so until Ryan picked it up and launched it with brilliant success as a latter-day aphorism. It has gone into the dictionaries of quotations (as said in advance of the operation to Monty) and, in the film, was solemnly delivered by Dirk Bogarde (Browning) to Sean Connery (Urquhart), as a retrospective view: 'Well, as you know I've always thought that we tried to go a bridge too far.'

The military historian Colonel Geoffrey S. Powell MC (author of *The Devil's Birthday: The Bridges to Arnhem*, 1984) summarized exactly why there is now a strong belief that Browning never said any such thing (1996): 'It was Nigel Hamilton in the third volume of his masterly biography of Montgomery, *Monty: The Field Marshal 1944–1976* (1986), a book based on Monty's own papers, who once and for all dealt with the myth of the expression "a bridge too far". He wrote: "Neither ... Urquhart, nor Brigadier Hackett ... ever heard Browning use the phrase ... Besides it was not in Browning's nature to speculate pessimistically ... Even if Browning *had* felt the operation to be too ambitious, he was not a man to say so."

'[In any case] Cornelius Ryan's book is littered with inaccuracies. His account of Browning's conversation with Monty, in which much is made of Browning's alleged remark is, of course, utterly imaginary as such a meeting never took place. But Ryan clearly based this imaginary interview on Urquhart's similar account on page 4 of *Arnhem*. For Urquhart's anecdote, I cannot fully account. Browning would not have passed on such a discouraging remark before the battle, one that forecast probably ruin to Urquhart's division. It seems more than likely that it arose in some post-battle and informal conversation, half remembered by Urquhart, and recounted by Browning as an excuse for the operation's failure.'

Clearly, at this date, no absolute verification is possible as no minutes of any meeting between Browning and Montgomery exist and Browning left no statement on the matter (having destroyed all his papers). Indeed, as Colonel Powell considers, 'It is a pity that no proper biography of Browning ever appeared, but Daphne du Maurier [his widow] denied aspirant authors access to his papers.' He did not die until 1965 which presumably would have enabled him to rebutt anything he did not like in Urquhart's 1958 book, but, as Colonel Powell indicates, the phrase did not become controversial until Cornelius Ryan got to work on it many years later.

BROWNING, Robert

English poet (1812–89)

2 The year's at the spring
And day's at the morn;
Morning's at seven;
The hill-side's dew-pearled;
The lark's on the wing;
The snail's on the thorn:
God's in his heaven –
All's right with the world!

'Pippa Passes' (1841). From P.G. Wodehouse, *Much Obliged, Jeeves* (1971): 'The snail's on the wing and the lark's on the thorn, or rather the other way round, as I've sometimes heard you say.'

3 What's become of Waring?

First line of poem 'Waring' (1842). Hence, the title of Anthony Powell's novel (1939).

4 Over my head his arm he flung
Against the world; and scarce I felt
His sword (that dripped by me and swung)
A little shifted in its belt.

'Count Gismond', St. 19 (1842). A 'lost' quotation pursued for over fifty years until traced to its source (1995) using the Chadwyck–Healey Poetry Full-Text Database (600–1900) on CD-ROM.

1 I sprang to the stirrup, and Joris, and he;
I galloped, Dirck galloped, we galloped all three.

'How They Brought the Good News from Ghent to Aix' (1845). Browning sets it in '16—' during the wars in the Netherlands, but, according to the *Browning Cyclopedia* (ed. Edward Berdoe, 1898): 'There is no actual basis in history for the incidents in this poem, though there is no doubt that in the war in the Netherlands such an adventure was likely enough.' So there is no point in asking what was the good news or what was the occasion.

Sellar and Yeatman (of *1066 and All That*) produced a splendid parody entitled 'How I Brought the Good News from Aix to Ghent (or Vice Versa)', which concludes with the messenger sending a telegram (in *Horse Nonsense*, 1933).

2 Never glad confident morning again.

'The Lost Leader' (1845). To be found very near the top of any list of over-used, mis-used quotations, this comes from Browning's poem in which Wordsworth is regretfully portrayed as a man who had lost his revolutionary zeal.

A correct – and devastating – use of the phrase came on 17 June 1963 when the British government under Prime Minister Harold Macmillan had been rocked by the Profumo scandal. In the House of Commons, Tory MP Nigel Birch said to Macmillan:

> I myself feel that the time will come very soon when my right hon. Friend ought to make way for a much younger colleague. I feel that that ought to happen. I certainly will not quote at him the savage words of Cromwell, but perhaps some of the words of Browning might be appropriate in his poem on 'The Lost Leader', in which he wrote:
>
> ... Let him never come back to us!
> There would be doubt, hesitation and pain.
> Forced praise on our part – the glimmer of twilight,
> Never glad confident morning again!'
>
> 'Never glad confident morning again!' – so I hope that the change will not be too long delayed.

Birch was right. A few months later Macmillan was out of office; a year later, so was the government.

In November 1983, on the twentieth anniversary of President Kennedy's assassination, Lord Harlech, former British Ambassador in Washington, paid tribute thus in *The Observer* Magazine: 'Since 1963 the world has seemed a bleaker place, and for me and I suspect millions of my contemporaries he remains the lost leader – "Never glad confident morning again".' Harlech may have wanted to evoke a leader who had been lost to the world, but surely it was a mistake to quote a *criticism* of one?

Also in November 1983, in *The Observer*, Paul Johnson wrote an attack (which he later appeared to regret) on Margaret Thatcher: 'Her courage and sound instincts made her formidable. But if her judgement can no longer be trusted, what is left? A very ordinary woman, occupying a position where ordinary virtues are not enough. For me, I fear it can never be "glad confident morning again".'

Still at it in 1988 was Shirley Williams. When part of the SDP united with the Liberals, she used the words about David Owen, the SDP's once and future leader.

3 What of soul was left, I wonder,
When the kissing had to stop?

'A Toccata at Galuppi's' (1855). Hence, *When the Kissing Had to Stop* (1960) by Constantine FitzGibbon, about a Russian takeover of Britain.

4 Ah, did you once see Shelley plain,
And did he stop and speak to you
And did you speak to him again?
How strange it seems, and new!

The first line of 'Memorabilia' (1855) is often misquoted as '*And* did you once see Shelley plain?'

BRUCE, Lenny

American satirist (1923–66)

5 I'm Super-jew!

Leaping out of a second-floor window. He sustained only a broken leg. Quoted in *The Observer* (21 August 1966).

BRUMMELL, Beau

English dandy (1778–1840)

6 Tell me, Alvanley, who is your fat friend?

A famous question to Lord Alvanley about the Prince Regent. Brummell, almost a dandy by profession, had fallen out with the Prince of Wales. He is said to have annoyed the Prince by ridiculing his mistress and also by saying once to his royal guest at dinner, 'Wales, ring the bell, will you?' When they met in London in July 1813, the Prince cut Brummell but greeted his companion. As the Prince walked off, Brummell put his question in ringing tones.

The nicely alliterative phrase 'fat friend' occurs as early as Shakespeare, *The Comedy of Errors* (V.i.414):

'There is a fat friend at your master's house.' But in the novel *Handley Cross* (1843) by R.S. Surtees, there is: 'When at length *our fat friend* got his horse and his hounds ... together again'; and in Anthony Trollope's *Castle Richmond* (1860): 'Is it not possible that one should have one more game of rounders? Quite impossible, *my fat friend*.' More recently, in 1972, there was a play by Charles Laurence called *My Fat Friend*. The play was about a fat girl and her experiences when she lost weight (it was originally going to be called *The Fat Dress*).

1 Yes, madam, I once ate a pea.

Having taken it into his head not to eat vegetables, Brummell was asked by a lady if he had never eaten any in his life. This is what he replied. Quoted in Daniel George, *A Book of Anecdotes* (1958) and, much earlier, in Charles Dickens, *Bleak House*, Chap. 12 (1852–3).

BRYAN, William Jennings

American Democratic politician (1860–1925)

2 We will answer their demand for a gold standard by saying to them: You shall not press down upon the brow of labour this crown of thorns. You shall not crucify mankind upon a cross of gold.

Speech to the Democratic Convention on 8 July 1896. One of the most notable examples of American oratory, it contained an impassioned attack on supporters of the gold standard. Bryan had said virtually the same in a speech to the House of Representatives on 22 December 1894. He won the nomination and fought the Presidential election against William J. McKinley who supported the gold standard. Bryan lost. The US formally went on to the gold standard in March 1900, under McKinley. Bryan championed a looser monetary policy based on silver. Somerset Maugham wrote in 1941 (included in *A Writer's Notebook*, 1949): 'Democracy seldom had a ruder shock than when a phrase – you shall not crucify mankind upon a cross of gold – nearly put an ignorant and conceited fool in the White House.'

A 'cross of gold'-type speech is sometimes called for when a politician (such as Edward Kennedy in 1980) is required to sweep a Convention with his eloquence.

3 No one ever made a million dollars honestly.

He later modified the sum to two million dollars, once he himself had made one. Unverified.

See also HOOVER 301:1.

BUCHAN, John (later Lord Tweedsmuir)

British politician and writer (1875–1940)

4 The Courts of the Morning.

Title of an adventure novel (1929) – a translation of *Los Patios de la Mañana*, a geographical hill feature in the fictitious South American republic of Olifa, where the book is set: 'In the Courts of the Morning there was still peace. The brooding heats, the dust-storms, the steaming deluges of the lowlands were unknown. The air was that of a tonic and gracious autumn slowly moving to the renewal of spring.' Whether the name has anywhere been given to actual hills, is not known.

5 An atheist is a man who has no invisible means of support.

Quoted in H.E. Fosdick, *On Being a Real Person* (1943) – not said *by* Fosdick as in *PDMQ* (1971).

BUCHANAN, James

American Democratic 15th President (1791–1868)

6 If you are as happy in entering the White House as I shall feel in returning to Wheatland [Pennsylvania], you are a happy man indeed.

To the incoming President, Abraham Lincoln, on the day of his retirement in 1861. Quoted in Asa E. Martin, *After the White House* (1951).

BUCKLE, Richard

English ballet critic (1916–)

7 John Lennon, Paul McCartney and George Harrison are the greatest composers since Beethoven, with Paul McCartney way out in front.

On the Beatles. Review in *The Sunday Times* (29 December 1963). *Compare* MANN 378:7 and PALMER 422:5.

BULMER-THOMAS, Ivor (formerly Ivor Thomas)

British Labour, then Conservative, MP (1905–93)

8 If ever he [Harold Wilson] went to school without any boots it was because he was too big for them.

Thomas made this jibe in a speech at the Conservative Party Conference (12 October 1949) – a remark often wrongly ascribed to Harold Macmillan. It followed a press dispute involving Wilson the previous year (*see* WILSON 574:4).

BULWER-LYTTON, Edward (1st Baron Lytton)

English novelist and politician (1803–73)

1 The pen is mightier than the sword.

According to a piece in the London *Standard* diary following the Gorbachev–Reagan summit in November 1987, Parker Pens broke new ground by placing an advertisement in the *Moscow News* to draw attention to the fact that the treaty had been signed with one of its fountain pens. The advertisement's Russian slogan, translated directly, was, 'What is written with the pen will not be chopped up with an axe', which the *Standard* thought was the equivalent of 'The pen is mightier than the sword'.

Unfortunately, the *Standard* announced that 'The pen is ...' was the most famous maxim attributed to Cardinal Richelieu. But no. That was merely a line said by Richelieu in Edward Bulwer-Lytton's play *Richelieu*, Act 2, Sc. 2 (1839):

> Beneath the rule of men entirely great,
> The pen is mightier than the sword.

– which is not quite the same as Richelieu himself having originated it. As for the idea, it was not, of course, Bulwer-Lytton's either. *CODP* finds several earlier attempts at expressing it, to which one might add this 'corollary' from Shakespeare's *Hamlet* (II.ii.344): 'Many wearing rapiers are afraid of goose-quills.' Cervantes, *Don Quixote* (Pt 1, Bk 4, Chap. 10) has, in Motteux's translation: 'Let none presume to tell me that the pen is preferable to the sword.'

BUNN, Alfred

English theatrical manager and librettist (c.1796–1860)

2 I dreamt I dwelt in marble halls
With vassals and serfs at my side,
And of all who assembled within those walls
That I was the hope and the pride.
I had riches too great to count –
Could boast of a high ancestral name;
But I also dream'd, which pleased me most,
That you loved me still the same.
I dream'd that suitors sought my hand,
That knights upon bended knee,
And with vows no maiden heart could withstand,
They pledged their faith to me.
And I dream'd that one of that noble host
Came forth my hand to claim;
But I also dream'd, which charmed me most,
That you lov'd me still the same.

Song, 'The Gypsy Girl's Dream', *The Bohemian Girl*, Act 2 (1843), with music by Michael Balfe. Arline, daughter of the Count, sings it to Thaddeus, 'a proscribed Pole'. The Balfe-Bunn work has been described as the most popular British opera of the nineteenth century. This song was parodied by Lewis Carroll in *Lays of Mystery, Imagination, and Humour* (1855): 'I dreamt I dwelt in marble halls,/And each damp thing that creeps and crawls/Went wobble-wobble on the walls.'

BUNNER, Henry Cuyler

American humorous writer (1855–96)

3 Shakespeare was a dramatist of note who lived by writing things to quote.

Quoted in *The Treasury of Humorous Quotations*, ed. by Evan Esar & Nicolas Bentley (1951), but otherwise unverified.

BUNYAN, John

English writer and preacher (1628–88)

4 It beareth the name of Vanity-Fair, because the town where 'tis kept, is lighter than vanity.

The Pilgrim's Progress, Pt 1 (1684). Hence, *Vanity Fair*, title of the novel (1847–8) by William Thackeray. Has also been used for magazines, notably the one published in New York from 1914–36.

5 So I awoke, and behold it was a dream.

Ib. Last words of Pt 1. The whole work is an allegory in the form of a dream.

6 A man that could look no way but downwards, with a muckrake in his hand.

Ib., Pt 2. 'In *Pilgrim's Progress*, the Man with the Muck-Rake is set forth as the example of him whose vision is fixed on carnal instead of on spiritual things. Yet he also typifies the man who in this life consistently refuses to see aught that is lofty, and fixes his eyes only on that which is vile and debasing.' So said President Theodore Roosevelt in a speech (14 April 1906). This led to the term 'muckraker' being applied to investigative journalists who seek out scandals, especially about public figures.

BURDETT, Winston

American journalist (twentieth century)

1 I don't want to be quoted, and don't quote me that I don't want to be quoted.

CBS news correspondent, quoted in Barbara Rowes, *The Book of Quotes* (1979). A circumspect journalist when on the receiving end of his colleagues' attentions.

BURGESS, Anthony

English novelist and critic (1917–93)

2 Who ever heard of a clockwork orange? ... The attempt to impose upon man, a creature of growth and capable of sweetness, to ooze juicily at the last round the bearded lips of God, to attempt to impose, I say, laws and conditions appropriate to a mechanical creation, against this I raise my sword-pen.

A Clockwork Orange (1962; film UK, 1971). This passage hints at the reason for the unusual title. The book describes an attempt to punish its criminal hero, Alex, by turning him into a 'mechanical man' through forms of therapy and brainwashing. But Burgess several times explained that he had taken the title from a cockney expression 'to be queer as a clockwork orange' (i.e., homosexual). This was not known to many but has been in use since the mid-1950s, according to Paul Beale in Partridge/*Slang*. As such, its relevance to the story, which has no overt homosexual element, is debatable.

3 The End of the World News.

The title of Burgess's novel (1982) derives from what BBC World Service newsreaders have sometimes said at the end of bulletins: 'That is the end of the world news' – leaving open the possibility that listeners had just been hearing the news of the end of the world.

BURGHLEY, 1st Lord (William Cecil)

English courtier and politician (1520–98)

4 What! all this for a song?

Burghley or Burleigh (the name is variously spelled) was Lord High Treasurer to Elizabeth I. He exclaimed this when told by the Queen to pay Edmund Spenser the sum of £100 for some poems. Related by Thomas Birch in 'The Life of Mr Edmund Spenser' in an edition of *The Faerie Queene*, 1751.

See also SHERIDAN 502:4.

BURGON, John William

English poet and clergyman (1813–88)

5 Match me such marvel, save in Eastern clime, –
A rose-red city – 'half as old as Time'!

This famous couplet from Burgon's poem 'Petra' (1845) palpably contains a quotation. It comes from the epilogue to the poem *Italy* (1838) by Samuel Rogers: 'By many a temple half as old as time.' Compare the parody contained in the travelogue sketch 'Balham – Gateway to the South', written by Frank Muir and Denis Norden in 1948 for a BBC Third Programme comedy show called *Third Division*:

> Broadbosomed, bold, becalm'd, benign
> Lies Balham foursquare on the Northern Line.
> Matched by no marvel save in Eastern scene,
> A rose-red city half as gold as green.

In 1959, this was re-recorded by Peter Sellers on his album *The Best of Sellers*.

BURKE, Edmund

Irish-born politician and philosopher (1729–97)

6 Parliament is a deliberative assembly of one nation, with one interest, that of the whole, where not local prejudices ought to guide but the general good, resulting from the general reason of the whole. You choose a member indeed; but when you have chosen him, he is not member of Bristol, but he is member of parliament.

Speech to the electors of Bristol (1774), establishing an important principle that an MP represents his constituency in parliament but does not solely or necessarily have to advance its interests.

7 Truth is stranger than fiction.

Pearson (1937) points out that if quoting Burke's *On Conciliation with America* (1775), this should properly be 'Fiction lags after truth'. By the time of Byron's *Don Juan*, 14:101 (1819–24), the saying was in the form: ''Tis strange, but true; for truth is always strange –/ Stranger than fiction.' By the mid-nineteenth century, the version 'Fact is stranger than fiction' had also emerged.

1 The people are the masters.

Speech, House of Commons (11 February 1780). *Compare* SHAWCROSS 500:7.

2 Not merely a chip off the old 'block', but the old block itself.

On Pitt the Younger's first speech (February 1781). Quoted in N.W. Wraxall, *Historical Memoirs of My Own Time* (1904 ed.)

3 The age of chivalry is past.

Should be 'The age of chivalry is gone', if alluding to Burke's *Reflections on the Revolution in France* (1790). The misquotation is probably caused by confusion with the proverb 'the age of miracles is past', which was current by 1602.

4 The only thing necessary for the triumph of evil is for good men to do nothing.

So Burke said, or at least is often quoted as having done. Bartlett (1968) cited it in a letter from Burke to William Smith (9 January 1795), but on checking found that this did not exist. In his book *On Language* (1980), William Safire describes his unavailing attempts to find a proper source. In the House of Commons on 23 April 1770, Burke said 'When bad men combine, the good must associate; else they will fall one by one, an unpitied sacrifice in a contemptible struggle' – which seems be heading somewhere in the right direction (also to be found in *Thoughts on the Cause of the Present Discontents*, 1770). But, for the moment, we have here another of those quotations which arrive apparently from nowhere, and gets quoted and re-quoted without justification. On the other hand, it is fair to assume that Burke would not have wished to disown it.

5 The great unwashed.

Meaning 'working-class people, the lower orders', this term is said (by Safire, 1978) to have been used originally by Burke (though untraced), and has also been attributed to Lord Brougham, perhaps echoing Shakespeare's reference to 'another lean unwash'd artificer' (*King John*, IV.ii.201). Bulwer-Lytton in *Paul Clifford* (1830) uses the full phrase. Thackeray has it in *Pendennis* (1848–50). Thomas Carlyle in his *History of the French Revolution* (1837) has: 'Man has set man against man, Washed against unwashed'.

6 Somebody has said, that a king may make a nobleman but he cannot make a gentleman.

Letter to William Smith (29 January 1795). *See* WILSON 577:2.

BURKE, Johnny

American songwriter (1908–64)

7 Every time it rains, it rains
Pennies from heaven.

Song 'Pennies from Heaven' (1937). Music by Arthur Johnston.

See also ROAD TO MOROCCO 456:7.

BURNAND, F.C. (later Sir Francis)

British editor (1836–1917)

8 It never was.

His reply when, as editor of *Punch* (1880–1906), he was asked why his organ wasn't as funny as it used to be.

BURNETT, W.R.

American author (1899–1982)

9 The Asphalt Jungle.

Title of Burnett's novel (1949; film US, 1950) about an elderly criminal carrying out one last robbery. This phrase was undoubtedly popularized by Burnett, but the *OED2* finds it in 1920, however. It is one of several phrases that suggest that there are urban areas where the 'law of the jungle' may apply. Next came *The Blackboard Jungle*, a novel (1954; film US, 1955) by Evan Hunter, on the educational system. A little after, in 1969, came references to 'the concrete jungle'.

BURNS, George

American comedian (1896–1996)

10 *Burns*: Say goodnight, Gracie.
Allen: Goodnight, Gracie.

Exchange with wife (Gracie Allen) – the customary ending of their TV series, *The George Burns and Gracie Allen Show* (1950–8).

11 Too bad that all the people who know how to run the country are busy driving taxicabs and cutting hair.

Remark attributed to him, by 1977. Also quoted in *Life* Magazine (December 1979).

12 The secret of acting is sincerity – and if you can fake that, you've got it made.

Usually attributed to Burns (as, for example, in Michael York, *Travelling Player*, 1991). Fred Metcalf in

The Penguin Dictionary of Modern Humorous Quotations (1987) has Burns saying, rather: 'Acting is about honesty. If you can fake that, you've got it made.' However, Kingsley Amis in a devastating piece about Leo Rosten in his *Memoirs* (1991) has the humorist relating 'at some stage in the 1970s' how he had given a Commencement address including the line: 'Sincerity. If you can *fake that* ... you'll have the world at your feet.' So perhaps the saying was circulating even before Burns received the credit. Or perhaps Rosten took it from him? An advertisement in *Rolling Stone*, *c.*1982, offered a T-shirt with the slogan (anonymous): 'The secret of success is sincerity. Once you can fake that you've got it made.'

1 When the man shows up at the door to return the pictures, you've got to go.

Asked by William Safire of *The New York Times* about the origin of this saying, Burns explained: 'You see, I'm an old vaudeville actor – I'm going back 65 or 70 years – and in those days, your contract had a cancellation clause in it. If the manager didn't like your act, he was able to cancel you after your first show. All the actors carried their own pictures, so after the first show, if the manager knocked on your door and gave you back your pictures, you started packing.' Burns (then in his nineties) added: 'When the guy knocks on my door with the pictures, I'm not going to answer.'

BURNS, John

British Labour politician (1858–1943)

2 I have seen the Mississippi. That is muddy water. I have seen the St Lawrence. That is crystal water. But the Thames is liquid history.

According to a *Daily Mail* report (25 January 1943) at Burns's death, this remark was made to an American who had spoken disparagingly of the River Thames. There are various versions of it. Denis Bridge commented (1994) that he used to live near Burns on North Side, Clapham Common, London. His father's version of the Burns remark went: 'The Mississippi is dirty water. The St Lawrence is cold, dirty water. But the Thames is liquid history.' The version I prefer is the one uttered with Burn's characteristic dropped aitch: 'The Thames is liquid 'istory!'

BURNS, Robert

Scottish poet (1759–96)

3 Wee, sleekit, cow'rin', tim'rous beastie.

'To a Mouse' (1785) – 'on turning her up in her nest with the plough, November 1785.' Sleekit = sleek.

4 The best laid plans o' mice an' men
Gang aft a-gley.

Ib. Hence, *Of Mice and Men*, title of a novel (1937; film US, 1939) by John Steinbeck. A-gley = off the right line, awry.

5 O wad some Pow'r the giftie gie us
To see oursels as others see us!
It wad frae mony a blunder free us,
And foolish notion.

'To a Louse' (1786). Hence, the peculiar resonance of the phrase 'to see ourselves as others see us'.

6 Man's inhumanity to man
Makes countless thousands mourn.

'Man was made to mourn' (1786), though the thought that lies behind it is, of course, a very old one. It provided John Arlott, the English journalist and radio cricket commentator (1914–91), with a bright comment on one occasion. At Lord's, a South African googly bowler named 'Tufty' Mann was tying a Middlesex tail-end batsman named George Mann into such knots that the crowd was reduced to laughter. When it occurred for the fourth time in a single over, Arlott, apparently without a moment's thought, reported, 'So what we are watching here is a clear case of Mann's inhumanity to Mann.' Reported in *The Daily Mail* (3 September 1980).

7 Fair fa' your honest, sonsie face,
Great chieftain o' the puddin'-race!

'To a Haggis' (1787). 'Sonsie' means 'comely, agreeable, plump'.

8 The Poetic Genius of my Country found me, as the prophetic bard Elijah did Elisha – at the *plough* – and threw her inspiring mantle over me. She bade me sing the loves, the joys, the rural scenes and rural pleasures of my natal Soil, in my native tongue. I tuned my wild, artless notes, as she inspired. She whispered me to come to this ancient metropolis of Caledonia, and lay my Songs under your honoured protection. I now obey her dictates ... I do not approach you, my Lords and Gentlemen, in the usual style of dedication, to thank you for past favours; that path is so hackneyed by prostituted Learning, that honest Rusticity is ashamed of it. Nor do I present this Address with the venal soul of a servile Author, looking

for a continuation of those favours: I was bred to the Plough, and am independent ...

'To the Noblemen and Gentlemen of the Caledonian Hunt' prefacing the 1787 'Edinburgh' edition of his poems. The Caledonian Hunt was an association of noblemen and country gentlemen who shared a keen interest in field sports, races, balls and social assemblies. This has been described as 'the start of the Burns myth'. It has also been written that Burns said this, obsequiously, only to please the Hunt who topped the subscribers' list.

A large, seated statue of Burns with the following version of the text below it is to be found in Victoria Embankment Gardens, London (a city he never visited): 'The Poetic Genius of my Country found me at the Plough and threw her inspiring Mantle over me. She bade me sing the Loves, the Joys, the Rural Scenes and Rural Pleasures of my Native Soil, in my Native Tongue. I tuned my Wild, Artless Notes as She inspired.'

1 O whistle, an' I'll come to you, my lad.

From the poem of that title (*c.*1788). *Compare* FLETCHER 240:1. *Oh, Whistle and I'll Come To You My Lad* became the title of a short story in *Ghost Stories of an Antiquary* (1904) by M.R. James, in which the wind is 'whistled up'.

2 Should auld acquaintance be forgot,
And never brought to min[d]?
Should auld acquaintance be forgot,
And days of o' lang syne.

(*Chorus*) For auld lang syne, my dear
For auld syne,
We'll take a cup o' kindness yet
For auld lang syne.

The song 'Auld Lang Syne' is traditionally massacred and half-remembered, if remembered at all, at farewell ceremonies and on New Year's Eve. It is not just inebriation that leads Sassenachs into gibbering incomprehensibility – there is widespread confusion as to what the words mean, how they should be pronounced and – indeed – what the correct words are.

In fact, Burns adapted 'Auld Lang Syne' from 'an old man's singing' in 1788. The title, first line and refrain had all appeared before as the work of other poets, mostly by the early 1700s. Nevertheless, what Burns put together is now the accepted version. 'For *the sake of* auld lang syne' should *not* be substituted at the end of verse and chorus. 'Auld lang syne' means, literally, 'old long since' i.e., 'long ago'. Hence, 'syne' should be pronounced with an 's' sound and not as 'zyne'.

3 We twa hae run about the braes,
And pou'd the gowans fine;
But we've wandered mony a weary fit,
Sin' auld lang syne.

Ib. A gowan is a daisy (Scots word recorded since the sixteenth century), indeed any white or yellow field flower. 'Pluck' would be more widely understood than 'pou' (the Scots version of 'pull'), which explains why P.G. Wodehouse uses it in the several allusions to 'pluck the gowans fine' in the Jeeves books. Sometimes, in any case, 'pu't' or 'pu'd the gowans fine' is printed in versions of the poem.

Incidentally, Wilkins Micawber quotes the line in Dickens, *David Copperfield*, Chap. 28, adding, 'I am not exactly aware ... what gowans may be, but I have no doubt that Copperfield and myself would frequently have taken a pull at them, had it been feasible.'

4 Some have meat and cannot eat,
Some cannot eat that want it:
But we have meat and we can eat,
Sae let the Lord be thankit.

'The Kirkudbright Grace' (1790). Also known as 'The Selkirk Grace' and, subsequently, always recited at Burns Night suppers and other celebrations.

5 A Workhouse! ah, that sound awakes my woes,
And pillows on the thorn my racked repose!
In durance vile here must I wake and weep,
And all my frowzy couch in sorrow steep.

'Epistle from Esopus to Maris' (1795–6). From P.G. Wodehouse, *The Code of the Woosters* (1938): 'It was nice to feel that I had got my bedroom to myself for a few minutes, but against that you had to put the fact that I was in what is known as durance vile and not likely to get out of it.'

6 Scots, wha hae wi' Wallace bled,
Scots, wham Bruce has aften led,
Welcome to your gory bed,
Or to victorie.

'Scots, Wha Hae' is the title given to, and a phrase from the first line of, a battle-song. It is sometimes subtitled 'Robert Bruce's March to Bannockburn' or 'Robert Bruce's Address to his army, before the battle of Bannockburn', and was published in 1799. 'Wha hae' is not an exclamation ('Scots wu-hey!') but simply means 'who have'. 'Wham' in the next line means 'whom'.

A further comment, from James Murray (creator of the *OED*) in 1912: 'Even Burns thought that Scotch was defiled by "bad grammar" and tried to conform his Scotch to *English* grammar! Transforming e.g., the

Scotch "*Scots 'at hae*" to *Scots wha hae* which no sober Scotch man in his senses ever naturally said.'

1 Nine inch will please a lady.

Title of poem included in *Bawdy Verse and Folksongs* 'written and collected by Robert Burns' (1982).

2 John, don't let the awkward squad fire over me.

Burns's dying words are said to have been these, presumably referring to his fear that literary opponents might metaphorically fire a volley of respect, as soldiers sometimes do, over a new grave – in their case by burbling inept and embarrassing paeans. Reported in A. Cunningham, *The Works of Robert Burns; with his Life* (1834).

As for the phrase 'awkward squad' on its own, Sloppy in *Our Mutual Friend* (1864–5) is described by Charles Dickens as 'Full-Private Number One in the Awkward Squad of the rank and file of life'. Of military origin and used to denote a difficult, uncooperative person, the phrase originally referred to a squad that consisted of raw recruits and older hands who were put in it for punishment, but seems to have been used in other contexts for quite some time.

See also SPECTOR 512:5.

BURROUGHS, Edgar Rice

American author (1875–1950)

3 Me Tarzan, you Jane.

A box-office sensation of 1932 was the first sound Tarzan film, *Tarzan the Ape Man*. It spawned a long-running series and starred Johnny Weismuller, an ex-US swimming champion, as Tarzan, and Maureen O'Sullivan as Jane. At one point the ape man whisks Jane away to his tree-top abode and indulges in some elementary conversation with her. Thumping his chest, he says, 'Tarzan!'; pointing at her, he says, 'Jane!' So, in fact, he does not say the catchphrase commonly associated with him, though Weissmuller did use the words in an interview for *Photoplay Magazine* (June 1932) – 'I didn't have to act in "Tarzan, the Ape Man" – just said, "Me Tarzan, you Jane"' – so it is not surprising the misquotation arose.

Interestingly, this great moment of movie dialogue appears to have been 'written' by the British playwright and actor Ivor Novello. In the original novel, *Tarzan of the Apes* (1914), by Edgar Rice Burroughs, the line does not occur (whatever it says in *PDMQ*, 1980), not least because, in the jungle, Tarzan and Jane are able to communicate only by writing notes to each other.

BURROUGHS, William S.

American novelist (1914–97)

4 Heavy metal.

The type of music known as Heavy Metal – very loud, amplified, clashing – was first described as such in 1968 when the group Steppenwolf used Burroughs's phrase 'heavy metal thunder' in their song 'Born To be Wild' (written by M. Bonfire). The Burroughs phrase appears in his science-fiction novel *The Ticket That Exploded* (1962); he also wrote in *Nova Express* (1964): 'At this point we got a real break in the form of a defector from The Nova Mob: Ukrainian Willy the Heavy Metal Kid.'

The use of the phrase 'heavy metal' in the sense of guns of large size and, figuratively, about human bodily or mental power dates back to the nineteenth century.

BURTON, Sir Richard

English explorer and writer (1821–90)

5 I struggled for 47 years, I distinguished myself in every way I possibly could. I never had a compliment nor a 'Thank you', nor a single farthing. I translated a doubtful book in my old age, and I immediately made sixteen thousand guineas. Now I know the tastes of England, we need never be without money.

Quoted in Isabel Burton, *Life of Captain Sir Richard F. Burton* (1893). He translated the *Kama Sutra* and *The Perfumed Garden*.

6 I wish I were a man: if I were, I would be Richard Burton. But as I am woman, I would be Richard Burton's wife.

In fact, said by his wife (*c.* October 1859). Quoted in *ib.*

7 Prostitutes for pleasure, concubines for service, wives for breeding ... A melon for ecstasy.

When the late Pearl Binder (Lady Elwyn-Jones) appeared with octogenarian aplomb on BBC Radio *Quote ... Unquote* in 1984, she chose as a favourite quotation what she claimed Burton had borrowed from Demosthenes: 'Prostitutes for pleasure, concubines for service, wives for breeding.' Alan Brien, who was in attendance, chimed in with, 'And a melon for ecstasy'.

What slightly off-colour, old joke did we have here? *A Melon for Ecstasy* was the title of a novel (1971) by John Fortune and John Wells, and presumably alluded to the same core remark. Apparently, the novelist John Masters ascribed to a 'Pathan tribesman', the saying 'A woman for duty, a boy for pleasure, a goat for ecstasy' whereas Stephen Fry in *Paperweight* (1992) credits this to the Greeks. Apropos the main quotation, compare John Gay, 'The Toilette' (1716): 'A miss for pleasure, and a wife for breed.'

BURTON, Richard

Welsh actor (1925–84)

1 Home is where the books are.

Caption to photograph of his library at Céligny in Melvyn Bragg, *Rich: The Life of Richard Burton* (1988). Burton was a great buyer of books and a voracious reader, so this may well be his own remark.

BURTON, Robert

English clergyman and writer (1577–1640)

2 As if they had heard that enchanted horn of Astolpho, that English duke in Ariosto, which never sounded but all his auditors were mad, and for fear ready to make away [with] themselves ... they are a company of giddy-heads, afternoon men.

The Anatomy of Melancholy (1621). This is the final part of the quotation from 'Democritus to the Reader' given by Anthony Powell as the epigraph to his novel with the title *Afternoon Men* (1931). The phrase also occurs earlier in this chapter in the sentence, 'Beroaldus will have drunkards, afternoon men, and such as more than ordinarily delight in drink, to be mad.'

See also ARNOLD 61:6.

BUSH, George

American Republican 41st President (1924–)

3 Voodoo economics.

Remark, during 1980 presidential primary campaign. It was his term for his then rival Ronald Reagan's economic policies, but it did not prevent Reagan from choosing Bush as his running-mate in due course. Bush commented: 'It's the only memorable thing I've ever said, and I've regretted saying it.'

4 In deep doodoo.

Remark variously used, before 1988, meaning, 'in the shit'. As Vice-President, Bush was asked what would happen to a Chinese official who was too friendly towards the Americans and, according to *The Wall Street Journal* (in 1986) replied: 'He would have been in deep doodoo.'

5 Oh, the vision thing.

As Bush debated with other potential Republican candidates for the presidency, he said: 'On vision – you have to have a vision. Mine is that education should be the No. 1 thing' – *The Washington Post* (15 January 1988). But, shortly before this, he had coined the phrase 'vision thing', unintentionally characterizing his own lack of an overarching view of what he might do with the presidency. His very use of the word 'thing' seemed to confirm his pragmatic, tongue-tied, earth-bound stance. *Time* Magazine had picked up the phrase by 27 January.

In 1993 *The Vision Thing* became the title of a BBC TV play by Mark Lawson about a British Prime Minister who did have visions and was consequently eased out of office.

6 My opponent won't rule out raising taxes, but I will. And the Congress will push me to raise taxes, and I'll say no, and they'll push again. And I'll say to them, read my lips, no new taxes.

Although popularized by Bush in his speech accepting the Republican nomination at New Orleans on 18 August 1988, the expression 'read my lips' was not new. According to William Safire in an article in *The New York Times* Magazine (September 1988), the phrase is rooted in 1970s rock music (despite there being a song with the title copyrighted by Joe Greene in 1957). The British actor/singer Tim Curry used the phrase as the title of an album of songs in 1978. Curry said he took it from an Italian-American recording engineer who used it to mean, 'Listen and listen very hard, because I want you to hear what I've got to say'. Several lyricists in the 1980s used the phrase for song titles. A football coach with the Chicago Bears became nicknamed Mike 'Read My Lips' Ditka. There has been a thoroughbred race horse so named. Safire also cites a number of American politicians, also in the 1980s. In the film *Breathless* (1983), a scrap dealer says it to the Richard Gere character, encouraging him to believe that there is no money in the yard worth taking.

Needless to say, Bush *did* have to raise taxes in due course.

7 I will keep America moving forward, always forward – for a better America, for an endless enduring dream and a thousand points of light.

From the same acceptance speech, and used many times throughout the 1988 campaign, the words 'thousand points of light' were put on his lips by speechwriter Peggy Noonan. But what did they mean? The phrase was said to symbolize individual endeavour, voluntary charity efforts, across the country (later, in June 1989, President Bush announced details of his 'Points of Light Programme, costing $25 million, to encourage a voluntary crusade to fight poverty, drugs and homelessness). But Bush never seemed too sure what he was saying. On one occasion, he called it '1,000 points of life'. Herblock, the cartoonist, drew a drunk at a bar pledging his vote to Bush because he had promised '1,000 pints of Lite'. Perhaps it was supposed to echo Shakespeare, *The Merchant of Venice* (V.i.90): 'How far that little candle throws his beams!/ So shines a good deed in a naughty world.' Light often comes in thousands: 'It was but for an instant that I seemed to struggle with a thousand mill-weirs and a thousand flashes of light' (Charles Dickens, *Great Expectations*, Chap. 54, 1860–1). In *Conducted Tour* (1981) Bernard Levin describes an English pantomime when parents were asked to take out matches and cigarette lighters – 'the vast shell of the Coliseum's auditorium was alive with a thousand tiny points of light'.

In her memoir *What I Saw at the Revolution* (1990), Noonan makes mention of several earlier uses of the phrase or parts of it. She does not appear to have been aware of C.S. Lewis's *The Magician's Nephew* (1955): 'One moment there had been nothing but darkness, next moment a thousand points of light leaped out ...', or of Thomas Wolfe's *The Web and the Rock* (1939): 'Instantly he could see the town below now, coiling in a thousand fumes of homely smoke, now winking into a thousand points of friendly light its glorious small design', though she had read it as a teenager. A speech by a turn-of-the-century engineer was also found urging the electrification of Venice so that it would be filled with 'a thousand points of light'.

Oddly, Noonan does not draw attention to one possible point of inspiration. Having admitted earlier that she is a fan of Auden's poem 'September 1, 1939' ('We must love one another or die'), she overlooks the lines:

> Defenceless under the night
> Our world in stupor lies;
> Yet, dotted everywhere,
> Ironic points of light
> Flash out wherever the Just
> Exchange their messages ...

1 America is never wholly herself unless she is engaged in high moral purpose. We as a people have such a purpose today. It is to make kinder the face of the nation and gentler the face of the world.

Inaugural Address (20 January 1989). The 'kinder/ gentler' theme had also appeared in the acceptance speech and during the campaign. Peggy Noonan suggests that Bush added the word 'gentler' to her 'I want a kinder nation' in the acceptance speech draft, but even so this was a familiar combination. In his 1932 autobiography, Clarence Darrow wrote: 'There may have lived somewhere a kindlier, gentler, more generous man than Eugene Debs, but I have not known him.' Charlie Chaplin in the film *The Great Dictator* (1940) urged: 'More than cleverness, we need kindness and gentleness.' In 1985 singer Roy Orbison said that Elvis Presley had 'made gentler and kinder souls of us all'.

2 I do not like broccoli and I haven't liked it since I was a little kid. I am President of the United States and I am not going to eat it any more.

Unverified statement (March 1990). Accordingly Bush banned broccoli from his plane, Air Force One. Outraged California farmers unloaded a 10-ton juggernaut of broccoli on the White House doorstep. Bush also said, 'I can't stand broccoli' and when this caused ructions among America's broccoli growers, he added: 'Wait till the country hears how I feel about cauliflower.' He also denounced carrots as being 'orange broccoli'.

See also WELLS 561:8.

BUTLER, Henry Montagu

English academic (1833–1918)

3 Would you, my dear young friends, like to be inside with the five wise virgins or outside, alone, and in the dark, with the five foolish ones?

A favourite story, to be taken with a pinch of salt, but if true, coming in the category of Sermons One Would Like To Have Heard Preached. Dr Butler, who was Headmaster of Harrow then, from 1886, Master of Trinity College, Cambridge, was preaching a sermon in the college chapel when he is supposed to have put this misguided rhetorical question. Quoted in Edward Marsh/Christopher Hassall, *Ambrosia and Small Beer* (1964).

BUTLER, Nicholas Murray

American teacher and writer (1862–1947)

4 An expert is one who knows more and more about less and less.

Remark in a Commencement address at Columbia University (of which he was President 1901–45). Quoted in *The Treasury of Humorous Quotations*, ed. by Evan Esar & Nicolas Bentley (1951).

BUTLER, R.A. (later Lord Butler)

English Conservative politician (1902–82)

1 That's Anthony for you – half mad baronet, half beautiful woman.

On Sir Anthony Eden, who had been described as the offspring of a mad baronet and a beautiful woman. Untraced quotation in David Carlton, *Anthony Eden* (1981).

2 The best Prime Minister we have.

In December 1955, Butler, passed over (not for the last time) for the Conservative Party leadership, was confronted by a Press Association reporter just as he was about to board an aircraft at London Airport. Criticism was growing over the performance of Anthony Eden, the Prime Minister selected in preference to him. The reporter asked, 'Mr Butler, would you say that this is the best Prime Minister we have?' Butler's 'hurried assent' to this 'well-meant but meaningless proposition' was converted into the above statement. 'I do not think it did Anthony any good. It did not do me any good either' (*The Art of the Possible*, 1971). In due course, Butler himself became known as 'the best Prime Minister we *never had*'.

3 Politics is the art of the possible.

Butler's memoirs entitled *The Art of the Possible* (1971) caused him to be credited with this view. However, in the preface to the paperback edition (1973) he pointed out that the thought appeared first to have been advanced in modern times by Bismarck in 1866–7 (in conversation with Meyer von Waldeck: '*Die Politik ist keine exakte Wissenschaft*'). Others who had touched on the idea included Cavour, Salvador de Madriaga, Pindar and Camus. To these might be added J.K. Galbraith's rebuttal: 'Politics is not the art of the possible. It consists in choosing between the disastrous and the unpalatable' (letter to President Kennedy, March 1962, quoted in *Ambassador's Journal*, 1969).

4 I think the Prime Minister has to be a butcher, and know the joints. That is perhaps where I have been not quite competent in knowing the ways that you cut up a carcass.

Interviewed on BBC TV by Kenneth Harris (transcript in *The Listener*, 28 June 1966). Possibly alluding to GLADSTONE 263:6.

BUTLER, Samuel

English author (1835–1902)

5 Dusty, cobweb-covered, maimed, and set at naught,
Beauty crieth in an attic, and no man regardeth.
O God! O Montreal!

'Psalm of Montreal' (1878). This poem arose from an incident in which a discobolus (a statue of a discus-thrower) in the Montreal Museum of Natural History was banished from public view. When asked why, a custodian replied that such things were 'rather vulgar'. Butler concluded that Montreal's inhabitants were as yet too busy with commerce to care greatly about the masterpieces of old Greek art.

6 It was very good of God to let Carlyle and Mrs Carlyle marry one another and so make only two people miserable instead of four, besides being very amusing.

Letter to Miss E.M.A. Savage (21 November 1884). In my very first quotation book I mistakenly attributed to Tennyson a view on the marriage of Thomas and Jane Carlyle. When it was suggested that the marriage had been a mistake – because with anyone but each other they might have been perfectly happy – I said that Tennyson had opined: 'I totally disagree with you. By any other arrangement *four* people would have been unhappy instead of *two*.' The remark should have been credited to Butler. My inaccurate version was taken up by *The Faber Book of Anecdotes* (1985).

7 It is bad enough to see one's own good things fathered on other people, but it is worse to have other people's rubbish fathered upon oneself.

Notebooks (*c.*1890). The perils of quoting and being worthy of quotation.

8 The little Strangs say the 'good words,' as they call them, before going to bed, aloud and at their father's knee, or rather in the pit of his stomach. One of them was lately heard to say "Forgive us our Christmasses, as we forgive them that Christmas against us".'

Ib. The true origin of this child's saying, occasionally ascribed elsewhere.

9 Greater luck hath no man than this, that he lay down his wife at the right moment.

Ib. Compare BIBLE 103:2.

1 'Tis better to have loved and lost than never to have lost at all.

The Way of All Flesh, Chap. 77 (1903). *Compare* TENNYSON 528:9.

2 Have you brought the cheque book, Alfred?

Butler, though dying, was engaged in the purchase of the freehold of a house in Hampstead. To Alfred Emery Cathie, his clerk, 'servant and friend', he said, 'Have you brought the cheque book, Alfred?' Butler took off his spectacles and put them down on the table. 'I don't want them any more,' he said, his head fell back, and he died (source: Philip Henderson, *Samuel Butler: the Incarnate Bachelor*, 1953.)

See also BELL 81:9.

BY ROCKET TO THE MOON

German film 1928. Directed by Fritz Lang (1890–1976).

3 Five – four – three – two – one.

It is said that the backward countdown to a rocket launch was first thought of by Lang. He considered it would make things more suspenseful if the count was reversed – 5–4–3–2–1 – so, in *By Rocket to the Moon* (sometimes known as *Frau im Mond* or 'The Woman in the Moon', from the German title) he established the routine for future real-life space shots.

BYRON, Lord

English poet (1788–1824)

4 When some proud Son of Man returns to
Earth,
Unknown to Glory, but upheld by Birth,
The sculptor's art exhausts the pomp of woe,
And storied urns record who rests below:
When all is done, upon the Tomb is seen,
Not what he was, but what he should have
been
... Ye! who perchance behold this simple urn,
Pass on – it honours none you wish to mourn:
To mark a friend's remains these stones arise;
I never knew but one – and here he lies.

On the memorial to Boatswain, his beloved Newfoundland dog, buried in the gardens of Newstead Abbey, Nottinghamshire (poem dated 30 November 1808). The poet at one time intended to be buried in the same vault as the dog.

5 Near this Spot are deposited the Remains of one who possessed Beauty without Vanity, Strength without Insolence, Courage without Ferocity, and all the Virtues of Man without his Vices. This praise, which would be unmeaning Flattery, if inscribed over human Ashes, is but a just Tribute to the Memory of *BOATSWAIN*, a *DOG* who was born in *Newfoundland*, May 1803, and died at *Newstead*, Nov. 18, 1808.

The main inscription on the memorial to Boatswain, once attributed to Byron himself, is now thought to have been written by John Cam Hobhouse, his close friend.

6 A man must serve his time to every trade
Save censure – critics all are ready made.
Take hackneyed jokes from Miller, got by rote,
With just enough of learning to misquote.

English Bards and Scotch Reviewers, l. 63 (1809). Joe Miller (1684–1738) lent his name (posthumously and unwittingly) to a book of old jokes compiled by John Mottley and called *Joe Miller's Jest-Book*. Accordingly, a 'Joe Miller' became the term for an old joke, as though it had come from the Mottley collection.

7 I awoke one morning and found myself famous.

On the success of the first two cantos of *Childe Harold* in 1812. Quoted in Thomas Moore, *The Letters and Journals of Lord Byron* (1830).

8 When one subtracts from life infancy (which is vegetation), – sleep, eating, and swilling – buttoning and unbuttoning – how much remains of downright existence? The summer of a dormouse.

Journal (7 December 1813). 'If I ever write an autobiography, Byron has found me the title' – Kenneth Tynan, letter of 17 November 1972. Hence, *The Summer of a Dormouse*, title of a novel (1967) by Monica Stirling. *ODQ* (1992) has 'all this buttoning and unbuttoning' from an anonymous '18th-century suicide note'.

9 I will keep no further journal ... to prevent me returning, like a dog, to the vomit of memory.

Ib. (19 April 1814). He did not, of course, keep to this. Compare: 'To write a diary every day is like returning to one's own vomit' – Enoch Powell, interview in *The Sunday Times* (6 November 1977). (The image of a dog returning to its vomit is biblical in origin: *see* BIBLE 96:3 and 105:9.)

1 The Assyrian came down like the wolf on the fold.

The Destruction of Sennacherib, St. 1 (1815). Byron based this poem on 2 Chronicles 32 and 2 Kings 19, where Sennacherib, king of Assyria, gets his comeuppance for besieging Jersualem in the manner so described in this line.

2 I remember a methodist preacher who on perceiving a profane grin on the faces of part of his congregation – exclaimed 'no *hopes* for *them* as *laughs*'.

Letter to Augusta Leigh (19 December 1816). In a note to *Hints from Horace*, Byron gave the name of the preacher as John Stickles.

3 So, we'll go no more a-roving
So late into the night,
Though the heart be still as loving,
And the moon be still as bright.

Poem (written in 1817). The second line is often misquoted as 'so far into the night.'

4 There was a sound of revelry by night.

Childe Harold's Pilgrimage, Canto 3, St. 11 (1818). Referring to the Duchess of Richmond's ball in Brussels on the night before the Battle of Waterloo (1815).

5 On with the dance! let joy be unconfined;
No sleep till morn, when Youth and Pleasure meet
Tho chase the glowing hours with flying feet.

Ib., Canto 3, St. 12. Hence, from *The Independent* (13 September 1996): 'Mr Kenyon will take a more relaxed attitude to the atmosphere of the last night [of the Proms] than his predecessor, who last year forbade "extraneous" noises. Mr Kenyon said: "I am a 'let joy be unconfined' man myself".'

6 Now Barabbas was a publisher.

The story has it that when John Murray, Byron's publisher, sent the poet a copy of the Bible in return for a favour, Byron sent it back with the words 'Now Barabbas was a robber' (St John 18:40, *see* BIBLE 103:4) altered to, 'Now Barabbas was a publisher ...' This story was included in Kazlitt Arvine's *Cyclopedia of Anecdotes of Literature and the Fine Arts* published in Boston, Massachusetts, in 1851. In 1981, the then head of the firm, John G. (Jock) Murray, told me that those involved were in fact the poet Coleridge and *his* publishers, Longmans. But when I asked for evidence in 1988, he could say only that, 'I have satisfied myself that it was not Byron'. The copy of Byron's Bible which exists has no such comment in it. He also drew my attention to the fact that in Byron's day publishers were more usually called booksellers.

Mencken, on the other hand, gave Thomas Campbell (1777–1844) as the probable perpetrator, so did Benham, and so did Samuel Smiles in *A Publisher and his Friends: Memoir and Correspondence of the late John Murray*, Vol. 1, Chap. 14 (1891). Certainly, Campbell seems to have taken the required attitude. At a literary dinner he once toasted Napoleon with the words: 'We must not forget that he once shot a bookseller' (quoted in G.O. Trevelyan, *The Life and Letters of Lord Macaulay*, 1876 – diary entry for 12 December 1848).

7 'Whom the gods love die young' was said of yore.

Don Juan, Canto 4, St. 12 (1819–24). Indeed, Menander the Greek and Plautus said it in times BC. *Whom the Gods Love* was the title of a film (UK, 1936) about Mozart. Related to this saying is what Euripides and other classical authors put in the form: 'Whom the Gods wish to destroy, they first make mad.' Sophocles in *Antigone* (*c.*450BC) quotes as a proverb: 'Whom Jupiter would destroy, he first makes mad.' *See* CONNOLLY 181:2.

8 There is a tide in the affairs of women,
Which, taken at the flood, leads – God knows where.

Ib. Canto 6, St. 2. *See* SHAKESPEARE 486:12.

9 Now Hatred is by far the longest pleasure;
Men love in haste, but they detest at leisure.

Ib. Canto 13, St. 6. Hence, the title of a novel *The Longest Pleasure* (1986) by Anne Mather.

10 Posterity will ne'er survey
A nobler grave than this.
Here lie the bones of Castlereagh.
Stop, Traveller ———.

'Epitaph' (1821). Byron wrote this epitaph on Viscount Castlereagh (1769–1822) apparently the year *before* the Foreign Secretary's death by suicide. Castlereagh is actually buried in Westminster Abbey and attracted the poet's enmity either because Byron supported Napoleon or on account of Castlereagh's assumed role in the Peterloo massacre of 1819 (which also inspired SHELLEY 501:7). In any case, the statesman was singularly unpopular: it is said that a great cheer went up when his coffin was carried into Westminster Abbey.

See also BURKE 130:7.

C

CAESAR, Julius

Roman general and politician (c.100–44BC)

1 Caesar's wife must be above suspicion.

It was Julius Caesar *himself* who said this of his wife Pompeia when he divorced her in 62BC. In North's translation of Plutarch's *Lives* – which is how the saying came into English in 1570 – Caesar is quoted thus: 'I will not, sayd he, that my wife be so much as suspected.' Pompeia was Caesar's second wife. According to Suetonius, in 61BC she took part in the women-only rites of the Feast of the Great Goddess. But it was rumoured that a profligate called Publius Clodius attended wearing women's clothes and that he had committed adultery with Pompeia. Caesar divorced Pompeia and at the subsequent inquiry into the desecration when asked why he had done so, he gave this response. He later married Calpurnia.

An example of the phrase in use occurs in Lord Chesterfield's letters (published 1774): 'Your moral character must be not only pure, but, like Caesar's wife, unsuspected.' This should not be confused with what a newly elected mayor (quoted by G.W.E. Russell in *Collections and Recollections*, 1898) once said. During his year of office, he said, he felt he should lay aside all his political prepossessions and be, like Caesar's wife, 'all things to all men'.

2 *Iacta alea est.*
The die is cast.

What Julius Caesar is supposed to have said when he crossed the Rubicon (a small stream on the east coast of northern Italy), marking the start of the war with Pompey (49BC). The stream marked the southern boundary of Cisalpine Gaul and crossing it meant the fateful decision had been made and there was no turning back. (Hence, the expression, 'to cross the Rubicon'.) Reported by Suetonius in *Lives of the Caesars*. Originally spoken in Greek, not Latin. The expression has been known in English since at least 1634. Here 'die' is the singular of 'dice'.

3 *Veni, vidi, vici.*
I came, I saw, I conquered.

According to Suetonius, *Lives of the Caesars*, this was an inscription displayed in Latin after Caesar's triumph over Pontus (a part of modern Turkey) in 47BC – a campaign that lasted only five days. Plutarch states that it was written in a letter by Caesar, announcing the victory of Zela (in Asia Minor), which concluded the Pontic (Black Sea) campaign. In North's 1579 translation of Plutarch, it says: 'Julius Caesar fought a great battle with King Pharnaces and because he would advertise one of his friends of the suddenness of this victory, he only wrote three words unto Anicius at Rome: *Veni, Vidi, Vici*: to wit, I came, saw, and overcame. These three words ending all with like sound and letters in the Latin, have a certain short grace, more pleasant to the ear, than can well be expressed in any other tongue.' Shakespeare alludes to Caesar's 'thrasonical brag' in four plays, including *Love's Labour's Lost* (IV.i.68) and *As You Like It* (V.ii.30).

4 *Et tu, Brute?*
And you, Brutus?

Julius Caesar's supposed dying words to Brutus, one of his assassins in 44BC, were made famous through Shakespeare's use of the Latin in the form, '*Et tu, Brute?* – Then fall Caesar!' in the play *Julius Caesar* (III.i.77). The Latin words are not found in any classical source, but they do occur in English drama just before Shakespeare. *The True Tragedie of Richard Duke of Yorke* (printed in 1595) has 'Et tu, Brute, wilt thou stab Caesar too?' The origin of the phrase lies probably in Suetonius's account of the assassination, in which Caesar is made to say in *Greek*, 'And thou, my son.' The 'son' has been taken literally, because, according to Suetonius, Caesar had had an intrigue with Brutus's mother and looked upon Brutus as his likely son.

Chips Channon wrote in his diary (7 April 1939): 'The Italians are occupying Albania ... "Et tu Benito?" – for Mussolini had only recently assured us that he had no territorial claims whatsoever on Albania.'

CAGNEY, James

American actor (1899–1986)

1 You dirty rat!

Although impersonators of James Cagney always have him saying 'You dirty rat!' it may be that he never said it like that himself. However, in Joan Wyndham's wartime diaries (*Love Lessons*, 1985) her entry for 1 October 1940 begins: 'Double bill at the Forum with Rupert. *Elizabeth and Essex*, and a gangster film where somebody actually *did* say "Stool on me would ya, ya doity rat!"' What film could this have been? Note her surprise that the line was uttered at all.

The nearest Cagney seems to have got to uttering the phrase with which he is most associated was in the films *Blonde Crazy* (1931) (where he says, 'You dirty, double-crossing rat') and *Taxi* (1931) (where he says, 'Come out and take it, you dirty yellow-bellied rat, or I'll give it to you through the door').

In a speech to an American Film Institute banquet on 13 March 1974, Cagney said to Frank Gorshin, a well-known impersonator: 'Oh, Frankie, just in passing: I never said [in any film] "Mmm, you dirty rat!" What I actually did say was "Judy! Judy! Judy!"' (*See* GRANT 270:2.)

See also WHITE HEAT 566:1.

CAINE, Michael

English actor (1933–)

2 Not many people know that.

It is rare for a personal catchphrase to catch on (as opposed to phrases in entertainment, films and advertising that are engineered to do so). But it has certainly been the case with the one that will always be associated with Caine. Peter Sellers started the whole thing off when he appeared on BBC TV's *Parkinson* show on 28 October 1972. The edition in question was subsequently released on disc ('Michael Parkinson Meets the Goons'), thus enabling confirmation of what Sellers said: '"Not many people know that" ... this is my Michael Caine impression ... You see Mike's always quoting from *The Guinness Book of Records*. At the drop of a hat he'll trot one out. "Did you know that it takes a man in a tweed suit five and a half seconds to fall from the top of Big Ben to the ground? Now there's not many people know that"!'

It was not until 1981–2 that the remark really caught on. Caine was given the line to say as an in-joke (in the character of an inebriated university lecturer) in the film *Educating Rita* (1983), and he put his name to a book of trivial facts for charity with the slight variant *Not a Lot of People Know That*! in 1984.

3 Been there, done that.

'Michael Caine was once asked if he had a motto: "Yeah – Been There, Done That. It'll certainly be on my tombstone. It'll just say, "Been There, Done That"' – quoted in Elaine Gallagher *et al*, *Candidly Caine* (1990). This is what might be called a T-shirt motto and certainly not original to Caine. Ian Dury used the phrase 'been there' in the song 'Laughter' (*The Ian Dury Songbook*, 1979) to indicate that a seduction has been accomplished, but the motto isn't solely restricted to sex. It can cover all human activity. About 1989 there were T-shirts for jaded travellers with the words: 'Been there, done that, got the T-shirt.'

See also NAUGHTON 407:8.

CALLAGHAN, James (later Lord Callaghan)

British Labour Prime Minister (1912–)

4 We say that what Britain needs is a new Social Contract. That is what this document is all about.

Referring to *Labour's Programme* (1972). While it was in Opposition from 1970–4, the British Labour Party developed the idea of a social 'compact' between government and trades unions. In return for certain 'social' measures, like price subsidies, the unions would moderate their wage demands. This, in turn, meant that unpopular voluntary or statutory incomes policies could be abandoned. The use of the words 'social contract' differed from that of Rousseau, Hobbes and Locke in that they were thinking in terms of a compact between a government and a whole people, rather than with just one section of it.

Coinage of the term 'social contract', in this specific sense, has been credited to Dennis (later Lord) Lyons (d.1978), a public relations consultant who advised the Labour Party in five general elections. Callaghan used the phrase at the Labour Party Conference on 2 October 1972. Anthony Wedgwood Benn had used the term in a 1970 Fabian pamphlet, *The New Politics*. (Jean-Jacques Rousseau's *Du contrat social* was published in 1762.)

1 *Bid ben, bid bont.*
He who commands, must be a bridge.

When Callaghan became Prime Minister in 1976, his first public engagement was at a luncheon in Cardiff before opening a new bridge over the River Taff. He said that he was to be guided by this Welsh proverb. 'I am to be a bridge between the Government and people, a bridge that links both together so that there is an easy understanding between us.' On 10 April 1976, *The Times* in its report of the speech managed to make a nonsense of the Welsh. Subsequently, in 1983, when George Thomas, former Speaker of the House of Commons, became Viscount Tonypandy, he took the words for his motto. They come indirectly from *The Mabinogion*, the collection of ancient Welsh folk stories, in which the tale is told of a king, leading an invasion of Ireland, who came to a river without a bridge. '"There is none," said he, "save that he who is chief, let him be a bridge. I will myself be a bridge." And then was that saying first uttered, and it is still used as a proverb. And then, after he had lain himself down across the river, hurdles were placed upon him, and his hosts passed through over him.' The Welsh form here is, apparently, '*A fo ben, bid bont*' – i.e., 'If he *be* a chief, let him be a bridge.'

2 Now, now, little lady, you don't want to believe all those things you read in the newspaper about crisis and upheavals, and the end of civilization as we know it. Dearie me, not at all.

This example of Callaghan's patronizing style when dealing, as Prime Minister, with the then Leader of the Opposition, Margaret Thatcher, was quoted in all seriousness by *Newsweek* Magazine. It was, in fact, a parody written by John O'Sullivan that had appeared in *The Daily Telegraph* (10 June 1976).

3 A great debate.

In a speech at Ruskin College, Oxford, in October 1976, Callaghan called for a 'national debate' on education policy, which also became known as a 'Great Debate'. Politicians like to apply the dignifying label 'great debate' to any period of discussion over policy. The rhyming phrase goes back to 1601, at least. 'The Conservative leaders now decided to bring a vote of no confidence against the Government [on its Defence Programme], and on February 15 [1951] the "Great Debate" as it was known in Tory circles was opened, by Churchill himself' (Martin Gilbert, *Never Despair*, 1988). From BBC TV, *Monty Python's Flying Circus* (4 January 1973): '*Stern music as the lights come on.* SUPERIMPOSED CAPTIONS: 'THE GREAT DEBATE' 'NUMBER 31' 'TV4 OR NOT TV4'.

4 A lie travels round the world while truth is putting on her boots.

In November 1976, Callaghan said in the House of Commons: 'A lie can be halfway round the world before the truth has got its boots on.' From time to time since, this has been credited to him as an original saying (as by *PDMQ*, 1980 and *ODMQ*, 1991). To Mark Twain has been attributed, 'A lie can travel half way round the world while the truth is putting on its shoes' – though this is probably no more than another example of the rule, 'When in doubt, say Mark Twain said it'.

A more certain user of the expression was C.H. Spurgeon (1834–92), the noted nineteenth-century Baptist preacher, though he even cited it as an 'old proverb' when saying: 'A lie will go round the world while truth is pulling its boots on' (*Gems from Spurgeon*, 1859). Benham (1948) suggests, however, that 'A lie travels round the world while Truth is putting on her boots' is 'probably [Spurgeon's] own' and ascribes it to his *John Ploughman's Almanack*.

The *Dictionary of American Proverbs* (1992) gives the variations: 'A lie can go around the world and back while the truth is lacing up its boots', 'A lie can travel round the world while the truth is tieing up its shoestrings', 'A lie can go a mile before truth can put its boots on' and 'A lie will travel a mile while truth is putting on its boots'.

5 Either back us or sack us.

Speech, Labour Party Conference (5 October 1977). This became a format phrase in British politics, usually suggested as something spoken by an individual rather than a whole government. From *The Independent* (25 October 1989): 'The Chancellor of the Exchequer was last night challenged by the Opposition to stand up to the Prime Minister, say "Back me or sack me" and end confusion over who is running the economy ... "It is time to say (to the Prime Minister) either back me or sack me" ... Mr Smith said.'

6 There I was waiting at the church ...

As speculation mounted over an October general election in 1978, Callaghan teased the Labour Party Conference in September by saying: 'The commentators have fixed the month for me, they've chosen the date and the day, but I advise them, "Don't count your chickens before they're hatched." Remember what happened to Marie Lloyd. She fixed the day and the date, and then she told us what 'appened. As far as I remember it went like this: "There was I, waiting at the church ... All at once, he sent me round a note. Here's the very note. This is what he wrote. "Can't get away to marry you today. My wife won't let me".'

Unfortunately, it wasn't Marie Lloyd's song. It was Vesta Victoria's. ('Waiting at the Church' had words by Fred W. Leigh, d.1924, and music by Henry W. Pether, d.1925). In the end, Callaghan did not call an election until the following May, by which time the 'winter of discontent' had undermined his chances of re-election. Given his record on misquotations, perhaps this was appropriate punishment.

1 Crisis, what crisis?

Callaghan may be said to have been eased out of office by a phrase he did not (precisely) speak. Returning from a sunny summit meeting in Guadeloupe to Britain's 'winter of discontent' on 10 January 1979, he was asked by a journalist at a London airport press conference (and I have been back to the original tapes to verify this): 'What is your general approach and view of the mounting chaos in the country at the moment?' Callaghan replied: 'Well, that's a judgement that you are making. I promise you that if you look at it from the outside (and perhaps you are taking rather a parochial view), I don't think that other people in the world would share the view that there is mounting chaos.'

Next day, *The Sun* carried the headline: 'Crisis? What crisis?' Callaghan lost the May 1979 general election. The editor of *The Sun* was given a knighthood by the incoming Prime Minister.

Some people insist on recalling that Callaghan said something much more like 'Crisis? What crisis?' on the TV news. When told that these words do not survive on film, these people begin to talk about conspiracy theories. But the impression he created was a strong one. In *The Diaries of Kenneth Williams* (1993), the comedian noted in his entry for 10 January (the day of Callaghan's return and not of the *Sun* headline, which he would not have seen anyway): 'Saw the news. Callaghan arrived back from Guadeloupe saying, "There is no chaos" which is a euphemistic way of talking about the lorry drivers ruining all production and work in the entire country, but one admires his phlegm.'

2 The minority parties have walked into a trap ... It is the first time in recorded history that turkeys have been known to vote for an early Christmas.

Speech, House of Commons (28 March 1979), from a recording rather than *Hansard*. During a debate which ended in a no confidence motion that sank his government and also led to a General Election defeat the next month, Callaghan derided the Liberal Party and the Scottish National Party in these terms. He described the phrase as a 'joke going about the House'.

See also DRYDEN 215:4.

CAMBRONNE, Baron Pierre de

French general (1770–1842)

3 *Merde!*

At the Battle of Waterloo in 1815, Cambronne, the commander of Napoleon's Old or Imperial Guard is *supposed* to have declined a British request for him to surrender with the words, '*La garde meurt mais ne se rend jamais/pas* [The Guards die but never/do not surrender].' However, it is quite likely that what he said, in fact, was, '*Merde! La garde meurt* ... [Shit! The Guards die ...]' At a banquet in 1835 Cambronne specifically denied saying the more polite version. That may have been invented for him by Rougemont in a newspaper, *L'Indépendent*.

In consequence of all this, *merde* is sometimes known in France as *le mot de Cambronne*, a useful euphemism when needed. Unfortunately for Cambronne, the words he denied saying were put on his statue in Nantes, his hometown.

CAMERON, James

Scottish journalist (1911–85)

4 I like the evening in India, the one magic moment when the sun balances on the rim of the world, and the hush descends, and ten thousand civil servants drift homeward on a river of bicycles, brooding on the Lord Krishna and the cost of living.

Writing in the *News Chronicle* in 1957 (included in *What a Way To Run the Tribe*, 1968).

CAMPBELL, Mrs Patrick

English actress (1865–1940)

5 It doesn't matter what you do, as long as you don't do it in the street and frighten the horses.

Although Ted Morgan's biography of Somerset Maugham (1980) actually attributes this to King Edward VII on the subject of the double standard of sexual morality, it is generally accepted as having been said by Mrs Pat. But what gave rise to the remark? Another version, as in Daphne Fielding's *The Duchess of Jermyn Street* (1964), is: 'It doesn't matter what you do *in the bedroom* as long as you don't do it in the street and frighten the horses.' Yet another (as in the *ODQ*, 1979) is, 'I don't mind where people *make love*, so long as they ...'

Margot Peters, in her otherwise painstakingly footnoted biography *Mrs Pat* (1984), gives no reason for stating her belief that it was 'when told of a *homosexual affair* between actors' that the actress uttered: 'I don't care what people do, as long as they don't do it in the street and frighten the horses.'

1 Do you know why God withheld the sense of humour from women? That we may love you instead of laughing at you.

To a man. Quoted in Leslie Robert Missen, *Quotable Anecdotes* (1966). As 'Women were born without a sense of humour – so they could love men, not laugh at them', quoted from Amsterdam in *Graffiti 2* (1980).

2 The deep, deep peace of the double-bed after the hurly-burly of the chaise longue.

On marriage. Quoted in Alexander Woollcott, 'The First Mrs Tanqueray', *While Rome Burns* (1934).

3 My Stella used to sing a song which I told her was silly, and she declared was funny – your last letter reminds me more of it than others –

He's mad, mad, mad,
He's clean gone off his nut
He cleans his boots with strawberry jam
He eats his hat whenever he can
He's mad, mad, mad.

Letter to Bernard Shaw (29 July 1912), included in *Bernard Shaw and Mrs Patrick Campbell: Their Correspondence* (1952). Stella was her daughter. Hence, *Boots With Strawberry Jam*, title of a musical (1968) with book and lyrics by Benny Green based on the correspondence.

4 You are a terrible man, Mr. Shaw. One day you'll eat a beefsteak and then God help all women.

On the grounds that he was a vegetarian. Quoted in Arnold Bennett, *The Journals* (18 June 1919). Alexander Woollcott, *While Rome Burns* (1934) has a slightly different version: 'Some day you'll eat a pork chop, Joey, and then God help all women.'

5 'Quoth the raven ...'

After a dull weekend, Mrs Pat took pen in hand and wrote this in the hostess's elaborate visitor's book. Also ascribed to John Barrymore. This version is from Bennett Cerf, *Shake Well Before Using* (1948). *See* POE 432:7.

CAMPBELL, Thomas

Scottish poet (1777–1844)

6 To live in hearts we leave behind
Is not to die.

'Hallowed Ground' (1825). This is probably the original of a sentiment frequently to be found on gravestones – for example, on that of RAF Aircraftsman 1st Class G.C.E. Hodges, who was killed in the Second World War on 18 September 1944, aged forty-two, and lies in Brookwood Military Cemetery, Surrey, it has: 'TO LIVE IN THE HEARTS/OF THOSE WE LOVE/IS NOT TO DIE.' Another variation is: 'He lives for ever in the hearts of those who loved him.'

7 What though my wingèd hours of bliss have been,
Like angel-visits, few and far between?

The Pleasures of Hope, 2, l. 378 (1799). 'Our semi-tautological phrase "few and far between" is a corrupt formulation by the nineteenth-century Scottish poet Thomas Campbell of an old folk saying to the effect that the visits of angels to our world are "brief and far between"' – *The Observer* (26 June 1988). Campbell, in any case, was echoing what the Scottish poet Robert Blair had written in *The Grave* (1743): 'Its Visits,/Like those of Angels, short, and far between.' William Hazlitt pointed this out.

The phrase 'few and far between' had existed before this in a different context. R. Verney wrote a letter in about July 1668 saying 'Hedges are few and between' (*Memoirs of the Verney Family*, IV.iii.89).

8 At last, when blind and seeming dumb,
He scolded, laughed, and spoke no more,
A Spanish stranger chanced to come
To Mulla's shore;

He hailed the bird in Spanish speech;
The bird in Spanish speech replied,
Flapped round his cage with joyous screech,
Dropt down, and died.

'The Parrot' (1840). The poem concerns a 'parrot from the Spanish Main' which ends up on the Island of Mull, in Scotland, and grows old. It refuses to speak until a sailor arrives from foreign parts, and then dies.

9 On Linden, when the sun was low,
All bloodless lay the untrodden snow,
And dark as winter was the flow
Of Iser, rolling rapidly.

'Hohenlinden' (1802). The fourth line features in several

anecdotes. In 1877, a writer to the New York *World* referred to a lost letter of John Keats to his brother George in which Keats reported that he had heard Charles Lamb say this to Thomas Campbell, having fallen downstairs (*Notes and Queries*, Vol. 206), though the writer himself did not believe in the existence of this letter. W.W. Keen, the American surgeon (1837–1932), included in his memoirs (1915–17) the anecdote of the learned butler who, as he was falling downstairs, replied to his master's inquiry as to what was going on: ''Tis I, sir, rolling rapidly.' A learned butler, indeed, to pun in such circumstances.

See also BYRON 139:6.

CAMUS, Albert

French novelist (1913–60)

1 Alas! after a certain age every man is responsible for the face he has.

The Fall (1956). *Compare* ORWELL 420:7.

CANNING, George

British Tory Prime Minister (1770–1827)

2 I called the New World into existence, to redress the balance of the old.

In a speech in the House of Commons on the affairs of Portugal (12 December 1826), Canning sought to justify his foreign policy in the face of French intervention to suppress Spanish liberal revolts. He said: 'If France occupied Spain, it was necessary ... to avoid the consequences of the occupation ... I sought materials for compensation in another hemisphere. Contemplating Spain as our ancestors had known her, I resolved that if France had Spain, it should not be Spain with the Indies.' *See also* ANONYMOUS 30:6.

CANTONA, Eric

French footballer (1966–)

3 When the seagulls follow the trawler, it is because they think sardines will be thrown into the sea.

Quoted in *The Observer* (2 April 1995). When a jail term for kicking a spectator was commuted to community service, Cantona said only this at a press conference and then walked out of it. He was referring to the undue interest paid in him by journalists. Compare what has been credited to Malcolm Muggeridge: 'Journalists follow authority as sharks follow a liner, dining on the scraps that are thrown overboard' (unverified); and to George Bernard Shaw: 'To the born editor, news is great fun, even as the capsizing of a boat in Sydney Harbour is great fun for the sharks' (in a letter to Kingsley Martin, quoted by Martin in a 1956 edition of Granada TV *What The Papers Say* and re-quoted in *The Listener*, 4 April 1976).

CANUTE

King of England, Norway and Denmark (c.995–1035)

4 Know all inhabitants of earth, that vain and trivial is the power of kings nor is anyone worthy of the name of king save Him whose nod heaven and earth and sea obey under laws eternal.

The name of Canute (or Knute or Cnut or Knut) is often evoked in a mistaken fashion. The tale is told of his having his throne carried down to the water's edge, his instructing the waves to go away from him and his failure thereat. The image is summoned up when one wants to portray pointless resistance to an idea, or clinging to an untenable position. However, it is wrong to paint Canute as a fool. After all, the whole point of the story was that Canute carried out the demonstration in order to show his courtiers that there were limits to his power. The original anecdote, pointing the correct moral, first appears in Henry of Huntingdon's *Historia Anglorum*, a twelfth-century manuscript, from which the above quotation is taken.

CAPOTE, Truman

American writer (1924–84)

5 That's not writing, that's typing.

On Jack Kerouac, attributed remark (1959). In Gerald Clarke, *Capote* (1988), '[It] isn't writing at all – it's typing' is given as his view of Beat Generation writers in general.

CARLYLE, Thomas

Scottish historian and philosopher (1795–1881)

6 The soul politic.

In contrast to the 'body politic' (the nation in its corporate character, the state), this phrase was used by Margaret Thatcher in speeches in the 1980s. But Carlyle had anticipated her in *Signs of the Times* (1829).

1 Silence is golden.

This encouragement to silence is from the German: '*Sprechen ist silbern, Schweigen ist golden*' and best known in Carlyle's English translation, 'Speech is silver(n), silence is golden' (*Fraser's Magazine*, June 1834). The original is sometimes given in the form, '*Reden ist Silber, Schweigen ist Gold*' (*Reden* = 'to speak'). Proverb research points to an Arab origin.

2 The whiff of grapeshot can, if needful, become a blast and tempest.

History of the French Revolution, Vol. 1, Bk 5, Chap. 3 (1837). Carlyle also uses the phrase 'whiff of grapeshot' as a chapter title (Vol. 3, Bk 7, Chap. 7) and on one other occasion (apparently quoting Napoleon). The expression refers to the ease with which Bonaparte and the artillery dispersed the Paris insurrection of the Vendémiaire in 1795, by firing at or over it.

3 The most terrified man in Paris or France is ... seagreen Robespierre ... 'A Republic?' said the Seagreen, with one of his dry husky *un*sportful laughs, 'What is that?' O seagreen Incorruptible, thou shalt see!

Ib., Vol. 2, Bk 5, Chap. 4. Accordingly, 'the seagreen incorruptible' became a nickname of Robespierre, the French revolutionary leader who established the Reign of Terror (1793–4) but was executed in it himself. There was no connection between Robespierre's greenness and his incorruptibility. He was green because of poor digestion, and he was incorruptible because he was a fanatic.

4 It were a real increase of human happiness, could all young men from the age of nineteen be covered under barrels, or rendered otherwise invisible; and there left to follow their lawful studies and callings; till they emerged, sadder and wiser, at the age of twenty-five.

A paean to youth from *Sartor Resartus* (1838).

5 Captains of industry.

Past and Present (1843). The apparent origin of this well-known phrase.

6 Genius is an infinite capacity for taking pains.

Carlyle did not quite say this in his life of *Frederick the Great* (1858–65) but, rather, 'Genius ... which means transcendent capacity of taking trouble, first of all'. Disraeli, Samuel Butler and Leslie Stephen are among those credited with the idea or simply with using it. By 1870, Jane Ellice Hopkins in *Work Amongst Working Men* was saying, 'Gift, like genius, I often think only means an infinite capacity for taking pains'.

James Agate in *Ego 6* (1944) calls Carlyle's remark, 'The most misleading pronouncement ever made by a great man' and suggests that a better definition of genius would be: 'That quality in a man which enables him to do things that other people cannot do, and without taking pains.' Indeed, it can be argued that 'taking pains' has nothing to do with genius at all. Mental, spiritual and physical energy may have more to do with it. *Compare* EDISON 220:5.

7 'Gad! she'd better!'

On hearing that Margaret Fuller said she 'accepted the universe'. Quoted in William James, *Varieties of Religious Experience* (1902).

CARROLL, Lewis (Charles Lutwidge Dodgson)

English writer (1832–98)

8 How doth the little crocodile
Improve his shining tail,
And pour the waters of the Nile
On every golden scale!

Alice's Adventures in Wonderland, Chap. 2 (1865). A parody of 'Against Idleness and Mischief' (1715) by Isaac Watts, which goes:

How doth the little busy bee
  Improve each shining hour,
And gather honey all the day
  From every opening flower!

It appears that Johnny Mercer (1909–76) found the title-lyric of his song 'My Shining Hour' (first sung in the film *The Sky's the Limit*, 1943) in the same place.

9 *Everybody* has won, and *all* must have prizes.

Ib., Chap. 3. The Dodo, at the end of the Caucus-Race. Hence, *All Must Have Prizes*, title of a book (1996) on the British education system by Melanie Phillips.

10 'You are old, father William,' the young man said,
'And your hair has become very white;
And yet you incessantly stand on your head –
Do you think, at your age, it is right?'

Alice's recitation from *ib.*, Chap. 5, is a parody of a much more sober piece – 'The Old Man's Comforts and How He Gained Them' (1799) by Robert Southey:

'You are old, father William,' the young man cried,
'The few locks which are left you are grey;
You are hale, father William, a hearty old man;
Now tell me the reason, I pray.'

1 Speak roughly to your little boy,
And beat him when he sneezes;
He only does it to annoy,
Because he knows it teases.

In *ib.*, Chap. 6. Said to be a parody of G.W. Langford (dates unknown) or David Bates, a mid-nineteenth century Philadelphian: 'Speak gently; it is better far/To rule by love than fear;/... Speak gently to the little child;/Its love be sure to gain ...'

2 She was a little startled by seeing the Cheshire Cat sitting on a bough of a tree a few yards off ... 'Well! I've often seen a cat without a grin,' thought Alice; 'but a grin without a cat! It's the most curious thing I ever saw in all my life!'

Ib. Hence, the expression 'to grin like a Cheshire Cat', meaning 'to smile very broadly'. The 'Cheshire Cat' is most famous from its appearances in *Alice* – where it has the ability to disappear leaving only its grin behind – but the beast had been known since about 1770. Carroll, who was born in Cheshire, probably knew that Cheshire cheeses were at one time moulded in the shape of a grinning cat. From Andrew Roberts, *Eminent Churchillians* (1994): 'British power was slowly disappearing during the Churchillian Era, leaving, like the Cheshire Cat, only a wide smile behind.'

3 Why is a raven like a writing desk?

In *ib.*, Chap. 7, the Hatter poses this riddle at the 'Mad Tea-Party', but Carroll stated positively that there was no answer. Nevertheless, various people have tried to supply one: 'a quill' – what a raven and a writing desk would have had in common in the last century (Christopher Brown of Portswood, Southampton); 'they both begin with the letter R' (Leo Harris); 'because it can produce a few notes, tho they are very flat; and it is never put with the wrong end in front' – these were Lewis Carroll's own possible solutions (1896 edition); 'because the notes for which they are noted are not noted for being musical notes' (Sam Loyd); 'Edgar Allan Poe' – he wrote on both a raven and a writing desk (Sam Loyd); 'because bills and tales (tails) are among their characteristics; because they both stand on their legs; conceal their steels (steals); and ought to be made to shut up' (Sam Loyd); 'because it slopes with a flap' (A. Cyril Pearson); 'because there is a "B" in "both"' (Dr E.V. Rieu). Some of these solutions are included in *The Annotated Alice*, ed. Martin Gardner (1960).

4 Twinkle twinkle little bat!
How I wonder what you're at! ...
Up above the world you fly,
Like a tea-tray in the sky.

The Hatter's song in *ib.* is a parody of Jane Taylor's poem 'The Star' (1806):

Twinkle, twinkle, little star.
How I wonder what you are!
Up above the world so high,
Like a diamond in the sky.

Compare ANONYMOUS 50:9.

5 Oh, 'tis love, 'tis love that makes the world go round.

This is the proverb the Duchess speaks in *ib.*, Chap. 9. W.S. Gilbert in *Iolanthe* (1882) has a song made up of proverbial sayings and includes:

In for a penny, in for a pound –
It's love that makes the world go round.

Ian Bradley in his *Annotated Gilbert and Sullivan* (Vol. 1) notes how a previous commentator wondered if this had to do with the old saying: 'It's drink that makes the world go round', and also finds it in *Our Mutual Friend* by Charles Dickens [published in the same year as *Alice*]. But earlier than these was a French song (published 1851, but recorded as early as 1700):

C'est l'amour, l'amour
Qui fait le monde/À la ronde.

There is an English song, 'Love Makes the World Go Round' by Noel Gay, but that was not written until *c.*1936.

6 Change lobsters again!

From the 'Lobster Quadrille' passage in *ib.*, Chap. 10. Hence, *Change Lobsters and Dance*, the English title of the autobiography (1974) of the film actress Lilli Palmer (called originally *Dicke Lilli, gutes Kind*). Perhaps deemed appropriate because Palmer quite frequently changed her marriage partners. The precise words for the title do not appear in *Alice*, though the instruction 'change lobsters' does.

7 'Will you walk a little faster?' said a whiting to a snail,
'There's a porpoise close behind us, and he's treading on my tail.'

Ib. A parody of 'Will you walk into my parlour ...' in 'The Spider and the Fly'. *See* HOWITT 303:7.

1 'Tis the voice of the Lobster: I heard him declare
You have baked me too brown, I must sugar my hair.

Ib. Alice's attempt to recite *The Sluggard*, an improving poem by Isaac Watts, which actually begins: ''Tis the voice of the sluggard; I heard him complain,/ "You have wak'd me too soon, I must slumber again"'.

2 It *was* a curious dream, dear, certainly; but now run in to your tea: it's getting late.

Ib., Chap. 12. Alice's sister to Alice, at the conclusion of the tale.

3 'Twas brillig, and the slithy toves
Did gyre and gimble in the wabe;
All mimsy were the borogoves,
And the mome raths outgrabe.

Through the Looking-Glass and What Alice Found There, Chap. 1 (1872). This opening stanza of the most famous of nonsense poems first appeared in a private periodical produced by Carroll in 1855. It is a parody of Anglo-Saxon poetry. Carroll gave the meanings of all the words and translated this stanza as: 'It was evening, and the smooth active badgers were scratching and boring holes in the hill-side; all unhappy were the parrots; and the grave turtles squeaked out' (quoted in *The Annotated Alice*, ed. Martin Gardner, 1960).

4 The Jabberwock, with eyes of flame,
Came whiffling through the tulgey wood,
And burbled as it came.

Ib. Carroll subsequently explained the name Jabberwock as meaning 'the result of much excited discussion'; whiffling is not a Carrollian invention but means something like blowing; tulgey (his invention) = thick, dense, dark; burbling, though an established word, was derived, according to Carroll, from an amalgam of 'bleat', 'murmur' and 'warble'.

5 'And hast thou slain the Jabberwock?
Come to my arms, my beamish boy!
O frabjous day! Callooh! Callay!'
He chortled in his joy.

Ib. Beamish (an old word) = shining brightly; frabjous (Carroll's invention) = fair and joyous; chortled (Carroll's invention, surprisingly perhaps) = chuckled and snorted.

6 'The time has come,' the Walrus said,
'To talk of many things:
Of shoes – and ships – and sealing-wax –
Of cabbages and kings.'

Ib., Chap. 4, the 'Walrus and the Carpenter' episode. As a result, the phrase 'cabbages and kings' was taken by the American writer O. Henry for the title of his first collection of short stories published in 1904, and there was a book entitled *Of Kennedys and Kings: Making Sense of the Sixties* by Harris Wofford (1980). It has been the title of more than one TV series, including the ITV version (1979–82) of the radio quiz *Quote ... Unquote*. However, the conjunction of 'cabbages' and 'kings' pre-dates Carroll. In Hesketh Pearson's *Smith of Smiths*, a biography of the Rev. Sydney Smith (1771–1845), he quotes Smith as saying about a certain Mrs George Groce: 'She had innumerable hobbies, among them horticulture and democracy, defined by Sydney as "the most approved methods of growing cabbages and destroying kings".'

7 But answer came there none –
And this was scarcely odd, because
They'd eaten every one.

Ib. 'But answer came there none' is a phrase that also appears in Scott (*The Bridal of Triermain*, 1813) and almost in Shakespeare ('But answer made it none', *Hamlet*, I.ii.215).

8 The rule is, jam tomorrow and jam yesterday – but never jam today.

Ib. Chap. 5. The White Queen wants Alice to be her maid and offers her twopence a week and jam every other day, except that she can never actually have any – it's never jam today. An early version of Catch-22. Nowadays, the phrase is used quite often in connection with the unfulfilled promises of politicians. But did Carroll adopt an older phrase?

Others recall being taught that this was an academic joke. In Latin there are two words meaning 'now': *nunc* and *iam*. The former is used in the present tense, whereas the latter is the correct word for past and future tenses, i.e., yesterday and tomorrow, so it is correct to say *iam* for tomorrow and *iam* for yesterday but never *iam* for today.

9 I sent a message to the fish:
I told them 'This is what I wish.'
The little fishes of the sea,
They sent an answer back to me.
The little fishes' answer was
We cannot do it, Sir, because –.

Ib., Chap. 6. Rhyme spoken by Humpty Dumpty which Alice does not quite understand.

1 He's an Anglo-Saxon Messenger – and those are Anglo-Saxon attitudes.

Ib., Chap. 7. Alice observes the Messenger, 'skipping up and down, and wriggling like an eel, as he came along'. When she expresses surprise, this is the King's explanation. Harry Morgan Ayres in *Carroll's Alice* (1936) suggests that the author may have been spoofing the Anglo-Saxon scholarship of his day.

Hence, *Anglo-Saxon Attitudes*, the title of Angus Wilson's novel (1956) about a historian investigating a possible archaeological forgery.

2 It's as large as life, and twice as natural!

Ib. Haigha says this of Alice. Until *Alice*, the expression was normally 'As large as life and *quite* as natural'.

3 'Friends, Romans and Countrymen, lend me your ears!'
(They were all of them fond of quotations:
So they drank to his health, and they gave him three cheers,
While he served out additional rations.)

The Hunting of the Snark, Fit the Second: The Bellman's Speech (1876). Initially alluding, of course, to SHAKESPEARE 486:9.

4 I am fond of children (except boys).

Letter to Kathleen Eschwege (1879), in Stuart Dodgson Collingwood, *The Life and Letters of Lewis Carroll* (1898). Carroll's fondness for little girls (not least Alice Liddell) has become notorious. Here he seems to be saying he is aware of his predilection.

5 Is all our Life, then, but a dream?

Introductory poem to *Sylvie and Bruno* (1889). In Poets' Corner, Westminster Abbey, Dodgson/Carroll is remembered by a stone (unveiled 17 December 1982) bearing this line. Compare the concluding line of the end-poem to *Through the Looking Glass*: 'Life, what is it but a dream?'

See also BUNN 129:2; SHAWCROSS 500:7.

CARSON, Rachel

American biologist (1907–64)

6 The Silent Spring.

Title of book (1962) – an early flowering of the environmental movement. The book aroused public awareness of the destruction of wildlife and the danger to the food chain caused by the use of dangerous pesticides, as in this passage: 'Over increasingly large areas of the United States, spring now comes unheralded by the return of birds, and the early mornings are strangely silent where once they were filled with the beauty of bird song.'

CARTER, Howard

English archaeologist (1873–1939)

7 As my eyes grew accustomed to the light, details of the room within emerged slowly from the mist, strange animals, statues and gold – everywhere the glint of gold ... Lord Carnarvon, unable to stand the suspense any longer, inquired anxiously, 'Can you see anything?' it was all I could do to get out the words, 'Yes, wonderful things.'

The Tomb of Tut-ankh-Amen (1933). The most exciting archaeological find of the twentieth century was that of the tomb of Tutankhamun in November 1921. Carter, backed by his patron, the 5th Earl of Carnarvon, had been digging fruitlessly for many years in Egypt's Valley of the Kings. Then he hit upon a flight of steps beneath the ruins of old workmen's huts. Carter wired for Carnarvon to join him. Three days of digging were needed to clear the entrance passage. On 26 November another sealed door appeared. It was through the hole which he made in this door that Carter glimpsed the treasure. He described the moment in a thrilling passage.

CARTER, Jimmy

American Democratic 39th President (1924–)

8 Why not the best?

Carter's official slogan, used as the title of a campaign book and song, as he ran for the presidency in 1976, originated with an interview he had had with Admiral Hyman Rickover when applying to join the nuclear submarine programme in 1948. 'Did you do your best [at Naval Academy]?' Rickover asked him. 'No, sir, I didn't *always* do my best,' replied Carter. Rickover stared at him for a moment and then asked: 'Why not?'

9 Jimmy who?

The question was posed when Carter came from nowhere (or at least from the Governorship of Georgia) to challenge Gerald Ford, successfully, for the US Presidency in 1976. It acquired almost the force of a slogan. *Jimmy Who?* was the title of a campaign biography published in 1976.

1 I've looked on a lot of women with lust. I've committed adultery in my heart many times. God recognises I will do this and forgives me.

Interviewed in *Playboy* (November 1976). The American electorate, perceiving a useful working relationship with the Almighty, voted in Carter as their President that same month.

2 He is competent, honest, trustworthy, a man of integrity. Bert, I'm proud of you.

Of Bert Lance (*q.v.*) (1931–), the director of Carter's Office of Management and Budget, as pressure mounted for him to be fired because of his banking activities in 1977. Carter had appointed Lance from the chairmanship of the Calhoun First National Bank in their mutual home state of Georgia, but irregularities in Lance's conduct were alleged and, after prolonged hearings, he was forced to resign. He was found not guilty on a list of charges but paid a fine to avoid a retrial on the remaining ones.

3 Hawae the lads!

On a visit to the northeast of England in 1977, President Carter (no doubt put up to it by the British Prime Minister, James Callaghan) used the traditional Geordie greeting when addressing a crowd. It means something like 'Come on, lads!' – a cry of encouragement – and also appears in the forms 'Haway' (or 'Howay') and 'Away' (or 'A-wee'). According to Frank Graham's *New Geordie Dictionary* (1979), it is a corruption of 'hadaway' as in 'hadaway wi'ye', which means the opposite, 'begone!'

4 I desire the Poles carnally.

On a visit to Poland. Quoted in the *Daily Mail* (29 December 1978). This was the inadequate translation into Polish by an American interpreter of Carter's 'I have come to learn your opinions and understand your desires for the future.'

5 [The] great President who might have been – Hubert Horatio Hornblower.

Speech accepting re-nomination, Democratic Convention, New York (15 August 1980) and unsuccessfully seeking to evoke the name of Hubert Horatio Humphrey.

CARTER, Lillian

American mother of President Carter (1898–1983)

6 Sometimes when I look at my children I say to myself, 'Lillian, you should have stayed a virgin.'

Remark quoted in *Woman* Magazine (9 April 1977), also recorded in the form, 'Wherever there's trouble – that's where Billy is! Sometimes ... I say to myself, "Lillian, you should have stayed a virgin"' – Bob Chieger, *Was It Good For You Too?* (1983).

CARTER, Sydney

English songwriter (1915–)

7 Dance then, wherever you may be,
I am the Lord of the Dance, said he,
And I'll lead you all wherever you may be,
And I'll lead you all in the dance, said he.

'Lord of the Dance' (1967), referring to Jesus Christ and employing the image of life as a dance. Hence, *Lord of the Dance*, title of a dance show (1996), choreographed by and featuring Michael Flatley.

CARTLAND, Barbara (later Dame Barbara)

English romantic novelist (1902–)

8 Of course they have, or I wouldn't be sitting here talking to someone like you.

When asked by an interviewer whether she thought British class barriers had come down. Attributed to Cartland by Jilly Cooper in *Class* (1979). The interviewer was Sandra Harris of the BBC Radio *Today* programme.

CARY, Phoebe

American poet (1824–71)

9 *'Tis a leak in the dyke!* The stoutest heart
Grows faint that cry to hear,
And the bravest man in all the land
Turns white with mortal fear ...
And the boy! he has seen the danger,
And, shouting a wild alarm,
He forces back the weight of the sea
With strength of his single arm.

'The Leak in the Dyke'. This verse account of the legendary Dutch boy – here called Peter – who saved the land from flooding contains an unusual feature: that he plugged the dyke with his arm rather than his finger. More usually, the tale is told of the boy 'who puts his finger in the dyke', as for example in Chap. 18 of another American work, *Hans Brinker, or the Silver*

Skates (1865) by Mary Mapes Dodge (who had never actually been to Holland). Her novel includes a recollection of this 'Hero of Haarlem', whose story, she suggests, had long been known to Dutch children. It is not clear whether she was making this up. What is clear, however, is that only as a result of the success of her book did various Dutch towns claim the boy as their own. A small statue was erected to him at Harlingen. Whatever the case, he was never more than a legend. Sometimes, erroneously, he is given the name 'Hans Brinker' out of confusion with the hero of Dodge's book. It is not possible to say which of the two versions (Cary's or Dodge's) came first.

Hence the figure of speech for someone who staves off a disaster through a simple (albeit temporary) gesture. From *The Times* (9 October 1986): 'To try to stand in front of the markets like the Little Dutch Boy with his finger in the dike would have been an act of folly if the Government were not convinced that the dike was fundamentally sound'; (27 July 1989): '"It was finger-in-the-dike stuff for us throughout the match," the Oxbridge coach, Tony Rodgers, said, "Ultimately the flood walls cracked."'

CASABLANCA

American film 1942. Script by Julius J. Epstein, Philip G. Epstein and Howard Koch, from an unproduced play* Everybody Comes To Rick's *by Murray Burnett and Joan Alison. With Humphrey Bogart as Rick, Ingrid Bergman as Ilsa, Dooley Wilson as Sam and Claude Rains as Capt. Louis Renault.

1 Play it again, Sam.

Of course, Humphrey Bogart never actually said this in the film when talking to Sam, played by Dooley Wilson. Sam is the night club pianist and reluctant performer of the sentimental song 'As Time Goes By'. At one point Ingrid Bergman, as Ilsa, *does* have this exchange with him:

Ilsa: Play it once, Sam, for old time's sake.
Sam: I don't know what you mean, Miss Ilsa.
Ilsa: Play it, Sam. Play, 'As Time Goes By.'

Later on Bogart, as Rick, also tries to get Sam to play it:

Rick: You know what I want to hear.
Sam: No, I don't.
Rick: You played it for her, [and] you can play it for me.
Sam: Well, I don't think I can remember it.
Rick: If she can stand it, I can. Play it.

All one can say is that the saying was utterly well established by the time Woody Allen thus entitled his play *Play It Again Sam* (1969; film US, 1972) about a film critic who is abandoned by his wife and obtains the help of Bogart's 'shade'. By listing it under Allen's name, Bartlett (1980 and 1992) might be thought to suggest that Allen coined the phrase. It would be interesting to know by which year it had really become established. Ian Gillies (1996) recalled that in 1943 the Jack Benny radio programme went to North Africa entertaining the troops. When he returned, two of the shows were based on the idea of a reporter asking him, 'When you toured North Africa, were you in Algiers?' and 'Were you in Casablanca?' Each led to a film parody. In that of *Casablanca*, Benny played the Bogart part and 'Rochester' (Eddie Anderson) Dooley Wilson. At one point Benny said, 'Sam, play that song for me again.'

2 Drop the gun, Louis.

Alistair Cooke writing in *Six Men* (1977) remarked of Bogart: 'He gave currency to another phrase with which the small fry of the English-speaking world brought the neighbourhood sneak to heel: "Drop the gun, Looey!"' Quite how Bogart did this, Cooke does not reveal. We have Bogart's word for it: 'I never said, "Drop the gun, Louie"' (quoted in Ezra Goodman, *Bogey: The Good-Bad Guy*, 1965).

It is just another of those lines that people would like to have heard spoken but that never were. Towards the end of the film what Rick says, is: 'Not so fast, Louis.' Ironically, it is *Louis* who says: 'Put that gun down.'

3 *Louis*: Major Strasser has been shot. Round up the usual suspects.

Soundtrack. In the final scene, 'Round up the usual suspects' is a line spoken by Renault, the Vichy French police chief in the Moroccan city, who is, in his cynical way, appearing to act responsibly in the light of the fact that a German officer, Major Strasser, has been shot. But Strasser was shot by Rick before Renault's very eyes.

It is remarkable that, of all the many memorable lines from *Casablanca*, it took until the early 1990s for this one to catch on. Indeed, as allusions go and referring to 'the people you would expect, the customary lot', it almost became a cliché – as was perhaps confirmed by the release of a film called *The Usual Suspects* (US, 1995) which involved a police identity parade.

Examples of the catchphrase in use range from straightforward quotation in 1983 to more recent unattributed allusions: 'All the usual suspects will be out at Fontwell tomorrow, when the figure-of-eight chase course will throw up its usual quota of specialist [racing] winners' – *Independent on Sunday* (17 January 1993). A BBC Radio Scotland discussion show was called *The Usual Suspects* in 1993 – a rather revealing title given that the journalists and hacks who take part are inevitably just the sort of people you would expect to hear invited on to such a show.

In 1992 Howard Koch appeared to concede the coining of the phrase to his co-scriptwriters Julius J. Epstein and Philip G. Epstein.

1 *Rick*: Louis, I think this is the beginning of a beautiful friendship.

Last words of film.

See also HUPFELD 152:1.

CASSANDRA (William Connor)

English journalist (1909–67)

2 As I was saying when I was interrupted, it is a powerful hard thing to please all the people all the time.

In September 1946, 'Cassandra' resumed his column in the *Daily Mirror* after the Second World War with quite a common form of words. In June of that same year, announcer Leslie Mitchell is also reported to have begun BBC TV's resumed transmissions with: 'As I was saying before I was so rudely interrupted.' The phrase sounds as if it might have originated in music-hall routines of the 'I don't wish to know that, kindly leave the stage' type. Compare A.A. Milne, *Winnie-the-Pooh* (1926): '"AS – I – WAS – SAYING," said Eeyore loudly and sternly, "as I was saying when I was interrupted by various Loud Sounds, I feel that –".' Fary Luis de León, the Spanish poet and religious writer, is believed to have resumed a lecture at Salamanca University in 1577 with, '*Dicebamus hesterno die ...* [We were saying yesterday].' He had been in prison for five years.

3 He is the summit of sex, the pinnacle of masculine, feminine and neuter. Everything that he, she and it can ever want ... This deadly, winking, sniggering, snuggling, chromium-plated, scent-impregnated, luminous, quivering, giggling, fruit-flavoured, mincing, ice-covered, heap of mother love.

On Liberace in the *Daily Mirror* (1956). The article formed the basis of a libel action which Liberace won. After his death it was revealed that he was a homosexual, the very point Cassandra might have been endeavouring to suggest through the use of such words as 'fruit-flavoured' and 'mincing'.

CASTLE, Ted (later Lord Castle)

English journalist (1907–79)

4 In Place of Strife.

This was Castle's suggested title for an ill-fated Labour government White Paper on industrial relations legislation put forward by his wife, Barbara Castle, Secretary of State for Employment, on 17 January 1969. It was clearly modelled on Aneurin Bevan, *In Place of Fear*, the title of a book about disarmament (1952); *see* BEVAN 89:1.

CASTLING, Harry

British songwriter (d.1930)

5 Let's all go down the Strand – have a banana!

From the song, 'Let's All Go Down the Strand' (1904), written with C.W. Murphy. The words 'Have a banana' were interpolated by audiences. Although not part of the original lyrics, they were included in later versions.

CATLIN, Wynn

Untraced (1930–)

6 Diplomacy is the art of saying 'Nice Doggie!' till you can find a rock.

Quoted in Laurence J. Peter, *Quotations for Our Time* (1977). Could this have anything to do with Wynelle Catlin, author of *Old Waffles* (1975) – Texas farm life fiction?

CATO the Elder (or 'the Censor')

Roman politician and orator (234–149BC)

7 *Delenda est Carthago.*
Carthage must be destroyed.

Cato punctuated or ended his speeches to the Roman Senate with this slogan for eight years, *c.*157BC, realizing the threat that the other state posed. It worked – Carthage was destroyed (in 146BC) and Rome reigned supreme, though Cato had not lived to see the effect of his challenge. He did have the decency to precede the slogan with the words '*ceterum censeo* [in my opinion]'.

8 Scipio is the soul of the council; the rest are vain shadows.

Quoted in Plutarch's *Life of Cato*. Alluded to, for example, in John Moore's *Portrait of Elmbury* (1945). He returns to Elmbury after four years' absence to find that his old classics master has been elected to the town council. 'You must show me proper respect,' he says, 'Scipio is the soul of the Council; the rest are vain shadows.'

CATULLUS

Roman poet (c.84–c.54BC)

1 *Vivamus, mea Lesbia, atque amemus.*
Let us love, my Lesbia, and let us love.

Carmina, No. 5, continuing, 'and let us reckon all the murmurs of more censorious old men as worth one farthing'.

2 *Odi et amo.*
I hate and I love.

Ib., No. 85, continuing, 'why I do so you may well ask. I do not know, but I feel it happen and am in agony'.

CAVELL, Edith

English nurse (1865–1915)

3 This I would say, standing as I do in view of God and Eternity: I realize that patriotism is not enough; I must have no hatred and bitterness towards anyone.

Bartlett (1992) is not alone in describing these, inaccurately, as her 'Last words [12 October 1915], before her execution by the Germans'. Cavell was a British Red Cross nurse who, without question, broke the rules of war by using her job to help Allied prisoners escape from German-occupied territory. She was condemned by a German court-martial for 'conducting soldiers to the enemy' and shot. Her 'message to the world' was not in the form of 'last words' spoken before the firing squad but was said the previous day (11 October 1915) to an English chaplain, the Rev. Stirling Gahan, who visited her in prison.

CERVANTES (Miguel de Cervantes Saavedra)

Spanish novelist (1547–1616)

4 Many a time we look for one thing, and light on another.

Don Quixote, Pt 1, Chap. 16. Numerous proverbial expressions took their first English form through Peter Motteux's translation (1700–3): for example, 'I have always heard it said, that to do a kindness to clowns, is like throwing water into the sea' (Pt 1, Chap. 23) and 'To withdraw is not to run away, and to stay is no wise action' (*ib.*)

5 *El Caballero de la Triste Figura.*
The Knight of the Doleful Countenance.

Ib., Pt 1, Chap. 19. Sancho Panza's description of Don Quixote. Smollett translates this as 'Knight of the Sorrowful Countenance' and Shelton, 'Knight of the Ill-favoured Face'.

CHALLONER, Richard

English bishop (1691–1781)

6 [Sanctity] does not so much depend upon doing extraordinary actions, as upon doing our ordinary actions extraordinarily well.

In a letter to *The Independent* Magazine (22 May 1993), David Pocock, pointed out that when, in an earlier issue, Stephen Bayley had written concerning Peter Boizot (founder of the Pizza Express restaurant chain in Britain), 'Doing ordinary things extraordinarily well is a true mark of genius', he had unwittingly misascribed Challoner's remark.

CHAMBERLAIN, Office of the Lord

British theatre censor until 1968

7 Omit 'You get all the dirt off the tail of your shirt.' Substitute 'You get all the dirt off the front of your shirt' ... Omit the song 'Plastic Mac Man' and substitute 'Oh you dirty young devil, how dare you presume to wet the bed when the po's in the room. I'll wallop your bum with a dirty great broom when I get up in the morning.'

Alterations ordered to script of *The Bed-Sitting Room* (1963) by John Antrobus and Spike Milligan. Quoted in Kenneth Tynan, *Tynan Right and Left* (1967).

CHAMBERLAIN, Joseph

English Liberal, then Conservative, politician (1836–1914)

8 We are not downhearted. The only trouble is, we cannot understand what is happening to our neighbours.

Speech at Smethwick (18 January 1906). Referring to a constituency which had not been part of a general electoral landslide.

CHAMBERLAIN, Neville

British Conservative Prime Minister (1869–1940)

1 How terrible, fantastic, incredible it is that we should be digging trenches and trying on gas-masks here because of a quarrel in a faraway country between people of whom we know nothing.

On Czechoslovakia. Radio broadcast (27 September 1938). An unverified suggestion has been made that he had been anticipated in this kind of shortsighted view of foreign affairs by Sir John Simon, as Foreign Secretary, in a House of Commons speech referring to the Japanese invasion of Manchuria in 1931.

2 This morning I had another talk with the German Chancellor, Herr Hitler, and here is the paper which bears his name upon it as well as mine ... 'We regard the agreement signed last night – and the Anglo-German Naval Agreement – as symbolic of the desire of our two peoples never to go to war with one another again.'

Speech, Heston airport (30 September 1938). On returning from signing the Munich agreement.

3 My good friends, this is the second time in our history that there has come back from Germany to Downing Street peace with honour. I believe it is peace for our time. Go home and get a nice quiet sleep.

Following the previous statement, Chamberlain spoke from a window at 10 Downing Street – 'Not of design but for the purpose of dispersing the huge multitude below' (according to his biographer Keith Feiling). Two days before, when someone had suggested the Disraeli phrase 'peace with honour', Chamberlain had impatiently rejected it. Now, according to John Colville, *Footprints in Time* (1976), Chamberlain used the phrase at the urging of his wife.

Chamberlain's own phrase 'peace for our time' is often misquoted as 'peace *in* our time' – as by Noël Coward in the title of his 1947 play set in an England after the Germans have conquered. Perhaps Coward, and others, were influenced by the phrase from the Book of Common Prayer, 'Give Peace in our time, O Lord'. The year before Munich, *Punch* (24 November 1937) showed 'Peace in our time' as a wall slogan.

4 This morning the British Ambassador in Berlin handed the German Government a final note stating that, unless we heard from them by eleven o'clock that they were prepared at once to withdraw their troops from Poland, a state of war would exist between us. I have to tell you that no such undertaking has been received, and that consequently this country is at war with Germany.

Radio broadcast from Downing Street, London (3 September 1939). This was the first occasion on which a people had been told by radio that its country was at war with another. Most of the British nation apparently heard the broadcast having been alerted that it would contain the news that it did. Chamberlain went on to say: 'You can imagine what a bitter blow it is to me that all my long struggle to win peace has failed ...' In the film *In Which We Serve* (1942), when sailors are shown listening to the broadcast on a wireless, this produces the response from one of them: 'It's not exactly a bank holiday for us ...'

5 Whatever may be the reason, whether it was that Hitler thought he might get away with what he had got without fighting for it, or whether it was that, after all, the preparations are not sufficiently complete, one thing is certain – he missed the bus.

Speech to Conservative Central Council (5 April 1940). Chamberlain made this boastful observation unwisely just as the 'phoney war' period (of little or no action) was coming to an end. Five days later Hitler invaded Norway. Chamberlain was ousted as Prime Minister within the month. Nevertheless, it is a notable use of the expression 'to miss the bus'. This first appears in the *OED2* in 1886 as 'to miss the omnibus', having probably developed from an earlier expression 'to miss the boat'.

CHAMFORT, Nicolas-Sébastien

French writer (1741–94)

6 Most anthologists of poetry or quotations are like those who eat cherries or oysters, first picking the best and winding up by eating everything.

Quoted in Prochnow & Prochnow, *Treasury of Humorous Quotations* (1969). A salutary reminder to all editors of dictionaries (and companions) of quotations.

CHANDLER, Raymond

American novelist (1888–1959)

7 The Big Sleep.

Title of novel (1939). A synonym for death.

1 She gave me a smile I could feel in my hip pocket.

Farewell, My Lovely (1940). But what does this line mean? A winning smile, presumably – but is the reference to the hip pocket meant to suggest something about money (where the wallet might be kept) or about guns or about the other things that men keep in their trousers?

2 Down these mean streets a man must go who is not himself mean; who is neither tarnished nor afraid.

Chandler wrote this of the heroic qualities a detective should have in 'The Simple Art of Murder' (in the *Atlantic Monthly*, December 1944, reprinted in *Pearls Are a Nuisance*, 1950). However, the phrase 'mean streets' was not original. In 1894 Arthur Morrison had written *Tales of Mean Streets* about impoverished life in the East End of London. The usage was well established by 1922 when the *Weekly Dispatch* was using the phrase casually: 'For him there is glamor in the mean streets of dockland.'

CHAPLIN, Charlie (later Sir Charles)

English-born film comedian (1889–1977)

3 All I need to make a comedy is a park, a policeman and a pretty girl.

My Autobiography (1964). Referring to film-making in about 1916.

CHAPMAN, George

English playwright (c.1559–1634)

4 I am ashamed the law is such an ass.

Revenge for Honour (published 1654). *Compare* DICKENS 206:10.

CHARLES I

English King (1600–49)

5 I go from a corruptible to an incorruptible crown, where no disturbance can have place.

Last words before his execution, quoted in David Hume, *History of England ...*, Chap. 22 (1778). He is also said to have remarked to Bishop Juxon, 'Remember.' Quoted in Barnaby Conrad, *Famous Last Words* (1961).

CHARLES II

English King (1630–85)

6 Let not poor Nelly starve.

Deathbed utterance, referring to his former mistress, Nell Gwyn. Recorded in Gilbert Burnet, *History of My Own Time* (1724).

7 He had been, he said, an unconscionable time dying; but he hoped that they would excuse it.

Last words, reported in Lord Macaulay, *History of England* (1849).

See also ROCHESTER 457:7.

CHARLES V

Holy Roman Emperor (1500–58)

8 I speak Spanish to God, Italian to women, French to men – and German to my horse.

Attributed remark. Alluded to in Lord Chesterfield, *Letters to His Son* (1832 ed.)

CHARLES

British Prince (1948–)

9 Yes ... whatever that may mean.

When asked if he was 'in love' upon getting engaged to Lady Diana Spencer. TV news interview (February 1981).

10 A kind of vast municipal fire station ... I would understand better this type of high-tech approach if you demolished the whole of Trafalgar Square, but what is proposed is like a monstrous carbuncle on the face of a much-loved and elegant friend.

Speech to the Royal Institute of British Architects (30 May 1984), describing the proposed design for a new wing of the National Gallery in London. It had an effect: the design was scrapped and replaced by another one.

The Prince's ventures into architectural criticism have not gone unnoticed, and the image of a 'monstrous carbuncle' ('a red spot or pimple on the nose or face caused by habits of intemperance' – *OED2*) has become part of the critical vocabulary. A report in *The Independent* (1 March 1988) about plans for a new lifeboat station dominating the harbour at Lyme Regis concluded by quoting a local objector: 'They've called this building a design of the age. What we've got here is a Prince Charles Carbuncle, and we don't like carbuncles down on Lyme harbourside.' The Prince's step-mother-in-law, the Countess Spencer, had earlier written in a book called *The Spencers on Spas* (1983) of how 'monstrous carbuncles of concrete have erupted in gentle Georgian squares'. In *Barnaby Rudge*, Chap. 54 (1841), Charles Dickens had written: 'Old John was so red in the face ... and lighted up the Maypole Porch wherein they sat together, like a monstrous carbuncle in a fairy tale.' Even before this, in 1821, William Cobbett had characterized the whole of London as 'the Great Wen of all', a 'wen' being a lump or protuberance on the body, a wart. *See also* COBBETT 176:1.

1 A glass stump.

Ib. Of a planned Mies van der Rohe office building in the City of London.

CHAUCER, Geoffrey

English poet (c.1343–1400)

2 Whan that Aprill with his shoures soote,
The droghte of March hath perced to the roote.

Opening words (in Middle English) of the General Prologue to *The Canterbury Tales* (*c.*1387). Nevill Coghill's 1951 translation of these lines runs: 'When in April the sweet showers fall/And pierce the drought of March to the root.'

CHAYEFSKY, Paddy

American playwright and screenwriter (1923–81)

3 I want you to get up right now and go to the window, open it and stick your head out and yell: 'I'm as mad as hell, and I'm not going to take this any more!'

Film *Network* (US, 1976) – in which Peter Finch plays a TV pundit-cum-evangelist who exhorts his viewers to get mad with these words. From *New Society* (25 November 1982): 'Some years ago the irascible Howard Jarvis, author of California's Proposition 13 (the one that pegged property taxes), coined the immortal political slogan: I'm mad as Hell and I'm Not Taking Any More.' Well, no, he obviously didn't. In 1978 Jarvis (1902–86), the California social activist, merely adopted the slogan and came to be associated with it. As a result, 57 per cent voted to reduce their property taxes. Dire warnings about the effect on government if tax revenues were pegged were not borne out and Proposition 13 paved the way for Reaganomics three years later. Jarvis entitled a book *I'm Mad as Hell* but duly credited Chayevsky with the coinage of his slogan. He added: 'For me, the words "I'm mad as hell" are more than a national saying, more than the title of this book; they express exactly how I feel and exactly how I felt about the ... countless other victims of exorbitant taxes.'

4 Altered States.

Title of novel (1978; film US, 1980, but Chayevsky's screen credit was in the form 'Sidney Aaron' because he had disowned the script). The novel/film was an sf thriller about genetic experimentation or, as one of the film guides puts it, about a 'psychophysiologist who hallucinates himself back into primitive states of human evolution, in which guise he emerges to kill'.

Could the phrase have anything to do with what Dr Albert Hofmann observed of his discovery, the psychedelic drug LSD? He noted in his diary for 1943: 'An intense stimulation of the imagination and an altered state of awareness of the world.'

CHER

American singer and actress (1946–)

5 Stripped, washed and brought to my tent.

Cher spent a certain amount of time in March 1988 denying, apropos some toy-boy lover, that she had ever ordered him, metaphorically speaking, to be stripped, washed and brought to her tent. The allusion here was not very precise. Presumably, the suggestion was that she had behaved as, say, an Arab prince might to an underling (either male or female). Perhaps she acquired the line from some film about sheiks and harems. Compare from Christopher Marlowe, 2 *Tamburlaine*, Act 4, Sc. 1 (1590): 'Then bring those Turkish harlots to my tent/And I'll dispose them as it likes me best.'

CHESTERFIELD, 4th Earl of

English politician and writer (1694–1773)

6 The pleasure is momentary, the position ridiculous, the expense damnable.

Chesterfield's alleged remark about sex is well known but has not been found in any of his works, not even in the letters of advice (1774) to his natural son for which he is best remembered. It may be that the original utterance was in French – by Voltaire, perhaps, or La Rochefoucauld – in the form '*Le plaisir est court et la position ridicule*'. It appears increasingly likely that the authorship has been imposed on Chesterfield as someone who had a reputation for handing out views like this. In fact, it doesn't sound like him.

The earliest source found to date is an unsigned piece in the journal *Nature* (Vol. 227, 22 August 1970). It begins: 'Lord Chesterfield once remarked of sexual intercourse "the pleasure is momentary, the position ridiculous, and the expense damnable".' Another example of an anonymous saying ascribed to a convenient author?

1 The chapter of knowledge is a very short, but the chapter of accidents is a very long one.

Letter to Solomon Dayrolles (16 February 1753). Possibly a phrase in general use even then, meaning 'a series of unforeseen happenings or misfortunes'. Hence, *A Chapter of Accidents*, title of the autobiography (1972) of Goronwy Rees. In 1837 John Wilkes was quoted by Southey as saying: 'The chapter of accidents is the longest chapter in the book'.

2 [Lord] Tyrawley and I have been dead these two years; but we don't choose to have it known.

When both Tyrawley and he were old and infirm. Quoted by Dr Johnson in Boswell, *Life of Johnson* (1791), for 3 April 1773, as an example of Chesterfield's wit.

3 Give Dayrolles a chair.

Last words. Mr Dayrolles called about half an hour before the Earl died. Quoted in W.H. Craig, *Life of Lord Chesterfield* (1907).

CHESTERTON, G.K.

English poet, novelist and critic (1874–1936)

4 'My country, right or wrong' is a thing no patriot would ever think of saying except in a desperate case. It is like saying, 'My mother, drunk or sober.'

The Defendant (1901). *See* DECATUR 198:4.

5 Am in Market Harborough. Where ought I to be?

This is often misquoted as 'Am in Wolverhampton' (for example, in *The 'Quote ... Unquote' Book of Love, Death and the Universe*, 1980, and several other places). Chesterton was noted for being disorganized and according to one biographer, Maisie Ward, in *Return to Chesterton* (1944), a hundred different places have been substituted for 'Market Harborough' in the telling of this story. Chesterton's wife, Frances, on this occasion cabled the answer 'Home', because, as she explained, it was easier to get him home and start him off again. Yes, Market Harborough was the original and is confirmed by Chesterton's own *Autobiography*, Chap. 16 (1936): 'Of those days the tale is told that I once sent a telegram to my wife in London, which ran: "Am in Market Harborough. Where ought I to be?" I cannot remember whether this story is true; but it is not unlikely or, I think, unreasonable.'

6 The human race, to which so many of my readers belong, has been playing at children's games from the beginning, and will probably do it till the end, which is a nuisance for the few people who grow up.

The Napoleon of Notting Hill, Chap. 1 (1904). Opening words, displaying typically Chestertonian good humour and argument in equal measure.

7 Individually, men may present a more or less rational appearance, eating, sleeping and scheming. But humanity as a whole is changeful, mystical, fickle and delightful. Men are men, but Man is a woman.

Ib. Chesterton is here echoing '*La donna è mobile*'. *See* PIAVE 430:8.

8 'Dr Polycarp was, as you all know, an unusually sallow bimetallist. "There," people of wide experience would say, "There goes the sallowest bimetallist in Cheshire".'

Ib., Chap. 3. A bimetallist was one who supported the unrestricted currency of both gold and silver at a fixed ratio to each other as coinage.

9 The Man Who Was Thursday.

Title of a short novel (1908), subtitled 'a Nightmare'. It was a fantasy with an anarchist background. The seven members of the Central Anarchist Council are named after the days of the week. Hence, all the many later newspaper headlines of 'The Man Who Was –' variety.

10 The prime truth of woman, the universal mother ... that if a thing is worth doing, it is worth doing badly.

'Folly and Female Education', *What's Wrong with the World* (1910). Obviously, a cynical variation of the proverbial 'If a job [*or* thing] is worth doing, it's worth doing well' – which *CODP* finds Lord Chesterfield using by 1746.

The father of someone I know always used to say: 'If a thing's worth doing, it's worth doing *well enough*.'

1 I tell you naught for your comfort,
Yea, naught for your desire,
Save that the sky grows darker yet
And the sea raises higher.

The Ballad of the White Horse (1911). Hence, *Naught for Your Comfort*, title of a book (1956) by Bishop Trevor Huddleston – a classic denunciation of apartheid in South Africa by an Anglican priest.

2 Are they clinging to their crosses, F.E. Smith? ...
Talk about the pews and steeples
And the cash that goes therewith!
But the souls of Christian peoples ...
Chuck it, Smith!'

Antichrist, or the Reunion of Christendom (1912). In this poem, Chesterton satirized the pontificating of F.E. Smith (later 1st Earl of Birkenhead) on the Welsh Disestablishment Bill. Hence, the popularizing, though not coinage, of the phrase 'Chuck it ——!' meaning, 'abandon that line of reasoning, that posturing'. Partridge/*Slang* guesses that it is of twentieth-century origin.

A more recent example from the BBC's *World at One* radio programme in May 1983 during the run-up to a general election: Labour politician Roy Hattersley complained that he was being questioned only on the 10 per cent of the Labour Party manifesto with which he disagreed. Robin Day, the interviewer, replied: 'Chuck it, Hattersley!'

3 I think I will not hang myself today.

'A Ballade of Suicide' (1915). This short poem is about a suicide who finds reasons for putting off the deed. In *Lyrics on Several Occasions* (1959), Ira Gershwin notes that the title of his song *I Don't Think I'll Fall in Love Today* (written in 1928) was inspired by this line.

4 The only way of catching a train I ever discovered is to miss the train before.

Quoted in *The Treasury of Humorous Quotations*, ed. by Evan Esar & Nicolas Bentley (1951). P. Daninos, 'Le Supplice de l'heure', *Vacances à tous prix* (1958) has: 'Chesterton taught me this: the only way to be sure of catching a train was to miss the one before it.'

5 Every good joke has a philosophical idea somewhere inside it.

Untraced. Possibly a rendering of the view put forward in his essay 'Cockneys and Their Jokes'.

6 It is the test of a good religion whether you can joke about it.

Quoted in *The 'Quote ... Unquote' Book of Love, Death and the Universe* (1980), but otherwise still awaiting verification.

7 Men with no right to their right reason,
Men with good reason to be wrong.

'The Queen of Seven Swords' (1926), but not included in *The Collected Poems* (1927). About the Reformation (in England).

8 When a man stops believing in God he doesn't then believe in nothing, he believes in anything.

Unverified, but widely quoted. The chief problem of verification is the immense number of GKC's books and newspaper articles that it could be in – if, indeed, it is. Aidan Mackey of the G.K. Chesterton Study Centre wrote in the March 1996 issue of *The Chesterton Society Newsletter*: 'I have been asked for the source by the BBC (twice), *The Sunday Telegraph*, by many writers and researchers, and by Mrs Thatcher's private office. I now believe that we must make a concerted effort to locate it, and to this end I seek help. I have been, very hastily, through 28 books but I work under pressure, and these should be checked again by at least one other reader ...

'It has been suggested to me that it is not a genuine quotation at all, but one which GKC had once or twice expressed, and that it has, with time, hardened into something else. However, I and others are certain that this is genuine. I am positive that I have read it in one of his books, not in a fugitive piece, and will even tempt fate by saying that the words [as above] are as near accurate as makes no difference.'

Another line of inquiry was opened by David Torvell (1996) who said he recognized the statement as coming from one of the 'Father Brown' stories: 'The context was a "locked-room murder" attributed to supernatural causes. Father Brown refused to accept what he regarded as atheist woolly-mindedness and successfully looked for human and mechanical agents.' This refers to 'The Miracle of Moon Crescent' from *The Incredulity of Father Brown* (1923): '"By the way," went on Father Brown, "don't think I blame you for jumping to preternatural conclusions. The reason's very simple, really. You all swore you were hard-shelled materialists; and as a matter of fact you were all balanced on the very edge of belief – of belief in almost anything".' To which one might add that in the adjacent story, 'The Oracle of the Dog', can be found: 'It's the first effect of not believing in God that you lose your common sense.'

Denis J. Conlon, Chairman of the Chesterton Society

commented (1996): 'There's general agreement that it does sound like the typical Father Brown aphorism, and GKC put many remarks about the superstitions of agnostics into his mouth. Unfortunately, not the one we are looking for, although one must always take into account that the stories as collected did vary a little from the versions originally published in magazines.

'I am beginning to think that it might have been something he said during one of his countless talks, lectures and debates. The earliest citation so far unearthed is in Emile Cammaerts's *Chesterton: The Laughing Prophet* first published in 1937, but Cammaerts does not give his source.'

What Cammaerts does do is to insert, in the middle of some direct quotation, the paraphrase, 'The first effect of not believing in God is to believe in anything.' It may be upon this that all the subsequent quoters have constructed their versions.

1 This is the sort of book we like
(For you and I are very small)
With pictures stuck in anyhow,
And hardly any words at all ...
You will not understand a word
Of all the words, including mine;
Never you trouble – you can see,
And all directness is divine –
Stand up and keep your childishness:
Read all the pedants' screeds and strictures;
But don't believe in anything
That can't be told in coloured pictures.

Written in a child's album and long untraced. It was quoted in *The Chesterton Review* (November 1981).

2 *Termino nobis donet in patria.*

The Latin text on Chesterton's grave in the Roman Catholic cemetery at Beaconsfield, Buckinghamshire, is taken from the final stanza of the Matins hymn for the Feast of Corpus Christi. The entire office was written by St Thomas Aquinas, and Chesterton was said to have known large parts of it by heart. As Father Ian Brady, editor of *The Chesterton Review*, pointed out (1992), the words would also have been familiar to Chesterton because they formed part of the hymn sung at the once-popular short devotional service of Benediction – a hymn that began with the words, '*O salutaris hostia*', and concluded with this prayer to the Holy Trinity:

Uni trinoque Domino
sit sempiterna gloria,
qui vitam sine termino
nobis donet in patria.

[Everlasting glory be to the Lord, Three in One, who gives us life without end in heaven.] In Maisie Ward's *Return to Chesterton* (1944), there is a letter from one of Chesterton's Beaconsfield friends in which Chesterton is quoted as saying that he regarded the phrase '*in patria*' as a perfect definition of heaven. 'Our native land,' he said, 'it tells you everything.' Father Brady added that perhaps the fact that Chesterton died on the Sunday within the Octave of Corpus Christi also influenced the choice of these words for his monument. The words were also an especial favourite of Chesterton's friend and colleague, Hilaire Belloc. It is said that Belloc was unable to hear the closing lines of the hymn without being moved to tears.

See also CORNFORD 183:11; TENNYSON 529:3.

CHEVALIER, Maurice

French entertainer (1888–1972)

3 I prefer old age to the alternative.

Remark (1960), on his 72nd birthday. Or 'Old age isn't so bad when you consider the alternative.' Quoted in Michael Freedland, *Maurice Chevalier* (1981).

CHILDERS, Erskine

English-born author and Irish patriot (1870–1922)

4 Take a step forward, lads. It will be easier that way.

Last words before being executed by firing squad (24 November 1922). Quoted in Andrew Boyle, *The Riddle of Erskine Childers* (1976). Childers's nonchalance also seems apparent from the fact that he managed to get a delay of an hour in his execution time in order to see the sunrise. He also shook hands with the firing squad.

CHRISTIE, Agatha (later Dame Agatha)

English detective novelist (1890–1976)

5 I believe that a well-known anecdote exists to the effect that a young writer, determined to make the commencement of his story forcible and original enough to catch the attention of the most blasé of editors, penned the first sentence: '"Hell!" said the Duchess'.

These are the opening lines of *The Murder on the Links* (1923). Later, *Hell! Said the Duchess* was the title of 'A Bed-time Story' (1934) by Michael Arlen. Partridge/*Catch Phrases* dates the longer phrase, 'Hell! said the Duchess when she caught her teats in the mangle', to *c.*1895 and says it was frequently used in the First World War.

Compare the suggested newspaper headline containing all the ingredients necessary to capture a reader's attention (sex, royalty, religion, etc.): 'Teen-age Dog-loving Doctor-priest in Sex-change Mercy-Dash to Palace' (a joke current by 1959 and quoted in *The Lyttelton Hart-Davis Letters*, Vol. 4, 1959). Hence, *PDMQ* (1980)'s attribution of 'Teenage sex-change priest in mercy dash to Palace' to Magnus Linklater in the BBC Radio programme *Between the Lines* (18 September 1976) is misleading.

Yet another version is: '"Hell!" said the Duchess, "I'm pregnant, whodunit?"'

1 An archaeologist is the best husband any woman can have; the older she gets, the more interested he is in her.

Attributed, for example, in Laurence J. Peter, *Quotations for Our Time* (1977). Christie was married to the archaeologist, Sir Max Mallowan, and so it seemed quite feasible when she was quoted as saying this in a news report (8 March 1954), also quoted in *The Observer* (2 January 1955). However, according to G.C. Ramsey, *Agatha Christie: Mistress of Mystery* (1967), she vehemently denied having said it, insisting that it would have been a very silly remark for anyone to make, and neither complimentary nor amusing.

Frank S. Pepper in his *Handbook of 20th Century Quotations* (1984) placed the remark in Christie's *Murder in Mesopotamia* (1936), but it is not be found in that book.

CHURCHILL, Caryl

English dramatist (1938–)

2 Serious Money.

Title of play (1987), meaning 'money in excessive amounts'. The *Longman Register of New Words* (1989) correctly surmised that this 'facetious usage seems to have started life among the fast-burning earners of the post-Big Bang, pre-Bust city of London, who when speaking of salaries in the six-figure bracket would concede that this was "serious money"'. The phrase was popularized when used as the title of Churchill's satirical play about the City. The *Register* also noted that the usage was likely to spread to other areas: 'Annie's – a bar favoured by serious drinkers' (*Sunday Times*, 28 August 1988), and so it did.

CHURCHILL, Lord Randolph

English politician (1849–94)

3 For the purposes of recreation he [Gladstone] has selected the felling of trees, and we may usefully remark that his amusements, like his politics, are essentially destructive ... The forest laments that Mr Gladstone may perspire.

Speech, Blackpool (24 January 1884). Gladstone's 'arboreal assaults' (in Roy Jenkins's phrase) became one of his central occupations, almost akin – though publicly better known – to his picking up fallen women.

4 Ulster will not be a consenting party; Ulster at the proper moment will resort to the supreme arbitrament of force; Ulster will fight and Ulster will be right.

Public letter to a Liberal-Unionist (7 May 1886). Hence, the slogan 'Ulster will fight and Ulster will be right' used by the Ulster Volunteers opposing Irish Home Rule (1913–14). From Randolph Churchill, *Youth: Winston Churchill* (1966): 'This famous slogan became the watchword of Ulster; it pithily explains why Ulster is still a part of the United Kingdom of Great Britain and Northern Ireland.'

5 An old man in a hurry.

On W.E. Gladstone. In an address to the electors of South Paddington (19 June 1886).

6 The duty of an opposition is to oppose.

In W.S. Churchill, *Lord Randolph Churchill* (1906). A political attitude cited when an opposition party appears to take up a contrary position just for its own sake. Harold Wilson's criticism of the EEC when in opposition to the Conservative government in the early 1970s was said to reflect it. When Labour returned to power it renegotiated Britain's terms of membership and put the results before a referendum in 1975.

CHURCHILL, Randolph

English journalist and politician (1911–68)

7 Isn't God a shit!

While reading the Bible from cover to cover in response to a bet. Quoted in Evelyn Waugh, *Diaries* (entry for 11 November 1944).

8 I should never be allowed out in private.

In a letter to a hostess whose dinner party he had

ruined with one of his displays of drunken rudeness. Quoted in Brian Roberts, *Randolph* (1984). In a letter to his father (16 October 1952), Randolph wrote: 'It is not for nothing that I coined the "mot" about myself: "Randolph should never be allowed out in private".'

See also THE TIMES 540:5.

CHURCHILL, Winston (later Sir Winston)

British Conservative Prime Minister (1874–1965)

1 The conditions of the Transvaal ordinance under which Chinese Labour is now being carried on do not, in my opinion, constitute a state of slavery. A labour contract into which men enter voluntarily for a limited and for a brief period, under which they are paid wages which they consider adequate, under which they are not bought or sold and from which they can obtain relief on payment of seventeen pounds ten shillings may not be a desirable contract ... but it cannot in the opinion of His Majesty's Government be classified as slavery in the extreme acceptance of the word without some risk of terminological inexactitude.

In 1906 the status of Chinese workers in South Africa was mentioned in the King's speech to Parliament as 'slavery'. An Opposition amendment of 22 February of the same year was tabled, regretting, 'That Your Majesty's ministers should have brought the reputation of this country into contempt by describing the employment of Chinese indentured labour as slavery'. Churchill, as Under-Secretary at the Colonial Office, replied by quoting what he had said in the previous election campaign. Subsequently, the phrase 'terminological inexactitude' has been taken, almost invariably, as a humorously long-winded way of indicating a 'lie', but the context shows that this is not the meaning. One of the first to misunderstand it, however, was Joseph Chamberlain (*q.v.*). Of 'terminological inexactitude' he said: 'Eleven syllables, many of them of Latin or Greek derivation, when one good English word, a Saxon word of a single syllable, would do!'

2 Nothing in life is so exhilarating as to be shot at without result.

The Malakand Field Force (1898), referring to his time in India. Quoted by Ronald Reagan after the attempt on his life in 1981. Compare Prince Andrew (*The Times*, 14 November 1983): 'Asked whether his Falklands experience had helped shape his character, the prince replied: "That is a very difficult question to answer. I think being shot at is one of the most character-forming things of one's life".'

3 He is one of those orators of whom it was well said, 'Before they get up, they do not know what they are going to say; when they are speaking, they do not know what they are saying; and when they have sat down, they do not know what they have said.'

On Lord Charles Beresford. Speech, House of Commons (20 December 1912). *Compare* GLADSTONE 264:3.

4 If you were my wife, I'd drink it.

To Lady Astor who had said, 'If you were my husband, I'd poison your coffee', (*c.*1912). Quoted in Consuelo Vanderbilt Balsan, *Glitter and Gold* (1952) and Elizabeth Langhorne, *Nancy Astor and Her Friends* (1974).

5 I can only say to you let us go forward together and put these grave matters to the proof.

Speech on Ulster (14 March 1914) – the first appearance of a Churchill stock phrase. Compare 'Let us go forward together in all parts of the Empire, in all parts of the Island' (speaking on the war, 27 January 1940); and 'I say, "Come then, let us go forward together with our united strength"' (in his 'blood, sweat and tears' speech, 13 May 1940). A cliché from then on. It occurs along with other rhetorical clichés during the 'Party Political Speech' (written by Max Schreiner) on the Peter Sellers comedy album *The Best of Sellers* (1958): 'Let us assume a bold front and go forward together.'

6 They say you can rat, but you can't re-rat.

On 'crossing the floor' of the House of Commons more than once. Reported in John Colville, *The Fringes of Power*, Vol.1 (1985), entry for 26 January 1941. The remark may date from 1923/4 when Churchill rejoined the Conservatives, having earlier left them to join the Liberals.

7 It is a good thing for an uneducated man to read books of quotations.

Ib., Chap. 9. He goes on: 'Bartlett's *Familiar Quotations* is an admirable work, and I studied it intently. The quotations when engraved upon the memory give you good thoughts. They also make you anxious to read the authors and look for more.'

8 [At Barnum's Circus] the exhibit on the programme I most desired to see was the one

described as the Boneless Wonder. My parents judged that the spectacle would be too revolting and demoralizing for my youthful eyes, and I have waited fifty years to see the boneless wonder sitting on the Treasury bench.

On Ramsay Macdonald. Speech, House of Commons (28 January 1931).

1 [It is] alarming and also nauseating to see Mr Gandhi, a seditious Middle Temple lawyer, now posing as a fakir of a type well-known in the East, striding half-naked up the steps of the vice-regal palace.

When Mahatma Gandhi was released from gaol to take part in a Round Table conference. Speech, Epping (23 February 1931).

2 Call that a maiden speech? It was a brazen hussy of a speech. Never did such a painted lady of a speech parade itself before a modest parliament.

To A.P. Herbert (1935). Quoted in Herbert's *Independent Member* (1950).

3 Saving is a very fine thing especially when your parents have done it for you.

Quoted in Fred Metcalf, *The Penguin Dictionary of Modern Humorous Quotations* (1987), but otherwise untraced.

4 I once went to bed with a man to see what it was like.

According to Ted Morgan, *Somerset Maugham* (1980), this was Churchill's reply when asked by Maugham if he had ever had any homosexual affairs. Maugham asked him who the man was. Churchill replied, 'Ivor Novello'. 'And what was it like?' 'Musical.' The source for this story was Alan Searle, one of Maugham's acolytes. Churchill's daughter, Mary Soames, questioned it when it was included in my *Dictionary of Twentieth Century Quotations* (1987), and it is surely of dubious veracity.

5 I cannot forecast to you the action of Russia. It is a riddle wrapped in a mystery inside an enigma.

Radio broadcast (1 October 1939). Not, as might appear, a general reflection on the Russian character but a specific response to the Soviet occupation of East Poland, undertaken in league with Germany, on 18 September.

6 I would say to the House, as I said to those who have joined this Government: I have nothing to offer but blood, toil, tears and sweat.

Speech to the House of Commons (13 May 1940) upon becoming Prime Minister. Note the order of the last five words. There are echoes in these of earlier speeches and writings. The combination makes an appearance in John Donne's line from *An Anatomy of the World* (1611): ''Tis in vain to do so or mollify it with thy tears or sweat or blood.' Byron follows with 'blood, sweat and tear-wrung millions' in 1823. Theodore Roosevelt spoke in an 1897 speech of 'the blood and sweat and tears, the labour and the anguish, through which, in the days that have gone, our forefathers moved to triumph'. The more usual order of the words was later enshrined in the name of the 1970s American band. Churchill seemed to avoid this configuration, however. In 1931, he had already written of the Tsarist armies: 'Their sweat, their tears, their blood bedewed the endless plain.'

Possibly the closest forerunner of Churchill's 'backs to the wall' exhortation was Giuseppe Garibaldi's impromptu speech to his followers on 2 July 1849 before Rome fell to French troops. The speech was not taken down at the time, so this version is made up of various accounts. Seated upon a horse in the Piazza of St Peter's, he declared: 'Fortune, who betrays us today, will smile on us tomorrow. I am going out from Rome. Let those who wish to continue the war against the stranger, come with me. I offer neither pay, nor quarters, nor provisions; I offer hunger, thirst, forced marches, battles and death [*fame, sete, marcie forzate, battaglie e morte*]. Let him who loves his country with his heart, and not merely his lips, follow me.' As precedents go, this is obviously quite a close one, and it is probable that Churchill had read G.M. Trevelyan's series of books about Garibaldi, published at the turn of the century, in which the lines occur. Having launched such a famous phrase, Churchill referred to it five more times during the course of the war, though he did not always use all four keywords or in the original order.

Indeed, right from the start, people seem to have had difficulty in getting the order of the words right. The natural inclination is to put 'blood', 'sweat' and 'tears' together. Joan Wyndham in *Love Lessons – A Wartime Diary* (1985) concludes her entry for 13 May 1940 with: 'Later we listened to a very stirring speech by Churchill about "blood, toil, sweat and tears".' There is a slight suspicion that this diary may have been 'improved' somewhat in the editing, but not, obviously, to the point of imposing accuracy. Boller & George's *They Never Said It* (1989), dedicated to exposing quotation errors, has Churchill saying, 'blood *and* toil, tears and sweat'.

1 You ask, what is our aim? I can answer in one word: victory, victory at all costs, victory in spite of all terror, victory, however long and hard the road may be.

Ib. Compare CLEMENCEAU 173:5.

2 We shall fight on the beaches, we shall fight on the landing grounds, we shall fight in the fields and in the streets, we shall fight in the hills; we shall never surrender.

At the end of May 1940 some 338,000 Allied troops were evacuated from the Dunkirk area of northern France – a formidable achievement celebrated as a victory although it was a retreat. In a speech to the House of Commons on 4 June, Churchill tried to check the euphoria. He ended thus, however, on a note of hope.

3 If we can stand up to [Hitler], all Europe may be free and the life of the world may move forward into broad, sunlit uplands.

Speech, House of Commons (18 June 1940). In Churchill's long speaking career there was one thematic device he frequently resorted to for his perorations. It appears in many forms but may be summarized as the 'broad, sunlit uplands' approach. In his collected speeches there are some thirteen occasions when he made use of this construction. 'The level plain ... a land of peace and plenty ... the sunshine of a more gentle and a more generous age' (1906); 'I earnestly trust ... that by your efforts our country may emerge from this period of darkness and peril once more in the sunlight of a peaceful time' (at the end of a speech on 19 September 1915 when Churchill's own position was precarious following the failure of the Gallipoli campaign); in his 'finest hour' speech, Churchill hoped that, 'the life of the world may move forward into broad, sunlit uplands' (1940); 'it is an uphill road we have to tread, but if we reject the cramping, narrowing path of socialist restrictions, we shall surely find a way – and a wise and tolerant government – to those broad uplands where plenty, peace and justice reign' (1951, prior to the general election).

4 What General Weygand called the Battle of France is over. I expect that the Battle of Britain is about to begin.

Ib. The urge to give names to battles – even before they are fought and won – is well exemplified by this coinage. The 'Battle of Britain' duly became the name by which the decisive overthrowing of German invasion plans by 'the Few' is known. The order of the day, read aloud to every pilot on 10 July, contained the words: 'The Battle of Britain is about to begin. Members of the Royal Air Force, the fate of generations is in your hands.' Another Churchill coinage – 'The Battle of Egypt' (speech, 10 November 1942) – caught on less well.

5 If we fail, then the whole world, including the United States, including all that we have known and cared for, will sink into the abyss of a new Dark Age made more sinister, and perhaps more protracted, by the lights of perverted science. Let us therefore brace ourselves to our duties, and so bear ourselves that, if the British Empire and its Commonwealth last for a thousand years, men will still say, This was their finest hour.

Ib. The various versions of this famous concluding passage raise questions as to precisely what Churchill did or did not say on this and other occasions. The first point to make about this (and almost every other Churchill speech) is that it was entirely premeditated. As Jock Colville, his secretary at the time, recalled in *Action This Day* (1968): 'The composition of a speech was not a task Churchill was prepared to skimp or to hurry; nor, except on some convivial occasion, was he willing to speak impromptu. He might improvise briefly, but only to elaborate or clarify, and he stuck closely to the text he had prepared ... Quick as was his wit and unfailing his gift for repartee, he was not a man to depart in the heat of the moment from the theme or indeed the words that he had laboriously conceived in set-speech form.'

Churchill dictated his speeches to a typist. The finished speech would be laid out on many sheets of paper, with plenty of spacing, and then the whole lot was fastened firmly together so that it wouldn't end up on the floor. He would read from detailed notes which were set out in what was known as Speech Form which meant rather like a hymn-sheet or, as someone said, like the psalms, and made them easier to read.

It would seem, however, that these 'notes' were almost a word-for-word text and this came in useful when (as on 18 June) he repeated his House of Commons speech in the evening for radio listeners to the BBC. But when one talks of Churchill's famous 'Finest Hour' speech one is, in fact, referring to any one of several versions: (1) the notes from which he spoke (2) the transcript of the parliamentary speech made by *Hansard* reporters (3) any transcripts made of the radio 'talk' (4) the version used when Churchill re-recorded some of his speeches for the Decca record company after the war was over. No wonder that published versions of the speeches differ in many details from each other and from Churchill's notes (which have been published).

It has to be said that these discrepancies are not very major, but they are interesting. At the peroration, did he say exactly what is in his notes and which is broadly speaking *Hansard*'s version and also what is to be found cited in the *ODQ* (1992) – namely, 'duty' for 'duties', 'lasts' for 'last'?

Or did he say what is to be found, for example, in the book *Churchill Speaks*, his 'Collected Speeches in Peace and War' (ed. by Robert Rhodes James, 1981) and which is given above? This version accords with what Churchill put in his *History of the Second War*, Vol. 2 (1949) and also with what he speaks on the Decca recording made after the war. This presumably met with his approval. It is also the version in Bartlett (1992). But we still cannot be sure it was what he said at the time. The *ODQ* also puts, rather, 'British *Commonwealth* and its *Empire*' in that order. If nothing else, this only goes to prove how difficult it is to quote correctly – even one of the most famous speeches of all.

The Finest Hours was the title of a documentary film (UK 1964) about Churchill's life.

1 Set Europe ablaze.

Instruction on the establishment of the Special Operations Executive to coordinate acts of subversion against enemies overseas. This ringing call was one of the last Churchillisms to become publicly known. E.H. Cookridge wrote in *Inside S.O.E.* (1966): 'The Special Operations Executive was born on 19 July 1940' on the basis of a memo from Winston Churchill '"to coordinate all action by way of subversion and sabotage against the enemy overseas". Or, as the Prime Minister later put it "to set Europe ablaze".' The title of the first chapter of Cookridge's book is 'Set Europe Ablaze'.

2 Never in the field of human conflict was so much owed by so many to so few.

On RAF pilots in the Battle of Britain. Speech, House of Commons (20 August 1940). Churchill's classic tribute was made well before the battle had reached its peak. There is a clear echo of Shakespeare's lines 'We few, we happy few, we band of brothers' in *Henry V*. Benham (1948) quotes Sir John Moore (1761–1809) after the fall of Calpi (where Nelson lost an eye): 'Never was so much work done by so few men.'

Another pre-echo may be found in Vol. 2 of Churchill's own *A History of the English-Speaking Peoples* (1956, but largely written pre-war). In describing a Scottish incursion in 1640 during the run-up to the English Civil War, he writes: 'All the Scots cannon fired and all the English army fled. A contemporary wrote that "Never so many ran from so few with less ado". The English soldiers explained volubly that their flight was not due to fear of the Scots, but to their own discontents.'

Earlier outings of the phraseology in Churchill's own speeches include: 'Never before were there so many people in England and never before have they had so much to eat' (Oldham by-election, 1899); and 'Nowhere else in the world could so enormous a mass of water be held up by so little masonry' (of a Nile dam, 1908).

The bookish phrase 'in the field of human conflict' tended to be dropped when Churchill's speech was quoted. It is interesting that Harold Nicolson, noting the speech in his diary, slightly misquotes this passage: '[Winston] says, in referring to the RAF, "never in the history of human conflict *has* so much been owed by so many to so few".' Much later, Terry Major-Ball was one of those who repeated the first of these errors in *Major Major* (1994): 'Never in the history of human conflict has a private soldier been so relieved,' he writes.

The immediate impact of Churchill's phrase was unquestionable, however, and is evidenced by a letter to him of 10 September from Lady Violet Bonham Carter (from the Churchill papers, quoted by Martin Gilbert in Vol. 6 of the official biography): 'Your sentence about the Air-war – "Never in the history [*sic*] of human conflict has [*sic*] so much been owed by so many to so few" – will live as long as words are spoken and remembered. Nothing so simple, so majestic & so true has been said in so great a moment of human history. You have beaten your old enemies "the Classics" into a cocked hat! Even my Father [H.H. Asquith] would have admitted that. How *he* would have loved it!'

By 22 September, Churchill's daughter, Mary, was uttering a *bon mot* in his hearing about the collapse of France through weak leadership: 'Never before has so much been betrayed for so many by so few' (recorded by John Colville, *The Fringes of Power*, Vol. 1, 1985).

3 Like the Mississippi, it just keeps rolling along. Let it roll. Let it roll on full flood, inexorable, irresistible, benignant, to broader lands and better days.

On cooperation with the US. In *Ib.* Alluding to HAMMERSTEIN 278:4.

4 Here is the answer which I will give to President Roosevelt ... Give us the tools, and we will finish the job.

Radio broadcast (9 February 1941). Towards the end of

his speech Churchill quoted the verse from LONGFELLOW 361:3 that President Roosevelt had sent him in January. Churchill's prime objective at this time (Pearl Harbor did not take place until December) was to bring the United States into the war or, at least, to wring every possible ounce of assistance out of it. Hence, the famous rallying cry with which he concluded. In May Churchill also replied to Roosevelt's quotation with his own taken from CLOUGH 175:3.

1 If Hitler invaded Hell, I would at least make a favourable reference to the Devil.

Remark (21 June 1941), recorded in John Colville, *The Fringes of Power*, Vol. 1 (1985). Churchill was justifying the fact that he – an arch anti-communist – was cooperating with the Soviet Union. His sole purpose was the destruction of Hitler.

2 As far as I can see, you have used every cliché except 'God is love' and 'Please adjust your dress before leaving'.

On a long-winded memorandum by Anthony Eden. This is quoted in Maurice Edelman, *The Mirror: A Political History* (1966) together with Churchill's comment: 'This offensive story is wholly devoid of foundation.' In 1941, Churchill took the unusual course of writing to Cecil King of the *Daily Mirror* about the matter. The columnist 'Cassandra' had used the story, though labelling it apocryphal and saying he had taken it from *Life* Magazine. *Reader's Digest* in August 1943 certainly carried this version by Allan A. Michie: 'Asked once to look over a draft of one of Anthony Eden's vague speeches on the post-war world, he sent it back to the Foreign Minister with this curt note: "I have read your speech and find that you have used every cliché known to the English language except 'Please adjust your dress before leaving'."'

3 [He is] like a female llama surprised in her bath.

On Charles de Gaulle. Quoted in Lord Moran, *The Struggle for Survival* (1966), which also includes his denial that he ever said it.

4 The Cross of Lorraine is the heaviest cross I have had to bear.

On Charles de Gaulle. In France the Resistance movement had a symbol – the Cross of Lorraine – and when Charles de Gaulle was told that Churchill had made this remark in reference to him, he commented: 'If we consider that the other crosses Churchill had to bear were the German army, submarine warfare, the bombing of Britain and the threat of annihilation, then when he says that the heaviest of all these was de Gaulle, it is quite a tribute to a man alone, without an army, without a country, and with only a few followers' (Romain Gary, *Life* Magazine, December 1958). According to Colonel Gilbert Rémy, *Ten Years with De Gaulle* (1971), the film producer Alexander Korda asked Churchill in 1948, 'Winston, did you really say that of all the crosses you ever had to bear, the heaviest was the Cross of Lorraine?' and Churchill replied, 'No, I didn't say it; but I'm sorry I didn't, because it was quite witty ... and so true!'

5 Now this is not the end. It is not even the beginning of the end. But it is, perhaps, the end of the beginning.

Speech, Mansion House, London (10 November 1942). Of the Battle of Egypt. The formula seems to have a particular appeal, judging by the number of times that it has been recalled. One occasion that comes to mind is when Ian Smith, the Rhodesian leader, broadcast a speech containing – or so it seemed at the time – a commitment to majority rule, after Dr Henry Kissinger's shuttle diplomacy in the autumn of 1976.

Note that Talleyrand went only half-way when he said, 'It is the beginning of the end [*Voilà le commencement de la fin*]' either after Napoleon's defeat at Borodino (1812) or during the Hundred Days (20 March – 28 June 1815).

In *F.E. Smith, First Earl of Birkenhead* (1983), John Campbell observes that Churchill was sitting next to F.E. when Smith addressed an all-party meeting in London on 11 September 1914. The battle of the Marne, he said, was not the beginning of the end, 'it is only the end of the beginning'. And, Campbell suggests, Churchill 'remembered and tucked [it] away for use again twenty-seven years later'.

6 The soft under-belly of the Axis.

The phrase 'soft under-belly', for a vulnerable part, appears to have originated with Churchill. Speaking in the House of Commons on 11 November 1942, he said: 'We make this wide encircling movement in the Mediterranean ... having for its object the exposure of the under-belly of the Axis, especially Italy, to heavy attack.' In his *The Second World War*, Vol. 4 (1951), he describes a prior meeting with Stalin in August 1942, at which he had outlined the same plan: 'To illustrate my point I had meanwhile drawn a picture of a crocodile, and explained to Stalin with the help of this picture how it was our intention to attack the soft belly of the crocodile as we attacked his hard snout.'

Somewhere, subsequently, the 'soft' and the 'underbelly' must have joined together to produce the phrase in the form in which it is now used.

1 In wartime, truth is so precious that she should always be attended by a bodyguard of lies.

Remark made to Stalin during the Teheran Conference (November 1943) on the subject of joint cover and deception schemes. Recounted in *The Second World War*, Vol. 5 (1952).

2 This is *your* victory.

Speech to crowds in London on VE-Day (8 May 1945).

3 No socialist Government conducting the entire life and industry of the country could afford to allow free, sharp, or violently-worded expressions of public discontent. They would have to fall back on some form of Gestapo.

Party political radio broadcast (4 June 1945). In the run-up to the general election that he lost, Churchill attempted to reinforce his view of a socialist future with a misjudged reference to the Gestapo. Evidently his wife had begged him to leave out the passage, but, in what was a significant miscalculation and a possible token of waning powers, Churchill went ahead and was duly much criticized by his political opponents, though he did also receive some support.

4 At the moment it seems quite effectively disguised.

On his defeat in the 1945 General Election, to his wife who had told him it might be a blessing in disguise. Quoted in his *The Second World War*, Vol. 6 (1954). Meaning 'a misfortune which turns out to be beneficial', this phrase has been in existence since the early eighteenth century.

Despite this comment, Churchill seems to have come round to something like his wife's point of view. On 5 September 1945 he wrote to her from an Italian holiday: 'This is the first time for very many years that I have been completely out of the world ... Others having to face the hideous problems of the aftermath ... It may all indeed be "a blessing in disguise".'

5 When the eagles are silent, the parrots begin to jabber.

A sort of proverb, possibly original to Churchill. Quoted in Sykes & Sproat, *The Wit of Sir Winston* (1965).

6 *Quand je regarde mon derrière, je vois qu'il est divisé en deux parties.*

Alleged remark in a Paris speech just after the Second World War. He told his audience that, looking back, he saw his career divided into two distinct and separate periods. So what he meant by his 'derrière' was not his backside but his past. Quoted on BBC Radio *Quote ... Unquote* (29 January 1979).

7 Neither the sure prevention of war, nor the continuous rise of world organisation will be gained without what I have called the fraternal association of the English-speaking peoples. This means a special relationship between the British Commonwealth and Empire and the United States.

Speech at Fulton, Missouri (5 March 1946). The term 'special relationship', used to describe affiliations between countries (the earliest *OED2* citation is for one between Britain and Galicia in 1929), but particularly referring to that supposed to exist between Britain and the US on the basis of historical ties and a common language, was principally promoted by Churchill in his attempts to draw the US into the 1939–45 war, though whether he used the phrase prior to 1941 is not clear. In the House of Commons on 7 November 1945, Churchill said: 'We should not abandon our special relationship with the United States and Canada about the atomic bomb.' In his Fulton speech, he also asked: 'Would a special relationship between the United States and the British Commonwealth be inconsistent with our over-riding loyalties to the World Organization [the UN]?'

8 From Stettin in the Baltic to Trieste in the Adriatic, an iron curtain has descended across the Continent.

Ib. A famous reference to an imaginary division between the Eastern and Western blocs in Europe, caused by the hard-line tactics of the Soviet Union after the Second World War. Churchill had already used the phrase 'iron curtain' in telegrams to President Truman and in the House of Commons.

Before him there were any number of uses, all alluding to the iron 'safety' curtains introduced in theatres as a fire precaution in the eighteenth century (and still sometimes referred to as 'the iron' in theatrical circles). In his novel *The Food of the Gods* (1904), H.G. Wells had written: 'An iron curtain had dropped between him [the scientist Redwood] and the outer world.' In the specific Soviet context, Ethel Snowden was using the phrase as early as 1920 in her book *Through Bolshevik Russia*. Describing her arrival in Petrograd with a Labour Party delegation, she said: 'We were behind the "iron curtain" at last!' Joseph Goebbels, Hitler's propaganda chief, wrote in an article for the weekly *Das Reich* (23 February 1945): 'Should the

German people lay down their arms, the agreements between Roosevelt, Churchill and Stalin would allow the Soviets to occupy all Eastern and South-Eastern Europe together with the major part of the Reich. An iron curtain would at once descend on this territory.' These remarks were reprinted in British newspapers at the time.

1 The Sinews of Peace.

Ib. Churchill's speech at Fulton had this title – an allusion to the phrase '*nervi belli pecunia*' from Cicero's *Philippics* where the 'sinews of war' meant 'money'. The 'sinews of peace' recommended by Churchill in dealing with the Soviet Union amounted to recourse to the newly formed United Nations Organization.

2 He dare not absent himself from his Cabinet at home. He knows full well that when the mouse is away the cats will play.

On Clement Attlee's reluctance to fly to Moscow and speak plainly to Stalin. Quoted in Harold Nicolson, *Diaries* (entry for 12 December 1946).

3 Madam, all babies look like me.

When a proud mother said her baby looked like him. Quoted in Sykes & Sproat, *The Wit of Sir Winston* (1965).

4 One is a majority.

Any number of British parliamentarians have used this expression to lessen the importance of achieving only a small majority in an election or parliamentary vote. It is fair to assume that a proportion of them attributed the phrase to Churchill (as Margaret Thatcher did in April 1988). The *Observer* Magazine had '"One vote is enough" – Churchill' in a compendium of election sayings on 5 April 1992. Possibly Churchill *did* say it, but if he did, he was quoting or alluding. It was Benjamin Disraeli who wrote, 'As for our majority ... one is enough' in Chapter 64 of his novel *Endymion* (1880). Accordingly, Andrew Roberts writes in *Eminent Churchillians* (1994): 'Despite Disraeli's famous comment, which Churchill made his own, that "One is Enough", the new Prime Minister felt himself politically insecure.'

Compare, from the US, 'One with the law is a majority' in Calvin Coolidge's Speech of Acceptance (27 July 1920) and 'One man with courage makes a majority', often ascribed to Andrew Jackson. Also, Wendell Phillips in a speech at Brooklyn on 1 November 1859 said: 'One, on God's side, is a majority.' Later, John F. Kennedy, when elected President in 1960, remarked: 'The majority is narrow, but the responsibility is clear. There may be difficulties with Congress, but a majority of one is still a majority.'

5 And you, madam, are ugly. But I shall be sober in the morning.

To Bessie Braddock MP who had told him he was drunk. Quoted in Sykes & Sproat, *The Wit of Sir Winston* (1965), without naming Braddock. She was named in Leslie Frewin, *Immortal Jester* (1973).

6 There, but for the grace of God goes God.

Churchill did not deny having made this remark about the Labour politician, Sir Stafford Cripps. It was quoted in Willans & Roetter, *The Wit of Winston Churchill* (1954) but had already been noted by Geoffrey Madan who died in July 1947 (see his *Notebooks*, published in 1981).

In so speaking, Churchill was adapting a remark made by John Bradford (who died in 1555) on seeing criminals going to their execution: 'There, but for the grace of God, goes John Bradford.' This is normally now rendered proverbially as 'There, but for the grace of God, go I.'

7 Who will relieve me of this Wuthering Height?

Of Sir Stafford Cripps at dinner. Quoted in Leslie Frewin, *Immortal Jester* (1973).

8 It [is] the first time that [I have] heard of a rat actually swimming out to join a sinking ship.

On Air Vice-Marshal Bennett who had joined the Liberals. Quoted in Malcolm Muggeridge, *Like It Was* (1981) – diary entry for 14 February 1948. Later, Ralph Yarborough said of John B. Connally's 1973 switch from Democratic to Republican party in pursuit of the presidential nomination: 'It is the only case on record of a man swimming toward a sinking ship' (quoted in *The Washington Post*, 18 January 1988).

9 A sheep in sheep's clothing.

On Clement Attlee. Quoted in Willans & Roetter, *The Wit of Winston Churchill* (1954). According to Safire (1980), however, Churchill told Sir Denis Brogan that he had said it not about Attlee but about Ramsay MacDonald, with rather more point. If so, it would appear that he was quoting a joke made by the humorous columnist 'Beachcomber' *c.*1936. Aneurin Bevan alluded to this same source *c.*1937 – 'Beachcomber once described Mr Ramsay MacDonald as ... It applies to many of the front-bench men with whom the Parliamentary Labour Party is cursed' (quoted in Michael Foot, *Aneurin Bevan*, Vol. 1, 1962).

Sir Edmund Gosse is supposed to have said the same

of T. Sturge Moore, the 'woolly-bearded poet', *c.*1906 – and was quoted as such by Ferris Greenslet in *Under the Bridge* (1943).

1 An empty taxi arrived at 10 Downing Street, and when the door was opened Attlee got out.

On Clement Attlee. Succeeded by the Labour leader after the 1945 general election, Churchill was obliged to oppose the man who had been his deputy in the wartime coalition. So this was another joke that went the rounds about the time. When John Colville told Churchill it was being attributed to him, he commented gravely, 'after an awful pause': 'Mr Attlee is an honourable and gallant gentleman, and a faithful colleague who served his country well at the time of her greatest need. I should be obliged if you would make it clear whenever an occasion arises that I never would make such a remark about him, and that I strongly disapprove of anybody who does.' This denial was reported in Kenneth Harris, *Attlee* (1982).

2 [Clement Attlee is] a modest man who has a good deal to be modest about.

Quoted in the *Chicago Sunday Tribune Magazine of Books* (27 June 1954), perhaps reviewing Willans & Roetter, *The Wit of Winston Churchill* (1954).

3 Don't talk to me about naval tradition. It's nothing but rum, sodomy, and the lash.

Quoted in Sir Peter Gretton, *Former Naval Person* (1968) – on the occasion when a naval officer objected that a wartime operation the Prime Minister was supporting ran against the traditions of the Royal Navy. In Harold Nicolson's diary (17 August 1950), this appears as: 'Naval tradition? Monstrous. Nothing but rum, sodomy, prayers and the lash.' Hence, *Rum, Bum and Concertina*, the title of a volume of George Melly's autobiography (1977), which he prefers to derive from 'an old naval saying': 'Ashore it's wine, women and song, aboard it's rum, bum and concertina'.

4 Bossom? What an extraordinary name. Neither one thing nor the other!

On Sir Alfred Bossom MP. Quoted in Willans & Roetter, *The Wit of Winston Churchill* (1954).

5 Do not criticize your government when out of the country. Never cease to do so when at home.

Attributed remark, but unverified. An unwritten rule for members of a political party in power – and also, to some extent – in opposition. Quite frequently ignored.

6 He's not as nice as he looks.

On Ian Mikardo MP. Said to have been spoken to Christopher Soames, Churchill's PPS. According to Matthew Parris, *Scorn* (1994): 'Sir Edward Heath told us that this remark was made after a debate in the House of Commons in which Mr Mikardo "pressed the Prime Minister about anti-Semitic practices at the Mid-Ocean Club, Bermuda, somewhat to the irritation of the Prime Minister".'

7 This is the sort of English up with which I will not put.

Marginal comment on document. Quoted in Sir Ernest Gowers, 'Troubles with Prepositions', *Plain Words* (1948).

8 In war, resolution; in defeat, defiance; in victory, magnanimity; in peace, goodwill.

Churchill's history *The Second World War* was published in six volumes between 1948 and 1954. He took as the motto of the work some words that had occurred to him just after the First World War, as Eddie Marsh, at one time his Private Secretary, recalled: 'He produced one day a lapidary epigram on the spirit proper to a great nation in war and peace ... (I wish the tones in which he spoke this could have been "recorded" – the first phrase a rattle of musketry, the second "grating harsh thunder", the third a ray of the sun through storm-clouds; the last, pure benediction).'

In 1941, Churchill said the words had been devised (and rejected) as an inscription for a French war memorial, in the form: 'In war fury, in defeat defiance ...' Perhaps he had been inspired by one of the Latin quotations he knew – '*parcere subiectis et debellare* [spare the conquered and subdue the proud]' – Virgil, *Aeneid*, Bk 6, l. 854. In *My Early Life* (1930) he had earlier given his rejected inscription just as it appears here in the head phrase.

9 The Gathering Storm.

Title of Vol. 1 of his history *The Second World War*, published in 1948. The phrase had already been used about the approach of the war by Anthony Eden. He used it in a speech to the National Association of Manufacturers in New York in 1938.

10 The years from 1931 to 1935, apart from my anxiety on public affairs, were personally very pleasant to me. I earned my livelihood by dictating articles which had a wide circulation ... I lived in fact from mouth to hand ... Thus I never had a dull or idle moment from morning till

midnight, and with my happy family around me dwelt at peace within my habitation.

Referring to his 'exile' at Chartwell in the 1930s, in Chap. 5 of *The Gathering Storm*, the first volume of Churchill's *The Second World War* (1948). Churchill would have known he was alluding to Ecclesiasticus 44:6: 'Rich men furnished with ability, living peaceably in their habitations' (from the passage beginning 'Let us now praise famous men', *see* BIBLE 100:3).

1 I felt as if I were walking with destiny, and that all my past life had been but a preparation for this hour and this trial.

On becoming Prime Minister in 1939. In *ib.* Hence, *A Walk With Destiny*, title of a TV drama documentary play by Colin Morris (1974). In the US, it was known as *The Gathering Storm* (*see above* 168:9).

2 I would kick him up the arse, Alfred.

On being asked what he would do if he saw Picasso walking ahead of him down Piccadilly. Quoted by Sir Alfred Munnings in a speech at the Royal Academy dinner (1949). A report in the *Times* Diary (29 March 1983) recalled that Munnings, as President, had invited Churchill, who had just been admitted to the Academy. He supposedly ruffled the politician's feathers by saying in his speech: 'Seated on my left is the greatest Englishman of all time. I said to him just now: "What would you do if you saw Picasso walking ahead of you down Piccadilly?" – and he replied: "I would kick him up the arse, Alfred".'

Alas, the BBC recording of the event fails to confirm that Munnings ever said this. Not a born speaker, to put it mildly, what he said was, 'Once he said to me, "Alfred, if you met Picasso coming down the street, would you join with me in kicking his something-something?" I said, "Yes, sir, I would!"'

The Times report also suggested that, 'as the laughter died, Munnings yelled at the top of his voice: "Blunt, Blunt [i.e., Sir Anthony Blunt, the art connoisseur later unmasked as a traitor] – you're the one who says he prefers Picasso to Sir Joshua Reynolds!"' If he did yell it he was very quiet about it, because the barb is not audible on the recording.

3 I am ready to meet my Maker. Whether my Maker is ready for the ordeal of meeting me is another matter.

On his 75th birthday. Speech (30 November 1949). Sometimes inaccurately described as his 'last words'.

4 It is not easy to see how things could be worsened by a parley at the summit, if such a thing were possible.

Quoted in *The Times* (15 February 1950). This was apparently the genesis of the term 'summit meeting/conference'.

5 Not dead ... but the candle in that great turnip has gone out.

When someone said that Stanley Baldwin 'might as well be dead'. Quoted in Harold Nicolson, *Diaries* (1968), entry for 17 August 1950.

6 Why do we need this peep-show?

On plans for commercial television in Britain. Attributed remark, *c.*1951, quoted in Asa Briggs, *Sound and Vision 1945–55* (1979). Alternatively, '... tuppenny Punch and Judy show', as quoted in Jo Gable, *The Tuppenny Punch and Judy Show* (1980).

7 The trees do not grow up to the sky.

A favourite proverb of Churchill's – but what does it mean? John Colville quotes him as saying it on 6 January 1953 in a situation where he is recommending a 'wait and see' policy. The full version seems to be, 'The trees are tall but they do not reach to the sky'. In other words, 'trees may be tall, but they're not that tall' or, metaphorically, 'no person is that important, however grand they may appear'. Later in the same year, on 9 November, in his speech to the Lord Mayor's Banquet, Churchill said: 'Another old saying comes back to my mind which I have often found helpful or at least comforting. I think it was Goethe who said, "The trees do not grow up to the sky". I do not know whether he would have said that if he had lived through this frightful twentieth century where so much we feared was going to happen did actually happen. All the same it is a thought which should find its place in young as well as old brains.'

Is this a case of ascribing to Goethe any foreign language quote of which the speaker doesn't really know the source? Wolfgang Mieder and George B. Bryan supply the answer in *The Proverbial Winston S. Churchill. An Index to Proverbs in the Works of Sir Winston Churchill* (1995). Listed are no fewer than thirteen occasions on which Churchill used the proverb in his writing or speeches. Mieder and Bryan note how close the meaning of the words is to 'Pride goeth before a fall' (Proverbs 16:18), how it derives from a German original '*Est ist dafür gesorgt, daß die Bäume nicht in den Himmel wachsen*' (though sometimes this is in the form '*God takes care that* the trees don't grow up to the sky'), and how although Goethe probably didn't originate it, he used the proverb in his autobiography *Dichtung und Wahrheit*

(1811). Earlier it occurs in Martin Luther's *Tischreden* (table talk) and in one of the collections of proverbs of Johannes Agricola (1528–48).

Of course, people *do* manufacture these folk proverbs. Anon. devised one for Khruschev himself: 'Great oafs from little ikons grow.' Lyndon Irving sent this one into a *New Statesman* competition (though it has been ascribed to Dr Walter Heydecker): 'No leg is too short to reach the ground' (a dachshund-comforting proverb, this one). In *Unauthorized Versions* (1990), Kenneth Baker says: 'I am reminded of a competition for the most meaningless Russian proverb, of which the winning entry was, "The tallest trees are closest to the sky".' This is probably a reference to the game played by Claud Cockburn who won it once (according to his son, Patrick, in *The Independent*, 29 May 1996) with the 'fine old Norwegian saying, "The tree is taller than the highest wave".'

1 Here at the summit of our worldwide community is a lady whom we respect because she is our Queen, and whom we love because she is herself.

Radio broadcast (2 June 1953) – after the coronation of Queen Elizabeth II.

2 In defeat unbeatable; in victory unbearable.

On Field Marshal Montgomery. Quoted in Edward Marsh, *Ambrosia and Small Beer* (1964).

3 I'd never heard of this place Guatemala until I was in my seventy-ninth year.

During his visit to the US (June 1954), recorded by Lord Moran in *The Struggle for Survival* (1966). Earlier, Moran recorded Churchill saying on 28 April 1953: 'I have lived seventy-eight years without hearing of bloody places like Cambodia.'

4 Talking jaw to jaw is better than going to war.

At a White House lunch (26 June 1954). *Compare* MACMILLAN 373:4.

5 Dead birds don't fall out of nests.

When, as an old man, a colleague told him his fly-buttons were undone. Alluded to in *The Lyttelton Hart-Davis Letters*, Vol. 2 (1979) – concerning 1957.

6 I have never accepted what many people have kindly said, namely that I inspired the nation. It was the nation and the race dwelling all round the globe that had the lion heart. I had the luck to be called upon to give the roar.

On his eightieth birthday. Speech, Westminster Hall (30 November 1954).

7 The portrait is a remarkable example of modern art. It certainly combines force and candour. These are qualities which no active member of either house can do without or should fear to meet.

Ib. For his birthday, both Houses of Parliament presented Churchill with a portrait painted by Graham Sutherland. He did not like it but accepted the portrait with a gracefully double-edged compliment. Lady Churchill's dislike of the portrait took a more practical form: she had it destroyed.

8 I look as if I was having a difficult stool.

Remark on the same portrait, quoted in Ted Morgan, *Somerset Maugham* (1980) but earlier in *The Lyttelton Hart-Davis Letters* (1978) – for 20 November 1955. Other versions of this criticism are: 'How do they paint one today? Sitting on a lavatory!' (said to Charles Doughty, secretary of the committee which organized the tribute), and 'Here sits an old man on his stool, pressing and pressing.'

9 I have always been a bit shy of the really extemporary speech ever since I heard it said that an extemporary speech was not worth the paper it was written on.

Speech in his constituency (18 November 1955). For another comment on Churchill's own attitude to impromptu speaking, *see above* 163:5.

10 I am not a pillar of the church but a buttress – I support it from the outside.

When Churchill was reproached for not going to church. Recalled by Montague Browne in a speech to the International Churchill Society, London (25 September 1985). Note, however, that it was said of John Scott, Lord Eldon (1751–1838): 'He may be one of its [the Church's] buttresses, but certainly not one of its pillars, for he is never found within it' (H. Twiss, *Public and Private Life of Eldon*, 1844). The *ODQ* (1992) adds that this remark was later attributed to Lord Melbourne.

11 I'm so bored with it all.

Last words – or, at least, his last comprehensible words. Quoted in Mary Soames, *Clementine* (1979).

See also BERNERS 87:8; BEVAN 89:4; HEALEY 286:4; KENNEDY 331:7; MARVELL 383:1; MURROW 404:2.

CIANO, Count Galeazzo

Italian politician (1903–44)

1 As always, victory finds a hundred fathers, but defeat is an orphan.

Mussolini's foreign minister (and son-in-law) made this diary entry on 9 September 1942 (translation published 1946). President Kennedy quoted the 'old saying' following the Bay of Pigs disaster in April 1961.

CIBBER, Colley

English playwright (1671–1757)

2 Off with his head – so much for Buckingham.

In his 1700 edition of Shakespeare's *Richard III*, Cibber extended III.iv.76 thus, by the last four words. It proved a popular and lasting emendation. The extra phrase was included in Laurence Olivier's film of Shakespeare's play (UK, 1955). In Boswell's *Life of Johnson* (1791) – for 15 May 1776 – John Wilkes is quoted as saying: 'If I had displeased the Duke [of Argyle], and he had wished it, there is not a Campbell among you but would have been ready to bring John Wilkes's head to him in a charger. It would have been only "Off with his head! So much for Aylesbury". I was then member for Aylesbury.'

In 'Private Theatres' (1835), one of the *Sketches by Boz*, Charles Dickens describes the roles on offer to amateur actors who at that time could pay to take certain roles in plays: 'For instance, the Duke of Glo'ster is well worth two pounds ... including the "off with his head!" – which is sure to bring down the applause, and it is very easy to do – "Orf with his ed" (very quick and loud; – then slow and sneeringly) – "So much for Bu-u-u-uckingham!" Lay the emphasis on the "uck"; get yourself gradually into a corner, and work with your right hand, while you're saying it, as if you were feeling your way, and it's sure to do.'

3 Perish that thought!

Ib., interpolation in Act 5. First recorded use of the expression, now usually 'perish the thought'. Another Act 5 interpolation is: 'Conscience avaunt, Richard's himself again:/Hark! the shrill trumpet sounds, to horse, away,/My soul's in arms, and eager for the fray.'

4 Stolen sweets are best.

The Rival Fools (1709). See also HUNT 305:3; TRENET 542:5.

CITIZEN KANE

American film 1941. Script by Herman J. Mankiewicz and Orson Welles. With Orson Welles as Kane, Dorothy Comingore as Susan and George Couloris as Thatcher.

5 *Kane*: Rosebud!

Soundtrack. His dying word, the first word in the film, and referred to *passim* as finding out what it meant to him is a theme of the picture. It is finally glimpsed written on the side of a snow-sledge – a powerful talisman of childhood innocence, or a 'symbol of maternal affection, the loss of which deprives him irrecoverably of the power to love or be loved' (Kenneth Tynan). Orson Welles himself issued a statement (14 January 1941) explaining: '"Rosebud" is the trade name of a cheap little sled on which Kane was playing on the day he was taken away from his home and his mother. In his subconscious it represented the simplicity, the comfort, above all the lack of responsibility in his home, and also it stood for his mother's love which Kane never lost.'

6 *Kane*: I've talked to the responsible leaders of the Great Powers – England, France, Germany, and Italy. They're too intelligent to embark on a project which would mean the end of civilization as we now know it. You can take my word for it: there'll be no war!

Soundtrack. A good example of the Hollywood cliché 'The end of civilization ...' in use.

7 *Kane*: Dear Wheeler, you provide the prose poems. I'll provide the war.

Soundtrack. Kane, replying to a war correspondent's message, 'Could send you prose poems about scenery but ... there is no war in Cuba'. This is based on an 1898 exchange between the newspaper artist Frederic Remington and his proprietor, William Randolph Hearst (1863–1951). Remington asked to be allowed home from Cuba because there was no war for him to cover. Hearst cabled: 'Please remain. You furnish the pictures and I will furnish the war.' Hearst was, of course, the model for Kane.

8 *Susan*: I'm the one who has to do the singing. I'm the one who gets the raspberries.

Soundtrack. Kane's wife is forced to sing in opera productions that he pays for. This is how she expresses her unhappiness at the hostile reception her inadequate voice receives.

CLARE, John

English poet (1793–1864)

1 Fields were the essence of the song
& fields & woods are still as mine
Real teachers that are all divine
So if my song be weak or tame
Tis I not they who bear the blame.

The first line of this quotation from Clare's 'Progress of Rhyme' is on his memorial tablet set in Poets' Corner, Westminster Abbey. The 'Northamptonshire Peasant Poet' died in an asylum for the insane.

CLARK, Brian

British playwright (1932–)

2 Whose Life Is It Anyway?

Title of play (1978; film US, 1981) about a paraplegic who resists his carers' determination to keep him alive. Hence, the format phrase 'whose —— is it anyway?' A BBC Radio 4/Channel 4 TV improvisatory game was given the title *Whose Line Is It Anyway?* (by 1989). By 1993, the *Independent* Magazine was campaigning for the abolition of it as a headline cliché. Among a blizzard of examples, it cited: 'WHOSE QUEEN IS IT ANYWAY?' (London *Evening Standard*, 18 March 1993) and 'WHOSE WOMB IS IT ANYWAY?' (*Northern Echo*, 9 November 1992).

3 Don't half-quote me to reinforce your own prejudices.

Kipling (1984) – put in the mouth of Rudyard Kipling.

CLARK, Kenneth (later Lord Clark)

English art historian (1903–83)

4 What could be more agreeable?

Remark attributed by *Private Eye* Magazine following TV series, *Civilisation* (1969), quoted in Auberon Waugh, *Four Crowded Years* (1976).

5 One may be optimistic, but one can't exactly be joyful at the prospect before us.

The end of *Civilisation*. Last words of the BBC TV series (1969) in which Clark interpreted western civilization mainly through its achievements in the visual arts.

6 Another Part of the Wood.

Title of the first volume of Clark's autobiography (1974) and taken from the stage direction to Act 3, Sc. 2 of Shakespeare's *A Midsummer Night's Dream*. Scene locations such as this were mostly not of Shakespeare's own devising but were added by later editors. Clark said he wished also to allude to DANTE 195:8. Lillian Hellman had earlier entitled one of her plays, *Another Part of the Forest* (1946).

CLARKE, Arthur C.

English writer (1917–)

7 Open the pod-bay doors, Hal!

In the script that Clarke wrote with Stanley Kubrick for the film *2001: A Space Odyssey* (UK, 1968), this is what the stranded astronaut, Dave Bowman (Keir Dullea), says to the errant computer. Not 'Open the pod door, Hal' as in *PDMQ* (1980).

CLARKE, Roy

British writer (1930–)

8 The Last of the Summer Wine.

Title of a long-running BBC TV comedy series (1974–) – about a trio of school friends in a Yorkshire village finding themselves elderly and unemployed. Not a quotation, according to its writer. In *Radio Times* (February 1983), Clarke described it as: 'Merely a provisional title which seemed to suit the age group and location. I expected it to be changed but no one ever thought of anything better.'

The phrase 'summer wine', on its own, had already been used in a song 'If I Thought You'd Ever Change Your Mind' by John Cameron, which was recorded in 1969 by Kathe Green ('... feed you winter fruits and summer wine ...')

'Last of the wine' had also been used earlier to describe things of which there is only a finite amount or of which the best is gone. From a programme note by composer Nicholas Maw for *The Rising of the Moon*, Glyndebourne Festival Opera (1970): 'In a recent television interview, Noël Coward was asked if he thought it still possible to write comedy for the stage. Did his own generation not have the "last of the wine"?' In the 1950s, Robert Bolt wrote a radio play and Mary Renault, a novel (1956) both with the title *The Last of the Wine*.

CLAUSEWITZ, Karl von

Prussian soldier (1780–1831)

1 War is nothing but a continuation of politics with the admixture of other means.

Vom Kriege (1832–4). Usually rendered as: 'War is the continuation of politics by other means.'

CLEAVER, Eldridge

American political activist (1935–)

2 If you're not part of the solution, you're part of the problem.

CODP's earliest citation for this (anonymous) modern proverb is Malcolm Bradbury's novel *The History Man* (1975). But there is little doubt that Cleaver said it in a 1968 speech in San Francisco. It may even be included in his *Soul on Ice* (1968). One form of Cleaver's remark is: 'What we're saying today is that you're either part of the solution or you're part of the problem.' Another: 'There is no more neutrality in the world. You either have to be part of the solution, or you're going to be part of the problem.'

Compare: 'If you're not part of the steamroller, you're part of the road' – attributed to Michael Eisner, Chairman of Walt Disney, in 1993.

CLEMENCEAU, Georges

French Prime Minister (1841–1929)

3 *J'Accuse.*
I accuse.

The Dreyfus Affair in France arose in 1894 when Captain Alfred Dreyfus, who was Jewish, was dismissed from the army on trumped-up charges of treason. Condemned to life imprisonment on Devil's Island, he was not reinstated until 1906. In the meantime, the case had divided France. The writer Émile Zola (1840–1902) came to the defence of Dreyfus with two open letters addressed to the President of the French Republic and printed in the paper *L'Aurore*. The first, under the banner headline, '*J'accuse* [I accuse]', was published on 13 January 1898, each paragraph beginning with the words; the second, more moderate in tone, on 22 January.

It is a small point, perhaps, but Clemenceau, who played a prominent part in the campaign with Zola, claimed in a letter (19 June 1902) that: 'It was I who gave the title "*J'accuse*" to Zola's letter.' He also said that he had written most of the second letter (source: D.R. Watson, *Clemenceau*, 1974.)

4 *La guerre, c'est une chose trop grave pour la confier à des militaires.*
War is too serious a business to be left to the generals.

In France Parliament had suspended its sittings at the outbreak of the First World War and the conduct of the war had been entrusted to the government and to Joffre and the General Staff. By 1915, however, opinion was changing. It may have been about this time that Clemenceau, who became French Prime Minister again in 1917, uttered this, his most famous remark. It is quoted in Suarez, *Soixante Années d'histoire française: la vie orgueilleuse de Clemenceau* (1932) and Hampden Jackson, *Clemenceau and the Third Republic* (1946).

The notion has also been attributed to Talleyrand (Briand quoted him as such to Lloyd George during the First World War) and, indeed, Clemenceau may have said it himself much earlier (in 1886 even). Subsequently, the format of the saying has been applied to many other professions. See BENN 84:3; DE GAULLE 199:6; MACLEOD 371:4. In 1990 Helmut Sihler, president of a West German chemical company, said: 'The environment is too important to be left to the environmentalists.'

5 My home policy? I wage war. My foreign policy? I wage war. Always, everywhere, I wage war.

Speech to the Chamber of Deputies (8 March 1918). *Compare* CHURCHILL 163:1.

6 We have won the war: now we have to win the peace, and it may be more difficult.

To General Mordacq (11 November 1918). Quoted in D.R. Watson, *Clemenceau* (1974).

7 The good Lord has only ten.

Remark about President Wilson's Fourteen Points at the Versailles Peace Conference (1918). Quoted in D. Wallechinsky & I. Wallace, *The People's Almanac* (1975). The 'points', set out in an address to Congress (8 January 1918), were Wilson's demands for a new world order following the First World War. They included proposals for 'open covenants of peace, openly arrived at', freedom of the seas, free trade and disarmament.

8 *Ah, si je pouvais pisser comme il parle!*
If I could piss the way he speaks!

On David Lloyd George. Quoted in A. Andrews, *Quotations for Speakers and Writers* (1969).

1 America is the only country in history which miraculously has gone directly from barbarism to degeneration without the usual interval of civilization.

So ascribed to Clemenceau by Hans Bendix in *The Saturday Review of Literature* (1 December 1945). No more substantial attribution appears to exist.

2 If you don't vote Socialist/Communist before you are twenty, you have no heart – if you do vote Socialist/Communist after you are twenty, you have no head.

The saying to this effect may derive from what Bennett A. Cerf attributed to Clemenceau in *Try and Stop Me* (1944). It is supposedly what Clemenceau said when told his son had just joined the Communist party: 'My son is twenty-two years old. If he had not become a Communist at twenty-two I would have disowned him. If he is still a Communist at thirty, I will do it then.'

Another suggested source is Dean Inge, the 'Gloomy Dean' of St Paul's (d.1954). And then there is the remark, attributed loosely to Benjamin Disraeli, in Laurence J. Peter's *Quotations for Our Time* (1977): 'A man who is not a Liberal at sixteen has no heart; a man who is not a Conservative at sixty has no head'.

Pass the Port Again (1980) has this version, ascribed to Maurice Maeterlinck: 'If a man is not a Socialist at twenty he has no heart. If he is a Socialist at thirty, he has no brain.' *The Oxford Book of Ages* (1985) ascribes to Aristide Briand (1862–1932) the similar: 'The man who is not a socialist at twenty has no heart, but if he is still a socialist at forty he has no head.'

Putting it another way, Will Durant, the American teacher, philosopher and historian (1885–1982), said, 'There is nothing in Socialism that a little age or a little money will not cure.' The American poet, Robert Frost, wrote in 'Precaution' (1936): 'I never dared be radical when young/For fear it would make me conservative when old.'

Compare what George Bernard Shaw said in a lecture at the University of Hong Kong in February 1933: 'Steep yourself in revolutionary books. Go up to your neck in Communism, because if you are not a red revolutionist at 20, you will be at 50 a most impossible fossil. If you are a red revolutionist at 20, you have some chance of being up-to-date at 40.'

3 Oh, to be seventy again!

Said to have been exclaimed on his eightieth birthday (i.e., in 1921) when walking down the Champs-Élysées with a friend and a pretty girl passed them (quoted by James Agate, *Ego 3*, 1938). The same remark is ascribed to Oliver Wendell Holmes Jr (1841–1935), the American jurist, on reaching his eighty-seventh year (by Fadiman & van Doren in *The American Treasury*, 1955). Bernard de Fontenelle (1657–1757), the French writer and philosopher, is said in great old age to have attempted with difficulty to pick up a young lady's fan, murmuring, 'Ah, if I were only eighty again!' (Pedrazzini & Gris, *Autant en apportent les mots*, 1969).

4 Buried standing, facing Germany.

His last wish as to how he was to be buried. Quoted in Barnaby Conrad, *Famous Last Words* (1961).

CLEVELAND, Grover

American Democratic 22nd and 24th President (1837–1908)

5 We love him for the enemies he has made.

A curious campaign slogan for Cleveland was derived from a speech made by Governor Edward Stuyvesant Bragg (1827–1912), when seconding Cleveland's presidential nomination (9 July 1884): 'They love him most for the enemies he has made.' With the slogan, however, Cleveland won the first of his two separate presidential terms. *Compare* ROOSEVELT 459:5.

CLINTON, Bill (William Jefferson Clinton)

American Democratic 42nd President (1946–)

6 When I was in England [as a Rhodes Scholar], I experimented with marijuana a time or two, and I didn't like it, and I didn't inhale and I never tried it again.

From a report in *The Washington Post* (31 March 1992). During his campaign for the Presidency, Clinton had to fend off criticisms that not only had he been to Oxford (anathema to the incumbent President, George Bush) but also had not fought in Vietnam and was generally associated with 1960s habits. While seeking the Democratic nomination, Clinton appeared on TV with a rival candidate, Jerry Brown. The two men were asked if they had ever violated state, federal or international laws. Under 'pinpoint questioning that closed all avenues of escape', according to the *Post*, he finally confessed to the above banality.

7 This ceremony is held in the depth of winter. But, by the words we speak and the faces we show the world, we force the spring.

It was unfair of the *Independent* Magazine (13 February 1993) to suggest that President Clinton had strayed into *Being There* territory during his Inaugural speech (20 January 1993) by using the 'exact words ... "After the winter comes the spring".' What Chauncey Gardiner, the platitudinous sage played by Peter Sellers in the 1980 film, said was: 'First comes spring and summer but then we have fall and winter. And then we get spring and summer again.' Clinton said, rather, in his opening paragraph what is printed above. That is not at all the same thing, though it may have been ill-advised of the new President to foster such a comparison.

1 Our democracy must be not only the envy of the world but the engine of our own renewal. There is nothing wrong with America that cannot be cured by what is right with America.

From the same Inaugural speech.

CLIVE, Lord (Robert)

English soldier and administrator (1725–74)

2 By God, Mr Chairman, at this moment I stand astonished at my own moderation.

Reply during Parliamentary cross-examination (1773). In R. Gleig, *The Life of Robert, First Lord Clive* (1848).

CLOUGH, Arthur Hugh

English poet (1819–61)

3 Say not the struggle naught availeth,
The labour and the wounds are vain,
The enemy faints not, nor faileth,
And as things have been, things remain ...

For while the tired waves, vainly breaking,
Seem here no painful inch to gain,
Far back, through creeks and inlets making,
Comes silent, flooding in, the main.

And not by eastern windows only,
When daylight comes, comes in the light,
In front, the sun climbs slow, how slowly,
But, westward, look, the land is bright.

'Say Not the Struggle Nought Availeth' (1855). In a radio broadcast on 3 May 1941, hinting at future American involvement in the war, Winston Churchill responded to the quotation (LONGFELLOW 361:3) sent to him by President Roosevelt by quoting from Clough. 'I have,' he said by way of introduction, 'some other lines which are less well known but which seem apt and appropriate to our fortunes tonight, and I believe they will be so judged wherever the English language is spoken or the flag of freedom flies.' He quoted the second two verses above in the form shown.

Hence, *The Land Is Bright*, title of a play (1941) by George S. Kaufman and Edna Ferber.

4 Thou shalt not kill; but need'st not strive
Officiously to keep alive.
Do not adultery commit;
Advantage rarely comes of it.
Thou shalt not steal; an empty feat,
When it's so lucrative to cheat ...

Clough's 'The Latest Decalogue' (1862) was an *ironical* version of the Ten Commandments – so the first two lines here were not serious advice to doctors (in which sense they have sometimes been quoted, however).

5 As I sat at the café, I said to myself,
They may talk as they please about what
 they call pelf,
They may sneer as they like about eating and
 drinking,
But help it I cannot, I cannot help thinking,
How pleasant it is to have money, heigh ho!
How pleasant it is to have money.

'Dipsychus' (1865). The poem was found in Clough's papers after his death and not published till then, which may perhaps explain why there are some rather free versions of it in circulation. Clough's 'The Latest Decalogue' and 'Say not the struggle nought availeth' were also only published posthumously.

On BBC Radio *Quote ... Unquote* (in 1980), Wynford Vaughan-Thomas recited a version that does not appear to come from Clough's original:

> Bring on the champagne and damn the expense,
> I've seen it observed by a person of sense
> The labouring classes would not last a day
> If fellows like us didn't eat, drink and pay!
> How pleasant it is to have money, heigh ho!
> How pleasant it is to have money.

COBB, Irvin S.

American humorist and writer (1876–1944)

6 Nothing trivial, I trust?

When Cobb was a reporter on the New York *World*, he had to work under Charles E. Chapin, whom he found to be a difficult boss. Arriving at the office one day, Cobb was told that Chapin was off sick and made this inquiry. Recounted in Ralph L. Marquard, *Jokes and Anecdotes* (1977), this may possibly be the origin of the oft-told tale. Recalled earlier as 'I've just learned about his illness; let's hope it's nothing trivial' in *The Treasury of Humorous Quotations*, ed. by Evan Esar & Nicolas Bentley (1951).

In Ulick O'Connor's *Oliver St John Gogarty* (1964), John Pentland Mahaffy is quoted as having said of the illness of Traill who had beaten him for the Provostship of Trinity College Dublin (in 1904): 'Nothing trivial, I hope.'

COBBETT, William

English radical writer (1762–1835)

1 But what is to be the fate of the great wen of all? The monster, called ... 'the metropolis of empire'?

In 'Rural Rides: The Kentish Journal' in *Cobbett's Weekly Political Register* (5 January 1822). Cobbett asked this of London. A 'wen' is a lump or protuberance on a body; a wart. *Compare* CHARLES 155:10.

COCKBURN, Alison

Scottish poet and songwriter (1713–94)

2 For the flowers of the forest are a'wade away.

'The Flowers of the Forest' (1765). 'Wade' means 'weeded', but sometimes the phrase is rendered as 'withered away'. The line also appears in 'The Flowers of the Forest' (1756) by the Scottish lyricist, Jean Elliot (1727–1805).

COCKBURN, Claud

English journalist (1904–81)

3 Small earthquake in Chile. Not many dead.

In his book *In Time of Trouble* (1956) (incorporated in *I Claud* ..., 1967), Cockburn claimed to have won a competition for dullness among sub-editors on *The Times* with this headline in the late 1920s: 'It had to be a genuine headline, that is to say one which was actually in the next morning's newspaper. I won it only once.' At Cockburn's death it was said, however, that an exhaustive search had failed to find this particular headline in the paper. It may just have been a smoking-room story. However, the idea lives on: it became (perhaps inevitably) the title of a book (1972) by Alastair Horne about the Allende affair (in Chile). The journalist Michael Green called a volume of memoirs *Nobody Hurt in Small Earthquake* (1990), and the cartoonist Nicholas Garland called his 'Journal of a year in Fleet Street', *Not Many Dead* (1990).

4 The Cliveden Set.

In news sheet *The Week* (17 June 1936). Insofar as it existed, the set was in favour of appeasement (*see* LOTHIAN 363:2) and took its name from the seat of Lord and Lady Astor, who were at the centre of it. Chips Channon wrote in his diary on 4 April 1938 (of a reception given by Lady Astor): 'The function will be criticised, since there is already talk of a so-called "Cliveden" set which is alleged to be pro-Hitler, but which, in reality, is only pro-Chamberlain and pro-sense'. On 8 May 1940, Channon added: 'I think [Lady Astor] is seriously rattled by the "Cliveden Set" allegations which were made against her before the war, and now wants to live them down.'

COCKS, Sir Barnett

English parliamentary official (1907–89)

5 A committee is a cul de sac down which ideas are lured and then quietly strangled.

Quoted in the *New Scientist* (8 November 1973). *Compare* TREE 542:4.

COFFIN, William Sloane

American clergyman (1924–)

6 Even if you win the rat-race, you're still a rat.

When consulted at his home in Vermont (July 1995), the Rev. Coffin said that to the best of his knowledge he did originate this statement in the above form. He thought up the quip 'in the 1950s or 1960s' when he was chaplain either at Williams College or at Yale University. He added the caveat that he originated the statement 'as far as I know'. The line is often attributed to the American actress Lily Tomlin who, in turn, ascribes it to the writer, Jane Wagner.

COHAN, George M.

American songwriter and entertainer (1878–1942)

7 The Yanks are coming
And we won't come back till it's over
Over there!

Song, 'Over There' (1917). Referring to the war in Europe.

8 I don't care what you say about me, as long as you say *something* about me, and as long as you spell my name right.

Quoted in J. McCabe, *George M. Cohan* (1973). See

other observations on publicity under ANONYMOUS 21:1.

COHEN, Sir Jack

British supermarket grocer (1898–1979)

1 Pile it high, sell it cheap.

Business motto. Hence, the title of Maurice Corina's book, *Pile It High, Sell It Cheap: The Authorised Biography* ... (1971).

COHN, Al

American musician (1925–88)

2 A gentleman knows how to play the accordion, but doesn't.

Cohn was a saxophonist. Unverified. However, *Reader's Digest* (March 1976) quoted *The Wall Street Journal*: 'A true gentleman is a man who knows how to play the bagpipes – but doesn't.' *Compare* ARISTOTLE 59:3.

COHN, Irving

American songwriter (1898–1961)

3 Yes, we have no bananas,
We have no bananas today.

Song 'Yes, We Have No Bananas' (1923), to music by Frank Silver (1892–1960). According to Ian Whitcomb in *After the Ball* (1972), the title line came from a cartoon strip by Tad Dorgan and not, as the composers were wont to claim, from a Greek fruit-store owner on Long Island. Alternatively, it was a saying picked up by US troops in the Philippines from a Greek pedlar. In Britain, Elders & Fyffes, the banana importers, embraced the song and distributed 10,000 hands of bananas to music-sellers with the slogan: 'Yes! we have no bananas! On sale here'.

COKE, Desmond

English writer and schoolteacher (1879–1931)

4 All rowed fast, but none so fast as stroke.

In *Sandford of Merton*, Chap. 12 (1903), Coke wrote: 'His blade struck the water a full second before any other: the lad had started well. Nor did he flag as the race wore on: as the others tired, he seemed to grow more fresh, until at length, as the boats began to near the winning-post, his oar was dipping into the water nearly twice as often as any other.' This is deemed to be the original of the modern proverbial saying.

The 'misquotation' is sometimes thought to have been a deliberate distortion of something written earlier than Coke, by Ouida, 'designed to demonstrate the lady's ignorance of rowing, or indeed of any male activity' – Peter Farrer in *Oxford Today* (Hilary, 1992).

COLEMAN, David

English broadcaster (1926–)

5 Juantorena opens wide his legs and shows his class.

Since the late 1970s, *Private Eye* Magazine has had a column with the title 'Colemanballs' devoted chiefly to the inanities of TV and radio sports commentators. The title was derived from the name of BBC TV's principal sports commentator at the time. Coleman was generally supposed to have committed any number of solecisms, tautologies and what-have-you in the cause of keeping his tongue wagging. Hearers who report his sayings have often been inaccurate. It is believed, however, that he did say, among other things, 'This man could be a black horse', 'There is only one winner in this race' and – of the footballer Asa Hartford who had a hole in the heart operation – 'He is a whole-hearted player'.

To be fair, however, the boob that started it all has been revealed as being perpetrated by another. At the 1976 Montreal Olympics it was said of the athlete Alberto Juantorena, competing in the 400 metres heats, that he 'opens wide his legs and shows his class'. It was not Coleman who said this but Ron Pickering (1930–91).

COLERIDGE, Samuel Taylor

English poet and writer (1772–1834)

6 It is an ancient Mariner,
And he stoppeth one of three ...

Water, water everywhere,
And all the boards did shrink;
Water, water, everywhere
Nor any drop to drink.

'The Rime of the Ancient Mariner' (1798). The last couplet here is often misquoted as 'Water, water, everywhere/And not a drop to drink'.

7 On awaking he ... instantly and eagerly wrote down the lines that are here preserved. At this moment he was unfortunately called out by a person on business from Porlock.

From Coleridge's introductory note to *Kubla Khan* (1816) describing how he, the poet, was interrupted in writing out the two or three hundred lines that had come to him in his sleep, when staying in Somerset. The incident happened in 1797 after Coleridge had taken opium and fallen asleep. Hence, the expression 'person from Porlock' to describe any kind of distraction, but especially from literary or other creative work.

1 In Xanadu did Kubla Khan
A stately pleasure-dome decree.

Kubla Khan. The 'stately pleasure-dome' has become a cliché of journalism and pop music. *The Pleasure Dome* was the title of a collection of Graham Greene's film criticism (1972). 'Welcome to the Pleasure Dome' was the title of an album and a song by Frankie Goes to Hollywood (1985). 'We would be turning ourselves into not just a non-reproductive society but an unproductive, hedonistic society. Here comes the stately pleasure dome' – *The Sunday Times* (1 May 1994). 'Politics govern artistic activity in France and Italy. President Mitterrand a stately pleasure dome decreed, and thence stem all the Bastille's problems' – *The Times* (12 September 1994).

2 And 'mid this tumult Kubla heard from far
Ancestral voices prophesying war!
The shadow of the dome of pleasure
Floated midway on the waves;
Where was heard the mingled measure
From the fountain and the caves.
It was a miracle of rare device,
A sunny pleasure-dome with caves of ice!

Ib. Ransacked by the architectural historian James Lees-Milne for titles of his published diaries: *Ancestral Voices* (1975), *Prophesying Peace* (1977), *Caves of Ice* (1983), *Midway on the Waves* (1985), *A Mingled Measure* (1994).

3 A savage place! as holy and enchanted
As e'er beneath a waning moon was haunted
By woman wailing for her demon-lover!
And from this chasm, with ceaseless turmoil seething,
As if this earth in fast thick pants were breathing,
A mighty fountain momently was forced.

Ib. The 'fast thick pants' have occasioned much schoolboy laughter over the years. C.S. Lewis evidently posed the question whether the pants were 'woollen or fur' (according to *My Oxford*, 1977).

4 That willing suspension of disbelief for the moment, which constitutes poetic faith.

Biographia Literaria, Chap. 14 (1817). The 'willing suspension of disbelief' for what is an essential part of much artistic experience, not just in poetry, has been called 'one of the most famous phrases ever coined' and describes the state of receptiveness and credulity required by the reader or 'receiver' of a work of literature, as well as the acceptance of dramatic and poetic conventions. In the original context, Coleridge was writing of two possible subjects for poetry: 'In this idea originated the plan of the Lyrical Ballads; in which it was agreed, that my endeavours should be directed to persons and characters supernatural, or at least romantic; yet so as to transfer from our inward nature a human interest and a semblance of truth sufficient to procure from these shadows of imagination that willing suspension of disbelief for the moment, which constitutes poetic faith.'

5 To see him act is like reading Shakespeare by flashes of lightning.

On Edmund Kean, the English actor (1787–1833). In *Table Talk* (1835), entry for 27 April 1823.

6 I wish our clever young poets would remember my homely definitions of prose and poetry; that is prose = words in their best order; poetry = the *best* words in the best order.

Ib., entry for 12 July 1827. Earlier Jonathan Swift had written in *A Letter to a Young Gentleman, Lately entered into Holy Orders* (9 January 1720): 'Proper words in proper places, make the true definition of a style.' Compare: 'Good prose is the selection of the best words; poetry is the best words in the best order; and journalese is any old words in any old order' – Anon. quoted by Adam Brewer in a letter to *The Times* (21 August 1987).

COLLINS, Michael

Irish politician (1890–1922)

7 Think what I have got for Ireland. Something which she has wanted these past seven hundred years. Will anyone be satisfied with the bargain? Will anyone? I tell you this – early this morning I signed my death warrant. I thought at the time how odd, how ridiculous – a bullet may just as well have done the job five years ago.

Letter (6 December 1921), written after he had signed a peace treaty with the British government. Subsequently, when head of the Irish provisional government, he was killed by his own compatriots in March

1922. In *Michael Collins*, Chap. 8 (1990), Tim Pat Coogan suggests that Collins had already made this point when, at 2.30 a.m. that morning: '[Lord] Birkenhead turned to Collins after putting his name to the document and said, "I may have signed my political death warrant tonight." The younger man replied, "I may have signed my actual death warrant".'

COLLINS, Norman

English broadcasting executive and novelist (1907–82)

1 London Belongs To Me.

Title of novel (1945; film UK, 1948 – known in the US as *Dulcimer Street*). Compare the later title *Paris Nous Appartient* [Paris Belongs To Us] (film France, 1961).

2 Steam radio.

Coinage attributed in Asa Briggs, *A History of Broadcasting in the United Kingdom*, Vol. 3 (1970).

COLMAN, George (the Younger)

English playwright (1762–1836)

3 Oh, London is a fine town,
A very famous city,
Where all the streets are paved with gold,
And all the maidens pretty.

The Heir-at-Law (1797). *See also* BIBLE 106:4.

4 Says he, 'I am a handsome man, but I'm a gay deceiver.'

Love Laughs at Locksmiths, Act 2 (1808). (By the time of Tennessee Williams's play, *The Glass Menagerie*, 1948, 'Gay Deceivers' had become a slang term for 'falsies'.)

COLSON, Charles

American Watergate conspirator (1931–)

5 I would walk over my grandmother if necessary [to get something done].

This was a view attributed to Colson rather than anything he ever actually said himself, but he subsequently muddied the water by appearing to endorse the sentiment. An article in *The Wall Street Journal* in 1971 had portrayed Colson, a special counsel of President Nixon, as someone who, in the words of another Washington official, would be prepared to walk over his grandmother if he had to. In 1972, when Nixon sought re-election as US President, Colson misguidedly sent a memo to campaign staff which stated: 'I am totally unconcerned about anything other than getting the job done ... Just so you understand me, let me point out that the statement ... "I would walk over my grandmother if necessary" is absolutely accurate.' This was leaked to *The Washington Post*.

Subsequently convicted for offences connected with Watergate and then emerging as a born-again Christian, Colson tried unavailingly to point out that he had never really said it. In his book *Born Again* (1977) he wrote: 'My mother failed to see the humour in the whole affair, convinced that I was disparaging the memory of my father's mother ... Even though both of my grandmothers had been dead for more than twenty-five years (I was very fond of both).' Such are the penalties for tangling with figures of speech.

In an earlier age – the 1880s – the editor of the *Pall Mall Gazette*, W.T. Stead, famous for his exposé of the child prostitution racket, said: 'I would not take libel proceedings if it were stated that I had killed my grandmother and eaten her.' Another even earlier image often invoked was of 'selling one's own grandmother'.

COMPTON-BURNETT, Ivy (later Dame Ivy)

English novelist (1884–1969)

6 Pushing forty? She's clinging on to it for dear life!

Of a certain woman. Erroneously ascribed to Dame Ivy in my book *Quote ... Unquote 3* (1983) as a result of a mishearing on BBC Radio *Quote ... Unquote* (5 January 1982) where it was, in fact, ascribed to 'one actress about another'. The error was, however, cheerfully repeated in *Collins Dictionary of Quotations* (1995).

CONABLE, Barber B., Jr

American Republican politician and banker (1922–)

7 I guess we have found the smoking pistol, haven't we?

The term 'smoking pistol/gun' was popularized during the Watergate affair. Conable said this of a tape of President Nixon's conversation with H.R. Haldeman, his chief of staff, on 23 June 1972, which contained a discussion of how the FBI's investigation of the Watergate burglary could be 'limited'. The phrase simply means 'incriminating evidence', as though a person found holding a smoking gun could be assumed to have committed an offence with it – as in Conan Doyle's Sherlock Holmes story 'The "Gloria Scott"' (1894): 'Then we rushed on into the captain's cabin ...

and there he lay ... while the chaplain stood, with a smoking pistol in his hand'.

CONFUCIUS

Chinese philosopher (551–479BC)

1 There is no spectacle more agreeable than to observe an old friend fall from a roof-top.

Sometimes it is a 'neighbour': 'Even a virtuous and high-minded man may experience a little pleasure when he sees his neighbour falling from a roof.' The earliest citation to hand dates only from 1970, and one suspects that, like so many other Confucian sayings, it has nothing whatever to do with the Chinese philosopher who, nevertheless, undoubtedly did exist and did say a number of wise things (some through his followers). Even when not prefaced by 'Confucius, he say ...' there is a tendency – particularly in the US – to ascribe any wry saying to him. In John G. Murray, *A Gentleman Publisher's Commonplace Book* (1996), the above precise form is ascribed to 'Kai Lung' – by which he presumably means Ernest Bramah's fictional Chinese philosopher.

With regard to this one, similar thoughts have occurred to others: 'Philosophy may teach us to bear with equanimity the misfortunes of our neighbours' – Oscar Wilde, *The English Renaissance of Art* (1882); 'I am convinced that we have a degree of delight, and that no small one, in the real misfortunes and pains of others' – Edmund Burke, *On the Sublime and Beautiful* (1756); and, especially, 'In the misfortune of our best friends, we find something that is not displeasing to us [*Dans l'adversité de nos meilleurs amis, nous trouvons toujours quelque chose qui ne nous deplaît pas*]' – Duc de La Rochefoucauld (1665).

2 I was complaining that I had no shoes till I met a man who had no feet.

Ascribed to Confucius in Patricia Houghton, *A World of Proverbs* (1981), but unverified. Has also been described as a 'Zen saying'. *Compare* BRAMAH 119:2. 'There was the man who complained because he had no shoes, until he met a man who had no feet' (quoted in Jacob M. Braude, *Speakers' Encyclopedia*, 1955); 'I had no shoes, and I murmured, till I met a man who had no feet' (described as 'Arabic' in Viscount Samuel, *A Book of Quotations*, 1947). It has also been attributed to R.W. Emerson. But, rather, Emerson's source may be the first appearance of the saying. In the *Rose Garden* or *Gulistany*, Sheik Muslih'ud-Din Sadi of Shiraz, who featured in thirteenth-century Persian classics, wrote: 'I had never complained of the vicissitudes of fortune, nor murmured at the ordinances of heaven, excepting on one occasion, that my feet were bare, and I had not wherewithal to shoe them. In this desponding state I entered the metropolitan mosque of Cufah, and there I beheld a man that had no feet. I offered up praise and thanksgiving for God's goodness to myself, and submitted with patience to my want of shoes.'

CONGREVE, William

English playwright (1670–1729)

3 See how love and murder will out.

The Double Dealer (1694). The proverb 'murder will out' (i.e., will be found out, will reveal itself) goes back at least to 1325, and 'truth will out' to 1439. Later, Hannah Cowley in *The Belle's Stratagem* (1782) has: 'Vanity, like murder, will out.'

4 Music has charms to soothe a savage breast.

The Mourning Bride (1697). Not 'hath charms' and not 'savage beast'.

5 Heaven has no Rage, like Love to Hatred turned,
Nor Hell a Fury, like a Woman scorned.

Ib. Hence, the expression, 'Hell hath no fury like a woman scorned'. The fury of a disappointed woman had been characterized along these lines before Congreve, but insofar as he coined this proverbial expression, it should be noted that his text is as above.

6 As I am a person I can hold out no longer.

The Way of the World, Act 5, Sc. 1. Lady Wishfort. Person = 'a person of distinction'. She uses the phrase in the form 'as I'm a person' several times in the course of the play.

CONNELL, James M.

Irish-born songwriter (1852–1929)

7 The people's flag is deepest red;
It shrouded oft our martyred dead,
And ere their limbs grew stiff and cold,
Their heart's blood dyed its every fold.
Then raise the scarlet standard high!
Within its shade we'll live or die.
Tho' cowards flinch and traitors sneer,
We'll keep the red flag flying here.

'The Red Flag' (1889). According to a record sleeve-note by the Workers' Music Association Ltd, Connell wrote in 1920 about 'a series of great struggles which got him into the mood which enabled him to write the song.' These were the Irish Land League, the Russian revolutionaries, the hanging of the Chicago anarchists and the English dockers' strike of 1889. Connell apparently intended the words to be sung to the jaunty tune of 'The White Cockade', a Scottish reel. Instead, in the British Labour Movement, it has traditionally been sung to the dirge-like German hymn tune, 'Der Tannenbaum' (known in Britain as 'Maryland'). *See also* SHAW 497:3.

CONNOLLY, Billy

Scottish comedian (1942–)

1 Still you can't worry too much about the future. Life is not a rehearsal.

Gullible's Travels (1983). But probably no more than a popular modern proverb. In December 1980 I spotted this in the Eight-O Club, Dallas, Texas, and included it in my *Graffiti 3* (1981): 'This is not a dress rehearsal, this is real life.' In John Julius Norwich's 1995 *Christmas Cracker*, the writer Sybille Bedford was quoted as having written this: 'You see, when one's young one doesn't feel part of it yet, the human condition; one does things because they are not for good; everything is a rehearsal. To be repeated ad lib, to be put right when the curtain goes up in earnest. One day you know that the curtain was up all the time. That *was* the performance.'

CONNOLLY, Cyril

English writer and critic (1903–74)

2 Whom the gods wish to destroy they first call promising.

Enemies of Promise (1938). *Compare* BYRON 139:7.

3 In the eighteenth century he would have become Prime Minister before he was thirty; as it was he appeared honourably ineligible for the struggle of life.

Ib. On Lord Dunglass (later Sir Alec Douglas-Home, British Prime Minister 1963–4) at Eton.

4 Imprisoned in every fat man a thin one is wildly signalling to be let out.

The Unquiet Grave (1944). Five years earlier, however, George Orwell had written 'I'm fat, but I'm thin inside. Has it ever struck you that there's a thin man inside every fat man, just as they say there's a statue inside every block of stone?' *See* ORWELL 419:5.

Great minds think alike. The coincidence was pointed out in a letter to *Encounter* in September 1975. Not to be outdone, Kingsley Amis twisted the idea round in 1963. *See* AMIS 18:4. And Timothy Leary was quoted in 1979 as having said: 'Inside every fat Englishman is a thin Hindu trying to get out.' *See also* WHITEHORN 566:3.

5 It is closing time in the gardens of the West and from now on an artist will be judged only by the resonance of his solitude or the quality of his despair.

In the final issue of *Horizon* Magazine (1949). Begun in 1940, this monthly review of literature became a leading cultural organ of its time. Malcolm Bradbury commented (1977): 'It ended in some desperation as Connolly noted a decline in the aesthetic, avant-garde impulse he favoured.'

6 She looked like Lady Chatterley above the waist and the gamekeeper below.

Of Vita Sackville-West. In Peter Quennell's *Customs and Characters* (1982), he says of the poet's appearance that it was 'strange almost beyond the reach of adjectives ... she resembled a puissant blend of both sexes – Lady Chatterley and her lover rolled into one, I recollect a contemporary humorist observing ... her legs, which reminded [Virginia] Woolf of stalwart tree trunks, were encased in a gamekeeper's breeches and top-boots laced up to the knee.'

Quennell may have been alluding to the rather more pointed remark that Vita looked 'like Lady Chatterley above the waist and the gamekeeper below'. In fact, by 'contemporary humorist' he probably meant Connolly, who went with him on a joint visit to Sackville-West at Sissinghurst in 1936. Certainly, that is the form in which Connolly's remark is more usually remembered.

7 He would not blow his nose without moralizing on conditions in the handkerchief industry.

The Evening Colonnade (1973). On George Orwell, whose copious essays and journalism were later to fill three sizeable volumes.

CONRAD, Joseph

Polish-born novelist (1857–1924)

8 I have lived, obscure, among the terrors and wonders of my time.

Quoted in Paul Ferris, *Sir Huge* (1990), but otherwise untraced.

See also ELIOT 225:7.

CONRAN, Shirley

English journalist and novelist (1932–)

1 Life is too short to stuff a mushroom.

Superwoman (1975). The epigraph to her home hints volume is in the tradition of such remarks. Richard Porson (1759–1808), Regius Professor of Greek at Cambridge, is quoted by Thomas Love Peacock in *Gryll Grange* (1861) as having said, 'Life is too short to learn German'.

CONWAY, Lord

Untraced

2 Wonderful in manifold glories are the great castle visions of Europe; Windsor from the Thames, Warwick or Ludlow from their riversides, Conway or Caernavon from the sea, Amboise from the Loire, Aigues Mortes from the lagoons, Carcassone, Coucy, Falaise and Château Gaillard – beautiful as they are and crowned with praise, are not comparable in beauty with Leeds, beheld among the waters on an autumnal evening when the bracken is golden and there is a faint blue mist among the trees – the loveliest castle, as thus beheld, in the whole world.

Quoted in Lord Geoffrey-Lloyd, *Leeds Castle* (1976). The phrase 'the loveliest castle in the world' has been used latterly as a promotional slogan for what is now a premier tourist site in Kent (this is not Leeds in Yorkshire).

COOK, Peter

English humorist (1937–95)

3 We exchanged many frank words in our respective languages.

Impersonating Harold Macmillan in the sketch 'T.V.P.M.', *Beyond the Fringe* (1961).

4 Yes, I could have been a judge but I never had the Latin, never had the Latin for the judging.

As a miner in 'Sitting on the Bench' in *ib.*

5 You know, I go to the theatre to be entertained ... I don't want to see plays about rape, sodomy and drug addiction ... I can get all that at home.

Caption to cartoon by Roger Law in *The Observer* (8 July 1962). However, the words 'I go to the theatre to be entertained. I want to be taken out of myself. I don't want to see lust and rape, incest and sodomy – I can get all that at home' also occur in the sketch 'Frank Speaking' credited to Cook and Alan Bennett in *Beyond the Fringe*. This sketch is also described as 'Lord Cobbold/The Duke' and credited to Cook and Jonathan Miller. By the time of Leslie Halliwell, *The Filmgoer's Book of Quotes* (1973), this was being quoted as: 'I don't like watching rape and violence at the cinema. I get enough of that at home!' *Compare* HITCHCOCK 296:5.

6 [Britain must be] about to sink sniggering beneath the watery main.

On the British satire boom of the early 1960s. Possibly from an interview in New York for BBC TV *Panorama* (1963).

7 Neither am I.

On being told that the person sitting next to him at a dinner party was 'writing a book'. Attributed to him in 1984, though he declined to claim it as original.

COOL HAND LUKE

American film 1967. Script by Donn Pearce and Frank Pierson. With Strother Martin as Captain and Paul Newman as Luke.

8 *Captain (to Luke)*: What we've got here is failure to communicate. Some men you just can't reach.

Soundtrack. The line 'What We've Got Here Is A [*sic*] Failure To Communicate' was used to promote the film. *What We Have Here Is A Failure To Communicate* was the title of a book (1975) by Barry Day.

COOLIDGE, Calvin

American Republican 30th President (1872–1933)

9 There is no right to strike against the public safety by anybody, anywhere, at any time.

Telegram to the President of the American Federation of Labour (14 September 1919). Coolidge was Governor of Massachusetts during a Boston police strike.

10 He was against it.

Coolidge went to church alone one Sunday because his wife was unable to accompany him. She asked on his return what the sermon was about. 'Sin,' he replied.

'But what did he say about it?' Coolidge said 'He was against it.' This story made an early appearance in John Hiram McKee, *Coolidge Wit and Wisdom* (1933). Mrs Coolidge said it was just the sort of thing he would have said. Coolidge himself said it would be funnier if it were true.

1 If you don't say anything, you won't be called on to repeat it.

Comment on the business of quotation. Quoted in Laurence J. Peter, *Quotations for Our Time* (1977).

2 You lose.

A story about Coolidge's taciturnity was told by his wife: a woman sat down next to him at a dinner party and said, 'You must talk to me, Mr Coolidge. I made a bet with someone that I could get more than two words out of you.' Coolidge replied: 'You lose.' This made an early appearance in Gamaliel Bradford, *The Quick and the Dead* (1931).

3 Poppa wins.

When a girl told him her father had bet her she could not get more than two words out of Coolidge. Quoted on BBC Radio *Quote ... Unquote* (7 June 1978).

4 Tat!

When a woman said 'I could give you tit for tat any time'. Quoted on BBC Radio *Quote ... Unquote* (2 March 1982).

5 They hired the money, didn't they?

Discussing the cancellation of the Allies' war debt in 1925. Quoted in John H. McKee, *Coolidge: Wit and Wisdom* (1933).

6 After all, the chief business of the American people is business.

Speech to the American Society of Newspaper Editors (17 January 1925). *ODQ* (1979) simply had, 'The business of America is business', but this was revised in the 1992 edition.

7 I do not choose to run.

That is not quite what Coolidge said, and, in any case, he didn't actually *say* it. Having been President since 1923, his words to newsmen on 2 August 1927 were 'I do not choose to run for President in 1928'. And rather than speak, 'Silent Cal' handed slips of paper with these words on them to waiting journalists. For some reason, the unusual wording of the announcement caught people's fancy and the phrase was remembered. In 1928, there was a silly song recorded in New York about a recalcitrant wristwatch. It was performed by Six Jumping Jacks with Tom Stacks (vocal) and was called 'I Do Not Choose To Run'. The dedication of Frank Nicholson's *Favorite Jokes of Famous People* (1928) is to: 'A famous man whose favorite joke is not included in this collection ... he did not choose to pun.'

8 Nothing in the World can take the place of persistence. Talent will not; nothing is more common than unsuccessful men with talent. Genius will not; unrewarded genius is almost a proverb. Education will not; the world is full of educated derelicts. Persistence and determination are omnipotent. The slogan 'press on' has solved and always will solve the problems of the human race.

Attributed. It was printed on the cover of the service sheet for his memorial service in 1933.

CORNFELD, Bernie

American businessman (1928–95)

9 Do you sincerely want to be rich?

Question posed to his salesmen, during training, by Cornfeld who made his name and fortune selling investment plans in the 1960s. His Investors Overseas Services crashed in 1970, ruining investors everywhere. He spent eleven months in a Swiss jail while awaiting fraud charges which were eventually dropped. The question was used as the title of a book about him by Charles Raw, *et al* (1971).

CORNFORD, Frances

English poet (1886–1960)

10 A young Apollo, golden-haired,
Stands dreaming on the verge of strife,
Magnificently unprepared
For the long littleness of life.

Poems, 'Youth' (1910). Of the poet Rupert Brooke (*q.v.*)

11 O why do you walk through the fields in gloves,
Missing so much and so much?
O fat white woman whom nobody loves.

'To a Fat Lady Seen from a Train' (1910). *The Oxford Companion to English Literature* (1985) describes this short poem as 'curiously memorable though undistinguished'. Part of the fascination must lie in the fact that we must all have wondered at some time about the people we glimpse from trains. It was Cornford's assumptions about the fat white woman, however, that caused G.K. Chesterton to provide the other side of the story. His 'The Fat White Woman Speaks' was published in *New Poems* (1932):

Why do you flash through the flowery meads,
Fat-headed poet that nobody reads;
And how do you know such a frightful lot
About people in gloves as such?

'Beachcomber' (J.B. Morton) also wrote a riposte, 'The Fat Lady Seen from a Train Replies to the Scornful Poet'.

CORNFORD, Francis

English academic (1874–1943)

1 Nothing should ever be done for the first time.

Microcosmographia Academica (1908). The precise wording is: 'Every public action, which is not customary, either is wrong, or, if it is right, is a dangerous precedent. It follows that nothing should ever be done for the first time.' Francis Cornford, who was married to Frances (*q.v.*), was Professor of Ancient Philosophy at Cambridge.

Compare: 'The conservative in financial circles I have often described as a man who thinks nothing new ought ever to be adopted for the first time' – Frank A. Vaderlip, *From Farm Boy to Financier* (1935).

CORNUEL, Anne-Marie Bigot de

French society hostess (1605–94)

2 No man is a hero to his valet.

In *Lettres de Mlle Aïssé à Madame C* (1787), letter of 1728. The apparent origin of this proverbial expression.

CORNWALL, Barry (B.W. Procter)

English poet (1787–1874)

3 The Sea! the Sea! the open Sea!
The blue, the fresh, the ever free!
Without a mark, without a bound,
It runneth the earth's wide regions 'round;
It plays with the clouds; it mocks the skies;
Or like a cradled creature lies.

'The Sea', *English Songs* (1851). Later set to music by the Chevalier Sigmund Neukomm (who died in 1858). Parodied in H.J. Byron's pantomime version of Aladdin (1861), with reference to tea-clippers:

The Tea! The Tea!
Refreshing Tea.
The green, the fresh, the ever free
From all impurity.

And at the back, consciously or not, must surely be an allusion to XENOPHON 586:1.

CORY, William

English poet and schoolmaster (1823–92)

4 At school you are engaged not so much in acquiring knowledge as in making mental efforts under criticism.

Cory, who was born William Johnson, was an assistant master of some distinction at Eton College but left under a cloud and changed his name to Cory. His view of education continues: 'A certain amount of knowledge you can indeed with average faculties acquire so as to retain; nor need you regret the hours you spent on much that is forgotten, for the shadow of lost knowledge at least protects you from many illusions. But you go to a great school not so much for knowledge as for arts and habits; for the habit of attention, for the art of expression, for the art of assuming at a moment's notice a new intellectual position, for the art of entering quickly into another person's thoughts, for the habit of submitting to censure and refutation, for the art of indicating assent or dissent in graduated terms, for the habit of regarding minute points of accuracy, for the art of working out what is possible in a given time, for taste, for discrimination, for mental courage, and for mental soberness.' The passage, which may be from Cory's 'Notes on Education', is quoted in *The Lyttelton Hart-Davis Letters*, Vol. 2 (1979).

5 Jolly boating weather,
And a hay-harvest breeze,
Blade on the feather,
Shade off the trees.
Swing, swing together,
With your bodies between your knees.

Cory wrote the 'Eton Boating Song' in 1863 and it was published two years later in *The Eton Scrap Book*, a school magazine. The phrase *Blade on the Feather* was taken as the title of a TV play (1980) by Dennis Potter, whose main character was an Old Etonian author and spy. 'On the feather' is a rowing term for when the oar's blade is returned horizontally at the end of a stroke, and out of the water.

1 He is one of those who like the palm without the dust.

In the 1860s Cory wrote this of one of his pupils, the future Prime Minister, Lord Rosebery, then aged fifteen. The comment was published in Johnson's *Letters and Journals* in 1897 and came to haunt Rosebery. As Robert Rhodes James notes in *Rosebery* (1963), it has been seized upon by countless persons as the key to the aristocratic politician's complex personality. The allusion is to Horace, the Roman author, who talked of 'the happy state of getting the victor's palm without the dust of racing'. '*Palma non sine pulvere* [no palm without labour]' is a motto of the Earls of Liverpool, among others.

COUÉ, Émile

French psychologist (1857–1926)

2 *Tous les jours, à tous (les) points de vue, je vais de mieux en mieux.*
Every day and in every way I am getting beter and better.

(Sometimes rendered 'every day in every way' ... *or* 'day by day in every way ...'). Coué was the originator of a system of 'Self-Mastery Through Conscious Auto-Suggestion', which had a brief vogue in the 1920s. His patients had to repeat the words over and over and they became a popular catchphrase of the time. Physical improvement did not necessarily follow. Couéism died with its inventor, though there have been attempted revivals. John Lennon alludes to the slogan in his song 'Beautiful Boy' (1980).

COWARD, Noël (later Sir Noël)

English entertainer and writer (1899–1973)

3 How strange, when I saw you acting in *The Glorious Adventure* [a film about the Great Fire of London], I laughed all the time!

To Lady Diana Cooper who told him she had not laughed once at his comedy *The Young Idea* (London, 1922). This exchange is quoted in *The Noël Coward Diaries* (note to 13 March 1946). The original of an anecdote that takes several forms – as told to me by an actress in 1979: 'Diana Wynyard said to Coward, "I saw your *Private Lives* the other night. Not very funny." He replied: "I saw your Lady Macbeth the other night – very funny!"'

Compare the story recounted in *Sheridaniana, or Anecdotes of the Life of Richard Brinsley Sheridan* (1826): the playwright Richard Cumberland took his children to see Sheridan's *The School for Scandal* and kept reprimanding them when they laughed at it – 'You should not laugh, my angels; there is nothing to laugh at.' When Sheridan was informed of this long afterwards, he commented: 'It was very ungrateful in Cumberland to have been displeased with his poor children for laughing at my comedy; for I went the other night to see his tragedy, and laughed at it from beginning to end.'

4 Just know your lines and don't bump into the furniture.

This advice to actors was attributed to Spencer Tracy by Bartlett (1980) but to Coward in the 1992 edition. In Leslie Halliwell, *The Filmgoer's Book of Quotes* (1973), Alfred Lunt is credited with the line: 'The secret of my success? I speak in a loud clear voice and try not to bump into the furniture'. In *Time* Magazine (16 June 1986), it was reported that President Reagan had offered a few hints on appearing before the cameras to a White House breakfast for Senators: 'Don't bump into the furniture,' he said, 'and in the kissing scenes, keep your mouth closed.' Coward seems to be the originator and Dick Richards, *The Wit of Noël Coward* (1968) has it that he said it during the run of his play *Nude With Violin* (1956–7).

5 I was photographed and interviewed and photographed again. In the street. In the park. In my dressing-room. At my piano. With my dear old mother. Without my dear old mother and on one occasion sitting up in an over-elaborate bed looking like a heavily-doped Chinese illusionist.

Quoted in Dick Richards, *The Wit of Noël Coward* (1968), but otherwise untraced.

6 Poor Little Rich Girl.

The title of the Coward song from Charlot's Revue (1926) is not original. The phrase had been used as the title of a Mary Pickford film of 1917 (which was remade in 1936).

7 A room with a view – and you
And no one to worry us
No one to hurry us.

Song, 'A Room With a View', *This Year of Grace* (1928). This had been preceded by the novel with the title by FORSTER 242:4.

8 Dear 338171 (May I call you 338?)

Writing to T.E. Lawrence in the RAF (when Lawrence

was hiding under the name 'Shaw'). Included in *Letters to T.E. Lawrence*, ed. D. Garnett (1938); letter dated 25 August 1930.

1 Very flat, Norfolk.

Private Lives, Act 1 (1930). Amanda is honeymooning with her second husband at the same hotel as her first, Elyot, is honeymooning with his new wife. In a wonderfully clipped conversation that nevertheless hints that they are probably still in love, Elyot remarks that he met his new wife at a house party in Norfolk. This is Amanda's famously dismissive response.

2 Strange how potent cheap music is.

Ib. Amanda. Some texts of the play (as quoted by Bartlett and the *ODQ*, for example) employ 'extraordinary', but 'strange' is what Gertrude Lawrence says on the record she made with Coward of the relevant scene in 1930. The line may be popular for two reasons. Coward's voice can be heard quite clearly in it and there is an in-joke – he, as playwright, is referring to one of his own compositions ('Someday I'll Find You'), which is being played at that moment.

3 Yes, moonlight is cruelly deceptive.

Ib., Act 3. In an exchange between Elyot and Amanda about the Taj Mahal. Her response is: 'And it didn't look like a biscuit box did it? I've always felt that it might.'

4 You're looking very lovely, you know, in this damned moonlight.

Ib. Elyot. Again, Coward himself on the 1930 recording (*Noel and Gertie* record album, CLP 1050) delivers this line differently from the published text – 'You're looking very lovely in this damned moonlight, *Amanda*' – and this is the way it is usually parodied.

5 Nothing to be fixed except your performance.

In response to a telegram from Gertrude Lawrence saying 'Nothing wrong that can't be fixed', concerning her part in *Private Lives*. Quoted in Lesley, Payn & Morley, *Noël Coward and his Friends* (1979).

6 Let's drink to the hope that one day this country of ours, which we love so much, will find dignity and greatness and peace again.

The toast from *Cavalcade* (1931). *See also* THATCHER 532:2.

7 In spite of the troublous times we are living in, it is still pretty exciting to be English.

Coward's curtain speech at the first night of *Cavalcade*, Drury Lane Theatre, London (1931).

8 In Bangkok at twelve o'clock
They foam at the mouth and run.
But mad dogs and Englishmen
Go out in the midday sun.

Song, 'Mad Dogs and Englishmen', *Words and Music* (1932). In *The Noël Coward Song Book* (1953), the composer wrote: 'I have sung it myself ad nauseam. On one occasion it achieved international significance. This was a dinner party given by Mr Winston Churchill on board HMS *Prince of Wales* in honour of President Roosevelt on the evening following the signing of the Atlantic Charter ... The two world leaders became involved in a heated argument as to whether "In Bangkok at twelve o'clock they foam at the mouth and run" came at the end of the first refrain or at the end of the second. President Roosevelt held firmly to the latter view and refused to budge even under the impact of Churchillian rhetoric. In this he was right and when, a little while later, I asked Mr Churchill about the incident he admitted defeat like a man.'

9 The Party's Over Now.

Title of song in *ib.* 'The Party's Over' was later (1956) the title of a song by Betty Comden and Adolph Green, to music by Jule Styne. *See also* CROSLAND 191:5.

10 I believe that since my life began
The most I've had is just
A talent to amuse.

Song, 'If Love Were All', *Bitter Sweet* (1932). *A Talent To Amuse* became the title of Sheridan Morley's biography of Coward in 1969. Compare this in Byron's *Don Juan*, Canto 13, St. 86 (1819–24): 'There was the *preux Chevalier de la Ruse*,/ Whom France and Fortune lately deign'd to waft here,/ Whose chiefly harmless talent was to amuse.' A collection of Nancy Mitford's writings, edited by Charlotte Mosley, was published as *A Talent to Annoy* in 1986.

11 Design for Living.

Title of play (1932). This, although dealing with what later would be called 'trendy' people, had nothing to do with fashion. It was about a *ménage-à-trois*, so the 'living' was in that sense. However, the phrase is often used in magazine journalism for headlines when the practical aspects of furniture and even clothes design are being discussed. The Flanders & Swann song 'Design for Living' in *At The Drop of a Hat* (1957) concerned trendy interior decorating and furnishing.

1 Dear Randolph, utterly unspoiled by failure.

On Randolph Churchill. Attributed by Leslie Thomas on BBC Radio, *Quote ... Unquote* (31 May 1978). Dick Richards, *The Wit of Noël Coward* (1968), has it that the remark was aimed, rather, at an unnamed playwright.

2 The Stately Homes of England
How beautiful they stand,
To prove the upper classes
Have still the upper hand.

Although this is one of Coward's best-known songs (from the show *Operette*, 1938), it is based on the ballad 'The Homes of England' (1827) by Mrs Felicia Dorothea Hemans:

The stately homes of England,
How beautiful they stand!
Amidst their tall, ancestral trees,
O'er all the pleasant land.

3 Like piddling on flannel.

His opinion of Mozart, after walking out of a Glyndebourne performance. Quoted in Cole Lesley, *The Life of Noël Coward* (1976).

4 Dear Mrs A., hooray hooray,
At last you are deflowered
On this as every other day
I love you. Noël Coward.

Telegram to Gertrude Lawrence on her marriage to Richard S. Aldrich. Quoted in Angus McGill & Kenneth Thomson, *Live Wires* (1982).

5 Soft, hysterical little actors
Ballet dancers, 'reserved' musicians,
Safe in your warm civilian beds.
Count your profits and count your sheep
Life is flying above your heads
Just turn over and try to sleep.
Lie in the dark and let them go
Theirs is a world you'll never know
Lie in the dark and listen.

Poem, 'Lie in the Dark and Listen' in *Collected Verse* (1984). W.F. Deedes wrote in *The Daily Telegraph* (28 September 1992): 'My advice to General Sir Michael Gray, Colonel Commandant of the Parachute Regiment, if he wants to make them wince at Broadcasting House [about a BBC TV play], is to send them a copy of Noël Coward's verse written during the last war with its cruel jibe at "Soft, hysterical little actors ..." which caused offence at the time to a certain galerie. But on no account, General, tell them I suggested it.'

Challenged by one of his readers (who had been unable to find it in Coward's lyrics) to give chapter and verse, Deedes said he couldn't. It was eventually traced to Coward's *Collected Verse* (as opposed to his lyrics, that is). 'Lie in the Dark and Listen' is an unusual, critical poem about those remaining at home in wartime while bomber crews fly overhead, off on another mission. On being told the news, Deedes gave, 'A thousand thanks. Failure to trace that line was seriously interfering with my sleep. Interesting verses; not quite Coward's style.'

6 A Month in the Wrong Country.

On an American production of Chekhov's *The Cherry Orchard* set in the Deep South. See *Noël Coward Diaries* for 4 September 1950.

7 Chase me, Charlie.

The title of a song from Coward's *Ace of Clubs* (1950) was not original. It had also been the title of a popular song current in 1900.

8 She said she didn't care a jot
If people quoted her or not.

Comment on the business of quotation. Song, 'Nina from Argentina', *Sigh No More* (1945).

9 Her lunch.

Watching the 1953 Coronation on TV, Coward was asked who the man was riding in a carriage with the portly Queen of Tonga. In fact, it was the Sultan of Kelantan. This famous story made an early appearance in Dick Richards, *The Wit of Noël Coward* (1968). It is often told differently and may well be apocryphal. About the only thing to be said for certain is that Coward did spend most of Coronation Day watching TV – he says so in his diaries. According to Ned Sherrin, *Theatrical Anecdotes* (1991), Coward always denied the story, 'not least because she [Queen Salote] was a personal friend and would have been very upset'. Sherrin suggests that Emlyn Williams was the perpetrator and, curiously, casts Emperor Haile Selassie in the role of 'the lunch' (he did not even attend the Coronation).

In his diary entry for Coronation Day, James Lees-Milne has the Coward story and wrongly identifies the man as Queen Salote's husband. The passage is included in the published diaries, *A Mingled Measure* (1994), but seems probably to have been inserted at a later date.

1 When Eve said to Adam 'Start calling me madam'
The world became far more exciting;
And turned to confusion the modern delusion
That sex is a question of lighting.

From Coward's introduction on the album 'Marlene Dietrich at the Café de Paris' (a recording of her London cabaret performance, 1954). Misquoted as 'sex is a question of *liking*' in *The Observer* (24 March 1992).

2 Passing a Leicester Square movie poster which proclaimed 'Michael Redgrave and Dirk Bogarde in *The Sea Shall Not Have Them*', [Coward] murmured, 'I don't see why not: everyone else has.'

Quoted by Sheridan Morley in the *Independent on Sunday* Magazine (12 November 1995). The film was released in 1954. *See also* HARRIS 283:1.

3 'Mrs So-and-So, a well-known figure in Café.' (Pause). 'Nescafé Society'.

Quoted in Alec Guinness, *Blessings in Disguise* (1985). Remark made to Guinness in Jamaica prior to the filming of *Our Man In Havana* (released 1959).

4 Edith, the line is 'On a clear day you can see Marlow. On a *very* clear day you can see Marlowe *and* Beaumont *and* Fletcher.'

Directing Edith Evans in a revival of *Hay Fever* (1964), when she kept saying a line as, 'On a very clear day you can see Marlow'. Quoted in Dick Richards, *The Wit of Noël Coward* (1968).

5 It made me feel that Albert had married beneath his station.

(Or, 'I never realised before that Albert married beneath him'). Coward's alleged comment on an inadequate portrayal of Queen Victoria was quoted in Kenneth Tynan, *Tynan on Theatre* (1964) and in *The Wit of Noël Coward* (ed. Dick Richards, 1968). However, James Agate has this in *Ego 6* (for 17 August 1943): 'At a luncheon party to-day I heard two women discussing historical films. One said, "My dear, they have a certain social value. Until I saw Anna Neagle and Anton Walbrook in the film about Queen Victoria [*Sixty Glorious Years*, 1938] I had no idea that the Prince Consort married beneath him!"' This may be no more than Agate purposely obscuring a source which was known to him, if indeed Coward was the originator. Coward makes no comment on the film in his published diaries.

6 She could eat an apple through a tennis racquet.

Come Into the Garden, Maud (1966). Coward often recycled witticisms from his own conversation in his plays, but this is a firm example of borrowing from another. A note in his diary for 10 December 1954 recorded: 'Lunched and dined with Darryl Zanuck who, David Niven wickedly said, is the only man who can eat an apple through a tennis racquet!' Compare the (American) proverbial expression, 'So buck-toothed he/she could eat a pumpkin through a picket fence', quoted in *Proverbium* (1989).

7 Too many Dear Boys, dear boy.

If the many people who have tried to imitate Coward's clipped delivery over the years are to be believed, the words he uttered most often in his career were 'Dear boy'. His friend Cole Lesley claimed, however, in *The Life of Noël Coward* (1978) that, 'He rarely used this endearment, though I expect it is now too late for me to be believed.' William Fairchild who wrote dialogue for the part of Coward in the film *Star!* (1968) was informed by the Master, after he had checked the script: 'Too many Dear Boys, dear boy.'

8 The doggie in front has suddenly gone blind, and the other one has very kindly offered to push him all the way to St Dunstan's.

To Laurence Olivier's five-year-old daughter, Tamsin, when she asked what two dogs were doing together. Quoted by Kenneth Tynan in *The Observer* (1 April 1973).

9 Goodnight, my darlings. I'll see you tomorrow.

Last words. Quoted in Cole Lesley, *The Life of Noël Coward* (1976).

COWLEY, Abraham

English poet and essayist (1618–67)

10 I never had any other Desire so Strong and so like to Covetousness, as that one which I have had always, that I might be Master at last of a small House and large Garden, with very moderate Conveniences joined to them, and there dedicate the Remainder of my Life to the Culture of them, and study of nature.

Introduction to poem *The Garden* (1664) and dedicated to John Evelyn, the diarist. 'Conveniences' here has the meaning 'material arrangements conducive to ease of action or saving of trouble' rather than the modern one.

1 God the first garden made, and the first city Cain.

Ib. Compare COWPER 189:4.

COWPER, William

English poet (1731–1800)

2 I am monarch of all I survey,
My right there is none to dispute;
From the centre all round to the sea
I am lord of the fowl and the brute.

'Verses Supposed to be Written by Alexander Selkirk' (*c.*1779). Selkirk was the original of 'Robinson Crusoe'. The first line is nowadays used as a light-hearted proprietorial boast. Kenneth Tynan, writing about Noël Coward (in *Panorama*, Spring 1952) said: 'He is, if I may test the trope, monocle of all he surveys'.

3 God moves in a mysterious way
His wonders to perform;
He plants his footsteps in the sea,
And rides upon the storm.

Hymn, 'Light Shining Out of Darkness', *Olney Hymns* (1779). Hence, the modern – often ironical – comment, 'God moves in a mysterious way ...' after some unexpected outcome to events.

4 God made the country, and man made the town.

'The Sofa', *The Task* (1785). *Compare* COWLEY 189:1.

5 England, with all thy faults, I love thee still –
My country!

'The Timepiece' in *ib.* Byron later made use of this in *Beppo*, st. 47 (1818): '"England! with all thy faults I love thee still,"/I said at Calais, and have not forgot it.'

6 Variety's the spice of life,
That gives it all its flavour.

'The Timepiece' in *ib.* The apparent origin of this proverb.

7 I was a stricken deer, that left the herd
Long since.

'The Garden' in *ib.* Hence, *The Stricken Deer*, title of a study of Cowper (1929) by David Cecil. The phrase 'stricken deer' appeared earlier in Shakespeare, *Hamlet*, III.ii.265 (1600–1).

8 Now stir the fire, and close the shutters fast,
Let fall the curtains, wheel the sofa round,
And, while the bubbling and loud-hissing urn
Throws up a steamy column, and the cups,
That cheer but not inebriate, wait on each,
So let us welcome peaceful ev'ning in.

'The Winter Evening' in *ib.* 'The cup that cheers' (the container is usually in the singular) means 'tea' (usually) in preference to alcohol.

CRAIK, Mrs (Dinah Maria Mulock)

English novelist (1826–87)

9 Each in his place is fulfilling his day, and passing away, just as that Sun is passing. Only we know not whither he passes; while whither we go we know, and the Way we know, the same yesterday, today and for ever.

Words to be found on the marble tablet to Mrs Craik in Tewkesbury Abbey. The quotation comes from the final chapter of the most celebrated of her novels, *John Halifax, Gentleman* (1857), which is set in and around Tewkesbury. Shortly before Halifax dies, Phineas Fletcher, the narrator, tells how new tenants of the old family house are going to turn it into an inn. Halifax says, 'What a shame! I wish I could prevent it. And yet, perhaps not ... Ought we not rather to recognize and submit to the universal law of change? how each in his place is fulfilling his day, and passing away ...'

CRANMER, Thomas

English archbishop and martyr (1489–1556)

10 This was the hand that wrote it, therefore it shall suffer first punishment.

During his trial for treason and heresy, Cranmer signed seven recantations of his faith. As he was being burned at the stake (in Oxford), he thrust his right hand first into the flames as it was this hand with which he had signed the recantations. Quoted in John Richard Green, *A Short History of the English People* (1874). Other versions include the exclamation, 'That unworthy hand!' and 'This hand hath offended!'

CRASTER, Mrs Edmund

English poet (d.1874)

11 A centipede was happy quite,
Until a frog in fun
Said, 'Pray, which leg comes after which?'
This raised her mind to such a pitch,

She lay distracted in a ditch
Considering how to run.

'The Puzzled Centipede'. Quoted in *PDQ* (1960). It is not clear whether the following verse (known by 1948) is by Mrs Craster or another hand:

While lying in this sorry plight
A ray of sunshine caught her sight,
And pondering its beauties long
She burst into a happy song:
Unthinking she began to run,
And quite forgot the croaker's fun.

CRAWFORD, Julia

Untraced

1 Kathleen Mavourneen! the grey dawn is breaking,
The horn of the hunter is heard on the hill.

'Kathleen Mavourneen', in *The Metropolitan Magazine* (1835). Could the second line have inspired STEVENSON's phrase in 521:3?

CRICK, Francis

English scientist (1916–)

2 We have discovered the secret of life!

On discovering the structure of DNA (1953) at the University of Cambridge's Cavendish Laboratory. Recounted by his partner James D. Watson in *The Double Helix* (1968) in the form: 'Thus I felt slightly queasy when at lunch Francis winged into the Eagle [a Cambridge pub] to tell everyone within hearing distance that we had found the secret of life.'

CRISP, Quentin

English celebrity (1908–)

3 There was no need to do any housework at all. After the first four years the dirt doesn't get any worse.

The Naked Civil Servant (1968). Crisp, a flamboyant and witty homosexual of the old school, suddenly became a celebrity as a result of a TV dramatization of his book in 1975. In consequence, he gave lectures and wrote several books containing his pronouncements.

4 I became one of the stately homos of England.

Ib. Alluding to Mrs Hemans's poem 'The Homes of England'; *see* COWARD 187:2.

CRITCHLEY, Julian (later Sir Julian)

English Conservative politician (1930–)

5 She [Margaret Thatcher] cannot see an institution without hitting it with her handbag.

In *The Times* (21 June 1982). Possibly the first use of the idea of 'handbagging' for the then Prime Minister's combative style of negotiation and dealing with institutions and colleagues. An inevitable joke to make about a woman and duly condemned as sexist by those who did not find it funny.

See also MORLEY 398:7.

CROKER, John Wilson

Irish politician and essayist (1780–1857)

6 We now are, as we always have been, decidedly and conscientiously attached to what is called the Tory, and which might with more propriety be called, the Conservative Party.

Quarterly Review (1830). Croker was the originator of the term 'Conservative'.

CROMER, Earl (Evelyn Baring)

English colonial administrator (1841–1917)

7 Love your country, tell the truth and don't dawdle.

The agent and consul-general in Egypt (1883–1907) offered this philosophy of life to the boys of the Leys School Cambridge. Quoted in James Morris, *Farewell the Trumpets* (1978). John G. Murray, *A Gentleman Publisher's Commonplace Book* (1996), has, rather: 'Field Marshal Sir William Robertson after the First World War made a speech at a school prize-giving: "Boys, I have a great deal to say to you but it won't take long: so remember it. Speak the truth. Think of others. Don't dawdle".'

CROMWELL, Oliver

English soldier and parliamentarian (1599–1658)

8 Put your trust in God, my boys, and keep your powder dry.

During his Irish campaign in 1649. There is some doubt whether he really said it at all, as it was ascribed to him long after his death by a certain Valentine Blacker (1778–1823) in an Orange ballad, *Oliver's Advice* (published 1856). The part about keeping one's powder dry is no more than sensible advice from the days when gunpowder had to be kept dry if it was to be used at all. The overall idiomatic injunction means, 'remain calm and prepared for immediate action', 'be prudent, practical, on the alert'.

Playing upon the word 'powder', *Keep Your Powder Dry* was the title of a 'female flagwaver' film (US 1945) about female WACS.

1 I desire you would use all your skill to paint my picture truly like me, and not flatter me at all; but remark all these roughnesses, pimples, warts, and everything as you see me; otherwise I will never pay a farthing for it.

According to Horace Walpole's *Anecdotes of Painting in England*, Vol. 3 (1763), this is what Cromwell said to the portrait painter, Sir Peter Lely. The anecdote was first recorded in 1721 and gave rise to the expression 'warts and all', for the plain, unvarnished truth. It is now thought more likely that Cromwell made the remark to Samuel Cooper, the miniaturist, whom Lely copied.

2 I beseech you, in the bowels of Christ, think it possible you may be mistaken.

From his Letter to the General Assembly of the Kirk of Scotland (3 August 1650). However strange it may sound to modern ears, the bowels were once thought to be the seat of tender and sympathetic emotions – kindness, mercy, pity, compassion and feeling. Hence, to refer to Christ's bowels was to heighten the imagery. John Wyclif wrote in 1382: 'I covet you all in the bowels of Christ ...' Bowels, in this sense, are often evoked in the Bible, mostly in the Old Testament – again, often with puzzling effect on modern sensibilities: 'My beloved put in his hand by the hole of the door, and my bowels were moved for him' (Song of Solomon 5:4).

CRONKITE, Walter

American broadcaster (1916–)

3 And that's the way it is.

Cronkite was the anchor of CBS TV's *Evening News* for nineteen years, for most of which he had used these words as his sign-off line. On the final occasion, before his retirement, he said: 'And that's the way it is, Friday March 6, 1981. Goodnight.'

CROSLAND, Anthony

English Labour politician (1918–77)

4 If it's the last thing I do, I'm going to destroy every fucking grammar school in England. And Wales, and Northern Ireland.

After a dinner with four teachers' associations (*c.*1965). Quoted in Susan Crosland, *Tony Crosland* (1982). As Education Secretary in Harold Wilson's Labour government, Crosland propelled the meritocratic move to destroy the old grammar schools and replace them with comprehensive schools, supposedly less dependent on privilege.

5 With its [the local government world's] usual spirit of patriotism and its tradition of service to the community's needs, it is coming to realize that, for the time being at least, the party is over.

Speech at a civic luncheon at Manchester (9 May 1975). A warning that Britain's local authorities should not carry on with lavish spending plans when the country's economy, as a whole, was in crisis. *Compare* COWARD 186:9.

CROSSMAN, Richard

English Labour politician (1907–74)

6 Already I realize the tremendous effort it requires not to be taken over by the Civil Service. My Minister's room is like a padded cell, and in certain ways I am like a person who is suddenly certified a lunatic and put safely into this great vast room, cut off from real life ... Of course, they don't behave *quite* like nurses because the Civil Service is profoundly deferential – 'Yes, Minister! No, Minister! If you wish it, Minister! Yes, minister.'

The Diaries of a Cabinet Minister, Vol. 1 (1975). *Yes Minister* was the title of a BBC TV comedy series (1980–5) about the relationship between British government ministers and the Civil Service. It has been said (for example, in *The Listener, c.*1985) that the title came from this description by Crossman, a minister in Labour governments of the 1960s and 1970s, of his first day in office as a Cabinet Minister, in October 1964. Antony Jay (co-author with Jonathan Lynn of the TV series) said in 1993: 'I think the Crossman attribution is probably fair. We didn't have it consciously in mind when we thought up the title, but the *Diaries* were one of our set texts and I feel that it was an echo of it that was running through our minds when we gave the series that title, though the original idea predated Crossman.'

CROWTHER, Leslie

English entertainer (1933–96)

1 Come on down!

The *ODMQ* (1991) credits Crowther with this catchphrase as host of the British TV game show *The Price is Right* (1984–8). But the phrase was already established when the show was imported from the US. In the American version (from 1956), the host (Bill Cullen was the first) would appear to summon contestants from the studio audience by saying '[name], come on down!'

CRUMB, Robert

American cartoonist (1943–)

2 Keep on truckin'.

This expression, meaning that you've got to 'persevere' or 'keep on keeping on', was described in Bartlett (1980) as the 'slogan of a cartoon character' created by Robert Crumb. Crumb drew semi-pornographic cartoons for a number of underground periodicals like *Snatch* in the 1960s and 1970s. He also created Fritz the Cat, later the subject of a full-length cartoon film. There were a number of records produced with the title in this period, and there was certainly a vogue for the phrase.

But it was probably not original to Crumb. There was a song called simply 'Truckin'' in 1935 (words by Ted Koehler and music by Rube Bloom), and the *OED2* finds that 'the truck' or 'trucking' was a jerky dance which emerged from Harlem in the summer of 1934. Partridge/*Catch Phrases* plumps for a suggestion that the phrase, while of Negro dance origin, came out of the great American dance marathons of the 1930s, though one of Partridge's contributors hotly disputes this.

Flexner (1982) discussing 'hoboes, tramps and bums' on the American railroad probably gets nearest to the source. He defines 'trucking it' thus: 'Riding or clinging to the trucking hardware between the wheels. This may have contributed to the jitterbug's use of *trucking* (also meaning to leave or move on in the 1930s) and to the 1960 students' phrase *keep on trucking*, keep moving, keep trying, keep "doing one's (own) thing" with good cheer.'

cummings, e.e.

American poet (1894–1962)

3 who knows if the moon's
a balloon, coming out of a keen city
in the sky – filled with pretty people?

'& N &' (1925). Hence, *The Moon's A Balloon*, title of David Niven's first volume of autobiography (1972).

4 nobody, not even the rain, has such small hands.

'somewhere I have never travelled' (1931). It is also said to be the epigraph of Tennessee Williams's play *The Glass Menagerie* (1945), though not in all editions. It also features in Woody Allen's film *Hannah and Her Sisters* (US, 1986) – where the Michael Caine character buys a book of e.e. cummings poetry for the Barbara Hershey character and urges her to read the poem (as a means to seducing her).

CURRAN, John Philpot

Irish judge (1750–1817)

5 The price of liberty is eternal vigilance.

Speaking on the night of election of the Lord Mayor of Dublin (10 July 1790), what Curran said precisely was: 'The condition upon which God hath given liberty to man is eternal vigilance; which condition if he break, servitude is at once the consequence of his crime, and the punishment of his guilt.' Not said by Thomas Jefferson, as is popularly supposed. The American abolitionist Wendell Phillips said in 1852: 'Eternal vigilance is the price of liberty.'

Compare 'The price of pedantry is eternal vigilance' – Oliver Mason, in a letter to *The Independent* (28 January 1987).

6 Like the silver plate on a coffin.

On Sir Robert Peel's smile. Quoted by Daniel O'Connell in a speech, House of Commons (26 February 1835).

CURZON, George (later 1st Marquess Curzon)

English Conservative politician (1859–1925)

7 Gentlemen do not take soup at luncheon.

Attributed remark (1912), quoted in E.L. Woodward, *Short Journey* (1942). Curzon was a snob and had an eccentric view of social behaviour. From the same source: 'Gentlemen never wear brown in London' (said to a fellow Cabinet member on the clothes of a colleague).

1 I never knew the lower classes had such white skins.

On seeing soldiers bathing in the First World War. Quoted in Kenneth Rose, *Superior Person* (1969).

2 This omnibus business is not what it is reported to be. I hailed one at the bottom of Whitehall and told the man to take me to Carlton House Terrace. But the fellow flatly refused.

On his first trip by bus. This is among the 'Curzonia' included in *The Oxford Book of Political Anecdotes* (1986), though it is not quite clear what the original source was. In fact, it is surely doubtful whether Curzon, the 'most superior person', *ever* went anywhere by bus. This may be yet another example of an old story being fixed on an obviously suitable subject. As always, the origin of the tale could lie in *Punch*. On 10 April 1901 there was a cartoon by Everard Hopkins with this caption: 'A GIRLISH IGNORANCE. *Lady Hildegarde, who is studying the habits of the democracy, determines to travel by Omnibus. Lady Hildegarde.* "CONDUCTOR, TELL THE DRIVER TO GO TO NO. 104, BERKELEY SQUARE, AND THEN HOME!"'

3 Ladies never move.

When instructing his second wife on the subject of love-making. Quoted in *The Oxford Book of Political Anecdotes* (1986). No precise source is given, however. The book of *New Statesmen* competition winners called *Salome Dear, Not With a Porcupine* (1982 – edited by Arthur Marshall) prefers, 'A lady does not move' (and proceeds to provide the circumstances in which it *might* first have been said).

Note, however, that a completely different source for the story is given by Rupert Hart-Davis in *The Lyttelton Hart-Davis Letters* (for 19 August 1956). When researching Cora, Lady Strafford, a thrice-married American, he discovered that: 'Before one of her marriages (perhaps the second – to Lord Strafford) she thought it would be a good thing to get a little sex-instruction, so she went over to Paris and took a few lessons from a leading cocotte. On her wedding night she was beginning to turn precept into practice when her bridegroom sternly quelled her by saying: "Cora, *ladies don't move!*"' Alas, he does not give a source for this version either.

CUST, Harry

English poet (1861–1917)

4 Not unto us, O Lord,
Not unto us the rapture of the day,
The peace of night, or love's divine surprise,
High heart, high speech, high deeds 'mid
  honouring eyes;
For at Thy word
All these are taken away.

'*Non Nobis*' in *Occasional Poems* (1918). Cust was heir to the childless 3rd Earl Brownlow but predeceased him, without leaving any legitimate children of his own. He was an MP, edited the *Pall Mall Gazette* and wrote poetry. 'High heart, high speech, high deeds' is written on his tomb in Belton Church, Leicestershire, which also bears a Greek inscription and the Latin motto '*OMNI DITIOR AESTIMATIONE* [richly endowed beyond all estimation]'.

D

DAILY EXPRESS

London-based newspaper, founded 1900

1 Britain will not be involved in a European war this year, or next year either.

A front-page headline (30 September 1938). Contrary to popular myth this was the only time the paper predicted as much in a headline though, occasionally, the view that 'There will be no European war' appeared in leading articles. While the statement turned out to be true up to the comma, Lord Beaverbrook, the paper's proprietor, unfortunately insisted on the 'or next year either'. He said: 'We must nail our colours *high* to the mast.' Something like the phrase 'Britain will not be involved in a European war' appeared eight times in the *Express* between September 1938 and August 1939 (A.J.P. Taylor, *Beaverbrook*, 1966).

A copy of the paper bearing the message '*Daily Express* holds canvass of its reporters in Europe. And ten out of twelve say NO WAR THIS YEAR' was later shown with ironic effect in Noël Coward's film *In Which We Serve* (1942). It was seen bobbing up and down amid the wreckage of a British destroyer that had been torpedoed by the Germans. As a result, Beaverbrook launched a campaign to try to suppress the film.

2 MARTIN BORMANN ALIVE.

Headline (25 November 1972). The paper claimed that Hitler's Deputy was still alive in South America.

3 CHARLES TO MARRY ASTRID – Official.

Headline (17 June 1977). Princess Marie Astrid – a Roman Catholic – was daughter of the Grand Duke of Luxembourg.

DAILY MIRROR

London-based newspaper, founded 1903

4 Forward with the people.

Slogan, from *c.*1935–59. Later, 'Forward with Britain'.

5 'The price of petrol has been increased by one penny' – Official.

Caption to cartoon by Philip Zec (6 March 1942). It showed a torpedoed sailor adrift on a raft. The caption was suggested by 'Cassandra' (William Connor). Together they led to the paper almost being suppressed by the government.

6 'Here you are – don't lose it again.'

Caption to cartoon by Philip Zec (8 May 1945 – Victory in Europe Day). The cartoon showed a wounded soldier bearing the slogan 'Victory and peace in Europe.'

7 Whose finger on the trigger?

'WHOSE FINGER?' was the actual front-page headline on 25 October 1951 – general election day – and the culmination of a campaign to ensure that the Labour government was re-elected and the Conservatives under Winston Churchill not allowed back. Earlier, on 21 September, the paper had asked, 'Whose finger do you want on the trigger when the world situation is so delicate?' The choice was between Churchill and Clement Attlee. Churchill's response (in a speech, 6 October 1951) was: 'I am sure we do not want any fingers upon any trigger. Least of all do we want a fumbling finger ... But I must tell you that in any case it will not be a British finger that will pull the trigger of a Third World War. It may be a Russian finger or an American finger, or a United Nations Organization finger, but it cannot be a British finger ... the control and decision and the timing of that terrible event would not rest with us. Our influence in the world is not what it was in bygone days.' As it happens, the *Mirror* was unable to stir the electorate and the Conservatives came back to power under Churchill. The Prime Minister then issued a writ for libel against the newspaper because he took the view that the slogan implied that he was a war-monger. The case was settled out of court.

1 Enough is enough.

Front page headline (10 May 1968) over an article by Cecil H. King, Chairman of the International Publishing Corporation, referring to the government of Harold Wilson. But it resulted in King's fall from power rather than the government's. *See also* MACMILLAN 373:5.

2 A good man fallen among politicians.

On Michael Foot, then Labour party leader. Editorial (28 February 1983). *See* BIBLE 102:8.

DAILY TELEGRAPH

London-based newspaper, founded 1855

3 Most Conservatives, and almost certainly some of the wiser Trade Union leaders, are waiting to feel the smack of firm government.

On the premiership of Sir Anthony Eden. Editorial comment (3 January 1956), written by Donald McLachlan.

4 A novel of today with a freshness and raw fury that makes 'Room at the Top' look like a vicarage tea-party.

Reviewing Alan Sillitoe's novel *Saturday Night and Sunday Morning* (1958). An early example of the 'makes ... look like a ...' type of criticism (not confined to this paper).

DALADIER, Édouard

French politician (1884–1970)

5 *C'est une drôle de guerre.*
It's a phoney war.

At first, when war was declared in September 1939, nothing happened. Chamberlain talked of a 'Twilight War' and on 22 December Daladier, the French Prime Minister, used this expression (spelled 'phony' in the US). On 19 January 1940, the *News Chronicle* had a headline: 'This is Not a Phoney War: Paris Envoy.' And Paul Reynaud employed the phrase in a radio speech on 3 April 1940: '"It must be finished", that is the constant theme heard since the beginning. And that means that there will not be any "phoney peace" after a war which is by no means a "phoney war".' Though speaking French, Reynaud used the phrase in English.

DALEY, Richard J.

American Democratic politician and Mayor of Chicago (1902–76)

6 Gentlemen, get the thing straight once and for all. The policeman isn't there to *create* disorder, the policeman is there to *preserve* disorder.

To the press, concerning riots during Democratic Convention, 1968. Audio source.

DALY, Daniel

American soldier (1874–1937)

7 Come on you sons of bitches! Do you want to live for ever?

According to Flexner (1976), Marine Sergeant Daly is remembered for having shouted this during Allied resistance at the Battle of Belleau Wood in June 1918 (during the First World War). Mencken (1942) has it from 'an American sergeant ... addressing soldiers reluctant to make a charge', in the form: 'What's the matter with you guys? Do you want to live forever?' Otherwise the saying remains untraced.

Whatever the case, Daly was not the first military man to use this form of encouragement. Frederick the Great (1712–86) demanded of hesitating guards at Kolin (18 June 1757), '*Ihr Racker/Hunde, wollt ihr ewig leben?* [Rascals/Dogs, would you live for ever?]' (or '*immer leben?*') Mencken concludes that the cry is 'probably ancient', anyway.

DANTE ALIGHIERI

Italian poet (1265–1321)

8 *Nel mezzo del cammin di nostra vita*
Mi ritrovai per una selva oscura,
Che la diritta via era smarrita.
In the middle of the journey of our life
I came to myself within a dark wood
Where the straight way was lost.

'Inferno', Canto 1, l. 1, *La Divina Commedia* (*c.*1320). *See* CLARK 172:6.

1 *Lasciate ogni speranza voi ch'entrate!*
All hope abandon, ye who enter here!

Ib., Canto 3, l. 9. Words written over the entrance to Hell. 'Abandon hope all ye who enter here!' is a popular though less accurate translation.

DANTON, Georges

French revolutionary leader (1759–94)

2 *De l'audace, encore de l'audace, toujours de l'audace!*
Boldness [*or* daring], more boldness, always boldness!

Speech to the Legislative Committee of General Defence (2 September 1792), reported in *Le Moniteur* (4 September). This was Danton's recipe for effective action against foreign invaders. He concluded: 'Thus will France be saved.'

DARROW, Clarence

American lawyer (1857–1938)

3 I have never wanted to see anybody die, but there are a few obituary notices I have read with pleasure.

Quoted in *The Treasury of Humorous Quotations*, ed. by Evan Esar & Nicolas Bentley (1951). The earliest source found for this frequently attributed remark.

DAUGHERTY, Harry

American Republican supporter (1860–1941)

4 [A group of senators]) bleary eyed for lack of sleep [will have to] sit down about two o'clock in the morning around a table in a smoke-filled room in some hotel and decide the nomination.

In *The New York Times* (21 February 1920). Daugherty's prediction concerning the 'smoke-filled room' refers to the choosing of the Republican Party's Presidential candidate in Chicago the following June, if – as in fact happened – the Convention failed to make up its mind. Daugherty, Warren Harding's (the eventual winner's) chief supporter, denied that he had ever used the phrase 'smoke-filled'. *ODMQ* (1991) cites a news report dated 12 June 1920 from Kirke Simpson of the Associated Press: '[Warren] Harding of Ohio was chosen by a group of men in a smoke-filled room early today as Republican candidate for President.' But this is clearly alluding to an already established phrase.

Suite 408–409–410 (previously rooms 804–5) of the Blackstone Hotel in Chicago became the 'smoke-filled room' – whoever coined it – a vivid phrase evoking cigar-smoking political bosses coming to a decision after much horse-trading.

DAVIES, Sir John

English poet (1569–1626)

5 What mean the mermaids when they dance and sing
But certain death unto the mariner?

'Orchestra, or a Poem of Dancing', St. 101 (1594). An early reference to the legendary capacity of mermaids to lure mariners to their deaths. They are generally shown singing alone, mirror in hand, combing their hair 'With a comb of pearl/On a throne', as Tennyson later put it. At Zennor in Cornwall 'for several centuries' there has been told the story of a mermaid's singing that so beguiled a church chorister and the squire's son, Matthew Trewhella, that he went off with her and was never seen again. It is said that their voices are still heard on calm nights. *See also* ELIOT 225:4.

DAVIES, Russell

Welsh journalist (1946–)

6 Nowadays [Robert] Mitchum doesn't so much act as point his suit at people.

Reviewing Mitchum's performance in the TV mini-series *The Winds of War*, in *The Sunday Times* (18 September 1983).

DAVIS, Bette

American film actress (1908–89)

7 Yes, I killed him. And I'm glad, I tell you. Glad, glad, glad!

In the 1940 film version of W. Somerset Maugham's *The Letter*, Davis plays a woman who has killed a man in what seems to have been self-defence. According to Leslie Halliwell in *The Filmgoer's Book of Quotes* (1973), she utters the memorable line – 'Yes, I killed him. And I'm glad, I tell you. Glad, glad, glad!' – but this is not to be found in the film. Might the line have been used on posters rather than in the film itself? After all, he notes in his book, 'They even used the line as a catch-phrase on the posters'. The line does not appear in Maugham's play. It is, however, mentioned in 'I Love a Film Cliché', a list song (1974) by Dick Vosburgh and

Peter Lomax from the show *A Day in Hollywood, A Night in the Ukraine* (1980).

1 I see – she's the original good time that was had by all.

On a starlet. Quoted in Leslie Halliwell, *The Filmgoer's Book of Quotes* (1973). In the form, 'There, standing at the piano, was the original good time who had been had by all', it has also been attributed to Kenneth Tynan at an Oxford Union debate in the late 1940s.

2 What a dump!

In the film *Beyond the Forest* (US, 1949). The phrase is memorably quoted by Elizabeth Taylor in the film of Edward Albee's *Who's Afraid of Virginia Woolf?* (US, 1966) as coming from a Bette Davis movie – and, indeed, a discussion of the phrase's film origins also occupies the opening minutes of the 1962 stage play. *Beyond the Forest* is the melodramatic film where Davis plays the discontented wife of a small-town doctor, has an affair, and comes to a sticky end. She also says of the small town in Wisconsin: 'If I don't get out of here, I'll just die! Living here is like waiting for the funeral to begin.'

The line 'what a dump!' had, however, already been used in Otto Preminger's 1945 film *Fallen Angel*. Dana Andrews suspected of murdering Linda Darnell, holes up in a seedy San Francisco hotel with his wife. Andrews exclaims, 'What a dump!' without, it must be admitted, the memorably explosive consonants of both Miss Davis and Miss Taylor.

But how much farther back can we take the phrase? Partridge/*Slang* with its famously wobbly dating suggests *c.*1919. A more definite indication comes from Eugene O'Neill's play *Ah Wilderness!* where at III.i.84 occurs 'Christ, what a dump!' That was in 1933.

3 Fasten your seatbelts. It's going to be a bumpy night.

Line delivered by Davis as Margo Channing in the film *All About Eve* (US, 1950). Script by Joseph L. Mankiewicz.

See also NOW VOYAGER 415:9.

DAVIS, Sammy, Jr

American entertainer (1925–90)

4 I'm a coloured, one-eyed Jew – do I need anything else?

Yes I Can (1966). Sometimes reported as being in answer to the question, 'What's your golf handicap?'

DAWSON OF PENN, Lord

English physician (1864–1945)

5 The King's life is moving peacefully towards its close.

On Monday, 20 January 1936, King George V lay dying at Sandringham (not Buckingham Palace, as stated in *ODQ*, 1992). At 9.25 p.m., Lord Dawson, the King's doctor, issued this bulletin which he had drafted on a menu-card. It was taken up by the BBC. All wireless programmes were cancelled and every quarter of an hour the announcer, Stuart Hibberd, repeated the medical bulletin until the King died at 11.55 p.m. and the announcement was made at 12.15. On the 21st, James Agate entered in his diary (*Ego 2*, 1936) that he 'heard afterwards that the Queen drafted this [bulletin]'.

It seems to be a difficult statement to get right. Harold Nicolson, the King's official biographer (1952), has 'to its close' rather than 'towards'. Chips Channon in his diary (entry for 20 January 1936) has: 'The life of the King is moving slowly to its close.' George Lyttelton wrote to James Agate to point out what he perceived to be an error in the passage already quoted from *Ego 2* (1936): 'Page 321. "The King's life is moving peacefully *to* (not 'towards') its close." I could swear to this. Surely the beauty of the sentence would be severely damaged by *ds* coming before "its"' (*Ego 6*, 1944).

But no. The above version, preceded by the words, 'This is London. The following bulletin was issued at 9.25 ...' has been checked against the BBC Sound Archives recording. Indeed, in *Ego 7* (for 23 May 1944), Agate authenticated the wording similarly. He told Lyttelton: 'In Noël Coward's film *This Happy Breed*, which I saw tonight, a lower middle-class family listens to the wireless on that January evening. You can distinctly hear Stuart Hibberd say, "The King's life is moving peacefully towards its close". The thing is obviously a record. *Now* what have you to say for yourself?' Lyttelton was reasonably contrite – but persuaded Hibberd to check with his diary just the same. *Compare* ASQUITH 62:8.

DAY LEWIS, C.

Anglo-Irish poet and critic (1904–72)

6 Eye of the wind, whose bearing in
A changeful sky the sage
Birds are never wrong about
And mariners must gauge.

When Peter Scott, the artist and naturalist, came to write his autobiography (published 1961), he set his heart on calling it *The Eye of the Wind*, but nowhere could he find a poem or passage of suitable prose containing the words. Eventually, in desperation, he asked Day Lewis to write a poem from which he could quote them.

The *OED2* has citations for the exact phrase going back to 1725 and for 'the wind's eye' to 1562. 'In the wind's eye' means 'in the direction of the wind'; 'into the wind's eye' means 'to windward'.

1 *Shall I be gone long?*
For ever and a day.
To whom there belong?
Ask the stone to say.
Ask my song.

An epitaph written for himself in 1944. It is now to be found on the poet's grave in the churchyard of St Michael, Stinsford, Dorset (near Thomas Hardy's heart). 'It directs the pilgrim back to the poems where he still breathes', according to Sean Day-Lewis in the biography of his father, *C. Day-Lewis*, 1980. (The hyphen was excluded from his pen name.)

DEAKIN, Ralph

English journalist (1888–1952)

2 Nothing is news until it has appeared in the columns of *The Times*.

In *I, Claud* (1967) Claud Cockburn described the 'Foreign and Imperial News Editor' of the London *Times*: 'Mr Deakin was believed to be the originator of the statement that nothing was news until it had appeared in the columns of *The Times*, and at that period he gave – from his shining shoes to the beautifully brushed bowler on the rack behind him – an impression of mental and physical discretion and complacency which could have been offensive had it not been, in its childish way, touching.'

The equivalent complacency, not to say pomposity, in the BBC was enshrined in the remark, 'The BBC does not have scoops' – thought to have been the philosophy of Tahu Hole (1908–85), an austere New Zealander who was Editor of BBC News from 1948 to 1958.

DEAN, John

American presidential counsel (1938–)

3 We have a cancer within, close to the Presidency, that is growing. It is growing daily.

At White House meeting with President Nixon (21 March 1973) – a warning on the growing threat to the Nixon administration of the Watergate scandal. Revealed in *The White House Transcripts* (1974).

DECATUR, Stephen

American naval officer (1779–1820)

4 My country, right or wrong!

Correctly, Decatur's toast at a public dinner in Norfolk, Virginia (April 1816) was: 'Our country! in her intercourse with foreign nations, may she always be in the right; but our country, right or wrong!' This is sometimes referred to as 'Decatur's Toast'. *Compare* CHESTERTON 157:4.

DE COUBERTIN, Baron Pierre

French founder of the modern Olympics Games (1863–1937)

5 The most important thing in the Olympic Games is not winning but taking part, just as the most important thing in life is not the triumph but the struggle. The essential thing in life is not conquering but fighting well.

Speaking on 24 July 1908 at a banquet for officials of the Olympic Games,which were being held that year in London, de Coubertin actually spoke in French: '*L'important dans ces olympiades, c'est moins d'y gagner que d'y prendre part ... L'important dans la vie ce n'est point le triomphe mais le combat.*' A few days previously, his view had been anticipated by the Bishop of Pennsylvania preaching in St Paul's Cathedral. He said: 'The important thing is not so much to have been victorious as to have taken part.'

De Coubertin repeated his words on many occasions and they later appeared on the electronic scoreboards during the opening ceremony of the Olympics (even if they were ignored by many of the participants). Thus was born a modern proverb. *Compare* RICE 454:6.

DEDERICH, Charles

American addiction specialist (1913–)

6 Today is the first day of the rest of your life.

Slogan (*c.*1969) – also known in the form 'Tomorrow is ...' and as a wall-slogan, graffito, etc. Attributed to Dederich, founder of the Synanon anti-drug and alcohol centres in the US. 'Today Is the First Day of the Rest of *My* Life' was apparently sung in a late 1960s musical *The Love Match* (by Maltby & Shire).

DEFOE, Daniel

English writer (1660–1731)

1 It happened one day, about noon, going towards my boat, I was exceedingly surprised with the print of a man's naked foot on the shore, which was very plain to be seen in the sand. I stood like one thunderstruck, or as if I had seen an apparition.

Robinson Crusoe (1719). *Compare* COWPER 189:2.

2 My man Friday.

Ib. Crusoe's name for the savage he encountered on his desert island. Hence, the term 'man Friday', later applied to any willing helper, and the subsequent 'girl Friday' to describe a female assistant with a wide range of duties (which was dismissed as a sexist term, in due course). The full original phrase can be seen alluded to in, for example, the film titles *My Man Godfrey* (US, 1936), about a tramp who becomes a butler, and *His Girl Friday* (US, 1940).

DE GAULLE, Charles

French general and President (1890–1970)

3 I, General de Gaulle, now in London, call on all French officers and men who are at present on British soil, or may be in the future, with or without arms ... to get in touch with me.

Broadcast appeal from London to Frenchmen betrayed by Pétain's armistice with the Germans. Translation of script broadcast 18 June 1940 (no recording exists).

4 *La France a perdu une bataille! Mais la France n'a pas perdu la guerre!*
France has lost a battle, but France has not lost the war!

This memorable line appeared in a proclamation dated 18 June 1940 and circulated later in the month, but it was not spoken in de Gaulle's famous broadcast appeal of that date, from London, to Frenchmen betrayed by Pétain's armistice with the Germans. Earlier, on 19 May 1940, Winston Churchill, in his first broadcast to the British people as Prime Minister, had said: 'Our task is not only to win the battle – but to win the war' (meaning the battle *for* Britain).

5 *Maintenant, elle est comme les autres.*
Now she is like the others.

Jean Lacouture in his biography (1965) of de Gaulle recorded the remark the future French President made at the graveside of his mentally disabled daughter, Anne, who died shortly before her twentieth birthday in 1948. Mme Yvonne de Gaulle had written to a friend when Anne was born: 'Charles and I would give everything, everything, health, fortune, promotion, career, if only Anne were a little girl like the others.' Hence, the particular nature of the later, poignant remark.

6 Politics is too important to be left to the politicians.

Quoted in Clement Attlee, *A Prime Minister Remembers* (1961). *See also* BENN 84:3; CLEMENCEAU 173:4; MACLEOD 371:4.

7 *La vieillesse est un naufrage.*
Old age is a shipwreck.

De Gaulle was referring particularly to Pétain when he made this observation in *Les Mémoires de Guerre* (1954). Compare other attributed sayings – J.M. Synge: 'Old age is a poor, untidy thing'; and Winston Churchill's reference to 'the surly advance of decrepitude'.

8 How can you govern a country which produces 246 different kinds of cheese?

There are many versions of de Gaulle's aphorisms but this is probably an accurate summing up of his view of the French people, although the number of cheeses varies. 246 is Ernest Mignon's version in *Les Mots du Général* (1962). The *ODQ* (1979) has 265 – the occasion given for this version is the 1951 election when de Gaulle's political party, though the largest, still did not have an overall majority.

Compare the older view of De la Reyniere (d.1838): '*On connoit en France 685 manières differentes d'accommoder les oeufs* [in France, there are 685 different ways of using eggs]'.

9 I always thought I was Jeanne d'Arc and Buonaparte – how little one knows oneself.

On being compared with Robespierre. Quoted in *Figaro Littéraire* (1958).

10 *Je vous ai compris ... Vive l'Algérie française!*
I have understood you ... Long live French Algeria!

De Gaulle became President in 1958 amid the turmoil created by resistance from French colonialists to the idea of Algerian independence. He eventually led his country in quite the opposite direction to the one expected of him, but from the beginning he spoke with a forked tongue. On 4 June he flew to Algiers and told a rally 'I have understood you' – which could have meant anything – at the same time as '*Vive l'Algérie française!*' – which could have been taken to imply that he supported the continuation of colonial rule.

1 *Europe des patries.*
A Europe of nations.

Widely taken as encapsulating de Gaulle's view of Europe but possibly not originated by him. Michel Debré used the phrase in a speech (15 January 1959) on taking office as the Prime Minister of France.

2 One does not arrest Voltaire.

Attributed remark (*c.*1960). On why he had not arrested Jean-Paul Sartre for urging French troops in Algeria to desert.

3 I can see her in about ten years from now on the yacht of a Greek petrol millionaire.

An attributed remark about Jackie Kennedy after de Gaulle had attended President Kennedy's funeral in 1963. In *Fallen Oaks* (1972), André Malraux recalls de Gaulle having said, rather, 'She is a star, and will end up on the yacht of some oil baron'. In 1968 she married Aristotle Onassis, the Greek shipping tycoon. When later reminded of his prediction, de Gaulle told Malraux: 'Did I say that? Well, well ... Fundamentally I would rather have believed that she would marry Sartre. Or you!'

4 *Vive le Québec libre!*
Long live free Quebec!

Speech, Montreal (25 July 1967). The Federal Canadian government found these words offensive and de Gaulle had to cut short his visit.

5 *La réforme, oui; la chienlit, non.*
Reform, yes, bed-shitting, no.

In private de Gaulle had a colourful way of describing his political opponents – for example, he would call them *pisse-vinaigres* ('vinegar pissers') and 'eunuchs of the Fourth Republic' or '*politichiens*'. Returning from a visit to Romania at the time of the May 1968 student uprising in France, he asked the Minister of Education: 'What about your students – still the *chienlit*?' Quite what this meant was much debated at the time. The polite dictionary definition is 'carnival masquerade' or 'ridiculous disguise' but if spelled 'chie-en-lit' it can mean 'bed-shitting' which seems more appropriate in the context. A day or two later, on 19 May, de Gaulle used the expression again at a Cabinet meeting while giving his view of the students' demands, as above. It was his Prime Minister, Georges Pompidou, who passed the remark to the press. One of the many banners appearing in the streets at the time responded with a cartoon of the President and the charge '*La chienlit c'est lui!*' This was outside the Renault factory at Billancourt where workers were staging a sit-in.

6 Where there is mystery, there is power.

Or 'Where there is no mystery there is no power.' This unverified statement was made by de Gaulle to André Malraux in the context of a discussion about the importance of politicians not exposing themselves too frequently on television. *Compare* BAGEHOT 71:5.

DE LA MARE, Walter

English poet and children's writer (1873–1956)

7 'Is there anybody there?' said the Traveller,
Knocking on the moonlit door;
And his horse in the silence champed the
grasses
Of the forest's ferny floor ...
'Tell them I came, and no one answered,
That I kept my word,' he said ...
Ay, they heard his foot upon the stirrup,
And the sound of iron on stone,
And how the silence surged softly backward,
When the plunging hoofs were gone.

'The Listeners' (1912). In a 1995 BBC TV poll to find Britain's favourite poem, this came third (behind Kipling's 'If' and Tennyson's 'The Lady of Shalott'). Its strong showing was put down to the fact that many of the voters must have learnt it at school.

DELANE, John Thaddeus

English newspaper editor (1817–79)

8 The first duty of the Press is to obtain the earliest and most correct intelligence of the events of the time, and instantly, by disclosing them to make them the common property of the nation.

In *The Times* (6 February 1852). Attributed to Delane (the paper's influential editor for thirty-six years) but in fact written by Robert Lowe and Henry Reeve. The correction was given by Harold Evans in a lecture on 4 March 1974.

DELAROCHE, Paul

French painter (1797–1856)

1 From today painting is dead.

On hearing of the invention of the 'daguerrotype', an early form of photography, in 1838.

DELDERFIELD, R.F.

English novelist (1912–72)

2 A Horseman Riding By.

Title of novel (1966). Just possibly an allusion to YEATS 588:1.

3 God is an Englishman.

The title of Delderfield's novel (published in 1970) might derive from a saying attributed to George Bernard Shaw (but untraced): 'The ordinary Britisher imagines that God is an Englishman.' But, however expressed, the arrogant assumption is almost traditional. Harold Nicolson recorded in his diary for 3 June 1942 that three years previously, R.S. Hudson, the Minister of Agriculture, was being told by the Yugoslav minister in London of the dangers facing Britain. 'Yes,' replied Hudson, 'you are probably correct and these things may well happen. But you forget that God is English.'

James Morris in *Farewell the Trumpets* has a Dublin balladeer at the time of the 1916 Easter Rising singing: 'God is not an Englishman and truth will tell in time.' The closing line of the Gilbert and Sullivan opera *HMS Pinafore* (1878) is 'That he is an Englishman!', but it is sung to such grandiose music that it tends to sound like, '*He* is an Englishman!' God's Englishness is also expressed in other ways: in a June 1977 edition of BBC Radio *Quote ... Unquote*, Anna Ford (a clergyman's daughter) mentioned the (apocryphal?) priest who prayed: 'Dear God, as you will undoubtedly have read in the leader column of *The Times* this morning ...'

And then God is sometimes included in other groups. R.A. Austen-Leigh's *Eton Guide* (1964) points out that on the south wall of Lower Chapel an inscription begins, 'You who in the chapel worship God, an Etonian like yourselves ...' When H.M. Butler, Master of Trinity College, Cambridge, said 'It was well to remember that, at this moment, both the Sovereign and the Prime Minister are Trinity men', Augustine Birrell replied: 'The Master should have added that he can go further, for it is obvious that the affairs of the world are built upon the momentous fact that God is also a Trinity man' (quoted by Harold Laski in a letter to Oliver Wendell Holmes, 4 December 1926).

In July 1987, on *Quote ... Unquote*, the actor Brian Glover drew attention to the adage: 'God was a Yorkshireman.' By way of contrast, there is apparently a Greek saying – presumably of reassurance – which states: 'Never mind, God isn't an Albanian.'

4 To Serve Them All My Days.

The title of Delderfield's 1972 novel about a schoolmaster sounds as if it *ought* to be a quotation, but contains no more than echoes of several religious lines: 'And to serve him truly all the days of my life' from the Catechism in the Book of Common Prayer; 'To serve thee all my happy days', from the hymn 'Gentle Jesus, meek and mild' in the Methodist Hymnal; the Devon carol, 'We'll bring him hearts that love him/To serve him all our days'; and, the Sunday school hymn: 'I must like a Christian/Shun all evil ways,/Keep the faith of Jesus,/And serve him all my days.'

DEMOSTHENES

Athenian orator and politician (384–322BC)

5 Action, action, action!

The three most important qualities in an orator. Quoted by Kenneth Tynan in 'A Tribute to Mr Coward' (1953). In Boswell's *Life of Johnson* (1791) – for 3 April 1773 – Dr Johnson 'repeated his usual paradoxical declamation against action in publick speaking. "Action can have no effect upon reasonable minds".' When Mrs Thrale pointed out Demosthenes's recipe, he retorted: 'Demosthenes, Madam, spoke to an assembly of brutes; to a barbarous people.'

DEMPSEY, Jack

American heavyweight boxer (1895–1983)

6 Honey, I just forgot to duck.

Dempsey said this to his wife, on losing his World Heavyweight title to Gene Tunney during a fight in Philadelphia (23 September 1926). In his *Autobiography* (1977), he recalled: 'Once I got to the hotel, Estelle managed to reach me by telephone, saying she'd be with me by morning and that she'd heard the news. I could hardly hear her because of the people crowding the phone. "What happened, Ginsberg?" (That was her pet name for me.) "Honey, I just forgot to duck."' The line was recalled by ex-sports commentator Ronald Reagan when explaining to *his* wife what had happened during an assassination attempt in 1981.

DENNIS, John

English playwright and critic (1657–1734)

1 A man who would make so vile a pun would not scruple to pick a pocket.

Quoted in *The Gentleman's Magazine* (1781). Possibly said of Dennis rather than by him.

2 See how the rascals use me! They will not let my play run and yet they steal my thunder!

Attributed remark, hence the expression 'to steal a person's thunder' meaning 'to get in first and do whatever the other wanted to make a big impression with', particularly with regard to ideas and policies. It is said to derive from an incident involving Dennis who had invented a device for making the sound of thunder in plays and had used it in an unsuccessful one of his own at the Drury Lane Theatre, London (*c.*1700). Subsequently, at the same theatre, he saw a performance of *Macbeth* and noted that the thunder was being produced in his special way. Another version of his remark is: 'That is *my* thunder, by God; the villains will play my thunder, but not my play.'

DENNIS, Nigel

English writer (1912–89)

3 A great American need not fear the hand of his assassin; his real demise begins only when a friend like Mr Sorensen closes the mouth of his tomb with a stone.

Reviewing *Kennedy* by Theodore C. Sorensen (1965) in *The Sunday Telegraph*. Quoted in A. Andrews, *Quotations for Speakers and Writers* (1969).

DENT, Alan

Scottish critic and writer (1905–78)

4 This is the tragedy of a man who could not make up his mind.

From the introduction to Dent's film adaptation of Shakespeare's *Hamlet* (1948). Laurence Olivier spoke the words but did not write them, as is suggested by the *ODQ* (1992). Dent's capsule comment was criticized on the grounds that *Hamlet* is not so much about a man who could not make up his mind as about one who could not bring himself to take necessary action.

DESANI, G.V.

Indian-born novelist (1909–)

5 Geography is everywhere.

In the days when humorous graffiti were all the rage, I was sent a photograph of a curious daub on a brick wall in the middle of a field in Bedworth, Warwickshire. It proclaimed: 'GEOGRAPHY IS EVERYWHERE – G.V. DESANI.' The identity of the given author of this profound thought puzzled me, but latterly I have learned that Desani actually exists. His novel *All About H. Hatterr* was published to acclaim in 1948. Until his retirement he was a visiting professor at the University of Austin, Texas. The last line of *Hatterr* is the (seemingly very Indian), 'Carry on, boys, and continue like hell!'

DE VALERA, Éamon

Irish President (1882–1975)

6 A land whose countryside would be bright with cosy homesteads, whose fields and villages would be joyous with the sounds of industry, with the romping of sturdy children, the contests of athletic youths and the laughter of comely maidens, whose firesides would be forums for the wisdom of serene old age.

On an ideal Ireland, in St Patrick's Day broadcast (1943).

7 It's my considered opinion that in the fullness of time history will record the greatness of Collins and it will be recorded at my expense.

Quoted in Tim Pat Coogan, *Michael Collins* (1990), and used as the epigraph of the film *Michael Collins* (US, 1996). De Valera and Collins were rival leaders at the time of the founding of the Irish Free State. Collins was assassinated (*see* COLLINS 178:7); de Valera went on to become the long-serving President of the Irish Republic. On this occasion, he was turning down a request to become Patron of the Michael Collins Foundation. The remark was relayed to Coogan by Collins's nephew, also called Michael Collins.

DEWAR, Sir James

Scottish physicist (1842–1923)

8 Minds are like parachutes. They only function when they are open.

Attributed in *ODQ* (1992). Sometimes quoted as 'Minds are like umbrellas ...'

DIAGHILEV, Serge

Russian ballet impresario (1872–1929)

1 *Étonne-moi!*
Astonish me!

Said to Jean Cocteau, the French writer and designer, in Paris in 1912. Cocteau had complained to Diaghilev that he was not getting enough encouragement and the Russian exhorted him with the words, 'Astound me! I'll wait for you to astound me.'

In Cocteau's *Journals* (published 1956), he comments: 'I was at the absurd age when one thinks oneself a poet, and I sensed in Diaghilev a polite resistance.' When Cocteau received the command he felt it was one he could, and should, obey. In due course, he may be said to have done so.

DIANA

British Princess of Wales (1961– 97)

2 Pretty amazing.

When asked in 1981 what her impression of Prince Charles had been on first meeting her future husband. This innocuous verdict on their encounter in a freshly ploughed field during 1977 briefly achieved catchphrase status. From a TV interview on the day of their engagement (24 February 1981). Quoted in Robert Lacey, *Princess* (1982).

3 There were three of us in this marriage, so it was a bit crowded.

Interviewed on BBC TV *Panorama* (20 November 1995). In answer to the question whether Camilla Parker Bowles was a factor in the breakdown of her marriage to the Prince of Wales.

4 I'd like to be a queen of people's hearts ... but I don't see myself being Queen of this country.

Ib. In answer to the question, 'Do you think you will ever be Queen?' From *The Independent* (18 December 1995): 'The Princess of Wales seems certain to land in next year's dictionaries of quotations for her wish to be "the queen of people's hearts".' It was a memorably spontaneous phrase. Or was it? Searching through the remaindered section of his record collection, Eagle Eye is stunned to find the lyrics from a 1987 composition by an amateur songwriter, Basilio Magno, who lives in Spain and is now 72. It is entitled Sweet Lady Di and includes the phrase: "She'll remain a queen in every Briton's heart".'

DÍAZ, Porfirio

Mexican President (1830–1915)

5 Poor Mexico! So far from God, so close to the United States.

Attributed in Bartlett (1980). *Compare* ANDREWES 19:4.

DIBDIN, Charles

English songwriter and playwright (1745–1814)

6 In every mess I finds a friend,
In every port a wife.

'Jack in his Element' (1790). An earlier version of this idea is in John Gay's *Sweet William's Farewell to Black-Eyed Susan* (1720): 'They'll tell thee, sailors, when away,/In ev'ry port a mistress find'. In Isaac Bickerstaffe's play *Thomas and Sally* (1761), there is mention of 'a wife in every port'. Later, the phrase tended to be 'a girl in every port', as in the title of a film (US, 1928) with Louise Brooks.

DIBDIN, Thomas

English songwriter (1771–1841)

7 Oh! what a snug little Island,
A right little, tight little Island!

Song, 'The Snug Little Island' from a musical play, *The British Raft* (1797), said to have been written in the late 1700s when Britain was threatened by Napoleonic invasion. In a letter (27 November 1816), Lord Byron wrote: 'I would never willingly dwell in the "tight little island."' *Tight Little Island* was the US title of the film (UK, 1948) of Compton Mackenzie's novel *Whisky Galore*.

DICKENS, Charles

English novelist (1812–70)

BARNABY RUDGE (1841)

8 He was not only a spectre at their licentious feasts; a something in the midst of their revelry and riot that chilled and haunted them; but out of doors he was the same.

This sentence from Chap. 16 is the earliest citation found of the expression 'spectre at the feast', meaning 'some ghost from the past that comes to unsettle some person or persons in the present'. Is the allusion simply to Banquo's ghost in Shakespeare's *Macbeth* (III.iv), or does it take in the Commendatore in Mozart's *Don Giovanni* and the writing on the wall at Belshazzar's Feast in the Book of Daniel (*see* BIBLE 99:1)?

A modern example from *The Independent* (3 June 1993): '"There was just one nomination for spectre at the feast", said one of the contributors to ... BBC1's chocolate box recollection of Coronation Day. He had the Duke of Windsor in mind (who didn't turn up in the end, to everyone's relief).'

But why '*spectre* at the feast' rather than 'ghost' or 'apparition' – because it is more euphonious?

BLEAK HOUSE (1852–3)

1 This is a London particular ... A fog, miss.

Chap. 3. The name 'London particular' was given to London's one-time notorious fogs because they were very characteristic of, or particular, to London. Possibly originally from a Madeira wine imported especially for the London market and thence applied to the fog because of its colour.

2 [Chadband] 'Why can't we not fly, my friends?' [Mr Snagsby] 'No wings.'

Chap. 19. Compare from Lord Berners, *First Childhood* (1934): 'My [model flying machine] elicited a reproof from the Headmaster, who happened to see it [*c.*1893]. "Men," he said, "were never meant to fly; otherwise God would have given them wings." The argument was convincing, if not strikingly, having been used previously, if I am not mistaken, by Mr Chadband.'

3 Self-praise is no recommendation.

Chap. 55. First recorded appearance of this proverbial expression. Also in *Our Mutual Friend*, Bk 4, Chap. 2 (1865).

A CHRISTMAS CAROL (1843)

4 'Bah,' said Scrooge. 'Humbug!'

Stave 1. Ebenezer Scrooge, an old curmudgeon, usurer and miser, has this view of the Christmas spirit until frightened into changing his ways by the appearance of a ghost and visions. The derivation of the word 'humbug' meaning 'deception, sham' is uncertain but it suddenly came into vogue *c.*1750.

5 'God bless us every one!' said Tiny Tim, the last of all.

Stave 3. Tiny Tim is the younger son in the Cratchit family and a cripple. The converted Scrooge is concerned to save him. Tiny Tim's exclamation is the sentimental highpoint of the story and is repeated as the last line of the story.

THE CRICKET ON THE HEARTH (1846)

6 The Cricket on the Hearth.

Title of Dickens's Christmas book for 1846. The cricket, so described, influences the main character to overcome a misunderstanding. Dickens probably took the idea from a ballad in what is known to be one of his favourite works – Goldsmith's *The Vicar of Wakefield* (1766):

> The cricket chirrups on the hearth,
> The crackling faggot flies.

Earlier, in Milton's 'Il Penseroso' (1632), there had been:

> Far from all resort of mirth,
> Save the cricket on the hearth.

DAVID COPPERFIELD (1850)

7 Barkis is willin'.

Chap. 5. Mr Barkis, a Yarmouth carrier, asks young David Copperfield to convey his willingness to marry Peggotty, in these words. Eventually they do marry.

8 'In case anything turned up,' which was his favourite expression.

Chap. 11. Of Wilkins Micawber, an optimistic failure, who lives on the breadline but is convinced that his fortunes will soon be on the mend. The character is based in part on Dickens's father. His financial analysis in Chap. 12 is impeccable: 'Annual income twenty pounds, annual expenditure nineteen nineteen and six, result happiness. Annual income twenty pounds, annual expenditure twenty pounds ought and six, result misery.'

9 My mother is likewise a very umble person. We live in a numble abode.

Chap. 16. Uriah Heep speaking. 'Humble abode' is a self-deprecating term for where one lives. Appropriately, two of the most unctuous characters in all literature use it. Heep, as here, and Mr Collins in Jane Austen's *Pride and Prejudice* (1813): 'The garden in which stands my humble abode, is separated only by a lane from Rosings Park, her ladyship's residence.'

10 Accidents will happen in the best-regulated families.

This proverbial expression is best remembered in the form delivered in Chap. 28: '"Copperfield," said Mr.

Micawber, "accidents will occur in the best-regulated families; and in families not regulated by ... the influence of Woman, in the lofty character of Wife, they must be expected with confidence, and must be borne with philosophy".' Dickens had earlier used the saying in *Pickwick Papers* (1836–7) and *Dombey and Son* (1844–6). However, the saying is not original to him. Sir Walter Scott wrote in Chapter 49 of *Peveril of the Peak* (1823): 'Nay, my lady ... such things will befall in the best regulated families.'

The *CODP* finds 'P. Atall' writing in *Hermit in America* (1819), 'Accidents will happen in the best regulated families'. Even earlier, George Colman in *Deuce is in Him* (1763) has the more basic, 'Accidents will happen'. *Compare* HERFORD 293:4.

1 I got to know what umbleness did, and I took to it. I ate umble pie with an appetite.

Chap. 39. Uriah Heep. The expression 'to eat humble pie', meaning 'to submit to humiliation' came about because the 'humbles' or 'umbles' were those less appealing parts of a deer (or other animal) which had been killed in a hunt. They would be given to those of lower rank and perhaps served as 'humble pie' or 'umble pie'. A coincidence then that 'humble pie' should have anything to do with being 'humble'. Recorded in use by 1830.

See also BURNS 134:2.

DOMBEY AND SON (1846–8)

2 When found, make a note of.

Chap. 15. The motto of Captain Cuttle. Also Chap. 19.

3 What the Waves were always saying.

Heading of Chap. 16. Nowhere in the novel does Dickens use the precise words, 'What are the *wild* waves saying?', though the book is fairly awash with the idea of a 'dark and unknown sea that rolls round all the world' (Chap. 1, end). At the end of Chap. 8, in Brighton, young Paul Dombey says to his sister, Florence, 'I want to know what it says ... The sea, Floy, what is it that it keeps on saying?' Then, a line or two later: 'Very often afterwards, in the midst of their talk, he would break off, to try to understand what it was that the waves were always saying; and would rise up in his couch to look towards that invisible region, far away.'

The quotation in question is actually the title line of a Victorian song with words by J.E. Carpenter (1813–85) and music by Stephen Glover (1813–70):

What are the wild waves saying,
Sister, the whole day long:
That ever amid our playing,
I hear but their low, lone song?
Not by the seaside only,
There it sounds wild and free;
But at night when 'tis dark and lonely,
In dreams it is still with me.

The song is a duet between the characters Paul and Florence Dombey and based on an incident in Dickens's novel. Compare this: an advertisement for Igranic wireless coils, dating from the early 1920s, which plays upon the idea of radio waves and asks, 'What are the wild waves saying?'

4 Said Mr Morfin, 'I have whistled, hummed tunes, gone accurately through the whole of Beethoven's Sonata in B, to let him know that I was within hearing, but he never heeded me.'

Chap. 53. Unfortunately, there is no Sonata in B by Beethoven – though there is a Piano Sonata in B flat major.

GREAT EXPECTATIONS (1860–1)

5 I had cherished a profound conviction that her bringing me up by hand gave her no right to bring me up by jerks.

Chap. 8. Included in Edward Gathorne-Hardy, *A New Garden of Bloomers* (1967). (Jerks = strokes with whip, lash.)

6 What larks!

Kenneth Tynan wrote to Cecil Beaton: 'Can you sing bass? Kensington's Boris Christoff – what larks!' (Letter, 1 January 1953). In *The Kenneth Williams Diaries* (1993) (entry for 30 August 1970), the actor writes: 'Tom played the piano and all the girls danced with us & I stuck me bum out and oh! what larks Pip!' Ned Sherrin dedicates his *Theatrical Anecdotes* (1991), 'For Judi [Dench] and Michael [Williams]: "What larks!"' Both these refer to the characteristic phrase of Joe Gargery, the blacksmith, who looks after his brother-in-law and apprentice, Pip, in the boy's youth. Chap. 13 has him saying 'calc'lated to lead to larks' and Chap. 57, 'And when you're well enough to go out for a ride – what larks!' The recent use of the phrase probably has more to do with the 1946 film of the book in which Bernard Miles played Joe. As he sees Pip off on a stage coach, he says, 'One day I'll come to see you in London and then, what larks, eh?' and similarly, after Pip's breakdown, 'You'll soon be well enough to go out again, and then – what larks!' Even here, the name Pip is not actually included in the phrase.

LITTLE DORRIT (1857)

1 Father is rather vulgar, my dear. The word Papa, besides, gives a pretty form to the lips. Papa, potatoes, poultry, prunes, and prism, are all very good words for the lips: especially prunes and prism.

Bk 2, Chap. 5. Amy Dorrit has just referred to her 'father', as such. Mrs General offers this list of 'P' words, which, she says, help the demeanour (rather than one's elocution).

2 Once a gentleman, and always a gentleman.

Bk 2, Chap. 28. Referring to Rigaud. The seemingly modern 'once a —— always a ——' format derives from an old series of proverbs, 'Once a knave/whore/captain, always a ...' Dr Johnson used 'once a coxcomb, and always a coxcomb' in an anecdote included in Boswell's *Life of Johnson* (1791) for the year 1770. S.T. Coleridge wrote an article with the title *Once a Jacobin Always a Jacobin* (21 October 1802). William Cobbett quoted 'once a parson always a parson' in his *Rural Rides* (for 11 October 1826).

MARTIN CHUZZLEWIT (1843–4)

3 When she sang, he sat like one entranced. She touched his organ, and from that bright epoch, even it, the old companion of his happiest hours, incapable as he had thought of elevation, began a new and deified existence.

Chap. 24. A passage one feels Dickens might have felt the need to improve, if he were writing today. It is included in Edward Gathorne-Hardy, *An Adult's Garden of Bloomers* (1966).

NICHOLAS NICKLEBY (1838–9)

4 As she frequently remarked when she made any such mistake, it would be all the same a hundred years hence.

Chap. 9. Mrs Squeers. *Compare* JOHNSON 318:13.

5 Language was not powerful enough to describe the infant phenomenon.

Chap. 23. 'The infant phenomenon' was the stage billing of Ninetta Crummles (who has been ten years old for at least five years). The term also appears earlier in *Pickwick Papers*, Chap. 26 (1836–7) when Sam Weller says to Master Bardwell: 'Tell her I want to speak to her, will you, my hinfant fernomenon?' This suggests that the phrase was in general use before this novel came to be written or was something Dickens had picked up from an actual case. In 1837, the eight-year-old Jean Davenport was merely billed as 'the most celebrated juvenile actress of the day'. George Parker Bidder (b.1806), who possessed extraordinary arithmetical abilities, had been exhibited round the country as a child, billed as 'the calculating phenomenon'.

6 All is gas and gaiters.

Chap. 49. The Gentleman in the Small-Clothes speaking. Gaiters (leg coverings below the knee) have traditionally been associated with bishops. Hence, *All Gas and Gaiters*, the title of a BBC TV comedy series about the clergy (1966–70).

THE OLD CURIOSITY SHOP (1840–1)

7 Does Little Nell die?

A query not from the book but *about* its child heroine, Nell Trent. She attempts to look after her inadequate grandfather and to protect him from various threats, but her strength gives out. According to one account, 'Does Little Nell die?' was the cry of 6,000 book-loving Americans who hurried to the docks in New York to ask this question of sailors arriving from England. Another version is that it was longshoremen demanding 'How is Little Nell?' or 'Is Little Nell dead?' As the novel was serialized, they were waiting for the arrival of the final instalment of the magazine to find out what had happened to the heroine. Little Nell's death came to typify the heights of Victorian sentimental fiction. Oscar Wilde later commented: 'One must have a heart of stone to read the death of Little Nell without laughing' (quoted in Ada Leverson, *Letters to the Sphinx from Oscar Wilde and Reminiscences of the Author*, 1930).

OLIVER TWIST (1837)

8 Please, sir, I want some more.

Chap. 2. Oliver requests more food in the workhouse.

9 Known by the *sobriquet* of 'The artful Dodger'.

Chap. 8. Jack Dawkins is the real name of the character thereafter referred to as the Dodger. He is a prominent member of Fagin's gang of young thieves. Eventually, he is convicted of theft and transported for life.

10 If the law supposes that ... the law is a ass – a idiot.

Chap. 51. Strictly speaking, if one is quoting Dickens, what Mr Bumble says, is not 'the law is *an* ass'. He is dismayed that the law holds him responsible for his wife's actions. *Compare* CHAPMAN 155:4.

OUR MUTUAL FRIEND (1864–5)

1 Our Mutual Friend.

The title refers to the novel's hero, John Harmon, who feigns death and whose identity is one of the mysteries of the plot. This is a rare example of Dickens using an established phrase for a title (he usually chooses the invented name of a character). 'Our mutual friend' was an expression established by the seventeenth century, but Dickens undoubtedly further encouraged its use. Some have objected that 'mutual friend' is a solecism, arguing that it is impossible for the reciprocity of friendship to be shared with a third party. Even before Dickens took it for a title, a correspondent was writing to the journal *Notes and Queries* in 1849 and asking: 'Is it too late to make an effective stand against the solecistic expression "mutual friend"?' *The Oxford Dictionary for Writers and Editors* (1981) points out that it is an expression used also by Edmund Burke, George Eliot and others, but 'the alternative "common" can be ambiguous'.

2 A fair day's wages for a fair day's work is ever my partner's motto.

Bk 1, Chap. 13. Not original to Dickens. T. Attwood in a speech in the House of Commons (14 June 1839) said: 'They only ask for a fair day's wages for a fair day's work', which is probably the first time the slogan was uttered. In any case, Benjamin Disraeli had used the slogan before Dickens in his novel *Sybil* (1845).

See also NASH 407:6.

PICKWICK PAPERS (1837)

3 It's over, and can't be helped, and that's one consolation, as they always say in Turkey, ven they cut the wrong man's head off.

Chap. 23. Sam Weller speaking. Hence, the term 'Wellerism' for a form of comparison in which a saying or proverbial expression is attributed to an amusingly inapposite source. For example, '"That's an antelope,' observed the small boy when he heard that his mother's sister had run away with the coachman.' Mieder & Kingsbury in their *Dictionary of Wellerisms* (1994) note that a Wellerism usually consists of three parts: a statement, a speaker who makes this remark, and a phrase or clause that places the utterance in a new light or an incompatible setting: '"Every little helps," quoth the wren when she pissed in the sea.' This last was recorded in 1605 and demonstrates that the type was known long before Dickens gave a fondness for uttering these jocular remarks to Sam Weller. Dickens did, however, popularize the form, which came to be known as 'Wellerism' (the word known by 1839).

A TALE OF TWO CITIES (1859)

4 It was the best of times, it was the worst of times, it was the age of wisdom, it was the age of foolishness, it was the epoch of belief, it was the epoch of incredulity, it was the season of light, it was the season of Darkness, it was the spring of hope, it was the winter of despair, we had everything before us, we had nothing before us, we were all going direct to Heaven, we were all going direct the other way.

Bk 1, Chap. 1. One of the most memorable opening sentences to a novel ever written. Hence, many allusions get made to it. For example, the headline 'Best Of Thames, Worst Of Thames' over a review of books about the current condition of London in *The Observer* (22 December 1996).

5 It is a far, far better thing that I do than I have ever done; it is a far, far better rest that I go to, than I have ever known.

Bk 3, Chap. 15. These words, appearing at the end of the novel, are sometimes said to be Sydney Carton's last words as he ascends the scaffold to be guillotined. But he does not actually speak them. They are prefaced with: 'If he had given any utterance to his [last thoughts], and they were prophetic, they would have been these ...'

One editor refers to this as, 'A complicated excursus into the pluperfect subjunctive.' In dramatizations, however, Carton has actually *said* the lines – as did Sir John Martin-Harvey in the play, *The Only Way* (1898) by F. Wills. One of the slogans devised by Dorothy L. Sayers in *Murder Must Advertise* (1933) was for margarine: 'It's a far, far butter thing ...'

DIDEROT, Denis

French philosopher (1713–84)

6 *L'esprit de l'escalier.*
Staircase wit.

Name given to witty ripostes that are only thought up afterwards, on the staircase to the way out. *Paradoxe sur le Comédien* (written 1773–8).

DIETZ, Howard

American writer and film executive (1896–1983)

1 *Ars Gratia Artis.*
Art for Art's sake.

Motto of Metro-Goldwyn-Mayer, devised *c.*1916. Recalled in *Dancing in the Dark* (1974).

2 A day away from Tallulah [Bankhead] is like a month in the country.

Ib. This remark has also been attributed to all the usual suspects – Parker, Ace, Kaufman, Woollcott and Benchley – but Dietz said he said it and Bankhead herself wrote in *Tallulah* (1952): 'How Dietz once remarked, "A day away from Tallulah is like a month in the country." Ever since he's enjoyed the reputation of a great wit.' Ouch.

3 More Stars Than There Are In Heaven.

Slogan for MGM, quoted in Leslie Halliwell, *The Filmgoer's Book of Quotes* (1973). Ascribed to Dietz in J.R. Colombo, *The Wit and Wisdom of the Movie Makers* (1979). The slogan appears on a poster for *Broadway Melody* (1929), the very first film musical.

4 That's Entertainment.

Title of song, *The Band Wagon* (1953). Hence, the title of the film celebration of Hollywood musicals *That's Entertainment* (US, 1974).

5 A ghost and a prince meet
And everyone ends in mincemeat.

Ib. Summary of *Hamlet.*

DIOGENES

Greek philosopher (c.400–c.325BC)

6 Stand out of my sun a little.

When asked by Alexander the Great if he lacked anything. Reported in Plutarch, *Parallel Lives*, in Thomas North's translation (1579). Sometimes rendered as 'Give me more light'.

DISNEY, Walt

American cartoon film-maker (1901–66)

7 All the world owes me a living.

The Grasshopper and the Ants (1934). This expression was so ascribed to Disney when it was used as the epigraph of Graham Greene's novel *England Made Me* (1935). The cartoon film in question – one of the first 'Silly Symphonies' – is based on the Aesop fable 'Of the ant and the grasshopper' (as it is called in Caxton's first English translation, 1484), which tells of a grasshopper asking an ant for corn to eat in winter. The ant asks, 'What have you done all the summer past?' and the grasshopper can only answer, 'I have sung'. The moral is that you should provide yourself in the summer with what you need in winter. Disney turns the grasshopper into a fiddler and gives him a song to sing (written by Larry Morey to music by Leigh Harline):

> Oh! the world owes me a living
> Deedle, diedle, doedle, diedledum.
> Oh! the world owes me a living
> Deedle, diedle, doedle, diedleum, etc.

This develops in time to:

> Oh, the world owes us a living ...
> You should soil your Sunday pants
> Like those other foolish ants,
> So let's play and sing and dance ...

And then, when the error of his ways has been pointed out to him, the grasshopper sings:

> I owe the world a living ...
> I've been a fool the whole year long.
> Now I'm singing a different song,
> You were right and I was wrong.

This song became quite well known and presumably helped John Llewellyn Rhys choose *The World Owes Me a Living* as the title for his 1939 novel about a redundant RFC hero who tries to make a living with a flying circus (filmed 1944). It is a little odd rendered in this form, because on the whole it is not something a person would say about himself. More usually, another would say, pejoratively, 'The trouble with you is, you think the world owes you a living.' The phrase *was* used before Disney. W.G. Sumner wrote in *Earth Hunger* (1896): 'The men who start out with the notion that the world owes them a living generally find that the world pays its debt in the penitentiary or the poorhouse.' Sumner was an American economist but the phrase may not have originated in the US.

8 I come from a land, from a faraway place
where the caravan camels roam.
Where they cut off your ear if they don't like
your face.
It's barbaric, but – hey – it's home.

From the opening song 'Arabian Nights' in the Disney cartoon film of *Aladdin* (1993) – produced long after Disney's death, of course. When the film opened in

Britain, in order not to offend Arab sensibilities, the lyrics had become: 'Where it's flat and immense and the heat is intense/It's barbaric but hey it's home.' The original lyric was written by Howard Ashman (music by Alan Menken), the amendment by Peter Schneider.

DISRAELI, Benjamin (1st Earl of Beaconsfield)

British Conservative Prime Minister (1804–81)

1 A dark horse, which had never been thought of ... rushed past the grandstand in sweeping triumph.

The Young Duke: A Moral Tale Though Gay (1831). Figuratively, the phrase 'dark horse' refers to a runner about whom everyone is 'in the dark' until he comes from nowhere and wins the race – of whatever kind. Possibly the phrase originated in Disraeli's novel.

2 Read no history: nothing but biography, for that is life without theory.

Contarini Fleming (1832). *Compare* EMERSON 229:8.

3 I will sit down now, but the time will come when you will hear me.

When Disraeli gave his maiden speech in the House of Commons (7 December 1837), he wanted to take the House by storm. His subject was the validity of certain Irish elections, but he was greeted with hisses, catcalls and hoots of laughter. The above was his concluding sentence.

4 'Two nations; between whom there is no intercourse and no sympathy; who are as ignorant of each other's habits, thoughts, and feelings, as if they were dwellers in different zones, or inhabitants of different planets; who are formed by a different breeding, are fed by a different food, are ordered by different manners, and are not governed by the same laws.' 'You speak of —' said Egremont, hesitatingly, 'THE RICH AND THE POOR.'

Sybil, or The Two Nations, Bk 2, Chap. 5 (1845). Disraeli did not speak of 'One Nation' – that was the title of a pamphlet published in 1950 by a group of Tories including Iain Macleod, Angus Maude and Enoch Powell. According to Alan Watkins in the *Independent on Sunday* (21 January 1996): 'The title was suggested by Maude, though some think the phrase was supplied to him by Macleod. The group, chiefly members who looked up to R.A. Butler, took their name from the pamphlet rather than the other way round.' Tony Blair, the Labour Party leader, revived the phrase in 1996.

5 The question is this: Is man an ape or an angel? Now I am on the side of the angels.

Speech on evolution to the Oxford Diocesan Society (25 November 1864).

6 I have climbed to the top of the greasy pole.

On becoming Prime Minister (1868). Quoted in W. Monypenny and G. Buckle, *The Life of Benjamin Disraeli* (1920).

7 When a man fell into his anecdotage it was a sign for him to retire from the world.

Lothair, Chap. 28 (1870). Earlier, however, his father, Isaac Disraeli, had noted in his *Curiosities of Literature* (1839): 'Among my earliest literary friends, two distinguished themselves by their anecdotical literature: James Petit Andrews, by his "Anecdotes, Ancient and Modern", and William Seward, by his "Anecdotes of Distinguished Persons". These volumes were favourably received, and to such a degree, that a wit of that day, and who is still a wit as well as poet, considered that we were far gone in our "Anecdotage".' The word 'anecdotage' in a less critical sense had been used by De Quincey in 1823 simply to describe anecdotes collectively.

8 You have it, madam.

In a letter to Queen Victoria (24 November 1875), Disraeli announced something of a coup: he had successfully bought Britain shares in the Suez Canal Company. Quoted in Robert Blake, *Disraeli* (1966).

9 Many thanks; I shall lose no time in reading it.

To an author who had sent him an unsolicited manuscript. Quoted in Wilfrid Meynell, *The Man Disraeli* (1903).

10 Everyone likes flattery; and when you come to Royalty you should lay it on with a trowel.

To Matthew Arnold. Quoted in G.W.E. Russell, *Collections and Recollections* (1898). The most notable example of Disraeli's own use of the trowel must be his saying 'We authors, Ma'am' to Queen Victoria when she published her Highland journals and on several other occasions (asserted by Monypenny and Buckle, *Life of Disraeli*, 1910–20).

The figure of speech 'To lay it on with a trowel', meaning 'to be generous in supplying something – usually when engaged in flattery', was an old one even in the nineteenth century. 'That was laid on with a trowel' appears in Shakespeare's *As You Like It*, I.ii.98 (1598) which the Arden edition glosses as 'slapped on thick and without nicety, like mortar'. The trowel in question is not a garden one, but of the kind used by painters for spreading paint thickly.

1 Great nations rise and fall. The people go from bondage to spiritual truth, to great courage, from courage to liberty, from liberty to abundance, from abundance to selfishness, from selfishness to complacency, from complacency to apathy, from apathy to dependence, from dependence back again to bondage.

This is generally attributed to Disraeli, though no source has been found. The historian A.F. Tytler (Lord Woodhouselee) (1747–1813) has also been credited with it.

2 The wisdom of the wise and the experience of the ages are perpetuated by quotations.

Comment on the art of quotation. Quoted in Laurence J. Peter, *Quotations for Our Time* (1977).

3 The Church of England is the Tory Party at prayer.

This description is often attributed to Disraeli. However, Robert Blake, the historian and author of *Disraeli* (1966) told *The Observer* (14 April 1985) that he could not say who had said it first and that a correspondence in *The Times* some years before had failed to find an answer. According to Robert Stewart's *Penguin Dictionary of Political Quotations* (1984), Agnes Maude Royden, the social reformer and preacher, said in an address at the City Temple, London (1917): 'The Church should no longer be satisfied to represent only the Conservative Party at prayer' – but even this sounds as though it was alluding to an already established saying.

4 Lord Salisbury and myself have brought you back peace – but a peace I hope with honour.

Speech on returning from the Congress of Berlin (16 July 1878). *Compare* CHAMBERLAIN 154:3.

5 A sophistical rhetorician, inebriated with the exuberance of his own verbosity, and gifted with an egotistical imagination that can at all times command an interminable and inconsistent series of arguments to malign an opponent and to glorify himself.

Of Gladstone, in a speech to a banquet in the Knightsbridge Riding School (27 July 1878), quoted in *The Times* (29 July). Commonly rendered in the form: 'Sir, you are intoxicated by the exuberance of your own verbosity'. In *Scouse Mouse* (1984), George Melly describes how this was ascribed to *Dr Johnson* by a headmaster called W.W. Twyne. A common mistake.

6 Posterity will do justice to that unprincipled maniac Gladstone – extraordinary mixture of envy, vindictiveness, hypocrisy and superstition; and with one commanding characteristic – whether Prime Minister or Leader of the Opposition, whether preaching, praying, speechifying or scribbling – *never a gentleman*.

Letter to Lord Derby (1878). Sometimes also given as said to Lady Derby in October 1876. Quoted in W. Monypenny and G. Buckle, *The Life of Benjamin Disraeli* (1920).

7 If, for instance, Mr Gladstone were to fall into the river, that would be a misfortune. But if anyone were to pull him out, that would be a calamity.

Asked to define the difference between a calamity and a misfortune. Almost certainly apocryphal. Quoted in Hesketh Pearson, *Lives of the Wits* (1962). A similar story is told concerning Napoleon III and Plon-Plon, once designated as his heir, concerning the difference between an accident and a misfortune (related in Felix Markham, *The Bonapartes*, 1975).

8 She is an excellent creature, but she never can remember which came first, the Greeks or the Romans.

On his wife, Mary Anne. Quoted in G.W.E. Russell, *Collections and Recollections* (1898).

9 Never complain, never explain.

Quoted in John Morley, *Life of Gladstone* (1903) – specifically about attacks in Parliament. The following must have been referring back to, or at least echoing, Disraeli: according to an article in the *Oxford Chronicle* (7 October 1893), a favourite piece of advice given to young men by Benjamin Jowett, who became Master of Balliol College, Oxford, in 1870, was, 'Never regret, never explain, never apologize.' *Compare* BALDWIN 73:7; FISHER 237:3; GRACIAN 268:8.

10 When I want to read a novel, I write one.

Quoted in W. Monypenny and G. Buckle, *The Life of Benjamin Disraeli* (1920). The earliest source found for this oft-repeated remark.

1 There are lies, damn lies – and statistics.

Although often attributed to Mark Twain – because it appears in his *Autobiography* (1924) – this should more properly be ascribed to Disraeli, as indeed Twain took trouble to do. On the other hand, the remark remains untraced among Disraeli's writings and sayings.

2 She would only ask me to take a message to Albert.

These are not Disraeli's last words. During his final illness, it was suggested that he might like to receive a visit from Queen Victoria. 'No, it is better not,' he replied, 'She would only ask me to take a message to Albert.' That is a perfectly genuine quotation and is confirmed by Robert Blake in his life, *Disraeli* (1966). The last authenticated words Disraeli uttered were: 'I had rather live but I am not afraid to die' (quoted in Wintle & Kenin, *The Dictionary of Biographical Quotation*, 1978).

See also CHURCHILL 167:4; SMITH 508:7.

DODD, Ken

English comedian and singer (1927–)

3 The trouble with Freud is that he never played the Glasgow Empire Saturday night.

On Freud's theory that a good joke will lead to great relief and elation. In the ATV programme *The Laughter Makers* (and so quoted in *The Times*, 7 August 1965). Dodd's remark has appeared in several versions since that date. For example, with the addition of 'after Rangers and Celtic had both lost' in *The Guardian* (30 April 1991).

DONATUS, Aelius

Roman grammarian (4th century AD)

4 Damn those who have made my remarks before me!

Quoted in *The Treasury of Humorous Quotations*, ed. by Evan Esar & Nicolas Bentley (1951). In the form 'Confound those who have said our remarks before us', quoted in St Jerome, *Commentary on Ecclesiastes*.

DONNE, John

English poet and divine (1572–1631)

5 Licence my roving hands, and let them go,
Behind, before, above, between, below.
O my America, my new found land,
My kingdom, safeliest when with one man manned.

'To His Mistress Going to Bed', *Elegies* (*c.*1595). The word-play in the third line was relatively topical. Newfoundland had been discovered by John Cabot in 1497 and had just been claimed for Queen Elizabeth I by Sir Humphrey Gilbert in 1583.

6 She, and comparisons are odious.

'The Comparison', in *ib. Compare* SHAKESPEARE 492:5.

7 Come live with me, and be my love,
And we will some new pleasures prove
Of golden sands, and crystal brooks,
With silken lines, and silver hooks.

'The Bait', *Songs and Sonnets* (1611). *Compare* MARLOWE 381:8.

8 Go, and catch a falling star
Get with child a mandrake root,
Tell me, where all past years are.
Or who cleft the Devil's foot.

'Song' in *ib.* Since at least 1563 a 'falling star' has been another name for a meteor or shooting star. Here, the catching is clearly just one of four impossible tasks. *Compare* EMERSON 230:2. 'Catch a falling star' was also the title of a 1958 song, popularized by Perry Como:

> Catch a falling star
> And put it in your pocket,
> Never let it fade away.

9 But I do nothing upon my self, and yet I am mine own *Executioner*.

'Meditation 12', *Devotions Upon Emergent Occasions* (1624). Hence, *Mine Own Executioner*, title of a novel (1945; film UK, 1947) by Nigel Balchin.

10 No man is an Island, entire of it self; every man is a piece of the Continent, a part of the main; if a clod be washed away by the sea, Europe is the less, as well as if a promontory were, as well as if a manor of thy friends or of thine own were; any man's death diminishes me, because I am involved in Mankind. And therefore never send to know for whom the bell tolls; it tolls for thee.

'Meditation 17' in *ib.* Hence, the title of the novel *For Whom the Bell Tolls* (1940; film US, 1943) by Ernest Hemingway, set in the Spanish Civil War. Hemingway's approach to the matter of choosing the title is described in a letter to Maxwell Perkins (21 April 1940) (included in *Ernest Hemingway Selected Letters 1917–1961*, ed. Carlos Baker, 1981): 'I think it has the magic that a title has to have. Maybe it isn't too easy to say. But maybe the book will make it easy. Anyway I have had thirty some titles and they were all possible but this is the first one that has made the bell toll for me. Or do you suppose that people think only of tolls as long distance charges and of Bell as the Bell of the telephone system? If so it is out. The Tolling of the Bell. No. That's not right.'

The same passage is the likely source for the modern funerary cliché, 'His death diminishes us all': 'Sir William's death diminishes us all' was how André Previn commented on the death of William Walton in March 1983. 'One must not be too hard on Mr Previn,' commented *The Guardian*. 'Music is his chosen medium, not words.'

1 John Donne, Anne Donne, Un-done.

Letter to his wife on his dismissal from the service of Sir George More, his father-in-law. Quoted in Izaak Walton, *The Life of Dr Donne*.

DOUGLAS, Kirk

American film actor (1916–)

2 My kids never had the advantage I had: I was born poor.

Remark, in several interviews, early 1980s.

DOUGLAS-HOME, Sir Alec (formerly Earl of Home, later Lord Home)

British Conservative Prime Minister (1903–95)

3 When I have to read economic documents I have to have a box of matches and start moving them into position to illustrate and simplify the points to myself.

Interviewed in *The Observer* (16 September 1962), when Foreign Secretary in Harold Macmillan's government. It was by such remarks as these that Douglas-Home projected an image of a likeable buffoon, which he was not (buffoon, that is – he was certainly likeable). When he became Prime Minister he still fostered the image: 'There are two problems in my life. The political ones are insoluble and the economic ones are incomprehensible' (speech, January 1964).

4 He [Home] is used to dealing with estate workers. I cannot see how anyone can say he is out of touch.

In fact, said by his daughter, Caroline (1937–) when he became Prime Minister. Quoted in the *Daily Herald* (21 October 1963).

5 As far as [being] the 14th Earl is concerned, I suppose Mr Wilson, when you come to think of it, is the 14th Mr Wilson.

TV interview (21 October 1963). In response to WILSON 575:4.

6 The Way the Wind Blows.

Title of memoirs (1976). He explains that it was what a gamekeeper said of his family's abilities: 'The Home boys always seem to know which way the wind blows', and he adds, '[He] was not thinking of me as a political trimmer, but simply stating a fact of our family life ... on the right interpretation of wind or weather depended the action of the day.' A proverbial expression of 1546 was 'I knew which way the wind blew.' *See also* DYLAN 217:9.

7 A large pipe and thick country tweeds gave the image of a yeoman squire living close to the soil. It was very clever, because in fact he was at his happiest in a room, preferably facing north, with the windows shut, reading Mary Webb.

On Stanley Baldwin, in *ib.*

DOWSON, Ernest

English poet (1867–1900)

8 They are not long, the weeping and the
laughter,
Love and desire and hate ...
They are not long the days of wine and roses;
Out of a misty dream
Our path emerges for a while, then closes
Within a dream.

'*Vitae Summa Brevis Spem Nos Vetar Incohare Longam*' (1896). Hence, *The Days of Wine and Roses*, title of a film (US, 1962) about an alcoholic (though the phrase is often used to evoke romance). Hence, also, *The Weeping and the Laughter*, the title of a novel (1988) by Noel Barber, and of autobiographies by J. Maclaren-Ross (1953) and Viva King (1976).

1 *Non Sum Qualis Eram.*
I am not what I was.

Title of poem (in full *Non Sum Qualis Eram Bonae Sub Regno Cynarae*) (1896), also known as 'Cynara'. She is a woman to whom the poet professes faithfulness even when consorting with others.

2 I have forgot much, Cynara! Gone with the wind.

Ib. Hence, *Gone With the Wind*, title of Margaret Mitchell's famous novel (1936; film US, 1939) where the phrase refers to the southern United States before the American Civil War, as is made clear by the on-screen prologue to the film: 'There was a land of Cavaliers and Cotton Fields called the Old South. Here in this patrician world the Age of Chivalry took its last bows. Here was the last ever seen of the Knights and their Ladies fair, of Master and Slave. Look for it only in books, for it is no more than a dream remembered, a Civilization gone with the wind.'

3 I have been faithful to thee, Cynara! in my fashion.

Ib. Compare 'Always True To You In My Fashion', the song by Cole Porter from *Kiss Me Kate* (1948) which echoes, consciously or unconsciously, this line.

4 For Lord I was free of all Thy flowers, but I chose the world's sad roses,
And that is why my feet are torn and mine eyes are blind with sweat.

Impenitentia Ultima (1896). In *Seven Pillars of Wisdom* (1926), T.E. Lawrence described being thrown to the ground from a camel: as he lay 'passively waiting for the Turks to kill me', he recalled the 'verses of a half-forgotten poem', but he does not own up to the source.

DOYLE, Sir Arthur Conan

Scottish-born writer (1859–1930)

5 'You have been in Afghanistan, I perceive.' 'How on earth did you know that?'

A Study in Scarlet, Chap. 1 (1888). The first exchange between Sherlock Holmes and Dr Watson.

6 It is cocaine ... a seven per cent solution. Would you care to try it?

The Sign of Four (1889). Hence, *The Seven Per Cent Solution*, title of a novel (1974; film US, 1976) by Nicholas Meyer, about Sherlock Holmes being treated by Sigmund Freud for a persecution complex and cocaine addiction.

7 Quick, Watson, the needle!

Not uttered by Holmes in the books but it is in the film *The Hound of the Baskervilles* (US, 1939).

8 It is quite a three-pipe problem, and I beg that you won't speak to me for fifty minutes.

'The Red-Headed League', *The Adventures of Sherlock Holmes* (1892). Holmes is saying that the case requires sufficient thought to accompany the smoking of three fills of his famous pipe.

9 The Napoleon of crime.

Of 'Ex-Professor Moriarty of mathematical celebrity', 'The Final Problem' in *The Memoirs of Sherlock Holmes* (1894). *Compare* ELIOT 227:2.

10 You know my methods, Watson.

'The Crooked Man', in *ib.* Partridge/*Catch Phrases* rightly includes Holmes's 'oft repeated phrase: "You know my methods, Watson, – apply them."' And adds: 'The phrase is extant.'

11 Elementary my dear Watson!

The Sherlock Holmes phrase appears nowhere in Conan Doyle's writings, though the great detective does exclaim just 'Elementary' to Dr Watson in 'The Crooked Man' in *ib.* Conan Doyle brought out his last Holmes book in 1927. His son Adrian (in collaboration with John Dickson Carr) was one of those who used the phrase in follow-up stories – as have adapters of the stories in film and broadcast versions. In the 1929 film *The Return of Sherlock Holmes* – the first with sound – the final lines of dialogue are:

Watson: Amazing, Holmes!
Holmes: Elementary, my dear Watson, elementary.

This may have put the catchphrase squarely in the language but it appears already to have been a phrase in 1915. In *Psmith Journalist*, Chap. 19, P.G. Wodehouse wrote: '"Elementary, my dear Watson, elementary," murmured Psmith. Even earlier, in *Psmith in the City* (1910), Psmith is already reaching towards the finished phrase: 'Then I am prepared to bet a small sum that he is nuts on Manchester United. My dear Holmes, how —! Elementary, my dear fellow, quite elementary.'

12 'Is there any other point to which you would wish to draw my attention?' 'To the curious incident of the dog in the night-time.' 'The

dog did nothing in the night-time.' 'That was the curious incident,' remarked Sherlock Holmes.

'Silver Blaze' in *The Memoirs of Sherlock Holmes* (1894). A much quoted example of an absence of fact that could provide an important clue in detection. Possibly most usually alluded to now as 'the dog that did not bark in the night'.

1 Come, Watson, come! The game is afoot.

'The Abbey Grange', *The Return of Sherlock Holmes* (1904). *Compare* SHAKESPEARE 484:5.

2 The vocabulary of Bradshaw is nervous and terse, but limited.

The Valley of Fear (1914). Understandably so, as Bradshaw's *Railway Guide* (1839–1961) was a timetable of train services, though it also included advertisements for hotels.

3 Matilda Briggs was not the name of a young woman ... It was a ship which is associated with the giant rat of Sumatra, a story for which the world is not yet prepared.

'The Sussex Vampire', *The Case Book of Sherlock Holmes* (1927). A tantalizing allusion to one of Holmes's successful cases – but the world never was able to be ready because Conan Doyle never wrote it. There is, however, a giant rat of Sumatra – *Rhizomys sumatrensis* – which can grow to a length of nineteen inches without the tail and weigh twenty pounds.

DRABBLE, Margaret

English novelist (1939–)

4 Sometimes it seems the only accomplishment my education ever bestowed on me, the ability to think in quotations.

A Summer Bird-Cage (1963). Comment on the business of quotation.

DRAKE, Sir Francis

English sailor and explorer (c.1540–96)

5 There must be a beginning of any great matter, but the continuing unto the end until it be thoroughly finished yields the true glory.

Dispatch to Sir Francis Walsingham before the Battle of Cadiz (1587). Hence, the title of a documentary film *The True Glory* (UK/US 1945) about the end of the Second World War. In a speech on 15 August 1945 about the surrender of Japan, Winston Churchill said: 'This is the true glory, and long will it gleam upon our forward path.' It was also a favourite phrase of Margaret Thatcher. She paraphrased it in a speech (21 May 1980) and alluded to the rest of Drake's dispatch in an address to the 1922 Committee of backbench MPs (19 July 1984): 'After reminding them of their success in the recent Euro-elections, and pointing out that few people during last year's general election could have foreseen a 19-week pit strike, she declared that it was not the beginning of the struggle that mattered. It was the continuation of the fight until it was truly concluded' (report in *The Guardian*, 20 July).

6 The singeing of the King of Spain's beard.

Drake's own phrase for his impish attack on the Spanish fleet and stores at Cadiz in 1587, which delayed the sailing of the Armada until the following year. Reported in Francis Bacon, *Considerations touching a War with Spain* (1629): 'I remember Drake, in the vaunting style of a soldier, would call the enterprise the singeing of the King of Spain's beard.'

7 There is plenty of time to win this game, and to thrash the Spaniards too.

An example of world-class insouciance. Possibly apocryphal, but this is what everyone would like to believe was said by Drake as he played bowls on Plymouth Hoe when the Armada was sighted (20 July 1588). So attributed in the *Dictionary of National Biography* (1917). His game of bowls was first mentioned in a prefix to the 1736 edition of Sir Walter Raleigh's *History of the World*. The saying, sometimes rendered as 'There is time to finish the game and beat the Spaniards afterwards', is 'the work of a later embroiderer', according to another source.

DRAPER, Ruth

American monologuist and entertainer (1884–1956)

8 Of course he [Dante] was a genius, wasn't he – like Shakespeare? ... He and Dante seem to have known *everything* ... known what would always be true ... Wonderful, I imagine that we're going to find that this is *full* of quotations.

Sketch, 'The Italian Lesson' (1930s?) Comment on the art of quotation.

DRAYTON, Michael

English poet (1563–1631)

1 Fair stood the wind for France
When we our sails advance,
Nor now to prove our chance
Longer will tarry ...

'Agincourt', *To the Cambro-Britons* (1619). Hence, *Fair Stood the Wind for France*, title of a story (1944) by H.E. Bates. Before Drayton, in Christopher Marlowe's *Edward II* (1593) there had been: 'Fair blows the wind for France'.

DRURY, Allen

American novelist (1918– 98)

2 Advise and Consent.

Title of novel (1959; film US, 1962) about Washington politics. Taken from Senate Rule 38: 'The final question on every nomination shall be, "Will the Senate advise and consent to this nomination?"' In the US Constitution (Art. 2, Sect. 2), dealing with the Senate's powers as a check on the President's appointive and treaty-making powers, the phrase is rather '*Advice* and consent'. Originally, George Washington as President went in person to the Senate Chamber (22 August 1789) to receive 'advice and consent' about treaty provisions with the Creek Indians. Vice-President Adams used the words, 'Do you advise and consent?' Subsequent administrations have sent written requests.

DRYDEN, John

English poet and playwright (1631–1700)

3 He was the man who, of all modern, and perhaps ancient poets, had the largest and most comprehensive soul ... He was naturally learn'd; he needed not the spectacles of books to read Nature: he looked inwards, and found her there ... He is many times flat, insipid; his comic wit degenerating into clenches, his serious swelling into bombast. But he is always great.

On Shakespeare, in *Essays of Dramatic Poesy* (1668).

4 A man so various that he seemed to be
Not one, but all mankind's epitome.
Stiff in opinions, always in the wrong;
Was everything by starts, and nothing long:
But, in the course of one revolving moon,
Was chemist, fiddler, statesman and buffoon.

Absalom and Achitophel (1681). In July 1978, the British Prime Minister, James Callaghan, as Rogue Quotationist, used this passage to attack Margaret Thatcher and the Conservative front bench in the House of Commons. Mrs Thatcher was at one time a chemist, but that is about the only link. Besides, Dryden was writing about a *man* in a work that dealt with the Exclusion Crisis with various public figures given biblical names. 'Zimri', described here, was George Villiers, 2nd Duke of Buckingham (1628–87). He was a politician, Cabal member and close friend of Charles II. It has been urged that it is his personal qualities rather than his political ones that are described in these lines.

5 Fairest Isle, all isles excelling,
Seat of pleasures, and of loves;
Venus here will chose her dwelling,
And forsake her Cyprian groves.

King Arthur, Act 5 (1691). Hence, *Fairest Isle*, a year-long celebration of British music and culture on BBC Radio 3 (1995).

6 Arms, and the man I sing, who, forced by fate,
And haughty Juno's unrelenting hate,
Expelled and exiled, left the Trojan shore.

Translation of Virgil's *Aeneid* (1697) – opening lines. Hence, *Arms and the Man*, title of a play (1894) by George Bernard Shaw. Between times, Thomas Carlyle, had suggested in *Past and Present* (1843) that a true modern epic was technological rather than military, and had written: 'For we are to bethink us that the Epic verily is not *Arms and the Man*, but *Tools and the Man*.' *See also* VIRGIL 551:6.

7 None but the brave deserves the fair.

Alexander's Feast (1697). Hence, *None But the Brave*, title of a film (US, 1965) about the Second World War. Earlier Sir Edwin Landseer's painting 'None But the Brave Deserve the Fair' (1838) had shown two stags fighting while anxious hinds look on.

8 'Tis sufficient to say, according to the proverb, here is God's plenty.

On Chaucer, in the Preface to *Fables Ancient and Modern* (1700).

9 Like pilgrims to th'appointed place we tend;
The world's an inn, and death the journey's
end.

Palamon and Arcite (1700). *See* SHERRIFF 503:4.

DUBČEK, Alexander

Czechoslovak politician (1921–92)

1 Give socialism back its human face.

Slogan used frequently in 1968 – sometimes 'Socialism [*or* Communism] with a human face' – when a brief flowering of independence in Czechoslovakia gave rise to the 'Prague Spring'. The phrase was first suggested to Dubček, Communist Party First Secretary, by Radovan Richta in a private conversation (according to Robert Stewart, *Penguin Dictionary of Political Quotations*, 1984). A party group in the Ministry of Foreign Affairs referred to Czech foreign policy acquiring 'its own defined face' (*Rudé právo*, 14 March 1968). The slogan was later applied to domestic affairs.

The experiment was quashed when the Soviet Union invaded the country in August 1968. Dubček was later removed from power.

DU BELLAY, Joachim

French poet (1522–60)

2 *Heureux qui comme Ulysse a fait un beau voyage.*
Happy he who, like Ulysses, has made a
great journey.

Les Regrets, Sonnet 31 (1558). Used as an inscription on the headstone of the grave of Sir Henry Channon (1897–1958), the American-born socialite and Conservative MP, who achieved posthumous fame through the publication of his diaries. He is buried at Kelvedon in Essex. Robert Rhodes James, editor of *Chips: The Diaries of Sir Henry Channon* (1967), refers to 'the words [from a sonnet] of Du Bellay which had been his special favourite'. The translation continues: 'Or like that man [Jason] who won the Fleece and then came home, full of experience and good sense, to live the rest of his time among his family.'

Much depends on the translation. Another: 'Happy the man who's journeyed much, like Ulysses./Or like the traveller who won the Golden Fleece,/And has returned at last, experienced and wise,/To end his days among his family in peace.' George Seferis (1900–71), 'On a Line of Foreign Verse', develops the idea: 'Fortunate he who's made the voyage of Odysseus./ Fortunate if on setting out he's felt the rigging/Of a love strong in his body, spreading there like/veins, where the blood throbs .../... To see once more the smoke/Ascending from his warm hearth and the dog grown/Old waiting by the door.'

DULLES, John Foster

American lawyer and Republican Secretary of State (1888–1959)

3 If ... the European Defence Community should not become effective; if France and Germany remain apart ... That would compel an agonizing reappraisal of basic United States policy.

Speech to the NATO Council, Paris (14 December 1953). Hence, 'agonizing reappraisal' became a political term for the process of reconsideration, possibly before a decision is made to make a U-turn, a reassessment of position that has probably been forced on the reappraiser.

4 The ability to get to the verge without getting into the war is the necessary art. If you cannot master it, you inevitably get into war. If you try to run away from it, if you are scared to go to the brink, you are lost.

Quoted in *Life* Magazine (16 January 1956). This was the origin of the term 'brinkmanship' popularized by Adlai Stevenson during the 1956 US Presidential campaign.

5 Yes, once ... many, many years ago. I thought I had made a wrong decision. Of course, it turned out that I had been right all along. But I was wrong to have *thought* I was wrong.

When asked if he had ever been wrong. Quoted in Henri Temuanka, *Facing the Music* (1973).

DUMAS, Alexandre (Dumas Père)

French novelist (1802–70)

6 *Tous pour un, un pour tous.*
All for one and one for all.

Motto of the Three Musketeers made famous in the novel *Les Trois Mousquetaires* (1844–5). Earlier, Shakespeare in his poem, *The Rape of Lucrece*, l. 141–4 (1594) had written:

> The aim of all is but to nurse the life
> With honour, wealth and ease, in waning age;
> And in this aim there is much thwarting strife
> That *one for all, or all for one* we gage [=pledge].

More prosaically, 'Each for all and all for each' has been used in Britain as a slogan of the Co-operative Wholesale Society.

DU MAURIER, Daphne (later Dame Daphne)

English novelist (1907–89)

1 Last night I dreamt I went to Manderley again.

Rebecca (1938). Opening words, spoken by the unnamed narrator who is the second wife of Mr de Winter. The story tells of the mystery surrounding her predecessor and is set in Manderley, a house that eventually meets its end, which is why she can only dream of going back to it.

DUNBAR, William

Scottish poet and priest (c.1460–c.1520)

2 *Timor mortis conturbat me.*
Fear of death disturbs me.

'Lament for the Makaris' [= makers = poets]. The poem is an elegy for life's transitoriness, as well as mourning the loss of Dunbar's fellow poets, including Chaucer and Gower.

3 London, thou art the flower of cities all!

In Praise of London. The authorship has been disputed and the poem is no longer thought to be by Dunbar.

DUNCAN, Isadora

American dancer and choreographer (1878–1927)

4 *Adieu, mes amis. Je vais à la gloire.*
Goodbye, my friends, I go on to glory.

Last words. Quoted in M. Desti, *Isadora Duncan's End* (1929). She was about to test-drive a Bugatti and was strangled when the scarf she was wearing caught in the spokes of a wheel.

DUNNING, John (Lord Ashburton)

English lawyer and politician (1731–83)

5 The influence of the Crown has increased, is increasing, and ought to be diminished.

Resolution passed by the House of Commons (6 April 1780), in protest at what was seen as the increasingly autocratic rule of King George III. As such, it marked the beginning of the House of Common's more positive role as a democratic legislature.

DURANT, Will

American writer (1885–1981)

6 There is nothing in Socialism that a little age or a little money will not cure.

Unverified. *Compare* CLEMENCEAU 174:2.

DUROCHER, Leo

American baseball manager (1906–91)

7 Nice guys finish last.

In his autobiography with the title *Nice Guys Finish Last* (1975), Durocher recalled that what he had said to reporters concerning the New York Giants in July 1946, was: 'All nice guys. They'll finish last. Nice guys. Finish last.' However, Frank Graham of the New York *Journal-American* had written down something slightly different: 'Why, they're the nicest guys in the world! And where are they? In seventh place!' Hence, the title of Ralph Keyes's book on misquotations *Nice Guys Finish Seventh* (1992).

DURY, Ian

British singer and songwriter (1942–)

8 Sex & Drugs & Rock & Roll.

Title of song (1977), written with Chaz Jankel. Also printed as 'sex'n'drugs'n'rock'n'roll'.

DYLAN, Bob

American singer and songwriter (1941–)

9 Keep a clean nose
Watch the plain clothes
You don't need a weather man
To know which way the wind blows.

Song, 'Subterranean Homesick Blues' (1965). Hence, 'Weathermen', original name of a violent radical group in the US (*fl.* 1969) which then became known as the Weather Underground.

10 I ain't gonna work on Maggie's Farm no more.

Song, 'Maggie's Farm' (1965). This was revived in the UK during the 1980s when Margaret Thatcher was Prime Minister.

1 All Along the Watchtower.

A 1968 Dylan song begins: 'All along the watchtower, princes kept the view.' This is probably after Isaiah 21:5, prophesying the fall of Babylon: 'Prepare the table, watch in the watchtower, eat, drink: arise ye princes, and anoint the shield.' (*The Watchtower*, magazine of Jehovah's Witnesses, presumably takes its name from the same source.)

2 If I had a good quote, I'd be wearing it.

When asked for 'a good quote' by a French journalist on a cold night. Quoted in *The Times* (July 1981).

DYSON, Will

Australian-born cartoonist (1883–1938)

3 Curious! I seem to hear a child weeping!

This caption to a cartoon in the *Daily Herald* appeared at the conclusion of the Versailles Peace Conference in 1919. The picture showed the 'Big Four' – President Wilson, Clemenceau, Orlando of Italy and Lloyd George – leaving the conference hall and hearing a child – signifying the next generation – bewailing the breakdown of their peace efforts. The headline is 'Peace and Future Cannon Fodder'; the caption has 'The Tiger' (Clemenceau) speaking; and the child is prophetically labelled '1940 Class'. If the biographical details of Dyson are correct as above, then he did not live to see his prophetic observation come true.

E

EASTWOOD, Clint

American film actor (1930–)

1 Go ahead, make my day!

This popular laconicism was originally spoken by Eastwood as a cop, himself brandishing a .44 Magnum, to a gunman he is holding at bay in *Sudden Impact* (1983). At the end of the film he says (to another villain, similarly armed), 'Come on, make my day'. In neither case does he add 'punk', as is sometimes supposed. (From *The Independent*, 14 July 1993: 'When Clint Eastwood said "Go ahead, punk, make my day" ...') – this may come from confusion with *Dirty Harry* (1971) in which Eastwood holds a .44 Magnum to the temple of a criminal and says 'Well, do ya [feel lucky], punk?'

In March 1985 President Ronald Reagan told the American Business Conference: 'I have my veto pen drawn and ready for any tax increase that Congress might even think of sending up. And I have only one thing to say to the tax increasers. Go ahead – make my day.' The phrase may have been eased into Reagan's speech by having appeared in a parody of the New York *Post* put together by editors, many of them anti-Reagan, in the autumn of 1984. Reagan was shown starting a nuclear war by throwing down this dare to the Kremlin (source: *Time* Magazine, 25 March 1985).

EBB, Fred

American songwriter (1932–)

2 Life is a cabaret, old chum.

Song, 'Cabaret' from the musical *Cabaret* (1966; film US, 1972), with music by John Kander.

3 Money makes the world go around.

Song, 'Money, Money' in *ib.* The modern proverbial phrase derives, apparently, from this musical. As with 'Tomorrow Belongs To Me' (below), we may have to thank the writers of *Cabaret* for either creating an instant 'saying' or, in this instance, for introducing to the English language something that has long been known in others. 'Money makes the world go around' is clearly built on the well-established proverb ''Tis love, that makes the world go round' (*see* CARROLL 147:5), but it is not recorded in either the *ODP* or the *CODP*. The nearest these get is, 'Money makes the mare to go'.

'Money makes the world go around' appears in the English language key to the 'Flemish Proverbs' picture by David Teniers the Younger (1610–90), at Belvoir Castle. The painting shows an obviously wealthy man holding a globe. The key may, however, be modern.

4 The babe in his cradle is closing his eyes, the blossom embraces the bee,
But soon says a whisper, 'Arise, arise',
Tomorrow belongs to me.
O Fatherland, Fatherland, show us the sign your children have waited to see,
The morning will come when the world is mine, Tomorrow belongs to me.

Song, 'Tomorrow Belongs to Me' in *ib.* Has this ever been used as an actual political slogan, either as 'Tomorrow belongs to me' or 'to us'? Harold Wilson in his final broadcast before the 1964 General Election said, 'If the past belongs to the Tories, the future belongs to us – all of us'. At a Young Conservative rally before the 1983 General Election, Margaret Thatcher asked: 'Could Labour have organized a rally like this? In the old days perhaps, but not now. For they are the Party of Yesterday. Tomorrow is ours.'

What one *can* say is that, in *Cabaret*, Ebb wrote a convincing pastiche of a Hitler Youth song, so much so that the song was denounced as a real Nazi anthem. Ebb told *The Independent* (30 November 1993): 'The accusations against "Tomorrow Belongs to Me" made me very angry ... "I knew that song as a child," one man had the audacity to tell me. A rabbinical person wrote me saying he had absolute proof it was a Nazi song.'

The *idea*, rather, seems likely to have been current in Nazi Germany. A popular song, '*Jawohl, mein Herr*', featured in the 1943 episode of the German film chronicle *Heimat* (1984), included the line, 'For from today, the world belongs to us'.

The nearest the slogan appears to have been actually used by any (admittedly right-wing) youth organization is referred to in this report from *The Guardian* (30 October 1987): 'Contra leader Adolfo Calero ... was entertained to dinner on Wednesday by Oxford University's Freedom Society, a clutch of hoorays ... [who] got "hog-whimpering" drunk ... and songs like "Tomorrow Belongs To Us" and "Miner, Cross that Picket Line" were sung on the return coach trip.'

The same paper, reporting a meeting addressed by the SDP leader, Dr David Owen (1 February 1988) noted: 'Down, sit down, he eventually gestured; his eyes saying Up, stay up. It reminded you of nothing so much as a Conservative Party conference in one of its most Tomorrow-belongs-to-us moods.' In each of these last two examples, it is the song from the musical that is being evoked, of course, rather than any Nazi original.

ECO, Umberto

Italian novelist (1932–)

1 *Il Nome della Rosa*.
The Name of the Rose.

Title of novel (1981). But what does it mean? Eco's own *Reflections on The Name of the Rose* (1985) explains how the title derives from the Latin hexameter with which the book ends: '*Stat rosa pristina nomine, nomina nuda tenemus*.' This comes from a satirical poem *De contemptu mundi* by the twelfth-century monk, Bernard of Cluny. Broadly speaking, the title has to do with the passing of things. The dying rose is merely another symbol of this – and only its name remains. Incidentally, Eco states in *Reflections*: 'A title must muddle the reader's ideas, not regiment them.'

EDDINGTON, Sir Arthur

British astrophysicist (1882–1944)

2 If as we follow the arrow we find more and more of the random element in the world, then the arrow is pointing towards the future; if the random element decreases the arrow points towards the past ... I shall use the phrase 'time's arrow' to express this one-way property of time which has no analogue in space.

The Nature of the Physical World (1928). Hence, *Time's Arrow: or the Nature of the Offence*, title of a novel (1991) by Martin Amis.

EDEN, Sir Anthony (later 1st Earl of Avon)

British Conservative Prime Minister (1897–1977)

3 A property-owning democracy.

See SKELTON 506:1.

4 We are not at war with Egypt. We are in an armed conflict; that is the phrase I have used. There has been no declaration of war.

Speaking in the House of Commons (1 November 1956) about Britain's response to the Egyptian takeover of the Suez Canal, Eden seemed curiously punctilious about his words, urging that it was not an act of war. Possibly he was obsessed by the thought of becoming a war-monger when, as he said in a TV and radio broadcast two days later: 'All my life I have been a man of peace, working for peace, striving for peace, and negotiating for peace. I have been a League of Nations man and a United Nations man. And I am still the same man, with the same convictions, and the same devotion to peace. I could not be other even if I wished, but I am utterly convinced that the action we have taken is right.'

EDISON, Thomas Alva

American inventor (1847–1931)

5 Genius is one per cent inspiration and ninety-nine per cent perspiration.

Quoted in *Life/Harper's Monthly Magazine* (September 1932), having originally been said by him *c.*1903. Earlier, the French naturalist, the Comte de Buffon (1707–88), was quoted in 1803 as having said, 'Genius is only a greater aptitude for patience.' *Compare* CARLYLE 146:6.

6 The phonograph is not of any commercial value.

Comment to his assistant, Samuel Insull. He had hopes that his invention would find a use in business rather than for entertainment. Quoted in Robert A. Conot, *A Streak of Luck* (1979) and Christopher Cerf, *The Experts Speak* (1984). Foresight of the commercial sort was not, apparently, one of Edison's characteristics: 'I have determined that there is no market for talking pictures' – remark (1926), quoted in Flexner (1982).

EDMONDS, J.M.

English poet and academic (1875–1958)

1 Went the day well? we died and never knew;
But well or ill, England we died for you.

'On Some who died early in the Day of Battle' in 'Four Epitaphs', published in *The Times* (6 February 1918). Later popularized in the form:

Went the day well?
We died and never knew.
But, well or ill,
Freedom, we died for you.

This appears as the anonymous epigraph on screen at the start of the 1942 British film *Went the Day Well?* (retitled *48 Hours* in the US). At the time the film was released, some thought it was a version of a Greek epitaph. Based on a story by Graham Greene entitled *The Lieutenant Died Last*, the film tells of a typical English village managing to repel Nazi invaders. The epigraph thus presumably refers to the villagers who die defending 'Bramley End'. In her 1992 British Film Institute monograph on the film Penelope Houston describes it as a quotation from an anonymous poem that appeared in an anthology of tributes to people killed in the war to which Michael Balcon, head of Ealing Studios, contributed a memoir of the dead director Pen Tennyson. But Edmonds was the poet. It is said that it was based on a suggestion given him by Sir Arthur Quiller-Couch who in turn got it from a Romanian folksong (*Notes and Queries*, Vol. 100).

2 When you go home, tell them of us and say,
'For your tomorrow these gave their today.'

'For a British graveyard in France', another suggested epitaph by Edmonds, which appeared in *The Times Literary Supplement* (4 July 1918). By the Second World War, however, it was frequently stated that 'the words are a translation from the Greek'. Famously, this version appeared on the 2nd British Division's memorial at Kohima War Cemetery, Assam (now Nagaland), in India (and on many other war graves round the world):

When you go home
Tell them of us and say
For your tomorrow
We gave our today.

Many people still appear to think that it is an allusion to the Greek poet Simonides (*q.v.*). The second line of Edmonds's original should not read 'for your tomorrows', as in *ODMQ* (1991) and *ODQ* (1992).

The BBC received a somewhat crusty letter from Edmonds (by this time a Fellow of Jesus College, Cambridge), dated 23 July 1953, in which he said, 'I thought the Greek origin of my epitaph used – and altered – at Kohima had been denied in print often enough; but here it is again. It is no translation, nor is it true to say it was suggested by one of the beautiful couplets which you will find in *Lyrica Graeca* (Loeb Classical Library), though I *was* at work on that book in 1917 when my Twelve War Epitaphs were first printed in *The Times* and its *Literary Supplement* ... The epitaph, of course, should be used only abroad. Used in England its "home" may be just round the corner – which makes the whole thing laughable.'

EDWARD III

English King (1312–77)

3 *Honi Soit Qui Mal Y Pense.*
Evil be to him who evil thinks.

The motto of the Order of the Garter, founded by Edward (*c.*1348), is traditionally said to derive from something uttered by him as he adjusted the Countess of Salisbury's garter when it fell down. The tale was current by the reign of Henry VIII and was included in Polydore Vergil's *Anglicae Historiae* (1534–55).

Accordingly, the version given by Sellar and Yeatman (*q.v.*) in their comic history *1066 and All That* (1930) is not so wide of the mark: 'Edward III had very good manners. One day at a royal dance he noticed some men-about-court mocking a lady whose garter had come off, whereupon to put her at her ease he stopped the dance and made the memorable epitaph: "*Honi soie qui mal y pense*" ("Honey, your silk stocking's hanging down").' Byron is also said to have re-translated the motto as, 'On his walk he madly puns.'

EDWARD VII

British King (1841–1910)

4 We are all socialists nowadays.

Edward is said to have said this, when Prince of Wales, in a speech at the Mansion House, London, on 5 November 1895 – though no record exists of him making any such speech on that day. His biographer, Sir Philip Magnus, makes no mention of him doing so either. The *ODQ* dropped the entry after pointing out in the Corrigenda to the 1941 edition that the saying should more correctly be ascribed to Sir William Harcourt (1827–1904). Harcourt is quoted as saying it in *Fabian Essays* (1889, edited by Bernard Shaw; i.e., six years before the supposed 1895 speech). Harcourt was Lord Rosebery's (Liberal) Chancellor of the Exchequer and an impassioned enemy of the House of

Lords. He introduced estate duty tax in his Budget of 1894. Oscar Wilde told an interviewer in the spring of 1894: 'We are all of us more or less Socialists nowadays' – Almy, 'New Views of Mr O.W.' in *Theatre* (1894). *Compare* THORPE 539:5.

1 Your apparatus is extremely impressive.

Remark to Hubert Booth, the inventor of the first domestic vacuum cleaner. Quoted in Channel 4 TV, *The Secret Life of the Vacuum Cleaner* (1989). The first electric one was so big it was put on a horse-drawn carriage and an 800-foot hose was run into the place being cleaned.

EDWARD VIII (later Duke of Windsor)

British King (1894–1972)

2 The young business and professional men of this country must get together round the table, adopt methods that have proved sound in the past, adapt them to the changing needs of the times and, whenever possible, improve them.

In a speech, as Prince of Wales, at the British Industries Fair in Birmingham (1927). Hence, the name 'Round Table' – although it may have some echoes of Arthurian knights working together – and the motto of the National Association of Round Tables of Great Britain and Ireland (in the form 'Adopt, adapt, improve'). The Round Table movement is a social and charitable organization for young professional and business men under the age of forty (after which age Rotary takes over).

3 Something must be done.

In November 1936 the King went to South Wales to tour the depressed areas and moved the public with his expressions of concern. At the Bessemer steel works at Dowlais, where 9,000 men had been made unemployed, hundreds sang an old Welsh hymn. Afterwards the King was heard to say to an official: 'These works brought all these people here. Something must be done to find them work' [or 'get them at work again']. Occasionally quoted as 'something ought to be done' and followed the next day by the promise, 'You may be sure that all I can do for you, I will', the King's words were taken as an indication of his concern for ordinary people and of his impatience with established authority.

Although his distress at what he saw in South Wales was no doubt genuine, the King's assurances might look less hollow if we did not now know that by then he had already informed his family and the Prime Minister of his decision to abdicate.

4 I have found it impossible to carry the heavy burden of responsibility and to discharge my duties as King as *I* would wish to do without the help and support of the woman I love.

Edward abdicated on 11 December 1936. That evening, before he left the country, 'His Royal Highness Prince Edward', as he was introduced, took the opportunity of broadcasting a message to his former subjects. Nothing in Edward's short reign became him like the leaving of it. He later commented (in *A King's Story*, 1951): 'It has become part of the Abdication legend that the broadcast was actually written by Mr Churchill. The truth is that, as he had often done before with other speeches, he generously applied the final brush strokes.' Such phrases as 'bred in the constitutional tradition by my father' and 'one matchless blessing ... a happy home with his wife and children' are the two most obvious of those strokes. They were applied to a basic text drawn up by Edward's lawyer, Walter Monckton. The BBC's chief, Sir John Reith, who introduced the broadcast from Windsor Castle, noted that he had 'never [seen] so many alterations in a script'.

The moving speech could be heard by all his subjects over the wireless, a unique event. However relieved people may subsequently have been that Edward's reign was not prolonged, for the moment they were touched, if not reduced to tears, by the courageous tones in which the broadcast was delivered and by the protestations of love and duty it included.

5 England ... the waste ... the waste.

These, if truly the Duke of Windsor's dying words, might seem to be appropriate, insofar as their meaning can be guessed at. Their provenance is, however, not recorded. A biographer of the Duchess of Windsor suggests rather that what the ex-King said on his deathbed in Paris was 'Darling' and 'Mama, mama, mama, mama'. On the other hand, Bryan & Murphy's *The Windsor Story* (1979) states that there were *no* last words.

See also GEORGE V 256:5.

EHRLICHMAN, John D.

American presidential aide (1925–)

6 It'll play in Peoria.

About 1968, during the Nixon election campaign, Ehrlichman is credited with devising this yardstick for judging whether policies would appeal to voters in 'Middle America'. He later told Safire (1978): 'Onomatopoeia was the only reason for Peoria, I suppose. And it ... exemplified a place, far removed from the media centres on the coasts where the national verdict is cast.' Peoria is in Illinois.

1 I think we ought to let him hang there. Let him twist slowly, slowly in the wind.

Richard Nixon's henchmen may have acted wrongly and, for much of the time, spoken sleazily. Occasionally, however, they minted political phrases that have lingered on. Ehrlichman, Nixon's Assistant for Domestic Affairs until he was forced to resign over Watergate in 1973, came up with one saying that caught people's imagination. In a telephone conversation with John Dean (Counsel to the President) on 7–8 March 1973 he was speaking about Patrick Gray (Acting Director of the FBI). Gray's nomination to take over the FBI post had been withdrawn by Nixon during Judiciary Committee hearings, although Gray had not been told of this. Ehrlichman suggested he be left in ignorance – and in suspense.

From *The Guardian* (28 January 1989): 'The foreign press observed with admiration the way President Bush stressed in words that he was not ditching the beleaguered Mikhail Gorbachev by playing his China card, while making it clear he was doing exactly that, and leaving the Soviet leader to twist a little longer in the wind.'

EHRMANN, Max

American writer (d.1945)

2 Go placidly amid the noise and haste, and remember what peace there may be in silence. As far as possible without surrender be on good terms with all persons. Speak your truth quietly and clearly; and listen to others, even the dull and ignorant; they too have their story. Avoid loud and aggressive persons, they are vexations to the spirit.

There can have been few bedroom walls during the great poster-hanging craze of the late 1960s which did not bear a copy of a text called 'Desiderata' ('things desired'), reputedly found in Old St Paul's Church, Baltimore, and dating from 1692. Les Crane spoke the words on a hit record in 1972. However, 'Desiderata' had nothing to do with Old St Paul's. That was a fanciful idea incorporated in the first US edition of the poster. Nor did 1692 come into it. The words were written by Max Ehrmann in *1927* and copyright was renewed in 1954 by Bertha K. Ehrmann. In 1983, the poster was still on sale as 'from 1692' but carrying the correct copyright lines.

EINSTEIN, Albert

German-born physicist (1879–1955)

3 $E = mc^2$.

Energy = mass x the speed of light squared. Statement, contained in a 72-page handwritten paper in which Einstein developed the Special Theory of Relativity in 1912. It was written for the *Handbuch der Radiologie*. No one knew that the manuscript existed until 1987 when it was sold for $1.2 million. Einstein conceived the idea of relativity in 1905, but the famous equation did not emerge until 1907–8.

4 When a man sits with a pretty girl for an hour, it seems like a minute. But let him sit on a hot stove for a minute – and it's longer than any hour. That's relativity.

Quoted in Barbara Rowes, *The Book of Quotes* (1979). On another occasion he said: 'It should be possible to explain the laws of physics to a barmaid.'

5 God does not play dice with the universe.

What he actually wrote (in German) to Max Born (on 4 December 1926) was simply: 'At any rate, I am convinced that *He* does not play dice.' This was his way of objecting to quantum mechanics, in which physical events can be known only in terms of probabilities. What he was saying was, there is no uncertainty in the material world. Compare: 'I cannot believe that God plays dice with the cosmos', so ascribed in *The Observer* (5 April 1954).

EISENHOWER, Dwight D.

American general and Republican 34th President (1890–1969)

6 I like Ike.

These words began appearing on buttons in 1947 as Eisenhower began to be spoken of as a possible presidential nominee (initially as a Democrat). By 1950, Irving Berlin was including one of his least memorable songs, 'They Like Ike', in *Call Me Madam*, and 15,000 people at a rally in Madison Square Gardens were urging Eisenhower to return from a military posting in Paris and run as a Republican in 1952, with the chant 'We like Ike'. It worked. The three sharp monosyllables and the effectiveness of the repeated 'i' sound made it an enduring slogan throughout the 1950s.

7 I shall go to Korea and try to end the war.

During the presidential election campaign, Eisenhower

made this promise in a speech on 24 October 1952. Between his election and inauguration, he did make a three-day visit to Korea but it had no discernible effect on the negotiations towards a truce.

1 You have broader considerations that might follow what you might call the 'falling domino' principle. You have a row of dominoes set up. You knock over the first one and what will happen to the last one is that it will go over very quickly.

The old metaphor of falling over 'like a stack of dominoes' was first used in the context of Communist takeovers by the American political commentator, Joseph Alsop. Then President Eisenhower said the above at a press conference (7 April 1954). In South-East Asia, the theory was proved true to an extent in the 1970s. When South Vietnam collapsed, Cambodia then fell to the Khmer Rouge and Laos was taken over by the Communist-led Pathet Lao. In 1989, when one eastern European country after another *renounced* Communism, there was talk of a 'reverse domino theory'.

2 In the councils of government, we must guard against the acquisition of unwarranted influence, whether sought or unsought, by the military-industrial complex. The potential for the disastrous rise of misplaced power exists and will persist.

Eisenhower's presidency was characterized by dull speech-making and convoluted extempore remarks. The only phrase for which he is remembered, if at all, occurred in his farewell address on 17 January 1961. The political scientist Malcolm Moos helped formulate the passage. Harry Truman, never able to say anything good about his successor, commented: 'Yes, I believe he did say something like that. I think somebody must have written it for him, and I'm not sure he understood what he was saying. But it's true.'

ELGAR, Sir Edward

English composer (1857–1934)

3 To my friends pictured within.

Dedication, 'The Enigma Variations' (1899). Each variation bears a dedication by name, nickname or initials to a friend or relative of the composer. Each of these has now been identified. For example, No. 9, 'Nimrod' portrays A.J. Jaeger of Novello's, the music publishers, and an old friend of Elgar's. *See also* KAZANTZAKIS 327:2.

4 My idea is that there is music in the air, music all around us, the world is full of it and you simply take as much as you require.

Quoted in R.J. Buckley, *Sir Edward Elgar* (1904). The phrase 'music in the air', of which this may be the first appearance, was taken as the title of (probably) more than one BBC radio series after the 1920s when music was rather 'on the air'. *Music in the Air* was also the title of a film (US, 1934) about an opera singer, based on a play by Oscar Hammerstein II and Jerome Kern.

5 Please play this tune as though you've never heard it before.

Remark to the London Symphony Orchestra, which was about to play his 'Land of Hope and Glory', *c.*1930. Audible on the album 'Elgar on Record' (HMV 7061).

6 The Starlight Express.

Title of incidental music composed for a play (1915) by Violet Pearn, based on Algernon Blackwood's *Prisoner in Fairyland*. In 1984, Andrew Lloyd Webber composed a musical called simply *Starlight Express*.

ELIOT, George (Mary Ann Evans)

English novelist (1819–80)

7 The first condition of human goodness is something to love; the second something to reverence.

'Amos Barton', in *Scenes of Clerical Life*, Chap. 10 (1858). When the novelist was commemorated in Poets' Corner, Westminster Abbey, this quotation was placed on her memorial. 'It is a quotation of which we are particularly fond,' said the Secretary of the George Eliot Fellowship, which was responsible for the worldwide appeal for funds to place the memorial stone in 1980, 'and it describes, we feel, George Eliot's own philosophy.'

8 Any coward can fight a battle when he's sure of winning; but give me the man who has pluck to fight when he's sure of losing. That's my way, sir; and there are many victories worse than defeat.

'Janet's Repentance' in *ib.*, Chap. 25. Sometimes remembered as: 'Give me the man, Sir, who fights when he is sure of losing. He's my kind of man, Sir, and there's many a victory worse than a defeat.'

9 The happiest women, like the happiest nations, have no history.

The Mill on the Floss, Bk 6, Chap. 3 (1860). Eliot adapted a proverbial expression to her own ends. In the form, 'Happy the people whose annals are blank in history-books!', the saying was ascribed to Montesquieu by Thomas Carlyle in his *History of Frederick the Great* (1858–65). In *The French Revolution – A History* (1838), Carlyle had written: 'A paradoxical philosopher, carrying to the uttermost length that aphorism of Montesquieu's, "Happy the people whose annals are tiresome," has said, "Happy the people whose annals are vacant".'

Theodore Roosevelt said in a speech (10 April 1899): 'It is a base untruth to say that happy is the nation that has no history. Thrice happy is the nation that has a glorious history. Far better it is to dare mighty things, to win glorious triumphs, even though checkered by failure, than to take rank with those spirits who neither enjoy much nor suffer much because they live in the grey twilight that knows neither victory nor defeat.' The earliest form of the proverb found by *CODP* is in Benjamin Franklin, *Poor Richard's Almanack* (1740): 'Happy that Nation, – fortunate that age, whose history is not diverting.'

1 Oh may I join the choir invisible
Of those immortal dead who live again
In minds made better by their presence.

Poem, 'Oh May I Join the Choir Invisible' (1867). The second two lines appear on Eliot's grave in Highgate Cemetery, London. A setting of the poem was sung by the graveside at her funeral.

2 The growing good of the world is partly dependent on unhistoric acts; and that things are not so ill with you and me as they might have been, is half owing to the number who lived faithfully a hidden life, and rest in unvisited tombs.

Middlemarch (1871), closing words; a commendation of quiet lives.

See also BIBLE 92:11.

ELIOT, T.S.

American-born English poet, playwright and critic (1888–1965)

3 No! I am not Prince Hamlet, nor was meant to be;
Am an attendant lord, one that will do
To swell a progress, start a scene or two.

'The Love Song of J. Alfred Prufrock', *Prufrock* (1917). Hence, *Not Prince Hamlet*, title of an autobiography (1989) by the critic and translator of plays, Michael Meyer.

4 I grow old ... I grow old ...
I shall wear the bottoms of my trousers rolled.

Shall I part my hair behind? Do I dare to eat a peach?
I shall wear white flannel trousers, and walk upon the beach.
I have heard the mermaids singing, each to each.

I do not think that they will sing to me.

Ib. Hence, the two film titles: *I've Heard the Mermaids Singing*, a Canadian film (1987) about a gauche girl who develops a crush on her (female) boss, and – even more allusively – *Eat the Peach* (Ireland, 1986). *To Eat a Peach* was the title of a novel by Calder Willingham (US, 1960s). *See also* DAVIES 196:5.

5 Webster was much possessed by death
And saw the skull beneath the skin;
And breastless creatures under ground
Leaned backwards with a lipless grin.

'Whispers of Immortality' (1920). Hence, *The Skull Beneath the Skin*, title of a crime novel (1982) by P.D. James.

6 April is the cruellest month, breeding
Lilacs out of the dead land, mixing
Memory and desire, stirring
Dull roots with spring rain.

The Waste Land (1922), opening words. Frequently misquoted, often with 'August' being substituted, possibly out of confusion with *August is a Wicked Month*, title of a novel (1965) by Edna O'Brien. Or, rather, the observation is much abused allusively: 'After the highs and lows of Christmas and the winter holidays, February always seems to me the cruellest month' (*The Daily Telegraph*, 15 February 1992); 'Sometimes March can be the cruellest month' (*Northern Echo*, 18 February 1992); 'August used to be the cruellest month' (*The Times*, 25 August 1992); 'June is the cruellest month in politics' (*The Times*, 5 June 1993); 'August has always been the cruellest month' (*The Times*, 25 August 1993).

7 And I will show you something different from either
Your shadow at morning striding behind you
Or your shadow at evening rising to meet you;
I will show you fear in a handful of dust.

Ib., Pt 1. As acknowledged, *A Handful of Dust*, the novel (1934) by Evelyn Waugh, takes it title from this. Compare, 'The heat of life in the handful of dust' in Joseph Conrad's novel *Youth* (1902). Earlier, a 'handful of earth' was a symbol of mortality.

1 O O O O that Shakespeherian Rag.
It's so elegant
So intelligent.

Ib., Pt 2. In *The Waste Land*, Eliot provides notes to explain the numerous allusions. However, he neglects to mention that l. 128–30 are taken from a popular song 'That Shakespearian Rag' published in 1912 by the Edward Marks Music Corp. (in the US) and written by Gene Buck, Herman Ruby and David Stamper. The chorus goes: 'That Shakespearian Rag, most intelligent, very elegant.' This was pointed out by Ian Whitcomb in *After the Ball* (1972).

2 When lovely woman stoops to folly and
Paces about her room again, alone,
She smooths her hair with automatic hand,
And puts a record on the gramophone.

Ib., Pt 3. From the *Observer* Magazine (28 November 1993): 'For some reason, T.S. Eliot's line "When lovely woman stoops to folly" comes to mind.' Yes, but as he acknowledged in the extensive notes to *The Waste Land*, it is a reference to the song in Goldsmith's *The Vicar of Wakefield* (1766):

> When lovely woman stoops to folly
> And finds too late that men betray,
> What charm can soothe her melancholy,
> What art can wash her guilt away?

Kate Hardcastle in Goldsmith's play *She Stoops to Conquer* (1773) also 'stoops' but not to folly, as the Epilogue points out:

> Well, having stooped to conquer with success,
> And gained a husband without aid from dress,
> Still as a Barmaid, I could wish it too,
> As I have conquered him to conquer you.

Mary Demetriadis once reworked the couplet for a *New Statesman* competition:

> When lovely woman stoops to folly
> The evening can be awfully jolly.

3 [The critic] must compose his differences with as many of his fellows as possible in the common pursuit of true judgement.

Essay, 'The Function of Criticism' (1923). Hence, *The Common Pursuit*, title of a book of essays by the critic F.R. Leavis (1952). In turn, it became the title of a play (1984) by Simon Gray about a group of Cambridge undergraduates and graduates who produce a literary magazine called *The Common Pursuit*.

4 We are the hollow men
We are the stuffed men
Leaning together ...
Between the idea
And the reality
Between the motion
And the act
Falls the shadow.

The Hollow Men (1925). Hence, *Falls the Shadow*, title of a novel (1996) by Gemma O'Connor.

5 This is the way the world ends
Not with a bang but a whimper.

Ib., last words. The phrase 'not with a bang but a whimper' is now widely used to express anticlimax and is frequently alluded to: from Richard Aldington, *The Colonel's Daughter* (1931): 'I wish you'd all shoot yourselves with a bang, instead of continuing to whimper.' From *The Times* (16 December 1959): 'Here the world ends neither with a bang nor a whimper, but with a slow, resigned sigh at its own criminal imbecility.'

Not With a Bang was the title of an ITV series (1990), and *The Observer* (8 July 1990) reported: 'After some 70 hours Ernest Saunders finally left the Southwark witness box on Thursday afternoon not with a bang or whimper but more with a chorus of the familiar refrains which had echoed ... '

The joke variation, 'This is the way to World's End/Not with a Banger but a Wimpy' is ascribed to his father-in-law, Professor Robert Gorham Davis of Columbia University, New York, by Michael Flanders in the introduction to a verse anthology *London Between the Lines* (1973).

'I should be glad,' Eliot remarked, a little ruefully, in 1964, 'to hear no more of a bang and a whimper.'

6 'A cold coming we had of it,
Just the worst time of the year
For a journey, and such a long journey:
The ways deep and the weather sharp,
The very dead of winter.'

'The Journey of the Magi' (1927) – opening words. As the quotation marks show, this is a conscious quotation of ANDREWES 19:3, though, in fact, a paraphrase.

7 Time present and time past
Are both perhaps present in time future,
And time future contained in time past.

'Burnt Norton' (1935), *Four Quartets*. Hence, one might suppose, *Time Present*, title of a play (1968) by John Osborne, except that the text is prefaced with 'a time to embrace and a time to refrain from embracing ...' from Ecclesiastes.

1 Sudden in a shaft of sunlight
Even while the dust moves
There rises the hidden laughter
Of children in the foliage.

Ib. Hence, *Hidden Laughter*, title of a play (1990) by Simon Gray.

2 Macavity, Macavity, there's no one like Macavity,
There never was a Cat of such deceitfulness and sauvity.
He always has an alibi, and one or two to spare:
At whatever time the deed took place – MACAVITY WASN'T THERE!
And they say that all the Cats whose wicked deeds are widely known
(I might mention Mungojerrie, I might mention Griddlebone)
Are nothing more than agents for the Cat who all the time
Just controls their operations: the Napoleon of Crime!

'Macavity: the Mystery Cat', *Old Possum's Book of Practical Cats* (1939). *Compare* DOYLE 213:9.

3 In my beginning is my end ...
In my end is my beginning.

'East Coker' (1940), *Four Quartets*. As to the second of these phrases, compare '*En ma fin git mon commencement*', a motto reputedly embroidered with an emblem of her mother by Mary, Queen of Scots (1542–87).

ELIZABETH I

English Queen (1533–1603)

4 The heart and stomach of a king.

What Elizabeth is supposed to have said in a speech to her army of 20,000 gathered at Tilbury during the approach of the Spanish Armada in 1588 is: 'My loving people, we have been persuaded by some that are careful for our safety to take heed how we commit ourselves to armed multitudes, for fear of treachery. But I assure you I do not desire to live to distrust my faithful and loving people. Let tyrants fear. I have always so behaved myself that, under God, I have placed my chiefest strength and safeguard in the loyal hearts and goodwill of my subjects; and therefore I am come amongst you, as you see, resolved, in the midst and heat of the battle, to live or die amongst you all, to lay down for my God, and for my kingdom, and for my people, my honour and my blood, even in the dust.

'I know I have the body of a weak and feeble woman, but I have the heart and stomach of a king, and of a king of England too; and think foul scorn that Parma or Spain, or any prince of Europe, should dare to invade the borders of my realm; to which, rather than any dishonour shall grow by me, I myself will take up arms, I myself will be your general, judge, and rewarder of every one of your virtues in the field. I know already for your forwardness you have deserved rewards and crowns; and we do assure you, in the word of a prince, they shall be duly paid you.'

In *History Today* (May 1988) Felix Barker contended that the Queen might never have used these words because of the absence of any contemporary accounts of her doing so. The sole source is an undated letter to the Duke of Buckingham (not published until 1691) from Leonel Sharp, a chaplain who was at Tilbury but who had a reputation for being 'obsequious and ingratiating' (according to the *DNB*). The only contemporary account of the speech is by a poet called James Aske, but it contains none of the above phrases. Why did no one else quote the good bits at the time, Felix Barker wondered, if they had in fact been used? For reasons of delicacy presumably, when Flora Robson came to give the speech in the film *Fire Over England* (1937), she found herself saying, 'But I have the heart and valour of a king' rather than the traditional 'heart and stomach'.

5 I would not open windows into men's souls.

Elizabeth is often cited as saying this, when in fact the phrase is most likely Francis Bacon's rationalization of her religious intolerance. In drafting a letter for her, he was attempting to say that the Queen, while not liking to do so, was forced into it by the people she had to deal with (source: letter from Professor William Lamont, University of Sussex, in *The Observer*, 13 November 1988). Sir Christopher Hatton (1540–91), Elizabeth's Lord Chancellor, is said to have commented, similarly: 'The queen did fish for men's souls, and had so sweet a bait that no one could escape her network.'

6 God may pardon you, but I never can.

Remark to the dying Countess of Nottingham, quoted in David Hume, *The History of England* ... (1759).

1 My lord, we have forgot the fart.

John Aubrey (1626–97) in his *Brief Lives* records that, 'the Earl of Oxford, Edward de Vere, making of his low obeisance to Queen Elizabeth, happened to let a fart, at which he was so abashed and ashamed that he went to travel, seven years.' On his return, the Queen welcomed him home with this remark. According to Sophia Hardy Wilson, writing to the *Independent* Magazine (3 July 1993), 'there is a similar story in the *Arabian Nights*, but in this case the traveller returns and meets a child and asks him how old he is, to which the child replies: "I was born in the year of the Great Fart".'

2 The word 'must' is not to be used to princes. Little man, little man! if your father had lived, he durst not have said so much.

To Robert Cecil on her death-bed (1603). Quoted in F. Chamberlin, *The Sayings of Queen Elizabeth* (1923).

3 All my possessions for a moment of time.

Last words (probably apocryphal). Quoted in Barnaby Conrad, *Famous Last Words* (1961).

ELIZABETH II

British Queen (1926–)

4 I should like to be a horse.

When a girl. Quoted in Frank S. Pepper, *Handbook of 20th Century Quotations* (1984).

5 Come on, Margaret!

To her sister, at end of radio talk to children evacuated to North America (13 October 1940).

6 I declare before you all that my whole life, whether it be long or short, shall be devoted to your service, and the service of our great imperial family to which we all belong.

On her 21st birthday. Radio broadcast from South Africa (21 April 1947).

7 My husband and I.

George VI had quite naturally spoken the words 'The Queen and I', but something in his daughter's drawling delivery turned her version into a joke. It first appeared during her second Christmas broadcast (made from New Zealand) in 1953 – 'My husband and I left London a month ago' – and still survived in 1962 – 'My husband and I are greatly looking forward to visiting New Zealand and Australia in the New Year.' By 1967 the phrase had become 'Prince Philip and I'. At a Silver Wedding banquet (20 November 1972), the Queen allowed herself a little joke: 'I think on this occasion I may be forgiven for saying "My husband and I".' Compare the title of the Rodgers and Hammerstein musical *The King and I* (1951).

8 I have to be seen to be believed.

Explaining the necessity for her to appear in public. Unverified.

9 She's more royal than we are.

On Princess Michael of Kent. Quoted in *Sunday* Magazine (14 April 1985). Compare the saying from the time of Louis XVI: *Il ne faut pas être plus royaliste que le roi* (You mustn't be more royalist than the king).

10 1992 is not a year I shall look back on with undiluted pleasure. In the words of one of my more sympathetic correspondents, it has turned out to be an *Annus Horribilis*.

Speaking at a lunch in the City of London on 24 November 1992 to mark her fortieth year on the British throne, the Queen reflected her current mood: she had a cold, part of Windsor Castle had been burned down four days previously, and the marriages of three of her children had collapsed or were collapsing. She states that she had the phrase from a correspondent, but it seems more likely that it was inserted by her private secretary and speechwriter, Sir Robert Fellowes. The more usual phrase is, of course, modern (as opposed to classical) Latin's *annus mirabilis* [wonderful year].

ELIZABETH THE QUEEN MOTHER

British Queen (1900–)

11 I'm glad we've been bombed. It makes me feel I can look the East End in the face.

Remark to policeman (13 September 1940) after the bombing of Buckingham Palace. Quoted in Betty Spencer Shew, *Queen Elizabeth, the Queen Mother* (1955). Cecil Beaton wrote in his diary that month: 'It is the genius of the Queen that has caused the palace to be bombed so that the East Enders should not feel they are alone in their misery' – quoted in Hugo Vickers, *Cecil Beaton* (1986).

12 The children will not leave unless I do. I shall not leave unless their father does, and the King will not leave the country in any circumstances whatever.

On whether her children would leave England after the bombing of Buckingham Palace. Quoted in D. Sinclair, *Queen and Country* (1980).

1 My favourite programme is 'Mrs Dale's Diary'. I try never to miss it because it is the only way of knowing what goes on in a middle-class family.

Untraced report from the London *Evening News*, quoted in Michael Bateman, *This England: selections from the* New Statesman *column 1934–1968* (1969).

2 The salmon are striking back.

When a fishbone lodged in her throat. Attributed in November 1982.

3 He is the only man since my dear husband died, to have the effrontery to kiss me on the lips.

On President Carter. Attributed in February 1983.

4 Do you think it's wise, darling? You know you've got to rule this afternoon.

To her daughter, when the Queen accepted a second glass of wine at lunch. Quoted in Compton Miller, *Who's Really Who* (1983).

ELLINGTON, Duke

American bandleader, pianist and composer (1899–1974)

5 There'll be some changes made.

In the early 1990s, Alistair Cooke asserted in three different *Letter from America* broadcasts on BBC Radio, that: '"There'll be some changes made", *as Duke Ellington used to say*.' In fact, Ellington never recorded the song with that title (written by Overstreet and Higgins in 1929). Most likely, Cooke was confusing it with the Mercer Ellington/Ted Person's 1939 composition 'Things Ain't What They Used To Be'.

ÉLUARD, Paul

French poet (1895–1952)

6 *Bonjour tristesse.*
Good-day sadness.

'À peine défigurée' (1932). Hence, *Bonjour Tristesse*, title of novel (1954; film UK, 1957) by Françoise Sagan.

EMERSON, Ralph Waldo

American poet and essayist (1803–82)

7 By the rude bridge that arched the flood,
Their flag to April's breeze unfurled,
Here once the embattled farmers stood,
And fired the shot heard round the world.

'Concord Hymn' (1837), written for the opening of the battle monument at Concord, Mass., site of the first armed resistance to the British in the American War of Independence.

8 There is properly no history; only biography.

'History' in *Essays* (1841). *Compare* DISRAELI 209:2.

9 All mankind love a lover.

'Love', in *ib*. Hence, the more modern rendering, 'All the world loves a lover'. In 1958 there was a popular song by Richard Adler and Robert Allen, 'Everybody Loves a Lover'. Compare the proverb, 'Everybody loves a Lord', which *CODP* finds by 1869.

10 If you maintain a dead church, contribute to a dead Bible-society, vote with a great party either for the government or against it ... under all these screens, I have difficulty to detect the precise man you are ... But do your [...] thing, and I shall know you.

Ib. The 1960s expression 'do your own thing' meaning 'establish your own identity'/'follow your star', is said to have been anticipated by Emerson in this way (e.g., in *Time* Magazine, 10 May 1982).

11 I hate quotations.

The *ODQ* (1979) had Emerson writing this in his journal for May 1849. Even toilers in the quotation vineyard feel like echoing this thought from time to time when they hear yet another person about to launch into some over-familiar line with, 'As the poet has it ...' or 'As George Bernard Shaw once said ...'

Oddly enough, and ironically, what the *ODQ* had (the entry was dropped from the 1992 edition) is a *misquotation*. What Emerson actually wrote was: '*Immortality*. I notice that as soon as writers broach this question they begin to quote. I hate quotation. Tell me what you know.' (*Journals and Miscellaneous Notebooks*, Vol. 6). So it is 'quotation' not 'quotations'. There is a difference.

12 Glittering generalities! They are blazing ubiquities.

An attributed remark, referring to Rufus Choate's criticism of the Declaration of Independence (in Choate's letter to the Maine Whig Central Committee, 9 August 1856) as being full of 'glittering generalities'.

1 The louder he talked of his honour, the faster we counted our spoons.

'Worship', *The Conduct of Life* (1860). Dr Samuel Johnson had anticipated this remark.

2 Hitch your wagon to a star.

'Civilization', *Society and Solitude* (1870). When a person is the vehicle of ideas (of the highest – justice, love, freedom, knowledge), he borrows their omnipotence.

3 Next to the originator of a good sentence is the first quoter of it.

'Quotation and Originality', *Letters and Social Aims* (1876). On the subject of this book. From the same source: 'By necessity, by proclivity – and by delight, we all quote.'

4 If a man write a better book, preach a better sermon, or make a better mousetrap than his neighbour, tho' he build his house in the woods, the world will make a beaten path to his door.

Sarah Yule claimed (in 1889) that she had heard Emerson say this in a lecture. Elbert Hubbard also claimed authorship. Either way, this is a remark alluded to whenever people talk of 'beating a path to someone's door' or a 'better mousetrap'. In his journal for February 1855, Emerson had certainly entertained the notion: 'If a man ... can make better chairs or knives ... than anybody else, you will find a broad hard-beaten road to his house, though it be in the woods.'

5 All my hurts
My garden spade can heal. A woodland walk,
A quest of river grapes, a mocking thrush,
A wild rose, a rock-loving columbine,
Salve my worst wounds.

On gardening. Quoted in Celia Haddon, *The Yearbook of Comfort and Joy* (1991).

EMMET, Robert

Irish politician (1778–1803)

6 Let no man write my epitaph; for as no man who knows my motives dare now vindicate them, let not prejudice or ignorance asperse them. Let them rest in obscurity and peace! Let my memory be left in oblivion, my tomb remain uninscribed, until other times and other men can do justice to my character. When my country takes her place among the nations of the earth, *then*, and *not till then*, let my epitaph be written.

Speech from the dock at his trial for leading a muddled insurrection against the British in July 1803. Tried and found guilty on 19 September. he was executed the next day. After this, his headless body was taken from Kilmainham gaol, Dublin, to one of the burial grounds at the Royal Hospital nearby, but the exact place of its burial is not known. Another theory is that Emmet lies in an unmarked grave in St Michan's churchyard or that of St Paul's. Hence, either way, there is still no epitaph over it.

EMPSON, William (later Sir William)

English poet and critic (1906–84)

7 Seven Types of Ambiguity.

Title of book (1930) of literary criticism. Empson defines the term 'ambiguity' broadly as referring to 'any verbal nuance, however slight, which gives room for alternative reactions to the same piece of language.' Accordingly, he discusses the use in literature of metaphors, puns, contradictory statements and so forth.

ENGLEBRECHT, H.C.

American author (1895–1939)

8 Merchants of Death.

This was the title of a book (1934), written jointly with F.C. Hanighen, about munitions makers who stood to profit from war. Later, the term was applied to dealers in drugs, tobacco and guns.

ERWIN, Dudley

Australian politician (1917–)

9 It is shapely, it wiggles, and it's name is Ainslie Gotto.

When asked the reason for his dismissal as Australian Air Minister in 1969, Erwin accused Ms Gotto, the secretary of Prime Minister John Gorton, of exerting undue influence. He said she ruled Gorton with 'ruthless authority'. Twelve years later, Ms Gotto – no longer involved in Australian politics – commented: 'That was another life ... I never wiggled, I was never aware of wielding power, and the rest was nonsense – the folklore of reporting' (*Daily Mail*, 18 June 1981).

EVANS, Edith (Dame Edith)

English actress (1888–1976)

1 Death is my neighbour now.

According to *PD20* (1995), this was a remark in a 'BBC radio interview, a week before her death [which was on] 14 October 1976'. Not the case, apparently. Evans's last broadcast was on 15 August 1976 – a choice of her favourite prose and poetry in the series *With Great Pleasure.* Far from making this remark herself, 'the last words she ever spoke in public' (according to Bryan Forbes, *Ned's Girl*, 1977) were from a poem 'Two Ways' 'by her great friend, Richard Church' (1893–1972):

Some are afraid of Death.
They run from him, and cry
Aloud, shrinking with fear
When he draws near.
Others take their last breath
As though it were a sigh
Of sheer content, or bliss
Beneath a lover's kiss.
Perhaps it is not much,
After life's labour,
That summoning touch
Of Death, our neighbour.

Compare *Death Is Now My Neighbour*, title of an Inspector Morse novel (1996) by Colin Dexter.

EVANS, Harold

English journalist and editor (1928–)

2 The camera cannot lie. But it can be an accessory to untruth.

Pictures on a Page (1978). In fact, 'the camera never lies/cannot lie' is a modern proverb and its origins are unrecorded. In the script for the commentary of a film ('Six Commissioned Texts', No. 1, 1962), W.H. Auden wrote: 'The camera's eye/Does not lie,/But it cannot show/The life within.'

EVARTS, William Maxwell

American lawyer and politician (1818–1901)

3 It was a brilliant affair; the water flowed like champagne.

On a dinner given by President Rutherford B. Hayes, who occupied the White House 1877–81 and was also a temperance advocate. Quoted in George F. Hoar, *Autobiography of Seventy Years* (1906).

EVELYN, John

English diarist (1620–1706)

4 He was universally beloved, hospitable, generous, learned in many things, skilled in music, a very great cherisher of learned men of whom he had the conversation.

Of Samuel Pepys on the day of his death, *Diary* (26 May 1703). *Compare* PEPYS 427:7.

EVERSLEY See SHAW-LEFEVRE

EWER, W.N.

English journalist (1885–1976)

5 How odd
Of God
To choose
The Jews.

A frequently misattributed rhyme – perhaps because it was composed in an informal setting and not published originally in written form – is the one by the foreign correspondent, W.N. Ewer. It was published subsequently in *The Week-End Book* (1924). In a letter to *The Observer* (13 March 1983), Alan Wykes, Honorary Secretary of the Savage Club in London, described the rhyme's origins: 'In the Savage Club, one of the guests was trying to make his mark with the Jewish pianist Benno Moiseiwitsch, who was not a man to be trifled with. "Is there," asked this Hooray Henry, "Any anti-Semitism in the club?" To this Benno snarled back: "Only amongst the Jews." Trilby Ewer, on the fringe of this conversation, thereupon coined the quatrain, which has since passed into history.'

There has been more than one corollary or rejoinder. This, published in 1924, was by Cecil Browne:

But not so odd
As those who choose
A Jewish God
Yet spurn the Jews.

Another, quoted in the early 1960s, went:

Who said he did?
Moses. But he's a yid.

F

FADIMAN, Clifton

American writer (1904–)

1 The mama of dada.

Of Gertrude Stein. *Party of One* (1955).

See also POWELL 437:6.

FAIRLIE, Henry

English journalist (1924–90)

2 I have several times suggested that what I call the 'Establishment' in this country is today more powerful than ever before. By the 'Establishment' I do not mean only the centres of official power – though they are certainly part of it – but rather the whole matrix of official and social relations within which power is exercised ... the 'Establishment' can be seen at work in the activities of, not only the Prime Minister, the Archbishop of Canterbury and the Earl Marshal, but of such lesser mortals as the Chairman of the Arts Council, the Director-General of the BBC, and even the editor of the *Times Literary Supplement*, not to mention dignitaries like Lady Violet Bonham Carter.

As a nickname for a conservative, partly hereditary, secretive, self-perpetuating ruling class, the term 'Establishment' was brought to prominence by Fairlie in a series of articles for *The Spectator* in 1955. On 23 September, he wrote the above. Hugh Thomas, editing a book on the phenomenon and called *The Establishment* (1959), stated: 'The word was, however, in use among the thoughtful at least a year previously; I recall myself employing it while passing the Royal Academy in a taxi in company with Mr Paul Johnson of the *New Statesman* in August 1954.' An earlier example of the phrase's use among the 'thoughtful' has, indeed, come to light in A.J.P. Taylor's *Essays in English History*. In one on William Cobbett (originally a review in the *New Statesman*, in 1953) he wrote: 'Trotsky tells how, when he first visited England, Lenin took him round London and, pointing out the sights, exclaimed: "That's *their* Westminster Abbey! That's *their* Houses of Parliament!" Lenin was making a class, not a national emphasis. By "them" he meant not the English, but the governing classes, the Establishment so clearly defined and so complacently secure.' *OED2* has other citations of the phrase in its modern sense going back to 1923, to which might be added one in George Eliot's *Daniel Deronda*, Bk 2, Chap. 12 (1876).

FARJEON, Herbert

English writer (1887–1945)

3 Glory, glory, hallelujah!
I'm the luckiest of females!
For I've danced with a man
Who's danced with a girl
Who's danced with the Prince of Wales!

Song, 'I've Danced With a Man Who's Danced With a Girl', *Picnic* (1927). Farjeon was a leading light in theatrical revue. Here he plays upon the extreme current popularity of the Prince of Wales who later became King Edward VIII and then the Duke of Windsor.

FARLEY, James

American Democratic politician (1888–1976)

4 As Maine goes, so goes Vermont.

In the 1936 US Presidential election, Farley was Franklin D. Roosevelt's campaign manager. On 4 November, Farley predicted that Roosevelt would carry all but two states – Maine and Vermont. The above is how he put it in a statement to the press, alluding to an earlier political maxim: 'As Maine goes, so goes the nation' (which Bartlett dates *c.*1888).

FAROUK I

Egyptian King (1920–65)

1 The whole world is in revolt. Soon there will be only five kings left – the King of England, the King of Spades, the King of Clubs, the King of Hearts and the King of Diamonds.

Remark to Lord Boyd-Orr (1948), quoted in *Life* Magazine (10 April 1950). Also recorded by Boyd-Orr in *As I Recall* (1966).

FARQUHAR, George

Irish playwright (1678–1707)

2 My Lady Bountiful.

The Beaux' Stratagem, Act 1, Sc. 1 (1707). Hence, the expression 'lady bountiful' (now only applied ironically) for a woman who is conspicuously generous to others less fortunate than herself (particularly within a small community or village.)

3 *Aimwell*: Then you understand Latin, Mr Boniface?
Boniface: Not I, sir, as the saying is, but he talks it so very fast that I am sure it must be good.

Ib., Act 3, Sc. 2. Boniface, the landlord, in Farquhar's play has a curious verbal mannerism. After almost every phrase, he adds, 'As the saying is ...' This was a well-established phrase even then. In 1548, Hugh Latimer in *The Sermon on the Ploughers* had: 'And I fear me this land is not yet ripe to be ploughed. For as the saying is: it lacketh weathering.' Nowadays, we are more inclined to use 'as the saying goes'.

FARRAGUT, David

American naval commander (1801–70)

4 Damn the torpedoes! Full speed ahead!

At the Battle of Mobile Bay (5 August 1864). During the American Civil War, Farragut fought on the Federal side and took part in the siege of Vicksburg. At Mobile Bay, he made a quick decision to chance passing through a minefield, suspecting that most of the torpedoes (= mines) were duds through long immersion. As a consequence, the Confederate boat *Tennessee* and two land forts were forced to capitulate. Farragut was appointed the US Navy's first vice-admiral in 1864 and its first Admiral in 1866.

FAULKNER, William

American novelist (1897–1962)

5 The nicest old lady I ever met.

On Henry James. Quoted in Edward Stone, *The Battle and the Books* (1964).

6 The long hot summer.

Coinage of this phrase follows the film title *The Long Hot Summer* (1958) and that of the spin-off TV series (1965–6). The film was based on 'The Hamlet', a story by Faulkner published in 1928 which contained the chapter heading 'The Long Summer' (*sic*). So it is not correct to say that Faulkner 'coined' the longer phrase. Bartlett (1980 and 1992) suggests that there was a film with the longer title in 1928. Some mistake surely?

The full phrase had appeared before all this – for example, in the opening chapter of Wilkie Collins, *The Woman in White* (1860): 'It was the last day of July. The long, hot summer was drawing to a close.' But the bright phrase rapidly turned into a journalist's cliché following the 1967 riots in the black ghettos of eighteen US cities, notably Detroit and Newark. In June of that year Martin Luther King warned: 'Everyone is worrying about the long hot summer with its threat of riots. We had a long cold winter when little was done about the conditions that create riots.'

FAWKES, Guy

English conspirator (1570–1606)

7 Desperate diseases require desperate remedies.

Commonly ascribed to Fawkes on 6 November 1605 (the day following his arrest for attempting to blow up the Houses of Parliament), 'A desperate disease requires a dangerous remedy' (*DNB* wording) was apparently said by him to James I, one of his intended victims. The King asked if he did not regret his proposed attack on the Royal Family. Fawkes replied that one of his objects was to blow the Royal Family back to Scotland. He was subsequently tried and put to death.

What he said, however, appears to have been a version of an established proverbial saying. In the form, 'Strong disease requireth a strong medicine', *ODP* traces it to 1539. In *Romeo and Juliet* (IV.i.68) (*c.*1595), Shakespeare has 'I do spy a kind of hope,/Which craves as desperate an execution/As that which we would prevent' – and alludes to the saying on two other occasions.

FEIRSTEIN, Bruce

American writer (1953–)

1 Real Men Don't Eat Quiche.

Title of book (1983) but used earlier as the title of an article in *Playboy* (1982).

FELDMAN, Marty

English comedian and writer (1933–83)

2 Am I speaking loud enough for you, judge? Sorry, am I waking you up?

To Judge Argyle during the *Oz* Magazine obscenity trial (summer 1971). Quoted in Tony Palmer, *The Trials of Oz* (1971).

FELLINI, Federico

Italian film director and writer (1920–93)

3 *La Dolce Vita.*
The Sweet Life.

The title of Federico Fellini's 1960 Italian film passed into the English language as a phrase suggesting high-society life of luxury, pleasure, and self-indulgence – a precursor of the Swinging Sixties. Meaning simply 'the sweet life', it is not clear how much of a set phrase it was in Italian before it was taken up by everybody else. Compare the long-established Italian phrase *dolce far niente* (sweet idleness).

FEYDEAU, Georges

French playwright (1862–1921)

4 In comedy there are only two main parts. He who slaps and he who gets slapped. It is never the one who slaps who gets the laughs.

On rejecting a request from Lucien Guitry to write a farce for him. Retold in *Ned Sherrin In His Anecdotage* (1994). One wonders what the connection is, if any, between this remark and *He Who Gets Slapped* – the English title of the play (1914) by the Russian dramatist Leonid Andreyev.

FIELD, Eric

English advertising practitioner (fl.1914)

5 Your King and Country need you.

Field Marshal Lord Kitchener was appointed Secretary of State for War on 6 August 1914, two days after the outbreak of the First World War. He set to work immediately, intent on raising the 'New Armies' required to supplement the small standing army of the day, which would not be adequate for a major conflict. In fact, advertising for recruits had started the year before, and the *month* before, Field of the Caxton Advertising Agency had received a call from a Colonel Strachey who 'swore me to secrecy, told me that war was imminent and that the moment it broke out we should have to start at once'. That night, Field wrote an advertisement with this slogan and only the royal coat of arms as illustration. The day after war was declared – 5 August – it appeared prominently in the *Daily Mail* and other papers.

The alliterative linking of 'king' and 'country' was traditional. Francis Bacon (1625) wrote: 'Be so true to thyself, as thou be not false to others; specially to thy King, and Country.' In 1913, J.M. Barrie included in his play *Quality Street*: 'If ... death or glory was the call, you would take the shilling, ma'am ... For King and Country.'

6 Your Country Needs You!

This version of Field's slogan, accompanied by the famous drawing of Kitchener with staring eyes and pointing finger, was taken up by the Parliamentary Recruiting Committee for poster use (issued 14 September 1914). The slogan and Alfred Leete's drawing were widely imitated abroad. In the US, James Montgomery Flagg's poster of a pointing Uncle Sam bore the legend 'I want *you* for US Army'. The British slogan also became a catchphrase used when telling a man he had been selected for a dangerous or disgusting task.

FIELD, Eugene

American critic (1850–95)

7 He played the King as though under momentary apprehension that someone else was about to play the ace.

Of Creston Clarke as King Lear. In a review attributed to him in the *Denver Tribune* (*c.*1880).

FIELDING, Henry

English novelist and judge (1707–54)

1 To fill up a work with these scraps may, indeed, be considered as a downright cheat on the learned world, who are by such means imposed upon to buy a second time in fragments and by retail, what they already have in gross, if not in their memories, upon their shelves.

Tom Jones, Bk 12, Chap. 1. On the quotation industry. Fielding, in one of his many addresses to the reader, is discussing why, when translating passages from the ancient classics, he does not give the original language or details of sources. The chapter heading is: 'Shewing what is to be deemed Plagiarism in a modern Author, and what is to be considered as lawful Prize.'

2 It hath been often said, that it is not death, but dying, which is terrible.

Amelia, Bk 3, Chap. 4 (1751). Clearly, from the 'it hath been often said', this is not something that is original to Fielding. It keeps on being said, too. The 1950s TV personality Gilbert Harding said to John Freeman in a *Face to Face* interview: 'I am not afraid of death. I am afraid of dying. I should be very glad to be dead, but I don't look forward to the actual process of dying.' In John Mortimer's *In Character* (1983), Cardinal Basil Hume quoted Monsignor Ronald Knox as having said, 'Everyone's afraid of dying but no one is afraid of being dead.' *See also* BACON 69:5; SMITH 509:5.

FIELD OF DREAMS

American film, 1989. Written and directed by Phil Alden Robinson. With Kevin Costner as Ray Kinsella.

3 If you build it, he will come.

Costner portrays an Iowa farmer who hears a voice (played by 'Himself', according to the credits) which tells him this repeatedly. So he creates a baseball pitch in his field so that 'Shoeless Joe' Jackson, the discredited Chicago White Sox player of 'Say it ain't so, Joe' fame (*see* ANONYMOUS 48:6), can come back from the dead and be rehabilitated. Subsequent messages received – and too complicated to explain here – are 'Ease his pain' and 'Go the distance'.

The Observer (5 June 1994) quoted James Cosgrove of AT&T as saying: 'In the movie *Field of Dreams* there is the phrase "If you build it, they will come".' Well no, there isn't.

A neater allusion to the original phrase occurs in the movie *Wayne's World 2* (1993), in which the ghost of rock star Jim Morrison inspires the teenagers to put on a rock concert called 'Waynestock'. When Morrison is asked whether big-name groups will actually show up, he intones, 'If you book them, they will come.'

FIELDS, Dorothy

American lyricist (1904–74)

4 I Can't Give You Anything But Love.

Title of song, written for *Delmar's Revels* (1927), but not performed until the following year. Music by Jimmy McHugh.

FIELDS, W.C.

American comedian (1879–1946)

5 On the whole I'd rather be in Philadelphia.

What the comedian actually submitted as a suggested epitaph to *Vanity Fair* Magazine in 1925 was: 'Here lies W.C. Fields. I would rather be living in Philadelphia.' This does not appear on his actual gravestone (which bears his name and dates only). The saying may have evolved from an older expression 'Sooner dead than in Philadelphia'.

One of the quips trotted out by President Reagan when he was lying in hospital, wounded by an assassin's bullet, in March 1981 was, 'All in all, I'd rather be in Philadelphia'. The following week, the London *Times* noted that historians of humour are unclear where Fields got the quip from: 'Some believe it was made originally by ... George Washington who became dissatisfied with New York after he was chosen President in 1789. As a result of this chance remark, which he may have made to Alexander Hamilton, the capital was moved to Philadelphia.

'A chronically restless man, Washington later made a joke that has survived less well: "Come to think of it, I'd rather be on the Potomac," he told Aaron Burr. It was then that the present-day capital was built and named after him.'

6 It ain't a fit night out for man or beast.

Film, *The Fatal Glass of Beer* (US, 1933). In a letter from Fields (8 February 1944) quoted in *W.C. Fields by Himself* (1974), he states that the catchphrase was first used by him in a sketch in Earl Carroll's *Vanities* and then as the title of a picture he made for Mack Sennett. He concluded: 'I do not claim to be the originator of this line as it was probably used long before I was born in some old melodrama.'

1 Never give a sucker an even break.

This saying has been attributed to various people but has largely become associated with Fields. He is believed to have ad-libbed it in the musical *Poppy* (1923) and certainly spoke it in the film version (1936). The words are not uttered, however, in the film called *Never Give a Sucker an Even Break* (1941). Bartlett (1992) attributes the saying to Edward Francis Albee (1857–1930).

2 Any man who hates children and dogs can't be all bad.

Or 'Anybody who hates dogs and babies can't be all bad'. Often ascribed to the comedian (for example, by *Radio Times*, 12 August 1965), it was, in fact, said *about* Fields by Leo Rosten (1908–97) at a Masquer's Club dinner (16 February 1939).

3 Not the way I play it.

When a gambler asks Fields as 'Cuthbert J. Twillie', 'Is this a game of chance?' Film, *My Little Chickadee* (US, 1939).

4 Elusive spondulicks.

A phrase used by Fields in the film *The Bank Dick* (1940). 'Spondulicks' or 'spondoolicks' or 'spondulacks' is an Americanism, current by the 1850s, for money, cash. Partridge/*Slang* convincingly suggests that the origin lies in the Greek word '*spondulikos*', from the noun '*spondulos*' – a species of shell used as money in prehistory and early history.

5 I was in love with a beautiful blonde once, dear. She drove me to drink. That's the one thing I'm indebted to her for.

Film, *Never Give a Sucker an Even Break* (US, 1941). Fields was a noted tippler, both on screen and off. Once, when asked why he did not drink water, he replied: 'Fish fuck in it', quoted in Leslie Halliwell, *The Filmgoer's Book of Quotes* (1973).

6 Boiled or fried?

When asked whether he liked children. Quoted on BBC Radio *Quote ... Unquote* (22 June 1977). Perhaps based on *Fields for President* (ed. Michael M. Taylor, 1971), in which the answer to the question whether he liked children is, 'I do if they're properly cooked'.

7 Horse sense is a good judgement which keeps horses from betting on people.

Quoted by Sam Ervin on record album *Senator Sam at Home* (1974).

8 Looking for loopholes.

To the actor Thomas Mitchell who came to visit Fields in a sanatorium during his last illness, was amazed to see him thumbing through the Bible, and asked, 'What are you doing?' Fields died on Christmas Day 1946 and his actual last words were: 'Goddamn the whole friggin' world and everyone in it but you, Carlotta' (a reference to his mistress). Quoted in the book, *Quote ... Unquote* (1978) – source unknown.

See also ANONYMOUS 39:2.

FILLMORE, Millard

American 13th President (1800–74)

9 Peace at any price.

'Peace at any price; peace and union' was the slogan of the American (Know-Nothing) Party in the 1856 US presidential election. The party supported ex-President Fillmore and the slogan meant that it was willing to accept slavery for blacks in order to avoid a civil war. Fillmore lost to James Buchanan.

It has been suggested that the phrase had been coined earlier (in 1820 or 1848) by Alphonse de Lamartine, the French foreign affairs minister in his *Méditations Poétiques* in the form '*La paix à tout prix*'. However, the Earl of Clarendon quoted an 'unreasonable calumny' concerning Lord Falkland in his *History of the Rebellion* (written in 1647): 'That he was so enamoured on peace, that he would have been glad the king should have bought it at any price.' When Neville Chamberlain signed his pact with Hitler in 1938, many praised him for trying to obtain 'peace at any price.'

FISHER, Lord (Jacky)

English admiral (1841–1920)

10 The British Navy always travels first class.

Quoted in Winston Churchill, *The Second World War,* Vol. 1 (1948). In fact, Churchill was reproducing a letter he had written to a later First Lord of the Admiralty in 1936, urging that the best possible warships should be prepared for any future engagements: 'It is terrible deliberately to build British battleships costing £7,000,000 apiece that are not the strongest in the world! As old Fisher used to say ...'

11 Fear God and Dread Nought.

His motto when elevated to the peerage (1909). Dreadnought was the name given to the class of British big-gun destroyer developed in the years prior to the

First World War. Fisher was sufficiently identified with the strategy that he could take this motto. Presumably it was the sailors on board who were to dread nought: the enemy was supposed to dread the battleship. The first destroyer of this class was so named in 1906 but there had been a tradition in the British navy of giving the name *Dreadnought* to battleships which went back to the reign of Queen Elizabeth I. A 'dreadnought' was also the name given to a stout outer garment worn in bad weather (known by 1806). *See also* WYNDHAM 585:3.

1 [Some day the Empire will go down because it is] Buggins's turn.

Letter (dated 8 January 1917), reprinted in *Memories* (1919). Fisher also used the expression in a letter in 1901, though he may not have originated it. The phrase gives the reason for a job appointment having been made – because it is somebody's turn to receive it rather than because the person is especially well qualified to do so. The name Buggins is used because it sounds suitably dull and humdrum. ('Joseph Buggins, Esq. J.P. for the borough' appears in one of G.W.E. Russell's *Collections and Recollections*, 1898. Trollope gave the name to a civil servant in *Framley Parsonage*, 1861. The similar sounding 'Muggins', self-applied to a foolish person, goes back to 1855, at least.)

2 You must be ruthless, relentless, and remorseless! *Sack the lot!*

On the ruinous cost of the Fleet and those responsible. Letter to *The Times* (2 September 1919).

3 Never contradict. Never explain. Never apologize.

Letter to *The Times* (5 September 1919). *Compare* DISRAELI 210:9.

4 Yours till charcoal sprouts.

Signing off correspondence. Quoted in Christopher Hassall, *Edward Marsh* (1959). His other salutations included, 'Yours till hell freezes' and 'Yours to a cinder.'

FITZGERALD, Edward

English poet (1809–93)

5 A book of verses underneath the bough,
A jug of Wine, a loaf of bread – and Thou
Beside me singing in the wilderness –
Oh, wilderness were paradise enow!

The Rubáiyát of Omar Khayyám, St. 12 (1879). Fitzgerald revised his poem so many times that it is difficult to settle for one version. The 1859 lines (St. 11) were: 'Here with a loaf bread beneath the bough,/A flask of wine, a book of verse – and Thou ...' Burnam (1980) makes the point that in Fitzgerald's somewhat free translation, the 'thou' could refer to either sex. In Victorian times, the assumption was female, but a literal translation would make it clear that the person being addressed was, in fact, a 'comely youth'.

In a sense, Fitzgerald mistranslated in both versions. The original Persian coupling was the traditional 'kebab' (meat on a skewer) and 'sherab' (wine), but Fitzgerald did not speak the language and relied on friends for help.

6 Ah, take the cash in hand and waive the rest;
Oh, the brave music of a *distant* drum!

Ib., St. 12 (1859). 'Nor heed the rumble of a distant drum!' is the 1879 version. A quotation scornfully applied by Aneurin Bevan to those who 'wanted to escape from awkward present conflicts altogether' and quoted by Michael Foot in his biography of Bevan.

7 I sometimes think that never blows so red
The rose as where some buried Caesar bled.

Ib., St. 20 (1859). Hence, *So Red the Rose*, title of a film (US, 1935).

8 The Moving Finger writes; and, having writ,
Moves on: nor all thy Piety nor Wit
Shall lure it back to cancel half a Line,
Nor all thy Tears wash out a Word of it.

Ib., St. 51 (1851). Hence, *The Moving Finger*, title of a 'Miss Marple' novel (1943) by Agatha Christie. Later the US title became *Murder In Our Midst*. Could this be because four other writers (including E. Phillips Oppenheim) had already used *The Moving Finger*?

9 Ah, moon of my delight that knows no wane
The moon of heaven is rising once again.
How oft hereafter rising shall one look
Through this same garden after us in vain.

Ib., St. 74 (1859). This version is one of the quotations displayed on plaques in the gardens of the Villa Cimbrone, Ravello, Italy.

10 Lost to a world in which I crave no part,
I sit alone and commune with my heart,
Pleased with my little corner of the earth,
Glad that I came – not sorry to depart.

From the translation of *Omar Khayyám* by Richard Le Gallienne (1866–1947) – i.e., not Fitzgerald's in which the lines do not appear. On a plaque in the garden of the Villa Cimbrone, Ravello, Italy. Compare Psalm 4:4: 'Commune with your own heart upon your bed, and be still'.

FITZGERALD, F. Scott

American novelist (1896–1940)

1 Tales of the Jazz Age.

Title of book (1922). Hence, the name given to the era of jazz – or when it first burst upon the world, as particularly described in Fitzgerald's works. From T. Griffith, *Waist-High Culture* (1960): 'In the years between the Armistice [1918] and the stock-market crash [1929], came the period we used to call ... the Jazz Age.'

2 Then wear the gold hat, if that will move her;
If you can bounce high, bounce for her too,
Till she cry 'Lover, gold-hatted, high-bouncing lover,
I must have you!'

As the epigraph to *The Great Gatsby* (1925), this is attributed to one 'Thomas Parke D'Invilliers'. He remains untraced, so one wonders whether perhaps it was Fitzgerald in disguise? He did, after all, write poetry himself, some of which has been published. As 'Thomas Parke D'Invilliers' appears as a poet character in Fitzgerald's *This Side of Paradise* (1920), this would appear definitely to be the case.

3 In a real dark night of the soul it is always three o'clock in the morning.

The Crack-Up (1936). *See* JOHN OF THE CROSS 315:1.

See also HEMINGWAY 290:2.

FITZPATRICK, James A.

American film-maker (1902–80)

4 And so we say farewell ...

The travelogues made by Fitzpatrick were a supporting feature of cinema programmes from 1925 onwards. With the advent of sound, the commentaries to 'Fitzpatrick Traveltalks' became noted for their closing words:

> And it's from this paradise of the Canadian Rockies that we reluctantly say farewell to Beautiful Banff ... And as the midnight sun lingers on the skyline of the city, we most reluctantly say farewell to Stockholm, Venice of the North ...
>
> With its picturesque impressions indelibly fixed in our memory, it is time to conclude our visit and reluctantly say farewell to Hong Kong, the hub of the Orient ...

Frank Muir and Denis Norden's notable parody of the genre – 'Bal-ham – Gateway to the South' – first written for radio *c.*1948 and later performed on record by Peter Sellers (1958) accordingly contained the words, 'And so we say farewell to the historic borough ...'

FITZSIMMONS, Bob

New Zealand-bred boxer in the US (1862–1917)

5 The bigger they are, the further they have to fall.

Referring to an opponent of larger build (James L. Jeffries), prior to a fight, in the *Brooklyn Daily Eagle* (11 August 1900). Also attributed to John L. Sullivan. Probably of earlier proverbial origin in any case and more usually, 'The bigger they come, the harder they fall.'

FLANDERS, Michael

English writer and entertainer (1922–75)

6 Eating people is wrong.

Song, 'The Reluctant Cannibal', *At the Drop of a Hat* (1957). Used as the title of a novel by Malcolm Bradbury (1959).

7 If God had intended us to fly, he'd never have given us the railways.

'By Air', *At the Drop of Another Hat* (1963). *See also* ANONYMOUS 35:4.

FLAUBERT, Gustave

French novelist (1821–80)

8 We shall find life tolerable once we have consented to be always ill at ease.

Quoted in *The Times* (23 June 1969) by Bryan Forbes, at that time newly appointed head of production at Elstree Studios: 'As an everyday working rule for anybody contemplating an existence in the British film industry, it is not without a certain valid cold comfort.' Forbes also notes that he had already used the quotation as an epigraph in his 'first pubished work', presumably *Truth Lies Sleeping* (1950). Otherwise untraced.

FLEMING, Ian

English novelist and journalist (1908–64)

1 [My name's] Bond – James Bond.'

Casino Royale (1953). Introduction, made well-known by more frequent use in the film versions of the Bond books. Fleming himself uses the full phrase in *Octopussy* (1966).

2 A martini, shaken not stirred.

This example of would-be sophistication became a running-joke in the immensely popular James Bond films of the 1960s and 1970s. However, the *idea* stems from the very first book in the series, *Casino Royale* (1953), in which Bond orders a cocktail of his own devising. It consists of one dry Martini 'in a deep champagne goblet', three measures of Gordon's gin, one of vodka – 'made with grain instead of potatoes' – and half a measure of Kina Lillet. 'Shake it very well until it's ice-cold.' Bond justifies this fussiness a page or two later: 'I take a ridiculous pleasure in what I eat and drink. It comes partly from being a bachelor, but mostly from a habit of taking a lot of trouble over details. It's very pernickety and old-maidish really, but when I'm working I generally have to eat all my meals alone and it makes them more interesting when one takes trouble.'

This characteristic was aped by the writers of the first Bond story to be filmed – *Dr No* (1962). A West Indian servant brings Bond a vodka and Martini and says: 'Martini like you said, sir, and not stirred.' Dr No also mentions the fad, though the words are not spoken by Bond himself. In the third film, *Goldfinger* (1964), Bond (played by Sean Connery) does get to say 'a Martini, shaken not stirred' – he needs a drink after just escaping a laser death-ray – and there are references to it in *You Only Live Twice* (1967) and *On Her Majesty's Secret Service* (1969), among others.

The phrase was taken up in all the numerous parodies of the Bond phenomenon on film, TV and radio, though – curiously enough – it may be a piece of absolute nonsense. According to one expert, shaking a dry Martini 'turns it from something crystal-clear into a dreary frosted drink. It should be stirred quickly with ice in a jug.'

The *ODMQ* (1991) claimed to have discovered the source for this remark actually in one of Fleming's novels – *Dr No* (1958) ('Bond said ... Martini – with a slice of lemon peel. Shaken and not stirred, please'), and this was taken up by Bartlett (1992). But it appears in the novels earlier than that: 'The waiter brought the Martinis, shaken and not stirred, as Bond had stipulated' (*Diamonds are Forever*, 1956).

3 You have a double-o number, I believe – 007, if I remember right. The significance of that double-o number, they tell me, is that you have had to kill a man in the course of some assignment.

Live and Let Die (1954). *See also below* 239:6.

4 Diamonds are Forever.

Title of book (1956), alluding to the advertising slogan 'A Diamond is Forever' for De Beers Consolidated Mines (since 1939).

5 From Russia with Love.

Title of novel (1957; film UK, 1963). As a format phrase, it has launched any number of allusions of the 'from —— with ——' variety. In *Keep Taking the Tabloids* (1983), Fritz Spiegl noted these headline uses: 'From the Rush Hour with Love', 'From Maggie without love!'. Compare *To Paris With Love* (film UK, 1954) and *To Sir With Love* (book by E.R. Braithwaite, 1959; film UK, 1967).

6 The licence to kill for the Secret Service, the double-o prefix, was a great honour.

Dr No (1958). Eventually there was a Bond film with the title *Licence to Kill* (UK, 1989). Compare this by William Godwin Jr (son of the philosopher-novelist) in *Blackwood's Edinburgh Magazine* (October 1833): 'My Lord of the thirty thousand acres expired on a couch of down ... each moment of his fluctuating existence watched by an obsequious practitioner, "licensed to kill", whose trade it is to assuage the pangs of death ...' The quotation marks make it look like an established joke at the expense of doctors.

7 You Only Live Twice.

Title of novel (1964). In an epigraph, Fleming puts: 'You only live twice:/Once when you are born/And once when you look death in the face' as 'after' Matsuo Bashō, the Japanese poet (1644–94).

8 My dear girl, don't flatter yourself. What I did this evening was for King and country. You don't think it gave me any pleasure, do you?

Not by Fleming. From the film script of *Thunderball* (1965), written by Richard Maibaum and John Hopkins.

9 Older women are best because they always think they may be doing it for the last time.

Quoted in John Pearson, *The Life of Ian Fleming* (1966).

Compare Benjamin Franklin's *Reasons for Preferring an Elderly Mistress* (1745): '8th and lastly. They are so grateful!'

See also KAEL 326:1; SHAKESPEARE 485:5.

FLETCHER, John

English playwright (1579–1625)

1 Whistle and she'll come to you.

Wit Without Money, Act 4, Sc. 4 (*c.*1614). *Compare* BURNS 133:1.

2 Nothing can cover his high fame but Heaven;
No pyramids set off his memories,
But the eternal substance of his greatness.

The False One (*c.*1620). This is the epitaph on the grave of Sir Thomas Beecham (1879–1961), the orchestral conductor. He was originally buried in Brookwood Cemetery, near Woking, but was re-interred at the parish cemetery of Limpsfield, Surrey, in April 1991. Beecham arranged music for several productions of Fletcher's plays and gave the Oxford Romanes Lecture on the playwright in 1956.

FO, Dario

Italian playwright (1926–)

3 Can't Pay Won't Pay.

The English title (1978) of the play *Non Si Paga! Non Si Paga!* (1974), as translated by Lino Pertile. In 1990 it was adopted as a slogan by those objecting to the British government's Community Charge or 'poll tax' and by other similar protest groups.

FOCH, Ferdinand

French soldier (1851–1929)

4 *Mon centre cède, ma droite recule, situation excellente. J'attaque!*
My centre gives way, my right retreats; situation excellent. I shall attack!

Remark to General Joffre, during the second Battle of the Marne (July/August 1918). In R. Recouly, *Foch*, 1919, the remark is given during the first Battle of the Marne, September 1914.

FOOT, Michael

British journalist and Labour politician (1913–)

5 Guilty Men.

Title of a tract 'which may rank as literature' (A.J.P. Taylor), written with Frank Owen and Peter Howard under the collective pseudonym 'Cato'. Published in July 1940, it taunted the appeasers who had brought about the situation where Britain had had to go to war with Germany. The preface contains this anecdote: 'On a spring day in 1793 a crowd of angry men burst their way through the doors of the assembly room where the French Convention was in session. A discomforted figure addressed them from the rostrum. "What do the people desire?" he asked. "The Convention has only their welfare at heart." The leader of the angry crowd replied, "The people haven't come here to be given a lot of phrases. They demand a dozen guilty men".'

The phrase 'We *name* the guilty men' subsequently became a cliché of popular 'investigative' journalism. The 'guilty men' taunt was one much used in the 1945 General Election by the Labour Party (and was referred to in a speech by Winston Churchill in the House of Commons, 7 May 1947).

6 I say this in the utmost affection ... he has passed from rising hope to elder statesman without any intervening period whatsoever.

Speech in the House of Commons (28 March 1979) – taken from a recording rather than *Hansard*. Foot, as Leader of the House, was ending the debate which resulted in the Labour government's defeat on a motion of no confidence (and led to its general election defeat the following month). The Liberals, led by the youngish David Steel, had until quite recently been part of the 'Lib-Lab' pact which had helped keep Labour in office. But then it collapsed.

Foot never relinquished his journalist's habit of using a good line whenever an opportunity presented itself. In 1952 he had written a profile of Peter Thorneycroft, the Conservative politician, who, he said, had, 'passed the stage of rising hope to elder statesman without any intervening period whatever.'

7 Is it always his desire to give his imitation of a semi-house-trained polecat?

This was Foot, when leader of Britain's Labour Party, talking about Norman Tebbit, the prickly Conservative Party Chairman. Foot said it at an eve-of-poll rally in Ebbw Vale in 1983. He noted that he had said it first in the House of Commons 'a few years ago' – indeed, on

2 March 1978. Foot lost the general election overwhelmingly. Tebbit continued to bite people in the leg for a few years more.

FOOT, Paul

English journalist (1937–)

1 If you don't know what's going on in Portugal, you must have been reading the papers.

Attributed in 1975. This was at the time when Portugal was undergoing political upheaval following a revolution against a dictatorship.

FORD, Gerald

American Republican 38th President (1913–)

2 I am a Ford, not a Lincoln. My addresses will never be as eloquent as Mr Lincoln's. But I will do my very best to equal his brevity and his plain speaking.

On becoming Vice-President. Speech, Washington (6 December 1973).

3 I believe that truth is the glue that holds government together, not only our government but civilization itself ... Our long national nightmare is over. Our Constitution works. Our great Republic is a government of laws and not of men. Here, the people rule.

On becoming President. Speech, Washington (9 August 1974).

4 There is no Soviet domination of Eastern Europe and there never will be under a Ford administration.

In a TV debate with Jimmy Carter, the Democratic challenger for the presidency (6 October 1976), Ford could be said to have scuppered his chances of a further term as President with this view. Pressed to elaborate, he said, 'I don't believe ... Romanians consider themselves dominated by the Soviet Union. I don't believe that the Poles consider themselves dominated by the Soviet Union. Each of those countries is independent, autonomous ... And the United States does not concede that those countries are under the domination of the Soviet Union.' After a couple of further clarifying statements, he finally admitted: 'I was perhaps not as precise as I should have been.'

5 If Abraham Lincoln were alive today he'd be turning in his grave.

Suggested as one of Ford's idiocies *c.*1975, but a traditional joke format. In Roger Woddis's poem 'Final Curtain' (written about and probably near the time of Watergate, 1973–4) he has:

George Washington's dead,
Like the pledge that I gave,
But if he were alive
He would turn in his grave.

A version attributed to Samuel Goldwyn is: 'If Roosevelt were alive today, he'd turn over in his grave' (*PDMQ*, 1971).

FORD, Henry

American industrialist (1863–1947)

6 GREAT WAR ENDS CHRISTMAS DAY. FORD TO STOP IT.

Initially, it was thought that the First World War would not last very long. Having started in August 1914, it would be 'over by Christmas'. The fact that this promise was not fulfilled did not prevent Ford from saying, as he tried to stop the war a year later: 'We're going to try to get the boys out of the trenches before Christmas. I've chartered a ship, and some of us are going to Europe.' He was not referring to American boys because the United States had not joined the war at this stage. The *New York Tribune* encapsulated it all in the above headline. Of almost every war since, it has been said that it would be 'over by Christmas'.

7 History is bunk.

In the course of a libel action against the *Chicago Tribune*, which came to court in the spring of 1919 – an editorial had described Ford as an 'anarchist' and an 'ignorant idealist' – the motor magnate found himself as much on trial as the defendant. Cross-examined for no fewer than eight days, Ford was continually tripped up by his ignorance. He could not say when the United States came into being. He suggested 1812 before 1776. He was asked about a statement reported by Charles N. Wheeler in an interview with Ford on 25 May 1916: 'History is more or less bunk. It's tradition.' Ford explained: 'I did not say it was bunk. It was bunk to me ... but I did not need it very bad.' The *Tribune* was found guilty of libel – and fined six cents.

8 Any colour as long as it's black.

To convey that there is no choice, this expression originated with Ford who is supposed to have said it about the Model T Ford which came out in 1909. Hill and Nevins in *Ford: Expansion and Challenge* (1957) have him saying: 'People can have it any colour – so long as it's black.' However, in 1925, the company had to bow to the inevitable and offer a choice of colours. Dr Harry Corbett of Bayswater, Australia, commented (1996): 'Initially, the T model was available in several colours but when Ford changed to a different painting technique the product used was only available in the colour black. The early finishing technique was a carryover from the carriage industry and resulted in curing times of up to four weeks. This meant that huge numbers of cars had to be stored during the finishing process. From what I can gather, Ford changed to a faster drying product – which was only available in black – to rid himself of the warehousing difficulties.'

FORREST, Nathan B.

American general (1821–77)

1 Firstest with the mostest.

To describe anything as 'the mostest' might seem exclusively American. However, *OED2* finds English dialect use in the 1880s and Partridge/*Slang* recognizes its use as a jocular superlative without restricting it to the US. As such, it is a consciously ungrammatical way of expressing extreme degree. Whether this was consciously the case with the Confederate general, Nathan B. Forrest, is very much in doubt. He could hardly read or write but he managed to say that the way to win battles was to be 'Firstest with the mostest', or that you needed to 'Git thar fustest with the mostest'. Bartlett (1992) gives this last as the usual rendering of the more formally reported words: 'Get there first with the most men'. In Irving Berlin's musical *Call Me Madam* (1950) there is a song with the title 'The Hostess with the Mostes' on the Ball'. One assumes that Berlin's use, like any evocation of 'the mostest' nowadays, refers back to Forrest's remark.

FORRO, Francis Stephen

Australian clergyman (1914–74)

2 Ah, yes, but they will make fine ancestors.

Response to a journalist's comments on the scruffiness of Hungarian refugees arriving at Mascot airfield, Sydney, in 1956. Quoted from Les A. Murray in *The Dictionary of Australian Quotations* (1984). Compare the untraced remark, 'Our greatest responsibility is to be good ancestors'.

FORSTER, E.M.

English novelist (1879–1970)

3 He was passionately in love with her; therefore she could do exactly as she liked. 'It mayn't be heaven below,' she thought, 'but it's better than Charles.'

Where Angels Fear to Tread, Chap. 3 (1905). The idea of marriage as a heaven or paradise below might seem to be a well-meaning nineteenth-century view of the matter, but in Nevill Coghill's translation (1951) of Chaucer's 'The Merchant's Tale', he puts: 'For wedlock is so easy and so clean/It is a very paradise on earth.' In Chaucer's original, the second line is: 'That in this world it is a paradys.' In his 'A Chapter on Ears', Charles Lamb quotes the lines of 'Dr [Isaac] Watts' (1674–1748): 'I have been there, and still would go;/'Tis like a little heaven below' – but here the reference is to chapels rather than marriage.

4 A Room With a View.

Title of novel (1908). *Compare* COWARD 185:7.

5 Only connect! That was the whole of her sermon. Only connect the prose and the passion, and both will be exalted, and human love will be seen at its height.

Epigraph to *Howard's End* (1910). Goronwy Rees wrote in *A Chapter of Accidents* (1972): 'It could be said that those two words, so misleading in their ambiguity, had more influence in shaping the emotional attitudes of the English governing class between the two world wars than any other single phrase in the English language.' The words also occur in the body of Forster's book (Chap. 22): 'Only connect! That was the whole of her sermon. Only connect the prose and the passion, and both will be exalted, and human love will be seen at its height. Live in fragments no longer. Only connect, and the beast and the monk, robbed of the isolation that is life to either, will die.' Forster's message was that barriers of all kinds must be dismantled if the harmony lacking in modern life was to be discovered.

6 Personal relations are the important thing for ever and ever, and not this outer life of telegrams and anger.

Ib., Chap. 19. Alluded to in Peter Hall's *Diaries* (1983) – entry for 30 December 1973: 'Jenny and Christopher to Paris to see their mother. The holidays feel over. Back into the world of telegrams and anger ...'

1 A Passage to India.

Title of novel (1924). Forster acknowledged that this was derived from a poem called 'Passage to India' (1871) in Walt Whitman's *Leaves of Grass.*

2 I hate causes, and if I had to choose between betraying my country and betraying my friend, I hope I should have the guts to betray my country.

'What I Believe', *Two Cheers for Democracy* (1938). This was quoted by the traitor Anthony Blunt when trying to persuade friends not to tell the British authorities what they knew about the 1951 defectors, Burgess and Maclean. Goronwy Rees (as above) replied to Blunt: 'Forster's antithesis was a false one. One's country [is] not some abstract conception which it might be relatively easy to sacrifice for the sake of an individual; it [is] itself made up of a dense network of individual and social relationships in which loyalty to one particular person formed only a single strand.' Blunt, Burgess and Maclean were part of the between-the-wars generation at Cambridge influenced by Forster's thinking.

FORTY-SECOND STREET

American film 1933. Script by James Seymour and Rian James. With Warner Baxter as Julian Marsh, the theatre producer, and Ruby Keeler as Peggy Sawyer, the chorus girl.

3 *Julian (to Peggy)*: You're going out a youngster – but you've got to come back a star!

Soundtrack. The origin of a notable show business cliché. Peggy is given her big break when she has to take over at short notice from the star of the show who has broken her leg.

FOSTER, Sir George

Canadian politician (1847–1931)

4 In these somewhat troublesome days when the great Mother Empire stands splendidly isolated in Europe.

A speech in the Canadian House of Commons (16 January 1896) was the occasion of the coining of the phrase 'splendid isolation', which was the headline in the London *Times* over its subsequent account. Foster was MP for North Toronto. 'A flattering Canadian conception of Britain's lonely magnificence' – Jan Morris in *Farewell the Trumpets* (1978). The 1st Lord Goschen picked up the phrase in a speech at Lewes (26 February 1896): 'We have stood here alone in what is called isolation – our splendid isolation, as one of our colonial friends was good enough to call it'.

FOWLER, H.W.

English lexicographer (1858–1933)

5 A writer expresses himself in words that have been used before because they give his meaning better than he can give it himself, or because they are beautiful or witty, or because he expects them to touch a chord of association in his reader, or because he wishes to show that he is learned and well read. Quotations due to the last motive are invariably ill-advised; the discerning reader detects it and is contemptuous; the undiscerning is perhaps impressed, but even then is at the same time repelled, pretentious quotations being the surest way to tedium.

A Dictionary of Modern English Usage (1926). On the art of quotation.

FOWLER, Sir Norman

English Conservative politician (1938–)

6 What *is* oral sex?

To civil servants during the anti-AIDS campaign he ran when Social Services Secretary, *c.*1986. Quoted in the *Independent on Sunday* (26 May 1991).

7 I have a young family and for the next few years I should like to devote more time to them while they are still so young.

Letter of resignation to the Prime Minister (3 January 1990). Margaret Thatcher replied the same day: 'I am naturally very sorry to see you go, but understand your reasons for doing so, particularly your wish to be able to spend more time with your family.' At the same time, Peter Walker also resigned from the Cabinet, giving as his reason that he wished to 'spend more time with my family' and the phrase became a cliché of political resignations.

FOX, Charles James

English Liberal politician (1749–1806)

8 No Greek: as much Latin as you like; never French in any circumstances: no English poet unless he has completed his century.

Fox's advice on the use of quotations in House of Commons speeches. Quoted in G.W.E. Russell, *Collections and Recollections* (1898).

FRANCIS OF ASSISI

Italian monk and saint (c.1181–1226)

1 Lord, make me an instrument of your peace.
Where there is hatred, let me sow love.
Where there is injury, pardon.
Where there is doubt, faith.
Where there is despair, hope.
Where there is darkness, light.
Where there is sadness, joy.
O Divine Master, grant that I may not so much seek
To be consoled as to console,
To be understood as to understand,
To be loved as to love.
For it is in giving that we receive,
It is in pardoning that we are pardoned,
It is in dying that we are born to eternal life.

Bartlett (1980) has a fuller version and a different translation, saying no more than that the words are 'attributed' to St Francis. In 1988, this was the version entitled 'Prayer for Peace' that was available (unattributed) in Britain on prayer cards. There was even a version on a tea-towel on sale at York Minster. At the Basilica of St Francis at Assisi, it was, of course, available in any number of languages (as above).

Actually, there is some doubt as to whether St Francis had anything to do with the prayer at all. The Rt Rev. Dr J.R.H. Moorman (1905–89), a former Bishop of Ripon, wrote to the *Church Times* stating that the prayer was written in France in 1912 (source: *The Observer*, 7 September 1986).

The prayer was quoted by Margaret Thatcher on becoming British Prime Minister (4 May 1979). According to Sir Ronald Millar, one of her speechwriters, it was he who at four o'clock on Mrs Thatcher's first morning as Prime Minister gave her the words to read out, 'ignoring the advice of harder-nosed associates who thought the sentiments too trite even for that emotional occasion' (*The Sunday Times*, 23 November 1980). It was inevitable that the quotation would in time be held against her.

FRANCIS II

Austrian Holy Roman Emperor (1768–1835)

2 But is he a patriot for me?

A distinguished servant of the Austrian Empire was being recommended to Francis II as a sterling patriot, so the last Holy Roman Emperor asked this. A. & V. Palmer, *Quotations in History* (1976), ascribing this to his other title of 'Francis I of Austria', add: 'Remark on being told of the patriotic qualities of a candidate for high office, *c.*1821'. Hence, the title of John Osborne's play *A Patriot for Me* (1965).

FRANKLIN, Benjamin

American politician and scientist (1706–90)

3 Fish and visitors smell in three days.

Poor Richard's Almanack (1736). In Whit Stillman's film *Barcelona* (1994), one of the characters – perhaps intentionally – misascribes this famous proverb to Dr Johnson. A pity that he didn't ascribe the saying to America's own Dr Johnson, Benjamin Franklin. Even so, *CODP* finds the idea (without the fish) in Plautus and the first English reference (with the fish) in Lyly's *Euphues* (1580). Wolfgang Mieder in *Proverbs Are Never Out of Season* (1993) has provided a useful corrective to the view that Franklin was a great coiner of proverbs. In fact, of the 1,044 proverbs in *Poor Richard's Almanack*, only 5 per cent can be said to have been coined by Franklin himself.

4 Here Skugg
Lies snug
As a bug
In a rug.

Letter to Miss Georgiana Shipley (26 September 1772) on the death of her pet squirrel. However, lest it be thought that, by its inclusion in dictionaries of quotations, Franklin originated the phrase 'snug as a bug in a rug', note that there are earlier uses. In an anonymous work *Stratford Jubilee* (commemorating David Garrick's Shakespeare Festival in 1769) we find:

> If she [a rich widow] has the mopus's [money]
> I'll have her, as snug as a bug in a rug.

Probably, however, it was an established expression even by that date, if only because in 1706 Edward Ward in *The Wooden World Dissected* had the similar 'He sits as snug a Bee in a Box' and in Thomas Heywood's play *A Woman Killed with Kindness* (1603) there is 'Let us sleep as snug as pigs in pease-straw.'

A little after Franklin's use: in the July 1816 edition of the *New Monthly Magazine*, among the curious epitaphs printed from Waddington in Yorkshire (now in Lancashire) was one, 'In memory of WILLIAM RICHARD PHELPS, late Boatswain of H.M.S. *Invincible*. He accompanied Lord Anson in his cruise round the world, and died April 21, 1789'. It reads:

When I was like you,
For years not a few,
On the ocean I toil'd,
On the line I have broil'd
In Greenland I've shiver'd,
Now from hardship deliver'd,
Capsiz'd by old death,
I surrender'd my breath.
And now I lie snug
As a bug in a rug.

1 We must indeed all hang together, or, most assuredly, we shall all hang separately.

At the signing of the Declaration of Independence (4 July 1776), though possibly not original.

2 Never pick a quarrel with someone who buys their ink in barrels.

Or, 'Never disagree with anyone who buys ink by the barrel' – i.e., with a journalist or professional arguer. This was attributed to Franklin by *The Observer* (27 July 1992) but remains unverified.

3 The body
of Benjamin Franklin, printer,
(Like the cover of an old book,
Its contents worn out,
And stript of its lettering and gilding)
Lies here, food for worms!
Yet the work itself shall not be lost,
For it will, as he believed, appear once more
In a new
And more beautiful edition,
Corrected and amended
By its Author!

An epitaph suggested for himself and written *c.*1728. Benham (1948) compares the Rev. Joseph Capen (nineteenth century), 'Lines on Mr John Foster': 'Yet at the resurrection we shall see/A fair edition, and of matchless worth,/Free from erratas, new in heaven set forth.' Benham also suggests that the idea was borrowed from the Rev. Benjamin Woodbridge, chaplain to Charles II, who wrote these 'Lines of John Cotton' (1652): 'O what a monument of glorious worth,/When in a new edition he comes forth,/Without erratas, may we think he'll be/In leaves and covers of eternity!'

In fact, Franklin lies with his wife under a simple inscription in Christ Church, Philadelphia: 'Benjamin and Deborah Franklin 1790.'

See also FLEMING 239:9.

FRASER, Malcolm

Australian Liberal Prime Minister (1930–)

4 Life is not meant to be easy.

Fraser was Prime Minister of Australia 1975–83. The phrase was very much associated with him and was used as the title of a biography by John Edwards in 1977. Douglas Aiton asked Fraser in an interview for the London *Times* (16 March 1981) if he had ever actually said it. Fraser replied, 'I said something very like it. It's from *Back to Methuselah* by Bernard Shaw ... A friend I was visiting in hospital asked me why I didn't give up politics and return to the good life [on his sheep farm]. I said life wasn't meant to be like that. That would be too easy. So that's what it grew from. I wouldn't mind a cent for every time it's been quoted or misquoted. It's the best thing I ever said.' Presumably, Shaw would agree.

Fraser's derivation of the line from Shaw was probably an afterthought, however. The play has, 'Life is not meant to be easy, my child; but take courage: it can be delightful.' In a Deakin lecture on 20 July 1971, which seems to have been his first public use of the phrase, Fraser made no mention of the source. Referring rather to Arnold Toynbee's analysis of history, Fraser said: 'It involves a conclusion about the past that life has not been easy for people or for nations, and an assumption for the future that that condition will not alter. There is within me some part of the metaphysic, and thus I would add that life is not meant to be easy.'

It is not, of course, a startlingly original view. In A.C. Benson's essays *The Leaves of the Tree* (1912), he quotes Brooke Foss Westcott, Bishop of Durham, as saying: 'The only people with whom I have no sympathy ... are those who say that things are easy. Life is not easy, nor was it meant to be.'

FREDERICK THE GREAT

Prussian King (1712–86)

5 *Une couronne n'est qu'un chapeau qui laisse passer la pluie.*
A crown is no more than a hat that lets in the rain.

Remark on declining a formal coronation (1740). Quoted in Alan and Veronica Palmer, *Quotations in History* (1976), but otherwise unverified.

6 My people and I have come to an agreement which satisfies us both. They are to say what

they please, and I am to do what I please.

Unverified.

See also DALY 195:7.

FREEMAN, Samuel

American jurist (fl.1862–90)

1 Never walk when you can ride, never sit when you can lie down.

Freeman apparently served in the US Supreme Court from 1862 to 1890. Claire Rayner, the British 'agony aunt', has a longer version according to the Sister Tutor who trained her as a nurse back in the 1950s: 'Nurse, never stand when you can sit, never sit when you can lie down, and never lie if there's any chance they might find you out.' Compare the letter Coleridge wrote to John Thelwall (14 October 1797): 'at other times I adopt the Brahman Creed, & say – It is better to sit than to stand, it is better to lie than to sit, it is better to sleep than to wake – but Death is the best of all!' (in E.L. Griggs, *Collected Letters of Samuel Taylor Coleridge*, Vol.1, 1956). *Compare* GEORGE V 256:5.

FRENCH, Marilyn

American novelist (1929–)

2 Whatever they may be in public life, whatever their relations with men, in their relations with women, all men are rapists, and that's all they are. They rape us with their eyes, their laws and their codes.

Said by a character whose daughter has been raped in *The Women's Room* (1977). From *The Observer* (3 March 1996): 'Talk to French about that quotation, and she seethes with exasperation. Because she never said those words. One of the characters in her first, massive bestseller *The Women's Room* did. And, she fumes: "Nobody holds up Iago's speeches and blames Shakespeare for them."'

FREUD, Sigmund

Austrian psychiatrist (1856–1939)

3 Two Jews were conversing about bathing. 'I take a bath once a year,' said one, 'whether I need one or not.'

Having been told a joke concerning Elizabeth I – that she would take a bath once a month 'whether she need it or no' – the search was on to find the origin. But it turned out to be a case of an old line becoming attached to a famous person. Certainly, the story has been told of people other than the Virgin Queen. Indeed, it is quoted as an anti-Semitic joke by Freud in *Jokes and their Relation to the Unconscious* (1905). He adds, helpfully, 'It is clear that this boastful assurance of his cleanliness only betrays his sense of uncleanliness'.

4 The artist has won – through his fantasy – what before he could only win *in* his fantasy: honour, power, and the love of women.

Introductory Lectures on Psycho-Analysis, No. 23 (1916).

5 The great question that has never been answered and which I have not yet been able to answer, despite my thirty years of research into the feminine soul, is 'What does a woman want?'

From a letter to Marie Bonaparte, quoted in Ernest Jones, *Sigmund Freud: Life and Work* (1955). The question became a rallying cry in the resurgence of feminism from the 1970s onwards. *What Do Women Want? Exploding the Myth of Dependency* was the title of a book by Luise Eichenbaum and Susie Orbach (1983). The same question is posed to the protagonist of Chaucer's 'The Wife of Bath's Tale' when the answer is: 'Wommen desiren to have sovereynetee/As wel over hir housbond as hir love,/And for to been in maistrie hym above.'

6 Sometimes a cigar is just a cigar.

This utterance remains untraced, but Ralph Keyes in *Nice Guys Finish Seventh* (1992) rather misses its point. Freud had nominated cigars as phallic symbols in dream symbolism but – as perhaps he never said – they were not *always* to be regarded as such. Sometimes, a cigar was just a cigar.

FRIEDMAN, Milton

American economist (1912–)

7 There is no such thing as a free lunch.

In the US the concept of the 'free lunch' dates back to at least 1840, according to Flexner (1976). It might have amounted to no more than thirst-arousing snacks like pretzels in saloon bars, but even so it was not strictly speaking 'free' because you had to buy a beer to obtain it. Quite at what point the saying 'There ain't no such thing as a free lunch' – meaning 'there's always a catch' or 'don't expect something for nothing' – arose is hard to say. The *ODMQ* (1991) found this in *The*

Moon is a Harsh Mistress, a science fiction novel (1966) by Robert A. Heinlein:

'Oh, "tanstaafl". Means "There ain't no such thing as a free lunch." And isn't,' I added, pointing to a FREE LUNCH sign across room, 'or these drinks would cost half as much. Was reminding her that anything free costs twice as much in the long run or turns out worthless.'

But it was misleading of the *ODMQ* to proffer this as if it were the original coinage when the observation that free lunches have hidden costs was already well established. In the epilogue to his *America* (1973) Alistair Cooke ascribes to 'an Italian immigrant, when asked to say what forty years of American life had taught him' – 'There is no free lunch'. The saying 'There is no such thing as a free lunch' is quoted by Burton Crane in *The Sophisticated Investor* (1959).

Milton Friedman, along with other economists of the University of Chicago school, gave the saying new life in the 1970s, using it in articles, lectures and as the title of a book (1975) to support his monetarist theories. But he did not coin the phrase either, even if it came to be much associated with him.

FROHMAN, Charles

American theatrical producer (1860–1915)

1 Why fear death? It is the most beautiful adventure of life.

These were Frohman's last words before going down with the *Lusitania* in 1915. The words were reported by survivors and quoted in I.F. Marcosson and D. Frohman, *Charles Frohman* (1916). Undoubtedly Frohman was alluding to the line 'To die will be an awfully big adventure' in J.M. Barrie's play *Peter Pan* (1904) which he had first produced on the London stage. *See* BARRIE 75:7.

2 For it is not right that in a house the muses haunt mourning should dwell. Such things befit us not.

These words are on the fountain monument to Frohman near the church (but outside the churchyard) of All Saints, Marlow, Buckinghamshire. Frohman used to spend weekends at Marlow and, indeed, expressed a wish to die and to be buried there. The monument shows a nude maiden in marble, and the inscription runs round the base. J. Camp in *Portrait of Buckinghamshire* (1972) comments: 'His memorial is a graceful tribute to the female form, and a reminder of the pleasure his stage presentations gave to so many on both sides of the Atlantic in late Victorian and Edwardian days.' The text is taken from a translation of fragments by Sappho, the Greek lyric poet of the late seventh century BC – also sometimes rendered as 'For it is not right that in the house of song ...' and taken to be her dying words. Henry T. Wharton in *Sappho* (1895) has the poet 'blaming her daughter' and translates the passage, 'For lamentation may not be in a poet's house: such things befit us not'. He also quotes Frederick Tennyson's version: 'In the home of the Muses/'Tis bootless to mourn.'

FROST, David (later Sir David)

English broadcaster (1939–)

3 Seriously, though, he's doing a grand job!

After a satirical attack in BBC TV's *That Was The Week That Was* (1962–3), Frost would proffer this pretend conciliation. It was taken up by clergymen and others, but Ned Sherrin, the show's producer, claims that the phrase was used on the programme no more than half a dozen times in all.

4 Hello, good evening, and welcome.

A greeting well known on both sides of the Atlantic derives from the period when Frost was commuting back and forth to host TV chat shows in London and New York, and in particular from ITV's *The Frost Programme* (1966). It may have been contrived to say three things where only one is needed, but it became an essential part of the Frost impersonator's kit (not to mention the Frost self-impersonator's kit). He was still saying it in 1983 when, with a small alteration, it became 'Hello, good *morning* and welcome!' at the debut of TV-am, the breakfast-TV station. The original phrase was used as the title of a BBC TV 'Wednesday Play' about a TV interrogator (16 October 1968), so was obviously well established by then.

The *ODMQ* (1991) wrongly ascribes *The Frost Programme* to BBC Television, whereas it was a Rediffusion production.

5 The chemistry thing is really important ... chemistry – sexual or otherwise – that is important.

In the period prior to the start of TV-am, the British breakfast television station, in 1983, Frost talked about hoped-for new approaches to on-screen presentation. He either invented the phrase 'sexual chemistry', or merely endorsed it when it was suggested to him by a reporter, to describe what it was important for presenters to have. 'Personal chemistry' to describe the attraction between two people had long been remarked where it existed in other walks of life. Shaw in *You*

Never Can Tell (1898) had: 'Not love: we know better than that. Let's call it chemistry ... Well, you're attracting me irresistibly – chemically.'

FROST, Robert

American poet (1874–1963)

1 Something there is that doesn't love a wall ...
My apple trees will never get across
And eat the cones under his pines, I tell him.
He only says, Good fences make good neighbours.

'Mending Wall', *North of Boston* (1914). The final thought is an old one, as Tom Burnam notes in *The Dictionary of Misinformation* (1975). E. Rogers (1640), in a letter quoted in the Winthrop Papers, wrote: 'A good fence helpeth to keepe peace between neighbours; but let us take heed that we make not a high stone wall, to keep us from meeting.' However, as Frost's poem makes clear, this is not the poet's point of view. It is the neighbour ('an old-stone savage armed') who says the line. Frost is pointing out that good fences do not necessarily make good neighbours at all: 'Before I built a wall I'd ask to know/What I was walling in or walling out.'

2 'Home is the place where, when you have to go there,
They have to take you in.'

From his poem 'The Death of a Hired Man' (1914). Note the quotation marks. *Compare* THATCHER 536:2.

3 Two roads diverged in a yellow wood,
And sorry I could not travel both
And be one traveller, long I stood
And looked down one as far as I could
To where it bent in the undergrowth ...

Two roads diverged in a wood, and I –
I took the one less travelled by,
And that has made all the difference.

'The Road Not Taken', *Mountain Interval* (1916). *The Road Less Travelled* was taken as the title of a popular work of psychotherapy by M. Scott Peck (1978).

4 The woods are lovely, dark and deep.
But I have promises to keep,
And miles to go before I sleep,
And miles to go before I sleep.

'Stopping by Woods on a Snowy Evening' (1923). Frost suffered misquotation at the hands of President Kennedy who used the poem as a rousing, uplifting end to speeches. However, until Jacqueline Kennedy pointed it out to her husband, he would frequently combine the poem with another (by Emerson) and say: 'I'll hitch my wagon to a star/But I have promises to keep.' Or he would work in the venue of his speech, as in 'Iowa is lovely, dark and deep' (source: Theodore C. Sorensen, *Kennedy*, 1965.)

Hence, *Promises to Keep*, title of a memoir (1971) by Chester Knowles, and of an unrelated film (US, 1985), and of a novel (1988) by George Bernau.

5 Some say the world will end in fire,
Some say in ice.
From what I've tasted of desire,
I hold with those who favour fire.

'Fire and Ice' (1923). Here fire = desire, ice = hate, either of which is strong enough to kill. The word combination has appealed to many. A.E. Housman in *A Shropshire Lad* (1896) has: 'And fire and ice within me fight/Beneath the suffocating night.' Dante's *Inferno* has: 'Into the eternal darkness, into fire and into ice.' Psalm 148:7 in the Book of Common Prayer has 'fire and hail'. Latterly, it has been used to refer to the death of the planet Earth by atomic warfare or a new ice age. The ice-skaters Jayne Torville and Christopher Dean had a routine with the title in the late 1980s.

6 The land was ours before we were the land's.
She was our land more than a hundred years
Before we were her people ...

'The Gift Outright' (1942): spoken from memory by Frost at President Kennedy's inauguration (20 January 1961).

7 Summoning artists to participate
In the august occasions of the state
Seems something artists ought to celebrate ...
It makes the prophet in us all presage
The glory of a next Augustan age
A golden age of poetry and power
Of which this noonday's the beginning hour.

At the inauguration of President Kennedy in January 1961, Frost attempted to read a specially commissioned poem, but couldn't see to read it, so he stopped after three lines and recited another poem 'The Gift Outright' from memory. Perhaps as well, given some of the lines above.

8 The brain is a wonderful organ. It starts working the moment you get up in the morning, and does not stop until you get into the office.

Quoted in Prochnow & Prochnow, *Treasury of Humorous Quotations* (1969). Sometimes rendered as '... until you get up to make a speech.'

FRYE, David

American impressionist and comedian (1934–)

1 He looks like the guy in a science fiction movie who is the first to see the Creature.

On Gerald R. Ford. Attributed in 1975.

FUCHIDA, Mitsuo

Japanese pilot (1902–)

2 Tora-tora-tora.

Fuchida was the leader of the Japanese attack on the US Pacific Fleet at Pearl Harbor (7 December 1941). On confirming that the fleet was indeed being taken by surprise at dawn, he uttered this code word to signal that the rest of the Japanese plan could be put into operation. 'Tora' means 'tiger' (source: Gordon W. Prange, *At Dawn We Slept*, Chap. 61, 1982). Hence, *Tora! Tora! Tora!*, title of a film (US, 1970) about the events leading up to Pearl Harbor.

FUKUYAMA, Francis

American government official (1953–)

3 What we may be witnessing is not the end of the Cold War but the end of history as such; that is, the end point of man's ideological evolution and the universalization of Western liberal democracy.

The 'end of history' was a concept promoted by Fukuyama in the summer 1989 edition of the American journal *National Interest* to describe western democracy's perceived triumph over Communism in eastern Europe. 'He gained a lot of publicity,' wrote Michael Ignatieff (*Independent on Sunday*, 22 October 1995) 'by stating the obvious: that the death of Communism had removed the last systematic challenge to the triumph of the capitalist system ... In fact, of course, History continued, not least because there is not one capitalist system but many, and the reckoning between them was far from over.'

The idea had been touched on before but for different reasons. From Graham Swift, *Waterland* (1983): 'Alluding rapidly to certain topics of the day ... the perilous and apparently unhaltable build-up of nuclear arms ... The only important thing about history, I think, sir, is that it's got to the point where it's probably about to end.' *Compare* SELLAR AND YEATMAN 473:13.

FULBRIGHT, J. William

American Democratic politician (1905–95)

4 A policy that can be accurately, though perhaps not prudently, defined as one of 'peaceful co-existence'.

Speech in the Senate (27 March 1964), but the phrase had long been current. In 1920 Lenin had spoken of 'peaceful cohabitation with the peoples, with the workers and peasants of all nations'. In the 1950s and 1960s, the possibility of fair competition between eastern and western ideologies was also much mooted, though whether the Soviets and the Americans meant quite the same thing by the phrase is somewhat doubtful.

5 We must dare to think 'unthinkable' thoughts. We must learn to explore all the options and possibilities that confront us in a complex and rapidly changing world. We must learn to welcome and not to fear the voices of dissent. We must dare to think about 'unthinkable' things because when things become unthinkable, thinking stops and action becomes mindless.

Ib. A little earlier, Herman Kahn had written a book with the title *Thinking the Unthinkable* (1962). The sort of thing Fulbright had in mind was collaboration with the Soviets on various schemes.

6 The Arrogance of Power.

Title of book (1967) questioning the basis of US foreign policy, particularly in Vietnam and the Dominican Republic. In the previous year, Fulbright, the Democratic chairman of the Senate Foreign Relations Committee, had given lectures establishing his theme: 'A psychological need that nations seem to have ... to prove that they are bigger, better or stronger than other nations.'

FULLER, R. Buckminster

American architect (1895–1983)

7 I am a passenger on the spaceship, Earth.

Operating Manual for Spaceship Earth (1969). The concept of planet Earth as a spaceship was designed to underline that we are travelling through space on our own, with our survival dependent upon a fragile economy and a polluted environment. The idea was not totally original: in 1965, Adlai Stevenson told UNESCO: 'We travel together, passengers on a little space ship, dependent on its vulnerable reserves of air and soil.' Marshall McLuhan added: 'There are no passengers on Spaceship Earth. Only crew.'

FULLER, Sam

American film writer and director (1912–97)

1 The film is like a battleground ... love ... hate ... action ... violence ... death ... in one word: emotions.

This is a maxim spoken by Fuller in a cameo appearance in Jean-Luc Godard's film *Pierrot le Fou* (France, 1966). He appears in the film as a visiting director and makes his pronouncement at a party. It has been wrongly attributed to Nicholas Ray.

FULLER, Thomas

English preacher and historian (1608–61)

2 Here lies Fuller's Earth.

A punning epitaph suggested for himself by the author of *The History of the Worthies of England*. T. Webb in *A New Select Collection of Epitaphs* (1775) mentions it. Fuller was buried in the church of which he had been rector, at Cranford, west London, but the grave no longer survives. His actual epitaph was a sober Latin text.

FULLER, Thomas

English writer and physician (1654–1734)

3 Be you never so high the law is above you.

Gnomologia (1732). During a landmark ruling in the British High Court in January 1977, Lord Denning quoted Fuller's words 'to every subject of this land, however powerful' in the matter of the 'South African mail boycott case'. He ruled that the Attorney-General, Sam Silkin, could not suspend or dispense with the execution of the law.

4 It is a silly game where nobody wins.

In *Ib.* I defiantly quote this every so often at the start of BBC Radio *Quote ... Unquote* in which, although it has the format of a quiz, no score is kept, there are no winners and absolutely no prizes.

FUNK, Walther

German Nazi minister (1890–1960)

5 *Kristallnacht.*
Night of Broken Glass.

A euphemistic but still chilling phrase attributed to Hitler's Minister of Economics, to describe the Nazi pogrom against Jews in Germany on the night of 9–10 November 1938. The cause of the pogrom was retaliation for the murder of a German diplomat by a Jew in Paris. Nazi hooligans were let loose on the streets during a night of terror in which 7,500 shops were looted, 101 synagogues were destroyed by fire and 76 demolished. In Nuremberg the synagogues were actually set on fire by the Fire Brigade.

G

GABOR, Zsa Zsa

Hungarian-born film actress (1919–)

1 You mean apart from my own?

In answer to the question 'How many husbands have you had?' Attributed, by 1976.

2 Of course, darling, return the ring – but keep the diamonds.

The source of this remark was sought as a quiz question in the *Sunday Express* Magazine (14 February 1988), but the answer was never revealed. When subsequently the question was posed through Godfrey Smith's column in *The Sunday Times* in 1992, there was a 'blizzard' of readers' letters all pointing to Gabor as the source. *The Little, Brown Book of Anecdotes* (1985) has, unsourced, that Gabor once appeared on a TV show and told a young woman who asked, 'I'm breaking my engagement to a very wealthy man who has already given me a sable coat, diamonds, a stove, and a Rolls-Royce. What should I do?' – ' Give back the stove.'

GAITSKELL, Hugh

English Labour politician (1906–63)

3 There are some of us ... who will fight and fight and fight again to save the party we love.

Speech as leader of the British Labour Party at the party conference (3 October 1960). When, against the wishes of the Party leadership, the conference looked like taking what Gaitskell called the 'suicidal path' of unilateral disarmament 'which will leave our country defenceless and alone', he was faced with making the most important speech of his life – for his leadership was at stake. Many delegates who were free to do so changed their votes, but the Party executive was still defeated. Nevertheless, Gaitskell reduced his opponents to a paper victory, and the phrase is often recalled in tribute to a great personal achievement. The coinage has been claimed by Brian Walden, the one-time Labour MP and broadcaster. *Compare* DANTON 196:2, which is sometimes rendered as: 'Dare! and dare! and dare again!'

4 It does mean, if this is the idea, the end of Britain as an independent European state ... it means the end of a thousand years of history.

In a speech to the Labour Party Conference (3 October 1962), Gaitskell gave this view of a proposal that Britain should join the European Economic Community. It is always dangerous these days to use the phrase 'thousand years'. Speaking on European unity (14 February 1948), Winston Churchill said: 'We are asking the nations of Europe between whom rivers of blood have flowed, to forget the feuds of a thousand years.' *See also* HITLER 298:2 and SMITH 508:1.

GALBRAITH, John Kenneth

Canadian-born American economist (1908–)

5 The Affluent Society.

Title of book (1958) about the effect of high living standards on economic theories that had been created to deal with scarcity and poverty. The resulting 'private affluence and public squalor' stemmed from an imbalance between private and public sector output. For example, there might be more cars and TV sets but not enough police to prevent them from being stolen. Martin Luther King in a 1963 letter from gaol used the phrase thus: 'When you see the vast majority of your twenty million Negro brothers smouldering in an airtight cage of poverty in the midst of an affluent society ... then you will understand why we find it difficult to wait.' The notion was not new to the mid-twentieth century, however. Tacitus, in his *Annals* (*c.*AD115), noted that 'many, amid great affluence, are utterly miserable', and Cato the Younger (95–46BC), when denouncing the contemporary state of Rome said: '*Habemus publice egestatem, privatim opulentiam*' [public want, private wealth].

The punning tag of 'effluent society', a commonplace by the 1980s, had appeared in Stan Gooch's poem 'Never So Good' in 1964.

1 The conventional wisdom.

In *ib.* Phrase devised to describe 'the beliefs that are at any time assiduously, solemnly and mindlessly traded between the pretentiously wise.'

2 The Great Wall, I've been told, is the only man-made structure on earth that is visible from the moon. For the life of me I cannot see why anyone would go to the moon to look at it, when, with almost the same difficulty, it can be viewed in China.

In *The Sunday Times* Magazine (23 October 1977) – a prime example of Galbraith's laconic style. At the time, China had not opened itself up to tourism. The idea of 'the Wall of China' being 'the only work of man visible from the moon' was current by August 1939 when it was mentioned in the *Fortnightly Review*.

See also BUTLER 137:3; TYNAN 547:2.

GALILEI, Galileo

Italian astronomer and physicist (1564–1642)

3 *Eppur si muove*
But it does move.

Muttered comment after his recantation of the theory that the earth moves around the sun, in 1632. First reported in an Italian history book (1757), the remark seems most unlikely ever to have passed Galileo's lips.

GALSWORTHY, John

English novelist (1867–1933)

4 Nobody tells me anything.

Stock phrase of James Forsyte in *The Man of Property* (1906) and *In Chancery* (1920).

GANDHI, Indira

Indian Prime Minister (1917–84)

5 Even if I die in the service of this nation, I would be proud of it. Every drop of my blood, I am sure, will contribute to the growth of this nation and make it strong and dynamic.

Speech, Bhubaneswar, Orissa (31 October 1984). Twenty-four hours later she was assassinated. The wording varied from report to report.

GANDHI, Mahatma

Indian politician (1869–1948)

6 That would be a good idea.

When asked what he thought of modern civilization. In *Good Work* (1979), E.F. Schumacher describes seeing a newsreel film of Gandhi's visit to England in 1930. Disembarking at Southampton he was swamped by journalists, one of whom put this question to him (sometimes reported as 'what do you think of *Western* civilization?') and got this reply.

GARBO, Greta

Swedish-born film actress (1905–90)

7 I want to be alone.

Garbo claimed (in *Life* Magazine, 24 January 1955) that 'I only said, "I want to be *let* alone"' – i.e., she wanted privacy rather than solitude. Oddly, as Alexander Walker observed in *Sex in the Movies* (1968): 'Nowhere in anything she said, either in the lengthy interviews she gave in her Hollywood days when she was perfectly approachable, or in the statements on-the-run from the publicity-shy fugitive she later became, has it been possible to find the famous phrase, "I want to be alone". What one can find, in abundance, later on, is "Why don't you let me alone?" and even "I want to be left alone", but neither is redolent of any more exotic order of being than a harassed celebrity. Yet the world prefers to believe the mythical and much more mysterious catch phrase utterance.'

What complicates the issue is that Garbo herself *did* employ the line several times on the screen. For example, in the 1929 silent film *The Single Standard* she gives the brush-off to a stranger and the subtitle declares: 'I am walking alone because I want to be alone.' And, as the ageing ballerina who loses her nerve and flees back to her suite in *Grand Hotel* (1932), she actually *speaks* it. Walker calls this 'an excellent example of art borrowing its effects from a myth that was reality for millions of people'.

The phrase was obviously well established by 1932 when the impressionist Florence Desmond spoke it on record in her sketch 'The Hollywood Party'. In 1935 Groucho Marx uttered it in *A Night at the Opera*. Then Garbo said, 'Go to bed, little father. We want to be alone,' in *Ninotchka* (1939). So it is not surprising that the myth has taken such a firm hold, and particularly since Garbo became a virtual recluse for the second half of her life.

1 I think I go home.

At one time, 'I tink I go home', spoken in a would-be Swedish accent, was as much part of the impressionist's view of Garbo as 'I want to be alone'. A caricatured Garbo was shown hugging Mickey Mouse in a cartoon film in the 1930s. She said, 'Ah tahnk ah kees you now' and 'Ah tink ah go home.' One version of how the line came to be spoken is told by Norman Zierold in *Moguls* (1969): 'After such films as *The Torrent* and *Flesh and the Devil*, Garbo decided to exploit her box-office power and asked Louis B. Mayer for a raise – from three hundred and fifty to five thousand dollars a week. Mayer offered her twenty-five hundred. "I tank I go home," said Garbo. She went back to her hotel and stayed there for a full seven months until Mayer finally gave way.'

Alexander Walker in *Garbo* (1980) recalls, rather, what Sven-Hugo Borg, the actress's interpreter, said of the time in 1926 when Mauritz Stiller, who had come with her from Sweden, was fired from directing *The Temptress*: 'She was tired, terrified and lost ... as she returned to my side after a trying scene, she sank down beside me and said so low it was almost a whisper, "Borg, I think I shall go home now. It isn't worth it, is it?"'

Walker comments: 'That catchphrase, shortened into "I think I go home", soon passed into the repertoire of a legion of Garbo-imitators and helped publicize her strong-willed temperament.'

GARCÍA LORCA, Frederico

Spanish poet (1899–1936)

2 Bullfight critics row on row
Crowd the vast arena full
But only one man's there who knows
And he's the man who fights the bull.

RQ (1989) reports that President Kennedy was fond of quoting these lines and attributing them thus, but adds that they are believed not to be by Lorca. The true source remains untraced.

GARDNER, Ava

American actress (1922–90)

3 *On the Beach* is a story about the end of the world, and Melbourne sure is the right place to film it.

Attributed remark (1959). As revealed, however, by *The Dictionary of Australian Quotations* (1984), it was in fact an invention of a Melbourne journalist, Neil Jillett (1933–). The manufacturing was recounted in the *Age* (Melbourne) of 14 January 1982.

GARDNER, Ed

American broadcaster (1901–63)

4 Opera is when a guy gets stabbed in the back and instead of bleeding he sings.

In the 1940s radio show *Duffy's Tavern*, quoted in *The Frank Muir Book* (1976). Has also been ascribed to Robert Benchley.

GARDNER, John W.

American government official (1912–)

5 As I said in another connection: 'An excellent plumber is infinitely more admirable than an incompetent philosopher. The society which scorns excellence in plumbing because plumbing is a humble activity and tolerates shoddiness in philosophy because it is an exalted activity will have neither good plumbing nor good philosophy. Neither its pipes nor its theories will hold water.'

Excellence: Can We Be Equal and Excellent Too? (1961): The alliterative comparison between the two professions is fairly commonplace. Maynard Keynes said that 'economists should not be regarded as philosophers, telling us the meaning of life, or even as doctors, laying down rules for healthy living, but as plumbers, who could fix things within their competence' – unverified, but quoted in the *Financial Times* (30 December 1991); 'Of course, this tends to downgrade the ambitions and claims of the advertisers; they are capitalism's plumbers rather than its philosophers' – *The Sunday Times* (17 June 1990).

GARFIELD, James A.

American Republican 20th President (1831–81)

6 My fellow citizens, the President is dead, but the government lives and God omnipotent reigns.

Speech, New York (15 April 1865) on Lincoln's assassination, when Garfield was a Congressman. Apparently, he was attempting to calm down a panicky New York crowd. Burke A. Hunsdale, *President Garfield and Education* (1882) has a different version: 'Fellow citizens! God reigns, and the Government at Washington still lives!' Garfield was himself assassinated the year he became President, in 1881.

1 From Log Cabin to White House.

Title of a biography (1881) of Garfield by the Rev. William Thayer. Earlier Presidents, such as Henry Harrison and Abraham Lincoln, had used their log-cabin origins as a prop in their campaigns. Subsequently, most presidential aspirants have sought a humble 'log cabin' substitute to help them on their way.

GARNER, John Nance

American Democratic Vice-President (1868–1967)

2 [The Vice-Presidency] isn't worth a pitcher of warm piss.

Usually bowdlerized to 'warm spit', as apparently it was by the first journalist who reported it and (invariably) by Alistair Cooke. Garner was Vice-President (1933–41) during F.D. Roosevelt's first two terms. Furthermore, Garner said, in 1963, that the job 'didn't amount to a hill of beans'.

Theo Lippman Jr in the *San Francisco Chronicle* (25 December 1992) provided this further Garner story: he was walking down the halls of the Capitol one day when the circus was in Washington. A fellow came up to him and introduced himself. 'I am the head clown in the circus,' he said. Very solemnly, Garner replied, 'And I am the Vice-President of the United States. You'd better stick around here a while. You might pick up some new ideas.'

GARRICK, David

English actor (1717–79)

3 Any fool can play tragedy, but comedy, sir, is a damned serious business.

Attributed, and in the form 'Comedy is a very serious thing', in conversation with the actor Jack Bannister. Hence, *A Damned Serious Business*, title of the later memoirs (1990) of Sir Rex Harrison, who does not, however, give a source for the observation. *Compare* GWENN 275:7.

GARROD, Heathcote William

English academic (1878–1960)

4 Madam, I am the civilization they are fighting to defend.

On being asked why he was not fighting to defend civilization in the First World War. Attributed by Dacre Balsdon in *Oxford Then and Now* (1970).

GASKELL, Elizabeth

English novelist and biographer (1810–65)

5 Miss Matty picked up her peas, one by one, on the point of the prongs ... Miss Pole sighed over her delicate young peas as she left them on one side of her plate untasted, for they *would* drop between the prongs. I looked at my host: the peas were going wholesale into his capacious mouth, shovelled up by his large round-ended knife. I saw, I imitated, I survived!

Cranford, Chap. 4 (1851–3). Describing a question of etiquette: how to eat green peas with only two-pronged forks.

GAUTIER, Théophile

French poet and novelist (1811–72)

6 The cat is a dilettante in fur.

Unverified. Christabel Aberconway's *Dictionary of Cat Lovers* (1950) contains the story of Gautier's cat Madame-Théophile which loved music but, 'high notes made her nervous, and she never failed to close the singer's mouth with her paw if the lady sang the high A. We used to try the experiment for the fun of the thing, and it never failed once. It was quite impossible to fool my dilettante cat on that note.' The story comes from his *Ménagerie intime* (1869) where the original French is, '*Il était impossible de tromper sur la note cette chatte dilettante.*' Then in Ruthven Tremain's *Animals' Who's Who* (1982), the same story appears somewhat condensed, with the text: 'At the high A she never failed to close the mouth of the singer with her soft paw ... [Those who tested her by hitting the note learned that] the dilettante in fur was not to be deceived.' So perhaps the 'fur' was an embellishment by one of the later re-tellers of the story.

GAVARNI, Paul

French caricaturist and illustrator (1801–66)

7 *Les enfants terribles.*
The terrible children.

Title of series of prints (1842). Subsequently the title of a novel (1929) by Jean Cocteau.

GAY, John

English poet and playwright (1685–1732)

1 A miss for pleasure, and a wife for breed.

'The Toilette' (1716). *Compare* BURTON 134:7.

2 Life is a jest, and all things show it;
I thought so once; and now I know it.

The couplet forms part of the inscription on the pedestal of Gay's monument in Westminster Abbey. The lines were written by Gay himself as 'My Epitaph' (1720).

3 It made Gay rich and Rich gay.

A popular view of *The Beggar's Opera*, first performed in London in 1728, expressed by Anon. Quoted in Samuel Johnson, 'John Gay', *Lives of the English Poets* (1779–81). The 'opera' was written by Gay and produced by John Rich, the manager of Covent Garden.

GEDDES, Sir Eric

British Conservative politician (1875–1937)

4 The Germans, if this Government is returned, are going to pay every penny; they are going to be squeezed as a lemon is squeezed – until the pips squeak. My only doubt is not whether we can squeeze hard enough, but whether there is enough juice.

Calls for reparations or 'indemnities' at the end of the First World War were fierce. Geddes, who had lately been First Lord of the Admiralty, said this in an electioneering speech at the Beaconsfield Club, Cambridge (10 December 1918). The previous night at the Guildhall, Cambridge, he had said the same thing in a slightly different way as part of what was obviously a stump speech: 'I have personally no doubt we will get everything out of her that you can squeeze out of a lemon and a bit more ... I will squeeze her until you can hear the pips squeak ... I would strip Germany as she has stripped Belgium.'

The slang term 'pip-squeak' for an insignificant, little person was current before this (by 1910). In the First World War it was also the name given to a high velocity German shell which made the noise in flight. Presumably Geddes constructed his idiom out of these elements. *See also* HEALEY 286:3.

GELDOF, Bob

Irish singer and songwriter (1954–)

5 Most people get into bands for three very simple rock and roll reasons: to get laid, to get fame, and to get rich.

In his autobiography *Is That It?* (1986), Geldof commented on the differences between his own band, the Boom Town Rats, and other punk outfits. One was that the Rats did not mind success: 'This was not what punk bands were supposed to do. They were certainly not supposed to delight in it. I continually annoyed the purists by saying in interviews, as I had done ever since the early days in Dublin, that what I wanted out of pop music was to get rich, get famous and get laid.' The above is an example from *Melody Maker* (27 August 1977).

6 I don't like Mondays.

Title of a hit song written and performed by Geldof and the Boom Town Rats (1979), derived from the excuse given by Brenda Spencer, a San Diego schoolgirl, for opening fire and killing an elementary school principal and a custodian, and wounding nine others in January 1979. A journalist rang her up and asked her why she was doing it and she replied, 'Something to do. I don't like Mondays.'

7 Do they know it's Christmas?

Title of a song written by Bob Geldof and Midge Ure in 1984. Performed by Band Aid – an ad hoc group of pop singers and musicians – it became the UK Christmas No. 1 record in 1984 and again in 1989. In 1984, by drawing attention to those suffering in the Ethiopian civil war and famine, it gave rise to the Band Aid concert in July 1985.

GENNEP, Arnold van

French ethnographer (1927–)

8 *Rites de passage*
Rites of Passage

Title of a book (1909) about the transitional stages through which man passes between birth and death. The most notable rite of passage is probably some experience (maybe of a ritual nature) that a boy has to go through before achieving manhood. It might have to do with a demonstration of his physical skills or involve some confirmation of his sexual maturity.

The concept is now well known, especially as the name given to a genre of films. From *Flicks* Magazine

(April 1994): 'Brad Pitt and Craig Sheffer play Paul and Norman in Robert Redford's *A River Runs Through It*, a nostalgic "rites of passage" drama ... it's only when they're fishing that they find the true harmony that eludes them elsewhere.'

Rites of Passage was the title of a novel (1980) by William Golding.

GEORGE II

British King (1683–1760)

1 Mad is he? Then I hope he will *bite* some of my other generals.

Replying to the Duke of Newcastle who had said that General Wolfe was a madman. Quoted in Henry Beckles Wilson, *The Life and Letters of James Wolfe* (1909).

GEORGE V

British King (1865–1936)

2 Wake up England!

In a speech at the Guildhall, London (5 December 1901) – four days before he was created Prince of Wales – the then Duke of York, on returning from an Empire tour, warned against taking the Empire for granted: 'To the distinguished representatives of the commercial interests of the Empire ... I venture to allude to the impression which seemed generally to prevail among our brethren overseas, that the old country must wake up if she intends to maintain her old position of pre-eminence in her Colonial trade against foreign competitors.' This statement was encapsulated by the popular press in the phrase 'Wake up, England!' which George did not precisely say himself. *Punch* was still using the phrase the following year (Vol. 123).

3 Today, 23 years ago, dear Grandmama died. I wonder what she would have thought of a Labour Government.

Diary entry for 22 January 1924. He had just asked Ramsay MacDonald to form the first Labour government.

4 My father was frightened of his mother, I was frightened of my father, and I'm damned well going to make sure that my children are frightened of me.

Quoted in Randolph Churchill, *Life of the Earl of Derby* (1959). Doubt has been cast on the likelihood of George V saying this.

5 Never miss an opportunity to relieve yourself; never miss a chance to sit down and rest your feet.

In *A King's Story* (1951), George's son and heir (who became the Duke of Windsor) wrote: 'Perhaps one of the only positive pieces of advice that I was ever given was that supplied by an old courtier who observed: "Only two rules really count. Never miss an opportunity to relieve yourself; never miss a chance to sit down and rest your feet".' The 'old courtier' may well in fact have been George V himself, to whom this advice has also been attributed directly. A correspondent who wished to remain anonymous told me in 1981 that a naval officer of her acquaintance who was about to accompany Prince George, Duke of Kent, on a cruise, was asked by George V to make sure that the Prince was properly dressed before going ashore. He also advised: 'Always take an opportunity to relieve yourselves.' Another correspondent suggested, rather, that King Edward VII had been the first to say this when he was Prince of Wales.

On the other hand, more than a century earlier, the 1st Duke of Wellington had said: 'Always make water when you can.'

6 Bugger Bognor!

What the King said in reply to a suggestion that his favourite watering place be dubbed Bognor Regis (*c.*1929). They are not his dying words, as often supposed – for example by Auberon Waugh in his *Private Eye* diary entry (9 August 1975) which stated: 'Shortly before the King died, a sycophantic courtier said he was looking so much better he should soon be well enough for another visit to Bognor, to which the old brute replied "Bugger Bognor" and expired.'

The dating is given by Kenneth Rose in his biography *George V* (1983) where it is linked to the King's recuperative visit to Bognor after his serious illness in the winter of 1928–9: 'A happier version of the legend rests on the authority of Sir Owen Morshead, the King's librarian. As the time of the King's departure from Bognor drew near, a deputation of leading citizens came to ask that their salubrious town should henceforth be known as Bognor Regis.

'They were received by Stamfordham, the King's private secretary, who, having heard their petition, invited them to wait while he consulted the King in another room. The sovereign responded with the celebrated obscenity, which Stamfordham deftly translated for the benefit of the delegation. His Majesty, they were told, would be graciously pleased to grant their request.'

1 No more coals to Newcastle, no more Hoares to Paris.

A rare example of a royal joke comes from the period just before George V's death. In December 1935, it was revealed that Sir Samuel Hoare, the Foreign Secretary, had come to an arrangement with Pierre Laval, his French counterpart, whereby Abyssinia was virtually to be consigned to the Italians behind the League of Nations' back. The Hoare-Laval Pact had been concluded in Paris when Sir Samuel was passing through on his way to a holiday in Switzerland. In the furore that followed he had to resign. The King may have been repeating a remark that was current anyway and it is surely unlikely that he made it direct to Hoare himself, despite Lord Avon's recollection of what the King told him (in *Facing the Dictators*, 1962).

2 How is the Empire?

This is the leading contender for the King's *actual* last, dying words. But, oddly enough, there are several others. On Monday 20 January 1936, a few members of the Privy Council gathered in the King's bedroom at Sandringham to witness the signing of a proclamation constituting a Council of State. The King was so weak it took a long time. To the Privy Councillors he murmured: 'Gentlemen, I am sorry for keeping you waiting like this – I am unable to concentrate.' These are sometimes given as his last words (in Barnaby Conrad, *Famous Last Words*, 1961, for example).

The King died just before midnight. The next day, Stanley Baldwin, the Prime Minister, broadcast a tribute which included a different version of the deathbed words: 'There is one thing I can tell you without any impropriety, for though much, and most indeed, of what passes near the end is sacred ... I think I may tell you this. The King was having brief intervals of consciousness, and each time he became conscious it was some kind enquiry or kind observation of someone, some words of gratitude for kindness shown. But he did say to his Secretary [Lord Wigram] when he sent for him, "How is the Empire?" – an unusual phrase in that form. And the Secretary said: "All is well, sir, with the Empire," and the King gave him a smile and relapsed once more into unconsciousness.'

Other accounts make it clear that the wonderfully imperial inquiry arose *before* the Privy Council meeting. One of them suggests that only the word 'Empire' was audible and the rest merely assumed by the King's Secretary. Lord Dawson, the King's physician, reported in his diary yet another version of the last words: 'God damn you.' Could this possibly relate to Margot Asquith's celebrated dictum? (62:8). *See also* DAWSON 197:5.

GEORGE VI

British King (1895–1952)

3 Abroad is bloody.

Quoted in W.H. Auden, *A Certain World* (1970). *Compare* MITFORD 395:1.

4 We're not a family; we're a firm.

Quoted in Peter Lane, *Our Future King* (untraced).

See also HASKINS 284:1; LINCOLN 356:2.

GEORGE, David Lloyd (later 1st Earl Lloyd George of Dwyfor)

British Liberal Prime Minister (1863–1945)

5 This is the leal and trusty mastiff which is to watch over our interests, but which runs away at the first snarl of the trade unions? A mastiff? It is the right hon. Gentleman's Poodle. It fetches and carries for him. It barks for him. It bites anybody that he sets it on to.

Lloyd George spoke in the House of Commons on 26 June 1907 in the controversy over the power of the upper House. He questioned the House of Lords' role as a 'watchdog' of the constitution and suggested that A.J. Balfour, the Conservative leader, was using the party's majority in the upper chamber to block legislation by the Liberal government (in which Lloyd George was president of the Board of Trade). As such it is encapsulated in the phrase 'Mr Balfour's poodle'.

6 Ninepence for fourpence.

A political slogan dating from 1908–9 when the Welfare State was being established in Britain. The phrase indicated how people stood to benefit from their contributions to the new National Health Insurance scheme. Associated with Lloyd George and said by A.J.P. Taylor (in *Essays in English History*) to have been snapped up from an audience interruption and turned into a slogan by him.

7 Sporting terms are pretty well understood wherever English is spoken .... Well, then. The British soldier is a good sportsman ... Germany elected to make this a finish fight with England ... The fight must be to a finish – to a knock out.

As Secretary of State for War, Lloyd George gave an interview to Roy W. Harris, President of the United Press of America. It was printed in *The Times* (29

September 1915). Lloyd George was asked to 'give the United Press, in the simplest possible language, the British attitude toward the recent peace talk'. Hence, the particular form of the above remarks. In his memoirs, Lloyd George entitled one chapter 'The Knockout Blow' – which is how this notion came to be popularly expressed.

1 What is our task? To make Britain a fit country for heroes to live in.

This is precisely what Lloyd George said in a speech at Wolverhampton (24 November 1918). It turned into the better known slogan 'A land fit for heroes' or, occasionally, 'A country fit for heroes.' By 1921, with wages falling in all industries, the sentiment was frequently recalled and mocked.

2 The world is becoming like a lunatic asylum run by lunatics.

In *The Observer* (8 January 1933). *See also* STALLINGS 515:6.

3 A good mayor of Birmingham in an off-year.

On Neville Chamberlain (who came to national politics after long experience in local government). Quoted in A.J.P. Taylor, *English History 1914–1945* (1965). Also, in the form: 'He might make an adequate Lord Mayor of Birmingham in a lean year', quoted in Leon Harris, *The Fine Art of Political Wit* (1965). In *Future Indefinite* (1954), Noël Coward ascribes to Lord Birkenhead (F.E. Smith), 'The most we can hope for from dear Neville is that he should be a good Lord Mayor of Birmingham in a lean year.'

Also attributed (and possibly more correctly) to Lord Hugh Cecil in the form 'He is no better than a Mayor of Birmingham, and in a lean year at that. Furthermore he is too old. He thinks he understands the modern world. What should an old hunk like him know of the modern world?' Quoted in Lord David Cecil, *The Cecils of Hatfield House* (1973).

4 Simon has sat on the fence so long that the iron has entered into his soul.

On Sir John Simon who had been Attorney-General and Home Secretary in Asquith's Liberal government but had resigned by the time Lloyd George became PM in 1916. He formed a division of the Liberal Party in the 1920s which Lloyd George scorned. Quoted in A.J.P. Taylor, *English History 1914–1945* (1965). Alluding to BIBLE 115:8.

5 When they circumcised Herbert Samuel they threw away the wrong bit.

Attributed by John Grigg in *The Listener* (7 September 1978). Samuel was a prominent Jewish Liberal politician around the time of the First World War.

6 He was brilliant to the top of his army boots.

On Sir Douglas Haig. Attributed. Haig became commander-in-chief of British forces during the First World War and had to contend with Lloyd George's distrust of him and the Prime Minister's desire to control strategy himself.

7 Lloyd George knew my father.

Even before Lloyd George's death in 1945, Welsh people away from home liked to claim some affinity with the Great Man. In time, this inclination was encapsulated in the singing of the words 'Lloyd George knew my father, my father knew Lloyd George' to the strains of 'Onward Christian Soldiers', which they neatly fit. In Welsh legal and Liberal circles the credit for this happy coinage has been given to Tommy Rhys Roberts QC (1910–75), whose father did indeed know Lloyd George. Arthur Rhys Roberts was a Newport solicitor who set up a London practice with Lloyd George in 1897. The partnership continued for many years, although on two occasions Lloyd George's political activities caused them to lose practically all their clients.

The junior Rhys Roberts was a gourmet, a wine-bibber and of enormous girth. Martin Thomas QC, a prominent Welsh liberal of the next generation, recalled (1984): 'It was, and is a tradition of the Welsh circuit that there should be, following the after-dinner speeches, a full-blooded sing-song. For as long as anyone can remember, Rhys Roberts's set-piece was to sing the phrase to the tune of "Onward Christian Soldiers" – it is widely believed that he started the practice ... By the 'fifties it had certainly entered the repertoire of Welsh Rugby Clubs. In the 'sixties, it became customary for Welsh Liberals to hold a Noson Lawen, or sing-song, on the Friday night of the Liberal Assemblies. It became thoroughly adopted in the party. I recall it as being strikingly daring and new in the late 'sixties for Young Liberals to sing the so-called second verse, "Lloyd George knew my mother". William Douglas-Home's play *Lloyd George Knew My Father* was produced in London in 1972. One of the leading Welsh Silks recalls persuading Rhys Roberts to see it with him.'

From Robert Robinson, *Landscape with Dead Dons* (1956): 'He had displayed a massive indifference to the rollicking scientists who would strike up *Lloyd George Knew My Father* in a spirit of abandoned wickedness.'

GERASIMOV, Gennady

Russian official spokesman (1935–)

1 We now have the 'Frank Sinatra Doctrine'. He had a song 'I Had It My Way' [*sic*]. So every country decides on its own which road to take.

Explaining the Kremlin's attitude to the breaking up of Communist eastern Europe, as Soviet Foreign Ministry spokesman. Remark made on American TV (25 October 1989).

GERSHWIN, Ira

American lyricist (1896–1983)

2 Someone To Watch Over Me.

Title of song, *Oh! Kay* (1926). Music by George Gershwin, as in all the following. Hence, *Someone To Watch Over Me*, title of film (US, 1987) about a bodyguard who falls for the woman he is minding.

3 I Got Plenty o' Nuthin'.

Title of song, *Porgy and Bess* (1935), written 'in collaboration with DuBose Heyward'. As Gershwin noted in his book *Lyrics on Several Occasions* (1959) this was one of the many poems by Dubose Heyward, the original author of *Porgy*, that was set to music in the opera. The collaboration extended to the other quotable songs from the opera.

4 They all laughed at Christopher Columbus
When he said the world was round;
They all laughed when Edison recorded
sound.

Song, 'They All Laughed' in *Shall We Dance* (1937). Said by Ira to have been inspired by the advertisement slogan 'They Laughed When I Sat Down At the Piano, But When I Started to Play ...' (for US School of Music piano tutor, from 1925).

GETTY, J. Paul

American oil tycoon (1892–1976)

5 I have fourteen other grandchildren and if I pay one penny now, then I'll have fourteen kidnapped grandchildren.

Explaining why he refused to pay ransom money to secure the release of his grandson (26 July 1973). Unverified. Andrew Barrow, *International Gossip* (1983) has a different version: 'I have fourteen other grandchildren. If I paid out a brass farthing for one I would have fourteen kidnapped grandchildren.'

6 The meek shall inherit the earth, but not the mineral rights.

Attributed, by 1981. Untraced. Compare F.E. Smith, 'Marquess Curzon', *Contemporary Personalities* (1924): 'We have the highest authority for believing that the meek shall inherit the earth; though I have never found any particular corroboration of this aphorism in the records of Somerset House' [once the depository for British wills and testaments]. Both alluding to Christ's sermon on the mount, St Matthew 5:5: 'Blessed are the meek: for they shall inherit the earth.'

7 If you can actually count your money, you are not really a rich man.

Quoted in Andrew Barrow, *Gossip* (1978). *Compare* MORGAN 398:4.

8 I want my lunch.

Last words. Quoted by Jean Rook in the *Daily Express* (9 June 1976), but otherwise unverified.

GIBBON, Edward

English historian (1737–94)

9 Such was the public consternation when the barbarians were hourly expected at the gates of Rome.

Nowadays, the phrase 'barbarians at the gates' is commonly used to describe a situation when the end of civilization is alleged to be at hand. In 1990 it was used as the title of a book about goings-on in Wall Street (subtitled 'The Fall of RJR Nabisco', by Bryan Burrough), suggesting that unregulated behaviour had broken out. It is just one of those ideas which seems always to have been there, but there is a good example (as above) in Bk 1 of Gibbon's *Decline and Fall of the Roman Empire* (1776–88). From *The Sunday Times* (19 June 1988): 'The ragbag, pseudo-scholarship on display here suggests that the barbarians are not at the gate, they are sitting in the professors' chairs.'

10 Twenty-two acknowledged concubines, and a library of sixty-two thousand volumes, attested the variety of his inclinations, and from the productions which he left behind him, it appears that the former as well as the latter were designed for use rather than ostentation.

Ib., Chap. 7. An example of Gibbon's stony-faced

sense of humour, on the Emperor Gordian. In a footnote, Gibbon adds: 'By each of his concubines, the younger Gordian left three or four children. His literary productions were by no means contemptible.'

1 After a powerful struggle, I yielded to my fate. I sighed as a lover, I obeyed as a son.

From *Memoirs of My Life and Writings*, Chap. 4, note, (1796). As a young man, Gibbon fell for Mlle Suzanne Curchod (later the wife of Jacques Necker, the French statesman) at Lausanne, Switzerland, in 1757. But he did not get married to her because of his father's objections. Possible sources for Gibbon's phrase have been found in Corneille's *Polyeucte*, '*J'en aurais soupiré, mais j'aurai obéi*' and, less plausibly, in Dryden's *Aureng-Zebe*, 'I to a Son's and Lover's praise aspire' (source: *Notes and Queries*, Vol. 234).

2 It was at Rome, on the fifteenth of October, 1764, as I sat musing amidst the ruins of the Capitol, while the barefoot friars were singing vespers in the Temple of Jupiter, that the idea of writing the decline and fall of the city first started to my mind.

Ib., Chap 6, note. On beginning his most famous history. In Chap. 8, with equal poignancy, Gibbon describes its completion: 'I will not dissemble the first emotions of joy on the recovery of my freedom, and, perhaps, the establishment of my fame. But my pride was soon humbled, and a sober melancholy was spread over my mind, by the idea that I had taken an everlasting leave of an old and agreeable companion.'

GIBBONS, Stella

English novelist (1902–89)

3 Something nasty in the woodshed.

Cold Comfort Farm (1933), *passim*. Hence, the phrase for any unnamed unpleasantness. In the novel, the phrase is used to refer to a traumatic experience in someone's background, e.g., from Chap. 10: 'When you were very small ... you had seen something nasty in the woodshed.' Hence, from Beryl Bainbridge's novel *Another Part of the Wood* (1968): 'They had all, Joseph, brother Trevor, the younger sister ... come across something nasty in the woodshed, mother or father or both, having it off with someone else.' Kyril Bonfiglioli entitled a novel *Something Nasty in the Woodshed* (1976).

GIBBS, Wolcott

American writer (1902–58)

4 Backward ran sentences until reeled the mind.

Parody of *Time* Magazine style in *More in Sorrow* (1958), which concludes with: 'Where it will all end, knows God.'

GIDE, André

French writer (1869–1951)

5 *Hugo – hélas!*
Hugo – alas!

On being asked to name the greatest poet of the 19th century. In *André Gide-Paul Valéry Correspondance 1890–1942*.

GILBERT, Fred

British composer and singer (1849–1903)

6 As I walk along the Bois de Boulogne with an independent air.

Song 'The Man Who Broke the Bank in Monte Carlo' (1900, though first performed by Charles Coborn in 1891). Hence, *With an Independent Air*, title of the autobiography (1977) of Howard Thomas, the British broadcasting executive and early participant in Independent Television.

GILBERT, Sir Humphrey

English navigator (1537–83)

7 We are as near to Heaven by sea as by land!

Quoted in Richard Hakluyt, *Third and Last Volume of the Voyages ... of the English Nation* (1600). Gilbert's ship sank on his return from Newfoundland where he had founded an English colony at St John's. He said this to put heart into his men as their ship *Squirrel* foundered. Compare what Friar Elstow is reported to have said when threatened with drowning by Henry VIII: 'With thanks to God we know the way to heaven, to be as ready by water as by land, and therefore we care not which way we go' (recounted by John Stow, *The Annals of England*, but not until 1615).

GILBERT, (Sir) W.S.

English writer and lyricist (1836–1911)

8 She may very well pass for forty-three
In the dusk with a light behind her!

Trial by Jury (1875). Music by Sir Arthur Sullivan, as for all the following. Ian Bradley writes in *The Annotated Gilbert and Sullivan*, Vol. 2 (1984): 'Gilbert had a thing about women in their forties. Poor Ruth in *The Pirates of Penzance* is mocked by Frederic for being forty-seven ... while Marco is warned by Gianetta in *The Gondoliers* not to address any lady less than forty-five.

1 I pray you, pardon me, ex-Pirate King,
Peers will be peers, and youth must have its fling

Ib. The proverb 'youth must have its fling', meaning 'let the young enjoy themselves while they can', also appears in Gilbert's lyrics for *The Mikado* (1885): 'But youth, of course, must have its fling'. Gilbert greatly enjoyed proverbs and, indeed, wrote two songs completely made up of them. In this instance, he appears to have created a more memorable version of the older proverbs 'Youth will have his course' (known from the sixteenth century) and 'Youth will be served' (though this latter did not appear until the early nineteenth century). In *The Water Babies* (1863), Charles Kingsley has:

When all the world is young lad
And all the trees are green:
... Young blood must have its course, lad
And every dog his day.

John Ray's *Compleat Collection of English Proverbs* (1670) has 'Youth will have its swing' (as a version of 'youth will have its course'), which means much the same as 'fling'.

2 Now Bach is decomposing.

In the archaeology of humour one is never really going to know who first cracked a joke. Nevertheless, as it can be dated, why not allow Gilbert to claim credit for originating a famous exchange? On a visit to the United States with Sullivan in 1879–80, Gilbert was told by a matron at a dinner party, 'Your friend Mr Sullivan's music is really too delightful. It reminds me so much of dear Baytch [Bach]. Do tell me: what is Baytch doing just now? Is he still composing?'

'Well, no, madam,' Gilbert returned, 'just now, as a matter of fact, dear Baytch is by way of decomposing.' This, at any rate, is how the joke appears in *Gilbert and Sullivan* by Hesketh Pearson (1947).

3 I can trace my ancestry back to a protoplasmal primordial atomic globule. Consequently, my family pride is something in-conceivable. I can't help it. I was born sneering.

The Mikado, Act 1 (1885). Spoken by Pooh-Bah, the corrupt official, who – contrary to the view of anti-evolutionists who think that such a descent is undignified – glories in it.

4 To sit in solemn silence in a dull, dark, dock,
In a pestilential prison, with a life-long lock,
Awaiting the sensation of a short, sharp, shock,
From a cheap and chippy chopper on a big black block.

Ib., Act 1. Other use: in a speech at the Conservative Party Conference (10 October 1979), William Whitelaw, as Home Secretary, outlined a new method of hard treatment for young offenders. They were to be given 'a short, sharp shock'. This expression had apparently been used by other Home Secretaries before him, however. Hence, *A Short Sharp Shock*, title of a play (1980) by Howard Brenton and Tony Howard (originally called *Ditch the Bitch*, referring to Margaret Thatcher).

5 Are you old enough to marry, do you think?
Won't you wait till you are eighty in the shade?

Ib., Act 2. Ko-Ko asks Katisha. There is also a song 'Charming Weather' in Lionel Monckton's *The Arcadians* (1908) with the lines, 'Very, very warm for May/Eighty in the shade they say,/Just fancy!' 'Eighty in the shade' is otherwise no more than a catchphrase used to express extreme temperature.

6 When I am lying awake at night, and the pale moonlight streams through the latticed casement, strange fancies crowd upon my poor mad brain, and I sometimes think that if we could hit upon some word for you to use whenever I am about to relapse – some word that teems with hidden meaning – like 'Basingstoke' – it might recall me to my saner self.

So says the character Mad Margaret in *Ruddigore* (1887). The mention of the place still raises a laugh, being one of those English names which, from sound alone, is irresistibly funny. Others would include Chipping Sodbury, Godalming, Scunthorpe, Wigan and Surbiton. More recently Neasden has joined the select band. However, it has been suggested that the modest Hampshire town had another claim upon the laughter of the original *Ruddigore* audience. Possibly the Conservative Party had recently held its annual conference there? Ian Bradley in his *Annotated Gilbert and Sullivan: 2* (1984) makes no mention of this theory and dismisses a suggestion that it was because

Basingstoke had a well-known mental hospital, on the grounds that this had not been built in 1887. He relays another theory that Gilbert's father had featured the town in his novel *The Doctor of Beauvoir*, and that his father and sister lived in Salisbury, which would have necessitated his passing through Basingstoke when paying visits.

A magazine called *Figaro* reporting on rehearsals for *Ruddigore* in December 1886 made mention of a character called Mad Margaret 'with that blessed word Barnstaple' – which suggests that Basingstoke was not Gilbert's first choice.

Basingstoke had already rated a mention in Shakespeare (*Henry IV, Part 2*, II.i.169), but with rather less comic result.

1 In a contemplative fashion,
And a tranquil frame of mind,
Free from every kind of passion,
Some solution let us find.
Let us grasp the situation,
Solve the complicated plot –
Quiet, calm deliberation
Disentangles every knot.

The Gondoliers, Act 2. When Harold Macmillan was Prime Minister (1957–63) he wrote this out in longhand as a motto for his Private Office and the Cabinet Room when at 10 Downing Street.

2 Funny without being vulgar.

A Quaker singer, David Bispham, noted in his *Recollections* (1920) that he had heard Gilbert say something like this to Sir Henry Beerbohm Tree about his Hamlet. On the stage of the Haymarket Theatre, London, after the first performance, Gilbert said: 'My dear fellow, I never saw anything so funny in my life, and yet it was not in the least vulgar.'

At the time, the line quickly went round in its abbreviated form, and apparently Tree put up a brave show of not being offended. He wrote to Gilbert on 25 March 1893:

'By the bye, my wife told me that you were under the impression that I might have been offended at some witticism of yours about my Hamlet. Let me assure you it was not so. On the contrary, it was I believe *I* who circulated the story. There could be no harm, as I knew you had not seen me act the part, and moreover, while I am a great admirer of your wit, I have also too high an opinion of my work to be hurt by it'.

Hesketh Pearson in his 1956 biography of Tree seems to think this letter shows the actor claiming not only to have circulated the story against himself but to have *invented* it. On the other hand, Pearson in his biography of Gilbert and Sullivan does report that Bernard Shaw told him that Gilbert complained shortly before his death (1911) of the way ill-natured witticisms had been fathered on him and instanced the description of Tree. There seems little doubt, though, that he did say it.

Shaw himself had used the phrase in a review of pantomime in *London Music* on 23 January 1897: 'Pray understand that I do not want the pantomime artists to be "funny without being vulgar". That is the mere snobbery of criticism. Every comedian should have vulgarity at his fingers' ends.'

J.B. Booth, in *Old Pink 'Un Days* (1924), recalled an exchange in a London theatre after Pavlova's successes when a large lady from Oldham or Wigan was attempting to pass herself off as a Russian dancer. 'What do you think of her?' asked one. Came the reply, 'Funny without being Volga.'

3 Sir, Saturday morning, although recurring at regular and well-foreseen intervals, always seems to take this railway by surprise.

From a letter to the station master at Baker Street station, London, on the Metropolitan Line. Quoted in John Julius Norwich, *A Christmas Cracker* (1973).

GILL, Eric

English sculptor, engraver and typographer (1882–1940)

4 Trousers and the Most Precious Ornament.

Title of book (1937). According to Fiona McCarthy, *Eric Gill* (1989), it is, 'A grand defence of male supremacy, a plea for the reconsideration of the penis, tucked away into men's trousers, "all sideways, dishonoured, neglected, ridiculed and ridiculous – no longer the virile member". The dishonoured penis was a terrible indictment of the world's lost potency, the onset of commercialization and destructiveness. In their craziness and funniness Gill's penis-power writings remind one of the cunt-power movement of the 1970s. This is Eric Gill in pursuit of Germaine Greer.'

GILLIATT, Penelope

British writer and critic (1933–93)

5 One of the most characteristic sounds of the English Sunday is the sound of Harold Hobson barking up the wrong tree.

Encore (November-December 1959). Hobson was for many years drama critic of *The Sunday Times*.

6 Sunday Bloody Sunday.

Title of film (1971) for which she wrote the screenplay In 1983, the Irish group U2 had a song with the title 'Sunday Bloody Sunday'; in 1973, the UK/US group Black Sabbath had released an album with the title *Sabbath Bloody Sabbath*. Since the nineteenth century there has been the exclamation 'Sunday, *bloody* Sunday!' to reflect frustration at the inactivity and boredom traditionally associated with the Sabbath. The term 'bloody Sunday', in the literal sense, has been applied to a number of occasions. On 13 November 1887 two men died during a baton charge on a prohibited socialist demonstration in Trafalgar Square, London. On 22 January 1905 hundreds of unarmed peasants were mown down when they marched to petition the Tsar in St Petersburg. In Irish history, there was a Bloody Sunday on 21 November 1920 when, among other incidents, fourteen undercover British intelligence agents in Dublin were shot by Sinn Fein. More recently, the name was applied to Sunday 30 January 1972 when British troops killed thirteen Catholics after a protest rally in Londonderry, Northern Ireland.

GILMOUR, Sir Ian (later Lord Gilmour)

British Conservative politician (1926–)

1 It does no harm to throw the occasional man overboard, but it does not do much good if you are steering full speed ahead for the rocks.

On being sacked as Deputy Foreign Secretary by Margaret Thatcher. Quoted in *Time* Magazine (September 1981).

GINSBERG, Allen

American poet and novelist (1926–97)

2 I saw the best minds of my generation destroyed by madness, starving hysterical
   naked,
dragging themselves through the negro streets
   at dawn looking for an angry fix,
angelheaded hipsters burning for the ancient
   heavenly connection to the starry dynamo
   in the machinery of the night.

From *Howl* (1956), a Jeremiad that has been described as the opening salvo of the Beat Generation. Ginsberg denounces the mechanistic dehumanization of a society whose God is Moloch, demanding human sacrifice.

3 Liverpool is at the present moment the centre of the consciousness of the human universe.

Attributed remark *c.*1964, when the Beatles were at their most famous. Quoted in *The Liverpool Scene*, ed. Edward Lucie-Smith (1967).

GISBORNE, Thomas

English preacher (1758–1846)

4 Turn, turn thy hasty foot aside,
Nor crush that helpless worm!
The frame thy wayward looks deride
Required a God to form.

The common lord of all that move,
From whom thy being flowed,
A portion of His boundless love
On that poor worm bestowed.

The sun, the moon, the stars, He made
For all his creatures free;
And spread o'er earth the grassy blade
For worms as well as thee.

Let them enjoy their little day,
Their humble bliss receive;
Oh I do not lightly take away
The life thou canst not give.

'The Worm' (undated). The poem appears in *The Children's Encyclopedia*, Vol 1 (1908–10). The lines 'The shape my scornful looks deride/Required a God to form' are quoted without attribution in G.K. Chesterton's novel *The Napoleon of Notting Hill* (1904).

GISCARD D'ESTAING, Valéry

French President (1926–)

5 During my seven years in office, I was in love with seventeen million French women.

Translated from *Le Pouvoir et la Vie* (1988). Giscard had the grace to concede: 'I know this declaration will inspire irony and that English language readers will find it very French.'

GLADSTONE, W.E.

British Liberal Prime Minister (1809–98)

6 The first essential for a Prime Minister is to be a good butcher.

Untraced. Quoted by Richard Nixon when interviewed (1977) by David Frost about Watergate. He was seeking to explain his reluctance to sack his aides Ehrlichman and Haldeman ... 'I suppose you could sum it all up the way one of your British Prime Ministers summed it up, Gladstone, when he said that the first requirement for a Prime Minister is to be a good butcher ... I will have to admit I was not a good butcher.' *See also* BUTLER 137:4.

1 My mission is to pacify Ireland.

On forming his first cabinet as Prime Minister (1 December 1968), according to H.C.G. Matthew, *Gladstone 1809–1874* (1986). In 1845, he had written in a letter to his wife, 'Ireland, Ireland! That cloud in the west, that coming storm, the vehicle of God's retribution.' He tried to resolve the Irish Question, but was ultimately unsuccessful in carrying a Home Rule Bill for Ireland.

2 Swimming for his life, a man does not see much of the country through which the river winds, and I probably know little of these years through which I busily work and live, beyond this, how sin and frailty deface them, and how mercy crowns them ... Farewell great year of opening, not of alarming, change: and welcome new year laden with promise and with care.

In his diary (31 December 1868). Reviewing his life at the end of a year, he blames the absorption of the political life for his missing out on other things. He also notes how important the month of December has been to him throughout his life: he was born on the 29th, became Chancellor of the Exchequer in 1853 and, this year, has just become Prime Minister for the first time.

3 When he rises to speak, he does not know what he is going to say. When he is speaking he does not know what he is saying, and when he sits down he does not know what he has said.

Of Lord Derby. Quoted in Kenneth Rose, *Superior Person* (1969). *Compare*: CHURCHILL 161:3

4 An account-book of the all-precious gift of Time.

On his diary. Quoted in John Morley's *Life of William Ewart Gladstone*, Vol.1 (1903). This was said when Gladstone was recommending to his son Herbert that he should 'keep a short journal of principal employments in each day: most valuable'. Gladstone himself kept such records every day for seventy years from June 1825. He rarely recorded opinions but made a note of every book he read and, chiefly, kept an almost minute by minute record of how he spent his time (presumably for the benefit of the Almighty).

5 Oh, William dear, if you weren't such a great man you would be a terrible bore.

Remarked *to* Gladstone by his wife Catherine. Quoted in Georgina Battiscombe, *Mrs Gladstone* (1956). Roy Jenkins in *Gladstone* (1995) describes this as 'a rarely illuminating expression of exasperated affection'.

See also ANONYMOUS 42:7.

GLASGOW, Ellen

American novelist (1874–1945)

6 In This Our Life.

Title of novel (1941, filmed US, 1942) about a neurotic girl who, according to one plot summary, 'steals her sister's husband, leaves him in the lurch, dominates her hapless family and is killed while on the run from the police'. Glasgow's novel gives no clue as to the relevance of the title, and does not even have a quotation as an epigraph, but the 'this our life' formula goes back to the sixteenth century at least. Within one scene, Shakespeare's *As You Like It* (II.i) has 'And this our life' and 'Yea, and of this our life'. Even earlier, the Preface to Thomas Cranmer's Book of Common Prayer (1549) employs the phrase 'in this our time'. So perhaps it was from some religious source? The Rev. Francis Kilvert, the diarist, used the expression 'in that her young life' on 26 March 1872. The exact phrase is in MEREDITH 390:1. It also occurs earlier in Thomas Carlyle's *Sartor Resartus* (1831): 'To me, in this our life ... which is an internecine warfare with the Time-spirit, other warfare seems questionable.' And exactly also in Thomas Heywood's poem *The Hierarchy of the Blessed Angels* (1635). All this would seem to indicate that it was just an old phrase rather than a quotation when used as the title of Glasgow's novel.

GLOUCESTER, William Henry, 1st Duke of

English Duke (1743–1805)

7 Another damned, thick, square book! Always scribble, scribble, scribble! Eh! Mr Gibbon?

Quoted in Henry Best, *Personal and Literary Memorials* (1829). Also ascribed to King George III and to a Duke of Cumberland.

GODARD, Jean-Luc

French film director (1930–)

1 *La photographie, c'est la vérité. Le cinéma: la vérité vingt-quatre fois par seconde.*
Photography is truth. And cinema is truth twenty-four times a second.

In film, *Le Petit Soldat* (France, 1960). The cinematographic version of 'the camera cannot lie'; *see* EVANS 231:2.

2 Movies should have a beginning, a middle and an end, but not necessarily in that order.

ODQ (1992) has this being said to Georges Franju and as quoted in *Time* Magazine (14 September 1981), but 'Every film should have a beginning, a middle and an end – but not necessarily in that order' was quoted in Len Deighton, *Close Up* (1972).

GODLEY, A.D.

English classicist (1856–1925)

3 What is this that roareth thus?
Can it be a motor bus?

There are many versions of Godley's macaronic, which begins thus. The *ODQ* (1992), which prints only part of it, gives the source as a letter Godley sent to C.R.L. Fletcher on 10 January 1914, reprinted in *Reliquiae* (1926). The magazine *Oxford Today* (Michaelmas 1992) took the trouble to find a complete, definitive version:

What is this that roareth thus?
Can it be a Motor Bus?
Yes, the smell and hideous hum
Indicat Motorem Bum!
Implet in the Corn and High
Terror me Motoris Bi:
Bo Motori clamitabo
Ne Motore caedar a Bo –
Dative be or Ablative
So thou only let us live:
Whither shall thy victims flee?
Spare us, spare us, Motor Be!
Thus I sang; and still anigh
Came in hordes Motores Bi,
Et complebat omne forum
Copia Motorum Borum.
How shall wretches live like us
Cincti Bis Motoribus?
Domine, defende nos
Contra hos Motores Bos!

The references to the Corn and High locate the poet in Oxford, where he taught most of his life. Motor buses were first introduced to Oxford in 1913, so Godley would seem to have developed a rapid dislike of them.

GOEBBELS, Joseph

German Nazi leader (1897–1945)

4 We can do without butter, but, despite all our love of peace, not without arms. One cannot shoot with butter, but with guns.

From the translation of a speech given in Berlin (17 January 1936). When a nation is under pressure to choose between material comforts and some kind of war effort, the choice has to be made between 'guns *and* butter'. Some will urge 'guns *before* butter'. Later that same year, Hermann Goering said in a broadcast, 'Guns will make us powerful; butter will only make us fat', so he may also be credited with the 'guns or butter' slogan. But there is a third candidate. Airey Neave in his book *Nuremberg* (1978) stated of Rudolf Hess: 'It was he who urged the German people to make sacrifices and coined the phrase: "Guns before butter".'

GOERING, Hermann

German Nazi leader (1893–1946)

5 When I hear the word Culture, I reach for my pistol.

Although Goering is often linked with this remark, it comes, in fact, from a play by an unsuccessful Nazi playwright, Hanns Johst (1890–1978), who was president of the Reich Chamber of Literature, a group of authors, translators and publishers which excluded those who refused to toe the party line. In 1933, he wrote *Schlageter*, a play about a martyr of the French occupation of the Ruhr after the First World War. A storm-trooper's line '*Wenn ich Kultur höre ... entsichere ich meinen Browning*' is more accurately translated as 'When I hear the word "culture", I release the safety catch of' – or 'I cock' – 'my Browning' (automatic rifle).

GOETHE, Johann Wolfgang von

German poet, novelist and playwright (1749–1832)

6 Then indecision brings its own delays,
And days are lost lamenting o'er lost days.
Are you in earnest? Seize this very minute;
What you can do, or dream you can, begin it;
Boldness has genius, power and magic in it.

Translation from *Faust* (1808). The last sentence is especially popular in motivational writings. It is spoken by the Manager in the 'Prelude at the Theatre' in John Anster's translation (1835). The original German, beginning '*Was heute nicht geschieht, ist morgen nicht getan* ...', is not very close to this. More directly, it reads: 'What is not done today is not done tomorrow, and not a day should be wasted. Resolve/determination should boldly/courageously grasp opportunity by the forelock; it will then not let it go, and continues to operate because it must.'

GOGARTY, Oliver St John

Irish writer (1878–1957)

1 I said, 'It is most extraordinary weather for this time of year.' He replied, 'Ah, it isn't this time of year at all.'

It Isn't This Time of Year at All (1954). The origin of a seminal Irish joke.

2 If a queen bee were crossed with a Friesian bull, would not the land flow with milk and honey?

Quoted on BBC Radio *Quote ... Unquote* (8 September 1984). Alluding to BIBLE 91:5.

GOLDMAN, William

American screenwriter (1931–)

3 Nobody knows anything.

On Hollywood film-making. *Adventures in the Screen Trade* (1983).

GOLDONI, Carlo

Italian playwright (1707–93)

4 The Servant of Two Masters.

English title of the play *Il Servitore Di Due Padroni* (1745). The presumed origin is 'No man can serve two masters' (Matthew 6:24 and Luke 16:13, *see* BIBLE 101:1). Compare: 'He who serves two masters has to lie to one of them' – Portuguese proverb; 'It is better to obey the laws of one master than to seek to please several' – Catherine the Great; 'Not bound to swear allegiance to any master, wherever the wind takes me I travel as a visitor' – Horace.

GOLDSMITH, Sir James

British businessman (1933–97)

5 If you pay peanuts, you get monkeys.

This remark – made in connection with the pay given to journalists on his short-lived news magazine *Now!* (*c.*1980) – is not original. The modern proverb was in use by 1966.

6 When you marry your mistress, you create a job vacancy.

Attributed in about 1978, when he married for the third time and also acquired another mistress by whom he had two children.

GOLDSMITH, Oliver

Irish-born playwright and writer (1730–74)

7 The Citizen of the World.

Title of a collection of letters by Goldsmith purporting to be those of Lien Chi Altangi, a philosophic Chinaman living in London and commenting on English life and characters. First published as 'Chinese Letters' in the *Public Ledger* (1760–1), and then again under the above title in 1762. *See also* BACON 69:7.

8 But soon a wonder came to light
That show'd the rogues they lied;
The man recover'd of the bite,
The dog it was that died.

'Elegy on the Death of a Mad Dog' (1766). Hence, *The Dog It Was That Died*, title of a radio play (1983) by Tom Stoppard.

9 There is no arguing with Johnson; for when his pistol misses fire, he knocks you down with the butt end of it.

Quoted in James Boswell, *The Life of Samuel Johnson* (1791) – for 26 October 1769.

10 Sweet Auburn, loveliest village of the plain,
Where health and plenty cheered the labouring swain ...
Ill fares the land, to hast'ning ills a prey,
Where wealth accumulates, and men decay ...
A bold peasantry, their country's pride,
When once destroy'd, can never be supplied.

The Deserted Village (1770). Goldsmith's view of the depopulation of villages caused by mercantilism and the drift to the cities. In many cases, the 'bold peasantry' had been forced into emigration. Later, a film by Bill Bryden about people leaving the island of St Kilda, off the west coast of Scotland, was given the title *Ill Fares the Land* (1982).

1 At church, with meek and unaffected grace,
His looks adorn'd the venerable place;
Truth from his lips prevailed with double sway,
And fools, who came to scoff, remained to pray.

Ib. Origin of the expression 'fools who come to scoff and remain to pray', meaning people who undergo some kind of conversion or change of heart. (From Clive James, *The Crystal Bucket*, 1981: 'I came to mock *Dallas* but stayed to pray.')

2 I love everything that's old: old friends, old times, old manners, old books, old wine; and I believe, Dorothy, you'll own I have been pretty fond of an old wife.

She Stoops to Conquer, Act 1, Sc. 1 (1773). Hardcastle, to his wife. Mistaken for an innkeeper, Hardcastle appears as the archetypal, reminiscent old bore.

3 I can't stay, I tell you. The Three Pigeons expects me down every moment. There's some fun going forward.

Ib. Tony Lumpkin to his mother. Hence, *There Is Some Fun Going Forward*, the somewhat unexpected title of a compilation album (material recorded 1969–72) from Dandelion Records, the label co-established by John Peel, the English disc jockey.

4 The very pink of perfection.

Ib., Act 1, Sc. 2. Miss Neville. The first use of this phrase. Mrs Malaprop's abuse of the 'the very pinnacle of politeness', three years later, may be related. *See* SHERIDAN 502:5.

5 As for murmurs, mother, we grumble a little now and then, to be sure. But there's no love lost between us.

Ib., Act 4, Sc. 1. Tony Lumpkin says this to his mother, Mrs Hardcastle. The editor of the New Mermaids edition (1979) states that Goldsmith coined the phrase 'No love lost', but this is true neither of the literal sense nor of the current ironic, opposite one. The *OED2* finds uses of the phrase in both senses over a century before Goldsmith's play.

See also DICKENS 204:6; ELIOT 226:2.

GOLDWATER, Barry M.

American Republican politician (1909–)

6 I would remind you that extremism in the defence of liberty is no vice. And let me remind you also that moderation in the pursuit of justice is no virtue.

Accepting his party's nomination for the presidency, San Francisco Convention (16 July 1964). Goldwater's extremist tag-line did him no good in the subsequent election. Lyndon Johnson beat him with a landslide and rejoined: 'Extremism in pursuit of the Presidency is an unpardonable vice. Moderation in the affairs of the nation is the highest virtue' (speech, New York, 31 October 1964). Perhaps Goldwater would have done better to quote Thomas Paine's *The Rights of Man* (1792), directly: 'A thing moderately good is not so good as it ought to be. Moderation in temper is always a virtue; but moderation in principle is always a vice.' To give him his due, Goldwater disclaimed any originality, saying the idea could be found in Cicero and in Greek authors.

7 In your heart you know I'm right.

Campaign slogan (1964) when Goldwater attempted to unseat President Lyndon Johnson in the 1964 US presidential election. Come-backs included: 'In your guts, you know he's nuts' and 'You know in your heart he's right – far right'.

GOLDWYN, Sam

Polish-born American film producer (1882–1974)

8 The reason so many people showed up at his funeral was because they wanted to make sure he was dead.

On Louis B. Mayer's funeral (quoted in Bosley Crowther, *Hollywood Rajah*, 1960). Probably apocryphal, if only because the funeral was, in fact, sparsely attended.

9 An oral [*or* verbal] contract isn't worth the paper it's written on.

Samuel Goldwyn Jr (interviewed by Michael Freedland in *TV Times*, 13 November 1982) has commented on the 'twenty-eight' genuine sayings attributed to his father and included this as one. Carol Easton in *The Search for Sam Goldwyn* (1976) claims that what he actually said about fellow mogul Joseph L. Mankiewicz was: 'His verbal contract is worth more than the paper it's written on.' The original attribution was by Alva

Johnston in *The Great Goldwyn* (1937) – who also cites: 'That's the way with these directors, they're always biting the hand that lays the golden egg.'

1 In two words – impossible!

Sam Goldwyn Jr has expressed doubts as to the authenticity of this one and, according to Alva Johnston, *The Great Goldwyn* (1937), the joke appeared in a humour magazine late in 1925, and was subsequently imposed upon Goldwyn. *H.L. Mencken's Dictionary of Quotations* (1942) has: 'I can answer in two words – im possible' and ascribes it to 'an American movie magnate, 1930.' Curiously, however, this is to be found in *Punch* (10 June 1931) – caption to a cartoon by George Belcher: 'Harassed Film-Producer. "This business can be summed up in two words: IM-POSSIBLE."'

2 We have all passed a lot of water since then.

Quoted in E. Goodman, *The Fifty Year Decline of Hollywood* (1961), but probably apocryphal. As also: 'Anyone who goes to a psychiatrist needs to have his head examined' – attributed in Norman Zierold, *Moguls* (1969).

3 Messages are for Western Union.

On films with a 'message'. Attributed in Arthur Marx, *Goldwyn* (1976) and earlier in Leslie Halliwell, *The Filmgoer's Book of Quotes* (1973). However, in his 1978 edition, Halliwell also attributes to Jack Warner: 'We'll make the pictures: let Western Union deliver the messages.'

4 Include me out.

This apparently arose when Goldwyn and Jack L. Warner were in disagreement over a labour dispute. Busby Berkeley, who had made his first musical for Goldwyn, was discovered moonlighting for Warner Brothers. Goldwyn said to Warner: 'How can we sit together and deal with this industry if you're going to do things like this to me? If this is the way you do it, gentlemen, include me out!'

Scott Berg, working on the official biography, told *The Sunday Times* (3 May 1981) that he claimed the ability to tell which Goldwynisms are genuine and suggested this one *might* be, as Goldwyn himself appeared to acknowledge when speaking at Balliol College, Oxford, on 1 March 1945: 'For years I have been known for saying "Include me out" but today I am giving it up for ever.' On the other hand, Boller & George, *They Never Said It* (1989) report Goldwyn as having denied saying it, claiming rather to have said to members of the Motion Picture Producers and Distributors of America: 'Gentlemen, I'm withdrawing from the association.'

5 Bon Voyage!

Waving from an ocean-going liner to friends on the quayside. Quoted in Lillian Hellman, *Pentimento* (1974).

6 Bloody and thirsty.

The story is told that when James Thurber was arguing with Goldwyn over the amount of violence that had crept into a film treatment of his story *The Secret Life of Walter Mitty*, eventually released in 1947, Goldwyn said, 'I'm sorry you felt it was too bloody and thirsty'. Thurber, with commendable presence of mind, replied, 'Not only did I think so, I was horror and struck.' For some reason, Boller & George, *They Never Said It* (1989), doubt whether this exchange took place, because 'Goldwyn secretaries would have weeded out the solecism'. But who says it was a written exchange? Arthur Marx in *Goldwyn: A Biography of the Man Behind the Myth* (1976), apparently.

GORDON, Adam Lindsay

Australian poet (1833–70)

7 I've had my share of pastime, and I've done
my share of toil,
And life is short.
... And none will weep when I go forth,
Or smile when I return.

The first line and a half are from 'The Sick Stockrider' (written 1869). The remaining two lines are from Macaulay, 'Virginia', *Lays of Ancient Rome* (1841).

GRACIAN, Baltasar

Spanish philosopher (1601–58)

8 Don't give explanations to those who haven't asked for them. And although they are asked for, it is folly to give them too eagerly. To offer excuses before they are called for is to incriminate yourself, and to bleed yourself when you are healthy is to attract malady and malice. Excusing yourself beforehand awakens suspicions that were fast asleep. The prudent person should never blink before the suspicions of others: that would be looking for offense. He should try to dissimulate with a firm, righteous manner.

'Manual of the Art of Discretion', Para. 246 (1646). An early formulation of the 'never complain, never explain' philosophy (*see* DISRAELI 210:9). 'Never complain' might just be said to be covered by this in para. 138: 'Leave things alone ... It takes little to muddy a stream. You can't make it grow clear by trying to, only by leaving it alone. There is no better remedy for disorder than leave it alone to correct itself.'

GRADE, Lew (later Lord Grade)

Russian-born British media tycoon (1906–99)

1 Are you buying or selling?

His reply to a small child who had asked, 'What does two and two make?' Apocryphal, according to Grade, but an essential piece of Gradiana. Quoted in *The Observer* during 1962.

2 Twelve! So who needs *twelve*? Couldn't we make do with *six*?

To Franco Zeffirelli who explained that the high cost of the TV film *Jesus of Nazareth* (1977) was partly because there had to be twelve apostles. Quoted in *Radio Times* (October 1983).

3 What about it? Do you want to crucify the boy?

When it was revealed that Robert Powell, the actor playing Christ in the film, was living with a woman to whom he was not married. Attributed.

4 It would have been cheaper to lower the Atlantic.

Grade produced a famously expensive and unsuccessful film *Raise the Titanic* (1980) and commented, ruefully, as here. Alas, on TV-am's *Frost on Sunday* (23 November 1987), Grade denied having said it. All he had actually managed was, 'I didn't raise the Titanic high enough'.

GRAHAM, Dr Billy

American evangelist (1918–)

5 I want you to get up out of your seats.

Frequent exhortation. *I'm Going to Ask You to Get Up Out of Your Seats* was the title of a BBC TV documentary directed by Richard Cawston (shown 24 November 1966). From the 1940s onwards, Dr Graham's slogan has been: 'Decide for Christ.'

GRAHAM, D.M.

(1911–)

6 That this House will in no circumstances fight for its King and Country.

Hitler came to power in January 1933. On 9 February, the Oxford Union Debating Society carried this motion by 275 votes to 153. Graham was the Librarian that term and worded the motion. It has been suggested that this pacifist rather than disloyal motion, although adopted by an unrepresentative group of young people, encouraged Hitler to believe that his programme of conquests would go unchallenged by the British. There appears to be no evidence that Hitler ever referred to the Oxford Union debate, though Goebbels and his propaganda ministry certainly knew of it. As a result, Churchill wrote in *The Second World War*, Vol. 1 (1948): 'In Germany, in Russia, in Italy, in Japan, the idea of a decadent, degenerate Britain took deep root and swayed many calculations.' Erich von Richthofen confirmed this view in *The Daily Telegraph* (4 May 1965): 'I am an ex-officer of the old Wehrmacht and served on what you would call the German General Staff at the time of the Oxford resolution. I can assure you, from personal knowledge, that no other factor influenced Hitler more and decided him on his course than that "refusal to fight for King and Country", coming from what was assumed to be the intellectual élite of your country.'

Sir John Colville, Churchill's Private Secretary during the war, recalled in a letter to *The Times* (12 February 1983): 'At Tubingen University in July 1933, I was contemptuously informed by a group of Nazi students that my contemporaries and I would never fight; and the Oxford debate was quoted in evidence.'

On the other hand, Sir Hugh Greene, Berlin correspondent of *The Daily Telegraph* (1934–9) commented in 1983: 'Obviously one did not have the opportunity of discussing the matter with Hitler personally, but one did talk from time to time with high Nazi officials and members of the German armed forces. I am sure that the subject was never mentioned. Why should Hitler concern himself with Oxford undergraduates when he could base his thinking on the attitude of British ministers?'

Mussolini is said, however, to have referred to the debate several times.

GRAHAM, Philip L.

American newspaper publisher (1915–63)

7 News [*or* journalism] is the first [rough] draft of history.

From *The Washington Post* (24 November 1985): 'The summit coverage was textbook stuff of the "journalism-as-first-draft-of-history" variety'; (28 February 1988): 'A daily newspaper such as the *Post* is, as someone once put it, the first rough draft of history'; (10 July 1988): 'The newspaper, *Post* executives have often reminded us, is merely a "first rough draft of history".' From the editor of Britain's ITN in *The Times* (21 December 1990): 'Journalism is the first draft of history.' From *The Times* (27 April 1991): 'When foreign governments want to know what matters are weighing on the minds of the US establishment, they have always turned to the *New York Times*, the sober "grey lady" which has been recording America's first draft of history for the past 140 years.' From *The Washington Post* (29 September 1991): 'Daily journalism is "the first rough draft of history", in the phrase of former *Washington Post* publisher, Philip Graham.'

The phrase has also been attributed to Ben Bradlee (1921–), a noted editor of *The Washington Post.*

GRAHAME, Kenneth

Scottish-born writer (1859–1932)

1 The Piper at the Gates of Dawn.

The Wind in the Willows, heading to Chap. 7 (1908). Grahame describes a lyrical, not to say mystical, experience that Mole and Ratty have when they hear the god Pan piping at dawn. Hence, the title of the first album recorded by Pink Floyd in 1967.

GRANT, Cary

English-born film actor (1904–86)

2 Judy ... Judy ... Judy!

Impersonators always put this line in Grant's mouth (as alluded to by CAGNEY 141:1), but Grant always denied that he had ever said it and had a check made of all his films. According to Richard Keyes, *Nice Guys Finish Seventh* (1992), Grant once said: 'I vaguely recall that at a party someone introduced Judy [Garland] by saying, "Judy, Judy, Judy," and it caught on, attributed to me.'

There may be another explanation. Impersonators usually seek a key phrase which, through simple repetition, readily gives them the subject's voice. It is possible that one of these impersonators found that saying 'Judy' helped summon up Grant's distinctive tones, and it went on from there. Besides, many an impersonator, rather than ape his subject, simply impersonates fellow impersonators.

GRANT, Ulysses S.

American soldier and 18th President (1822–85)

3 No terms except unconditional and immediate surrender can be accepted. I propose to move immediately upon your works.

Message to Simon Bolivar Buckner under siege at Fort Donelson during the American Civil War (16 February 1862). First recorded use of the 'unconditional surrender' demand.

4 I know only two tunes. One of them is 'Yankee Doodle' and the other isn't.

When, as President, Grant (who was tone-deaf) had to attend a concert. Afterwards he declined to say he had enjoyed it, giving this reason. Quoted in Louis Untermeyer, *A Treasury of Laughter* (1946).

GRAVES, John Woodcock

British huntsman and songwriter (1795–1886)

5 Yes, I ken John Peel, and Ruby too,
Ranter and Ringwood, Bellman and True,
From a find to a check, from a check to a view,
From a view to a death in the morning.

Song 'D'ye ken John Peel' (1832). Hence, the title of Anthony Powell's 1933 novel *From a View to a Death.* Compare *A View to a Kill*, title of a James Bond film (UK, 1985). The original title of the short story by Ian Fleming (published in 1960 in *For Your Eyes Only*) was '*From* a View To a Kill'.

In foxhunting terminology, a 'check' is a loss of scent, a 'view (halloo)' is the huntsman's shout when a fox breaks cover, and a 'kill' or a 'death' is self-explanatory. This verse from Graves's song also provided the title of a film (UK, 1988) based on a novel by Desmond Lowden, *Bellman and True.* Although Bellman and True are mentioned in the list of hounds, the book and film are about a bellman in the criminal sense: that is, a man who disables alarm systems so that robberies can take place.

GRAVES, Robert

English poet (1895–1985)

6 Goodbye To All That.

Title of autobiography (1929). Apparently, 'all that', meaning 'all that sort of thing', was in the language before it was popularized by Graves in the title of his farewell to participation in the First World War and to any unhappy period in his private life. But the cod volume of English history *1066 And All That* by Sellar and Yeatman, appearing the following year, 1930, further popularized it.

1 Far away is close at hand
Close joined is far away,
Love shall come at your command
Yet will not stay.

'Song of Contrariety' (1923). Hence, 'Far away is close at hand in images of elsewhere', the very noticeable graffiti text painted in large letters which stood by the side of the track outside Paddington railway station in London (late 1970s). It became quite famous and puzzled many people. No one is ever likely to know who wrote it. 'Peter Simple' in *The Daily Telegraph* attributed it to 'the Master of Paddington' and when he (Michael Wharton) came to write a volume of autobiography in 1995, he called it *Far Away Is Near at Hand*.

2 The White Goddess.

Title of book (1948) in which Graves claims that worship of the ancient goddess of fertility and the moon was the origin of poetry.

GRAY, Thomas

English poet (1716–71)

3 Where ignorance is bliss,
'Tis folly to be wise.

'Ode on a Distant Prospect of Eton College' (1747). Hence, the proverbial expression. There was a BBC radio show in the late 1940s with the title *Ignorance is Bliss* and a film *Folly To Be Wise* (UK, 1952).

4 The curfew tolls the knell of parting day,
The lowing herd wind slowly o'er the lea,
The ploughman homeward plods his weary way,
And leaves the world to darkness and to me.

Now fades the glimmering landscape on the sight,
And all the air a solemn stillness holds,
Save where the beetle wheels his droning flight,
And drowsy tinklings lull the distant folds.

'Elegy Written in a Country Churchyard' (1751). One of the most quoted poems in the English language, feeding numerous phrases into allusive speech. From P.G. Wodehouse, *Right Ho, Jeeves* (1934): '"But what can I say about the sunset?" asked Gussie. "Well, Jeeves got off a good one the other day. I met him airing the dog in the park one evening, and he said, 'Now fades the glimmering landscape on the sight, sir, and all the air a solemn stillness holds.' You might use that".' *See also* JOHNSON 320:10; WOLFE 579:5.

5 Beneath those rugged elms, that yew-tree's shade,
Where heaves the turf in many a mouldering heap,
Each in his narrow cell for ever laid,
The rude forefathers of the hamlet sleep.

Ib. See also BISHOP 109:5.

6 Let not ambition mock their useful toil,
Their homely joys, and destiny obscure;
Nor grandeur hear with a disdainful smile,
The short and simple annals of the poor.

The boast of heraldry, the pomp of pow'r,
And all that beauty, all that wealth e'er gave,
Awaits alike th'inevitable hour,
The paths of glory lead but to the grave.

Ib. Hence, *Paths of Glory*, title of a novel (1935; film US, 1957) by Humphrey Cobb. *See also* WASHINGTON 556:2.

7 Can honour's voice provoke the silent dust,
Or flatt'ry soothe the dull cold ear of death?

Ib. Hence, *Silent Dust*, title of a film (UK, 1949) based on a play called *The Paragon*.

8 Full many a flower is born to blush unseen,
And waste its sweetness on the desert air.

Ib. Taken up by the poet Charles Churchill: 'Nor waste their sweetness in the desert air' appears in *Gotham* (1764).

9 Far from the madding crowd's ignoble strife,
Their sober wishes never learn'd to stray;
Along the cool sequestered vale of life
They kept the noiseless tenor of their way.

Ib. Hence, the title of Thomas Hardy's novel *Far From the Madding Crowd* (1874; film UK, 1967). 'Madding' here means 'frenzied, mad' – not 'maddening'.

GRAYSON, Victor

British Labour politician (1881–?1920)

10 Never explain: your friends don't need it and your enemies won't believe it.

Attributed (in 1977) to the MP who simply disappeared without trace, it may be no more than a posthumously imposed reworking of HUBBARD 303:8.

GRAZIANO, Rocky

American boxer (1922–90)

1 Somebody Up There Likes Me.

Title of the autobiography of this World Heavyweight Boxing Champion (1947–8) and the subsequent film (US, 1956).

GREELEY, Horace

American editor and politician (1811–72)

2 Go West, young man!

An early example of a misattribution that refuses to be corrected. The originator of the saying was John Babsone Lane Soule, who first wrote it in the Terre Haute, Indiana, *Express* in 1851 when, indeed, the thing to do in the United States was to head westwards, where gold and much else lay promised. However, Horace Greeley repeated it in *his* newspaper, the New York *Tribune*, and, being rather more famous, a candidate for the Presidency, and all, it stuck with him. Greeley reprinted Soule's article to show where he had taken it from, but to no avail. The original sentence was, 'Go west, young man, and grow up with the country'. To 'go west' meaning 'die' is a completely separate coinage. It dates back to the sixteenth century and alludes to the setting of the sun.

3 The moment a newspaperman tires of his own campaign is the moment the public begins to notice it.

Attributed to Greeley by the British journalist and editor, Harold Evans, in the *Independent on Sunday* (29 December 1991). A version has also been encountered in connection with Richard Nixon's view of a politician getting over his policies: 'When you get tired of saying it, that's when they're just beginning to listen.'

GREEN, Benny

English writer and broadcaster (1927–98)

4 Live music is an anachronism, and now is the winter of our discothèque.

Remark, by 1976. Alluding to SHAKESPEARE 493:5.

GREEN, Hannah (Joanne Greenberg)

American novelist (1932–)

5 I Never Promised You A Rose Garden.

Title of novel (1964; film US, 1977). This expression presumably means: 'It wasn't going to be roses, roses all the way between us – or a bed of roses – but maybe what we have is still acceptable.' A song 'Rose Garden' by Joe South had the line in 1968 and was a hit for Lyn Anderson in 1971. Fernando Collor de Mello, the then President of Brazil, said in a TV address to his shaken countrymen (reported 26 June 1990): 'I never promised you a rose garden ... following the example of developed countries, we are also cutting state spending.'

GREENE, Graham

English novelist, playwright and screenwriter (1904–91)

6 Fame is a powerful aphrodisiac.

Quoted in *Radio Times* (10 September 1964). *Compare* BELLOW 83:2 and KISSINGER 340:3.

See also WELLES 559:2.

GREENE, Hugh Carleton (later Sir Hugh Greene)

English broadcasting executive (1910–87)

7 Although ... the BBC does try to attain the highest standards of impartiality, there are some respects in which it is not neutral, unbiased or impartial. That is, where there are clashes for and against the basic moral values – truthfulness, justice, freedom, compassion, tolerance. Nor do I believe that we should be impartial about certain things like racialism, or extreme forms of political belief.

From an address entitled 'The Conscience of the Programme Director' given to the International Catholic Association for Radio and Television in Rome (9 February 1965). At that time, Greene was Director-General of the BBC. Elsewhere it was confirmed that the BBC was also not impartial about crime. It was against it.

GREGORY, Lady (Augusta)

Irish writer (1852–1932)

8 The Rising of the Moon.

Title of one-act play (1907). Shared by a film (Ireland, 1957) and by an opera (Glyndebourne, 1970) with libretto by Beverley Cross and music by Nicholas Maw. All these works (with Irish themes) borrow the title of an Irish patriotic song. This was written by John Keegan Casey (1846–70) and called, precisely, 'The Rising of the Moon A.D. 1798': 'And a thousand blades were flashing/At the risin' of the moon'. The phrase came to be synonymous with the rising of the Irish themselves.

GRELLET, Stephen

French missionary (1773–1855)

1 I expect to pass through this world but once; any good thing therefore that I can do now, or any kindness that I can show to any fellow-creature, let me do it now; let me not defer or neglect it, for I shall not pass this way again.

Born Etienne de Grellet du Mabillier, in France, he eventually settled in the US. Now sometimes referred to as a Quaker 'saint', he is widely quoted as having said this. It is not to be found in any of his writings, however, and has been attributed to others. Benham (1907) exhaustively explores the alternatives and mentions William C. Gannett in *Blessed be Drudgery* (1897) as having: 'The old Quaker was right ...' (and then quoting as above).

Arthur Marshall, in *Life's Rich Pageant* (1984), quotes Maurice Bowra (1898–1971), the Oxford don, as having said at lunch in the Reform Club (with a bishop sitting within earshot): 'I expect to pass through this world but once and therefore if there is anybody that I want to kick in the crutch I had better kick them in the crutch *now*, for I do not expect to pass this way again.'

GRENFELL, Joyce

English entertainer (1910–80)

2 George – don't do that.

'Nursery School Sketches' (1953). This line came from the sketch in which Grenfell played a slightly harassed but unflappable teacher. Part of its charm lay in the audience's never knowing precisely what it was that George was being asked not to do. When the nursery school sketches were re-printed in a book called *George – Don't Do That* (1977), the line appeared in the one entitled 'Free Activity Period'.

3 When you've got over the disgrace of the single life, it's more airy.

Quoting her own diary entry about an Irish woman in BBC Radio, *Something Sensational To Read In the Train* (1970). Also in *Joyce Grenfell Requests the Pleasure* (1976).

4 The sordid topic of coin.

A delightful term for the matter of payment due or cash. Not from any sketch but mentioned by her in discussing a woman who inspired the creation of one of her characters. In *Joyce Grenfell Requests the Pleasure* (1976), she writes about the wife of an Oxbridge vice chancellor who featured in three monologues called 'Eng. Lit.'. The character was based partly on Grenfell's own expression while cleaning her teeth, partly on the playwright Clemence Dane (Winifred Ashton) and partly on the idiosyncratic speech patterns of Hester Alington, wife of the Dean of Durham, and a distant relative of Grenfell's husband. 'On a postcard addressed to a shoe-shop in Sloane Street she had written: "Gently fussed about non-appearance of dim pair of shoes sent to you for heeling" ... And when Viola [Tunnard, Grenfell's accompanist] and I went to Durham to perform in aid of one of her charities she introduced the paying of our expenses: "My dears, we have not yet touched on the sordid topic of coin ..."'

5 If I should go before the rest of you
Break not a flower nor inscribe a stone,
Nor when I'm gone speak in a Sunday voice
But be the usual selves that I have known.

Weep if you must,
Parting is hell,
But life goes on,
So sing as well.

Poem (date unknown) included in the book *Joyce By Herself and Her Friends*, published in 1980 after her death. It was read at her funeral.

See also STOPPARD 521:9.

GREY, Sir Edward (later Viscount Grey of Fallodon)

British Liberal politician (1862–1933)

6 The lamps are going out all over Europe; we shall not see them lit again in our lifetime.

Grey was Foreign Secretary at the outbreak of the 1914–18 war and with this statement tolled the knell for the era that was about to pass. In *Twenty-five Years* (1925), he recounted: 'A friend came to see me on one of the evenings of the last week – he thinks it was on Monday August 3. We were standing at a window of my room in the Foreign Office. It was getting dusk, and the lamps were being lit in the space below on which we were looking. My friend recalls that I remarked on this with the words ...'

GRIFFITH, D.W.

American film director (1874–1948)

1 Move those ten thousand horses a trifle to the right. And that mob out there, three feet forward.

Directing an epic film. Quoted in Josef Von Sternberg, *Fun In a Chinese Laundry* (1965).

2 Speaking movies are impossible. When a century has passed, all thoughts of our so-called 'talking pictures' will have been abandoned. It will never be possible to synchronize the voice with the picture.

Remark (1926) quoted in Flexner (1982).

See also WHITMAN 567:2.

GRIFFITH-JONES, Mervyn

British lawyer (1909–79)

3 Is it a book that you would even wish your wife or your servants to read?

When Penguin Books Ltd was tried at the Old Bailey in October 1960 for publishing an unexpurgated edition of D.H. Lawrence's novel *Lady Chatterley's Lover* (1928), the jury and the public at large were entertained by the social attitudes revealed by Griffith-Jones, senior prosecuting counsel, especially by the question posed in his opening address on the first day of the trial.

Gerald Gardiner, in his closing speech for the defence, commented: 'I cannot help thinking that this was, consciously or unconsciously, an echo from an observation which had fallen from the Bench in an earlier case: "It would never do to let members of the working class read this." I do not want to upset the Prosecution by suggesting that there are a certain number of people nowadays who as a matter of fact don't *have* servants. But of course that whole attitude is one which Penguin Books was formed to fight against.'

The publishers were found not guilty of having published an obscene book, and from the trial is usually dated the permissive revolution in British sexual habits (if not in social attitudes).

GRIMOND, Jo (later Lord Grimond)

British Liberal politician (1913–93)

4 In bygone days, commanders were taught that when in doubt, they should march their troops towards the sound of gunfire. I intend to march my troops towards the sound of gunfire.

Speech, Liberal Party Assembly, Brighton (14 September 1963). At the subsequent general election a year later, the Liberal vote was doubled.

5 Our teeth are in the real meat.

On the chance of a pact with the Labour government. Speech, Liberal Party Assembly (1965).

GROMYKO, Andrei

Soviet politician (1909–89)

6 This man has a nice smile, but he has got iron teeth.

Proposing Mikhail Gorbachev as Soviet Communist Party leader in a speech (11 March 1985).

GROSSMITH, George and Weedon

English humorous writers (1847–1912) and (1854–1919)

7 I left the room with silent dignity, but caught my foot in the mat.

The Diary of a Nobody, Chap. 12 (1894). The nobody in question is Charles Pooter, an assistant in a mercantile firm, whose mundane doings and thoughts, described with a total lack of humour, gave rise to the term 'Pooterish' for anyone who displays similar characteristics coupled with a lack of awareness. From Chap. 13: 'I am a poor man, but I would gladly give ten shillings to find out who sent me the insulting Christmas card I received this morning.'

GUEDALLA, Philip

British writer (1889–1944)

8 History repeats itself. Historians repeat each other.

'Some Historians', *Supers and Supermen* (1920). Also ascribed to A.J. Balfour.

9 The work of Henry James has always seemed divisible by a simple dynastic arrangement

into three reigns: James I, James II, and the Old Pretender.

'Men of Letters: Mr Henry James', *Collected Essays* (1920). Guedalla also used this device in his introduction to *The Queen and Mr Gladstone* (1933). There were really three Queen Victorias, he wrote: 'The youngest of the three was Queen Victoria I ... distinguished by a romping sort of innocence ... She was succeeded shortly after marriage by Victoria II ... [bearing] the unmistakable impress of her married life ... [Then] the Queen became Queen-Empress ... her third and final manner.'

GUINAN, Texas

American nightclub hostess (1884–1933)

1 Hello, sucker!

Customary greeting to clients. Quoted in W. & M. Morris, *Dictionary of Word and Phrase Origins* (1971 ed.).

2 Big butter-and-egg man.

Her description of a small-town businessman trying to prove himself a big shot in the city. Quoted in *ib.*

3 Fifty million Frenchmen can't be wrong.

A good deal of confusion surrounds this phrase. As a slightly grudging expression it appears to have originated with American servicemen during the First World War, justifying support for their French allies. The precise number of millions was variable. Partridge/*Catch Phrases* suggests that it was the last line of a First World War song 'extolling the supreme virtue of copulation, though in veiled terms'. Partridge may, however, have been referring to a song with the title (by Rose, Raskin & Fisher), which was not recorded by Sophie Tucker until 15 April 1927. Cole Porter's musical *Fifty Million Frenchmen* opened in New York on 27 November 1929. An unrelated US film with this three-word title was released in 1931.

Where the confusion has crept in is that Guinan was refused entry into France with her girls in 1931 and said: 'It goes to show that fifty million Frenchmen *can* be wrong.' She returned to America and renamed her show *Too Hot for Paris*. Perversely, the *ODQ* (1979, 1992) has her saying 'Fifty million Frenchmen *can't* be wrong' in the *New York World-Telegram* on 21 March 1931, and seems to be arguing that she originated the phrase as she had been using it 'six or seven years earlier'.

Bernard Shaw also held out against the phrase. He insisted: 'Fifty million Frenchmen can't be right.'

GUINNESS, Sir Alec

English actor (1914–)

4 Always remember before going on stage, wipe your nose and check your flies.

Quoted in Kenneth Williams, *Just Williams* (1985). *Time* Magazine (11 May 1987) preferred 'Blow your nose and check your fly'.

GUNN, Thom

English-born poet (1929–)

5 He turns revolt into style.

Poem, 'Elvis Presley' (1957). Hence, *Revolt into Style*, the title of a book about the pop arts in Britain (1970) by George Melly.

GURNEY, Dorothy Frances

English poet (1858–1932)

6 The kiss of the sun for pardon,
The song of the birds for mirth,
One is nearer God's Heart in a garden
Than anywhere else on earth.

'God's Garden', *Poems* (1913). The text most likely to be found inscribed on a stone as a garden ornament.

GWENN, Edmund

British actor (1875–1959)

7 It is. But not as hard as farce.

On his deathbed, when someone said to him that dying 'must be very hard'. Quoted in *Time* Magazine (30 January 1984). *Compare* GARRICK 254:3.

GWYN, Nell

English actress and courtesan (1650–87)

8 Pray, good people, be civil. I am the Protestant whore.

Remark at Oxford during the Popish Terror (1681). Quoted in B. Bevan, *Nell Gwyn* (1969). *See also* CHARLES II 155:6.

H

HACKNEY, Alan

British comedy writer (1924–)

1 Miles of cornfields, and ballet in the evening.

Of Soviet Russia. Novel, *Private Life* (1958), filmed as *I'm All Right, Jack* (UK, 1959).

HAGGARD, Sir Henry Rider

English writer (1856–1925)

2 She who must be obeyed.

The original 'she' in Haggard's novel *She* (1887) was the all-powerful Ayesha, 'who from century to century sat alone, clothed with unchanging loveliness, waiting till her lost love is born again'. But also, 'she was obeyed throughout the length and breadth of the land, and to question her command was certain death'.

From the second of these two quotations we get the use of the phrase by barrister Horace Rumpole regarding his formidable wife in the 'Rumpole of the Bailey' stories by John Mortimer (in TV plays from 1978 and novelizations therefrom). Hence, too, one of the many nicknames applied to Margaret Thatcher – 'She-Who-Must-Be-Obeyed', used, for example, by Denis Healey in a speech to the House of Commons (27 February 1984).

HAIG, Alexander

American general and Republican politician (1924–)

3 I'll have to caveat my response, senator, and I'll caveat that.

When Haig was being examined at his confirmation hearings in the Senate for the Secretaryship (1981), he came out with this curious use of noun as verb, presumably meaning, 'I'll say that with this warning'. (Perhaps that is why he called his memoirs *Caveat*?) Subsequently, his way with the language became known as 'Haigspeak', 'Haigese' and 'Haigravation'. Multi-syllabic jargon and verbal distortions flowed from his mouth. An aide asked him for a pay increase. Haig replied: 'Because of the fluctuational predisposition of your position's productive capacity as juxtaposed to government standards, it would be momentarily injudicious to advocate an increment.' The perplexed aide replied, 'I don't get it'. Haig said, 'That's right' (*The Times*, 29 January 1983).

4 As of now, I am in control [here] at the White House.

After the assassination attempt on President Reagan in March 1981, Secretary of State Haig made this claim while the President was in an operating theatre and the Vice-President was flying back to the White House. *The New York Times* reported that Haig's 'voice was trembling and his face perspiring'. In fact, he had made the claim without authority, and it was open to question whether he was entitled to make it at all. *The Times* (1 April 1981) presciently noted, 'The phrase may come back to haunt him'.

In his memoirs, *Caveat: Realism, Reagan & Foreign Policy* (1984), Haig admitted that he had been wrong to say that 'constitutionally ... you have the President, the Vice-President and the Secretary of State in that order'. He should have said 'traditionally', as the Secretary of Defense was third in line, at least on defence matters. It is only fair to point out that Haig also added to his statement the words, 'pending return of the Vice-President'.

But the physical aspect counted against him – 'My appearance became a celebrated media happening. It is now far too late to correct the impressions made' – and he never ran for President as at one time seemed probable.

HAIG, Sir Douglas (later 1st Earl Haig)

British soldier (1861–1928)

1 A very weak-minded fellow, I'm afraid, and, like the feather pillow, bears the marks of the last person who has sat on him!

Letter to his wife (14 January 1918), about the 17th Earl of Derby, generally considered an uninspiring choice as Secretary for War (1916–18). Lloyd George, as Prime Minister, took over Derby's responsibilities the following March. Haig's private papers were made public in an edition edited by Robert Blake in 1952.

2 With our backs to the wall, and believing in the justice of our cause, each one of us must fight on to the end.

The expression 'backs to the wall', meaning 'up against it', dates back to at least 1535, but it was memorably used when the Germans launched their last great offensive of the First World War. On 12 April 1918 Haig, as British Commander-in-Chief on the Western Front, issued an order for his troops to stand firm: 'Every position must be held to the last man: there must be no retirement.' A.J.P. Taylor in his *English History 1914–1945* (1966) commented: 'In England this sentence was ranked with Nelson's last message. At the front, the prospect of staff officers fighting with their backs to the walls of their luxurious chateaux had less effect.'

HAILSHAM, Viscount (later Quintin Hogg, later Lord Hailsham)

British Conservative politician (1907–)

3 A great party is not to be brought down because of a squalid affair between a woman of easy virtue and a proved liar.

On the Profumo affair. Interview, BBC TV (13 June 1963) – this version taken from a recording.

4 If the British public falls for this, I say it will be stark, staring bonkers.

On Labour policies during a General Election. Press conference, London (12 October 1964).

HALBERSTAM, David

American journalist (1934–)

5 The Best and the Brightest.

In Halberstam's book with this title (1972) the phrase applies to the young men from business, industry and the academic world whom John F. Kennedy brought into government in the early 1960s but who were ultimately responsible for the quagmire of American involvement in the Vietnam War. The alliterative combination is almost traditional: 'Political writers, who will not suffer the best and brightest of characters ... to take a single right step for the honour or interest of the nation' (*Letters of Junius*, 1769); 'Best and brightest, come away!' (Shelley, 'To Jane: The Invitation', 1822; originally the letter poem 'The Pine Forest of the Cascine Near Pisa'); 'Brightest and best of the sons of the morning' (*see* HEBER 288:2); 'The best, the brightest, the cleverest of them all!' (Trollope, *Dr Thorne*, Chap. 25, 1858).

HALDEMAN, H.R.

American government official (1926–93)

6 Once the toothpaste is out of the tube, it is awfully hard to get it back in.

Remark to John Dean on the Watergate affair (8 April 1973) and reported in *Hearings Before the Select Committee on Presidential Campaign Activities: Watergate and Related Activities* (Vol. 4, 1973). The remark has been wrongly attributed to his colleague, John D. Ehrlichman, and to President Nixon, but it is probably not an original expression in any case.

HALL, Archibald

British butler (1924–)

7 It was easy after the first one. After that I was trying for *The Guinness Book of Records*.

On being convicted of five murders. Quoted in *The Observer* (5 November 1978).

HALL, Jerry

American model (1956–)

8 My mother said it was simple to keep a man – you must be a maid in the living room, a cook in the kitchen and a whore in the bedroom. I said I'd hire the other two and take care of the bedroom bit.

Quoted in *The Observer* (6 October 1985). Hall, who eventually married the pop singer Mick Jagger, was putting her own gloss on an old saying. Compare: 'They say a woman should be a cook in the kitchen and a whore in bed. Unfortunately, my wife is a whore in the kitchen and a cook in bed.' This was quoted by Peter Porter on BBC Radio *Quote ... Unquote* (31 July 1979) from *Exploring English Character* (1955) by Geoffrey Gorer, in which readers of the *Sunday People* were invited to take part in a survey about their sex lives. This was collected from a 'working class, Sunderland' man.

HALL, Sir Peter

English theatre director (1930–)

1 We do not necessarily improve with age: for better or worse we become more like ourselves.

Quoted in *The Observer* (*c.*1988). Almost a proverbial expression by this time. In my *Eavesdroppings* (1981), I quoted this from Miss Bernice Hanison of Haywards Heath: 'On the London Underground, I heard one of those carrying, well-bred, female voices saying to her companion: "I don't know about you, but as we get older I always find we get more and more like ourselves".'

HALM, Friedrich (Baron von Münch-Bellinghausen)

German playwright (1806–71)

2 Two minds with but a single thought,
Two hearts that beat as one.

What Pearson (1937) says Halm actually wrote near the end of Act 2 of *Der Sohn der Wildnis* is, 'Two *souls* with but a single thought ...' (as in Maria Lovell's translation of the play, as *Ingomar the Barbarian*, 1854). The original German is, indeed, '*Zwei Seelen und ein Gedanke*'. But the 'two minds' version is the one that entered the English language. Partridge/*Catch Phrases* draws attention to the similar phrase 'Great minds think alike' – which may have influenced the English form.

Compare the variation 'two minds with *not* a single thought': Kenneth Horne contributed an article entitled 'TMWNAST' to the *Radio Times Annual* (1954): 'The title of this article is how Murdoch and I would write it in our script if it were a catchphrase ... It is quite true that when Murdoch and I get together to write our epic stuff we are two minds with not a single thought.'

HAMILTON, Richard

English painter (1922–)

3 Just What Is It That Makes To-Day's Home So Different, So Appealing?

Dating from 1956, this is the title of what is held to be the first British 'pop art' painting. Hamilton produced a small collage of magazine photographs of, for example, a Charles Atlas muscleman carrying a baseball bat (with 'POP' written on it), a female nude, and various 'modern' artefacts like a TV set and a tape-recorder. A painting on the wall comes from a comic book called *Young Romance* and out of the window there is a neon cinema sign advertising an Al Jolson film. (The *first* recorded use of the word 'Pop' *in* art is in Eduardo Paolozzi's picture 'I Was a Rich Man's Plaything' (*c.*1947) which is a modest collage of advertisements and the cover of *Intimate Confessions*. A pistol, pointed at a pin-up, is going 'Pop!')

Possibly Hamilton also found his title in a magazine or an advertisement? Whatever the case, it lingers. From the heading to an article in *The Sunday Times* (16 January 1994): 'Just what is it that makes today's Catholicism so different, so appealing, to aristocratic Anglicans? Cristina Odone, the editor of the Catholic Herald, explains.'

HAMMERSTEIN II, Oscar

American lyricist (1895–1960)

4 Ol' Man River
He just keeps rollin' along.

'Ol Man River', *Show Boat* (1927). Music by Jerome Kern. *See also* CHURCHILL 164:3.

5 Some enchanted evening ...
You may see a stranger across a crowded room.

Song, 'Some Enchanted Evening', *South Pacific* (1949). Music by Richard Rodgers. *See also* PYM 443:4.

HAMPTON, Christopher

English playwright (1946–)

6 Masturbation is the thinking man's television.

The Philanthropist (1970). An amusing variant on the 'thinking man's/person's/woman's ——' theme. As long ago as 1931, Pebeco toothpaste in the US was being promoted as 'The Toothpaste for Thinking People'. However, Frank Muir set the more recent trend (now almost a cliché) when in the 1960s he talked of British broadcaster Joan Bakewell as 'the thinking man's crumpet'. Much later, Chantal Cuer, a French-born broadcaster in Britain, said she had been described as 'the thinking man's croissant'. And how about these for originality? 'Frank Delaney – the thinking man's Russell Harty' (*The Sunday Times*, 16 October 1983); 'Frank Delaney – the thinking man's Terry Wogan' (*The Guardian*, 17 October 1983); 'the thinking woman's Terry Wogan, TV's Frank Delaney' (*Sunday Express*, 30 October 1983). And still it goes on: Janet Suzman, the actress, has been described as 'the thinking man's Barbara Windsor'. From *The Independent* (28 January 1989): 'One member of the Government said: "[Kenneth Clark's] the thinking man's lager lout."' From *The Observer* (29 January 1989): 'It was chaired by Nick Ross, the thinking woman's newspaper boy.' Also, from *The Observer* (13 September 1987): 'His performance as a trendy and hung-up LA painter in *Heartbreakers* made him the thinking woman's West Coast crumpet' – which brings us back to more or less where we started. In February 1989, the American magazine *Spy* drew up a long list of examples of American variations on the theme: *Hobbies* Magazine in 1977 had described Descartes as 'the thinking man's philosopher'; *Boating* Magazine (1984) described the Mansfield TDC portable toilet as 'the thinking man's head'; *Horizon* (1965) called Lake Geneva 'the thinking man's lake'; and *Esquire* (1986) had called actor William Hurt 'the thinking man's asshole'.

1 *Philip (bewildered)*: I'm sorry. (*Pause.*) I suppose I am indecisive. (*Pause.*) My trouble is, I'm a man of no convictions. (*Longish pause.*) At least, I think I am.

Ib. This re-emerged later as a graffito: 'I used to be indecisive – but now I'm not so sure' – contributed by Brian Johnston to BBC Radio *Quote ... Unquote* (21 August 1979), but see also PERTWEE 429:4.

2 Asking a working writer what he thinks about critics is like asking a lamp-post how it feels about dogs.

For some reason this is frequently misascribed to John Osborne (e.g., in Metcalf, *The Penguin Dictionary of Modern Humorous Quotations*, 1987). Hampton's view was quoted originally in *The Sunday Times* Magazine of 16 October 1977. This misattribution may have come about because Osborne was the more famously combative of the two playwrights.

HANCOCK, John

American merchant and politician (1737–93)

3 There! I guess King George [*or* John Bull] will be able to read that!

Hancock, from Boston, was one of (if not) the first to sign the Declaration of Independence in 1776. His signature is quite the largest on the document and he is variously reported to have made it that way 'so the King of England could read it without spectacles' or as above. Hence, 'John Hancock' is an American nickname for a signature or autograph.

HANCOCK'S HALF-HOUR

British radio and TV series (BBC), from 1954 onwards (also called simply* Hancock *on TV). Scripts by Alan Simpson and Ray Galton. Starring Tony Hancock (1924–68).

4 Ha-harr, Jim, lad.

Stock routine. Impersonating Robert Newton as Long John Silver in the film *Treasure Island* (1950).

5 Mis-ter *Chris*-tian ... I'll have you *hung* from the *high*-est *yard*-arm in the *Navy*.

Stock routine. An impersonation of Charles Laughton as Captain Bligh in the film *Mutiny on the Bounty* (1935). In fact, the nearest Laughton gets to saying this is when he addresses Fletcher Christian: 'I'll live to see you – all of you – hanging from the highest yard arm in the British fleet.'

HANDEL, George Frideric

German-born British composer (1685–1759)

6 Art thou troubled?
Music will soothe thee.

From aria in the opera *Rodelinda* (1725), with libretto by Antonio Salvi (1742–?).

7 I did think I did see all heaven before me and the great God himself.

When Handel had completed composing Part 2 of *Messiah*, which includes the Hallelujah Chorus, his servant found him at the table, tears streaming from his eyes. This was his comment. Quoted in Derek Watson, *Dictionary of Musical Quotations* (1991). *Messiah* was composed between 22 August and 14 September 1741 and first performed the following April.

8 See, the conquering hero comes!
Sound the trumpets, beat the drums!

Lines written by Thomas Morell, English clergyman (1703–84), which occur both in Handel's oratorio *Judas Maccabaeus* (1747) and also in *Joshua* (1748). Hence, presumably, *Hail the Conquering Hero*, title of a film (US, 1944).

HANFF, Minnie Maud

American advertising copywriter (1880–1942)

1 Vigor, Vim, Perfect Trim;
Force made him, Sunny Jim.

From a jingle for Force breakfast cereal (1903). The name, character and appearance of 'Sunny Jim' were invented by two young American women – Miss Hanff and a Miss Ficken – and the name has passed into the language. One might say, 'Ah, there you are ... I've been looking for you, Sunny Jim', even if the person isn't called Jim. Lady Cynthia Asquith writing in her diary (13 July 1918) says: 'I like McKenna [a politician]. He is such a "Sunny Jim" and ripples on so easily.' So it is a name applied to a cheerful person, but it can also be used in a slightly patronizing way. Thus it was applied to James Callaghan, when British Prime Minister, who was nothing if not patronizing in return with his air of a bank manager who knew best (an *Observer* headline of 18 March 1979 stated, 'Sunny Jim tires of wheeler-dealing').

The Force Food Company was founded in 1901. A London office was established the following year. In the US, the product has now disappeared from sale but in 1970, the A.C. Fincken Company re-launched it in the UK.

2 High o'er the fence leaps Sunny Jim,
Force is the food that raises him.

Hanff wrote numerous little rhymes to promote the cereal. This one dates from 1920.

HANRAHAN, Brian

English broadcast journalist (1949–)

3 I'm not allowed to say how many planes [Harrier jets from HMS *Hermes*] joined the raid, but I counted them all out and I counted them all back.

Report broadcast by BBC TV News (1 May 1982). Hanrahan was attempting to convey the success of a British attack on Port Stanley airport during the Falklands War. As Alasdair Milne commented in *DG: The Memoirs of a British Broadcaster* (1988), it was, 'An elegant way of telling the truth without compromising the exigencies of military censorship.'

HARBACH, Otto

American lyricist (1873–1963)

4 Smoke Gets in Your Eyes.

Title of song, *Roberta* (1933).

See also MACMILLAN 374:4.

HARBEN, Joan

English actress (1909–53)

5 It's being so cheerful as keeps me going.

Harben would utter this catchphrase in the character of 'Mona Lott', a gloomy laundrywoman with a dreary, flat voice, in *ITMA*, the BBC's immensely popular radio comedy show (1939–49). When told to 'keep her pecker up' by the star of the show, Tommy Handley, she would reply, 'I always do, sir, it's being so cheerful as keeps me going'. Her family was always running into bad luck, so she had plenty upon which to exercise her cheerfulness. Scripts for the show were by Ted Kavanagh and Handley himself. The catchphrase had earlier appeared in a *Punch* cartoon during the First World War (27 September 1916): 'Wot a life. No rest, no beer, no nuffin. It's only us keeping so cheerful as pulls us through.'

HARBURG, E.Y.

American lyricist (1898–1981)

6 It's only a paper moon,
Sailing over a cardboard sea,
But it wouldn't be make-believe
If you believed in me.

Song, 'It's Only a Paper Moon', *The Great Magoo* (1932). Written with Harold Arlen and Billy Rose. Hence, *Paper Moon*, title of a film (US, 1973).

7 Once I built a rail-road,
Now it's done.
Brother, can you spare a dime?

Song, 'Brother Can You Spare a Dime', *New Americana* (1932). Music by Jay Gorney. Became the anthem of the Great Depression in the United States (1929–39).

8 Somewhere over the rainbow, skies are blue,
And the dreams that you dare to dream really
do come true.

Song, 'Over the Rainbow', *The Wizard of Oz* (1939). Music by Harold Arlen. *See* BAUM 77:3.

1 Follow the Yellow Brick Road.

Title of song in *ib.* Hence, 'Goodbye Yellow Brick Road', the title of a song (1973) by Bernie Taupin and Elton John. *See also* BAUM 77:4.

See also SCHULTZ 470:4.

HARDING, Gilbert

English broadcaster (1907–60)

2 Sole purpose of visit.

In written answer to US immigration question, 'Is it your intention to overthrow the government of the United States by force?' (late 1940s). Quoted in Wallace Reyburn, *Gilbert Harding: A Candid Portrayal* (1978).

3 If, sir, I possessed the power of conveying unlimited sexual attraction through the potency of my voice, I would not be reduced to accepting a miserable pittance from the BBC for interviewing a faded female in a damp basement.

To Mae West's manager who had suggested he might sound a bit more 'sexy' when interviewing her for the BBC. Quoted by Wynford Vaughan-Thomas in *Gilbert Harding by His Friends* (1961).

HARDING, Warren G.

American Republican 29th President (1865–1923)

4 America's present need is not heroics but healing, not nostrums but normalcy, not revolution but restoration, not agitation but adjustment, not surgery but serenity, not the dramatic but the dispassionate, not experiment but equipoise, not submergence in internationality but sustainment in triumphant nationality.

The slogans 'Back to Normalcy' and 'Return to Normalcy with Harding' were both based on a word extracted from a speech Harding made in Boston, Massachusetts (14 May 1920). Out of such an alliterative bog stuck the word 'normalcy', a perfectly good Americanism, though it has been suggested that Harding was actually mispronouncing the word 'normality'. He himself claimed that 'normalcy' was what he had meant to say, having come across it in a dictionary.

HARDY, Oliver

American film comedian (1892–1957)

5 Well, here's another nice mess you've gotten me into.

Hardy's exasperated cry to his partner Stan Laurel (1890–1965) after some piece of ineptitude was spoken in several of their films. Oddly, both *ODMQ* (1991) and *ODQ* (1992) place the saying under Laurel's name while acknowledging that it was always said *to* him. It is one of the few film catchphrases to register because there was a sufficient number of Laurel and Hardy features for audiences to become familiar with it. Latterly, it has often been remembered as 'another fine mess', possibly on account of one of the duo's thirty-minute features (released in 1930) being entitled *Another Fine Mess*. *The Independent* (21 January 1994) carried a letter from Darren George of Sheffield – clearly a Laurel and Hardy scholar – which stated that 'nice mess' was what was 'invariably' spoken and that in *Another Fine Mess* 'the duo inexplicably misquote themselves'.

HARDY, Thomas

English novelist and poet (1840–1928)

6 'Justice' was done, and the President of the Immortals (in Aeschylean phrase) had ended his sport with Tess.

Tess of the D'Urbervilles, Chap. 59 (1891). From the concluding paragraph, after Tess has been hanged. Hardy never missed an opportunity to over-emphasize what he was doing – here writing a tragedy of classical proportions in a rural setting. The note of pretentiousness also appears in the subtitle to *Under the Greenwood Tree* – he has to call it, 'A Rural Painting of the Dutch School'.

7 Done because we are too menny.

Jude the Obscure, Pt 6, Chap. 2 (1896). A child's suicide note, explaining why he has killed himself and two others.

8 A time there was ...
Before the birth of consciousness,
When all went well ...
But the disease of feeling germed,
And primal rightness took the tinct of wrong.

'Before Life and After' (1909). Hence, *A Time There Was*, title of a 'suite on English folk tunes' (1974) by Benjamin Britten. Also *A Time There Was: a profile of Benjamin Britten* (1980), for London Weekend Television.

1 In Time of 'The Breaking of Nations'.

Title of poem (1917) about war. It was conceived at the time of the Franco-Prussian but not written until the First World War. The phrase 'breaking of nations' sounds biblical but, apparently, is not.

HARE, Augustus

English clergyman and writer (1792–1834)

2 God is a gentleman and no gentleman cares to be praised to his face.

Somerset Maugham once quoted Hare's explanation of why he omitted all passages glorifying God when he read aloud to his household from the Prayer Book. Unverified. Possibly a confusion with his nephew Augustus Hare (1834–1903), biographer and writer of guide books.

HARE, David

English playwright (1947–)

3 Paris by Night.

The title of Hare's film (1988) is derived from a promotional tag for tourism in the French capital, in use since at least the 1950s. A London West End revue had the somewhat nudging phrase for its title in 1955. In 1943 there had been a US film *Paris After Dark*. From the 1930s onwards there was also a cheap perfume, available from Woolworth and manufactured by Bourjois (*sic*), called 'Evening in Paris', which also traded on the city's reputation for sophisticated pleasures.

4 Racing Demon.

The title of a play (1990) about the Church of England came from the name of a 'patience' card game played by several players, each with his own pack of cards.

5 Murmuring Judges.

The title of a play (1991) about the British criminal justice system came from an old legal expression meaning to speak ill of the judiciary. So, to 'murmur' a judge is to complain or grumble against his actions. In Scottish law it is still an offence to do so.

HARGREAVES, William

English songwriter (1846–1919)

6 I'm Burlington Bertie
I rise at ten thirty and saunter along like a toff,
I walk down the Strand with my gloves on my hand,
Then I walk down again with them off.

From the song, 'Burlington Bertie from Bow' (1915), and not to be confused with the earlier 'Burlington Bertie' (1900) by Harry B. Norris. That song, performed by Vesta Tilley, is about a 'swell'. Hargreaves was writing about a more down-at-heel character (for his wife Ella Shields, the male impersonator, to perform). It is a kind of parody but is probably better known now than the original.

HARLOW, Jean

American film actress (1911–37)

7 Would you be shocked if I put on something more comfortable?

'Do you mind if I put on something more comfortable?' and 'Excuse me while I slip into something more comfortable' are just two of the misquotations of this famous line. 'Pardon me while I slip into something more comfortable' was perpetrated by Denis Gifford in *The Independent* (22 July 1995). What Jean Harlow as Helen actually says to Ben Lyon as Monte in *Hell's Angels* (1930) is, of course, by way of a proposition and she duly exchanges her fur wrap for a dressing gown.

HARRIS, Joel Chandler

American writer (1848–1908)

8 Tar-baby ain't sayin' nuthin', en Brer Fox, he lay low.

'The Wonderful Tar-Baby Story', *Uncle Remus and His Legends of the Old Plantation* (1881). In Kenneth Harris's biography of Clement Attlee (1982), he says at one point that the former British Prime Minister was, 'lying low, like Brer Rabbit, and saying nuffin''. This is a fairly common conflation of what Harris originally actually wrote. In fact, the phrase 'en Brer Fox, he lay low' is a phrase repeated rhythmically throughout the piece, as Frank Muir has noted, 'like a line in a Blues song'.

HARRIS, John

English author (1916–)

1 The Sea Shall Not Have Them.

Title of novel (1953; film UK, 1954) about air-sea rescue operations during the Second World War. But was it ever the actual motto of an air-sea rescue unit? Apparently it was. In Harris's original book, there is a note explaining it as 'the motto of Air-Sea Rescue High-Speed Launch Flotillas.' *See also* COWARD 188:2.

HARRISON, George

English pop singer and musician (1943–)

2 In Spite of All the Danger.

Title of song written by Harrison with Paul McCartney, recorded in 1958 and revealed on the album *The Beatles Anthology I* (1995).

3 As far as I'm concerned, there won't be a Beatles reunion as long as John Lennon remains dead.

Quoted in *The Independent* Magazine (28 October 1995).

HARRISON, Tony

English poet (1937–)

4 Yan Tan Tethera.

Title of opera (1986), libretto by Harrison, music by Harrison Birtwistle, about a shepherd who moves down from the north of England to Wiltshire and enters into rivalry with a local shepherd. The title refers to an old shepherd's spell 'Yan, tan, tethera, 1–2–3, Sweet Trinity, Keep us. And our sheep'. The method of counting Yan = 1, T(y)an = 2, Tethera = 3, Methera = 4, Pimp = 5, and so on, is one used, for example, by old-time Yorkshire shepherds and farmers. James Agate in *Ego 3* (1938) calls them 'Cymric numerals still used by shepherds in counting sheep' and gives this version of 1–20: 'Yan tan tethera pethera pimp, sethera lethera hovera bovera dik, yan-a-dik tan-a-dik tethera-dik pethera-dik bumfit, yan-a-bumfit tan-a-bumfit tethera-bumfit pethera-bumfit figgit.'

HART, Lorenz

American lyricist (1895–1943)

5 Thou swell, thou witty, thou sweet, thou grand.

Song 'Thou Swell' in *A Connecticut Yankee* (1927) with music by Richard Rodgers. Hence, *Thou Swell Thou Witty*, title of his collected lyrics, ed. by Dorothy Hart (1976).

6 We'll have Manhattan ...

Song, 'Manhattan', *Garrick Gaieties* (1925). Music by Richard Rodgers. Hence, *I'll Take Manhattan*, title of a novel (1986) by Judith Krantz. Although acknowledging the Rodgers and Hart song, it only alludes to it.

HARTLEY, L.P.

English novelist (1895–1972)

7 The past is a foreign country: they do things differently there.

The Go-Between (1953), opening words. Compare Christopher Morley's earlier statement: 'Life is a foreign language: all men mispronounce it' –*Thunder on the Left*, Chap. 14 (1925).

HARVEY, F.W.

English poet (1888–1957)

8 From troubles of the world
I turn to ducks
Beautiful comical things.

'Ducks' (1919).

See also SHAKESPEARE 477:2.

HAŠEK, Jaroslav

Czechoslovakian writer (1883–1923)

9 When a man buys a motor car, he doesn't always know what he is letting himself in for.

The Good Soldier Svejk (*c.*1923). Svejk's charwoman tells him of the assassination of Franz Ferdinand, the event that triggered the First World War, as the Archduke drove through Sarajevo in a motor car. Svejk deduces the above from this occurrence. Hašek's humour is oblique at the best of times (some would say imperceptible) and another translator renders this passage much more meekly, thus: 'Yes, of course, a gentleman like him can afford it, but he never imagines that a drive like that might finish up badly.'

HASKINS, Minnie Louise

English teacher and writer (1875–1957)

1 And I said to the man who stood at the Gate of the Year, 'Give me a light that I may tread safely into the unknown'. And he replied, 'Go out into the darkness, and put your hand into the Hand of God. That shall be to you better than light, and safer than a known way.'

Introduction to poem, *The Desert* (1908). If one were to look for an equivalent British example of President Reagan's quoting of J.G. Magee's 'High Flight' poem at the time of the Challenger disaster in 1986 (375:8) – that is to say, an outstanding choice of quotation in a head of state's speech – the most obvious, and possibly only, candidate would be found in King George VI's Christmas radio broadcast of 1939.

The King, hampered by a severe speech impediment, was scarcely a man noted for what he said. Yet when he quoted an obscure poet that year, he captured the public imagination as few other Royals had done (and certainly not since). He concluded his message by quoting (anonymously) words written by Haskins, a retired lecturer at the London School of Economics.

One can imagine how the nation collectively responded to the King's difficult delivery of the words, especially given that this was the first Christmas of the war. The King added: 'May that Almighty Hand guide and uphold us all.'

Haskins did not hear the broadcast herself but was soon inundated with writing offers. Her reprinted poem sold 43,000 copies, she was ushered into *Who's Who* and merited an obituary in *The Times* – all testimony to the power of being quoted by the right person at the right time. One assumes that the King's speech was written for him by a member of the Royal Household. According to the King's official biographer, John Wheeler-Bennett, the poem had merely been 'sent to him shortly before the text of his broadcast was completed'.

HASSALL, Christopher

English writer (1912–63)

2 She's genuinely bogus.

On Edith Sitwell. Quoted in *PDMQ* (1971).

HAVERS, Sir Michael (later Lord Havers)

British Conservative politician (1923–92)

3 [He] maintained his denial. He was then offered the immunity from prosecution. He sat in silence for a while. He got up, he looked out of the window, poured himself a drink and after a few minutes confessed. Later [he] co-operated, and [he] continued to co-operate. That's how the immunity was actually given and how Blunt responded.

On the immunity from prosecution offered to the spy, Sir Anthony Blunt, in April 1964. What happened when Blunt was interviewed by the security service at his home. From a recording of Havers's speech, as Attorney-General, in the House of Commons (21 November 1979) rather than from *Hansard*.

HAWKER, R.S.

English clergyman (1803–75)

4 And shall Trelawny die?
Here's twenty thousand Cornish men
Will know the reason why.

The refrain from Hawker's 'Song of the Western Men' (1845) refers to Bishop Sir Jonathan Trelawny of Bristol. In 1688 Trelawny was sent to the Tower by King James II with six other bishops on charges of seditious libel. They were acquitted. Hawker said he took the whole refrain from an old Cornish ballad, but, if so, it has not been discovered.

HAWKESWORTH, John

English TV playwright (1920–)

5 By the Sword Divided.

Hawkesworth gave this title to a BBC TV historical drama series (1983–5) set in the English Civil War. He commented (1991): 'When I first wrote down the idea for a story about the Civil War I called it 'The Laceys of Arnescote' ... [but] I decided the title didn't convey the sort of Hentyish swashbuckling style that we were aiming at, so I thought again. The title "By the Sword Divided" came to me as I was walking along a beach in Wales.'

The phrase sounds like a quotation but apparently is not. In dealing with the Civil War period, Macaulay in his *History of England*, Chaps. 1–2 (1848), came close with: 'Thirteen years followed during which England was ... really governed by the sword'; 'the whole nation was sick of government by the sword'; 'anomalies and abuses ... which had been destroyed by the sword'.

HAY, Ian

British novelist and playwright (1876–1952)

1 TO
THE MEMBERS
OF
THE MOST RESPONSIBLE
THE LEAST ADVERTISED
THE WORST PAID
AND
THE MOST RICHLY REWARDED
PROFESSION
IN THE WORLD.

Dedication of book, *The Lighter Side of School Life* (1914). Apart from his war novels, Hay's best known works are concerned with public school life. Curiously, he does not appear ever to have taught at such a school himself.

2 The First Hundred Thousand.

Title of war novel (1915), subtitled 'Adventures of a typical regiment in Kitchener's army'. The book begins with a poem (Hay's own, presumably):

We're off a hundred thousand strong.
And some of us will not come back.

A.J.P. Taylor in his *English History 1914–45*, describing a period of 'patriotic frenzy' in the Great War, says that the 'spirit of 1915 was best expressed by Ian Hay, a writer of light fiction, in *The First Hundred Thousand* – a book which treated soldiering as joke, reviving "the best days of our lives" at some imaginary public school'.

3 What do you mean, funny? Funny-peculiar, or funny ha-ha?

Hay's play *Housemaster*, Act 3 (first performed 1936 – not the novel published in the same year, where it does not appear) is usually given as the origin of this popular expression. However, in the American Meriel Brady's novel *Genevieve Gertrude*, Chap. 7 (1928) there is this:

'I liked that song, myself,' he said, 'even if it isn't classical. It's funny, anyhow.'
Genevieve Gertrude raised her hand.
'Do you mean funny peculiar, or funny ha-ha?' she inquired politely.
...''Cause,' explained his mentor gravely, 'our teacher don't allow us to say funny when we mean peculiar. It's bad English, you know.'

There is also a tantalizing play on words to be found in Mary Vivian Hughes, *A London Family Between the Wars*, Chap. 6 (1940) – referring to the 1920s:

'Haven't you brought me any funny stories this time?'
'Not much. There's one thing I heard – "not sunny but pecoola" as you used to say when you were tiny.'

The first, if not the second, of these quotes is clear proof that the phrase existed before Ian Hay popularized it further.

HAYES, J. Milton

British writer (1884–1940)

4 There's a one-eyed yellow idol to the North of Khatmandu;
There's a little marble cross below the town;
And a brokenhearted woman tends the grave of 'Mad' Carew,
While the yellow god for ever gazes down.

'The Green Eye of the Yellow God' (1911), written with Cuthbert Clarke. This recitation piece (often misascribed to Kipling) has been much parodied, though it can hardly have been written in total seriousness in the first place. The British music-hall comedian Billy Bennett (1887–1942) once performed 'The Green Tie of the Little Yellow Dog' before King George V: 'There's a cock-eyed yellow poodle to the North of Gongapooch, [Hindustani for 'arseholes']/There's a little hot-cross-bun that's turning green,/There's a double-jointed wop-wop doing tricks in who-flung-dung,/ And you're a better man than I am Gunga-Din.'

HAYWARD, Abraham

English essayist (1801–84)

5 He writes too often and too fast ... If he persists much longer in this course, it requires no gift of prophecy to foretell his fate – he has risen like a rocket, and he will come down like a stick.

Of Charles Dickens. Hayward was reviewing *Pickwick Papers* for *The Quarterly Review* (October 1838). Not entirely original: Tom Paine had said of Edmund Burke, 'As he rose like the rocket, he fell like the stick' – *Letter to the Addressers on the late Proclamation* (1792).

HAZLITT, William

English essayist (1778–1830)

1 The Spirit of the Age.

Hazlitt's book of essays (1825) was devoted to examinations of the work and characters of contemporary writers. The phrase had earlier been used by Shelley in a letter of 1820: 'It is the spirit of the age, and we are all infected with it.' David Hume had used it in 1752 (according to *Notes and Queries*, Vol. 236). Later, *The Pall Mall Gazette* was stating (6 August 1891): 'The Spirit of the Age is against those who put party or programme before human needs.' In 1975 the title *Spirit of the Age* was given to a BBC TV series on the history of architecture, with Alec Clifton-Taylor.

2 A nickname is the heaviest stone that the devil can throw at a man.

'On Nicknames', *The Edinburgh Magazine* (1818). In fact, Hazlitt was referring more to political labels than personal nicknames.

HEALEY, Denis (later Lord Healey)

British Labour politician (1917–)

3 I warn you that there are going to be howls of anguish from the 80,000 people who are rich enough to pay over 75 per cent on the last slice of their income.

Speech to the Labour Party Conference (1 October 1973), when Shadow Chancellor, explaining that Labour's programme would cost money and the only way to raise it was through taxation. He promised increased income tax and a wealth tax if the party won the next election (it never materialized). Not 'howls of anger', as quoted in *The Sunday Telegraph* (October 1980). In his autobiography *The Time of My Life* (1989), Healey said the phrase 'make the rich howl with anguish' still 'hangs round my neck like Wilson's phrase "the pound in your pocket", and Heath's election promise to cut prices "at a stroke". I never said either that I would "squeeze the rich until the pips squeak", though I did quote Tony Crosland using this phrase of Lloyd George's in reference to property speculators, not to the rich in general.'

Phrase of Lloyd George's? Surely, he meant GEDDES 255:4.

4 That part of his speech was rather like being savaged by a dead sheep.

Speech, House of Commons (14 June 1978). As Chancellor of the Exchequer, on being attacked by Sir Geoffrey Howe in a debate over his Budget proposals. In 1987 Alan Watkins of *The Observer* suggested that Sir Roy Welensky, of Central African Federation fame, had earlier likened an attack by Iain Macleod to being *bitten* by a sheep. We had to wait until 1989 and the publication of Healey's memoirs to be told that, 'the phrase came to me while I was actually on my feet; it was an adaptation of Churchill's remark that an attack by Attlee was "like being savaged by a pet lamb". Such banter can often enliven a dull afternoon.'

The Churchill version remains untraced, but he was noted for his Attlee jokes (and busily denied that he had ever said most of them, *see* CHURCHILL 167:9). In 1990, the victim of Healey's phrase, Geoffrey Howe, also claimed that it wasn't original. 'It came from a play', he said sheepishly. A profile of Healey in *The Sunday Telegraph* (3 November 1996) suggested that he had appropriated the phrase 'dead sheep' without acknowledgement from the journalist Andrew Alexander.

5 Mrs Thatcher is doing for monetarism what the Boston Strangler did for door-to-door salesmen.

Speech, House of Commons (15 December 1979). Once he got hold of a good line, Healey was never one to let it go. It may be instructive to note, however, what happened to this one by way of subsequent use and attribution. From *Today* (24 May 1987): 'Liberal David Steel said earlier this year: "Mrs Thatcher seems to have done for women in politics what the Boston Strangler did for door-to-door salesmen".' From *The Independent* (20 January 1989): 'Mr Healey also had a pithy word for President Reagan: "He has done for monetarism what the Boston Strangler did for door-to-door salesmen".' From *The Washington Post* (16 October 1991): 'Shields introduced Hatch, the starched shirt of the Senate hearings, as "the man who has done for bipartisanship what the Boston Strangler did for door-to-door salesmen".' From *The Sunday Times* (9 February 1992): 'Denis Healey ... claimed to have tried to do for economic forecasters what the Boston Strangler did for door-to-door salesmen ...'

6 When you are in a hole, stop digging.

On US politicians having got themselves into a hole over the arms race. Remark, September 1983; also attributed to him in *The Observer* (May 1988). However, on 7 January 1983, the *Financial Times* quoted Kenneth Mayland, an economist with the First Pennsylvania Bank, as saying: 'The first rule of holes; when you're in one, stop digging.' So, was it an established proverb that Denis Healey simply picked up and made his own (as he has been somewhat inclined to do with other people's jokes and phrases)?

1 I plan to be the Gromyko of the Labour party for the next thirty years.

Remark on several occasions (1984), referring to Andrei Gromyko (1909–89) who served as Soviet foreign minister from 1957 almost until his death. Healey had been defeated in his attempt to become leader of the Labour Party and was hoping to emulate Gromyko's long-running influence (rather than his grim visage).

2 You mustn't take out a man's appendix while he's moving a grand piano.

Quoted as a 'favourite aphorism' of Healey's in Philip Ziegler, *Mountbatten* (1985). Given Healey's magpie tendencies when it comes to a good joke or line, it may be assumed not to be of his own invention.

HEALY, Tim

Irish politician (1855–1931)

3 He is not a man to go tiger-shooting with.

This jibe was reputedly fired at the somewhat weak and vacillating Lord Rosebery by Healy, the Irish Nationalist leader who sat in the Westminster Parliament (1880–1918). It is quoted by Robert Rhodes James in *Rosebery* (1963). If not the first use of this slur, it is the most famous. In 1961, Lord Montgomery was quoted as saying: '[Chairman] Mao has a very fine strong face. He's the sort of man I'd go in the jungle with.' In 1970, I was told of a university appointments secretary who would add his own comments on the bottom of application forms he was forwarding to employers on behalf of students. On one he wrote: 'This chap would be splendid to shoot tigers with.'

HEANEY, Seamus

Irish poet (1939–)

4 Is there a life before death? That's chalked up
In Ballymurphy. Competence with pain,
Coherent miseries, a bite and sup,
We hug our little destiny again.

'Whatever You Say Say Nothing', *North* (1975). But as if this underlines the saying's Irish origins too well, bear in mind that 'Is there life before death?' had earlier been the epigraph to Chap. 9 of Stephen Vizinczey's novel *In Praise of Older Women* (1966). There, it is credited to 'Anon. Hungarian'.

HEATH, Edward (later Sir Edward)

British Conservative Prime Minister (1916–)

5 The full-hearted consent of the Parliament and people of the new member countries.

On 5 May 1970, a month and a half before he became Prime Minister, Heath addressed the Franco-British Chamber of Commerce in Paris. Looking ahead to the forthcoming enlargement of the EEC through British, Irish and other membership, he said that this would not be in the interests of the Community, 'except with the full-hearted consent ...' The statement, penned by Douglas Hurd, then a Heath aide, was seized upon subsequently by those seeking a referendum on EEC entry.

6 This would, at a stroke, reduce the rise in prices, increase productivity and reduce unemployment.

A press release (No. G.E.228), from Conservative Central Office, dated 16 June 1970, was concerned with tax cuts and a freeze on prices by nationalized industries. The phrase 'at a stroke', though never actually spoken by Heath, came to haunt him, when he became Prime Minister two days later.

7 We were returned to office to change the course of history of this nation – nothing less. If we are to achieve this task we will have to embark on a change so radical, a revolution so quiet and yet so total, that it will go far beyond the programme for a parliament to which we are committed and on which we have already embarked, far beyond the decade and way into the 80s.

Speech, Conservative Party Conference (October 1970) – shortly after his government had been formed. A 'quiet revolution' is a subtle change which does not draw attention to itself. The phrase was written by Barry Day (an advertising man) who was Heath's speechwriter at the time but had earlier been used to describe the operations of the Liberal government in the Canadian province of Quebec, led by Jean Lesage (1960).

8 It is the unpleasant and unacceptable face of capitalism, but one should not suggest that the whole of British industry consists of practices of this kind.

In 1973 it was revealed that a former Tory Cabinet minister, Duncan Sandys, had been paid £130,000 in compensation for giving up his £50,000 a year consultancy with the Lonrho company. The money was to be paid, quite legally, into an account in the Cayman Islands to avoid British tax. This kind of activity did not seem appropriate when the government was promoting a counterinflation policy. Replying to a question from Jo Grimond MP in the House of Commons on 15 May, Heath, as Prime Minister, created a format phrase that has since been used to describe the 'unnacceptable face of' almost anything. In the text from which he spoke (said to have been prepared by his then aide, Douglas Hurd), it apparently had 'facet'.

See also ANONYMOUS 49:5.

HEATH, Robert

English poet (seventeenth century)

1 Things of so small concern or moment, who
Would stuff his Diary with, or care to know?
As what he wore, thought, laugh'd at, where he walked,
When farted, where he pissed, with whom he talked.

'Satyr 1', *Clarastella* (1650). Not a very encouraging view of diary keeping.

HEBER, Reginald

English bishop and hymn writer (1783–1826)

2 Brightest and best of the sons of the morning!
Dawn on our darkness and lend us Thine aid!

Hymn (1811). *Compare* HALBERSTAM 277:5.

3 What though the spicy breezes
Blow soft o'er Ceylon's isle;
Though every prospect pleases,
And only man is vile.

This was what Heber originally wrote in the hymn 'From Greenland's icy mountains' (1821), leading up to the lines about 'the heathen in his blindness' bowing down 'to wood and stone'. Later, however, he changed 'Ceylon's' to 'Java's'. Sir Peter Kemp, writing to *The Independent* Magazine (15 May 1993), said that he had been told there were two reasons for this change: Java, with its accent on the first syllable, goes better with the tune that is usually used. Secondly, 'the Colonial Office of the day objected to Bishop Heber's traducing of a part of the Empire and insisted on the change'. Heber became Bishop of Calcutta in 1823.

John Lloyd of Haverfordwest, Pembrokeshire, challenged the second point (1994): 'I gravely doubt this: even if a Colonial Office existed at the time, both Calcutta, where Heber was Bishop, and Ceylon, would have been within the competence of the India Office. The intervention, as I heard the story when I was in the East, was from one of Heber's clergy, who pointed out that Ceylon was in Heber's Diocese – Calcutta being the Diocese for the whole of British India at the time – and it would be prudent, if he had to refer to heathen who, in their blindness, bowed down to wood and stone, to locate them somewhat further away.

'The more appealing anecdote about the hymn is that Heber showed it to his father-in-law, the Dean of St Asaph, seeking approval for his little three-verse masterpiece, the peroration of which concludes verse three. The Dean is said to have said, "It is very good, but if you think you can get the collection up in three verses, you are mistaken". This resulted in Heber adding the fourth verse, which is clearly repetitious of the earlier three.'

HEIN, Piet

Danish poet, designer and inventor (1905–96)

4 Losing one glove is sorrow enough
But nothing compared with the pain
Of losing one glove
Discarding the other
Then finding the first one again.

Translation of one of his aphoristic *Grooks*, though as Hein lived from 1969 to 1976 in Britain, it may have been written in English originally. In 1996, on BBC Radio *Quote ... Unquote*, Jonathan Cecil quoted the following as a 'Danish proverb', which may conceivably have been what Hein versified or is simply a prose remembering of what he wrote: 'It is terrible to lose a right-handed glove and to have to throw the left-handed glove away. But it is even more terrible to lose a right-handed glove and to throw the left-handed glove away and then to find the right-handed glove.'

HEINE, Heinrich

German poet (1797–1856)

5 *Dieu me pardonnera, c'est son métier.*
God will pardon me. It is his profession.

Last words. Quoted in Alfred Meissner, *Heinrich Heine: Erinnerungen* (1856). Has also been attributed to Voltaire and to Catherine the Great.

HELLER, Joseph

American novelist (1923–)

1 Catch-22.

The title of Heller's novel (1961; film US, 1970), about a group of US fliers in the Second World War, has become a widely used catchphrase. 'It was a Catch-22 situation,' people will say, as if resorting to a quasi-proverbial expression like 'Heads you win, tails I lose' or 'Damned if you do, damned if you don't'. What Heller did was to affix a name to the popular view that 'there's always a catch', some underlying law that defeats people by its brutal, ubiquitous logic. Oddly, Heller had originally called it 'Catch-18'. In the book, the idea is explored several times. Captain Yossarian, a US Air Force bombardier, does not wish to fly any more missions. He goes to see the group's MO, Doc Daneeka, about getting grounded on the grounds that he is crazy:

Daneeka: There's a rule saying I have to ground anyone who's crazy.

Yossarian: Then why can't you ground me? I'm crazy.

Daneeka: Anyone who wants to get out of combat duty isn't really crazy.

This is the catch – 'Catch-22'.

2 Some men are born mediocre, some men achieve mediocrity, and some men have mediocrity thrust upon them. With Major Major it was all three.

Catch-22, Chap. 9. Alluding to SHAKESPEARE 495:10.

HELLMAN, Lillian

American playwright and writer (1905–84)

3 The Watch on the Rhine.

The title of a play (1941; film US, 1943) comes from the poem '*Die Wacht am Rhein*' by Max Schnekenburger (1840), set to music by Karl Wilhelm (1854), which became a German national song. There was a British parody in the First World War: 'When We've Wound Up the Watch on the Rhine'.

4 To hurt innocent people whom I knew many years ago in order to save myself is, to me, inhuman and indecent and dishonorable. I cannot and will not cut my conscience to fit this year's fashions.

Letter to Chairman, House Committee on un-American Activities, Washington (19 May 1952). Quoted in *Scoundrel Time* (1976).

HELMSLEY, Leona

American hotelier (1920–)

5 We don't pay taxes. Only the little people pay taxes.

In August 1989, Helmsley, New York's self-styled 'hotel queen', was found guilty of evading more than $1 million in taxes. During the trial her housekeeper, Elizabeth Baum, recounted how Helmsley had made this unfortunate observation (quoted in *The New York Times*, 2 July 1989). Helmsley received a four-year jail term and a $7 million fine for tax fraud.

HELPMANN, Sir Robert

Australian dancer and choreographer (1909–86)

6 The trouble with nude dancing is that not everything stops when the music stops.

After the opening night of *Oh, Calcutta!*. Quoted in *The Frank Muir Book* (1976). Also in the form: 'No. You see there are portions of the human anatomy which would keep swinging after the music had finished', when asked if the fashion for nudity on stage would extend to dance (Elizabeth Salter, *Helpmann*, 1978).

HEMANS, Felicia

English poet (1793–1835)

7 The boy stood on the burning deck
Whence all but he had fled;
The flame that lit the battle's wreck
Shone round him o'er the dead.

'Casabianca' (1849). A famous recitation poem and based on a true incident. During the Battle of the Nile (1798), Louis de Casabianca was commander of the French ship *L'Orient*. His son, aged about thirteen, remained at his post when the vessel caught fire and perished with it.

See also COWARD 187:2.

HEMINGWAY, Ernest

American novelist (1899–1961)

8 The Sun Also Rises.

Title of novel (1926). *See* BIBLE 96:5.

1 Grace under pressure.

In an interview with *The New Yorker* (30 November 1929), Hemingway gave this as a definition of 'guts'. It was based on the Latin '*fortiter in re, suaviter in modo*' and was later invoked by John F. Kennedy at the start of his book *Profiles in Courage* (1956).

2 *F. Scott Fitzgerald*: The very rich are different from you and me.
Hemingway: Yes, they have more money.

In Tom Burnam, *More Misinformation* (1980), the facts are neatly established about this famous exchange said to have occurred between Hemingway and F. Scott Fitzgerald. In his short story 'The Rich Boy' (1926) Fitzgerald had written: 'Let me tell you about the very rich. They are different from you and me.' Twelve years later in *his* short story 'The Snows of Kilimanjaro' (1938) Hemingway had the narrator remember 'poor Scott Fitzgerald', his awe of the rich and that 'someone' had said, 'Yes, they have more money'.

When Fitzgerald read the story, he protested to Hemingway who dropped Fitzgerald's name from further printings. In any case, the put-down 'Yes, they have more money' had not been administered to Fitzgerald but to Hemingway himself. In 1936, Hemingway said at a lunch with the critic Mary Colum: 'I am getting to know the rich.' She replied: 'The only difference between the rich and other people is that the rich have more money.'

Also discussed in *Scott and Ernest* (1978) by Mathew J. Bruccoli. Compare: 'The Rich aren't like us – they pay less taxes' – Peter de Vries, in *The Washington Post* (30 July 1989).

3 Did the earth move for you?

Jokily addressed to one's partner after sexual intercourse, this appears to have originated as 'Did thee feel the earth move?' in Hemingway's *For Whom the Bell Tolls* (1940). It is not spoken in the 1943 film version, however. Headline from *The Sport* (22 February 1989): 'SPORT SEXCLUSIVE ON A BONK THAT WILL MAKE THE EARTH MOVE.' From the same novel comes the other interesting inquiry on the subject of kissing: 'Where do the noses go? I always wondered where the noses would go.'

4 The Old Man and the Sea.

Title of novel (1952; film US, 1958), presumably alluding to 'The Old Man *of* the Sea', the name of a troublesome character in *The Arabian Nights* who climbed on the back of Sinbad the Sailor and was hard to dislodge, hence, the phrase for 'a burden'.

5 If you are lucky enough to have lived in Paris as a young man, then wherever you go for the rest of your life, it stays with you, for Paris is a moveable feast.

Epigraph, *A Moveable Feast* (1964). In the ecclesiastical world, a moveable feast is one that does not fall on a fixed date but, like Easter, occurs according to certain rules.

See also JACKSON 310:1.

HENDERSON, Leon

American economist (1895–1986)

6 Having a little inflation is like being a little pregnant.

Quoted by J.K. Galbraith in *A Life in Our Times* (1981). Henderson was appointed by President Roosevelt to the National Defense Advisory Commission in 1940.

HENDRIX, Jimmy

American rock musician (1942–70)

7 Once you're dead, you're made for life.

This attributed remark, dating from *c.*1968, was certainly prescient in Hendrix's own case. His success was enhanced following his early death in September 1970. Within six weeks he had a No. 1 hit in the UK with 'Voodoo Experience'. *The Independent* (21 April 1995) added the sentence 'It's funny the way most people love the dead' before the remark.

The pattern of a surge of interest – indeed, *increased* popularity – after death has been accorded to any number of pop stars who have died relatively young. Elvis Presley in 1977 and John Lennon in 1980 benefited similarly. A graffito (reported in *Time* Magazine, 8 April 1985) following Presley's death commented: 'Good career move.' *Compare* VIDAL 551:2.

HENLEY, W.E.

English poet (1849–1903)

8 In the fell clutch of circumstance,
I have not winced nor cried aloud:
Under the bludgeonings of chance
My head is bloody, but unbowed.

'Invictus. In Memoriam R.T. Hamilton Bruce' (1875). Hence, 'bloody but unbowed' has become a phrase in general use, often as an unascribed quotation, meaning 'determined after having suffered a defeat.' 'Bloody but unbowed, veteran discount retailers Gerald and Vera Weisfeld have hit out at the new £56m rescue deal agreed between struggling Poundstretcher owner Brown & Jackson and South African group Pepkor' – *Daily Mail* (10 May 1994).

1 It matters not how strait the gate,
How charged with punishments the scroll,
I am the master of my fate:
I am the captain of my soul.

Ib. Winston Churchill said in a speech to the House of Commons (9 September 1941): 'Today we may say aloud before an awe-struck world, "We are still masters of our fate. We are still captain of our souls".' Compare P.G. Wodehouse, 'Lord Emsworth and the Girl Friend', *Blandings Castle and Elsewhere* (1935): 'It is always unpleasant for a proud man to realize that he is no longer captain of his soul; that he is to all intents and purposes ground beneath the number twelve heel of a Glaswegian head-gardener.'

2 Madam Life's a piece in bloom
Death goes dogging everywhere:
She's the tennant of the room,
He's the ruffian on the stair.

'To W.R.' (1877). Hence, *The Ruffian On the Stair*, title of a radio play (1964) by Joe Orton.

3 What have I done for you,
England, my England?
What is there I would not do,
England, my own?

'Pro Rege Nostro', *For England's Sake* (1900). Hence, many allusions: *England My England*, title of a book of short stories by D.H. Lawrence (1922); A.G. MacDonell's satire on country life, *England, Their England* (1933); a posthumous book of George Orwell's essays, *England, Your England* (1953); and *England, Our England*, title of a revue by Keith Waterhouse and Willis Hall (London, 1962).

4 The nightingale has a lyre of gold,
The lark's is a clarion call,
And the blackbird plays but a boxwood flute,
But I love him best of all.

'XVIII to A.D.' (undated). A 'lost' quotation until traced to its source (1997) using the Chadwyck-Healey Poetry Full-Text Database (600–1900) on CD-ROM.

HENRI IV (Henri of Navarre)

French King (1553–1610)

5 *Paris vaut bien une messe.*
Paris is well worth a mass.

Said either by Henri or his minister Sully (in conversation with him), though no real evidence exists. Henri had led the Protestant forces in the Third Huguenot War (1569–72) as King of Navarre, but in 1589 he marched on Catholic-held Paris and became King of France. In 1593 he renounced Protestantism and converted to Catholicism, hence this cynical if pragmatic remark, which was first recorded in 1622.

In 1681 Hardouin de Péréfixe commented in *Histoire de Henry le Grand*: 'The Politiques ... said to him that of all canons, the Canon of the Mass was the best to reduce the towns of his kingdom.'

6 *Je veux qu'il n'y ait si pauvre paysan en mon royaume qu'il n'ait tous les dimanches sa poule au pot.*
I will make sure that there will be no labourer in my kingdom without the means of having a chicken in his pot.

A remark recorded by a contemporary lawyer, Pierre de l'Estoile. Péréfixe (1681) later recorded it in the above French version. 'A chicken in every pot' accordingly became one of the earliest political slogans. In 1928, running for the US Presidency, Herbert Hoover said, 'The slogan of progress is changing from the "full dinner pail" to the full garage' and by 1932 this was sometimes interpreted as 'a chicken in every pot and two cars in every garage'. In 1960 John F. Kennedy misquoted Hoover as having uttered the slogan 'Two chickens for every pot' in 1928.

7 *Toujours perdrix.*
Always partridge.

(Or, in Latin, *semper perdrix*), meaning 'too much of a good thing'. The King was reproved by his confessor for his marital infidelities, so he ordered the priest to be fed on nothing but partridge. When the priest complained that it was 'always partridge', the King replied it was the same if you had only one mistress.

HENRY II

English King (1133–89)

8 Will no man rid me of this turbulent priest?

Henry II's rhetorical question regarding Thomas Becket – which was unfortunately acted upon by the Archbishop's murderers in 1170 – is ascribed to 'oral tradition' by *ODQ* (1979) in the form: 'Will no one revenge me of the injuries I have sustained from one turbulent priest?' The King, who was in Normandy, had received reports that the Archbishop was ready 'to tear the crown from' his head. 'What a pack of fools and cowards I have nourished in my house,' he cried, according to another version, 'that not one of them will avenge me of this turbulent priest!' Yet another version has, 'of this upstart clerk'.

An example of the phrase used allusively in conversation was played on tape at the conspiracy-to-murder trial involving Jeremy Thorpe MP in 1979. In one recording, Andrew Newton speaking of the alleged plot said: 'They feel a Thomas à Becket was done, you know, with Thorpe sort of raving that would nobody rid me of this man.'

HENRY IV

English King (1367–1413)

1 Lauds be given to the Father of heaven, for now I know that I shall die here in this chamber, according to the prophecy of me declared, that I should depart this life in Jerusalem.

The last words of Henry IV, according to Raphael Holinshed's *The Chronicles of England, Scotland and Ireland* (1587). He had just been told that he was lying in the Jerusalem Chamber of Westminster Abbey. He had been preparing for an expedition to the Holy Land and was visiting the Abbey on the eve of his departure when taken ill. Shakespeare in *Henry IV, Part 2* takes this situation almost word for word from the chronicle (*see* 483:11). After the dissolution of the Abbey, the Jerusalem Chamber became the meeting place of the Dean and Chapter. Its name derives from mention of Jerusalem in inscriptions round the fireplace or from the original tapestry hangings.

HENRY VIII

English King (1491–1547)

2 The King found her so different from her picture ... that ... he swore they had brought him a Flanders mare.

On seeing Anne of Cleves, his fourth wife, for the first time. Quoted by Tobias Smollett, *A Complete History of England* (1759).

3 The things I've done for England.

In Sir Alexander Korda's film *The Private Life of Henry VIII* (1933), Charles Laughton as the King is just about to get into bed with one of his many wives when, alluding to her ugliness, he sighs: 'The things I've done for England.' The screenplay was written by Lajos Biro and Arthur Wimperis. There is no historical precedent.

The phrase caught on, to be used ironically when confronted with any unpleasant task. In 1979, Prince Charles on a visit to Hong Kong sampled curried snake meat and, with a polite nod towards his ancestor, exclaimed: 'Boy, the things I do for England.'

HENRY, O.

American writer (1862–1910)

4 Turn up the lights [*or* put up the shades], I don't want to go home in the dark.

Attributed last words, alluding to the song 'I'm Afraid to Go Home in the Dark.'

HENRY, Patrick

American statesman (1736–99)

5 I know not what course others may take; but as for me, give me liberty or give me death!

Henry was the foremost opponent of British rule and the leading orator of American independence. His speech in the Virginia Convention (23 March 1775) helped carry the vote for independence. He became Governor of the new state and was four times re-elected. Compare Joseph Addison, *Cato*, Act, Sc. 5 (1713): 'Chains or conquest, liberty or death.'

HENRY, Philip

English clergyman (1631–96)

6 All This and Heaven Too.

Title of a novel (1939, film US, 1940) by Rachel Field. As acknowledged in the book, Matthew Henry, the nonconformist divine and Bible commentator (d.1714), attributed the saying to his minister father in his *Life of Mr Philip Henry* (1698). Compare the title *All This and World War II* (film US, 1976) and the *Daily Express* front page headline on Coronation Day (2 June 1953): 'ALL THIS – AND EVEREST TOO' – announcing the fact that a British-led expedition had been the first to conquer the world's highest mountain.

HEPBURN, Katharine

American film actress (1909–)

1 Not any more.

The great actress was once observed shovelling snow outside her New York residence. 'Hey, aren't you Joan Crawford?' someone called out. This was her reply. Source untraced. Almost any famous person worth his or her salt has at some time, apparently, been asked the question, 'Hey, didn't you used to be —— ——?' In addition, the English actor Ernest Thesiger kept on acting to a ripe old age and enjoyed telling the story of the person who had asked him, 'Excuse me, but *weren't* you Ernest Thesiger?' To which he replied: 'Madam, I was.' Related in Michael Pertwee, *Name Dropping* (1974), Derek Salberg, *My Love Affair With the Theatre* (1978) and Donald Sinden, *The Everyman Book of Theatrical Anecdotes* (1987).

2 He gives her class and she gives him sex.

On what made the screen partnership of Fred Astaire and Ginger Rogers work. Quoted in Leslie Halliwell, *The Filmgoer's Book of Quotes* (1973), but otherwise unsubstantiated.

See also STAGE DOOR 515:2.

HERACLITUS

Greek philosopher (c.540–c.480BC)

3 The past and present
Are as one –
Accordant and discordant
Youth and age
And death and birth –
For out of one came all
From all comes one.

Edith Sitwell (*q.v.*) is buried in St Mary's churchyard extension, Weedon Lois, Northamptonshire, under a headstone designed by Henry Moore. It bears this, her own version of words from Heraclitus, which she had quoted in the concluding lines of her poem 'The Wind of Early Spring'.

HERFORD, Oliver

American humorist (1863–1935)

4 Actresses will happen in the best-regulated families.

Quoted in *The Treasury of Humorous Quotations*, ed. by Evan Esar & Nicolas Bentley (1951). *See* DICKENS 204:10.

HERODOTUS

Greek historian (c.485–425BC)

5 Neither snow nor rain nor heat nor gloom of night stays these couriers from the swift completion of their appointed rounds.

Words inscribed on the stone face of the New York City Post Office, being adapted from the *Histories* of Herodotus. He is describing how King Cyrus the Great of Persia set up what is thought to have been the first organized system of mounted messengers (in the sixth century BC). But the New York inscription has given rise to the comment, 'Well, what is it then?'

HERRICK, Robert

English poet and clergyman (1591–1674)

6 Be she showing in her dress,
Like a civil wilderness;
That the curious may detect
Order in a sweet neglect.

Herrick *twice* refers to types of 'disorder in the dress'. The above comes from 'What Kind of Mistress He Would Have' (1648). In 'Delight in Disorder', he writes:

> A sweet disorder in the dress
> Kindles in clothes a wantonness ...

He concludes that such distractions bewitch him more than 'when Art/Is too precise in every part'.

7 Gather ye rosebuds while ye may.

'To the Virgins, to Make Much of Time' (1648). *Compare* PORTER 435:6.

HEWART, Gordon (later Viscount Hewart)

British lawyer and politician (1870–1943)

8 Justice should not only be done, but should manifestly and undoubtedly be seen to be done.

The origin of this noted legal observation is contained in a ruling by Hewart (King's Bench Reports, 1924). A man named McCarthy in Hastings had been accused of dangerous driving. There had been an accident in which people were injured. He was convicted, but it was later discovered that a partner in the firm of solicitors who had demanded damages against him was also clerk to the Hastings justices. As Robert Jackson noted (*The Chief*, 1959), no one believed that the clerk had acted improperly during the case but the circumstances warranted an application by McCarthy's solicitor for the conviction to be quashed in a Divisional Court. Hewart ruled in his favour in the case of Rex *v*. Sussex Justices (9 November 1923).

When a fellow-judge joked that 'be seen' was a misprint for 'seem', Hewart made it clear that justice must always be seen to be done in view of the defendant and of the world. *Compare* MORTON 401:3.

1 If it's only wind, I'll call it ...

F.E. Smith, 1st Earl of Birkenhead, taunted Hewart, when Lord Chief Justice, about the size of his stomach. 'What's it to be – a boy or a girl?' Replied Hewart: 'If it's a boy I'll call him John. If it's a girl I'll call her Mary. But if, as I suspect, it's only wind, I'll call it F.E. Smith.'

I printed that anecdote in my book *Quote ... Unquote* (1978). The story had come to me the previous year from a *Quote ... Unquote* listener who said it had been told to her brother 'by a stranger in a bus queue in Harrogate in 1923'. Smith died in 1930, Hewart in 1943.

According to Humphrey McQueen in *Social Sketches of Australia* (1978), the Antipodean version has Sir George Houstoun Reid (1845–1918) replying, in answer to the question, apropos his stomach, 'What are you going to call it, George?': 'If it's a boy, I'll call it after myself. If it's a girl, I'll call it Victoria after our Queen. But if, as I strongly suspect, it's nothing but piss and wind, I'll call it after you.'

According to *Pass the Port Again* (1981 ed.) the exchange occurred between Lord Haldane and Winston Churchill, as also in John Parker, *Father of the House* (1982), in which the exchange is specifically located at the Oxford Union in 1926. *The Faber Book of Anecdotes* (1985) has the US version: President William Taft (1857–1930) making the retort to Senator Chauncey Depew (1834–1928).

HILL, Charles (later Lord Hill)

British doctor, politician and broadcaster (1904–89)

2 Black-coated workers.

Referring to prunes as laxatives, this term was popularized by Hill as the Radio Doctor from 1941 onwards in an early morning BBC programme *The Kitchen Front*. He noted in his autobiography *Both Sides of the Hill* (1964): 'I remember calling on the Principal Medical Officer of the Board of Education ... At the end of the interview this shy and solemn man diffidently suggested that the prune was a black-coated worker and that this phrase might be useful to me. It was.' Earlier, Chips Channon (8 April 1937) had used the phrase in a literal sense concerning the clerical and professional class when he wrote: 'The subject was "Widows and Orphans" the Old Age Pensions Bill, a measure which affects Southend and its black-coated workers' (*Chips: The Diaries of Sir Henry Channon*, ed. Robert Rhodes James, 1967).

HILL, Joe

Swedish-born songwriter and industrial organizer in US (1879–1915)

3 Work and pray, live on hay,
You'll get pie in the sky when you die.

'The Preacher and the Slave' in *Songs of the Workers* (1911), published by Industrial Workers of the World. Sung to the turn of 'In the Sweet By and By', this added 'pie in the sky' to the list of common expressions. Hill contributed songs, essays and letters to the IWW's Industrial Workers and Solidarity from 1910 until his execution (on a murder charge) (Flexner, 1982). *See also* ALI 16:2.

HILL, Patty Smith

American teacher (1868–1946)

4 Happy Birthday to You.

Originally entitled 'Good Morning to All' and published in *Song Stories for Children* (1893), Hill's well-known song with this title was eventually copyrighted in 1935. The music was written by her sister, Mildred J. Hill (1859–1916). What we have here is the 'most frequently sung phrase in English', according to *The Guinness Book of Records* (which also lists 'For He's a Jolly Good Fellow' and 'Auld Lang Syne' as the top songs of all time). 'Happy Birthday to You' was the first line of the second stanza of the original song. It has had a chequered legal history because of the widespread belief that it is in the public domain and, therefore, out of copyright. It is not.

HILL, Rowland

English preacher (1744–1833)

5 Why must the devil have all the best tunes?

According to E.W. Broome's biography of Hill, what he said was: 'I do not see any good reason why the devil should have all the good tunes.' He was referring to Charles Wesley's defence of the practice of setting hymns to the music of popular songs. The phrase is now used generally to rebut the necessity for the virtuous and worthy to be dull and dreary. This Rev. Hill is not to be confused with Sir Rowland Hill, originator of the English penny postage system.

A perhaps better known – but later – use of the phrase concerns William Booth (1829–1912), the founder of the Salvation Army. It was his practice to use established tunes to accompany religious lyrics. In this way, more than eighty music-hall songs acquired religious lyrics, 'Champagne Charlie is My Name', for example, became 'Bless His Name He Sets Me Free'. When Booth was challenged on the suitability of such a process, he was doubtful at first, but then exclaimed, 'Why should the Devil have all the best tunes!'

Reference to the Booth use is made by the composer Percy Grainger in the Preface to *Spoon River* (1930): 'Salvation Army Booth objected to the devil having all the good tunes. I object to jazz and vaudeville having all the best instruments!'

HILLARY, Edmund (later Sir Edmund)

New Zealand mountaineer (1919–)

1 Well, we knocked the bastard off!

The first two climbers to reach the summit of the world's highest mountain, Mount Everest, in the Himalayas, were Hillary and his Sherpa guide, Tenzing Norgay. They were members of the British-led expedition in 1953. In his autobiography *Nothing Venture, Nothing Win* (1975), Hillary described what happened when they came down from the summit on 29 May: 'George [Lowe] met us with a mug of soup just above camp, and seeing his stalwart frame and cheerful face reminded me how fond of him I was. My comment was not specially prepared for public consumption but for George ... He nodded with pleasure ..."Thought you must have!"'

Among the frequent misrenderings of the remark is, 'We done the bugger!' – as in *PDMQ* (1971) where it is even ascribed to Tenzing Norgay (who did not even speak English).

HILLEBRAND, Fred

American songwriter (1893–1963)

2 Home, James, and don't spare the horses!

A catchphrase used jocularly, as if talking to your driver, telling someone to get a move on. From the title of a song (1934) by Hillebrand and recorded by Elsie Carlisle in that year and by Hillebrand himself in 1935. The component 'Home, James!' had existed long before – in the works of Thackeray, for example.

HILLINGDON, Lady (Alice)

Wife of 2nd Baron Hillingdon (1857–1940)

3 Close your eyes and think of England.

The source that Partridge/*Catch Phrases* (1977) gives for this saying – in the sense of advice to women when confronted with the inevitability of sexual intercourse, or jocularly about doing almost anything unpalatable – is the *Journal* (1912) of Lady Hillingdon: 'I am happy now that Charles calls on my bedchamber less frequently than of old. As it is, I now endure but two calls a week and when I hear his steps outside my door I lie down on my bed, close my eyes, open my legs and think of England.'

There *was* a Lady Hillingdon who married the 2nd Baron in 1886 and he was, indeed, called Charles. He was Conservative MP for West Kent (1885–92) and, according to *Who Was Who* owned 'about 4,500 acres' when he died (in 1919). A portrait of Lady Hillingdon was painted by Sir Frank Dicksee PRA in 1904. The rose 'Climbing Lady Hillingdon' was also probably named after her.

But where her journals are, if they ever existed, is unknown. Jonathan Gathorne-Hardy also quotes the 'journal' in *The Rise and Fall of the British Nanny* (1972), but just to complicate matters, he refers to her as Lady 'Hilling*ham*', though *ODMQ* (1991) and *ODQ* (1992) in picking up this reference do not appear to have noticed.

Salome Dear, Not With a Porcupine (ed. Arthur Marshall, 1982) has it instead that the newly wedded Mrs Stanley Baldwin is supposed to have declared: 'I shut my eyes tight and thought of the Empire.' We may discount Bob Chieger's assumption in *Was It Good for You, Too?* (1983) that 'Close your eyes and think of England' was advice given to Queen Victoria on *her* wedding night. In 1977 there was a play by John Chapman and Anthony Marriott at the Apollo Theatre, London, with the title *Shut Your Eyes and Think of England.*

Sometimes the phrase occurs in the form 'lie back and think of England' but this is a conflation with 'she should lie back and enjoy it'.

HILLS, Denis

English teacher and writer (1913–)

4 A village tyrant ... a black Nero.

On President Idi Amin of Uganda. Hills was sentenced to death for treason on account of these words in his book *The White Pumpkin* (1975) but was pardoned and freed after the intervention of the Queen and the Foreign Secretary. The 'village tyrant' taunt was not new. In his biography *Aneurin Bevan*, Vol. 2 (1975), Michael Foot describes the setting up of the National Health Service in the late 1940s and quotes Dr Roland Cockshut, one of the leading spokesmen on the BMA Council, as saying: 'We might have been going to meet Adolf Hitler ... [but] he is no village tyrant, but a big man on a big errand.'

HILTON, James

English novelist (1900–54)

1 Random Harvest.

The novel (1941; film US, 1942) takes its title, as Hilton acknowledges, from an error in German wartime propaganda when it was claimed an attack had been launched on the British town of 'Random'. This was on the basis of a British communiqué which had stated that 'bombs were dropped at random'.

HIPPOCRATES

Greek physician (c.460–357BC)

2 *Ars longa vita brevis.*
Life is short, the art long.

Aphorisms. As a suggested epitaph for one Thomas Longbottom who died young, '*Ars longa, vita brevis*' was contributed to BBC Radio *Quote ... Unquote* (17 May 1978). In the same edition, Richard Stilgoe suggested rather that *Punch* in its early days had reproduced the death announcement of a man called 'Longbottom' and put over it the headline 'Vita brevis'. Unverified. Hence, also, 'Ars Longa, Vita Sackville-West', which was used as a chapter heading in the book *Quote ... Unquote* (1978).

HIROHITO

Japanese Emperor (1901–89)

3 The war situation has developed not necessarily to Japan's advantage.

Radio broadcast announcing Japan's surrender (15 August 1945). Most Japanese had never heard the Emperor's voice before, but here he was on the radio, explaining what had happened in the war, particularly after the bombing of Hiroshima.

HITCHCOCK, Alfred

British-born film director (1899–1980)

4 Actors are cattle.

In *Saturday Evening Post* (22 May 1943). He later denied this: 'What I said was actors should be *treated* like cattle' (quoted in Leslie Halliwell, *The Filmgoer's Book of Quotes*, 1973).

5 Television has brought murder back into the home – where it belongs.

Quoted in *The Observer* (1965). *Compare* COOK 182:5; MILLER 391:3.

HITCHCOCK, Raymond

American comedian (c.1870–1929)

6 All dressed up and nowhere to go.

The phrase comes from a song popularized by Hitchcock in *The Beauty Shop* (New York, 1914) and *Mr Manhattan* (London, 1915):

> When you're all dressed up and no place to go,
> Life seems dreary, weary and slow.
> My heart has ached as well as bled
> For the tears I've shed,
> When I've had no place to go
> Unless I went back to bed ...

The words gained further emphasis when they were used by newspaper editor William Allen White to describe the Progressive Party following Theodore Roosevelt's decision to retire from presidential competition in 1916. He said the party was: 'All dressed up with nowhere to go.'

The *OED2* has this phrase starting life in a song by 'G. Whiting' (1912), 'When You're All Dressed Up and Have No Place to Go', but Lowe's *Directory of Popular Music* ascribes it to Silvio Hein and Benjamin Burt.

Cole Porter wrote a parody in 1914 concluding with the words '... and don't know Huerto Go'.

HITLER, Adolf

German Nazi leader (1889–1945)

7 It was no secret that this time the revolution would have to be bloody ... When we spoke of it, we called it 'The Night of the Long Knives [*Die Nacht der langen Messer*]'.

During the weekend of 29 June to 2 July 1934, there

occurred in Nazi Germany the Night of the Long Knives. On this original occasion, Hitler, aided by Himmler's black-shirted SS, liquidated the leadership of the brown-shirted SA. The SA, undisciplined storm-troopers, had helped Hitler gain power but were now getting in the way of his dealings with the German army. Some eighty-three were murdered on the pretext that they were plotting another revolution. Hitler's explanation (above) to the Reichstag on 13 July does not make it clear whether he himself coined the phrase. Indeed, it seems that he may have been alluding to an early Nazi marching song.

Hence, the phrase 'Night of the Long Knives' now in common use for any kind of surprise purge in which no actual blood is spilt. Compare, *Verschwörung der langen Messer* ('conspiracy of the long knives', translating the much older Welsh phrase *twyll y cyllvyll hirion*), which had previously been used as the name of a premeditated massacre of unarmed and unprepared men. To be precise it described the supposed murder by Hengist and his Saxons of a party of British nobles at a peace conference, as described by Nennius, Geoffrey of Monmouth and various other pseudo-historical sources. The German phrase is used in Geoffrey of Monmouth's *Historia Regum Britanniae* (ed. San-Marte, 1854).

1 War is the father of all things.

To add to his many other atrocities, Hitler was apparently a misquoter. In *The War Path: Hitler's Germany 1933–9* (1978), David Irving says that Hitler's favourite quotation was the above, which he attributed to Karl von Clausewitz. But, according to Irving, it was in fact uttered by 'Heracles'. Unverified.

In a speech at Chemnitz (2 April 1938), Hitler said: 'Man has become great through struggle ... Struggle is the father of all things.'

2 And now before us stands the last problem that must be solved and will be solved. It is the last territorial claim which I have to make in Europe, but it is the claim from which I will not recede and which, God willing, I will make good ... With regard to the problem of the Sudeten Germans, my patience is now at an end.

Speech, Berlin Sportpalast (26 September 1938). When Hitler appeared to be about to invade Czechoslovakia in order to retrieve the territory of the German-speaking Sudetenland, the British Prime Minister, Neville Chamberlain, went to see him and the so-called Munich agreement was signed before the end of the month.

3 Well, he seemed such a nice old gentleman, I thought I would give him my autograph as a souvenir.

On Neville Chamberlain and the Munich agreement (1938). Attributed in the *PDMQ* (1971).

4 A last appeal to reason.

On 19 July 1940 Adolf Hitler made a speech to the Reichstag. Following, as it did, the Fall of France and the May Blitz on London, it somewhat surprisingly appeared to contain an offer of peace to the British (though Hitler tried to draw a distinction between ordinary British folk and their war-mongering leaders, principally Winston Churchill).

The speech and the peace proposal, although reported prominently in *The Times* next morning, were largely ignored, and the Germans were much annoyed by the British rejection of the peace offer that followed, notably by Lord Halifax, the Foreign Secretary, within the next few days. In an attempt to appeal to the British people, literally over the heads of the leadership, copies of the speech were dropped on England by the Luftwaffe in a leaflet-raid on the night of 1–2 August. The Imperial War Museum displays an actual copy of the tabloid newspaper-sized leaflet dropped over Somerset a little later, on 11 August. It is headed 'A LAST APPEAL TO REASON / BY / ADOLF HITLER / Speech before the Reichstag 19th July 1940', and makes very tedious reading.

A correspondent wrote (1988): 'I saw a copy myself at the time and tried to read it. Nearly half was taken up, I remember, by long lists of appointments, transfers and promotions in the German armed forces and civil administration ... Needless to say, public opinion generally regarded the leaflet as beneath contempt. I remember hearing about an item on the subject in a cinema newsreel, which ended by showing a pair of hands cutting up the leaflet into small rectangles, threading a string through the corners, and hanging the bundle on a hook on a tiled wall. Very explicit for those prudish days: the audience, I was told, roared approval.'

5 *Nacht und Nebel.*
Night and Fog.

Name of a 1941 decree issued over Hitler's signature describing a simple process: anyone suspected of a crime against occupying German forces was to disappear into 'night and fog'. Such people were thrown into the concentration camp system, in most cases never to be heard of again. Alain Resnais, the French film director, made a cinema short about a concentration camp and called it *Nuit et Brouillard* (1955). Possibly, too, there is an echo in the title of Woody Allen's film *Shadows and Fog* (1992).

The phrase comes from Wagner's opera *Das Rheingold* (1869). '*Nacht und Nebel niemand gleich*' is the spell that Alberich puts on the magic Tarnhelm, which renders him invisible and omnipresent. It means approximately, 'In night and fog no one is seen' or 'Night and fog is the same as being no one, a non-person' or 'Night and fog make you no one instantly'.

1 The Final Solution [*Endlösung*] of the Jewish Problem.

A euphemistic term given by Nazi officials from the summer of 1941 onwards to Hitler's plan to exterminate the Jews of Europe. A directive (drafted by Adolf Eichmann) was sent by Hermann Goering to Reinhard Heydrich on 31 July 1941: 'Submit to me as soon as possible a draft showing ... measures already taken for the execution of the intended final solution of the Jewish question.' Gerald Reitlinger in *The Final Solution* (1953) says that the choice of phrase was probably, though not certainly, Hitler's own. Before then it had been used in a non-specific way to cover other possibilities, such as emigration. It is estimated that the 'final solution' led to the deaths of up to six million Jews.

2 This war ... is one of those elemental conflicts which usher in a new millennium and which shake the world once in a thousand years.

Speech, Reichstag (26 April 1942). The 'thousand years' principle was well established by this time. On 5 September 1934, Adam Wagner, Gauleiter of Bavaria, had told the Nuremberg rally (at which Hitler was present): 'By the National Socialist revolution, the German form of life has been definitely settled for the next thousand years.'

3 *Brennt Paris?*
Is Paris burning?

Following the D-Day landings on the northern coast of France in 1944, the next target was the liberation of Paris. The Allied forces managed to reach the French capital ahead of German Panzer divisions which would have tried to destroy the city. When Hitler put the above inquiry to Jodl at Oberkommando der Wehrmacht at Rastenberg (25 August 1944) – after Paris had been recaptured by the Allies – he received no reply. Later, the phrase was used as the title of a book by Collins and Lapierre (1965) and of a film (US, 1965).

HOBART, Alice Tisdale

American novelist (1882–1967)

4 Oil for the Lamps of China.

Hobart's novel with this title (1933; film US, 1935) was an exposé of American oil companies and their habit of sending bright young men to the Far East and dropping them when they were used up. The phrase is an old expression, used when winning anything or receiving a windfall. Other similar expressions include 'corn in Egypt' and 'little fishes are sweet'.

HOBBES, Thomas

English philosopher (1588–1679)

5 No arts; no letters; no society; and which is worst of all, continual fear and danger of violent death; and the life of man, solitary, poor, nasty, brutish, and short.

This description of life was given by Thomas Hobbes in *Leviathan, or the Matter, Form, and Power of a Commonwealth, Ecclesiastical and Civil*, Chap. 13 (1651). In this treatise of political philosophy, Hobbes sees man not as a social being but as a selfish creature. The state of nature in which he resides is thus.

The last portion of this bleak view has fallen victim to over-quoting, as Philip Howard, Literary Editor of *The Times*, noted on 15 August 1984. He warned of the danger that: 'We become so fond of hackneyed quotation that we trot it out, without thinking, at every opportunity.' He gave, as his example, 'the onc about the life of man being "solitary, poor, nasty, brutish, and short," just to let everybody know that I am an intellectual sort of chap who reads Hobbes in the bath'.

Curiously, later that year, on 1 November, when *The Times* had a first leader on the assassination of Mrs Indira Gandhi, it began by observing that world figures know all too sickeningly well 'the continual fear and danger of violent death' that Thomas Hobbes identified as a condition of man. And added: 'With that awful daily awareness, now goes for some a reminder of his definition of life as nasty, brutish and short.'

HOFFNUNG, Gerard

English cartoonist and musician (1925–59)

6 Have you tried the famous echo in the Reading Room of the British Museum?

Suggestion to tourists visiting Britain for the first time. Speech, Oxford Union debating society (4 December 1958). On the motion 'Life begins at 38'. The same speech also included Hoffnung's recitation of a supposed letter from a Tyrolean landlord: 'Standing among savage scenery, the hotel offers stupendous revelations. There is a French widow in every bedroom (affording delightful prospects).'

HOGBEN, Lancelot

English scientist (1895–1975)

1 This is not the age of pamphleteers. It is the age of engineers. The spark-gap is mightier than the pen. Democracy will not be salvaged by men who talk fluently, debate forcefully and quote aptly.

Epilogue, *Science for the Citizen* (1938). The art of quotation cannot put off the end of civilization – according to this scientist anyway.

HOGG, James

Scottish poet (1770–1835)

2 Where the pools are bright and deep
Where the gray trout lies asleep,
Up the river and o'er the lea
That's the way for Billy and me.

'A Boy's Song' (1838). Hogg was known as the Ettrick Shepherd because he was indeed a shepherd born in Ettrick Forest. Of some eminence, he was offered a knighthood, which he declined, thinking it would be incompatible with his shepherd status.

HOLLAND, Henry Fox (1st Baron Holland)

English Whig politician (1773–1840)

3 If Mr Selwyn calls again, shew him up; if I am alive I shall be delighted to see him; and if I am dead, he would like to see me.

Deathbed words, concerning George Selwyn who, apparently, enjoyed executions and corpses. Quoted in J.H. Jesse, *George Selwyn and his Contemporaries* (1844).

HOLLAND, Henry Scott

English Anglican clergyman (1847–1918)

4 Death is nothing at all ... I have only slipped away into the next room.

Hardly a day passes without newspaper reports of memorial services noting that 'so-and-so read from the works of Canon Henry Scott Holland'. The passage in question is the one beginning, 'Death is nothing at all', and judging by its popularity, the words have a message capable of comforting many who are bereaved. It comes from a sermon on death entitled 'The King of Terrors' which Holland delivered in St Paul's Cathedral (of which he was a Canon) on 15 May 1910, at which time the body of King Edward VII was lying in state at Westminster. The context is important:

> There is another aspect altogether which death can wear for us. It is that which first comes to us, perhaps, as we look down upon the quiet face, so cold and white, of one who has been very near and dear to us. There it lies in possession of its own secret. It knows it all. So we seem to feel. And what the face says in its sweet silence to us as a last message from one whom we loved is: 'Death is nothing at all. It does not count. I have only slipped away into the next room. Nothing has happened. Everything remains exactly as it was. I am I, and you are you, and the old life that we lived so fondly together is untouched, unchanged. Whatever we were to each other, that we are still. Call me by the old familiar name. Speak of me in the easy way which you always used. Put no difference into your tone. Wear no forced air of solemnity or sorrow. Laugh as we always laughed at the little jokes that we enjoyed together. Play, smile, think of me, pray for me. Let my name be ever the household word that it always was. Let it be spoken without an effort, without the ghost of a shadow upon it. Life means all that it ever meant. It is the same as it ever was. There is absolute and unbroken continuity. What is this death but a negligible accident? Why should I be out of mind because I am out of sight? I am but waiting for you, for an interval, somewhere very near, just around the corner. All is well. Nothing is hurt; nothing is lost. One brief moment and all will be as it was before. How we shall laugh at the trouble of parting when we meet again!'
>
> So the face speaks. Surely while we speak there is a smile flitting over it; a smile as of gentle fun at the trick played us by seeming death ...

The sermon was published posthumously in a collection entitled *Facts of the Faith* (1919).

There is a basic similarity of thought contained in a sermon by a Dean of St Paul's, with whose works one assumes Holland must have been familiar, John Donne. Preaching about death (as he did so often), on Easter Day 1627, Donne said in St Paul's (the earlier building): 'Though death have divided us ... yet we do live together already, in a Holy Communion of Saints ... If the dead, and we, be not upon one floor, nor under one story, yet we are under one roof. We think not a friend lost, because he is gone into another room, nor because he is gone into another Land; And into another world, no man is gone; for that Heaven, which God created, and this world, is all one world.'

HOLLANDER, Nicole

American illustrator and cartoonist (late twentieth century)

1 Can you imagine a world without men? No crime and lots of happy, fat women

Syndicated comic strip 'Sylvia' (1981). The line 'A world without men would be one containing a bunch of fat, happy women – and no crime' was uttered in a Fox TV show called *Living Single* (August 1993). It has also been attributed to Marion Smith.

HOLMES, Oliver Wendell, Jr

American judge (1841–1935)

2 The question in every case is whether the words used are used in such circumstances and are of such a nature as to create a clear and present danger that they will bring about the evils that Congress has a right to prevent.

Ruling in the US Supreme Court in the case of Schenk *v.* United States (1919). This concerned free speech and included Holmes's claim that the most stringent protection of same would not protect a man in falsely shouting fire in a theatre and causing panic. Hence, *Clear and Present Danger*, title of film (US, 1994) about a CIA agent in conflict with his political masters in Washington.

HOME See DOUGLAS-HOME

HOMER

Greek poet (eighth century BC)

3 But night is already at hand; it is well to yield to the night.

This is but one translation of a passage from *The Iliad* (Bk 7, l. 264). Others include: 'And now 'tis late; we must submit to night' and 'The light is failing. We should do well to take the hint.' Either way, in the original Greek, Maurice Baring used to say that it was the most beautiful line in Homer. Hence, perhaps, *Yield to the Night*, title of a film (UK, 1956) – the actress Diana Dors's finest hour as a condemned murderess – based on a novel by Joan Henry.

HOOD, Thomas

English poet (1799–1845)

4 There is a silence where hath been no sound,
There is a silence where no sound may be,
In the cold grave – under the deep, deep sea.

Sonnet, 'Silence'. These were the last words heard in the film *The Piano* (1993) by the New Zealand writer and director, Jane Campion. They are 'spoken' by the dumb heroine who has just consigned her piano to the bottom of the sea and who has also come near to death herself by being dragged down with it.

HOOK, Theodore

English writer, hoaxer and joker (1788–1841)

5 I beg your pardon, sir, are you anyone in particular?

Said to an imposing gentleman, after bowing low to him. Quoted in W.D. Adams, *Treasury of Modern Anecdote* (1886). Hook or not, 'Please, are you anybody?' was the caption to a cartoon by Lewis Baumer in *Punch* (16 February 1938). It showed a little girl with an autograph book approaching an impressive gentleman.

HOOVER, Herbert

American Republican 31st President (1874–1964)

6 When a great many people are unable to find work, unemployment results.

Quoted in W.E. Woodward, *A New American History* (1936). Hoover was not such a klutz as this unfortunate statement of the obvious might suggest. He was, however, brought down by his resistance to governmental help for the unemployed following the 1929 world slump.

7 We are challenged with a peacetime choice between the American system of rugged individualism and a European philosophy of diametrically opposed doctrines – doctrines of paternalism and state socialism.

So said Hoover, running for the Presidency in a speech in New York on 22 October 1928. Six years later he commented: 'While I can make no claim for having introduced the term "rugged individualism", I should have been proud to have invented it. It has been used by American leaders for over half a century in eulogy of those God-fearing men and women of honesty whose stamina and character and fearless assertion of rights led them to make their own way in life.'

1 The grass will grow in the streets of a hundred cities, a thousand towns.

From a speech (31 October 1932) on proposals 'to reduce the protective tariff to a competitive tariff for revenue'. The image had earlier been used by William Jennings Bryan in his 'Cross of Gold' speech (128:2): 'Burn down your cities and leave our farms, and your cities will spring up again as if by magic; but destroy our farms and the grass will grow in the streets of every city in the country.' And from Anthony Trollope, *Doctor Thorne*, Chap. 15 (1858): '"Why, luke at this 'ere town," continued he of the sieve, "the grass be a-growing in the very streets; – that can't be no gude".'

HOPE, Anthony (Sir Anthony Hope Hawkins)

English novelist (1863–1933)

2 Oh, for an hour of Herod!

At the first night of J.M. Barrie's play *Peter Pan* (1904). Quoted in Denis Mackail, *The Story of JMB* (1941). Compare: 'There are moments when one sympathizes with Herod' – Saki, 'Reginald on House-Parties' (1904).

3 His foe was folly & his weapon wit.

This is inscribed on W.S. Gilbert's memorial on the Victoria Embankment, London, and the line was provided in 1915 by Hope who recalled: 'Whilst on the committee of the Authors' Society I had something to do with the memorial. The words on the memorial are mine, except that I put them first into prose – "Folly was his foe, and wit his weapon", – then somebody (I forget who) pointed out that transposed they would make a line, and this was adopted.'

4 TO
THE BEAUTIFUL MEMORY
OF KENNETH GRAHAME
HUSBAND OF ELSPETH
AND
FATHER OF ALASTAIR
WHO PASSED THE RIVER
ON THE 6TH OF JULY 1932
LEAVING
CHILDHOOD & LITERATURE
THROUGH HIM
THE MORE BLEST
FOR ALL TIME.

Epitaph on the grave of Kenneth Grahame, author of *The Wind in the Willows*, in St Cross churchyard, Oxford. Hope was his cousin. The use of the phrase 'passing the river' for death is absolutely appropriate for an author who wrote so enchantingly of the river bank and 'messing about in boats'. It may also be taken to allude to the classical use of crossing the rivers of Styx, Acheron, Lethe and so on, as a symbol of death, but chiefly to the Christian use. In John Bunyan's *The Pilgrim's Progress* (1678) Christian passes through the River of Death (which has no Bridge) and quotes Isaiah 43:2, 'When thou passest through the waters, I will be with thee, and through the Rivers, they shall not overflow thee.'

HORACE

Roman poet (65–8BC)

5 *Atque inter silvas Academi quaerere verum.*
And seek for truth in the groves of Academe.

Epistles, II.ii.45. Hence, the phrase 'groves of Academe' for the academic community or the world of university scholarship. *The Groves of Academe* was the title of a novel (1952) by Mary McCarthy.

6 *Nil desperandum.*
Never despair.

Odes, I.vii.27. Literally, 'there is nought to be despaired of'. Also translated as 'never say die'. The context is '*nil desperandum est Teucro duce et auspice Teucro* [nothing is to be despaired of with Teucer as leader and protector]'. Hence, *nil carborundum* ... (as in the title of a play by Henry Livings, 1962), though this alludes rather to the cod-Latin phrase *illegitimi non carborundum*, supposed to mean 'Don't let the bastards grind you down', used by US General 'Vinegar Joe' Stilwell as his motto during the Second World War, though it is not suggested that he devised it. Partridge/*Catch Phrases* gives it, rather, as '*illegitimis*' and its origins in British army intelligence very early on in the same war. Something like the phrase has also been reported from 1929. 'Carborundum' is, in fact, the trade name of a very hard substance composed of silicon carbide, used in grinding. Perhaps because it is a made-up one, the phrase takes many forms, e.g.: 'nil illegitimis ...', 'nil bastardo illegitimi ...', 'nil bastardo carborundum ...' etc. When the Rt Rev. David Jenkins, the Bishop of Durham, was unwise enough to make use of the phrase at a private meeting in March 1985, a cloth-eared journalist reported him as having said, 'Nil desperandum illegitimi ...'

1 *Dum loquimur, fugerit invida*
Aetas: carpe diem, quam minimum credula postero.
While we are talking, envious time is fleeing:
seize the day, put no trust in the future.

Odes, I.xi.7. Accordingly, '*carpe diem*' has become a motto meaning 'enjoy the day while you have the chance' or 'seize the opportunity, make the most of the present time'.

2 *Eheu fugaces, Postume, Postume,*
Labuntur anni.
Ah me, Postumus, Postumus, the fleeting years are slipping by.

Odes, II.xiv.1. Note how Byron quotes this cry: 'It is three minutes past twelve ... and I am now thirty-three! *Eheu, fugaces, Posthume, Posthume, / Labuntur anni*, – but I don't regret them so much for what I have done, as for what I *might* have done' (*Diary*, 22 January 1821).

3 *Dulce et decorum est pro patria mori.*
It is sweet and honourable to die for one's country.

Odes, III.ii.13. '*Pro patria mori*' is an epitaph frequently put on the graves of those killed on active service. It has also been used as a family motto. *See* OWEN 421:5.

4 *Parcentes ego dexteras voli; sparge rosas*
Fling roses: the stingy hand at feasts, I hate.

Odes, III.xix.21. In the gardens of the Villa Cimbrone, Ravello, southern Italy, are several plaques bearing quotations including this one.

5 *Quamquam ridentem dicere verum*
Quid vetat?
Why should one not speak the truth, laughing?

Satires, I.i.24. Another translation: 'Why should truth not be impress'd/Beneath the cover of a jest.' Used as a justification of satire.

6 Even Homer nods.

Meaning 'even the greatest, best and wisest of us can't be perfect all the time, and can make mistakes', this phrase was not, naturally, coined by Homer himself. Current by the eighteenth century at least is the form: 'Let Homer, who sometimes nods, sleep soundly upon your shelf for three or four years' (letter of Lord Chesterfield to Lord Huntingdon, 31 August 1749). Mencken has 'Even Homer sometimes nods' as an English proverb derived from Horace, *Ars Poetica* (*c.*8BC): 'I am indignant when worthy Homer nods' – and familiar since the seventeenth century. Longinus (*c.*AD213–273) evidently added: 'They say that Homer sometimes nods. Perhaps he does – but then he dreams as Zeus might dream.'

See also CORY 185:1; GOLDONI 266:4.

HOUSMAN, A.E.

English poet (1859–1936)

7 In summertime on Bredon
The bells they sound so clear;
Round both the shires they ring them
In steeples far and near,
A happy noise to hear.

Here of a Sunday morning
My love and I would lie,
And see the coloured counties,
And hear the larks so high
About us in the sky.

A Shropshire Lad, No. 21 (1896). *See* KINGSMILL 336:3 for a parody.

8 Into my heart an air that kills
From yon far country blows;
What are those blue remembered hills,
What spires, what farms are those?

Ib., No. 40. Hence, *Blue Remembered Hills*, title of a TV play about childhood (1979) by Dennis Potter.

9 When summer's end is nighing
And skies at evening cloud,
I muse on change and fortune
And all the feats I vowed
When I was young and proud.

Last Poems, No. 39 (1922). Hence, *Change and Fortune*, the title of the memoirs (1980) of the former Labour cabinet minister, Douglas Jay (later Lord Jay).

10 I had a visit not long ago from Clarence Darrow, the great American barrister for defending murderers. He had only a few days in England but he could not return home without seeing me, because he had so often used my poems to rescue his clients from the electric chair. Loeb and Leopold owe their life sentence partly to me; and he gave me a copy of his speech, in which, sure enough, two of my pieces are misquoted.

From a letter to Basil Housman (dated 29 December 1927), included in *The Letters of A.E. Housman* (1971).

1 If a line of poetry strays into my memory, my skin bristles so that the razor ceases to act.

Lecture, *The Name and Nature of Poetry*, Cambridge (9 May 1933). A classic definition of poetry.

2 Some can gaze and not be sick,
But I could never learn the trick.
There's this to say for blood and breath,
They give a man a taste for death.

Additional Poems, No. 16 (1937). Hence, *A Taste for Death*, the title of a crime novel (1986) by P.D. James.

3 That is indeed very good. I shall have to repeat that on the Golden Floor.

So Housman said to his doctor who had told him a risqué story to cheer him up before he died (quoted in *The Daily Telegraph*, 21 February 1984). 'Golden floor' is an expression for heaven, possibly derived from 'threshing floor', as in various Old Testament verses. Current by 1813 (Shelley, 'Queen Mab'), the phrase also occurs in the Harvest Festival hymn 'Come ye thankful people, come'.

HOWE, Sir Geoffrey (later Lord Howe)

British Conservative politician (1926–)

4 I have more than one pair of trousers.

In November 1982, when Howe was Chancellor of the Exchequer, he was travelling by rail on an overnight sleeper and had his trousers stolen. He merely commented, 'I have more than one pair of trousers', and it was left to an anonymous colleague – probably a fellow member of the Cabinet – to say, 'I am thrilled about the loss of your trousers ... because it revealed your human face'. This was repeated by Lady Howe in a magazine interview two years later.

5 I no longer believe it possible to resolve that conflict [of loyalty to the Prime Minister and to the interests of the nation] from within this Government. That is why I have resigned ... The time has come for others to consider their own response to the tragic conflict of loyalty with which I have myself wrestled for perhaps too long.

Speech, House of Commons (13 November 1990). Resigning as Leader of the House and Deputy Prime Minister, Howe's statement precipitated the fall of the Prime Minister, Margaret Thatcher, the following month.

HOWE, Julia Ward

American preacher (1819–1910)

6 Mine eyes have seen the glory of the coming of the Lord:
He is trampling out the vintage where the grapes of wrath are stored.

'The Battle Hymn of the Republic' (1862). Written at the height of the Civil War after Howe had seen President Lincoln reviewing Union troops outside Washington in 1861. She thought they should have an anthem more suitable to sing than 'John Brown's Body' – but fitted her words to the earlier tune. Hence, *The Grapes of Wrath*, title of the novel (1939; film US, 1940) by John Steinbeck.

HOWITT, Mary

English writer (1799–1888)

7 'Will you walk into my parlour?' said a spider to a fly.

'The Spider and the Fly' (1834). Often misquoted as 'said the spider to the fly'. There have been several musical settings of this poem, but even in the Rolling Stones song called 'The Spider and the Fly' (written by Nanker and Phelge, recorded 1971) the lyric states correctly: 'Don't say Hi! like a spider to a fly' and 'I said my, my, my, like a spider to a fly,/Jump right ahead in my web.' *See* CARROLL 147:7.

HUBBARD, Elbert

American writer and editor (1856–1915)

8 Never Explain – your friends do not need it and your enemies will not believe you anyway.

The Motto Book (1907). *Compare* GRAYSON 271:10.

9 Life is just one damned thing after another.

In *The Philistine* (December 1909). Also attributed to Frank Ward O'Malley (1875–1932), though the saying may pre-date them both. Became a general expression of dismay at a series of misfortunes (also rendered as 'ODTAA'). John Masefield published his novel *Odtaa* in 1926.

10 Editor: a person employed by a newspaper

whose business it is to separate the wheat from the chaff and to see that the chaff is printed.

The Roycroft Dictionary (1914). *See* STEVENSON 520:5.

HUBBARD, Frank McKinney ('Kin')

American humorist (1868–1930)

1 If there's one thing above all a vulture can't stand, it's a glass eye.

Attributed, but unverified. Possibly from *Abe Martin's Sayings and Sketches* (1915). Abe Martin was a folksy, humorous character whose sayings, originally published in the *Indianapolis News* from 1892, were later collected annually.

2 None but the brave can live with the fair.

Attributed. Alluding to DRYDEN 215:7.

HUGHES, Howard

American industrialist and film producer (1905–76)

3 That man's ears make him look like a taxi-cab with both doors open.

On Clark Gable. Quoted in Charles Higham & Joel Greenberg, *Celluloid Muse* (1969).

HUGHES, Robert

Australian-born art critic (1938–)

4 The Shock of the New.

Title of TV series and book (1980) about modern art. As acknowledged, this was taken from the title of Ian Dunlop's 1972 book on 'seven historic exhibitions of modern art'. Compare Thomas Crawford's use of the idea in *Longer Scottish Poems* (1987), in connection with the best efforts of Robert Burns – which represent, 'the perfection of the old achieving the shock and immediacy of the new.'

HUGHES, Ted

English Poet Laureate (1930–98)

5 It took the whole of Creation
To produce my foot, each feather:
Now I hold Creation in my foot.

'Hawk Roosting', *The Hawk in the Rain* (1957). For a parody of Hughes's bleak vision, of which this is a prime example, *see* LARKIN 344:5. A veil is best drawn over his later work as Poet Laureate, for example lines, 'The helicopter picked you up,/The pilot it was me' – 'The Honey Bee and the Thistle' (1986), written to mark the wedding of the Duke and Duchess of York.

HUGHES, Thomas

English novelist (1822–96)

6 It's more than a game. It's an institution.

Of cricket. *Tom Brown's Schooldays* (1857).

HUGO, Victor

French novelist (1802–85)

7 *On résiste à l'invasion des armées; on ne résiste pas à l'invasion des idées.*
An invasion of armies can be resisted, but not an idea whose time has come.

Histoire d'Un Crime (written 1852, published 1877), conclusion. This quotation has been popularly re-translated as: 'No army can withstand the strength of an idea whose time has come' (Mencken, 1942); 'There is one thing stronger than all the armies in the world; and that is an idea whose time has come' (in the *Nation*, 15 April 1943). Compare: 'Stronger than an army is a quotation whose time has come' – W.I.E. Gates, quoted in Laurence J. Peter, *Quotations for Our Time* (1977).

HUME, David

Scottish philosopher (1711–76)

8 It is much more likely that human testimony should err, than that the laws of nature should be violated.

In *My Early Life*, Chap. 9 (1930), Winston Churchill quotes this passage without attribution. Many readers assume that it must be from Hume but have been unable to find the exact words in that man's works. The Rev. Dr L.M. Brown of Edinburgh offered this instead, from Thomas Paine's *The Age of Reason* (1793): 'If we are to suppose a miracle to be something so entirely out of course of what is called nature, that she must go out of that course to accomplish it, and we see an account of such a miracle by the person who said he saw it, it raises a question in the mind very easily decided; which is, is it more probable that nature should go out of her course, or that a man should tell a lie? We have never seen, in our time, nature go out of her course ... it is therefore at least millions to one that the reporter of a miracle tells a lie.'

Dr Brown commented: 'It is perhaps not impertinent to remark that this argument, though deserving serious consideration, is not so unanswerable as Thomas Paine seems to imagine.' Churchill's quotation may simply be his own paraphrase of Paine or Hume. Compare James Boswell, *Life of Johnson* (for 21 July 1763): 'I mentioned Hume's argument against the belief of miracles, that it is more probable that the witnesses to the truth of them are mistaken, or speak falsely, than that the miracles should be true'; and again (for 22 September 1777): 'Hume's argument against miracles, "That it is more probable witnesses should lie, or be mistaken, than that they should happen".'

There is also a letter of Lord Byron (13 September 1811): 'As to miracles, I agree with Hume that it is more probable men should lie or be deceived, than that things out of the course of nature should so happen.'

HUMPHREY, Hubert

American Democratic Vice-President (1911–78)

1 Here we are the way politics ought to be in America, the politics of happiness, the politics of purpose and the politics of joy.

Speech in Washington (27 April 1968). 'The Politics of Joy' became a slogan in Humphrey's presidential bid that year.

2 It was once said that the moral test of government is how that government treats those who are in the dawn of life, the children; those who are in the twilight of life, the elderly; and those who are in the shadows of life, the sick, the needy and the handicapped.

From a speech at the dedication of the Hubert H. Humphrey building (1 November 1977), but the source of the 'once said' remains untraced.

HUNT, Leigh

English writer and editor (1784–1859)

3 Stolen sweets are always sweeter,
Stolen kisses much completer.

'Song of fairies robbing an orchard' (1830). The idea that 'stolen pleasures are sweetest' really goes back to Proverbs 9:17: 'Stolen waters are sweet'. *Compare* CIBBER 171:4; TRENET 542:5.

4 ... I pray thee then,
Write me as one that loves his fellow-men.

'Abou Ben Adhem' (1838). Hence, 'WRITE ME AS ONE/THAT LOVES HIS FELLOW MEN', inscribed on Hunt's grave in Kensal Green Cemetery, London.

5 Jenny kissed me when we met,
Jumping from the chair she sat in;
Time, you thief, who love to get
Sweets into your list, put that in:
Say I'm weary, say I'm sad,
Say that health and wealth have missed me,
Say I'm growing old, but add,
Jenny kissed me.

'Rondeau' (1838). The 'Jenny' was Jane Carlyle, wife of Thomas Carlyle. Hunt was a neighbour of theirs in Cheyne Row, Chelsea, and had been told that she was anxious about him during a flu epidemic. So he went to see her and the nature of her greeting was uncharacteristic. She was not the kissing sort.

HUPFELD, Herman

American songwriter (1894–1951)

6 You must remember this, a kiss is still a kiss,
A sigh is just a sigh;
The fundamental things apply,
As time goes by.

Song, 'As Time Goes By', *Everybody's Welcome* (1931). Also in the film CASABLANCA (1943). Hence, *You Must Remember This*, the title of a novel (1987) by Joyce Carol Oates.

HUSSEIN, Saddam

Iraqi President (1937–)

7 The great, the jewel and the mother of battles has begun.

Said at the start of the Gulf War (6 January 1991, quoted in *The Independent*, 19 January 1991). Although, as a result, 'the mother of ——' became a catchphrase format in the West, Hussein was simply using the commonplace Arabic 'mother of' construction.

HUTCHINS, Robert M.

American educator (1899–1977)

8 Whenever I feel like exercise, I lie down until the feeling passes.

Untraced, but apparently said by the former University of Chicago President rather than all the other candidates (Wilde, Twain, W.C. Fields and so on). Ascribed by J.P. McEvoy in *Young Man Looking Backwards* (1938). However, Hutchins's biographer, Harry S. Ashmore, ascribes it to *McEvoy* and says that it was merely one of many sayings Hutchins collected to use when appropriate. In the film *Mr Smith Goes to Washington* (US, 1939), Thomas Mitchell speaks the line: 'Every time I think of exercise, I have to lie down till the feeling leaves me.'

HUXLEY, Aldous

English novelist and writer (1894–1963)

1 The proper study of mankind is books.

Crome Yellow (1921). Alluding to POPE 434:3.

2 The Gioconda Smile.

Title of short story (included in *Mortal Coils*, 1922, and dramatized, 1948). It refers to Leonardo da Vinci's portrait of a young woman, known as 'Mona Lisa' (*c.*1503), now in the Louvre, Paris, which has a curious, enigmatic, unsmiling smile, almost a smirk. '*La Gioconda*' and '*La Joconde*', the titles by which the painting is also known, may either be translated as 'the jocund lady', as might be expected, or refer to the sitter's actual surname. She may have been the wife of Francesco del Giocondo (whose name does, however, derive from 'jocund').

The smile was already being mentioned by 1550 in Giorgio Vasari's life of the painter. Vasari probably made up the story that Leonardo employed 'singers and musicians or jesters' to keep the sitter 'full of merriment'. Any number of nineteenth-century writers were fascinated by the smile, some seeing it as disturbing and almost evil. More recently, Lawrence Durrell commented: 'She has the smile of a woman who has just dined off her husband', and Cole Porter included 'You're the smile/On the Mona Lisa' in his list song 'You're the Top!' (1934). Ponchielli's opera *La Gioconda* (1876), after Victor Hugo's drama, and a D'Annunzio play (1898) are not connected with da Vinci's portrait (except in that they feature jocund girls).

3 I looked down by chance, and went on passionately staring by choice, at my own crossed legs. Those folds in the trousers – what a labyrinth of endlessly significant complexity! And the texture of the grey flannel – how rich, how deeply, mysteriously sumptuous!

Huxley's famous description of a discovery he had made using mescaline occurs in *The Doors of Perception* (1954) and caused much amusement when quoted in the druggy 1960s.

4 An intellectual is someone who has found something more interesting to think about than sex.

Quoted in Robert Irwin, *Exquisite Corpse* (1996), otherwise untraced.

HUXLEY, Thomas Henry

English biologist (1825–95)

5 Try to learn something about everything and everything about something.

Attributed, but possibly something said by Lord Brougham (*q. v.*).

I

IBARRURI, Dolores ('La Pasionaria')

Spanish Communist leader (1895–1989)

1 Fascism will not pass, the executioners of October will not pass.

Radio speech given in Madrid (18 July 1936). As '*No pasarán* [They shall not pass]' it became a Republican slogan in the Spanish Civil War (1936–9). *Compare* PÉTAIN 429:5.

2 It is better to die on your feet than to live on your knees.

Said in a radio speech from Paris calling on the women of Spain to help defend the Republic (3 September 1936). According to her autobiography (1966), she had used these words earlier, on 18 July, when broadcasting in Spain (see above). Emiliano Zapata (*c.*1877–1919), the Mexican guerrilla leader, had used the expression before her in 1910: 'Men of the South! It is better to die on your feet than to live on your knees! [... *mejor morir a pie que vivir en rodillas*]'. Franklin D. Roosevelt picked up the expression in his message accepting an honorary degree from Oxford University (19 June 1941): 'We, too, are born to freedom, and believing in freedom, are willing to fight to maintain freedom. We, and all others who believe as we do, would rather die on our feet than live on our knees.'

IBSEN, Henrik

Norwegian playwright (1828–1906)

3 You should never have your best trousers on when you go out to fight for freedom and truth.

An Enemy of the People (1882). Mieder & Co. in *A Dictionary of American Proverbs* (1992) have it, anonymously, as a proverb: 'Never wear your best trousers when you go out to fight for freedom.'

4 But, good God, people don't do such things!

Hedda Gabler (1890). Judge Brack on Hedda's suicide. Last words of the play.

INGE, William

English clergyman and theologian (1860–1954)

5 [Having] ceased to be a pillar of the Church, [he was] now two columns of the *Evening Standard.*

Quoted in Alfred Noyes, *Two Worlds for Memory* (1953). Sometimes rendered as 'a lot of pillars of society end up as columns in the *News of the World*'.

INGHAM, Sir Bernard

English civil servant (1932–)

6 A semi-detached member of the Cabinet.

Phrase employed by 'Downing Street sources' (understood to be Ingham) in May 1986 to describe John Biffen (then Leader of the House of Commons) who was subsequently sacked from Margaret Thatcher's Cabinet. It meant that Biffen was not a wholehearted member.

7 Kill the Messenger.

Ingham was Chief Press Secretary to the Prime Minister, Margaret Thatcher, from 1979 to 1990. The somewhat surprising title of his memoirs (1991) was an apparent allusion to what reputedly happened to messengers bringing bad news in classical times. Ingham's implication would seem to be that press officers get blamed for their master's – or in his case, mistress's – doings, just as the media are often blamed for the news which they report rather than initiate. As early as Sophocles, *Antigone* (l. 277), a sentinel was saying to Creon: 'None love the messenger who brings bad news.' Compare the maltreatment of messengers in several Shakespeare plays: in *Antony and Cleopatra*, a messenger says: 'The nature of bad news infects the teller' (I.ii.92) and Cleopatra threatens a messenger with a knife and the messenger says, 'It is never good to bring bad news' (II.v.85).

As for precisely 'killing the messenger', the American journal *RQ* (read by reference librarians) has been agonizing over this question since 1981. One suggested original is the biblical story of David killing the man who brought the news of Saul's death in 2 Samuel 1:1–15 (though he was killed not for the news but for boasting he had killed Saul himself). Another is Plutarch's 'Life of Lucius Lucullus' in *Lives of the Noble Grecians and Romans*, which in Sir Thomas North's translation (1579) has the marginal note: 'Tigranes slue the first messenger that brought the newes of Lucullus approach' and the line: 'Now for Tigranes, the first man that ventured to bring him newes of Lucullus comming, had no joy of it: for he cut off his head for his labor.'

INGRAMS, Richard

English writer and editor (1937–)

1 The only thing I really mind about going to prison is the thought of Lord Longford coming to visit me.

On the prospect of having to go to gaol (1976) as a result of litigation concerning *Private Eye*, the magazine he then edited. Ingrams has no recollection of having made this remark but is happy to accept responsibility for it (BBC Radio *Quote ... Unquote*, 26 December 1976).

2 Publish and be sued.

Personal motto, suggested on BBC Radio *Quote ... Unquote* (4 May 1977).

INNES, Hammond

British novelist (1913–)

3 I'm replacing some of the timber used up by my books. Books are just trees with squiggles on them.

On growing trees. Interview, *Radio Times*, (18–24 August 1984).

INSKIP, Sir Thomas (later Viscount Caldecote)

English lawyer and politician (1876–1947)

4 Dictators have only become impossible through the invention of the microphone.

Untraced. What did he mean – that no one would take them seriously if their voices could be heard, or that broadcasting information would reveal the truth about them? Compare what Shimon Peres, when Israeli Foreign Minister, said at a Davos meeting (quoted in the *Financial Times*, 31 January 1995): 'Television has made dictatorship impossible, but democracy unbearable.'

IONESCO, Eugène

Romanian-born playwright (1912–94)

5 To the recent query, 'If you could ask one question about life, what would the answer be?' Eugène Ionesco responded, 'No'.

Quoted in *Esquire* (December 1974). Ionesco settled in France in 1940 and achieved fame as the writer of 'Theatre of the Absurd' plays including *The Bald Prima Donna* (1950) and *Rhinoceros* (1960).

IRISH REPUBLICAN ARMY

6 *Tiocfaidh Ar La.*
Our day will come.

Slogan. Also (in English) the title of a song sung by Ruby and the Romantics (1963).

7 Thatcher will now realize that Britain cannot occupy our country, torture our prisoners and shoot our people in their own streets and get away with it. Today we were unlucky. But remember, we only have to be lucky once. You will have to be lucky always.

Quoted in *The Irish Times* (13 October 1984). This message was contained in an anonymous telephone call to a Dublin radio station following the unsuccessful IRA attempt to blow up Margaret Thatcher and other government leaders at a Brighton hotel.

IRVING, Washington

American writer (1783–1859)

1 The almighty dollar, that great object of universal devotion throughout our land.

'The Creole Village', *Wolfert's Roost* (1855), first printed in *Knickerbocker* Magazine (12 November 1836). Mark Twain took up the theme in his *Notebooks* (pub. 1935): 'We Americans worship the almighty dollar! Well, it is a worthier god than Hereditary Privilege.' *Compare* 21:2.

ISHERWOOD, Christopher

English-born American writer (1904–86)

2 I am a camera with its shutter open, quite passive, recording, not thinking.

'A Berlin Diary', *Goodbye to Berlin* (1939), opening words. According to Peter Parker in the *Dictionary of National Biography 1986–1990*, 'the famous sentence ... (to Isherwood's increasing irritation) was often quoted as a summation of his fictional method.'

J

JACKSON, T.J. 'Stonewall'

American general (1824–63)

1 Let us cross over the river, and rest under [the shade of] the trees.

Dying words, after the Confederate general in the American Civil War had been shot in error by his own troops (May 1863). *Across the River and Into the Trees* was the title of a novel (1950) by Ernest Hemingway. Accordingly, E.B. White's noted parody of Hemingway's style (collected 1954) was called 'Across the Street and Into the Grill'. Often used allusively: 'Then we began to notice, as we lazily cropped the grass that it was greener across the river at Shepperton Studios than at Pinewood. It was time for The Archers and their followers to move across the river and into the trees' – Michael Powell, *Million-Dollar Movie* (1992).

JACOBS, Joe

American boxing manager (1896–1940)

2 We was robbed!

Believing that his client, Max Schmeling, had been cheated of a heavyweight title by Jack Sharkey (21 June 1932), Jacobs shouted this protest into a microphone. Quoted in Peter Heller, *In This Corner* (1975).

3 I should have stood in bed.

Jacobs left his sick-bed to attend the baseball World Series in October 1935. He bet on the losers. Quoted in John Lardner, *Strong Cigars and Lovely Women* (1951). Leo Rosten in *Hooray for Yiddish* (1983) puts his own gloss on the expression: 'The most celebrated instance of this usage was when Mike [*sic*] Jacobs, the fight promoter, observing the small line at his ticket window, moaned, "I should of stood in bed!" *Stood* is a calque for the Yiddish *geshtanen*, which can mean both "stood" and "remained". Mr Jacobs' use of "of" simply followed the speech pattern of his childhood.'

JAGGER, Mick and RICHARD, Keith

English rock musicians and songwriters (1943–) and (1943–)

4 Mother's Little Helper.

Title of song (1966). Referring to a tranquillizer.

5 It's Only Rock 'n' Roll.

Title of song (1974). Hence, the expression meaning 'It doesn't matter; the importance should not be exaggerated'. In a 1983 *Sunday Express* interview, Tim Rice was quoted as saying, 'It would be nice if [the musical *Blondel*] is a success but I won't be upset if it isn't. It is only rock 'n' roll after all and it doesn't really matter a hoot.'

JAMES I (James VI of Scotland)

Anglo-Scottish King (1566–1625)

6 No bishop, no King.

To a delegation of Presbyterians from the Church of Scotland, who were seeking religious toleration in England. Quoted in *Sum and Substance of the Conference* (1604).

7 Have I three kingdoms and thou must needs fly into my eye?

To a fly. Quoted in John Selden *Table Talk* (1689). The three kingdoms were presumably England, Scotland and Ireland. Compare Laurence Sterne, *Tristram Shandy*, Bk 2, Chap. 12 (1759–67): '"I'll not hurt thee," says my uncle Toby, rising from his chair, and going across the room with the fly in his hand ... lifting up the sash, and opening his hand as he spoke ... "go, poor devil, get thee gone, why should I hurt thee? – This world surely is wide enough to hold both thee and me".'

1 Dr Donne's verses are like the peace of God; they pass all understanding.

Archdeacon Plume (1630–1704) recorded this remark of James I's about the poet and cleric, John Donne. Alluding to Philippians 4:7 (*see* BIBLE 104:10).

See also WILSON 577:2.

JAMES II

English King (1633–1701)

2 When King James II observed that the new St Paul's Cathedral was amusing, awful and artificial, he implied that Sir Christopher Wren's creation was 'pleasing, awe-inspiring, and skilfully achieved.'

Simeon Potter, *Our Language* (1976). Unverified remark employing three adjectives that were complimentary once but are pejorative now. In William Kent's *An Encyclopedia of London* (1937), it is Charles II who in 1675 is credited with approving a new design for St Paul's because it was 'very artificial, proper and useful'. Other monarchs up to Queen Anne have also been credited with the saying, or something like it.

JAMES, Carwyn

British sports coach (1929–83)

3 Get your retaliation in first.

'The Government was trying to get its retaliation in first, as we realised it would. The phrase, by the way, comes from the late Carwyn James, the coach to the British Isles rugby team who beat New Zealand in 1971. It is now freely used by people who would be hardput to tell the difference between a rugby ball and a boiled egg. James, who liked Chekhov and gin-and-tonic, would have been pleased to be remembered in the dictionaries of quotation as well as in the record books' – Alan Watkins, *Independent on Sunday* (18 February 1996). Also recorded in *The Guardian* (7 November 1989) and applied to other sports, possibly before this.

JAMES, Henry

American novelist (1843–1916)

4 Cats and monkeys, monkeys and cats – all human life is there.

'The Madonna of the Future' (1879). What is the connection, if any, with the *News of the World*, which used 'All human life is there' to promote itself *c.*1958–9? In 1981 Maurice Smelt, the advertising copywriter, explained: '"All human life is there" was my idea, but I don't, of course, pretend that they were my words. I simply lifted them from *The Oxford Dictionary of Quotations*. I didn't bother to tell the client that they were from Henry James, suspecting that, after the "Henry James – who he?" stage, he would come up with tiresome arguments about being too high-hat for his readership. I did check whether we were clear on copyright, which we were by a year or two ... I do recall its use as baseline in a tiny little campaign trailing a series that earned the *News of the World* a much-publicized but toothless rebuke from the Press Council. The headline of that campaign was: "'I've been a naughty girl', says Diana Dors". The meiosis worked, as the *News of the World* knew it would. They ran an extra million copies of the first issue of the series.'

5 So here it is at last, the distinguished thing.

After suffering a stroke (2 December 1915), James reported that he had heard a voice saying this (as recounted in Edith Wharton, *A Backward Glance*, 1934). These are not his dying words, however. He did not die until 28 February. His last recorded words, said to Alice James, were, 'Tell the boys to follow, to be faithful, to take me seriously' (H. Montgomery Hyde, *Henry James at Home*, 1969).

JAMES, William

American psychologist (1842–1910)

6 We do not weep because we are sad, we are sad because we weep.

Summary of a passage from Chap. 25 ('The Emotions) from *The Principles of Psychology* (1890): 'My theory is that the bodily changes follow directly the perception of the exciting fact, and that our feeling of the same changes as they occur *is* the emotion. Common-sense says, we lose our fortune, are sorry and weep ... the hypothesis here to be defended says that this order of sequence is incorrect ... and that the more rational statement is that we feel sorry because we cry, angry because we strike, afraid because we tremble, and not that we cry, strike or tremble, because we are sorry, angry or fearful as the case may be.' This is the classical statement of what became known as the James-Lange theory of emotion, because it was proposed almost simultaneously by James and by the Danish physiologist Carl Lange.

JAY, Douglas (later Lord Jay)

English Labour politician (1907–96)

1 Fair Shares for All, is Labour's Call.

His slogan for the Battersea North by-election (June 1946), which he won. In *Change and Fortune* (1980), Jay wrote: 'My excellent agent ... asked me to send him a brief rhyming North Battersea slogan. I suggested "Fair Shares for All is Labour's Call"; and from this by-election "Fair Shares for All" spread in a few years round the country.' The *OED2* has no citation of the phrase 'fair shares' before this date, although 'fair share' was common in the nineteenth century.

2 For in the case of nutrition and health, just as in the case of education, the gentleman in Whitehall really does know better what is good for people than the people know themselves.

The Socialist Case (1947). From Tam Dalyell's obituary of Lord Jay in *The Independent* (7 March 1996): 'It is one of the misfortunes of life that a public figure can forever be associated with one inaccurate remark, taken out of context, and never intended to carry an immortal interpretation. For half a century Douglas Jay suffered as the originator of the sinister aphorism "the man in Whitehall knows best" ... [where, in fact, he said,] "the Gentleman in Whitehall is usually right".' As will be apparent, even Dalyell in trying to set the record straight, got it wrong.

In *The Downing Street Years* (1993), Margaret Thatcher commented on Jay's view: 'A disinterested civil service, with access to the best and latest information, was better able to foresee economic eventualities and to propose responses to them than were the blind forces of the so-called "free market". Such a philosophy was explicitly advocated by the Labour Party. It gloried in planning, regulation, controls and subsidies.'

JAY, Peter

English journalist and diplomat (1937–)

3 As we walked the White Cliffs overlooking the English Channel during the weekend he [James Callaghan] was taking over the Government ... [he said] he saw his role as being like that of Moses ... to lead the people away from the fleshpots of Egypt into the desert and in the direction of the promised land ... even if it were never to be given to him to see that land ... [It was] the language of realism and statesmanship.

Speech as British Ambassador, Washington (August 1977). Callaghan was his father-in-law.

4 A mission to explain.

IBA public meeting, Croydon (1980) and many times thereafter. Phrase encapsulating his programme philosophy for the TV-am breakfast television station of which he was the Chief Executive.

5 Remember above all that together we can – being so nice and so talented – work it out.

Pep-talk to TV-am staff (November 1982), quoted in Michael Leapman, *Treachery* (1984).

See also BIRT 109:4.

JEFFERSON, Thomas

American polymath and 3rd President (1743–1826)

6 We hold these truths to be self-evident; that all men are created equal; that they are endowed by their creator with certain unalienable rights; that among these are life, liberty, and the pursuit of happiness.

From the Declaration of Independence (4 July 1776), which Jefferson drafted. Note, not 'inalienable'. George Mason had already drafted the Virginia Declaration of Rights (1774) which stated that 'all men are by nature equally free and independent and have certain inherent rights'.

7 You retire from the great theatre of action with the blessings of your fellow citizens.

From the President of Congress's remarks at the resignation of George Washington as commander-in-chief (23 December 1783), probably penned by Jefferson. On that occasion, Washington himself said: 'Having now finished the work assigned me, I retire from the great theatre of action'. *Compare* WALPOLE 555:2.

8 A little rebellion now and then is a good thing.

Letter to James Madison (30 January 1787). When he addressed both houses of parliament on a visit to Britain in June 1982, President Reagan recalled that Margaret Thatcher had earlier quoted these words apropros a portrait of George III in the British embassy in Washington, coupled with the thought that Britons and Americans would wish to let bygones be bygones.

1 Avoid all foreign entanglements.

Not quite what Jefferson said in his first inaugural address (4 March 1801) – rather, 'Peace, commerce, and honest friendship with all nations, entangling alliances with none ...' – but a cornerstone of American foreign policy for generations.

2 The price of liberty is eternal vigilance.

See CURRAN 192:5.

3 Peace is our passion.

In a letter to Sir John Sinclair (30 June 1803). Compare 'Peace is our profession', slogan of the US Strategic Air Command (by 1962).

4 Government is best which governs least.

Quoted in Fawn M. Brodie, *Thomas Jefferson: An Intimate History* (1974), but otherwise untraced.

5 No one more sincerely wishes the spread of information among mankind than I do, and none has greater confidence in its effect upwards, supporting free and good government.

Quoted in 1810 and reported in *The President Speaks* (1984) but otherwise untraced.

6 Advertisements contain the only truths to be relied on in a newspaper.

Letter to Nathaniel Macon (1819). Compare BEVAN 90:1.

7 To attain all this [universal republicanism], however, rivers of blood must yet flow, and years of desolation pass over; yet the object is worth rivers of blood, and years of desolation.

Letter to John Adams (4 September 1823). *Compare* POWELL 437:7.

8 HERE WAS BURIED
THOMAS JEFFERSON
AUTHOR OF THE
DECLARATION
OF
AMERICAN INDEPENDENCE,
OF THE
STATUTE OF VIRGINIA
FOR
RELIGIOUS FREEDOM,
AND FATHER OF THE
UNIVERSITY OF VIRGINIA.

Jefferson devised his own epitaph, 'because by these, as testimonials I have lived, I wish most to be remembered'. He omitted that he had been US President for two terms. His draft, of course, left the date of death to be inserted. The epitaph is now to be found inscribed on an obelisk over Jefferson's grave in the family cemetery near his house, Monticello, Virginia.

JENKIN, Patrick (later Lord Jenkin)

British Conservative politician (1926–)

9 People can clean their teeth in the dark.

Advice to members of the public as Energy Minister, during Britain's 'Three-Day Week' energy crisis in 1974 (caused by a coal miners' strike). Interviewed on BBC Radio 1 *Newsbeat* on 15 January, Jenkin appealed to householders to save energy and reduce the consumption of electricity: 'You don't even [need to] do your teeth with the light on. You can do it in the dark.' He was photographed using his electric razor by candlelight.

JENKINS, David

English Anglican bishop (1925–)

10 After all, a conjuring trick with bones only proves that somebody's clever at a conjuring trick with bones.

Discussing the Resurrection on BBC Radio (28 October 1984), as reported in *The Guardian* (29 October).

JENKINS, Roy (later Lord Jenkins)

Welsh-born Labour, then Social Democrat, then Liberal Democrat politician (1920–)

11 The permissive society has been allowed to become a dirty phrase. A better phrase is the civilised society.

Speech, Abingdon (19 July 1969). Jenkins was speaking having been Home Secretary in a Labour government (1965–7). He had a notably liberal record, presiding over or setting the tone for liberalization of divorce and anti-homosexual laws, the abolition of theatre censorship and much else. It is impossible to say precisely when the phrase 'permissive society' had come to be applied to Britain in the 1969s – the *OED2*'s first citation dates only from January 1968.

1 The experimental plane may well finish up a few fields from the end of the runway. If that is so, the voluntary occupants will have only inflicted bruises or worse upon themselves. But the reverse may occur and the experimental plane soar into the sky.

On the possibility of the creation of a new centre party. Speech, Commons Press Gallery lunch (8 June 1980).

2 The politics of the left and centre of this country are frozen in an out-of-date mould which is bad for the political and economic health of Britain and increasingly inhibiting for those who live within the mould. Can it be broken?

Ib. The following year, when the Social Democratic Party was established, there was much talk of 'breaking the mould of British politics' – i.e., doing away with the traditional two-party system. In a speech to the SDP Conference at Cardiff in October 1982, its President, Shirley Williams, specifically said: 'That is why we must break the mould of politics.' This was by no means a new way of describing political change and abolishing an old form of government in a way that prevented its being reconstituted. Indeed, Jenkins had quoted Andrew Marvell's 'Horatian Ode Upon Cromwell's Return from Ireland' (1650) – 'And cast the kingdoms old,/Into another mould' – in his book *What Matters Now*, as early as 1972.

In his *English History 1914–1945* (1965) A.J.P. Taylor had written: 'Lloyd George needed a new crisis to break the mould of political and economic habit.' The image evoked, as in the days of the Luddites, was of breaking the mould from which iron machinery is cast so completely that the machinery has to be re-cast from scratch.

JEROME, Jerome K.

English writer (1859–1927)

3 Love is like the measles; we all have to go through it.

Idle Thoughts of an Idle Fellow (1886). *Compare* BILLINGS 108:2 and JERROLD 314:5.

4 I like work: it fascinates me. I can sit and look at it for hours.

Three Men In a Boat, Chap. 3 (1889). As Jerome also wrote *Idle Thoughts of an Idle Fellow*, how appropriate that the inscription on his grave in St Mary's churchyard, Ewelme, Oxfordshire, is: 'For we are labourers together with God' (1 Corinthians 3:9).

JERROLD, Douglas

English writer (1803–57)

5 Love's like the measles – all the worse when it comes late in life.

'Love', *The Wit and Opinions of Douglas Jerrold* (1859). *Compare* BILLINGS 108:2 and JEROME 314:3.

JESSEL, George

American entertainer (1898–1981)

6 Same old story: you give 'em what they want and they'll fill the theatre.

On the large number of mourners at film producer Harry Cohn's funeral (in 1958) – quoted by Lillian Hellman in *Scoundrel Time* (1976). Earlier quoted, as said on TV by Red Skelton (1910–97), in Philip French, *The Movie Moguls* (1969). An unattributed version appears in Oscar Levant, *The Unimportance of Being Oscar* (1968).

JOAD, C.E.M.

English philosopher (1891–1953)

7 It all depends what you mean by ...

The Brains Trust was a discussion programme first broadcast by the BBC in 1941, taking its title from President Roosevelt's name for his circle of advisers (in America, more usually '*brain* trust'). Joad was a regular participant, who became a national figure and was often called 'Professor', though he was not entitled to be. His discussion technique was to jump in first and leave the other speakers with little else to say. Alternatively, he would try to undermine arguments by using the phrase for which he became famous. When the chairman once read out a question from a listener, Mr W.E. Jack of Keynsham – 'Are thoughts things or about things?' – Joad inevitably began his answer with, 'It all depends what you mean by a "thing".'

His broadcasting career ended rather abruptly when he was found travelling by rail using a ticket that was not valid. The BBC banished him.

JOFFRE, Joseph Jacques Césaire

French general (1852–1931)

8 Troops that can advance no farther must, at any price, hold on to the ground they have conquered and die on the spot rather than give way.

Joffre, as French Commander-in-Chief, issued his order for the start of the (first) Battle of the Marne on 5 September 1914. In his memoirs (1932), he recalled that his staff was installed in an ancient convent of the Order of Cordeliers, 'and my own office was in what had formerly been a monk's cell. It was from here that I directed the Battle of the Marne and it was in this room that, at half past seven next morning, I signed the following order addressed to the troops ...' The text was apparently written by General Maurice Gustave Gamelin (1872–1958). Together, the French and British managed to push the Germans back along the 200-mile front of the Marne river, preventing the enemy from reaching Paris as it had threatened to do.

JOHN OF THE CROSS

Spanish mystic, poet and saint (1542–91)

1 *La Noche oscura del alma.*
The dark night of the soul.

Treatise based on his poem 'Songs of the Soul Which Rejoices at Having Reached Union with God by the Road of Spiritual Negation' (*c.*1578). Hence, the phrase denoting mental and spiritual suffering prior to some big step. *See* FITZGERALD 238:3. Douglas Adams wrote *The Long Dark Tea-time of the Soul* (1988).

JOHN, Augustus

Welsh artist (1878–1961)

2 We have become, Nina, the sort of people our parents warned us about.

This was recorded about the time Michael Holroyd's two-volume biography of John appeared (1974–5), but it is not in that book. It was quoted, in this precise form, on BBC Radio *Quote ... Unquote* in January 1977. Holroyd confirms it *was* addressed to Nina Hamnett (1890–1956), the painter and something of a figure in London Bohemia, but says that he encountered it only *after* he had written his biography. He first used it in 1981 in his entry on John in *Makers of Modern Culture*. In the 1996 revision of the biography, he gives it as: 'We are the sort of people our fathers warned us against.'

When my version appeared in the second *Quote ... Unquote* book, Bernard Davis wrote in 1981 from Turkish Cyprus, saying: 'An acquaintance of mine, York-Lodge, a close friend of Claud Cockburn and Evelyn Waugh, was continually saying, "We are the sort of people our parents warned us against", and claiming it as his own. This was about 1924.'

It was probably a common expression dating from between the wars, if not before. The saying was reported as graffiti from New York City in the early 1970s ('We are the people our parents warned us about') and a placard carried at a demonstration by homosexuals in New York in 1970 asserted, 'We're the people our parents warned us against'. In 1968, Nicholas Von Hoffman brought out a book on hippies with the title *We Are the People Our Parents Warned Us Against.*

JOHNSON, Arte

American entertainer (1934–)

3 Very interesting ... but stupid!

Catchphrase, NBC TV *Rowan and Martin's Laugh-In* (1967–73). Although I used this as the title of a 'book of catchphrases from the world of entertainment' (1980), because it seemed to describe the contents, it was not strictly speaking the fixed form of the catchphrase. For no accountable reason, Johnson used to appear on *Laugh-In* as a bespectacled German soldier wearing a helmet. He would sometimes peer through a potted plant and comment on the proceedings with the thickly accented words, 'Verrrry interesting ... but it stinks!' or 'but stupid!' or whatever.

An enormous hit on US television from its inception in 1967, *Laugh-In* lasted until 1973 and was briefly revived, without Rowan and Martin and with little success, in 1977. The original was a brightly coloured, fast-moving series of sketches and gags, with a wide range of stock characters, linked together by the relaxed charm of Dan Rowan (1922–87) and Dick Martin (1923–).

In *ODMQ* (1991) this catchphrase is wrongly ascribed to Rowan and Martin themselves.

JOHNSON, Burges

American writer (1877–1963)

4 I wish poor Bella's knees were made to bend,
I truly am as sorry as can be.
I hope that You won't mind, and that You'll send
The blessings that each dolly asks of Thee.
And, Lord, I pray that You will just pretend
This is my dollies' talking 'stead of me.

Poem, 'Hear My Dollies' Prayer', *c.*1909 – or, at least, it was printed that year on a picture postcard showing a little girl praying at her bedside, flanked by her dolls, all kneeling except 'Poor Bella' whose knees have not been 'made to bend'. Remembered nostalgically by many.

JOHNSON, Hiram

American all-party senator (1866–1945)

1 The first casualty when war comes is truth.

Speech to the US Senate (*c.*1917), but untraced. According to *PDMQ* (1971) this was 'quoted in Johnson, *Common English Quotations*'. Curiously, yet another namesake – Samuel – said much the same thing less pithily in *The Idler* (11 November 1758) : 'Among the calamities of war, may be justly numbered the diminution of the love of truth, by the falsehoods which interest dictates and credulity encourages.' At the time of the First World War, Arthur (later Lord) Ponsonby is also reported to have said: 'When war is declared, truth is the first casualty.' Hence, *The First Casualty*, title of a book (1975) by Phillip Knightley on propaganda in wartime.

JOHNSON, Lyndon B.

American Democratic 36th President (1908–73)

2 Come now, let us reason together.

Frequent exhortation. Based on Isaiah 1:18.

3 I've got his pecker in my pocket.

When Senate Majority leader. Quoted in David Halberstam, *The Best and the Brightest* (1972) – in which there also occurs Johnson's definition: 'I want loyalty. I want him to kiss my ass in Macy's window at high noon and tell me it smells like roses. I want his pecker in my pocket.'

4 All I have, I would have given gladly not to be standing here today.

On becoming President following the assassination of John F. Kennedy. Speech to Congress (27 November 1963).

5 In your time we have the opportunity to move not only toward the rich society and the powerful society but upward to the Great Society.

Speech, University of Michigan (May 1964). Richard N. Goodwin suggested the name for Johnson's policy platform in the US. After tentative use in over a dozen speeches, the phrase was first elevated to capital letters in this speech at Ann Arbor. According to Hugh Sidey, *A Very Personal Presidency* (1986), Goodwin stumbled on the phrase one midnight in early March 1964 when working as a part-time speechwriter. Even when Goodwin was taken on full time, Johnson was reluctant to admit that the writer had a hand in the President's speeches.

6 We Americans know, although others appear to forget, the risks of spreading conflict. We still seek no wider war.

Broadcast address (4 August 1964). 'No wider war' is misleadingly reminiscent of the German phrase *Nie wieder Krieg* [Never again war], a slogan of the 1920s-30s. 'No more war' and 'Never again', although recurring slogans, were probably not much heard before the twentieth century. At the UN in 1965 Pope Paul VI quoted President Kennedy 'four years ago' to the effect that 'mankind must put an end to war, or war will put an end to mankind ... No more war, never again war.' (The Pope said this in Italian.) Earlier, the phrase was used by Winston Churchill at the end of a letter to Lord Beaverbrook in 1928 (quoted in Martin Gilbert's biography of Churchill, Vol. 5.) A.J.P. Taylor in his *English History 1914–45* suggests that the slogan was 'irresistible' at the end of the First World War. David Lloyd George had said in a newspaper interview (*The Times*, 29 September 1916): '"Never again" has become our battle cry.' Churchill in his *The Second World War* (Vol. 1) said of the French: 'with one passionate spasm [they cried] never again.'

In *Goodbye to Berlin* (1939), Christopher Isherwood describes a Nazi book burning. The books are from a 'small liberal pacifist publisher'. One of the Nazis holds up a book called '*Nie wieder Krieg* [Never again war]' as though it were 'a nasty kind of reptile'. 'No More War!' a fat, well-dressed woman laughs scornfully and savagely. 'What an idea!'

Later, in the mid-1960s, 'Never again' became the slogan of the militant Jewish Defence League – in reference to the Holocaust. A stone monument erected near the birthplace of Adolf Hitler at Braunau, Austria, in 1989 (the centenary of his birth) bore the lines 'For Peace, Freedom and Democracy – Never Again Fascism [*Nie wieder Faschismus*] – Millions of Dead are a warning'.

7 We are not about to send American boys nine or ten thousand miles away from home to do what Asian boys ought to be doing for themselves.

Broadcast address (21 October 1964). *Compare* ROOSEVELT 460:1.

8 For the world which seems to lie out before us like a land of dreams.

In the summer of 1965 the poet Robert Lowell had outraged Johnson by refusing to attend a Festival of the Arts at the White House, in protest at America's involvement in the Vietnam War. A few weeks later, in an address to a gathering of students, Johnson said: 'Robert Lowell, the poet, doesn't like everything around here. But I like one of his lines where he wrote ...'

Unfortunately for Johnson, the above was not a line of Lowell's but from Matthew Arnold's 'Dover Beach'. Lowell had used the line as an epigraph to his book *The Mills of the Kavanaughs*. Also, Arnold did not write 'lie out', simply 'lie'. Stand up the speeechwriter who landed the President in this soup.

1 You let a bully come into your front yard, the next day he'll be on your porch.

On Vietnam. Quoted in *Time* Magazine (15 April 1984). A remark he made on several occasions.

2 That Gerald Ford. He can't fart and chew gum at the same time.

Quoted in Richard Reeves, *A Ford Not a Lincoln* (1975) and J.K. Galbraith, *A Life in Our Times* (1981). This is the correct version of the euphemistic: 'He couldn't walk and chew gum at the same time.'

3 I'd much rather have that fellow inside my tent pissing out, than outside my tent pissing in.

On why he kept J. Edgar Hoover at the FBI. Quoted in David Halberstam, *The Best and the Brightest* (1972). The same sentiment is attributed to Laurence Olivier about employing Kenneth Tynan, a critic, at the National Theatre, in John Dexter, *The Honourable Beast* (1993).

4 Did y'ever think, Ken, that making a speech on economics is a lot like pissing down your leg? It seems hot to you, but it never does to anyone else.

Quoted in J.K. Galbraith, *A Life in Our Times* (1981), but otherwise untraced, as also Johnson's view: 'An economist is a man who couldn't tell the difference between chicken salad and chicken shit.'

5 Son, they are all my helicopters.

When told by an officer that he was walking towards the wrong helicopter, with the words, 'That's your helicopter over there, sir'. Quoted in Hugh Sidey, *A Very Personal Presidency* (1968).

6 It is true that a house divided against itself is a house that cannot stand. There is a division in the American house now and believing this as I do, I have concluded that I should not permit the Presidency to become involved in the partisan divisions that are developing in this political year. Accordingly, I shall not seek, and I will not accept, the nomination of my party for another term as your President.

Unable to cope with the Vietnam War, Johnson surprised everyone by announcing in a TV address on 31 March 1968 his intention not to stand again as President. Even an hour before the broadcast he did not know whether he would use the extra portion about his retirement. Apart from the biblical reference to a 'house divided' (St Mark 3:25 – *see* BIBLE 102:4 – which perhaps had come to Johnson by way of a Lincoln speech in 1858 on the circumstances that had led to the American Civil War), there is also an echo of General Sherman's words to the Republican convention in 1884 (*see* 503:3).

JOHNSON, Paul

English journalist and writer (1928–)

7 The hunting fraternity are notoriously lascivious and, in the season, the night air of Melton Mowbray is loud with the sighs of adulterers.

'Hunting and Humbug', *New Statesman* (12 July 1963). Quoted by Alan Whicker in his notable TV film 'Death in the Morning', which won a BAFTA award in 1964. Melton Mowbray, in Leicestershire – near where the Pytchley, Quorn and Belvoir hunt – has a more savoury reputation for its pork pies.

JOHNSON, Philander Chase

American writer (1866–1939)

8 Cheer up! the worst is yet to come!

Everybody's Magazine (May 1920). It seems that the idea was probably formed long before. It was possibly quoted by Mark Twain in a letter to his wife (1893/4). *See* 545:3.

JOHNSON, Dr Samuel

English writer and lexicographer (1709–84)

9 He was a vicious man, but very kind to me. If you call a dog HERVEY, I shall love him.

Quoted in James Boswell, *Life of Johnson* (1791), relating to 1737. Not long before his death, Johnson recalled the friendship of the Hon. Henry Hervey, who had been in the army at Lichfield (Johnson's birthplace) and had later introduced him into London society.

1 There mark what ills the scholar's life assail,
Toil, envy, want, the patron, and the jail.

The Vanity of Human Wishes (1749). An early shot in Johnson's war against patrons; *see also* below 318:6 and 318:9.

2 His fall was destined to a barren strand,
A petty fortress and a dubious hand;
He left the name, at which the world grew pale,
To point a moral, or adorn a tale.

Of Charles XII of Sweden, in *ib.*

3 I'll come no more behind your scenes, David; for the silk stockings and white bosoms of your actresses excite my amorous propensities.

To David Garrick. In Boswell's *Life* (1791), relating to 1750. In Appendix G to the *Life* John Wilkes recalls this statement in the form: '... the silk stockings and white bosoms of your actresses do make my genitals to quiver.'

4 What, is it you, you dogs! I'll have a frisk with you.

Boswell, *Life of Johnson* (1791), relating to 1753. When his friends Beauclerk and Langton, who had been drinking, knocked Johnson up at three o'clock in the morning, this was his happy response.

5 They teach the morals of a whore, and the manners of a dancing master.

Quoted in Boswell, *Life of Johnson* (1791), relating to 1754. On Lord Chesterfield's famous *Letters* to his natural son.

6 Is not a Patron, my Lord, one who looks with unconcern on a man struggling for life in the water, and, when he has reached ground, encumbers him with help?

From Johnson's magisterial and rebuking letter to the Earl of Chesterfield (February 1755). When Johnson's *Dictionary* was nearing publication, Chesterfield (who might have fancied it would be dedicated to him) attempted to insinuate himself into the learned doctor's favour, having done nothing to help until that time. Johnson made it clear to him what the position was in a devastating letter. Reproduced in Boswell, *Life of Johnson* (1791).

7 What is obvious is not always known, what is known is not always present. Sudden fits of inadvertency will surprise vigilance; slight avocations will seduce attention, and casual eclipses of the mind will darken learning.

Preface, *A Dictionary of the English Language* (1755) – a magnificent disclaimer for any errors.

8 Every quotation contributes something to the stability or enlargement of the language.

Ib. Here Johnson is referring to the citations – the examples of words used in context by other authors – rather than to quotations when employed to illustrate or decorate a theme. This method reached its greatest fulfilment in the extensive citations used by the later *Oxford English Dictionary* (1884–1928).

9 *Lexicographer.* A writer of dictionaries, a *harmless drudge*.

Johnson's celebrated definition in *ib.* Other definitions in his *Dictionary* are noted for their playfulness or subjectiveness, e.g.: '*Network.* Anything reticulated or decussated at equal distances, with interstices between the intersections'; '*Oats.* A grain, which in England is generally given to horses, but in Scotland supports the people'; and '*Patron.* Commonly a wretch who supports with insolence, and is paid with flattery.'

10 Ignorance, Madam, pure ignorance.

Largely working alone on his great *Dictionary* (1755), Johnson committed one or two errors. In the first edition he wrongly defined the word 'pastern' as 'the knee of a horse'. In fact, in a horse, it is rather the equivalent of the *ankle* in humans. It was corrected in later editions but when a woman asked how he had come to make this mistake, he splendidly forebore to give an elaborate defence (as reported in Boswell's *Life*, for 1755).

11 If a man does not make new acquaintance as he advances through life, he will soon find himself left alone. A man, Sir, should keep his friendship *in constant repair*.

Remark to Sir Joshua Reynolds, in Boswell, *Life of Johnson* (1791), relating to 1755.

12 No, *you* smell, *I* stink.

In response to someone who had said to Johnson, 'You smell!' Probably apocryphal.

13 Consider, Sir, how insignificant this will appear a twelvemonth hence.

In *ib.*, relating to 6 July 1763. When Boswell talked of

some temporary setback as a serious distress, Johnson laughed and promulgated this excellent piece of advice. *Compare* DICKENS 206:4.

1 Sir, let me tell you, the noblest prospect which a Scotsman ever sees, is the high road that leads him to England!

In *ib.*, relating to 6 July 1763. Johnson no doubt enjoyed baiting the Scotsman Boswell in this fashion, but his biographer records how 'this unexpected and pointed sally produced a roar of applause.'

2 Sir, a woman's preaching is like a dog's walking on his hinder legs. It is not done well; but you are surprised to find it done at all.

A saying of Johnson's often invoked to describe something about which there is little complimentary to be said. In Boswell's *Life* (1791), relating to 31 July 1763, when Boswell mentions that, 'I had been that morning at a meeting of the people called Quakers, where I had heard a woman preach.'

3 So far is it from being true that men are naturally equal, that no two people can be half an hour together, but one shall acquire an evident superiority over the other.

In *ib.* (1791), relating to 15 February 1766 – 'on his favourite subject of subordination.'

4 Not at all, Sir. On the contrary, were he not to marry again, it might be concluded that his first wife had given him a disgust to marriage; but by taking a second wife he pays the highest compliment to the first, by shewing that she made him so happy as a married man, that he wishes to be so a second time.

In response to Boswell's remark that a gentleman who married a second time showed disregard of his first wife. Boswell, *Life of Johnson* (1791), relating to 30 September 1769.

5 It matters not how a man dies, but how he lives. The act of dying is not of importance, it lasts so short a time.

In *ib.*, for 27 October 1769: 'To my question, whether we might not fortify our minds for the approach of death, he answered, in a passion, "No, Sir, let it alone ..."' This neatly provided an epitaph on a later memorial in the crypt of St Paul's Cathedral, London:

GORDON HAMILTON-FAIRLEY
DM FRCP
FIRST PROFESSOR OF CLINICAL ONCOLOGY
1930–1975
KILLED BY A TERRORIST BOMB
It matters not how a man dies but how he lives.

Professor Hamilton-Fairley was head of the medical oncology unit at St Bartholomew's Hospital, London, and one of Britain's leading cancer experts. He was killed in Campden Hill Square, London, as he passed a car containing an IRA bomb intended for his next door neighbour, Hugh Fraser, a Conservative MP.

6 It was the triumph of hope over experience.

When told that a gentleman who had been very unhappy in marriage, married immediately after his wife died. One of the anecdotes collected by Johnson's friend, the Rev. Dr Maxwell, and inserted by Boswell in the *Life of Johnson* (1791) in the year 1770. Johnson had a very positive view of marriage (though it is sometimes forgotten that he was himself married for a while), hence, his remark 'Even ill assorted marriages were preferable to cheerless celibacy' (in *ib.*) and 'Marriage has many pains, but celibacy has no pleasures (*Rasselas*, 1759).

7 No, Sir, do *you* read books *through*?

When Mr Elphinston pressed Johnson on whether he had read a new book. In *ib.*, for 19 April 1773.

8 Read over your compositions, and where ever you meet with a passage which you think is particularly fine, strike it out.

Recalling the advice of a college tutor. In *ib.*, for 30 April 1773. This has survived in the modern sayings 'kill your darlings' and 'throw away your babies', advice often given to aspiring journalists (and in use by the 1960s).

9 A man may write at any time, if he will set himself doggedly to it.

Quoted in Boswell, *Journal of a Tour to the Hebrides* (1785), relating to 16 August 1773. Boswell recalls the remark when discussing Johnson's ready production of the twice-weekly paper *The Rambler* when he had much else on his mind and was also afflicted by natural indolence. Also in the *Life* (at March 1750).

10 When once you have thought of big men and little men, it is very easy to do all the rest.

On Swift's *Gulliver's Travels*, in *ib.*, for 24 March 1775.

1 Patriotism is the last refuge of a scoundrel.

In *ib.*, for 7 April 1775. Boswell adds that, of course, he means 'pretended patriotism which so many, in all ages and countries, have made a cloak for self-interest.'

2 Nothing odd will do long. *Tristram Shandy* did not last.

In *ib.*, for 21 March 1776. Sterne's novel had been published in 1759–67. While wrong in one sense, it is clear that Johnson had the measure of the work.

3 Sir, you have but two topicks, yourself and me. I am sick of both.

A rebuff to Boswell who, however, merely says that it was delivered to a 'gentleman' who asked another 'a variety of questions' about Dr Johnson. In *ib.*, for May 1776.

4 BOSWELL: 'That, Sir, was great fortitude of mind.' JOHNSON: 'No, Sir; stark insensibility.'

In *ib.*, an exchange dated 20 March 1776 but referring to 1728 when Johnson entered Pembroke College, Oxford. His tutor asked him why he had not been attending instruction and Johnson replied 'with as much *nonchalance* as I am now talking to you' that he had been sliding in Christ Church meadow.

5 *OLIVARII GOLDSMITH, Poetae, Physici, Historici, qui nullum fere scribendi genus non tetigit, nullum quod tetigit non ornavit.*

Of Oliver Goldsmith, A Poet, Natural Philosopher, and Historian, who left no species of writing untouched by his pen, and touched none that he did not adorn.

Goldsmith's epitaph in Poets' Corner, Westminster Abbey, was written by Johnson, but not without dissent among Goldsmith's other friends and admirers. As James Boswell records in his *Life of Johnson* (16 May 1776), the 'Epitaph gave occasion to a *Remonstrance* to the MONARCH OF LITERATURE'. Various emendations were suggested to Johnson's draft and presented to him in the form of a round robin. Sir Joshua Reynolds took it to Johnson 'who received it with much good humour, and desired Sir Joshua to tell the gentlemen, that he would alter the Epitaph in any manner they pleased, as to the sense of it; but *he would never consent to disgrace the walls of Westminster Abbey with an English inscription.*' Johnson argued further that, 'the language of the country of which a learned man was a native, is not the language fit for his epitaph, which should be in an ancient and permanent language. Consider, Sir; how you should feel, were you to find at Rotterdam an epitaph upon Erasmus *in Dutch*!'

And so it remained in Latin, despite the protest from Goldsmith's friends. The above is an extract only.

6 Sir, when a man is tired of London, he is tired of life; for there is in London all that life can afford.

In *ib.*, 20 September 1777. One of the worst examples of 'quote abuse' I have ever come across was something attributed to Robert Moses, a New York Parks Commissioner, by Barbara Rowes in *The Book of Quotes* (1979): 'Every true New Yorker believes with all his heart that when a New Yorker is tired of New York, he is tired of life.'

7 There are no snakes to be met with throughout the whole island.

As a joke, Johnson used to boast of being able to repeat a complete chapter of *The Natural History of Iceland* by a Dane called Horrebow (1758). He would then say this sentence which is, indeed, the entire contents of Chapter 72 of Horrebow's book. In Boswell's *Life* (1791), for 13 April 1778. Sometimes, in telling the story, *Ireland* rather than Iceland is mistakenly put into the joke, presumably out of confusion with the fact that St Patrick traditionally did drive all the snakes out of that country by ringing a bell.

8 I am willing to love all mankind, *except an American.*

Boswell, *Life of Johnson* (1791), for 15 April 1778. Johnson was not a supporter of the American Revolution – the Declaration of Independence had been signed less than two years previously. He went on to characterize Americans as 'Rascals – Robbers – Pirates'.

9 I would rather praise it than read it.

'Congreve', *The Lives of the English Poets* (1779–81). Johnson said this about the novel *Incognita* (1691). Congreve went on to become better known, of course, as a playwright.

10 In the character of his [Gray's] Elegy I rejoice to concur with the common reader ... The churchyard abounds with images which find a mirror in every mind, and with sentiments to which every bosom returns an echo.

'Thomas Gray' in *ib.* Hence, *The Common Reader*, the title of two volumes of Virginia Woolf's collected essays, published in 1925 and 1932.

1 An exotic and irrational entertainment, which has been always combated, and always has prevailed.

'John Hughes', in *ib.* This is not Dr Johnson's definition of 'opera' in his *Dictionary* (1755), as is often supposed. He is referring in particular to *Italian* opera. Johnson was self-admittedly unmusical but had no objection to *English* opera.

In Kenneth Clark's *Civilisation* (1969, and in the TV original), he says: 'Opera, next to Gothic architecture, is one of the strangest inventions of western man. It could not have been foreseen by any logical process. Dr Johnson's much quoted definition, which as far as I can make out he never wrote, "an extravagant and irrational entertainment", is perfectly correct; and at first it seems surprising that it should have been brought to perfection in the age of reason.' Clark is quite right that Johnson did not call it an 'extravagant and irrational entertainment' but how interesting that he did not go so far as to check and find out what Johnson *did* say.

In his *Dictionary* Johnson does not in fact define the word 'opera' himself, but merely quotes Dryden: 'An *opera* is a poetical tale or fiction, represented by vocal and instrumental musick, adorned with scenes, machines and dancing.'

2 At this man's table I enjoyed many cheerful and instructive hours ... with David Garrick, whom I hoped to have gratified with this character of our common friend; but what are the hopes of man! I am disappointed by that stroke of death, which has eclipsed the gaiety of nations, and impoverished the public stock of harmless pleasure.

Johnson was Garrick's great friend (and one-time schoolteacher in Lichfield) and they continued to see each other when Garrick had become the foremost actor of the age. The 'epitaph' appears in the life of Edmund Smith, one of Johnson's *Lives of the English Poets* (published in 1779, the year of the actor's death). Eva Maria, Garrick's widow, had the words engraved below his memorial bust in the south transept of Lichfield Cathedral. John Wilkes had his doubts about the tribute and made an 'attack' on the phrase about eclipsing the gaiety of nations. Boswell relayed this to Johnson, who replied: 'I could not have said more nor less, for 'tis truth; "eclipsed", not "extinguished", and his death did eclipse; 'twas like a storm.'

'But why *nations*?' Boswell continued. 'Did his gaiety extend farther than his own nation?' Johnson deftly tossed in the Scots ('if we allow the Scotch to be a nation, and to have gaiety') but Boswell pressed on, 'Is not *harmless pleasure* very tame?' To which Johnson replied: 'Nay, Sir, harmless pleasure is the highest praise. Pleasure is a word of dubious import; pleasure is in general dangerous, and pernicious to virtue; to be able therefore to furnish pleasure that is harmless, pleasure pure and unalloyed, is as great a power as men can possess.' Boswell's initial account of this exchange appears in his journal for 24 April 1779 and appears in substantially the same form in his *Life of Johnson* at this date.

When Charles Dickens died in 1870, Thomas Carlyle wrote: 'It is an event world-wide, a *unique* of talents suddenly extinct, and has "eclipsed" (we too may say) "the gaiety of nations".'

3 BOSWELL: 'Should you not like to see Dublin, Sir?' JOHNSON: 'No, Sir! Dublin is only a worse capital.' BOSWELL: 'Is not the Giant's Causeway worth seeing?' JOHNSON:'Worth seeing? yes; but not worth going to see.'

Boswell, *Life of Johnson* (1791), for 12 October 1779. Johnson always had an aversion to visiting Ireland. In fact, he never went there, though the strength of his views as here – and next – might lead one to suppose that he had.

4 Dublin, though a place much worse than London, it is not so bad as Iceland.

In a note to Boswell's *Life* (not first edition). It comes from the continuation of a letter from Mrs Smart, but is not actually printed in the *Life*. Johnson never visited either place.

5 Sir, your wife, *under pretence of keeping a bawdy-house*, is a receiver of stolen goods.

Johnson's response when a man attacked him with some coarse raillery. In the *Life of Johnson* (1791) – for 1780 – Boswell reproduces some *Johnsoniana* collected by Bennet Langton. When the 'contests' in abusive language conducted between passers by on the River Thames are mentioned, this example is adduced, though it is not clear whether Johnson himself was on the river when he uttered this squelch.

6 The woman had a bottom of good sense.

In *ib.*, for 20 April 1781. Boswell comments, 'The word *bottom* thus introduced, was so ludicrous when contrasted with his gravity, that most of us could not forbear tittering and laughing.' Johnson did not take kindly to this and demanded, 'Where's the merriment? ... I say the *woman* was *fundamentally* sensible.' Boswell adds: 'We all sat composed as at a funeral.'

1 [Quotation] is a good thing; there is a community of mind in it. Classical quotation is the *parole* of literary men all over the world.

In *ib.*, for 8 May 1781. Comment on the art of quotation. *Parole* = the way of speaking, conversing.

2 Sir, there is no settling the point of precedency between a louse and a flea.

Johnson's reply when asked to decide which of two poets – Derrick and Smart – was the better. Recounted in Boswell's *Life* (1791) for 1783. It was, in fact, a standard figure of speech at that time for pedantically nit-picking comparisons. It had earlier been used by John Eachard and, in Latin, by Daniel Heinsius (according to *Notes and Queries*, Vol. 239).

3 The Empress of Russia has ordered the *Rambler* to be translated into the Russian language: so I shall be read on the banks of the Volga.

Boswell, *Life of Johnson* (1791), for 15 May 1784. Unfortunately, it turns out not to have been true but Boswell records the immense satisfaction Johnson had on receiving the information.

4 Madam, a fool would have swallowed that.

To his shocked companion after spitting out a hot potato at dinner. Untraced and also ascribed to Winston Churchill and others. Known by 1950.

5 An odd thought strikes me: we shall receive no letters in the grave.

In Boswell, *Life of Johnson* (1791), a remark from the last few weeks of his life in December 1784.

JOHNSTON, Sir Charles

English diplomat, poet and translator (1912–86)

6 Then Petra flashed by in a wink.
It looked like Eaton Square – *but pink.*

'Air Travel in Arabia', in *Poems and Journeys* (1979). The source for this couplet proved elusive at one time, but this is it.

JOLSON, Al

American entertainer (1888–1950)

7 Wait a minute, wait a minute. You ain't heard nothin' yet! You wanna hear 'Toot, Toot, Tootsie'? All right, hold on.

It seems that when Jolson exclaimed this in the first full-length talking picture *The Jazz Singer* (1927), he was not just ad-libbing – as is usually supposed – but was promoting the title of one of his songs. He had recorded 'You Ain't Heard Nothing Yet', written by Gus Kahn and Buddy de Sylva, in 1919. In addition, Martin Abramson in *The Real Story of Al Jolson* (1950) suggests that Jolson had also uttered the slogan in San Francisco as long before as 1906. Interrupted by noise from a building site across the road from a café in which he was performing, Jolson had shouted, 'You think that's noise – you ain't heard nuttin' yet!'

Listening to the film soundtrack makes it clear that Jolson did not add 'folks' at the end of his mighty line, as Bartlett (1992), the *PDMQ* (1980) and the *ODQ* (1979) all say he did. Rather curiously, A.J.P. Taylor in *English History 1914–1945* (1965) seems to think that the ad-libbed words were 'Come on, Ma, listen to this.'

JONG, Erica

American novelist (1942–)

8 The zipless fuck is the purest thing there is. And it is rarer than the unicorn. And I have never had one.

Fear of Flying (1973). Jong coined the phrase 'zipless fuck' for a 'brief and passionate sexual encounter' (*OED2*) and, in her novel, explained her choice of the word 'zipless', 'because when you come together zippers fell away like petals'.

JONSON, Ben

English playwright and poet (1572–1637)

9 Ramp up my genius, be not retrograde;
But boldly nominate a spade a spade.

The Poetaster, Act 5, Sc. 1 (1601). *See* PLUTARCH 432:5.

10 Soul of the Age!
The applause, delight, the wonder of our stage!

'To the Memory of My Beloved, the Author, Mr William Shakespeare' (1623). This work contains most of Jonson's eminently quotable tributes to, and comments about, Shakespeare: 'How far thou didst our Lyly outshine,/Or sporting Kyd, or Marlowe's mighty line'; 'Thou hadst small Latin, and less Greek'; 'He was not of an age, but for all time!'; and 'Sweet Swan of Avon!'

11 I remember the players have often mentioned it as an honour ... that in his writing (whatso-

ever he penned) he never blotted out a line. My answer hath been 'Would he had blotted out a thousand.' Which they thought a malevolent speech.

Timber, or Discoveries made upon Men and Matter (1641). Also on Shakespeare. This work includes the remark: 'For I loved the man, and do honour his memory, on this side of idolatry.'

1 O Rare Ben Johnson.

Jonson's epitaph in Westminster Abbey was composed in the year he died. According to Abbey tradition (recounted in the *Official Guide*, 1988 revision), Jonson died in poverty and was buried upright to save space. So he was, in the north aisle of the nave, with a small square stone over him. The stone, with the inscription spelled as above, was set upright in the north aisle wall in 1821 to save it from being worn away, and it may still be found there. (There is also a wall plaque 'O RARE BEN IOHNSON', erected before 1728, in Poets' Corner.)

Another tradition, according to John Aubrey, had it that the original epitaph was 'done at the charge of Jack Young, afterwards knighted, who, walking here when the grave was covering, gave the fellow eighteen pence to cut it'. The inscription has also been ascribed to the playwright, Sir William D'Avenant (1608–68) who succeeded Jonson as unofficial Poet Laureate. His own gravestone set in the floor of Poets' Corner reads, 'O RARE S. WILLIAM DAVENANT' (or 'O rare Sir Will. Davenant' as Aubrey has it, 'in imitation of that on Ben Johnson').

Either way, the spelling is not at fault – 'Jonson' is merely an alternative that has become accepted. An attempt has been made to suggest that what the epitaphist meant to say was '*Orare Ben Jonson*' – 'pray for Ben Jonson' – but this is questionable Latin.

JORDAN, Louis

American singer, musician and songwriter (1908–75)

2 Is You Is Or Is You Ain't My Baby?

Title of song (1943), written with Billy Austin. It suffered a revival in *c.*1990 when commercials for a British credit card included the jingle, 'Does you does or does you don't take Access?'

JOSEPH II

Holy Roman Emperor (1741–90)

3 Too many notes.

The Emperor's comments were directed at Mozart's opera *Die Entführung aus dem Serail* [The Abduction from the Seraglio], first performed in 1782. Unwilling to concede the point, Mozart replied that it had 'just as many as are necessary'. Franz Xaver Niemetschek's biography of the composer (1798) provides the context: 'The monarch, who at heart was charmed by this deeply stirring music, said to Mozart nevertheless: "Too beautiful for our ears and an extraordinary number of notes, dear Mozart." "Just as many, Your Majesty, as are necessary," he replied with that noble dignity and frankness which so often go with great genius.'

James Agate, *Ego 6* (1942) has the opera as *Le Nozze di Figaro* and Mozart's reply as: 'Not one too many, your Majesty.'

JOSEPH, Jenny

English poet (1932–)

4 When I am an old woman I shall wear purple
With a red hat which doesn't go, and doesn't suit me,
And I shall spend my pension on brandy and summer gloves
And satin sandals, and say we've no money for butter.

'Warning' in *New Poems* (P.E.N. anthology, 1965). In a 1996 poll by BBC TV to find Britain's most popular post-war poem, this came top. Indeed, it is widely known and can be found printed on tea-towels and other gift-fodder, often without acknowledging the poet. The success of the poem apparently irritates Jenny Joseph, who does not regard it as typical of her work.

JOYCE, James

Irish novelist (1882–1941)

5 Snow was general all over Ireland ... His soul swooned slowly as he heard the snow falling faintly through the universe and faintly falling, like the descent of their last end, upon all the living and the dead.

'The Dead', *Dubliners* (1916), the concluding words of this, the most notable of the collection of short stories. Gabriel, reflecting on a loveless marriage to Gretta, thinks in particular of the snow falling on the grave of Michael Furey who – Gretta has just admitted – died for her. The prospect of death 'in the full glory of some passion' seems preferable to fading and withering dismally with age.

1 The snotgreen sea. The scrotumtightening sea.

Ulysses, Chap. 1 (1937). Evidence from the first chapter of Joyce's inventive way with words.

2 riverrun, past Eve and Adam's, from swerve of shore to bend of bay, brings us by a commodius vicus of recirculation back to Howth Castle and Environs.

The first words of *Finnegans Wake* (1939). The last line of the book, 'A way a lone a last a loved a long the', is also part of this opening and forms a circular whole with it.

3 No, it did a lot of other things, too.

When a young man accosted him in Zurich and asked, 'May I kiss the hand that wrote Ulysses?' Quoted in Richard Ellman, *James Joyce* (1959).

4 Envoy: Love me, love my umbrella.

Giacomo Joyce (*c*.1914). The final fragment in this posthumously published work.

JOYCE, William

Irish-American propagandist (1906–46)

5 Germany calling, Germany calling.

Joyce broadcast Nazi propaganda from Hamburg during the Second World War, was found guilty of treason (on the technicality that he held a British passport at the beginning of the war) and was hanged in 1946. He had a threatening, sneering, lower middle class delivery, which made his call-sign sound more like 'Jarmany calling'. Although Joyce was treated mostly as a joke in wartime Britain, he is credited with giving rise to some unsettling rumours. No one seemed to have heard the particular broadcast in question, but it got about that he had said the clock on Darlington Town Hall was two minutes slow, and so it was supposed to be.

His nickname of 'Lord Haw-Haw' was inappropriate as he did not sound the slightest bit aristocratic. *That* sobriquet had been applied by Jonah Barrington, the *Daily Express* radio correspondent, to Joyce's predecessor who *did* speak with a cultured accent but lasted only a few weeks from September 1939. This original was Norman Baillie-Stewart. He is said to have sounded like Claud Hulbert or one of the Western Brothers. An imaginary drawing appeared in the *Daily Express* of a Bertie Woosterish character with a monocle and receding chin. Baillie-Stewart said that he understood there was a popular English song called 'We're Going to Hang Out the Washing on the Siegfried Line' which ended 'If the Siegfried Line's still there'. 'Curiously enoff,' he said, 'the Siegfried Line is still thcy-ah.'

JUDGE, Jack

British entertainer (1878–1938)

6 It's a long way to Tipperary
It's a long way to go;
It's a long way to Tipperary
To the sweetest girl I know!
Goodbye Piccadilly! Farewell, Leicester
 Square!
It's a long, long way to Tipperary,
But my heart's right there.

Song, 'Tipperary' (1912). Billed as written with Harry Williams (1858–1930), but Judge later claimed to have written both words and music and given a credit to Williams in payment of a loan. The most popular song among British soldiers during the early part of the First World War, though some say it was sung more in the music-halls back home than at the Front. It tells of an Irishman on a visit to London who longs for the green fields of home. 'Goodbye Piccadilly! Farewell Leicester Square' was soon interpreted, however, as the British soldiers' farewell to the fleshpots of home. At the slightest encouragement, the writer John Julius Norwich will sing a French version (source unknown):

C'est à Tip – Tip, à Tipperary
 Où nous allons, mes amis.
Et c'est chic, chic à Tipperary
Mais, mon Dieu, c'est loin d'ici.
 Où est-ce Tipperary?
 Je m'en fous, et vous aussi,
C'est pour Tip – Tip – Tip, pour Tipperary
Que nous quittons Paris.

JUMBO

American film 1962. With Jimmy Durante.

7 *Sheriff*: Where are you going with that elephant?
Durante: What elephant?

Soundtrack. The film was based on the 1935 Rodgers–Hart–Hecht–MacArthur stage show *Jumbo* in which Durante delivered the same joke. It was specifically credited to Charles Lederer.

JUNG, Carl

Swiss psychologist (1875–1961)

1 Liverpool is the pool of life.

Returning to my home town in 1982, I was intrigued to find a sign in Mathew Street – sacred site of the erstwhile Cavern Club – saying: 'Liverpool is the pool of life./C.J. JUNG 1927'. An agreeable compliment, but is there any record of the Swiss psychologist ever having set foot in the fair city? None. His *Memories, Dreams, Reflections* (1963) makes clear that he was simply describing a dream he had had. He saw a round pool, and in the middle of it a small island. While everything round about was obscured by rain, fog, smoke and dimly-lit darkness, the little island blazed with sunlight. 'I had had a vision of unearthly beauty,' Jung says, 'and that was why I was able to live at all. Liverpool is the "pool of life". The "liver", according to an old view, is the seat of life – that which "makes to live".'

Unfortunately, even here, Jung is basing his supposition on fanciful etymology, presumably just hearing the name 'Liverpool', and never having been there. The derivation of the place name is 'pool with clotted water', rather more to the point than 'pool of life'.

The sign had been taken down by 1987. A somewhat wobbly allusion occurs in Beryl Bainbridge, *An Awfully Big Adventure* (1989): 'O'Hara reminded him that Jung had considered Liverpool the centre of the Universe. "How interesting," said Potter. "I take it he didn't live here."'

JUNOR, John (later Sir John)

Scottish journalist and editor (1919–97)

2 I think we should be told.

By 1980, *Private Eye* Magazine was running a regular parody of the opinion column written by Junor for the *Sunday Express*. It frequently included the would-be campaigning journalist's line, 'I think we should be told'. In 1985, Sir John – as he was by then – told me that he had never once used the phrase in his column.

3 Pass the sick-bag, Alice.

An expression of contempt from the same parodies, but one that Sir John did, however, admit to having used – though only once.

JUVENAL

Roman satirist (c.AD 60–c.130)

4 *Sed quis custodiet ipsos*
Custodes?
But who is to guard the guards themselves?

Satires, No. 6. A key question to be asked of people in any sort of authority – who are *they* answerable to?

5 *Panem et circenses.*
Bread and circuses.

Ib., No. 10 – on what the citizen is chiefly concerned about, having been bribed by whoever is in office with public entertainments and free food, as a way of avoiding popular discontent.

6 *Mens sana in corpore sano.*
A sound mind in a healthy body.

Ib., No. 10. One of the most famous of proverbial Latin sayings and much used as a motto – e.g., of Chelsea College of Physical Education, Eastbourne, and Summer Fields School, Oxford.

K

KAEL, Pauline

American film critic (1919–)

1 Kiss Kiss Bang Bang.

Title of book (1968) of collected criticism. She says the words came from an Italian poster – 'perhaps the briefest statement imaginable on the basic appeal of movies'. Usually, they are taken to refer to the James Bond movies. Indeed, Bond's creator Ian Fleming himself described his books in a letter (*c.*1955) to Raymond Chandler as 'straight pillow fantasies of the bang-bang, kiss-kiss variety'. John Barry, composer of music for most of the Bond films, named one of his themes 'Mr Kiss Kiss Bang Bang' for *Thunderball* (1965).

2 She's playing herself – and it's awfully soon for that.

Of Barbra Streisand in *What's Up, Doc?* In *Deeper into Movies* (1973).

KARR, Alphonse

French novelist and editor (1808–90)

3 *Plus ça change, plus c'est la même chose.*
The more things change, the more they remain the same.

Les Guêpes (1849). The presumed origin of the phrase. *Compare* LAMPEDUSA 343:2.

KAUFMAN, George S.

American playwright (1889–1961)

4 Everything I've ever said will be credited to Dorothy Parker.

Quoted in Scott Meredith, *George S. Kaufman and the Algonquin Round Table* (1974). The lament of the unjustly misappropriated.

5 Excuse me for interrupting but I actually thought I heard a line I wrote.

At rehearsal of the Marx Brothers film *Animal Crackers* for which he wrote the script. In *ib.*

6 Massey won't be satisfied until somebody assassinates him.

Of Raymond Massey's off-stage interpretation of Abraham Lincoln. In *ib.* Also in Howard Teichman, *George S. Kaufman* (1973).

7 Well, let's say I'm not against it ...

When stopped at the stage door and asked if he was 'with the show'. In *ib.*

8 Guido Nadzo is nadzo guido.

Of an actor called Guido Nadzo. In *ib.* Also attributed to Brooks Atkinson.

9 God finally caught his eye.

Of a dead waiter. In *ib.* As 'By and by/God caught his eye' this has been attributed to David McCord (1897–?), in 'Remainders' from *Bay Window Ballads* (1935).

10 Under an assumed name.

When a poor bridge partner asked how he should have played a hand. In *ib.*

11 You Can't Take It With You.

Title of play (1936), written with Moss Hart, from the saying that suggests that there is no point in holding on to money as it will be no good to you when you are dead (as in the expression 'there are no pockets in shrouds'). An early appearance is in Captain Marryat's *Masterman Ready* (1841). An American version is: 'You can't take your dough when you go.' 'You can always take one with you' was a slogan suggested by Winston Churchill when invasion by the Germans threatened in 1940.

KAUFMAN, Gerald

British Labour politician (1930–)

1 The longest suicide note [ever penned] in history.

As a Labour Shadow Cabinet member, on the party's 1983 General Election manifesto. Quoted in Denis Healey, *The Time of My Life* (1989).

KAZANTZAKIS, Nikos

Greek novelist (1883–1957)

2 I hope for nothing, I fear nothing, I am free.

Translation of the inscription on his grave at Iraklion, Crete. He was buried by the southern bastion of the city when the Orthodox Church refused him sacred ground as a non-believer (source: Hagg & Lewis, *Guide to Greece*, 1986). Compare, from Torquato Tasso, *Jerusalem Delivered* (1580–1): '*Brama assai, poco spera, e nulla chiede* [He desired much, he hoped little, and asked for nothing]' which, in turn, was written by Edward Elgar at the end of his score for 'The Enigma Variations' (1899) in the form: 'I long for much, I hope for little, I ask for nothing.'

KEARNEY, Denis

Irish-born American labour leader (1847–1907)

3 Horny-handed sons of toil.

Kearney used this expression describing labourers who bear the marks of their work in a speech at San Francisco (*c.*1878). He was leading a 'workingman's protest movement against unemployment, unjust taxes, unfair banking laws, and mainly against Chinese labourers' (Flexner, 1982). Earlier, the American poet J.R. Lowell had written in 'A Glance Behind the Curtain' (1843): 'And blessèd are the horny hands of toil.' The 3rd Marquess of Salisbury, the British Conservative Prime Minister, had also used the phrase earlier in *The Quarterly Review* (October 1873).

KEATING, Paul

Australian Labour Prime Minister (1944–)

4 I learned about self-respect and self-regard for Australia, not about some cultural cringe to a country [Britain] which decided not to defend the Malaysian peninsula, not to worry about Singapore, and not to give us our troops back to keep ourselves free from Japanese domination. This was a country that you people [the Opposition] wedded yourselves to. Even as they walked out on you and joined the Common Market, you were looking for your MBEs and your knighthoods. You take Australia right back down the time tunnel to the cultural cringe where you've always come from.

Speech in Parliament at Canberra (27 February 1992). The phrase 'cultural cringe', referring to the belief that one's own country's culture is inferior to that of others, was not coined by Keating, although it is certainly well-established in Australia. The Australian critic Arthur Angell Phillips (1900–85) wrote in *Meanjin* (1950): 'Above our writers – and other artists – looms the intimidating mass of Anglo-Saxon culture. Such a situation almost inevitably produces the characteristic Australian Cultural Cringe – appearing either as the Cringe Direct, or as the Cringe Inverted, in the attitude of the Blatant Blatherskite, the God's-own-country and I'm-a-better-man-than-you-are Australian bore.'

KEATS, John

English poet (1795–1821)

5 My ear is open like a greedy shark,
To catch the tunings of a voice divine.

'Imitation of Spenser' (1817). In the novel *Gaudy Night* (1935) by Dorothy L. Sayers, Lord Peter Wimsey quotes the shark remark and describes it as 'the crashing conclusion of a sonnet by Keats'.

6 Much have I travelled in the realms of gold,
And many goodly states and kingdoms seen ...

Then felt I like some watcher in the skies
When a new planet swims into his ken;
Or like stout Cortez when with eagle eyes
He star'd at the Pacific – and all his men
Look'd at each other with a wild surmise –
Silent, upon a peak in Darien.

'On First Looking Into Chapman's Homer' (1817). There are two minor errors of fact here. It was, in fact, Balboa, a companion of Cortés, who became the first European to set eyes on the Pacific Ocean at Darien on the Isthmus of Panama in 1513. Nor was he silent: he exclaimed, '*Hombre!*', an expression of surprise, the equivalent of the modern 'Man, look at that!'

1 And other spirits there are standing apart
Upon the forehead of the age to come:
These, these will give the world another heart,
And other pulses. Hear ye not the hum
Of mighty workings?

Sonnet 'Addressed to the Same' (i.e., Benjamin Robert Haydon) (1817). Hence, *Another Heart and Other Pulses* (1984), title of Michael Foot's account of his leadership of the British Labour Party during the 1983 General Election.

2 I had a dove and the sweet dove died;
And I have thought it died of grieving.

'I had a dove and the sweet dove died' (written 1818). *See* PYM 443:4.

3 A thing of beauty is a joy forever.

Endymion, Bk 1, l. 1 (1818). *Compare* ROWLAND 463:3.

4 For lo!
He cannot see the heavens, nor the flow
Of rivers, nor hill-flowers running wild
In pink and purple chequer, nor, up-pil'd,
The cloudy rack slow journeying in the west,
Like herded elephants.

Ib., Bk 2, l. 289. Of course, it was quite likely that Keats had seen an individual elephant but one wonders how he had any idea of what a *herd* would look like? But then, he was a poet.

5 Oh, what can ail thee knight at arms
Alone and palely loitering?
The sedge has withered from the lake
And no birds sing! ...

For she looked at me as she did love
And made sweet moan.

... La belle dame sans merci
Thee hath in thrall.

'La belle dame sans merci' (1820). Keats took the title of his tale of a knight fatally in thrall to an elfin woman from a fifteenth-century poem *La belle dame sans mercy*. In *The White Goddess* (1948), Robert Graves argues that La Belle Dame represents 'Love, Death by Consumption ... and Poetry all at once'.

6 My heart aches, and a drowsy numbness pains
My sense, as though of hemlock I had
drunk.

'Ode to a Nightingale' (1820). In a poll to find Britain's favourite poem, conducted by the BBC TV programme *Bookworm* in 1995, this one came ninth.

7 Already with thee! tender is the night.

Ib. Hence, *Tender is the Night*, title of a novel (1943; film US, 1961) by F. Scott Fitzgerald.

8 Season of mists and mellow fruitfulness,
Close bosom-friend of the maturing sun;
Conspiring with him how to load and bless
With fruit the vines that round the thatch-
eaves run.

'To Autumn' (1820). In a poll to find Britain's favourite poem, conducted by the BBC TV programme *Bookworm* in 1995, this one came sixth.

9 You I am sure will forgive me for sincerely remarking that you might curb your magnanimity and be more of an artist, and 'load every rift' of your subject with ore.

Letter to Shelley (August 1820). The quotation marks are taken to indicate a reference to Edmund Spenser's *The Faerie Queene*, Bk 2, Canto 7, St. 28 (1596): 'And with rich metal loaded every rift.'

10 Here lies One
Whose Name was writ in Water.

Keats's own choice of epitaph on his anonymous grave in the English cemetery, Rome. A few days before he died, Keats said that on his gravestone there should be no mention of his name or country. As he lay dying, listening to the fountain outside on the Spanish Steps in Rome, it is said he kept being reminded of the lines from Beaumont and Fletcher's play *Philaster*: 'All your better deeds/Shall be in water writ, but this in marble.' Robert Gittings in his biography of Keats (1968) comments: 'The quotations that may have suggested this phrase are many; but the gentle sound of the fountain, which had been his companion for so many nights as he lay in the narrow room above the square, may have seemed the right symbol for his end.'

One of the possible sources? Shakespeare, in *Henry VIII* (IV.ii.45) has: 'Men's evil manners live in brass; their virtues/We write in water.'

The self-written epitaph of Robert Ross, a friend of Oscar Wilde's, was: 'Here lies one whose name was writ in hot water' (source: Osbert Sitwell, *Noble Essences*, 1950).

KELLY, Ned

Australian outlaw (1855–80)

1 Ah well, I suppose it has come to this! ... Such is life!

Last words, quoted in Frank Clune, *The Kelly Hunters* (1958). Kelly was the son of a transported Irish convict and himself became a horse thief. He was hanged in Melbourne. The last phrase Partridge/*Slang* calls a 'world-old, world-wide truism' and Partridge/*Catch Phrases* adds 'world-weary'. W.J. Temple wrote in his diary (7 April 1796): 'This interruption is very teasing; but such is Life.' From Charles Dickens, *Martin Chuzzlewit*, Chap. 29 (1846): '"Sairey," says Mrs Harris, "sech is life. Vich likeways is the hend of all things!"' The British pop singer and political clown Lord David Sutch felicitously entitled his autobiography *Life As Sutch* (1992).

KELLY, Walt

American cartoonist (1913–73)

2 We have met the enemy and he is us.

Kelly's syndicated comic strip featured an opossum called Pogo. This phrase was used in a 1970 Pogo cartoon used on the 1971 Earth Day poster. Kelly had taken some time to get round to this formulation. In his introduction to *The Pogo Papers* (1953) he wrote: 'Resolve then, that on this very ground, with small flags waving and tinny blasts on tiny trumpets, we shall meet the enemy, and not only may he be ours, he may be us.'

There may be an allusion here to what US Captain Oliver Hazard Perry (1785–1819) said at the Battle of Lake Erie (10 September 1813): 'We have met the enemy and he is ours' or 'and they are ours'.

KEMPIS See *THOMAS À KEMPIS*

KENNEDY, Edward M.

American Democratic politician (1932–)

3 For me, a few hours ago, this campaign came to an end. For all those whose cares have been our concern, the work goes on, the cause endures, the hope still lives, and the dream shall never die.

Having failed to win his party's nomination for the presidency. Speech at Democratic Convention (13 August 1980).

4 *Jestem Poliakiem.*
I am a Pole.

Statement, Gdansk (1987). Standing next to Lech Walesa.

5 The man who was never there [when controversial issues were discussed in the Reagan administration] ... Where was George?

On George Bush. Speech, Democratic Convention, Atlanta, (July 1988). Congressman Tony Coelho also hit upon this taunt.

KENNEDY, Jimmy

Ulster songwriter (1902–84)

6 If you go down in the woods today
You're sure of a big surprise ...
For every bear that ever there was
Will gather there for certain because
Today's the day the teddy bears have their
picnic.

Song, 'The Teddy Bears' Picnic' (1932). Written to existing music by John W. Bratton.

KENNEDY, John F.

American Democratic 35th President (1917–63)

7 I just received the following wire from my generous Daddy – 'Dear Jack. Don't buy a single vote more than is necessary. I'll be damned if I'm going to pay for a landslide'.

Speech, Washington, DC (1958). Quoted in Bill Adler, *The Wit of President Kennedy* (1964) and Theodore Sorensen, *Kennedy* (1965).

8 We stand today on the edge of a New Frontier ... But the New Frontier of which I speak is not a set of promises – it is a set of challenges. It sums up not what I intend to offer the American people, but what I intend to ask of them.

Accepting the Democratic nomination in Los Angeles (15 July 1960). Theodore C. Sorensen in *Kennedy* (1965), suggests that Kennedy had a hand in coining the slogan for the forthcoming administration: 'I know of no outsider who suggested the expression, although the theme of the Frontier was contained in more than one draft.' In 1964 Harold Wilson said in a speech in Birmingham: 'We want the youth of Britain to storm the new frontiers of knowledge.'

The last sentence of Kennedy's speech above is a clear pre-echo of a theme in his Inaugural speech.

1 Do you realize the responsibility I carry? I'm the only person standing between Nixon and the White House.

Remark (13 October 1960), quoted in Arthur M. Schlesinger Jr, *A Thousand Days* (1965).

2 It was easy. They sank my boat.

When asked how he became a war hero. In *ib.*

3 Let the word go forth from this time and place, to friend and foe alike, that the torch has been passed to a new generation of Americans, born in this century, tempered by war, disciplined by a hard and bitter peace, proud of our ancient heritage, and unwilling to witness or permit the slow undoing of those human rights to which this nation has always been committed, and to which we are committed today at home and around the world. Let every nation know, whether it wishes us well or ill, that we shall pay any price, bear any burden, meet any hardship, support any friend, oppose any foe to assure the survival and the success of liberty.

Inaugural address, Washington, DC (20 January 1961). As preparation, Kennedy told Sorensen to read all the previous inaugural speeches and suggestions were solicited from the likes of Adlai Stevenson, J.K. Galbraith and Billy Graham. Kennedy laid down basic rules: the speech was to be as short as possible, to deal almost exclusively with foreign affairs, to leave out the first person singular and to emulate Lincoln's Gettysburg address by using one-syllable words wherever possible.

The sentence beginning 'Let every nation ...' was later inscribed on the Kennedy memorial at Runnymede, near London.

4 To those old allies whose cultural and spiritual origins we share, we pledge the loyalty of faithful friends. United, there is little we cannot do in a host of co-operative ventures.

Ib. Sorensen says 'no Kennedy speech underwent so many drafts ... Kenneth Galbraith suggested "co-operative ventures" with our allies in place of "joint ventures", which sounded like a mining partnership.'

5 To our sister republics south of our border, we offer a special pledge: to convert our good words into good deeds, in a new alliance for progress, to assist free men and free governments in casting off the chains of poverty.

Ib. The 'Alliance for Progress', used as the name of Kennedy's Latin American policy, had first been mentioned by him in October 1960. Speechwriter Richard Goodwin said he took it from the title of a Spanish American magazine, *Alianzo. Alianza para Progreso* was officially launched in March 1961.

6 To those nations who would make themselves our adversary, we offer not a pledge but a request: that both sides begin anew the quest for peace, before the dark powers of destruction unleashed by science engulf all humanity in planned or accidental self-destruction.

Ib. Walter Lippmann suggested that references to the Communist bloc be changed from 'enemy' to 'adversary'.

7 Let us never negotiate out of fear, but let us never fear to negotiate.

Ib. The contrapuntal form of words became a hallmark of Kennedy speech-making.

8 All this will not be finished in the first one hundred days. Nor will it be finished in the first one thousand days, nor in the life of this Administration, nor even perhaps in our lifetime on this planet. But let us begin.

Ib. The phrase 'hundred days' is used to refer to a period of intense political action (often immediately upon coming to power). The allusion is to the period during which Napoleon ruled between his escape from Elba and his defeat at the Battle of Waterloo in 1815. Hence, the title of Arthur M. Schlesinger's memoir, *A Thousand Days* (1965), referring also to the 1,056 days of Kennedy's presidency. *Compare* WILSON 575:6.

9 And so, my fellow Americans, ask not what your country can do for you; ask what you can do for your country.

Ib. Kennedy's speech employed a number of phrases that had been used by the President (and others) before. The 'Ask not ...' idea, for example, had been used by him three times during the election campaign. In a TV address during September 1960, Kennedy had said, 'We do not campaign stressing what our country is going to do for us as a people. We stress what we can for the country, all of us.' In his memoir *A Thousand Days* (1965), Arthur M. Schlesinger, a Kennedy aide, traced the President's interest in the 'Ask not' theme back to a notebook he had kept in 1945 which included the Rousseau quotation, 'As soon as any man says of the affairs of state, What does it matter to me?, the state may be given up as lost.'

Other antecedents that have been cited include Kahlil Gibran, writing in Arabic after the First World War: 'Are you a politician asking what your country can do for you or a zealous one asking what you can do for your country? If you are the first, then you are a parasite; if the second, then you are an oasis in the desert.' Warren G. Harding said at the Republican National Convention in Chicago (1916): 'We must have a citizenship less concerned about what the government can do for it and more anxious about what it can do for the nation.' The Mayor of Haverhill, Massachusetts, said at the funeral of John Greenleaf Whittier (1892): 'Here may we be reminded that man is most honoured, not by that which a city may do for him, but by that which he has done for the city.' Oliver Wendell Holmes's Memorial Day Address 1884 contained the words: 'It is now the moment when by common consent we pause to become conscious of our national life and to rejoice in it, to recall what our country has done for each of us, and to ask ourselves what we can do for our country in return.'

In Britain, meanwhile, in October 1893, the Hon. St John Broderick MP told an audience in the Tennant Hall, Leeds: 'Clergymen do well to preach the neglected doctrine that the first duty of a citizen is to consider what he can do for the state and not what the state will do for him.'

It was Kennedy's inverted use of 'Ask not', however, that made what was obviously not a new concept eminently memorable.

1 My fellow citizens of the world, ask not what America will do for you, but what together we can do for the freedom of man.

Ib. Dean Rusk suggested that the other peoples of the world be challenged to ask 'what together we can do for freedom' instead of 'what you can do for freedom'.

2 I believe that this nation should commit itself to achieving the goal, before this decade is out, of landing a man on the moon and returning him safely to earth.

Supplementary State of the Union message to Congress (25 May 1961). Unusually for a political target this one was achieved, within the decade, in July 1969.

3 I wonder how it is with you, Harold? If I don't have a woman for three days, I get a terrible headache.

To Harold Macmillan. Remark, quoted in Alistair Horne, *Macmillan 1957–1986* (1989).

4 Some men are killed in a war and some men are wounded, and some men never leave the country ... It's very hard in military or personal life to assure complete equality. Life is unfair.

Remark at news conference (21 March 1962). *Compare* FRASER 245:4.

5 I think it's the most extraordinary collection of talent, of human knowledge, that has ever been gathered together at the White House – with the possible exception of when Thomas Jefferson dined alone.

Speech at dinner for Nobel prize winners (29 April 1962). Jefferson (*q.v.*) was the great American polymath.

6 We don't see the end of the tunnel, but I must say I don't think it is darker than it was a year ago, and in some ways lighter.

Press conference (12 December 1962). Numerous politicians had earlier used the expression 'The light at the end of the tunnel', but it became a catchphrase of the Vietnam War.

7 He mobilized the English language and sent it into battle.

At a ceremony granting honorary US citizenship to Sir Winston Churchill on 9 April 1963 (at which Churchill was not present), Kennedy used this phrase, but it was not his own. In a broadcast to mark Churchill's eightieth birthday in 1954, Edward R. Murrow had said: 'He mobilized the English language and sent it into battle to steady his fellow countrymen and hearten those Europeans upon whom the long dark night of tyranny had descended.' The borrowing was not surprising, as the veteran broadcaster had been drafted to help with Kennedy's speeches.

1 All free men, wherever they may live, are citizens of Berlin, and, therefore, as a free man, I take pride in the words *Ich bin ein Berliner*.

On 26 June 1963, Kennedy proclaimed a stirring slogan outside the City Hall of West Berlin in the then newly divided city. Ben Bradlee noted in *Conversations with Kennedy* (1975) that the President had to spend 'the better part of an hour' with Frederick Vreeland and his wife before he could manage to pronounce this and the other German phrases he used. It detracts only slightly to know that the President need only have said, '*Ich bin Berliner*' to convey the meaning 'I am a Berliner'. It could be argued that the '*ein*' adds drama because he was saying not 'I was born and bred in Berlin' or 'I live in Berlin', but 'I am one of you'. But by saying what he did, he drew attention to the fact that in Germany '*ein Berliner*' is a doughnut.

2 Yesterday, a shaft of light cut into the darkness.

Speech (26 July 1963). For the first time an agreement had been reached on bringing the forces of nuclear destruction under international control. A nuclear Test Ban Treaty had been initialled by the US, USSR and UK.

3 According to the ancient Chinese proverb, 'A journey of a thousand miles must begin with a single step'.

Ib. According to Burton Stevenson, *Book of Proverbs* (1949), it is a saying of Lao-Tze and is Maxim 64 in *Tao-teh-king* (The Way of Virtue) (*c.*550BC). Sometimes also said to be an Arab proverb.

4 Forgive but never forget.

Remark attributed by Ted Sorensen in 1968 TV interview. This thought later turned up in an elaborated form in the 'Personal Conduct' section of *The Second Sin* (1973) by Thomas Szasz, the Hungarian-born psychiatrist: 'The stupid neither forgive nor forget; the naïve forgive and forget; the wise forgive but do not forget.' Any earlier appearances of this probably proverbial view remain unfound.

KENNEDY, Joseph P.

American politician and businessman (1888–1969)

5 When the going gets tough, the tough get going.

On the election of John F. Kennedy as US President in 1961, attention was focused on several axioms said to come from the Boston-Irish political world and more precisely from Joseph P. Kennedy, his father. At this distance, it would be impossible to say for sure whether this wealthy, ambitious businessman / ambassador / politician originated the expressions, but he certainly instilled them in his sons. This one is quoted in J.H. Cutler, *Honey Fitz* (1962).

6 Don't get mad, get even.

Quoted in Ben Bradlee, *Conversations with Kennedy* (1975) and attributed to 'the Boston-Irish political jungle'. *Don't Get Mad Get Even* became the title of a book (1983), 'a manual for retaliation' by Alan Abel.

7 If you want to make money, go where the money is.

Quoted in Arthur M. Schlesinger, *Robert Kennedy and His Times* (1979), as also: 'Kennedys don't cry', a family rendering of his 'We don't want any crying in this house'. Other similar sayings included: 'Only winners come to dinner' and 'We don't want any losers around here. In this family we want winners. Don't come in second or third – that doesn't count – but win' (sometimes shortened to 'Kennedys always come first').

KENNEDY, Robert F.

American Democratic politician (1925–68)

8 My thanks to all of you. And now it's on to Chicago and let's win there.

Speech, Los Angeles (4 June 1968) after winning the California primary. His last public remark before being murdered.

See also SHAW 499:4.

KENYATTA, Jomo

Kenyan President (c.1889–1978)

9 Originally, the Africans had the land and the English had the Bible. Then the missionaries came to Africa and got the Africans to close their eyes and fold their hands and pray. And when they opened their eyes, the English had the land and the Africans had the Bible.

This saying was attributed to Kenyatta on BBC Radio *Quote ... Unquote* (13 October 1984), but later in *The Observer*, 'Sayings of the Week' (16 December 1984) had Desmond Tutu, Bishop of Johannesburg, saying it. A version relating to the American Indians had earlier been said by Chief Dan George (d.1982):

'When the white man came we had the land and they had the Bibles; now they have the land and we have the Bibles' – *Bloomsbury Dictionary of Quotations* (1987).

KEPPEL, Alice (Mrs George Keppel)

English mistress of King Edward VII (1869–1947)

1 Things were done better in *my* day.

Remark made on the day of Edward VIII's abdication, according to Janet Flanner writing in the magazine *Travel & Leisure* and quoted by Bryan & Murphy, *The Windsor Story* (1979). Flanner (1892–1978) was Paris correspondent for *The New Yorker* (1925–75).

What Keppel meant to convey was, 'The King didn't have to abdicate in order to carry on. He married properly and then took whoever he fancied as mistresses.' The remark has also been attributed to Miss Maxine Elliott, the Edwardian actress and another former mistress of Edward VII's, in the form, 'We did it better in my day'. According to Andrew Barrow, *Gossip* (1978), Elliott said it to Winston Churchill at a dinner with the Duke and Duchess of Windsor near Cannes on 7 January 1938.

Compare a similar lament from STERNE 519:3: 'They order, said I, this matter better in France', which, by 1818, had become in Lady Morgan's *Autobiography* (not published until 1859): 'So you see, my dear Olivia, they manage these things better in France.' In a letter to former President Eisenhower (20 July 1965), Harold Macmillan moaned: 'Naturally, people consult me, but they never take my advice, so I give it without much sense of responsibility. Yes, indeed, we managed things much better in our time.'

KERMAN, Joseph

American musicologist and critic (1924–)

2 Tosca, that shabby little shocker.

Description of Puccini's opera *Tosca*, in *Opera as Drama* (1956). 'This must be the most often quoted remark in all musicology' – *The Sunday Times* (10 March 1991). In Kerman's 1989 revision of the book, he cites Bernard Shaw's evaluation (previously unknown to him) of Sardou's Tosca play: 'Such an old-fashioned, shiftless, clumsily constructed, emptyheaded turnip ghost of a shocker.'

KEROUAC, Jack

American novelist (1922–69)

3 The Beat Generation.

The Guardian (4 April 1988) announced in an obituary: 'Although a novelist, poet and lecturer at many universities, John Clellon Holmes was chiefly known for giving the Beat Generation its name. The phrase first appeared in his 1952 novel *Go*.' The headline to the piece (by William J. Weatherby) was, 'The naming of a generation'. This came as news to those who had believed until then that it was Kerouac who was not only the presiding genius of that phenomenon of the 1950s but had given the name to it. Indeed, in the book *The Origins of the Beat Generation* and in *Playboy* (June 1959), Kerouac admitted to borrowing the phrase from a broken-down drug addict called Herbert Huncke.

Turning to Randy Nelson's *The Almanac of American Letters* (1981), we discover a description of the moment of coinage. He reports Kerouac as saying: 'John Clellon Holmes ... and I were sitting around trying to think up the meaning of the Lost Generation and the subsequent existentialism and I said, "You know, this is really a beat generation": and he leapt up and said, "That's it, that's right".' Holmes actually attributed the phrase directly to Kerouac in *The New York Times* Magazine of 16 November 1952.

When these versions were put to Weatherby in 1988, he replied: 'I based my comment on what Holmes told me close to the end of his life. It's possible his memory was shadowed by then or he had oversimplified the past, but the majority view seems to be he fathered the phrase or at least it emerged in a conversation in which he was involved. I don't believe Kerouac himself thought it up or even cared much for it.'

KEY, Francis Scott

American lawyer (1779–1843)

4 O, say, can you see, by the dawn's early light,
What so proudly we hailed at the twilight's last gleaming.

'The Star-Spangled Banner' (1814) – latterly a kind of national anthem. Hence, *Twilight's Last Gleaming*, title of a film (US/West Germany, 1977).

KEYNES, John Maynard (later Lord Keynes)

English economist (1883–1946)

5 *In the long run* we are all dead.

A Tract on Monetary Reform (1923). Explaining how always to be considering the 'long run' is a 'misleading guide to current affairs'.

6 When he's alone in a room, there's nobody there.

On David Lloyd George. So quoted by Baroness Asquith in BBC TV *As I Remember* (30 April 1967). However, James Agate in *Ego 5* (for 30 September 1941): 'Sat next to Lady Oxford, who was in great form ... "Lloyd George? There is no Lloyd George. There is a marvellous brain; but if you were to shut him in a room and look through the keyhole there would be nobody there".' So, it is strange that Baroness Asquith who was familiar with most of her stepmother's witticisms should have chosen to attribute this one to Keynes. Unless, of course, Lady Oxford (Margot Asquith) had simply appropriated Keynes's observation unacknowledged.

1 This goat-footed bard, this half-human visitor to our age from the hag-ridden magic and enchanted woods of Celtic antiquity.

On David Lloyd George, in *Essays and Sketches in Biography* (1933).

KHRUSCHEV, Nikita

Soviet Communist Party leader (1894–1971)

2 If anyone believes that our smiles involve abandonment of the teaching of Marx, Engels and Lenin he deceives himself. Those who wait for that must wait until a shrimp learns to whistle.

On the likelihood of the Soviet Union rejecting communism. Speech at Moscow (17 September 1955). Hence, *When Shrimps Learn to Whistle – Signposts for the Nineties*, title of a book (1990) by Denis Healey.

3 [He promoted a] cult of personality.

Denouncing Stalin. Speech to 20th Party Congress (25 February 1956).

4 We say this not only for the socialist states who are more akin to us. We base ourselves on the idea that we must peacefully co-exist. About the capitalist states, it doesn't depend on you whether or not we exist. If you don't like us, don't accept our invitations, and don't ask us to come and see you. Whether you like it or not, history is on our side. We will bury you. *[Applause from colleagues. Laughter from Mr Gomulka.]*

Said to western diplomats at a Moscow reception for the Polish leader Wladislaw Gomulka at the Polish Embassy in Moscow (18 November 1956). The last two sentences were not reported at the time by either *Pravda* or *The New York Times* but they were by *The Times* of London (on 19 November 1956), perhaps because the previous night at a Kremlin reception the British Ambassador, Sir William Hayter, had walked out when Khruschev described Britain, France and Israel as 'fascists' and 'bandits' (over the Suez affair).

'We will bury you' can also be translated as 'We will be present at your funeral', i.e., outlive you, and Khruschev made several attempts in later years to make plain that he meant 'outstrip' or 'beat' in the economic sense, rather than anything more threateningly literal. The remark may have been exaggerated by western commentators.

5 If you cannot catch a bird of paradise, better take a wet hen.

Quoted in *Time* Magazine (6 January 1958). Khruschev became famous for his citing of folksy Russian proverbs (always assuming they were genuine and he had not made them up himself). Another one, 'If you start throwing hedgehogs under me, I shall throw two porcupines under you' (quoted in *The New York Times*, 7 November 1963).

KIAM, Victor

American businessman (1926–)

6 I liked the shaver so much I bought the company.

Slogan for Remington electric razors, current in TV advertisements in the UK from *c.*1985.

KIERKEGAARD, Sören

Danish philosopher (1813–55)

7 The lowest depth to which people can sink before God is defined by the word 'journalist'. If I were a father and had a daughter who was seduced I should not despair over her; I would hope for her salvation. But if I had a son who became a journalist and continued to be one for five years, I would give him up.

Untraced, but being quoted by 1980.

8 Life must be lived forwards, but it can only be understood backwards.

Quoted as an epigraph by John Mortimer in his novel *Paradise Postponed* (1986) and used as a promotional line for George Melly's volume of autobiography

Scouse Mouse (1984), this obscure thought can be found in Kierkegaard's *Journals and Papers*, Vol. 1 (1843): 'Philosophy is perfectly right in saying that life must be understood backward. But then one forgets the other clause – that it must be lived forward.'

KILMER, Joyce

American poet and journalist (1886–1918)

1 I think that I shall never see
A poem lovely as a tree.

'Trees' (1913). Famously set to music by Rasbach. *Compare* NASH 407:5.

KING, Martin Luther, Jr

American clergyman and Civil Rights leader (1929–68)

2 I have a dream that one day this nation will rise up and live out the true meaning of its creed – 'We hold these truths to be self-evident that all men are created equal'. I have a dream ...

The largest protest rally in US history took place on 28 August 1963, when nearly 250,000 people joined the March on Washington. The Civil Rights demonstration reached its climax near the Lincoln Memorial with a sixteen-minute speech by King in which he applied the repetitions and rhythms of a revivalist preacher to a clear challenge on the lack of Negro progress since the Emancipation Proclamation of exactly one hundred years before. King used his familiar technique of delivering almost ritualistic invocations of the Bible and American lore in a sob-laden voice. He summoned up themes and phrases from his own speeches dating back to 1956. In Detroit, as recently as the 23 June, he had used the 'I have a dream' motif: 'I have a dream this evening that one day we will recognize the words of Jefferson that all men are created equal ...'

3 Free at last, free at last, thank God Almighty, we are free at last!

His peroration (in both the Washington and Detroit speeches) came, as he acknowledged, from an old Negro spiritual. On his grave in South View Cemetery, Atlanta, Georgia, is carved a slightly altered version of these words: 'Thank God Almighty, I'm free at last.'

4 I've been to the mountain top ... I've looked over, and I've seen the promised land. I may not get there with you, but I want you to know tonight that we as a people will get to the promised land. So, I'm happy tonight. I'm not worried about anything. I'm not fearing any man. Mine eyes have seen the glory of the coming of the Lord.

On the night before he was assassinated, King said this in a speech at Memphis (3 April 1968). Did he have a premonition? The original 'promised land' (not called as such in the Bible, but referring to Canaan, western Palestine, and by association, Heaven) was promised to the descendants of Abraham, Isaac and Jacob. In Numbers 14:39–40: 'Moses told these sayings unto all the children of Israel ... And they rose up early in the morning and gat them up into the top of the mountain, saying, Lo, we be here, and will go up unto the place which the Lord hath promised.'

KING, Philip

English playwright (1904–79)

5 Sergeant, arrest several of these vicars!

Tom Stoppard once claimed this as the funniest line anywhere in English farce. Alas, King's *See How They Run* (first performed in 1944) does not have quite that line in it. For reasons it would be exhausting to go into, the stage gets filled with various people who are, or are dressed up as, vicars, and the order is given: 'Sergeant, arrest most of these people.'

KINGSLEY, Charles

English novelist and poet (1819–75)

6 There are more ways of killing a cat than choking her with cream.

Westward Ho!, Chap. 22 (1855). The first recorded appearance of what may be a Devonshire proverb.

7 Be good, sweet maid, and let who will be clever;
Do lovely things, not dream them, all day long;
And so make Life, and Death, and that For Ever,
One grand sweet song.

'A Farewell. To C.E.G.' (1856). From P.G. Wodehouse, *Thank You, Jeeves* (1934): 'He greets you as if you were a favourite son, starts agitating the cocktail shaker before you know where you are, slips a couple into you with a merry laugh, claps you on the back, tells you a dialect story about two Irishmen named Pat and Mike, and, in a word, makes life one grand, sweet song.'

1 For men must work, and women must weep,
And there's little to earn, and many to keep,
Though the harbour bar be moaning.

'The Three Fishers' (1858). 'Bar', here, means 'a ridge of sand, mud, shingle' but the line has given rise to many a pun. '[Lord Simon] was not popular with his fellow barristers who proclaimed, "There'll be no moaning at the Bar when he puts out to sea"' – John Colville, *The Fringes of Power*, Vol. 2 (1985). *Compare* TENNYSON 530:4.

2 When all the world is young, lad,
And all the trees are green ...
Young blood must have its course, lad,
And every dog his day.

'Young and Old', song from *The Water Babies* (1863). *Compare* BIBLE 100:1.

KINGSMILL, Hugh

English writer (1889–1949)

3 'Tis Summer Time on Bredon,
And now the farmers swear;
The cattle rise and listen
In valleys far and near,
And blush at what they hear.

But when the mists in autumn
On Bredon top are thick,
The happy hymns of farmers
Go up from fold and rick,
The cattle then are sick.

One of 'Two Poems after A.E. Housman', *The Table of Truth* (1933). *Compare* HOUSMAN 302:7.

4 [Friends are] God's apology for relations.

Quoted in Michael Holroyd, *The Best of Hugh Kingsmill* (1970). Hence, the title *God's Apology* for Richard Ingrams's book about Kingsmill and his circle (1977). The origin of the saying has been said to lie in a Spanish proverb.

KINNOCK, Neil

Welsh-born Labour politician (1942–)

5 And it's a pity that people had to leave theirs on the ground at Goose Green in order to prove it.

In reply to heckler's comment, 'At least Mrs Thatcher has got guts'. TVS election programme 'The South Decides' (5 June 1983).

6 I warn you, if Margaret Thatcher wins on Thursday, I warn you not to be ordinary. I warn you not to be young. I warn you not to fall ill. And I warn you not to get old – if Thatcher wins on Thursday.

Speech, Bridgend (7 June 1983), two days before a British general election. Checked against a sound recording. Labour lost the election but Kinnock's fine speech may well have contributed to his becoming the party's leader four months later.

There is a mild, ironical, echo – almost certainly unconscious – of a passage from Bernard Shaw's bibliographical appendix to *The Intelligent Woman's Guide to Socialism and Capitalism* (1928) in which Shaw recalls a point he had made in the various prefaces to his plays: 'I ... made it quite clear that ... under Socialism you would not be allowed to be poor. You would be forcibly fed, clothed, lodged, taught, and employed whether you liked it or not ... Also you would not be allowed to have half a crown an hour when other women had only two shillings, or to be content with two shillings when they had half a crown. As far as I know I was the first Socialist writer to whom it occurred to state this explicitly as a necessary postulate of permanent civilization; but as nothing that is true is ever new I daresay it had been said again and again before I was born.'

7 I'll tell you what happens with impossible promises. You start with far-fetched resolutions. They're then pickled into a rigid dogma or code ... And you end in the grotesque chaos of a Labour council – a *Labour* council – hiring taxis to scuttle round a city handing out redundancy notices to its own workers ... I am telling you, you can't play politics with people's jobs.

To militants within the Labour Party. Speech, Labour Party Conference, Bournemouth (1 October 1985). Checked against a sound recording.

8 I would die for my country ... but I could never let my country die for me.

Speech on nuclear disarmament, Labour Party Conference, (30 September 1986).

1 Why am I the first Kinnock in a thousand generations to be able to get to university? Why is Glenys [his wife] the first woman in her family in a thousand generations to be able to get to university? Was it because *all* our predecessors were 'thick'? ... Of course not. It was because there was no platform upon which they could stand ... no method by which the communities could translate their desires for those individuals into provision for those individuals.

Speech, Llandudno (15 May 1987), and also used in a Party Political Broadcast (21 May). Later in that year it was famously plagiarized by US Senator Joe Biden, who was shaping up to run for the Democratic ticket in the 1988 presidential election. At other times, Biden had credited Kinnock with the words but not on 23 August when he said: 'Why is it that Joe Biden is the first in his family ever to go to university? ... Is it because our fathers and mothers were not so bright? ... It's because they didn't have a platform upon which to stand.' His rivals duly pounced, the speeches were reproduced side by side, and Biden, who had little chance of winning any primaries, was soon out of the race.

KIPLING, Rudyard

English poet and novelist (1865–1936)

2 And a woman is only a woman, but a good Cigar is a Smoke.

Poem, 'The Betrothed' (1886). Lest Kipling, as usual, take more blame than he should for what one of his characters says – now seen as an outrageous example of male chauvinism – it is worth pointing out that the man in question (the poem is in the first person) is choosing between his cigars and his betrothed, a woman called Maggie. The situation arose in an actual breach of promise case, *c.*1885, in which the woman had said to the man: 'You must choose between me and your cigar.'

The poem ends: 'Light me another Cuba – I hold to my first-sworn vows. / If Maggie will have no rival, I'll have no Maggie for Spouse!'

3 But that's another story ...

Plain Tales from the Hills (1888). A catchphrase popular around 1900 derives from Kipling, though not exclusively – earlier it had appeared in Laurence Sterne's *Tristram Shandy* (1760), intended to prevent one of the many digressions with which that novel is full.

4 The Man Who Would Be King.

Title of a story (1888; film US, 1975) about two adventurers in India in the 1880s who find themselves accepted as kings by a remote tribe. Compare *The Man Born To Be King* – Jesus Christ – a verse drama for radio (1942) by Dorothy L. Sayers (a title already used by William Morris for a part of his poem *The Earthly Paradise* (1868–70); and 'the lad that's born to be king' in 'The Skye Boat Song' (1908) by Sir Harold Edwin Boulton.

5 Oh, East is East, and West is West, and never the twain shall meet,
Till Earth and Sky stand presently at God's great Judgement Seat;
But there is neither East nor West, Border, nor Breed, nor Birth,
When two strong men stand face to face, though they come from the ends of the earth!

'The Ballad of East and West' (1889). Kipling had a curious knack for coining popular phrases, of which 'East is East and West is West' is but one. George Orwell noted in *Horizon* (February 1942): 'Kipling is the only English writer of our time who has added phrases to the language. The phrases and neologisms which we take over and use without remembering their origin do not always come from writers we admire ... [but] Kipling deals in thoughts that are both vulgar and permanent.'

6 We know that the tail must wag the dog, for the horse is drawn by the cart;
But the Devil whoops, as he whooped of old: 'It's clever, but is it Art?'

'The Conundrum of the Workshops' (1890). Possibly the origin of the 'But is it Art?' question.

7 For the wind is in the pine trees, and the temple-bells they say:
'Come you back you British soldier; come you back to Mandalay!'
... On the road to Mandalay
Where the flyin'-fishes play,
An' the dawn comes up like thunder outer China 'crost the Bay!

'Mandalay' (1892). Famously set to music by Oley Speaks (1874–1948) in 1907.

8 Ship me somewheres east of Suez, where the best is like the worst,

Where there ain't no Ten Commandments
  an' a man can raise a thirst.

Ib. Hence, 'East of Suez' as a phrase to denote, especially, the British Empire as it was in India and the East, which was usually reached through the Suez Canal (opened in 1869). John Osborne entitled a play set on a 'sub-tropical island, neither Africa nor Europe', *West of Suez* (1971).

1 Gentlemen rankers out on the spree,
Damned from here to Eternity.

'Gentlemen-Rankers' (1892). Hence, *From Here to Eternity*, title of the novel (1951; film US, 1953) by James Jones.

2 He wrapped himself in quotations – as a beggar would enfold himself in the purple of emperors.

'The Finest Story in the World', *Many Inventions* (1893). One way of looking at the art of quotation.

3 There are nine and sixty ways of constructing
  tribal lays,
And – every – single – one – of – them – is –
  right!

'In the Neolithic Age' (1893). In the article mentioned at 337:5, George Orwell notes that, in his book *Adam and Eve*, John Middleton had incorrectly ascribed this quotation to Thackeray, and adds: 'This is probably what is known as a "Freudian error". A civilized person would prefer not to quote Kipling – i.e., would prefer not to feel that it was Kipling who had expressed his thought for him.'

4 When 'Omer smote 'is bloomin' lyre,
He'd 'eard men sing by land and sea;
An' what he thought 'e might require,
'E went an' took – the same as me!

'When 'Omer Smote 'Is Bloomin' Lyre', introduction to the Barrack-Room Ballads in 'The Seven Seas' (1896).

5 The tumult and the shouting dies;
The captains and the kings depart:
Still stands Thine ancient sacrifice,
An humble and a contrite heart.
Lord God of hosts, be with us yet,
Lest we forget – lest we forget!

From Kipling's poem 'Recessional' (1897), written as a warning on Queen Victoria's Jubilee Day that while empires pass away, God lives on. Kipling himself may have agreed to the adoption of 'Lest we forget' as an epitaph during his work for the Imperial War Graves Commission after the First World War. Another use to which the phrase has been put: it was the title of the Fritz Lang film *Hangmen Also Die* (US, 1943) when it was re-issued. The alliterative coupling of captains and kings had been used earlier by Tennyson in 'A Dream of Fair Women' (1832): 'Melting the mighty hearts/Of captains and of kings.' Hence, *Captains and the Kings*, title of a novel (1972) by Taylor Caldwell (about an immigrant orphan boy who founds a US political dynasty – based on the Kennedy family) and *The Tumult and the Shouting*, title of the autobiography (1954) of Grantland Rice.

Margaret Thatcher had a seemingly inexhaustible supply of quotations – never more so than when she had just returned in triumph to 10 Downing Street. She quoted 'Recessional' on being re-elected for a third term in June 1987. So much did she enjoy it that she repeated the words at that year's Conservative Party Conference. *See also* KNOX 341:1.

6 A fool there was and he made his prayer
(Even as you and I!)
To a rag and a bone and hank of hair
(We called her the woman who did not care)
But the fool he called her his lady fair –
(Even as you and I!)

'The Vampire' (1897). Hence, the film title *A Fool There Was* (US 1914). It was through this film that Theda Bara popularized the notion of the female 'vamp'.

7 Lalun is a member of the most ancient profession in the world.

'On the City Wall', *In Black and White* (1888). The first reference found to prostitution, in these terms. Latterly, it has perhaps been more commonly referred to as 'the world's oldest profession'. From Alexander Woollcott, *Shouts and Murmurs* (1922): 'The Actor and the Streetwalker ... the two oldest professions in the world – ruined by amateurs.'

8 Nursed the pinion that impelled the steel.

'An Unsavoury Interlude' (1899) in *Stalky & Co.* Little Hartopp quotes about King that he 'nursed the pinion that impelled the steel' but does not explain the allusion. It is from Byron, *English Bards & Scotch Reviewers*, l. 846 (1809).

9 The book was amazing, and full of quotations that one could hurl like a javelin.

In the *Stalky & Co.* stories, the lads fall to reading 'Uncle Remus'.

1 Each to his choice, and I rejoice
The lot has fallen to me
In a fair ground – in a fair ground –
Yea, Sussex by the sea!

'Sussex' (1902). Kipling lived there. But the phrase 'Sussex by the sea' also occurs in a song with this title (words and music by W. Ward-Higgs, d.1936):

We plough and sow and reap and mow,
And useful men are we ...
You may tell them all that we stand or fall
For Sussex by the sea.

That song was not published until 1908, so it looks as though Kipling got there first. (Incidentally, the English county has since been cut in two. It is still by the sea, however.)

2 The flannelled fools at the wicket or the muddied oafs at the goals.

'The Islanders' (1902) – where the 'fools' are, of course, cricketers. Hence, *Flanelled Fool*, title of book (1967), 'a slice of life in the 30s', by the critic, T.C. Worsley.

3 The Cat That Walked By Himself.

Title of story in *The Just-So Stories.* 'I am the cat that walks alone' was a favourite expression of Lord Beaverbrook (see 79:5).

4 Five and twenty ponies
Trotting through the dark –
Brandy for the Parson
'Baccy for the Clerk;
Laces for a lady, letters for a spy,
And watch the wall, my darling, while the Gentlemen go by!

'A Smuggler's Song', *Puck of Pook's Hill* (1906). Hence, *Brandy for the Parson*, title of a film comedy (UK, 1951) about smuggling.

5 If you can keep your head when all about you
Are losing theirs and blaming it on you ...
If you can meet with Triumph and Disaster
And treat those two impostors just the same ...

If you can talk with crowds and keep your virtue,
Or walk with Kings – nor lose the common touch ...

The poem 'If –' from *Rewards and Fairies* (1910) is one of the most plundered and parodied poems in the language: the second two lines are inscribed over the doorway to the Centre Court at Wimbledon; 'As someone pointed out recently, if you can keep your head when all about you are losing theirs, it's just possible you haven't grasped the situation' – Jean Kerr, *Please Don't Eat the Daisies* (1958); also, 'If you can keep your girl when all about you/Are losing theirs and blaming it on you ...' – an anonymous verse, source untraced, of the kind that says it is written 'with apologies to Rudyard Kipling Esq.'

It is also the most popular poem in the language – or, at least, is the one people most often mention when asked what their favourite poem is. It came top of a British poll taken by the BBC TV programme *Bookworm* in 1995. In *The Ultimate Spin Doctor* (1996), Mark Hollingsworth recounts how, when Tim Bell first met Margaret Thatcher in 1978, she asked him what his favourite poem was. He, of course, replied 'If' – which accorded with her view – and she concluded that they would get on very well together. He became her advertising and public relations adviser.

6 If you can fill the unforgiving minute
With sixty seconds' worth of distance run,
Yours is the Earth and everything that's in it,
And – which is more – you'll be a Man, my son!

Ib. Hence, *The Unforgiving Minute*, title of the autobiography (1978) of Beverley Nichols.

7 For the female of the species is more deadly than the male.

'The Female of the Species' (1911). Hence, *The Female of the Species* (UK, 1917) and *Deadlier Than the Male*, title of film (UK, 1967), and a survey of women crime-writers (1981) by Jessica Mann. A much-quoted line, though sometimes the quoter takes the teeth out of the remark. In 1989, Margaret Thatcher said: 'The female of the species is rather better than the male.'

8 And that is called paying the Dane-geld;
But we've proved it again and again,
That if once you have paid him the Dane-geld
You never get rid of the Dane.

'Dane-Geld', one of the 'Songs written for C.R.L. Fletcher's "A History of England"' (1911). Danegeld was an English tax levied between 991 and 1012 to buy peace from the Danes.

9 So when the world is asleep, and there seems no hope of her waking
Out of some long, bad dream that makes her mutter and moan,

Suddenly, all men arise to the noise of fetters breaking,
And every one smiles at his neighbour and tells him his soul is his own!

'The Dawn Wind' – 'the fifteenth century' in *ib.* Margaret Thatcher was a great quoter – Kipling was top of her source list – though sometimes she misquoted, twisted or ignored the fact that she was speaking someone else's lines. When a newspaperman queried the source of the above lines, which Mrs Thatcher had used to indicate how things were going in her 1979 election campaign, it was duly reported that the Prime-Minister-to-be had recalled his request in the small hours of the morning and taken the trouble to write him a note explaining their provenance.

1 As it will be in the future, it was at the birth of Man –
There are only four things certain since Social Progress began: –
That the Dog returns to his vomit and the Sow returns to her Mire,
And the burnt Fool's bandaged finger goes wabbling back to the Fire.

Ib. Compare BIBLE 96:3 and 105:9.

2 Jane lies in Winchester, blessèd be her shade!
Praise the Lord for making her, and her for all she made.
And, while the stones of Winchester – or Milsom Street – remain,
Glory, Love, and Honour unto England's Jane!

'Jane's Marriage' (1926), in which he speculates on which man loved Jane Austen and concludes that it was Captain Wentworth in *Persuasion*. Milsom Street is not in Winchester but in Bath, the location of so many incidents in Austen's novels.

See also BALDWIN 72:4.

KISSINGER, Henry

American Republican politician (1923–)

3 Power is the ultimate aphrodisiac.

An unverified remark, diagnosing his success as a 'swinger'. Also, in the form 'power is the great aphrodisiac', this was quoted in *The New York Times* (19 January 1971). *Compare* BELLOW 83:2 and NAPOLEON 406:6.

4 We are [all] the President's men and we must behave accordingly.

Saying at the time of the 1970 Cambodia invasion. Quoted in Kalb and Kalb, *Kissinger* (1974). Hence, *All the President's Men*, title given by Carl Bernstein and Bob Woodward to their first book on Watergate (1974; film US, 1976). It might seem also to allude to the lines from the nursery rhyme 'Humpty Dumpty' (first recorded in 1803):

All the king's horses
And all the king's men,
Couldn't put Humpty together again.

There was also a Robert Penn Warren novel (and film US, 1949) based on the life of southern demagogue Huey 'Kingfish' Long and called *All the King's Men*.

See also NANSEN 405:4.

KITCHEN, Fred

British entertainer (1872–1950)

5 Meredith, we're in!

The catchphrase originated as a shout of triumph in a music-hall sketch called 'The Bailiff' (or 'Moses and Son') performed by Kitchen, the leading comedian with Fred Karno's company. The sketch was first seen about 1907, and the phrase was used each time a bailiff and his assistant looked like gaining entrance to a house. Kitchen is reputed to have had it put on his gravestone.

KLINGER, Friedrich Maximilian von

German playwright (1752–1831)

6 *Sturm und Drang.*
Storm and stress.

Title of play (1777). Hence, the name given to the German literary movement of the late eighteenth century which chiefly consisted of violently passionate dramas by the likes of Goethe and Schiller. Said to have been applied by Goethe himself.

KNOX, Ronald

English priest and writer (1888–1957)

7 As no less than three of [these poems] wear the aspect of a positively last appearance [i.e., a promise not to write more], they have been called in the words of so many eminent preachers 'ninthlies and lastlies'.

Knox's *Juxta Salices* (1910) includes a group of poems he had written when still at Eton and is prefaced with the above. The expression 'ninthlies and lastlies' – or at least the idea behind it – is, as he indicates, not original. 'In Ambush', published 1898, one of Kipling's *Stalky & Co.* stories has: 'Ninthly, and lastly, they were to have a care and to be very careful.' The *OED2* has Thomas B. Aldrich writing in *Prudence Palfrey* (1874–85) of: 'The poor old parson's interminable ninthlies and finallies,' and there is a 'fifthly and lastly' dated 1681. Benjamin Franklin, in 1745, concluded his *Reasons for Preferring an Elderly Mistress* with: 'Eighth and lastly. They are so grateful!!' Ultimately, the origin for all this must be the kind of legal nonsense-talk parodied by Shakespeare's Dogberry in *Much Ado About Nothing* (*c*.1598): 'Marry, sir, they have committed false report; moreover, they have spoken untruths; secondarily, they are slanders; *sixthly and lastly*, they have belied a lady; thirdly, they have verified unjust things; and to conclude, they are lying knaves.'

1 The tumult and the shouting dies,
The captains and the kings depart,
And we are left with large supplies
Of cold blancmange and rhubarb tart.

'After the Party', included in Laurence Eyres, *In Three Tongues* (1959). *Compare* KIPLING 338:5.

See also REAGAN 448:3.

KOCH, Ed

American politician (1924–)

2 How'm I doin'?

Koch was Mayor of New York City in 1977–89. He helped balance the city's books after a period of bankruptcy by drastically cutting services. His catchphrase during this period was 'How'm I doing?', which he called out to people as he ranged around New York. 'You're doing fine, Ed', they were supposed to shout back. A 1979 cartoon in *The New Yorker* showed a woman answering the phone and saying to her husband: 'It's Ed Koch. He wants to know how he's doin'.' A booklet of Koch's wit and wisdom took the phrase as its title. An old song with the same title was disinterred. Unfortunately for him, Koch's achievements did not carry him forward to the State Governorship as he had hoped. Voters concluded that he wasn't doin' very well at all.

KOESTLER, Arthur

Hungarian-born writer (1905–83)

3 Darkness at Noon.

Title of novel (1940) about the imprisonment, trial and execution of a Communist who has betrayed the Party. It was originally going to be called *The Vicious Circle.* Though originally written in German and translated for Koestler, the book's title appears always to have been rendered in English (Koestler was dealing with a London publisher). As such, it echoes Milton's *Samson Agonistes* (1671): 'O dark, dark, dark, amid the blaze of noon.' *Darkness at Noon, or the Great Solar Eclipse of the 16th June 1806* was the title of an anonymous booklet published in Boston, Mass. (1806).

KREISLER, Fritz

Austrian-born American violinist (1875–1962)

4 In that case, madam, my fee will be only two thousand dollars.

To a society hostess who had jibbed at his fee of $5,000 for a recital, adding that he would not be expected to mingle with the guests. Quoted by Bennett A. Cerf in *Try and Stop Me* (1944). Also ascribed to Nellie Melba and other famous musicians and singers.

KUNDERA, Milan

Czech-born French novelist (1929–)

5 The Unbearable Lightness of Being.

English title of Kundera's novel (1984; film US, 1987). In Czech it is *Nesnesitelná lehkost bytí* (which means, more literally, 'the unbearable easiness/facility of being'). An allusion: 'The unbearable rightness of being PC [politically correct]', headline in *The Guardian* (24 September 1992).

KURNITZ, Harry

American screenwriter (c.1907–68)

6 Lynn is the evil of two Loessers.

On the first wife (with whom he was having a feud) of the composer Frank Loesser. Quoted in *The Observer* (31 March 1968).

L

LAMB, Lady Caroline

English wife of 2nd Viscount Melbourne (1785–1828)

1 Mad, bad, and dangerous to know.

Diary entry on first meeting Lord Byron at a ball in March 1812. Quoted in Elizabeth Jenkins, *Lady Caroline Lamb* (1932).

LAMB, Charles

English writer (1775–1834)

2 Mary, where are all the naughty people buried?

As a boy in the 1780s, to his sister, on observing the fulsome epitaphs in a churchyard in the 1780s. Quoted in Leonard Russell, *English Wits* (1940). William Wordsworth, in the second of his essays on epitaphs (possibly written about 1812), recalls the story (old even in his day, one imagines) of the person who, tired of reading so many fulsome epitaphs on 'faithful wives, tender husbands, dutiful children and good men of all classes', exclaimed, 'Where are all the *bad* people buried?' Perhaps he was referring to Lamb? Whoever first made the comment, Wordsworth argues that there is a lot to be said for having, 'in an unkind world, one enclosure where the voice of Detraction is not heard ... and there is no jarring tone in the peaceful concert of amity and gratitude'.

3 Gone before
To that unknown and silent shore.

'Hester' (1803). *Compare* NORTON 415:4.

4 The greatest pleasure I know, is to do a good action by stealth, and to have it found out by accident.

'Table Talk by the late Elia' in *The Athenaeum* (4 January 1834). *Compare* POPE 434:9.

LAMBTON, John, 1st Earl of Durham

English Whig politician (1792–1840)

5 He said he considered £40,000 a year a moderate income – such a one as a man *might jog on with.*

Letter from Thomas Creevey to Miss Elizabeth Ord (1821) in *The Creevey Papers* (1903).

LAMONT, Norman (later Lord Lamont)

English Conservative politician (1942–)

6 The turn of the tide is sometimes difficult to discern ... What we are seeing is the return of that vital ingredient – confidence. The green shoots of economic spring are appearing once again.

Speech to the Conservative Party Conference at Blackpool (9 October 1991). As Chancellor of the Exchequer he was earnestly endeavouring to convince his audience that Britain was coming out of a recession. It had not obviously done so before he was relieved of his responsibilities in 1993. John Smith, on his election as Labour leader (18 July 1992) commented: 'You don't have to be a paid-up member of the Royal Horticultural Society to know that the Chancellor's green shoots and his promised recovery are as far away as ever.' In *The Independent* (30 November 1993), Lamont reflected: 'My wife tried to talk me out of that phrase, but only because I used it in October, the wrong season for green shoots.'

Compare this use: in a letter to a lover (6 May 1962), the poet Philip Larkin wrote: 'Spring comes with your birthday, and I love to think of you as somehow linked with the tender green shoots I see on all the trees and bushes ... and I wish I could be with you and we could plunge into bed.'

1 We give the impression of being in office but not in power.

Lamont was sacked as Chancellor of the Exchequer in June 1994 and caused a slight stir in the House of Commons during his 'resignation' statement, by saying this of the government. A nice dig, but not new. As A.J.P. Taylor noted in his *English History 1914–45* (1965), writing of Ramsay MacDonald as Prime Minister of a minority government in 1924: 'The Labour government recognized that they could make no fundamental changes, even if they knew what to make: they were "in office, but not in power".'

LAMPEDUSA, Giuseppe Di

Italian writer (1896–1957)

2 If we want everything to remain as it is, it will be necessary for everything to change.

The Leopard (1957) – at the end, where the Prince muses on the future. In an introductory title to the film (Italy/US, 1963), this is given as the Prince's credo, but translated into English as 'Things will have to change in order that they can remain the same.' *Compare* KARR 326:3.

3 One year of flames and thirty of ashes.

Of marriage. Unverified.

LANCASTER, Osbert (later Sir Osbert)

English cartoonist (1908–86)

4 Stockbroker's Tudor.

Term for bogus Tudor architecture in *Pillar to Post* (1938).

5 It's an odd thing, but now one knows it's profoundly moral and packed with deep spiritual significance a lot of the old charm seems to have gone.

Maudie Littlehampton on the book *Lady Chatterley's Lover* during its trial on obscenity charges. Caption to cartoon in the *Daily Express* (1961).

LANCE, Bert

American Democratic politician (1931–)

6 If it ain't broke, don't fix it.

On government reorganization as President Carter's Director of the Office of Management. Quoted in *The Nation's Business* (27 May 1977) – what may be the first citation of a modern proverb, if not its actual coinage. Has also been ascribed to the motor magnate Henry Ford and picked up by Margaret Thatcher as an argument against unnecessary governmental intervention.

See also CARTER 150:2.

LANCHESTER, Elsa

British film actress (1902–86)

7 She looked as though butter wouldn't melt in her mouth. Or anywhere else.

On Maureen O'Hara. In *News Summaries* (30 January 1950).

LANDOWSKA, Wanda

Polish-born harpsichordist (1877–1959)

8 Oh, well, you play Bach *your* way. I'll play him *his*.

Remark to fellow musician. Quoted in Harold C. Schonberg, *The Great Pianists* (1963). Also in *The 'Quote ... Unquote' Book of Love, Death and the Universe* (1980).

LANG, Andrew

Scottish poet and scholar (1844–1912)

9 He uses statistics as a drunken man uses lamp-posts – for support rather than illumination.

Quoted in *The Treasury of Humorous Quotations*, ed. by Evan Esar & Nicolas Bentley (1951). Lang seems to be the actual originator of this oft-quoted joke.

LANG, Julia

British broadcaster (1921–)

10 Are you sitting comfortably? Then I'll [*or* we'll] begin.

This way of beginning a story on *Listen With Mother*,

BBC radio's daily spot for small children, was used from the programme's inception in January 1950. Lang, the original presenter, recalled in 1982: 'The first day it came out inadvertently. I just said it. The next day I didn't. Then there was a flood of letters from children saying, "I couldn't listen because I wasn't ready".' It remained a more or less essential part of the proceedings until the programme was threatened with closure in 1982.

In *The Times* obituary of Frieda Fordham, an analytical psychologist (18 January 1988), it was claimed that *she* had actually coined the phrase when advising the BBC's producers.

LAO-TZU

Chinese philosopher and founder of Taoism (c.604–531BC)

1 Heaven and Earth have no pity; they regard all things as straw dogs.

Tao Te Ching. Hence, *Straw Dogs*, title of film (UK 1971).

LARKIN, Philip

English librarian and poet (1922–85)

2 The Less Deceived.

Title of his second collection of verse (1955) in which the poem 'Deceptions' tells of a 'ruined' Victorian girl: '... for you would hardly care/That you were less deceived, out on that bed ...' (than the man who had ruined her). Probably an allusion to *Hamlet*. Ophelia thought that Hamlet loved her and in this she was the 'more deceiv'd' (III.i.119).

3 Sexual intercourse began
In nineteen sixty-three
(Which was rather late for me) –
Between the end of the *Chatterley* ban
And the Beatles' first LP.

'Annus Mirabilis', in *High Windows* (1974). In fact, the Chatterley ban (i.e., on the publication of D.H. Lawrence's novel) ended in 1961; the Beatles' first LP was *Please, Please Me* (released 22 March 1963). Two cultural landmarks.

4 They fuck you up, your mum and dad.
They may not mean to, but they do.
They fill you up with the faults they had
And add some extra, just for you.

... Man hands on misery to man.
It deepens like a coastal shelf.
Get out as early as you can,
And don't have any kids yourself.

'This Be the Verse' in *ib.* Larkin later mourned the popularity of this poem, which, he said, would 'clearly be my "Lake Isle of Innisfree". I fully expect to hear it recited by a thousand Girl Guides before I die' – letter of 6 June 1982 (*Selected Letters*, 1992). *Compare* YEATS 587:1.

5 The sky split apart in malice
Stars rattled like pans on a shelf.
Crow shat on Buckingham Palace
God pissed Himself ...

Larkin's idea of how Ted Hughes (*q.v.*), later to be Poet Laureate (a job that Larkin shrank from), would have celebrated Elizabeth II's Silver Jubilee in 1977. The piece is included in *Selected Letters of Philip Larkin* (1992).

LASKI, Harold

English political scientist (1893–1950)

6 In that state of resentful coma that they dignified by the name of research.

In one of his letters to Oliver Wendell Holmes Jr (dated 10 October 1922, published 1953), Laski recounted how he had recently spoken at a Conference on Workers' Education at Oxford: 'I made an epigram in my address which pleased me. A trade-unionist attacked Oxford for being slow to respond to the workers' demand for education. I said that I was amazed at the speed of the response in dons who spent most of their days in ...' Laski was so pleased with his epigram that he used it soon afterwards in *three* other letters to Holmes without any apparent awareness that he was repeating himself.

In *The Lyttelton Hart-Davis Letters* (for 27 October 1955), it is suggested that 'Laski produced it – mendaciously – as his own in a letter to Judge Holmes'. If the remark was not his own, the originator remains untraced.

In *Geoffrey Madan's Notebooks* (ed. Gere & Sparrow, 1981 – but Madan died in 1947) there is the uncredited quotation: '"Research" is a mere excuse for idleness.' Compare what Benjamin Jowett (1817–1893) said: '"Research!" the Master exclaimed. "Research!" he said. "A mere excuse for idleness; it has never achieved, and will never achieve any results of the slightest value"' (Logan Pearsall Smith, *Unforgotten Years*, 1938).

1 De mortuis nil nisi bunkum.

Quoted in *PDMQ* (1971). Based on the maxim '*de mortuis nil nisi bonum* [meaning, speak nothing but good of the dead – or not at all]', this remark of Laski's is to the effect that one may – or, rather, one does – only speak emptily, or nonsense, or rubbish about the dead.

THE LAST FLIGHT

American film 1931. Script by John Monk Saunders. With Richard Barthelmess.

2 It seemed like a good idea at the time.

Soundtrack. On why some American airmen in Europe had gone bull-fighting, with the result that one was gored to death. Leslie Halliwell in *The Filmgoer's Book of Quotes* (1973) suggests that this was the first time the film catchphrase was used.

LATIMER, Hugh

English bishop and martyr (1485–1555)

3 Be of good comfort, Master Ridley, and play the man. We shall this day light such a candle, by God's grace in England, as I trust shall never be put out.

On being burned at the stake with Nicholas Ridley in Oxford. Quoted in Barnaby Conrad, *Famous Last Words* (1961).

LAUDER, Sir Harry

Scots entertainer (1870–1950)

4 It's a braw brecht moonlecht necht.

Song, 'Just a Wee Deoch-an-Duoris' (1912). In fact, though Lauder did write some of his own songs – and though he did indeed popularize this one – the words are by R.F. Morrison, to music by Whit Cunliffe. Later, the line was notably interpolated in 'Hoots Mon', an instrumental and a UK No. 1 hit, by Lord Rockingham's XI (1958).

See also PUNCH 441:2.

LAW, Andrew Bonar

Canadian-born British Conservative Prime Minister (1858–1923)

5 I must follow them; I am their leader.

Quoted in Edward Raymond, *Mr Balfour* (1920). *See* LEDRU-ROLLIN 347:7.

6 Tranquillity.

Slogan for the 1922 General Election which he won. It is said to have emerged from an exchange with the future Lord Swinton, then a party official. Law: 'They tell me that we have to have what is called a slogan. What shall we have for this election?' Swinton: 'Well, I know what the country is feeling, they don't want to be buggered about.' Law: 'The sentiment is sound ... let us call it "Tranquillity".' Another version of this story is given by Swinton in *I Remember* (1948).

LAWRENCE, D.H.

English novelist and poet (1885–1930)

7 Curse the blasted, jelly-boned swines, the slimy, the belly-wriggling invertebrates, the miserable sodding rotters, the flaming sods, the snivelling, dribbling, dithering, palsied, pulseless lot that make up England today.

On a publisher's rejection of *Sons and Lovers*. Letter to Edward Garnett (3 July 1912).

8 Nothing but old fags and cabbage-stumps of quotations from the Bible and the rest, stewed in the juice of deliberate, journalistic dirty-mindedness.

Of James Joyce, in a letter to Aldous Huxley (15 August 1928).

9 *Homo sum!* the Adventurer.

Essay 'Climbing down Pisgah', published posthumously. It is quoted on Lawrence's memorial (1985) in Poets' Corner, Westminster Abbey. At a ceremony in the Abbey to mark Lawrence's birthday in September 1987, Professor James T. Boulton gave an address in which he explained his choice of this epitaph. He quoted Lawrence as saying, 'Man is nothing ... unless he adventures. Either into the unknown of the world, of his environment. Or into the unknown of himself.' Boulton added: 'The very essence of man and human life, in Lawrence's view, is bound up with the act of knowing and the nature of knowledge ... That commitment to adventure, in Lawrence's view, is what should motivate all human beings.' *See also* TERENCE 530:6.

LAWRENCE, T.E.

English soldier and writer (1888–1935)

1 I loved you, so I drew these tides of men into
my hands
and wrote my will across the sky in stars
to earn you freedom, the seven pillared
worthy house,
that your eyes might be shining for me
when we came.

Epigraph, *The Seven Pillars of Wisdom* (1926) and with the dedication 'To S.A.' This has been taken to refer to Selim Ahmed, an Arab friend who died in 1918. The innocent suggestion that 'S.A.' stands for 'Saudi Arabia' is thus a little wide of the mark.

2 All men dream: but not equally. Those who dream by night in the dusty recesses of their minds wake in the day to find that it was vanity; but the dreamers of the day are dangerous men, for they may act their dream with open eyes, to make it possible. This I did.

An elusive quotation from *ib.* It is included in the 'Introductory Chapter', originally 'Chapter 1' and suppressed from the first edition.

3 I am proudest of my thirty fights in that I did not have any of our own blood shed. All our subject provinces to me were not worth one dead Englishman.

Introductory Chapter from *ib.* Compare other 'not worth one ——' constructions: Bismarck said of possible German involvement in the Balkans: 'Not worth the healthy bones of a single Pomeranian grenadier'; 'Thomas P. "Tip" O'Neill ... said the bombing should stop because "Cambodia is not worth one American life"' (1973) – quoted in William Shawcross, *Sideshow* (1986); 'I don't believe the unity of Ireland is worth a single death' – Lord (Gerry) Fitt, quoted in *The Observer* (4 August 1985).
See also BIBLE 95:8.

LAWTON, Lord Justice (Sir Frederick)

British judge (1911–)

4 Wife beating may be socially acceptable in Sheffield but it is a different matter in Cheltenham.

Quoted in *The 'Quote ... Unquote' Book of Love, Death and the Universe* (1980). Unverified.

LAZARUS, Emma

American poet (1849–87)

5 Give me your tired, your poor,
Your huddled masses yearning to breathe
free,
The wretched refuse of your teeming shore,
Send these, the homeless, tempest-tossed, to
me:
I lift my lamp beside the golden door.

'The New Colossus' (1883), inscribed on the Statue of Liberty, New York. Although Lazarus was not an immigrant herself – she was born in New York – she championed oppressed Jewry. Her sonnet echoed George Washington's letter to newly arrived immigrants in December 1782: 'The bosom of America is open to receive not only the Opulent and respectable Stranger; but the oppressed and persecuted of all Nations and Religions.'

LEAR, Edward

English poet and artist (1812–88)

6 How pleasant to know Mr Lear!
Who has written such volumes of stuff!
Some think him ill-tempered and queer,
But a few think him pleasant enough.

Preface, *Nonsense Songs* (1871). Hence *How Pleasant to Know Mr Lear*, title of a one-man biographical show by Charles Lewsen (1968).

7 On the coast of Coromandel
Where the early pumpkins blow,
In the middle of the woods,
Lived the Yonghy-Bonghy-Bó.
Two old chairs, and half a candle;–
One old jug without a handle,–
These were all his worldly goods.

'The Courtship of the Yonghy-Bonghy-Bó' (1871). This poem was itself parodied in 1943 by Sir Osbert Sitwell who wrote: 'On the coast of Coromandel / Dance they to the tunes of Handel'.

The alliterative phrase 'on the coast of Coromandel' has long been around (not surprising when one considers that Coromandel is mostly coast and nothing else). The coast was the scene of the Franco-British struggle for supremacy in India in the eighteenth century. The *OED2* has citations from 1697, 'On the coast of Coromandel ... they call them catamarans' and from 1817, 'The united fleet appeared on the coast of Coromandel', and several others. The phrase had also been used earlier by Macaulay in his essay 'Frederick the Great' (1842).

1 Below the high Cathedral stairs,
Lie the remains of Agnes Pears.
Her name was Wiggs; it was not Pears.
But Pears was put to rhyme with stairs.

This is but one form of the 'forced rhyme' epitaph. It occurs in Lear's diary (entry for 20 April 1887). With 'Susan Pares' replacing 'Agnes Pears', the rhyme was first published without date in *Queery Leary Nonsense* (1911), edited from manuscripts by Lady Constance Strachey. The most usual form ends: 'Her name was Smith; it was not Jones;/But Jones was put to rhyme with Stones.'

LEARY, Dr Timothy

American hippie guru (1920–96)

2 Turn on, tune in, drop out.

Title of lecture (1966), summing up his philosophy of 'the game of life'. Later Leary ascribed the phrase to Marshall McLuhan.

LEAVIS, F.R.

English literary critic (1895–1978)

3 Not only not a genius, he is intellectually as undistinguished as it is possible to be.

On C.P. Snow. Quoted in *The Guardian* (April 1978).

4 Milton is as mechanical as a bricklayer.

Quoted in *The Guardian* (April 1978). Leavis was noted for his attacks on Milton. He also said once in reply to someone who asked him if he had read a book by a writer he disliked, 'To read it would be to condone it.'

LE CARRÉ, John

English novelist (1931–)

5 The Spy Who Came In from the Cold.

Title of novel (1963), about a spy from the West getting even with his East German counterpart around the time of the erection of the Berlin Wall. Hence the journalistic format, not to say cliché, 'the —— who came in from the cold'. After this, any person or any thing, coming in from any kind of exposed position, or returning to favour, might be described as 'coming in from the cold'. From the *Financial Times* (21 March 1984): '[London Stock Exchange) Oils and leading Engineerings were well to the fore. Stores also joined in the recovery, while Life Insurances came in from the cold after a particularly depressing spell before and after the abolition of Life Assurance premium relief.' On 22 June 1990 Douglas Hurd, British Foreign Secretary, speaking in Berlin, said: 'We should not forget the reason for which Checkpoint Charlie stood here for so many years but no one can be sorry that it is going. At long last ... we are bringing "Charlie" in from the cold.' In *Keep Taking the Tabloids* (1983), Fritz Spiegl noted these much earlier headline uses: 'Explorer comes in from cold', 'Stranger who flew in from the cold', 'Spy who came in from the Cold War', 'Dartmoor sheep come in from the cold', 'Quarter that came in from the cold'.

LE CORBUSIER (Charles Edouard Jeanneret)

French architect (1887–1965)

6 *La maison est une machine à habiter.*
A house is a machine for living in.

Vers une Architecture (1923). Some feel that Le Corbusier's description of the purpose of a house is a rather chilling one but in the context of his expanded explanation, it is not so bleak. He wrote in *Almanach de l'Architecture* (1925): 'The house has [three] aims. First it's a machine for living in, that is, a machine destined to serve as a useful aid for rapidity and precision in our work, a tireless and thoughtful machine to satisfy the needs of the body: comfort. But it is, secondly, a place intended for meditation and thirdly a place whose beauty exists and brings to the soul that calm which is indispensable.'

Compare from Leo Tolstoy, *War and Peace*, Bk 10, Chap. 29 (1865–9): '*Notre corps est une machine à vivre* [Our body is a machine for living].'

LEDRU-ROLLIN, Alexandre Auguste

French politician (1807–74)

7 I must follow them for I am their leader.

Ledru-Rollin became Minister of the Interior in the provisional government during the 1848 Paris revolution. He was looking from his window one day as a mob passed by and he said: '*Eh, je suis leur chef, il fallait bien les suivre* [Ah well, I'm their leader, I really ought to follow them].' It is said that 'he gave offence by his arbitrary conduct' (of which this would seem to be a prime example) and had to resign.

The remark was being quoted by 1857 and is now a frequently invoked form of political abuse. Winston Churchill is supposed to have said of Clement Attlee: 'We all understand his position. "I am their leader, I must follow them".' *See also* LAW 345:5.

LEE, Henry ('Light-Horse Harry')

American soldier and politician (1756–1818)

1 A citizen, first in war, first in peace, and first in the hearts of his countrymen.

Funeral Oration on the death of General Washington (1800) – from a Resolution presented to the US House of Representatives on Washington's death in December 1799.

LEE, Robert E.

American Confederate general (1807–70)

2 I determined to avoid the useless sacrifice of those whose past services have endeared them to their countrymen.

Lee put this in 'General Order No. 9', a written address dated 10 April 1865, at the conclusion of the American Civil War. He was explaining to the Confederate troops he was leading why he had surrendered to General Grant at Appomattox Court House, Virginia, the previous day. The army of North Virginia had been compelled to yield to overwhelming numbers and Lee also said, 'It is our duty to live. What will become of the women and children of the South if we are not here to protect them?'

In March 1976 the British Labour politician Roy Jenkins was quoted as saying, 'I am determined to avoid the useless sacrifice' when, not making progress in his bid for the party leadership, he withdrew from the race. In his memoirs, *A Life at the Centre* (1991), Jenkins states: 'I quoted (or more probably misquoted) Lee's message' and then goes on to quote a substantial passage from Lee's order, though pointedly omitting the actual 'useless sacrifice' phrase.

LEE, Gypsy Rose

American striptease entertainer (1913–70)

3 God is love – but get it in writing.

Unverified. Compare what US Secretary of State George Schultz commented after the Washington summit between Mikhail Gorbachev and Ronald Reagan in December 1987: '"Trust but verify" is really an ancient saying in the United States, but in a different guise. Remember the storekeeper who was a little leery of credit, and he had a sign in his store that said, IN GOD WE TRUST – ALL OTHERS CASH?' Referring to the verification procedures over arms reductions signed by the leaders in Washington, Shultz said, 'This is the cash.' *See also* ANONYMOUS 36:7.

LEHMAN, Ernest

American writer (1920–)

4 Sweet Smell of Success.

Title of novel and film (1957) and the origin of the phrase. *Compare* OLIVIER 418:5.

LEHMANN, Rosamond

English novelist (1901–90)

5 The trouble with Ian [Fleming] is that he gets off with women because he can't get on with them.

Quoted in John Pearson, *The Life of Ian Fleming* (1966). Apparently, Lehmann was borrowing a line from Elizabeth Bowen, although this is unverified.

LEJEUNE, C.A.

English film critic (1897–1973)

6 Me no Leica.

A small joke, but a good one. There was a vogue for dismissive one-line criticisms of plays and films, especially in the 1930s, '40s and '50s, when suitable opportunities presented themselves. It was either when Christopher Isherwood's Berlin stories were turned first into a play, *I am a Camera* (1951), or subsequently into a film (1955), that one critic summed up his/her reaction with the words 'Me no Leica'. This has been variously attributed to Caroline Lejeune, George Jean Nathan, Walter Kerr and Kenneth Tynan. It is a comment on the transitory nature of much criticism that one cannot say for sure who did originate the joke.

Another short review of Lejeune's is said to have been of the film *My Son My Son* (US, 1940). She put: 'My Son My Son, my sainted aunt!' As for *No Leave No Love* (US, 1946), she wrote: 'No comment'.

1 It makes me want to call out, Is there an apple in the house?

On Charlton Heston's performance as a doctor. Unverified.

LEMAY, Curtis E.

American general and air force chief (1906–90)

2 My solution to the problem would be to tell them frankly that they've got to draw in their horns and stop their aggression, or we're going to bomb them back into the Stone Age.

On the North Vietnamese. *Mission with LeMay* (1965).

LENIN, N. (Vladimir Ilyich Ulyanov)

Russian revolutionary and Soviet leader (1870–1924)

3 *Shag vpered dva shaga nazad.*
One Step Forward Two Steps Back.

In 1904, Lenin wrote a book about 'the crisis within our party' under this title. Note that in *Conducted Tour* (1981), Bernard Levin refers to Lenin's 'pamphlet' under the title *Four Steps Forward, Three Steps Back.* Vilmos Voigt pointed out in *Proverbium Yearbook of International Proverb Scholarship* (1984) that just after the publication of his work, Lenin referred to the 'current German form, *Ein Schritt vorwärts, zwei Schritte zurück* [one step forwards, two steps back]', and Voigt wondered what precisely the source of Lenin's phrase was and in which language.

4 Communism is Soviet power plus the electrification of the whole country.

Report to the 8th Congress (1920). Could this have been alluded to in *The Electrification of the Soviet Union,* the title of an opera with libretto by Craig Raine and music by Nigel Osborne, first presented at Glyndebourne in 1986? The opera is based on a novella by Boris Pasternak called *The Last Summer*, but the only hints in the published text are two quotations: 'And the neat man/To their east who ordered Gorki to be electrified' (W.H. Auden) and 'Next, he introduced electricity to Ethiopia, first in the palaces and then in other buildings'.

5 Those who make revolutions by halves are digging their own graves.

Sometimes attributed to Lenin, this had been said earlier by the French revolutionary Saint-Just to the National Convention in 1794, in the form: '*Ceux qui font des révolutions à moitié n'ont fait que se creuser un tombeau.*' George Büchner quoted it, too, in *Dantons Tod* (1835) but ascribed it to Robespierre: '*Wer eine Revolution zur Hälfte vollendet, gräbt sich selbst sein Grab.*'

6 Who, whom? We or they?

Questions to show that there are two categories of people – those who do and those to whom it is done. Quoted in Fitzroy Maclean, *Disputed Barricade* (1957).

7 A good man fallen among Fabians.

On Bernard Shaw. Quoted in Arthur Ransome, *Six Weeks in Russia in 1919* (1919). *See* BIBLE 102:8.

8 Give us the child for eight years and it will be a Bolshevik forever.

Lenin *may* have said this to the Commissars of Education in Moscow in 1923, but the earliest source is tainted – it is *100 Things You Should Know About Communism* published by the Committee on un-American Activities in 1951.

Compare, however, 'Give us a child until it is seven and it is ours for life', a saying usually attributed to the Jesuits, founded in 1534 by St Ignatius Loyala, but possibly wished on them by their opponents. Another version is: 'Give us the child, and we will give you the man.' *Lean's Collecteana*, Vol. 3 (1903) has, as a 'Jesuit maxim', 'Give me a child for the first seven years, and you may do what you like with him afterwards'.

Muriel Spark in her novel *The Prime of Miss Jean Brodie* (1962) has her heroine, a teacher, say: 'Give me a girl at an impressionable age and she is mine for life.'

See also BEVAN 89:7.

LENNON, John

English singer and songwriter (1940–80)

9 Would the people in the cheaper seats clap your hands. And the rest of you – if you'd just rattle your jewellery.

To audience at Royal Variety Performance (4 November 1963). From soundtrack of the TV recording.

10 Christianity will go. It will vanish and shrink. I needn't argue about that. I'm right and I'll be

proved right. We're more popular than Jesus now.

In interview with Maureen Cleave of the London *Evening Standard* (4 March 1966). The remark lay dormant for several months, but when the Beatles paid a visit to the US it was reprinted and caused an outcry. The Beatles were burned in effigy and their records banned by radio stations in Bible-belt states. Lennon subsequently withdrew the remark: 'I just said what I said – and I was wrong' (press conference, Chicago, 11 August 1966).

An interesting pre-echo occurs in a remark by Zelda Fitzgerald, recorded in Ernest Hemingway's *A Moveable Feast* (1964): 'Ernest, don't you think Al Jolson is greater than Jesus?'

1 Life is what happens to you while you're busy making other plans.

In the lyrics of Lennon's song 'Beautiful Boy' (included on his 'Double Fantasy' album, 1980), this is one of two quotations (the other is the slogan 'Every day in every day I'm getting better and better', *see* COUÉ 185:2). So it is wrong to credit Lennon with either line, as has been done.

Barbara Rowe's *The Book of Quotes* (1979) ascribes the 'Life is ...' saying to Betty Talmadge, divorced wife of Senator Herman Talmadge, in the form 'Life is what happens to you when you're making other plans.' Dr Laurence Peter in *Quotations for Our Time* (1977) gives the line to 'Thomas La Mance', who remains untraced.

2 And so, dear friends, you'll just have to carry on. The dream is over ... nothing's changed. Just a few of us are walking around with longer hair.

On the split-up of the Beatles and the end of the 1960s. Unverified. 'And so dear friends' is in the song 'God' (1970).

3 Reality is for people who can't cope with drugs.

Katharine Whitehorn confidently ascribed this to Lennon in *The Observer* (29 January 1995). Rosalie Maggio, editor of *Quotations By Women* (1996) commented that 'Lily Tomlin said, "Reality is a crutch for people who can't cope with drugs" on the television show *Rowan and Martin's Laugh-In* in the 1960s' but concluded that the coinage should be attributed rather to Jane Wagner, the American writer, actor, director and producer (1935–) in *Appearing Nitely* (1977).

4 Love is the answer.

'Mind Games' (1973). The line itself became the title of a song written by Ralph Cole and performed by Island Lighthouse (1974). The question 'Is love the answer?' occurs in Liz Lochhead's poem 'Riddle-Me-Ree' (1984). A much-alluded to view: 'Love is the answer, but while you are waiting for the answer, sex raises some pretty good questions' – Woody Allen, 1975; 'If love is the answer, could you rephrase the question?' – Lily Tomlin, 1979; both quoted in Bob Chieger, *Was It Good For You Too?* (1983).

See also next entry.

LENNON, John and McCARTNEY, Paul (later Sir Paul)

English singers and songwriters (1940–80) and (1942–)

5 Yeh-yeh-yeh.

'She Loves You' (1963). 'Yeh' as a common corruption of 'yes' has been current (and derived from the US) since the 1920s. But whether spelt 'yeh-yeh-yeh', as in the published lyrics, or 'yeah-yeah-yeah' (which captures the Liverpudlian pronunciation better), this phrase became a hallmark of the Beatles after its use in their song 'She Loves You'. The record they made of the song was in the UK charts for 31 weeks from August 1963 and was for 14 years Britain's all-time best-selling 45 r.p.m. record. Though most commonly associated with the Beatles, the phrase was not new. Some of the spadework in Britain had been done by the non-Liverpudlian singer Helen Shapiro, who had a hit in September 1961 with 'Walking Back to Happiness', which included the refrain 'Whoop Bah Oh Yeah Yeah'. The Beatles had toured with Shapiro topping the bill before their own careers took off. Following the Beatles' use, there was a French expression in the early 1960s – *yé yé* – to describe fashionable clothing.

6 It's been a hard day's night.

The title of the Beatles' first feature film *A Hard Day's Night* (UK, 1964) was apparently chosen towards the end of filming when Ringo Starr used the phrase to describe a 'heavy' night out (according to Ray Coleman, *John Lennon*, 1984). What, in fact, Ringo must have done was to use the title of the Lennon and McCartney song (presumably already written if it was towards the end of filming) in a conversational way. Indeed, Hunter Davies in *The Beatles* (1968) noted: 'Ringo Starr came out with the phrase, though John had used it earlier in a poem.' It certainly sounds like a Lennonism and may have had some limited general use subsequently as a catchphrase meaning that the speaker has had 'a very tiring time'.

1 It was twenty years ago today, that
Sgt. Pepper taught the band to play.

Song, 'Sgt. Pepper's Lonely Hearts Club Band' (1967) and title track of record album. Hence, *It Was Twenty Years Ago Today*, title of a book (1987) by Derek Taylor about the making of the album.

2 Being for the Benefit of Mr Kite.

Title of song on *Sgt. Pepper's Lonely Hearts Club Band* (1967), from a standard nineteenth-century phrase used in advertising 'testimonial' performances. Compare the title of Chap. 48 of *Nicholas Nickleby* (1838–9) by Charles Dickens: 'Being for the benefit of Mr Vincent Crummles, and Positively his last Appearance on this Stage.' As for the lyrics, largely written by John Lennon, though credited jointly to him and Paul McCartney, they derive almost word for word, as Lennon acknowledged, from the wording of a Victorian circus poster he bought in an antique shop. Or that was the story, until Derek Taylor revealed in *It Was Twenty Years Ago Today* (1987) that the poster was 'liberated' from a café during the filming of promotional clips for the 'Penny Lane/Strawberry Fields Forever' record. Headed 'Pablo Fanque's Circus Royal' in the Town Meadows, Rochdale, the poster announces:

Grandest Night of the Season!
And Positively the
Last Night But Three!
Being for the Benefit of Mr. Kite,
(late of Wells's Circus) and
Mr. J. Henderson,
the Celebrated Somerset Thrower!
Wire Dancer, Vaulter, Rider, &c.
On Tuesday Evening, February 14th, 1843.

('Somerset' is an old word for somersault.)

3 Picture yourself in a boat on a river with
tangerine trees and marmalade skies.
Somebody calls you, you answer quite slowly
a girl with kaleidoscope eyes.

Song, 'Lucy in the Sky with Diamonds' on *ib.*, which gave rise to the memorable mishearing by an old lady, 'The girl with colitis goes by ...' (quoted in the book *Babes and Sucklings*, 1983).

4 A Day in the Life.

Title of song on *ib.*, presumably taking its name from that type of magazine article and film documentary which strives to depict twenty-four hours in the life of a particular person or organization. In 1959, Richard Cawston produced a TV documentary which took this form, with the title *This is the BBC*. In 1962, the English title of a novel (film UK, 1971) by Alexander Solzhenitsyn was *One Day in the Life of Ivan Denisovich*. Lennon and McCartney's use of the phrase for the description of incidents in the life of a drug-taker may have inspired the subsequent *Sunday Times* Magazine feature 'A Life in the Day' and the play *A Day in the Death of Joe Egg* by Peter Nichols (1967; film UK, 1971).

5 I heard the news today oh boy
four thousand holes in Blackburn, Lancashire
and though the holes were rather small
they had to count them all
now they know how many holes it takes
to fill the Albert Hall.

Ib. The inspiration for these lines can be traced directly to the *Daily Mail* (17 January 1967). Lennon had the newspaper propped up on his piano as he composed. The original brief story, topping the 'Far & Near' column stated: 'There are 4,000 holes in the road in Blackburn, Lancashire, or one twenty-sixth of a hole per person, according to a council survey. If Blackburn is typical there are two million holes in Britain's roads and 300,000 in London.'

6 Eleanor Rigby picks up the rice in the church
where a wedding has been,
lives in a dream.
Waits at the window, wearing the face that
she keeps
in a jar by the door,
Who is it for?
All the lonely people, where do they all come
from?

Song 'Eleanor Rigby' (1967).

7 Magical Mystery Tour.

Title of film (1967). Hence, the phrase now given to a winding journey, caused by the driver not knowing where he is going. A 'Mystery Tour' is a journey undertaken in a coach from a holiday resort when the passengers are not told of the intended destination (and known as such probably from the 1920s onwards). The 'magical' derives from the Beatles' title for a largely unsuccessful attempt at making their own film. In *Next Horizon* (1973), Chris Bonington writes: 'Climbing with Tom Patey was a kind of Magical Mystery Tour, in which no one, except perhaps himself, knew what was coming next.' From the *Daily Express* (12 April 1989): 'On and on went the city bus driver's magical mystery tour. Passengers point out their way home – and get a lift to the door.' From McGowan & Hands's

Don't Cry for Me, Sergeant-Major (1983) (about the Falklands war): 'Then at Midnight *Canberra* slipped out, or as Lt Hornby so eloquently put it, "buggered off on the second leg of our magical mystery tour".'

LEONARD, Elmore

American novelist (1925–)

1 Erotic is when you do something sensitive and imaginative with a feather. Kinky is when you use the whole chicken.

Attributed to Leonard by William Rushton in 1987, but otherwise untraced. However, in a BBC TV *Moving Pictures* profile of Roman Polanski (reviewed in *The Guardian*, 25 November 1991), Peter Coyote ascribed the remark to Polanski in the form: 'Eroticism is using a feather, while pornography is using the whole chicken.' Another version uses 'perverted' instead of 'kinky'.

LEONCAVALLO, Ruggiero

Italian composer and librettist (1858–1919)

2 *Vesti la giubba*!
On with the motley!

I Pagliacci (1892). '*Giubba*' in Italian, means simply 'jacket' (in the sense of costume), and 'the motley' is the old English word for an actor or clown's clothes, originally the many-coloured coat worn by a jester or fool (as mentioned several times in Shakespeare's *As You Like It*). The popularity of the phrase in English probably dates from Enrico Caruso's 1902 recording of the aria, which became the first gramophone record eventually to sell a million copies.

Partridge/*Catch Phrases* suggests that, as a result, 'on with the motley!' is what one says to start a party or trip to the theatre. It may also mean 'on with the show, in spite of what has happened'. In the opera, the Clown has to 'carry on with the show' despite having a broken heart. So it might be said jokingly nowadays by anyone who is having to proceed with something in spite of difficulties. Laurence Olivier used the phrase in something like its original context when describing a sudden dash home from Ceylon during a crisis in his marriage to Vivien Leigh: 'I got myself on to a plane ... and was in Paris on the Saturday afternoon. I went straight on home the next day as I had music sessions for *The Beggar's Opera* from the Monday; and so, on with the motley' (*Confessions of an Actor*, 1982).

See also RABELAIS 445:4.

LERMONTOV, Mikhail

Russian novelist and poet (1814–41)

3 Land of the unwashed, goodbye!
Land of the masters, land of knaves!
You, in neat blue uniforms!
You who live like cringing slaves!
In my exile I may find
Peace beneath Caucasian skies, –
Far from slanderers and tsars,
Far from ever-spying eyes.

From a Lermontov poem written *c.*1840, expressing his exasperation with Mother Russia. It was quoted by Nicholas Daniloff, an American journalist accused of spying, on his release from imprisonment in the Soviet Union (October 1986).

LERNER, Alan Jay

American songwriter and playwright (1918–86)

4 I talk to the trees
But they don't listen to me.

Song, *Paint Your Wagon* (1951; film US, 1969). Music by Frederick Loewe, as for all the following collaborations:

5 My Fair Lady.

Title of musical (1956; film US, 1964). It was understandable when Lerner and Loewe wished to make a musical out of Shaw's *Pygmalion* that they should seek a new title. After all, not even in Shaw's Preface (only in his Afterword) does he allude to the relevance of the Greek legend to his story of a Covent Garden flower-girl who gets raised up and taught to 'speak proper' just like a Mayfair lady.

Lerner and Loewe turned, it seems, to the refrain of a nursery rhyme (first recorded in the eighteenth century):

> London Bridge is broken down,
> Broken down, broken down,
> London Bridge is broken down,
> My fair lady.

It has also been suggested that they were drawn to the title because 'my fair lady' is how a cockney flower-seller would pronounce the phrase 'Mayfair lady'.

6 The rain in Spain stays mainly in the plain.

Song, 'The Rain in Spain' in *ib.* According to Jonathan Cecil (1996), this elocutionary phrase was invented by

Anthony Asquith, director of the 1938 film version of *Pygmalion*. It received Shaw's approval. Actually in the film it is used with 'mainly in the *plains*' (*see* SHAW 499:1). However, Rosemary Hewett suggested (1996) that the phrase was actually suggested by Professor Edmund Tilley who was the adviser on phonetics for the production. She added that the set for Higgins's study was based on the one Prof. Tilley had when he was at Robert College, Constantinople.

Whatever the case, the rhyming of 'rain' and 'Spain' is a venerable activity. In *Polite Conversation* (1738), Jonathan Swift has this exchange:

I see 'tis raining again.
Why then, Madam, we must do as they do in Spain.
Pray, my Lord, how is that?
Why, Madam, we must let it rain.

'Rain, rain, go to Spain' was a proverbial expression current by 1659.

1 How To Handle a Woman.

Title of song in *Camelot* (1960; film US, 1967). In *Crying With Laughter* (1993), the British comedian Bob Monkhouse describes convincingly how the title was derived from a remark he once made about Erich Maria Remarque's way of handling the tantrums of his wife, Paulette Godard.

2 Camelot ...
Where once it never rained till after sundown
By eight a.m. the morning fog had flown
Don't let it be forgot
That once there was a spot
For one brief shining moment that was known
As Camelot ...

Title song of *ib. Camelot* was first produced on Broadway in December 1960 just before President Kennedy took office. Hence, the name 'Camelot' came to be applied to the romantic concept of his presidency. As Lerner wrote in *The Street Where I Live* (1978), when Jackie Kennedy quoted the lines in an interview with *Life* Magazine after her husband's assassination in 1963: '*Camelot* had suddenly become the symbol of those thousand days when people the world over saw a bright new light of hope shining from the White House ... For myself, I have never been able to see a performance of *Camelot* again.'

In 1983, on the twentieth anniversary of President Kennedy's death, William Manchester wrote a memorial volume with the title *One Brief Shining Moment*.

LESTER, Alfred

English comedian (1872–1925)

3 Always merry and bright.

Lester – who was always lugubrious – was especially associated with this phrase. He played 'Peter Doody', a jockey in the Lionel Monckton / Howard Talbot / Arthur Wimperis musical comedy *The Arcadians* (1909). He had it as his motto in a song, 'My Motter'. *Punch* quoted the phrase on 26 October 1910. Somerset Maugham in a letter to a friend (1915) wrote: 'I am back on a fortnight's leave, very merry and bright, but frantically busy – I wish it were all over.' An edition of *The Magnet* from 1920 carries an advertisement for a comic called *Merry and Bright*. P.G. Wodehouse used the phrase in *The Indiscretions of Archie* (1921).

Larry Grayson suggested (1981) that it was later used as the billing for Billy Danvers, the red-nosed music-hall comedian (d.1964). However, there may have been confusion with Danvers's undoubted bill-matter 'Cheeky, Cheery and Chubby' (*c.*1918).

LETTS, Winifred Mary

English poet (1882–1972)

4 I saw the spires of Oxford
As I was passing by,
The gray spires of Oxford
Against a pearl-gray sky;
My heart was with the Oxford men
Who went abroad to die.

'The Spires of Oxford (As Seen from the Train)', *Hallow-e'en* (1916). This is the first verse of a four-verse poem on the Oxford men who had gone to fight in the First World War.

LEVANT, Oscar

American pianist and actor (1906–72)

5 Strip the phoney tinsel off Hollywood and you'll find the real tinsel underneath.

In the early 1940s. Quoted in Leslie Halliwell, *The Filmgoer's Book of Quotes* (1973).

6 *Romance on the High Seas* was Doris Day's first picture; that was before she became a virgin.

Memoirs of an Amnesiac (1965). *Compare* MARX 384:1.

LEVER, William Hesketh (1st Viscount Leverhulme)

English soapmaker and philanthropist (1851–1925)

1 Half the money I spend on advertising is wasted, and the trouble is I don't know which half.

Quoted by David Ogilvy in *Confessions of an Advertising Man* (1963), this observation has also been fathered on John Wanamaker and, indeed, on Ogilvy himself. Ogilvy says 'as the first Lord Leverhulme (and John Wanamaker after him) complained ...' Leverhulme remains the most likely originator – he made his fortune through the manufacture of soap from vegetable oils instead of from tallow. Ogilvy had Lever Brothers as a client and could presumably have picked up the remark that way. However, Wanamaker, who more or less invented the modern department store in the US, was active by the 1860s and so possibly could have said it first.

LÉVIS, Duc de

French writer and soldier (1764–1830)

2 *Noblesse oblige.*
Nobility has its obligations.

Maximes et réflexions (1812). That is to say, privileged ancestry entails responsibility and honourable behaviour. Some hope. Hence, however, *Noblesse Oblige* (1956), title of a book by Nancy Mitford, subtitled 'An enquiry into the identifiable characteristics of the English aristocracy'.

3 *Gouverner, c'est choisir.*
To govern is to make choices.

Ib. As 'to govern is to choose', this was ascribed to Pierre Mendès-France, the French politician (1907–82), by Nigel Lawson, the former Chancellor of the Exchequer in a speech to the House of Commons (25 March 1991). He was attacking the British government, from which he had resigned, about the extent it was making consultations without making clear-cut decisions on certain issues. Could he have made a mistake? The remark is so ascribed to Mendès-France in *PDMQ* (1971).

LEWIS See DAY LEWIS, C.

LEWIS, C.S.

English scholar, religious writer and novelist (1898–1963)

4 Then Aslan [the great Lion] turned to them and said: '... You are – as you used to call it – in the Shadow Lands – dead. The term is over; the holidays have begun. The dream is ended: this is the morning.'

The Last Battle (1956) – the final 'Narnia' book. Hence, the title *Shadowlands* of a BBC TV film (1985), a play (1979) and a film (UK, 1993) by William Nicholson, all about Lewis's late-flowering relationship with the woman who became his wife and died shortly after of cancer. In Act 1 of the play, the meaning of the term 'shadowlands' seems to have been transferred from death to what has not been attained in life: 'For believe me, this world that seems to us so substantial, is no more than the shadowlands. Real life has not begun yet.'

In Nicholson's script for the film (UK, 1993), the Lewis character says: 'Shadows ... It's one of my stories. We live in the shadowlands. The sun is always shining, somewhere else, round a bend in the road, over the brow of a hill.'

LEWIS, Sinclair

American novelist (1885–1951)

5 It Can't Happen Here.

Title of novel (1935), adapted for the stage the following year, warning against fascism in the United States. A self-deluding catchphrase, a short-sighted response to external threats. Appropriately, Kevin Brownlow and Andrew Mollo's film about what would have happened if the Germans had invaded England in 1940 was entitled *It Happened Here* (UK, 1963).

LEY, Robert

German Nazi official (1890–1945)

6 *Kraft durch Freude.*
Strength through joy.

A German Labour Front slogan was coined *c.*1933 by Ley, the head of this Nazi organization which provided regimented leisure.

LEYBOURNE, George

English songwriter (d.1884)

1 He'd fly through the air with the greatest of ease
A daring young man on the flying trapeze.

Song, 'The Man on the Flying Trapeze' (1868). Music by Alfred Lee. The person referred to was Jules Léotard (d.1880), the French trapeze artist. He also gave his name to the tight, one-piece garment worn by ballet dancers, acrobats and other performers. *The Daring Young Man on the Flying Trapeze* was the title of a volume of short stories (1934) by William Saroyan.

LIBERACE (Wladziu Valentino Liberace)

American pianist and entertainer (1919–87)

2 I cried all the way to the bank.

The flamboyant pianist discussed criticism of his shows in his *Autobiography* (1973): 'I think the people around me are more apt to become elated about good reviews (or depressed by bad ones) than I am. If they're good I just tell them, "Don't let success go to your head." When the reviews are bad I tell my staff that they can join me as I cry all the way to the bank.' Liberace gave currency to this saying long before 1973, however (see *Collier's* Magazine, 17 September 1954), and he may not have invented it.

Richard Keyes, in *Nice Guys Finish Seventh* (1992), suggests that the accepted version is now 'I *laughed* all the way to the bank', which is questionable. Whatever the form, it became a catchphrase meaning that the speaker is in a position to ignore criticism.

It has been suggested that Liberace's use of the phrase dates back to his 1959 libel action in London against the *Daily Mirror* whose columnist 'Cassandra' (William Connor) had described him as 'fruit-flavoured' (see 152:3). This was taken to imply that he was homosexual. Liberace won the case and £8,000. However, as early as June 1954, Liberace was apparently saying in response to critics after a concert in New York: 'What you said hurt me very much. I cried all the way to the bank' (quoted in Nat Shapiro, *An Encyclopedia of Quotations about Music*, 1977).

LINCOLN, Abraham

American Republican 16th President (1809–65)

3 If you once forfeit the confidence of your fellow citizens, you can never regain their respect and esteem. You may fool all the people some of the time; you can even fool some of the people all the time; but you can't fool all of the people all the time.

There is so much Lincolniana – and so much that can't be verified – but this has the authentic ring about it, although it has also been ascribed to Phineas T. Barnum. The saying first appeared in Alexander K. McLure, *Lincoln's Yarns and Stories* (1904).

4 To give victory to the right, not bloody bullets, but peaceful ballots only, are necessary.

Speech (18 May 1858). Usually rendered as 'the ballot is stronger than the bullet'.

5 People who like this sort of thing will find this the sort of thing they like.

What has been called 'the world's best book review' (by Hilary Corke in *The Listener* (28 April 1955) can only loosely be traced back to Lincoln. G.W.E. Russell had it in his *Collections and Recollections* (1898). Bartlett has steadily ignored it in recent years.

As recounted by S.N. Behrman in *Conversations with Max* (1960), Max Beerbohm once mischievously invented a classical Greek source for the remark, and passed it off in a letter to the press under Rose Macaulay's signature. *See also* BEERBOHM 80:1.

6 In giving freedom to the slave, we assure freedom to the free – honorable alike in what we give and what we preserve. We shall nobly save or meanly lose the last, best hope of earth.

Referring to the act of giving freedom to the slaves, the phrase 'last, best hope of earth' comes from Lincoln's Second Annual Message to Congress (1 December 1862). It is not '*on* earth', but has been endlessly quoted and alluded to by later Presidents and politicians. One example: in President Kennedy's inaugural speech (1961), the United Nations was 'our last best hope'.

7 Four score and seven years ago our fathers brought forth [up]on this continent a new nation, conceived in liberty, and dedicated to the proposition that all men are created equal. Now we are engaged in a great civil war, testing whether that nation or any nation so conceived and so dedicated can long endure. We are met on a great battlefield of that war. We have come to dedicate a portion of that field, as a final resting place for those who here gave their lives that that nation might live. It is altogether fitting and proper that we should do

this. But, in a larger sense, we cannot dedicate – we cannot consecrate – we cannot hallow – this ground. The brave men, living and dead, who struggled here, have consecrated it far above our poor power to add or detract. The world will little note nor long remember what we say here, but it can never forget what they did here. It is for us, the living, rather to be dedicated here to the unfinished work which they who fought here have thus far so nobly advanced. It is rather for us to be here dedicated to the great task remaining before us – that from these honored dead we take increased devotion to that cause for which they gave the last full measure of devotion; that we here highly resolve that these dead shall not have died in vain; that this nation, under God, shall have a new birth of freedom; and that government of the people, by the people, [and] for the people, shall not perish from the earth.

The Federal victory at the Battle of Gettysburg in the American Civil War foreshadowed the ultimate defeat of the Confederacy. But what immortalized the battle was Lincoln's address, as President, at the dedication of the battlefield cemetery at Gettysburg on 19 November 1863. Lincoln's prophecy that the world would 'little note nor long remember' what he said seemed likely to be true, judging by initial reaction to the speech. One American paper spoke of the President's 'silly remarks'. *The Times* of London (as did many American papers) ignored the speech in its report of the ceremony. Later *The Times* was to say: 'Anything more dull and commonplace it wouldn't be easy to reproduce.' The *Chicago Tribune* wrote, however, that the words would, 'Live among the annals of man'. There is a legend that Lincoln jotted down the Gettysburg Address on the back of an envelope on a train going to the battlefield, but the structure of the words is so tight that this seems unlikely and Burnam (1980) suggests that there were some five drafts of the speech. Also, the Associated Press was apparently given an advance copy. He spoke it mostly from memory.

The text, as above, though now (literally) carved in stone, is only an approximation of what Lincoln actually said. Gore Vidal in writing his novel *Lincoln* (1984) chose to draw instead on the notes made by Charles Hall of the Boston *Daily Advertiser* who had the advantage of actually hearing the speech delivered, but the differences are very minor.

Thirty-three years before Lincoln delivered the Gettysburg Address, Daniel Webster had spoken of 'The people's government, made for the people, made by the people, and answerable to the people' (Second Speech on Foote's Resolution, 26 January 1830).

According to Bartlett (1992), Theodore Parker, a clergyman, had used various versions of this credo in anti-slavery speeches during the 1850s. Lincoln's law partner William H. Herndon gave him a copy of Parker's speeches. Before composing Gettysburg, Lincoln marked the words 'democracy is direct self-government, over all the people, by all of the people, for all of the people' in a Parker sermon dating from 1858.

1 God must have loved the common people; he made so many of them.

There is no evidence that Lincoln said this. James Morgan in a book called *Our Presidents* (1928) was the first to put it in his mouth.

2 He ain't heavy, he's my brother.

King George VI concluded his 1942 Christmas radio broadcast by reflecting on the European allies and the benefits of mutual cooperation, saying: 'A former President of the United States of America used to tell of a boy who was carrying an even smaller child up a hill. Asked whether the heavy burden was not too much for him, the boy answered: "It's not a burden, it's my brother!" So let us welcome the future in a spirit of brotherhood, and thus make a world in which, please God, all may dwell together in justice and peace.'

Benham (1948) suggests that the American President must have been Lincoln – though it has not been possible to trace a source for the story. In fact, the King's allusion seems rather to have been a dignification of an advertising slogan and a charity's motto. As a headline, 'He ain't heavy ... he's my brother' may have been used first by Jack Cornelius of the BBD&O agency in a 1936 American advertisement for the 'Community Chest' campaign ('35 appeals in 1'). But it is difficult to tell what relationship this has, if any, with the similar slogan used to promote the Nebraska orphanage and poor boys' home known as 'Boys Town'.

In the early 1920s the Rev. Edward J. Flanagan – Spencer Tracy played him in the film *Boys Town* (1938) – admitted to this home a boy named Howard Loomis who could not walk without the aid of crutches. The larger boys often took turns carrying him about on their backs. One day, Father Flanagan is said to have seen a boy carrying Loomis and asked whether this wasn't a heavy load. The reply: 'He ain't heavy, Father ... he's m'brother.' In 1943, a 'two brothers' logo (similar to, though not the same as, the drawing used in the Community Chest campaign) was copyrighted for Boys Town's exclusive use. Today, the logo and the motto (in the 'Father/m'brother' form) are registered service marks of Father Flanagan's Boys' Home (Boys Town).

It seems likely that the saying probably *does* predate the Father Flanagan story, though whether it goes back to Lincoln is anybody's guess. More recent applications have included the song with the title, written by Bob Russell and Bobby Scott, and popularized by the Hollies in 1969. Perhaps the brief Lennon and McCartney song 'Carry that Weight' (September 1969) alludes similarly? – 'Boy – you're gonna carry that weight,/Carry that weight a long time.'

1 You cannot bring about prosperity by discouraging thrift. You cannot strengthen the weak by weakening the strong. You cannot help small men up by tearing big men down. You cannot help the wage earner by pulling down the wage payer. You cannot further the brotherhood of man by encouraging class hatred. You cannot help the poor by destroying the rich. You cannot establish sound security on borrowed money. You cannot keep out of trouble by spending more than you earn. You cannot build character and courage by taking away man's initiative and independence. You cannot help men permanently by doing for them what they could and should do for themselves.

That Lincoln never said any of this is a fact that few people seem obliged to accept, especially if they are proponents of free enterprise. The playwright Ronald Millar described in *The Sunday Times* (23 November 1980) what had happened when he wrote his first speech for Margaret Thatcher as Prime Minister: 'I dashed off a piece including the quote from Abraham Lincoln, "Don't make the rich poorer, make the poor richer." I gave her the first draft and she immediately delved into her handbag for a piece of yellowing paper on which was written the very same Lincoln quotation. "I take it everywhere with me," she said. And from then on I've worked for her whenever she's asked me.'

Ex-President Ronald Reagan attributed the line, 'You cannot strengthen the weak by weakening the strong' to Lincoln in an address to the Republican Convention in August 1992. When it was pointed out that this had in fact been uttered by 'a Rev. William Boetcker of Pennsylvania', a spokeswoman for Mr Reagan 'said it was not really his fault; he had found the line, attributed to Lincoln, in a handbook of quotes' (*The Independent*, 20 August 1992). On the other hand, if he had referred to the Congressional Research Service's authoritative *Respectfully Quoted*, he would have found that President Calvin Coolidge had said, 'Don't expect to build up the weak by pulling down the strong' in a speech to the Massachusetts State Senate on 7 January 1914.

The misattribution to Lincoln of all or part of the 'Ten Points' was most likely first made by a member of the US Congress, but the list has been widely distributed since the 1940s. In *Harper's* Magazine (May 1950), Albert A. Woldman claimed that the quotation came rather from *The Industrial Decalogue*, a pamphlet published in 1911 by one William Boetcker (sometimes described as the Rev. William J. H. Boetcker).

It is possible that Lincoln did say: 'I don't believe in a law to prevent a man getting rich; it would do more harm than good', and, 'That some should be rich shows that others may become rich, and hence is just encouragement to industry and enterprise.'

2 I have always plucked a thistle and planted a flower where I thought a flower would grow.

In William H. Herndon's biography of Lincoln (1888) there is quoted a statement by Joshua F. Speed, a friend of the President, dated 6 December 1866, in which he relates a good turn done not long before the assassination. Lincoln released two draft-dodgers from gaol as a result of a mother's and a wife's pleas. '"The mother spoke out in all the features of her face [said Lincoln]. It is more than one can often say that in doing right one has made two people happy in one day. Speed, die when I may, I want it said of me by those who know me best, that I always plucked a thistle and planted a flower when I thought a flower would grow". What a fitting sentiment [Speed adds]! What a glorious recollection!'

See also SIMON 505:1; STEVENSON 520:2.

LINDNER, R.M.

American psychologist (1914–56)

3 Rebel Without a Cause.

According to *ODMQ* (1991), with the subtitle 'The hypnoanalysis of a criminal psychopath', this was the title of a book published by Lindner in 1944. In *ODQ* (1992) he is described as a 'novelist'. The phrase became famous later when used as the title of a film (1955), for which the screenplay credit is given to Stewart Stern 'from an original story by the director, Nicholas Ray'. *The Motion Picture Guide* (1990) gives the provenance of the script, however, as 'based on an adaptation by Irving Shulman of a story line by Ray inspired from the story *The Blind Run* by Dr Robert M. Lindner.'

The film's study of adolescent misbehaviour had little to do with what one would now think of as psychopathic but it helped popularize the phrase 'rebel without a cause' to describe a certain type of alienated youth of the period. It was the film that projected its star, James Dean, to status as chief 1950s rebel, a position confirmed when he met his premature end soon after.

LINKLATER, Eric

Scottish writer (1899–1974)

1 At my back I often hear Time's winged chariot changing gear.

Juan in China (1937). Alluding to MARVELL 383:3.

LITTLE CAESAR

American film 1930. Script by various. With Edward G. Robinson as Rico.

2 *Rico*: Mother of Mercy, is this the end of Rico?

Dying words. Soundtrack. Rico is a gangster (modelled on Al Capone). He meets his end on some church steps, hence the 'Mother of Mercy' cry.

LITVINOV, Maxim

Soviet politician (1876–1951)

3 Peace is indivisible.

Said on several occasions and at the League of Nations in Geneva (1 July 1936).

LIVINGSTONE, David

Scottish missionary and explorer (1813–73)

4 The most wonderful sight I had witnessed in Africa ... It had never been seen before by European eyes; but scenes so lovely must have been gazed upon by angels in their flight.

On Victoria Falls in what was to become Rhodesia and is now Zimbabwe. *Missionary Travels and Researches* (1857). In fact, the falls had been seen by Portuguese eyes before Livingstone's. He renamed them after his sovereign – 'the only English name I have affixed to any part of country.' Sometimes this passage is said to come from his journal of the 1855 expedition, but that contains only his more prosaic impressions. This was written up when he returned home for a book of his travels.

5 All I can add in my solitude is, may heaven's rich blessing come down on everyone, American, English, or Turk – who will help heal this open sore of the world.

These words (referring to the slave trade) are quoted on Livingstone's gravestone in Westminster Abbey. They are taken from a letter he had addressed to the *New York Herald* (1 May 1872). 'Loneliness' rather than 'solitude' may have been in the original.

LLEWELLYN, Richard

Welsh novelist (1907–83)

6 None But the Lonely Heart.

Title of novel (1943; film US, 1944). Apparently an original coinage, but compare, 'None But the Weary Heart', the English title often given to a song by Tchaikovsky (Op. 6, No. 6). The lyrics of this song have been translated into English as, 'None but the weary heart can understand how I have suffered and how I am tormented'. It originated as 'Mignon's Song' in the novel *Wilhelm Meister* by Goethe – '*Nur wer die Sehnsucht kennt* [Only those who know what longing is]' – which was translated into Russian by Mey.

LLOYD, Harold

American film comedian (1893–1971)

7 I am just turning forty and taking my time about it.

On being asked his age when he was 77. Quoted in *The Times* that same year (1970).

LLOYD, Marie

English music-hall entertainer (1870–1922)

8 She sits among the cabbages and peas.

Line from song supposedly made famous by Marie Lloyd, but untraced. According to the story, when forbidden by a watch committee (local guardians of morals) to sing 'She sits among the cabbages and peas,' she substituted, 'She sits among the cabbages and leeks.' The story was told, for example, by John

Trevelyan, the British film censor (*TV Times*, 23 April–9 May 1981). There is some doubt as to whether the song really exists beyond the confines of this story – and whether it has any connection with a song written in 1929, after Lloyd's death, called 'Mucking About the Garden'. This was written by Leslie Sarony, the British entertainer (1897–1985), using the *nom de plume* 'Q. Cumber' or 'Q. Kumber'. Unfortunately, I have been unable to find the sheet music (published by Lawrence Wright) to see if it really does contain the immortal line, 'She sits among the cabbages and peas/Watching her onions grow', as has been suggested. The only recording I have heard of the song, by George Buck, does not have the couplet. I suspect that the recording by Sarony himself with Tommy Handley and Jack Payne (on Columbia 5555), which I have not heard, does not have it either.

LOCKHART, John Gibson

Scottish writer and critic (1794–1854)

1 It is a better and a wiser thing to be a starved apothecary than a starved poet; so back to the shop Mr John, back to 'plasters, pills, and ointment boxes.'

Reviewing *Endymion* by John Keats in *Blackwood's Edinburgh Magazine* (August 1818).

LOESSER, Frank

American songwriter (1910–69)

2 See What the Boys in the Back Room Will Have.

Title of song, *Destry Rides Again* (1939). *See also* BEAVERBROOK 78:4.

3 Finally found a fellow
He says 'Murder!' – he says!
Every time we kiss he says 'Murder!' – he says!
Is that the language of love?

Song, '"Murder" He Says', *Happy Go Lucky* (1943). *Murder He Says* then became the title of a film (US, 1945).

4 How To Succeed in Business Without Really Trying.

Title of musical (1961). Taken from Shepherd Meade's non-fiction guidebook of that title.

LOGUE, Christopher

English poet (1926–)

5 Come to the edge.
We might fall.
Come to the edge.
It's too high!
COME TO THE EDGE!
And they came,
and he pushed,
and they flew.

'Come to the Edge', *New Numbers* (1969). In a profile of Tom Stoppard (*The New Yorker*, 19 December 1977), Kenneth Tynan described the playwright addressing a class of drama students in Santa Barbara: 'What is the real dialogue that goes on between the artist and his audience? [Stoppard asks at the end]. By way of reply, he holds the microphone close to his mouth and speaks eight lines by the English poet Christopher Logue ... A surge of applause. In imagination, these young people are all flying.'

Many people have, however, seen the lines attributed to the surrealist French poet Guillaume Apollinaire (1880–1918). For example, Anthony Powell in his *Journals 1982–1986* (1995, entry for 26 October 1982) has: 'At Royal Academy Banquet [not of this date] when [Margaret Thatcher] spoke, quoting Guillaume Apollinaire in a speech (something about a man walking blindfold over a cliff), passage I did not recognise, tho' I know Apollinaire's works fairly well ... Mrs T knew roughly about Apollinaire, a bit vague about quotation (which I still can't find).'

Accordingly, in 1995, I asked Christopher Logue for his comments. He had an intriguing explanation for the confusion: 'In 1961 or '62, Michael English and I were asked by Michael Kustow to design a poster / poem for an Apollinaire exhibition he was mounting at the ICA [Institute of Contemporary Arts in London].

'I wrote "Come to the Edge" and put the words "Apollinaire said" at the beginning of it; a cross between a title and a first line. On the poster, the poem, plus "Apollinaire said:" framed an illustration of clouds. Later, when the poem was reprinted, I dropped the trope. Last year, though, the US "magician" David Copperfield projected a garbled version of the poem on to a screen as part of his show, as well as printing it in his "tour-book" – the show's programme. I believe the poem has been reprinted in at least one US book without my permission. Maybe it had the trope attached to it still.' Indeed, a David Copperfield TV special shown in the UK in 1995 concluded with an approximation of the poem ... attributed to Apollinaire.

LOMBARDI, Vince

American football coach (1913–70)

1 Winning isn't everything. It's the only thing.

Various versions of this oft-repeated statement exist. Lombardi, coach and general manager of the Green Bay Packers team from 1959 onwards, claimed *not* to have said it in this form but, rather, 'Winning is not everything – but making the effort to win is' (interview 1962). The first version of Lombardi's remarks to appear in print was in the form, 'Winning is not the most important thing, it's everything'. One Bill Veeck is reported to have said something similar. Henry 'Red' Sanders, a football coach at Vanderbilt University, *does* seem to have said it, however, *c.*1948, and was so quoted in *Sports Illustrated* (26 December 1955). John Wayne, playing a football coach, delivered the line in the 1953 film *Trouble Along the Way*.

Compare 'Winning in politics isn't everything; it's the only thing' – a slogan for the infamous 'Committee to Re-Elect the President' (Nixon) in 1972.

LONG, Huey

American politician (1893–1935)

2 I looked around at the little fishes present and said, 'I'm the Kingfish.'

Quoted in Arthur M. Schlesinger Jr, *The Politics of Upheaval* (1960). Long was known by the nickname 'Kingfish'.

3 Everyman a king but no man wears a crown.

The Louisiana Governor (and demagogue) found this slogan for his Share-the-Wealth platform – which he espoused from 1928 until his assassination – in William Jennings Bryan's 'Cross of Gold' speech (1896) – *see* BRYAN 128:2. He suggested that only 10 per cent of the American people owned 70 per cent of the wealth. As Safire (1978) points out, the full slogan used 'everyman' as one word.

LONGFELLOW, Henry Wadsworth

American poet (1807–82)

4 Life is real! Life is earnest!
And the grave is not the goal;
Dust thou art, to dust returnest,
Was not spoken of the soul ...

Lives of great men all remind us
We can make our lives sublime,
And, departing, leave behind us
Footprints on the sands of time.

Let us, then, be up and doing,
With a heart for any fate;
Still achieving, still pursuing,
Learn to labour and to wait.

'A Psalm of Life' (1838). Longfellow is probably the most parodied poet. There are several parodies of this poem – *see* ANONYMOUS 37:1 – and this was told in 1996:

> Lives of criminals remind us
> We can make our lives sublime
> And, in parting, leave behind us
> Fingerprints on the files of crime.

5 The Wreck of the Hesperus.

Title of poem (1839) about an actual incident involving a schooner off the coast of New England. Hence, the expression, 'to look/feel like the wreck of the *Hesperus*', meaning, 'in a mess, in a sad state' – known in the US and UK since the nineteenth century.

6 The shades of night were falling fast,
As through an Alpine village passed
A youth, who bore, 'mid snow and ice,
A banner with the strange device,
Excelsior!

'Excelsior' (1841). The poem, of which this is the first verse, became a favourite recitation of the parlour poetry school and was also set to music more than once. It has been suggested that Longfellow was inspired by the ungrammatical motto on the State shield of New York (which is the comparative or past participle or *excelsus*, rather than, presumably what was intended, *excelsius* ('more loftily'), the comparative of the adverb *excelse*). Strange device, indeed. The poem gave rise to a delightful parody 'The Shades of Night', which was written, apparently, by A.E. Housman:

> The shades of night were falling fast,
> And the rain was falling faster,
> When through an Alpine village passed
> An Alpine village pastor ...

7 Thy fate is the common fate of all,
Into each life some rain must fall,
Some days must be dark and dreary.

'The Rainy Day' (1842). Hence, 'Into each life some rain must fall,/But too much is falling in mine' from the song 'Into Each Life A Little Rain Must Fall' (as it is sometimes worded, but which also contains 'some rain' in the lyrics). Written by Allan Roberts and Doris Fisher (1944).

1 Underneath the spreading chestnut tree
The village smithy stands;
The smith a mighty man is he
With large and sinewy hands
And the muscles of his brawny arms
Are strong as iron bands.

'The Village Blacksmith' (1842) – one of the most parodied and plundered of verses. In the nineteenth century there were musical settings by several composers but that by W.H. Weiss (1820–67) was the most popular (in 1854). There was then a lull until a song was written called 'The Chestnut Tree' in 1938. This was a joint effort by Jimmy Kennedy, Tommie Connor and Hamilton Kennedy:

Underneath the Spreading Chestnut Tree
I loved her and she loved me.
There she used to sit upon my knee
'Neath the Spreading Chestnut Tree.

There beneath the boughs we used to meet,
All her kisses were so sweet.
All the little birds went tweet tweet tweet
'Neath the Spreading Chestnut Tree.

The actual blacksmith only manages to make an appearance in this song by exclaiming 'Chest ... nuts!' – which gave rise to interesting gestures by performers. Instructions as to how to do these were given on the sheet music for this 'novelty singing dance sensation'.

In George Orwell's novel *1984* (1948), there is another variation:

Under the spreading chestnut tree
I sold you and you sold me:
There lie they, and here lie we
Under the spreading chestnut tree.

2 And the night shall be filled with music
And the cares that infest the day
Shall fold their tents, like the Arabs,
And as silently steal away.

'The Day is Done' (1844). At the conclusion of his case for the defence in the Jeremy Thorpe trial (1979), Mr George Carman QC said to the Old Bailey jury: 'I end by saying in the words of the Bible: "Let this prosecution fold up its tent and quietly creep away".' His client should not have got off after that.

3 Sail on, Oh Ship of State!
Sail on, Oh Union, strong and great.
Humanity with all its fears,
With all the hope of future years,
Is hanging breathless on thy fate!

'The Building of the Ship' (1849). On 20 January 1941, before the US had entered the Second World War, President Roosevelt sent a letter to the British Prime Minister, Winston Churchill, containing this extract (with minor differences in spelling and punctuation) from Longfellow's poem. He commented: 'I think this verse applies to your people as it does to us.' (For Churchill's response, *see* CLOUGH 175:3.)

4 There was a little girl
Who had a little curl
Right in the middle of her forehead,
When she was good
She was very, very good,
But when she was bad she was horrid.

'There Was a Little Girl' (*c.*1850), said to have been composed and sung to his second daughter when she was a babe in arms. Thus was born a much-invoked description.

5 Lo! in that hour of misery
A lady with a lamp I see
Pass through the glimmering gloom,
And flit from room to room.
And slow, as in a dream of bliss
The speechless sufferer turns to kiss
Her shadow, as it falls
Upon the darkening walls.

'Santa Filomena' (1857). Florence Nightingale (1820–1910), philanthropist and nursing pioneer, was dubbed 'the lady with a lamp' in commemoration of her services to soldiers at Scutari during the Crimean War (1854–6). She inspected hospital wards at night, carrying a lamp – a Turkish lantern consisting of a candle inside a collapsible shade. The phrase appears to have been coined by Longfellow in his poem which was written very shortly after the events described.

On her death, Moore Smith & Co. of Moorgate, London, published a ballad with the title 'The Lady with *the* Lamp', which begins:

The Lady with the Lamp –
Let this her title be
Remembered through the ages
That will dawn and flee.

Straight to an Empire's heart
Her noble way she trod.
She lives, she lives for ever
Now she rests, she rests with God.

The film biography (1951), with Anna Neagle as Miss

Nightingale, was called *The Lady with a Lamp* and was based on a play by Reginald Berkeley.

1 Though the mills of God grind slowly, yet they grind exceeding small.

Longfellow's translation of a line of verse (1654) by Friedrich von Logau, a German poet – in turn, a translation of a verse in Latin. The meaning of this saying is that the ways in which reforms are brought about, crime is punished, and so on, are often slow, but the end result may be perfectly achieved.

2 The heights by great men reached and kept
Were not attained by sudden flight,
But they, while their companions slept,
Were toiling upward in the night.

'The Ladder of St Augustine' (1858). Inspirational lines that must have adorned many a motivational speech-day or commencement speech.

3 Between the dark and the daylight,
When the night is beginning to lower,
Comes a pause in the day's occupations,
That is known as the Children's Hour.

'The Children's Hour' (1859). This became the name for the period between afternoon tea and dressing for dinner, particularly in Edwardian England. When the long-running and fondly remembered BBC radio programme *Children's Hour* began in 1922, it was known as '*The* Children's Hour', which suggests that it ultimately derived from the title of Longfellow's poem. Lillian Hellman also wrote a play called *The Children's Hour* (1934), variously filmed, about a schoolgirl's allegations of her teachers' lesbianism.

4 Ships that pass in the night, and speak each other in passing;
Only a signal shown and a distant voice in the darkness;
So on the ocean of life we pass and speak one another,
Only a look and a voice; then darkness again and silence.

'The Theologian's Tale: Elizabeth', Pt 4, *Tales of a Wayside Inn* Pt 3 (1874). The origin of the expression 'ships that pass in the night' referring to acquaintance (with people) that is of only short duration.

LONGWORTH, Alice Roosevelt

American political hostess (1884–1980)

5 If you haven't got anything nice to say about anyone, come and sit by me.

Embroidered on a cushion at Longworth's Washington, DC, home. The daughter of Theodore Roosevelt, she had a reputation for barbed wit, but many of her 'sayings' were not entirely original.

6 [Calvin Coolidge] looked as if he had been weaned on a pickle.

She admitted hearing this 'at my dentist's office. The last patient had said it to him and I just seized on it. I didn't originate it – but didn't it describe him exactly?' (*The New York Times*, 25 February 1980). It first appeared as an 'anonymous remark' quoted in Longworth's *Crowded Hours* (1933).

7 [Thomas E. Dewey] looks like the bridegroom on the wedding cake.

A description that helped destroy Dewey when he stood against President Truman in 1948 came from one Grace Hodgson Flandrau. Longworth admitted: 'I thought it frightfully funny and quoted it to everyone. Then it began to be attributed to me.' Sometimes just 'the man on the wedding cake', Dewey did indeed have a wooden appearance, and a black moustache.

8 One part mush and two parts Eleanor.

On Franklin Roosevelt. Or, 'one-third sap, two-thirds Eleanor'. In *The New York Times* (*op. cit.*), Longworth denied saying any such thing.

LOOS, Anita

American novelist (1893–1981)

9 Gentlemen Prefer Blondes.

Title of novel (1925), to which a sequel was added: *But Gentlemen Marry Brunettes* (1928). Irving Berlin wrote a song with the title very shortly after this (sung in London in the revue *RSVP*, 23 February 1926). And a B.G. de Sylva and Lewis Gensler song, with the same title, was performed on Broadway in *Queen High* (2 November 1926).

10 Kissing your hand may make you feel very good but a diamond and safire bracelet lasts forever.

Ib. This was the inspiration for the Jule Styne/Leo

Robin song 'Diamonds Are a Girl's Best Friend' in the 1949 stage musical and 1953 film based on the book.

LORCA See GARCÍA LORCA

LORENZ, Edward

American meteorologist (1917–)

1 Predictability: Does the Flap of a Butterfly's Wings in Brazil Set Off a Tornado in Texas?

Title of a paper on predictability in weather forecasting delivered to the American Association for the Advancement of Science, Washington, DC (29 December 1979). Apparently, Lorenz originally used the image of a seagull's wing flapping. What is now called 'The Butterfly Effect' – how small acts lead to large – appeals to chaos theorists. J. Gleick gives another example in *Chaos: Making a New Theory* (1988), also from weather forecasting: 'The notion that a butterfly stirring the air today in Peking can transform storm systems next month in New York.'

LOTHIAN, 11th Marquess of

British Conservative politician (1882–1940)

2 The only lasting solution is that Europe itself should gradually find its way to an internal equilibrium and a limitation of armaments by political appeasement.

Letter to *The Times* (4 May 1934). Hence, the term 'appeasement' given to the policy of conciliation and concession towards Nazi Germany, around 1938. The word had been used in this context since the end of the First World War. On 14 February 1920 Winston Churchill was saying in a speech: 'I am, and have always been since the firing stopped on November 11, 1918, for a policy of peace, real peace and appeasement.' The 1930s use of the term probably dates from Lothian's letter, however. *See also* COCKBURN 176:4.

LOUIS XIV

French King (1638–1715)

3 *L'état c'est moi.*

I am the state.

Alleged remark to parliament on 13 April 1655, but there is no contemporary evidence for it. Some of his personal edicts were being challenged in the interests of the state. Louis is said to have strode into the chamber wearing his hunting clothes and brandishing a riding crop.

4 *Dieu, a-t-il donc oublié ce que j'ai fait pour lui?*

Has God forgotten then what I have done for him?

Alleged remark after the Battle of Malplaquet (1709). An allied army under Marlborough defeated the French in the last pitched battle of the War of the Spanish Succession.

LOUIS XVI

French King (1754–93)

5 *Rien.*

Nothing.

His complete diary entry made at Versailles on the evening of 14 July 1789 – the day of the storming of the Bastille. In fact, he wrote '*Rien*' on most of the days that July and put only one-line entries most of the time, anyway. A similar story has been told that on 4 July 1776, when the American Declaration of Independence was signed, King George III wrote in his diary: 'Nothing of importance happened today.' There appears to be absolutely no evidence for this.

6 Frenchmen, I die innocent: it is from the scaffold and near appearing before God that I tell you so. I pardon my enemies: I desire that France ...

Louis's last words before execution (21 January 1793) are given here as reported by Thomas Carlyle in *The French Revolution – A History*, III.ii.8 (1837). The remainder of the last sentence was drowned out by the sound of drumming, but others have it that he went on: 'Pray God that my blood fall not on France!' or 'I hope that my blood may cement the happiness of the French people'.

LOUIS XVIII

French King (1755–1824)

7 *L'exactitude est la politesse des rois.*

Punctuality is the politeness of kings.

Quoted in *Souvenirs de J. Lafitte* (1844). By 1834, however, this proverb was being cited in the form 'punctuality is the politeness of princes' (and not ascribed to Louis XVIII).

LOUIS, Joe

American boxer (1914–81)

1 He can run, but he can't hide.

In the *New York Herald Tribune* (9 June 1946), before a World Heavyweight Championship fight with the quick-moving Billy Conn (whom he beat by a knockout on 19 June).

In the wake of the hijacking of a TWA airliner to Beirut in the summer of 1985, President Reagan issued a number of warnings to international terrorists. In October, he said that America had 'sent a message to terrorists everywhere. The message: "You can run, but you can't hide".' Coming from a former sports commentator, the allusion was clear, but one suspects that the saying possibly pre-dates Louis in any case.

LOVELACE, Richard

English poet (1618–58)

2 Stone walls do not a prison make,
Nor iron bars a cage.

'To Althea, From Prison' (1649). When combined with a phrase from SHAKESPEARE 475:7, this produced a delightfully lunatic allusion in *The Kenneth Williams Letters* (1994): 'I must say I fell about at your line – "Age shall not wither her, nor iron bars a cage" – how true that is even today' – Kenneth Williams to John Hussey (2 October 1971). However, others recall this in the BBC radio show *Much Binding in the Marsh*, which ran from 1947 to 1953.

LOVELL, James

American astronaut (1928–)

3 OK, Houston, we have had a problem here ...
Houston, we have had a problem.

The Apollo 13 space mission took off at 13.13 Houston time on 11 April 1970. Two days into the mission – i.e., on the 13th – and 200,000 miles from Earth, an oxygen tank exploded, seriously endangering the crew. Lovell, the commander, noted the happening with notable understatement. It is hard to decipher precisely what he said from the recording of the incident. *The Times* (15 April) had, 'Hey, we've got a problem.' Asked to repeat this, Lovell said: 'Houston, we've had a problem. We've had a main bus interval' (indicating a fault in the electrical system). Emergency procedures allowed the crew to make a safe return to earth. The words have also been ascribed to another crew member, John L. Swigert Jr (as in *Time* Magazine, 10 January 1983). A TV movie in 1974 was entitled *Houston, We've Got a Problem*. In the feature film *Apollo 13* (US, 1995), based on a book by Lovell, Swigert gets to say, 'Hey, we've got a problem here' and Lovell follows this with, 'Houston, we have a problem'.

LOW, David

British political cartoonist (1891–1963)

4 Very well, alone.

Caption to cartoon in the London *Evening Standard* (18 June 1940) reflecting the mood of the British nation following the Fall of France. The cartoon showed a British soldier confronting a hostile sea and a sky full of bombers.

LOWELL, James Russell

American poet (1819–91)

5 New occasions teach new duties: Time makes
ancient good uncouth;
They must upward still, and onward, who
would keep abreast of truth.

'The Present Crisis' (1844). Probably the first formulation of the phrase 'onwards and upwards'. The first lines of the nineteenth-century hymn 'Onward! Upward!' (words by F.J. Crosby, music by Ira D. Sankey), are:

Onward! upward! Christian soldier.
Turn not back nor sheath thy sword;
Let its blade be sharp for conquest
In the battle for the Lord.

Sankey also set the words of Albert Midlane in 'Onward, Upward, Homeward!', of which the refrain is:

Onward to the glory!
Upward to the prize!
Homeward to the mansions
Far above the skies!

Or could the words be from a motto? The Davies-Colley family of Newfold, Cheshire, have them as such in the form 'Upwards and Onwards'. Now it has become a light-hearted catchphrase. 'Nicholas Craig' in *I, An Actor* (1988) asks of young actors: 'Will you be able to learn the language of the profession and say things like "onwards and upwards", "Oh well, we survive" and "Never stops, love, he *never stops*".'

See also KEARNEY 327:3.

LOWELL, Robert

American poet (1917–77)

1 If we see light at the end of the tunnel,
It's the light of the oncoming train.

'Since 1939' (1977), but probably not original. The *ODQ* (1992) has Paul Dickson citing 'Rowe's Rule: the odds are five to six that the light at the end of the tunnel is the headlight of an oncoming train' (*The Washingtonian*, November 1978). On BBC Radio *Quote ... Unquote* (1980), John Lahr said it had been a favourite remark of his father, the actor, Bert Lahr (d.1967).

LUCAS, George

American film director and writer (1944–)

2 May the Force be with you.

Film, *Star Wars* (US, 1977), scripted by Lucas. A benediction and valediction used several times. At one point, Ben Obi-Wan Kenobi (Alec Guinness) explains what it means: 'The Force is what gives the Jedi its power. It's an energy field created by all living things. It surrounds us, it penetrates us, it binds the galaxy together.'

The phrase turned up in Cornwall a short while after the film was released in Britain – as a police force recruiting slogan. Later, President Reagan, promoting his 'Star Wars' weapon system, said: 'It isn't about fear, it's about hope, and in that struggle, if you'll pardon my stealing a film line, "The force is with us".'

Compare 'The Lord be with you' from Morning Prayer in the Anglican Book of Common Prayer.

3 The Empire Strikes Back.

Title of film (US, 1980). This was the fictional 'evil empire' vaguely alluded to by Ronald Reagan in his remarks about the Soviet Union (449:6). The phrase caught on in other ways, too. In *c.*1981, the proprietors of an Indian restaurant in Drury Lane, London, considered it as a name before rejecting it in favour of 'The Last Days of the Raj'. In 1982, *Newsweek* Magazine gave it as the title of a cover story about Britain's attempt to recapture the Falkland Islands.

LUCE, Clare Boothe

American writer and diplomat (1903–87)

4 Stuffed Shirts.

There seems to be an urge among obituary writers to credit the recently deceased with the coining of phrases, even when the facts do not really support it. Patrick Brogan writing of Mrs Luce in *The Independent* (12 October 1987) stated: 'She wrote a series of articles poking fun at the rich and pompous, coining for them the descriptive phrase "stuffed shirts", a title she used for her first book.' That book was published in 1933, but the *OED2* has an example of the phrase dating from 1913 (when Luce was a mere ten), which makes it clear that by then it was already current US usage. So though she may have re-popularized the phrase she certainly did not coin it.

5 Nature abhors a virgin – a frozen asset.

Quoted in Fred Metcalf, *Penguin Dictionary of Modern Humorous Quotations* (1987). *Compare* RABELAIS 445:1.

See also PARKER 424:9.

LUDENDORFF, Erich

German general (1865–1937)

6 Lions led by donkeys.

On British troops in the First World War. Sometimes misascribed to Ludendorff, whereas the real credit for the phrase should go to General Max Hoffman (1869–1927), who succeeded Ludendorff as chief of the German general staff in 1916. Alan Clark in a book called *The Donkeys* (1961) quotes a slightly different version of the exchange as its epigraph:

> *Ludendorff*: The English soldiers fight like lions.
> *Hoffman*: True. But don't we know that they are lions led by donkeys.

Clark gives the source as Field Marshal von Falkenhayn's memoirs – but the exchange remains untraced. One wonders if Clark might have invented it himself?

LUMLEY, Joanna

English actress (1946–)

7 I had no wish to tiptoe into old age alone.

Explaining the reason for her re-marriage. So quoted in *The Observer* 'Sayings of the Week' column on 23 November 1986. On 4 January 1987, *The Observer* stated that Ms Lumley claimed she had never actually made the remark to the *Daily Mail* journalist who had attributed it to her in an interview (and in a headline) the previous November. In fact, it transpired that the journalist had not even put the remark in her copy – it was added in the editing stage.

LUTHER, Martin

German Protestant theologian (1483–1546)

1 *Hier stehe ich. Ich kann nicht anders. Gott helfe mir. Amen.*

Here I stand. I can do no other. God help me. Amen.

Speech at the Diet of Worms (18 April 1521). Attributed. Following Luther's attack on the doctrinal system of the Church of Rome, a papal bull was issued against him. He burned it in Wittenberg. When the Emperor Charles V convened his diet at Worms, an order was issued for the destruction of Luther's books and he was summoned to justify himself before the diet.

LUTYENS, Sir Edwin

English architect (1869–1944)

2 The piece of cod passeth all understanding.

When Lutyens's son, Robert, was attempting to write a book about his father, they met for lunch at the Garrick Club in London so that Sir Edwin could make known his views on the project and its author. When the matter was broached, however, Sir Edwin, embarrassed, merely exclaimed, 'Oh, my!' Then, as the fish was served, he looked at his son over the *two* pairs of spectacles he was wearing and made the above comment. Recounted in Robert Lutyens, *Sir Edwin Lutyens* (1942). *Compare* BIBLE 104:10; JAMES I 311:1.

3 The answer is in the plural and they bounce.

Said to have been the response given by Lutyens to a Royal Commission (quoted without source in *PDMQ*, 1971). However, according to Robert Jackson, *The Chief* (1959), when Gordon (later Lord) Hewart was in the House of Commons, he was answering questions on behalf of David Lloyd George. For some time, one afternoon, he had given answers in the customary brief parliamentary manner – 'The answer is in the affirmative' or 'the answer is in the negative'. After one such noncommittal reply, several members arose to bait Hewart with a series of rapid supplementary questions. He waited until they had all finished and then replied: 'The answer is in the plural!'

LYTE, H.F.

English clergyman and hymnwriter (1793–1847)

4 Change and decay in all around I see;
O Thou, who changest not, abide with me.

Hymn 'Abide With Me' (*c.*1847). Possibly inspired by Luke 24:29: 'Abide with us: for it is toward evening, and the day is far spent.'

M

McALPINE, Sir Alfred

British civil engineer (1881–1944)

1 Keep Paddy behind the big mixer.

Attributed last words, presumably encouraging the use of Irish labour in British building works. Unverified. Could it rather have been said by Robert McAlpine, another member of the family?

MacARTHUR, Douglas

American general (1880–1964)

2 I shall return.

MacArthur was forced by the Japanese to pull out of the Philippines and left Corregidor on 11 March 1942. On 20 March he made his commitment to return when he arrived by train at Adelaide. He had journeyed southwards across Australia and was just about to set off eastwards for Melbourne. So, although he had talked in these terms before leaving the Philippines, his main statement was delivered not there but on Australian soil. At the station, a crowd awaited him and he had scrawled a few words on the back of an envelope: 'The President of the United States ordered me to break through the Japanese lines and proceed from Corregidor to Australia for the purpose, as I understand it, of organizing the American offensive against Japan, a primary object of which is the relief of the Philippines. I came through and I shall return.'

MacArthur had intended his first words to have the most impact – as a way of getting the war in the Pacific a higher priority – but it was his last three words that caught on. The Office of War Information tried to get him to amend them to '*We* shall return', foreseeing that there would be objections to a slogan which seemed to imply that he was all-important and that his men mattered little. MacArthur refused. In fact, the phrase had first been suggested to a MacArthur aide in the form '*We* shall return' by a Filipino journalist, Carlos Romulo. 'America has let us down and won't be trusted,' Romulo had said. 'But the people still have confidence in MacArthur. If he says he is coming back, he will be believed.' The suggestion was passed to MacArthur who adopted it – but adapted it.

MacArthur later commented: '"I shall return" seemed a promise of magic to the Filipinos. It lit a flame that became a symbol which focused the nation's indomitable will and at whose shrine it finally attained victory and, once again, found freedom. It was scraped in the sands of the beaches, it was daubed on the walls of the *barrios*, it was stamped on the mail, it was whispered in the cloisters of the church. It became the battle cry of a great underground swell that no Japanese bayonet could still.'

As William Manchester wrote in *American Caesar* (1978): 'That it had this great an impact is doubtful ... but unquestionably it appealed to an unsophisticated oriental people. Throughout the war American submarines provided Filipino guerrillas with cartons of buttons, gum, playing cards, and matchboxes bearing the message.

On 20 October 1944, MacArthur *did* return. Landing at Leyte, he said, against a background of still continuing gunfire: 'People of the Philippines, I have returned ... By the grace of Almighty God, our forces stand again upon Philippine soil.'

3 In war there is no substitute for victory.

Speech to Congress (19 April 1951). President Truman sacked MacArthur from his command of UN forces in Korea for repeatedly criticizing the administration's policy of non-confrontation with China. Even so, Truman had to allow MacArthur a hero's return home and a chance to address Congress.

4 The world has turned over many times since I took the oath on the Plain at West Point, and the hopes and dreams have long since van-

ished. But I still remember the refrain of one of the most popular barrack ballads of that day, which proclaimed, most proudly, that old soldiers never die. They just fade away. And like the old soldier of that ballad, I now close my military career and just fade away – an old soldier who tried to do his duty as God gave him the light to see that duty. Goodbye.

Ib., conclusion. In fact, the ballad quoted by MacArthur, and which he dated as 'turn of the century', was a British Army song of the First World War. It is a parody of the gospel hymn 'Kind Words Can Never Die'. J. Foley copyrighted a version of the parody in 1920. The more usual form of the words is, 'Old soldiers never die – they simply fade away.'

MACAULAY, Thomas (1st Baron Macaulay)

English historian, poet and politician (1800–59)

1 The gallery in which the reporters sit has become a fourth estate of the realm.

In 1828, Macaulay wrote this in *The Edinburgh Review* of the Press representatives in the House of Commons – i.e., 'fourth estate' after the Lords Spiritual, the Lords Temporal, and the Commons – but a number of others have also been credited with the coinage. Edmund Burke, for example, is said to have pointed at the press gallery and remarked: 'And yonder sits the fourth estate, more important than them all.'

The phrase was originally used to describe various forces outside Parliament – such as the Army (as by Falkland in 1638) or the Mob (as by Fielding in 1752). When William Hazlitt used it in 'Table Talk' in 1821, he meant not the press in general but just William Cobbett. Two years later, Lord Brougham is said to have used the phrase in the House of Commons to describe the press in general. So when Macaulay wrote, it was obviously an established expression. Then Carlyle used it several times – in his article on Boswell's *Life of Johnson* in 1832, in his *History of the French Revolution* in 1837 and in his lectures 'On Heroes, Hero-Worship, & the Heroic in History' in 1841. But he attributed the phrase to Burke (who died in 1797). It has been suggested that the BBC (or the broadcast media in general) now constitute a *fifth* estate, as also, at one time, did the trades unions.

2 It was about the lovely close of a warm summer day,
There came a gallant merchant-ship full sail to Plymouth Bay.

Poem, 'The Armada' (1833), describing how the news of the Spanish Armada in 1588 was flashed across England from beacon to beacon.

3 As every schoolboy knows.

Robert Burton wrote 'Every schoolboy hath the famous testament of Grunius Corocotta Porcellus at his fingers' ends' in *The Anatomy of Melancholy* (1621) and Bishop Jeremy Taylor used the expression 'every schoolboy knows it' in 1654. In the next century, Jonathan Swift had 'to tell what everybody schoolboy knows'. But the most noted user of this rather patronizing phrase was Macaulay who would say things like, 'Every schoolboy knows who imprisoned Montezuma, and who strangled Atahualpa' (essay on 'Lord Clive', January 1840).

4 Lars Porsena of Clusium
By the nine gods he swore
That the great house of Tarquin
Should suffer wrong no more.

'Horatius', *Lays of Ancient Rome* (1842). Hence, *Lars Porsena, or the Future of Swearing and Improper Language*, title of a short study (1920) by Robert Graves.

5 We know of no spectacle so ridiculous as the British public in one of its periodical fits of morality.

'Moore's *Life of Byron*', in *Essays Contributed to the Edinburgh Review.* (1843). A frequently paraded observation, not least during the Profumo scandal in Britain in 1963. Has been misattributed to Oscar Wilde, whose treatment might well have been another occasion for quoting it.

McAULIFFE, Anthony C.

American general (1898–1975)

6 Nuts!

In December 1944, the Germans launched a counter-offensive in what came to be known as the Battle of the Bulge. 'Old Crock' McAuliffe was acting commander of the American 101st Airborne Division and was ordered to defend the strategic town of Bastogne in the Ardennes forest. This was important because Bastogne stood at a Belgian crossroads through which the advancing armies had to pass. When the Americans had been surrounded like 'the hole in a doughnut' for seven days, the Germans said they would accept a surrender. On 23 December, McAuliffe replied: 'Nuts!'

The Germans first of all interpreted this one word reply as meaning 'crazy' and took time to appreciate what they were being told. Encouraged by McAuliffe's spirit, his men managed to hold the line and thus defeat the last major enemy offensive of the war.

McAuliffe recounted the episode in a BBC broadcast on 3 January 1945: 'When we got [the surrender demand] we thought it was the funniest thing we ever heard. I just laughed and said, "Nuts", but the German major who brought it wanted a formal answer; so I decided – well, I'd just say "Nuts", so I had it written out: "QUOTE, TO THE GERMAN COMMANDER: NUTS. SIGNED, THE AMERICAN COMMANDER UNQUOTE".'

When Agence France Presse sought a way of translating this it resorted to, '*Vous n'êtes que de vieilles noix* [You are only old fogeys]' – although '*noix*' in French slang also carries the same testicular meaning as 'nuts' in English. When McAuliffe's obituary came to be written, *The New York Times* observed: 'Unofficial versions strongly suggest that the actual language used by the feisty American general was considerably stronger and more profane than the comparatively mild "Nuts", but the official version will have to stand.'

MacCARTHY, Sir Desmond

English writer and critic (1877–1952)

1 [Journalists are] more attentive to the minute hand of history than to the hour hand.

Quoted by Kenneth Tynan in a 1958 article collected in *Curtains* (1961), but otherwise unverified.

McCARTHY, Mary

American writer (1912–89)

2 I once said in an interview that every word she writes is a lie, including 'and' and 'the'.

On Lillian Hellman, in *The New York Times* (16 February 1980). The remark was probably made on the TV *Dick Cavett Show* (25–26 January 1980). It prompted a $2 million lawsuit but Hellman died before a judgement.

McCARTNEY, Paul *See* LENNON, JOHN, AND McCARTNEY, PAUL

McCORMICK, Peter Dodds

Scottish-born Australian songwriter (1834–1916)

3 Australia's sons, let us rejoice,
For we are young and free,
We've golden soil and wealth for toil,
Our home is girt by sea;
Our land abounds in nature's gifts
Of beauty rich and rare;
In hist'ry's page, let ev'ry stage
Advance Australia Fair,
In joyful strains then let us sing
Advance Australia fair.

The song 'Advance Australia Fair' was first performed in Sydney in 1878, but the alliterative phrase 'Advance Australia' had existed much earlier when Michael Massey Robinson wrote in the *Sydney Gazette* (1 February 1826): '"ADVANCE THEN, AUSTRALIA",/ Be this thy proud gala/ ... And thy watch-word be "FREEDOM FOR EVER!"'

'Advance Australia' became the motto of the Commonwealth of Australia when the states united in 1901. In the 1970s and 1980s, as republicanism grew, it acquired the force of a slogan and was used in various campaigns to promote national pride (sometimes as 'Let's Advance Australia'). In 1984, 'Advance Australia Fair' superseded 'God Save the Queen' as the national anthem. The first line became 'Australians all let us rejoice ...' McCormick's second verse was mostly ignored:

When gallant Cook from Albion sailed
To trace wide oceans o'er,
True British courage bore him on
Till he landed on our shore.
Then here he raised Old England's flag,
The standard of the brave.
With all her faults we love her still
Britannia rules the wave.
In joyful strains then let us sing,
Advance Australia Fair.

McCOY, Horace

American writer (1897–1955)

4 They Shoot Horses, Don't They?

Title of novel (1935; film US, 1969). Meaning, 'Well, if he was a horse, they'd shoot him, such is his condition.' McCoy may have originated this modern proverbial expression.

McCRAE, John

Canadian poet (1872–1918)

5 In Flanders fields the poppies blow
Between the crosses, row on row,
That mark our place; and in the sky

The larks, still bravely singing, fly
Scarce heard amid the guns below.

From 'In Flanders Fields', written after the second Battle of Ypres and sent anonymously to *Punch* where it was published on 8 December 1915. McCrae was a Canadian academic turned volunteer medical officer. He himself died of wounds in a Normandy hospital in May 1918. His poem was the inspiration for the Poppy Day appeals which became an annual event from 1921, raising money for ex-servicemen. These appeals have been described as the best marketing idea in the history of charities.

1 If ye break faith with us who die
We shall not sleep, though poppies grow
On Flanders fields.

McCrae's own reputed last words ('Tell them this: If ye break faith with us who die we shall not sleep') are taken from the last lines of the same poem.

McCULLERS, Carson

American novelist (1917–67)

2 The Heart Is a Lonely Hunter.

Title of novel (1940; film US, 1968), about a deaf mute. Taken from 'The Lonely Hunter' – 'My heart is a lonely hunter that hunts on a lonely hill' – by the Scottish novelist and poet William Sharp (1855–1905).

McENROE, John

American tennis champion (1959–)

3 Man, you cannot be serious.

To umpire at Wimbledon (June 1981). By this date, McEnroe, eventually holder of three Wimbledon singles titles, had become celebrated for his 'Superbrat' behaviour towards umpires and linesmen, telling them 'You are the pits' and such like. 'You cannot be serious!' was elevated to catchphrase status through various show biz take-offs, including Roger Kitter's record, 'Chalk Dust – The Umpire Strikes Back' (UK, 1982).

McGILL, Donald

English comic postcard artist (1875–1962)

4 Can't see my little Willy.

McGill drew his first comic postcard in 1905 and, judging by the style and appearance of one of his most famous cards, it probably dates from within the next ten to fifteen years. The card shows a fat man with an enormous stomach (or 'corporation') which prevents him from seeing the small boy seated at his feet. The double-entendre in the caption is signed prominently by the artist.

'I've lost my little Willie!' (which rather obscures the joke) was used as the title of a 'celebration of comic postcards' (1976) by Benny Green. This book title may have been taken from the caption to a re-drawing of the idea by another cartoonist.

5 'Do you like Kipling?'
'I don't know, you naughty boy, I've never kippled.'

This caption to one of McGill's postcards – undated, but possibly from the 1930s – might just be the origin of a little joke. However, J.K. Stephen (1859–92) had already seen the possibilities in the name in his poem 'To R.K.' which ends:

When the Rudyards cease from kipling
And the Haggards ride no more.

McGONAGALL, William

Scottish poet (c.1830–1902)

6 Beautiful Railway Bridge of the Silv'ry Tay!
Alas, I am very sorry to say
That ninety lives have been taken away
On the last Sabbath day of 1879,
Which will be remember'd for a very long time.

'The Tay Bridge Disaster' (1890). McGonagall is usually considered to be the most splendidly bad poet in the world. He really did exist.

McGOVERN, George

American Democratic politician (1922–)

7 I am one thousand per cent for Tom Eagleton and I have no intention of dropping him from the ticket.

On his vice-presidential running mate. Attributed in 1972. He dropped him shortly afterwards.

MACHIAVELLI, Niccolò

Florentine politician and philosopher (1469–1527)

8 There is nothing more difficult to take in hand, nor perilous to conduct, or more uncertain in its success, than the introduction of a new order of things, because the innovator has for

enemies all those who have done well under the old conditions, and lukewarm defenders in those who may do well under the new.

The Prince Chap. 6 (1532). Marmaduke Hussey, a beleaguered Chairman of the BBC, admitted in an interview with the *Independent on Sunday* (16 December 1991) that he clung to this quotation which was 'provided by an ally [I] turned to for advice'.

McKINNEY, Joyce

American beauty queen (1950–)

1 I loved Kirk so much, I would have skied down Mount Everest in the nude with a carnation up my nose.

A former Miss Wyoming, McKinney was charged in an English court with kidnapping Kirk Anderson, a Mormon missionary and her ex-lover. She allegedly abducted Mr Anderson to a remote country cottage where he was chained to a bed and forced to make love to her. In Epsom Magistrates' Court (6 December 1977) McKinney told a stunned jury of her feelings in the matter.

MACKINTOSH, Sir James

Scottish historian and philosopher (1765–1832)

2 The commons, faithful to their system, remained in a wise and masterly inactivity.

Vindiciae Gallicae (1791). Mackintosh was writing about the 'third estate' at the first session of the Estates General summoned in France in 1789. Alan Watkins in *The Observer* (19 February 1989) ascribed the phrase to the 3rd Marquess of Salisbury (the British Prime Minister), when writing of 'Mr Nigel Lawson's display of masterly inactivity'. In the US Vice-President John C. Calhoun told the South Carolina legislature in 1831: 'If the Government should be taught thereby, that the highest wisdom of a State is a "wise and masterly inactivity", an invaluable blessing will be conferred. Benham (1948) compares Horace – '*strenua nos exercet inertia* [strenuous inertia urges us on]'.

MACLEISH, Archibald

American poet (1892–1982)

3 To see the earth as it truly is, small and blue and beautiful in that eternal silence where it floats, is to see ourselves as riders on the earth together, brothers on that bright loveliness in the eternal cold – brothers who know they are truly brothers.

Written for *The New York Times* (25 December 1968) after an Apollo space mission returned with a photograph that showed the earth as seen from beyond the moon. Macleish revised the wording to provide an epigraph for his *Riders on the Earth* (1978): 'To see the earth as we now see it, small and blue and beautiful in that eternal silence where it floats, is to see ourselves as riders on the earth together; brothers on that bright loveliness in the unending night – brothers who *see* now they are truly brothers.'

MACLEOD, Iain

British Conservative politician (1913–70)

4 History is too serious to be left to historians.

Quoted in *The Observer* (16 July 1961). *See also* BENN 84:3; CLEMENCEAU 173:4; DE GAULLE 199:6.

5 It is some measure of the tightness of the magic circle on this occasion that neither the Chancellor of the Exchequer nor the Leader of the House of Commons had any inkling of what was happening.

On the method of choosing the Conservative Party leader in 1963. Article in *The Spectator* (17 January 1964). Sometimes rendered as 'magic circle of Old Etonians'. Macleod was describing the way in which the leader, although supposedly just 'emerging', was in fact the choice of a small group of influential Tory peers and manipulators. In the present case, they ensured that Alec Douglas-Home succeeded Harold Macmillan over the claims of R.A. Butler. Macmillan had said: 'I hope that it will soon be possible for the customary process of consultation to be carried out within the party about its future leadership.

A year or two later, and as a result of this experience, the Tory leadership came to be decided instead by a ballot of Conservative MPs.

6 The nanny state.

On over-protective government, in *Spectator* articles (1960s). Unverified. In the 1980s this derogatory term came to be adopted by Thatcherites, who deplored the socialist, Welfare State support for a public they believed should be left to sink or swim in the face of the normal forces acting upon society.

7 We now have the worst of both worlds – not just inflation on the one side or stagnation on

the other side, but both of them together. We have a sort of 'stagflation' situation.

Speech, House of Commons (17 November 1965). Coinage of another standard term in British politics, for stagnant demand coupled with severe inflation.

MACLEOD, Norman

Scottish theologian (1812–72)

1 Courage brother! do not stumble,
Though thy path be dark as night;
There's a star to guide the humble;
Trust in God, and do the Right.

From 'Trust in God'. This may be the source of the expression 'Trust in God, and do the right', which has been much used subsequently as a gravestone inscription. For example, it appears on the grave of Douglas, 1st Earl Haig (1861–1928), in the ruins of Dryburgh Abbey, Berwickshire (Borders). Haig was Commander-in-Chief of British forces in France and Flanders for most of the First World War. The headstone, at Haig's request, is identical to those in the cemeteries of France. A notice near the grave suggests that the wording of the epitaph was that used on many graves of First World War dead of lower rank. ('For God and the right' is another form of this motto-like idea.)

McLUHAN, Marshall

Canadian writer (1911–80)

2 The new electronic interdependence recreates the world in the image of a global village.

The Gutenberg Galaxy (1962). Hence, *David Frost's Global Village*, title of an occasional Yorkshire TV series (from 1979) in which Frost discussed global issues with pundits beamed in by satellite.

3 The medium is the message.

Understanding Media (1964). McLuhan's basic tenet: that the form of the media has a more significant effect on society than anything they have to say.

See also LEARY 347:2.

McMAHON, Ed

American broadcaster (1923–)

4 Here's Johnny!

Said with a drawn-out, rising inflection on the first word, this was McMahon's introduction to Johnny Carson on NBC TV's *Tonight* show in the US (from 1961 until the early 1990s). In full, what McMahon (a former circus clown) said was: [Drum roll] 'And now ... heeeeere's Johnny!' It was emulated during Simon Dee's brief reign as a chat-show host in Britain during the 1960s. The studio audience joined in the rising inflection of the announcer's 'It's Siiiiimon Dee!' Jack Nicholson, playing a psychopath, chopped through a door with an axe and cried 'Here's Johnny!' in the film *The Shining* (1981).

MACMAHON, Comte Maurice de

French general (1808–93)

5 *J'y suis et j'y reste.*
Here I am, and here I stay.

Said at the taking of the Malakoff fortress during the Crimean War (8 September 1855). In his home at the Château de Sully is an engraving of Macmahon standing on the parapet of a Russian gun position at Sebastopol, which has just been captured after heavy opposition. An English sailor, approaching the general to warn him that the position is mined, receives the reply: '*Libre à vous porter où vous voulez, quant à moi, j'y suis et j'y reste* [Up to you to go where you like, as for me, here I am and here I stay].'

MACMILLAN, Harold (later 1st Earl of Stockton)

English Conservative Prime Minister (1894–1986)

6 The Middle Way.

Title of book (1938), setting out the arguments for a middle course in politics, that is to say, one occupying 'the middle ground' between extremes. Not unexpectedly, the phrase had been used before – indeed, it dates back to the thirteenth century. *See also* ADAMS 12:5. Winston Churchill ended an election address on 11 November 1922 by saying: 'What we require now is not a period of turmoil, but a period of stability and recuperation. Let us stand together and tread a sober middle way.' The 'Middle Way' is also believed to be a tenet of Buddhism.

7 There ain't gonna be no war.

As Foreign Secretary to Prime Minister Eden, Macmillan attended a four-power summit conference at Geneva where the chief topic for discussion was German reunification. Nothing much was achieved but the 'Geneva spirit' was optimistic and on his return to London he breezily said this to a press conference on 24 July 1955. The phrase is, without doubt, a direct quote from the *c.*1910 music-hall song, which was sung in a raucous cockney accent by a certain Mr Pélissier (1879–1913) in a show called 'Pélissier's Follies' during the reign of Edward VII:

There ain't going to be no waar
So long as we've a king like Good King Edward.
'E won't 'ave it, 'cos 'e 'ates that sort of fing.
Muvvers, don't worry,
Not wiv a king like Good King Edward.
Peace wiv honour is 'is motter [*snort*] –
Gawd save the King!

Sir David Hunt confirmed (1988) that it was the Pélissier song that Macmillan had in mind. In fact, he (Hunt) had sung it to him on one occasion. Coincidentally, some time before December 1941, an American called Frankl *did* write a song called, precisely, 'There Ain't Gonna Be No War'.

1 A Foreign Secretary – and this applies also to a prospective Foreign Secretary – is always faced with this cruel dilemma. Nothing he can say can do very much good, and almost anything he may say may do a great deal of harm. Anything he says that is not obvious is dangerous; whatever is not trite is risky. He is forever poised between the cliché and the indiscretion.

Speech, House of Commons (27 July 1955). In *Newsweek* Magazine (30 April 1956), Macmillan was also quoted as having said that his life as Foreign Secretary was 'forever poised between a cliché and an indiscretion.' *Compare* RUNCIE 464:1.

2 Let's be frank about it. Most of our people have never had it so good. Go around the country, go to the industrial towns, go to the farms, and you'll see a state of prosperity such as we have never had in my lifetime – nor indeed ever in the history of this country. What is beginning to worry some of us is 'Is it too good to be true?' or perhaps I should say 'Is it too good to last?' For amidst all this prosperity, there is one problem that has troubled us, in one way or another, ever since the war. It is the problem of rising prices. Our constant concern is: Can prices be steadied while at the same time we maintain full employment in an expanding economy? Can we control inflation?'

Speech at Bedford (20 July 1957). 'You've never had it so good' is a phrase that will forever be linked with Macmillan's name but, as will be clear from the above, his first use of the idea was in the context not of a boast but a warning.

Macmillan is said to have appropriated the phrase from Lord Robens (a former Labour minister who had rejected socialism and who had used the phrase in conversation with the Prime Minister not long before). However, as 'You Never Had It So Good', it had been a slogan used by the Democrats in the 1952 US Presidential election. As early as 1946, *American Speech* (Vol. 21) was commenting on that phrase: 'This is a sardonic response to complaints about the Army; it is probably supposed to represent the attitude of a peculiarly offensive type of officer.'

In his memoirs, Macmillan commented: 'For some reason it was not until several years later that this phrase was taken out of its context and turned into a serious charge against me, of being too materialistic and showing too little of a spiritual approach to life ... curiously enough these are the inevitable hazards to which all politicians are prone.'

Given the way the phrase came to dog him, it would have been surprising if it had ever been used as an official Tory party slogan. It was rejected – in so many words – for the 1959 general election by the Conservatives' publicity group, partly because it 'violated a basic advertising axiom that statements should be positive, not negative'. There was, however, an official poster that came very close with, 'You're Having It Good, Have It Better'.

3 I thought the best thing to do was to settle up these little local difficulties, and then turn to the wider vision of the Commonwealth.

Statement at London Airport, as Prime Minister, before leaving for a tour of the Commonwealth (7 January 1958). A characteristically airy reference to the fact that his entire Treasury team, including the Chancellor of the Exchequer, had resigned over a disagreement about budget estimates. So 'little local difficulties' became a phrase used to demonstrate a dismissive lack of concern.

4 Jaw-jaw is better than war-war.

On 30 January 1958 in Canberra, Australia, Macmillan consciously echoed a saying of Winston Churchill's – 'To jaw-jaw is always better than to war-war' – which Churchill had uttered at a White House luncheon in Washington, DC, on 26 June 1954.

5 What matters is that Mr Macmillan has let Mr [Selwyn] Lloyd know that at the Foreign

Office, in these troubled times, enough is enough.

Report, *The Times* (1 June 1959). Having fed this view to the newspaper, Macmillan was prevented by the fuss it caused from firing Lloyd and the Foreign Secretary remained in place for a further year. This helped popularize the phrase 'enough is enough' – a basic expression of exasperation often employed in political personality clashes – though usually without result. *Compare* DAILY MIRROR 195:1.

1 Exporting is fun.

A Macmillan slogan that misfired, though in this instance he never actually said it. The phrase was included in a 1960 address to businessmen, but when Macmillan came to read the passage he left out what was later considered to be a rather patronizing remark. The press, however, printed what was in the advance text of the speech as though he had actually said it.

Compare the earlier Labour slogan, 'We must export – or die', which arose out of a severe balance of payments problem under the Labour government in 1945–6.

2 The most striking of all the impressions I have formed since I left London a month ago is of the strength of this African national consciousness. In different places it may take different forms, but it is happening everywhere. The wind of change is blowing through this continent. Whether we like it or not, this growth of national consciousness is a political fact.

Speaking to both houses of the South African parliament on 3 February 1960, Macmillan gave his hosts a message they cannot have wanted to hear. The phrase 'wind of change' – though not, of course, original – was contributed to the speechwriting team by the diplomat (later Sir) David Hunt. The *OED2* acknowledges that the use of the phrase 'wind(s) of change' increased markedly after this speech. When Macmillan sought a title for one of his volumes of memoirs he plumped for the more common, plural usage – *Winds of Change. Compare* BALDWIN 73:2.

3 As usual, the Liberals offer a mixture of sound and original ideas. Unfortunately none of the sound ideas is original and none of the original ideas is sound.

Speech to London Conservatives (7 March 1961). Compare what is ascribed to Dr Samuel Johnson: 'Your manuscript is both good and original; but the part that is good is not original, and the part that is original is not good.' Quoted in *The Treasury of Humorous Quotations*, ed. by Evan Esar & Nicolas Bentley (1951).

4 She didn't say yes, she didn't say no ...

The song 'She Didn't Say Yes' by Otto Harbach and Jerome Kern from the musical *The Cat and the Fiddle* (1931) was memorably quoted by Macmillan when Prime Minister in October 1962. Speaking to the Conservative Party Conference at Llandudno he referred to the Labour Party's attitude to the government's attempts (from July 1961) to open negotiations for Britain's entry to the European Common Market: 'What did the socialists do? ... They solemnly asked Parliament not to approve or disapprove, but to "take note" of our decision. Perhaps some of the older ones among you [oh, wonderful Macmillanism!] will remember that popular song –

"She didn't say yes, she didn't say no,
She didn't say stay, she didn't say go.
She wanted to climb, but dreaded to fall,
She bided her time and clung to the wall".'

Private Eye – perhaps inspired by a recent American record that had taken President Kennedy's inaugural speech and added a music track – put out a record of Macmillan 'singing' the song to a tinny 1960s backing. Very droll it was, too, and now sadly evocative of a bygone era.

5 Power? It's like a Dead Sea fruit; when you achieve it, there's nothing there.

Quoted in *Queen* Magazine (22 May 1963). Compare Thomas Moore, *Lalla Rookh* (1817): 'Like Dead Sea fruits, that tempt the eye,/But turn to ashes on the lips!' In *Brewer's Politics* (1995), Macmillan's saying is delightfully misquoted as, 'like a *seafront*; when you achieve it, there's nothing there.'

6 I was determined that no British Government should be brought down by the action of two tarts.

Attributed remark (13 July 1963), referring to the Profumo Affair, quoted in Anthony Sampson, *Macmillan* (1967). Alternatively, 'I was not going to have the British Government pulled down by the antics of a whore.'

7 I hope that it will soon be possible for the customary processes of consultation to be carried on within the party about its future leadership.

On his resignation as Prime Minister. Statement (read

by R.A. Butler) to Conservative Party Conference (10 October 1963).

1 There are three bodies no sensible man directly challenges: the Roman Catholic Church, the Brigade of Guards and the National Union of Mineworkers.

Quoted in *The Observer* (22 February 1981). *Compare* BALDWIN 73:6.

2 Mogadon Man.

Of Sir Geoffrey Howe. Ascribed by Anthony Howard in *The Independent* (29 July 1989).

3 Although at my age I cannot interfere or do anything about it, it breaks my heart to see what is happening in our country today. A terrible strike is being carried on by the best men in the world. They beat the Kaiser's army and they beat Hitler's army. They never gave in.

Maiden speech in the House of Lords (13 November 1984). The strike referred to was by miners. How their forebears managed to win two world wars was not made clear. In fact, some miners who remained at home engaged in strikes while the First World War was still being fought.

4 [The sale of assets is common with individuals and the state when they run into financial difficulties ...] First of all the Georgian silver goes, and then all that nice furniture that used to be in the saloon. Then the Canalettos go.

Summarized as 'selling off the family silver', meaning 'to dispose of valuable assets which, once gone, cannot be retrieved', this allusion was memorably used in a speech to the Tory Reform Group by Macmillan, by then Earl of Stockton, on 8 November 1985. He was questioning the government's policy of privatizing profitable nationalized industries.

5 Memorial services are the cocktail parties of the geriatric set.

Quoted in Alastair Horne, *Macmillan 1957–1986* (1989). In Ruth Dudley Edwards, *Harold Macmillan: a life in pictures* (1983), Macmillan (who is purported to have written the picture captions) states: 'I rather agree with Ralph Richardson [the actor] that Memorial Services are the "cocktail parties of the geriatric set".'

MAETERLINCK, Maurice

Belgian poet and playwright (1862–1949)

6 The living are just the dead on holiday.

Quoted in *The Treasury of Humorous Quotations*, ed. by Evan Esar & Nicolas Bentley (1951). Unverified. In his play *L'Oiseau Blue* (1909) there is the line, 'There are no dead.' In a 1980 episode of BBC TV's *Dr Who* ('Destiny of the Daleks'), scripted by Terry Nation, there is the question: 'Who was it that said the living are the dead on holiday?'

MAFFEY, Sir John (later 1st Baron Rugby)

British diplomat (1877–1969)

7 This temperamental country [Ireland] needs quiet treatment and a patient, consistent policy. But how are you to control Ministerial incursions into your china shop? Phrases make history here.

As British Ambassador in Dublin, in a letter to the Dominions Office in London (21 May 1945), quoted in Robert Fisk, *In Time of War* (1985). Maffey's official title was UK Representative to Eire, which he was from 1939–49. John Betjeman, the poet, was his Press Attaché (1941–3).

MAGEE, John Gillespie

Anglo-American air force pilot and poet (1922–41)

8 Oh! I have slipped the surly bonds of Earth,
And danced the skies on laughter-silvered
wings;
... And, while with silent lifting mind I've trod
The high untrespassed sanctity of space,
Put out my hand, and touched the face of
God.

From 'High Flight', a sonnet written by Magee, a pilot with the Royal Canadian Air Force in the Second World War. He came to Britain, flew in a Spitfire squadron, and was killed at the age of nineteen on 11 December 1941 during a training flight from the airfield near Scopwick, Lincolnshire (where the first and last lines appear on his grave). Magee had been born in Shanghai of an American father and an English mother who were missionaries. He was educated at Rugby and at a school in Connecticut. The sonnet was written on the back of a letter to his parents which stated, 'I am enclosing a verse I wrote the other day. It started at 30,000 feet, and was finished soon after I landed.' The parents were living in Washington, DC, at the time of his death and, according to *Respectfully Quoted* (1989), the poem came to the attention of the Librarian of Congress, Archibald MacLeish, who acclaimed Magee as the first poet of the war.

'High Flight' was published in 1943 in a volume called *More Poems from the Forces* (which was 'Dedicated to the USSR'). Copies of the poem – sometimes referred to as 'the pilot's creed' – were widely distributed and plaques bearing it were sent to all R.C.A.F. airfields and training stations. It became very much the pilot's poem the world over. The lines became even more famous when President Reagan quoted them on 28 January 1986 in his TV broadcast to the nation on the day of the space shuttle *Challenger* disaster.

Two footnotes: in his lyrics for the English version of the musical *Les Misérables* (1985), Herbert Kretzmer blended Magee's words with something from Evelyn Waugh's *Brideshead Revisited* ('to know and love another human being is the root of all wisdom') to produce the line: 'To love another person is to see the face of God.' Magee's original words are curiously reminiscent of Oscar Wilde's lines prefixed to his *Poems* (Paris edition, 1903):

> Surely there was a time I might have trod
> The sunlit heights, and from life's dissonance
> Struck one clear chord to reach the ears of God.

MAGRITTE, René

Belgian Surrealist painter (1898–1967)

1 *Ceci n'est pas une pipe.*
This is not a pipe.

Written beneath the profile of a tobacco pipe in an oil painting called '*La trahison des images* [the treachery of images]' (1929). His interest was in words as images and in achieving a realization in paint of his belief that 'everything tends to suggest that there is little connection between an object and what represents it.' Magritte also painted '*Ceci est un morceau de fromage*' in which a painting of a piece of cheese is shown inside a glass cheese dome.

MAGUIRE, William H.

American sailor (1890–1953)

2 Praise the Lord and pass the ammunition!

Said in 1941, and subsequently used as the title of a song by Frank Loesser (1942). The authorship of this saying is disputed. It may have been said by an American naval chaplain during the Japanese attack on Pearl Harbor. Lieut. Howell M. Forgy (1908–83) is one candidate. He was on board the US cruiser New Orleans on 7 December 1941 and encouraged those around him to keep up the barrage when under attack. His claim is supported by a report in *The New York Times* (1 November 1942).

Another name mentioned is that of Captain W.H. Maguire. At first Captain Maguire did not recall having used the words but a year later said he might have done. Bartlett favours Maguire and makes no mention of Forgy. Either way, the expression may actually date from the time of the American Civil War.

MAJOR, John

British Conservative Prime Minister (1943–)

3 The harsh truth is that if the policy isn't hurting it isn't working. I know there is a difficult period ahead but the important thing is that we cannot and must not fudge the determination to stop inflation in its tracks.

Major had to deliver this speech at Northampton (27 October 1989) on suddenly becoming Chancellor of the Exchequer following the resignation of Nigel Lawson. It had probably been written for his predecessor. In 1996, the Conservative Party tried to capitalize on this 'harsh truth' by producing poster advertisements declaring, 'YES, IT HURTS. YES, IT WORKS.'

Adlai Stevenson said in his speech accepting the Democratic Presidential nomination (26 July 1952): 'Let's talk sense to the American people. Let's tell them the truth, that there are no gains without pains.' 'No pain(s), no gain(s)' is, indeed, a proverb more commonly known in the US and in the form 'no pain, no gain' was used by Jane Fonda in her fitness workouts (by 1984).

4 Well – who would have thought it?

What Major is alleged to have said when opening his first Cabinet meeting. Invariably, bathos is the hallmark of Major's sayings – as in, 'Gentlemen, I think we had better start again, somewhere else', which is what he said after an IRA mortar-bomb attack on Downing Street had caused a large explosion during a Cabinet meeting on 2 February 1991. For a while, he also had a verbal mannerism, 'Oh, yes ... oh, yes.'

5 We Conservatives have always passed our values on, from generation to generation. I believe that personal prosperity should follow

the same course. I want to see wealth cascading down the generations.

Speech, Conservative Party Conference (11 October 1991). This wish proved fruitless for those old people who found that, under Mr Major's government, they had to sell off their property and spend their savings to pay for long-term health care.

1 Fifty years on from now, Britain will still be the country of long shadows on county [cricket] grounds, warm beer, invincible green suburbs, dog lovers and – as George Orwell said – old maids bicycling to Holy Communion through the morning mist.

In a speech on 22 April 1993 to the Conservative Group for Europe, Major sought to show that though the future of Britain lay within Europe, the character of Britain would survive 'unamendable in all essentials'. As his speechwriter acknowledged (for one finds it hard to think that Major spotted it himself), one of Major's lyrical certainties was derived from George Orwell's essay, 'The Lion and the Unicorn: Socialism and the English Genius: Part 1: England Your England', published in *Horizon* (December 1940). The socialist Orwell was, rather, talking about specifically *English* civilization – actually 'old maids *biking* to Holy Communion through the mists of the autumn morning' – which was 'somehow bound up with solid breakfasts and gloomy Sundays, smoky towns and winding roads, green fields and red pillar-boxes'. Orwell also talked rather of the beer being bitterer, the grass greener, and mentioned 'the queues outside the Labour Exchanges' which, for some reason, Major forbore to do.

2 The message from this Conference is clear and simple. We must go back to basics ... The Conservative Party will lead the country back to those basics, right across the board: sound money, free trade; traditional teaching; respect for the family and the law.

A political cliché now but the alliterative phrase (sometimes 'back to *the* basics') may first have surfaced in the US where it was the mid-1970s slogan of a movement in education to give priority to the teaching of the fundamentals of reading, writing and arithmetic. On 8 October 1993, however, Major launched it as a slogan in a speech to the Conservative Party Conference. This text has been checked against a recording of the speech. A number of government scandals in the ensuing months exposed the slogan as hard to interpret or, at worst, suggested a going back to 'the bad old days'.

MALLARMÉ, Stéphane

French poet (1842–98)

3 *Prélude à l'après-midi d'un faune.*
Prelude to the afternoon of a fawn.

Title of poem (*c.*1865). Debussy took the title for his own orchestral work (1894).

MALLORY, George Leigh

English mountaineer (1886–1924)

4 Because it's there.

Mallory disappeared in 1924 on his last attempt to scale Mount Everest. The previous year, during a lecture tour of the US, he had frequently been asked why he wanted to achieve this goal. On one such occasion he replied: 'Because it's there.'

In 1911, at Cambridge, A.C. Benson had urged Mallory to read Carlyle's life of John Sterling – a book that achieved high quality simply 'by being *there*'. Perhaps that is how the construction entered Mallory's mind. On the other hand, Tom Holzel and Audrey Salkeld in *The Mystery of Mallory and Irvine* (1986) suggest that 'the four most famous words in mountaineering' may have been invented for the climber by a reporter named Benson in *The New York Times* (18 March 1923). A report in the *Observer* (2 November 1986) noted that Howard Somervell, one of Mallory's climbing colleagues in the 1924 expedition, declared forty years later that the 'much-quoted remark' had always given him a 'shiver down the spine – it doesn't smell of George Mallory one bit'. Mallory's niece, Mrs B.M. Newton Dunn, claimed in a letter to *The Daily Telegraph* (11 November 1986) that the mountaineer had once given the reply to his sister (Mrs Newton Dunn's mother) 'because a silly question deserves a silly answer'.

The saying has become a catchphrase in situations where the speaker wishes to dismiss an impossible question about motives and also to express his acceptance of a challenge that is in some way daunting or maybe foolish. In September 1962 President Kennedy said: 'We choose to go to the moon in this decade, and do the other things, not because they are easy but because they are hard; because that goal will serve to organize and measure the best of our energies and skills ... Many years ago the great British explorer George Mallory, who was to die on Mount Everest, was asked why did he want to climb it, and he said, "Because it is there". Well, space is there, and ... the moon and the planets are there, and new hopes for knowledge and peace are there.'

There have been many variations (and misattributions). Sir Edmund Hillary repeated it regarding his own attempt on Everest in 1953. It was quoted in John Hunt, *The Ascent of Everest* (1953) which may have contributed to the remark's modern popularity.

MALORY, Sir Thomas

English writer (d.1471)

1 *Hic jacet Arthurus, rex quondam rexque futurus.* Here lies Arthur, the once and future king.

This is what, according to Malory in *Le Morte d'Arthur* (1469–70), was written on the tombstone of the legendary King. Hence, the title of T.H. White's Arthurian romance, *The Once and Future King* (1958). If a King Arthur did exist (possibly in the sixth century AD), there is a notice in the ruins of Glastonbury Abbey, Somerset, which claims to mark the site of his tomb – but no inscription is available.

MANDELA, Nelson

South African nationalist leader and President (1918–)

2 The struggle is my life.

'Letter from the underground' (1961). Quoted beneath the bronze bust of the then prisoner, installed outside the Royal Festival Hall, London (1985).

MANDELA, Winnie

South African political activist (1934–)

3 Together, hand in hand, with our matches and our necklaces, we shall liberate this country.

Remark, quoted in *The Observer* (20 April 1986). The 'necklaces' were car tyres filled with petrol.

MANKIEWICZ, Herman J.

American screenwriter (1897–1953)

4 I think that's what they call professional courtesy.

When a Hollywood agent told him how he had been swimming unscathed in shark-infested waters. Quoted by Dick Vosburgh on BBC Radio, *Quote ... Unquote* (31 July 1979).

5 It's all right, Arthur. The white wine came up with the fish.

Having left the table to be sick, at a formal dinner in the home of the producer Arthur Hornblow Jr. Attributed to Mankiewicz in Max Wilk, *The Wit and Wisdom of Hollywood* (1972). Also attributed to Howard Dietz.

See also CITIZEN KANE 171:5–8.

MANKIEWICZ, Joseph L.

American film producer and writer (1909–93)

6 My native habitat is the theatre. I toil not, neither do I spin. I am a critic and a commentator. I am essential to the theatre – as ants to a picnic, as the boll weevil to a cotton field.

Spoken by George Sanders as the critic 'Addison de Witt'. Film, *All About Eve* (1950). The allusion in the second sentence is to BIBLE 101:2.

See also DAVIS 197:3.

MANN, William

British music critic (1924–89)

7 The outstanding English composers of 1963 must seem to have been John Lennon and Paul McCartney ... the slow sad song about 'That Boy' ... is expressively unusual for its lugubrious music, but harmonically it is one of their most interesting, with its chains of pandiatonic clusters ... so natural is the Aeolian cadence at the end of 'Not a Second Time' (the chord progression which ends Mahler's *Song of the Earth*) ... autocratic but not by any means ungrammatical attitude to tonality ... the quasi-instrumental vocal duetting ... the melismas with altered vowels ...

Reviewing the music of the Beatles in *The Times* (27 December 1963). Not to be confused with BUCKLE 128:7 and PALMER 422:5.

MANNING, Olivia

English novelist (1908–80)

8 Fortunes of War.

Manning's Balkan trilogy of novels and her Levant trilogy form a single narrative with this overall title and the BBC TV adaptation of the six books was called *Fortunes of War* (1985). The earliest citation in *OED2* for the phrase 'fortunes of war' is 1880, but it had long been known in the singular: 'After uncertain fortune of war, on both sides' was written by John Selden in 1612; Charles Dickens, *Sketches by Boz*, Chap. 12 (1833–6) has this cry from a street game: 'All the fortin of war! this time I vin, next time you vin'; the war memorial at the cemetery of El Alamein (following the battle of 1942) is dedicated 'to whom the fortune of war denied a known and honoured grave'.

THE MAN OF LA MANCHA

American musical play (1965; film 1972). Lyrics by Joe Darion, music by Mitch Leigh, based on a play by Dale Wasserman.

1 To dream the impossible dream,
To fight the unbeatable foe,
To bear with unbearable sorrow,
To run where the brave dare not go.

Song, 'The Impossible Dream'. *See also* NIXON 413:1.

MAO ZEDONG (Mao Tse-tung)

Chinese revolutionary and Communist leader (1893–1976)

2 Every Communist must grasp the truth, Political power grows out of the barrel of a gun.

In *Quotations from Chairman Mao Tse-tung* (1966), dated 6 November 1938. The 'little red book' of the Great Helmsman's 'thoughts' was issued during the ideological purge known as the Cultural Revolution (1966–9). It seems likely to have had the widest circulation of any book of quotations ever produced – and certainly of that devoted to one author. Back in 1960, Lin Piao, Minister of Defence, had produced a set of sayings which Mao revised. Next Lin started printing quotations from Mao in the *Liberation Army Daily*. In 1964 a pocket edition was produced for soldiers to carry about with them in their packs and this formed the basis of the first regular edition of the *Quotations* published on 1 August 1965. While not pithy or particularly well expressed, even in translation, the quotations echoed themes that Mao had promoted over a much longer period. As far as one can tell, Mao thought his own 'thoughts' and did not need to have his writings and speeches ghosted. After all, in his younger days he had been a prolific writer on public affairs and wrote poetry almost all his life. To him, therefore, can be ascribed many of the slogans and catchwords of Chinese communism.

3 All reactionaries are paper tigers. In appearance, the reactionaries are terrifying, but in reality they are not powerful.

In *ib.*, from interview with US journalist (1946). A 'paper tiger' is a person who appears outwardly strong but is, in fact, weak. *Paper Tiger* was also the title of a film (UK, 1975) about a coward (David Niven) who pretended to be otherwise until he was finally put to the test. In *Kai Lung Unrolls His Mat* (1928), Ernest Bramah writes: 'Even a paper leopard can put a hornless sheep to flight', and as early as 1900 Bramah uses the precise expression in *The Wallet of Kai Lung*: 'If it is the wish of this illustriously-endowed gathering that this exceedingly illiterate paper tiger should occupy their august moments with a description of ... Chee Chou ...' It should be stressed that Bramah was a lover of chinoiserie rather than an expert Sinologist, and must undoubtedly have come across the phrase in English or some other western language rather than in Chinese.

4 'He who is not afraid of death by a thousand cuts dares to unhorse the emperor' – this is the indomitable spirit needed in our struggle to build socialism and communism.

In *ib.*, though Mao appears to be using a proverbial saying. An eastern source for the phrase may be hinted at in what Jaffar the villainous magician (Conrad Veidt) says in the 1940 film version of *The Thief of Baghdad*: 'In the morning they die the death of a thousand cuts.' The film comedy *Carry on Up the Khyber* (1968) has the phrase, too. Now, the phrase 'death of/by a thousand cuts' is used to mean 'the destruction of something by the cumulative effect of snipping rather than by one big blow'.

5 I hope that everybody will express his opinions openly. It's no crime to talk, and nobody will be punished for it. We must let a hundred flowers bloom and a hundred schools of thought contend and see which flowers are the best and which school of thought is best expressed, and we shall applaud the best blooms and the best thoughts.

Mao's statement at a meeting of officials and party leaders in May 1956 invited intellectual criticism of the regime and outlined an experiment allowing freedom of dissent. A period of self-criticism was duly launched on 27 February 1957 in a major speech to an audience of 1,800 influential Chinese. It had the title 'On the Correct Handling of Contradictions Among the People', but Mao found that his proposal did not have the support of the whole party and the press. When the official text was published on 19 June in the *People's Daily*, the horticultural image was given a sinister and revealing twist: 'Only by letting poisonous weeds show themselves above ground can they be uprooted.'

The campaign ran from 1 May, but so great was the amount of criticism stirred up that it was ended by 7 June and reprisals taken against some of those who had spoken out. These people were attacked as bourgeois rightists. Leaders of student riots were executed. Understandably, therefore, the passage about 'flowers blooming' is not included in the little red book of *Quotations from Chairman Mao Tse-tung* (1966).

1 The Great Leap Forward.

Name for enforced industrialization (1958).

2 People of the world, unite and defeat the US aggressors and all their running dogs!

In a 'Statement Supporting the People of the Congo Against US Aggression' (28 November 1964), Mao provided a vivid weapon in the coinage 'running dogs', for use against the 'lackeys' of the US during the Vietnam War. Edgar Snow had earlier recorded him using the term in 1937.

3 Don't be a gang of four.

Apparently, on one occasion, Mao gave this warning to Jiang Qing, his unscrupulous wife, and her colleagues. They became labelled as the Gang of Four in the mid-1970s when they were tried and given death sentences for treason and other crimes (later commuted to life imprisonment). The other three members were Zhang Chunqiao, a political organizer in the Cultural Revolution; Wang Hogwen, a youthful activist; and Yao Wenyuan, a journalist.

4 A fat man should not play the concertina.

Attributed on BBC Radio *Quote ... Unquote* (10 May 1978). Perhaps attributed to Mao simply as a change from Confucius?

MARIE-ANTOINETTE

Queen of France (1755–93)

5 *Qu'ils mangent de la brioche.*
Let them eat cake.

This remark is commonly ascribed to Marie-Antoinette, an Austrian disliked by the French people, after she had arrived in France to marry King Louis XVI in 1770. More specifically she is supposed to have said it during the bread shortage of 1789, though no evidence exists that she did.

The saying is to be found in Book 6 of Rousseau's *Confessions*, published posthumously in 1781–8 but written during the 1760s. Rousseau's version, referring to an incident in Grenoble about 1740, goes: 'At length I recollected the thoughtless saying of a great princess who, on being informed that the country people had no bread, replied, "Let them eat cake".' The *ODQ* (1979) notes that Louis XVIII in his *Relation d'un Voyage à Bruxelles et à Coblentz en 1791* (published 1823) attributes to Marie-Thérèse (1638–83), wife of Louis XIV, 'Why don't they eat pastry? [*Que ne mangent-ils de la croûte de pâté?*]'

Tom Burnam, *The Dictionary of Misinformation* (1975) adds that Alphonse Karr, writing in 1843, recorded that a Duchess of Tuscany had said it in 1760 or before. Later, it was circulated to discredit Marie-Antoinette. Similar remarks are said to date back to the thirteenth century, so if Marie-Antoinette did ever say it, she was quoting.

MARKS, Leo

English bookseller and cryptographer (1920–)

6 The life that I have is all that I have,
And the life that I have is yours.
The love that I have of the life that I have
Is yours and yours and yours.

A sleep I shall have
A rest I shall have,
Yet death will be but a pause,
For the peace of my years in the long green grass
Will be yours and yours and yours.

'Code Poem for the French Resistance' (*c.*1941). The poem was of the type written to be used as the basis for codes used by Special Operations Executive agents in the Second World War. It could also be used as an *aide-mémoire* for these codes, and Marks, who was in charge of agents' cyphers, considered it better for security if the poems were original. He composed dozens of them. This one was specifically written for use by Violette Szabo, the British wartime spy, who was eventually captured, tortured and executed by the Gestapo. Hence, its use in the biographical film *Carve Her Name With Pride* (1958). Leo is the son of the owner of Marks & Co., the booksellers featured in Helene Hanff's book *84, Charing Cross Road* (1971).

MARLBOROUGH, Sarah Duchess of

English wife of the 1st Duke (1660–1744)

1 His Grace returned from the wars today and pleasured me twice in his top-boots.

The *ODQ* (1979) put, 'The Duke returned from the wars today and did pleasure me in his top-boots', acknowledging 'oral trad. Attr. in various forms'. When and where the remark first appeared in print is impossible to say. One source is I. Butler, *Rule of Three* (1967). Another is James Agate, *Ego 4* (for 28 July 1938) who, talking of pageants, writes: 'How can yonder stout party hope to be Sarah, Duchess of Marlborough – "His Grace returned from the wars this morning and pleasured me twice in his top-boots" – when we know her to be the vicar's sister and quite unpleasurable?'

MARLOWE, Christopher

English playwright (1564–93)

2 Holla, ye pampered jades of Asia!
What, can ye draw but twenty miles a day ... ?

Tamburlaine, Pt 2, Act 4, Sc. 3. Misquoted by Pistol in Shakespeare, 483:7.

3 Thus methinks should men of judgement frame
Their means of traffic from the vulgar trade,
And, as their wealth increaseth, so enclose
Infinite riches in a little room.

The Jew of Malta, Act 1, Sc. 1 (*c.*1592). 'The OED database is one of the wonders of the modern world – to paraphrase Christopher Marlowe, "infinite riches in a little ROM"' – Erich Segal in *The Times Literary Supplement* (1992).

4 Fornication? But that was in another country: and besides, the wench is dead.

Ib., Act 4, Sc. 1. Barabas to Barnadine. Hence, *The Wench Is Dead*, title of a crime novel (1989) by Colin Dexter. This phrase is also used as the epigraph of T.S. Eliot's 'Portrait of a Lady' (1917).

5 Was this the face that launched a thousand ships,
And burnt the topless towers of Ilium?
Sweet Helen, make me immortal with a kiss!
Her lips suck forth my soul: see where it flies.
Come, Helen, come, give me my soul again.
Here will I dwell, for heaven is in those lips,
And all is dross that is not Helena.

Doctor Faustus, Act 5 Sc. 1 (*c.*1594), referring to Helen of Troy. Marlowe's mighty line had almost appeared in his *Tamburlaine the Great*, Pt 2, Act 2, Sc. 4 (1587): 'Helen, whose beauty ... /Drew a thousand ships to Tenedos.' Accordingly, Shakespeare must have been alluding to Marlowe when in *Troilus and Cressida*, II.ii.82 (*c.*1601) he wrote of Helen:

> Why she is a pearl
> Whose price hath launch'd above a thousand ships.

He also alludes to it in *All's Well That Ends Well*.

The consistent feature of these mentions is the figure of a 'thousand', which was a round number probably derived from the accounts of Ovid and Virgil. Tom Burnam, *Dictionary of Misinformation* (1975), quotes from Lucian's 'The Dialogues of the Dead' (*c.*AD90): 'This skull is Helen ... Was it then for this that the thousand ships were manned from all Greece?'

Much alluded to and played upon. Chips Channon records (23 April 1953) in the House of Commons: '[Aneurin] Bevan looked at poor, plain Florence Horsburgh [Independent MP for the Combined English Universities] and hailed her with the words "That's the face that sank a thousand scholarships".'

'Make me immortal with a kiss!' had also made an earlier appearance – in Marlowe's *Dido, Queen of Carthage*, Act 4, Sc. 4 (1594), in which Dido says of Aeneas: 'For in his looks I see eternity,/And he'll make me immortal with a kiss.'

6 My men, like satyrs grazing on the lawns,
Shall with their goat-feet dance an antic hay.

Edward II, Act 1, Sc. 1 (1593). Gaveston speaking. Antic hay = a grotesque country dance. Hence, the title of Aldous Huxley's novel *Antic Hay* (1923).

7 Whoever lov'd that lov'd not at first sight?

A 'saw' (saying) from Marlowe's poem *Hero and Leander*, which was published in 1598, though probably written in 1593, the year of his death. Phebe, the shepherdess in Shakespeare's *As You Like It* (probably written in 1598), quotes the line (III.v.82).

8 Come live with me, and be my love,
And we will all the pleasures prove.

'The Passionate Shepherd to his Love' (date unknown), a translation of Lucan's *Pharsalia*.

See also DONNE 211:7.

MARQUIS, Don

American writer (1878–1937)

1 Publishing a volume of verse is like dropping a rose petal down the Grand Canyon and waiting for the echo.

Quoted in *The Treasury of Humorous Quotations*, ed. by Evan Esar & Nicolas Bentley (1951). E. Anthony, *O Rare Don Marquis* (1962) has it as: 'Writing a book of poetry is ...'

MARRYAT, Frederick

English novelist (1792–1848)

2 We always took care of number one.

Scenes and Adventures in the Life of Frank Mildmay (1829). That is, we always gave ourselves priority, we are self-centred. An early appearance of this phrase. Compare: 'Whenever a person proclaims to you "In worldly matters I'm a child" ... you have got that person's number and it's Number One' – Charles Dickens, *Bleak House*, Chap. 57 (1853).

3 If you please, ma'am, it was a very little one.

Of an illegitimate baby. *Mr Midshipman Easy*, Chap. 3 (1836). The joke dates from before 1638, however.

MARSHALL, Arthur

English writer and entertainer (1910–89)

4 It's all part of life's rich pageant.

The origin of this happy phrase – sometimes 'pattern' or 'tapestry' is preferred to 'pageant' – was the subject of an inquiry by Michael Watts of the *Sunday Express* in 1982. The earliest he came up with was from a record called 'The Games Mistress', written and performed by Marshall *c.*1935. The monologue concludes: 'Oh My! Bertha's got a bang on the boko. Keep a stiff upper lip, Bertha dear. What, knocked a tooth out? Never mind, dear – laugh it off, laugh it off. It's all part of life's rich pageant.' Consequently, Marshall called his autobiography, *Life's Rich Pageant* (1984), but it seems a touch unlikely that he really originated the phrase. In 1831, Thomas Carlyle had talked of 'the fair tapestry of human life'.

5 The animated meringue.

Of Barbara Cartland, the romantic novelist noted for her white make-up. Remark recalled by Marshall on *Quote ... Unquote*, BBC Radio (December 1979). Far from taking offence, Miss Cartland sent him a telegram of thanks.

6 There is nothing like a morning funeral for sharpening the appetite for lunch.

Life's Rich Pageant (1984). It was quoted at his own (pre-lunch) memorial service in 1989.

MARSHALL, Thomas R.

American Democratic Vice-President (1854–1925)

7 What this country needs is a really good five cent cigar.

Said to John Crockett, the chief clerk of the Senate, during a tedious debate in 1917 and quoted in *The New York Tribune* (4 January 1920). Another version is that it was said to Henry M. Rose, assistant Secretary of State. The remark is mentioned in a caption in *Recollections of Thomas R. Marshall* (1925). At about that time, 'Owls' cigars cost six cents and 'White Owls', seven cents.

MARSTON, John

English poet and playwright (1576–1634)

8 'My kingdom for a horse' – look thee I speak play scraps.

From his play *What You Will* (1607) – a clear example of quotation by a contemporary of Shakespeare. Marston's play is thought to have appeared in 1601 and Shakespeare's *Richard III* in 1591. ('What You Will' is also, of course, the subtitle of Shakespeare's *Twelfth Night*, written in 1601.) *See* SHAKESPEARE 493:8.

MARTIAL

Spanish-born Latin epigrammatist (c.AD 40–c.104)

9 *Rus in urbe.*
Country in the town.

Epigrammata, Bk 12, No. 57. Remark applied, for example, to a garden that provides rustic simplicity within the sophistication of the town. In May 1969 I visited a friend who had a cottage in the country near Bradford-on-Avon, but it wasn't a very rustic place. Indeed, it had almost a suburban or even urban aspect to it. And so I pronounced it 'urbs in rure'. Subsequently, I found exactly the same joke in *Punch* for 3 July 1901 and that the inverted phrase was used as the title of a *Punch* cartoon on 28 September 1904.

MARVELL, Andrew

English poet and politician (1621–78)

1 *He* nothing common did nor mean
Upon that memorable scene.

On the execution of Charles I. 'An Horatian Ode upon Cromwell's Return from Ireland' (written 1650). Quoted by Winston Churchill concerning Edward VIII's conduct at the Abdication in 1936 (also in his 'Finest Hour' speech, House of Commons, 18 June 1940).

2 Had we but world enough, and time,
This coyness, lady, were no crime.

'To His Coy Mistress' (pub. 1681). Hence, *World Enough and Time* (1950), title of a novel by Robert Penn Warren.

3 But at my back I always hear
Time's wingèd chariot hurrying near:
And yonder all before us lie
Deserts of vast eternity.

Ib. Compare LINKLATER 358:1.

4 O let our voice his praise exalt,
Till it arrive at Heaven's vault:
Which thence (perhaps) rebounding, may
Echo beyond the Mexique Bay.

'Bermudas' (*c.*1653). Hence, *Beyond the Mexique Bay*, title of a travel book (1934) by Aldous Huxley.

See also JENKINS 314:2.

MARX, Chico

American comedian (1886–1961)

5 You can't fool me. There ain't no Sanity Clause!

Fiorello (Chico) replies thus, in Christmassy fashion, when Otis B. Driftwood (Groucho Marx) says in the film *A Night at the Opera* (1935): 'If any of the parties participating in this contract is shown not to be in their right mind, the entire agreement is automatically nullified. That's what they call a sanity clause.' Chico says he is the manager of a tenor whom Groucho would like to sing with the New York Opera Company and they go through the contract in this fashion.

6 But I wasn't kissing her. I was whispering in her mouth.

When his wife had caught him kissing a chorus girl. Quoted in Groucho Marx & Richard Anobile, *The Marx Brothers Scrapbook* (1974).

MARX, Groucho

American comedian (1895–1977)

7 Please accept my resignation. I don't care to belong to any club that will have me as a member.

Zeppo Marx recalled that this was about The Friars Club, a theatrical organization, for which his brother did not have much use. Hector Ace added that Groucho had some misgivings about the quality of the members – 'doubts verified a few years later when an infamous card-cheating scandal erupted there'. The wording varies, but the one here is taken from Arthur Sheekman's introduction to *The Groucho Letters* (1967). The actual letter unfortunately does not survive. In *Groucho and Me* (1959), he himself supplied the version: 'PLEASE ACCEPT MY RESIGNATION. I DON'T WANT TO BELONG TO ANY CLUB THAT WILL ACCEPT ME AS A MEMBER.' Woody Allen in *Annie Hall* (1977) appears to suggest that the joke first appeared in Freud.

8 Since my daughter is only half-Jewish, could she go in the water up to her knees?

When excluded from a beach club on racial grounds. Quoted in *The Observer* (21 August 1977).

9 My regiment leaves at dawn.

A line spoken by Groucho in the film *Monkey Business* (1931), preceded by the words, 'Come, Kapellmeister, let the violas throb!' Presumably this is a cliché of operetta, but no precise example has been traced. It was certainly the situation in many romantic tangles, even if the line itself was not actually spoken.

10 There'll always be a lamp in the window for my wandering boy.

A line spoken by Groucho in the film *Horse Feathers* (1932). What is it? Probably a bringing together of two clichés from popular fiction and parlour poetry. 'Where is my wand'ring boy tonight?' is the first line of a poem/song written and composed by the (presumably American) Rev. R. Lowry in 1877. Under the title 'Where Is Your Boy Tonight?' it is No. 303 in Ira D. Sankey's *Sacred Songs and Solos*. No mention of a lamp in the window, however. Putting a light or lamp in a window is a traditional sign of devotion to or of showing support for a cause. In a speech in Scotland on 29 November 1880 Lord Rosebery said of Gladstone:

'From his home in Wales to the Metropolis of Scotland there has been no village too small to afford a crowd to greet him – there has been no cottager so humble that could not find a light to put in his window as he passed.'

Groucho returned to the theme in *At the Circus* (1939). About to become a ring-master, he is being helped by Chico into a tail-coat which he finds rather tight. 'You'd have to be a wizard to get into this coat,' he says. Chico: 'That's-a-right, it belonged to a wizard.' At this point, a pigeon flies out of the tail pocket. Chico: 'It's a homing pigeon.' And Groucho says: 'Then there'll always be a candle burning in my pocket for my wandering pigeon.'

1 I've been around so long, I knew Doris Day before she was a virgin.

Quoted in Leslie Halliwell, *The Filmgoer's Book of Quotes* (1973), but *see* LEVANT 353:6. I suspect it was Levant's remark, rather than a simple case of two men with but a single thought.

2 From the moment I picked up your book until I laid it down I was convulsed with laughter. Someday I intend reading it.

Quoted in Hector Arce, *Groucho* (1979). Concerning *Dawn Ginsbergh's Revenge* (1928) by S.J. Perelman.

3 Show me a rose and I'll show you a girl named Sam.

Song, 'Show me a Rose'. In fact, written by Harry Ruby and Bert Kalmar, though popularized by Groucho.

4 I never go to movies where the hero's bust is bigger than the heroine's.

On the films of Victor Mature. Quoted in Leslie Halliwell, *The Filmgoer's Book of Quotes* (1973). Probably regarding Mature's appearance in *Samson and Delilah* (1949).

5 They say a man is as old as the woman he feels. In that case I'm eighty five ... I want it known here and now that this is what I want on my tombstone: Here lies Groucho Marx, and Lies and Lies and Lies. P.S. He never kissed an ugly girl.

The Secret Word is Groucho (1976). Presumably Groucho was alluding to the proverb 'A man is as old as he feels, and a woman as old as she looks' (known by 1871).

See also ANIMAL CRACKERS 19:8–9; ANONYMOUS 23:3.

MARX, Karl

German political theorist (1818–83)

6 Religion ... is the opium of the people.

A Contribution to the Critique of Hegel's Philosophy of Right, Introduction (1843–4). A catchphrase suggesting that religion is like a drug releasing people from the reality of their lives. Compare the modern graffito (observed in Harrow, *c.*1979): 'Nicholas Parsons [a TV quizmaster] is the neo-opiate of the people.'

7 A spectre is haunting Europe – the spectre of communism.

The Communist Manifesto (1848), opening paragraph. Written with Friedrich Engels.

8 The workers have nothing to lose in this [revolution] but their chains. They have a world to gain. Workers of the world, unite!

Ib., closing words. *See also* 385:2.

9 History repeats itself – the first time as tragedy, the second time as farce.

In *The Eighteenth Brumaire of Louis Napoleon* (1852). Marx provides the context: 'Hegel says somewhere that all great events and personalities in world history reappear in one fashion or another. He forgot to add: the first time as tragedy, the second as farce.' Hence, the title of a book on the theatre, by the playwright David Edgar, *The Second Time As Farce* (1988).

10 Prominent because of the flatness of the surrounding countryside.

This aspersion is to be found cast against John Stuart Mill, the English philosopher and social reformer, in *Das Kapital*, Vol. 1, Chap. 16 (1867). After having demolished one of Mill's arguments, Marx says: 'On a level plain, simple mounds look like hills; and the insipid flatness of our present bourgeoisie is to be measured by the altitude of its "great intellects".'

11 From each according to his ability, to each according to his needs.

Usually attributed to Marx, but not from either *Das Kapital* or *The Communist Manifesto*. The slogan appears in his *Critique of the Gotha Programme* (1875) in which he says that after the workers have taken power, capitalist thinking must first disappear. Only then will the day come when society can 'inscribe on its banners: from each according to his ability, to each according to his needs'.

John Kenneth Galbraith commented in *The Age of Uncertainty* (1977): 'It is possible that these ... twelve words enlisted for Marx more followers than all the hundreds of thousands in the three volumes of *Das Kapital* combined.'

There is some doubt whether Marx originated the slogan or whether he was quoting Louis Blanc, Morelly or Mikhail Bakunin. The latter wrote: 'From each according to his faculties, to each according to his needs' (declaration, 1870, by anarchists on trial after the failure of their uprising in Lyons).

Also, Saint-Simon (1760–1825), the French reformer, had earlier said: 'The task of each be according to his capacity, the wealth of each be according to his works.' And, much earlier, Acts 4:34–35 had: 'Neither was there any among them that lacked: for as many as were possessors of lands or houses sold them, and brought the prices of things that were sold, and laid them down at the apostles feet: and distribution was made unto every man according as he had need.'

1 The ferocious chastity of Irishwomen.

In a letter to Friedrich Engels (who had two Irish mistresses). Untraced. Hence, *Ferocious Chastity* (1987), a stage recital on the lot of Irish women by Gemma O'Connor.

2 The philosophers have only interpreted the world in various ways. The point however is to change it.

Theses on Feuerbach (1888). Marx, though German-born, lived in London from 1849 onwards. He was buried in Highgate Cemetery on 17 March 1883. His ill-kept grave remained in a far corner of the cemetery until 1956 when the Soviet Communist Party paid for a monolithic black marble block to be installed, with two quotations inscribed upon it: 'Workers of all lands unite' from 384:8 (at the top) and this quotation below it.

MARY I

English Queen (1516–58)

3 When I am dead and opened, you shall find Calais lying in my heart.

'Bloody Mary' or 'Mary Tudor', who ruled 1553–8, reputedly said this, according to *Holinshed's Chronicles* (1577). She was referring to the re-capture by the French of Calais in 1558, a notable defeat for England, as the town had been an English possession for more than two hundred years and was its last territory in France. *Compare* SELLAR AND YEATMAN 473:10.

MARY

British Queen of King George V (1867–1953)

4 Well, Prime Minister, here's a pretty kettle of fish.

Queen Mary's eldest son reigned for less than a year as Edward VIII. He abdicated in order to marry the American divorcee, Wallis Simpson. For most of 1936, the British public was kept in ignorance of the manoeuvres going on behind the scenes to resolve this crisis. The Prime Minister, Stanley Baldwin, steered matters to their conclusion. He subsequently told his daughter of a meeting he had had with Queen Mary as the storm grew: 'I had a tremendous shock. For, instead of standing immobile in the middle distance, silent and majestic, she came trotting across the room *exactly like a puppy dog*: and before I had time to bow, she took hold of my hand in both of hers and held it tight. "Well, Prime Minister," she said, "here's a pretty kettle of fish"' (quoted in Frances Donaldson, *Edward VIII*, 1974).

Years later, meeting Queen Mary at a dinner party, Noël Coward boldly asked, 'Is it true, Ma'am, that you said, "Here's a pretty kettle of fish?"' She replied, 'Yes, I think I did.' (Cole Lesley, *The Life of Noël Coward*, 1978).

In the form, 'This is a nice kettle of fish, isn't it?', the Queen's remark was noted on 17 November 1936 in the diary of Nancy Dugdale whose husband was Baldwin's Parliamentary Private Secretary. Extracts from the diary were published in *The Observer* (7 December 1986).

5 No more bloody wars, no more bloody medals.

To a soldier who had exclaimed 'No more bloody wars for me' as she presented medals during the First World War. Attributed by Robert Lacey on BBC Radio *Quote ... Unquote* (19 February 1979).

MASCHWITZ, Eric

English songwriter (1901–69)

6 The sigh of midnight trains in empty stations ...
The smile of Garbo and the scent of roses ...
These foolish things
Remind me of you.

Song, 'These Foolish Things' (1936) – once cited by John Betjeman as evidence of poetry in popular culture. The song was originally published as by 'Holt Marvell' (with music by Jack Strachey) because

Maschwitz had to conceal his identity as a BBC executive. This has led to such oddities as the *PDMQ* (1980) crediting the whole song to Strachey alone. In the *ODQ* (1992), it is still credited to 'Holt Marvell', as also in the *ODMQ* (1991), where the music credit is shared between Jack Strachey and 'Harry Link', whoever he might be.

Picked up by Michael Sadleir for a book called *These Foolish Things* in 1937 and by Bertrand Tavernier as the title of a film (1990) which included the song on the soundtrack.

1 A Nightingale Sang in Berkeley Square.

Title of a song first sung in the revue *New Faces* (1940). Music by Manning Sherwin. As Maschwitz acknowledged in his autobiography *No Chip on My Shoulder* (1957), the title was derived from a short story called 'When the Nightingale Sang in Berkeley Square' in Michael Arlen's *These Charming People* (1923). Nightingales are last reported to have sung in Berkeley Square in 1850 (according to Victoria Glendinning, *Trollope*, 1992).

MASEFIELD, John

English Poet Laureate (1878–1967)

2 I must down to the sea again, to the lonely sea and the sky.

In Masefield's poem 'Sea Fever' (1902), this line – *without* any 'go' before 'down' – was apparently as he originally intended it, though the original manuscript is lost. An early draft of the poem has 'I must down' – indeed, it pursues a different course, beginning, 'I must down to the roads again, to the vagrant life.' The repeated line was 'I must down' in the first published version of *Salt Water Ballads* in 1902. Heinemann Collected Editions of Masefield's poetry had 'down' (in 1923, 1932 and 1938) but changed to 'go down' in 1946. *Selected Poems* in 1922 and 1938 both had 'go down'. No one knows why this divergence occurred, but the pull of Psalm 107 ('They that *go down to the sea* in ships, that do their business in great waters') may have been a factor. John Ireland's musical setting of the poem has had the 'go' since its first publication (1915). Some editions of the poem also have a plural 'seas again'. Curiously, the *ODQ* suggests that the 1902 original 'I must down to the seas' was 'possibly a misprint'.

Most of this information is drawn from an article by Agnes Whitaker in *The Times* (5 December 1980). She comments on 'the inspired economy' of 'I must down' and adds: 'It is disconcerting that standard editions, and works of reference which we treat almost like sacred texts, should contradict each other, especially over such an immensely well-known poem.'

Note also, *The Lonely Sea and the Sky* – title given to the memoirs (1964) of Sir Francis Chichester, the solo round-the-world yachtsman.

See also HUBBARD 303:9.

MASON, Donald

American Navy pilot (1913–)

3 Sighted sub, sank same.

Radio message (28 January 1942), from a US Navy flyer after he had dropped a depth charge on a surfaced Japanese submarine in the South Pacific. 'This concise message was one of the first good news to come after Pearl Harbor and was given wide publicity as showing the good spirit of our armed forces' – Flexner (1976).

MATHEW, Sir James

Irish judge (1830–1908)

4 In England, Justice is open to all, like the Ritz hotel.

Attributed to Mathew by R.E. Megarry in *Miscellany-at-Law* (1955). However, the thought is old enough. In *Tom Paine's Jests* (1794) there is: 'A gentleman haranguing on the perfection of our law, and that it was equally open to the poor and rich, was answered by another, "So is the London Tavern".' In William Hazlitt's *The Spirit of the Age* (1825), this jest was specifically ascribed to the radical politician John Horne Tooke (1736–1812).

MATTHEWS, A.E.

English actor (1869–1960)

5 I always wait for *The Times* each morning. I look at the obituary column, and if I'm not in it, I go to work.

Quoted in Leslie Halliwell, *The Filmgoer's Book of Quotes* (1973). Matthews's own obituary appeared on 26 July 1960. Several people have used the line subsequently. In *The Observer* (16 August 1987), William Douglas-Home, the playwright, was quoted as saying: 'Every morning I read the obits in *The Times*. If I'm not there, I carry on.'

MAUDLING, Reginald

British Conservative politician (1917–77)

1 I don't think one can speak of defeating the IRA, of eliminating them completely, but it is the design of the security forces to reduce their level of violence to something like an acceptable level.

At the end of visit to Northern Ireland as Home Secretary (15 December 1971). Remembered, and used against him, as 'an acceptable level of violence'.

2 There comes a time in every man's life when he must make way for an older man.

On being replaced in the Shadow Cabinet by a man four years his senior. Reported in *The Guardian* (20 November 1976). He also said at that time: 'I have never been sacked before. I was appointed by Winston Churchill and I am now being dismissed by Margaret Thatcher. Life goes on. The world changes.'

MAUGHAM, W. Somerset

English novelist and short-story writer (1874–1965)

3 In every play a stranger comes into the room, opens a window to let in fresh air and everyone dies of pneumonia.

Of Ibsen. Quoted by Robin Bailey on BBC Radio *Quote ... Unquote* (27 July 1985). Unverified.

4 Of Human Bondage.

Title of novel (1915). From the title of one of the books in Spinoza's *Ethics* (1677).

5 The Moon and Sixpence.

Maugham took the title of his 1919 novel from a review of an earlier book – *Of Human Bondage* (1915) – in *The Times Literary Supplement*. It had said that the main character was: 'Like so many young men ... so busy yearning for the moon that he never saw the sixpence at his feet' (source: Ted Morgan, *Somerset Maugham*, 1980).

6 I [Death] was astonished to see him in Baghdad, for I had an appointment with him tonight in Samarra.

Sheppey, Act 3 (1933). Hence, the expression 'an appointment in Samarra', meaning an appointment with Death or one which simply cannot be avoided. Presumably a tale acquired by Maugham from some other source, in which a servant is jostled by Death in the market at Baghdad. Terrified, he jumps on a horse and rides to Samarra (a city in northern Iraq) where he thinks Death will not be able to find him. When the servant's master asks Death why he treated him in this manner, Death replies that he had merely been surprised to encounter the servant in Baghdad ... 'I had an appointment with him tonight in Samarra.' The novel *Appointment in Samarra* (1934) by John O'Hara alludes to the incident.

7 The Trembling of a Leaf.

Title of collection of short stories (1921). From Sainte-Beuve: 'Extreme happiness separated from extreme despair by a trembling leaf, is that not life?' (source: Ted Morgan, *Somerset Maugham*, 1980).

8 The Razor's Edge.

Title of a novel (1944; film US, 1946). It comes from the Katha-Upanishad: 'The sharp edge of a razor is difficult to pass over; thus the wise say the path to Salvation is hard' (source: Ted Morgan, *Somerset Maugham*, 1980).

9 I stand in the very first row of the second-raters.

Said by *The Oxford Companion to English Literature* (1985) to be in his autobiography *The Summing Up* (1938), this view has not been found there. Compare the similar self-estimation of Arnold Bennett (quoted in *The Lyttelton Hart-Davis Letters* for 18 January 1956), 'My work will never be better than third-rate, judged by the high standards, but I shall be cunning enough to make it impose on my contemporaries', and the view of Maugham as 'a good writer of the second rank' put forward by Karl G. Pfeiffer in his *Somerset Maugham, a Candid Portrait* (1959).

10 To eat well in England, all you have to do is take breakfast three times a day.

This oft-quoted view appears in Ted Morgan, *Somerset Maugham* (1980) as the response to a friend's statement that he 'hated the food in England': 'What rubbish. All you have to do is eat breakfast three times a day.'

11 At a dinner party one should eat wisely but not too well, and talk well but not too wisely.

Written in 1896 but not reproduced until *A Writer's Notebook* (1949).

1 They are scum.

Of state-aided undergraduates. In *The Sunday Times* (25 December 1955) – a review of Kingsley Amis's novel *Lucky Jim*, which was to be published the following month.

See also BEERBOHM 79:10; DAVIS 196:7.

MAUROIS, André

French novelist and biographer (1885–1967)

2 In defeat he thought only of future victories.

Prometheus: The Life of Balzac, Chap. 8 (1965). Maurois is describing the young Balzac at a time when he was harassed by creditors and facing bankruptcy: 'He still had reserves of exuberance and hopefulness ... he lived in the future, a triumphant future teeming with houris and riches.'

MAXTON, Jimmy

Scottish Independent Labour Party politician (1855–1946)

3 Sit down, man. You're a bloody tragedy.

To Ramsay MacDonald on the occasion of the last speech he made in the House of Commons. Quoted in *PDMQ* (1971).

4 If my friend cannot ride two horses – what's he doing in the bloody circus?

Said of a man who had proposed disaffiliation of the ILP from the Labour Party and quoted in G. McAllister, *James Maxton* (1935). Maxton had been speaking in a debate at a Scottish Conference of the ILP in 1931 and been told he could not be a member of two parties – or ride two horses – at the same time. Hence, the more general expression, 'If you can't ride two horses at once, you shouldn't be in the circus'.

MEAD, Margaret

American anthropologist (1901–78)

5 Never doubt that a small group of thoughtful citizens can change the world. Indeed, it's the only thing that ever has.

Quoted in *The Utne Reader* (1992), but otherwise untraced.

MEARNS, Hughes

American writer (1875–1965)

6 As I was walking up the stair
I met a man who wasn't there.
He wasn't there again today.
I wish, I wish he'd stay away.

Lines written for an amateur play, *The Psycho-Ed* (1910).

MELBOURNE, 2nd Viscount

English Whig Prime Minister (1779–1848)

7 A damned bore.

Of the Prime Ministership. We have only Charles Greville's word for it, but when William IV offered the prime ministership to Melbourne in 1834, 'He thought it a damned bore and was in many minds what he should do – be minister or no'. His secretary urged him to accept, however, with the words: 'Why damn it, such a position was never occupied by any Greek or Roman, and if it only last two months, it is well worth while to have been Prime Minister of England.' The words were quoted by Clement Attlee while ironically congratulating Anthony Eden on becoming Prime Minister (in 1955) when an election was imminent (source: Robert Blake in *The Prime Ministers*, Vol. 2, 1975.)

MELVILLE, Herman

American novelist (1819–91)

8 I would prefer not to.

Bartleby (1853). Characteristic response to any request, by the scrivener, Bartleby.

MENCKEN, H.L.

American journalist and linguist (1880–1956)

9 Dear Reader, You may be right.

Standard reply to readers' letters when he was editor of *The American Mercury*. Attributed.

10 Mr Mencken has just entered a trappist monastery in Kentucky and left strict instructions that no mail was to be forwarded. The enclosed is returned therefore for your archives.

Rejection slip when editor of *The American Mercury*. Attributed.

1 If after I depart this vale you ever remember me and have thought to please my ghost, forgive some sinner and wink your eye at some homely girl.

Mencken suggested this epitaph for himself in *Smart Set* (December 1921). After his death, it was inscribed on a plaque in the lobby of the offices of the Baltimore *Sun* newspapers (with which he had been associated most of his working life).

2 No one ever went broke underestimating the intelligence of the American people.

In fact what Mencken wrote (about journalism) in the *Chicago Tribune* (19 September 1926), was: 'No one in this world, so far as I know ... has ever lost money by underestimating the intelligence of the great masses of the plain people. Nor has anyone ever lost public office thereby.'

3 The only really happy people are married women and single men.

Quoted in *The 'Quote ... Unquote' Book of Love, Death and the Universe* (1980), but otherwise unverified.

4 Here, indeed, was his one really notable talent. He slept more than any other President, whether by day or by night ... Nero fiddled, but Coolidge only snored ... He had no ideas, and he was not a nuisance.

On President Coolidge, in *The American Mercury* (April 1933).

5 Only presidents, editors, and people with tapeworms have the right to use the editorial 'we'.

Precise wording and source untraced. Sometimes in the form: 'There are two kinds of people entitled to refer to themselves as "we". One is an editor, the other is a fellow with a tapeworm.' Also attributed to Bill Nye and Mark Twain.

MENDELSSOHN, Felix

German composer (1809–47)

6 Calm Sea and Prosperous Voyage.

The pleasing title of this overture (Op. 27, 1832) was taken from two poems by Goethe, with whom Mendelssohn was personally acquainted. One '*Meeresstille*', the other, '*Glükliche Fahrt*'. (Beethoven also made a choral and orchestral setting of these poems.) Nowadays one might wish a 'calm sea and a prosperous voyage' to a friend off on a sea cruise, but *Meeresstille* refers to that more sinister prospect for anyone on a vessel with sails – a becalmed sea.

MENZIES, Sir Robert

Australian Liberal Prime Minister (1894–1978)

7 Considering the company I keep in this place, that is hardly surprising.

When accused by a member of Parliament of harbouring a superiority complex. Quoted in *Time* Magazine (29 May 1978).

8 If I were the Archangel Gabriel, madam, I'm afraid you would not be in my constituency.

In answer to a heckler who cried, 'I wouldn't vote for you if you were the Archangel Gabriel'. Quoted in R. Robinson, *The Wit of Sir Robert Menzies* (1966).

MERCER, Johnny

American lyricist (1909–76)

9 You're much too much and just too very very
To ever be in Webster's dictionary.

Song, 'Too Marvellous for Words', *Ready, Willing and Able*, (1937). A pity about the split infinitive. Webster also features in another song lyric; *see* ROAD TO MOROCCO 456:7.

10 I could eat alphabet soup and *shit* better lyrics.

On seeing a British musical (1975), possibly *Jeeves* – lyrics by Alan Ayckbourn (after Tim Rice had withdrawn from the production), music by Andrew Lloyd Webber. Unverified.

See also CARROLL 146:8.

MERCHANT, Vivien

English actress (1929–83)

11 He didn't need to take a change of shoes; he can always wear hers; she has very big feet you know.

On her husband, Harold Pinter, when he left her for Lady Antonia Fraser. Quoted in *The Observer* (21 December 1975).

MEREDITH, George

English novelist and poet (1828–1909)

1 Ah, what a dusty answer gets the soul
When hot for certainties in this our life!

Modern Love (1862). *See* GLASGOW 264:6.

2 The lark ascending.

Title of poem (1881) – taken by Vaughan Williams for his orchestral piece (1914).

MERMAN, Ethel

American entertainer (1908–84)

3 Call me Miss Birdseye. This show is frozen.

To Irving Berlin when he wanted to change a song lyric in *Call Me Madam* (1950). Quoted in *The Times* (13 July 1985).

MERTON, R.K.

American sociologist (1910–)

4 The self-fulfilling prophecy is, in the beginning, a *false* definition of the situation evoking a new behavior which makes the originally false conception come *true*.

Social Theory and Social Structure (1949). Coinage of the phrase 'self-fulfilling prophecy' meaning 'anticipation of an outcome which only serves to bring it about'. 'Panic buying of spirits ... caused largely by forecasts of the shortage – a self-fulfilling prophecy' – *The Times* (7 December 1973).

METTERNICH, Prince

Austrian statesman (1773–1859)

5 When Paris sneezes, Europe catches cold.

Untraced. This comment, said to date from 1830, cannot be found in his *Mémoires*, for example. Another form is: 'When France has a cold, all Europe sneezes.'

6 *Italien ist ein geographischer Begriff.*
Italy is a geographical concept.

Discussing the Italian question with Palmerston in 1847 (also in a letter dated 19 November 1849). Italy was indeed no more than a group of individual states until Victor Emmanuel II was proclaimed King in 1861.

MICHAELIS, John

American general (1912–85)

7 You're not here to die for your country. You're here to make those so-and-sos die for theirs.

A famous rallying cry to the 27th Infantry (Wolfhound) Regiment, which Michaelis commanded during the Korean War. Quoted in *Time* Magazine (11 November 1985). *See also* PATTON 426:1.

MIDLER, Bette

American singer and actress (1944–)

8 These days, you fuck someone, your arm drops off.

On sex in the age of AIDS. Quoted in *The Independent* (12 November 1988).

MIKES, George

Hungarian-born writer in Britain (1912–87)

9 Continental people have sex life; the English have hot-water bottles.

How To Be An Alien (1946). Later, in *How To Be Decadent* (1977), Mikes commented: 'Things have progressed. Not on the continent, where people still have sex lives; but they have progressed here because the English now have electric blankets. It's a pity that electricity so often fails in this country.'

MILLAIS, Sir John Everett

English painter (1829–96)

10 The Boyhood of Raleigh.

Title of painting (1870) showing the young Sir Walter Raleigh with a friend being told stories by an old seagoing man. The man gestures towards the sea as he talks. The picture is now in the Tate Gallery, London.

MILLER, Arthur

American playwright (1915–)

11 For a salesman, there is no rock bottom to the life ... He's a man way out there in the blue, riding on a smile and a shoeshine ... A salesman is got to dream, boy. It comes with the territory.

'Requiem' at the end of *Death of a Salesman*, Act 1

(1948). Since at least 1900, 'territory' has been the American term for the area a salesman covers. Miller's use may, however, be a possible origin for the late twentieth-century expression, 'It comes/goes with the territory', meaning 'it's all part and parcel of something, what is expected'. From *The Washington Post* (13 July 1984): '[Geraldine Ferraro as prospective Vice-President] will have to be judged on her background, training and capacity to do the job. That goes with the territory.' From the film *Father of the Bride* (1991): Steve Martin says: 'I'm a father. Worrying comes with the territory.' From the London *Evening Standard* (17 February 1993): 'Why go on about the latest "award-winning documentary maker"? If you get a documentary on television, you win an award: it goes with the territory.'

1 [Roslyn:] 'How do you find your way back in the dark?' Gay nods, indicating the sky before them: 'Just head for that big star straight on. The highway's under it; take us right home.'

From Miller's novel *The Misfits* (1961). In his screenplay (the same year), the last line of the film, spoken by Clark Gable, becomes: 'The highway's under it. It'll takes us right home.' This is sometimes given as Gable's own 'last line', as he died shortly after the filming was completed.

2 Why should I go? She won't be there.

When asked if he would attend his ex-wife Marilyn Monroe's funeral (1962). Attributed.

MILLER, Jonathan

English entertainer, writer and director (1934–)

3 It is my aim to get the violence off the streets and into the churches where it belongs.

Spoken as a trendy vicar in 'Man Bites God' in *Beyond the Fringe.* (1961) (script credited to whole cast). *Compare* COOK 182:5 and HITCHCOCK 296:5. Also 'Get Bingo out of the supermarkets and into the churches where it really belongs' – performed on CBS TV *Rowan and Martin's Laugh-In* and included on the record album *Laugh-In '69* (1969).

MILLER, Max

American journalist (1899–1967)

4 I Cover the Waterfront.

Title of book (1932) about Miller's experiences as a 'waterfront reporter' on the *San Diego Sun* during the late 1920s and early 1930s. Filmed (US 1933) as a story about a journalist who exposes a smuggling racket. Hence, 'cover' is in the journalistic sense. The song with the title (by Johnny Green and Ed Heyman), sung notably by Billie Holiday, was originally unconnected with the film – written merely to cash in on the association – and sounds as if it might be about laying paving stones or some other activity. However, so successful was it that it was subsequently added to the soundtrack. Since the film, the phrase 'to cover the waterfront' has meant 'to cover all aspects of a topic' or merely 'to experience something'. A woman going in to try a new nightclub in the film *Cover Girl* (1944) says: 'This is it. We cover the waterfront.' In *The Wise Wound* (1978) by Penelope Shuttle and Peter Redgrove, 'she's covering the waterfront' is listed among the many slang expressions for menstruation.

MILLIGAN, Spike

Irish entertainer and writer (1918–)

5 Contraceptives should be used on every conceivable occasion.

Milligan speaks this line in his script for BBC Radio *The Last Goon Show of All* (1972). Also reported as graffiti from Michigan in Haan & Hammerstrom *Graffiti in the Big Ten* (1981).

6 The Army works like this: if a man dies when you hang him, keep hanging until he gets used to it.

Attributed by Richard Ingrams on BBC Radio *Quote ... Unquote* (4 May 1977).

7 My favourite quotation is eight pounds ten for a second-hand suit.

When asked for his favourite quotation on BBC Radio *Quote ... Unquote* (1 January 1979).

See also O'REILLY 419:2.

MILLS, Nat and Bobbie

English entertainers (1900–93) and (d.1955)

8 Let's get *on* with it!

Mr and Mrs Mills were a variety act that flourished in the 1930s and 1940s portraying 'a gumpish type of lad and his equally gumpish girlfriend'. Nat recalled (in 1979): 'It was during the very early part of the war. We were booked by the BBC to go to South Wales for a *Workers' Playtime*. Long tables had been set up in front of the stage for the workers to have lunch on before the broadcast. On this occasion, a works foreman went round all the tables shouting, "Come on, let's get on with it", to get them to finish their lunch on time. I was informed he used this phrase so many times, the workers would mimic him among themselves. So I said to Bobbie, "You start the broadcast by talking to yourself and I'll interject and say, 'Let's get on with it'". Lo and behold it got such a yell of laughter we kept it in all our broadcasts. Even Churchill used our slogan to the troops during the early part of the war.'

MILNE, A.A.

English writer (1882–1956)

1 Sydney Smith, or Napoleon or Marcus Aurelius (somebody about that time) said that after ten days any letter would answer itself. You see what he meant.

Untraced. In fact, it was Arthur Binstead in *Pitcher's Proverbs* (1909), who said, 'The great secret in life ... [is] not to open letters for a fortnight. At the expiration of that period you will find that nearly all of them have answered themselves.'

2 Little boy kneels at the foot of the bed,
Droops on the little hands, little gold head;
Hush! Hush! Whisper who dares!
Christopher Robin is saying his prayers.

'Vespers' in *When We Were Very Young* (1924). *Compare* MORTON 401:1.

3 Worraworraworraworraworra.

The House at Pooh Corner (1928). This is the noise ('not a growl, and it isn't a purr') made by Tigger, who is the bouncy tiger. However, 'wurra-wurra-wurra' also occurs in Thackeray's *The Rose and the Ring*, Chap. 15 (1856). Here it seems to denote eating noises – but from the same corner of the animal kingdom. Count Hogginarmo jumps into a circus ring, and then: 'Wurra wurra wurra wur-aw-aw-aw!!! In about two minutes, the Count Hogginarmo was GOBBLED UP by those lions: bones, boots and all, and there was an end of him.' Earlier still, on 26 January 1788, when Captain Arthur Phillip's fleet landed at what would later be called Sydney Harbour in Australia, it was greeted by Aborigines crying, '*Warra, warra!*' (meaning, 'Go away!')

See also STOPPARD 521:9.

MILNER, Alfred (1st Viscount Milner)

British imperialist (1854–1925)

4 If we believe a thing to be bad, and if we have a right to prevent it, it is our duty to try to prevent it, and to damn the consequences.

On the peers and the Budget. In a speech in opposition to Lloyd George's Finance Bill at Glasgow (26 November 1909).

MILNES, Richard Monckton (1st Baron Houghton)

English politician and writer (1809–85)

5 My exit is the result of too many entrées.

Dying words (or, at least, suggested dying words) of this notable *gourmand*. Quoted in Barnaby Conrad, *Famous Last Words* (1961).

MILTON, John

English poet (1608–74)

6 Come, knit hands, and beat the ground,
In a light fantastic round.

Comus, l. 143 (1637). *Compare* BROOKER 122:6.

7 Sabrina fair,
Listen where thou art sitting
Under the glassy, cool, translucent wave,
In twisted braids of lilies knitting
The loose train of thy amber-dropping hair.

Ib., l. 859. Billy Wilder's 1954 film *Sabrina*, based on a play by Samuel Taylor, was about the daughter (Audrey Hepburn) of a chauffeur who gets wooed by both the two brothers who employ her father. Known simply as *Sabrina* in the US, the film was released as *Sabrina Fair* in Britain. This could have been because the distributors thought that English cinema-goers would relish an allusion to the poetic name for the river Severn, as applied to the nymph in Milton's masque *Comus*. On the other hand, the distributors might have been sending them a message that the film had nothing at all to do with Sabrina, a busty (41–18–36) model, who was at that time featured on TV shows with Arthur Askey, the comedian.

Alas, this second theory does not fit, as Norma Sykes (her real name) did not start appearing until 1956 and, in fact, actually took her stage-name from the title of the film. So, it must have been the allusion to Milton after all.

1 To sport with Amaryllis in the shade,
Or with the tangles of Neaera's hair?
Fame is the spur that the clear spirit doth raise
(That last infirmity of noble mind)
To scorn delights, and live laborious days.

Lycidas, l. 68 (1638). Hence, *Fame Is the Spur*, title of a novel (1940, film UK 1946) by Howard Spring about an aspiring politician.

2 Look homeward, Angel, now, and melt with ruth.

Ib., l. 163. Ruth = pity, the quality of being compassionate. Hence, *Look Homeward, Angel!*, the title of a novel (1929) by Thomas Wolfe and a song by Johnnie Ray (1957).

3 At last he rose, and twitched his mantle blue:
Tomorrow to fresh woods and pastures new.

Ib., l. 192. Often remembered as 'Tomorrow to fresh *fields* and pastures new'. The misquotation probably gained hold because of the alliteration – always a lure in phrase-making. There may be tautology in the fields and pastures, but how likely is it that a shepherd would lead his flock into a wood where the sheep would be liable to get lost, lose their wool on bushes, eat poisonous plants and so on?

4 A good book is the precious life-blood of a master spirit, embalmed and treasured up on purpose to a life beyond life.

From *Areopagitica* (1644). A sentiment used for many years to promote the Everyman's Library series of classic reprints. *Compare* ANONYMOUS 29:2 and SIDNEY 504:3.

5 Come, and trip it as ye go
On the light fantastic toe ...

'L'Allegro', l. 33 (1645). *Compare* BROOKER 122:6.

6 Far from all resort of mirth,
Save the cricket on the hearth.

'Il Penseroso', l. 81 (1645). *Compare* DICKENS 204:6.

7 Blest pair of sirens, pledges of heav'n's joy,
Sphere-born harmonious sisters.

'At a Solemn Music' (1645) – the sirens are 'Voice' and 'Verse'. Notably set to music (1887) by Sir Hubert Parry.

8 Cromwell, our chief of men, who through a cloud,
Not of war only, but detractions rude,
Guided by faith and matchless fortitude,
To peace and truth thy glorious way has ploughed.

Sonnet, 'To the Lord General Cromwell' (written 1652). Hence, *Cromwell: Our Chief of Men*, title of Antonia Fraser's biography (1973). Fraser's book was known, however, as *Cromwell the Lord Protector* in the US.

9 Of man's first disobedience, and the fruit
Of that forbidden tree, whose mortal taste
Brought death into the world, and all our woe,
With loss of Eden.

Paradise Lost, Bk 1, l. 1 (1667). Milton's sonorous opening statement of his theme – Adam's disobedience and the Fall.

10 Thick as autumnal leaves that strow the brooks
In Vallombrosa, where the Etrurian shades
High over-arched embower.

Ib., Bk 1, l.302. Describing Satan's legions – 'Angel forms, who lay entranced...'

11 Let none admire
That riches grow in hell; that soil may best
Deserve the precious bane.

Ib., Bk 1, l. 690. Hence, *Precious Bane*, title of the novel (1924) by Mary Webb.

12 God is thy law, thou mine; to know no more
Is woman's happiest knowledge and her praise.
With thee conversing I forget all time.

Ib., Bk 4, l. 637. Eve to Adam, a delicate compliment. As 'With Thee conversing we forget all time, and toil, and care,/Labour is rest, and pain is sweet,/If Thou my God, art there' it became a hymn by Charles Wesley (No. 460 in *The Methodist Hymnal*).

13 Wherefore with thee
Came not all hell broke loose.

Ib., Bk 4, l.917. The Archangel Gabriel speaks to Satan. Hence, 'all hell broke loose', a popular descriptive catchphrase for when chaos occurs. Milton had been anticipated in this by the author of a Puritan pamphlet, *Hell Broke Loose: or, a Catalogue of Many of the Spreading Errors, Heresies and Blasphemies of These Times, for Which We are to be Humbled* (1646). Also in Robert Greene's play *Friar Bacon and Friar Bungay* (*c.*1589), the character Miles has the line: 'Master, master, master up! Hell's broken loose.' As an idiomatic phrase it was certainly well established by 1738 when Swift compiled his *Polite Conversation*. When there is 'A great Noise below', Lady Smart exclaims: 'Hey, what a clattering is there; one would think Hell was broke loose.'

1 Unmoved,
Unshaken, unseduced, unterrified,
His Loyalty he kept, his Love, his Zeal;
Nor number, nor example with him wrought
To swerve from truth, or change his constant
mind.

Ib., Bk 5, l. 898. A quotation to be found on the memorial tablet to the Liberal Prime Minister, H.H. Asquith, in Westminster Abbey. The lines were chosen 'after much thought by his family', according to Asquith's biographer, Roy Jenkins.

2 Ask for this great deliverer now, and find him
Eyeless in Gaza, at the mill with slaves.

Samson Agonistes, l. 40 (1671). Hence, *Eyeless in Gaza* (1936), title of a book by Aldous Huxley.

MINNEY, R.J.

English writer (1895–1979)

3 Carve Her Name With Pride.

As Michael Powell comments in *Million-Dollar Movie* (1992), the title of Minney's book (1956; film UK, 1958), 'sounds like a quotation, and probably is'. But I think not. Minney makes no reference to the title in his somewhat soupy biography of Violette Szabo, the wartime agent who was executed by the Germans and became the first British woman to receive the George Cross (gazetted posthumously in 1946). The notion of carving an epitaph is, of course, an old one. Robert Browning has 'If ye carve my epitaph aright' in his poem 'The Bishop Orders His Tomb' (1845).

MINOW, Newton N.

American government official (1926–)

4 Keep your eyes glued to that set until the station signs off. I can assure you that you will observe a vast wasteland.

On American TV watched from morn till night. Speech, National Association of Broadcasters (9 May 1961).

MITCHELL, Margaret

American novelist (1900–49)

5 My dear, I don't give a damn.

Gone With the Wind, Chap. 57 (1936). Popularly remembered, however, as in the last scene of the film (US, 1939) where Scarlett O'Hara is finally abandoned by her husband, Rhett Butler. Although Scarlett believes she can win him back, there occurs the controversial moment when Rhett replies to her entreaty:

Scarlett: Where shall I go? What shall I do?
Rhett: Frankly, my dear, I don't give a damn.

These words were allowed on to the soundtrack only after months of negotiation with the Hays Office, which controlled film censorship. In those days the word 'damn' was forbidden in Hollywood under Section V (1) of the Hays Code, even if it was what Mitchell had written in her novel (though she hadn't included the 'frankly'). Sidney Howard's original draft was accordingly changed to: 'Frankly, my dear, I don't care.' The scene was shot with both versions of the line, and the producer, David Selznick, argued at great length with the censors over which was to be used. He did this not least because he thought he would look a fool if the famous line was excluded. He also wanted to show how faithful the film was to the novel. Selznick argued that the *Oxford Dictionary* described 'damn' not as an oath but as a vulgarism, that many women's magazines used the word, and that preview audiences had expressed disappointment when the line was omitted. The censors suggested 'darn' instead. Selznick finally won the day – but because he was technically in breach of the Hays Code he was fined $5000. The line still didn't sound quite right: Clark Gable, as Rhett, had to put the emphasis unnaturally on 'give' rather than on 'damn'.

6 After all, tomorrow is another day.

The last words of the film, spoken by Vivien Leigh as Scarlett O'Hara, are: 'Tara! Home! I'll go home, and I'll think of some way to get him back. After all, tomorrow is another day!' The last sentence is as it appears in Mitchell's novel, but the idea behind it is proverbial. In John Rastell's *Calisto and Melebea* (*c.*1527) there occurs the line: 'Well, mother, tomorrow is a new day'.

See also DOWSON 213:2.

MITFORD, Nancy

English author (1904–73)

7 She said that all the sights in Rome were called after London cinemas.

Pigeon Pie (1940). Compare the caption to a cartoon by Bert Thomas in *Punch* (12 January 1921): 'The Profiteer's Lady (in Rome): "Wot *was* the Coliseum, 'Enry? A cinema?"'

1 I loathe abroad, nothing would induce me to live there ... and, as for foreigners, they are all the same, and they all make me sick.

The Pursuit of Love, Chap. 10 (1945). Compare 'Frogs ... are slightly better than Huns or Wops, but abroad is unutterably bloody and foreigners are fiends', from *ib.*, Chap. 15. Mitford wrote both these passages in the character of 'Uncle Matthew'. This no great opinion of foreigners is put down to his four years in France and Italy between 1914 and 1918. It certainly does not reflect her own view – she lived in France for many years until her death. *Compare* GEORGE VI 257:3.

2 Love in a Cold Climate.

Title of novel (1949). This caused Evelyn Waugh to write to Mitford (10 October): '[It] has become a phrase. I mean when people want to be witty they say I've caught a cold in a cold climate and everyone understands.' The title was suggested by Bennett Cerf, the book's American publisher.

Earlier, Robert Southey, the poet, writing to his brother Thomas (28 April 1797) had said: 'She has made me half in love with a cold climate.'

3 I love children – especially when they cry, for then someone takes them away.

Attributed on BBC Radio *Quote ... Unquote* (26 April 1978), but unverified.

See also ROSS 461:7.

MITTERRAND, François

French socialist President (1916–96)

4 She has the eyes of Caligula and the lips of Marilyn Monroe.

Of Margaret Thatcher. Attributed, for example, by Anthony Powell in his *Journals 1982–1986* (1995 – entry for 28 March 1985). In Hugo Young, *One of Us* (1989), the remark is attributed to Mitterand when briefing his new European Minister, Roland Dumas (which would have been in 1983) and is given in French: '*Cette femme Thatcher! Elle a les yeux de Caligule, mais elle a la bouche de Marilyn Monroe.*'

MIZNER, Wilson

American playwright (1876–1933)

5 [Always] be nice to people on your way up, because you'll meet 'em on your way down.

Quoted in Alva Johnston, *The Legendary Mizners* (1953). Also ascribed to Jimmy Durante and others.

MOLA, Emilio

Spanish Nationalist general (1887–1937)

6 *La quinta columna.*
The fifth column.

In October 1936, during the Spanish Civil War, Mola was besieging the Republican-held city of Madrid with four columns. He was asked in a broadcast whether this was sufficient to capture the city and he replied that he was relying on the support of the *quinta columna* [the fifth column], which was already hiding inside the city and which sympathized with his side. Hence, the term 'fifth columnists' meaning 'traitors, infiltrators'. It was also the title of Ernest Hemingway's only play (1938).

MONDALE, Walter

American Democratic Vice-President (1928–)

7 Where's the beef?

A slogan borrowed by Mondale in 1984, when he was seeking the Democratic presidential nomination, to describe what he saw as lack of substance in the policies of his rival for the nomination, Gary Hart. Hence, a classic example of an advertising slogan turning into a political catchphrase. The Wendy International hamburger chain promoted its wares in the US, from 1984, with TV commercials, one of which showed elderly women eyeing a small hamburger on a huge bun – a Wendy competitor's product. 'It certainly is a big bun,' asserted one. 'It's a very big fluffy bun,' the second agreed. But the third asked, 'Where's the beef?' Mondale took it from there.

MONROE, Marilyn

American film actress (1926–62)

8 I had the radio on.

When asked if she had really posed for a calendar (1947) with nothing on. Quoted in *Time* Magazine (11 August 1952).

1 Isn't there another part of the matzoh you can eat?

On being served matzoh balls for supper at Arthur Miller's parents. Oral tradition, no doubt apocryphal. Gore Vidal merely cites 'the dumb starlet [who] would ask, What do they do with the rest of the matzoh?' in *The New York Review of Books* (17/31 May 1973).

2 I'm not worried about the money, I just want to be *wonderful* ...

What Monroe is supposed to have said when she was asked if all the haggling over money and contracts in the movie business ever got her down. Quoted by Peter Potter in *All About Money* (1988).

MONSARRAT, Nicholas

English novelist (1910–79)

3 You English ... think we know damn nothing *but I tell you we know damn all.*

The Cruel Sea (1951). Compare this: in the second volume of David Niven's autobiography to which he gave the title *Bring On the Empty Horses* (1975), he talked of Michael Curtiz, the Hungarian-born American film director (1888–1962). During the filming of *The Charge of the Light Brigade* (1936), Curtiz ordered the release of a hundred riderless steeds by shouting: 'Bring on the empty horses!' David Niven and Errol Flynn fell about with laughter at this. Curtiz rounded on them and said, 'You and your stinking language! You think I know f*** nothing. Well, let me tell you, I know f*** all!' In fact, this is a frequently told tale and may pre-date Curtiz as well.

MONTAGU, Lady Mary Wortley

English writer (1689–1762)

4 This world consists of men, women and Herveys.

Alluding to Lord Hervey of Ickworth (d.1743), with whom she had some sort of literary friendship. Attributed by Lord Wharncliffe in *The Letters and Works of Lady Mary Wortley Montagu* (1837). According to the *DNB*, Hervey had loose morals, was 'effeminate in appearance as well as in habits' but had eight children.

5 It has all been very interesting.

Lady Mary's wonderful 'dying words' (as given, for example, in Barnaby Conrad, *Famous Last Words*, 1961) have, unfortunately, not been authenticated. Robert Halsband in his *Life of Lady Mary Wortley Montagu* (1956) remarks that 'they are nowhere unequivocally recorded' and notes that the source – Iris Barry's *Portrait of Lady Mary Montagu* (1928) – is 'clearly fictitious'.

MONTAIGNE, Michel de

French essayist (1533–92)

6 I quote others only the better to express myself.

Essays, Bk 1, Chap. 26 (1580). This might be more accurately rendered as: 'I do not speak the minds of others except to speak my own mind better.'

7 It could be said of me that in this book I have only made up a bunch of other men's flowers, and provided nothing of my own but the string to bind them.

Ib., Bk 3, Chap. 12. Hence, *Other Men's Flowers*, title of a poetry anthology by Lord Wavell (1944).

MONTEFIORE, Hugh

British Anglican clergyman (later bishop) (1920–)

8 Why did He not marry? Could the answer be that Jesus was not by nature the marrying sort?

At conference, Oxford (26 July 1967). Compare Anthony Powell's autobiographical volume *Infants of the Spring* (1976), in which he writes of an entertainer called Varda that she 'had been married for a short time to a Greek surrealist painter, Jean Varda, a lively figure ... but not the marrying sort'. It is not quite clear what is to be inferred from this. However, when Hugh Montefiore used the phrase about Jesus, people were outraged at the suggestion that He might have been a homosexual.

Usually encountered in the negative sense, 'marrying sort' has nevertheless existed in its own right. From Shaw's *Pygmalion* (1916): (Professor Higgins to Liza) 'All men are not confirmed old bachelors like me and the Colonel. Most men are the marrying sort (poor devils!)'

MONTGOMERY, Bernard (later 1st Viscount Montgomery of Alamein)

English field marshal (1887–1976)

9 Here we will stand and fight; there will be no further withdrawal ... We are going to finish

with this chap Rommel once and for all. It will be quite easy. There is no doubt about it. He is definitely a nuisance. Therefore we will hit him a crack and finish with him.

One of the most effective exhortations of the war was given by Montgomery as he took command of the Eighth Army on 13 August 1942. Two months before the Battle of El Alamein, he electrified his officers with a private pep talk. A recording of the speech was made after the war and was based on shorthand notes made at the time.

1 Who is this chap? He drinks, he's dirty, and I know there are women in the background!

On Augustus John who had been sent to paint him (*c.*1944). Quoted in *The Times Literary Supplement* (21 March 1975). Hence, *Women in the Background*, title of a novel (1996) by Barry Humphries.

2 I have heard some say ... [homosexual] practices are allowed in France and in other NATO countries. We are not French, and we are not other nationals. We are British, thank God!

Speech, House of Lords (24 May 1965). Commenting on a bill to relax the laws against homosexuals.

3 Consider what the Lord said to Moses – and I think he was right.

For a time, it seemed that this was something that Montgomery – that blushing violet – had *actually* said. Then it was traced to a line in a sketch called 'Salvation Army' performed by Lance Percival as an army officer but with a Montgomery accent on BBC TV's *That Was the Week That Was* (1962–3). Hence, it is simply a joke, though totally in character.

Compare *The Lyttelton Hart-Davis Letters* (Vol. 4, relating to 1959), where the same joke occurs in the form, 'Did you hear of the parson who began his sermon: "As God said – and rightly ...".' No mention of Montgomery. Compare also a remark made by Donald Coggan, Archbishop of Canterbury, on 7 June 1977, during a sermon for the Queen's Silver Jubilee service at St Paul's Cathedral: 'We listened to these words of Jesus [St Matthew 7:24] a few moments ago.' Then he exclaimed: 'How right he was!'

One is reminded irresistibly of Lorenz Hart's stripper's song 'Zip' from *Pal Joey* (1940):

> I was reading Schopenhauer last night,
> And I think that Schopenhauer was right.

Compare, yet further, what William Jackson, Bishop of Oxford, once preached (according to *The Oxford Book of Oxford*, 1978): 'St Paul says in one of his Epistles – and I partly agree with him.'

MONTY PYTHON'S FLYING CIRCUS

British TV comedy series (BBC), from 1969–74. Written and performed by John Cleese (as Announcer and Praline), Eric Idle (as Nudge), and others.

4 *Announcer*: And now for something completely different.

Catchphrase, usually delivered by Cleese as a dinner-jacketed BBC announcer, seated before a microphone on a desk in some unlikely setting, the phrase was taken from a slightly arch 'link' much loved by magazine programme presenters. These people were thus deprived of a very useful phrase. When introducing BBC Radio 4's breakfast-time *Today* programme in the mid-1970s, I sorely regretted this. After all, if you are introducing a magazine programme there is not much else you can say to get from an interview with the Prime Minister to an item about beer-drinking budgerigars. The children's BBC TV series *Blue Peter* is sometimes said to have provoked the *Python* use of the phrase.

It was first delivered by Eric Idle in the second edition of *Python* (on 12 October 1969), though it had also featured in some of the same team's earlier series *At Last the 1948 Show* (ITV, 1967). Used as the title of the comedy team's first cinema feature in 1971.

5 *Norman*: Nudge, nudge, wink, wink. Know what I mean? Say no more!

Catchphrase of prurient character later known as 'Nudge', who accosted people with remarks like, 'Is your wife a goer, then? Eh, eh?' The phrases were spoken in any order (first, on 19 October 1969). Hence, titles of my books *Nudge Nudge, Wink Wink* (1986) and *Say No More!* (1987).

6 *Praline*: It's not pining, it's passed on. This parrot is no more. It's ceased to be. It's expired. It's gone to meet its maker. This is a late parrot. It's a stiff. Bereft of life it rests in peace. It would be pushing up the daisies if you hadn't nailed it to the perch. It's rung down the curtain and joined the choir invisible. It's an ex-parrot.

'Parrot sketch' (7 December 1969), in which a man who has just bought a parrot that turns out to be dead, registers a complaint with the pet shop owner. From this came the later expression 'dead parrot' for anything one wished to describe as 'undoubtedly moribund, quite incapable of resuscitation'. Somewhat belatedly, in early 1988, there were signs of the phrase becoming an established idiom when it was applied to a controversial policy document drawn up as the basis for a merged Liberal/Social Democratic Party. Then *The Observer* commented (8 May 1988): 'Mr Steel's future – like his document – was widely regarded as a "dead parrot". Surely this was the end of his 12-year reign as Liberal leader?' In October 1990, Margaret Thatcher belatedly came round to the phrase (fed by a speechwriter, no doubt) and called the Liberal Democrats a 'dead parrot' at the Tory Party Conference. When the Liberals won a by-election at Eastbourne the same month, the Tory party chairman Kenneth Baker said the 'dead parrot' had merely 'twitched'.

MOORE, Clement Clarke

American scholar (1779–1863)

1 'Twas the night before Christmas, when all
through the house
Not a creature was stirring, not even a mouse;
The stockings were hung by the chimney
with care,
In hopes that St Nicholas soon would be there.

'A Visit from St Nicholas' (1823). Written for his children at Christmas 1822 and then published in the Troy *Sentinel*.

MOORE, George

Irish novelist (1852–1933)

2 The difference between my quotations and those of the next man is that I leave out the inverted commas.

Quoted in Laurence J. Peter, *Quotations for Our Time* (1977), but unverified. Moore also said the similarly untraced: 'Taking something from one man and making it worse is plagiarism' – quoted in Bentley and Esar, *A Treasury of Humorous Quotations* (1951).

MOORE, Thomas

Irish poet (1779–1852)

3 Oh! ever thus, from childhood's hour,
I've seen my fondest hopes decay;
I never lov'd a tree or flow'r,
But 'twas the first to fade away.
I never nurs'd a dear gazelle,
To glad me with its soft black eye,
But when it came to know me well,
And love me, it was sure to die!

'The Fire Worshippers', Pt 1, in *Lalla Rookh* (1817). *See* PYM 443:4.

MORGAN, J.P., Jr

American banker (1867–1943)

4 If you have to ask the price you can't afford it.

Morgan succeeded his father as head of the US banking house of Morgan. The story has it that a man was thinking of buying a yacht similar to Morgan's and asked him how much it cost in annual upkeep. Morgan replied with words to this effect. Quoted in Bennett A. Cerf, *Laughing Stock* (1945). *Compare* GETTY 259:7.

MORGANFIELD, McKinley (Muddy Waters)

American lyricist and blues singer (1915–83)

5 Got My Mojo Workin'.

Title of song. In 1960, Muddy Waters, the American blues singer was singing a song with the refrain, 'Got my mojo workin', but it just don't work on you.' He knew what he was singing about because he had written the song under his real name, McKinley Morganfield. *The Dictionary of American Slang* (1975) defines 'mojo' simply as 'any narcotic' but a sleeve note to an album entitled *Got My Mojo Workin'* (1966) by the jazz organist Jimmy Smith is perhaps nearer to the meaning of the word in the song. It describes 'mojo' as 'magic – a spell or charm guaranteed to make the user irresistible to the opposite sex'. Word known by 1926. Indeed, it seems that 'mojo' could well be a form of the word 'magic' corrupted through Black pronunciation, though the *OED2* finds an African word meaning 'magic, witchcraft' that is similar. The *OED2* derives the narcotic meaning of the word from the Spanish *mojar*, 'to celebrate by drinking'.

MORLEY, Lord (3rd Earl of Morley)

English Liberal politician and writer (1838–1923)

6 That most delightful way of wasting time.

Of letter-writing. 'Life of George Eliot', *Critical Miscellanies* (1886).

7 Although in Cabinet all its members stand on an equal footing, speak with equal voice, and, on the rare occasions when a division is taken,

are counted on the fraternal principle of one vote, yet the head of the Cabinet is *primus inter pares*, and occupies a position which, so long as it lasts, is one of exceptional and peculiar authority.

Life of Walpole (1889). Lord Morley may have been the first to use the phrase *primus inter pares* [first among equals] in this context, but the otherwise anonymous Latin saying has also been used about the position of politicians in a number of countries and also of the Pope. *The Oxford Dictionary of Colloquial English* (1985) defines it as an idiom meaning 'the one of a group who leads or takes special responsibility but who neither feels himself, nor is held by others to be, their superior'. The Round Table in Arthurian legend was meant to show not only that there was no precedence among the knights who sat at it but also that King Arthur was no more than first among equals.

Used specifically regarding the British Prime Minister within the Cabinet, the phrase cannot predate Sir Robert Walpole (in power 1721–42) who is traditionally the first to have held that position. *First Among Equals* was the title of Jeffrey Archer's novel (1984) about the pursuit of the British Prime Ministership. In 1988 Julian Critchley MP (*q.v.*) was quoted as having referred to Margaret Thatcher as '*prima donna inter pares*'.

MORRIS, Desmond

English biologist and writer (1928–)

1 The Naked Ape.

Title of book (1967). Morris begins: 'There are one hundred and ninety-three living species of monkeys and apes. One hundred and ninety-two of them are covered with hair. The exception is a naked ape self-named *Homo sapiens*.'

MORRIS, Jan (formerly James Morris)

Welsh writer (1926–)

2 There's romance for you! There's the lust and dark wine of Venice! No wonder George Eliot's husband fell into the Grand Canal.

Venice (1960). Closing words. After George Eliot's long unmarried relationship with G.H. Lewes, in 1880 she wed John Walter Cross who was twenty years her junior. As Morris has already observed, Cross did indeed once fall, 'with an ignominious plop, from their hotel window into the Grand Canal beneath.'

3 DEDICATED GRATEFULLY TO THE WARDEN AND FELLOWS OF ST ANTONY'S COLLEGE, OXFORD. EXCEPT ONE.

Dedication of *The Oxford Book of Oxford* (1978). Compare the wish attributed to W.C. Fields: 'A Merry Christmas to all my friends except two.'

4 Say farewell to the trumpets!
You will hear them no more.
But their sweet sad silvery echoes
Will call to you still
Through the half-closed door.

Some book, film and TV titles are quasi-quotations or are, rather, quasi-poetic in sound – titles like *By the Sword Divided, Carve Her Name With Pride, To Serve Them All My Days, A Horseman Riding By, God Is an Englishman*, and so on. (All of these are dealt with elsewhere in this book.) Morris has admitted that, having thought up the title *Farewell the Trumpets* (1978) for the final volume of her *Pax Britannica* trilogy, she then wrote a poem to quote it from. The poem duly appears as the book's epigraph.

MORRIS, William

English poet and craftsman (1834–96)

5 Forget six counties overhung with smoke,
Forget the snorting steam and piston stroke,
Forget the spreading of the hideous town;
Think rather of the pack-horse on the down,
And dream of London, small, and white,
and clean.

Prologue to *The Earthly Paradise* (1868–70). Morris's friend, Edward Burne-Jones, once commented: 'You cannot find short quotations in him, he must be taken in great gulps' (Georgiana Burne-Jones, *Memorials of Edward Burne-Jones*, 1904).

See also BELL 81:9.

MORRISON, Herbert (later Lord Morrison)

British Labour politician (1888–1965)

6 Go to it!

On 22 May 1940, Morrison, as Minister of Supply, concluded a radio broadcast calling for a voluntary labour force with these words. They echoed the public mood after Dunkirk and were subsequently used as a wall-poster slogan – in vivid letters – in a campaign run by the S.H. Benson agency (which later indulged in self-parody on behalf of Bovril, with 'Glow to it' in 1951–2). 'Go to it', meaning 'to act vigorously, set to with a will', dates from the early nineteenth century at least. In Shakespeare, *King Lear* (IV.vi.112), it means something else:

> Die for adultery! No:
> The wren goes to't, and the small gilded fly
> Does lecher in my sight.

MORRISON, Herbert

American broadcaster (1905–89)

1 Oh, the humanity!

'Toward us, like a great feather ... is the *Hindenburg*. The members of the crew are looking down on the field ahead of them getting their glimpses of the mooring mast ...' On 6 May 1937 radio commentator Morrison was describing the scene at the Naval airbase in Lakehurst, New Jersey, as the German airship made its first arrival there that year (having made ten round trips to the US the previous year). 'It is starting to rain again ... the back motors of the ship are just holding it just enough to keep it from – It's burst into flames! ... It's crashing, terrible! ... Folks, this is terrible, this is one of the worst catastrophes the world ever witnessed ... It's a terrific sight, ladies and gentlemen, the smoke and the flames now. And the plane is crashing to the ground ... Oh, the humanity! All the passengers! ... I can't talk, ladies and gentlemen ...' (transcribed from a recording).

A few seconds later Morrison managed to continue describing what *Time* Magazine called 'the worst and most completely witnessed disaster in the history of commercial aviation'. Although the *Hindenburg* was destroyed (virtually ending airships as a commercial venture), there were survivors.

MORTIMER, John

English author, playwright and lawyer (1923–)

2 Clinging to the Wreckage.

Title of autobiography (1982) – explained in an epigraphic paragraph or two: 'A man with a bristling grey beard [a yachtsman, said:] "I made up my mind, when I bought my first boat, never to learn to swim ... When you're in a spot of trouble, if you can swim you try to strike out for the shore. You invariably drown. As I can't swim, I cling to the wreckage and they send a helicopter out for me. That's my tip, if you ever find yourself in trouble, cling to the wreckage!"' Mortimer concludes: 'It was advice that I thought I'd been taking for most of my life.'

3 In the beginning was the Word. It's about the only sentence on which I find myself in total agreement with God.

Quoted in *The Observer* (1 July 1984). Alluding to John 1:1: 'In the beginning was the Word, and the Word was with God, and the Word was God.'

4 The shelf life of the modern hardback writer is somewhere between the milk and the yoghurt.

Quoted in *The Observer* (28 June 1987) and picked up by *ODMQ* (1991). As he had, in fact, said at the time, Mortimer was quoting the American humorous columnist Calvin Trillin (1935–), who had said, rather, 'A shelf life somewhere between butter and yoghurt' in *The New York Times* on 14 June 1987.

5 Champagne socialist.

The *ODQ* (1992) attributes to Mortimer this description of himself and, indeed *The Sunday Telegraph* (3 July 1988) stated that 'he once described himself as a "champagne socialist"'. The phrase might, it is true, have been coined with Mortimer in mind – he likes a bottle or two, goes around calling everyone 'darling' and doesn't see why the good things in life should be denied him just because he is a 'bit Left', but to what extent he has applied the phrase to himself, if at all, is not totally clear. From *The Independent* (2 September 1991): '[On the set of his latest television serial *Titmuss Regained*] Mortimer relaxed in the catering bus with a bottle of Moët (apparently determined not to disappoint those who think of him as a champagne socialist).'

The earliest use of the phrase found to date is in connection with that other larger-than-life character, the late tycoon and criminal, Robert Maxwell. From *The Times* (2 July 1987): 'Robert Maxwell, *Daily Mirror* newspaper tycoon and possibly the best known Czech in Britain after Ivan Lendl, has long been renowned for his champagne socialist beliefs.' At around that time, the phrase was also applied to socialist figures such as Clive Jenkins and Derek Hatton.

But maybe the phrase has even earlier beginnings: a similarly alliterative phrase was applied to a more admirable and larger-than-life socialist, Aneurin Bevan. Randolph Churchill (who was something of a champagne Conservative) recalled in the *Evening Standard* (8 August 1958), how Brendan Bracken had once 'gone for' Bevan: '"You Bollinger Bolshevik, you ritzy Robespierre, you lounge-lizard Lenin," he roared at Bevan one night, gesturing, as he went on, somewhat in the manner of a domesticated orang-utan. "Look at you, swilling Max's champagne and calling yourself a socialist".'

MORTON, J.B. (Beachcomber)

British humorous writer (1893–1979)

1 Hush, hush
Nobody cares!
Christopher Robin
Has
Fallen
Down–
Stairs.

'Now We are Sick', *By the Way* (1931). Parodying MILNE 392:2.

2 The man with the false nose had gone to that bourne from which no hollingsworth returns.

'Another True Story', *Gallimaufry* (1936). Alluding to Shakespeare *Hamlet* (III.i.79) – 'the undiscover'd country, from whose bourn/No traveller returns' (480:3). Bourne & Hollingsworth was a noted London department store.

3 Justice must not only be seen to be done but has to be seen to be believed.

Attributed by Peter Cook on BBC Radio *Quote ... Unquote* (5 June 1980) – and, consequently, to Cook himself.

4 Wagner is the Puccini of music.

PDMQ (1971) attributes this to Beachcomber and Rupert Hart-Davis concurs, saying that the announcement 'summed up the jargon-bosh of art- and music-critics beautifully' (*Lyttelton Hart-Davis Letters* for 5 February 1956). But no precise source is available. On the other hand, James Agate in *Ego 6* (for 13 October 1943) has: 'I do not doubt the sincerity of the solemn ass who, the other evening, said portentously: "Wagner is the Puccini of music!"' As Agate was addressing a group of 'school-marms' and as he generally had an after-dinner speaker's way with attribution, it may well still have been a Beachcomber coinage.

MORTON, Rogers

American government official (1914–79)

5 I'm not going to do anything to rearrange the furniture on the deck of the *Titanic*.

Refusing any last-ditch attempts to rescue President Ford's re-election campaign. He was Ford's campaign manager. Quoted in *The Times* (13 May 1976).

MORTON, Thomas

English playwright (c.1764–1838)

6 Approbation from Sir Hubert Stanley is praise indeed.

A Cure for the Heartache, Act 5, Sc. 2 (1797). This became a reasonably common proverbial phrase. P.G. Wodehouse uses the expression in *Psmith Journalist*, Chap. 15 (1915) and *Piccadilly Jim* Chap. 18 (1918). It is alluded to in Dorothy L. Sayers, *Gaudy Night*, Chap. 15 (1935): 'At the end of the first few pages [Lord Peter Wimsey] looked up to remark: "I'll say one thing for the writing of detective fiction: you know how to put your story together; how to arrange the evidence." "Thank you," said Harriet drily; "praise from Sir Hubert is praise indeed".'

7 Speed the Plough.

Title of play (1798), but a very old phrase indeed: in the form 'God speed the plough', it was what one would say when wishing someone luck in any venture (and not just an agricultural one). The phrase was in use by 1500 at least and is also the title of a traditional song and dance. *Speed-The-Plow* was the title of a play (1988) by David Mamet, about two Hollywood producers trying to get a project off the ground.

8 What will Mrs Grundy say?

Repeated question in *ib.* Hence, the expression 'Mrs Grundy' for 'a censorious person; an upholder of conventional morality'. Compare the later names of Mrs Ormiston Chaunt, an actual woman who campaigned in the late nineteenth century against immorality in the music-hall, and Mrs (Mary) Whitehouse who attempted to 'clean up' British TV from 1965 onwards.

MOSLEY, Oswald

English politician (1896–1980)

9 The only methods we shall employ will be English ones. The good old English fist.

Quoted in the *Manchester Guardian* (28 May 1931). Having been successively a Conservative, Independent and Labour MP (also serving as a minister in the 1929 Labour government), Mosley resigned and became leader of the British Union of Fascists. The union's meetings and marches (particularly in the East End of

London) often involved violent incidents. Here, Mosley was explaining how these occasions would be policed.

1 I am not, and never have been, a man of the right. My position was on the left and is now in the centre of politics.

Letter to *The Times* (26 April 1968). When Mosley published his autobiography in 1968, a forceful debate arose in Britain as to what precisely he had advocated in the 1930s and whether or not he had encouraged the use of violent methods. This letter may be seen as an example of the extensive self-justification that Mosley went in for during the latter part of his life.

MOUNTBATTEN OF BURMA, Earl

British military commander and Viceroy (1900–79)

2 In my experience, I have always found that you cannot have an efficient ship unless you have a happy ship, and you cannot have a happy ship unless you have an efficient ship. That is the way I intend to start this commission, and that is the way I intend to go on – with a happy and efficient ship.

From Mountbatten's initial address to the crew of HMS *Kelly* after he became the destroyer's captain in 1939. When Noël Coward wrote the script of his film *In Which We Serve* (1942), based on Mountbatten's association with HMS *Kelly* and its sinking during the Battle of Crete, the speech was adopted *verbatim*. Coward delivered it.

3 I can't think of a more wonderful thanksgiving for the life I have had than that everyone should be jolly at my funeral.

TV interview, broadcast after his assassination (August 1979).

MOYNIHAN, Daniel Patrick

American Democratic politician (1927–)

4 The time may have come when the issue of race could benefit from a period of 'benign neglect'. The subject has been too much talked about ... We may need a period in which negro progress continues and racial rhetoric fades.

As a counsellor to President Nixon, Moynihan quoted the phrase in a memorandum dated 2 March 1970. This was leaked to *The New York Times* and the inevitable furore ensued, though all he was suggesting was that racial tensions would be lessened if people on both sides were to lower their voices a little. He was quoting an 1839 remark by an Earl of Durham to Queen Victoria regarding Canada. It had done so well 'through a period of benign neglect' by the mother country that it should be granted self-government.

MOZART, Wolfgang Amadeus

Austrian composer (1756–91)

5 I write [music] as a sow piddles.

Quoted by Laurence J. Peter in *Quotations for Our Time* (1977). Source untraced, but using imagery of which Mozart was typically fond. Compare John Aubrey's memoir of Dr Kettle who, 'was wont to say that "Seneca writes, as a boare doth pisse", *scilicet*, by jirkes' (*Brief Lives*, from *c.*1690).

6 Didn't I say before that I was writing this *Requiem* for myself?

The last recorded words of Mozart concern the *Requiem* which he left unfinished when he died. He certainly seems to have said this on his last day alive, according to the biography (1828) by Georg Nikolaus Nissen based on that by Franz Xaver Niemetschek (1798) for which Mozart's widow Constanze supplied much material.

MUGGERIDGE, Kitty

English writer (1903–94)

7 He rose without trace.

Of David Frost. A notable remark, made *c.*1965. Curiously delighting in it, Frost provides the context in the first volume of his autobiography (1993). Malcolm Muggeridge (Kitty's husband) had predicted that after *That Was the Week That Was*, Frost would sink without trace. She said, 'Instead, he has risen without trace'.

MUGGERIDGE, Malcolm

English writer and broadcaster (1903–90)

8 Twilight of empire ... a phrase which occurred to me long ago.

Diaries (entry for 21 December 1947). Referring to Britain at any time after the death of Queen Victoria in 1901, but particularly when the colonies started moving towards independence. A phrase fashioned, presumably, after 'twilight of the gods' (German *Götterdämerung*).

1 Frumpish and banal.

On Queen Elizabeth II. Magazine article (October 1957).

2 He looked, I decided, like a letter delivered to the wrong address.

On Evelyn Waugh. 'My Fair Gentleman', in *Tread Softly* ... (1996).

3 He was not only a bore; he bored for England.

On Anthony Eden. 'Boring for England', in *ib.*

4 Very much like the Church of England. It is doctrinally inexplicable but it goes on.

On *Punch* (which he had once edited). Attributed in A. Andrews, *Quotations for Speakers and Writers* (1969).

5 To succeed pre-eminently in English public life it is necessary to conform either to the popular image of a bookie or of a clergyman; Churchill being a perfect example of the former, Halifax of the latter.

The Infernal Grove (1973). To James Callaghan has, however, been ascribed the view: 'Prime Ministers tend either to be bookmakers or bishops, and they take it in turn.'

See also THE TIMES 540:5.

MÜNSTER, Count Georg

Hanoverian diplomat (1794–1868)

6 Despotism tempered by assassination.

So replied Lord Reith, the BBC's first Director-General, when asked by Malcolm Muggeridge in the TV programme *Lord Reith Looks Back* (1970) what he considered the best form of government. The phrase was not original. For example, *Quotations for Speakers and Writers* (1969) quotes the remark of a Russian noble *to* Count Münster on the assassination of Emperor Paul I in 1800: 'Despotism tempered by assassination, that is our Magna Carta.' The *ODQ* (1992) prefers a direct quote from Count Münster's *Political Sketches of the State of Europe, 1814–1867* (1868): 'An intelligent Russian once remarked to us, "Every country has its own constitution; ours is absolutism moderated by assassination".' Bartlett (1980) attributes 'Absolutism tempered by assassination' direct to the earlier Ernst Friedrich Herbert von Münster (1766–1839).

The dates are rather important. How else is one to know whether Thomas Carlyle in his *History of the French Revolution* (1837) was alluding to the saying, when he wrote: 'France was long a despotism tempered by epigrams'? In a speech to the International Socialist Congress (Paris, 17 July 1889), the Austrian, Victor Adler, followed up with: 'The Austrian government ... is a system of despotism tempered by casualness.'

Notes and Queries, Vol. 202 (1957) has earlier sources, including Mme de Staël.

MURDOCH, Iris (later Dame Iris)

English novelist and philosopher (1919–)

7 A bad review is even less important than whether it is raining in Patagonia.

Quoted in a profile in *The Times* (6 July 1989), but otherwise unverified.

MURRAY, Sir James

Scottish lexicographer (1837–1915)

8 The traditional practice of dictionary makers is 'to copy shamelessly from one dictionary to another'.

When *The Century Dictionary* (1889) seemed to plagiarize Murray's work, it was his friends who reminded him of this. He did not necessarily subscribe to it himself. Quoted in Elizabeth Murray, *Caught in the Web of Words* (1977).

9 Have thy tools ready. God will find thee work.

According to Elizabeth Murray in *ib.*, this was his favourite text. It supposedly came from Charles Kingsley, and Murray hung it in his bedroom.

MURROW, Edward R.

American broadcaster (1908–65)

10 This ... is ... London.

Standard beginning to his wartime reports (1940s), a greeting that became familiar to American radio listeners to reports given by Murrow from London. It was a natural borrowing from BBC announcers who had been saying 'This is London calling' from the earliest days of station 2LO in the 1920s. One of them, Stuart Hibberd, entitled a book of his broadcasting diaries, *This Is London* (1950). Murrow added the distinctive pauses.

1 Goodnight ... and good luck.

Stock phrase in broadcasting, particularly on *See It Now* which has been called 'the prototype of the in-depth quality television documentary' (CBS TV, 1951–8).

2 He [Churchill] mobilized the English language and sent it into battle to steady his fellow countrymen and hearten those Europeans upon whom the long dark night of tyranny had descended.

Broadcast (30 November 1954). *See* KENNEDY 331:7.

3 Anyone who isn't confused doesn't really understand the situation.

Ascribed to Murrow on the subject of Vietnam by Walter Bryan, *The Improbable Irish* (1969). Then applied to the situation in Northern Ireland. There were a number of such sayings.

See also ANONYMOUS 21:7.

MUSSOLINI, Benito

Italian fascist leader (1883–1945)

4 I will make the trains run on time and create order out of chaos.

Efficiency may be the saving grace of a fascist dictatorship, but did Mussolini ever actually make this boast? Or did he merely claim afterwards that this is what he had done? One of his biographers (Giorgio Pini, 1939) quotes Mussolini exhorting a stationmaster: 'We must leave exactly on time ... From now on everything must function to perfection.' The improvement was being commented on by 1925. In that year, HRH Infanta Eulalia of Spain wrote in *Courts and Countries after the War* that 'the first benefit of Mussolini's direction in Italy' is when you hear that 'the train is arriving on time'. Quite *how* efficient the trains really were, is open to doubt. Perhaps they just ran *relatively* more on time than they had done before. But they had managed all right for the famous 'March on Rome' (October 1922) which – despite its name – was largely accomplished by train.

5 That garrulous monk.

On Hitler. Quoted in Winston Churchill, *The Second World War*, Vol.1 (1948).

6 It is better to have lived one day as a tiger than a thousand years as a sheep.

'Tibetan saying' quoted by Jim Ballard, husband of the British climber Alison Hargreaves who was killed on K2 in August 1995. It may have been one of her favourite sayings but, in fact, it is better known as a slogan of Mussolini's in the form: '*È meglio vivere un giorno di leone* [lion] *che cent' anni da pecora.*' (*c.*1930, quoted in Denis Mack-Smith, *Mussolini's Roman Empire*, 1967). Another form: from the film *The King of Comedy* (US, 1983): 'Look, I figure it this way: better to be a king for a night than a schmuck for a lifetime.'

MUSSOLINI, Vittorio

Italian airforce pilot and son of Benito (1916–97)

7 I dropped an aerial torpedo right in the centre, and the group opened up like a flowering rose. It was most entertaining.

On a bombing raid in Abyssinia. *Voli sulle Ambe* (1937).

N

NABOKOV, Vladimir

Russian-born novelist (1899–1977)

1 Lolita, light of my life, fire of my loins. My sin, my soul. Lo-lee-ta: the tip of the tongue taking a trip of three steps down the palate to tap, at three, on the teeth. Lo. Lee. Ta.

Lolita (1955), opening words. In *The Independent* Magazine (26 October 1996), the screenwriter Andrew Davies selected this as 'My Favourite Opening Paragraph', adding: 'There's a certain tantalising purity about it ... There's a lot of play on the actual sound of the words. It's an exquisitely sensual piece of writing.'

NAIPAUL, V.S. (later Sir Vidia)

Trinidadian novelist (1932–)

2 In a Free State.

Title of a novel (1971), set in a 'free state' in Africa, this phrase had earlier been used as the title of a sketch performed on record by Peter Sellers (1959). The latter is a take-off of an interview with a drunken Brendan Behan, the playwright, and thus the title here alludes to the Irish 'Free State'.

THE NAKED CITY

American film 1948. Script by Malvin Wald and Albert Matz.

3 *Narrator*: There are eight million stories in the naked city. This has been one of them.

Soundtrack. Last lines. Also used in TV series (1958–63) of the same name.

NANSEN, Fridtjof

Norwegian explorer (1861–1930)

4 The cold of the polar regions was nothing to the chill of an English bedroom.

Quoted in *The Laughing Diplomat* (1939) by Daniele Varè. Nansen made several voyages in the Arctic regions. He was also the first Norwegian ambassador to London (1906–8), which is when he presumably acquired his knowledge of the bedrooms.

5 The difficult is what takes a little time; the impossible is what takes a little longer.

Quoted – as said by Nansen – in *The Listener* (14 December 1939). Bartlett (1980) places this slogan specifically with the US Army Service Forces, but the idea has been traced back to Charles Alexandre de Calonne (1734–1802), who said: '*Madame, si c'est possible, c'est fait; impossible? cela se fera* [if it is possible, it is already done; if it is impossible, it will be done]' – quoted in J. Michelet, *Histoire de la Révolution Française* (1847). Henry Kissinger once joked: 'The illegal we do immediately, the unconstitutional takes a little longer' (quoted in William Shawcross, *Sideshow*, 1979).

NAPOLEON I

French Emperor (1769–1821)

6 *L'Angleterre est une nation de boutiquiers.*
England is a nation of shopkeepers.

Most of Napoleon's attributed sayings are, like Abraham Lincoln's, impossible to verify now. This remark was quoted by Barry E. O'Meara in *Napoleon in Exile* (1822). Earlier, however, Samuel Adams, the American Revolutionary leader, *may* have said in his *Oration in Philadelphia* (1 August 1776): 'A nation of shop-keepers are very seldom so disinterested.' In the same year, Adam Smith was writing in *The Wealth of Nations*: 'To found a great empire for the sole purpose of raising up a people of customers, may at first sight appear a project fit only for a nation of shopkeepers.'

1 **Every soldier has the baton of a field marshal in his knapsack.**

This is the anglicized form of a saying frequently attributed to Napoleon. E. Blaze in *La Vie Militaire sous l'Empire* (1837) has it thus: '*Tout soldat français porte dans sa giberne le bâton de maréchal de France*' (which should be more accurately translated as, 'Every French soldier carries in his cartridge-pouch the baton of a marshal of France'). This was how the saying first appeared in English in 1840. The meaning is: 'Even the lowliest soldier may have leadership potential.'

Mencken (1942) ascribes the saying to Louis XVIII (1755–1824), and, indeed, the French king who reigned after Napoleon said in a speech to cadets at Saint-Cyr (9 August 1819): 'Remember that there is not one of you who does not carry in his cartridge-pouch the marshal's baton of the Duke of Reggio; it is up to you to bring it forth.'

2 **An iron hand in a velvet glove.**

Napoleon is supposed to have said, 'Men must be led by an iron hand in a velvet glove', but this expression is hard to pin down as a quotation. Thomas Carlyle wrote in *Latter-Day Pamphlets* (1850): 'Soft speech and manner, yet with an inflexible rigour of command ... "iron hand in a velvet glove", as Napoleon defined it.' The Emperor Charles V (1519–56) may have said it earlier. Sometimes an iron 'fist' rather than 'hand' is evoked. Either way, the image is of unbending ruthlessness or firmness covered by a veneer of courtesy and gentle manners.

3 **From the sublime to the ridiculous there is but one step.**

Nowadays most often used as a phrase without the last five words. The proverbial form most probably came to us from the French. Napoleon is said to have uttered on one occasion (probably to the Polish ambassador, De Pradt, after the retreat from Moscow in 1812): '*Du sublime au ridicule il n'y a qu'un pas.*'

However, Thomas Paine had already written in *The Age of Reason* (1795): 'The sublime and the ridiculous are often so nearly related, that is difficult to class them separately. One step above the sublime, makes the ridiculous; and one step above the ridiculous, makes the sublime again.' Indeed, the chances are that 'from the sublime to the ridiculous' may have been a standard turn of phrase in the late eighteenth century. 'Dante, Petrarch, Boccacio, Ariosto, make very sudden transitions from the sublime to the ridiculous' (Joseph Warton, *Essay on the Genius and Writings of Pope*, Vol. 2, 1772).

4 **An army marches on its stomach.**

Attributed remark, encapsulating a report in E.A. de Las Cases, *Mémorial de Ste-Hélène* (1823).

5 **Not tonight, Josephine.**

Napoleon did not, as far as we know, ever say the words that have become popularly linked with him. The idea that he had had better things to do than satisfy the Empress Josephine's famous appetite, or was not inclined or able to do so, must have grown up during the nineteenth century. There was also a saying, attributed to Josephine, apparently, '*Bon-a-parte est Bon-à-rien* [Bonaparte is good for nothing]', which may be relevant.

A knockabout sketch filmed for the Pathé Library in *c.*1932 has Lupino Lane as Napoleon and Beatrice Lillie as Josephine. After signing a document of divorce (which Napoleon crumples up), Josephine says, 'When you are refreshed, come as usual to my apartment.' Napoleon says (as the tag to the sketch), 'Not tonight, Josephine,' and she throws a custard pie in his face.

The film *I Cover the Waterfront* (US 1933) has been credited with launching the phrase, though it merely popularized it. A British song with the title had appeared in 1915 (sung by Florrie Forde and written by Worton David and Lawrence Wright) and an American one (sung by Ada Jones and Billy Murray) was recorded on an Edison wax cylinder (?1901–10). Neither of these songs is about the historical Josephine: the British one is about a man who has promised his mother he will not kiss his bride before their wedding day and the American one is about a stenographer. The saying may well have been established in music-hall and vaudeville by the end of the previous century.

6 **[Women] belong to the highest bidder. Power is what they like – it is the greatest of all aphrodisiacs.**

Attributed to Napoleon by Constant Louis Wairy (his valet) in *Mémoires de Constant, premier valet de l'empereur* (1830–1). *Compare* KISSINGER 340:3.

7 **In victory you deserve it: in defeat you need it.**

A saying of Napoleon's (unverified) on the subject of champagne. On the other hand, 'Aid is ... like champagne: in success you deserve it, in failure you need it' is ascribed to Lord Bauer (1915–), British economist, in *Lords of Poverty* (1989) by Graham Hancock.

1 Plans are nothing, but planning is everything.

Attributed to Napoleon, but unverified. He does, however, appear to have said: 'Unhappy the general who comes on the field of battle with a system.' This is said to be included in his *Maxims 1804–15.* A favourite saying of Dwight D. Eisenhower (quoted by Richard M. Nixon in *Six Crises*, 1962) was: 'In preparing for battle I have always found that plans are useless but planning is indispensable.'

2 I shall return with the violets in the spring.

Leaving for Elba on his first journey into exile (1814). 'Someone heard Napoleon murmur as he left Fontainebleau for Elba that when the violets returned next spring he too would be back' – Elizabeth Longford, *Wellington: The Years of the Sword* (1969). He duly returned in March 1815.

3 *France – armée – tête d'armée – Joséphine.*

Napoleon died on St Helena in 1821 saying either this (Tristan de Montholon, who reported it, says he heard Napoleon say it twice) or '*Mon Dieu! La nation Française. Tête d'armée* [My God! The French nation. Head of the army].'

NASBY, Petroleum V. (David Ross Locke)

American humorist (1833–88)

4 The late unpleasantness.

Ekkoes from Kentucky (1868). A euphemism for a previous war or recent hostilities. 'Nasby' referred to the recently ended Civil War as 'the late onpleasantniss' and the coinage spread. It still survives: 'Here, for instance, is Dan Rather, America's father-figure, on the hot-line to Panama during the late unpleasantness [an invasion]' (*The Independent*, 20 January 1990).

NASH, Ogden

American poet (1902–71)

5 I think that I shall never see
A billboard lovely as a tree.
Perhaps unless the billboards fall,
I'll never see a tree at all.

'Song of the Open Road', *Happy Days* (1933). *Compare* KILMER 335:1.

6 Every Englishman is convinced of one thing, viz.
That to be an Englishman is to belong to the most exclusive club there is.

'England Expects', *I'm a Stranger Here Myself* (1938). Possibly the first encapsulation of a frequently used format. Compare the similar views expressed about membership of the British Parliament. 'Mr Twemlow' in Charles Dickens, *Our Mutual Friend*, Bk 2, Chap.3 (1864–5) says of the House of Commons: 'I think ... that it is the best club in London.' And Winston Churchill called it 'the best club in Europe' (quoted in Leon Harris, *The Fine Art of Political Wit*, 1965). This last phrase was also used (as though well-established) by Lady Astor in a talk on the BBC Empire Service in November 1937.

NATHAN, George Jean

American drama critic (1882–1958)

7 The test of a real comedian is whether you laugh at him before he opens his mouth.

In *The American Mercury* (September 1929). Now a cliché. Fred Lawrence Guiles said of Stan Laurel in *Stan* (1980): 'Very early on in his stage career Stan had made an interesting discovery: he found that audiences laughed at him before he ever said or did anything.' In November 1987 Robert McLennan of the SDP said of Barry Humphries as Sir Les Patterson: 'Like all great comic creations, he makes you laugh before he opens his mouth.'

NAUGHTON, Bill

English playwright (1910–92)

8 It seems to me if they ain't got you one way then they've got you another. So what's it all about, that's what I keep asking myself, what's it all about?

Alfie (1966) – the film script of his earlier radio and stage play. The phrase 'What's it all about, Alfie?' was chiefly popularized by Burt Bacharach and Hal David's song. This was not written for the film, which had a jazz score, with no songs, by Sonny Rollins, but Cher recorded it and this version was added to the soundtrack for the American release of the picture. Cilla Black then recorded it in Britain and Dionne Warwick in the US.

When Michael Caine, who played Alfie in the film, published his autobiography in 1992, it was naturally entitled *What's It All About?*

NEALE, J.M.

English clergyman and hymn writer (1818–66)

1 Art thou weary, art thou languid,
Art thou sore distressed?
'Come to me,' saith One, 'and coming
Be at rest!'

Hymn. Neale was a leading post tractarian and founder of an order of nuns. He wrote many well-known hymns or translated them from the Latin.

NELSON, Horatio (Viscount Nelson)

English admiral (1758–1805)

2 The Nelson touch.

Denoting any action bearing the hallmark of Horatio Nelson, his quality of leadership and seamanship, this term was coined by Nelson himself before the Battle of Trafalgar (1805): 'I am anxious to join the fleet, for it would add to my grief if any other man was to give them the Nelson touch.' In a letter to Lady Hamilton (1 October 1805), he wrote that when he came to explain it to his men, 'it was like an electric shock'. *The Oxford Companion to Ships and the Sea* (1976) describes various manoeuvres to which the term could be applied, but adds: 'It could have meant the magic of his name among officers and seamen of his fleet, which was always enough to inspire them to great deeds of heroism and endurance.' The British title of the film *Corvette K-225* (US, 1943) was *The Nelson Touch*.

3 I owe all my success in life to having been always a quarter of an hour before my time.

I.e., early. Chiefly in sea battles rather than in private life, one expects. We have this statement by courtesy of Samuel Smiles in *Self-Help* (1859). In *The Dictionary of War Quotations* (1989) the wording is: 'I have always been a quarter of an hour before my time, and it has made a man of me.'

4 Before this time tomorrow I shall have gained a peerage, or Westminster Abbey.

At the Battle of the Nile (1798), reported in Robert Southey, *The Life of Nelson* (1860 edition). Earlier, at the Battle of Cape St Vincent (1797), he is reported to have said: 'Westminster Abbey or victory!' Both of these echo Shakespeare, *Henry VI, Part 3* (II.ii.174): 'And either victory, or else a grave.'

5 I have only one eye – I have a right to be blind sometimes ... I really do not see the signal!

At the Battle of Copenhagen in 1803, Nelson 'put the telescope to his blind eye', as the modern allusion would have it – that is to say he made sure he did not see what he did not want to see (a signal ordering him to desist from action) and had a decisive victory. His exact words, according to Robert Southey's *Life of Nelson* (1813) were as above.

Alan Watkins, writing in *The Observer* (27 June 1993): 'Mr [John] Major then indulged in some misquotation of his own involving Lord Nelson, who is supposed to have said at the Battle of Copenhagen: "I really do not see the signal," though the more popular version is: "Danger? I see no danger." Mr Major took the latter version and replied, referring to the press: "Assault? I see no assault".' (Is Watkins right about the popularity of the 'danger' version?)

6 England expects that every man will do his duty.

At 11.30 a.m. on 21 October 1805 the British Fleet approached Napoleon's combined French and Spanish fleets before the Battle of Trafalgar. Nelson told one of his captains: 'I will now amuse the fleet with a signal.' At first, it was to be, 'Nelson confides that every man will do his duty'. But it was suggested that 'England' would be better than 'Nelson'. Flag Lieutenant Pasco then pointed out that the word 'expects' was common enough to be in the signal book, whereas 'confides' would have to be spelled out letter by letter and would require seven flags, not one.

When Admiral Lord Collingwood saw the signal coming from HMS *Victory*, he remarked: 'I wish Nelson would stop signalling, as we all know well enough what we have to do.'

Mencken (1942) finds an American saying from 1917 – during the First World War – 'England expects every American to do his duty.' In Britain, at about the same time, there was a recruiting slogan: 'England Expects that Every Man will Do His Duty and Join the Army Today.'

7 Kiss me, Hardy.

What exactly did Nelson say as he lay dying on HMS *Victory* at Trafalgar in 1805, having been severely injured by a shot fired from a French ship? It has been asserted that, according to the Nelson family, he was in the habit of saying 'kismet' (fate) when anything went wrong. It is therefore not *too* unlikely that he said, 'Kismet, Hardy' to his Flag Captain, and that witnesses misheard, but there is no real reason to choose this version.

In fact, the recording angel had to work overtime when Nelson lay dying, he said so much. The first reliable report of what went on was by Dr Beatty, the ship's surgeon, included in *Despatches and Letters of Lord Nelson* (ed. Nicholas, 1846):

> Captain Hardy now came to the cockpit to see his Lordship a second time. He then told Captain Hardy that he felt that in a few minutes he should be no more, adding in a low tone, 'Don't throw me overboard, Hardy.' The Captain answered, 'Oh, no, certainly not.' Then replied his Lordship, 'You know what to do. Take care of my dear Lady Hamilton. Kiss me, Hardy.' The Captain now knelt and kissed his cheek, when his Lordship said, 'Now I am satisfied. Thank God I have done my duty.'

This seems to be quite a reasonable description and, if Hardy did actually kiss him (a gesture that surely couldn't be mistaken), why should Nelson not have asked him to? Was there something wrong with a naval hero asking for this gesture from another man? Robert Southey in his *Life of Nelson*, published earlier, in 1813, also supports the 'kiss me' version (his account is almost identical to Beatty's). In Ludovic Kennedy's *On My Way to the Club* (1989), he recalls his own investigations into the matter: 'I was delighted to receive further confirmation from a Mr Corbett, writing from Hardy's home town of Portesham [in 1951]. He said that Nelson's grandson by his daughter Horatia had recently paid him a visit, at the age of over ninety. "He told me he had asked his mother what exactly had happened when Nelson was dying. She said she herself had asked Hardy, who replied, 'Nelson said, "Kiss me, Hardy" and I knelt down and kissed him'".'

It is also possible to argue that 'kiss' can mean no more than 'touch' – a reasonable and usual request from a dying man who needs some last physical contact.

NERO

Roman Emperor (AD37–68)

1 *Qualis artifex pereo!*
What a great artist dies with me!

As he drove a dagger into his throat rather than be taken alive. Nero had poetic and artistic ambitions (hence the expression about him fiddling while Rome burned – probably he was playing the lyre.) Quoted in Suetonius, *Lives of the Caesars*. Quoted in Barnaby Conrad, *Famous Last Words* (1961).

NERVAL, Gérard de

French poet (1808–55)

2 Well, you see, he doesn't bark and he knows the secrets of the sea.

Explaining his penchant for taking a lobster for a walk in the gardens of the Palais Royal, Paris, on a long blue leash (pink, in some versions). Théophile Gautier, *Portraits et Souvenirs Littéraires* (1875), has an elaborate version of the explanation, which translates as: 'Why should a lobster be any more ridiculous than a dog? Or any other animal that one chooses to take for a walk? I have a liking for lobsters; they are peaceful, serious creatures; they know the secrets of the sea; they don't bark, and they don't gnaw upon one's *monadic* privacy like dogs do. And Goethe had an aversion to dogs, and he wasn't mad.' An unanswerable conclusion, surely?

NESBIT, E(dith)

English writer (1858–1924)

3 You had no right to write the Preface if you were not going to write the book.

To Bernard Shaw, after an empty flirtation (1887). Quoted in Michael Holroyd, *Bernard Shaw*, Vol. 1 (1988).

NEVINS, Allan

American writer and teacher (1890–1971)

4 The former allies had blundered in the past by offering Germany too little and offering even that too late, until finally Nazi Germany had become a menace to all mankind.

In *Current History* (May 1935). On 13 March 1940 the former Prime Minister David Lloyd George said in the House of Commons: 'It is the old trouble – too late. Too late with Czechoslovakia, too late with Poland, certainly too late with Finland. It is always too late, or too little, or both.' From there the phrase passed into more general use, though usually political. From the *Notting Hill & Paddington Recorder* (25 January 1989): 'Junior Transport Minister, Peter Bottomley, came to West London last week to unveil plans for a £250 million relief road that will cut a swathe through the heart of the area ... But Hammersmith and Fulham councillors are furious about the government consultation exercise which they claim is "too little too late".'

From *The Guardian* (30 January 1989): 'The Home Office is preparing a video to warn prisoners of the dangers [of AIDs] – but is it too little, too late?'

NEWBOLT, Sir Henry

English poet (1862–1938)

5 The Island Race.

Title of book of poems (1898) – though not of any actual poem – the first prominent appearance of the phrase. The characterization of Britain as an 'island race' understandably reached its apogee in the Second World War, but at big patriotic moments there has always been a tendency to draw attention to the fact of Britain being an island, from John of Gaunt's 'sceptr'd isle' in Shakespeare's *Richard II* onwards. Winston Churchill said, 'We shall defend our Island, whatever the cost may be' in his 'We shall fight on the beaches' speech of 4 June 1940. The flag-waving film *In Which We Serve* (1942) refers specifically to the 'island race'. Churchill used the phrase as the title of Bk 1, Vol. 1 of his *History of the English-Speaking Peoples* (1956). In *The Second World War*, Vol. 5 (1952) he also quotes the 'island *story*' phrase from Tennyson's 'Ode on the Death of the Duke of Wellington' (1852):

> Not once or twice in our rough island story
> The path of duty was the way to glory.

1 There's a breathless hush in the Close to-night – ...
'Play up! play up! and play the game!'

'Vitaï Lampada', in *ib.* The title of the poem refers, roughly speaking, to 'the torch of tradition', which the generations hand on like runners. Newbolt combines a cricket match with some military action in the desert to produce an imperial-sounding message.

See also TENNYSON 529:5.

NEWTON, Sir Isaac

English scientist (1642–1727)

2 O Diamond! Diamond! thou little knowest the mischief done!

To his dog who is said to have knocked over a candle and set fire to Newton's papers, thus destroying the labour of many years. Probably apocryphal, though recounted by 1772. Another version renames the dog: 'Ah, poor Fidele, what mischief hast thou done!' From P.G. Wodehouse, *The Code of the Woosters* (1938): 'I don't know if you were ever told as a kid that story about the fellow whose dog chewed up the priceless manuscript of the book he was writing. The blow-out, if you remember, was that he gave the animal a pained look and said: "Oh, Diamond, Diamond, you – or it may have been thou – little know – or possibly knowest – what you – or thou – has – or hast – done." I heard it in the nursery, and it has always lingered in my mind.'

3 If I have seen further it is by standing on the shoulders of giants.

In a letter to Robert Hooke (5 February 1676). Hooke had claimed to have discovered first the gravitational law of inverse squares, and Newton was attempting to conciliate him. Long before, in 1159, Bernard of Chartres, the French philosopher, had been quoted as saying, 'We are like dwarfs on the shoulders of giants, so that we can see more than they ... not by virtue of any sharpness of sight on our part ... but because we are carried high and raised up by their giant size.' The proverbial expression 'A dwarf on a giant's shoulders sees the further of the two' appears to have been established by the fourteenth century.

NEWTON, John

English hymnwriter (1725–1807)

4 Amazing grace! how sweet the sound,
That saved a wretch like me!
I once was lost, but now am found,
Was blind, but now I see.

Most people are familiar with 'Amazing Grace' from the great popular success it had when sung and recorded by Judy Collins in the early 1970s, but it is quite wrong for record companies to label the song 'Trad.' – as, for example, on the CD 'Amazing Grace' (Philips 432–546–2), by Jessye Norman. It was a hymn written in the seventeenth century by Newton, a reformed slave-trafficker. He (together with the poet William Cowper), wrote the Olney Hymnbook of 1779, and this is but one example from that work.

The slightly complicated thing is that the *tune* to which 'Amazing Grace' now gets sung *is* a traditional tune – it is an old American one – but that is hardly any excuse for denying Newton his credit for the words. (Some people say that before it was an anonymous American tune, however, it was an anonymous Scottish tune.)

NEW YORK SUN *See* SUN, THE

NICHOLAS

Christian prelate and saint (fl.AD350)

5 God be glorified!

One of the numerous legends associated with St Nicholas, patron saint of Greece and Russia, and popularly known as 'Santa Claus', concerns his birth. It is said that he leapt from his mother's womb and cried out, 'God be glorified!' In Benjamin Britten's cantata *St Nicholas* (1948), which has a libretto by Eric Crozier, he can be heard saying it.

NICHOLSON, Vivian

English pools winner (1936–)

1 I'm going to spend, spend, spend, that's what I'm going to do.

Nicholson and her husband Keith, a trainee miner, were bringing up three children on a weekly wage of £7 in Castleford, Yorkshire. Then, in September 1961, they won £152,000 on Littlewoods football pools. Arriving in London by train to collect their prize (recounted in her autobiography *Spend, Spend, Spend*, 1977), she made this off-the-cuff remark to reporters. It made newspaper copy (as in the *Daily Herald*, 28 September 1961) and was used as the title of a TV play. The win was the prelude to misfortune. Keith died in a car crash and Viv worked her way through a succession of husbands until all the money had gone.

NICOLSON, Harold (later Sir Harold)

English writer and politician (1886–1968)

2 We shall have to walk and live a Woolworth life hereafter.

On life after the Second World War. *Harold Nicolson: Diaries and Letters*, Vol. 2 (1967), entry for 4 June 1941.

3 It was like playing squash with a dish of scrambled eggs.

Letter to his sons (18 March 1943). On trying to engage in debate with Nancy Astor in the House of Commons. She was famous for not being able to stick to the point.

4 The BBC's unerring instinct for the second-rate.

Letter to Lady Violet Bonham Carter, in *ib.*, 28 August 1943. He was threatening to resign as a governor of the BBC over the appointment of William Haley as Editor-in-Chief. Compare his own low view of the activity in which he had some success: 'The gift of broadcasting is, without question, the lowest human capacity to which any man could attain' – quoted in *The Observer* (5 January 1947).

5 He is all right as a gay young midshipman. He may be all right as a wise old King. But the intervening period ... is hard to manage or swallow. For seventeen years he did nothing at all but kill animals and stick in stamps.

On writing the official biography of King George V. Letter to his wife in *Harold Nicolson: Diaries and Letters*, Vol. 3 (1968), for 17 August 1949.

NIEBUHR, Reinhold

American Protestant theologian (1892–1971)

6 God give us the grace to accept with serenity the things that cannot be changed;
Give us the courage to change what should be changed;
Give us the wisdom to distinguish one from the other.

Bartlett (1980) calls this 'The Serenity Prayer', dates it 1934, and in the 15th (but not 16th edition) notes that it was, 'written for a service in the Congregational church of Heath, Massachusetts, where Dr Niebuhr spent many summers. The prayer was first printed in a monthly bulletin of the Federal Council of Churches, Enormously popular, it has been circulated in millions of copies.' One place where it could be found was Dale Carnegie's book *How To Stop Worrying and Start Living* (1944), in which Niebuhr is described as Professor of Applied Christianity at New York's Union Theological Seminary.

But there is a question mark over the authorship. The prayer was immensely popular in Germany after the Second World War and was credited to the eighteenth-century theologian 'Friedrich Oetinger'. This name was actually a pseudonym of Theodor Wilhelm, a writer who later admitted that he had simply translated Niebuhr's words.

Curiously, another version has been attributed to one Johann Christoph Oetinger (that name again), a deacon in Weinsberg from 1762 to 1769: '*Gib mir Gelassenheit, Dinge hinzunehmen, die icht nicht ändern kann, Den Mut, Dinge zu ändern, die ich ändern kann, und die Weisheit, das eine vom andern zu untersheiden.*'

Niebuhr was often asked where he had found the prayer but, in January 1950, he was telling *The A.A. Grapevine*: 'It may have been spooking around for years, even centuries, but I don't think so. I do honestly believe that I wrote it myself.' He stuck to this line and accepted copyright fees from Hallmark Cards from 1962. And yet, *American Notes and Queries* (June 1970) stated that 'Niebuhr has acknowledged, more than once, both in seminar and publicly that he was not the original author of the Serenity Prayer.'

God, give us the serenity to see that it doesn't really matter who wrote it. It exists, and many people obviously find it very helpful.

A shortened version has been adopted by Alcoholics Anonymous, the self-help group which has two million members and 67,000 groups in 114 countries: 'God grant me the serenity to accept the things I cannot change; the courage to change the things I can; and the wisdom to know the difference.'

NIEMÖLLER, Martin

German Protestant pastor and theologian (1892–1984)

1 When Hitler attacked the Jews, I was not a Jew, therefore, I was not concerned. And when Hitler attacked the Catholics, I was not a Catholic, and therefore, I was not concerned. And when Hitler attacked the unions and the industrialists, I was not a member of the unions and I was not concerned. Then, Hitler attacked me and the Protestant church – and there was nobody left to be concerned.

Attributed to Niemöller by *The Congressional Record* (14 October 1968), though it has not been documented. Niemöller did, however, speak out against Hitler until he was silenced in 1937. The following year he was put in Sachsenhausen Concentration Camp, and then sent to Dachau. He spent four years in solitary confinement before being liberated by the Allies in 1945. Sometimes another version is given: 'In Germany, first they came for the Jews. I was silent. I was not a Jew. Then they came for the Communists. I was silent. I was not a Communist. Then they came for the trade unionists. I was silent. I was not a trade unionist. Then they came for me. There was no one left to speak for me.'

NIGHTINGALE, Florence

English nurse (1820–1910)

2 Too kind, too kind.

When given the Order of Merit in 1907. Quoted in E. Cook, *Life of Florence Nightingale* (1913). In *Eminent Victorians* (1918) Lytton Strachey suggests that Nightingale *murmured* the words and adds, 'she was not ironical'. Not her last words, as sometimes suggested.

NIXON, Richard M.

American Republican 37th President (1913–94)

3 Would you buy a used car from this man?

Although attributed by some to Mort Sahl and by others to Lenny Bruce, and though the cartoonist Herblock denied that he was responsible (*The Guardian*, 24 December 1975), this is just a joke *about* Nixon and one is no more going to find an origin for it than for most such. As to *when* it arose, this is Hugh Brogan, writing in *New Society* (4 November 1982): 'Nixon is a double-barrelled, treble-shotted twister, as my old history master would have remarked; and the fact has been a matter of universal knowledge since at least 1952, when, if I remember aright the joke, "Would you buy a second-hand car from this man?" began to circulate.' It was a very effective slur and, by 1968, when the politician was running (successfully) for President, a poster of a shifty-looking Nixon with the line as caption was in circulation.

Now used of anybody one has doubts about. *The Encyclopedia of Graffiti* (1974) even finds: 'Governor Romney – would you buy a *new* car from this man?' In August 1984, John de Lorean said of himself – after being acquitted of drug-dealing – 'I have aged 600 years and my life as a hard-working industrialist is in tatters. Would you buy a used car from me?'

4 Regardless of what they say about it, we are going to keep it ... I don't believe I ought to quit because I am not a quitter.

TV address (23 September 1952). Nixon was defending himself, when running as a vice-presidential candidate, against charges that he had been operating a secret fund. He denied that any of the money had been put to his personal use: every penny had gone on campaign expenses. Then he proceeded to throw dust in the eyes of viewers by mentioning a dog called 'Checkers' that had been given to his daughters. Was that a politically acceptable gift? He rejected any idea of disappointing his daughters by returning it. Never mind that the problem was not the dog but the 'secret fund', the so-called 'Checkers' speech saved the day for Nixon.

5 Just think about how much you're going to be missing. You won't have Nixon to kick around any more, because, gentlemen, this is my last press conference.

To the press, on losing the California gubernatorial election (7 November 1962), following his two terms as Eisenhower's Vice-President. Nixon was reluctant to appear and concede defeat before newsmen, feeling that they had given him a tough time during the campaign. But he did, and bade them what turned out to be a temporary farewell. President Kennedy's comment was that Nixon must have been 'mentally unsound' to make the statement: 'Nobody could talk like that and be normal.' In 1982 John Ehrlichman attributed the Nixon performance to a 'terrible hang-over'.

6 I have a secret plan to end the [Vietnam] war.

Attributed remark during the 1968 presidential election. William Safire, *On Language* (1980) declares that Nixon never said it. Compare David Halberstam, *The Best and the Brightest*, 'A Final Word' (1972): 'He did not spell out his policies, in large part because he had none. He contented himself with telling audiences that he had a plan to end the war, even touching his breast pocket as if the plan were right there in the jacket ... The truth was that he had no plan at all.'

1 I see another child tonight. He hears a train go by. At night he dreams of faraway places where he'd like to go. It seems like an impossible dream.

Speech accepting the Republican presidential nomination at Miami (8 August 1968). Nixon suddenly switched to the third person. He told of a boy growing up with limited prospects in a small town in southern California. The climax came when Nixon let the audience know that *he* was that small boy whose 'impossible dream' had become a reality. William Safire, then a Nixon speechwriter, recalled how proud his boss was of that ending, and what Nixon had had to say about it: 'I'd like to see [Rockefeller] or Romney or Lindsay do a moving thing like that "impossible dream" part, where I changed my voice. Reagan's an actor, but I'd like to see him do it' (quoted in *The Washington Post*, 6 May 1984).

The phrase was taken from a song called 'The Impossible Dream' (*see* MAN OF LA MANCHA 379:1).

2 And this certainly has to be the most historic phone call ever made.

Talking to Apollo 11 astronauts on the moon (20 July 1969).

3 This is the greatest week in the history of the world since the Creation.

On the USS *Hornet* welcoming the Apollo 11 astronauts home from the first moon landing on 24 July 1969. Dr Billy Graham, the evangelist, told him shortly afterwards: 'Mr President, I know exactly how you felt, and I understand exactly what you meant, but, even so, I think you may have been a little excessive.'

4 The great silent majority of my fellow Americans.

Still trying to extricate the US from Vietnam, Nixon gave a TV address on 3 November 1969 designed to show it would be wrong to end the war on less than honourable terms or to be swayed by anti-war demonstrations. He himself wrote some paragraphs calling for the support of a particular section of American opinion. The notion of a large unheard body of opinion – sometimes called the 'silent centre' or 'Middle America' – was not new but Nixon's appeal ushered in a period of persecution of the 'vocal minority'.

Ironically, the phrases 'silent majority' and 'great majority' were used in the nineteenth century to describe *the dead*. *Harper's New Monthly Magazine* had 'The silent majority' as a heading in September 1874. The dying words of Lord Houghton in 1884 were: 'Yes, I am going to join the Majority and you know I have always preferred Minorities.' *Compare* BROWNE 125:4.

5 I don't give a shit about the lira.

In conversation (23 June 1972), revealed in transcripts of the Watergate tapes (published as *The White House Transcripts*, 1974).

6 I feel it could be cut off at the pass.

One of the milder sayings to have emerged from the Watergate tapes was 'to cut something/someone off at the pass'. This was a re-cycled phrase from Western films where the cry would be uttered, meaning 'to intercept, ambush' (sometimes in the form 'head 'em off at the pass'). As said by Nixon it meant simply 'we could use certain tactics to stop them'. The phrase occurred in a crucial exchange in the White House Oval Office on 21 March 1973 between the President and his Special Counsel, John Dean:

> *RN*: You are a lawyer, you were a counsel ... What would you go to jail for?
> *JD*: The obstruction of justice.
> *RN*: The obstruction of justice?
> *JD*: That is the only one that bothers me.
> *RN*: Well, I don't know. I think that one ... I feel it could be cut off at the pass, maybe, the obstruction of justice.

7 I don't give a shit what happens. I want you all to stonewall it, let them plead the Fifth Amendment, cover-up or anything else, if it'll save it, save the plan.

On the Watergate cover-up this conversation (22 March 1973) was revealed in one of the transcripts of recordings Nixon himself had ordered to be made of his day-to-day conversations. These enabled the world to know that the holder of the highest office, a head of state, could talk like a sleazy racketeer.

8 There can be no whitewash at the White House.

TV address (30 April 1973), quoted in Carl Bernstein & Bob Woodward, *All The President's Men* (1974).

1 People have got to know whether or not their President is a crook. Well, I am not a crook. I've earned everything I have got.

Concerning a charge of tax avoidance. Press conference (17 November 1973).

2 You fellows, in your business, you have a way of handling problems like this. Somebody leaves a pistol in the drawer. I don't have a pistol.

To General Alexander Haig (7 August 1974). Quoted in Bob Woodward & Carl Bernstein, *The Final Days* (1976).

3 I have never been a quitter. To leave office before my term is completed is abhorrent to every instinct in my body. But as President I must put the interests of America first ... Therefore, I shall resign the presidency, effective at noon tomorrow.

Broadcast (8 August 1974). For his earlier use of the 'quitter' theme, *see* above 412:4.

4 This country needs good farmers, good businessmen, good plumbers, good carpenters ...

Even in his rambling, maudlin farewell address to White House staff on 9 August 1974, Nixon seemed unable to resist an inept reference to 'plumbers', a code word for those who had broken into the Watergate building 'to plug leaks' and had started off the whole tawdry affair. Presumably, Nixon did not realize what he was saying.

5 When the President does it, that means it is not illegal.

TV interview with David Frost (19 May 1977). *Compare* BLACKSTONE 110:6.

6 I brought myself down. I gave them a sword and they stuck it in and they twisted it with relish. And I guess if I'd been in their position I'd have done the same thing.

Ib. Hence, *I Gave Them A Sword*, title of a book (1978) by David Frost about the Nixon interviews.

See also GREELEY 272:3.

NOBLE, Vernon

English writer and broadcaster (1908–87)

7 This would I wish to be said of me:
he loved children, cats and dogs,
and beauty in all its guises –
a face, a figure, picture and poem
and the texture and colour of clouds;
not afraid of the verb 'to love'
and the use of it, sometimes perhaps
too often, and sometimes not enough,
but always with meaning at the time.
He suffered the pains of the world,
blunderingly trying to remedy them.
He could forgive others more easily
than he could forgive himself.
he tried hard in all his endeavours,
and lamented that he lost the game,
but enjoyed playing it; and lastly,
he was at all times aware of God.

'Request', *Days of Our Years* (1983). At Noble's request this poem was read at the Quaker gathering to mark his death.

NOEL, Thomas

English poet (1799–1861)

8 Rattle his bones over the stones;
He's only a pauper, whom nobody owns!

'The Pauper's Drive' (1841). A popular nineteenth-century recitation. The poem concludes: 'Bear soft his bones over the stones!/Though a pauper, he's one whom his Maker yet owns.' Quoted in *Parlour Poetry* (ed. Michael R. Turner, 1967).

NORTH, Christopher (Professor John Wilson)

Scottish literary critic (1785–1854)

9 His Majesty's dominions, on which the sun never sets.

Noctes Ambrosianae in *Blackwood's Magazine* (April 1829). Hence, the idea of 'the empire upon which the sun never sets', referring to the British Empire, which was so widespread at its apogee that the sun was always up on some part of it. Earlier, the idea had been widely applied to the Spanish Empire. In 1641 the English explorer and writer Captain John Smith (of Pocahontas fame) asked in *Advertisements for the Unexperienced* ...: 'Why should the brave Spanish soldier brag the sun never sets in the Spanish dominions, but ever shineth on one part or other we have conquered for our king?'

1 Laws were made to be broken.

In *ib.* (May 1830). Probably more likely to be given nowadays in the form, 'Rules are meant to be broken'.

See also ANONYMOUS 36:4.

NORTHCLIFFE, 1st Viscount

British newspaper proprietor (1865–1922)

2 When I want a peerage, I shall buy one like an honest man.

Quoted in *PDMQ* (1971) and Tom Driberg, *Swaff* (1974). An unlikely remark, even if meant in jest. Northcliffe was created a Baron in 1905 and a Viscount in 1917. His battles with David Lloyd George, the principal purveyor of pay-as-you-rise ennoblement, raged throughout the First World War.

3 News is what someone, somewhere doesn't want published ... all the rest is advertising.

Unquestionably Northcliffe's view, but unverified. *Compare* SWAFFER 524:5.

NORTON, Caroline

English novelist and poet (1808–77)

4 For death and life, in ceaseless strife,
Beat wild on this world's shore,
And all our calm is in that balm –
Not lost but gone before.

Poem, 'Not Lost But Gone Before'. Hence, the standard epitaph now imprinted on countless graves. According to Benham (1907), 'Not lost but gone before' was the title of a song published in Smith's *Edinburgh Harmony* (1829) – perhaps a setting of Norton's poem?

But the idea was not new. From *Human Life* (1819) by Samuel Rogers:

> Those whom he loved so long and sees no more,
> Loved, and still loves – not dead – but gone before.

According to Mencken (1942), the phrase occurs in one of Alexander Pope's epitaphs for 'Elijah Fenton, Easthampstead England' (*c.*1731), although this one is not included in *Pope's Poetical Works*:

> 'Weep not,' ye mourners, for the dead,
> But in this hope your spirits soar,
> That ye can say of those ye mourn,
> They are not lost but gone before.

And to Philip Henry (1631–96) is ascribed the couplet:

> They are not *amissi*, but *praemissi*;
> Not lost but gone before.

Seneca wrote: '*Non amittuntur sed praemittuntur*' ('They are not lost but sent before'). So the concept is, indeed, a very old one. The simple phrase 'gone before' meaning 'dead' was well established in English by the early sixteenth century.

NOVALIS

German poet and novelist (1772–1801)

5 Every man is potentially hero and genius; only inertia keeps men mediocre.

Probably from *Heinrich von Ofterdingen* (1802).

NOVELLO, Ivor

Welsh-born composer and actor (1893–1951)

6 Keep the Home Fires Burning.

Title of song (1915). Originally entitled 'Till the Boys Come Home'. The words were, in fact, written by Lena Guilbert Ford.

7 And Her Mother Came Too.

Title of song, *A to Z* (1922). The words were, in fact, written by Dion Titheradge.

8 Blaze of lights and music calling, Music weeping,
rising, falling, Like a rare & precious diamond
His brilliance still lives on.

Lines on Novello's memorial tablet in the crypt of St Paul's Cathedral, London. They were written by Lynn S. Maury of the Ivor Novello Memorial Society, which mounted an eight-year campaign to have a plaque placed in the cathedral.

See also BURROUGHS 134:3.

NOW VOYAGER

American film 1942. Based on the novel by Olive Higgins Prouty. With Bette Davis as Charlotte Vale.

9 *Charlotte*: Let's not ask for the moon – we have the stars.

Soundtrack. Closing words.

See also WHITMAN 567:5.

NYE, Edgar Wilson 'Bill'

American humorist (1850–96)

1 I have been told that Wagner's music is better than it sounds.

In Mark Twain's *Autobiography* (published posthumously in 1924) he ascribes this to Nye who had pre deceased him in 1896. Given the dates involved here, it is curious that Lewis Baumer was providing this caption to a *Punch* cartoon (20 November 1918): (Two women talking) – 'Going to hear some Wagner.' 'What! – do you like the stuff?' 'Frankly, no; but I've heard on the best authority that his music's very much better than it sounds.'

See also MENCKEN 389:5.

O

OATES, Captain Lawrence Edward ('Titus')

English explorer (1880–1912)

1 I am just going outside, and I may be some time.

Oates walked to his death on Captain R.F. Scott's 1912 expedition. Beaten to the South Pole by the Norwegian explorer, Roald Amundsen, the small party fell victim to terrible weather conditions on the return journey to its ship. One man died, and Oates, suffering from scurvy, from an old war wound and from frostbitten and gangrenous feet, realized that he would be next. He presumably thought that without him slowing them down, the remaining three members of the party might stand a better chance of survival. He did not bother to spend the couple of hours' painful effort needed to put on his boots. He made his classic stiff-upper-lip understatement, went out in his stockinged feet and did not return.

It was inevitable in time that iconoclasts would review the evidence and wonder whether, in the light of Oates's expressed criticisms of Scott, his action was truly voluntary or whether it was the result of silent hints from the expedition leader. As the only record of what Oates said was contained in Scott's diary (published as *Scott's Last Expedition*, 1923), it has been suggested that the words were Scott's invention. But it was an act perfectly in character and there would have been no need for any invention.

Not only did Oates define courage for a generation, he unwittingly provided a joke expression or catch-phrase to be used when a person is departing from company for whatever reason. When Trevor Griffiths came to write a TV drama series about Scott's expedition called *The Last Place on Earth* (1985), he accordingly substituted the line: 'Call of nature, Birdie.'

2 Hereabouts died a very gallant gentleman.

Scott wrote in his diary: 'We knew that poor Oates was walking to his death, but though we tried to dissuade him, we knew it was the act of a brave man and an English gentleman.' Oates's actual epitaph, composed later by E.L. Atkinson and Apsley Cherry-Garrard (and recorded in the latter's *The Worst Journey in the World*, 1922) took up this theme and was placed on a cairn marking the spot from where he walked. The epitaph continues: 'Captain L.E.G. Oates of the Inniskilling Dragoons. In March 1912, returning from the Pole, he walked willingly to his death in a blizzard, to try and save his comrades, beset by hardship. This note is left by the Relief Expedition. 1912.'

O'CASEY, Sean

Irish playwright (1884–1964)

3 The whole worl' is in a state o' chassis.

Juno and the Paycock (1924). Said several times during the play by Jack Boyle – also last words of the play.

4 English literature's performing flea.

On P.G. Wodehouse and quoted by Wodehouse in a book entitled *Performing Flea* (1953). Wodehouse comments: 'I believe he meant to be complimentary, for all the performing fleas I have met impressed me with their sterling artistry and that indefinable something which makes the good trouper.'

OCHS, Adolph S.

American newspaper proprietor (1858–1935)

5 All the news that's fit to print.

Slogan devised by Ochs when he bought *The New York Times*, and used in every edition since – at first on the editorial page, on 25 October 1896, and from the following February on the front page near the masthead.

It became the paper's war-cry in the battle against formidable competition from the *World*, the *Herald* and the *Journal*. It has been parodied by Howard Dietz as 'All the news *that fits* we print' – which, at worst, sounds like a slogan for the suppression of news. However, no newspaper prints everything.

O'CONNOR, Edwin

American novelist (1918–68)

1 The Last Hurrah.

Title of novel (1956; film US, 1958) about an ageing Boston-Irish politician making his last electoral foray. Hence, the expression 'last hurrah' for a politician's farewell.

O'HARA, John

American writer (1905–70)

2 George [Gershwin] died on July 11, 1937, but I don't have to believe that if I don't want to.

Quoted in *Newsweek* Magazine (15 July 1940). From *The Observer* (13 October 1996): 'At Clem Thomas's funeral recently, in his address he [Cliff Morgan] paraphrased an American poet. "Clem is dead," he said, "but I don't have to believe it".' Well, not a poet exactly ...

O'KEEFE, Patrick

American advertising practitioner (1872–1934)

3 Say it with flowers.

This slogan was originally devised for the Society of American Florists and invented in 1917 for its chairman, Henry Penn of Boston, Massachusetts. Major Patrick O'Keefe, head of an advertising agency, suggested: 'Flowers are words that even a babe can understand' – a line he had found in a poetry book. Penn considered that too long. O'Keefe, agreeing, rejoined: 'Why, you can say it with flowers in so many words.' Later came several songs with the title (source: Julian Lewis Watkins, *The 100 Greatest Advertisements*, 1959).

OLIVIER, Sir Laurence (later Lord Olivier)

English actor (1907–89)

4 Dear boy, why not try acting?

To Dustin Hoffman during the filming of *Marathon Man* (*c.*1975), Hoffman having stayed up for three nights in order to portray a sleepless character. A much told story, e.g., in *The Times* (17 May 1982).

5 Success smells like Brighton.

Quoted in *Peter Hall's Diaries* (1983, in an entry for 1977). Unless it was a remark Olivier was fond of making, this quotation comes from a TV interview he gave to Kenneth Tynan in the BBC series *Great Acting* (26 February 1966). Talking of the tumultuous reception of his stage *Richard III* (1944), Olivier said: 'There was something in the atmosphere ... There is a phrase "the sweet smell of success" ... I have had two experiences like that and it just smells like Brighton and oyster bars and things like that.'

O'NEILL, Eugene

American playwright (1888–1953)

6 The Iceman Cometh.

Title of play (1946) about a saloon harbouring alcoholics who would, of course, be looking forward to having some to put in their drinks. The phrase was of endless fascination to the British, to whom the concept of the 'iceman' was all but unknown and the 'cometh' wonderfully affected. In *Salad Days* (1954), there is the line: 'The spaceman cometh!' and there was a song 'The Gas-Man Cometh' by Michael Flanders and Donald Swann (1963). Perhaps the 'cometh' was biblical in origin, as in 'behold this dreamer cometh' (Genesis 37:19).

ONO, Yoko

Japanese-born artist (1933–)

7 Woman Is the Nigger of the World.

Title of song (1972) by her husband John Lennon – from a remark she had made in an interview with *Nova* Magazine (1968). Compare Zora Neale Hurston, *Their Eyes Were Watching God* (1937): 'De nigger woman is de mule uh de world so fur as Ah can see.'

OPPENHEIMER, J. Robert

American physicist (1904–67)

8 I am become death, the destroyer of worlds.

Quoting from the *Bhagavad Gita*, at the explosion of the first atomic bomb, New Mexico (16 July 1945). Recalled in Giovanitti & Freed, *The Decision to Drop the Bomb* (1965).

ORCZY, Baroness

Hungarian-born writer (1865–1947)

1 We seek him here, we seek him there,
Those Frenchies seek him everywhere.
Is he in heaven? – Is he in hell?
That demmed, elusive Pimpernel?

The Scarlet Pimpernel, Chap. 12 (1905). The Scarlet Pimpernel is the *nom de guerre* of a seemingly foppish Englishman, Sir Percy Blakeney, who helps French aristocrats to escape the guillotine in the 1790s. He makes up this rhyme to point up the French government's predicament.

O'REILLY, P.J.

British lyricist (early twentieth century)

2 Drake is going west, lads.

Song, 'Drake Goes West' (1910), with music by Wilfrid Sanderson. Alluded to in Noël Coward's 1952 song 'There Are Bad Times Just Around the Corner':

In Dublin they're depressed, lads,
Maybe because they're Celts
For Drake is going West, lads,
And so is everyone else.

Spike Milligan has also used the line in parody:

Drake is going West, lad
Howard is going East
But little Fred just lies in bed
Lazy little beast.

ORTON, Joe

English playwright (1933–67)

3 Prick Up Your Ears.

Title for unmade film, suggested by his lover and murderer Kenneth Halliwell. Eventually used by John Lahr for his biography of Orton (1978) and by Alan Bennett for a film about Orton and Halliwell (UK, 1987).

4 *Mike*: There's no word in the Irish language for what you were doing.
Wilson: In Lapland they have no word for snow.

The Ruffian on the Stair (rev. ed. 1967). What they were doing was, naturally, of a homosexual nature. The observation about Lapland amounts to artistic licence: rather the reverse is believed to be the case. Far from having no word for snow, the Laps have any number to describe all the different types of snow.

ORWELL, George

English novelist and journalist (1903–50)

5 I'm fat, but I'm thin inside. Has it ever struck you that there's a thin man inside every fat man, just as they say there's a statue inside every block of stone?

Coming Up for Air (1939). *See also* AMIS 18:4; CONNOLLY 181:4; WHITEHORN 566:3.

6 It is commonly said that every human being has in him the material for one good book, which is true in the same sense as it is true that every block of stone contains a statue.

In *New Statesman and Nation* (7 December 1940). The 'commonly said' points to a proverbial expression, but no earlier use has been found, though Italo Svevo is said to have produced a James Joyce citation. Presumably, the idea behind the saying is that all people have one story that they alone can tell – namely, the story of their life. The 'every block of stone' remark has been attributed rather loosely to Aristotle and Michelangelo. Pope wrote in *The Dunciad*, Bk 4, l. 270: '... and hew the Block off, and get out the Man'. A note to this line, signed by Pope and William Warburton, reads: 'A notion of Aristotle, that there was originally in every block of marble, a Statue, which would appear on the removal of the superfluous parts.' More recently, James Sutherland has added, 'This notion is usually credited to Michelangelo. I have failed to trace it in Aristotle' (1963 ed. of *The Dunciad*). Diogenes Laertius had access, however, to works of Aristotle now lost, and in his *Vitae Philosophorum*, 5:33, he wrote: 'This realization, according to [Aristotle], is twofold. Either it is potential, as that of Hermes in the wax, provided the wax be adapted to receive the proper mouldings, or as that of the statue implicit in the bronze; or again it is determinate, which is the case with the completed figure of Hermes or the finished statue' (trans. R.D. Hicks).

The Michelangelo may be a corruption of something from *Rime* (his collected poems) (*c.*1538):

Non ha l'ottimo artista alcun concetto
ch'un marmo solo in sè non circoscriva
col suo soverchio, e solo a quello arriva
la man che ubbidisce all'intelletto

– which, when translated, means: 'The best artist has not any project/idea which a single piece of marble does not contain in its plethora; and it is only attained by the hand that obeys the mind.' Longfellow translated it thus: 'Nothing the greatest artist can conceive/That every marble block doth not confine/Within itself; and only its design/The hand that follows intellect can achieve.'

1 Its atmosphere is something halfway between a girls' school and a lunatic asylum.

On the BBC. Diary entry for 14 March 1942, quoted in *The Collected Essays, Journalism and Letters of George Orwell*, Vol. 2 (1968).

2 [Attlee] reminds me of nothing so much as a recently dead fish before it has had time to stiffen.

Diary entry for 19 May 1942 in *ib.* Clement Attlee was deputy Prime Minister at that time.

3 Mr Blunden is no more able to resist a quotation than some people are to refuse a drink.

Reviewing a book by Edmund Blunden. In the *Manchester Evening News* (20 April 1944).

4 Four legs good, two legs bad.

Animal Farm (1945). The slogan with which the animals seize control from their human master.

5 All animals are equal, but some are more equal than others.

A fictional slogan from *ib.*, which was a commentary on the totalitarian excesses of Communism. It had been anticipated: Hesketh Pearson recalled in his biography of the actor/manager Sir Herbert Beerbohm Tree (1956) that Tree wished to insert one of his own epigrams in a play called *Nero* by Stephen Phillips (1906). It was: 'All men are equal – except myself.' In Noël Coward's *This Year of Grace* (1928) there is the exchange: Pellet: 'Men are all alike' Wendle: 'Only some more than others'.

The saying alludes, of course, to Thomas Jefferson's 'All men are created equal and independent', from his 'rough draft' of the American Declaration of Independence (1776). It has the makings of a formula phrase in that it is more likely to be used to refer to humans than to animals. Only the second half of the phrase need actually be spoken, the first half being understood: 'You-Know-Who [Mrs Thatcher] is against the idea [televising parliament]. There aren't card votes at Westminster, but some votes are more equal than others' (*The Guardian*, 15 February 1989).

6 BIG BROTHER IS WATCHING YOU.

Slogan from *Nineteen Eighty-Four* (1949). In a dictatorial state, every citizen is regimented and observed by a spying TV set in the home. The line became a popular catchphrase following the sensational BBC TV dramatization of the novel (1954). Aspects of the Ministry of Truth in the novel were derived not only from Orwell's knowledge of the BBC (where he worked) but also from his first wife Eileen's work at the Ministry of Food, preparing 'Kitchen Front' broadcasts during the Second World War (*c.*1942–4). One campaign there used the slogan 'Potatoes are Good for You' and was so successful that it had to be followed by 'Potatoes are Fattening'.

7 At 50, everyone has the face he deserves.

Notebook entry for 17 April 1949, when he was forty-six and had only one year to live, quoted in *The Collected Essays*, Vol. 4 (1968). *Compare* CAMUS 145:1.

See also MAJOR 377:1; WELLINGTON 560:4.

OSBORNE, Charles

Australian-born writer and arts administrator (1927–)

8 If a third of all the novelists and maybe two-thirds of all the poets now writing dropped dead suddenly the loss to literature would not be great.

Osborne was thus quoted in *The Observer* (3 November 1985) from remarks he had made at a (British) Arts Council press conference. It was only later – as he confirmed in 1991 – that Osborne became aware that Rebecca West had uttered a similar sentiment at the 1962 Edinburgh Festival Writers' Conference: 'It would be no loss to the world if most of the writers now writing had been strangled at birth' (a remark recorded, for example, in Stephen Spender, *Journals 1939–83*, 1985).

OSBORNE, John

English playwright (1929–94)

9 They spend their time mostly looking forward to the past.

Look Back in Anger, Act 2, Sc. 1. Hence, the title *Looking Forward to the Past*, the title of a history chat show on BBC Radio 4 (current 1991).

10 This is a letter of hate. It is for you my countrymen. I mean those men of my country who have defiled it ... There is murder in my brain

and I carry a knife in my heart for everyone of you. Macmillan, and you, Gaitskell, you particularly ... Till then, damn you, England. You're rotting now, and quite soon you'll disappear.

'A Letter To My Fellow Countrymen' in *Tribune* (18 August 1961). Written from the South of France.

1 Don't clap too hard – it's a very old building.

The Entertainer (1957), but an old music-hall joke.

O'SHAUGHNESSY, Arthur

English poet (1844–81)

2 We are the music makers,
We are the dreamers of dreams ...
Yet we are the movers and shakers
Of the world for ever, it seems.

'Ode' (1874), set to music by Edward Elgar as *The Music Makers* (1912). Hence, the modern expression 'movers and shakers' to describe people of power and influence. From J.F. Burke's novel, *Death Trick* (1975): 'Beniamino Tucci was known as the Little Godfather of the Upper West Side. A mover and shaker with many interests.' From *The Economist* (7 November 1987): 'Many of the advertised movers and shakers [in President Reagan's administration] soon resign in disgust, or bolt back to the private sector once their Washington experience can be cashed in.'

OWEN, David (later Lord Owen)

English Labour then Social Democrat politician (1938–)

3 We are fed up with fudging and mudging, with mush and slush.

Speech, Labour Party Conference, Blackpool (2 October 1980). 'To fudge and mudge', meaning 'to produce the appearance of a solution while, in fact, only patching up a compromise', was a verb that often arose in discussions of the Social Democratic Party and the Liberal Party in Britain during the 1980s. Owen, one of the SDP's founders, had used it earlier in his previous incarnation, as a member of the Labour Party.

OWEN, Robert

Welsh-born socialist reformer (1771–1858)

4 All the world is queer save thee and me, and even thou art a little queer.

On breaking up with his business partner, W. Allen, at New Lanark (1828). Attributed.

OWEN, Wilfred

English poet (1893–1918)

5 If you could hear, at every jolt, the blood
Come gargling from the froth-corrupted lungs,
Obscene as cancer, bitter as the cud
Of vile, incurable sores on innocent tongues, –
My friend, you would not tell with such high
zest
To children ardent for some desperate glory,
The old Lie: Dulce et decorum est
Pro patria mori.

'Dulce et decorum est' (written 1917) in *Poems* (1920). Compare HORACE 302:3. In a poll to find Britain's favourite poem, conducted by the BBC TV programme *Bookworm* in 1995, this one came eighth.

P Q

PAINE, Albert Bigelow

American writer (1861–1937)

1 The Great White Way.

Title of novel (1901), later becoming a sobriquet for Broadway, the main theatre zone of New York City – alluding to the brightness of the illumination. For a while, Broadway was also known as 'the Gay White Way', though for understandable reasons this is no longer so.

PAINE, Tom

English-born American revolutionary and political theorist (1737–1809)

2 We have it in our power to begin the world over again.

Common Sense, originally published in 1776. The words were quoted by Ronald Reagan, first at the end of his 'Evil empire' speech (at Orlando, Florida, 8 March 1983), then in a televised Presidential campaign debate with his challenger, Walter Mondale (7 October 1984). Possibly they were also alluded to in Reagan's 'Farewell Address to the Nation' (11 January 1989): 'Once you begin a great movement, there's no telling where it will end. We meant to change a nation, and instead, we changed a world.'

Paine's words were also quoted by Margaret Thatcher on a visit to the White House in November 1988. An odd choice of quotation, when Paine had done his best to end any possibility of a 'special relationship' between Britain and America. The passage continues: 'Independence is the only bond that can tie and keep us [Americans] together ... Let the names of Whig and Tory be extinct.'

3 The Rights of Man.

Title of book (1791). A treatise on government that forced Paine to flee England the following year but earned him an honoured place as a theoretician of the French revolution, then in progress. Compare the title *The Rites of a Man* – 'Love, Sex and Death in the Making of the Male' – a book (1991) by Rosalind Miles.

See also HAYWARD 285:5.

PAKULA, Alan J.

American film director (1928–)

4 Love and Pain and the Whole Damned Thing

Title of film (US 1972), script by Alvin Sargent. *Love, Pain and the Whole Damn Thing* was used as the English title of a short story collection by the German writer and film director, Doris Dorrie (1989).

PALMER, Tony

English film-maker and critic (1935–)

5 If there is still any doubt that Lennon and McCartney are the greatest songwriters since Schubert ...

Reviewing the Beatles' 'White Album' in *The Observer* (November 1968). Compare BUCKLE 128:7 and MANN 378:7.

PALMERSTON, Lord

British Prime Minister (1784–1865)

6 Die, my dear doctor? That's the *last* thing I shall do.

Deathbed words. Quoted in E. Latham, *Famous Sayings and their Authors* (1961).

PANKHURST, Emmeline and Christabel

English suffragette leaders (mother and daughter) (1858–1928) and (1880–1958)

1 Votes for Women.

Both Pankhursts, founders of the Women's Social and Political Union, have described how this battle-cry emerged. This is a synthesis of their recollections: in October 1905 a large meeting at the Free Trade Hall, Manchester, was to be addressed by Sir Edward Grey, who was likely to attain ministerial office if the Liberals won the forthcoming general election. The WSPU was thus keen to challenge him in public on his party's attitude to women's suffrage in Britain: 'The question was painted on a banner in large letters ... How should we word it? "Will you give women suffrage?" – we rejected that form, for the word "suffrage" suggested to some unlettered or jesting folk the idea of suffering. "Let them suffer away!" – we had heard the taunt. We must find another wording and we did!

'It was so obvious and yet, strange to say, quite new. Our banners bore this terse device: "WILL YOU GIVE VOTES FOR WOMEN?"' The plan had been to let down a banner from the gallery as soon as Grey stood up to speak. Unfortunately, the WSPU had failed to obtain the requisite number of tickets. It had to abandon the large banner and cut out the three words which would fit on a small placard. 'Thus quite accidentally came into existence the slogan of the suffrage movement around the world.'

Alas, Sir Edward Grey did not answer the question and it took rather more than this slogan – hunger-strikes, suicide, the First World War – before women got the vote in Britain in 1918. In the US, the Nineteenth Amendment, extending female franchise on a national scale, was ratified in time for the 1920 elections.

Other uses to which the slogan was put: a newspaper with the title *Votes for Women* was launched in October 1907. At a meeting in the Royal Albert Hall, someone boomed 'Votes for Women' down an organ pipe. The International Labour Party used to refer to it as 'Votes for Ladies'. In due course, some feminists were to campaign with the slogan 'Orgasms for women'.

PARKER, Dorothy

American writer (1893–1967)

2 Guns aren't lawful;
Nooses give;
Gas smells awful;
You might as well live.

'Resumé', *Enough Rope* (1927). Hence, *You Might As Well Live*, title of a biography of Parker (1970) by John Keats.

3 Scratch an actor and you'll find an actress.

Quoted in Leslie Halliwell, *The Filmgoer's Book of Quotes* (1973). Hence, *Scratch an Actor*, title of book (1969) by Sheilah Graham, the Hollywood gossip columnist. Maybe out of confusion with 'Scratch a lover, and find a foe' from 'The Ballade of Great Weariness' in *ib.*

4 This is not a novel to be tossed aside lightly. It should be thrown with great force.

Quoted in R.E. Drennan, *Wit's End* (1973). In Matthew Parris, *Scorn* (1994), this is said to refer to Benito Mussolini's novel *Claudia Particella, L'Amante del Cardinale: Grande Romanzo dei Tempi del Cardinal Emanuel Madruzzo.* When this was published in the US as *The Cardinal's Mistress*, Parker did review it devastatingly (15 September 1928), but not actually including this put down.

5 And it is that word 'hummy', my darlings, that marks the first place in *The House at Pooh Corner* at which Tonstant Weader fwowed up

On A.A. Milne's *The House at Pooh Corner* in her column 'Constant Reader', in *The New Yorker* (20 October 1928).

6 Outspoken by whom?

When told that she was 'very outspoken'. Quoted by Ralph L. Marquard, *Jokes and Anecdotes for All Occasions* (1977).

7 Where does she find them?

In reply to comment, 'Anyway, she's always very nice to her inferiors'. Quoted in *The Lyttelton Hart-Davis Letters*, Vol. 1 (1978). Told sometimes regarding Clare Boothe Luce.

8 How can they tell?

In 1933, when told that President Calvin Coolidge had died, Parker produced this, one of her two or three most quoted remarks. It is recorded in Bennett Cerf, *Try and Stop Me* (1944). As 'How do they know?', it appears in Malcolm Cowley, *Writers at Work*, Series 1 (1958). In that form it is also attributed to Wilson Mizner (Alva Johnston, *The Legendary Mizners*, 1953). The lack of contemporary sources and its omission, for example, from the Keats biography (see below) makes one wonder if the remark has drifted to Parker from Mizner.

1 Go to the Martin Beck Theatre and watch Katharine Hepburn run the whole gamut of emotions from A to B.

Reviewing *The Lake* (1933), for which *see also* STAGE DOOR 515:2. This is only attributed. G. Carey in *Katharine Hepburn* (1985) has the famous quip merely as a remark made in the intermission on the first night. Some would say that Parker went on and stated that Hepburn put some distance, 'between herself and a more experienced colleague [Alison Skipworth] lest she catch acting from her.'

2 GOOD WORK, MARY. WE ALL KNEW YOU HAD IT IN YOU.

Telegram to Mrs Robert Sherwood, when delivered of a baby. Quoted in Alexander Woollcott, *While Rome Burns* (1934).

3 This is on me. Excuse my dust. If you can read this you are standing too close.

Suggested epitaphs, *c.*1925. In *ib.*

4 Brevity is the soul of lingerie – as the Petticoat said to the Chemise.

In *ib.* Said to have been written as a caption for *Vogue* in 1916. *Compare* SHAKESPEARE 479:4.

5 If, with the literate, I am
Impelled to try an epigram,
I never seek to take the credit;
We all assume that Oscar said it.

'A Pig's Eye View of Literature' (1937). A law of quotations encapsulated by, nevertheless, probably the most quoted woman of the twentieth century.

6 Oh, life is a glorious cycle of song,
A medley of extemporanea;
And love is a thing that can never go wrong
And I am Marie of Roumania.

'Comment', *Not So Deep as a Well* (1937). An expression of disbelief found in a recent detective novel – Val McDermid's *Clean Break* (1995): 'If what you had nicked off your wall is a Monet, I am Marie of Romania'. The rather more pressing question is, what was so funny about Marie of Roumania (1875–1938) that she got brought into the verse? Well, she was one of Queen Victoria's grandchildren and became the queen of King Ferdinand I. She paid a famous visit to the US in 1926 and, apparently, carried on rather like a cross between Imelda Marcos and Fergie, the present Duchess of York. No doubt this was what captured Parker's amused attention.

7 How do people go to sleep? I'm afraid I've lost the knack ... I might repeat to myself, slowly and soothingly, a list of quotations beautiful from minds profound; if I can remember any of the damn things.

'The Little Hours', *Here Lies* (1939). A further use for quotations.

8 He really needs to telephone, but he's too embarrassed to say so.

When a man asked to be excused to go to the men's room. In John Keats, *You Might as Well Live* (1970).

9 Pearls before swine.

To Clare Booth Luce, when going through a swing-door together, Luce had used the customary phrase 'Age before beauty'. Mrs Luce described this account as completely apocryphal in answer to a question from John Keats in *ib.*

10 There, but for a typographical error is the story of my life.

When someone said, 'They're ducking for apples' at a Hallowe'en party. In *ib.*

11 [Enough space] to lay a hat – and a few friends.

On her requirements for an apartment. In *ib.*

12 Because he spills his seed on the ground.

On naming her canary 'Onan'. In *ib.* Alluding to Genesis 38:9.

13 It serves me right for putting all my eggs in one bastard.

When pregnant. In *ib.*

14 You can lead a whore to culture but you can't make her think.

Challenged to compose a sentence including the word 'horticulture'. In *ib.*

See also TYNAN 546:5.

PARKINSON, C. Northcote

English author and historian (1909–93)

1 It is a commonplace observation that work expands so as to fill the time available for its completion.

First promulgated in *The Economist* (19 November 1955), what later became known as 'Parkinson's Law' was concerned with the pyramidal structure of bureaucratic organizations. A pre-echo may be found in the eighteenth-century Lord Chesterfield's letters: 'The less one has to do, the less time one finds to do it in.'

PARNELL, Charles Stewart

Irish nationalist politician (1846–91)

2 No man has a right to fix the boundary of the march of a nation: no man has a right to say to his country – thus far shalt thou go and no further.

Speech, Cork (1885). The limit-setting phrase was of earlier coinage, however. George Farquhar, the (Irish-born) playwright has this in *The Beaux' Stratagem*, Act 3, Sc. 2 (1707): 'And thus far I am a captain, and no farther.' And then again, Job 38:11 has: 'Hitherto shalt thou come, but no further: and here shall thy proud waves be stayed.'

PASCAL, Blaise

French philosopher and mathematician (1623–62)

3 I have made this letter longer only because I have not had time to make it shorter.

Lettres Provinciales, No. 16 (1657). *Compare* WILSON 578:3.

4 If Cleopatra's nose had been shorter the whole face of the earth would have changed.

Pensées, 2.62 (1670). That is to say, if the Queen of Egypt had not attracted both Julius Caesar and Mark Antony, and become embroiled with the affairs of the Roman empire, history might have taken a different course.

5 *Tous le malheur des hommes vient d'une seule chose qui est de ne savoir pas demeurer en repos dans une chambre.*
All the troubles of men are caused by one single thing, which is their inability to stay quietly in a room.

Ib., 2.139. The last word has been mistranslated as 'bedroom', which puts a rather different complexion on it.

6 The heart has its reasons which reason knows nothing of.

Ib., 4.277. Hence, *The Heart Has Its Reasons*, title of the memoirs (1956) of the Duchess of Windsor.

PATER, Walter

English critic (1839–94)

7 She is older than the rocks among which she sits; like the vampire, she has been dead many times, and learned the secrets of the grave; and has been a diver in deep seas, and keeps their fallen day about her; and trafficked for strange webs with Eastern merchants: and, as Leda, was the mother of Helen of Troy, and as Saint Anne, the mother of Mary; and all this has been to her but as the sound of lyres and flutes, and lives only in the delicacy with which it has moulded the changing lineaments, and tinged the eyelids and the hands.

Of the Mona Lisa. From 'Leonardo da Vinci', *Studies in the History of the Renaissance* (1873).

PATERSON, 'Banjo'

Australian poet (1864–1941)

8 Oh! there once was a swagman camped in a Billabong
Under the shade of a Coolabah tree;
And he sang as he looked at his old billy boiling,
'Who'll come a-waltzing Matilda with me?'

[Swagman = itinerant labourer carrying his swag, or bundle; Billabong = dead water, backwater; billy = cooking-pot]. Song, 'Waltzing Matilda' (written in 1894 but not published until 1903). The title 'Waltzing Matilda' comes from the Australian phrase for carrying your 'Matilda' or back-pack as a tramp does. *The Macquarie Dictionary* (1981) suggests a derivation from the German *walzen*, to move in a circular fashion 'as of apprentices travelling from master to master', and German *Mathilde*, a female travelling companion or bed-roll (from the girl's name). All this has the status of an unofficial Australian national anthem so Australians can get quite abusive when discussing the meaning of the song. The above verse is as shown in

The Dictionary of Australian Quotations (ed. Murray-Smith, 1984). Note, however, this different transcription in *ODQ* (1992):

Once a jolly swagman camped by a billabong,
Under the shade of a coolibah tree;
And he sang as he watched and waited till his 'Billy' boiled:
'You'll come a-waltzing, Matilda, with me.'

PATTON, George S., Jr

American general (1884–1945)

1 I want you to remember that no bastard ever won a war by dying for his country. He won it by making the other poor dumb bastard die for his country.

From script of the film *Patton* (US, 1970). Based on his actual words? *Compare* MICHAELIS 390:7.

See also ANONYMOUS 48:7.

PAUL, Leslie

Irish social philosopher (1905–85)

2 Angry Young Man.

Any writer from the mid-1950s who showed a social awareness and expressed dissatisfaction with conventional values and with the Establishment – John Osborne, Kingsley Amis and Colin Wilson among them – was likely to be labelled with this phrase. Paul had called his autobiography *Angry Young Man* in 1951, but the popular use of the phrase stems from *Look Back in Anger*, the 1956 play by John Osborne, which featured an anti-hero called Jimmy Porter. Other earlier uses of phrases like it, though not necessarily with precisely this sense, include, by H.G. Wells, *Brynhild* (1937): 'I am Angry Man ... almost professionally'; by Rebecca West in *Black Lamb and Grey Falcon* (1941): 'The angry young men run about shouting'; by J.B. Priestley, *Magicians* (1954): 'He's the contemporary Angry Little Man.'

The phrase did not occur in Osborne's play but was applied to the playwright by George Fearon in publicity material from the Royal Court Theatre, London. Fearon later told *The Daily Telegraph* (2 October 1957): 'I ventured to prophesy that this generation would praise his play while mine would, in general, dislike it ... "if this happens," I told [Osborne], "you would become known as the Angry Young Man". In fact, we decided then and there that henceforth he was to be known as that.'

In Osborne's *Almost a Gentleman* (1991), he pours the inevitable scorn on Fearon, and quotes him as saying, 'I suppose you're really – an angry young man ... aren't you?', and comments: 'He was the first one to say it. A boon to headline-writers ever after.'

PAYN, James

English novelist and poet (1830–98)

3 I had never had a piece of toast
Particularly long and wide,
But fell upon the sanded floor,
And always on the buttered side.

In *Chamber's Journal* (2 February 1884). This may be no more than a proverbial expression versified (prefiguring Murphy's Law) and is, in any case, probably a parody of MOORE 398:3. However, in A.D. Eichardson, *Beyond Mississippi* (1867) there had already been: 'His bread never fell on the buttered side.'

PAYNE, J.H.

American actor and songwriter (1791–1852)

4 Mid pleasures and palaces though we may roam,
Be it ever so humble, there's no place like home.

Song, 'Home, Sweet Home' from the opera *Clari, or, The Maid of Milan* (1823). The origin of the expression 'no place like home'.

PEACOCK, Thomas Love

English novelist and poet (1785–1866)

5 A book that furnishes no quotations is, *me judice*, no book – it is a plaything.

Crotchet Castle, Chap. 9 (1831). The quotationist's credo.

PEAKE, Mervyn

English novelist, poet and artist (1911–68)

6 To live at all is miracle enough.

Title line of poem (*c.*1949). Peake is chiefly known for his grotesque Gothic fantasies *Titus Groan* (1946) and *Gormenghast* (1950). His work as a war artist had taken him to Belsen and he was profoundly affected by this experience. This poem, it will be noted, was written quite soon afterwards. The title line is also inscribed on Peake's gravestone at Burpham, West Sussex.

PEARSON, Hesketh

English biographer (1887–1964)

1 Misquotation is ... the pride and privilege of the learned. A widely-read man never quotes accurately for the rather obvious reason that he has read too widely.

Common Misquotations (1937). Pearson was, apparently, the first person to compile a dictionary solely devoted to misquotations. It is a slim volume and slightly muddies its own water by claiming that certain sayings are commonly misquoted when they are not and by condemning variants of proverbs (which surely cannot be said to have a correct form). Pearson truly observed, however: 'Misquotations are the only quotations that are never misquoted.'

PENIAKOFF, Vladimir

Belgian-born soldier and writer (1897–1951)

2 Spread alarm and despondency.

Meaning, 'have a de-stabilizing effect, purposely or not'. During the Second World War, Lieutenant-Colonel Peniakoff ran a small raiding and reconnaissance force on the British side which became known as 'Popski's Private Army'. In his book *Private Army* (1950), he wrote: 'A message came on the wireless for me. It said "Spread alarm and despondency" ... The date was, I think, May 18th, 1942'. When a German invasion was thought to be imminent at the beginning of July 1940, Winston Churchill had issued an 'admonition' to 'His Majesty's servants in high places ... to report, or if necessary remove, any officers or officials who are found to be consciously exercising a disturbing or depressing influence, and whose talk is calculated to spread alarm and despondency'. Prosecutions for doing this did indeed follow. The phrase goes back to the Army Act of 1879: 'Every person subject to military law who ... spreads reports calculated to create unnecessary alarm or despondency ... shall ... be liable to suffer penal servitude.'

PEPYS, Samuel

English civil servant and diarist (1633–1703)

3 And so to bed.

Pepys's famous signing-off line for his diary entries occurs first on 15 January 1660. However, on that occasion, these are not quite his last words. He writes: 'I went to supper, and after that to make an end of this week's notes in this book, and so to bed'. Then he adds: 'It being a cold day and a great snow, my physic did not work so well as it should have done.' Usually, the phrase is the last thing he writes, though sometimes he just puts, 'So to bed.' The fame of the phrase 'And so to bed' is in part due to its use as the title of a play by J.B. Fagan (1926), which was turned into a musical by Vivian Ellis (1951).

Both Mencken (1942) and Bartlett (1980) give the date of its first appearance as 22 July 1660 (when the phrase in fact is just 'So to bed'); the *ODQ* (1992) also has, misleadingly, 20 April 1660. The reason for this confusion is that these books *may* have been dealing with incomplete or inaccurate transcriptions of Pepys's shorthand that were superseded by the Latham/Matthews edition of 1970–83.

Indeed, the first time I read the diaries – in an old Dent's Everyman's Library edition (1906, revised 1953) – I was more than a little surprised that the full phrase 'And so to bed' was *nowhere* to be found. It couldn't have been excised on the grounds of taste, could it?

4 My Lord told me that among his father's many old sayings that he had writ in a book of his, this is one: that he that doth get a wench with child and marries her afterward it is as if a man should shit in his hat and then clap it upon his head.

Diary (7 October 1660). Pepys's patron (also his first cousin once removed) was the politician, naval commander and diplomat, Edward Mountagu, created 1st Earl of Sandwich in 1660. His father had been a royalist, whereas Mountagu espoused the parliamentarian cause. The book in question remains untraced.

5 I went out to Charing Cross, to see Major-General Harrison hanged, drawn and quartered; which was done there, he looking as cheerful as any man could do in that condition.

Ib. (13 October 1660). Thomas Harrison was one of the regicides. Pepys reflects that not only had he seen King Charles I beheaded but now he had seen 'the first blood shed in revenge for the blood of the King.'

6 A good honest and painful sermon.

Ib. (17 March 1661). Painful here = painstaking. It was preached by 'a stranger' but Pepys does not reveal upon what text.

7 In fine, a most excellent person he is and must be allowed a little for a little conceitedness;

but he may well be so, being a man so much above others.

On John Evelyn. *Ib.* (5 November 1665). *Compare* EVELYN 231:4.

1 Strange to say what delight we married people have to see these poor fools decoyed into our condition.

Ib. (25 December 1665). On Christmas Day, Pepys saw 'a wedding in the church, which I have not seen many a day', and was particularly struck by how merry the young couple was with each other.

2 And so I betake myself to that course, which is almost as much to see myself go into my grave – for which, and all the discomforts that will accompany my being blind, the good God prepare me!

Ib., closing words (31 May 1669). In fact, he was able to keep on working and did not die for another thirty years or so.

PERCIVAL, Horace

English actor (d.1961)

3 Don't forget the diver!

This – of all the many catchphrases sired by BBC radio's *ITMA* show – is the one with the most interesting origin. It was spoken by Percival as 'the Diver' and was derived from memories that the star of the show, Tommy Handley, had of an actual one-legged man who used to dive off the pier at New Brighton, Merseyside, in the 1920s. 'Don't forget the diver, sir, don't forget the diver,' the man would say, collecting money. 'Every penny makes the water warmer, sir.' The radio character first appeared in 1940 and no lift/elevator descended for the next few years without somebody using the Diver's main catchphrase or his other one, 'I'm going down now, sir!'

But who was the original diver? James Gashram wrote to *The Listener* (21 August 1980):

> My grandfather McMaster, who came from a farm near the small village of Rathmullen, in County Donegal, knew Michael Shaughnessy, the one-legged ex-soldier, in the late 1890s, before he left for the Boer War and the fighting that cost him his leg. About 1910, Shaughnessy, then married to a Chester girl, settled in Bebington on the Wirral peninsula ... Before the internal combustion engine, [he] used to get a lift every weekday from Bebington to New Brighton in a horse-drawn bread-cart owned by the Bromborough firm of Bernard Hughes. The driver of that cart, apparently, was always envious of the 'easy' money Shaughnessy got at New Brighton – sometimes up to two pounds a day in the summer – and would invariably say to him on the return to Bebington, 'Don't forget the *driver*'. Shaughnessy rarely did forget. It was many years later, some time in the early 1930s, that, remembering the phrase so well, he adapted it to his own purposes by changing it to 'Don't forget the diver', and shouted it to the people arriving from Liverpool.

As for 'I'm going down now, sir', bomber pilots in the Second World War are said to have used this phrase when about to make a descent. From *ITMA*'s VE-Day edition:

> *Effects*: *Knocking*
> *Handley*: Who's that knocking on the tank?
> *The Diver*: Don't forget the diver, sir – don't forget the diver.
> *Handley*: Lumme, it's Deepend Dan. Listen, as the war's over, what are you doing?
> *The Diver*: I'm going down now, sir.
> *Effects*: *Bubbles*.

PERELMAN, S.J.

American humorist (1904–79)

4 I've got Bright's Disease. And he's got mine.

Caption to cartoon in *Judge* (16 November 1929). The disease of the kidneys was first described in 1827 by Dr Richard Bright, who is not to be blamed for the intrinsic humour in naming diseases after specific people.

5 'Oh, son, I wish you hadn't become a scenario writer!' she sniffed.
'Aw, now, Moms,' I comforted her, 'it's no worse than playing the piano in a call house.'

'Strictly from Hunger' – which later became the title of his second book (1937). Quoted in Leslie Halliwell, *The Filmgoer's Book of Quotes* (1973) as: 'Movie scriptwriting is no worse than playing piano in a call house.' A common enough comparison at the time. Flexner (1976) has as a saying from the Depression: 'Don't tell my mother I'm in politics – she thinks I play the piano in a whorehouse.'

Jacques Seguela (1934–) wrote a book with the title: *Don't Tell Mother I Work in Advertising – She Thinks I'm a Piano-player in a Brothel* (1979).

PERKINS, Carl

American singer and songwriter (1932–98)

1 It's a-one for the money
Two for the show
Three to get ready
Now go, cat, go,
But don't you step on my blue suede shoes.

Song, 'Blue Suede Shoes' (1956). The start of this song 'Blue Suede Shoes' (immortalized by Elvis Presley) is based on the form of words that children traditionally use at the start of races. A British version dating from 1888 is, 'One for the money, two for the show, three to make ready, and four to go.' Another version from 1853, is, 'One to make ready, and two to prepare; good luck to the rider, and away goes the mare.'

PERKINS, Frances

American politician (1882–1965)

2 Call me madam.

When Perkins was appointed Secretary of Labor by President Roosevelt in 1933, she became the first US woman to hold Cabinet rank. It was said that when she had been asked *in Cabinet* how she wished to be addressed, she had replied: 'Call me Madam.' She denied that she had done this, however. It was *after* her first Cabinet meeting that reporters asked how they should address her. The Speaker-elect of the House of Representatives, Henry T. Rainey, answered for her: 'When the Secretary of Labor is a lady, she should be addressed with the same general formalities as the Secretary of Labor who is a gentleman. You call him "Mr Secretary". You will call her "Madam Secretary". You gentlemen know that when a lady is presiding over a meeting, she is referred to as "Madam Chairman" when you rise to address the chair' (quoted in George Martin, *Madam Secretary – Frances Perkins*, 1976). Some of the reporters put this ruling into Perkins's own mouth and that presumably is how the misquotation occurred.

Hence, however, *Call Me Madam*, the title of Irving Berlin's musical, first performed on Broadway in 1950, starring Ethel Merman as a woman ambassador appointed to represent the US in a tiny European state. This was inspired by the case of Pearl Mesta, the society hostess, whom President Truman had appointed as ambassador to Luxembourg.

PERÓN, Eva

Argentinian actress and wife of Juan Perón (1919–52)

3 Quite so. But I have not been on a ship for fifteen years and they still call me 'Admiral'.

This was an Italian admiral's response when Eva Perón complained to him that she had been called a 'whore' on a visit to northern Italy. Cited in an article 'The Power Behind the Glory', *Penthouse* Magazine (UK, August 1977).

See also RICE 455:3.

PERTWEE, Boscoe

Untraced

4 I used to be indecisive, but now I'm not so sure.

M.M. Harvey of Andover sent this quotation to BBC Radio *Quote ... Unquote* in 1977, but it has proved impossible to trace a source or, indeed, the existence of its author. *Compare* HAMPTON 279:1.

PÉTAIN, Henri Philippe

French marshal and politician (1856–1951)

5 *Ils ne passeront pass.*
They shall not pass.

Slogan popularly supposed to have been coined by Pétain, the man who defended Verdun with great tenacity in 1916. He is said to have uttered it on 26 February that year. However, the first official record of the expression appears in the Order of the Day for 23 June 1916 from General Robert Nivelle (1856–1924) to his troops at the height of the battle. His words were '*Vous ne laisserez pas passer* [You will not let them pass]'. Alternatively, Nivelle is supposed to have said these words to General Castelnau on 23 January 1916. To add further to the mystery, the inscription on the Verdun medal was '*On ne passe pas*'. One suspects that the slogan was coined by Nivelle and used a number of times by him but came to be associated with Pétain, the more famous 'Hero of Verdun'.

The slogan saw further service. Later, as '*No pasarán*', it was used on the Republican side during the Spanish Civil War.

PETER, Laurence J.

Canadian writer (1919–90)

6 In a hierarchy every employee tends to rise to his level of incompetence.

The Peter Principle – Why Things Always Go Wrong (with

R. Hull) (1969). Intoning his principle on TV (1982), he added '... and stays there'.

1 The noblest of all dogs is the hot-dog; it feeds the hand that bites it.

Quotations for Our Time (1977). Although compiling a book of quotations, Peter inserted several observations of his own. This is one of the brightest. The next one, probably not: 'When you see yourself quoted in print and you're sorry you said it, it suddenly becomes a misquotation.'

PETRONIUS

Roman satirist (d. AD 65)

2 We trained hard; but it seemed that every time we were beginning to form into teams we would be reorganised. I was to learn later in life that we tend to meet any new situation by reorganising; and a wonderful method it can be for creating the illusion of progress while producing confusion, inefficiency and demoralisation.

Gaius Petronius (also known as Petronius Arbiter in Nero's court) is said to have written this in the 'Trimalchio's Feast' section of the *Satyricon* (written in AD66), but it has not been found in the (admittedly variable) text. Indeed, doubts have been cast on the authenticity of this quotation. One suggestion is that it dates only from 1945. In *The Observer* (7 July 1996) Mark Tully quoted the statement but described Gaius Petronius rather as a Roman *centurion*.

PEYREFITTE, Roger

French diplomat and novelist (1907–)

3 Word was brought to Georges that the Ambassador would like to see him. As he went up the stairs, he thought of the advice which his first chief had given him, to be 'colourless, odourless, and tasteless'.

Diplomatic Diversions, Pt 1, Chap. 3 (1953). Translation of *Les Ambassades* (1952). Quoted in contempt of diplomats or civil servants.

PHILIP, Prince (Duke of Edinburgh)

Greek-born consort of Queen Elizabeth II (1921–)

4 Dontopedology is the science of opening your mouth and putting your foot in it. I've been practising it for years.

Speech to the General Dental Council, quoted in *Time* Magazine (21 November 1960).

5 Just at the moment we are suffering a national defeat comparable to any lost military campaign and, what is more, it is self-inflicted ... I think it is time we pulled our finger out.

This kind of remark (made to businessmen on 17 October 1961) helped give the Queen's husband a reputation for plain speaking, which contrasted with the customary anodyne statements put into royal mouths by cautious courtiers.

6 I never see any home cooking – all I get is fancy stuff.

Quoted in *The Observer* (December 1962). When this remark appeared in the *PDMQ* (1971) it had to be corrected, at the Prince's request, lest it reflect badly on the Buckingham Palace chefs. He said he had been referring to meals consumed away from the Palace.

7 The *Daily Express* is a bloody awful newspaper.

Said at a 1962 press reception in Rio de Janeiro, this view was later qualified in answer to a question from Willie Hamilton (in the MP's book, *My Queen and I*, 1975): 'I was having a private conversation with a journalist who claimed that the *Daily Express* was a splendid newspaper. My reply was spontaneous and never intended for publication ... I can say that the reasons [for my remark] no longer exist.'

PIAVE, Francesco Maria

Italian librettist (1810–76)

8 *La donna è mobile.*
Woman is fickle.

The Duke of Mantua's aria in Act 3 of Verdi's opera, *Rigoletto* (1851): 'Woman is wayward/As a feather in the breeze/Capricious is the word'. *See also* CHESTERTON 157:7.

PICASSO, Pablo

Spanish artist (1881–1973)

9 *Je ne cherche pas, je trouve.*
I do not seek, I find.

On painting. Picasso evidently explained this remark to the effect that if you looked for something you knew what you were looking for, whereas when he began a painting he never knew what would happen. Quoted in *PDMQ* (1971) – this would appear to be a version of what Picasso said in an interview with *The Arts* in 1923: 'To search means nothing in painting. To find is the thing.'

PINTER, Harold

English playwright (1930–)

1 (Pause.)

Stage direction in *The Room* (1957) and *The Birthday Party* (1957) and characteristic of all his subsequent work.

2 'But what would you say your plays were *about*, Mr Pinter?'
'The weasel under the cocktail cabinet.'

'Exchange at a new writers' brains trust', quoted in John Russell Taylor, *Anger and After* (1962).

PITKIN, William

American teacher (1878–1953)

3 Life Begins at Forty.

Title of book (1932), in which Pitkin, who was Professor of Journalism at Columbia University, dealt with 'adult reorientation' at a time when the problems of extended life and leisure were beginning to be recognized. Based on lectures Pitkin had given, the book was a hearty bit of uplift: 'Every day brings forth some new thing that adds to the joy of life after forty. Work becomes easy and brief. Play grows richer and longer. Leisure lengthens. Life's afternoon is brighter, warmer, fuller of song; and long before shadows stretch, every fruit grows ripe ... Life begins at forty. This is the revolutionary outcome of our new era ... TODAY it is half a truth. TOMORROW it will be an axiom.' It rapidly became a well-established catchphrase. Helping it along was a song with the title by Jack Yellen and Ted Shapiro (recorded by Sophie Tucker in 1937).

The phrase seems to have caught on everywhere with great rapidity. *Life Begins at Oxford Circus* was the title of a Crazy Gang show at the London Palladium in 1935.

PITT, William (1st Earl of Chatham) (Pitt the Elder)

British Prime Minister (1708–78)

4 The atrocious crime of being a young man, which the honourable gentleman has, with such spirit and decency, charged upon me, I shall neither attempt to palliate nor deny; but content myself with wishing that I may be one of those whose follies cease with their youth, and not of those who continue ignorant in spite of age and experience.

Speech, House of Commons (6 March 1741), in response to Sir Robert Walpole.

5 The lungs of London.

Of its parks. Quoted by William Windham, in a speech in the House of Commons (1808).

PITT, William (Pitt the Younger)

British Prime Minister (1759–1806)

6 Yes, I know I am young and inexperienced but it is a fault I am remedying every day.

In a 1987 election broadcast, James Callaghan quoted this response in support of Neil Kinnock, the then leader of the British Labour Party. It remains untraced, though 'Pitt the Younger', becoming Britain's youngest Prime Minister at the age of twenty-four undoubtedly did have to justify himself. Another version is that when King George III commented on his extraordinary youth, Pitt replied: 'Time, Your Majesty, will take care of that.' His father had similarly had to justify his own youth (though he was not to become Prime Minister until middle age), see above 431:4.

7 Roll up that map; it will not be wanted these ten years.

Commenting on the map of Europe after the Battle of Austerlitz (1805). Quoted in Lord Stanhope, *Life of the Rt Hon. William Pitt* (1862). He was correct almost to the month: Napoleon's hold over Europe lasted only until 1815.

8 Oh, my country! how I leave my country!

Pitt's last recorded words refer to the breaking up of the English coalition in the wake of the defeat of Austro-Russian forces by Napoleon at the Battle of Austerlitz in 1805. Often given as '... how I love my country!' In the 1862 edition of Stanhope's life of Pitt it is 'love'; in the 1879 edition, 'leave'. Alternatively, popular tradition has it that his actual last spoken words were, 'I think I could eat one of Bellamy's veal pies'. Quoted in Barnaby Conrad, *Famous Last Words* (1961).

PLINY the Elder

Roman politician (AD23–79)

1 *Semper aliquid novi Africam adferre.*
Africa always brings [us] something new.

Historia Naturalis, Bk 8. Pliny's version of what was originally a Greek proverb. Often rendered '*Ex Africa semper aliquid novi* [there is always something new out of Africa]'. Hence, *Out of Africa* (film US/UK, 1985) based in part on Isak Dinesen's 1938 book (originally, in Danish, *Den Afrikanske Farm*), and a whole spate of 'out of ...' constructions. In 1986, *The Independent* launched a series of weekly columns entitled 'Out of Europe/Asia/etc'. The same year, Ruth Prawer Jhabvala and Tim Piggot-Smith both brought out books called *Out of India*.

PLOMER, William

British writer and poet (1903–73)

2 Patriotism is the last refuge of the sculptor.

Quoted in *The Lyttelton Hart-Davis Letters*, Vol. 2 (1979, for 13 October 1956). *Compare* JOHNSON 320:1.

PLOWDEN, Edmund

English lawyer (1518–85)

3 'The case is altered', quoth Plowden.

Proverbial expression derived from a law case in which Plowden himself featured. A Roman Catholic, Plowden was arrested some time after 1570 for the treasonable offence of attending a surreptitious mass. He defended himself and was able to prove that the priest who had presided over the mass in question was an *agent provocateur*. Accordingly, he argued that a true mass could not be celebrated by an impostor – so 'the case is altered' – and was acquitted.

Another, less likely, origin is given by Henry G. Bohn in *A Hand-Book of Proverbs* (1855): 'Plowden being asked by a neighbour of his, what remedy there was in law against his neighbour for some hogs that had trespassed his ground, answered, he might have very good remedy; but the other replying, that they were his [i.e., Plowden's] hogs, Nay then, neighbour, (quoth he), the case is altered.'

The phrase was much quoted. In Shakespeare's *King Henry VI, Part 3*, IV.iii.30 (1590–1) there occurs the following exchange:

King Edward: Why, Warwick, when we parted,
Thou call'dst me King.
Warwick: Ay, but the case is alter'd:
When you disgrac'd me in my embassade,
Then I degraded you from being King,
And come now to create you Duke of York.

It occurs in Thomas Kyd, *Soliman and Perseda*, II.i.292 (1592) and Ben Jonson's play *The Case Is Altered* (1598–9). The dying Queen Elizabeth I is sometimes quoted as having said in 1603: 'I am tied, I am tied, and the case is altered with me' (Elizabeth Jenkins, *Elizabeth the Great*, 1958). From all this, The Case Is Altered is also the name given to a number of public houses in Britain though the name is sometimes erroneously said to be a corruption of the Spanish *casa alta* (high house).

PLUTARCH

Greek philosopher and biographer (c.AD 46–c.120)

4 Ingratitude towards their great men is the mark of strong peoples.

Quoted by Churchill in *The Second World War*, Vol. 1 (1948), reflecting on his own defeat at the hands of the British electorate in 1945 following his successful leadership of the country during the Second World War.

5 Macedonians had not the wit to call a spade by any other name than a spade.

Apophthegmata – as translated from Greek to Latin by Erasmus. What was rather a trough, basin, bowl, or boat in the original Greek ended up as a 'spade' and passed into English giving us the expression 'to call a spade a spade', meaning 'to speak bluntly, to call things by their proper names without resorting to euphemisms'. The phrase was into the language by 1580.

POE, Edgar Allan

American novelist and poet (1809–49)

6 Thy Naiad airs have brought me home,
To the glory that was Greece
And the grandeur that was Rome.

'To Helen' (1831). Hence, *The Grandeur That Was Rome*, title of a BBC TV series (*c.*1960), presented by the archaeologist Sir Mortimer Wheeler.

7 Take thy beak from out my heart, and take thy
form from off my door!
Quoth the Raven, 'Nevermore'.

'The Raven' (1845). In the Courtauld Institute Gallery, London, there is a painting of a nude by Gauguin with the title 'Nevermore'. What bird would you say features in it? Well, no, not a raven, it is a devil's bird. You might expect it to allude to Poe's poem, but Gauguin quite clearly stated that this was not the case.

POLLOK, Robert

Scottish poet and clergyman (1798–1827)

1 To set as sets the morning star, which goes
Not down behind the darkened west, nor hides
Obscured among the tempests of the sky,
But melts away into the light of heaven.

The Course of Time, Bk 5 (1827) – published in the year of his early death from consumption. This passage is quoted anonymously in Thomas Hardy, *A Pair of Blue Eyes*, Chap. 29 (1873). It was alluded to ('She sets as sets the morning star ...') in John Brown's moving essay about the child author 'Pet Marjorie' Fleming (who died aged eight) in *Horae Subsecivae* (1858–62).

POMPADOUR, Madame de

Mistress of Louis XV of France (1721–64)

2 *Après nous le déluge.*
After us, the flood.

Remark to Louis XV on 5 November 1757 after Frederick the Great had defeated the French and Austrian armies at the Battle of Rossbach. It carries with it the suggestion that nothing matters once you are dead and has also been interpreted as a premonition of the French Revolution. Bartlett notes that this 'reputed reply' by the King's mistress was recorded by three authorities, though a fourth gives it to the King himself. Bartlett then claims the saying was not original anyway but was 'an old French proverb'. However, the *ODP* has as an English proverb, 'After us the deluge', deriving from Mme de Pompadour. Its only citation is Burnaby's 1876 *Ride to Khiva*: 'Our rulers did not trouble their heads much about the matter. "India will last my time ... and after me the Deluge".' Metternich, the Austrian diplomat and chancellor, may later have said '*après moi le déluge*', meaning that everything would grind to a halt when he stopped controlling it. The deluge alluded to in both cases may be a dire event like the Great Flood or 'universal deluge' of Noah's time.

PONTE, Lorenzo da

Italian librettist (1749–1838)

3 *Così fan tutte.*
That's what all women do.

Title of Mozart's opera (1790), which may also be translated as 'women are like that'. The phrase had appeared earlier in Da Ponte's libretto for *Le nozze di Figaro* (1778). In that opera, Don Basilio sings, '*Così fan tutte le belle, non c'è alcuna novità* [That's what all beautiful women do, there's nothing new in that]'.

POPE, Alexander

English poet (1688–1744)

4 Where'er you walk, cool gales shall fan the glade,
Trees, where you sit, shall crowd into a shade:
Where'er you tread, the blushing flow'rs shall rise,
And all things flourish where you turn your eyes.

'Summer', *Pastorals* (1709). Not to be confused with 'Where e'er you walk', a famous tenor aria from Handel's opera *Semele* (1744), for which the libretto was by William Congreve out of Ovid's *Metamorphoses*.

5 A little learning is a dang'rous thing;
Drink deep, or taste not the Pierian spring.

An Essay on Criticism, l. 215 (1711). Hence, *A Little Learning*, title of Evelyn Waugh's autobiographical volume (1964).

6 To err is human; to forgive, divine.

Ib., l. 525. Though crisply expressed, not an original thought. Henry Wotton's translation of J. Yver's *Courtly Controversy* (1578) has: 'To offend is human, to repent divine, to persevere devilish.'

7 For fools rush in where angels fear to tread.

Ib., l. 625. Hence, *Where Angels Fear To Tread*, title of a novel (1906) by E.M. Forster. *Fools Rush In* was the title of a play (1947; film UK, 1949) by Kenneth Horne. The phrase 'Fools rush in' was also the bill matter of the British comedians Morecambe and Wise in the 1950s.

8 With varying vanities, from ev'ry part,
They shift the moving toyshop of the heart.

On women. *The Rape of the Lock*, Canto 1, l. 99 (1714).

Hence, *The Moving Toyshop*, title of Edmund Crispin's detective thriller (1946) which begins with the apparent disappearance of a toyshop in Oxford.

1 Nature, and Nature's Laws lay hid in Night:
GOD said, *Let Newton be!* and all was Light.

'Epitaph: Intended for Sir Isaac Newton' (1730), in Westminster Abbey. Sir John Squire later suggested this response (in his *Poems*, 1926):

> It did not last: the Devil howling 'Ho!
> Let Einstein be!' restored the status quo.

2 Hope springs eternal in the human breast:
Man never Is, but always To be blest.

An Essay on Man, Epistle 1, l. 95 (1733). The origin of the proverbial expression, 'Hope springs eternal'.

3 Know then thyself, presume not God to scan;
The proper study of mankind is man.

Ib., Epistle 2, l. 1. *Compare* HUXLEY 306:1.

4 Worth makes the man, and want of it, the fellow:
The rest is all but leather or prunella.

Ib., Epistle 4, l. 203. Pope distinguishes between a cobbler (the leather) and a parson (prunella is the material from which clerical gowns were made). But through misinterpretation came about the expression 'leather and prunella', meaning something to which the speaker is entirely indifferent. In George Eliot's *Middlemarch*, Chap. 43 (1871–2), Lydgate says, 'Ladislaw is a sort of gypsy; he thinks nothing of leather and prunella' – suggesting that he cares nothing for social rank.

5 A wit's a feather, and a chief's a rod;
An honest man's the noblest work of God.

Ib., Epistle 4, l. 247. The American agnostic, Robert C. Ingersoll (1833–99) concluded in *The Gods* (1876): 'An honest God is the noblest work of man.'

6 Shall then this verse to future age pretend
Thou wert my guide, philosopher, and friend?

Ib., Epistle 4, l. 389. 'Guide, philosopher and friend' has subsequently become an ingratiating form of address. From P.G. Wodehouse, *The Inimitable Jeeves* (1923): 'Right from the first day he came to me, I have looked on [Jeeves] as a sort of guide, philosopher, and friend.'

7 Who breaks a butterfly upon a wheel?

'An Epistle to Dr Arbuthnot', l. 305 (1735). Meaning 'who goes to great lengths to accomplish something trifling?' As 'Who Breaks a Butterfly on a Wheel', it was famously used as the headline to a leading article in *The Times* (1 July 1967) when Mick Jagger, the pop singer, was given a three-month gaol term on drugs charges.

8 Let the two Curls of Town and Court, abuse
His father, mother, body, soul, and muse.
Yet why? that Father held it for a rule,
It was a sin to call our neighbour fool.

Ib. Self-justificatory lines. In a series of pamphlets Edmund Curll had depicted Pope's father as being, variously, a lowly 'Mechanic, a Hatter, a Farmer, nay a Bankrupt'. Further, 'the following line, "Hard as thy Heart, and as thy Birth obscure" had fallen from a ... Courtly pen, in certain *Verses to the Imitator of Horace*'. Pope's eighteenth-century editors went to some trouble in footnotes to show that, on the contrary, Pope's father was 'of a Gentleman's family in Oxfordshire' and not to be sneered at. The 'Courtly pen' was probably that of Lord Hervey (1696–1743), though he may have been joined in the attack by Lady Mary Wortley Montagu who had fallen out with Pope by this time.

9 Let humble Allen, with an awkward shame,
Do good by stealth, and blush to find it fame.

Epilogue to the Satires, *Imitations of Horace* (1738). *Compare* LAMB 342:4.

10 I am his Highness' dog at Kew;
Pray tell me, sir, whose dog are you?

'Epigram Engraved on the Collar of a Dog which I gave to his Royal Highness' – Frederick, Prince of Wales – 1738.

PORSON, Richard

English scholar (1759–1808)

11 There were moments when his memory failed him; and he would forget to eat dinner, though he never forgot a quotation.

Edith Sitwell, *English Eccentrics* (1933). Just prior to this remark she has described how Porson, Regius Professor of Greek at Cambridge, set about a young man in a hackney coach who had produced inaccurate quotations to impress the ladies.

See also CONRAN 182:1.

PORTER, Cole

American composer and lyricist (1891–1964)

1 And when they ask us, how dangerous it was,
Oh, we'll never tell them, no, we'll never tell them:
We spent our pay in some café
And fought wild women night and day,
'Twas the cushiest job we ever had.
And when they ask us, and they're certainly going to ask us,
The reason why we didn't win the Croix de Guerre,
Oh, we'll never tell them, oh, we'll never tell them
There was a front, but damned if we knew where.

These words became famous during the First World War and were brought to a new audience in the stage show *Oh What a Lovely War* (1963; film UK, 1969). As such, they were a parody of the song 'They Didn't Believe Me' by Jerome Kern and Herbert Reynolds (M.E. Rourke) (1914), which goes:

> And when I told them how beautiful you are
> They didn't believe me, they didn't believe me.
> Your lips, your arms, your cheeks, your hair,
> Are in a class beyond compare,
> You're the loveliest girl that one can see.
>
> And when I tell them, and I'm certainly goin' to tell them,
> That I'm the man whose wife one day you'll be
> They'll never believe me, they'll never believe me,
> That from this great big world you've chosen me.

The parody was thought to be anonymous until Robert Kimball, editor of the *Complete Lyrics of Cole Porter* (1983), was going through the composer's voluminous papers and came across the words in the 'oldest compilation Porter had preserved of his works, a set of typed miscellaneous lyrics'.

In fact, Porter's version is slightly different from the one given above – e.g., line 2 is 'We never will tell them, we never will tell them'; line 5, ''Twas the wonderfulest war you ever knew', etc. So, we do not have 100 per cent proof that Porter wrote the parody, but it is an intriguing possibility. Note how the words 'night and day', which he was to couple in his most famous song in 1932, make an early appearance together here.

2 Night and day you are the one.

Song, 'Night and Day', *Gay Divorce* (1932). Hence, *Night and Day*, title of play (1978) by Tom Stoppard.

3 I get no kick from champagne.
Mere alcohol doesn't thrill me at all,
So tell me why should it be true
That I get a kick out of you?

Song, 'I Get a Kick Out of You' in *Anything Goes* (1934). According to Robert Kimball, editor of the *Complete Lyrics of Cole Porter* (1983), 'any substitutes for the lines that begin "Some get a kick from cocaine" are incorrect.'

4 You're the nimble tread of the feet of Fred Astaire,
You're Mussolini,
You're Mrs Sweeny,
You're Camembert.

Porter's 'list' song 'You're the Top' in *ib.* has understandably had to be revised since it was first published. Of this segment, in due course, Mussolini was topped rather than the tops, and Mrs Charles Sweeny (as she had been since 1933), became the infamous Margaret, Duchess of Argyll (who died in July 1993).

5 So goodbye, dear, and amen.

Title of song in *Jubilee* (1935). Hence, *Goodbye Baby and Amen*, title of a book of photographs (1969) by David Bailey and Peter Evans, subtitled 'A Saraband for the Sixties'.

6 Gather ye autographs while ye may.

Title of song in *ib.*, but dropped from show. *See* HERRICK 293:7.

7 Brush up your Shakespeare
Start quoting him now.

'Brush Up Your Shakespeare' in *Kiss Me Kate* (1948). Observing the play-within-a-play (a production of *The Taming of the Shrew*) are two gangsters. At one point they hymn the art of Shakespearean quotation – including a pun on the name 'Coriolanus', which is best left unexplained here.

8 Always True to You in my Fashion.

Title of song in *ib. See* DOWSON 213:3.

9 Paris Loves Lovers.

Title of song in *Silk Stockings* (1955). Compare the line 'Paris is for lovers' spoken in the previous year's Billy Wilder film *Sabrina* (*Sabrina Fair* in the UK). It almost has the ring of an official slogan, though this was long before the days of such lines as 'I Love New York' (1977) and 'Virginia is for Lovers' (1981).

PORTER, Peter

Australian-born poet (1929–)

1 In Australia
Inter alia,
Mediocrities
Think they're Socrates.

Unpublished clerihew. Quoted in *The Dictionary of Australian Quotations* (1984). Porter commented on BBC Radio *Quote ... Unquote* (28 November 1989) that writing these lines had meant he had recently been denied a grant by the Australian government.

POTTER, Dennis

English TV playwright (1935–94)

2 Vote, Vote, Vote, for Nigel Barton.

Potter was a frequent borrower for the titles of his plays – *Blade on the Feather, Blue Remembered Hills, Pennies from Heaven, Where the Buffalo Roam, Follow the Yellow Brick Road, Cream in My Coffee* and *Lipstick on My Collar* (all from songs). But the title of this BBC 'Wednesday Play' (1965) about a Labour politician is possibly less obvious. It echoes the election song (usually sung by children to the tune of 'Tramp, tramp, tramp, the boys are marching' and known by 1880):

Vote, vote, vote for (Billy Martin),
  Chuck old (Ernie) out the door –
If it wasn't for the law
  I would punch him on the jaw,
And we don't want (Ernie) any more.

According to Iona and Peter Opie, *The Lore and Language of Schoolchildren* (1959), Sir Anthony Eden said in 1955: 'I remember how in the old days the boys used to go round singing in chorus:

'Vote, vote, vote for So-and-so;
Punch old So-and-so in the eye;
When he comes to the door,
We will knock him on the floor,
And he won't come a-voting any more!'

3 The trouble with words is that you never know whose mouths they've been in.

In *The Guardian* (15 February 1993). Hence, *The Trouble with Words* (1994), title of a book by John Simmons. But Potter was not the first to say it. In a *c.*1950 piece entitled 'Four Eccentrics', Kenneth Tynan, after applying Carew's elegy on John Donne to the actress Hermione Gingold, added: 'But I believe I can hear her rebuking me; very coldly, with magisterial authority. She is saying: "Take those words out of your mouth: you don't know *where* they've been".'

POTTER, Stephen

English humorist (1900–69)

4 How to be one up – how to make the other man feel that something has gone wrong, however slightly.

Defining 'One-Upmanship'. *Lifemanship* (1950).

5 'Yes, but not in the South', with slight adjustments will do for any argument about any place, if not about any person.

Ib., the second volume of Potter's not solely humorous exploration of the art of 'One-Upmanship', which he defined as 'how to make the other man feel that something has gone wrong, however slightly'. In discussing ways of putting down experts while in conversation with them, Potter introduces the above 'blocking phrase' with which to disconcert, if not totally silence, them. In a footnote, he remarks: 'I am required to state that World Copyright of this phrase is owned by its brilliant inventor, Mr Pound' – though which 'Pound' he does not reveal. Indeed, the blocking move was known before this. Richard Usborne wrote of it in a piece called 'Not in the South' included in *The Pick of 'Punch'* (1941). He introduced a character called Eustace who had found a formula 'for appearing to be a European, and world, pundit. It was a formula that let me off the boredom of finding out facts and retaining knowledge.' It was to remark, 'Not in the South.'

6 If you have nothing to say, or, rather, something extremely stupid and obvious, say it, but in a 'plonking' tone of voice – i.e. roundly, but hollowly and dogmatically.

Ib. Although 'plonking' had been used in Yorkshire dialect for 'large', this would appear to be the first appearance of the term, as defined.

7 Talk of the 'imperial decay' of your invalid port. 'Its gracious withdrawal from perfection, keeping a hint of former majesty, withal, as it hovers between oblivion and the divine *Untergang* of infinite recession.'

How to promote a Cockburn '97, clearly past its best. *One-Upmanship* (1952).

POUND, Ezra

American poet (1885–1972)

1 Winter is icummen in,
Lhude sing Goddamm,
Raineth drop and staineth slop,
And how the wind doth ramm!
Sing: Goddamm.

'Ancient Music' (1917). Based on 'Sumer is icumen in,/Lhude sing cuccu!', the anonymous 'Cuckoo Song' (*c.*1250).

POWELL, Anthony

English novelist (1905–)

2 A Dance to the Music of Time.

The overall title of Powell's novel sequence (published 1951–75 and giving a panoramic view of postwar Britain) is given in the first novel, *A Question of Upbringing*. The narrator, Nicholas Jenkins, looking at workmen round a bucket of coke in falling snow, is put in mind of the painting with this title by Nicolas Poussin, which hangs in the Wallace Collection, London. There it is known as *Le 4 stagioni che ballano al suono del tempo* – a title bestowed by Giovanni Pietro Bellori. Sometimes, however, the painting is known, less interestingly, as '*Ballo della vita humana* [The Dance of Human Life]'.

3 Books Do Furnish a Room.

Title of the tenth volume (1971) of *A Dance to the Music of Time*. According to the blurb on the dust-jacket of the first edition: 'The book's title is taken to some extent from the nickname of one of the characters, Books-do-furnish-a-room Bagshaw, all-purpose journalist and amateur of revolutionary theory, but the phrase also suggests an aspect of the rather bleak post-war period – London's literary world finding its feet again.'

The notion of books being looked upon as furniture – and the consequent taunt to people who regard them as such – is an old one. Lady Holland in her *Memoir* (1855) quotes the Rev. Sidney Smith as joking: 'No furniture so charming as books.' And Edward Young in *Love of Fame: The Universal Passion*, Satire II (1725–8) has: 'Thy books are furniture.'

4 To Keep the Ball Rolling.

Overall title given to Powell's autobiographical sequence (1976–82). He says it comes from Joseph Conrad's *Chance* (1913): 'To keep the ball rolling I asked Marlow if this Powell was remarkable in any way. "He was not exactly remarkable," Marlow answered with his usual nonchalance. "In a general way it's very difficult to become remarkable. People won't take sufficient notice of one, don't you know".'

See also BURTON 135:2.

POWELL, Colin

American general (1937–)

5 First we are going to cut it off, then we are going to kill it.

As chairman of the US Joint Chiefs of Staff, on allied strategy for defeating the Iraqi army in the Gulf War. Quoted in *The Independent* (26 January 1991).

POWELL, Enoch

English Conservative then Ulster Unionist politician (1912–98)

6 Milk is rendered immortal in cheese.

In a broadcast talk in 1967, I quoted Powell as having said this but have no idea where I got it from. If, indeed, Powell did say this, he had been anticipated by Clifton Fadiman (1904–) in *Any Number Can Play* (1957), where he wrote of: 'Cheese – milk's leap toward immortality.'

7 As I look ahead, I am filled with foreboding. Like the Roman, I seem to see 'the River Tiber foaming with much blood'.

With these words, on 20 April 1968, Enoch Powell, the Conservative Opposition Spokesman for Defence, concluded a speech in Birmingham on the subject of immigration. The next day, he was dismissed from the Shadow Cabinet for a speech 'racialist in tone and liable to exacerbate racial tensions'. What became known as the 'Rivers of Blood' speech certainly produced an astonishing reaction in the public, unleashing anti-immigrant feeling that had been largely pent up until this point. Later, Powell said that he should have quoted the remark in Latin to emphasize that he was evoking only a classical prophecy of doom and not actually predicting a bloodbath. In Virgil's *Aeneid* (Bk 6, l. 87) the Sibyl of Cumae prophesies: '*Et Thybrim multo spumantem sanguine cerno.*'

But 'Rivers of blood' was quite a common turn of phrase in English before Powell made it notorious. *See* JEFFERSON 313:7. Speaking on European unity (14 February 1948), Winston Churchill said: 'We are asking the nations of Europe between whom rivers of blood have flowed, to forget the feuds of a thousand years.'

1 All political lives, unless they are cut off in mid-stream at a happy juncture, end in failure, because that is the nature of politics and of human affairs.

Joseph Chamberlain (1977). Leader of the Liberal Unionists in the 1890s, Chamberlain never became Prime Minister and had to retire from public life through ill-health, with his tariff reforms (giving preferential treatment to colonial imports) not yet in place. Powell may also have had himself in mind when writing this concluding passage.

2 Every quotation is out of context because the context of everything is everything and you can't transmit that ... To be the most misquoted is to be the most quoted [man in British politics] and I'll settle for the combination.

On BBC Radio *PM* programme (December 1978). Powell had just been voted the Best Political Speaker (or some such title) in an informal poll on the radio programme.

PRESSBURGER, Emeric

Hungarian-born screenwriter (1902–88)

3 Killing a Mouse on Sunday.

Title of novel (1961) about a survivor from the Spanish Civil War who comes out of retirement twenty years afterwards to kill a brutal police chief. The title is from Richard Braithwaite, *Barnaby's Journal* (1638), describing Banbury, 'the most Puritan of all Puritan towns':

To Banbury came I, O profane one!
Where I saw a Puritane one
Hanging of his cat on Monday
For killing of a mouse on Sunday.

When the novel was filmed, the title became, less obscurely, *Behold a Pale Horse* (1964; *see* BIBLE 106:1). In *Million-Dollar Movie* (1992), Michael Powell, Pressburger's long-time film collaborator, describes how 'the title was certainly no help ... Emeric had discovered that great tempter, *The Oxford Dictionary of Quotations* ... I was worried about the title. I said so ... "It is a cat and mouse story, Michael." "Great! ... why not call it *Cat and Mouse*?" "I have called it *Killing a Mouse on Sunday*, Michael".'

PRIESTLEY, J.B.

English novelist and playwright (1894–1984)

4 *Ruby*: Me mother says if God had intended men to smoke He'd have put chimneys in their heads.
Ormonroyd: Tell your mother from me that if God had intended men to wear clothes He'd have put collar studs at back of their necks.

When We Are Married (1938). *Compare* ANONYMOUS 35:4.

5 Let the People Sing.

Title of novel by Priestley, written so that it could first be broadcast by the BBC in (of all months) September 1939. The story, about people fighting to save a village hall from being taken over by commercial interests, was later made into a film (1942). Characters in the story write a song that goes:

Let the people sing,
And freedom bring
An end to a sad old story.
Where the people sing,
Their voices ring
In the dawn of the people's glory.

In December 1939 another song was recorded with this title (music by Noel Gay, lyrics by Ian Grant and Frank Eyton) and featured in the 1940 revue *Lights Up*. Later, ENSA, the forces' entertainment organization, used it as its signature tune. On 1 April 1940 the BBC started a long-running series of programmes – again with this title – featuring 'songs of the moment, songs of the past, songs of sentiment, songs with a smile, songs with a story, songs of the people'. The phrase almost took on the force of a slogan. Angus Calder in *The People's War* (1969) wrote of Ernest Bevin, the Minister of Labour from October 1940: 'Bevinism in industry was symbolized by the growing understanding of the value of music and entertainment in helping people to work faster ... There were the BBC's *Workers' Playtime* and *Music While You Work* which "progressive" management relayed over loudspeakers several times a day ... "Let the People Sing", it might be said, was the spiritual essence of Bevinism.' The phrase appears to have originated with Priestley, though one might note the similarity to the hymns 'Let all on earth their voices raise' and 'Let all the world in every corner sing'.

6 [They] made an excursion to hell and came back glorious.

On the 'little holiday steamers' used in the rescue from

Dunkirk. 'Postscript to the News', BBC radio (5 June 1940).

1 The Admass.

I.e., the public to which advertisers address themselves. The term was coined by Priestley in *Journey Down a Rainbow* (written with Jacquetta Hawkes, 1955): 'This is my name for the whole system of an increasing productivity ... plus high-pressure advertising and salesmanship, plus mass communication, and the creation of the mass mind, the mass man.'

2 If the day ever comes when Shakespeare is no longer acted, read and studied, quoted and loved, Western Man will be near his end.

Closing words of Chap. 4, 'England and Shakespeare' in Priestley's *Literature and Western Man* (1960).

See also WAUGH 557:2.

PROCTER, Ann Adelaide

English poet and hymn writer (1825–64)

3 Seated one day at the organ
I was weary and ill at ease,
And my fingers wandered idly
Over the noisy keys ...
But I struck one chord of music,
Like the sound of a great Amen.

'A Lost Chord', *Legends and Lyrics* (1858). Famously set to music by Sir Arthur Sullivan as '*The* Lost Chord' in the 1870s – described as 'the most popular ballad of the nineteenth century'.

PROFUMO, John

English Conservative politician (1915–)

4 There was no impropriety whatsoever in my acquaintanceship with Miss Keeler.

When rumours surfaced of a relationship between the Secretary of State for War and Christine Keeler, a 'model' who had also been sharing her favours with a Soviet military attaché in London, Profumo made a statement to the House of Commons on 22 March 1963. It later became clear that there *had* been 'impropriety' (apart from adultery, there was the possibility of a security risk) and Profumo resigned. For many, his 'misleading' of (or 'lie' to) the House was considered a worse crime than anything else he had done.

5 I shall not hesitate to issue writs for libel and slander if scandalous allegations are made or repeated outside the House.

Ib. Subsequently, 'I shall not hesitate to issue writs' became, through the offices of *Private Eye* Magazine, a catchphrase associated with Harold Wilson who became British Prime Minister in 1964. He was famously ready to say he would have recourse to the law, though he did not always do so.

PROUDHON, Pierre-Joseph

French social reformer (1809–65)

6 Property is theft.

Qu'est-ce que la propriété? (1840).

See also TOLSTOY 541:1.

PROUST, Marcel

French novelist (1871–1922)

7 *A La Recherche du Temps Perdu.*
In search of lost time.

Title of novel sequence (1913–27). Also translated as 'Remembrance of Things Past'. A captivating title, which expresses perfectly what the novels are about: the artist deriving creative energy from the memory of past experiences.

8 I raised to my lips a spoonful of the tea in which I had soaked a morsel of the cake ... suddenly the memory returns. The taste was of the little crumb of madeleine which on Sunday mornings at Combray ... my aunt Léonie used to give me, dipping it first in her own cup of real or of lime-flower tea.

'Du Côté du chez Swann', *A La Recherche du Temps Perdu* (1913) in the C.K. Scott Moncrieff translation. The key moment in the novel and, if truth be told, the only one most people know about.

See also BERESFORD 86:5.

PRYDE, James

British artist (1866–1941)

9 My god, they've shot the wrong person!

At the unveiling of an unlifelike statue of Nurse Edith Cavell outside the National Portrait Gallery in London (1920). Quoted on BBC Radio *Quote ... Unquote* (1977).

PUCCINI, Giacomo

Italian composer (1858–1924)

1 *Che gelida manina.*
Your tiny hand is frozen.

Opera, *La Bohème*, Act 1 (1896). Rodolfo to Mimi. Puccini did not write his own libretti. This one was by Giuseppe Giacosa and Luigi Ilica.

2 *Nessun dorma! Nessun dorma!*
... All'alba vincerò!
Vincerò! Vincerò!
No man shall sleep! No man shall sleep!
... At dawn I shall win!
I shall win! I shall win!

Opera, *Turandot*, Act 3 (1926). Calaf refers to his secret (his name) which he does not think anyone will find out before dawn. The song as sung by Luciano Pavarotti gained widespread popularity when it was chosen to accompany British television coverage of the 1990 football World Cup, held that year in Italy. The idea of winning was aptly transferred from torture, beheading and sex in old Peking to the playing field. *Turandot*'s libretto was by Giuseppe Adami and Renato Simoni after a play by Carlo Gozzi.

PUDNEY, John

English poet (1909–77)

3 Do not despair
For Johnny-head-in-air;
He sleeps as sound
As Johnny underground ...

'For Johnny' (1942), said to have been written by Pudney on the back of an envelope during the Blitz. The lines were subsequently used in the film *The Way to the Stars* (1945) in which they were recited following the death of their supposed author, an RAF pilot.

The character 'Johnny Head-in-Air' originally appeared in English translations of *Struwwelpeter* (1845), the collection of verse tales by Heinrich Hoffmann.

PULP FICTION

American film 1994, written and directed by Quentin Tarantino. With Ving Rhames as Marsellus Wallace.

4 *Marsellus*: I'm gonna git Medieval on your ass.

About to take revenge on a man who has raped him. Soundtrack and published script.

PUNCH

London-based humorous weekly periodical, founded 1841

5 *Peccavi* – I have Sindh.

In Vol. 6 (18 May 1844), *Punch* suggested that Caesar's '*Veni, vidi, vici*' was beaten for brevity by 'Napier's dispatch to Lord Ellenborough, *Peccavi*.' *ODQ* credits the joke to Catherine Winkworth (1827–78). She was a young girl, so it was sent into *Punch* on her behalf. Later, she became a noted translator of hymns.

It seems, however, that the supposed remark was soon taken as genuine, even at *Punch* itself. On 22 March 1856, the magazine (confusing sender and receiver in the original) included the couplet:

> '*Peccavi* – I've Scinde,' wrote Lord Ellen, so proud.
> More briefly Dalhousie wrote – '*Vovi* – I've Oude.'

'*Peccavi*' is the Latin phrase for 'I have sinned'. The *OED* sees it as part of the expression 'to cry *peccavi*', an acknowledgement or confession of guilt. The earliest citation given by the *OED* is Bishop John Fisher's Funeral Sermon at St Paul's for Henry VII (1509): 'King David that wrote this psalm, with one word speaking his heart was changed saying *Peccavi*.' This refers to Psalm 41:4: 'I said, Lord, be merciful unto me: heal my soul, for I have sinned against thee.' But the phrase occurs in a number of other places in the Bible, mostly in the Old Testament – for example, 'And Saul said unto Samuel, I have sinned' (1 Samuel 15:24.)

The Latin word is often thought to have furnished the above famous pun. Here is Charles Berlitz's version in *Native Tongues* (1982): 'Sir Charles Napier, a British officer in India, was given command of an expedition to annex the kingdom of Sind in [1843] ... To announce the success of his mission, he dispatched to the headquarters of the British East India Company a one-word message, the Latin word *peccavi*, which means "I have *sinned*".' Alas, Napier did no such thing.

6 Advice to persons about to marry, – Don't.

Vol. 8 (1845). What is probably the most famous of all *Punch* jokes appeared on the January page of the 1845 Almanack. R.G.G. Price in his history of the magazine, wonders whether it is perhaps 'the most famous joke ever made' and remarks that 'it needs an effort to realize how neat, ingenious and profound it must have seemed at the time'. It was based on an advertisement put out by a house furnisher of the day and was probably contributed by Henry Mayhew, better known for his serious surveys of *London Labour and the London Poor*, though others also claimed to have thought of it.

1 Collapse of stout party.

A catchphrase that one might use as the tagline to a story about the humbling of a pompous person. It has long been associated with the magazine *Punch* and was thought to have occurred in those wordy captions that used to be given to its cartoons. But, as Ronald Pearsall explains in his book *Collapse of Stout Party* (1975): 'To many people Victorian wit and humour is summed up by *Punch* when every joke is supposed to end with "Collapse of Stout Party", though this phrase tends to be as elusive as "Elementary, my dear Watson" in the Sherlock Holmes sagas.'

At least the *OED2* has managed to find a reference to a 'Stout Party' in the caption to a cartoon in the edition of *Punch* dated 25 August 1855.

2 Mun, a had na' been the-ere abune twa hoours when – *Bang* – went *Saxpence!*

Vol. 54 (5 December 1868). Said by a Scotsman who has just been on a visit to London, in caption to a cartoon. Hence, the expression, 'bang went sixpence!', a lightly joking remark about one's own or another person's unwillingness to spend money. The saying was repopularized by Sir Harry Lauder, the professional stage Scotsman.

3 When is a door not a door? When it's ajar.

Ib. Seemingly one of the oldest punning riddles. *Punch* in its 'comic chronology' (17 December 1872, i.e., its *Almanack for 1873*) has 'AD1001 invention of the riddle "When is a door not a door?"'

4 GOOD ADVERTISEMENT. I used your soap two years ago; since then I have used no other.

Vol. 86 (26 April 1884). Caption to a cartoon by Harry Furniss showing a grubby tramp writing a testimonial. It was taken up, with permission, by Pears' Soap and widely used in advertisements during the 1880s and 1890s. The slogan was changed slightly to: 'Two years ago I used your soap *since when* I have used no other!'

Pears' soap also used a signed testimonial (with picture) from Lillie Langtry, the actress and mistress of King Edward VII (when he was Prince of Wales). Hers read: 'Since using Pears' Soap for the hands and complexion *I have discarded all others.*' This advertisement is undated but may possibly predate the *Punch* cartoon.

5 Dropping the Pilot.

Vol. 98 (29 March 1890). Meaning 'to dispense with a valued leader', this phrase comes from the caption to a cartoon by Sir John Tenniel which showed Kaiser Wilhelm II leaning over the side of a ship as his recently disposed-of chancellor, Otto von Bismarck, dressed as a pilot, walked down the steps to disembark. Bismarck had been forced to resign following disagreements over home and foreign policy. The phrase was also used as the title of a poem on the same subject. From *The Independent* (12 May 1990): 'Kenneth Baker, the Conservative chairman, yesterday called on Tories to stop idle speculation about the party leadership ... "We have moved through difficult waters ... We should not, we must not, we will not drop the pilot".'

6 Oh no, my Lord, I assure you! Parts of it are excellent.

Vol. 109 (1895). Caption to cartoon in which a bishop is saying: 'I'm afraid you've got a bad egg, Mr Jones.' The nervous young curate, keen not to say anything critical, flannels this reply. Hence, the expression 'like the curate's egg', meaning 'patchy, good in parts'.

7 A LITTLE LEARNING
Teacher And who was JOAN OF ARC?
Scholar Please, sir, NOAH's wife.

Vol. 122 (29 January 1902). 'Noah's wife was called Joan of Ark' was listed as one of 'British children's answers to church school questions' in a US publication called *Speaker's Idea File* (1993). But how old did the compilers think it to be? About as old as the Ark itself is the fact of the matter.

8 Look here, Steward, if this is coffee, I want tea; but if this is tea, then I wish for coffee.

Vol. 123 (23 July 1902). This was the caption to a cartoon by G.D. Armour. Frequently misascribed. On BBC Radio *Quote ... Unquote* (4 September 1979), a panellist ascribed it to Charles de Gaulle. Robert Byrne in *The 637 Best Things Anybody Ever Said* (1982) gives it to Abraham Lincoln.

9 What a very pretty woman your wife must be.

Vol. 127 (3 August 1904). Caption to a cartoon. Spoken to a father by someone looking at his child.

10 *MR BINKS*: 'ONE OF MY ANCESTORS FELL AT WATERLOO.'
LADY CLARE: 'AH? WHICH PLATFORM?'

Vol. 129 (1 November 1905). Caption to cartoon by F.H. Townsend. To this joke is often added the further response, 'Ha, ha! As if it mattered which platform!'

Shamelessly misattributed over the years. *The Best of Myles* reprints as an 'overheard' this from Flann O'Brien's Dublin newspaper column [early 1940s]: 'D'you know that my great-grandfather was killed at Waterloo ... Which platform?' A.L. Rowse writes of Lord David Cecil in *Friends and Contemporaries* (1989): 'Anything for a laugh – simplest of jokes. I think of him now coming into my room [at Christ Church in the early 1920s], giggling and sputtering with fun. Someone had said, "My grandfather was killed at Waterloo" "I'm so sorry – which platform?"'

1 Well, mum, sometimes I sits and thinks and then again I just sits.

Vol. 131 (24 October 1906). Caption to a cartoon by Gunning-King headed 'Change of Occupation' which shows a vicar's wife talking to an old, somewhat rustic gentleman who has been laid up with an injured foot. She is sympathizing with him and saying: 'Now that you can't get about, and are not able to read, how do you manage to occupy the time?' This is his reply.

Until recently this well-known saying did not feature in any dictionary of quotations. So where did it originate? On first being asked about it, people would invariably say, 'Oh, that's what my father used to say'. Pressed as to its possible origin, they would come up with a bewildering variety of suggestions – Lewis Carroll, Laurel and Hardy, Winnie-the-Pooh, Uncle Remus (it could certainly be made to sound southern American) and Mark Twain. One person thought it could be found 'in Chapter 8, probably' of *Pickwick Papers* by Charles Dickens [concerning Joe, 'the fat boy'], but it could not. Several others were absolutely positive that it came from that little American book *The Specialist* (1930) by Charles Sales, the one about a man who specializes in the building of outdoor privies. The connection with sitting and thinking seemed highly likely, but, no, it does not rate a mention.

Then came reference to the novel *Anne of the Island* (1915) by L.M. Montgomery, the Canadian writer who had earlier written *Anne of Green Gables*. At one point in the book, an old woman who drives a mail-cart remarks: 'O' course it's tejus [tedious]. Part of the time I sits and thinks and the rest I jest sits.' Was this the first outing for what was clearly to become a much used and popular saying? No, it was not. Such evidence-sifting probably seems a shade preposterous ... not least because the answer (when you know it) is a very obvious one.

2 Mummy, what's that man *for*?

Vol. 131 (14 November 1906). Caption to cartoon drawn by F.H. Townsend, who was art editor of the magazine at the time. It shows the remark being said by a small boy to his mother about a man carrying a bag of golf clubs. This is probably the origin of the widely used jibe, 'What is that lady/gentleman *for*?' – a remark, out of the mouth of a not-quite babe or suckling, which becomes a convenient stick with which to beat anyone the speaker wishes to reduce in importance. It is particularly useful when taunting politicians. For example, 'It was an anonymous little girl who, on first catching sight of Charles James Fox, is supposed to have asked her mother: "what is that gentleman for?" One asks the same question of Mr [Douglas] Hurd. Why is he where he is in this particular government? He has never been wholly in sympathy either with Mrs Thatcher or with her version of Conservatism.' – Alan Watkins, *The Observer* (29 May 1988); but *see* SHAW-LEFEVRE 501:1.

Compare 'I am reminded of the small boy who once pointed at Hermione Gingold and asked, "Mummy, what's that lady for?"' – Michael Billington (possibly quoting Kenneth Tynan) in *The Guardian* (21 July 1988).

'"What," a little girl is supposed to have asked her mother, pointing at Sir John Simon, a pre-war Chancellor, "is that man for?" What, she might now ask, pointing at the Labour faithful assembling in Brighton today, is that party for?' – editorial, the *Independent on Sunday* (29 September 1991).

3 The quality of Mersea is not strained.

Vol. 181 (19 August 1931). Writing to James Agate from Liverpool on 17 April 1942, John Gielgud, the actor, who was touring in *Macbeth*, noted: 'There was a very nice misprint in the *Liverpool Echo* on Wednesday, paying tribute to our broad comedian George Woodbridge, who plays the Porter, as "an engaging Portia". I could not forbear to murmur that the quality of Mersey is not strained.' Well, this was an early appearance of the 'Mersey' joke, in *Ego 5* (1942). It had already appeared, though, in *Punch*. *See* SHAKESPEARE 490:10.

PUSHKIN, Aleksandr

Russian poet and novelist (1799–1837)

4 I loved you and it may be that my love within my soul has not yet altogether died away; howbeit, it will not trouble you any more, I do not wish to sadden you in any way. I loved you in silence and without hope, worn out now with jealousy and now with shamefastedness; I loved you so truly and so tenderly as may God grant you may be loved by some other one.

Poem 'I Loved You' (1829). As featured in Maurice Baring's introduction to *The Oxford Book of Russian Verse* (1925). Of this short poem, Baring says: 'Russian literature in the hands of an artist such as Pushkin reminds one constantly of Greek art. Pushkin's eight lines could only have been written either in Russian or in Greek.' He then gives this prose translation.

PUTNAM, Israel

American general (1718–90)

1 Don't one of you fire until you see the white of their eyes.

To his men at Bunker Hill (1775). Quoted in R. Frothingham, *History of the Siege of Boston* (1873). Also attributed to William Prescott.

PUZO, Mario

American novelist (1920–)

2 He's a businessman. I'll make him an offer he can't refuse.

Puzo's 1969 Mafia novel *The Godfather* gave to the language a new expression which, as far as can be established, was Puzo's own invention. Johnny Fontane, a singer, desperately wants a part in movie and goes to see his godfather, Don Corleone, seeking help. All the contracts have been signed and there is no chance of the studio chief changing his mind. Still, the godfather promises Fontane he will get him the part, with these words. In the 1971 film, the exchange was turned into the following dialogue:

> *Corleone*: In a month from now this Hollywood big shot's going to give you what you want.
> *Fontane*: Too late, they start shooting in a week.
> *Corleone*: I'm going to make him an offer he can't refuse.

3 A lawyer with his briefcase can steal more than a thousand men with guns.

Ib. In *The Godfather Papers* (1969) Puzo singled out this as the most quoted line from the novel. 'I've had people in France, Germany and Denmark quote that line to me with the utmost glee,' he said. 'And some of them are lawyers.' Puzo mentioned it to the head of the studio, the producer, director and everyone on the film, but the line did not get spoken in it.

PYM, Barbara

English novelist (1913–80)

4 Some Tame Gazelle.

Title of novel (1950). Pym's stories of quiet lives lived in a narrow band of middle-class society in most cases had quotations for their titles. Sometimes it was indicated in the book what the source was: *The Sweet Dove Died* (1978) (John Keats), *A Glass of Blessings* (1958) (George Herbert), *Less Than Angels* (1955) (Alexander Pope), *Civil to Strangers* (unpublished) (John Pomfret) and the short story 'So, Some Tempestuous Morn' (Matthew Arnold). At other times Pym kept mum. The short story 'Across a Crowded Room' is presumably Oscar Hammerstein II, of all people – see 278:5 – but very 1950s. *A Few Green Leaves* (1980) could be anything or nothing, as also *Excellent Women* (1952).

Some Tame Gazelle replaced 'Some Sad Turtle' and derives from a poem called 'Something to Love' by Thomas Haynes Bayly (1797–1839), a minor English poet:

> Some tame gazelle, or some gentle dove:
> Something to love, oh, something to love!

5 No Fond Return of Love.

Title of novel (1961). Behind it is an interesting story, which is related in Hazel Holt's memoir of Pym. Rejecting 'A Thankless Task' Pym decided she needed a title with 'love' in it, so sat down and worked her way through *The Oxford Book of English Verse* until she came to 'Prayer for Indifference' by the eighteenth-century Irish poet Fanny (Frances) Greville (*c.*1724–89). She adapted the first line:

> I ask no kind return of love,
> No tempting charm to please;
> Far from the heart those gifts remove
> That sigh for peace and ease.

6 What is the future of my kind of writing? ... Perhaps in retirement ... a quieter, narrower kind of life can be worked out and adopted. Bounded by English literature and the Anglican Church and small pleasures like sewing and choosing material for this uncertain summer.

Diary entry (6 March 1972), in Holt & Pym, *A Very Private Life* (1985). This was written when one of her novels had been rejected (Pym is famous for having fallen out of favour and for then being rediscovered). The phrase 'this uncertain summer' is quintessential Pym and sounds as if it ought to have served her as a title. It had been used by Sir James E. Smith in *The English Flora* (1824–8): 'It may be observed that our uncertain summer is established by the time the Elder is in full flower.'

Compare *Uncertain Glory*, the title of a film (US, 1944) and taken probably from Shakespeare's *Two Gentlemen of Verona* (I.iii.85): 'O, how this spring of love resembleth/The uncertain glory of an April day.'

See also ALEXANDER 15:7.

QUAYLE, Dan

American Republican Vice-President (1947–)

1 Space is almost infinite. As a matter of fact, we think it *is* infinite.

As head of the Space Council. Remark, quoted in *The Guardian* (8 March 1989). George Bush's surprise choice for running mate in the 1988 election, Quayle soon became noted, when in office, for his eccentric and often idiotic statements. Of the Nazi holocaust (quoted in the same source), he said: 'It was an obscene period in our nation's history ... No, not in our nation's but in World War II. We all lived in this century; I didn't live in this century but in this century's history.'

R

RABELAIS, François

French writer (c.1494–c.1553)

1 Nature abhors a vacuum.

Gargantua (1535). Rabelais quotes the maxim in its original Latin form '*natura abhorret vacuum*'. Galileo (1564–1642) asserted it as the reason mercury rises in a barometer. *See also* BROWN 123:5; LUCE 365:4.

2 *Fais/Fay ce que voudras.*
Do what you will/do as you please.

Gargantua and Pantagruel, Bk 1 (1532). An appealing motto and one that has been adopted by more than one free-living soul. In the eighteenth century it became the motto of the Monks of Medmenham, better known as the Hell Fire Club. Sir Francis Dashwood founded a mock-Franciscan order at Medmenham Abbey in Buckinghamshire in 1745, and the members of the Club were said to get up to all sorts of disgraceful activities, orgies, black masses and the like. The politician John Wilkes was of their number. The motto was written up over the ruined door of the abbey.

Aleister Crowley (1875–1947), the satanist, who experimented in necromancy and the black arts, sex and drugs, also picked up the motto. Newspapers called him the 'Wickedest Man in the World', though he fell short of proving the claim. Of his 'misunderstood commandment', Germaine Greer comments in *The Female Eunuch* (1970): '*Do as thou wilt* is a warning not to delude yourself that you can do otherwise, and to take full responsibility for what you do. When one has genuinely chosen a course for oneself it cannot be possible to hold another responsible for it.'

3 *Adieu paniers, vendanges sont faites.*
Farewell baskets, the grapes are gathered.

Ib. One of those peculiar lines that get turned into catchphrases. Friar Jean des Entommeurs is exhorting his fellow monks to stop praying and repel the soldiers who are vandalizing their vineyard – a call to arms.

4 The comedy is ended.

The dying words of Rabelais are supposed to have been: '*Je m'en vais chercher un grand peut-être; tirez le rideau, la farce est jouée* [I am going to seek a grand perhaps; bring down the curtain, the farce is played out].' The attribution is made, hedged about with disclaimers, in Jean Fleury's *Rabelais et ses oeuvres* (1877) (also in the life of Rabelais by Motteux, who died in 1718). In Lermontov's novel *A Hero of Our Time* (1840), a character says: '*Finita la commedia*', and Leoncavallo's opera *Pagliacci* (1892) ends '*La commedia è finita*'. *Compare* BEETHOVEN 80:5.

RALEIGH, Sir Walter

English explorer and courtier (c.1552–1618)

5 But true love is a durable fire
In the mind ever burning;
Never sick, never old, never dead,
From itself never turning.

Poem 'Walsingham' (undated). *A Durable Fire* was the title given to a volume of the letters of Duff and Diana Cooper 1913–50 (published 1983).

6 Give me my scallop-shell of quiet,
My staff of faith to walk upon,
My scrip of joy, immortal diet,
My bottle of salvation,
My gown of glory, hope's true gage,
And thus I'll take my pilgrimage.

'The Passionate Man's Pilgrimage' or 'His Pilgrimage' (1604). There is some doubt about the authorship. The scallop shell was the emblem worn by pilgrims to identify themselves as such. More particularly, it was the emblem of St James of Compostela and was adopted, according to Erasmus, because the seashore was close to the end of the pilgrimage route to the saint's shrine.

1 'Tis a sharp remedy, but a sure one for all ills.

Feeling the edge of the axe which was to behead him. David Hume, *History of Great Britain* (1754).

2 So the heart be right, 'tis no matter which way the head lies. What dost thou fear? Strike man, strike!

When asked how he wished to place his head on the block. Quoted in W. Stebbing, *Sir Walter Raleigh* (1891).

RANDOLPH, David

American conductor and writer (1914–)

3 *Parsifal* is the kind of opera that starts at six o'clock. After it has been going three hours, you look at your watch and it says 6.20.

Quoted in *The American Treasury*, ed. Clifton Fadiman (1955), but otherwise unverified.

RANDS, William Brighty

English journalist and poet (1823–82)

4 When Love arose in heart and deed
To wake the world to greater joy,
'What can she give me now?' said Greed,
Who thought to win some costly toy.

'The Flowers', *Lilliput Levee* (1864). Rands was sometimes known as the 'laureate of the nursery'. His books were originally published anonymously or pseudonymously.

RANSOME, Arthur

English novelist and journalist (1884–1967)

5 BETTER DROWNED THAN DUFFERS IF NOT DUFFERS WON'T DROWN.

Swallows and Amazons, Chap. 1 (1930). A telegram from the father of one of the children in the novel. It is interpreted as meaning: 'Daddy thinks none of us shall get drowned and that if any of us do get drowned, it's good riddance.'

RAPHAEL, Frederic

English novelist and screenwriter (1931–)

6 *Robert (to Diana)*: Your idea of fidelity is not having more than one man in the bed at the same time ... You're a whore, baby, that's all, just a whore, and I don't take whores in taxis.

Film, *Darling* (UK, 1965), with Dirk Bogarde as Robert Gold and Julie Christie as Diana Scott.

7 He glanced with disdain at the big centre table where the famous faces of the Cambridge theatre were eating a loud meal. 'So this is the city of dreaming spires,' Sheila said. 'Theoretically speaking that's Oxford,' Adam said. 'This is the city of perspiring dreams.'

The Glittering Prizes (1976). *See* ARNOLD 61:3.

RATTIGAN, Terence (later Sir Terence)

English playwright (1911–77)

8 The Way to the Stars.

Title of film (UK, 1945), set near an RAF airfield during the Second World War, and which reworked most of Rattigan's stage play *Flare Path*. It presumably alludes to the RAF motto '*Per ardua ad astra* [through striving/struggle to the stars]', first proposed in 1912. However, the words '*Macte nova virtute, puer, sic itur ad astra*' from Virgil's *Aeneid* (Bk 9, l. 641) are often translated as: 'Go to it with fresh courage, young man; this is the way to the stars' – the words of Ascanius, son of Aeneas, before battle. In the US, perhaps to avoid any such questions, the film was called *Johnny in the Clouds*, after the line 'Johnny Head-in-air' (*see* PUDNEY 440:3), which is recited in the film.

9 A nice, respectable, middle-class, middle-aged maiden lady, with time on her hands and the money to help her pass it ... Let us call her Aunt Edna ... Aunt Edna is universal, and to those who may feel that all the problems of the modern theatre might be solved by her liquidation, let me add that ... she is also immortal.

Preface, *Collected Plays*, Vol. II (1953). During the revolution in English drama of the 1950s the term 'Aunt Edna' was used by the new wave of angry young dramatists and their supporters to describe the more conservative theatregoer – the type who preferred comfortable three-act plays of the Shaftesbury Avenue kind. Ironically, the term had been coined in self-defence by Rattigan, one of the generation of dramatists they sought to replace.

RATUSHINSKAYA, Irina

Ukrainian poet (1954–)

1 Grey is the Colour of Hope.

Title of book (1988), referring to the colour of the author's uniform as an inmate of a Soviet labour camp. On her twenty-ninth birthday, Ratushinskaya was sentenced to seven years in the camp, to be followed by five years' internal exile. Her 'crime' was her poetry. She was released (after intensive campaigning) in 1986, just prior to the Reykjavik summit meeting between Presidents Reagan and Gorbachev. Compare: 'Citizens to arms! ... Let us take as our emblem green cockades, green the colour of hope' – Camille Desmoulins, French revolutionary leader, speech (14 July 1789).

RAY, John

English botanist and paroemiologist (1627–1705)

2 Misery loves company.

Bartlett (1992) lists this proverb, along with five others, under Ray's name. This is surely misleading as the whole point of any proverb book – not least Ray's own *A Collection of English Proverbs* (1670) – is that it represents traditional expression of wisdom rather than an individual's. Of course, some proverb collectors and scholars (notably Benjamin Franklin) did coin proverbs and slip them into their collection, but there is no reason to believe that Ray did so.

The *ODP* does not include this proverb, anyway, though *CODP* finds earlier citations *c.*1349 and 1578.

RAY, Man

French artist and photographer (1890–1976)

3 *La photographie n'est pas l'art.*
Photography is not art.

Quoted in *The Independent* (3 March 1995). Misleadingly it has been translated as 'Art is not photography'.

RAYMOND, Ernest

English novelist (1888–1974)

4 Tell England, ye who pass this monument,
We died for her, and here we rest content.

Tell England, Bk 2, Chap. 12 (1922): 'We had walked right on to the grave of our friend. His name stood on a cross with those of six other officers, and beneath was written in pencil the famous epitaph ... The perfect words went straight to Doe's heart. "Roop," he said, "if I'm killed you can put those lines over me".'

The book (film UK, 1931) was about a group of English public school boys who end up at Gallipoli. Quite where the epitaph originated is hard to say. In *Farewell the Trumpets* (1978) James Morris finds it on a memorial from the Boer War at Wagon Hill, Ladysmith, in the form:

Tell England, ye who pass this monument,
We, who died serving her, rest here content.

Presumably, this memorial was erected *before* the First World War and *before* Raymond's book popularized the couplet.

Whatever the case, the words clearly echo the epitaph by the ancient Greek poet Simonides (*q.v.*) on the Spartans who died at Thermopylae (delaying the vastly greater Persian army at the cost of their own lives): 'Tell the Spartans, stranger, that here we lie, obeying their orders.' Indeed, Diana Raymond, the novelist's widow, wrote in 1992: 'I (and all the family) always understood from Ernest that he had taken the lines from the epitaph for the Spartans who died at Thermopylae, substituting "England" for "Sparta" and making his own translation. This leaves the problem of the Boer War memorial at Ladysmith. Either two people had the same idea; or else Ernest had somewhere at the back of his mind without realising it a memory of this. I rather think the first answer is the right one; he was very accurate in his references.'

READE, Charles

English novelist (1814–84)

5 Make 'em laugh, make 'em cry, make 'em wait.

A suggested recipe for writing novels to be published in serial form (as done by Charles Dickens and many others in the nineteenth century). Reade, who wrote *The Cloister and the Hearth* (1861), came up with it – or at least he did according to the *PDQ* (1960). Kenneth Robinson in his biography *Wilkie Collins* (1951) attributes the remark to Reade's contemporary.

REAGAN, Ronald

American film actor, Republican governor and 40th President (1911–)

6 Win this one for the Gipper!

Bridging his film and political careers, this Reagan slogan refers to George Gipp, a character he had played in *Knute Rockne – All-American* (1940). Gipp was a real-life football star who died young. At half-time in a 1928 army game, Rockne, the team coach, had recalled something Gipp had said to him: 'Rock, someday when things look real tough for Notre Dame, ask the boys to go out there and win one for me.' Reagan used the slogan countless times. One of the last was at a campaign rally for Vice-President George Bush in San Diego, California, on 7 November 1988. Reagan's peroration included these words: 'So, now we come to the end of this last campaign ... And I hope that someday your children and grandchildren will tell of the time that a certain President came to town at the end of a long journey and asked their parents and grandparents to join him in setting America on the course to the new millennium ... So, if I could ask you just one last time. Tomorrow, when mountains greet the dawn, would you go out there and win one for the Gipper? Thank you, and God bless you all.'

1 Randy – where's the rest of me?

Film *King's Row* (1941) in which Reagan plays the part of Drake McHugh, and Ann Sheridan appears as Randy Monaghan. A famous moment occurs when Drake, on waking to find that his legs have been amputated by a sadistic doctor, poses this pained question. *Where's the Rest of Me?* was used by Reagan as the title of an early autobiography (1965).

2 Sex is best in the afternoon after coming out of the shower.

To Viveca Lindfors. Remark (1949), quoted in Bob Chieger, *Was It Good For You Too?* (1983).

3 An alimentary canal with a big appetite at one end and no responsibility at the other.

On government. Bartlett (1992) came under particular attack for its treatment of Reagan, the erstwhile 'Great Communicator'. While noting two of Reagan's many borrowings in footnotes ('Go ahead, make my day' and 'Evil empire'), it listed only *three* original sayings. Adam Meyerson, raising the topic in *The Washington Post* (14 February 1993), thought the choice of only three Reaganisms (compared with *twenty-eight* apiece for John F. Kennedy and Franklin Roosevelt) was politically motivated and intended to diminish the former President. Supporters of Bartlett responded with the suggestion that Reagan relied so much on borrowings from old movie scripts and on the scribblings of speechwriters like Peggy Noonan that his famous lines did not deserve Bartlett's form of immortality. But neither Kennedy nor Roosevelt produced his mighty lines unaided, and the rule in compiling such dictionaries should always be to recognize the person who actually went out there and spoke the lines (however arrived at) – in other words the person who popularized them. For the record: the *ODQ* (1992) includes *five* Reaganisms (completely different from Bartlett's). *Chambers Dictionary of Modern Quotations* (1993) contains *fifteen* entries under 'Reagan', together with four cross-references to his borrowings.

In *Speaking My Mind* (1989), the book of Reagan's selected speeches, there is not a single mention of Peggy Noonan or any other speechwriter. The drafts which are reproduced in the book – spattered with emendations in the President's own hand – seem designed to convince that he really was 'speaking his own mind'.

Of the three sayings Bartlett did include, the above is a gag dating from 1965, when Reagan was campaigning for Governor of California. Bartlett gives no indication that this might be no more than a gag-writer's re-working of the definition of a baby long ascribed to Ronald Knox (*q.v.*) in the form 'a loud voice at one end and no sense of responsibility at the other'. It was so ascribed in the 1976 BBC Reith Lectures, though Frank S. Pepper's *Handbook of 20th Century Quotations* (1984) gives the 'baby' version to 'E. Adamson'.

4 A shining city on a hill.

In a speech on 14 October 1969 Reagan quoted Governor Winthrop of the Massachusetts Bay Colony who told new settlers in 1630: 'We shall be as a city upon a hill, the eyes of all people are upon us.' It was meant as a warning as much as a promise. Winthrop did not use the word 'shining'. A writer in *The Observer* (8 March 1987) recalled Reagan using it as early as 1976 when he had just lost the Republican nomination to Gerald Ford. He told his supporters he would be back, they would win in the end and once again America would be a 'shining city on a hill'. Later, when President, Reagan was often to use the image to describe the US as a land of security and success. He used the phrase particularly during his bid for re-election as President in 1984. In return, at the Democratic Convention, New York Governor Mario Cuomo remarked that a shining city might be what Reagan saw 'from the veranda of his ranch' but he failed to see despair in the slums. 'There is despair, Mr President, in the faces that you don't see, in the places that you don't visit in your shining city ... This nation is more a tale of two cities than it is just a shining city on a hill.'

If anything, the image is biblical. Matthew 5:14 has: 'A city that is set on a hill cannot be hid ... Let your light so shine before men that they may see your good works' (*see* BIBLE 100:7); the 'holy hill' of Zion is a 'sunny mountain' according to one etymology; the New Jerusalem is the jewelled city lit by the glory of

God in Revelation (source: letter to *The Observer* from Alan MacColl, University of Aberdeen, 15 March 1987.)

1 Don't you cut me off. I am paying for this microphone.

Just prior to a broadcast debate at Nashua, New Hampshire, during the presidential primary there in 1980, Reagan turned the tables on George Bush (then also a challenger) by insisting that the other Republican candidates be allowed to participate. Reagan won the dispute over who should speak in the debate by declaring 'Don't you cut me off, I am paying for this microphone, Mr Green!' Never mind that the man's name was actually 'Breen', the line in the form, 'Don't you shut me off, I'm paying for this broadcast' had earlier been delivered by Spencer Tracy in the film *State of the Union* (1948). This borrowing was pointed out by Christopher J. Matthews writing in *The Washington Post* (6 May 1984), and by *Time* Magazine (8 February 1988).

2 There you go again!

To President Carter during TV debate (29 October 1980). When Carter claimed that Reagan would dismantle federal health support for the elderly, Reagan – with his later familiar sideways nod of the head – came up with this line which struck a chord with voters.

3 Please tell me you're Republicans.

To surgeons, as he entered the operating room after an attempted assassination (30 March 1981). Quoted in *Time* Magazine (13 April 1981).

4 What makes you think I'd be happy about that?

When told by an aide that the government was running normally, on the same occasion. In *ib.*

5 Congressional Medal of Honor, posthumously awarded.

Reagan told a meeting (undated) of the Congressional Medal of Honor Society about an aircraft gunner who couldn't leave his post when his plane was crashing. He was told by his commanding officer that he would win a 'Congressional Medal of Honor, posthumously awarded'. No such incident happened in real life, though it did in the film *Wing and a Prayer* (1944). In 1985, Michael Rogin, a professor of political science at Berkeley, explored Reagan's other borrowings of film lines in a presentation entitled 'Ronald Reagan: The Movie'.

6 In your discussions of the nuclear freeze proposals, I urge you to beware the temptation of pride – the temptation blithely to declare yourselves above it all and label both sides equally at fault, to ignore the facts of history and the aggressive impulses of an evil empire.

The Soviet Union was so described by Reagan in a speech to the National Association of Evangelicals at Orlando, Florida (8 March 1983). The inspiration for this turn of phrase was made clear later the same month (23 March) when Reagan first propounded his 'Star Wars' proposal as part of a campaign to win support for his defence budget and arms-control project. The proposal, more properly known by its initials SDI (for Strategic Defence Initiative), was to extend the nuclear battleground into space. The President did not use the term 'Star Wars' but it was an inevitable tag to be applied by the media, given his own fondness for adapting lines from the movies. The film *Star Wars* and the sequel *The Empire Strikes Back* had been released in 1977 and 1980, respectively.

In the controversy over Reagan's poor showing in Bartlett (1992) (see above), it was argued that Bartlett was wrong in ascribing the phrase 'evil empire' to George Lucas, the creator of *Star Wars*. Apparently, in that film it appears only in the form 'evil galactic empire'.

An alternative version, 'the most evil enemy mankind has ever known in his long climb from the swamp to the stars' was quoted by *The Guardian* (30 May 1988) on the occasion of Reagan's visit to the Soviet Union.

Compare from *The Independent* (19 May 1990): 'Frank Salmon, an East End protection racketeer who built an "evil empire" on violence and fear, was yesterday jailed for 7½– years at the Old Bailey.'

7 Where do we find such men?

In 1984, on the fortieth anniversary of the D-Day landings, President Reagan visited Europe and made a speech in which he eulogized those who had taken part in the event. 'Where do we find such men?' he asked. On a previous occasion he had said: 'Many years ago in one of the four wars in my lifetime, an admiral stood on the bridge of a carrier watching the planes take off and out into the darkness bent on a night combat mission and then found himself asking, with no one there to answer – just himself to hear his own voice – "Where do we find such men?"' But the very first time he had used the line he had made it clear where it came from and that it was fiction. The line comes from James Michener's novel *Bridges at Toko-Ri*, later filmed (1954) with William Holden who asks, 'Where do we get such men?' Over the years, fiction became fact for

Reagan. Perhaps he could not, or was unwilling, to distinguish between the two (source: Rogin, as above.)

1 It's morning again in America.

Slogan for Reagan's 1984 re-election campaign. Coined by Hal Riney (1932–), an American advertising executive (source: *Newsweek* Magazine, 6 August 1984.)

2 My fellow Americans, I am pleased to tell you that I have signed legislation to outlaw Russia for ever. We begin bombing in five minutes.

During microphone test prior to radio broadcast. Audio recording (13 August 1984).

3 I will not make age an issue of this campaign. I am not going to exploit for political purposes my opponent's youth and inexperience.

On his challenger, Walter Mondale, during 1984 election. TV debate (22 October 1984).

4 This is not the end of anything, this is the beginning of everything.

In victory speech on re-election. Quoted in *The Times* (8 November 1984).

5 You ain't seen nothing yet!

On the same occasion, and during the preceding campaign. Quoted in the *Daily Express* (8 November 1984). *Compare* JOLSON 322:7.

6 They are the moral equivalent of our Founding Fathers and the brave men and women of the French Resistance. We cannot turn away from them, for the struggle here is not right versus left; it is right versus wrong.

On the Nicaraguan Contras. Speech (1 March 1985), said to have been written by Pat Buchanan.

7 There is no limit to what a man can do and where he can go if he doesn't mind who gets the credit.

The propensity for American Presidents to clutter their desks with plaques bearing uplifting messages dates back to the days of Harry S Truman at least. His 'the buck stops here' motto was apparently of his own devising. Jimmy Carter either retrieved the original or had a copy made and displayed it near his own desk when he was in the Oval Office. Enter Ronald Reagan. According to the *Daily Mail* (18 April 1985): 'Besides a calendar, a pen set, a clock and a horseshoe, the First Desk is now home to no fewer than eight inspirational messages. They range from the consoling "Babe Ruth struck out 1,330 times", through the boosting "Illegitimi Non Carborundum" ... to the altruistic "there is no limit ..."'

8 Do we get to win this time?

So says John Rambo (a hunk bringing home American prisoners left behind in the Vietnam War) in the film *Rambo: First Blood Part Two* (US, 1985 – a sequel to *First Blood*, 1982). The terms 'Ramboesque', 'Rambo-like' and 'Ramboism' were rapidly adopted for mindless, forceful heroics. When Reagan quoted this line in a speech (undated), he did have the grace to credit it for once rather than pass it off as one of his own.

9 We are not going to tolerate these attacks from outlaw states run by the strangest collection of misfits, looney tunes, and squalid criminals since the advent of the Third Reich.

On the hijacking of a US plane by Shi'ite Muslims, in a broadcast (8 July 1985). Meaning 'mad person' or, as an adjective, 'mad', the phrase 'looney tune' refers to the cinema cartoon comedies called Looney Tunes, which have been produced by Warners since the 1940s. The phrase was already established and had been used, for example, in the Mel Brooks film *High Anxiety* (1977).

10 The future doesn't belong to the fainthearted; it belongs to the brave.

TV address on the space shuttle *Challenger* disaster (28 January 1986). Written by Peggy Noonan. *See also* MAGEE 375:8.

11 There's a coincidence today. On this day 390 years ago, the great explorer Sir Francis Drake died aboard ship off the coast of Panama. In his lifetime the great frontiers were the oceans, and a historian later said, 'He lived by the sea, died on it, and was buried in it.' Well, today we can say of the *Challenger* crew: Their dedication was, like Drake's, complete.

Ib. The identity of the historian remains untraced. However, G.M. Trevelyan is supposed to have said of *Nelson* that he was, 'Always in his element and always on his element.' Compare what Mencken (1942) has as a 'Japanese proverb': 'If you were born at sea, you will die on it.' Isadora Duncan wrote in *My Life* (1928): 'I was born by the sea, and I have noticed that all the great events of my life have taken place by the sea' – she also died by the sea, at Nice. Kenneth Grahame wrote in *The Wind in the Willows*, Chap. 1 (1908): 'And you really live by the river? ... By it and with it and on it and in it.'

1 There is nothing better for the inside of a man than the outside of a horse.

When *Time* Magazine quoted President Reagan as saying this (28 December 1987), it received many letters from readers saying such things as: 'This quotation bears a striking resemblance to a remark made by the California educator and prep school founder Sherman Thacher: "There's something about the outside of a horse that's good for the inside of a boy"'; and, 'Rear Admiral Grayson, President Woodrow Wilson's personal physician put it ... "The outside of a horse is good for the inside of a man"'; and, 'Lord Palmerston said it.'

Time sensibly replied (19 January 1988): 'Everyone is right. The origin of the saying is unknown. It is one of the President's favorite expressions.'

2 I now begin the journey that will lead me into the sunset of my life.

Statement revealing that he had Alzheimer's Disease, 1994. Quoted in *The Daily Telegraph* (5 January 1995).

See also DEMPSEY 201:6; EASTWOOD 219:1; LOUIS 364:1; MAGEE 375:8.

REDMOND, John

Irish politician (1856–1918)

3 If I believed that there was the smallest reasonable chance of success, I would have no hesitation in advising my fellow-countrymen to endeavour to end the present system of armed revolt.

Speech, House of Commons (12 April 1905). Redmond was a champion of Home Rule.

REED, Henry

English poet and playwright (1914–86)

4 As we get older we do not get any younger.
Seasons return, and today I am fifty-five,
And this time last year I was fifty-four,
And this time next year I shall be sixty-two.

'Chard Whitlow', *A Map of Verona* (1946). In parody of T.S. Eliot.

5 To-day we have naming of parts.
Yesterday
We had daily cleaning.
And tomorrow morning,
We shall have what to do after firing. But to-day,
To-day we have naming of parts.

'Lessons of the War' in *ib.* Has been described as the most substantial poem to have emerged from the Second World War. How different it is in tone from those that came out of the First World War.

REED, John

American writer (1887–1920)

6 Ten Days that Shook the World.

Title of book (on Russian Revolution) (1919). Also used as the alternative, English, title of Sergei Eisenstein's 1927 film *October*.

REED, Thomas B(rackett)

American politician (1839–1902)

7 A statesman is a successful politician who is dead.

Remark *c.*1880, quoted in Henry Cabot Lodge, *The Democracy of the Constitution* (1915). Reed was in the House of Representatives.

REES, Nigel

English writer and broadcaster (1944–)

8 When in doubt, ascribe all quotations to George Bernard Shaw.

'Rees's First Law of Quotations', *Quote ... Unquote 3* (1983). Quoted in Des MacHale, *Wit* (1996). The law's first qualification is: 'Except when they obviously derive from Shakespeare, the Bible or Kipling.' The first corollary is: 'In time, all humorous remarks will be ascribed to Shaw whether he said them or not.' To which one might now add that Shaw can on occasions be replaced by Wilde, Chesterton or Churchill. All quotations in translation, on the other hand, should be attributed to Goethe (with 'I think' obligatory).

9 To be a bore is to have halitosis of the mind, as someone should probably have said before me.

Best Behaviour (1992). Compare Harold L. Ickes on Huey Long: 'The trouble with Senator Long is that he is suffering from halitosis of the intellect. That's presuming Emperor Long has an intellect' – quoted in Arthur M. Schlesinger, *The Politics of Upheaval* (1960).

REES-MOGG, William (later Lord Rees-Mogg)

English journalist and editor (1928–)

1 The arts are to Britain what sunshine is to Spain.

'Sayings of the Week' in *The Observer* credited this to Sir William (as he then still was and Chairman of the Arts Council of Great Britain) on 31 March 1985. On 22 September the same year, it gave the credit to Luke Rittner, secretary-general of the same organization. Clearly a popular saying thereabouts.

REEVES, Rosser

American advertising agent (1910–84)

2 Each advertisement must say to each reader: 'Buy *this* product, and you will get *this specific benefit*' ... The proposition must be one that the competition either cannot, or does not, offer. It must be unique ... The proposition must be so strong that it can move the mass millions ... These three points are summed up in the phrase: 'UNIQUE SELLING PROPOSITION.' This is a U.S.P.

Reality in Advertising, Chap. 13 (1960). The term was coined by Reeves at the Ted Bates & Company agency which he helped found in 1940 and turn into one of the largest in the world. He described the term USP as 'a theory of the ideal selling concept ... a verbal short-hand of what makes a campaign work.'

REGER, Max

German composer (1873–1916)

3 I am sitting in the smallest room of my house. I have your review before me. In a moment it will be behind me.

In 1906 Reger wrote what might appear to be the original of a famous type of abusive remark in a letter to the music critic Rudolph Louis. It is quoted in N. Slonimsky, *Lexicon of Musical Invective* (1953), having been translated from the German. Ned Sherrin, in *Theatrical Anecdotes* (1991), reports the similar reply from Oscar Hammerstein (grandfather of the lyricist) to a creditor: 'I am in receipt of your letter which is now before me and in a few minutes will be behind me.' (In the *Evening Standard*, 30 January 1992, Milton Shulman ascribed it to Noël Coward ...)

There seems every chance that the real originator of the remark was John Montagu, 4th Earl of Sandwich. N.A.M. Rodger in *The Insatiable Earl* (1993) suggests that when William Eden (later Lord Auckland) defected from Sandwich in 1785 he wrote him a letter: 'Contemporaries repeated with relish Sandwich's terse reply ... "Sir, your letter is before me, and will presently be behind me".' Rodger gives his source as J.H. Jesse, *George Selwyn* (1843–4) and adds, helpfully, 'Manufactured lavatory paper was not known in the eighteenth century.'

REICH, Charles

American author (1928–)

4 The extraordinary thing about this new consciousness [an anti-urban counter-culture] is that it has emerged out of the wasteland of the Corporate State. For one who thought the world was irretrievably encased in metal and plastic and sterile stone, it seems a remarkable greening of America.

The Greening of America (1971) – explaining his title.

REITH, John (later Lord Reith)

Scottish-born broadcasting administrator (1889–1971)

5 It was in fact the combination of public service motive, sense of moral obligation, assured finance and the brute force of monopoly which enabled the BBC to make of broadcasting what no other country has made of it.

Into the Wind (1949). Reith's dour approach to broadcasting – he was, from 1922, the BBC's first Director-General – set the standard and tone of British broadcasting in its early days and beyond. When he wrote these words, however, momentum was building for the 'brute force of monopoly' to be overturned by the introduction of commercial television (which eventually arrived in 1955). Commercial radio did not operate in the UK until 1973.

6 I was inordinately ambitious, I suppose, to be *fully stretched* ... inordinately ambitious to be of service.

BBC TV, *Lord Reith Looks Back* (1967). Reith was describing his youthful determination to achieve something recognizable. Initially, he was an engineer before being drawn into broadcasting, about which he then knew nothing.

7 I hear you.

To Malcolm Muggeridge in *ib.* Using a Scots expression meaning that a remark is not worth considering or is untrue.

See also MÜNSTER 403:6.

REMARQUE, Erich Maria

German novelist (1897–1970)

1 All Quiet on the Western Front.

Title given to the English translation of Remarque's novel *Im Westen nichts Neues* (1929, film US, 1930). 'All Quiet on the Western Front' had been a familiar phrase of the Allies in the First World War, used in military communiqués and newspaper reports and also taken up jocularly by men in the trenches to describe peaceful inactivity. Partridge/*Catch Phrases* hears in it echoes of 'All quiet on the Shipka Pass' – cartoons of the 1877–8 Russo-Turkish War, which Partridge says had a vogue in 1915–16, though he never heard the allusion made himself. For no very good reason, Partridge rules out any connection with the US song 'All Quiet Along the Potomac'. This, in turn, came from a poem called 'The Picket Guard' (1861) by Ethel Lynn Beers – a sarcastic commentary on General George Brinton McClellan's policy of delay at the start of the Civil War. The phrase (alluding to the Potomac River which runs through Washington, DC) had been used in reports from McClellan's Union headquarters and put in Northern newspaper headlines.

REPINGTON, Charles à Court

English soldier and journalist (1858–1925)

2 The First World War 1914–18.

Title of book (1920). Presumably this helped popularize the name for the war, ominously suggesting that it was merely the first of a series. Indeed, it was thought to be a shocking title because it presupposed another war.

Known at first as the 'European War', the conflict became known quite rapidly as the 'Great War'. By 10 September 1918, as he later described in his book, Repington was referring to it in his diary as the 'First World War', thus: 'I saw Major Johnstone, the Harvard Professor who is here to lay the bases of an American History. We discussed the right name of the war. I said that we called it now *The War*, but that this could not last. The Napoleonic War was *The Great War*. To call it *The German War* was too much flattery for the Boche. I suggested *The World War* as a shade better title, and finally we mutually agreed to call it *The First World War* in order to prevent the millennium folk from forgetting that the history of the world was the history of war.'

The *OED2* finds 'Great War' in use by 1914 (though earlier in 1887), but does not find 'First World War' until 1931.

REUBEN, David

American doctor and author (1933–)

3 Everything You Always Wanted To Know About Sex But Were Afraid To Ask.

Title of book (1970). The use of the format was popularized even further when Woody Allen entitled a film *Everything You Always Wanted To Know About Sex, But Were Afraid To Ask* (US, 1972) – though, in fact, he simply bought the title of the book and none of its contents. The format soon became a cliché and almost any subject you can think of has been inserted into the sentence.

REUTHER, Walter

American labour leader (1907–70)

4 If it looks like a duck, walks like a duck and quacks like a duck, then it just may be a duck.

Usually ascribed to Reuther during the McCarthyite witch-hunts of the 1950s. He came up with it as a test of whether someone was a Communist. Then it came to be applied elsewhere – but usually in politics: 'Mr Richard Darman, the new [US] Budget director, explained the other day what "no new taxes" means. He will apply the duck test. "If it looks like a duck, walks like a duck and quacks like a duck, it's a duck"' – *The Guardian* (25 January 1989). Curiously, it has also been attributed to Cardinal Cushing.

REVERE, Paul

American patriot (1735–1818)

5 The British are coming! The British are coming!

Doubt has been cast on Revere's reputed cry to warn people of approaching British troops during the American War of Independence. On his night ride of 18 April 1775, from Boston to Lexington, it is more likely that he cried 'The regulars are out' and, besides, there were many other night-riders involved. Hence, however, *The Russians Are Coming, The Russians Are Coming*, the title of a film (US, 1966).

REYNOLDS, Sir Joshua

English painter (1723–92)

1 I should desire that the last words which I should pronounce in this Academy, and from this place, might be the name of – Michael Angelo.

As the first President of the Royal Academy (1768). *Discourses on Art*, No. 15 (1790).

RHODES, Cecil

British-born South African colonialist (1853–1902)

2 Remember that you are an Englishman, and have consequently won first prize in the lottery of life.

The source for this statement (much quoted in this form by Sir Peter Ustinov – in *Dear Me*, 1977, for example) is a book called *Jottings from an Active Life* (1928) by Colonel Sir Alexander Weston Jarvis. Jarvis wrote of Rhodes: 'He was never tired of impressing upon one that the fact of being an Englishman was the greatest prize in the lottery of life, and that it was the thought which always sustained him when he was troubled.'

Hence, Tom Stoppard's attribution of the words to Kipling (quoted in 1989) is probably incorrect.

3 So much to do, so little done, goodbye, God bless you.

From 'Dr Robinson's sermon at Westminster' (presumably at a memorial service) comes this report of Rhodes's dying words. Also reported in Lewis Mitchell, *Life of Rhodes* (1910). The gist of what Rhodes said before he breathed his last on 26 March 1902 was indeed 'So much to do, so little done', though this is sometimes quoted with the phrases reversed. It was a theme that had obviously preoccupied him towards the end of his life. He said to Lord Rosebery: 'Everything in the world is too short. Life and fame and achievement, everything is too short.'

Tennyson had already anticipated him. *In Memoriam* (1850) has these lines in section lxxiii:

So many worlds, so much to do,
So little done, such things to be.

The actual last words of Rhodes were much more prosaic: 'Turn me over, Jack.'

RHYS, Jean

British novelist (1894–1979)

4 Wide Sargasso Sea.

Title of novel (1966). This, in modern parlance, is a 'prequel' to Charlotte Brontë's *Jane Eyre*. It recounts the previous history of Mr Rochester's mad wife before she was incarcerated in Thornfield Hall. She is described as being Antoinette Cosway, a Creole heiress from the West Indies. The Sargasso Sea, in the North Atlantic, is made up of masses of floating seaweed, creating sluggish waters.

RIBBLESDALE, Lord

English peer (1854–1925)

5 It [is] gentlemanly to get one's quotations very slightly wrong. In that way one unprigs oneself and allows the company to correct one.

Quoted in Lady Diana Cooper, *The Light of Common Day* (1959). On the art of gentle misquotation.

RICE, Grantland

American sports journalist and poet (1880–1954)

6 For when the One Great Scorer comes to
mark against your name,
He writes – not that you won or lost – but how
you played the Game.

'Alumnus Football', *Only the Brave and Other Poems* (1941). The fourteen verse poem is little better than doggerel and concerned with 'Life's big game' upon the 'Field of Fame'. The last two lines, all that is ever quoted, are in the voice of 'the wise old coach, Experience': 'Keep coming back, and though the world may romp across your spine,/Let every game's end find you still upon the battling line;/For when the One Great Scorer ...'

A number of odd aspects to this couplet have been pointed out. First, in quotation dictionaries the initial word is sometimes given as 'But' or 'And'. Second, there are versions with '*write* against your name' and 'He *marks* – not that you ...' Third, on the gravestone at Eyam, Derbyshire, of Harry Bagshaw, the Derbyshire and MCC cricketer who died in January 1927, the verse is inscribed (under the heading 'WELL PLAYED') with 'to *write* against your name' and 'He *writes* – not that you ...' Fourth, in *The Manor School*, a boys' school story by one H. (Helen) Elrington (first published in 1927), the lines are given as the book's epigraph in a 'But', 'to write', 'He writes' and '*But that* you played the game' version. In addition, the name 'H. Elrington' is placed after the words, as though she were claiming authorship. Is her claim to have penned the lines fraudulent? What might have happened is that Grantland Rice's poem was first published in the New York *Tribune* – this is a fact, though there is no date for it. Rice was certainly active in writing for its sports pages in the early 1920s. His prose characterization of some footballers as 'The Four Horsemen' and a poem describing the footballer 'Red' Grange as 'The Galloping Ghost' both appeared in the *Trib* over the same weekend in October 1924.

The 'One Great Scorer' lines became known in Britain but without acknowledgement to their author who was not known here – hence, their unattributed appearance on the Bagshaw grave and under the novelist's own name in H. Elrington's book, both as it happens in 1927.

In Alan Bennett's parody of an Anglican sermon in the revue *Beyond the Fringe* (1961), the lines are (deliberately?) misascribed to that 'Grand old Victorian poet, W.E. Henley' (who wrote, rather, 'It matters not how strait the gate ... I am the master of my fate'; *see* 291:1).

See also DE COUBERTIN 198:5.

RICE, Sir Stephen

Irish lawyer and politician (1637–1715)

1 I will drive a coach and six horses through the Act of Settlement.

Rice, a Roman Catholic Chief Baron of the Irish Exchequer, used the courts in Dublin to get his own back on an act of settlement (1662) and was quoted as having said this by W. King, *The State of the Protestants of Ireland* (1672). It is presumably the origin of the expression 'to drive a coach and horses through something', meaning 'to overturn something wantonly, and to render it useless'. It is clear that by the late seventeenth century, this was based on a common metaphor (usually mentioning *six* horses) for something large: in Sir John Vanbrugh's play *The Relapse*, Act 2 (1696), there is: *Seringe* (*viewing his wound*) 'Oons, what a gash is here! Why, sir, a man may drive a coach and six horses into your body.' The modern equivalent probably involves a bus or a tank. In 1843, Charles Dickens wrote in *A Christmas Carol*: 'You may talk vaguely about driving a coach-and-six up a good old flight of stairs, or through a bad young Act of Parliament ...' (which might seem to allude to the Rice example).

RICE, Tim (later Sir Tim)

English lyricist (1944–)

2 Jesus Christ Superstar!

Title of musical (1970), with music by Andrew Lloyd Webber. Based on a 1960s Las Vegas billing, 'Tom Jones – Superstar'.

3 Don't Cry for Me, Argentina.

Title of song, *Evita* (1976). There is an unexplained conjunction between this line and the inscription (in Spanish) that appears on Eva Perón's bronze tomb in Recoleta cemetery, Buenos Aires. It begins with words to the effect, 'Do not cry for me when I am far away'. The tomb also bears the words: 'I will come again, and I will be millions.' According to Nicholas Fraser, co-author of *Eva Perón* (1980): 'She never said this, but that doesn't keep it from being true.' Besides, Eva's body was not returned to Argentina until 1976 and the inscription (of which there is more than one) in Recoleta cemetery bears a date 1982. Could it have been inspired by the song rather than the other way round? Hence, whatever the case, *Don't Cry for Me, Sergeant Major*, title of a book (1983) by Robert McGowan and Jeremy Hands, giving an 'other ranks' view of the Falklands conflict between Britain and Argentina.

RICE-DAVIES, Mandy

English 'model and showgirl' (1944–)

4 Well, he would, wouldn't he?

An innocuous enough phrase but one still used allusively because of the way it was spoken by Rice-Davies during the Profumo affair in 1963 (Secretary of State for War John Profumo carried on with Rice-Davies's friend Christine Keeler who was allegedly sharing her favours with the Soviet military attaché). The *ODQ* (1992) describes Rice-Davies as a 'courtesan', which is rather quaint. She was called as a witness when Stephen Ward, was charged under the Sexual Offences Act. During the preliminary Magistrates Court hearing on 28 June 1963, she was questioned about the men she had had sex with. When told by Ward's defence counsel that Lord Astor – one of the names on the list – had categorically denied any involvement with her, she replied, chirpily: 'Well, he would, wouldn't he?'

The court burst into laughter, the expression passed into the language and is still resorted to because – as a good catchphrase ought to be – it is bright, useful in various circumstances and tinged with innuendo.

'Oscar Wilde said the Alps were objects of appallingly

bad taste. He would, wouldn't he?' wrote Russell Harty in *Mr Harty's Grand Tour* (1988).

RICHARD, Keith See JAGGER, MICK RICHARD, KEITH

RICHARDS, Frank

English writer (1875–1961)

1 The fat greedy owl of the Remove.

Of Billy Bunter. 'The Greyfriars Photographer' in *The Magnet*, Vol. 3, No. 72 (1909). Bunter, the archetypal fat schoolboy, may be called an 'owl' because his round spectacles give him that appearance. The 'Remove' was the name given at one time to a class or division in English public schools (e.g., at Eton by 1718). The term may derive from the act of promoting a pupil from one class or division to a higher one.

2 Yarooh! ... I say you fellows! ... You beast!

The cries of Billy Bunter in the Greyfriars School stories (1908–40), *passim*. Catchphrases presumably based by Richards on schoolboy slang of the late nineteenth century.

3 The rottenfulness is terrific!

Passim in *ib.* Said by Hurree Jamset Ram, the basic format for these remarks was 'the ——fulness is terrific'.

RICHELIEU, Cardinal

French prelate and politician (1585–1642)

4 If you give me six lines written by the hand of the most honest of men, I will find something in them which will hang him.

Usually ascribed to Richelieu but it may have been said, rather, by one of his agents (according to an 1867 French source).

See also BULWER-LYTTON 129:1.

RIIS, Jacob

Danish-born American journalist (1849–1914)

5 How the Other Half Lives.

Title of book (1890) describing the conditions in which poor people lived in New York City. This might appear to have given us the expression meaning 'how people live who belong to different social groups (but especially the rich)'. Indeed, the expression seems basically to have referred to the poor but has since been used about any 'other half'. Riis alluded to the basic saying in these words: 'Long ago it was said that "one half of the world does not know how the other half lives".' *OED2* finds this proverb in English (by 1607), and in French, in *Pantagruel* by Rabelais (1532). Alan Ayckbourn entitled a play (1970) *How the Other Half Loves*.

RIPLEY, Robert Leroy

American journalist (1893–1949)

6 Believe it or not!

This exclamation was used as the title of a long-running syndicated newspaper feature, and radio and TV series in the US. Ripley created an illustrated strip, *Ripley's Believe It or Not* (in *c.*1923), but one feels the phrase must have existed before, though citations are lacking.

ROAD TO MOROCCO

American film 1942. With Bob Hope and Bing Crosby.

7 Like Webster's Dictionary
We're Morocco bound.

Song, 'Road to Morocco'. Written by Johnny Burke, with music by Jimmy van Heusen. One of the neatest puns in popular music. Noah Webster's *An American Dictionary of the English Language* (2 vols., 1828, and subsequent editions) presumably was issued in morocco-leather bookbinding – but hardly more noticeably so than other quality books of the period.

ROBERTS, Allan

American songwriter (1905–66)

8 You Always Hurt the One You Love.

Title of song (1944) written to music by Doris Fisher (1915–). *Compare* WILDE 570:4.

ROBIN, Leo

American songwriter (1899–1985)

9 Thanks for the Memory.

Title of song, *The Big Broadcast of 1938*, written with Ralph Rainger. Became Bob Hope's signature tune.

See also LOOS 362:10.

ROBINSON, John

English Anglican bishop (1919–83)

1 What I think is clear is that what Lawrence is trying to do is to portray the sex relationship as something essentially sacred ... as in a real sense an act of holy communion.

On D.H. Lawrence's *Lady Chatterley's Lover*, when giving evidence in Regina *v.* Penguin Books Ltd (27 October 1960).

ROBSON, Bobby

British football manager (1933–)

2 The first ninety minutes are the most important.

In a football match. Quoted as title of TV documentary (1983). He was manager of the England football team.

ROCHE, Sir Boyle

Irish politician (1743–1807)

3 Mr Speaker, I smell a rat; I see him forming in the air and darkening the sky; but I'll nip him in the bud.

Attributed remark in the Irish Parliament. In an untraced book – Wills, *The Irish Nation* – it is conceded that the chamberlain to the vice-regal court (in Dublin), as Roche later became, had a 'graceful address and ready wit', but, additionally, 'it was usual for members of the cabinet to write speeches for him, which he committed to memory, and, while mastering the substance, generally contrived to travesty the language and ornament with peculiar graces of his own'. Could this be the reason for Roche's peculiar sayings?

The *DNB* adds that 'he gained his lasting reputation as an inveterate perpetrator of "bulls" [i.e., ludicrous, self-contradictory propositions, often associated with the Irish]'.

4 How could the sergeant-at-arms stop him in the rear, while he was catching him at the front? Could he like a bird be in two places at once?

Supposedly said in the Irish parliament. This version is from *A Book of Irish Quotations* (1984). Brewer suggests that he was quoting from 'Jevon's play *The Devil of a Wife*' (untraced) and that what he said was, 'Mr Speaker, it is impossible I could have been in two places at once, unless I were a bird' – adding that the phrase was probably of even earlier origin.

5 Why should we put ourselves out of our way to do anything for posterity; for what has posterity done for us? (*Laughter*). I apprehend you gentlemen have entirely mistaken my words, I assure the house that by posterity I do not mean my ancestors but those who came immediately after them.

Said in the Irish parliament? Quoted in *A Book of Irish Quotations* (1984). Benham (1948), claiming that it is 'erroneously attributed' to Roche, notes that the words occur in John Trumbull's poetic work *McFingal* (1775) and that Mrs Elizabeth Montagu had earlier written in a letter (1 January 1742): 'The man was laughed at as a blunderer who said in a public business "We do much for posterity; I would fain see them do something for us".' This obviously alludes to the true originator, ADDISON 13:6.

'Why should I write for posterity – what has posterity ever done for me?' – attributed to Oscar Wilde in *The Independent* (9 November 1996). Compare 'Posterity is Right Around the Corner' (1976) by E.Y. Harburg (1898–1981):

Why should I write for posterity?
What, if I may be free
To ask a ridiculous question,
Has posterity done for me?

ROCHEFOUCAULD-LIANCOURT, Duc de la

French courtier (1747–1827)

6 *Non, Sire, c'est une grande révolution.*
No, Sir, a big revolution.

In reply to Louis XVI's comment '*C'est une grande révolte* [It's a big revolt]' on the fall of the Bastille (15 July 1789). Quoted in F. Dreyfus, *La Rochefoucauld-Liancourt* (1903).

ROCHESTER, John Wilmot, 2nd Earl of

English poet (1647–80)

7 Here lies a great and mighty king
Whose promise none relies on;
He never said a foolish thing,
Nor ever did a wise one.

A familiar jesting epitaph on Charles II, quoted in *Thomas Traherne: Remarks and Collections* (1885–1921). Other versions include, 'Here lies our sovereign Lord the King ...' and 'Here lies our mutton-eating king' (where 'mutton' = prostitute). Charles II's reply is said to have been: 'This is very true: for my words are my own, and my actions are my ministers' (also in *Traherne* ...).

ROCKEFELLER, Nelson

American Republican governor and Vice-President (1908–79)

1 The brotherhood of man under the fatherhood of God.

When Governor Rockefeller was competing against Barry Goldwater for the Republican presidential nomination in 1964, reporters latched on to a favourite saying of the candidate and rendered it with the acronym 'BOMFOG'. In fact, according to Safire (1978), they had been beaten to it by Hy Sheffer, a stenotypist on the Governor's staff who had found the abbreviation convenient for the previous five or six years.

The words come from a much-quoted saying of John D. Rockefeller II (1874–1960), the Governor's father: 'These are the principles upon which alone a new world recognizing the brotherhood of man and the fatherhood of God can be established ...' Later, 'BOMFOG' became an acronym for any pompous, meaningless generality and was also used by feminists to denote use of language that demeaned women by reflecting patrician attitudes. The individual phrases 'brotherhood of man' and 'fatherhood of God' do not appear before the nineteenth century.

ROCKNE, Knute

American football coach (1888–1931)

2 Show me a good and gracious loser and I'll show you a failure.

Attributed remark (1920s).

See also REAGAN 447:6.

ROGERS, Will

American humorist (1879–1935)

3 I never met a man I didn't like.

The folksy American 'cowboy comedian' of the 1920s and 1930s suggested this epitaph for himself (by 1926). It is a little more believable in context: 'When I die, my epitaph or whatever you call those signs on gravestones is going to read: "I joked about every prominent man of my time, but I never met one I dident [*sic*] like." I am so proud of that I can hardly wait to die so it can be carved. And when you come to my grave you will find me sitting there, proudly reading it.'

According to Paula McSpadden Love, *The Will Rogers Book* (1972), the utterance was first printed in the *Boston Globe* (16 June 1930). However, the *Saturday Evening Post* (6 November 1926) had: 'I bet you if I had met him [Trotsky] and had a chat with him, I would have found him a very interesting and human fellow, for I never yet met a man that I didn't like.'

4 See what'll happen if you don't stop biting your finger-nails.

On the Venus de Milo. Quoted in Bennett Cerf, *Shake Well Before Using* (1948).

ROHE, Ludwig Mies van der

German-born architect (1886–1969)

5 Less is more.

Statement about design meaning that less visual clutter makes for a more satisfying living environment. It was quoted at Rohe's death in the *New York Herald Tribune*. Robert Browning had used the phrase in a different artistic context in 'Andrea del Sarto' (1855).

6 God is in the details.

The architect's obituary in *The New York Times* (1969) attributed this saying to Mies but it also appears to have been a favourite of the German art historian Aby Warburg (though E.M. Gombrich, his biographer, is not certain that it originated with him). In the form *Le bon Dieu est dans le détail*, it has also been attributed to Gustave Flaubert (1821–80). Subsequently, there has arisen the saying 'The devil is in the detail', which has been described as a maxim of the German pop musician, Blixa Bargeld. He probably did not invent it himself as it is mentioned in Lutz Röhrich's *Lexikon der sprichwörtlichen Redensarten* (1994) as '*Der Teufel steckt im Detail*'.

ROLAND, Madame

French revolutionary (1756–93)

7 The more I see of men, the more I like dogs.

Attributed remark in *ODQ* (1979). However, A. Toussenel wrote in *L'Esprit des bêtes* (1847): 'The more one gets to know of men, the more one values dogs.'

8 O Liberty! how many crimes are committed in thy name!

Mme Roland was about to be executed by the guillotine during the French Revolution (on 8 November 1793). According to Robert Chambers, *Book of Days* (1864), she addressed her remark to a gigantic statue of Liberty erected near it.

ROONEY, Mickey

American film actor (1920–)

1 Let's put on a show!

This is often taken to be a staple line from the films that the young Rooney made with Judy Garland from 1939 onwards. The expression apparently had several forms – 'Hey! I've got it! Why don't we put on a show?'/'Hey kids! We can put on the show in the backyard!'/'Let's do the show right here in the barn!' – though it is difficult to give a precise citation.

In *Babes in Arms* (1939) Rooney and Garland play the teenage children of retired vaudeville players who decide to put on a big show of their own. Alas, they do not actually say any of the above lines, though they do express their determination to 'put on a show'. In *Strike Up the Band* (1940), Rooney has the line: 'Say, that's not a bad idea. We could put on our own show!' – though he does not say it to Garland. In whatever form, the line has become a film cliché, now used only with amused affection.

2 Had I been brighter, the ladies been gentler, the Scotch been weaker, had the gods been kinder, had the dice been hotter, this could have been a one-sentence story: Once upon a time I lived happily ever after.

Attributed remark in 1965, probably in his autobiography, *I.E.*

ROOSEVELT, Franklin D.

American Democratic 32nd President (1882–1945)

3 He is the Happy Warrior of the political battlefield.

Alfred E. Smith, the Democrat politician, had this nickname bestowed on him by Roosevelt in 1924. Smith ran against Herbert Hoover for the Presidency in 1928 but did not win. He subsequently fell out with Roosevelt when the latter became President. The phrase comes from WORDSWORTH 582:8.

4 I pledge you, I pledge myself to a New Deal for the American people.

So said Roosevelt to the 1932 Democratic Convention that had just nominated him. The 'New Deal' slogan became the keynote to the election campaign, but it was not new to politics. In Britain, David Lloyd George had talked of a 'New deal for everyone' in 1919. Woodrow Wilson had had a 'New Freedom' slogan, and Teddy Roosevelt had talked of a 'Square Deal'. Abraham Lincoln had used 'New deal' on occasions. The FDR use was engineered by either Samuel Rosenman or Raymond Moley. 'I had not the slightest idea that it would take hold the way it did,' Rosenman said later, 'nor did the Governor [Roosevelt] when he read and revised what I had written ... It was simply one of those phrases that catch public fancy and survive.' On the other hand, Moley claimed: 'The expression "new deal" was in the draft I left at Albany with Roosevelt ... I was not aware that this would be the slogan for the campaign. It was a phrase that would have occurred to almost anyone.'

5 I ask you to judge me by the enemies I have made.

Quoted in *The Observer* (16 October 1932). *Compare* CLEVELAND 174:5.

6 Let me assert my firm belief that the only thing we have to fear is fear itself.

Roosevelt took the Presidential oath of office on 4 March 1933 and then delivered his first Inaugural address. The classic sentence did not appear in Roosevelt's first draft but appears to have been inserted by him the day before the speech was delivered. As for inspiration: a copy of Thoreau's writings was with him at this time containing the line 'Nothing is so much to be feared as fear'. Raymond Moley asserted later, however, that it was Louis Howe who contributed the 'fear' phrase, having picked it up from a newspaper advertisement for a department store.

In fact, any number of precedents could be cited – the Duke of Wellington ('the only thing I am afraid of is fear'), Montaigne ('The thing of which I have most fear is fear'), Bacon ('Nothing is terrible except fear itself'), the Book of Proverbs 3:25 ('Be not afraid of sudden fear') – but in the end what matters is that Roosevelt had the wit to utter it on this occasion.

7 There is a mysterious cycle in human events. To some generations much is given. Of other generations much is expected. This generation of Americans has a rendezvous with destiny.

Speech, Democratic convention (1936). Later, in a TV address on behalf of Senator Barry Goldwater (27 October 1964), Ronald Reagan told viewers: 'You and

I have a rendezvous with destiny. We will preserve for our children this, the last best hope of man on earth.'

1 And while I am talking to you mothers and fathers, I give you one more assurance. I have said this before, but I shall say it again and again and again: Your boys are not going to be sent into any foreign wars.

Campaign speech delivered in Boston, Massachusetts (30 October 1940). In a sense, Roosevelt kept his promise. American boys were never sent into any foreign wars. The US went to war in December 1941 after the Japanese attack on Pearl Harbor and only later were American forces sent to Europe and elsewhere. *Compare* JOHNSON 316:7.

2 And who voted against the appropriations for an adequate national defense? MARTIN, BARTON and FISH.

A slogan for crowd repetition, from election speeches (1940). Seeking to blame Republicans for US military unpreparedness, Roosevelt cited three Congressmen – Joseph Martin, Bruce Barton (later of the advertising agency Batten, Barton, Durstine & Osborn) and Hamilton Fish. The speech in which the phrase first arose was written by Judge Samuel I. Rosenman and Robert E. Sherwood, the dramatist. Crowds loved to join the rhythmic line echoing 'Wynken, Blynken and Nod'.

3 Yesterday, December 7th 1941, a date which will live in infamy, the United States of America was suddenly and deliberately attacked by naval and air forces of the Empire of Japan.

Thus Roosevelt began his address to Congress, the day after Pearl Harbor. In the draft it had said, 'a date which will live in world history' and 'simultaneously'. With such strokes did he make his speech seeking a declaration of war against Japan the more memorable. However, Palmer, *Quotations in History* (1976) has 'date *that shall* live in infamy'. Cole & Lass, *The Dictionary of 20th-Century Allusions* (1991) has '*day that* will live in infamy'.

ROOSEVELT, Theodore

American Republican 26th President (1858–1919)

4 I wish to preach not the doctrine of ignoble ease but the doctrine of the strenuous life.

In a speech at the Appomattox Day celebration of the Hamilton Club (Chicago, 10 April 1899) which helped swell Roosevelt's reputation and swept him into the vice-presidency in the election of 1900, and then into the White House following the assassination of President McKinley.

5 There is a homely adage – 'Speak softly and carry a big stick – you will go far'.

In 2 September 1901, just a few days before the assassination of President McKinley, Roosevelt said this at the Minnesota State Fair. He went on, 'If the American nation will speak softly and yet build and keep at a pitch of the highest training a thoroughly efficient navy, the Monroe Doctrine [which sought to exclude European intervention in the American continent] will go far.' Note that he did not claim the 'adage' to be original.

6 Good ... to the last drop.

Visiting Joel Cheek, perfector of the Maxwell House coffee blend, in 1907, the President drank a cup and passed this comment. The slogan has been in use ever since, despite those who have inquired, 'What's wrong with the last drop then?' Professors of English have considered the problem and ruled that 'to' can be inclusive and need not mean 'up to but not including'.

7 I am strong as a bull moose.

After two terms as President, Roosevelt withdrew from Republican politics and then, in 1912, unsuccessfully tried to make a come-back as a Progressive ('Bull Moose') candidate. The popular name stemmed from a remark Roosevelt had made when he was standing as Vice-President in 1900. Writing to Mark Hanna, he said, 'I am strong as a bull moose and you can use me to the limit.'

8 Foolish fanatics ... the men who form the lunatic fringe in all reform movements.

Autobiography (1913). Referring to any group of extremists, usually in politics. Roosevelt popularized, if he did not coin, the term.

See also BUNYAN 129:6.

ROSE, Billy

American impresario and songwriter (1899–1966)

9 Does the Spearmint Lose Its Flavour on the Bedpost Overnight?

The 1924 song with this title is usually credited to Marty Bloom and Ernest Breuer 'with assistance from'

Rose. 'Chewing-gum' was substituted for 'Spearmint' when the song was revived in Britain in 1959, lest it seem to be advertising a particular brand.

1 The Night is Young (and You're So Beautiful).

Title of a song (1936), written with Irving Kahal. The previous year 'The Night Is Young (And So Are We)' had been written by Oscar Hammerstein II and Sigmund Romberg and included in the film *The Night is Young*. Hence, the popularity of the expression, 'The night is young!' – the sort of thing one would say when attempting to justify another drink. From Frank Brady, *Citizen Welles* (1989): 'At three in the morning, when a few people decided to leave, Orson, stepping into the role of clichéd host from a Grade B movie, would not hear of it: "You're not leaving already, my friends. The night is still young. Play, Gypsies! Play, play, play!"'

The expression was known before all this, however. In Sir Walter Besant's *Dorothy Forster*, Chap. 11 (1884) there is: 'They ... left the table when the night was yet young, and the bottle just beginning'; Max Beerbohm, *Seven Men* (1919) has: 'He looked at the clock. I pointed out that the night was young.'

ROSEBERY, 5th Earl of

British Liberal Prime Minister (1847–1929)

2 I have three ambitions in life: to win the Derby, marry an heiress, and become Prime Minister.

A legend grew up that Rosebery had said this. Robert Rhodes James comments in *Rosebery* (1963) that, 'although it is quite possible that he did once make such an observation, it is extremely unlikely that it was meant seriously'. Rhodes James also quotes Algernon Cecil in *Queen Victoria and Her Prime Ministers* (1953) as saying: 'At London dinner-parties half a century ago it was rare for Rosebery to be mentioned without some allusion being made to his three declared ambitions ... Aprocryphal or not, it gives if not Rosebery's measure of a man, yet certainly the measure of him given by the men of his time.'

Nevertheless, he achieved his ambitions in the sense that he did win the Derby thrice (twice while Prime Minister), he married Hannah Rothschild, an heiress, and – managing to overcome his aristocratic disdain for accepting almost anything that was offered him – he succeeded Gladstone as Prime Minister in 1894. But the Liberal Party was falling apart anyway, Rosebery was prey to insomnia and inaction, and he was out of office after a year. He was forty-eight and, despite his undoubted personal qualities, never held high office again.

3 To your tents, O Israel!

A famous – and possibly apocryphal – story concerns Rosebery saying this one evening when he felt his Rothschild relatives had kept him up long enough. The phrase was later used by G.B. Shaw as the title of a diatribe in *The Fortnightly Review* (November 1893), expressing Fabian disillusion with Gladstone's Liberal Party on such radical matters as Irish Home Rule. Michael Holroyd in *Bernard Shaw* (Vol. 1) calls it 'the Biblical call to revolt'. It is a quotation from 1 Kings 12:16.

4 I am leaving tonight; Hannah and the rest of the heavy baggage will follow later.

Rhodes James (as above) describes this as one of Rosebery's 'alleged *mots*'.

5 I must plough my furrow alone.

Rosebery said this in a speech at the City Liberal Club (19 July 1901) on breaking away from his Liberal Party colleagues. A famous declaration of independence, but it seems likely that the expression had been used by others before him. He added: 'Before I get to the end of that furrow it is possible that I may find myself not alone ... If it be so, I shall remain very contented in the society of my books and my home.' So it was to be.

6 What is the advice I have to offer you? ... You have to clear your slate. It is six years since you were in office ... The primary duty of the Liberal party is to wipe its slate clean.

Speech to Liberal audience at Chesterfield (16 December 1901). Sir Henry Campbell-Bannerman replied at Leicester (19 February 1902): 'I am no believer in the doctrine of the clean slate.'

ROSS, Alan S.C.

British academic (1907–80)

7 U and Non-U. An Essay in Sociological Linguistics.

Title of essay in *Noblesse Oblige*, ed. Nancy Mitford (1956). Ross had first used 'U' to denote 'upper class' verbal usage and 'Non-U' to denote incorrect, non-upper class usage, in a 1954 article.

ROSS, Harold

American editor (1892–1951)

8 *The New Yorker* will not be edited for the little old lady from Dubuque.

When Ross founded the magazine in 1925, he made

this declaration. Dubuque, Iowa, thus became involved in another of those yardstick phrases on account of its being representative of Middle America (like 'It'll play in Peoria', *see* 226:6). A man called 'Boots' Mulgrew who lived there used to contribute squibs to the Chicago *Tribune* signed 'Old Lady in Dubuque'. Ross, presumably, had heard of this line and consciously or otherwise developed it to describe the sort of person he was not creating the magazine for. (On the other hand, Malcolm Muggeridge once quoted a writer on the *Daily Express* who explained the huge readership of Beaverbrook newspapers in the UK by saying, 'I write for one little old reader'.)

1 Who he?

James Thurber in *The Years with Ross* (1959), describes how Ross would customarily add this query to manuscripts (though not for publication) on finding a name he did not know in an article (sometimes betraying his ignorance). He said the only two names everyone knew were Houdini and Sherlock Holmes. The phrase echoes the Duke of Wellington's peremptory 'Who? Who?' on hearing the names of ministers in Lord Derby's new administration (1852).

Re-popularized by *Private Eye* in the 1980s, this editorial interjection after a little-known person's name showed some signs of catching on: 'This month, for instance, has been the time for remembering the 110th anniversary of the birth of Grigori Petrovsky. Who he?' – *New Statesman*, 26 February 1988. A book with the title *Who He? Goodman's Dictionary of the Unknown Famous* was published in 1984 and the actress Billie Whitelaw entitled her memoirs *Billie Whitelaw ... Who He?* (1995).

ROSSETTI, Christina

English poet (1830–95)

2 Remember me when I am gone away,
Gone far away into the silent land;
When you can no more hold me by the hand,
Nor half turn to go yet turning stay.
Remember me when no more day by day
You tell me of our future that you planned;
Only remember me; you understand
It will be late to counsel then or pray.

Yet if you should forget me for a while
And afterwards remember, do not grieve;
For if the darkness and corruption leave
A vestige of the thoughts that once I had,
Better by far you should forget and smile
Than that you should remember and be sad.

'Remember' (1862). One of the two or three most popular readings at funerals and memorial services.

3 In the bleak mid-winter
Frosty wind made moan,
Earth stood hard as iron,
Water like a stone.

'Mid-Winter' (1875). Known particularly as a Christmas carol sung to the tune 'Cranham' by Gustav Holst. Hence, *In the Bleak Midwinter*, title of film (UK, 1996), written and directed by Kenneth Branagh, about a theatrical group putting on a production of *Hamlet* in December.

ROSSINI, Gioachino

Italian composer (1792–1868)

4 Wagner has beautiful moments but awful quarters of an hour.

Letter (April 1867), quoted in E. Naumann, *Italiensiche Tondichter* (1883). In his *Reminiscences, Inscriptions & Anecdotes* (1913), the musician Francesco Berger attributed this to the pianist Hans von Bülow: 'Some one observed, "Well, you must admit that he has some heavenly moments." "I don't dispute the *heavenly moments*," said he, "but he has some *devilish ugly half-hours*".' Rossini is also supposed to have said: 'One can't judge Wagner's opera *Lohengrin* after a first hearing, and I certainly don't intend hearing it a second time' – quoted in *The Frank Muir Book* (1976).

5 Give me a laundry-list and I will set it to music.

Quoted in *The Treasury of Humorous Quotations* (Esar & Bentley, 1951), but otherwise unverified.

ROTTEN, Johnny (John Lydon)

English pop singer (1957–)

6 Love is two minutes fifty-two seconds of squishing [*or* squelching] noises. It shows your mind isn't clicking right.

Of recent *bons mots*, one of the most quoted – but variously so – is the opinion of Johnny Rotten, who was at one time with the notorious punk group, the Sex Pistols. Jonathon Green's *Dictionary of Contemporary Quotations* (1982) has the version: 'Love is two minutes fifty-two seconds of squishing noises. It shows your mind isn't clicking right.' But, in the previous year, my *Graffiti 3* had had a photograph taken in London (1980) of a wall bearing the legend: 'Love is three minutes of squelching noises. (Mr J. Rotten).'

Auberon Waugh in *Private Eye* (18 November 1983) settled for 'two and a half minutes of squelching' but provided the interesting gloss that, in an interview with Christena Appleyard in the *Mirror*, Rotten had wished to amend his aphorism: 'It is more like five minutes now, he says, because he has mastered a new technique.' McConville and Shearlaw in *The Slanguage of Sex* (1984) claim that as a result of Rotten's statement, 'squelching' became an expression for sexual intercourse. They suggest that he had referred to 'two minutes of squelching noises' in *New Musical Express* in 1978.

ROUSSEAU, Jean-Jacques

French philosopher (1712–78)

1 *L'homme est né libre, et partout il est dans les fers.* Man was born free, and everywhere he is in chains.

Du Contrat Social, Chap. 1 (1762).

See also CALLAGHAN 141:4.

ROUTH, Dr Martin

English scholar (1755–1854)

2 Always verify your references.

In 1949 Winston Churchill gave an inaccurate account to the House of Commons of when he had first heard the words 'unconditional surrender' from President Roosevelt. Subsequently, in his *The Second World War*, Vol. 4 (1951), Churchill wrote: 'It was only when I got home and searched my archives that I found the facts as they have been set out here. I am reminded of the professor who in his declining hours was asked by his devoted pupils for his final counsel. He replied, "Verify your quotations".'

Well, not exactly a 'professor', and not exactly his dying words, and not 'quotations' either. Martin Routh was President of Magdalen College, Oxford, for sixty-three years. Of the many stories told about Routh, Churchill was groping towards the one where he was asked what precept could serve as a rule of life to an aspiring young man. Said Routh: 'You will find it a very good practice *always to verify your references, Sir!*'

This story was first recorded in this form in July 1878, as Churchill and his amanuenses might themselves have verified. In 1847, Routh gave the advice to John Burgon, later a noted Dean of Chichester, who ascribed it in an article in the *Quarterly Review* (and subsequently in his *Lives of Twelve Good Men*, 1888 ed.) Perhaps Churchill was recalling instead the Earl of Rosebery's version, given in a speech on 23 November 1897: 'Another confirmation of the advice given by one aged sage to somebody who sought his guidance in life, namely, "Always wind up your watch and verify your quotations".'

ROWLAND, Helen

American columnist and writer (1875–1950)

3 Somehow a bachelor never quite gets over the idea that he is a thing of beauty and a boy forever.

A Guide to Men (1922). Compare the comment of Flann O'Brien (1911–66) on the supposed youthfulness of the Irish police force: 'A thing of duty is a boy forever.' Both alluding to KEATS 328:3.

ROWLAND, Richard

American film executive (?1881–1947)

4 The lunatics have taken over the asylum.

Quoted in Terry Ramsaye, *A Million and One Nights* (1926). Attributed remark when the United Artists film company was established in 1919 by Charles Chaplin, Mary Pickford, Douglas Fairbanks and D.W. Griffith, to exploit their own talent. Rowland was one of their erstwhile employers at Metro.

See also GEORGE 258:2; STALLINGS 515:6.

RUBIN, Jerry

American Yippie leader (1938–94)

5 Don't trust anyone over thirty.

Attributed by Flexner (1982). Actually, this appears to have been first uttered by Jack Weinberg at Berkeley in 1964/5 during a free speech demonstration. Bartlett (1992) finds Weinberg (1940–) saying in an interview on the free speech movement, 'We have a saying in the movement that we don't trust anybody over thirty'. In 1970 Weinberg told *The Washington Post* (23 March) that he did not actually believe the statement but had said it in response to a question about adults manipulating the organization. In 1969, Spiro Agnew included 'Thou shalt not trust anybody over thirty' as one of his 'Ten Commandments of Protest'.

RUNCIE, Robert (later Lord Runcie)

English Archbishop of Canterbury (1921–)

1 My advice was delicately poised between the cliché and the indiscretion.

On discussions with the Prince and Princess of Wales prior to marrying them. Quoted in *The Times* (14 July 1981). *Compare* MACMILLAN 371:3.

2 I have done my best to die before this book is published.

Letter to Humphrey Carpenter quoted in the biographer's *Robert Runcie, The Reluctant Archbishop* (1996). Runcie had cooperated with Carpenter (indeed, had invited him to write the biography), believing that the book would not actually be published until after his death.

RUNYON, Damon

American writer (1884–1946)

3 He is without strict doubt a Hoorah Henry, and he is generally figured as nothing but a lob as far as doing anything useful in this world is concerned.

'Tight Shoes' in *Take It Easy* (1938). Jim Godbolt adapted this to 'Hooray Henry' in 1951 to describe a sub-species of British upper-class twit.

4 The race is not always to the swift nor the battle to the strong, but that's the way to bet.

Quoted in *The Treasury of Humorous Quotations*, ed. by Evan Esar & Nicolas Bentley (1951). Alluding to BIBLE 97:2.

RUSHDIE, Salman

Indian-born novelist (1947–)

5 Naughty but nice.

Before achieving fame and misfortune as a novelist, Rushdie worked as a freelance advertising copywriter in London. In 1988, appearing on BBC Radio's *Desert Island Discs*, he claimed to have originated the use of the phrase 'Naughty but nice' to promote fresh cream in cakes for the National Dairy Council (from 1977 onwards). Advertisements being collaborative efforts, agencies – in this case Ogilvy & Mather – are reluctant to concede creative triumphs to particular individuals. Whatever his contribution on this one, however, Rushdie certainly did not coin the phrase 'Naughty but nice'. A 1939 US film had the title. It was about a professor of classical music who accidentally wrote a popular song. Curiously, *ODMQ* (1991) gives the coinage of the phrase to Jerry Wald and Richard Macaulay, writers of the film, on this basis. But Partridge/*Slang* glosses it as 'a reference to copulation since *c.*1900 ex a song that Minnie Schult sang and popularized in the USA, 1890s'. Indeed. There have since been various songs with the title, notably one by Johnny Mercer and Harry Warren in *The Belle of New York* (film, 1952). Compare also the similarly alliterative, 'It's Foolish But It's Fun' (Gus Kahn/Robert Stolz) sung by Deanna Durbin in *Spring Parade* (1940).

RUSK, Dean

American Democratic politician (1909–94)

6 We're eyeball to eyeball and the other fellow just blinked.

In the missile crisis of October 1962, the US took a tough line when the Soviet Union placed missiles on Cuban soil. After a tense few days, the Soviets withdrew. Secretary of State Rusk was speaking to an ABC news correspondent, John Scali, on 24 October and said: 'Remember, when you report this, that, eyeball to eyeball, they blinked first.' Columnists Charles Bartlett and Stewart Alsop then helped to popularize this in the above form (though sometimes 'I think' is inserted before 'the other fellow').

'Eyeball to eyeball' is a black American serviceman's idiom. Safire (1978) quotes a reply given by the all-black 24th Infantry Regiment to an inquiry from General MacArthur's HQ in Korea (November 1950) – 'Do you have contact with the enemy?' 'We is eyeball to eyeball.'

RUSKIN, John

English art critic (1819–1900)

7 All violent feelings ... produce ... a falseness in ... impressions of external things, which I would generally characterize as the 'Pathetic fallacy'.

Modern Painters, Vol. 3 (1856). Hence, the concept of the 'pathetic fallacy' – the attribution of human feelings to nature or, to put it another way, the belief that nature reflects human feelings when this is expressed, usually in literature. So, a thunderstorm may be represented as echoing some human drama played out beneath it.

1 There was a rocky valley between Buxton and Bakewell ... divine as the vale of Tempe; you might have seen the gods there morning and evening, – Apollo and the sweet Muses of the Light ... You enterprised a railroad ... you blasted its rocks away ... And now, every fool in Buxton can be at Bakewell in half-an-hour, and every fool in Bakewell at Buxton.

'Joanna's Cave', *Praeterita* (1885–9). An early attack on the pointlessness of much travel.

2 I have seen, and heard, much of Cockney impudence before now; but never expected to hear a coxcomb ask two hundred guineas for flinging a pot of paint in the public's face.

On Whistler's painting 'The Falling Rocket, or Nocturne in Black and Gold', in a letter (18 June 1877) and included in *Fors Clavigera: Letters to the Workers and Labourers of Great Britain* (1871–84). Whistler (an American) brought an action for libel and was awarded a farthing in damages. He was bankrupted by his legal costs; Ruskin could not pay his own either and had to be helped by friends. *See* WHISTLER 565:6.

RUSSELL, Bertrand (3rd Earl Russell)

English mathematician and philosopher (1872–1970)

3 Better Red than dead.

A slogan used by some (mainly British) nuclear disarmers. *Time* Magazine (15 September 1961) gave 'I'd rather be Red than dead' as a slogan of Britain's Campaign for Nuclear Disarmament. Russell wrote in 1958: 'If no alternative remains except Communist domination or the extinction of the human race, the former alternative is the lesser of two evils'. The counter-cry 'Better dead than red' may also have had some currency. (In the film *Love With a Proper Stranger* (US, 1964) Steve McQueen proposed to Natalie Wood with a picket sign stating 'Better Wed Than Dead'.)

4 Three passions, simple but overwhelmingly strong, have governed my life: the longing for love, the search for knowledge, and unbearable pity for the suffering of mankind.

'What I have lived for', Prologue, *The Autobiography of Bertrand Russell*, Vol. 1 (1967). Russell continued: 'I have sought love, first, because it brings ecstasy – ecstasy so great that I would often have sacrificed all the rest of life for a few hours of this joy. I have sought it, next, because it relieves loneliness – that terrible loneliness in which one shivering consciousness looks over the rim of the world into the cold unfathomable lifeless abyss. I have sought it, finally, because in the union of love I have seen, in a mystic miniature, the prefiguring vision of the heaven that saints and poets have imagined. This is what I sought, and though it might seem too good for human life, this is what – at last – I have found.'

RUSSELL, Sir William Howard

British journalist (1820–97)

5 The ground flies beneath their horses' feet; gathering speed at every stride, they dash on towards that thin red streak topped with a line of steel.

So Russell wrote in a report dated 25 October and published in *The Times* (14 November 1854) when describing a Russian charge repulsed by the British 93rd Highlanders. This was the first stage of the Battle of Balaclava in the Crimean War (the Charge of the Light Brigade followed a few hours later). The *ODQ* (1979, 1992) has 'tipped' here instead of 'topped'.

By the time he wrote his book *The British Expedition to the Crimea* (1877), Russell was putting: 'The Russians dashed on towards *that thin red line tipped with steel*' [his italics]. Thus was created the jingoistic Victorian phrase 'the thin red line', standing for the supposed invincibility of British infantry tactics.

Compare Kipling's poem 'Tommy' from *Departmental Ditties* (1890) which goes: 'But it's "Thin red line of 'eroes" when the drums begin to roll.'

S

SABATINI, Rafael

Italian-born novelist (1875–1950)

1 Born with the gift of laughter and a sense that the world was mad.

Over the inside gate at Yale University's Hall of Graduate Studies is inscribed this slight variation of the first line from Sabatini's popular novel *Scaramouche* (1921), though understandably Yale savants did not immediately recognize it as such. How this not very highly regarded literary figure came to have his work displayed in such an illustrious setting was subsequently explained in a letter to *The New Yorker* (8 December 1934) from a young architect, John Donald Tuttle. He had chosen the line, he said, as a form of protest against the neo-gothic he had been forced to use on the building. 'As a propitiatory gift to my gods for this terrible thing I was doing, and to make them forget by appealing to their sense of humour, I carved the inscription over the door' (quoted in Burnam, 1980).

SACKS, Oliver

British-born neurologist (1933–)

2 The Man Who Mistook His Wife for a Hat.

Title of book (1985) describing various instances of brain disorders. The title refers to a case in which the patient could not recognize everyday objects. Also the title of an opera (1991) by Michael Nyman (based on the book).

SACKVILLE-WEST, V(ita)

English novelist and poet (1892–1962)

3 They rustle, they brustle, they crackle, and if you can crush beech nuts under foot at the same time, so much the better. But beech nuts aren't essential. The essential is that you should tramp through very dry, very crisp, brown leaves – a thick drift of them in the Autumn woods, shuffling through them, kicking them up ... walking in fact 'through leaves'.

In a BBC radio talk 'Personal Pleasures' (1950), Sackville-West explained the origin of an expression 'through leaves', used in her family to express pure happiness. That is, the sort of happiness enjoyed by young children shuffling through drifts of dry autumn leaves. It spread, at least as far as James Lees-Milne, later to become the biographer of Vita's husband, Harold Nicolson. In a diary entry for 9 January 1949, he wrote: 'I made a little more progress with my book this weekend, but no "through leaves" as I should like. Laboured, factual and stodgy stuff churned itself out' (*Midway on the Waves*, 1985).

SAHL, Mort

American satirist (1926–)

4 Let my people go!

During viewing of lengthy film, *Exodus*. As told on his record album 'The New Frontier' (1961). Another version is that Sahl, invited by the director, Otto Preminger, to a preview, stood up after three hours and said, 'Otto – let my people go!' (alluding to BIBLE 91:6).

SAINT-SIMON, Comte Henri de

French social reformer (1760–1825)

5 The future belongs to us. In order to do great things one must be enthusiastic.

Quoted in Barnaby Conrad, *Famous Last Words* (1961), otherwise unverified.

SAKI (H.H. Munro)

English writer (1870–1916)

1 When I was at Poona in '76.

'Reginald', *Reginald* (1904); a phrase typical of an old British India hand. Included in Partridge/*Catch Phrases* as 'Gad, sir, when I was in Poona'.

2 Women and elephants never forget an injury.

'Reginald on Besetting Sins' in *ib.* The basic expression 'an elephant never forgets' is what one might say of one's self when complimented on remembering a piece of information forgotten by others. As such, it is based on the view that elephants are supposed to remember trainers, keepers and so on, especially those who have been unkind to them. A song with the title 'The Elephant Never Forgets' was featured in the play *The Golden Toy* by Carl Zuckmayer (London, 1934) and recorded by Lupino Lane. *Stevenson's Book of Proverbs, Maxims and Familiar Phrases* (1949) has it that the modern saying really derives from a Greek proverb: 'The camel [*sic*] never forgets an injury' – which is exactly how Saki uses it.

3 Put that bloody cigarette out!

Last words. Quoted in A.J. Langguth, *The Life of Saki* (1981). During a night march on Beaumont-Hamel in the First World War, it was said by Lance-Sergeant Munro to one of his men who had just lit up. He was killed by a German sniper.

See also HOPE 301:2.

SALINGER, J.D.

American novelist (1919–)

4 The Catcher in the Rye.

Title of novel (1951) about the emergent seventeen-year-old Holden Caulfield. As explained in Chap. 22, it comes from a vision he has of standing in a field of rye below a cliff where he will catch any children who fall off. He wishes to protect innocent children from disillusionment with the world of grown-ups. The opening words of the novel have become famous: 'If you really want to hear about it, the first thing you'll probably want to know is where I was born and what my lousy childhood was like, and how my parents were occupied and all before they had me, and all that David Copperfield kind of crap.'

SALISBURY, 3rd Marquess of

British Conservative Prime Minister (1830–1903)

5 We are part of the community of Europe and we must do our duty as such.

Speech at Caernavon (10 April 1888). Sometimes misattributed to Gladstone and Lloyd George – and on one occasion to both.

6 By office boys for office boys.

Of the *Daily Mail.* Quoted in H. Hamilton Fyfe, *Northcliffe, an Intimate Biography* (1930). *Compare* THACKERAY 531:3.

See also KEARNEY 327:3; SALISBURY (next) 467:7.

SALISBURY, 5th Marquess of

British Conservative politician (1893–1972)

7 The present Colonial Secretary has been too clever by half. I believe he is a very fine bridge player. It is not considered immoral, or even bad form to outwit one's opponents at bridge. It almost seems to me as if the Colonial Secretary, when he abandoned the sphere of bridge for the sphere of politics, brought his bridge technique with him.

On Iain Macleod. Speech, House of Lords (1961). To say that someone is 'too clever by half' is to show that you think they are more clever than wise and are over-reaching themselves. As such, this is a fairly common idiom. The remark seems to run in the family. The 3rd Marquess (*q.v.*) had anticipated him in a debate on the Irish Church Resolutions in the House of Commons on 30 March 1868, when he said of an amendment moved by Disraeli: 'I know that with a certain number of Gentlemen on this side of the House this Amendment is popular. I have heard it spoken of as being very clever. It is clever, Sir; it is too clever by half.'

Rodney Ackland's version of an Alexander Ostrovsky play was presented as *Too Clever by Half* at the Old Vic, London, in 1988. Of Dr Jonathan Miller, the polymath, in the mid-1970s, it was said, 'He's too clever by three-quarters.'

SANDBURG, Carl

American poet (1878–1967)

8 Sometime they'll give a war and nobody will come.

The origin of this light joke appears to lie in Sandburg's epic poem *The People, Yes* (1936). It became popular in the 1960s – especially as a graffito – at the time of protests against the Vietnam War. Charlotte Keyes (1914–) wrote an article in *McCall's* Magazine (October 1966), which was given the title 'Suppose They Gave a War, and No One Came?' A US film (1969) was called *Suppose They Gave a War and Nobody Came?*

It is also well known in German as '*Stell dir vor, es gibt Krieg, und keiner geht hin* [Suppose they gave a war and nobody came]'. Ralf Bülow in the journal *Der Sprachdienst* (No. 27, 1983) traced it back not only to Sandburg but also to Thornton Wilder. They both lived in Chicago in the early 1930s. Bülow recounts a Wilder anecdote which Sandburg may have picked up. In the same edition of *Der Sprachdienst*, Reinhard Roche comments on how German journalists and others have ascribed the remark to Bertolt Brecht because of his poem '*Wer zu Hause bleibt, wenn der Kampf beginnt* [Who will be away from home when the war begins?]' and argues that 'much more philological caution is needed before assigning certain popular expressions to literary figures'.

SARTRE, Jean-Paul

French philosopher and writer (1905–80)

1 *L'Enfer, c'est les Autres.*
Hell is other people.

Huis Clos (1944). Subsequently, T.S. Eliot, *The Cocktail Party* (1950) had: 'What is hell?/Hell is oneself.'

SATIE, Erik

French composer (1866–1925)

2 When I was young, I was told: 'You'll see, when you're fifty.' I am fifty and I haven't seen a thing.

In a letter to his brother, quoted in Pierre-Daniel Templier, *Erik Satie* (1932).

SAYERS, Dorothy L.

English novelist (1893–1957)

3 Far from it, as the private said when he aimed at the bulls-eye and hit the gunnery instructor.

Unnatural Death (1927). This Wellerism (*see* DICKENS 207:3) may not be original to Sayers. However, it was a literary form she enjoyed using. Compare, from *The Unpleasantness at the Bellona Club* (1928): '*Au contraire*, as the man said in the Bay of Biscay when they asked if he'd dined.' In this, Sayers had been anticipated by G.K. Chesterton in *The Man Who Was Thursday* (1907/8): '"Au contraire", as the man said when asked if he'd dined on the boat.' In his *Autobiography* (1936), Chesterton has this as, '... lunched on the boat.'

4 The Nine Tailors.

Title of novel (1934) in which 'Tailor Paul' is the name of one of the church bells of Fenchurch St Paul which play a significant part in the plot. The saying 'Nine Tailors Make A Man' is quoted on the last page of the novel. So what we have in the title is a blend of various elements. In bell-ringing it was possible to indicate the sex of the dead person for whom the bells were being tolled. 'Nine tailors' or 'nine tellers' (strokes) meant a man. The bell-ringing use of the phrase does, however, echo an actual proverb, 'It takes nine tailors to make a man', which apparently came from the French, *c.*1600. The meaning here would seem to be that a man should buy his clothes from various sources. Or it was something said in contempt of tailors (in that they were so feeble that it would take nine of them to equal one normal man).

G.L. Apperson, the proverb collector, showed in 1929 that, until the end of the seventeenth century, there was some uncertainty about the number of tailors mentioned. In *Westward Hoe* by John Webster and Thomas Dekker (1607) it appeared as three.

5 *Placetne, magistra?*
Does it please you, O mistress?

Lord Peter Wimsey proposing to Harriet Vane in *Gaudy Night* (1936). She replies '*Placet* [It pleases]'.

See also KIPLING 337:4.

SCALPONE, Al

American writer (1913–)

6 The family that prays together stays together.

Devised by Al Scalpone for the Roman Catholic Rosary Crusade in the US. The crusade began in 1942 and the slogan was first broadcast on 6 March 1947, according to Father Patrick Peyton, *All For Her* (1967). The slogan is quoted in Joseph Heller, *Catch-22* (1961) which is set in the period 1944–5, but this may simply be an anachronism. The source of many humorous variants: 'the family that shoots together loots together', 'the family that flays together stays together' etc.

SCHACHT, Hjalmar

German banker (1877–1970)

1 I wouldn't believe Hitler was dead, even if he told me so himself.

Attributed remark on 8 May 1945. Quoted on BBC Radio *Quote ... Unquote* (15 June 1977). Schacht was Hitler's Central Bank Governor.

SCHELLING, Friedrich von

German philosopher (1775–1854)

2 *Architektur ist überhaupt die erstarrte Musik.* Architecture in general is frozen music.

Die Philosophie der Kunst (1809) in which von Schelling also describes architecture as 'music in space'. He had already used the 'frozen' phrase in a lecture in 1802–3. Goethe, perhaps aware of this, states in *Gespräche mit Eckermann* (23 March 1829), 'I have found among my papers a sheet ... in which I call architecture frozen music.' In *Maximen und Reflexionen* Goethe attributes the saying, rather, to a 'noble philosopher' – he probably meant Schelling. Madame de Staël wrote in *Corinne* (1807) about St Peter's in Rome: '*La vue d'un tel monument est comme une musique continuelle et fixée.*' As she was in touch with leading German intellectuals – she met Goethe in 1804 – she may well have known Schelling's phrase. In the reflection following his maxim, Goethe does not refer to Madame de Staël, but he does mention Saint Peter's as a building in which this sensation can be experienced. Schopenhauer said in *Die Welt als Wille und Vorstellung* (written 1814–18) that for thirty years people had kept repeating the witticism about architecture being 'frozen [*gefrorene*] music' – the first mention of 'frozen'; *erstarrte* actually means something more like 'fixed' or 'petrified'.

SCHLIEMANN, Heinrich

German archaeologist (1822–90)

3 I have looked upon the face of Agamemnon.

On discovering a gold death mask at an excavation in Mycenae. Quoted in W. Durant, *The Story of Civilization: The Life of Greece* (1939). So Schliemann in a telegram to the King of the Hellenes in August 1876. He had just found the well-preserved body of a high-ranking man wearing a golden burial mask in the grave circle at Mycenae. Removing the mask, he found eyes, mouth and flesh still intact. But was it really Agamemnon, the King of Mycenae in the thirteenth century BC, and leader of the Achaean coalition that fought against Troy? Alas, there seems little chance. Agamemnon's burial place is not known, and the mask, having now been dated with accuracy, proves to be of someone even more ancient. Still, it was a wonderful telegram to have sent.

When finally persuaded that the mask pre-dated Agamemnon, Schliemann said, 'All right, let's call him Schulze.'

SCHOENBERG, Arnold

German composer (1874–1951)

4 Very well, I can wait.

When told his violin concerto needed a soloist with six fingers. Quoted in *PDMQ* (1971) and Nat Shapiro, *An Encyclopedia of Quotations About Music* (1978).

SCHROEDER, Patricia

American Democratic politician (1940–)

5 After carefully watching Ronald Reagan, he is attempting a great break-through in political technology – he has been perfecting the Teflon-coated Presidency. He sees to it that nothing sticks to him.

Speech in the US House of Representatives (2 August 1983). 'Teflon' is the proprietary name for polytetrafluoroethylene (first produced 1938, US patent 1945), a heat-resistant plastic chiefly known as the name given to a range of cookware coated with it that 'won't scratch, scar or mar' (1965). Hence, when President Reagan exhibited an ability during his first term (1981–5) to brush off any kind of 'dirt' or scandal that was thrown at him (chiefly through the charm of his personality), this was the epithet to apply to him. *Time* Magazine wrote (7 July 1986): 'Critics say that he is coated with Teflon, that no mess he makes ever sticks to him. That is perfectly true.' As his second term wore on, however, and as happens with an old non-stick frying-pan, the story was a little different.

Schroeder made the observation first, but it turned into a political cliché used by many.

SCHULBERG, Budd

American writer (1914–)

6 What Makes Sammy Run?

Title of novel (1941) about how a 'dynamic but vicious opportunist achieves success'. It provided an alternative phrase to 'what makes so-and-so tick?'

1 *Terry (to Charley)*: I coulda had class! I coulda been a contender! I coulda been somebody – instead of a bum, which is what I am! Let's face it. It was you, Charley!

Film, *On the Waterfront* (US, 1954). Schulberg's script was performed by Marlon Brando as Terry and Rod Steiger as Charley, his brother. It has become a much-quoted line, not least because of Brando's delivery. Brando plays a dockyard worker fighting corruption. In this speech, he laments what has happened to his former career as a boxer and blames it on his brother's betrayal. It continues: 'So what happens? He gets the title shot outdoors in the ball park – and whadda I get? A one-way ticket to Palookaville.'

SCHULTZ, Charles M.

American cartoonist (1922–)

2 Good grief, Charlie Brown!

A stock phrase from the 'Peanuts' strip. The behaviour of Charlie Brown frequently elicits this exclamation from other characters.

3 It Was a Dark and Stormy Night.

Title of book (1960s). In it, the line is given to the character Snoopy in his doomed attempts to write the Great American Novel. As a scene-setting, opening phrase, this appears to have been irresistible to more than one story-teller over the years and has now become a joke. It was used in all seriousness by the English novelist Edward Bulwer-Lytton at the start of *Paul Clifford* (1830). At some stage, the phrase also became part of a jokey children's 'circular' story-telling game, 'The tale without an end'. Iona and Peter Opie in *The Lore and Language of Schoolchildren* (1959) describe the workings thus: 'The tale usually begins: "It was a dark and stormy night, and the Captain said to the Bo'sun, 'Bo'sun, tell us a story,' so the Bo'sun began ..." And such is any child's readiness to hear a good story that the tale may be told three times round before the listeners appreciate that they are being diddled.'

4 Happiness Is a Warm Puppy.

Title of book (1962). Samuel Johnson had declared in 1766, 'Happiness consists in the multiplicity of agreeable consciousness,' but he was not the first to have a go at defining happiness, nor the last. In 1942, along came E.Y. Harburg with the lyrics to his song 'Happiness is a Thing Called Joe'. However, it was Schultz who really launched the 'Happiness is ——' format. In *c.*1957 he had drawn a strip 'centring around some kid hugging Snoopy and saying in the fourth panel that "Happiness is a warm puppy."' This became the title of a best-selling book in 1962 and let loose a stream of promotional phrases using the format, including 'Happiness is egg-shaped', 'Happiness is a cigar called Hamlet', 'Happiness is a warm ear-piece' (UK ad slogans); 'Happiness is seeing Lubbock, Texas, in the rear view mirror' (line from a Country and Western song); 'Happiness is a Warm Gun' (song title), 'Happiness is Wren-shaped', and many, many more. By which time one might conclude that 'Happiness is ... a worn cliché'.

SCHUMACHER, E.F.

German-born British economist (1911–77)

5 Small is Beautiful. A study of economics as if people mattered.

Title of book (1973), the first phrase of which provided a catchphrase and a slogan for those who were opposed to the expansionist trend in business and organizations that was very apparent in the 1960s and 1970s and who wanted 'economics on a human scale'. However, it appears that Schumacher very nearly did not bother with the phrase. According to his daughter and another correspondent (*The Observer*, 29 April and 6 June 1984), the book was going to be called 'The Homecomers'. His publisher, Anthony Blond, suggested 'Small*ness* is Beautiful', and then Desmond Briggs, the co-publisher, came up with the eventual wording.

SCOTT, C.P.

British editor (1846–1932)

6 Comment is free, but facts are sacred.

Scott was the influential editor of the *Manchester Guardian* for more than fifty-nine years – the longest editorship of a national newspaper anywhere in the world. In a signed editorial on 5 May 1921, marking the paper's centenary, he wrote: 'The newspaper is of necessity something of a monopoly, and its first duty is to shun the temptations of monopoly. Its primary office is the gathering of news. At the peril of its soul it must see that the supply is not tainted. Neither in what it gives, nor in what it does not give, nor in the mode of presentation, must the unclouded face of truth suffer wrong. Comment is free, but facts are sacred.' This passage was seized upon fairly quickly by politicians and journalists who, broadly speaking, held Scott in high regard. A man of forthright ideas and integrity, he is said to have expressed surprise when it was suggested to him that not all readers immediately turned to the leader page first of all.

1 Television? No good will come of this device. The word is half Greek and half Latin.

Quoted in *PDMQ* (1971), otherwise unverified.

SCOTT, Paul

English novelist (1920–78)

2 The Jewel in the Crown.

Title of novel (1966). It would be reasonable to suppose that the 1984 television adaptation of Paul Scott's 'Raj Quartet' of novels had something to do with the popularity of this phrase, now meaning, 'a bright feature, an outstanding part of anything'. This first of Scott's novels gave its name to the whole TV series. 'The Jewel in *Her* Crown' [my italics] is the title of a 'semi-historical, semi-allegorical' picture referred to early on in the book. It showed Queen Victoria, 'surrounded by representative figures of her Indian Empire: Princes, landowners, merchants, moneylenders, sepoys, farmers, servants, children, mothers, and remarkably clean and tidy beggars ... An Indian prince, attended by native servants, was approaching the throne bearing a velvet cushion on which he offered a large and sparkling gem.' (In fact, Victoria, like Disraeli, who is also portrayed, never set foot in India.)

Children at the school where the picture was displayed had to be told that 'the gem was simply representative of tribute, and that the jewel of the title was India herself'. The picture must have been painted *after* 1877, the year in which Victoria became Empress of India. It was probably an actual picture, though the painter's name is untraced.

The *OED2* refers only to the 'jewels of the crown' as a rhetorical phrase for the colonies of the British Empire, and has a citation from 1901. The specifying of India as *the* jewel is understandable. The Kohinoor, a very large oval diamond of 108.8 carats from India, had been part of the British crown jewels since 1849.

Many writers have used the phrase in other contexts. In *Dombey and Son*, Chap. 39 (1846–8), Charles Dickens writes: 'Clemency is the brightest jewel in the crown of a Briton's head.' Earlier, in *The Pickwick Papers*, Chap. 24 (1836–7), he has (of Magna Carta): 'One of the brightest jewels in the British crown.' In the poem 'O Wert Thou in the Cauld Blast', Robert Burns has: 'The brightest jewel in my crown/Wad be my queen, wad be my queen.' And then again, Laurence Olivier was quoted in *The Scotsman* (19 July 1957) as saying: 'I have always had the greatest admiration for the work of the BBC ... By far its most valuable jewel in its crown is the Third Programme, and that is going to be cut up, we are told.'

SCOTT, Robert Falcon

English explorer (1868–1912)

3 Great God! This is an awful place and terrible enough for us to have laboured without the reward of priority.

Scott contrived masterly epitaphs for himself and his companions by keeping at his diary as he slowly froze to death. All these jottings were quickly published in *Scott's Last Expedition: Journals* (1913). The above was written on reaching the South Pole and finding that the Norwegian explorer, Roald Amundsen, had beaten him to it.

4 Had we lived, I should have had a tale to tell of the hardihood, endurance, and courage of my companions which would have stirred the hearts of every Englishman. These rough notes and our dead bodies must tell the tale.

Towards the end, he addressed this 'Message to the public'.

5 It seems a pity, but I do not think I can write more. R. SCOTT. For God's sake look after our people.

The last entry in the diary, with the writing tapering away, was for 29 March 1912.

SCOTT, Sir Walter

Scottish novelist and poet (1771–1832)

6 If thou would'st view fair Melrose aright,
Go visit it by the pale moonlight.

The Lay of the Last Minstrel, Canto 2, St. 1 (1805). *Compare* ANONYMOUS 56:4.

7 O Caledonia! stern and wild,
Meet nurse for a poetic child!
Land of brown heath and shaggy wood,
Land of the mountain and the flood.

Ib. Caledonia was the Roman name for part of northern Britain. This is the most famous poetic use of the word to describe the modern Scotland.

8 O, young Lochinvar is come out of the west,
Through all the wide Border his steed was
the best.

Marmion, Canto 5, St. 12 (1808). Lochinvar, the hero of a ballad, claims his 'fair Ellen' just as she is about to be married to another. He puts her on his horse and rides off. Hence, the phrase 'Young Lochinvar' to describe any dashing, heroic figure but especially a young male eloper.

1 O what a tangled web we weave,
When first we practise to deceive.

Ib, Canto 6, St. 17. The origin of the modern proverbial expression.

2 O Woman! in our hours of ease,
Uncertain, coy, and hard to please ...
When pain and anguish wring the brow,
A ministering angel thou!

Ib., Canto 6, St. 30. Alluded to in P.G. Wodehouse, *Jeeves in the Offing*, Chap. 16 (1960): 'Like the woman in the poem I was mentioning, she sometimes inclined to be a toughish egg in hours of ease, she could generally be relied on to be there with the soothing solace when one had anything wrong with one's brow.'

3 The Heart of Midlothian.

Title of novel (1818). It refers to the nickname of the Tolbooth or prison which once stood on a site near St Giles' Cathedral in Edinburgh. Heart of Midlothian (or 'Hearts') football team (founded 1873), apparently took its name from a ballroom used by the players in the early days, which in turn had taken its name from the novel.

4 I offered Richard the services of my Free Lances.

Ivanhoe (1820), coining the word 'freelance', redolent of the Middle Ages when an unattached soldier for hire – a mercenary – would have been appropriately called a 'free lance'. Thus what is only a nineteenth-century invention came to be used to describe any self-employed person, especially a writer or journalist.

5 My own right hand shall do it.

In his journal for 22 January 1826 Scott is reflecting on the fact that he has just been saddled with thousands of pounds' worth of debts. He is going to raise the money by writing and not by involving anyone else. On another occasion (recorded in Lord Cockburn, *Memorials of His Time*, 1856) he said, 'This right hand shall work it all off'. And so he did.

6 That young lady has a talent for describing the involvements and feelings and characters of ordinary life which is to me the most wonderful thing I ever met with. The Big Bow-Wow strain I can do myself like any now going; but the exquisite touch, which renders ordinary commonplace things and characters interesting, from the truth of the description and the sentiment, is denied to me.

On Jane Austen, in his journal (14 March 1826). He had just been reading *Pride and Prejudice* and was lamenting that she had died so young. Scott may have taken his use of 'bow-wow' (dog-like, barking, snarling) from what Lord Pembroke is quoted as saying in Boswell's *Journal of a Tour to the Hebrides* (1785): 'Dr Johnson's sayings would not appear so extraordinary, were it not for his *bow-wow way*.'

See also ANONYMOUS 25:6.

SEDGWICK, John

American general (1813–64)

7 They couldn't hit an elephant at this dist——.

Last words before being shot by a sniper at the Battle of Spotsylvania in the American Civil War. Sedgwick was with the Union Army. Quoted in J. Green *Famous Last Words* (1979).

SEEGER, Pete

American songwriter (1919–)

8 Where have all the flowers gone?

Title of song (1961). Becoming a format phrase and cliché in journalistic hands. In *Keep Taking the Tabloids* (1983), Fritz Spiegl noted these headline uses: 'Where Have All The Guitars Gone', 'Where have all the Letters Gone'.

SEGAL, Erich

American writer (1937–)

9 Love means never having to say you're sorry.

Film, *Love Story* (1970) and also used as a promotional tag for it. Ryan O'Neal says it to Ray Milland, playing his father. He is quoting his student wife (Ali MacGraw) who has just died. Segal, who wrote the script, also produced a novelization of the story in which the line appears as the penultimate sentence, in the form 'Love means *not ever* having to say you're sorry'. A graffito (quoted 1974) stated: 'A vasectomy means never having to say you're sorry'; the film *The Abominable Dr Phibes* (UK, 1971) was promoted with the slogan: 'Love means never having to say you're ugly.'

SELFRIDGE, H. Gordon

American-born store owner (1858–1947)

1 The customer is always right.

Selfridge was an American who, after a spell with Marshall Field & Co, came to Britain and introduced the idea of the monster department store. It appears that he was the first to say 'the customer is always right' and many other phrases now generally associated with the business of selling through stores. The hotelier César Ritz (1850–1918) was being quoted by 1908 as saying, '*Le client n'a jamais tort* [The customer is never wrong]'. *CODP*'s earliest citation is from Carl Sandburg's *Good Morning, America* (1928), introduced by the words, 'Behold the proverbs of a nation'.

2 There are —— shopping days to Christmas.

This may have been coined by Selfridge. At least, when he was still in Chicago he sent out an instruction to heads of departments and assistants at the Marshall Field store there: 'The Christmas season has begun and but twenty-three more shopping days remain in which to make our holiday sales record.' Another similar coinage was 'The Bargain Basement', also originally at Marshall Field's and then (from 1912) in London (source: A.H. Williams, *No Name On The Door*, 1957).

3 Complete satisfaction or money cheerfully refunded.

Another of his slogans, quoted in *ib.* Selfridge apparently made it the text of one of his staff sermons and added: 'If a customer wants to try on fourteen pairs of gloves and then decides not to buy – why, that's all right by me.'

4 This famous store needs no name on the door.

Slogan. In about 1925 Selfridge removed the name-plates from his Oxford Street, London, store (opened in 1909). His publicity director, George Seal, thought up this rhyme and it was used on the firm's notepaper as a caption to a picture of the building. There was no other heading.

5 'Business as usual' must be the order of the day.

Speech (26 August 1914). In the context of the early days of the First World War, the traditional store-keeper's slogan (as might be used after a fire or similar) was first used by H.E. Morgan, an associate of Selfridge's. Winston Churchill also took up the cry. It was used until it was shown to be manifestly untrue and hopelessly inappropriate.

SELLAR, W.C. and YEATMAN, R.J.

British humorists (1898–1951) and (1897–1968)

6 1066 and All That.

Title of book (1930). *Compare* GRAVES 270:6.

7 A Good Thing.

Comment *passim* in *ib.* As in Chap. 1: 'The Roman Conquest was, however, a *Good Thing*, since the Britons were only natives at the time.'

8 Expostulate (chiefly) on
(a) The Curfew
(b) Gray's Energy in the Country Churchyard.

Ib., Chap. 21, Test Paper II, Up to the End of Henry III. Note the tribute to the poet Gray's exertions at Stoke Poges.

9 'Honi soie qui mal y pense' ('Honey, your silk stocking's hanging down').

Ib., Chap. 24. *See* EDWARD III 221:3.

10 A post-mortem examination revealed the word 'CALLOUS' engraved on her heart.

Ib., Chap. 32. *Compare* MARY 385:3.

11 The Cavaliers (Wrong but Wromantic) and the Roundheads (Right but Repulsive).

Ib., Chap. 35. A characterization of the opposing forces in the English Civil War, which is worthy of being taken seriously.

12 [Gladstone] spent his declining years trying to guess the answer to the Irish Question; unfortunately, whenever he was getting warm, the Irish secretly changed the question.

Ib., Chap. 57. The phrase 'Irish question' appears, incidentally, to have been coined by Benjamin Disraeli. In a speech to the House of Commons (16 February 1844): 'I want to see a public man come forward and say what the Irish question is ... Thus you have a starving population, an absentee aristocracy, and an alien Church, and in addition the weakest executive in the world ... That is the Irish question in its integrity.' *Compare* BISMARK 110:5.

13 AMERICA was thus clearly top nation, and History came to a.

Ib., Chap. 62. In Test Paper V, Up to the End of

History, Sellar and Yeatman may have been parodying a currently fashionable theory that history had come to an end, which has been found in the works of Robert Graves and others, but this remains unverified. *Compare* FUKUYAMA 249:3.

1 Oh to be in England now that Dean Nuisance is on a Hellenic cruise.

Garden Rubbish and Other Country Bumps (1936). Captain Pontoo speaking. Dean Nuisance is the archetypal gardening bore, or something even worse: the gardening expert who gives advice without ever getting his hands dirty, and who regards all gardening as a kind of spiritual experience.

SENECA

Roman philosopher and poet (c.4 BC–AD 65)

2 *Ecce par Deo dignum, vir fortis cum mala fortuna compositus.*
Behold a thing worthy of a God, a brave man matched in conflict with adversity.

From *De Providentia*, Sect. 4. An oft-alluded to and variously rendered remark. Robert Burton's *Anatomy of Melancholy* (1621) has: 'Seneca thinks the gods are well pleased when they see great men contending with adversity.' Oliver Goldsmith's *The Vicar of Wakefield* (1766) has: 'The greatest object in the universe, says a certain philosopher, is a good man struggling with adversity; yet there is a still greater, which is the good man that comes to relieve it.' The Rev. Sydney Smith's 'Sermon on the Duties of the Queen' (preached in St Paul's Cathedral, undated but possibly *c.*1837) has: 'A wise man struggling with adversity is said by some heathen writer to be a spectacle on which the gods might look down with pleasure.' It is ignored by Bartlett and *ODQ*.

SENNETT, Mack

Canadian-born comedy filmmaker (1880–1960)

3 An idea going in one direction meets an idea going in the opposite direction.

Defining a joke. Untraced.

4 It's got to *move*!

Summing up the nature of his comedy technique; quoted in Leslie Halliwell, *The Filmgoer's Book of Quotes* (1973).

SEYLER, Athene (later Dame Athene)

British actress (1889–1990)

5 Whenever I see his fingernails, I thank God I don't have to look at his feet.

Of Hannen Swaffer, journalist. Remark, quoted in Bryan Forbes, *Ned's Girl* (1977).

SHACKLETON, Sir Ernest

Irish explorer (1874–1922)

6 Men wanted for hazardous journey. Small wages, bitter cold, long months of complete darkness, constant danger, safe return doubtful. Honour and recognition in case of success.

Nominated by Julian L. Watkins in his book *The 100 Greatest Advertisements* (Chicago, 1949/59) for the simplicity and 'deadly frankness' of its copy is this small advertisement, said to have appeared in London newspapers in 1900, signed 'Ernest Shackleton'. Watkins reports Shackleton as saying: 'It seemed as though all the men in Great Britain were determined to accompany me, the response was so overwhelming.' Shackleton led three expeditions to the Antarctic in 1907–9, 1914–17 and 1921–22. His biographer, Roland Huntford, suggests that the advertisement would have been published before the 1914 expedition but casts doubt on it ever appearing. Shackleton had no need to advertise for companions, he says.

SHAFFER, Peter

English playwright (1926–)

7 As old Martin describes the ordeal, the men climb the Andes.

The Royal Hunt of the Sun, Act 1, Sc. 8 (1964). An ambitious stage direction in an epic play about the conquest of Peru, Atahuallpa, the Inca sun god, and the Spanish explorer Pisarro. It is said that John Dexter agreed to direct the play only when he saw this challenge. From Robert Stephens, *Knight Errant* (1995): 'Dexter's production was a work of sheer inspiration, sparked off by the famously unhelpful but challenging stage direction of "They cross the Andes".'

SHAKESPEARE, William

English playwright and poet (1564–1616)

The text of all the works is as in the Arden Shakespeare (2nd Series), except for the Sonnets, which are as in the Oxford Shakespeare (1988).

ALL'S WELL THAT ENDS WELL (1603)

1 All's Well That Ends Well.

Title. The Rev. Francis Kilvert's diary entry for 1 January 1878 has: 'The hind axle broke and they thought they would have to spend the night on the road ... All's well that ends well and they arrived safe and sound.' So, is the allusion to the title of Shakespeare's play or to something else? In fact, it was a proverbial expression before Shakespeare. *CODP* finds, 'If the ende be wele, than is alle wele' in 1381, and points to the earlier form, 'Wel is him that wel ende mai'.

A curious footnote is that the title was very nearly also bestowed on Leo Tolstoy's *War and Peace* (1863–9). *See* TOLSTOY 541:1.

2 'Twere all one
That I should love a bright particular star
And think to wed it, he is so above me.

I.i.83. Although one can see the point of Michael Coveney entitling his biography of the actress Dame Maggie Smith, *A Bright Particular Star* (1993), in the play the words are said by a woman (Helena) about a man (Bertram).

3 I know a man that had this trick of melancholy sold a goodly manor for a song.

III.ii.8. The expression 'for a song' was proverbial in Shakespeare's day. 'I bought it for a song' occurs in *Regulus* (1694) by John Crowne. Possibly also from the 'trifling cost' (Brewer) of ballad sheets sold in olden days. Hence, 'to go for a song', meaning 'to be sold very cheaply, if not for free'. *Going for a Song* was the title of a BBC TV antiques programme (from 1968).

ANTONY AND CLEOPATRA (1607)

4 Where's my serpent of old Nile?

I.v.25. Cleopatra suggests what Antony must be thinking (when he is away from her).

5 My salad days,
When I was green in judgement, cold in blood,
To say as I said then!

I.v.73. Cleopatra. Hence, *Salad Days*, title of a musical (1954) by Julian Slade and Dorothy Reynolds.

6 The barge she sat in, like a burnished throne,
Burned on the water ...
For her own person,
It beggared all description.

II.ii.191. Enobarbus of Cleopatra. Hence, the expression 'beggars all description', meaning 'is indescribable' and originating with the meaning of the verb 'to beggar' in the sense 'exhausting the resources of'.

7 Age cannot wither her, no custom stale
Her infinite variety.

II.ii.235. Enobarbus on Cleopatra. *See also* LOVELACE 364:2.

8 Let's have one other gaudy night: call to me
All my sad captains; fill our bowls once more;
Let's mock the midnight bell.

III.xiii.183. Antony. Hence, conceivably, *Gaudy Night*, title of a detective novel (1935) by Dorothy L. Sayers, making play on the word 'gaudy', meaning an Oxford college celebration.

9 I have yet
Room for six scotches more.

IV.vii.9. Scarus's apparently jocular remark is quite the reverse of its modern meaning. A 'scotch' is a cut, or small incision – so when he meets Antony on the battlefield he is boasting of his bravery.

10 Shall I abide
In this dull world, which in thy absence is
No better than a sty? ...
O! withered is the garland of the war,
The soldier's pole is fall'n; young boys and girls
Are level now with men; the odds is gone,
And there is nothing left remarkable
Beneath the visiting moon.

IV.xv.67. Cleopatra laments Antony's death. Rosemary Anne Sisson entitled a novel *Beneath the Visiting Moon* (1986).

11 I wish you all joy of the worm.

V.ii.259. Clown. Worm = asp.

12 Give me my robe, put on my crown; I have
Immortal longings in me.

V.ii.279. Cleopatra. Immortal longings = longings for immortality.

AS YOU LIKE IT (1598)

1 I will tell you the beginning, and if it please your ladyships, you may see the end, for the best is yet to do.

I.ii.104. Le Beau. Hence, *Beginning*, the title of an autobiography (1989) by the youthful actor Kenneth Branagh – which might not appear to be a quotation at first glance, but is, and is suitably modest.

2 Sweet are the uses of adversity ...
And this our life, exempt from public haunts,
Finds tongues in trees, books in the running brooks,
Sermons in stones, and good in everything.

II.i.12. Duke Senior. *Compare* WILDE 571:3.

3 Under the greenwood tree
Who loves to lie with me.

II.v.1. Amiens singing. Hence, *Under the Greenwood Tree*, title of a novel (1872) by Thomas Hardy.

4 And so from hour to hour, we ripe and ripe,
And then, from hour to hour, we rot and rot:
And thereby hangs a tale.

II.vii.28. Jaques, reporting the words of a motley fool (Touchstone). As a story-telling device, 'thereby hangs a tale' is still very much in use to indicate that some tasty tit-bit is about to be revealed. It occurs a number of times in Shakespeare, e.g., *The Merry Wives of Windsor* (I.iv.143) and *The Taming of the Shrew* (IV.i.50). In *Othello* (III.i.8), the Clown says, 'O, thereby hangs a tail', emphasizing the innuendo that may or may not be present in the other examples.

5 If ever you have look'd on better days ...
True it is that we have seen better days.

II.vii.113 & 120. Orlando and Duke Senior. Hence, 'to have seen better days', meaning 'to have been more successful, prosperous than at present', as in 'The whole town bears evident marks of having seen better days' – Robert Forsyth, *The Beauties of Scotland* (1806).

6 All the world's a stage,
And all the men and women merely players:
They have their exits and their entrances;
And one man in his time plays many parts,
His acts being seven ages. At first the infant,
Mewling and puking in the nurse's arms.
And then the whining schoolboy, with his satchel,
And shining morning face, creeping like snail
Unwillingly to school ...

II.vii.139. Jaques speaking. Probably the second most famous speech in all Shakespeare. Hence, *All the World's a Stage*, title of a BBC TV history of the theatre (1984).

7 And then the justice,
In fair round belly with good capon lined,
With eyes severe, and beard of formal cut,
Full of wise saws and modern instances.

Ib. Modern instances = trite examples or cases recently presided over.

8 Blow, blow, thou winter wind,
Thou art not so unkind
As man's ingratitude.

II.vii.174. Amiens singing. Unkind = cruel, contrary to nature.

9 Thou art in a parlous state, shepherd.

III.ii.42. Touchstone. An early appearance of the pairing 'parlous state'.

10 Whoever lov'd that lov'd not at first sight?

III.v.82. Phebe quoting. *See* MARLOWE 381:7.

11 A poor virgin, sir, an ill-favoured thing, sir, but mine own.

V.iv.57. Touchstone speaking. In 1985 the painter Howard Hodgkin won the £10,000 Turner prize for a work of art called 'A Small Thing But My Own'. It was notable that he chose the word 'small' rather than 'poor'. In Shakespeare, Touchstone is not talking about a work of art but about Audrey, the country wench he woos. The line is nowadays more likely to be used (in mock-modesty) about a thing rather than a person. A pun: 'Do you know Sir Arthur Evans's reported remark on finding a fragment of pottery in Crete – "an ill-favoured thing, but Minoan"?'

12 He uses his folly like a stalking horse and under the presentation of that he shoots his wit.

V.iv.105. Duke Senior. A figurative use of the term 'stalking horse'. Originally, this was a device used in hunting to get close to game which apparently sees no danger in a four-legged beast (and recorded since 1519). The wooden horse at Troy was an even more devastating form of equine deception. Since the mid-1800s in the United States, the phrase has been used in politics about a candidate put forward to test the water on behalf of another candidate. Latterly in Britain (since about 1989) the term has been applied to an MP who stands for election as leader of his party with no hope of getting the job. His role is to test the water on behalf of other stronger candidates and to see whether the incumbent leader is challengeable.

CORIOLANUS (1608)

1 Despising
For you the city, thus I turn my back.
There is a world elsewhere.

III.iii.133. Coriolanus. Lord Byron alludes to this in a letter dated 8 February 1816: 'I mean to go abroad the moment packages will permit – "There is a world beyond Rome."' In a second letter of the same date he quotes Shakespeare directly.

2 The gods look down, and this unnatural scene
They laugh at.

V.iii.184. Coriolanus. The Gods (or God) laughing is a phenomenon frequently to be observed in many areas of literature. In the first book of Homer's *Iliad* there is a scene in the gods' dwelling on Olympus which has the gods roaring with laughter. This was caused by the spectacle of the crippled god of fire and metallurgy, Hephaestus, with his bobbing gait carrying round the wine-cup to serve them. Homer says that this caused 'uncontrollable laughter' among the gods. This passage gave rise to the expression 'Homeric laughter', meaning an irresistible belly laugh which is cosmically dominant. That is to say, the laughter is epic rather than of the sort that Homer might have produced. It is interesting that here the laughter is directed at a cripple, reminding us that, even among the gods, there is very little laughter that is not cruel.

The Jewish God also laughs. A book called *The Day God Laughed* (1978) by Hyam Maccoby contains the story about Rabbi Eliezer disputing with the Sages who refuse to accept any sign that God approves his interpretation of Jewish law. The prophet Elijah comments on God's involvement in this dispute: 'He was laughing, and saying, "My children have defeated me, my children have defeated me".' Maccoby adds that this story was dismissed as one of the imbecilities of the Talmud in the medieval Disputation of Paris, when the Talmud was put on trial by Christians.

The Christian God laughs lots of times – not least in the works of G.K. Chesterton, especially in his poem 'The Fish':

For I saw that finny goblin
Hidden in the abyss untrod;
And I knew there can be laughter
On the secret face of God.
Blow the trumpets, crown the sages,
Bring the age by reason fed!
('He that sitteth in the heavens,
he shall laugh' – the prophet said.)

Then there is the poem by Sir Laurence Jones, 'Lines to a Bishop who was shocked (AD 1950) at seeing a pier-glass [mirror] in a bathroom'. When the Bishop sees his nakedness, the poem ends:

You shrink aghast, with pained and puzzled eyes,
While God's loud laughter peals about the skies.

The poem 'Ducks' by F.W. Harvey (1888–1957) ends:

Caterpillars and cats are lively and excellent puns:
All God's jokes are good – even the practical ones!
And as for the duck, I think God must have smiled a bit
Seeing those bright eyes blink on the day he fashioned it.
And He's probably laughing still at the sound that came out of its bill!

Laughter in Paradise was the title of a 1951 film about a dead man's revenge on the beneficiaries of his will. The original idea (as in the headword quotation) also occurs in a Cole Porter song 'I Love Him But He Didn't Love Me' (1929), whose verse begins:

The gods who nurse
This universe
Think little of mortals' cares.
They sit in crowds
On exclusive clouds
And laugh at our love affairs.

Additionally, a song of the 1940s called 'Tonight' (also known as 'Perfidia'), written by Milton Leeds to music by Alberto Dominguez, has: 'While the Gods of love look down and laugh at what romantic fools we mortals be.' There is here a more obvious allusion to the situation in Shakespeare's *A Midsummer Night's Dream* (III.ii.115) when the sprite Puck says to Oberon, King of the Fairies: 'Lord, what fools these mortals be!' It is but a short step from this to *The Stars Look Down*, the title of the novel (1935, filmed UK, 1939) by A.J. Cronin.

CYMBELINE (1609–10)

3 Boldness be my friend!
Arm me, Audacity, from head to foot.

I.vii.18. What Iachimo says when he sets off to pursue Imogen. Hence, *Boldness Be My Friend*, title of a book (1953) by Richard Pape about his exploits in the Second World War. In 1977, Richard Boston wrote a book called *Baldness Be My Friend*, partly about his own lack of hair.

1 Hark! hark! the lark at heaven's gate sings.

II.iii.20. *See* BLAKE 112:4.

2 Golden lads and girls all must,
As chimney-sweepers, come to dust.

IV.ii.262. Guiderius singing. Hence, possibly, the expression 'golden youth', meaning 'a young man or woman with obvious talent who is expected to do well in life and career.' Also in the form 'gilded youth', a fashionable young man or men (usually), dedicated to the pursuit of pleasure (possibly based on the French *jeunesse dorée*). 'What avail his golden youth, his high blood ... if they help not now?' Benjamin Disraeli, *Coningsby* (1844).

HAMLET (1600–1)

3 For this relief much thanks.

I.i.8. Francisco to Barnardo, the two sentinels at the very beginning of the play. 'Relief' here in the sense of relieving another person of guard duty, nothing lavatorial. In *The Lyttelton Hart-Davis Letters* (for the 1960s), reference is made to the phrase being used as the title of a book about a Victorian sanitary engineer (Thomas Crapper, presumably), but if any such volume was published, it remains untraced.

4 O! that this too too sullied flesh would melt,
Thaw and resolve itself into a dew ...
How weary, stale, flat, and unprofitable
Seem to me all the uses of this world ...
Frailty, thy name is woman!

I.ii.129. Hamlet. The Arden edition describes the choice of the word 'sullied' (= dirty, soiled, tarnished) as 'the most debated reading in the play in recent years.' The First Folio has 'solid'.

5 Methinks I see my father ... in my mind's eye,
Horatio.

I.ii.184. Hamlet. Hence, 'in the mind's eye', meaning 'in the imagination'. However, this is a traditional metaphor dating back to Plato.

6 A was a man, take him for all in all;
I shall not look upon his like again.

I.ii.187. Hamlet of his late father. Now a cliché of tribute and obituary. Dorothy Parker on Isadora Duncan's book *My Life* in *The New Yorker* (14 January 1928): 'She does not whine, nor seek pity. She was a brave woman. We shall not look upon her like again.' In *Joyce Grenfell Requests the Pleasure* (1976), the actress recalls being rung by the United Press for a comment on the death of Ruth Draper, the monologist: 'My diary records: "I said we should not see her like again. She was a genius." Without time to think, clichés take over and often, because that is why they have become clichés, they tell the truth.'

7 A countenance more in sorrow than in anger.

I.ii.231. Horatio describing a feature of the Ghost of Hamlet's father. 'More in sorrow than in anger' now means that you are doing something – like meting out punishment – in a rational rather than hot-headed way. From *The Independent* (23 April 1992): 'I told an Essex Girl Joke. A young woman turned on me as if I came from another, less advanced planet, and, more in sorrow than in anger, said she didn't think what I'd said was frightfully right-on.'

8 This above all: to thine own self be true,
And it must follow, as the night the day,
Thou canst not then be false to any man.

I.iii.78. Polonius, verging on the pompous. It would appear to have provided the somewhat unlikely title *This Above All* for a film (UK, 1942) based on a novel by Eric Knight about a conscientious objector/deserter in World War Two who sees the light. The lines from *Hamlet* are read out from a copy of Shakespeare and become the last words of the film.

9 Though I am native here
And to the manner born.

I.iv.14. Hamlet. Hence, *To the Manor Born*, the title of a TV comedy series (1979–81), created by Peter Spence, about a lady of the manor. Shakespeare may have intended a play on the word 'manor', too.

10 It is a custom
More honour'd in the breach than in the
observance.

I.iv.16. The Prince is telling Horatio that the King's drunken revelry is a custom that would be *better* 'honour'd' if it were not followed at all. Now an expression usually taken to mean that whatever custom is under consideration has fallen into sad neglect.

11 Something is rotten in the state of Denmark.

I.iv.90. Hamlet. Now, as 'there is something rotten in the state of Denmark', a common way of expressing that all is not well in some situation.

12 But that I am forbid
To tell the secrets of my prison-house,
I could a tale unfold whose lightest word

Would harrow up thy soul, freeze thy young blood,
Make thy two eyes, like stars, start from, their spheres,
Thy knotted and combinèd locks to part,
And each particular hair to stand on end,
Like quills upon the fretful porpentine.

I.v.13. The Ghost of Hamlet's father talking to the Prince. Porpentine = porcupine. 'His face was flushed, his eyes were bulging, and ... his hair was standing on end – like quills upon the fretful porpentine, as Jeeves once put it when describing to me the reactions of Barmy Fotheringay-Phipps on seeing a dead snip, on which he had invested largely, come in sixth in the procession at the Newmarket Spring Meeting.' So says Bertie Wooster in *The Code of the Woosters* (1938) by P.G. Wodehouse, using one of his favourite Shakespearean images – from *Hamlet*, though Wooster probably isn't aware of this. From *Jeeves in the Offing* (1949): '[Jeeves], do you recall telling me once about someone who told somebody he could tell him something which would make him think a bit? Knitted socks and porcupines entered into it, I remember.' In 1986 some of the more literate regulars of the Porcupine pub in Charing Cross Road, London, would talk of repairing to 'the Fretters'.

1 Murder most foul, as in the best it is,
But this most foul, strange and unnatural.

I.v.27. The Ghost. Hence, *Murder Most Foul*, title of a film (UK, 1964) based on the Agatha Christie novel *Mrs McGinty's Dead* (1952), with Miss Marple substituted for Hercule Poirot.

2 There are more things in heaven and earth, Horatio,
Than are dreamt of in your philosophy.

I.v.174. Hamlet. Not some philosophy of Horatio's in particular, but philosophy in general.

3 To put an antic disposition on.

I.v.180. Hamlet's announcement that he is going to affect madness. Antic = grotesque, strange or odd.

4 Brevity is the soul of wit.

II.ii.90. Polonius. Meaning, that the cleverest and most effective statements are made in relatively few words. *Compare* PARKER 424:4.

5 Though this be madness, yet there is method in it.

II.ii.205. An aside by Polonius about Hamlet. Hence, the expression 'there is method in my/his/her madness'.

6 He that plays the king shall be welcome.

II.ii.318. Hamlet is talking to Rosencrantz and obviously toying with the idea of having the actors play out recent events at Elsinore. *He That Plays the King* was used as the title of a book of theatre criticism (1950) by Kenneth Tynan. The thriller *To Play the King* (1992) by Michael Dobbs, concerning a clash between a British Prime Minister and a King, might seem to allude to this, but probably owes more to 'playing the king' in chess or cards (as is shown by the other titles in the trilogy, *House of Cards* and *Final Cut*). Shakespeare quite frequently uses the 'play the ——' formula, and not just about kings.

7 I am mad north-north-west. When the wind is southerly, I know a hawk from a handsaw.

II.ii.374. Hamlet speaking. Hence, *North by Northwest*, title of Alfred Hitchcock's film thriller (US, 1959) in which Cary Grant has to feign madness as Hamlet does. There may also be an allusion to a slogan of Northwest Airlines.

8 Buzz, buzz.

II.ii.389. Hamlet speaking, when told by Polonius, 'The actors are come hither, my lord'. One commentator describes it as 'a contemptuous exclamation dismissing something as idle gossip or (as here) stale news'. Hence, *Buzz, Buzz!*, title given to a collection of his reviews (1918) by James Agate, the dramatic critic.

9 Then came each actor on his ass.

II.ii.391. Hamlet says this to Polonius who has just announced the arrival of the actors. It is thought that Shakespeare might have been quoting a line from a ballad. Michael MacLiammoir, the Irish actor, used the phrase *Each Actor on His Ass* as the title of one of his volumes of memoirs (1960).

10 For the play, I remember, pleased not the million, 'twas caviare to the general.

II.ii.431. Hamlet. The general = the general public. The Arden Shakespeare notes that when the play was written, caviare was a novel delicacy. It was probably inedible to those who had not yet acquired a taste for it. Hence, 'caviare to the general', a famously misunderstood phrase meaning 'of no interest to common folk'. It has *nothing* to do with giving expensive presents of caviare to unappreciative military gentlemen. Lord Jenkins, Chancellor of Oxford University, apparently committed this solecism in an obituary of Lord Zuckerman in *The Independent* (2 April 1993): 'Solly Zuckerman's taste was sharp and astringent, "Caviar for the general" (on the whole he liked generals in spite of his scepticism for conventional military wisdom), but once acquired it never palled.'

1 O, what a rogue and peasant slave am I.
Is it not monstrous that this player here,
But in a fiction, in a dream of passion,
Could force his soul so to his own conceit ...
And all for nothing!
For Hecuba!
What's Hecuba to him, or he to her,
That he should weep for her?

II.ii.544. The sorrows of Hecuba are depicted in several Greek tragedies and, as Hamlet discusses with the players what play they might perform to catch his uncle out, the Prince reflects on an aspect of the actor's craft. Acting can make the other actors (and the audience) weep but what is the point of doing so? He, Hamlet, has a much better motive for using the art. Michael MacLiammoir, the Irish actor, reduced the words to *All for Hecuba*, the title of a volume of memoirs (1946).

2 The play's the thing
Wherein I'll catch the conscience of the king.

II.ii.600. Hamlet speaking. Hence, the somewhat watered down use of 'the play's the thing' in contexts where theatre or drama as a whole is being promoted.

3 To be or not to be, that is the question:
Whether 'tis nobler in the mind to suffer
The slings and arrows of outrageous fortune,
Or to take arms against a sea of troubles
And by opposing end them? To die – to sleep,
No more; and by a sleep to say we end
The heart-ache and the thousand natural shocks
That flesh is heir to: 'tis a consummation
Devoutly to be wish'd. To die, to sleep;
To sleep, perchance to dream – ay, there's the rub:
For in that sleep of death what dreams may come
When we have shuffled off this mortal coil,
Must give us pause – there's the respect
That makes calamity of so long life.
For who would bear the whips and scorns of time,
Th' oppressor's wrong, the proud man's contumely,
The pangs of dispriz'd love, the law's delay,
The insolence of office, and the spurns
That patient merit of th'unworthy takes,
When he himself might his quietus make
With a bare bodkin? Who would fardels bear,
To grunt and sweat under a weary life,
But that the dread of something after death,
The undiscovered country, from whose bourn
No traveller returns, puzzles the will,
And makes us rather bear those ills we have
Than fly to others that we know not of?
Thus conscience doth make cowards of us all,
And thus the native hue of resolution
Is sicklied o'er with the pale cast of thought,
And enterprises of great pitch and moment
With this regard their currents turn awry
And lose the name of action.

III.i.56. Hamlet's soliloquy beginning thus is one of the most quoted passages in all literature. It is constantly alluded to, especially in the titles of works by other writers. A small selection: *To Be Or Not To Be* was used as the title of a film comedy (US 1942, 1983) about Polish actors under the Nazis. *Slings and Arrows* was a post-Second World War revue in London, with Hermione Gingold. *Outrageous Fortune* was the title of a film (US, 1987), loosely about rival actresses aspiring to be in a production of *Hamlet*. *Perchance to Dream* was the title of a musical by Ivor Novello (1945). *Mortal Coils* was the title of a collection of short stories (1922) by Aldous Huxley. A thriller by Cyril Hare was entitled *With a Bare Bodkin* (1982). There is a natural history book by John Hay called *The Undiscovered Country* (1982), and that title was also used for Tom Stoppard's 1980 adaptation of a play by Arthur Schnitzler. Graham Greene had a novel *The Name of Action* (1930).

4 O! what a noble mind is here o'erthrown ...
The glass of fashion, and the mould of form.

III.i.152. Ophelia is lamenting Hamlet's apparent madness and decline. This is what he once was: a person upon whom others modelled themselves and who dictated what fashion should be. *The Glass of Fashion* was used as the title of a play by Sydney Grundy, first staged at the Globe, London, in the 1880s; also as the title of book (1954) by Cecil Beaton.

5 O! it offends me to the soul to hear a robustious periwig-pated fellow tear a passion to tatters ... I would have such a fellow whipped

for o'erdoing Termagant. It out-Herods Herod.
Pray you, avoid it.

III.ii.8. The Prince is instructing the actors not to go over the top. Hence, 'to out-Herod Herod', a literary allusion, often adapted in the form 'to out something something' and meaning to go beyond the extremes of tyranny (or whatever activity is under consideration) as usually perceived. The allusion is to Herod's slaughter of all the children of Bethlehem (Matthew 2:16). Termagant and Herod both featured in medieval mystery plays as noisy, violent types.

1 Give me that man
That is not passion's slave, and I will wear him
In my heart's core, in my heart of heart.

III.ii.71. Hamlet. Hence, 'in my heart of hearts', meaning 'in my deepest and most hidden thoughts and feelings' – apparently a coinage of Shakespeare's.

2 *Hamlet*: Lady, shall I lie in your lap?
Ophelia: No, my lord.
Hamlet: I mean, my head upon your lap.
Ophelia: Ay, my lord.
Hamlet: Do you think I meant country matters?
Ophelia: I think nothing, my lord.
Hamlet: That's a fair thought to lie between maids' legs.

III.ii.115. Shakespeare's bawdy is sometimes obscure, but few can miss that 'country matters' means physical love-making or fail to note the pun in the first syllable – which also occurs in John Donne's poem 'The Good-Morrow' (1635), and William Wycherley's *The Country Wife* (1675). *Country Matters* was the title of a British TV drama series (ITV, 1972) presenting an anthology of stories by H.E. Bates and A.E. Coppard, linked only by their setting in the English countryside. One presumes that the producers knew what they were doing in calling it this.

3 The lady doth protest too much, methinks.

III.ii.225. Gertrude's line is often evoked to mean, 'There is something suspicious about the way that person is complaining more than is natural'. However, what Hamlet's mother is actually doing is giving her opinion of 'The Mousetrap', the play-within-a-play. What she means to say is that the Player Queen is promising more than she is likely to be able to deliver. Gertrude uses the word 'protest' in the sense of 'state formally' not 'complain'.

4 *Hamlet*: Methinks it is like a weasel.
Polonius: It is backed like a weasel.
Hamlet: Or like a whale.
Polonius: Very like a whale.

III.ii.373. The Prince is teasing Polonius about the shape of a cloud. Hence, the title of John Osborne's 1980 TV play *Very Like a Whale* about a captain of industry in emotional turmoil.

5 'Tis now the very witching time of night,
When churchyards yawn and hell itself breathes out
Contagion to this world.

III.ii.379. Hamlet. The modern phrase 'witching hour (of midnight)' seems to have grown out of a blend of such lines as this from *Hamlet* and 'It was now the witching hour consecrated to ghost and spirit' – Lord Lytton, *Rienzi* (1835). *The Witching Hour* was the title of a play be Augustus Thomas (*c.*1915; filmed US, 1921 and 1934). From the *Daily Mirror* (3 December 1994): '9.45pm, Drop into The Midnight Shop (223 Brompton Road, SW3), which, as its name suggests, stays open until the witching hour. It claims to be London's original late-night store, and is a well-stocked grocers and delicatessen.'

6 An eye like Mars to threaten and command.

III.iv.57. Hamlet, describing a feature of his father's portrait. *See* WODEHOUSE 579:3.

7 For 'tis the sport to have the engineer
Hoist with his own petard.

III.iv.208. Hamlet. A petard was a newly invented device in Shakespeare's day, used for blowing up walls, and so on with gunpowder. Thus the image is of the operative being blown up into the air by his own device. Hence, 'hoist with one's own petard', meaning 'to be caught in one's own trap', has nothing to do with being stabbed by one's own knife (poniard/poignard = dagger) or hanged with one's own rope. Compare the more recent expression 'to score an own goal'.

8 Hamlet, this deed, for thine especial safety –
... must send thee hence
With fiery quickness.

IV.iii.40. King Claudius means that the commission or document sending him to England is for his own safety (ironically: as it turns out, Hamlet is supposed to be killed on the journey). Hence, 'for thine especial safety', the motto on the safety curtain at the Theatre Royal, Drury Lane, London.

1 They say the owl was a baker's daughter.

IV.v.43. So says Ophelia, mystifyingly. The reference is to an old English legend about Christ going into a baker's shop and asking for something to eat. A piece of cake is put in the oven for Him, but the baker's daughter says it is too large and cuts it in half. The dough swells up to an enormous size, she exclaims 'Woo! Woo!' and is turned into an owl.

2 When sorrows come, they come not single spies,
But in battalions.

IV.v.78. Hence, *Single Spies*, title of stage double bill (1988) by Alan Bennett, consisting of his plays *An Englishman Abroad* and *A Question of Attribution* about Guy Burgess and Anthony Blunt (who were indeed both single and spies).

3 There's rosemary, that's for remembrance.

IV.v.173. Ophelia. Hence, *This For Remembrance*, title of the autobiography (1978) of Rosemary Clooney, the American singer.

4 Alas, poor Yorick. I knew him, Horatio, a fellow of infinite jest, of most excellent fancy.

V.i.178. Hamlet speaking, when the Gravedigger produces the skull of Yorick, the late King's jester. To make it easier to quote, presumably, the form 'I knew him *well*, Horatio' has crept into popular use.

5 It did me yeoman's service.

V.ii.36. Hamlet. Hence, the phrase 'yeoman service' meaning 'useful service as rendered by a faithful servant'. 'Sir, Your correspondent, Frank McDonald, who has given yeoman service to the protection of our environment ...' – letter to the editor, *The Irish Times* (9 June 1994).

6 The rest is silence.

V.ii.363. Hamlet's dying words. A 1959 German film of *Hamlet* was given the English language title *The Rest is Silence*.

7 Goodnight, sweet prince,
And flights of angels sing thee to thy rest.

V.ii.364. Horatio at Hamlet's death. Also to be found on the grave of Douglas Fairbanks (1883–1939), the actor of swashbuckling film roles, chiefly in the silent cinema. 'Inscribed on the white marble sarcophagus at the head of a 125-foot lagoon in Hollywood Cemetery' – Barnaby Conrad, *Famous Last Words* (1961).

8 The ears are senseless that should give us hearing,
To tell him his commandment is fulfilled,
That Rosencrantz and Guildernstern are dead.

V.ii.374. The line is spoken by one of the English ambassadors after Hamlet has arranged for the killing of his two old student friends (who had been set up by his uncle Claudius to kill *him*). Hence, *Rosencrantz and Guildernstern Are Dead*, the title of a play (1966) by Tom Stoppard, concerning two of the minor characters in *Hamlet*. The two characters are also referred to in a play by W.S. Gilbert, *Rosencrantz and Guildernstern* (1891).

9 Hamlet, revenge!

The title of a detective novel (1937) by Michael Innes comes *not* from Shakespeare's play but from an earlier one (which is lost to us) on the same theme. Thomas Lodge saw it in 1596 and noted the pale-faced 'ghost which cried so miserably at the theatre, like an oyster-wife, Hamlet, revenge'.

HENRY IV, PART 1 (1597)

10 Let not us that are squires of the night's body be called thieves of the day's beauty: let us be Diana's foresters, gentlemen of the shade, minions of the moon.

I.ii.25. Falstaff to Prince Hal. Minions of the moon = night-time robbers. In 1984, a French film was released in the English-language market with the title *Favourites of the Moon*. It was a quirky piece about Parisian crooks, petty and otherwise, whose activities overlapped in one way or another, but the English title hardly seemed relevant to the subject. Not surprisingly, as it was a translation back into English. The original French title was *Les Favoris de la Lune* and, as a caption acknowledged, this was a French translation of the original Shakespearean phrase.

11 By heaven, methinks it were an easy leap
To pluck bright honour from the pale-fac'd moon.

I.iii.199. Hotspur. Oddly misquoted in an official British government booklet about Combined Operations, 1940–2: 'The tradition of combined operations, which began in the reign of Elizabeth, is rapidly reaching its fullest manifestation in the reign of George VI. Men of the Commandos still go out in the night-time with darkened faces, "To win bright honour from the palefaced moon," but they are not alone.'

1 The turkeys in my panier are quite starved.

II.i.26. First Carrier. As the events of the play cannot have occurred later than 1413 (when King Henry IV died), it was anachronistic of Shakespeare to have had anyone mention turkeys. These were not discovered until 1518 in Mexico, from whence they were introduced to Europe. However, the term 'turkey-cock' had been in known in England since the Crusades (referring to what we now called guinea-fowl), so perhaps this is not an error after all. And yet, the earliest *OED2* citation for 'turkey-cock' is 1541 and it is not apparent whether this term was abbreviated to 'turkey' in 1597, when *Henry IV, Part I* was first performed.

2 I tell you, my lord fool, out of this nettle, danger, we pluck this flower, safety.

II.iii.9. Hotspur commenting on a letter he is reading. Hence, 'to grasp the nettle', meaning 'to summon up the courage to deal with a difficult problem'. The latter part was quoted by Neville Chamberlain as he was about to fly off to Germany in September 1938 on a trip to see Hitler which resulted in the Munich Agreement. This led the *Sheffield Star* to comment: 'Our Prime Minister carries a pocket Shakespeare with him wherever he travels. He put Shakespeare on the map with a quotation from *Henry IV* when he set out for the Munich conference' – quoted in Michael Bateman, *This England* (1969).

3 I would 'twere bed-time, Hal, and all were well.

V.i.125. Falstaff to Prince Hal before the battle of Shrewsbury. 'Would it were bedtime and all were well' is how the phrase came to be used – as in Oliver Goldsmith, *She Stoops to Conquer,* I.ii (1773).

4 But thoughts, the slaves of life, and life, time's fool,
And time, that takes survey of all the world,
Must have a stop.

V.iv.80. Hotspur. Hence, *Time Must Have a Stop*, title of a novel (1944) by Aldous Huxley.

5 The better part of valour is discretion

V.iv.119. Falstaff cynically reinterprets an old maxim and this is how the words are still used, as well as in this form. Sometimes rendered as 'Discretion is the better part of valour'.

HENRY IV, PART 2 (1597)

6 He hath eaten me out of house and home; he hath put all my substance into that fat belly of his.

II.i.72. Mistress Quickly of Falstaff. Hence, the expression 'to eat someone out of house and home', meaning 'to eat so much that the houseowner who has provided the fare for the guest(s) is in a seriously depleted state as a result'. Never said in complete seriousness. Parents might say to their children, 'You would eat us out of house and home you would.' Apparently it was a proverbial expression by the time Shakespeare used it.

7 Shall pack-horses,
And hollow pamper'd jades of Asia,
Which cannot go but thirty miles a day,
Compare with Caesars ...?
Let the welkin roar.

II.iv.160. Pistol. *Compare* MARLOWE 381:2.

8 Uneasy lies the head that wears a crown.

III.i.31. King Henry. Hence, *Uneasy Lies the Head*, title of autobiography (1962) by King Hussein of Jordan.

9 We have heard the chimes at midnight, Master Shallow.

III.ii.209. Falstaff. A film compressing both parts of *Henry IV* (1966) and directed by Orson Welles was entitled *Chimes at Midnight*.

10 Thy wish was father, Harry, to that thought.

IV.v.2. King Henry to Prince Hal who has presumed that his father was dead.

11 *King*: Doth any name particular belong
Unto the lodging where I first did swoon?
Warwick: 'Tis called Jerusalem, my noble lord.
King: Laud be to God! Even there my life must end.
It hath been prophesied to me, many years,
I should not die but in Jerusalem,
Which vainly I suppos'd the Holy Land.
But bear me to that chamber; there I'll lie;
In that Jerusalem shall Harry die.

IV.v.232. *Compare* HENRY IV 292:1.

12 Let me but bear your love, I'll bear your cares.

V.ii.58. Hal in his first speech as King Henry V. The line is placed, unattributed, below the statue of Queen Victoria in Piccadilly, Manchester. Neal Ascherson commented in *The Independent* (1995) on the incongruity, '[Of] the suggestion that this ancient queen, by then a hermit who seldom left her dusty palaces, was still as hungry to be loved as a young princess, still as eager to purchase love with royal sympathy and good works.'

1 Under which king, Besonian? Speak or die!

V.iii.110. Pistol exclaims this to Justice Shallow who has just said he has some special authority under the King. Besonian literally means 'raw recruit', but here means 'ignoramus'.

HENRY V (1599)

2 O, for a Muse of fire, that would ascend
The brightest heaven of invention;
A kingdom for a stage, princes to act
And monarchs to behold the swelling scene! ...
Can this cockpit hold
The vasty fields of France? or may we cram
Within this wooden O the very casques
That did affright the air at Agincourt?

Prologue, l. 1. Chorus speaking, in a notable appeal to the audience of the Elizabethan stage to use its imagination. 'Cockpit' reminds us that theatres like the Globe (which had probably not quite been completed when this play was written) were but a short step from that less enlightened form of entertainment. 'Wooden O' is a straightforward reference to the round shape of the wooden theatre building. Casques = helmets.

3 Nay, sure, he's not in hell: he's in Arthur's bosom, if ever man went to Arthur's bosom.

II.iii.9. The Hostess (formerly Mistress Quickly) is talking of the dead Falstaff. Her malapropism is for *Abraham's* bosom, meaning the place where the dead sleep contentedly. From Luke 16:23: 'And it came to pass, that the beggar died, and was carried by the angels into Abraham's bosom.' The person alluded to is Abraham, the first of the Hebrew patriarchs.

4 A' parted ev'n just between twelve and one, ev'n at the turning o' th' tide: for after I saw him fumble with the sheets and play with flowers and smile upon his fingers' end, I knew there was but one way; for his nose was as sharp as a pen, and a'babbled of green fields.

II.iii.17. The Hostess, continuing to relate the death of Falstaff. One of the most pleasing touches to be found in all of Shakespeare may not have been his at all. The 1623 Folio of Shakespeare's plays renders the last phrase as 'and a Table of green fields', which makes no sense, though some editors put 'as sharp as a pen, on a table of green field' (taking 'green field' to mean green cloth.)

The generally accepted version was inserted by Lewis Theobald in his 1733 edition. As the 1954 Arden edition comments: '"Babbled of green fields" is surely more in character with the Falstaff who quoted the Scriptures ... and who lost his voice hallooing of anthems. Now he is in the valley of the shadow, the "green pasture" of Psalm 23 might well be on his lips.'

Shakespeare may well have handwritten 'babld' and the printer read this as 'table' – a reminder that the text of the plays is far from carved in stone and a prey to mishaps in the printing process as are all books and newspapers.

5 Once more unto the breach, dear friends, once more,
Or close the wall up with our English dead ...
Stiffen the sinews, conjure up the blood ...
I see you stand like greyhounds in the slips,
Straining upon the start. The game's afoot:
Follow your spirit.

III.i.1. King Henry 'before Harfleur'. From this, Sherlock Holmes, in the stories by Sir Arthur Conan Doyle, had a way of saying: 'Come, Watson, come! The game is afoot' – as in 'The Adventure of the Abbey Grange' (1904).

6 Cry 'God for Harry, England, and Saint George!'

III.i.34. King Henry concludes. Hence, *Cry God for Larry*, title of a book (1969) by Virginia Fairweather about Sir Laurence Olivier who notably portrayed King Henry in a 1944 film of the play.

7 Behold, as may unworthiness define,
A little touch of Harry in the night.

Ib., l. 46. Referring to the king's wandering about, disguised, in the English camp on the eve of the Battle of Agincourt. Hence, *A Little Touch of Schmilsson In the Night.* This was the title of a record album (US, 1973) by the singer Nilsson. Nilsson/Schmilsson is a Yiddish reduplication of no great meaning (as in the joke 'Oedipus, Schmoedipus – what does it matter so long as he loves his mother?') Nilsson's first name is 'Harry', which takes us back to the king.

8 'Tis not the balm, the sceptre and the ball,
The sword, the mace, the crown imperial
... That beats upon the high shore of this world.

IV.i.266. King Henry. 'Crown Imperial' was the title given to Sir William Walton's march, which was composed for the Coronation of King George VI in 1936. 'Orb and Sceptre' followed for that of Queen Elizabeth II in 1953. In a television interview, Walton said that if he lived to write a march for a third coronation it would be called 'Sword and Mace'.

Oddly enough, the orchestral parts of 'Crown Imperial' bear a different quotation: 'In beauty bearing the crown imperial' from the poem 'In Honour of the City' by William Dunbar. This is what Walton must have begun with, subsequently discovering the Shakespeare sequence.

1 Old men forget; yet all shall be forgot,
But he'll remember with advantages
What feats he did that day.

IV.iii.49. King Henry. Hence, *Old Men Forget*, title of the memoirs (1953) of Duff Cooper, 1st Viscount Norwich.

2 We few, we happy few, we band of brothers ...
And gentlemen in England now a-bed
Shall think themselves accurs'd they were not here.

IV.iii.60. King Henry before the Battle of Agincourt. Hence, *Gentlemen in England*, title of novel (1985) by A.N. Wilson.

HENRY VI, PART 1 (1591)

3 Henry the Fifth, too famous to live long!

I.i.6. The Duke of Bedford at Henry V's funeral.

HENRY VI, PART 2 (1590–1)

4 Seal up your lips and give no words but mum.

I.ii.89. Hume speaking. Hence, 'mum's the word' meaning 'we are keeping silent on this matter'. No mother is invoked here: 'mum' is just a representation of 'Mmmm', the noise made when lips are sealed. The word 'mumble' obviously derives from the same source.

5 *Commons (Within)*: [i.e., a rabble offstage] An answer from the King, or we will all break in!
King: Go, Salisbury, and tell them all from me,
I thank them for their tender loving care.

III.ii.277. When people use the expression 'tender loving care' nowadays, it is a pretty fair bet that they are not quoting Shakespeare. However, he does use the three words in the same order. In its modern sense, the *OED2* recognizes the phrase as a colloquialism denoting, 'especially solicitous care such as is given by nurses' and cites *The Listener* (12 May 1977): 'It is in a nurse's nature and in her tradition to give the sick what is well called "TLC", "tender loving care", some constant little service to the sick.' But there is a much earlier use of the phrase, in this sense, in the final chapter, 'T.L.C. TREATMENT', of Ian Fleming's novel *Goldfinger* (1959). James Bond says to Pussy Galore, 'All you need is a course of TLC.' 'What's TLC?' she asks. 'Short for Tender Loving Care Treatment,' Bond replies. 'It's what they write on most papers when a waif gets brought in to a children's clinic.' This may point to an American origin. Indeed, a correspondent in the US recalls being told in the 1940s that there was a study done in foundling hospitals where the death rate was very high, which showed that when nurses picked up the babies and cuddled them more frequently, the death rate went down. This led to the prescription, 'TLC *t.i.d.*' (three times a day).

6 The first thing we do, let's kill all the lawyers.

IV.ii.73. Dick the Butcher (one of Jack Cade's rebels).

7 And Adam was a gardener.

IV.ii.128. Cade. After Genesis 2:15 and 3:23. In *Hamlet* (V.i.31), Shakespeare refers to gardening as 'Adam's profession'.

HENRY VI, PART 3 (1590–1)

8 Why, I can smile, and murder whiles I smile.

III.ii.182. Richard, Duke of Gloucester speaking. Incorporated in Laurence Olivier's film of *Richard III* (1955) and also by Ian McKellen in his film of the same (1996) for which the line was used as a promotional slogan on posters, in the form, 'I can smile ... and murder while I smile.'

HENRY VIII (1612)

9 Had I but serv'd my God with half the zeal
I serv'd my king, he would not in mine age
Have left me naked to mine enemies.

III.ii.455. Cardinal Wolsey. *See* WOLSEY 580:5.

JULIUS CAESAR (1599)

10 Beware the ides of March.

I.ii.18. Soothsayer. In the Roman calendar, this was the 15 March. The 'Ides' was also the fifteenth day of May, July and October, and the thirteenth day of all other months.

11 I, as Aeneas, our great ancestor,
Did from the flames of Troy upon his shoulder
The old Anchises bear, so from the waves of Tiber

Did I the tired Caesar.

I.ii.111. Cassius describing how he once rescued Caesar from drowning. According to Greek mythology, Anchises and Aphrodite had a son, Aeneas. The story of Aeneas rescuing his father is told in Virgil's *Aeneid*. Shakespeare also alludes to this incident in *King Henry VI, Part 2* (V.ii.63). In his diary for 15 October 1940, Harold Nicolson is describing what happened when a bomb fell on the Carlton Club in London: 'They saw through the fog the figure of Quintin Hogg escorting old Hailsham [his father, Lord H.] from the ruins, like Aeneas and Anchises' (*Harold Nicolson: Diaries and Letters*, Vols.1–3, ed. Nigel Nicolson, 1966–8).

1 The fault, dear Brutus, is not in our stars,
But in ourselves, that we are underlings.

I.ii.138. Cassius speaking. Hence, *Dear Brutus*, title of a play (1917) by J.M. Barrie.

2 Let me have men about me that are fat,
Sleek-headed men, and such as sleep a-nights.
Yond Cassius has a lean and hungry look;
He thinks too much: such men are dangerous.

I.ii.189. Caesar. Hence, film titles *Such Men Are Dangerous* (US, 1930) and *Such Women Are Dangerous* (US, 1934).

3 For mine own part, it was Greek to me.

I.ii.280. Casca. The apparent origin of the expression 'It's all Greek to me', meaning, 'I don't understand'.

4 Against the Capitol I met a lion,
Who glaz'd upon me, and went surly by.

I.iii.20. Casca. Together with 'A lioness hath whelped in the streets,/And graves have yawn'd and yielded up their dead' (II.ii.17), this probably leads to *A Lion Is In the Streets*, title of film (US, 1953), based on the Huey Long story.

5 Yon grey lines
That fret the clouds are messengers of day.

II.i.103. Cinna. Hence, *Messengers of Day*, the title of Vol.2 (1978) of Anthony Powell's autobiography *To Keep The Ball Rolling*.

6 *Brutus*: Peace! count the clock.
Cassius: The clock hath stricken three.

II.i.192. An anachronism, as mechanical clocks were not invented until the thirteenth century.

7 *Et tu, Brute?* Then fall, Caesar!

III.i.77. Caesar's dying words. *See* CAESAR 140:4.

8 Cry havoc and let slip the dogs of war.

III.i.273. Antony. Hence, the titles of the 1943 US film *Cry Havoc* and Frederick Forsyth's novel *The Dogs of War* (1974; film UK, 1980).

9 Friends, Romans, countrymen, lend me your ears;
I come to bury Caesar, not to praise him.
The evil that men do lives after them,
The good is oft interred with their bones.

III.ii.75. Antony. Hence, *The Evil That Men Do*, title of film (US, 1984).

10 See what a rent the envious Casca made.

III.ii.177. Antony. Hence, *Envious Casca*, title of a crime novel (1941) by Georgette Heyer.

11 This was the most unkindest cut of all.

III.ii.185. Antony. The origin of the expression for a wounding act or piece of behaviour which is especially hurtful because of the person who does it.

12 There is a tide in the affairs of men,
Which, taken at the flood, leads on to fortune;
Omitted, all the voyage of their life
Is bound in shallows and in miseries.

IV.iii.217. Brutus. Hence, *Taken at the Flood*, title of a Hercule Poirot novel (1948) by Agatha Christie (though re-titled *There Is a Tide* in the US). *See* BYRON 139:8.

13 To tell thee thou shalt see me at Philippi.

IV.iii.282. Caesar's ghost to Brutus. From P.G. Wodehouse, *Thank You, Jeeves* (1934): '"We shall meet at Philippi, Jeeves." "Yes, sir." "Or am I thinking of some other spot?" "No, sir, Philippi is correct." "Very good, Jeeves." "Very good, sir".'

14 This was the noblest Roman of them all ...
His life was gentle, and the elements
So mix'd in him, that Nature might stand up
And say to all the world, 'This was a man!'

V.v.68. Antony speaking about Brutus. 'This was a man' is the epitaph on the fictional 'Cassius Hueffer', one of the characters who speaks from beyond the grave in *Spoon River Anthology* (1915) by the American poet, Edgar Lee Masters. 'Hueffer' comments on his gravestone: 'Those who knew me smile/As they read this empty rhetoric/ ... Now that I am dead I must submit to an epitaph/Graven by a fool!'

KING JOHN (1596)

1 Therefore, to be possess'd with double pomp,
To guard a title that was rich before,
To gild refined gold, to paint the lily,
To throw a perfume on the violet,
To smooth the ice, or add another hue
Unto the rainbow, or with taper-light
To seek the beauteous eye of heaven to garnish,
Is wasteful and ridiculous excess.

IV.ii.11. Salisbury speaking. Hence, the expression 'to gild the lily', meaning 'to attempt to improve something that is already attractive and risk spoiling it'. Arden notes that 'to gild gold' was a common expression in Shakespeare's time.

2 This England never did, nor never shall,
Lie at the proud foot of a conqueror,
But when it first did help to wound itself ...
Come the three corners of the world in arms
And we shall shock them! Nought shall make us rue
If England to itself do rest but true!

V.vii.113. Philip the Bastard. Last words of play. Hence, *This England*, title of a book (1969) by Michael Bateman, made up of selections from the *New Statesman* column of that name 1934–1968. *See also* below, 492:14.

KING LEAR (1605)

3 Edmund the base
Shall top th'legitimate – : I grow, I prosper;
Now, gods, stand up for bastards!

I.ii.20. The Bastard Edmund speaking of himself. Hence, *God Stand Up for Bastards*, title of a book (1973) by David Leitch, which is a study of the author's upbringing and the circumstances of his birth.

4 How sharper than a serpent's tooth it is
To have a thankless child!

I.iv.286. Lear. Alluded to in P.G. Wodehouse, *The Inimitable Jeeves*, Chap. 17 (1924): '"I might have known you would muck it up," said young Bingo. Which, considering what I had been through for his sake, struck me as a good bit sharper than a serpent's tooth.'

5 I have seen better faces in my time
Than stands on any shoulder that I see
Before me at this instant.

II.ii.90. Kent. Hence, *Faces in My Time*, the title of Vol. 3 (1980) of Anthony Powell's autobiography *To Keep The Ball Rolling*.

6 I am a man
More sinn'd against than sinning.

III.ii.59. Lear. Hence, the expression meaning 'to be less guilty or responsible than other people who have done wrong' – an example being prostitutes.

7 He that has and a little tiny wit,
With hey, ho, the wind and the rain,
Must make content with his fortunes fit,
Though the rain it raineth every day.

III.ii.74. Fool. *Compare Twelfth Night* at 496:1.

8 Child Rowland to the dark tower came,
His word was still: Fie, foh, and fum,
I smell the blood of a British man.

III.iv.179. Edgar mouthing snatches of verse in his assumed madness. Shakespeare, in turn, was quoting a line from an older ballad (a 'child(e)' was a candidate for knighthood). In certain Scottish ballads of uncertain date, Childe Roland is the son of King Arthur who rescues his sister from a castle to which she has been abducted by fairies. In the *Chanson de Roland* (French, twelfth century) and other tellings of the legend, he is the nephew of Charlemagne. Shakespeare probably combined material from two completely different sources – the first line from a ballad about Roland, the second two from the old story of Jack the Giant-killer.

Later, Shakespeare's use was quoted by Robert Browning in the poem 'Childe Roland to the Dark Tower Came' (1855), which concludes with the lines:

> Dauntless the slug-horn to my lips I set,
> And blew. 'Childe Roland to the Dark Tower came.'

In Thomas Nashe's play *Have with you to Saffron-walden* (1596), there occurs this line: 'O, tis a precious apothegmatical Pedant, who will find matter enough to dilate a whole day of the first invention of *Fy, fa, fum*, I smell the blood of an Englishman' – which just goes to show how well-established is the business of phrase origin finding. Note how it is 'Englishman' rather than 'British man'.

Pearson (1937) has it the line is often misquoted as 'I smell the blood of an Englishman'.

9 *Lear*: We'll go to supper i'th'morning.
Fool: And I'll go to bed at noon.

III.vi.83. The Fool's last words. Hence, *I'll Go To Bed at*

Noon, the title of a book (1944), subtitled 'A Soldier's Letters to His Sons', by the actor Stephen Haggard, published posthumously. Haggard had played the Fool in the 1940 Old Vic production with John Gielgud.

1 Out, vile jelly!

III.vii.81. Cornwall putting out Gloucester's remaining eye.

2 *Gloucester*: Is't not the king?
Lear: Ay, every inch a king.

IV.vi.107. *See below* 491:11.

3 The wheel is come full circle.

V.iii.173. Edmund the Bastard speaking. He is referring to the Wheel of Fortune, being at that moment back down at the bottom where he was before it began to revolve. A modern example of the phrase in use: Chips Channon writes in his diary (13 October 1943): 'I turned on the wireless and heard the official announcement of Italy's declaration of war on Germany. So now the wheel has turned full circle'.

4 Howl, howl, howl! O! you are men of stones ...
She's gone for ever!

V.iii.256. Lear at Cordelia's death.

5 Her voice was ever soft,
Gentle and low, an excellent thing in woman.

V.iii.271. Lear on Cordelia.

6 O! let him pass; he hates him
That would upon the rack of this tough
world
Stretch him out longer.

V.iii.312. Kent. Hence, *The Rack*, the title of a novel (1958) by the English writer A.E. Ellis (Alan Beesley) (d.1971) about the ordeal of a man in a sanatorium. The last page of the novel explains how the title was arrived at: 'He picked up [Benjamin] Haydon's *Journal* and turned to the entry which the latter had made just before killing himself: "22nd. God forgive me. Amen. Finis of B.R. HAYDON. 'Stretch me no more on this rough world' – Lear." Something was grotesquely wrong. He opened his Shakespeare ... "The rack,' he murmured. "Haydon forgot the rack".' (He also changed 'tough' to 'rough'.)

7 The oldest hath borne most: we that are young
Shall never see so much, nor live so long.

V.iii.324. Edgar speaking. Last words of play.

LOVE'S LABOUR'S LOST (1592–3)

8 Berowne is like an envious sneaping frost
That bites the first-born infants of the spring.

I.i.101. King Ferdinand. Hence, probably, *Infants of the Spring*, the title of Vol. I (1976) of Anthony Powell's autobiography *To Keep the Ball Rolling*. Powell does not indicate a source. Perhaps he was thinking rather of *Hamlet* (I.iii.39):

> The canker galls the infants of the spring
> Too oft before their buttons be disclos'd.

9 *Honorificabilitudinitatibus*.

V.i.37. Costard speaking. The longest word in Shakespeare appears to be a schoolmasterly joke, not original to him. The context allows it no meaning, just length, though it has something to do with honourableness. The *OED2* does not list it as a headword, preferring 'honorificabilitudinity' (honourableness). Samuel Johnson noted that it was 'often mentioned as the longest word known'. At twenty-seven letters it was overtaken, in time, by 'antidisestablishmentarianism' with twenty-eight, and by 'floccipaucinihilipilification', with twenty-nine, meaning, 'the action of estimating as worthless', which was first used in 1741, and is the longest word actually in the *OED2*. Scientific words of forty-seven and fifty-two letters have also been invented, but don't really count.

Those seeking to prove that Francis Bacon wrote Shakespeare's plays claimed that the twenty-seven letter word was, in fact, an anagram – '*Hi ludi, F Baconis nati, tuiti orbi*' ('These plays, born of F Bacon, are preserved for the world') – which surely deserves some sort of prize for ingenuity, if nothing else.

MACBETH (1606)

10 What bloody man is that?

I.ii.1. Duncan speaking of a 'bleeding Captain'. Often quoted jokingly as though it was a pejorative comment.

11 If you can look into the seeds of time,
And say which grain will grow, and which
will not,
Speak then to me.

I.iii.58. Banquo is talking to the witches. Demons were said to have the power of predicting which grain would grow and which would not. *The Seeds of Time* was used by John Wyndham as title of a collection of short stories (1969).

12 Come what come may,

Time and the hour runs through the roughest day.

I.iii.148. Macbeth's aside. Hence, *Time and the Hour*, title of a novel (1975) by Faith Baldwin.

1 Nothing in his life
Became him like the leaving it; he died
As one that had been studied in his death,
To throw away the dearest thing he ow'd,
As 'twere a careless trifle.

I.iv.7. Malcolm on the murdered Thane of Cawdor. Sometimes adapted and used figuratively to describe the way a person has relinquished a position with dignity. A cliché by 1900.

2 Yet do I fear thy nature:
It is too full o'th'milk of human kindness,
To catch the nearest way.

I.v.16. Lady Macbeth on compassion. The origin of the phrase 'milk of human kindness'.

3 Letting 'I dare not' wait upon 'I would,'
Like the poor cat i'th adage.

I.vii.44. Lady Macbeth. The proverbial expression referred to is 'The cat would eat fish, and would not wet her feet'. In P.G. Wodehouse's Jeeves stories, this quotation is a source of endless allusion. For example: 'That is the problem that is torturing me, Jeeves. I can't make up my mind. You remember that fellow you've mentioned to me once or twice, who let something wait upon something? You know who I mean – the cat chap' – *The Code of the Woosters* (1938).

4 We fail?
But screw your courage to the sticking-place,
And we'll not fail.

I.vii.60. Lady Macbeth. Alluded to in P.G. Wodehouse, *Joy in the Morning*, Chap. 13 (1974): 'That will give you eight minutes to screw your courage to the sticking-point, one minute to break window and one to make get-away.'

5 This is a sorry sight.

II.ii.20. Macbeth. Hence, the expression 'a sorry sight', meaning 'It is a miserable, sad, pitiable sight'. Apparently a coinage of Shakespeare's.

6 After life's fitful fever he sleeps well.

III.ii.23. Macbeth speaking of the murdered King Duncan. Curiously, this quotation appears on the grave in Warrington Cemetery of George Formby Sr (d.1921), for whom it has a certain relevance. He was a music-hall comedian who invented the Wigan Pier joke and one of his catchphrases was 'Coughin' well tonight' – often tragically true. He had a convulsive cough, the result of a tubercular condition which eventually killed him.

7 But now, I am cabin'd, cribb'd, confin'd, bound in
To saucy doubts and fears.

III.iv.23. Macbeth to the First Murderer – sometimes misrendered as 'Cribbed, cabined and confined'.

8 Double, double toil and trouble:
Fire, burn: and cauldron, bubble.

IV.i.10. All the Witches speaking. Hence, *Double Double Oil and Trouble*, title of a crime novel (1978) by Emma Lathen.

9 By the pricking of my thumbs,
Something wicked this way comes.

IV.i.44. Said by the Second Witch as Macbeth approaches. It was an old superstition that sudden pains in the body were signs that something was about to happen. Hence, *By the Pricking of My Thumbs*, title of a thriller (1968) by Agatha Christie and *Something Wicked This Way Comes*, title of a novel (1962; film US, 1983) by Ray Bradbury.

10 O Hell-kite! – All?
What, all my pretty chickens, and their dam,
At one fell swoop?

IV.iii.219. Macduff, told that his wife and children have all been slaughtered. Hence, 'at one fell swoop' meaning 'at one time, in a single movement'. 'Fell' here means 'fierce' and originally had a 'deadly' connotation. Indeed, the image in the full phrase is of a hawk swooping on its prey. Apparently, a Shakespearean coinage.

11 Out, damned spot! out, I say!

V.i.33. Lady Macbeth. In Thomas Bowdler's *The Family Shakespeare* (1818) – with all those words omitted 'which cannot be read aloud in a family' – this becomes 'Out crimson spot ...'

12 I have liv'd long enough: my way of life
Is fall'n into the sere, the yellow leaf.

V.iii.22. Macbeth. Note how Byron takes up the phrase: 'My days are in the yellow leaf;/The flowers and fruits of love are gone' – 'On This Day I Complete my Thirty-Sixth Year' (1824). He died three months later.

1 To-morrow, and to-morrow, and to-morrow,
Creeps in this petty pace from day to day,
To the last syllable of recorded time;
And all our yesterdays have lighted fools
The way to dusty death. Out, out, brief candle!
Life's but a walking shadow; a poor player,
That struts and frets his hour upon the stage,
And then is heard no more: it is a tale
Told by an idiot, full of sound and fury,
Signifying nothing.

V.v.19. Macbeth speaking. Almost every phrase from this speech seems to have been used as title material. A slight exaggeration, but *Tomorrow and Tomorrow* was a film in 1932; *All Our Yesterdays* was the title of Granada TV's 1960–73 programme devoted to old newsreels and *All My Yesterdays* of the actor Edward G. Robinson's memoirs (1974); *The Way to Dusty Death* was the title of a novel by Alastair Maclean (1973); *Brief Candles* was the title of a novel (1930) by Aldous Huxley; *Told By an Idiot* was a novel by Rose Macaulay (1923); 'full of sound and fury' is echoed in the title of William Faulkner's novel *The Sound and The Fury* (1929).

2 They have tied me to the stake, I cannot fly,
But, bear-like, I must fight the course.

V.vii.1. Macbeth. Compare *King Lear* (III.vii.54) where Gloucester, shortly before his eyes are put out, says: 'I am tied to th'stake, and I must stand the course'.

3 Let fall thy blade on vulnerable crests;
I bear a charmed life.

V.viii.11. Macbeth. Hence, 'a charmed life', an expression for a life in which luck and ease are in full measure. *Charmed Life* is the title of a book by Mary McCarthy (1956). 'Actually, the goaltender led a charmed life. Most of the danger was involved with the fellow who played between point and cover-point.' *Globe and Mail* (Toronto) (16 May 1967).

4 Lay on, Macduff;
And damn'd be he that first cries, 'Hold enough!'

V.viii.33. Macbeth. It would be interesting to know at what stage people started saying '*Lead* on, Macduff' to mean, 'You lead the way, let's get started.' Partridge/*Catch Phrases* has an example from 1912, but it probably started long before then. There has been a change of meaning along the way. Macbeth uses the words 'lay on' as defined by *OED2* as: 'to deal blows with vigour, to make vigorous attack, assail.' The shape of the phrase was clearly so appealing that it was adapted to a different purpose.

MEASURE FOR MEASURE (1604)

5 O cunning enemy, that, to catch a saint,
With saints doth bait thy hook! ...
But this virtuous maid
Subdues me quite. Ever till now
When men were fond, I smil'd and wonder'd how.

II.ii.180. Angelo. *Compare* 'Set a thief to catch a thief' under ANONYMOUS 49:4.

THE MERCHANT OF VENICE (1596)

6 What news on the Rialto?

I.iii.33. Shylock. *See* WODEHOUSE 579:3.

7 The devil can cite Scripture for his purpose.

I.iii.93. Antonio speaking – because Shylock has just been doing so. Hence, the expression meaning that 'an ill-disposed person may turn even good things to his advantage'.

8 All that glisters is not gold,
Often have you heard that told.

II.vii.65. Morocco reading the scroll in the golden casket. Meaning, 'appearances can be deceptive', the proverb was common by Shakespeare's time. *CODP* quotes a Latin version – '*Non omne quod nitet aurum est* [not all that shines is gold]' – and also an English one, in Chaucer. The now obsolete word 'glisters', rather than 'glitters' or 'glistens', was commonly used in the saying from the seventeenth century onwards. In poetic use, Thomas Gray, for example, used 'glisters' in his 'Ode on the Death of A Favourite Cat drowned in a tub of Gold Fishe' (1748).

Pearson (1937) has Spenser, 'Gold all is not that doth golden seem', then Shakespeare, then Middleton 'All is not gold that glisteneth' and Dryden 'All ... that glitters is not gold'.

9 What's here? the portrait of a blinking idiot
Presenting me a schedule!

II.ix.54. Arragon speaking on opening the silver casket. Hence, 'blinking idiot' meaning a very stupid person (with twinkling or half-opened eyes). Apparently an original coinage by Shakespeare.

10 The quality of mercy is not strain'd,
It droppeth as the gentle rain from heaven
Upon the place beneath: it is twice blest,
It blesseth him that gives and him that takes.

IV.i.180. Portia. Origin of the expression 'the quality of mercy (is not strained)'.

1 A Daniel come to judgement! yea, a Daniel!

IV.i.219. Shylock. Alluding to the story of Susannah and the Elders in the Apocrypha. Daniel was a young youth who, by a cunning ploy, saved Susannah from death after she had been condemned to death by the Elders after she had rejected their advances. Hence, the expression 'a Daniel come to judgement' for someone who displays unusual wisdom for their years.

2 The man that hath no music in himself,
Nor is not moved with concord of sweet sounds,
Is fit for treasons, stratagems, and spoils ...
Let no such man be trusted.

V.i.83. Lorenzo. From P.G. Wodehouse, *Thank You, Jeeves* (1934): '"Jeeves," I called down the passage, "What was it Shakespeare said the man hadn't music in himself was fit for?" "Treasons, stratagems, and spoils, sir." "Thank you, Jeeves."'

THE MERRY WIVES OF WINDSOR (1601)

3 We have a nay-word how to know one another: I come to her in white, and cry 'mum'; she cries 'budget'; and by that we know one another.

V.ii.6. Slender's ludicrous planned elopement with Anne Page is to be carried out by their finding each other in the crowd with this exchange of greetings. The Arden Shakespeare adds the gloss: 'An appropriately childish greeting. "Mumbudget" ... was used of an inability or a refusal to speak ...' *OED* conjectures, with convincing citations, that it was "the name of some children's game in which silence was required". Thomas Hardy later uses "to come mumbudgeting" in the sense of "to come secretly".' In Ngaio Marsh's *A Wreath for Riviera* (1949), Inspector Alleyn whispers, 'You cry mum and I'll cry budget' when hiding from a villain.

A MIDSUMMER NIGHT'S DREAM (1594)

4 That which, withering on the virgin thorn,
Grows, lives, and dies, in single blessedness.

I.i.77. Theseus. Hence, *Single Blessedness*, title of a book (1976) by Margaret Adams, about women remaining unmarried.

5 Ay me! for aught that ever I could read,
Could ever hear by tale or history,
The course of true love never did run smooth.

I.i.132. Lysander. Origin of the expression 'the course of true love (never did run smooth)'.

6 Ill met by moonlight, proud Titania.

II.i.60. Oberon. Hence, *Ill Met By Moonlight*, title of a film (UK, 1956, based on a book by W. Stanley Moss) about British agents in Crete during the German occupation. In the US the film was called *Night Ambush*.

7 Lord, what fools these mortals be.

III.ii.115. Puck. *See above* 477:2.

8 I have a reasonable good ear in music. Let's have the tongs and the bones.

IV.i.28. Bottom to Titania, referring to the most primitive of instruments, the tongs and the bones (knackers or clappers, rattled together). When Lord Harewood, the noted opera lover and administrator, wrote his autobiography (1981) he gave it as title, *The Tongs and the Bones* and put the lines as epigraph to the book.

9 I never heard
So musical a discord, such sweet thunder.

IV.i.117. Hippolyta. Hence, *Such Sweet Thunder*, title of Duke Ellington's Shakespeare suite (1956).

10 We do not come, as minding to content you,
Our true intent is. All for your delight,
We are not here ...

V.i.113. When Quince reads the prologue of the play-within-a-play, he mispunctuates it. Hence, 'Our true intent is all for your delight' were the words written over the entrance to the first Butlin's holiday camp to be opened, at Skegness, in 1936. One wonders how many of the campers who passed under it recognized it as a great 'unspoken' line from Shakespeare? It is also a motto that has cropped up on the programmes of countless British repertory theatres.

11 Well roared, Lion!

V.i.254. Demetrius to the Lion in the play. One of two Shakespearean quotations on the memorial plaque to Sir Donald Wolfit (1902–68), last of the actor-managers, in St Paul's Church, Covent Garden, London. The other is 'Is't not the King? Ay, every inch a King' from *King Lear* (488:2).

12 This passion, and the death of a dear friend, would go near to make a man look sad.

V.i.277. Theseus. A forerunner of the modern format 'that and a —— will get you ——', an American expression of the obvious where the object mentioned is clearly of no value: 'That, and a dollar, will get you a cup of coffee', 'That, and a token, will get you on the subway' ...

1 Come, trusty sword,
Come, blade, my breast imbrue!

V.i.330. Thisbe. Lines from the play-within-a-play and thus a consciously archaic use of the phrase 'trusty sword'. Phrase known by 1558; also in Edmund Spenser – 'His trusty sword, the servant of his might' (1596).

See also CLARK 172:6.

MUCH ADO ABOUT NOTHING (1598)

2 *Don Pedro*: You were born in a merry hour ...
Beatrice: A star danced, and under that I was born.

II.i.316. The actress Gertrude Lawrence entitled her autobiography *A Star Danced* (1945).

3 Is it not strange, that sheeps' guts should hale souls out of men's bodies?

II.iii.59. Benedick. Shakespeare got it right. Sheep, horse, ass, but *not* cat intestines are used in the making of strings for musical instruments. The name 'catgut' was possibly introduced as a pejorative way of describing the sound made by badly played violin strings, whatever their actual source.

4 Sigh no more, ladies, sigh no more,
Men were deceivers ever:
One foot in sea, and one on shore,
To one thing constant never.

II.iii.65. Balthasar's song. Hence, *Sigh No More*, title of a revue (1945) by Noël Coward.

5 Comparisons are odorous.

III.v.15. Dogberry. 'Comparisons are odious' had been a established proverbial expression by *c.*1440. *Compare* DONNE 211:6.

OTHELLO (1604)

6 But I will wear my heart upon my sleeve,
For doves to peck at: I am not what I am.

I.i.64. Iago. 'Daws' instead of 'doves' in the First Folio (1623).

7 Put money in thy purse.

I.iii.340. Iago to Rodrigo. Michael MacLiammoir, the Irish actor, took the phrase for a volume of his diaries (1952), recounting the time he spent playing Iago to Orson Welles's Othello, in the 1951 film.

8 To suckle fools and chronicle small beer.

II.i.160. Iago to Desdemona. Small beer = trivialities.

9 Excellent wretch, perdition catch my soul,
But I do love thee, and when I love thee not,
Chaos is come again.

III.iii.91. Othello on Desdemona. Hence, the title of the rock musical *Catch My Soul* (1970), based on the play.

10 O farewell ...
Pride, pomp, and circumstance of glorious war!

III.iii.356. Othello. Hence, 'Pomp and Circumstance', the title of five marches by Sir Edward Elgar (Nos. 1–4 composed 1901–7, and No. 5 in 1930).

11 Nay, we must think
Men are not gods.

III.iv.146. Desdemona. In 1936, a film about an actor playing Othello who nearly strangles his wife was called *Men Are Not Gods*.

12 Here is my journey's end, here is my butt,
And very sea-mark of my utmost sail.

V.ii.268. Othello. *See* SHERRIFF 503:4.

13 Speak of them as they are; nothing extenuate,
Nor set down aught in malice; then must you speak
Of one that lov'd not wisely, but too well.

V.ii.343. Othello. Origin of the saying 'loved not wisely but too well'.

RICHARD II (1595)

14 This royal throne of kings, this scepter'd isle,
This earth of majesty, this seat of Mars,
This other Eden, demi-paradise ...
This happy breed of men, this little world,
This precious stone set in the silver sea ...
This blessed plot, this earth, this realm, this England.

II.i.40. John of Gaunt. Hence, *This England*, title of a film (UK, 1941), known in Scotland as *Our Heritage* [*sic*] – but *see also* above, 487:2; *The Demi-Paradise*, title of a film (UK, 1943), known in the US as *Adventure for Two*. *This Happy Breed*, title of a play (1943; film UK 1944) by Noël Coward. All patriotic flag-wavers (like the speech itself) and designed to promote England in the Second World War.

1 The caterpillars of the commonwealth.

II.iii.165. Bolingbroke. Referring to the conspirators Bushy, Bagot and co. Caterpillars = parasites.

2 O, call back yesterday, bid time return.

III.ii.69. Salisbury. Hence, *Call Back Yesterday*, title of a volume of memoirs (1953) by Hugh Dalton.

3 Let's talk of graves, of worms, and epitaphs.

III.ii.145. King Richard. Hence, *Let's Talk of Graves of Worms and Epitaphs*, title of a crime novel (1975) by Robert Player.

4 For God's sake, let us sit upon the ground
And tell sad stories of the death of kings ...
For within the hollow crown
That rounds the mortal temples of a king
Keeps Death his court.

III.ii.155. King Richard. Hence, *The Hollow Crown*, title of the Royal Shakespeare Company's entertainment (1962) based on Shakespeare's kings and queens.

RICHARD III (1592–3)

5 Now is the winter of our discontent
Made glorious summer by this sun of York ...

I.i.1. Richard speaking. Hence, the title of John Steinbeck's novel *The Winter of Our Discontent* (1961). *See also* THE SUN 523:2.

6 I am not in the giving vein today.

IV.ii.116. Richard to Buckingham. Two lines later he says, 'I am not in the vein'.

7 The king's name is a tower of strength.

V.iii.12. Richard. *See also* TENNYSON 529:4. In the Bible God is often referred to as a 'strong tower'.

8 A horse! a horse! My kingdom for a horse!

V.iv.7/13. Richard's twice-repeated cry in his last desperate moments. The actual Richard III's last words when he met Henry Tudor at the Battle of Bosworth on 23 August 1485 were, 'I will die King of England. I will not budge a foot ... Treason! treason!' That was how it was reported by John Rowe, who presumably picked it up from someone who had actually been at the battle, for he was not. Evidently, Richard then rushed on the future Henry VII and was killed.

Shakespeare's memorable cry may have been inspired by lines in other plays written about the time he wrote his (*c.*1591). The only indication that Richard III might have had a similar concern at the actual battle is contained in the book of Edward Hall's chronicle called 'The tragical doynges of Kyng Richard the thirde' (1548) where it states: 'When the loss of the battle was imminent and apparent, they brought to him a swift and light horse to convey him away.' *See also* MARSTON 382:8.

9 The bloody dog is dead

V.v.2. Richmond. *See* ANONYMOUS 24:4.

See also CIBBER 171:2–3.

ROMEO AND JULIET (1594)

10 The strangers all are gone.

I.v.143. The Nurse. Hence, the title of Vol. 4 (1982) of Anthony Powell's autobiographical sequence *To Keep the Ball Rolling*.

11 O Romeo, Romeo, wherefore art thou Romeo?

II.ii.33. Juliet. In this famous – and famously misunderstood – line, 'wherefore' does not mean 'where'. Juliet is not *looking for* Romeo from her balcony. It means 'for what reason'.

12 What's in a name? That which we call a rose
By any other word would smell as sweet.

II.ii.43. Juliet. There is an implicit comparison here with Romeo as a rose. Hence, 'a rose by any other name', the expression indicating that the name of someone or something is unimportant and that the quality or nature of that person or thing is the important factor.

13 A plague o' both your houses.

III.i.92. Mercutio speaking, wounded. Origin of the curse on all parties in a dispute.

14 Give me my Romeo; and when I shall die,
Take him and cut him out in little stars,
And he will make the face of heaven so fine
That all the world will be in love with night,
And pay no worship to the garish sun.

III.ii.21. Juliet. Some texts have 'he shall die'.

SONNETS (1592–5)

15 To the only begetter of these ensuing sonnets, Mr W.H.

Dedication (1609), inserted by Thomas Thorpe, the publisher. The identity of Mr W.H. is still disputed.

1 Shall I compare thee to a summer's day?
Thou art more lovely and more temperate.
Rough winds do shake the darling buds of May,
And summer's lease hath all too short a date.

Sonnet 18. Hence, the titles of two modern novels. In H.E. Bates, *The Darling Buds of May* (1958), Charlie the tax inspector recites the poem when he is drunkenly pursuing the lovely daughter, Mariette. John Mortimer's *Summer's Lease* (1988) was about the goings-on in a villa rented by English visitors to Tuscany.

2 When, in disgrace with fortune and men's eyes,
I all alone beweep my outcast state.

Sonnet 29. Hence, *Fortune and Men's Eyes*, title of a play (1967) by John Herbert, about homosexuals.

3 Full many a glorious morning have I seen
Flatter the mountain tops with sovereign eye,
Kissing with golden face the meadows green,
Gilding pale streams with heavenly alchemy.

Sonnet 33. From P.G. Wodehouse, *The Code of the Woosters* (1938): 'I remember Jeeves saying to me once, apropos of how you can never tell what the weather's going to do, that full many a glorious morning had he seen flatter the mountain tops with sovereign eye then turn into a rather nasty afternoon.'

4 That time of year thou mayst in me behold
When yellow leaves, or none, or few, do hang
Upon those boughs which shake against the cold,
Bare ruined choirs where late the sweet birds sang.

Sonnet 73. Compare *Lucrece*, l. 871: 'The adder hisses where the sweet birds sing'.

5 From you have I been absent in the spring.

Sonnet 98. Hence, *Absent in the Spring*, title of a thriller (1948), written by Agatha Christie under the name Mary Westmacott.

6 When in the chronicle of wasted time
I see descriptions of the fairest wights.

Sonnet 106. Hence, *Chronicles of Wasted Time*, title of Malcolm Muggeridge's two volumes of autobiography (1972–3).

7 My nature is subdued
To what it works in, like the dyer's hand.

Sonnet 111. Hence, *The Dyer's Hand*, title of a collection of essays and lectures (1962) by W.H. Auden.

8 My mistress' eyes are nothing like the sun.

Sonnet 130. Hence, *Nothing Like the Sun*, title of a novel (1964) by Anthony Burgess, about the life of Shakespeare and of a record album by Sting (1987).

THE TAMING OF THE SHREW (1592–3)

9 And do as adversaries do in law,
Strive mightily, but eat and drink as friends.

I.ii.277. Tranio. The apparent coining of 'striving mightily', a florid expression for great endeavour.

10 Come on, and kiss me Kate.

V.ii.181. Petruchio to Katherina. Hence, *Kiss Me Kate*, title of the Cole Porter musical (1948; film US, 1953) based around a touring company's production of *The Taming of the Shrew*.

THE TEMPEST (1612)

11 The still-vex'd Bermoothes.

I.ii.229. Ariel. Bermoothes = Bermuda.

12 Full fadom five thy father lies;
Of his bones are coral made;
Those are pearls that were his eyes:
Nothing of him that doth fade,
But doth suffer a sea-change
Into something rich and strange.

I.ii.399. Fadom = fathom. When Ariel sings of a sea-change he does actually mean a change caused by the sea. Now, invariably, the expression is used simply as a grandiloquent and irrelevant way of saying 'change'. *Rich and Strange* was the title of a film (UK 1932) by Alfred Hitchcock.

13 Our revels now are ended ...
And, like this insubstantial pageant faded,
Leave not a rack behind. We are such stuff
As dreams are made on; and our little life
Is rounded with a sleep.

IV.i.148. Prospero. It is definitely 'dreams are made on' not 'made of' (though Shakespeare did use the 'of' form elsewhere). So, well done, the writer of the *Guardian* headline (9 May 1988): 'Stuff that dreams are made on' and, rather less well done, Humphrey Bogart as Sam Spade in *The Maltese Falcon* (1941): 'What is it?' he is asked before speaking the last line of the picture, and replies: 'The stuff that dreams are made of.' Absolutely no marks to the cast of the 1964 Cambridge Footlights revue, *Stuff What Dreams Are Made Of.*

1 This rough magic
I here abjure; and, when I have requir'd
Some heavenly music – which even now I do, –
To work mine end upon their senses, that
This airy charm is for, I'll break my staff,
Bury it certain fadoms in the earth,
And, deeper than did ever plummet sound
I'll drown my book.

V.i.49. Prospero. Hence, *This Rough Magic* – title of a 'suspenseful novel about British residents on a Greek island' – (1964) by Mary Stewart.

2 O brave new world,
That has such people in't!

V.i.183. Miranda's exclamation. 'Brave new world' has subsequently become a phrase for a future state, particularly one where progress has produced a nightmarish utopia. Nowadays a slightly ironic term for some new or futuristically exciting aspect of modern life. Aldous Huxley used it as the title of his novel *Brave New World* in 1932.

TROILUS AND CRESSIDA (1601–2)

3 Launch'd above a thousand ships.

II.ii.82. Troilus. *See* MARLOWE 381:5.

4 Time hath, my lord, a wallet at his back
Wherein he puts alms for oblivion.

III.iii.145. Ulysses. Hence, *Alms for Oblivion*, title of a novel sequence (1964–84) by Simon Raven.

TWELFTH NIGHT (1600)

5 If music be the food of love, play on,
Give me excess of it, that, surfeiting,
The appetite may sicken, and so die.

I.i.1. Orsino. Hence, the title of Simon Brett's 'Charles Paris' crime novel, *Sicken and So Die* (1995).

6 O mistress mine, where are you roaming?
... Journeys end in lovers meeting ...
What is love? 'Tis not hereafter,
Present mirth hath present laughter.

II.iii.40. Clown's/Feste's song. Hence, *Present Laughter*, title of play (1942) by Noël Coward.

7 Dost thou think because thou art virtuous, there shall be no more cakes and ale?

II.iii.114. Sir Toby Belch to Malvolio. The Arden Shakespeare comments that cakes and ale were 'traditionally associated with festivity, and disliked by Puritans both on this account and because of their association with weddings, saints' days, and holy days'. In due course, 'cakes and ale' became a synonym for enjoyment, as in the expression 'Life isn't all cakes and ale' (or 'beer and skittles', for that matter).

On 4 May 1876, Francis Kilvert wrote in his diary: 'The clerk's wife brought out some cakes and ale and pressed me to eat and drink. I was to have returned to Llysdinam to luncheon ... but as I wanted to see more of the country and the people I decided to let the train go by, accept the hospitality of my hostess and the cakes and ale which life offered, and walk home quietly in the course of the afternoon' – a neat demonstration of the literal and metaphorical uses of the phrase.

Hence, also, *Cakes and Ale*, the title of a novel (1930) by W. Somerset Maugham.

8 Come away, come away death,
And in sad cypress let me be laid.

II.iv.51. From the Clown's/Feste's song. Probably referring to a coffin made of cypress wood, or a shroud of Cyprus lawn, i.e., linen. Hence, *Sad Cypress* – title of a Hercule Poirot novel (1940) by Agatha Christie.

9 But let concealment, like a worm i'th'bud.
Feed on her damask cheek ...
And with a green and yellow melancholy
She sat like Patience on a monument,
Smiling at grief.

II.iv.112. Viola. Origin of the expression 'like Patience on a monument' for anyone waiting uncomplainingly.

10 But be not afraid of greatness. Some are born great, some achieve greatness, and some have greatness thrust upon 'em.

II.v.144. Malvolio reading from a letter. *Compare* HELLER 289:2.

11 Daylight and champaign discovers not more!

II.v.160. Malvolio, having finished the letter, exclaiming that its meaning is as clear as daylight. Champaign = flat open country (and not the drink). Other texts have the word as 'champain' and 'champian'. Hence, *Daylight and Champain*, title of a collection of essays (1937) by the historian, G.M. Young.

12 There is no darkness but ignorance.

IV.ii.43. Clown/Feste to Malvolio when he is incarcerated. From the *Independent on Sunday* (27 October 1996): 'Words that, like so many of the Bard's dazzlingly plain throwaways, have somehow ricocheted down the centuries and struck quite unexpected targets. If you look at the statue of Shakespeare in Leicester Square, you will find them carved into the scroll that dangles from his stone hand. If you browse through Ezra Pound's *Pisan Cantos* (written when the poet, like Malvolio, was locked up), you will find the same phrase, charged with rancour and nostalgia, used to evoke Edwardian London. You will not, however, find Feste's maxim in Trevor Nunn's screenplay for *Twelfth Night...*'

1 When that I was and a little tiny boy,
With hey, ho, the wind and the rain ...
'Gainst knaves and thieves men shut their gate,
For the rain it raineth every day.

V.i.398. Clown's/Feste's song. *Compare King Lear* at 487:7.

THE TWO GENTLEMEN OF VERONA (1592–3)

2 O, how this spring of love resembleth
The uncertain glory of an April day,
Which now shows all the beauty of the sun,
And by and by a cloud takes all away.

I.iii.84. Proteus. Hence, *Uncertain Glory*, title of a film (US, 1944). *Compare* PYM 443:6.

VENUS AND ADONIS (1592–3)

3 Who see his true-love in her naked bed,
Teaching the sheets a whiter hue than white.

L. 397. The possible origin of 'whiter than white', meaning 'of extreme purity, innocence or virtue'.

THE WINTER'S TALE (1611)

4 Our ship hath touch'd upon
The deserts of Bohemia.

III.iii.1. Antigonus. A supposed geographical error on Shakespeare's part. Bohemia (now part of the Czech Republic) does not have a coast. However, at certain points in history it *did* have an outlet on the Adriatic.

5 *Exit, pursued by a bear.*

III.iii.58. A famous stage direction. It refers to the fate of Antigonus who is on the sea coast of Bohemia (see above). Most of Shakespeare's stage directions are additions by later editors, but this one may be original. The bear used could have been a real one (as bear-baiting was common in places adjacent to Shakespeare's theatres) or portrayed by a man in costume.

6 GOOD FREND FOR IESUS SAKE FORBEARE,
TO DIGG THE DUST ENCLOASED HEARE:
BLESTE BE YE MAN [THA]T SPARES THES STONES,
AND CURST BE HE [THA]T MOVES MY BONES.

Inscription on Shakespeare's grave in Holy Trinity church, Stratford-upon-Avon. According to S. Schoenbaum, *William Shakespeare: A Documentary Life* (1975), several seventeenth century sources suggest that Shakespeare wrote his own epitaph. However, perhaps the point is rather that he may have *chosen* it rather than *composed* it. By the nineteenth century, Halliwell Phillips was curtly dismissing this 'wretched doggerel', but James Walter in *Shakespeare's True Life* (1890) was asking, 'Who dares question the words being those of the great dramatist himself?' Walter seemed to accept that because the words were 'there chiselled when the great one was laid in his grave', they must, therefore, have been written by him.

Hesketh Pearson in his biography argues that Shakespeare chose to phrase his wish simply and clearly, and not in the words of a King Lear, because of a very real fear that his remains would be removed.

7 Item, I give unto my wife my second best bed, with the furniture.

From his will (1616). 'Second best' here means 'next in quality to the first; and need not necessarily suggest that Shakespeare was snubbing his wife with this bequest. Peter Levi, *The Life and Times of William Shakespeare* (1988), has this comment: 'Much crazy speculation has been raised on this small foundation. It is true that most wills provide for widows and this does not, but the reason is obvious. John Hall and Susanna [son-in-law and daughter] were to move into New Place [the Stratford-on-Avon home] and look after Anne Shakespeare as they were uniquely fitted to do. The "second best bed" was William and Anne's old marriage bed. The grander New Place bed in the best bedroom must go to John Hall and Susanna, but William remembered at the last moment to reserve his wife's bed, in which she no doubt habitually slept, for her own.' Garry O'Connor, *William Shakespeare* (1991), adds: 'Anne had asked for this, which otherwise would have gone to Susanna. A correspondent in *The Times* in 1977 suggests that this is roughly similar to a modern testator who, having disposed of the bulk of his estate, turns to his solicitor and says, "And don't forget to leave Anne the mini".'

SHANKLY, Bill

Scottish football manager (1914–81)

1 Some people think football is a matter of life and death. I don't like that attitude. I can assure them it is much more serious than that.

Quoted in *The Guardian*, 'Sports Quotes of the Year' (24 December 1973), but otherwise unverified.

SHANKS, Edward

English poet (1892–1953)

2 O memory, take and keep
All that my eyes, your servants, bring you
home!

These lines appear twice in a poem called 'Memory' by Shanks who edited *Granta* at Cambridge, served in the First World War, wrote novels and criticism and was the first winner of the Hawthornden Prize for Poetry. The full text is in *Poems of Today* (2nd Series), an anthology popular in schools, especially in the 1920s.

SHAW, Bernard

Irish playwright and critic (1856–1950)

3 The funeral march of a fried eel.

On the song, 'The Red Flag'. Quoted in W.S. Churchill, *Great Contemporaries* (1937).

4 The Devil can quote Shakespeare for his own purposes.

Quoted in *The Treasury of Humorous Quotations*, ed. by Evan Esar & Nicolas Bentley (1951). Alluding to SHAKESPEARE 490:7.

5 I often quote myself; it adds spice to my conversation.

Quoted in *ib.* Shaw, with some justification, on a self-quotation habit.

6 England and America are two countries separated by the same language.

Quoted in *ib.* and in *Readers' Digest*, by 1942. *See* WILDE 568:8.

7 A man who never missed an occasion to let slip an opportunity.

Shaw said this of Lord Rosebery presumably in the 1890s when he was briefly Liberal Prime Minister, though it remains untraced. Robert Rhodes James in *Rosebery* (1963) has the slightly different 'man who never missed a chance of missing an opportunity', which, he says, expresses the point of view of 'the political extrovert who turns aside with contempt from hesitation, pusillanimity, and doubt'.

8 Oh, you are a very poor soldier – a chocolate cream soldier!

Arms and the Man, Act 1 (1894). Shaw's play was later turned into a musical known as *The Chocolate Soldier* (New York, 1909 – after the original German *Der Tapfere Soldat* [*Brave Soldier*], 1908). The story concerns Captain Bluntschli, a Swiss officer, who gets the better of a professional cavalry soldier. As shown here, Shaw's phrase for Bluntschli was, rather, 'the chocolate *cream* soldier'. Ian Fleming, the creator of James Bond, was nicknamed the *chocolate sailor* during the Second World War because as a Commander of the RNVR he never actually went to sea.

9 I quite agree with you, sir, but what can two do against so many?

Responding to a solitary boo amongst the mid-act applause at the first performance of *Arms and the Man* (1894). Quoted in St John Irvine, *Bernard Shaw: His Life, Work and Friends* (1956).

10 He who can, does. He who cannot, teaches.

Man and Superman (1903), 'Maxims for Revolutionists' included with published text. A development of this thought was popular as a graffito (reported, for example, from Middlesex Polytechnic in 1979): 'and those who can't teach lecture on the sociology of education degrees.'

Yet a further development is encompassed by A.B. Ramsay in 'Epitaph on a Syndic' from his *Frondes Salicis* (1935):

No teacher I of boys or smaller fry,
No teacher I of teachers, no, not I.
Mine was the distant aim, the longer reach,
To teach men how to teach men how to teach.

11 The golden rule is that there are no golden rules.

Ib. Quoted by G.K. Chesterton in *Heretics* (1905).

12 Wot prawce Selvytion nah [What price salvation now]?

Major Barbara (1907). *See also* STALLINGS 515:7.

1 With the single exception of Homer, there is no eminent writer, not even Sir Walter Scott, whom I can despise so entirely as I despise Shakespear when I measure my mind against his ... It would positively be a relief to me to dig him up and throw stones at him.

Dramatic Opinions and Essays, Vol. 2 (1907). Quoting a view already stated in *The Saturday Review* (1896).

2 Dearest liar: I have found you out.

Letter to Mrs Patrick Campbell (4 January 1913), included in *Bernard Shaw and Mrs Patrick Campbell: Their Correspondence* (1952). Mrs Pat had claimed that Shaw had written critically of her but when he re-read his articles he discovered they were full of praise. Hence, *Dear Liar*, title of a play (1960) by Jerome Kilty, based on the correspondence.

3 *Liza*: My aunt died of influenza: so they said ... But it's my belief (as how) they done the old woman in.

Pygmalion, Act 3 (1914). The words 'as how' were inserted by Mrs Patrick Campbell in her performances as Eliza Doolittle and were also incorporated in the 1938 film.

4 *Freddy*: Are you walking across the Park, Miss Doolittle? If so –
Liza: Walk! Not bloody likely. (*Sensation*). I am going in a taxi.

Ib. Shaw's play is about the conversion of an illiterate, ill-spoken flower girl (Eliza Doolittle) by a professor of phonetics (Henry Higgins). It uses the same theme as part of Tobias Smollett's novel *Peregrine Pickle* (1751) in which Pickle trains a girl and then introduces her into exclusive and elegant circles. From Chap. 95: 'One evening, being at cards with a certain lady, whom she detected in the very fact of unfair conveyance, she taxed her roundly with the fraud, and brought upon herself such a torrent of sarcastic reproof, as overbore all her maxims of caution, and burst open the flood-gates of her own natural repartee, twanged off with the appellations of b—— and w——, which she repeated with great vehemence ... to the terror of her antagonist and the astonishment of all present: nay, to such an unguarded pitch was she provoked, that starting up, she snapt her fingers, in testimony of disdain, and, as she quitted the room, applied her hand to that part which was the last of her that disappeared, inviting the company to kiss it, by one of its coarsest denominations.'

Here, obviously, is the origin of the celebrated tea-party scene in Act III of Shaw's play. Audience anticipation for the first performance in London on Saturday 11 April 1914 had been whipped up by that morning's edition of the *Daily Sketch*: '*PYGMALION* MAY CAUSE SENSATION!! Mr Shaw introduces a certain forbidden word. WILL MRS PATRICK CAMPBELL SPEAK IT? Has the censor stepped in or will the word spread? If he does not forbid it then anything might happen!! It is a word which the *Daily Sketch* cannot possibly print and tonight it is to be uttered on the stage.'

When the phrase was finally uttered, the audience gasped – 'their intake of breath making a sound that could have been mistaken for a protracted hiss,' according to Shaw's biographer, Hesketh Pearson (1942). 'This never happened again because all future audiences knew what was coming and roared with laughter.' Then there was laughter which continued for a minute and a quarter according to the stage manager's stopwatch.

Although the play was well received by the critics, the press rumbled on about the language it used. *The Times* in its review (13 April 1914), said: 'O, greatly daring Mr Shaw! You will be able to boast you are the first modern dramatist to use this word on the stage! But really, was it worth while? There is a whole range of forbidden words in the English language; a little more of your usage and we suppose that they will be heard, too. And then goodbye to the delights of really intimate conversation.'

The *Daily Mirror* sought the view of a number of bishops. Sydney Grundy, theatre critic of the *Daily Mail*, said there was no harm in Shaw's 'incarnadine adverb' when informed by genius but 'on his pen it is poison'. The Theatrical Managers' Association wrote to Sir Herbert Beerbohm Tree, who was presenting the play as well as playing Professor Higgins, saying that a member had complained of the phrase and that 'with a view to retaining the respect of the public for the theatre' they wanted him to omit the words. He declined. A revue opened at the Alhambra shortly afterwards with the title *Not ****** Likely*. In time, the euphemistic alternative 'Not Pygmalion likely!' emerged.

Shaw concluded: 'By making a fashionable actress use bad language in a fashionable theatre, I became overnight more famous than the Pope, the King, the Kaiser and the Archbishop of Canterbury.'

Pygmalion was filmed with Wendy Hiller in 1938, and thus the word 'bloody' was heard for the first time in the cinema. By the time *My Fair Lady* – the musical version – was filmed in 1964, the shock effect of 'bloody' was so mild that Eliza was given the line 'Come on, Dover, move your bloomin' arse!' in the Ascot racing sequence. Which takes us right back to *Peregrine Pickle* ...

1 The rain in Spain stays mainly in the plains.

Ib. 1938 film version only. *See also* LERNER 352:6.

2 In Hampshire, Hereford and Hertford, Hurricanes hardly ever happen.

Ib. Introduced for the film and adopted for *My Fair Lady*.

3 Where the devil are my slippers, Eliza?

Last words (spoken by Higgins) in the 1938 film version (and of the musical adaptation *My Fair Lady* – in the order 'Eliza, where the devil are my slippers?') but not in Shaw's original stage text. The intention appears to be for Higgins to hint at some romantic interest in Eliza. Shaw always opposed this. Even his published text of the film script (1941) shuns the line. And although Higgins ask for his slippers twice during the course of Act IV of the original play, the words are not addressed to Eliza.

4 You see things; and you say 'Why?' But I dream things that never were; and I say 'Why not?'

Back to Methuselah (1921). A saying that has often wrongly been ascribed to both John and Robert Kennedy (because they both used it in numerous political speeches) is, in fact, also from Shaw. In the play, it is spoken by The Serpent, in an attempt to seduce Eve. President Kennedy quoted it correctly (and acknowledged Shaw) in his address to the Irish Parliament in Dublin in June 1963. Robert's version tended to be: 'Some men see things as they are and say "Why?" I dream things that never were and say, "Why not?"' In this form it was attributed to Robert (Shaw going unmentioned) in the address delivered by Edward Kennedy at his brother's funeral in 1968.

So frequently was the saying invoked by Robert Kennedy as a peroration that, on the campaign trail, the words 'As George Bernard Shaw once said ...' became a signal for reporters to dash for the press bus. Once he forgot to conclude with the Shaw quote, according to Arthur M. Schlesinger in *Robert Kennedy and His Times* (1979), and several reporters missed the bus. On another occasion it came on to rain and Kennedy told the crowd: 'It's silly for you to be standing in the rain listening to a politician ... As George Bernard Shaw once said, "Run for the buses".'

5 Nobel Prize money is a lifebelt thrown to a swimmer who has already reached the shore in safety.

Attributed to Shaw, but unverified. Shaw won the Nobel prize for Literature in 1925. Here he is merely paraphrasing Samuel Johnson's pointed remark to Lord Chesterfield. *See* JOHNSON 318:6.

6 All Americans are blind and deaf – and dumb.

A whopping journalistic misquotation dating from the 1930s. Shaw *did* meet Helen Keller, the American writer who heroically overcame deafness and blindness. According to Hesketh Pearson's 1942 biography of Shaw, he rather paid her the compliment: 'I wish all Americans were as blind as you.'

7 What if the child inherits my beauty and your brains?

There may be some truth in the story that Shaw was once approached by a woman who thought herself to be a fine physical specimen and suggested that they combine to make a baby, saying: 'You have the greatest brain in the world and I have the most beautiful body; so we ought to produce the most perfect child.' His reply: 'Yes, but fancy if it were born with my beauty and your brains?'

Alas, this was not said to Isadora Duncan or any of the other women who have been woven into the tale. Hesketh Pearson in *Bernard Shaw* (1942) said the request came from 'a woman in Zurich', though no trace of a letter containing it has ever been found.

8 *G.K. Chesterton*: To see you, Mr Shaw, one would think there was a famine in the land. *G.B. Shaw*: And looking at you, Mr Chesterton, one would know who to blame.

This celebrated fat man/thin man exchange was the subject of a letter to *The Guardian* from a Mr Robert Turpin of Plymouth (14 May 1985): 'I first heard the story from a great-uncle of mine who knew both Shaw and Chesterton and actually attended the meeting at which the exchange took place.' (If so, the great-uncle was privileged to be one of those rare people to have been present at the cracking of an immortal joke.)

Caution immediately sets in, however – especially as the paper also carried a letter from Peter Black, the journalist, saying he had first encountered the story in Australia involving the portly Prime Minister, Sir Robert Menzies. The *PDMQ* (1980) meanwhile, had cast Lord Northcliffe, the well-built press baron, in the Chesterton role.

The most reliable version must surely be that which appears in *Thirty Years With GBS* (1951) by Blanche Patch, Shaw's secretary: 'One look at you, Mr Shaw, and I know there's famine in the land.' 'One look at you, *Mr Hitchcock*, and I know who caused it.' This was, of course, Alfred Hitchcock, the film director.

1 The trouble, Mr Goldwyn, is that you are only interested in art and I am only interested in money.

Telegraphed version of the outcome of a conversation between Shaw and the film producer Sam Goldwyn. It appears to have been recounted first in Alva Johnson, *The Great Goldwyn* (1937). It has been said that this witticism was, in fact, the creation of Howard Dietz but that Shaw approved it.

2 A perpendicular expression of a horizontal desire.

On dancing. Quoted in the *New Statesman* (23 March 1962).

3 Youth is too precious/important to be wasted on the young.

Attributed in Copeland, *10,000 Jokes, Toasts, & Stories* (1939) in the form '[Youth is] far too good to waste on children'. *The Treasury of Humorous Quotations* (ed. by Evan Esar & Nicolas Bentley, 1951) has it from Shaw in the form, 'Youth is a wonderful thing; what a crime to waste it on children.' But where is it to be found in all of Shaw?

In the film *It's a Wonderful Life* (US, 1946), a proverbial-sounding line is uttered: 'Youth is wasted on the wrong people'. Later, in Sammy Cahn's lyrics for the song 'The Second Time Around' (1960; music by Jimmy Van Heusen) there is what is presumably no more than a quotation:

> It's that second time you hear your love song sung,
> Makes you think perhaps, that
> Love like youth is wasted on the young.

4 The question of who are the best people to take charge of children is a very difficult one; but it is quite certain that the parents are the very worst.

Everybody's Political What's What? (1944). In fact, Shaw is quoting William Morris, the designer. *Compare* BELL 81:9.

5 We don't stop playing because we grow old, we grow old because we stop playing.

Unverified. Quoted in *The Independent* (29 October 1996). Another version: 'People do not cease to play because they grow old, people grow old because they cease to play' – promotional material for book, *Serious Play: A Leisure Wellness Guidebook* (1994) by Martin Kimeldorf.

6 A dramatic critic ... is a man who leaves no turn unstoned.

Attributed in *The New York Times* (5 November 1950). Hence, *No Turn Unstoned* (1982), title of a book of 'the worst ever theatrical reviews' compiled by Diana Rigg. However, she ascribes it to the Rev. Joseph McCulloch in the form, 'A critic is a man who leaves no turn unstoned.'

See also CAMPBELL 144:3–4; FRASER 245:4; LENIN 349:7; WILDE 570:9.

SHAWCROSS, Sir Hartley (later Lord Shawcross)

English jurist and Labour politician (1902–)

7 We are the masters now!

It might have seemed in poor taste for a Labour minister to crow this. After all, it had been into the mouth of an imperialist that George Orwell had earlier put these words in his novel *Burmese Days* (1934): 'No natives in this Club! It's by constantly giving way over small things like that that we've ruined the Empire ... The only possible policy is to treat 'em like the dirt they are ... We've got to hang together and say, "We are the masters, and you beggars ... keep your place".'

So quite why Shawcross, Attorney-General in Britain's first post-war Labour government, did say something like it bears some examination. For a start, it was not said, as one might expect, on the day new Labour MPs swarmed into the House of Commons just after their sweeping election victory in 1945. It was said on 2 April 1946, almost nine months later. Then again, what Shawcross said was, 'We are the masters at the moment' – though understandably the more pungent variant has passed into the language. A look at *Hansard* reveals precisely why he chose this form of words. He was winding up for the government in the third reading of the Trade Disputes and Trade Unions Bill and drew attention to what he saw as the Conservative Opposition's lack of support for a measure it had promised to introduce if it won the election:

> [We made this an issue at the election] when he invited us to submit this matter to the verdict of the people ... I realise that the right hon. Member for Woodford [Winston Churchill] is such a master of the English language that he has put himself very much in the position of Humpty-Dumpty in *Alice* ... 'When I use a word,' said Humpty-Dumpty, 'it means just what I intend it to mean, and neither more nor less.' 'But,' said Alice, 'the question is whether you can make a word mean different things.' 'Not so,' said Humpty-Dumpty, 'the question is which is to be the master. That's all.'
>
> We are the masters at the moment, and not only at the moment, but for a very long time to come, and as hon. Members opposite are not prepared to implement the pledge which was given by their

leader in regard to this matter at the General Election, we are going to implement it for them.

At the end of the debate, the votes cast were: Ayes 349; Noes 182. When the House met again after the 1950 General Election – at which the Conservatives just failed to oust Labour – Churchill commented: 'I like the appearance of these benches better than what we had to look at during the last four and a half years. It is certainly refreshing to feel, at any rate, that this is a Parliament where half the nation will not be able to ride rough-shod over the other half ... I do not see the Attorney-General in his place, but no one will be able to boast "We are the masters now".'

So, by this time, the popular version of the words had already emerged. *Compare* BURKE 131:1.

SHAW-LEFEVRE, Charles (Viscount Eversley)

English lawyer and politician (1794–1888)

1 What is that fat gentleman in such a passion about?

As a child, on hearing Charles James Fox speak in the House of Commons. Quoted in G.W.E. Russell, *Collections and Recollections* (1898). *Compare* PUNCH 442:2.

SHELLEY, Percy Bysshe

English poet (1792–1822)

2 The winds of heaven mix for ever
With a sweet emotion.

'Love's Philosophy' (written 1819). The phrase 'wind(s) of heaven' might seem to suggest the movements and changes in our lives, as directed by heaven, but it may simply be poetic usage for 'winds' rather than religious. From George Eliot, *Silas Marner* (1861): 'Life ... when it is spread over a various surface, and breathed on variously by the multitudinous currents from the winds of heaven to the thoughts of men.' Eliot is also quoted as having said in 1840: 'O how luxuriously joyous to have the wind of heaven blow on one after being stived in a human atmosphere.' *The Wind of Heaven* was a drama by Emlyn Williams, first performed in 1945.

3 Hail to thee, blithe spirit!
Bird thou never wert.

'To a Skylark' (1819). Hence, *Blithe Spirit*, title of Noël Coward's comedy (1941; film, UK 1945) about a spiritualist.

4 Many a green isle needs must be
In the deep wide sea of misery,
Or the mariner, worn and wan,
Never thus could voyage on.

'Lines Written in the Euganean Hills' (1818). Palgrave's notes to *The Golden Treasury* delicately put it: 'The leading idea of this beautiful description of a day's landscape in Italy is expressed with *an obscurity not infrequent with its author*' (my italics). 'It appears to be, – On the voyage of life are many moments of pleasure, given by the sight of Nature, who has power to heal even the worldliness and the uncharity of man.'

5 If winter comes, can spring be far behind?

'Ode to the West Wind' (1819). Hence, *If Winter Comes*, title of a film (US, 1948) based on a novel by A.S.M. Hutchinson.

6 And yours I see is coming down.

The Cenci, V.iv.162 (1819). In fact, referring to hair.

7 I met murder on the way
He had a mask like Castlereagh ...

'The Mask of Anarchy', St. 2 (1819). *See* BYRON 139:10.

8 O world! o life! o time!
On whose last steps I climb,
Trembling at that where I had stood before;
When will return the glory of your prime?
No more – Oh, never more!

'A Lament' (1821). Thomas Hardy thought this one of the finest passages in all English poetry.

9 The cemetery is an open space among the ruins, covered in winter with violets and daisies. It might make one in love with death, to think that one should be buried in so sweet a place.

On Keats's burial place in the English cemetery in Rome. Preface to *Adonais* (1821), his elegy on the death of Keats. Shelley's own remains were to be buried there, in due course, not far away from his fellow poet's.

10 I weep for Adonais – he is dead!
O, weep for Adonais! though our tears
Thaw not the frost which binds so dear a head ...
Peace, peace! He is not dead, he doth not
sleep –
He hath awakened from the dream of life.

Ib. Famously quoted by Mick Jagger of the Rolling Stones at a concert in Hyde Park, London, following the death of his colleague, Brian Jones (July 1969).

SHERIDAN, Philip Henry

American general (1831–88)

1 The only good Indian is a dead Indian.

Sheridan, mostly a cavalry commander on the Federal side in the American Civil War, is supposed to have said this at Fort Cobb in January 1869, but exhaustive study by Wolfgang Mieder (in *The Journal of American Folklore*, No. 106; 1993) has shown that this particular racial slur may already have been proverbial and have been wished on Sheridan unjustly. For example, the previous year, during a debate on an 'Indian Appropriation Bill' in the House of Representatives (28 May 1868), James Michael Cavanaugh (1823–79), a congressman from Montana, had said: 'I will say that I like an Indian better dead than living. I have never in my life seen a good Indian (and I have seen thousands) except when I have seen a dead Indian.'

Mieder adds that, though Sheridan was known as a bigot and Indian hater, Charles Nordstrom's account of the Fort Cobb incident in 1869 is of questionable authenticity: 'A chief of the Comanches, on being presented to Sheridan, desired to impress the General in his favor, and striking himself a resounding blow on the breast, he managed to say: "Me, Toch-a-way; me good Injun." A quizzical smile lit up the General's face as he set those standing by in a roar by saying: "The only good Indians I ever saw were dead".'

Sheridan repeatedly denied having made any such a statement, but, whatever the case, an imperishable formula had been devised: 'The only good X is a dead X' is still with us.

SHERIDAN, Richard Brinsley

English dramatist and politician (1751–1816)

2 I was struck all of a heap.

The Duenna, Act 2, Sc. 2 (1775). Not, in fact, an original phrase for 'astounded'. 'Struck of a heap' was current by 1741 and Shakespeare has 'all on a heap'.

3 Behold thy votaries submissive beg,
That thou will deign to grant them all they ask;
Assist them to accomplish all their ends,
And sanctify whatever means they use
To gain them!

The Critic, Act 2 Sc. 2 (1779). A prayer from the play within the play.

4 Burghley's nod.

Nothing to do with the actual Burghley. Within Sheridan's play *The Critic* (1779) is a mock-tragedy on the Spanish Armada. In Act 3 Sc. 1, Burghley is represented as too preoccupied with affairs of state to be able to say anything, so he shakes his head and the character Puff explains what he means: 'Why by that shake of the head, he gave you to understand that even though they had more justice in their cause and wisdom in their measures – yet, if there was not a greater spirit shown on the part of the people – the country would at last fall a sacrifice to the hostile ambition of the Spanish monarchy ...' 'The devil! – did he mean all that by shaking his head?' 'Every word of it – if he shook his head as I taught him.'

Hence, also, the expression, 'To be as significant as the shake of Lord Burghley's head.'

5 He is the very pineapple of politeness!

The Rivals, Act 3, Sc. 3 (1775). Mrs Malaprop speaking – after whom 'malapropisms' are called. 'Her select words [are] so ingeniously *misapplied*, without being *mispronounced*' (Act 2, Sc. 2). She was not the first character to have such an entertaining affliction: Shakespeare's Dogberry and Mistress Quickly are similarly troubled. After the French phrase *mal à propos* ('awkward, inopportune'). In this instance, she is attempting to say 'the very pinnacle of politeness' (but *see* GOLDSMITH 267:4).

6 If I reprehend any thing in this world, it is the use of my oracular tongue, and a nice derangement of epitaphs!

Ib. Hence, *A Nice Derangement of Epitaphs*, title of a novel (1988) by Ellis Peters, about a medieval monk detective, Father Cadfael.

7 A man may surely be allowed to take a glass of wine by his own fireside.

On being found drinking a glass of wine in the street, when watching the Drury Lane Theatre, which he owned, burning down (24 February 1809). Reported in T. Moore, *Life of Sheridan* (1825).

8 The Right Honourable Gentleman is indebted to his memory for his jests, and to his imagination for his facts.

Replying to Mr Dundas in the House of Commons. Quoted in Moore, *op. cit.*

SHERMAN, William T.

American general (1820–91)

1 Hold the fort, for I am coming.

The phrase 'hold the fort' has two meanings: 'Look after this place while I'm away' and 'Hang on, relief is at hand'. In the second sense, there is a specific origin. In the American Civil War, General Sherman signalled words to this effect to General John M. Corse at the Battle of Allatoona, Georgia (5 October 1864). What he actually semaphored from Keneshaw Mountain was: 'Sherman says hold fast. We are coming' (Mencken, 1942) or 'Hold out. Relief is coming' (Bartlett, 1980).

The phrase became popularized in its present form as the first line of a hymn or gospel song written by Philip Paul Bliss *c.*1870 ('Ho, My Comrades, See the Signal!' in *The Charm*). This was introduced to Britain by Moody and Sankey during their evangelical tour of 1873 (and not written by them, as is sometimes supposed):

'Hold the fort, for I am coming,'
  Jesus signals still;
Wave the answer back to heaven,
  'By thy grace we will.'

More recently, perhaps thanks to a pun on 'union' (as in the American 'Union' and as in 'trade union'), the song has been adapted as a trade union song in Britain:

Hold the fort, for we are coming
Union men be strong
Side by side keep pressing onward.
Victory will come.

2 War is hell.

All he may actually have said in a speech at Columbus, Ohio (11 August 1880) was: 'There is many a boy here today who looks on war as all glory, but, boys, it is all hell.'

3 I will not accept if nominated, and will not serve if elected.

Message to the Republican national Convention in 1884, sent by telegraph to General Henderson when Sherman was being urged to stand as the Republican candidate for the presidency. This version was recalled by Sherman's son in an addendum to his father's *Memoirs* (4th edition, 1891). Perhaps most usually rendered in the form: 'If nominated, I will not run. If elected, I will not serve.' Sometimes, the message is extended to: 'If asked I will not stand. If drafted I will not run. If elected I will not serve.'

SHERRIFF, R.C.

English playwright (1896–1975)

4 Journey's End.

The title of Sherriff's play (1929), set in the trenches of the First World War, might seem to nod towards Shakespeare – 'Journeys end in lovers meeting' (*Twelfth Night*, II.iii.44) or 'Here is my journey's end' (*Othello*, V.ii.268) – or towards Dryden, 'The world's an inn, and death the journey's end' ('Palamon and Arcite'). But it is impossible to be certain. In his autobiography, *No Leading Lady* (1968), Sherriff wrote of the titles he rejected, like 'Suspense' and 'Waiting', and then adds: 'One night I was reading a book in bed. I got to a chapter that closed with the words: "It was late in the evening when we came at last to our Journey's End". The last two words sprang out as the ones I was looking for. Next night I typed them on a front page for the play, and the thing was done.' He does not say what the book was.

SHUBERT, Lee

American impresario (1875–1953)

5 Audiences don't like plays where people write letters with feathers.

On costume drama. Unverified. Also ascribed to Max Gordon, Broadway producer, and to a Missouri cinema owner about costume epics, mid-1930s.

SHULTZ, George

American Republican politician (1920–)

6 Don't just do something, stand there.

Objecting to government meddling, as Labor Secretary, in a speech (1970), quoted in Safire (1978).

See also LEE 348:3.

SIBELIUS, Jean

Finnish composer (1865–1957)

7 Pay no attention to what the critics say. No statue has ever been put up to a critic.

Remark, attributed by 1937. Quoted in Bengt de Törne, *Sibelius: A Close-Up* (1937).

SICKERT, Walter

German-born English painter (1860–1942)

1 Come again when you can't stay so long.

As a young man, Denton Welch paid a visit to Sickert and later wrote a description of the oddities he had encountered. The great man persecuted and terrified him and, during tea, danced in front of him wearing boots such as deep sea divers wear ... 'to see how Denton would react to the experience' (in Edith Sitwell's phrase). As Welch left the house, Sickert said the above to him. Welch's 'Sickert at St Peter's' appeared in *Horizon*, Vol. 6, No. 32 (1942). In *Taken Care of* (1965), Edith Sitwell comments on the article but gives the tag as 'Come again – when you have a little less time'. Either way, this farewell was not originated by Sickert. Indeed, Welch ends his article by saying, 'And at these words a strange pang went through me, for it was what my father had always said as he closed the book, when I had finished my bread and butter and milk, and it was time for bed'.

SIDNEY, Sir Philip

English soldier and poet (1554–86)

2 Thy necessity is yet greater than mine.

Wounded at the Battle of Zutphen (1586), Sidney was 'thirsty with excess of bleeding' and called for something to drink. As he was putting the bottle to his lips, he saw a wounded soldier who eyed it enviously. 'Which Sir Philip perceiving, took the bottle from his head, before he drank, and delivered it to the poor man with these words' – a story reported by Fulke Greville, Lord Brooke, *Life of Sir Philip Sidney* (1652).

3 A tale which holdeth children from play, and old men from the chimney corner.

One of the quotations used to promote the Everyman's Library series of classic reprints. It is from *The Defense of Poetry* (1595): 'With a tale forsooth he [the poet] cometh unto you, with a tale which ...' *Compare* ANONYMOUS 29:2 and MILTON 393:4.

SIEYÈS, Emmanuel Joseph

French prelate and revolutionary leader (1748–1836)

4 *J'ai vécu.*
I lived [= survived].

When the Abbé Sieyès, who played an important part in the French Revolution and then lapsed into 'philosophic silence', was asked *c.*1795 what he had done during the Reign of Terror, this was his reply. Recorded by 1836.

SIGNORET, Simone

French film actress (1921–85)

5 Nostalgia Isn't What It Used To Be.

Title of autobiography (1978). From a graffito chalked up on a wall in New York City. As 'Nostalgia ain't what it used to be', the remark has been attributed to the American novelist Peter de Vries.

SIMENON, Georges

Belgian novelist (1903–89)

6 I have made love to ten thousand women.

Simenon's best known remark arose parenthetically in an interview *he* was conducting with an old friend, Federico Fellini, to publicize the latter's new film *Casanova*. Not in a calculated, premeditated or publicity seeking way, he suddenly said: 'You know, Fellini, I think that in my life I have been even more of a Casanova than you. I did the sum a year or two ago and since the age of 13 and a half I have had 10,000 women. It was not at all a vice, I suffer from no sexual vice, but I have a need to communicate. And even the 8,000 prostitutes who must be included in this total of 10,000 women were human beings, female human beings.' The interview was published in *L'Express* (21 February 1977) and the claim attracted worldwide publicity. Later, his second wife Denyse said: 'The true figure is no more than twelve hundred' (*The Sunday Times*, 20 February 1983). Patrick Marnham in *The Man Who Wasn't Maigret* (1992) calls this 'Simenon's last publicity coup ... and in some ways his greatest coup of all'.

SIMON, Carly

American singer and songwriter (1945–)

7 You're so vain, you probably think this song is about you.

Song, 'You're So Vain' (1972). It is usually assumed that the subject of the song was, in fact, the film actor Warren Beatty.

SIMON, Guy

English writer (1944–)

1 Jimmy Carter had the air of a man who had never taken any decisions in his life. They had always taken him.

In *The Sunday Times* (5 June 1978). Compare from A.A. Milne, *The House at Pooh Corner*, Chap. 9 (1928): '[Pooh speaking] Because Poetry and Hums aren't things which you get, they're things which get *you*. And all you can do is to go where they can find you'; a letter (4 April 1864) from Abraham Lincoln to A.G. Hodges: 'I claim not to have controlled events, but confess plainly that events have controlled me.'

SIMON, Paul

American singer and songwriter (1942–)

2 The mother and child reunion is only a motion away.

Song, 'Mother and Child Reunion' (1972). Professor Simon Frith of the University of Strathclyde confidently stated in *The Independent* (22 January 1993) that this was a reference to abortion. Lesley Bennett responded the following day: 'Paul Simon told me (in 1968 or 1969) that "Mother and Child Reunion" was the name of a dish he had eaten in Chinatown in San Francisco. The dish was a combination of chicken with egg; the reunion, presumably, happened when they were eaten and digested together.'

SIMONIDES

Greek poet (c.556–468BC)

3 Go, tell the Spartans, thou who passest by,
That here obedient to their laws we lie.

Quoted in Herodotus, *Histories*, Bk 7. Hence, *Go Tell the Spartans*, title of film (US, 1978). *See also* RAYMOND 447:4.

SIMS, George R.

English journalist and playwright (1847–1922)

4 It is Christmas Day in the Workhouse.
And the cold bare walls are bright
With garlands of green and holly,
And the place is a pleasant sight.

The poem 'In the Workhouse – Christmas Day' (1879) became a popular late-Victorian recitation. It tells of a pauper rising up to challenge the 'guardians' who have come to watch the Christmas feast. He chides them for turning away a dying woman the previous year – his wife. Nowadays it is probably better known as the result of several parodies. One from the First World War (and included in the stage show *Oh What a Lovely War*, 1963) goes:

It was Christmas day in the cookhouse,
The happiest day of the year,
Men's hearts were full of gladness
And their bellies full of beer,
When up spoke Private Shorthouse,
His face as bold as brass,
Saying, 'We don't want your Christmas pudding
You can stick it up your ...'

Tidings of comfort and joy, comfort and joy,
Oh, tidings of comfort and joy!

Hence, the further version performed by the music-hall comedian, Billy Bennett (d.1942).

It was Christmas Day in the cookhouse.
The troops had all gone to bed.
None of them had any Christmas pudding
'Cause the sergeant had done what they said.

SITWELL, Edith (later Dame Edith)

English poet (1887–1964)

5 I do not want Miss Mannin's feelings to be hurt by the fact that I have never heard of her ... At the moment I am debarred from the pleasure of putting her in her place by the fact that she has not got one.

On novelist Ethel Mannin. Quoted in John Pearson, *Façades* (1978). Used by Sitwell subsequently about various other targets.

6 I enjoyed talking to her, but thought *nothing* of her writing. I considered her 'a beautiful little knitter'.

On Virginia Woolf. Letter to G. Singleton (11 July 1955).

SITWELL, Sir Osbert

English writer (1892–1969)

7 Great Morning.

The title of one of his volumes of memoirs (1947) may derive from foxhunting. Compare Shakespeare, *Troilus and Cressida* (IV.iii.1): 'It is great morning; and the hour prefix'd/For her delivery to this valiant Greek'; and *Cymbeline* (IV.ii.61): 'It is great morning' – in both of which cases, the meaning is 'broad daylight'. Compare also the title of J.B. Priestley's 1946 novel, *Bright Day*.

SKELTON, Noel

British Conservative politician (1880–1935)

1 To state as clearly as may be what means lie ready to develop a property-owning democracy, to bring the industrial and economic status of the wage-earner abreast of his political and educational, to make democracy stable and four-square.

Article in *The Spectator* (19 May 1923), printed in *Constructive Conservatism* (1924). The phrase 'property-owning democracy' was later popularized by Anthony Eden (at Conservative Conference, Blackpool, 3 October 1946) and Winston Churchill (5 October 1946) and came to be associated with them, though Skelton undoubtedly coined the phrase.

SMART, Christopher

English poet (1722–71)

2 He *walks* as if he had fouled his small-clothes, and *looks* as if he smelt it.

Said about Thomas Gray, the poet. Quoted in Christopher Devlin, *Poor Kit Smart* (1961) from *Facetiae Cantabrigienses*, which appears to have been some kind of nineteenth-century Cambridge University rag.

SMITH, Alexander

Scottish poet and essayist (1830–67)

3 Summer has leapt upon Edinburgh like a tiger.

A Summer in Skye (1865). Described by Sir Harold Hobson as, 'the perfect opening sentence'.

SMITH, Alfred E.

American politician (1873–1944)

4 Nobody shoots at Santa Claus.

In American politics, this is sometimes said about the folly of attacking government benefit programmes. Former Governor Smith said in 1933: 'No sane local official who has hung up an empty stocking over the municipal fireplace is going to shoot Santa Claus just before a hard Christmas.' Later Santa Claus came to represent the free lunch, the government handout, the something-for-nothing – and again, any politician had to take his courage in both hands to knock it.

5 UNPACK.

The *ODQ* (1992) has this as a telegraph message in 1932 to the Pope whom Smith had hoped would come to live in the United States, in the event of Smith's campaign for the presidency proving successful. Rather it was a joke told *about* Smith, as in the form, 'What did Al Smith telegraph to the Pope after he lost the election?' 'Unpack.' As Smith stood for the Presidency in 1928 (and lost to Herbert Hoover), it seems that this joke took a little time to emerge.

6 No matter how thin you slice it, it's still baloney.

Said by Smith about Roosevelt's New Deal during campaign speeches in 1936. Roosevelt had supported him in 1928 but they fell out when Roosevelt himself ran for the presidency. The *PDMQ* (1980), on the other hand, has Brendan Gill, *Here at the New Yorker* (1975), ascribing the remark to Rube Goldberg.

7 The kiss of death.

On William Randolph Hearst's support for Governor Al Smith's opponent, Ogden Mills. Safire (1978) defines the political use of the phrase as 'unwelcome support from an unpopular source, occasionally engineered by the opposition'. The 'kiss of death' derives from the kiss of betrayal given by Judas to Christ which foreshadowed the latter's death. In the Mafia, too, a kiss from the boss is an indication that your time is up. Compare *Kiss of Death*, the title of a gangster film (US, 1947).

In Britain, Winston Churchill used the phrase in the House of Commons on 16 November 1948. Nationalization and all its methods were a 'murderous theme'; the remarks of Government spokesman about the control of raw materials, 'about as refreshing to the minor firms as the kiss of death'.

See also ROOSEVELT 459:3.

SMITH, Bessie

American blues singer (1894–1937)

8 Any Woman's Blues.

Title of a song (*c.*1929). Hence, title of a novel (1990) by Erica Jong.

SMITH, Cyril (later Sir Cyril)

British Liberal politician (1928–)

1 If the fence is strong enough I'll sit on it.

Quoted in *The Observer* (15 September 1974). Member of Parliament for Rochdale (1972–92), 'Big Cyril' weighed something like twenty-five stones.

SMITH, Dodie

English novelist and playwright (1896–1990)

2 The family – that dear octopus from whose tentacles we never quite escape.

Play, *Dear Octopus* (1938) – explaining the title.

SMITH, Edward

English sea captain (d.1912)

3 Be British, boys, be British.

Smith's reputed last words were said to his crew some time in the hours between the *Titanic* hitting the iceberg and his going down with the ship. Michael Davie in *The Titanic: the full story of the tragedy* (1986) describes the evidence for this as 'flimsy', but obviously the legend was well established by 1914 when the statue to him in Lichfield was erected. It has 'Be British' as part of the inscription. *See also* WRIGHT 584:6.

SMITH, F.E. (1st Earl of Birkenhead)

British Conservative politician and lawyer (1872–1930)

4 *Judge*: You are extremely offensive, young man. *Smith*: As a matter of fact, we both are, and the only difference between us is that I am trying to be, and you can't help it.

In 2nd Earl of Birkenhead, *The Earl of Birkenhead* (1933). One can hardly believe that Smith really said some of the things he is supposed to have said to judges. If there is any truth in this story – as in the two following – one suspects it was polished up by Smith himself in the re-telling.

5 Possibly not, My Lord, but far better informed.

To judge who complained that he was no wiser at the end than when he had started hearing one of Smith's cases. Quoted in *ib.*

6 *Judge*: What do you suppose I am on the bench for, Mr Smith?
Smith: It is not for me, your honour, to attempt to fathom the inscrutable workings of Providence.

Quoted in Winston Churchill, *Great Contemporaries* (1937).

7 Mr George Robey is the Darling of the music-halls, m'lud.

To Mr Justice Darling who had asked, as judges do, who George Robey the comedian was. Quoted in A.E. Wilson, *The Prime Minister of Mirth* (1956).

8 Try taking a couple of aspirates.

When J.H. Thomas, the Labour MP, complained he ''ad a 'eadache'. Quoted in John Campbell, *F.E. Smith, First Earl of Birkenhead* (1983) in a form which has Thomas saying, 'Ooh, Fred, I've got an 'ell of an 'eadache' (told to the author by Lady Gaselee).

9 Winston has devoted the best years of his life to preparing his impromptu speeches.

On Winston Churchill. Quoted in the book *Quote ... Unquote* (1978), but otherwise unverified.

10 The world continues to offer glittering prizes to those who have stout hearts and sharp swords.

Rectorial Address at Glasgow University (7 November 1923) in which he suggested that the only way to preserve the peace was to prepare for war. His subject was 'Idealism in International Politics'. John Campbell in his biography of Birkenhead (1983) comments that 'for ever after, his career was seen, as it still is, as exemplifying the single-minded pursuit of "glittering prizes", from cups and scholarships to office, wealth and fame. This was not at all the context in which F.E. coined the phrase.' Campbell states additionally that there were other instances of Smith's using the phrase – 'but it seems clear from [an earlier] Montreal speech that F.E. was neither plagiarizing not consciously coining an epigram.' To the Canadian Bar Association at Montreal he had said (3 September 1923): 'The glittering counter of world-dominion ... The world still holds precious and incalculable prizes for those who have the will to conquer and the manhood to die.'

Hence, *The Glittering Prizes*, the title of a BBC TV drama series (1976) by Frederic Raphael, about the fortunes of a group of Cambridge graduates.

11 Good God, do you mean to say this place is a club?

On being approached by the Secretary of the Athenaeum whose lavatory Smith was in the habit of using on his way to the office. Discussed by Campbell (*op.cit.*) who claims to have established that it must have been, rather, the National Liberal Club.

SMITH, Ian

Rhodesian Prime Minister (1919–)

1 Let me say again, I don't believe in black majority rule ever in Rhodesia. Not in a thousand years.

Radio broadcast in Rhodesia (20 March 1976). It came about in 1979.

SMITH, Logan Pearsall

American writer (1865–1946)

2 Thank heavens, the sun has gone in, and I don't have to go out and enjoy it.

These are sometimes quoted as though they were Logan Pearsall Smith's last (dying) words – as in *A Dictionary of Famous Quotations* (1962), for example. They are not, though the misunderstanding is understandable. They appear in 'Last Words' in *All Trivia* (1933). Smith did not die until 1946 when, according to James Lees-Milne, *Caves of Ice* (1983), his actual last words were, 'I must telephone to the Pope-Hennesseys'.

SMITH, Samuel Francis

American clergyman and poet (1808–95)

3 My country, 'tis of thee,
Sweet land of liberty,
Of thee I sing:
Land where my fathers died,
Land of the pilgrims' pride,
From every mountain-side
Let freedom ring.

'America' (1832). Hence, *Of Thee I Sing* was the title of a musical (1931) by Gershwin/Gershwin/Kaufman/Ryskind, about the US presidency (title song: 'Of Thee I Sing, Baby'). Smith's verse is sung to the tune of the British National Anthem. This verse was quoted by Martin Luther King just before the peroration of his 'I have a dream speech' (1963).

SMITH, Stevie

English poet (1902–71)

4 A Good Time Was Had By All.

Title of a collection of her poems (1937). Eric Partridge asked her where she had taken the phrase from and she duly replied: from parish magazines where reports of church picnics or social evenings invariably ended with the phrase.

5 Nobody heard him, the dead man,
But still he lay moaning:
He was much further out than you thought
And not waving but drowning.

'Not Waving, But Drowning' (1957). Hence, the modern proverbial expression used to describe any sort of situation where a gesture may be misinterpreted. When Hugh Whitemore's play *Stevie* opened in London (1977), a critic wrote that any poet 'who could encapsulate the whole irony of existence in a poem's title' deserved more than our trifling attention. In a poll to find Britain's favourite poem, conducted by the BBC TV programme *Bookworm* in 1995, this one came fourth.

SMITH, Sydney

English clergyman, essayist and wit (1771–1845)

6 If you choose to represent the various parts in life by holes upon a table, of different shapes, – some circular, some triangular, some square, some oblong, – and the persons acting these parts by bits of wood of similar shapes, we shall generally find that the triangular person has got into the square hole, and a square person has squeezed himself into the round hole.

Lecture 9, *Sketches of Moral Philosophy* (1804). An early formulation of the 'square peg in a round hole' idea, meaning 'someone badly suited to his job or position'. The better known phrase was in use by 1836. Later, James Agate in *Ego 5* (1942) was writing: 'Will somebody please tell me the address of the Ministry for Round Pegs in Square Holes?'

7 My idea of heaven is eating *pâté de foie gras* to the sound of trumpets.

The source usually given for this famous remark is Hesketh Pearson, *The Smith of Smiths*, Chap. 10 (1934). The *ODQ* (1979), citing Pearson, put it as '——'s idea of heaven ...', as though Smith were quoting another. By 1992 the *ODQ* was putting it in Smith's own mouth. In fact, Pearson's version is quite clearly '*His* idea of heaven ...', without saying whose. Bartlett, although managing to include 25 of his sayings, does not include the quotation in any form.

What we have here is quite clearly *not* Smith's own conception of bliss. Although he was by far the wittiest clergyman of the nineteenth century and possibly of all time, he was certainly not frivolous in matters of religion. Indeed, he proudly claimed never to have made jokes on that subject.

The whole matter is discussed and neatly sorted out by Alan Bell in his short biography, *Sydney Smith* (1980): 'Probably the joke was made more than once, just as he preached a good sermon several times ... [the form] "——s idea of heaven" was Saba's [his daughter and biographer, Lady Holland's] suggestion to the editor of *Recollections of the Table-Talk of Samuel Rogers* (1887), and it seems to have been made not merely to protect the reputation of a clergyman from having made humorous speculations about the hereafter. The remark is surely best applied to Sydney's friend and fellow-wit, Henry Luttrell, one of the best-known gourmets of the period, the very man whom Sydney had described as having a "soup-and-pattie look". When this friend was thought to be dying, Sydney wrote to Lady Davy that he was "going gently downhill, trusting that the cookery in another planet may be at least as good as in this; but not without apprehensions that for misconduct here he may be sentenced to a thousand years of tough mutton, or condemned to a little eternity of family dinners".'

A further curiosity: Smith died in 1845 but presumably uttered his remark a good few years before that. In Benjamin Disraeli's novel *The Young Duke*, we can read this, however: 'All paradise opens! Let me die eating ortolans to the sound of soft music.' And that was published in 1831.

1 It is long, yet vigorous, like the penis of a jackass.

Of an article submitted by Lord Brougham to Smith's *Edinburgh Review*. Quoted in Matthew Parris, *Scorn* (1994).

2 As if St Paul's had come down and littered.

Of the Royal Pavilion at Brighton. Quoted in Peter Virgin, *Sydney Smith* (1994). 'It was as though St Paul's had gone down to the sea and pupped' is another version.

3 No furniture so charming as books, even if you never open them, or read a single word.

Quoted in Lady Holland, *A Memoir of Sydney Smith* (1855). *Compare* POWELL 437:3.

4 Avoid shame, but do not seek glory. Nothing so expensive as glory.

Ib. Hence, *The Expense of Glory*, title of a biography of John Reith (1993) by Ian McIntyre.

5 Death must be distinguished from dying, with which it is often confused.

Quoted in Hesketh Pearson, *The Smith of Smiths* (1934). *Compare* FIELDING 235:2.

6 Going to marry her! Impossible! You mean a part of her; he could not marry her all himself ... There is enough of her to furnish wives for a whole parish ... You might people a colony with her; or give an assembly with her; or perhaps take your morning's walk round her, always provided there were frequent resting-places, and you were in rude health.

To a young Scot who was about to marry an Irish widow twice his age and twice his size. Quoted in *ib.*, Chap. 11.

SMOLLETT, Tobias

Scottish novelist (1721–71)

7 I am again your petitioner, in behalf of that great Cham of literature, Samuel Johnson.

Smollett's nickname for Dr Samuel Johnson occurred in a letter to John Wilkes (16 March 1759), reproduced in James Boswell, *Life of Johnson* (1791). 'Cham' is a form of 'khan' (as in Genghis Khan) meaning 'monarch' or 'prince'.

SNAGGE, John

English broadcaster (1904–96)

8 I don't know who's ahead – it's either Oxford or Cambridge.

Radio commentary on the Oxford and Cambridge University Boat Race (1949). Snagge was best known as a BBC radio announcer with a formidably authoritative voice, made for giving news of great events, introducing the sovereign's Christmas broadcast and such like. On this occasion, his commentator's lapse into the obvious had to be pointed out to him afterwards. Cambridge won.

SNOW, C.P. (later Lord Snow)

English novelist and scientist (1905–80)

9 Corridors of Power.

Title of novel (1964). This phrase was reasonably well established for the machinations of government, especially the bureaucrats and civil servants of Whitehall, by the time Snow used it, but he undoubtedly popularized it. Earlier, he had written in his novel *Homecomings* (1956): 'The official world, the corridors of power, the dilemmas of conscience and egotism – she disliked them all.'

1 Two Cultures and the Scientific Revolution.

For a time, the title of Snow's 1959 Rede Lecture at Cambridge on the gap between science and literature and religion gave another much used phrase to the language. 'The Two Cultures' became a catchphrase in discussions of the inability of the two camps to speak a common language or, indeed, to understand each other at all.

SNOWDEN, Philip (1st Viscount Snowden)

English politician (1864–1937)

2 This is not Socialism. It is Bolshevism run mad.

An early political sensation on British radio was made in a broadcast during the 1931 General Election. On 17 October, Snowden, who had been Chancellor of the Exchequer in the 1929 Labour government and who now held the same post in the National government, said this of the Labour Party's plans in a radio broadcast. He also said: 'I hope you have read the Election programme of the Labour Party. It is the most fantastic and impracticable programme ever put before the electors.' The plans were, of course, similar to the ones he had himself devised in 1929. He later commented: 'My effort was universally believed to have had great influence on the result of the Election. The Labour Party gave me the credit, or, as they put it, the discredit of being responsible for the tragic fate which overtook them.'

SOCRATES

Greek philosopher (469–399BC)

3 Crito, we owe a cock to Aesculapius; please pay it and don't forget it.

Last words, quoted in Plato, *Phaedo.* Said to the friend with whom he had been conversing after drinking hemlock. A cock was the usual offering made to Aesculapius, the Greek god of medicine and healing, to return thanks for a recovery from illness.

SOLON

Athenian statesman and poet (c.640–c.556BC)

4 *De mortuis nil nisi bonum.*
Of the dead, speak kindly or not at all.

Sometimes ascribed to Solon (*c.*600BC). 'Speak not evil of the dead' was also a saying of Chilo(n) of Sparta (one of the Seven Sages, also sixth century BC). Later Sextus Propertius (d.AD2) wrote: '*Absenti nemo non nocuisse velit* [Let no one be willing to speak ill of the absent].' Sometimes simply referred to in the form '*de mortuis ...*', it is a proverb which appears in some form in most European languages.

SOLZHENITSYN, Alexander

Russian writer (1918–)

5 The Gulag Archipelago 1918–56.

Title of a factual account (1974) of the Stalinist terror. It alludes to the system of Soviet labour camps. The acronym GULAG is derived from *Glavnoye Upravleniye ispravitelno-trudovykh Lagerei* [main administration of correctional labour camps].

SOME LIKE IT HOT

American film 1959. Script by Billy Wilder and I.A.L. Diamond. With Joe E. Brown as Osgood.

6 *Osgood*: Well, nobody's perfect.

Last line of the film. Soundtrack. Addressed to 'Daphne' (Jack Lemmon, in drag) who has just confessed that he is not a woman and is thus unable to marry the wealthy Osgood.

SOMOZA, Anastasio

Nicaraguan dictator (1925–80)

7 Indeed, you won the elections, but I won the count.

Quoted in *The Guardian* (17 June 1977). Ironically, this remark had been anticipated by Tom Stoppard in his play *Jumpers* (1972): 'It's not the voting that's democracy, it's the counting.'

SONDHEIM, Stephen

American songwriter (1930–)

8 Everything's coming up roses.

Title of song in *Gypsy* (1959), with music by Jule Styne. But did the expression exist before this? It is possibly adapted from the expression, 'to come out smelling of roses', but there do not seem to be any examples even of *that* before the date of the Sondheim coinage.

1 Send in the Clowns.

Title of song in *A Little Night Music* (1973), words and music by Sondheim. The tradition that the 'show must go on' grew out of circus. Whatever mishap occurred, the band was told to go on playing and the cry went up 'send in/on the clowns' – for the simple reason that panic had to be avoided, the audience's attention diverted, and the livelihood of everybody in the circus depended on not having to give the audience its money back. Perhaps 'send in' was right for the circus, 'send on' for the stage?

Similarly, 'the show must go on' seems primarily a circus phrase, though no one seems able to turn up a written reference much before 1930. In 1950, the phrase was spoken in the film *All About Eve* and, in the same decade, Noël Coward wrote a song which posed the question '*Why* Must the Show Go On?'

2 Shepherd's pie and peppered
With genuine shepherds on top.

Sweeney Todd (1979). Sondheim attempts to fashion a lyric out of an amusing notion. Not the first to do so, as witness this cartoon caption from *Punch* (30 January 1918):

> *Bobbie (who is eating shepherd's pie, and has been told not to be wasteful)* 'Mummie, *must* I eat this? It's such a *partickerly* nasty bit of the shepherd?'

3 Sunday in the Park with George.

Title of musical (1983), derived from that of a painting 'Sunday on the Island of La Grande Jatte' and the name of the painter, Georges Seurat, who first exhibited it at the 1886 Impressionist Exhibition.

SOPHOCLES

Greek playwright and poet (c.496–406BC)

4 To die would be good, but never to have been born would be better.

Chorus in play, *Oedipus at Colonus* – but sometimes remembered in a German translation. Friedrich Hölderlin quoted the words on the title page of his novel *Hyperion* (1797). They occur also in Heinrich Heine's *Ruhelechzend* ('Yearning for Rest') (*c.*1853–6) – '*Der Tod ist gut, doch besser wär's/Die mutter hätt uns nie geboren* [Death is good, but it is better Mother had never given birth to us]' – and in his poem 'Morphine' – '*Gut ist der Schlaf, /Der Tod ist besser, /Das beste wäre, / Nie geboren sein* [Sleep is good. Death is better. Best it were never to have been born]'. Friedrich Nietzsche wrote similarly in *The Birth of Tragedy* (1872), attributing the words to Silenus, the companion of Dionysus.

Sophocles may have been anticipated by Aeschylus. In a fragment of an otherwise lost play, there is a passage that has been translated as: 'Death is rather to be chosen than a toilsome life; and not to be born is better than to be born to misery' (Loeb Classical Library ed. of Aeschylus, Vol. 2, p. 502, 1926).

5 Someone asked Sophocles, 'How is your sex-life now? Are you still able to have a woman?' He replied, 'Hush, man; most gladly am I rid of it all, as though I had escaped from a mad and savage master.'

When jazz singer George Melly was on BBC Radio *Quote ... Unquote* in 1989 he quoted a 'Greek philosopher' who, on being asked if he was upset at losing his sexual appetite, replied: 'Upset, certainly not. It's like being unchained from a lunatic.' In a 1988 epistle from *The Kenneth Williams Letters*: 'Understand exactly what Plato meant when he said that after the sexual compulsion vanished with age, he felt "released from a demon".' Williams – the late comic actor – was half-right. It was in fact Sophocles who said it but as reported by Plato in *The Republic* (Bk. 1, l. 329b).

It all depends on the translation from the Greek, of course. Another is: 'I have left it behind me and escaped from the madness and slavery of passion ... a release from slavery to all your many passions.'

SOUTHERN, Terry

American novelist (1924–95)

6 While the hopeless ecstasy of his huge pent-up spasm began ... sweet Candy's melodious voice rang out through the temple in truly mixed feelings: 'GOOD GRIEF – IT'S DADDY!'

Candy (1958), last lines. Written with Mason Hoffenberg and originally published as by 'Maxwell Kenton'.

7 She says, 'Listen, who do I have to fuck to get *off* this picture?'

Blue Movie (1970). Also attributed to Shirley Wood of NBC TV in the 1960s as 'Who do you have to fuck to get out of show business?' But, more likely, it originated with some anonymous Hollywood starlet of the 1930s.

SOUTHEY, Robert

English Poet Laureate (1774–1843)

1 It was a summer evening,
Old Kaspar's work was done,
And he before his cottage door
Was sitting in the sun,
And by him sported on the green
His little grandchild Wilhelmine ...

'The Battle of Blenheim' (1798) – Southey's subtle tract on the futility of war, which ends:

> 'But what good came of it at last?'
> Quoth little Peterkin.
> 'Why that I cannot tell,' said he,
> 'But 'twas a famous victory.'

See also CARROLL 146:10; MITFORD 395:2.

SPARROW, John

English scholar (1906–92)

2 Never lend a book; never give a book away; never read a book.

The 'book collector's caveat', which Sparrow was fond of quoting, according to his obituary in *The Independent* (4 February 1992).

3 This stone with not unpardonable pride,
Proves by its record what the world denied:
Simon could do a natural thing – he died.

Suggested epitaph for Sir John (later Viscount) Simon (1873–1954), lawyer and Liberal politician. 'Lord Simon has died ... John Sparrow wrote this epitaph many years ago ... But then John Simon helped John Sparrow to become Warden of All Souls, and the latter came to regret his epigram' – *Harold Nicolson's Diaries and Letters 1945–1962* (entry for 11 January 1954). In Sparrow's *Grave Epigrams and Other Verses* (1981), 'Simon' is replaced by '*Nemo*'.

4 Without you, Heaven would be too dull to bear,
And Hell would not be Hell if you are there.

Epitaph for Sir Maurice Bowra (1898–1971), first published in *The Times Literary Supplement* (23 June 1972) as a poem, 'C.M.B.' It was reprinted, in this altered form, in Sparrow's *Grave Epigrams and Other Verses* (1981):

> Send us to Hell or Heaven or where you will,
> Promise us only, you'll be with us still:
> Heaven, without you, would be too dull to bear,
> And Hell will not be Hell if you are there.

Bowra was a noted Oxford personality and Warden of Wadham. Sparrow was part of his circle, the Warden of All Souls, and a connoisseur of inscriptions and epitaphs. Bowra's actual grave in St Cross churchyard bears his name in suitably bold letters but no epitaph.

SPECTOR, Phil

American record producer (1940–)

5 To Know Him Is To Love Him.

Song title (1958). In *The Picture of Dorian Gray* (1890), Oscar Wilde had: 'To see him is to worship him, to know him is to trust him.' Blanche Hozier wrote to Mabell, Countess of Airlie, in 1908: 'Clementine is engaged to be married to Winston Churchill. I do not know which of the two is more in love. I think that to know him is to like him.'

Thus the format existed before Spector. The words have a biblical ring to them, but whether Spector was ever aware of the words of No. 3 in *CSSM Choruses* (3rd ed., 1928, by the Children's Special Service Mission, London) we may never know. Written by R. Hudson Pope, it goes:

> All glory be to Jesus
> The sinner's only Saviour ...
> To know Him is to love Him,
> To trust him is to prove Him.

Robert Burns (1759–96) came very close to the phrase on a couple of occasions – in 'Bonnie Lesley': 'To see her is to love her/And love but her for ever', and in 'Ae Fond Kiss': 'But to see her was to love her,/Love but her, and love for ever.' Besides, the words have often been used in an epitaph context. Fitz-Greene Halleck (1795–1867) wrote 'On the death of J.R. Drake':

> Green be the turf above thee,
> Friend of my better days;
> None knew thee but to love thee
> Nor named thee but to praise.

Samuel Rogers (1763–1855) wrote of 'Jacqueline':

> Oh! she was good as she was fair.
> None – none on earth above her!
> As pure in thought as angels are,
> To know her was to love her.

It appears that Spector acquired the title of his song from the gravestone of his father, a suicide, where it read: 'To Have Known Him Was To Have Loved Him'. Quoted in John Tobler & Stuart Grundy, *The Record Producers* (1982).

SPENCER, Herbert

English philosopher (1820–1903)

1 To play billiards well is the sign of a misspent youth.

Under Spencer, the *ODQ* (1979) had: 'It was remarked to me by the late Mr Charles Roupell ... that to play billiards was a sign of an ill-spent youth.' On the other hand, in the archives of the Savile Club in London it is recorded that Robert Louis Stevenson, who was a member from 1874 to 1894, propounded to Spencer that 'proficiency in this game [note: probably billiards, because it was said in the Savile billiards room] is a sign of a misspent youth' (mentioned in 'Words', *The Observer*, 4 May 1986).

Other clubs also claim the honour and some people would supply the word 'snooker' or 'bridge' instead of 'billiards'. A keen billiards player, Spencer was displeased when the saying kept being ascribed to him in newspapers. He had quoted it from someone else. So he dictated a denial to Dr David Duncan, who edited his *Life and Letters* (1908) from which the *ODQ* quotation was taken. *ODQ* (1992) puts the remark under Roupell and describes him as an 'official referee of the British High Court of Justice'.

Benham (1948) notes that a similar view had earlier appeared in *Noctes Ambrosianae* in March 1827.

2 This survival of the fittest which I have here sought to express in mechanical terms is that which Mr Darwin has called 'natural selection, or the preservation of favoured races in the struggle for life.'

Principles of Biology (1864–7). In other words, Spencer, in talking of evolution and the 'survival of the fittest', was pointing to the survival of the most suitable, not of the most physically fit.

SPENCER, Sir Stanley

English painter (1891–1959)

3 Painting is saying 'Ta' to God.

Quoted in letter to *The Observer* from his daughter Shirin (7 February 1988).

SPENSER, Edmund

English poet (c.1552–99)

4 That we spent, we had:
That we gave, we have:
That we left, we lost.

Epitaph of 'the Earl of Devonshire', quoted in *The Shepheardes Calendar*, 'May', l.70 (1579). Compare:

What wee gave, wee have;
What wee spent, wee had;
What wee left, wee lost.

This is the epitaph on Edward Courtenay, Earl of Devon (d.1419) and his wife, at Tiverton.

5 Sweet Thames, run softly, till I end my song.

This line is repeated at the end of each verse of Spenser's *Prothalamion* (1596). In *Handbook of 20th Century Quotations* (ed. Frank S. Pepper, 1984) it is attributed to T.S. Eliot in *The Waste Land* (1922). As with ELIOT 226:1–2, this is another example of Eliot's magpie-like use of quotation misleading readers who do not plunge in among his fairly copious notes. Eliot quotes it at his l. 176.

6 Sleep after toil, port after stormy seas,
Ease after war, death after life does greatly please.

The Faerie Queen, Bk 1, Canto 9, St. 40 (1590–6). Popular as a gravestone inscription. It was put, for example, on the bronze statue of Admiral Robert Blake (1599–1657) at Bridgwater, Somerset. It also appears on the tombstone of the Polish-born novelist Joseph Conrad (1857–1924) in the cemetery of St Thomas's Roman Catholic Church, Canterbury. The quotation had been used by Conrad as the epigraph to his last complete work, *The Rover*.

SPINOZA, Baruch

Dutch philosopher (1632–77)

7 Peace is not an absence of war, it is a virtue, a state of mind, a disposition for benevolence, confidence, justice.

Theological-Political Treatise (1670). Hence, *Absence of War*, title of play (1993) by David Hare, which concerned a leader of the British Labour Party losing yet another General Election and asked whether a socialist government could ever gain power without compromising its principles.

SPOONER, William

English clergyman and academic (1844–1930)

8 Kinquering congs their titles take.

Spoonerism, the accidental transposing of the beginnings of words, is named after a former Warden of

New College, Oxford, and the term had been coined by 1900. Many of Spooner's reported efforts must be apocryphal. 'A half-warmed fish' is one of the more likely ones. 'Kinquering congs ...' – announcing the hymn in New College Chapel (1879) – sounds reasonable (it was reported in the Oxford *Echo*, 4 May 1892). It was alluded to in *Punch* (Vol. 122, 1902) in a joke about the current Ping Pong craze – 'Ponquering Pings their titles take' – and Spooner is mentioned by name.

1 Sir, you have tasted two whole worms; you have hissed all my mystery lectures and been caught fighting a liar in the quad; you will leave Oxford by the next town drain.

A surely apocryphal spoonerism, but reported in *The Oxford University What's What* (1948). Aprocryphal, too, are probably the following: 'Let us drink a toast to the queer old dean', quoted in *PDQ* (1960); 'The Minx by Spoonlight' – the most remarkable sight in Egypt – quoted in Julian Huxley, *Memories* (1970); 'It popped on its little drawers' (of a cat falling from a window), quoted in William Hayter, *Spooner* (1977). 'Yes indeed, the Lord *is* a shoving leopard', quoted in Brewer (1989).

2 I remember your name perfectly; but I just can't think of your face.

Not all Spooner's eccentric remarks are strictly speaking Spoonerisms. Here we have a transposition of whole words. Quoted in *PDQ* (1960).

3 Through a dark glassly ...

Attributed by James Laver, in conversation with the author (5 December 1969). Described by Hayter (in *op. cit*) as one of the more likely spoonerisms.

4 Was it you or your brother who was killed in the war?

Not a Spoonerism, but an eccentric remark. A joke well-established at New College by 1963 was that Spooner had once inquired of an undergraduate (*c.*1918), 'Now, tell me, was it you or your brother who was killed in the war?' But Frank Muir in *The Oxford Book of Humorous Prose* cites this from John Taylor's *Wit and Mirth* (1630): 'A nobleman (as he was riding) met with a yeoman of the country, to whom he said, "My friend, I should know thee. I do remember I have often seen thee." "My good lord," said the countryman, "I am one of your honour's poor tenants, and my name is T.I." "I remember thee better now" (saith my lord) "There were two brothers but one is dead. I pray thee, which of you doth remain alive?"'

5 It is no further from the north coast of Spitsbergen to the North Pole than it is from Land's End to John of Gaunt.

A malapropism spoken to Julian Huxley and recalled by him in *SEAC* (Calcutta) (27 February 1944). Also quoted in William Hayter, *Spooner* (1977).

6 Poor soul – very sad; her late husband, you know, a very sad death – eaten by missionaries – poor soul!

Quoted in William Hayter, *Spooner* (1977). A further malapropism, demonstrating that Spooner's talent did not just lie with Spoonerisms.

SPRING-RICE, Sir Cecil

English diplomat and poet (1859–1918)

7 I vow to thee, my country – all earthly things above –
Entire and whole and perfect, the service of my love.

'I Vow to Thee, My Country' (1918). Notably set to music by Gustav Holst in 1921, using the central melody from 'Jupiter', No. 4 of his *The Planets*.

8 And there's another country, I've heard of long ago –
Most dear to them that love her, most great to them that know.

Ib. Hence, *Another Country*, title of a play (1981; film UK, 1984) by Julian Mitchell, showing how the seeds of defection to Soviet Russia were sown in a group of boys at an English public school. In this original context, the 'other country' is Heaven, rather than the Soviet Union, of course. As the playwright has confirmed, the title was *not* taken from MARLOWE 381:4.

SQUIRE, Sir John

English poet, essayist and critic (1884–1958)

9 I'm not so think as you drunk I am.

'Ballade of Soporific Absorption' in Maurice Baring, *One Hundred and One Ballades* (1931).

See also POPE 434:1.

STAËL, Madame de

French writer (1766–1817)

1 *Tout comprendre rend très indulgent.*
To be totally understanding makes one very indulgent.

Corinne (1807). Possibly best remembered in the form '*Tout comprendre, c'est tout pardonner* [To know everything is to forgive everything].'

STAGE DOOR

US film 1937. Script by Morrie Ryskind and Anthony Veiller, based on a play by Edna Ferber and George S. Kaufman. With Katharine Hepburn as Terry.

2 *Terry (in a play within the film)*: The Calla lilies are in bloom again. Such a strange flower, suitable to any occasion. I carried them on my wedding day, and now I place them here in memory of something that has died.

Soundtrack. These lines were taken from a 1933 Broadway play called *The Lake* in which Hepburn had starred. It had been a flop.

STALIN, Joseph

Soviet Communist leader (1879–1953)

3 Oho! The Pope! How many divisions has he got?

Quoted in Winston Churchill, *The Second World War*, Vol. 1 (1948). Pierre Laval, French Foreign minister, asked Stalin in 1935, 'Can't you do something to encourage religion and the Catholics in Russia? It would help me so much with the Pope'. This was Stalin's reply.

4 He who is not with us is against us.

A view popularly ascribed to the Soviet leader. *Time* Magazine (11 August 1986) also noted a corollary attributed to the Hungarian Communist Party leader, Janos Kadar (1912–89): 'He who is not against us is with us.' In fact, Stalin was quoting Jesus Christ who said: 'He that is not with me is against me' (Luke 11:23) and Kadar was also quoting Christ who provided the corollary: 'He that is not against us is for us' (Luke 9:50). It is not surprising that Stalin quoted Scripture. He went from a church school at Guri to the theological seminary at Tiflis to train for the Russian Orthodox priesthood.

5 The trouble with free elections is, you never know who is going to win.

This has been attributed to Leonid Brezhnev, but not traced. It is, however, just the kind of thing Stalin might have said at the Potsdam Conference in 1945 when Winston Churchill's fate in the British General Election hung in the balance. Molotov has also been suggested.

STALLINGS, Laurence

American writer (1894–1968)

6 Hollywood – a place where the inmates are in charge of the asylum.

Quoted in Laurence J. Peter, *Quotations for Our Time* (1977). *See also* GEORGE 258:2; ROWLAND 463:4.

7 What Price Glory?

Title of play (1924; film US, 1952) about the stupidity of war, written with Maxwell Anderson. Further popularized the 'what price ——?' format phrase, questioning the sacrifices and compromises that may have to be made in order to carry out any sort of mission. Format known by 1893. *See* SHAW 497:12. *What Price Hollywood?* was the title of a film (US, 1932).

STANLEY, Sir Henry Morton

British explorer and journalist (1841–1904)

8 Dr Livingstone, I presume?

The most famous greeting was put by Stanley to the Scottish explorer and missionary Dr David Livingstone at Ujiji, Lake Tanganyika, on 10 November 1871. Stanley had been sent by the *New York Herald* to look for Livingstone who was missing on a journey in central Africa. In *How I Found Livingstone* (1872), Stanley described the moment: 'I would have run to him, only I was a coward in the presence of such a mob – would have embraced him, only, he being an Englishman, I did not know how he would receive me; so I did what cowardice and false pride suggested was the best thing – walked deliberately to him, took off my hat and said: "Dr Livingstone, I presume?" "YES," said he, with a kind smile, lifting his cap slightly.'

One unhelpful suggestion is that Stanley was making a tongue-in-cheek reference to a moment in Sheridan's *School for Scandal*, Act 5, Sc. 1 (1777) in which, after much mutual confusion, two of the main characters finally get to meet with the line, 'Mr Stanley, I presume.' But, really, it was not such a remarkable salutation after all. In the American Civil War, General

Robert E. Lee, when he entered Maryland at Williamsport on 25 June 1863, was greeted by the spokesman of a women's committee of welcome with the words, 'This is General Lee, I presume?'

In the 1960s, when Robert F. Kennedy was campaigning south of Atlanta, he said to one of the rare white men he met: 'Dr Livingstone, I presume.'

1 Through the Dark Continent.
Through Darkest Africa.

In 1878, Stanley published a book of reportage *Through the Dark Continent* and followed it, in 1890, with *Through Darkest Africa.* It is presumably from these two titles that we get the expressions 'dark continent' and 'darkest ——' to describe not only Africa but almost anywhere remote and uncivilized. Flexner (1982) suggests that 'In darkest Africa' was a screen subtitle in a silent film of the period 1910–14.

STANSHALL, Vivian

English entertainer and eccentric (1942–95)

2 And looking very relaxed – Adolf Hitler on vibes.

Written and spoken by Stanshall in a number called 'The Intro and the Outro' (1967), performed by the Bonzo Dog Band.

3 The Canyons of Your Mind.

Title of 1968 hit record, written and performed by Stanshall: 'In the canyons of your mind ... I will wander through your brain to the ventricles of your heart, my dear ... I'm in love with you again.' Somewhat oddly, it came from a phrase in the Val Doonican hit 'Elusive Butterfly' (1966) written by Bob Lind (who had recorded it himself in 1965).

STANTON, Charles E.

American soldier (1859–1933)

4 Lafayette, we are here.

Nine days after the American Expeditionary Force landed in France, Stanton, a member of General Pershing's staff, stood at the tomb of Lafayette in the Picpus cemetery in Paris, and declared, 'Here and now, in the presence of the illustrious dead, we pledge our hearts and our honour in carrying this war to a successful issue. Lafayette, we are here!' This graceful tribute to the Marquis de Lafayette (1757–1834) who enlisted with the American revolutionary armies in 1777 and forged a strong emotional link between the United States and France, was delivered by Colonel Stanton on 4 July 1917 and repeated on 14 July. According to *The New York Tribune* (6 September 1917), Stanton may have spoken all or some of his remarks in French – *Lafayette, nous voilà!* As Bartlett (1968 and 1980) points out, the remark has also been attributed to General Pershing though he disclaimed having said 'anything so splendid'. There is evidence, however, that he may have pronounced the phrase before Stanton and that Stanton merely picked it up.

STANTON, Edwin McMasters

American lawyer and politician (1814–69)

5 Now he belongs to the ages.

Of Abraham Lincoln – on hearing of his death (15 April 1865). Quoted in I.M. Tarbell, *The Life of Abraham Lincoln* (1900).

STANTON, Frank L.

American journalist and poet (1857–1927)

6 Sweetest li'l feller, everybody knows;
Dunno what to call him, but he's mighty lak' a rose!

Song 'Mighty Lak' a Rose' (1901), music by Ethelbert Nevin. By 1991, when the singer Elvis Costello was entitling one of his albums (but no title song) 'Mighty Like a Rose', the southern American intonation of the original had clearly been dispensed with. There is a parody:

Sweetest little feller,
Wears his sister's clothes.
Don't know what to call him,
But we think he's one of those.

STAR TREK

American science-fiction TV series, first aired 1966–9, then the basis of several motion pictures for the cinema. It was created by Gene Roddenberry (1921–91).

7 Space – the final frontier. These are the voyages of the starship *Enterprise*. Its five year mission: to explore strange new worlds, to seek out new life and new civilizations, to boldly go where no man has gone before.

From the introductory voice-over commentary to the TV series. Though short-lived, the show nevertheless acquired a considerable after-life through countless repeats (not least in the UK) and through the activities of 'Trekkies'. In one of the feature films (1988) that belatedly spun off from the series, the split infinitive remained but feminism, presumably, had decreed that it should become 'to boldly go where no *one* has gone before'.

1 Beam me up, Scotty!

In fact, 'Beam us up, Mr Scott' appears to be the nearest thing to this catchphrase ever actually spoken in the series (in an episode called 'Gamesters of Triskelion'). According to 'Trekkies', Captain Kirk (William Shatner) never actually said to Lieutenant Commander 'Scotty' Scott, the chief engineer, 'Beam me up, Scotty!' – meaning that he should transpose body into matter, or some such thing. Another actual phrase that has been used is, 'Enterprise, beam us up' and, we are told, that in the fourth episode, 'Scotty, beam me up' *may* have been said. Somebody has probably written a doctoral thesis on all this.

2 It's life, Jim, but not as we know it.

This is Mr Spock's line from the song 'Star Trekkin'' by the Firm – a No. 1 hit record in the UK (June 1987) in which impersonators of the main *Star Trek* characters simply intone would-be lines from the show to music. As far as one knows, this line was never actually spoken in any of the TV episodes or films. Other lines from this song include: 'There's Klingons on the Starboard Bow' and 'It's worse than that, he's dead, Jim.'

The catchphrase had a certain vogue in the UK in the early 1990s. A 1995 poster advertisement in London stated 'It's direct insurance, but not as we know it, Jim'. A headline from *The Independent* (19 April 1996): 'It's the weekend, Jim, but not as we know it.'

STEEL, David (later Sir David)

British Liberal politician (1938–)

3 I have the good fortune to be the first Liberal leader for over half a century who is able to say to you at the end of our annual assembly: go back to your constituencies and prepare for government.

Speech, Liberal Party Assembly, Llandudno (18 September 1981). Rallying-cry in the first flush of enthusiasm for the alliance with the newly formed SDP. However, by the time of the next general election (1983), squabbling had broken out between the two parties and the Falklands War had given the incumbent Conservative government an unassailable advantage.

STEELE, Sir Richard

Irish-born essayist (1672–1729)

4 A modest fellow never has a doubt from his cradle to his grave.

The Tatler, No. 52 (1709). Possibly the earliest appearance of the phrase 'cradle to the grave'. Soon after came:

A sunbeam in a winter's day,
Is all the proud and mighty have
Between the cradle and the grave.

John Dyer, *Grongar Hill* (1726).

STEFFENS, Lincoln

American journalist (1866–1936)

5 I have seen the future and it works.

Steffens was a muck-raking journalist who paid a visit to the newly formed Soviet Union as part of the William C. Bullitt diplomatic mission of 1919. As did a number of the first visitors to the new Soviet system, he returned home with an optimistic view. His phrase for it was this. However, in his *Autobiography* (1931), he phrases it a little differently. '"So you've been over into Russia?" said Bernard Baruch, and I answered very literally, "I have been over into the future, and it works".' Bullitt said Steffens had been rehearsing this formula even before he went to the Soviet Union. Later, he tended to use the shorter, more colloquial form himself.

Philip Toynbee wrote of the US in *The Observer* (27 January 1974): 'I have seen the future and it does not work.'

STEIN, Gertrude

American poet (1874–1946)

6 Rose is a rose is a rose is a rose.

Stein's poem 'Sacred Emily' (1913) is well-nigh impenetrable to most readers, but somehow it has managed to give a format phrase to the language. If something is incapable of explanation, one says, for example, 'a cloud is a cloud is a cloud'. What Stein wrote, however, is frequently misunderstood. She did not say 'A rose is a rose is a rose', but 'Rose is a rose is a rose is a rose' (i.e., upper case R and no indefinite article at the start and three not two repetitions). The Rose in question was not a flower but an allusion to the English painter, Sir Francis Rose, 'whom she and I regarded,' wrote Constantine Fitzgibbon, 'as the peer of Matisse and Picasso, and whose paintings – or at least painting – hung in her Paris drawing-room while a Gauguin was relegated to the lavatory' (letter to *The Sunday Telegraph*, 7 July 1978). Stein also refers to 'Jack Rose' (not a 'Jack' rose) earlier in the poem.

In John Malcolm Brinnin, *The Third Rose* (1959), Stein is quoted as saying: 'Now, listen! I'm no fool. I know that in daily life we don't go around saying "is a ... is ... is ..." Yes, I'm no fool; but I think that in that line the rose is red for the first time in English poetry for a hundred years.'

Note: *ODMQ* (1991) and *ODQ* (1992) have: 'Rose is a rose is a rose is a rose, is a rose.' And, perversely, Sir Harold Acton wrote in *Memoirs of an Aesthete* (1948) of a letter from Stein: 'A silver rose adorned the writing-paper with the motto "a rose is a rose is a rose". (She had not yet discovered Francis Rose, who must have made her doubt this opinion.)'

1 To write is to write is to write is to write is to write is to write is to write is to write.

Unverified. Possibly a confusion of the 'rose' line above with another dictum of hers: 'The way to say it, is to say it' – quoted by Robert Graves in *Modern Language Quarterly*, No. 27.

2 I Love You Alice B. Toklas.

The film comedy (US, 1968) with this title was about a lawyer (Peter Sellers) amid the Flower People of San Francisco in the 1960s. Alice B. Toklas (who came, as it happens, from San Francisco) was Stein's secretary and lover, for whom Stein 'ghosted' *The Autobiography of Alice B. Toklas* (1933). *The Alice B. Toklas Cookbook* (1954) – a mixture of memoirs and culinary hints – was, however, written by Toklas herself. Popular in the 1960s – perhaps in an 'alternative' edition – it seems to have contained recipes for marijuana cookies, hash brownies and such like.

3 The lost generation.

This phrase refers to the large number of promising young men who lost their lives in the First World War, and also, by extension to those who were not killed in the war but who were part of a generation thought to have lost its values. Stein recorded and popularized the remark made by a French garage owner in the Midi just after the war. Rebuking an apprentice who had made a shoddy repair to her car, he said: 'All you young people who served in the war' are from 'a lost generation [*une génération perdue*]'. Ernest Hemingway used this as the epigraph to his novel *The Sun Also Rises* (1926) and referred to it again in *A Moveable Feast* (1964).

4 What *is* the answer? ... In that case, what is the question?

Last words. Quoted in D. Sutherland, *G.S., a Biography of her Work* (1951). There is more than one version of what she said.

STEINBECK, John

American writer (1902–68)

5 A man got to do what he got to do.

The Grapes of Wrath (1939). The earliest appearance traced of the expression 'a man's gotta do what a man's gotta do', though probably not original to Steinbeck.

6 Unless the bastards have the courage to give you unqualified praise, I say ignore them.

On critics. Quoted in J.K. Galbraith, *A Life in Our Times* (1981).

STEINEM, Gloria

American feminist writer (1934–)

7 A woman without a man is like a fish without a bicycle.

Elaine Partnow's *The Quotable Woman 1800–1981* (1982) attributes this saying to Steinem but gives no hint as to why it makes such a very dubious attribution, though it is reasonable to assume that the words must have crossed Ms Steinem's lips at some stage. It is, after all, probably the most famous feminist slogan of recent decades. Bartlett (1992) lists it anonymously as a 'feminist slogan of the 1980s'.

So, if not from Steinem, whence came the saying? Mrs C. Raikes of Moseley, Birmingham contributed it to BBC Radio *Quote ... Unquote* (1977), adding: 'I felt you had to share in this pearl of wisdom I found yesterday on a lavatory wall in Birmingham University. Written in German, it translates as ...' Indeed, the chances are that the saying may have originated in West Germany where it is known in the form, '*Eine Frau ohne Mann ist wie ein Fisch ohne Velo!*' Compare, however, what Arthur Bloch in *Murphy's Law ...* (also 1977) calls 'Vique's Law': 'A man without religion is like a fish without a bicycle.' In 1979, Arthur Marshall contributed the interesting variant: 'A woman without a man is like a moose without a hatrack.' In Haan & Hammerstrom, *Graffiti in the Big Ten* (1981) is 'Behind every successful man is a fish with a bicycle.'

8 We are becoming the men we wanted to marry.

In *Ms* (July/August 1982). *Compare* JOHN 315:2.

STERNE, Laurence

Irish novelist and clergyman (1713–68)

1 This world surely is wide enough to hold both thee and me.

Tristram Shandy, Bk 2, Chap. 12 (1760–67). *See under* JAMES I 310:7.

2 'L—d!' said my mother, 'what is all this story about?' — 'A cock and a bull,' said Yorick, 'And one of the best of its kind, I ever heard.'

Ib., Bk 9, Chap. 33. Last words. As for where the phrase 'cock and bull story' comes from, suggested origins include: old fables in general which have animals talking, going right back to Aesop – confirmed perhaps by the equivalent French phrase *'coq à l'âne'* (literally, 'cock to donkey') – someone who hated having to listen to such fables was probably the first to dub them as such; Samuel Fisher's 1660 story about a cock and a bull being transformed into a single animal – which people may have thought pretty improbable; somehow from the Cock and Bull public houses, which are but a few doors apart in Stony Stratford, Buckinghamshire; generally confused tales told first in one pub, the Cock, and then retold in another, the Bull.

The *OED2*'s earliest citation of the precise form as it is now used comes (later than Sterne) from the Philadelphia *Gazette of the United States* (1795): 'A long cock-and-bull story about the Columbianum' (a proposed national college). Motteux's 1700 translation of Cervantes, *Don Quixote* (Pt 1, Bk 3, Chap. 17) has: 'don't trouble me with your foolish stories of a cock and a bull'.

3 They order, said I, this matter better in France.

A Sentimental Journey (1768). First sentence. *Compare* KEPPEL 333:1.

4 God tempers the wind to the shorn lamb.

In *Ib.*, we find: 'How she had borne it ... she could not tell – but God tempers the wind, said Maria, to the shorn lamb.' That is to say, God arranges matters so as not to make them unduly harsh for the unfortunate. As such, this is possibly one of the most preposterously untrue of all proverbial sayings. For a proverb it is, not an original remark of Sterne's, as is sometimes supposed, though Sterne's wording is how it is now used. *CODP* finds a French version in 1594.

Winston Churchill, *My Early Life* (1930) (in the chapter entitled 'The Fourth Hussars'), remembers a widely read colonel who could not pronounce his r's: 'When, for instance, on one occasion I quoted, "God tempers the wind to the shorn lamb", and Brabazon asked "Where did you get that fwom?" I had replied with some complacency that, though it was attributed often to the Bible, it really occurred in Sterne's *Sentimental Journey*.'

Brewer (1989) points out that Sterne erred in putting 'lamb' where earlier it had said 'sheep' – lambs are never shorn.

STEVENSON, Adlai

American Democratic politician (1900–65)

5 A heartbeat away from the Presidency.

The traditional description of the position of the US Vice-President and, as Safire (1978) puts it, 'a reminder to voters to examine the shortcomings of a vice-presidential candidate'. The earliest use of the phrase Safire finds is Stevenson beginning an attack on Richard Nixon in 1952 with, 'The Republican vice-presidential candidate, who asks you to place him a heartbeat from the Presidency'. Jules Witcover entitled a book on Vice-President Spiro Agnew's enforced resignation in 1973, *A Heartbeat Away*. The phrase was much in evidence again when George Bush selected Dan Quayle as his running-mate in 1988.

6 Dragged kicking and screaming into the twentieth century.

For a well-known phrase, this is curiously little documented and has proved impossible to track to source. The earliest example found in this precise form comes from an article by Kenneth Tynan written in 1959 and collected in *Curtains* (1961): 'A change, slight but unmistakable, has taken place; the English theatre has been dragged, as Adlai Stevenson once said of the Republican Party, kicking and screaming into the twentieth century.'

Tony Benn declared during a by-election in May 1961: 'It is given to Bristol in this election to wrench the parliamentary system away from its feudal origins, and pitchfork it kicking and screaming into the twentieth century.' Nobel prize winning chemist, Sir George Porter, said in a speech in September 1986: 'Should we force science down the throats of those that have no taste for it? Is it our duty to drag them kicking and screaming into the twentieth century? I am afraid it is.'

Obviously, it is a 'format' phrase that lends itself to subtle modification. From *The Daily Telegraph* (11 September 1979): 'Mr Ian McIntyre, whose ambition was to bring Radio 4 kicking and screaming into the 1970s'; from *The Washington Post* (19 January 1984): 'All [President Reagan] said before he was dragged kicking and screaming into the East Room was that he wouldn't call the Soviet Union an "evil empire" any more'; and from the same paper (19 December 1988): 'Still, Jones and Hawke, prodded by other corporate-minded partners, have dragged Arnold & Porter – sometimes kicking and screaming – into a 21st century mode of thinking, which they believe will position the firm to compete with firms that already have more than 1,000 lawyers.'

The nascent form can be found in a 1913 article by J.B. Priestley in *London Opinion*: '[By listening to ragtime] he felt literally dragged out of the nineteenth into the twentieth century.' (His use of 'literally' suggests that the idea of dragging from one century to another was already an established one.)

1 I have been thinking that I would make a proposition to my Republican friends ... That if they will stop telling lies about the Democrats, we will stop telling the truth about them.

Presidential campaign remark (10 September 1952), but it was originated by Republican Senator Chauncey Depew about the *Democrats* earlier in the century. Depew was a senator in 1899–1911.

2 Someone asked me as I came down the street, how I felt, and I was reminded of a story that a fellow townsman used to tell – Abraham Lincoln. They asked him how he felt once after an unsuccessful election. He felt like a little boy who had stubbed his toe in the dark. He said that he was too old to cry, but it hurt too much to laugh.

Stevenson's remark after his presidential electoral defeat (5 November 1952). The actual Lincoln remark appeared in *Frank Leslie's Illustrated Weekly* (22 November 1862) after a defeat in the New York elections: '[I feel] somewhat like the boy in Kentucky who stubbed his toe while running to see his sweetheart. The boy said he was too big to cry, and far too badly hurt to laugh.'

3 Eggheads of the world unite; you have nothing to lose but your yolks.

Attributed. In a speech at Oakland (1 February 1956) he said, rather, 'Eggheads of the world, arise – I was even going to add that you have nothing to lose but your yolks.' 'Egghead' as a synonym for 'intellectual' had been popularized by the columnist Joseph Alsop during the 1952 US presidential campaign.

4 She would rather light a candle than curse the darkness, and her glow has warmed the world.

An eloquent tribute paid by Stevenson to Eleanor Roosevelt when the former First Lady died in November 1962. Possibly he had been inspired to do so by what she had written in *My Day* (based on her newspaper column): 'Even a candle is better than no light at all.' However, Stevenson was merely quoting the motto of the Christopher Society, which came, in turn, from a Chinese proverb. 'Better to light a candle than curse the darkness' was also quoted by Peter Benenson, the founder of Amnesty International, at a Human Rights Day ceremony on 10 December 1961 and provided Amnesty International with its symbol of a burning candle (encircled by barbed wire).

5 An editor is one who separates the wheat from the chaff and prints the chaff.

Attributed in Bill Adler, *The Stevenson Wit* (1966), but *see* HUBBARD 303:10.

See also ANONYMOUS 46:5.

STEVENSON, Sir Melford

British judge (1902–87)

6 A totally incomprehensible choice for any free human being to make.

On living in Manchester, to the husband in a divorce case. Quoted in *The Daily Telegraph* (11 April 1979).

STEVENSON, Robert Louis

Scottish writer (1850–94)

7 For my part, I travel not to go anywhere, but to go. I travel for travel's sake. The great affair is to move.

'Cheylard and Luc', *Travels With a Donkey* (1879). Stevenson also put this view in the words: 'To travel hopefully is a better thing than to arrive, and the true success is to labour' – 'El Dorado', *Virginibus Puerisque* (1881). Subsequently, the thought emerged in the form 'the journey not the arrival matters' (an expression used as the title of an autobiographical volume by Leonard Woolf, 1969). 'Getting there is half the fun' may have been used to advertise Cunard steamships in the 1920s and 1930s. It was definitely used to promote the Peter Sellers film *Being There* (1980) in the form: 'Getting there is half the fun. Being there is all of it.' In *Up the Organisation* (1970), Robert Townshend opined of getting to the top: 'Getting there isn't half the fun – it's all the fun.'

1 Pieces of eight, pieces of eight!

Treasure Island (1883). Cry of Long John Silver's parrot 'Captain Flint'. 'Pieces of eight' were coins.

2 A Penny Plain and Twopence Coloured.

Title of a noted essay in *The Magazine of Art* (1884) on the toy theatres or 'juvenile drama' of his youth. The expression referred to the prices of characters and scenery you could buy either already coloured or in black and white to colour yourself. Stevenson popularized the phrase in several pieces but it undoubtedly existed before. George Augustus Sala, *Twice Round the Clock* (1859) has: 'The Scala [theatre, Milan] ... with its rabbit-hutch-like private boxes, whose doors are scrawled over with the penny plain and twopence coloured-like coats of arms of the ... Lombardian nobility.' *Tuppence Coloured* (on its own) was the title of a theatrical novel by Patrick Hamilton (1927) and of a revue (with Joyce Grenfell and others) in 1947.

3 Under the wide and starry sky
Dig the grave and let me lie.
Glad did I live and gladly die,
And I laid me down with a will.

This be the verse you grave for me:
Here he lies where he longed to be;
Home is the sailor, home from the sea
And the hunter home from the hill.

Stevenson's gravestone on Mount Vaea, Somoa, wrongly transcribes his poem 'Requiem' in *Underwoods* (1887) as above. The penultimate line should read 'Home is the sailor, *home from sea*', without the definite article. But this is a common quotation error. In *Across the Plains* (1892), Stevenson had composed an epitaph of which any man 'need not be ashamed': '*Here lies one who meant well, tried a little, failed much.*'

Compare *Home Is the Hero*, title of a film (UK, 1959) based on Walter Macken's play. 'Home Comes the Hero' is the title of Chap. 22 of *Tom Moore* (1977) by Terence de Vere White. Otherwise the origin of this form of the phrase remains untraced.

4 Steel-true and blade-straight
The great artificer
Made my mate.

Poem 'My Wife', *Songs of Travel* (1896). Rather curiously, it is quoted as:

STEEL TRUE
BLADE STRAIGHT

on the grave of Sir Arthur Conan Doyle (1859–1930), the creator of Sherlock Holmes, in All Saints' churchyard, Minstead, Hampshire. Presumably, the widow – who was a spiritualist, if that is relevant – chose the epitaph.

STONE, Irving

American novelist (1903–89)

5 The Agony and the Ecstasy.

Title of novel (1961; film, US 1965), about Michelangelo and the Sistine Chapel. Apparently, an original coinage. Compare what William Faulkner said in his speech accepting the Nobel Prize for Literature (10 December 1950) – whatever was 'worth the agony and the sweat' was worth writing about.

STOPPARD, Tom (later Sir Tom)

British playwright (1937–)

6 The bad ended unhappily, the good unluckily. That is what tragedy means.

Rosencrantz and Guildenstern Are Dead, Act 2 (1966). *Compare* WILDE 569:12.

7 McFee ... whose chief delusion is that Edinburgh is the Athens of the North ... McFee's dead ... He took offence at my description of Edinburgh as the Reykjavik of the South.

Jumpers (1972). Compare John Betjeman's earlier remark in a letter to Michael Rose (25 September 1955): 'As someone said, "We have often heard Cork called the Venice of Ireland, but have never heard Venice called the Cork of Italy".'

8 It seems pointless to be quoted if one isn't going to be quotable ... It's better to be quotable than honest.

Quoted in *The Guardian* (21 March 1973). A reflection on quotability.

9 If I knew, I'd go there.

In answer to the journalists' clichéd question 'Where do you get your ideas from?' Source – probably a *Guardian* interview. But compare what Joyce Grenfell wrote in *Joyce Grenfell Requests the Pleasure* (1976). She stated that this was her reply to the question, 'Where do you get the ideas for your monologues?'

Earlier, A.A. Milne said of writing his articles for *Punch*: 'Ideas may drift into other minds, but they do not drift my way. I have to go and fetch them. I know no work manual or mental to equal the appalling heart-breaking anguish of fetching an idea from nowhere' (quoted in Ann Thwaite, *A.A. Milne*, 1990). Later, the novelist Terry Pratchett was profiled in *The Observer* (8 November 1992): '"Where do you get your incredible ideas from?" asked a boy. (Someone always does.) "There's this warehouse called Ideas Are Us," Pratchett replied.'

1 He's someone who flies around from hotel to hotel and thinks the most interesting thing about any story is the fact that he has arrived to cover it.

Of a foreign correspondent. *Night and Day*, Act 1 (1978).

2 Every member of the orchestra carries a conductor's baton in his knapsack.

Every Good Boy Deserves Favour (1978). *Compare* NAPOLEON 406:1.

STORY, Jack Trevor

British novelist (1917–91)

3 Live Now, Pay Later.

Title of screenplay (1962) based on the novel *All on the Never Never* by Jack Lindsay. As a simple graffito, the same line was recorded in Los Angeles (1970) in *The Encyclopedia of Graffiti* (1974). The same book records a New York subway graffito on a funeral parlour ad: 'Our layaway plan – die now, pay later.' 'Book now, pay later' was used in an advertisement in the programme of the Royal Opera House, Covent Garden, London, in 1977.

Back to 1962: in that year, Daniel Boorstin in *The Image* made oblique reference to travel advertisements using the line, 'Go now, pay later'. Was Hire Purchase ever promoted with 'Buy now, pay later'? It seems likely. These lines – in the US and UK – seem to be the starting point for a construction that has been much used and adapted since.

STOWE, Harriet Beecher

American novelist (1811–96)

4 I s'pect I growed. Don't think nobody ever made me.

Uncle Tom's Cabin (1852). The little slave girl, Topsy, asserts that she has no mother or father, replies thus, on being asked who made her. Hence, the rephrased expression: 'Like Topsy – she just growed.'

STRACHEY, Lytton

English biographer (1880–1932)

5 I would try to get between them.

During the First World War Strachey had to appear before a military tribunal to put his case as a conscientious objector. He was asked by the chairman what, in view of his beliefs, he would do if he saw a German soldier trying to violate his sister. With an air of noble virtue, the homosexual Strachey replied, 'I would try to get between them'. A correspondent suggests that it was much more likely that Strachey would have said something more grandiloquent – 'I would interpose my body' or some such – but the source for this anecdote is Robert Graves in *Goodbye To All That* (1929) and his version is the one given above.

6 If this is dying, then I don't think much of it.

Last words, quoted in Michael Holroyd, *Lytton Strachey*, Vol. 2 (1968). If he truly said this, it seems to prove that Strachey's customary mordant wit did not desert him on his deathbed and became a mortal wit.

SULLIVAN, Brendan V.

American lawyer (1942–)

7 I'm not a potted plant ... I'm here as the lawyer. That's my job.

Answering criticism from Senator Daniel Inouye that he interrupted too much and that his client, Oliver North, should be the one to speak up. During the 1987 hearings into the 'Iran-*contra*' affair (after which North was found guilty of taking part in illegal military and security actions). Quoted in *The New York Times* (10 July 1987).

SULTAN Salman Al-Saud

Saudi Arabian Prince and air force pilot (1956–)

8 From space the world has no boundaries.

The Prince was the first Arab in space: he flew as a member of the American *Discovery* shuttle crew in June 1985. He recited the Koran, spoke to his uncle King Fahd from the space craft and made the above observation, which was variously reported. *The Washington Post* (12 July 1985) had: 'Prince Sultan, who just went up in the space shuttle and made the statement about no boundaries in space.' *The Daily Telegraph* (6 July 1985) quoted his less crisp actual words. When asked about the Beirut hostage crisis, he had replied:

'Looking at it from up here, with trouble all over the world, not just in the Middle East, it looks very strange as you see the boundaries and borderlines disappearing. Lots of people who are causing some of these problems ought to come up here and take a look.'

THE SUN

American New York-based newspaper, founded 1833

1 If you see it in the *Sun*, it's so.

In 1897 a New York girl called Virginia O'Hanlon wrote a letter to the *Sun* which went, in part: 'Dear Editor: I am 8 years old. Some of my little friends say there is no Santa Claus. Papa says, "If you see it in the *Sun* it's so." Please tell me the truth, is there a Santa Claus?' The newspaper replied, in a famous piece, 'Your little friends are wrong ... there is a Santa Claus ... Not believe in Santa Claus! You might as well not believe in fairies!' After his death in 1906, it was revealed that Francis P. Church had written the editorial.

THE SUN

British London-based newspaper, founded 1964

2 WINTER OF DISCONTENT. Lest we forget ... the *Sun* recalls the long, cold months of industrial chaos that brought Britain to its knees.

This was the headline to a feature (30 April 1979) in the run-up to the general election which swept Margaret Thatcher and the Conservatives to power and was probably the first major use of this phrase to characterize the industrial unrest of the winter of 1978–9. It alludes to *Richard III* (SHAKESPEARE 493:5), which begins, famously, with Gloucester's punning and original metaphor, even if the editor of the Arden Shakespeare does describe the entire image as 'almost proverbial'. Probably made all the more memorable by Laurence Olivier's delivery of these lines in the 1955 film, the phrase 'winter of discontent' suffered the unpleasant fate of becoming a politician's and journalist's cliché following the winter of 1978–9 when British life was disrupted by all kinds of industrial protest against the Labour government's attempts to keep down pay rises. Most notably, rubbish remained uncollected and began to pile up in the streets and a gravediggers' strike in one area reportedly left bodies unburied.

This 'winter of discontent' (as it is still referred to many years later) may perhaps have contributed to the Conservative victory at the May 1979 general election. The question has been asked, who first referred to it as such? *The Sun*'s earlier use of the phrase was the crucial one. (Sir) Larry Lamb, editor at the time, recalled in a Channel 4 TV programme *Benn Diaries II* (29 October 1989) that he introduced the phrase 'in a small way' during the winter itself (it was imitated by others), then 'in a big way' during the election. James Callaghan, the Prime Minister who was destroyed by the phrase, seems to have claimed that he used the phrase first (recalled in a TV programme, December 1991).

There is little new under the *Sun*, of course. J.B. Priestley, writing of earlier much harder times in *English Journey* (1934) ended his fourth chapter with: 'The delegates have seen one England, Mayfair in the season. Let them see another England next time, West Bromwich out of season. Out of all seasons except the winter of discontent.'

3 GOTCHA!

Front page headline (4 May 1982). How *The Sun* 'celebrated' the sinking of the Argentine cruiser *General Belgrano* during the Falklands war, but the headline was retained for the first edition only. Other 'gung-ho' *Sun* headlines of the time included: 'STICK IT UP YOUR JUNTA' (20 April) – its attitude towards a negotiated settlement – and 'THE SUN SAYS KNICKERS TO ARGENTINA' and 'UP YOURS, GALTIERI', which sound so unlikely they must have appeared. The *Sun* posture was memorably parodied at the time by *Private Eye*, which suggested the headline: 'KILL AN ARGIE AND WIN A METRO.'

4 FREDDIE STARR ATE MY HAMSTER – Comic put a live pet in sandwich, says beauty.

Front page headline (13 March 1986). The paradigm of British tabloid journalism.

5 IF KINNOCK WINS TODAY WILL THE LAST PERSON IN BRITAIN PLEASE TURN OUT THE LIGHTS.

Front page headline on the day of a British general election (9 April 1992). Something of an old joke. As 'Would the last person to leave the country please switch off the lights' appeared in the book *Graffiti 2* (1980). Earlier, in Israel (*c*.1966), when due to the political situation many people decided to leave the country, the story ran that at Lydda Airport near Tel Aviv a notice had been put up: 'Will the last to leave kindly turn out the light' (source: Maxime Rodinson, *Israel and the Arabs*, 1969).

SUNSET BOULEVARD

American film 1950. Script by Charles Brackett, Billy Wilder and D.M. Marshman Jr. With Gloria Swanson as Norma Desmond and William Holden as Joe Gillis.

1 *Joe*: You're Norma Desmond – used to be in silent pictures – used to be big.
Norma: I *am* big. It's the pictures that got small.

Soundtrack. A famously derisive line spoken by a film star who has been brought low by the advent of sound in the cinema.

2 *Norma*: All right, Mr De Mille. I'm ready for my close-up.

Last line. Soundtrack. The musical (1993), with book by Christopher Hampton and music by Andrew Lloyd Webber, has rather the spoken line, 'And now, Mr De Mille, I'm ready for my close-up.

SURTEES, R.S.

English novelist and journalist (1805–64)

3 Women never look so well as when one comes in wet and dirty from hunting.

Mr Sponge's Sporting Tour, Chap. 21 (1853). A possibly ambivalent statement, but it is definitely from the man's point of view.

SVEVO, Italo

Italian novelist (1861–1928)

4 There are three things I always forget. Names, faces, and – the third I can't remember.

Quoted in *PDMQ* (1971). Otherwise untraced.

SWAFFER, Hannen

English journalist (1879–1962)

5 Freedom of the press in Britain is freedom to print such of the proprietor's prejudices as the advertisers don't object to.

In conversation with Tom Driberg, *c.*1928 (recalled in Driberg's *Swaff*, 1974). Driberg suspected that Swaffer began to take this view *c.*1902.

6 *Yes and No* – No!

A comedy by Kenneth Horne with the title *Yes and No* featuring Steve Geray and Magda Kun opened at the Ambassadors Theatre, London, in the autumn of 1938. It occasioned probably the shortest theatrical notice of all time. Swaffer wrote: '*Yes and No* (Ambassadors) – No!' (source: letter from Bill Galley in *The Sunday Telegraph*, 24 March 1970).

On BBC Radio *Quote ... Unquote* (1993), Tony Hawks ascribed something similar to Dorothy Parker about the André Charlot musical show *Yes!* which was presented in London in 1923. Her one-word review had apparently been 'No!' – though this joke may have been foisted upon her.

See also NORTHCLIFFE 415:3.

SWIFT, Jonathan

Anglo-Irish writer and clergyman (1667–1745)

7 Italian effeminacy and Italian nonsense ... wholly unsuitable to our northern climate and to the genius of the people.

On opera. Quoted in Gary Schmidgall, *Literature as Opera* (1977), but otherwise untraced.

8 Instead of dirt and poison we have rather chosen to fill our hives with honey and wax; thus furnishing mankind with the two noblest of things, which are sweetness and light.

Preface, *The Battle of the Books* (1704). *Compare* ARNOLD 61:7.

9 Many a true genius appears in the world – you may know him by this sign, that the dunces are all in confederacy against him.

Thoughts on Various Subjects (1706). Hence, *A Confederacy of Dunces*, the title of a novel (1980) by John Kennedy Toole.

10 I cannot but conclude the bulk of your natives to be the most pernicious race of little odious vermin that nature ever suffered to crawl upon the surface of the earth.

'A Voyage to Brobdingnag', *Gulliver's Travels* (1726). The King to Gulliver – about the British.

11 And he gave it for his opinion, that whoever could make two ears of corn or two blades of grass to grow upon a spot of ground where only one grew before, would deserve better of mankind, and do more essential service to his country than the whole race of politicians put together.

Ib. Compare VEBLEN 549:7.

1 This breed of Struldbruggs was peculiar to their country ... He observed long life to be the universal desire and wish of mankind. Only in this island, the appetite for living was not so eager, from the continual example of the Struldbruggs before their eyes.

'A Voyage to Laputa, etc.', in *ib.* The Struldbruggs who live for ever are to be found on the island of Luggnagg.

2 So, naturalists observe, a flea
Hath smaller fleas that on him prey;
And these have smaller fleas to bite 'em,
And so proceed *ad infinitum.*
Thus every poet, in his kind,
Is bit by him that comes behind.

Referring to literary critics. 'On Poetry, a Rhapsody' (1733). Hence, the better remembered lines from *A Budget of Paradoxes* by Professor Augustus de Morgan (1806–71):

Great fleas have little fleas
Upon their backs to bite 'em,
And little fleas have lesser fleas,
And so *ad infinitum.*
And the great fleas themselves in turn
Have greater fleas to go on,
While these again have greater still,
And greater still, and so on.

3 Good God! what a genius I had when I wrote that book.

Of *A Tale of a Tub.* Quoted in Sir Walter Scott's edition of *The Works of Swift* (1814).

4 Here lies the body of Jonathan Swift, Professor of Holy Theology, for thirty years Dean of this cathedral church, where savage indignation can tear his heart no more. Go, traveller, and if you can, imitate one who with his utmost strength protected liberty. He died in the year 1745, on the 19th of October, aged seventy-eight.

Swift wrote this epitaph for himself (originally in Latin) and it may be found on a tablet in St Patrick's Cathedral, Dublin, where he lies buried and where he served as Dean 1713–45. The inscription includes the key phrase: '*Ubi saeva indignatio ulterius cor lacerare nequit*'. Said W.B. Yeats: 'Swift sleeps under the greatest epitaph in history.'

See also COLERIDGE 178:6.

SWINBURNE, Algernon

English poet (1837–1909)

5 Thou hast conquered, O pale Galilean.

'Hymn to Proserpine' (1866). Pale Galilean = Jesus Christ. At one time, 'Galilean' (meaning a native of Galilee, but by extension, Christ or any Christian) was a term of abuse used by pagans.

6 From too much love of living,
From hope and fear set free,
We thank with brief thanksgiving
Whatever gods may be
That no life lives forever;
That dead men rise up never;
That even the weariest river
Winds somewhere safe to sea.

'The Garden of Proserpine', St. 1 (1866). The hero of Jack London's autobiographical novel *Martin Eden* (1909) reads this stanza aloud before drowning himself.

7 All our past proclaims our future:
Shakespeare's voice and Nelson's hand,
Milton's faith and Wordsworth's trust in this
our chosen and chainless land,
Bear us witness: come the world against her,
England yet shall stand.

'England: An Ode', Pt 2, St. 5, in *Astrophel and Other Poems* (1894). *Compare* SHAKESPEARE 487:2.

T

TAGORE, Rabindranath

Bengali poet and philosopher (1861–1941)

1 O Tajmahal, thy white marble is a solitary tear-drop on the cheek of time!

Of the Taj Mahal. *Bal ka* (1914–16), in translation. James Callaghan, the British Prime Minister, on a visit to India in January 1978 quoted the line as 'A tear-drop on the cheek of destiny'.

TALLEYRAND, Charles Maurice de

French statesman (1754–1838)

2 *C'est une nouvelle, ce n'est pas un évènement.*
It is not an event, it is an item of news.

Remark when the news of Napoleon's death at St Helena in 1821 reached Europe. Ignored by Bartlett and the *ODQ*, this quotation does, however, appear in Benham (1907). Quoting the 5th Earl of Stanhope's *Conversations with the Duke of Wellington* (for 1 November 1831), Elizabeth Longford, *Wellington: Pillar of State* (1972) places the remark at 'a Parisian party ... at Mme Craufurd's ... [and] Wellington and Talleyrand were there to hear the startled cries'. J.F. Bernard's *Talleyrand* (1973) dates this occasion to 14 July 1821: 'Madame Crawford broke the silence with a cry: "Oh, good God! What an event!" She was answered by the prince's [Talleyrand's] quiet, deep voice, from a corner of the room: "No, madame. It is no longer an event. It is only a bit of news."'

3 What does he mean by that?

On the death of the Turkish ambassador to France. Unverified. Alluded to in Ben Pimlott, *Harold Wilson*, Chap. 29 (1992). However, another version is that it was said in the form, 'Died, has he? Now I wonder what he meant by that?', *about* Talleyrand and *by* King Louis Philippe. Also unverified.

TATE, Nahum

English hymn writer (1652–1715)

4 Thus on the fatal banks of Nile,
Weeps the deceitful crocodile.

Dido and Aeneas, Act 3 (1689); Tate's libretto for Henry Purcell's opera. Dido sings the words about Aeneas just after he has told her he is leaving her. The corresponding scenes in Virgil (*Aeneid*, Bk 4, l. 305ff and 365ff) do not use this metaphor, so presumably it is Tate's own.

5 As pants the hart for cooling streams
When heated in the chase.

Psalm 42, *New Versions of the Psalms* (1696). With Nicholas Brady (1659–1726).

TAYLOR, Ann and Jane

English writers (1782–1866) and (1783–1824)

6 Who ran to help me when I fell,
And would some pretty story tell,
Or kiss the place to make it well?
My Mother.

One of the verses from 'My Mother' *Original Poems for Infant Minds* (1804). Sometimes this is attributed to Ann Taylor only. A parody that was widely known by at least 1978, goes:

> Who took me from my bed so hot
> And placed me shivering on the pot,
> Nor asked me whether I should or not?
> My Mother!

See also CARROLL 147:4.

TAYLOR, Bert Leston

American journalist (1866–1921)

1 A bore is a man who, when you ask him how he is, tells you.

The So-Called Human Race (1922), but almost a proverbial observation.

TAYLOR, Jeremy

English divine (1613–67)

2 *Si fueris Romae, Romano vivito more; si fueris alibi, vivito sicut ibi.*
If you are at Rome, live in the Roman style; if you are elsewhere, live as they live elsewhere.

Ductor Dubitantium (1660). Usually rendered: 'When in Rome, do as the Romans do.' Possibly based on earlier by St Ambrose (in *c.*AD400).

TEBBIT, Norman (later Lord Tebbit)

English Conservative politician (1931–)

3 [My father] did not riot. He got on his bike and looked for work. And he kept on looking till he found it.

Having just been appointed British Employment Secretary, Tebbit addressed the Conservative Party Conference on 15 October 1981. He related how he had grown up in the 1930s when unemployment was all around and made the above comment. This gave rise to the pejorative catchphrase 'on your bike' or 'get on your bike' from the lips of Mr Tebbit's opponents, and gave a new twist to a saying Partridge / *Slang* dates from *c.*1960, meaning 'go away' or 'be off with you'. Tebbit later pointed out that he had not been suggesting that the unemployed should literally get on their bikes.

4 Nobody with a conscience votes Conservative.

When Tebbit had this view ascribed to him by *The Guardian* in January 1987, he extracted 'substantial damages' from the newspaper. But it often proves difficult to bury such remarks and remove them completely from the record. When the *New Statesman* repeated the attribution in error in the summer of 1992, Lord Tebbit, as he had now become, received further libel damages.

5 Some thought my willingness to stand toe to toe against the more thuggish elements of the Labour Party and slug it out blow for blow rather vulgar. Others, especially in the country at large, seemed delighted at the idea of a Tory MP unwilling to be strangled by the old school tie.

Upwardly Mobile (1988). The *OED2*'s oldest citation for the very British phrase 'old school tie' – symbolizing the supposed freemasonry among those who have been educated at public (i.e., private) schools in Britain – dates from 1932 (in a piece by Rudyard Kipling). The strangulation element appears to have crept in more recently. In Frederic Raphael's script for the film *Nothing But the Best* (UK, 1964), the Denholm Elliott character says to the Alan Bates character, 'From now on, no one will be able to accuse you of being strangled by the old school tie' (this is just a moment before Bates strangles Elliott with just such an article of clothing). From BBC radio's *Round the Horne* (7 April 1968): 'It's painful to be strangled by the old school tie'. *The Times* (27 September 1986) had: '[Trevor Howard] broke new ground, away from the English studio stereotypes of silly-ass eccentrics or decent but wooden chaps strangled by a combination of old school tie and stiff upper lip.'

TEMPLE, William

English theologian and Archbishop (1881–1944)

6 Personally, I have always looked on cricket as organized loafing.

Remark to parents when headmaster of Repton School. Quoted in *PDMQ* (1971).

TENNYSON, Alfred (1st Baron Tennyson)

English Poet Laureate (1809–92)

7 Below the thunders of the upper deep;
Far, far beneath in the abysmal sea,
His ancient, dreamless, uninvaded sleep
The Kraken sleepeth.

'The Kraken' (1830), about a mythical sea-monster, sleeping in the depths, waiting only to rise and die. The word 'kraken' is of Norwegian origin, and the monster was supposed to be of gigantic size and found off the coast of Norway. Hence, *The Kraken Wakes*, title of a science fiction novel (1953) by John Wyndham.

8 You must wake and call me early, call me early, mother dear;
Tomorrow'll be the happiest time of all the glad New-year;
Of all the glad New-year, mother, the maddest merriest day;

For I'm to be Queen o' the May, mother, I'm
  to be Queen o' the May.

'The May Queen' (1832). When Tennyson entered the Sheldonian Theatre in Oxford to receive an honorary degree of DCL, his long hair was in poetic disorder, dishevelled and unkempt. A voice cried out to him, 'Did your mother call you early, dear?' (recounted by Julian Charles Young in a diary note, 8 November 1863).

1 And through the field the road runs by
To many-towered Camelot.

'The Lady of Shalott' (1832, rev. 1842). In a poll to find Britain's favourite poem, conducted by the BBC TV programme *Bookworm* in 1995, this one came second.

2 Out flew the web and floated wide;
The mirror crack'd from side to side;
'The curse is come upon me,' cried
The Lady of Shalott.

Ib. Hence, *The Mirror Crack'd from Side to Side*, title of a Miss Marple crime novel (1962) by Agatha Christie.

3 Howe'er it be, it seems to me,
'Tis only noble to be good.
Kind hearts are more than coronets,
And simple faith than Norman blood.

'Lady Clara Vere de Vere' (1833). Hence, *Kind Hearts and Coronets*, title of film (UK, 1949), about an aristocratic English family.

4 Having known me, to decline ...

Locksley Hall, L.43 (1842). This curious unattributed fragment is a quotation that gets interrupted in Anthony Hope's novel *The Dolly Dialogues*, Chap. 22 (1894). Clearly, it must have been something that was known to any well-read person of the 1890s.

5 ... I dipped into the future far as human eye
  could see,
Saw the Vision of the world, and all the wonder that would be.

Saw the heavens fill with commerce, argosies
  of magic sails,
Pilots of the purple twilight, dropping down
  with costly bales;

Heard the heavens fill with shouting, and
  there rain'd a ghastly dew
From the nations' airy navies grappling in
  the central blue.

Ib., l. 119. A rejected lover returns to his one-time home by the sea and, among other things, complains of the modern world of steamships and railways. He also makes an eerie prediction of commerce and warfare being extended to the skies. Sir John Colville's published diaries of his time as Winston Churchill's private secretary (*The Fringes of Power*, paperback editions 1986–7) reveal the wartime Prime Minister quoting 'Tennyson's prescient lines about aerial warfare' (19 March 1941) without actually saying what the lines are.

6 We are not now that strength which in old days
Moved earth and heaven; that which we are,
  we are;
One equal temper of heroic hearts,
Made weak by time and fate, but strong in will
To strive, to seek, to find, and not to yield.

'Ulysses', l. 44 (1842). The line 'To strive, to seek ...' appears on a memorial to Captain Scott, Captain Oates and others, at the South Pole. It was chosen by Apsley Cherry-Garrard, author of *The Worst Journey in the World* (1922).

7 O Swallow, Swallow, flying, flying South,
Fly to her, and fall upon her gilded eaves,
And tell her, tell her, what I tell to thee.
O tell her, Swallow, thou that knowest each,
That bright and fierce and fickle is the South,
Dark and true and tender is the North.

Ib., Pt 4, l. 75 (song added 1850). Sometimes used, semi-humorously, to emphasize the qualities of those from the North of England or Scotland. If anything, however, the contrast is really between the North and the South of *Europe*.

8 The moan of doves in immemorial elms.

Ib., Pt 7, l. 203. Hence, 'immemorial elms' as a cliché of quotation. 'The PM ... dreams of Britain where we all drink warm beer in the shadow of immemorial elms, and nuns bicycle to church through the mist, and Denis Compton is still at the crease on the final day of the Oval test match' – *The Observer* (19 February 1995); 'I have driven for hours around those winding lagoon-like car parks, lovingly landscaped between clumps of immemorial elms, trying to find the exit' – *The Times Higher Education Supplement* (31 March 1995).

9 'Tis better to have loved and lost
Than never to have loved at all.

In Memoriam A.H.H., Canto 27 (1850). *Compare* BUTLER 138:1.

1 Though Nature, red in tooth and claw
With ravine, shrieked against his creed.

Ib., Canto 56. Origin of the phrase 'red in tooth and claw'.

2 So many worlds, so much to do,
So little done, such things to be.

Ib., Canto 73. *Compare* RHODES 454:3.

3 Revered, beloved – you that hold
A nobler office on the earth
Than valour, power of brain, or birth,
Could give the warrior kings of old.

'To the Queen' – the new Poet Laureate's first poem to his sovereign in March 1851. G.K. Chesterton quotes the last three lines in *The Napoleon of Notting Hill*, Chap. 3 (1904) as though they had been written by his character, Mr Quin: '... to quote a poem that I wrote in my youth ...'

4 O fall'n at length that tower of strength
Which stood four-square to all the winds that blew!

'Ode on the Death of the Duke of Wellington' (1852). *See also* SHAKESPEARE 493:7.

5 Not once or twice in our rough island story
The path of duty was the way to glory.

Ib. The probable origin of the 'island story' phrase. *Our Island Story, a child's history of England* (*c.*1910) by H.E. Marshall (stories and fables from King Arthur to Queen Victoria, addressed to two Australian children) was an immensely popular history book in the early twentieth century. *Compare* NEWBOLT 409:5.

6 Forward the Light Brigade!
Was there a man dismay'd?
Not tho' the soldier knew
Someone had blundered:
Their's not to make reply,
Their's not to reason why,
Their's but to do and die:
Into the valley of Death
Rode the six hundred.

['Their's' is as written.] 'The Charge of the Light Brigade' (1854). The Charge of the Light Brigade took place at Balaclava, near Sebastopol, on 25 October 1854, during the Crimean War. Owing to a misunderstood order, 247 officers and men out of 637 were killed or wounded. Tennyson's famous poem about it was published in *The Examiner* newspaper on 9 December that same year. According to Christopher Ricks's edition of the poems, Tennyson wrote this on 2 December 1854, 'in a few minutes, after reading ... *The Times* in which occurred the phrase *someone had blundered*, and this was the origin of the metre of his poem'. In fact, *The Times* had spoken rather (in a leader on 13 November) of 'some hideous blunder'. Advised to be careful because controversy would offend the War Office, Tennyson allowed the 'someone had blundered' line to be deleted when his next collection of poems was published (*Maud, and Other Poems*, 1855). But when he heard that the Society for the Propagation of the Gospel intended to circulate this *revised* poem to the troops, he had copies of the *uncut* version printed and sent to the Crimea.

7 And chalk and alum and plaster, are sold to the poor for bread.

Maud, I.i.x (1855). It is extraordinary how frequently Tennyson turns out to be the author of 'lost quotations' and half-remembered bits of verse. In 1992, this was traced to its source via the *OED2* on CD-Rom, where it is to be found as a citation for the word 'alum' (though incorrectly given as '*while* chalk and alum'. A correspondent had sought a source for the words her mother used to sing to a hymn tune.

8 Come into the garden, Maud,
For the black bat, night, has flown.

Ib., I.xxii.1. The first line, immensely famous, was further popularized in the musical setting of the lines by Michael Balfe in 1856.

9 For why is all around us here
As if some lesser god had made the world,
But had not force to shape it as he would.

'The Passing of Arthur' (l.13–15) in *Idylls of the King* (1859). Hence, *Children of a Lesser God*, the title of Marc Medoff's play (1979, film US, 1986), about a relationship between a deaf girl and her speech therapist. Medoff's suggestion, presumably, is that people with a disability like deafness could be said to be the work of a 'lesser god'.

10 The old order changeth, yielding to the new,
And God fulfils himself in many ways,
Lest one good custom should corrupt the world.

Ib., l. 407. The meaning of the third line has puzzled some readers. Tennyson himself indicated that what he meant was 'e.g., chivalry, by formalism of habit or by any other means'.

1 The woods decay, the woods decay and fall,
The vapours weep their burthen to the ground,
Man comes and tills the field and lies beneath,
And after many a summer dies the swan.

'Tithonus' (1860). Hence, *After Many A Summer*, title of a novel (1939) by Aldous Huxley.

2 Flower in the crannied wall,
I pluck you out of the crannies,
I hold you here, root and all, in my hand,
Little flower – but *if* I could understand
What you are, root and all, and all in all,
I should know what God and man is.

'Flower in the Crannied Wall' (1869). A 'lost' quotation sought in 1989 by a biochemist who said that it summed up his own philosophy.

3 Landscape-lover, lord of language
more than he that sang the Works and Days,
All the chosen coin of fancy
flashing out from many a golden phrase.

'To Virgil' (1882), 'written at the request of the Mantuans for the nineteenth centenary of Virgil's death'. The rush of alliteration in the first line of this stanza possibly introduces the phrase 'lord of language'. Subsequently it has been otherwise bestowed. 'Ah, Madame Melba, I am the Lord of Language and you are the Queen of Song, and so I suppose I shall have to write you a sonnet' – Oscar Wilde, quoted in Nellie Melba, *Melodies and Memories* (1925). In *De Profundis* (published 1905), Wilde wrote of his mother's death: 'I, once a lord of language, have no words in which to express my anguish and shame.'

From this phrase may also have come such compliments as 'master of language' and 'lord of words'. The latter was used, for example, to describe the broadcaster, Sir Huw Wheldon, and the playwright, Samuel Beckett, at their deaths in 1986 and 1989, respectively. 'The Word-Lord' is a heading in *Punch* (9 June 1915).

4 Sunset and evening star,
And one clear call for me!
And may there be no moaning of the bar,
When I put out to sea.

'Crossing the Bar' (1889). *Compare* KINGSLEY 336:1.

5 A louse in the locks of literature.

Of the critic, Churton Collins. Quoted in Evan Charteris, *Life and Letters of Sir Edmund Gosse* (1931).

TERENCE

Roman playwright (c.190–159BC)

6 *Homo sum; Humani, nil a me alienum puto.*
I am a man; I count nothing human foreign to me.

Heauton Timoroumenos. See also LAWRENCE 345:9.

TERESA OF AVILA

Spanish mystic and saint (1515–82)

7 Let nothing disturb thee,
Let nothing affright thee,
All passeth away,
God alone will stay,
Patience obtaineth all things.
Who God possesseth, is lacking in nothing
God alone sufficeth.

In *The Art of the Possible* (1971), R.A. Butler recalled how he quoted all but the last two of these lines to Winston Churchill when the Prime Minister retired in 1955, adding 'This, like St Augustine, I have learned'. But, no, this is commonly known as 'St Teresa's prayer', and Stephen Clissold in his biography of her (published in 1979) tells of the circumstances in which it was written.

8 Alas, O Lord, to what a state dost Thou bring those who love thee!

The Interior Castle (1577), translated by the Benedictines of Stanbrook (1921). This has also been rendered as, when caught in a great flood on the road to Burgos, she exclaimed: 'Lord if this is how you treat your friends, no wonder they are so few.'

THE TERMINATOR

American film 1984. With Arnold Scharzenegger as the Terminator.

9 I'll be back!

A phrase that caught on following its menacing use by Schwarzenegger playing a time-travelling robot who terminates his opponents with extreme prejudice. The phrase is spoken only once within the film but caught on because it so perfectly caught the central threat and menace of the story.

Coincidentally, the last words of the film *Pimpernel Smith* (UK, 1941) are: 'I'll be back ... we'll all be back.' These are spoken by Leslie Howard as a professor of archaeology who goes into war-torn Europe to rescue refugees.

TEY, Josephine

British crime novelist (1896–1952)

1 The beasts that talk,
The streams that stand,
The stones that walk,
The singing sand ...
That guard the way
To Paradise.

The Singing Sands (1952), in which the whole plot hinges on this fragment of verse scribbled on a newspaper by a dying man. The detective in question – Inspector Grant – is reduced to putting an advertisement in *The Times* to find the source, and thinks: 'It will serve me right if someone writes to say that the thing is one of the best-known lines of some Xanadu concoction of Coleridge's, and that I must be illiterate not to have known it.' But it does not appear to be an actual quotation.

'Singing sands' in itself is a long-established term for sands that appear to make a noise. The caption to a cartoon in *Punch* (22 August 1923): 'Lord Curzon's forthcoming book of travel, his publishers state, will contain "a full and picturesque study of the Singing Sands, i.e., the sand slopes and dunes which in remote and often inaccessible parts of Asia, Arabia and even America, give forth sounds which resemble the noise of trumpets and drums".'

THACKERAY, William Makepeace

English novelist (1811–63)

2 'Revenge may be wicked, but it's natural,' answered Miss Rebecca. 'I'm no angel.' And, to say the truth, she certainly was not.

Vanity Fair, Chap. 1 (1847–8). An early appearance of the self-deprecatory phrase, 'I'm no angel'. *Compare*: *I'm No Angel* (film US, 1933) and *We're No Angels* (film US, 1954).

3 The *Pall Mall Gazette* is written by gentlemen for gentlemen.

Pendennis, Chap. 32 (1848–50). *Compare* SALISBURY 467:6.

THATCHER, Sir Denis

English businessman and husband of Margaret Thatcher (1915–)

4 I like everything my beloved wife likes. If she wants to buy the top brick of St Paul's, then I would buy it.

Quoted in *The Observer* (7 April 1985) and probably taken from an interview in the *Sunday Express*. Partridge/*Slang* suggests that the phrase 'to give someone the top brick off the chimney' means 'to be the acme of generosity, with implication that foolish spoiling, or detriment to the donor would result, as in "his parents'd give that boy the ..." or "she's that soft-hearted, she'd give you ...".' Partridge's reviser, Paul Beale, who inserted this entry, commented that he had heard the phrase in the early 1980s but that it was probably in use much earlier.

Indeed, when Anthony Trollope was standing for Parliament in 1868, he described a seat at Westminster as 'the highest object of ambition to every educated Englishman' and 'the top brick of the chimney'. In *Nanny Says*, Joyce Grenfell's and Sir Hugh Casson's collection of nanny sayings (1972) is included, 'Very particular we are – it's top brick off the chimney or nothing'. Presumably, Denis Thatcher was reworking this saying for his own ends. Unconsciously, he may have been conflating it with another kind of reference, such as is found in Charles Dickens, *Martin Chuzzlewit*, Chap. 38 (1844): 'He would as soon as thought of the cross upon the top of St Paul's Cathedral taking note of what he did ... as of Nadgett's being engaged in such an occupation.'

THATCHER, Margaret (later Baroness Thatcher)

British Conservative Prime Minister (1925–)

5 No woman in my time will be Prime Minister or Chancellor or Foreign Secretary – not the top jobs. Anyway, I wouldn't want to be Prime Minister. You have to give yourself 100%.

Interview, *The Sunday Telegraph* (26 October 1969). Mrs Thatcher was notably dismissive of her chances of achieving high office – before the opportunity presented itself. A little later, when Secretary of State for Education, she was interviewed on the BBC TV programme *Val Meets the VIPs* (1973) and said: 'I do not think there will be a woman Prime Minister in my lifetime ... I would not wish to be Prime Minister, dear. I have not enough experience for that job. The only full ministerial position I've held is Minister of Education and Science. Before you could even *think* of being Prime Minister, you'd need to have done a good deal more jobs than that.'

1 Ladies and gentlemen, I stand before you tonight in my green chiffon evening gown, my face softly made up, my fair hair gently waved ... the Iron Lady of the Western World. Me? A cold war warrior? Well, yes – if that is how they wish to interpret my defence of values, and freedoms fundamental to our way of life.

Speech in her Finchley constituency (31 January 1976). Earlier, on 19 January, Mrs Thatcher had said in a speech that 'The Russians are bent on world dominance ... the Russians put guns before butter'. Within a few days the Soviet Defence Ministry newspaper *Red Star* (in an article signed by Captain Y. Gavrilov) had accused the 'Iron Lady' of seeking to revive the Cold War. The article wrongly suggested that she was popularly known by this nickname in the UK at that time, though a headline over a profile by Marjorie Proops in the *Daily Mirror* of 5 February 1975 had been 'The Iron Maiden'. Now, in her Finchley speech, she made the 'Iron Lady' sobriquet her own.

2 Let us make this a country safe to work in. Let us make this a country safe to walk in. Let us make it a country safe to grow up in. Let us make it a country safe to grow old in. And [the message of the 'other' Britain] says, above all, may this land of ours, which we love so much, find dignity and greatness and peace again.

Televised party political broadcast on 30 April 1979, the eve of her first election win. Thatcher smuggled in an unacknowledged quote from Noël Coward's play *Cavalcade* (1931). In the original, the toast is: 'That one day this country of ours, which we love so much, will find dignity and greatness and peace again.' The hand of Sir Ronald Millar, the playwright and her principal speechwriter, may presumably be detected in this.

3 I would just like to remember some words of St Francis of Assisi which I think are really just particularly apt at the moment – 'Where there is discord, may we bring harmony; where there is error may we bring truth; where there is doubt, may we bring faith; and where there is despair, may we bring hope.'

Outside 10 Downing Street on becoming Prime Minister (4 May 1979). *See* FRANCIS OF ASSISI 244:1.

4 There is no easy popularity in that [harsh economic measures already set in train by the government] but I believe people accept there is no alternative.

Speech to the Conservative Women's Conference, London (21 May 1980). An early appearance of the famously nannyish phrase 'there is no alternative' that became a rallying cry of the Thatcher government. It provides a good example of how it can be more difficult tracing the origins of recent quotations than of older ones. By the early 1980s, everyone in Britain knew the phrase, but how had it arisen? If she had said it in the House of Commons it would have been possible to search through the parliamentary record *Hansard* (the electronic version makes computer-searching very simple). But she had not, apparently. So one was faced with searching through newspapers for a mention of the phrase, except that most British newspapers were not being transferred on to computer databases until the mid-1980s.

Perhaps she had said it at one of her meetings with Parliamentary lobby correspondents? But these occasions are never directly reported and if she had said it at one, the political correspondents consulted were unable to remember.

In 1984 Dr David Butler, the psephologist, appoached me regarding the phrase because he was revising his *British Political Facts*. Some more asking around was done and no progress was made. Patrick Cosgrave, an adviser to Mrs Thatcher before she became Prime Minister, suggested that, perhaps, the phrase had not actually been coined by her, but simply picked up, in the way she had of seizing on ideas she fancied.

Butler wrote to Downing Street and received a letter from Mrs Thatcher's then political secretary espousing a similar view: 'I am not sure that the Prime Minister ever actually used the phrase ... and my suspicion, shared by others, is that TINA was coined by those who were pressing for a change of policy.'

This only took us further away than ever from a satisfactory conclusion. Then, in 1986, and in the time-honoured fashion, I happened to stumble upon a report of Mrs Thatcher speech to the Conservative Women's Conference, marking the end of her first year in office, as above. So, there, she *had* said it, and publicly, too. I don't know whether this was the first time – in fact, I think she may well have said it at some stage in 1979 – but at last here was a reference.

A correspondent suggested a comparison with the old Hebrew catchphrase '*ain breira*' ('there is no choice'). The acronym TINA, said to have been coined by Young Conservatives, was flourishing by the time of the Party Conference in September 1981.

5 To those waiting with bated breath for that favourite media catchphrase, the U-turn, I

have only one thing to say. You turn if you want to. The lady's not for turning.

Speech to the Conservative Party Conference at Brighton (11 October 1980). Here Mrs Thatcher comes up with what is, in a sense, her best remembered formally spoken 'line'. While not convincing the hearer that she could have alluded unaided to the title of the play *The Lady's Not for Burning* (1948) by Christopher Fry, the cry had the curiously insidious memorability that most effective slogans need to have. Again, one detects the hand of Sir Ronald Millar in all this. Indeed, in *The Sunday Times* (23 November 1980), he confirmed that he had coined the phrase, but also reported that he would have 'preferred his friend the prime minister to have said "the lady's not for turning" with an elided "'s" exactly as in the original title of Christopher Fry's play.' Which is odd, because any recording of the speech will confirm that she did *not* say, 'The lady is not', but 'the lady's not ...' (just as she was told).

1 **As the poet said, 'One clear morn is boon enough for being born', and so it is.**

Interview on BBC Radio with Pete Murray (7 March 1982). The occasion was when, tearfully, she described her fears while it had seemed that her son Mark was lost on a Trans-Sahara car rally. She realized then, she said, that all the little things people worried about really were not worth it. Here Mrs Thatcher is relying on that old standby 'As the poet said ...' to disguise forgetfulness or genuine ignorance of the source.

I was puzzled by the quotation and wrote to Downing Street for illumination, my letter plopping on the mat just as the Falklands War broke out. When that little difficulty was resolved, I received back a photocopy of an anonymous poem which had presumably been carried about in the Thatcher handbag for many a year. Subsequently, in *Woman's Own* (17 November 1984), it was revealed that the poem had been taken from something called 'Love's Tapestry Calendar 1966':

Life owes me nothing:
  One clear morn
Is boon enough
  for being born;
And be it ninety years
  or ten,
No need for me
  to question when.
While life is mine,
  I'll find it good
And greet each hour
  with gratitude.

2 **Failure? Do you remember what Queen Victoria once said? 'Failure? – the possibilities do not exist.'**

TV news interview (5 April 1982) at the start of the war in the Falklands. Mrs Thatcher evoked the spirit of Queen Victoria with the remark that had been made at the end of 'Black Week' in 1899, during the Boer War: 'We are not interested in the possibilities of defeat; they do not exist.' *Time* Magazine (December 1982) ascribed the words to Mrs Thatcher as though they were not a quotation. *See also* VICTORIA 550:6.

3 **Just rejoice at that news and congratulate our forces and the Marines. Goodnight. Rejoice!**

Remark to newsmen outside 10 Downing Street (25 April 1982) on the recapture of South Georgia – wording confirmed by TV recordings made at the time. Usually rendered as 'Rejoice, rejoice!' From the next day's *Daily Telegraph* (26 April 1982): 'A triumphant Prime Minister declared "Rejoice, rejoice" last night ...'. Much later, this is Julian Critchley MP writing in *The Observer* (27 June 1993): 'Shortly after Mrs Thatcher's defenestration in November 1990, I ran into [Sir Edward] Heath in a Westminster corridor. I quoted a Spanish proverb: if you wait by the river long enough, the body of your enemy will float by. Heath broke into a broad grin: "Rejoice, rejoice", was his reply.'

Either way, can one detect signs of her Methodist upbringing? Although 'Rejoice, rejoice!' is quite a common expression, each verse of Charles Wesley's hymn 'Rejoice! the Lord is King' ends: 'Rejoice, again I say, rejoice' (a hymn played at the 1983 Conservative Party Conference). There was also a nineteenth-century hymn (words by Grace J. Frances), 'Rejoice, Rejoice, Believer!' The refrain of 'O Come, O Come Emmanuel' (a hymn translated by J.M. Neale) goes, 'Rejoice! Rejoice! Emmanuel/Shall come to thee, O Israel'. But, as P. Daniel of York points out, the ultimate source is Philippians 4:4: 'Rejoice in the Lord alway: and again I say, Rejoice.'

4 **Let me make one thing absolutely clear. The NHS is safe with us.**

Speech to Conservative Party Conference, Brighton (8 October 1982).

5 **Victorian values ... those were the values when our country became great, not only internationally but at home.**

Interview on ITV's *Weekend World* (17 January 1983). In the General Election of that year and thereafter, Margaret Thatcher and other Cabinet ministers frequently commended the virtue of a return to Victorian values. The phrase appears to have been coined for her by Brian Walden in this TV interview. It was *he* who suggested to *her* that she was trying to restore 'Victorian values'. She replied: 'Very much so. Those were the values when our country became great. But not only did our country become great internationally, also much advance was made in this country – through voluntary rather than state action.' Mrs Thatcher also said in an LBC radio interview on 15 April: 'I was brought up by a Victorian grandmother. We were taught to work jolly hard. We were taught to prove ourselves; we were taught self-reliance; we were taught to live within our income ... You were taught that cleanliness is next to godliness. You were taught self-respect. You were taught always to give a hand to your neighbour. You were taught tremendous pride in your country. All of these things are Victorian values. They are also perennial values.' On 23 April *The Daily Telegraph* quoted Dr Rhodes Boyson, the Minister for Schools, as saying: 'Good old-fashioned order, even Victorian order, is far superior to illiterate disorder and innumerate chaos in the classroom,' and Neil Kinnock, then Chief Opposition Spokesman on Education, as saying: 'Victorian Britain was a place where a few got rich and most got hell. The "Victorian values" that ruled were cruelty, misery, drudgery, squalor and ignorance.'

In her book *The Downing Street Years* (1993), Margaret Thatcher comments: 'I never felt uneasy about praising "Victorian values" or – the phrase I originally used – "Victorian virtues".'

1 Some say Maggie may, or others say Maggie may not. I can only say that when the time comes, I shall decide.

Speech (April 1983), when wishing to appear coy about whether she would be calling a General Election soon. An unwise allusion to a character in the Liverpool song 'Maggie May', which dates from at least 1830. She is a prostitute who steals sailors' trousers, but, as the song goes on to relate: 'A policeman came and took that girl away./For she robbed a Yankee whaler,/She won't walk down Lime Street any more.'

A number of groups (including the Beatles) revived the song at the time of Liverpool's resurgence in the early 1960s. Lionel Bart and Alun Owen wrote a musical based on her life and called *Maggie May* in 1964.

2 Oh, the Right Honourable Gentleman is afraid of an election is he? Afraid, afraid, afraid, frightened, frit, couldn't take it, couldn't stand it!

A challenge to the prominent Labour minister, Denis Healey, in the House of Commons (20 April 1983). Healey had suggested that she was preparing to 'cut and run' regarding a general election. 'Frit', as an abbreviation for 'fright/frightened' is still widely used in the North Midlands – including Grantham where she was born. The first recorded use of the word was by the Northamptonshire poet, John Clare. In 'The Village Minstrel' (1821), he wrote:

> The coy hare squats nesting in the corn,
> Frit at the bow'd ear tott'ring over her head.

The chief surprise in Mrs Thatcher using the word was that hitherto she had successfully concealed her linguistic roots.

3 We had to fight the enemy without in the Falklands. We always have to be aware of the enemy within which is more difficult to fight and more dangerous to liberty.

Speech to the 1922 Committee (19 July 1984). The expression 'enemy within' refers to an internal rather than external threat. It has been suggested that it is a shortened version of 'the enemy/traitor within the gate(s)' – 'one who acts, or is thought to act, against the interests of the family, group, society, etc. of which he is a member' – but, whatever the case, it is a phrase with a long history. In 1940 Winston Churchill said of the BBC that it was 'an enemy within the gates, doing more harm than good'. A 1957 film had a title *The Enemy Below* and a 1978 TV film *The Enemy at the Door*.

On 22 January 1983, *The Economist* wrote of the industrial relations scene in Britain: 'The government may be trusting that public outrage will increasingly be its ally. Fresh from the Falklands, Mrs Thatcher may even relish a punch-up with the enemy within to enhance her "resolute approach" further.'

Seven months later, Mrs Thatcher was using exactly the same phrase and context regarding the British miners' strike. She 'told Tory MPs that her government had fought the enemy without in the Falklands conflict and now had to face an enemy within ... she declared that the dockers and pit strikers posed as great a threat to democracy as General Galtieri, the deposed Argentine leader' (*The Guardian*, 20 July 1984).

Earlier, in 1980, Julian Mitchell had used the phrase as the title of a play about anorexia. It was also the title of a Tony Garnett BBC TV play in 1974 and of a stage play by Brian Friel in 1962. A book (1960) by Robert F. Kennedy about 'organized corruption' in the US labour movement had the title, as did one by John Watner during / about the Second World War (untraced). The earliest *OED2* citation dates from 1608: 'The enemy within ... sporteth herself in the consumption of those vital parts, which waste and wear away by yielding to her unpacifiable teeth' – Edward Topsell, *The Historie of Serpents*. Compare also Cicero on the Catilinarian conspiracy to launch a *coup d'état*: '*Intus est hostis*' (*In Catilinam*, II.v.11).

1 In church on Sunday morning – it was a lovely morning and we haven't had many lovely days – the sun was coming through a stained glass window and falling on some flowers, falling right across the church. It just occurred to me that this was the day I was meant not to see.

Mrs Thatcher expressed her feelings on having escaped death in an IRA bomb explosion at Brighton. In a TV interview she referred to Sunday 14 October 1984. *The Observer* (21 October) reported the final phrase as 'the day I was not meant to see'. *The Daily Telegraph* (17 October) had already affirmed that 'the day I was meant not to see' was the correct version, adding: 'Since they are words which may well enter future anthologies, we should get the record straight.' In 1995, *Brewer's Politics* was giving the phrase as, 'this was *a* day I was not meant to see.'

2 We must try to find ways to starve the terrorists of the oxygen of publicity on which they depend.

Speech to American Bar Association meeting in London (15 July 1985). While the phrase 'oxygen of publicity' did not seem new at the time, this usage certainly popularized the term. Coinage of the phrase has been ascribed to Britain's then Chief Rabbi, Lord Jakobovits.

3 Stop being moaning minnies.

Remark during visit to Tyneside (11 September 1985). Mrs Thatcher was reported as accusing those who complained about the effects of unemployment of being 'Moaning Minnies'. In the ensuing uproar, a Downing Street spokesman had to point out that it was the reporters attempting to question her, rather than the unemployed, upon whom Mrs Thatcher had bestowed the title.

As a nickname, it was by no means an original coinage. Anyone who complains is a 'moaner' and a 'minnie' is a word that can be used to describe a lost lamb which finds itself an adoptive mother. From *The Observer* (20 May 1989): 'Broadcasters are right to complain about the restrictions placed on them for the broadcasting of the House of Commons ... But the Moaning Minnies have only themselves to blame.'

The original 'Moaning Minnie' was something quite different. In the First World War a 'Minnie' was the slang name for a German *Minenwerfer*, a trench mortar or the shell that came from it, making a distinctive moaning noise. In the Second World War the name was applied to air-raid sirens, which also made that noise.

4 Is he one of us?

Attributed remark when reviewing candidates for appointments (by 1985). From *The Independent* (28 January 1989): 'Mr [Kenneth] Clarke also failed the is-he-one-of-us? test applied by Mrs Thatcher to favoured colleagues.' Hence, *One of Us*, the title of Hugo Young's political study of Mrs Thatcher (1989).

5 I hope to go on and on.

On her future as Prime Minister. In BBC Radio interview with John Cole (11 May 1987) after she had called a General Election, possibly repeating an earlier remark. This is precisely what she said in answer to Cole's question whether she expected this to be her last election as party leader. In Cole's memoir, *As It Seemed to Me* (1995), he cannot resist stating that what she said was – as popularly rendered – that she intended 'to go on and on and on'.

6 There is no such thing as Society. There are individual men and women, and there are families. And no government can do anything except through people, and people must look to themselves first. It's our duty to look after ourselves and then to look after our neighbour.

Interview, *Woman's Own* (31 October 1987) – which, in her memoirs (*op. cit.*), she says 'caused a storm of abuse at the time'. What she meant was that no one could escape moral responsibility for their actions by transferring that responsibility to an abstraction. Much-alluded to: from the film *Trainspotting* (UK, 1996): 'There was no such thing as society and, even if there was, I most certainly had nothing to do with it.'

7 We have become a grandmother.

Remark to news reporters (3 March 1989). From this use of the royal 'we' stemmed a conviction in some observers that all was not well with Mrs Thatcher. She survived in office for only another year and a half.

8 The President of the Commission, M. Delors, said at this conference the other day that he wanted the European Parliament to be the

democratic body of the Community, he wanted the Commission to be the Executive, and he wanted the Council of Ministers to be the Senate. No. No. No.

Speech, House of Commons (30 October 1990) on her return from the Rome summit. It has been said that the stridency of her attack on this occasion contributed to the resignation of the Deputy Prime Minister, Sir Geoffrey Howe, the following month and her own removal from office the month after that.

1 It's a funny old world.

In *The Independent* (23 November 1990), Margaret Thatcher was reported as having exclaimed 'It's a funny old world' (with tears in her eyes) at the previous day's Cabinet meeting at which she announced she had been ousted from the Prime Ministership. This is a fairly common expression of reluctant acceptance of some blow that fate has delivered. In the 1934 film *You're Telling Me*, W.C. Fields delivers the line, 'It's a funny old world – a man's lucky if he gets out of it alive.'

2 Home is where you come to when you have nothing better to do.

Interview, *Vanity Fair* (May 1991). The meaning of this observation was disputed. Her view was that she had spoken as if addressing her children – this was the traditional attitude of children towards their homes – and had not been describing her own feelings about home. All she had meant to say was that the children's home was always there. *Compare* FROST 248:2. In *The Observer* (20 September 1987), Bette Davis, the actress, was quoted by Katharine Whitehorn as having said: 'Home is only where you go to when you've nowhere to go.'

See also DRAKE 214:5; KIPLING 339:5 and 339:7.

THAT WAS THE WEEK THAT WAS

British TV satire series (BBC), 1962–3. Title also used in the US.

3 That Was the Week That Was.

Title. *See* BIRD 108:7.

4 Well, it was satire, wasn't it? ... You can say bum, you can say po, you can say anything ... Well, he said it! The thin one! He said bum one night. I heard him! Satire!

Sketch, 'Close Down' (by Keith Waterhouse and Willis Hall).

THING, The

American film 1951, (known in the UK as The Thing From Another World).

5 *Last speech*: I bring you warning – to every one listening to the sound of my voice. Tell the world, tell this to everyone wherever they are: *watch the skies*, watch everywhere, keep looking – *watch the skies!*

The key phrase was later used to promote the film *Close Encounters of the Third Kind* (1977) and was the original title of that film.

THOMAS à KEMPIS

German religious writer (1379–1471)

6 *Nam homo proponit, sed Deus disponit.*
Man proposes and God disposes.

De Imitatione Christi, I, 19 (*c.*1420); the first appearance of the idea in this form. It derives from an old proverb found in Greek, Hebrew and Latin. Proverbs 16:9 in the Bible has it in the form: 'A man's heart deviseth his way; but the Lord directeth his steps.'

'Man Proposes, God Disposes' was the title of an extraordinary painting (1864) by Sir Edwin Landseer, showing two polar bears amid the wreckage of a ship caught in Arctic ice. In 1987, Liza Minelli said 'Man plans and God laughs' in a TV interview, which sounds like a modern development of the old proverb.

7 *O quam cito transit gloria mundi.*
O, how quickly the world's glory passes away.

Ib. More usually rendered as '*sic transit gloria mundi* [so passes away the glory of the world]'. This expression is used at the coronation ceremony of Popes when a reed surmounted with flax is burned and a chaplain intones: '*Pater sancte, sic transit gloria mundi*' to remind the new Holy Father of the transitory nature of human vanity. *ODQ* (1992) says, however, that it was used at the crowning of Alexander V at Pisa in July 1409, and is of earlier origin, which, if so, would mean that it was à Kempis who was doing the a-quoting.

8 Everywhere I have sought rest and not found it, except sitting in a corner by myself with a little book.

Quoted by Allen Andrews in *Quotations for Speakers and Writers* (1969). Benham (1948) has that, 'according to his biographer', Thomas à Kempis inscribed these words in his books: '*Im omnibus requiem quaesivi, et nusquam invei nisi in een hoecksken met een boecksken, id est angello cum libello* [In all things have I sought rest and have never found it except in a little nooklet with a booklet, that is in a small corner with a small book].'

THOMAS, Dylan

Welsh poet (1914–53)

1 And Death Shall Have No Dominion.

Title of poem (1936) on immortality; a straightforward allusion to Romans 6:9: 'Christ being raised from the dead dieth no more: death hath no more dominion over him.'

2 Portrait of the Artist as a Young Dog.

Title of a book (1940) of mostly autobiographical short stories, probably after *Portrait of the Artist as a Young Man*, the novel (1914–15) by James Joyce, also largely autobiographical. It alludes to the customary way of describing self-portraits in art – e.g., 'Portrait of the Artist with Severed Ear' (Van Gogh).

3 In my craft or sullen art
Exercised in the still night
When only the moon rages
And the lovers lie abed
With all their griefs in their arms ...

Not for the proud man apart
From the raging moon I write
On these spindrift pages.

'In my craft or sullen art' (1945). The phrase 'raging moon' may be an original coinage to Thomas. The nearest the *OED2* gets is 'raging *noon*'. *The Raging Moon* was the title of a film (UK,1970, from a novel by Peter Marshall) about physically disabled people.

4 Time held me green and dying
Though I sang in my chains like the sea.

'Fern Hill' (1946). Part of the inscription on Thomas's memorial in Poets' Corner, Westminster Abbey (unveiled on St David's Day 1982). The second line is also quoted on the statue of him and on a stone monument, both in Swansea. On Thomas's modest grave in the Welsh town of Laugharne there is but a wooden cross, bearing his name, dates and 'RIP'.

5 Do not go gentle into that good night.
Rage, rage against the dying of the light.

'Do Not Go Gentle Into That Good Night' (1951). Probably inspired by Thomas's observation of his dying father. A combative man in earlier years, he was now, in his eighties, 'soft and gentle at the last'. The poet urges him not to acquiesce in the process of dying.

6 The land of my fathers [Wales] – my fathers can have it.

Quoted in *Adam* (December 1953). 'Land of My Fathers' (1860) is the Welsh national anthem.

7 In pursuit of my life-long search for naked women in wet mackintoshes.

When asked, 'Why have you come to America, Mr Thomas?' Quoted in Constantine Fitzgibbon, *Dylan Thomas*, Chap. 8 (1965). Another version from the *Evening Standard* (2 May 1995): 'Asked by the hack pack the reason for his visit to [New York] his succinct reply was: "Naked women in wet macs".'

8 I've had eighteen straight whiskies. I think that's the record.

Thomas made this dying boast to his girlfriend, Liz Reitell, after a drinking bout in New York. Quoted in Barnaby Conrad, *Famous Last Words* (1961). These were not his last words, although he went into a coma shortly afterwards and died. His biographers have subjected the bout to much scrutiny and have watered it down to a mere four or five whiskies. He often exaggerated.

THOMAS, Edward

English poet (1878–1917)

9 Yes; I remember Adlestrop –
The name, because one afternoon
Of heat the express-train drew up there
Unwontedly. It was late June ...

And for that minute a blackbird sang
Close by, and round him, mistier,
Farther and farther, all the birds
Of Oxfordshire and Gloucestershire.

'Adlestrop', *Poems* (1917). An evocative description of a moment on a hot summer's day in Oxfordshire. Adlestrop station was, in fact, in Gloucestershire, though close to the county border.

THOMAS, J(ames) H(enry)

British trade unionist and politician (1874–1949)

10 You don't take a ham sandwich to the Lord Mayor's banquet, do you?

When asked whether his wife was accompanying him on an official visit to Paris. Unverified.

See also SMITH 507:8.

THOMPSON, Francis

English poet (1859–1907)

1 Look for me in the nurseries of heaven.

'To My Godchild Francis M.W.M.' (1913). This is the text chosen for Thompson's grave in the Roman Catholic annexe to Kensal Green Cemetery, London.

2 The angels keep their ancient places;
Turn but a stone and start a wing!
'Tis ye, 'tis your estranged faces,
That miss the many-splendoured thing.

'The Kingdom of God' (1913). Hence, *Love Is a Many-Splendored Thing*, the novel (1952; film US, 1955) by Han Suyin.

THOMPSON, Hunter S.

American writer (1939–)

3 Fear and Loathing in Las Vegas.

Title of book (1972) based on his articles in *Rolling Stone* (11/25 November 1971) describing a visit to the gambling resort while under the influence of a variety of mind-expanding drugs. Apart from having a much-quoted title, the book is a prime example of what Thompson calls 'gonzo journalism', in which the writer chronicles his own role in the events he is reporting and doesn't worry too much about the facts. The word may be the same as Italian *gonzo* [a fool; foolish].

THOMPSON, William Hale 'Big Bill'

American politician (1867–1944)

4 [I'd] punch King George in the snoot.

On what he would do if George V were ever to set foot in Chicago (not that there was much chance of the king ever doing so). Quoted in Kenneth Allsop, *The Bootleggers* (1961). No direct quotation exists of whatever it was Thompson said when running for a third term as mayor in 1927 – 'poke in the snoot', 'bust in the snoot' are other reported versions – but his Anglophobia is not in question. 'I wanta make the King of England keep his snoot out of America ... That's what Big Bill wants' – quoted in Lloyd Wendt & Herman Kogan,*Big Bill of Chicago* (1953).

THOMPSON, William Hepworth

English scholar (1810–86)

5 What time he can spare from the adornment of his person he devotes to the neglect of his duties.

Of Sir Richard Jebb, later Professor of Greek at Cambridge. Quoted in M.R. Bobbit, *With Dearest Love to All* (1960).

THOMSON, James

Scottish poet (1700–48)

6 When Britain first, at Heaven's command,
Arose from out the azure main,
This was the charter of the land,
And guardian angels sung this strain:
'Rule, Britannia, rule the waves;
Britons never will be slaves.'

Alfred: a Masque (1740), which had another author called Mallet, but Thomson is thought to have written this bit. The music was by Dr Thomas Arne. Invariably misquoted. Of the several recordings of this famous patriotic song, few can match that by Cilla Black (on PCS 7103). I suspect it was recorded when Swinging London was at its height and the Union Jack flag was plastered patriotically over everything from mini-skirts to tea-mugs. Anyway, what she is heard to sing is:

> Rule, Britannia,
> Britannia rules the waves.
> Britons never, never, never
> Shall be slaves.

Of course, Cilla Black is not alone in preferring to sing 'rules' and 'shall'. Annually, at the Last Night of the Proms, several hundred other people can be heard singing her version – and drowning out those who may feel like sticking to Thomson.

There is a difference, however, between a poetic exhortation – 'rule' – and a boastful assertion in – 'rules'. As for the difference between 'will' and 'shall', life is really too short to go on about that at any length. But an interesting defence of the Cilla Black reading comes from Kingsley Amis and James Cochrane in *The Great British Songbook* (1986): 'When what a poet or lyric-writer wrote differs from what is habitually sung, we have generally preferred the latter ... Britons never "shall" be slaves here, not "will" as James Thomson, a Scot following Scottish usage, naturally had them.'

THOMSON, Roy (later Lord Thomson)

Canadian-born industrialist (1894–1976)

1 You know, it's just like having a licence to print your own money.

To a neighbour in Edinburgh just after the opening of Scottish Television (a commercial TV company he had founded) in August 1957. Quoted in Russell Braddon, *Roy Thomson* (1965). Cautioned not to repeat this brash statement, he flew to Canada and repeated the bon mot in an interview with *Time* Magazine. 'In fact it was current in America before he used it. Having more important things to do he did not repudiate the authorship' – L. Marsland Gander [TV critic] in *The Sunday Telegraph* (6 June 1982).

2 Editorial is what keeps the ads apart.

Attributed remark. *Compare* NORTHCLIFFE 415:3.

THOREAU, Henry David

American writer (1817–62)

3 If a man does not keep pace with his companions, perhaps it is because he hears a different drummer. Let him step to the music which he hears, however measured or far away.

Walden (1854). Hence, presumably, *Different Drummer*, a ballet (1984) choreographed by Kenneth MacMillan; *The Different Drum* (1987), a work of popular psychotherapy by M. Scott Peck; and *Different Drummer*, a BBC TV series (1991) about eccentric American outsiders.

THORNDIKE, Sybil (later Dame Sybil)

English actress (1882–1976)

4 Divorce? Never. But murder often!

When asked if she had ever considered divorce during her long marriage to Sir Lewis Casson. Unverified. The British Liberal politician David Steel apparently once said of his ally Dr David Owen on one occasion: 'I am reminded of Dame Sybil Thorndike's comment on her long marriage. She considered divorce never, murder frequently. With Dr Owen it is murder, occasionally.' Also attributed to Elizabeth Longford, historian wife of the 7th Earl of Longford, in John G. Murray, *A Gentleman Publisher's Commonplace Book* (1996).

THORPE, Jeremy

English Liberal politician (1929–)

5 Bunnies *can* (and *will*) go to France. Yours affectionately, Jeremy. I miss you.

Letter to Norman Scott (13 February 1961). Thorpe was a flamboyant politician who became leader of the Liberal Party but then had to resign in 1976 because Scott, a former male model, spread rumours that the two of them had had a homosexual affair. It was further alleged that Thorpe had plotted to have Scott murdered, though this charge was overturned at the Old Bailey in 1979.

In an earlier bid to defuse the situation (*c.* 1976), Thorpe had allowed publication of a letter which ended as above. Scott explained the 'bunnies' as referring to Scott as a frightened rabbit – this was how Thorpe had described him on the night he had seduced Scott. The saying became part of the folklore surrounding the scandal.

In R.W. Holder's *The Oxford Dictionary of Euphemisms* (1995) 'bunny' is defined as a 'homosexual who takes the female role', though whether this usage was current in 1961 is not clear (Partridge/*Slang* does not have it.)

6 Greater love hath no man than this, that he lay down his friends for his life.

Comment on the 'Night of the Long Knives', when Harold Macmillan sacked half his Cabinet (13 July 1962). Quoted in D.E. Butler & A. King, *The General Election of 1964* (1965). Alluding to John 15:13 (*see* BIBLE 103:2).

7 We believe that the only way in which the maximum degree of national cooperation can be achieved is for a government of national unity to be formed.

Letter to Edward Heath (4 March 1974). Later in the year, the phrase became a central theme in the Conservatives' October general election campaign.

8 Looking around the House, one realises that we are all minorities now.

After a general election that resulted in no party having a clear majority. Speech, House of Commons (6 March 1974), alluding to 'We are all socialists nowadays', EDWARD VII 221:4.

THURBER, James

American cartoonist and writer (1894–1961)

1 I suppose that the high-water mark of my youth in Columbus, Ohio, was the night the bed fell on my father.

My Life and Hard Times (1933). The chapter in which this line occurs is simply called 'The Night the Bed Fell'.

TIME

American news magazine, founded 1923

2 World War II began last week at 5.20 a.m. (Polish time) Friday, September 1, when a German bombing plane dropped a projectile on Puck, fishing village and air base in the armpit of the Hel Peninsula.

September 1939. Others, more cautiously, were talking only of 'the war in Europe' at this time.

THE TIMES

British London-based newspaper, founded 1788

3 We shall not pretend that there is nothing in his long career which those who respect and admire him would wish otherwise.

On the accession of King Edward VII. Leading article (23 January 1901).

4 IT *IS* A MORAL ISSUE.

Title of leading article about the Profumo affair (11 June 1963).

5 At social gatherings he was liable to engage in heated and noisy arguments which could ruin a dinner party, and made him the dread of hostesses on both sides of the Atlantic. The tendency was exacerbated by an always generous, and occasionally excessive alcoholic intake.

From the obituary of Randolph Churchill (7 June 1968). *Times* obituaries are traditionally unsigned but this one – which, not before time, pushed forward the boundaries of what it was possible to say about the recently dead – is believed to have been written by Malcolm Muggeridge.

6 But the truth is that when it comes to the heat [*sic*] of the matter, to the courage that supports a nation, Lord George-Brown drunk is a better man than the Prime Minister [Harold Wilson] sober.

Leading article (4 March 1976), after Brown had announced that he was quitting the Labour Party and after an incident in which he was photographed falling in the gutter outside the Houses of Parliament. *The Times* Magazine (23 May 1993), while mentioning that Woodrow Wyatt claimed to have made the remark earlier – in 1963 – also revealed that William Rees-Mogg had actually come up with the sentence, as editor, in 1976: 'I wrote it. I remember it well. Bernard Levin was sitting in my outer office. I showed it to Bernard and said: "I don't really think I can print that, do you?" Bernard replied: "If you *don't* print it, I shall never speak to you again." Perhaps Woodrow's memory is playing him up.' *See also* BROWN 124:1.

See also COCKBURN 176:3; LINCOLN 355:7; POPE 434:7.

THE TIMES LITERARY SUPPLEMENT

British London-based journal, founded 1902

7 As a contribution to natural history, the work is negligible.

Reviewing Kenneth Grahame's *The Wind in the Willows* (22 October 1908). Quoted in Peter Green, *Kenneth Grahame* (1959).

TO HAVE AND HAVE NOT

US film 1945. Script by Jules Furthman and William Faulkner after Ernest Hemingway's novel. With Lauren Bacall as 'Slim' and Humphrey Bogart as 'Steve'.

8 If you want anything – just whistle.

This is not a direct quotation (though often given as such). What Bacall actually says *to* Bogart (and not the other way round, as in *PDMQ*, 1980) is: 'You know you don't have to act with me, Steve. You don't have to say anything, and you don't have to do anything. Not a thing. Oh, maybe just whistle. You know how to whistle, don't you, Steve? You just put your lips together and blow.'

TOLKIEN, J.R.R.

English novelist and academic (1892–1973)

9 Farmer Giles of Ham.

Title of story (1949). 'Farmer Giles' as the personification of the (British) farmer, possibly derives from the subject of Robert Bloomfield's poem *The Farmer's Boy*

(1800) (although he is a labourer rather than a farmer). Coincidentally or not, Isaac Bickerstaff in *The Maid of the Mill* (1765) has: 'I am determined farmer Giles shall not stay a moment on my estate, after next quarter day.' Accordingly, 'farmers' is rhyming slang for piles (haemorrhoids).

TOLSTOY, Leo

Russian novelist (1828–1910)

1 War and Peace.

English title of novel (1865–8). According to Henry Troyat's biography, Tolstoy did not decide on a title until very late. '*The Year 1805* would not do for a book that ended in 1812. He had chosen *All's Well That Ends Well* [*see* SHAKESPEARE 475:1], thinking that would give the book the casual, romantic tone of a long English novel'. Finally, the title was 'borrowed from Proudhon' – *La Guerre et la Paix* (1862).

2 Life is everything. Life is God. Everything changes and moves and that movement is God. And while there is life there is joy in consciousness of the divine. To love life is to love God. Harder and more blessed than all else is to love this life in one's sufferings, in innocent sufferings.

Ib. An expression of Pierre's pantheistic belief – which Tolstoy himself held.

3 Shakespeare's plays are bad enough, but yours are even worse.

To Anton Chekhov. Remark, quoted in Henri Troyat, *Tolstoy* (1965). Whilst unkind to Chekhov, this is an example of Tolstoy's obsessive dislike for Shakespeare. He resented him because Shakespeare subsumed himself in his characters, was not didactic, and – chiefly perhaps – because Shakespeare just was not Tolstoy.

TOMALIN, Nicholas

English journalist (1931–73)

4 The only qualities essential for real success in journalism are rat-like cunning, a plausible manner, and a little literary ability.

In *The Sunday Times* Magazine (26 October 1969). Tomalin was writing on careers in journalism, and his view, though a touch self-serving, has continued to be quoted admiringly by other journalists. He himself was killed while covering the Arab-Israeli war in 1973.

TOPLADY, Augustus Montague

English clergyman (1740–78)

5 Rock of Ages, cleft for me,
Let me hide myself in Thee.

Hymn, first published in *The Gospel Magazine* (1775). Brewer (1989) recounts two stories of its composition: one, that it was written while seated by a great cleft in the rock near Cheddar, Somerset; two, that it was written on the ten of diamonds between two rubbers of whist at Bath.

The phrase 'rock of ages' is said to be the actual meaning in Hebrew of the words 'everlasting strength' at Isaiah 26:4.

TOYNBEE, Arnold

English historian (1889–1975)

6 No annihilation without representation.

Pressing for a greater British voice in UNO (1947). Attributed by *PDMQ* (1971). Toynbee was, of course, echoing the cry 'No taxation without representation', the North American colonists' anti-British slogan of the 1760s and in the years before the War of Independence. In the form 'Taxation without representation is tyranny', its coinage has been attributed to the lawyer and statesman James Otis. In 1763 he opposed British taxation on the grounds that the colonies were not represented in the House of Commons.

TRAIN, Jack

English actor (1902–66)

7 I don't mind if I do!

Catchphrase of 'Colonel Chinstrap' in BBC radio show *ITMA* (first appeared 1940–1). Spoken whenever a drink was even so much as hinted at, originally in the form, 'Thanks, I will!' The Colonel was based on an elderly friend of the announcer, John Snagge. He was a typical ex-Indian Army type, well-pleased with himself. The phrase had existed before, of course. *Punch* carried a cartoon in 1880 with the following caption:

> *Porter*: Virginia Water!
> *Bibulous old gentleman (seated in railway carriage)*: Gin and water! I don't mind if I do!

ITMA, however, secured the phrase a place in the language, as the Colonel doggedly turned every hint of liquid refreshment into an offer:

> *Tommy Handley*: Hello, what's this group? King John signing the Magna Carta at Runnymede?
> *Chinstrap*: Rum and mead, sir? I don't mind if I do!

TRAPIDO, Barbara

English novelist (1941–)

1 Brother of the More Famous Jack.

Title of novel (1982). It refers neither to characters in the book nor to Robert and John F. Kennedy. No, Chapter 4 has: 'Yeats, William Butler ... Brother of the more famous Jack, of course.' The Irish poet W.B. Yeats did indeed have a brother, Jack, who was a leading artist. Often alluded to. From Robert Stephens, *Knight Errant* (1995): 'The stars were Claude Hulbert, brother of the more famous Jack, his wife Delia Trevor, and another fine comedian called Sonny Hale.' From Michael Kerrigan, *Who Lies Where* (1995): 'Bankside was, of course, theatreland in the seventeenth century. Edmund Shakespeare, brother of the more famous William, is buried here.'

TRAVERS, Ben

English playwright (1886–1980)

2 There's a lot of promiscuity around these days and I'm all for it.

Remark, *c.*1980, quoted in *Telegraph Sunday Magazine*. Travers, noted for his farces, enjoyed a revival in his last years. In *A-Sitting on the Gate* (1978), he wrote: 'The year 1976 during which I reached my ninetieth birthday was by far the most eventful and rewarding of my lifetime, for two of my farces were revived and I found myself the rather bewildered old author of three simultaneous London successes (*The Bed*, *Plunder* and *Banana Ridge*)'.

TREE, Sir Herbert Beerbohm

English actor-manager (1853–1917)

3 Ladies, just a little more virginity, if you don't mind.

To unsuitable American actresses who had been assembled to play ladies-in-waiting to a queen. Quoted in Alexander Woollcott, *Shouts and Murmurs* (1923).

4 A committee should consist of three men, two of whom are absent.

Quoted in Hesketh Pearson, *Beerbohm Tree* (1956). Also attributed to Lord Mancroft (1914–87) in some anthologies. On the other hand, *The Treasury of Humorous Quotations*, ed. by Evan Esar & Nicolas Bentley (1951), has E.V. Lucas (1868–1938) saying, 'The best committee is a committee of two when one is absent.' Hendrik Van Loon wrote in *America* (1927): 'Nothing is ever accomplished by a committee unless it consists of three members, one of whom happens to be sick and the other absent.' Anon. said: 'A committee of one gets things done.'

On the same subject: to J.B. Hughes (in Prochnow & Prochnow, *Treasury of Humorous Quotations*, 1969) is attributed the remark, 'If Moses had been a committee the Israelites would still be in Egypt'. (Or, 'never would have got across the Red Sea' in a remark attributed in 1965 to General Booth, founder of the Salvation Army.)

The anonymous observation, 'A camel is a horse designed by a committee' (quoted, for example, in American *Vogue*, 1958) bears an interesting resemblance, surely, to 'A donkey is a horse translated into Dutch' – which Georg Christoph Lichtenberg (1742–99) had in his *Aphorisms*.

John Le Carré included in the novel *Tinker, Tailor, Soldier, Spy* (1974), the observation, 'A committee is an animal with four back legs'. *See also* ALLEN 16:7; COCKS 176:5.

TRENET, Charles

French singer and songwriter (1913–)

5 *Baisers Volés.*
Stolen Kisses.

Title of film (France, 1968) by François Truffaut, taken from a phrase in the song, '*Que Reste-t-il de Nos Amours*' (1943), written and performed by Trenet (and which is featured in the film). In English, there had earlier been the song 'A Stolen Kiss' (1923) by R. Penso; also a ballad, undated, by F. Buckley, 'Stolen Kisses are the Sweetest'. *See also* CIBBER 171:4; HUNT 305:3.

TRINDER, Tommy

English comedian (1909–89)

6 Overpaid, overfed, oversexed and over here.

On American troops in Britain during the Second World War. Quoted in *The Sunday Times* (4 January 1976). This was Trinder's full-length version of a popular British expression of the early 1940s. He certainly did not invent it although he may have done much to popularize it. Partridge/*Catch Phrases* makes no mention of Trinder and omits the 'overfed'.

As 'over-sexed, over-paid and over here' it is said also to have been a popular expression about American troops in Australia 1941–5 (according to *The Dictionary of Australian Quotations*, 1984) and to have been revived there during the Vietnam War.

TROLLOPE, Anthony

English novelist (1815–82)

1 Three hours a day will produce as much as a man ought to write.

Autobiography, Chap. 15 (1883). The book was published posthumously and did Trollope much harm in the short term by showing that he was rather more interested in the money he made from his books than his Victorian contemporaries might have thought proper. Its last words: 'Now I stretch out my hand, and from the further shore I bid adieu to all who have cared to read any among the words that I have written.'

TROTSKY, Leon

Russian revolutionary (1879–1940)

2 The literary 'fellow travellers' of the Revolution.

Literature and Revolution (1923). Trotsky was referring to non-Communist writers who sympathized with the Revolution. Later, the phrase came to mean anyone who sympathized with Communism without actually being a member of the Party.

3 You are pitiful isolated individuals; you are bankrupts; your role is played out. Go where you belong from now on – into the dustbin of history!

History of the Russian Revolution, Vol. 3, Chap. 10 (1933). Sometimes 'dustheap' or 'scrapheap of history' is put instead. Was it with reference to the fate of the decrees emanating from Kerensky's Provincial government in the Winter Palace in 1917? Or was it to the fate of his opponents (as suggested by E.H. Carr in his *Socialism in One Country* (1958)? The latter, in fact, and specifically referring to the Mensheviks (the moderates who opposed Lenin and the Bolsheviks' call for the overthrowing of the Tsar by revolution).

Earlier, in a similar coinage, Charles Dickens reflected on Sir Robert Peel's death in 1850: 'He was a man of merit who could ill be spared from the Great Dust Heap down at Westminster.' *See also* BIRRELL 109:2.

TRUMAN, Harry S

American Democratic 33rd President (1884–1972)

4 I don't know whether you fellows ever had a load of hay fall on you, but when they told me yesterday what had happened, I felt like the moon, the stars, and all the planets had fallen on me.

Remark to journalists, on succeeding F.D. Roosevelt (13 April 1945). Quoted in *Newsweek* Magazine (23 April 1945).

5 This is the greatest thing in history.

On the Hiroshima atom bomb. Remark (6 August 1945). Quoted in A.J.P. Taylor, *English History 1914–1945* (1965).

6 The son of a bitch isn't going to resign on me, I want him fired.

To Omar Bradley of General MacArthur. Quoted in Merle Miller, *Plain Speaking: An Oral Biography of Harry S Truman* (1974). Truman's language was notably salty for the period. His wife had to reprimand him for frequent recourse to 's.o.b.'s'. In 1951 he sacked General Douglas MacArthur from his command of UN forces in Korea for insubordination and repeatedly criticizing the administration's policy of non-confrontation with China. Truman added this remark, lest the General hear of the decision and jump the gun.

7 If you can't stand the heat, get out of the kitchen.

Looking back in 1960, Truman said: 'Some men can make decisions and some cannot. Some men fret and delay under criticism. I used to have a saying that applies here, and I note that some people have picked it up.' When Truman announced that he would not stand again as President, *Time* Magazine (28 April 1952) had him give a 'down-to-earth reason for his retirement, quoting a favourite expression of his military jester Major General Harry Vaughan', namely, 'If you can't stand the heat, get out of the kitchen'. The attribution is usually given to Truman himself but it may not be what he said at all. 'Down-to-earth' is not quite how I would describe this remark, whereas 'If you can't stand the stink, get out of the shit-house' would be. I have only hearsay evidence for this, but given Truman's reputation for salty expressions, it is not improbable.

Bartlett (1980) quotes Philip D. Lagerquist of the Harry S Truman Library as saying, 'President Truman has used variations of the aphorism ... for many years, both orally and in his writings' (1966). Note the 'variations'.

8 The buck stops here.

Truman had a sign on his desk bearing these words, indicating that the Oval Office was where the passing of the buck had to cease. It appears to be a saying of his own invention. 'Passing the buck' is a poker player's expression. It refers to a marker that can be passed on by someone who does not wish to deal. Later, Jimmy Carter restored Truman's motto to the Oval Office. When President Nixon published his memoirs (1978), people opposed to its sale went around wearing buttons which said, 'The book stops here'.

1 The biggest mistake in politics is to take your friends for granted and try to buy your enemies.

Said after he defeated Thomas Dewey in the 1948 Presidential election. Quoted in *The Observer* (7 July 1996).

2 It's a recession when your neighbour loses his job: it's a depression when you lose yours.

Quoted in *The Observer* (13 April 1958). Often reassigned to other politicians.

3 He not only doesn't give a damn about the people; he doesn't know how to tell the truth. I don't think the son of a bitch knows the difference between telling the truth and lying.

Of Richard Nixon. Quoted in Merle Miller, *op. cit.* (1974). Barbara Rowes, *The Book of Quotes* (1979) adds the extra: 'Richard Nixon is a no-good lying bastard. He can lie out of both sides of his mouth at the same time, and if he ever caught himself telling the truth, he'd lie just to keep his hand in.'

4 What's a statesman anyway? I'll tell you what he is – he's just a politician no one is afraid of any more.

Quoted in *The Observer* (11 May 1986). Another definition is: 'A statesman is a defunct politician.' *See also* REED 451:7.

TUCKER, Sophie

Russian-born American entertainer (1884–1966)

5 Keep breathing.

Asked, at the age of eighty, the secret of longevity. Quoted in *The Quotable Woman* (1978).

6 I've been rich and I've been poor. Believe me, honey, rich is better.

Unverified. Henry McNulty wrote (in 1995): 'Although Ms. Tucker was born in Russia, she grew up in Hartford, Connecticut, and is considered a "hometown girl" by Hartfordites. So as you can imagine, the files at the *Hartford Courant* newspaper, where I am an editor, are full of stories about, and comments by, Sophie Tucker.

'I have diligently gone through all the stories that appeared in the *Courant* from 1922 until her death in February 1966. There was absolutely no mention of the "I've been rich" quotation – not even in her obituary. I also checked the lengthy obituaries in *The New York Times* and the (now defunct) *Hartford Times*. Again, no mention of this comment, and you'd think there would have been if she'd said it. I then studied Ms. Tucker's 1945 autobiography *Some of These Days* (named after one of her signature tunes.) But again, although she wrote extensively of her early poverty, there was no I've-been-rich-and-poor comment. (In fact, the book is amazingly free of the wisecracks she is so known for.) So I have nothing conclusive to provide except, I suppose, negative evidence (and fortunately, no one else will have to pore through her autobiography). My guess is that this is one of those comments that sounds like something "the last of the Red Hot Mamas" *would* have said, so it is attributed to her whether she said it or not.

'The most recent edition of *Bartlett's Familiar Quotations* [1992], by the way, has a version of the quote calling it "attributed" to Ms. Tucker. They report it as: "I have been poor and I have been rich. Rich is better." This rather more formal version, leaving out "believe me, honey" makes me think, again, that this is something that Sophie Tucker *ought to have said*, and various people quote it as they imagine she would have said it. Whether she did so is still in question, but if votes are being counted, I vote no.'

Incidentally, in *PD20* (1995) there are the following two entries: 'I've been rich, and I've been poor and believe me, rich is better' – Joe E. Lewis (d.1971), quoted in Barbara Rowes, *The Book of Quotes* (1979). 'I've been rich and I've been poor; believe me rich is better' – spoken by Gloria Grahame in the film *The Big Heat* (US, 1953), screenplay by Sydney Boehm from the story by William P. McGivern. Further evidence, perhaps, that it is a modern proverb that somehow became attached to Tucker, maybe without reason.

TURNER, J.M.W.

English painter (1775–1851)

7 The Fallacies of Hope.

Poem (*c.*1812). Turner liked not only to give titles to his pictures – 'The Fighting Téméraire', 'Slavers throwing overboard the dead and dying – typhoon coming on', and so on, but to append portions of verse as citations or captions. As one of his biographers, Jack Lindsay, explained (1966): 'He wanted the extra heightening of consciousness which the verses provided.' However, if the verses did not quite fit his ideas, he happily rewrote them, be they by Shakespeare or Gray or whoever. He also wrote his own poetry so that he could quote from it in these captions, including a work which survives only in fragments, 'The Fallacies of Hope'. There are some who believe that the poem never actually existed.

Kenneth Clark used the phrase as the title of one of the parts of his *Civilisation* TV series (1969) and explained how Ruskin had said of Turner that he was indeed 'without hope' – especially in the face of Nature's cruelty and indifference. Turner also wrote: 'Hope, hope, fallacious hope, where is thy market now?'

Unfortunately, Turner was considerably less of a poet than he was a painter. Under his painting 'Queen Mab's Grotto', he appended supposed lines from *A Midsummer Night's Dream* – 'Frisk it, frisk it, by the moonlight beam' (which appear nowhere in Shakespeare) and from his own 'Fallacies of Hope' – 'Thy orgies, Mab, are manifold'. That should give sufficient flavour of his written art.

1 The sun is God!

Dying words. Quoted in Barnaby Conrad, *Famous Last Words* (1961).

TWAIN, Mark (Samuel Langhorne Clemens)

American writer (1835–1910)

2 Earned a precarious living by taking in one another's washing.

Customarily ascribed (with slight hesitancy) to Mark Twain. In *The Commonweal* (6 August 1887) an article entitled 'Bourgeois Versus Socialist' signed by William Morris ends: 'A bourgeois paradise will supervene, in which everyone will be free to exploit – but there will be no one to exploit ... On the whole, one must suppose that the type of it would be that town (surely in America and in the neighbourhood of Mark Twain) that I have heard of, whose inhabitants lived by taking in each other's washing.'

Two years later, George Bernard Shaw wrote that 'The inhabitants [of Bayreuth] either live in villas on independent incomes or else by taking in one another's washing and selling confectionery, scrap books and photographs' (from *The Hawk*, 13 August 1889). Slightly after this, 'E.W.C.' wrote in *Cornish Notes & Queries* (First Series) (1906): 'I have certainly heard the phrase in connection with the Scilly Islands. And some go so far, and are so rude, as to suggest "Hence their name".' Similarly, in the forward to his *Poems 1938–1945*) (1946), Robert Graves declared: 'I write poems for poets, and satires or grotesques for wits ... The moral of the Scilly Islanders who earned a precarious livelihood by taking in one another's washing is that they never upset their carefully balanced island economy by trying to horn into the laundry trade of the mainland; and that nowhere in the Western Hemisphere was washing so well done.'

Benham (1960) lists the well-known joke with the attribution 'origin unknown', and adds: 'It is said that a society was formed (*circa* 1900) for the purpose of discovering the origin of the phrase, but without result.'

3 Cheer up! The worst is yet to come.

In a letter from Twain to his wife (1893/4) included in *The Love Letters of Mark Twain*. Also in *Those Extraordinary Twins* (1894). Partridge/*Catch Phrases* manages no more than 'a US c.p. of ironic encouragement since *c.*1918'. The most usual attribution, though, is to the American writer Philander Johnson (1866–1939) in his *Shooting Stars* (*c.*1920), *see* 317:8. The similar expression, 'Cheer up ... you'll soon be dead!' appears in several British entertainments in the period 1909–18. The original non-ironic line, 'The worst is yet to come', occurs in Tennyson's *Sea Dreams* (1864).

The worst pun on the phrase concerns the man who was eating a German meal but was encouraged to continue with the words, 'Cheer up, the *wurst* is yet to come!'

4 When I was a boy of fourteen, my father was so ignorant I could hardly stand to have the old man around. But when I got to be twenty-one, I was astonished at how much he had learned in seven years.

Attributed in *Reader's Digest* (September 1939). As Burman (1980) points out, if Twain ever said this (or words to the effect: it is untraced), there was more than a hint of poetic licence about it. His own father died when Twain was eleven.

5 The report of my death was an exaggeration.

Twain's reaction to a false report, quoted in the *New York Journal* (2 June 1897). Frequently over-quoted and paraphrased ever since, this has become the inevitable remark to invoke when someone's death has been wrongly reported (most usually one's own). It is also now employed in the sense of, 'You thought I was finished, but look at me now' (for example, by George Bush in February 1988 regarding the decline in his political fortunes). Variations include: 'Reports of my death have been greatly exaggerated' or 'are premature'.

A headline from *The Independent* (13 November 1993): 'Reports of Queen Mother's death exaggerated Down Under'.

1 Everybody talks about the weather but nobody does anything about it.

Was this said by Twain or by Charles Dudley Warner (1829–1900)? It first appeared in an unsigned editorial in the *Hartford Courant* (24 August 1897) in the form – 'A well-known American writer said once that, while everybody talked about the weather, nobody seemed to do anything about it' – but the quip has often been assigned to Twain who lived in Hartford (Connecticut) at the time. In 1993 Henry McNulty, an Associate Editor and the Reader Representative on the *Courant* (which is 'the Oldest Newspaper of Continuous Publication in America') guided me through the minefield of attribution: 'For many years the *Courant*, quite understandably, has taken the position that Warner, not Twain, made this remark. (Example: a 1947 *Courant* article on the subject was headlined, "Sorry, Mark, But Charlie Really Said It".) But after studying what various experts have had to say, I am now in favour of attributing it to Twain until new evidence turns up.

'As far as I know, the "weather" remark has not been found in any of Twain's writings, so I suppose it's fair to say that *in print*, the *Courant* is the original source. But who wrote the *Courant* editorial? Then, as now, they were unsigned. In 1897, Warner was the *Courant*'s editor, so it is certain that the editorial was approved (or at least seen) by him; but did he actually write it? No one knows, and there is no way to tell for sure today.

'Assuming that Warner wrote the editorial, one possibility is that the reference was to himself. He certainly was well-known at the time; he was a prolific writer; and the phrase "Politics makes strange bedfellows" is one from one of his eighteen books. It's not impossible that this was just a further quip, a wink to his friends. But if not, the most likely suspect would be Mark Twain. Warner and Twain were friends, neighbors and literary collaborators (they wrote *The Gilded Age*). Again, the "well-known American writer" phrasing would very likely be an in-joke, since of course every *Courant* reader would be familiar with Twain.

'Some years later, several people indeed attributed the remark to Warner. Charles Hopkins Clark, editor of the *Courant* after Warner's death in 1900, is reported to have said, "I guess it's no use. They still believe Mark Twain said it, despite all my assurances that it was Warner." That seems conclusive, but could his statement be colored both by the passage of time and by the fact that he and Warner were friends and colleagues?

'In July 1989, the New York State Bar Journal addressed the problem in a column entitled "Legal Lore". The Bar Journal decided to attribute the remark to both men. "Mark Twain ... probably did make the oral comment first to his billiard companion, Charles Dudley Warner," it said. "But ... Warner deserves the credit for having first put into writing this well-weathered statement."

'In the absence of any genuinely new historical evidence, this seems to me to be the best solution. I suppose one can't blame the *Courant* for insisting for all these years that Warner, not Twain, was the sole author of the quip, but I'm afraid that owes more to chauvinism than to scholarship.'

2 Golf is a good walk spoiled.

So attributed by Laurence J. Peter in *Quotations for Our Time* (1977). The German author Kurt Tucholsky (1890–1935) wrote: '*Golf, sagte einmal jemand, ist ein verdorbener Spaziergang* [Golf, someone once said, is a walk spoiled].' Otherwise unverified.

3 Always do right. This will gratify some people, and astonish the rest.

Talk to young people, Brooklyn (16 February 1901). President Truman kept this saying on his desk.

4 What a good thing Adam had. When he said a good thing he knew nobody had said it before.

Notebooks (published 1935). A surely unnecessary worry for a highly quotable author to have.

See also DISRAELI 211:1.

TYNAN, Kenneth

English critic (1927–80)

5 And I'll stay off Verlaine, too; he was always chasing Rimbauds.

Tynan used this quip in his very early days as a (schoolboy) critic. It earned him a rebuke from James Agate (recounted in *Ego 8*, for 20 July 1945), who wrote: 'To say that "Verlaine was always chasing Rimbauds" is just *common*. Like cheap scent.' Whether Tynan knew it or not, he had been anticipated by Dorothy Parker who wrote the 'chasing Rimbauds' line, in 'The Little Hours', *Here Lies* (1939).

6 Forty years ago he was Slightly in Peter Pan,

and you might say that he has been wholly in Peter Pan ever since.

On Noël Coward (1953), collected in *Curtains* (1961). He went on: 'Even the youngest of us will know, in fifty years' time, exactly what we mean by "a very Noël Coward sort of person."'

1 What, when drunk, one sees in other women, one sees in Garbo sober.

On Greta Garbo (1953), in *ib.* One of the finest compliments Tynan ever paid, just as his description of Anna Neagle (in that same year) is among his most withering: 'She sings, shaking her voice at the audience like a tiny fist.'

2 They say *The New Yorker* is the bland leading the bland. I don't know if I'm bland enough.

To a journalist before leaving England to join the magazine as its drama critic (1958). Quoted in Kathleen Tynan, *The Life of Kenneth Tynan* (1987). At about the same time, J.K. Galbraith was writing in *The Affluent Society* (1958): 'These are the days when ... in minor modification of the scriptural parable, the bland lead the bland.' In Leslie Halliwell, *The Filmgoer's Book of Quotes* (1973), an anonymous definition of television is given as 'the bland leading the bland'. All these quips allude, of course, to BIBLE 101:8.

3 I think so certainly ... I doubt if there are any rational people to whom the word 'fuck' would be particularly diabolical, revolting or totally forbidden. I think that anything that can be printed or said can also be seen.

In answer to a question whether he would allow 'a play to be put on at the National Theatre in which, for instance, sexual intercourse took place on the stage?' Interviewed on BBC TV *BBC3* programme (13 November 1965). This was the first time the f-word had been spoken, noticeably, in a British broadcast.

4 Oh! Calcutta!

Title of Tynan's sexually explicit stage revue (1969) – it derives from a curious piece of word play, being the equivalent of the French '*Oh, quel cul t'as* [Oh, what a lovely bum you've got]'. French *cul* is derived from the Latin *culus* 'buttocks' but, according to the context, may be applied to the female vagina or male anus. In her *Life of Kenneth Tynan* (1987), Kathleen Tynan states that she was writing an article on the surrealist painter Clovis Trouille, one of whose works was a naked odalisque lying on her side to reveal a spherical backside. The title was 'Oh! Calcutta! Calcutta!': 'I suggested to Ken that he call his erotic revue *Oh! Calcutta!* ... I did not know at the time that it had the further advantage of being a French pun.'

5 I do not see the EEC as a great love affair. It is more like nine middle-aged couples with failing marriages meeting at a Brussels hotel for a group grope.

Quoted in the *Observer* (11 May 1975). Also attributed to E.P. Thompson.

6 The Sound of Two Hands Clapping.

Title of a collection of Tynan's critical writings (1975). As he acknowledged, it derives from a Zen koan ('a riddle used in Zen to teach the inadequacy of logical reasoning'): 'We know the sound of two hands clapping. But what is the sound of one hand clapping?' This koan is said to appear as the epigraph of J.D. Salinger's *For Esmé – With Love and Squalor* (1953), though not in all editions.

U V

UHLAND, Johann Ludwig

German lyric poet (1787–1862)

1 Take, O boatman, thrice thy fee:
Take, I give it willingly:
For, invisible to thee,
Spirits twain have crossed with me.

An anonymous translation given in Benham (1907) – where also the poet's name is given as John Louis Upland. In *Mary Barton* (1848), Mrs Gaskell gives the lines in the original language: *'Nimm, nur, Fährmann, nim die Miethe, / Die ich gerne dreifach biete! / Zween, die mit mir überfuhren, / Waren geistige Naturen.'* Lewis Carroll, in *Sylvie and Bruno Concluded*, Chap. 3 (1893), quotes the above English version, but does not name the poet.

UMBERTO I

Italian King (1844–1900)

2 It is one of the incidents of the profession.

Of an attempt on his life. Attributed in A. Andrews, *Quotations for Speakers and Writers* (1969).

UPTON, Ralph R.

American engineer (early twentieth century)

3 Stop; look; listen.

Notice at US railroad crossings 1912. Quoted in R. Hyman, *A Dictionary of Famous Quotations* (1967). This rather esoteric piece of information stayed with me for many years, until suddenly confirmation started flooding in. The date was confirmed by Meredith Nicholson in *A Hoosier Chronicle* (1912): 'Everybody's saying "Stop, Look, Listen!" ... the white aprons in the one-arm lunch rooms say it now when you kick on the size of the buns.' The originator was confirmed by *Notes and Queries*, Vol. 195 (1950) saying that it was devised by Upton to replace the former 'Look out for the locomotive'. And any number of allusions testify to its popularity. A show with the title *Stop! Look! Listen!* (with music by Irving Berlin) opened on Broadway (27 December 1915); in 1916, George Robey introduced one of his greatest popular songs, 'I Stopped, I Looked, I Listened' in *The Bing Boys Are Here*, in London; a 1936 cheesecake advertisement for a New York supplier of artists' materials had the slogan 'Stop, Look and Kiss 'em'.

VANBRUGH, Sir John

English playwright and architect (1664–1726)

4 Under this stone, Reader, survey
Dead Sir John Vanbrugh's house of clay.
Lie heavy on him, Earth! for he
Laid many heavy loads on thee!

This epitaph was not written by Vanburgh, nor was it ever actually placed on his grave. It was written by Dr Abel Evans (1679–1737) thinking of Blenheim Palace, though it has also been ascribed to the architect, Nicholas Hawksmoor. The above version is the one in John Booth, *Metrical Epitaphs* (1868). *A Collection of Epitaphs* ... (1806) has: 'Lie *light* upon him earth! tho' he/Laid many a heavy load on thee.' (Compare, on Pelham: 'Lie heavy on him, land, for he/Laid many a heavy tax on thee'.)

Benham (1907) compares the Latin, '*Sit tibi terra gravis!* [May the earth be heavy upon thee]', which contrasts with '*Sit tibi terra levis!* [Let the earth lie light upon you]', sometimes abbreviated to 'S.T.T.L.'

VANDIVER, Willard D.

American politician (1854–1932)

1 I come from a state that raises corn and cotton and cockleburs and Democrats, and frothy eloquence neither convinces nor satisfies me. I am from Missouri. You have got to show me.

Vandiver was a representative in Congress from Columbia, Missouri, from 1897 to 1905. When he was a member of the House Naval Committee and was inspecting the Navy Yard at Philadelphia in 1899, he good-humouredly made the above statement when speaking at a dinner. 'I'm from Missouri' quickly became a way of showing scepticism and demanding proof. Missouri, accordingly, became known as the 'Show Me' state. The date of the speech is sometimes given as 1902, the speaker's name as Vandiner.

VARIETY

American show business newspaper, founded 1905

2 WALL ST. LAYS AN EGG.

Headline on the Wall Street crash (30 October 1929).

3 STICKS NIX HICKS PIX.

Headline meaning that cinema-goers in rural areas were not attracted to films with bucolic themes (17 July 1935).

4 EGGHEAD WEDS HOURGLASS.

Headline on the marriage of playwright Arthur Miller to Marilyn Monroe (1956). Quoted in Leslie Halliwell, *The Filmgoer's Book of Quotes* (1973).

VAUVENARGUES, Luc de Clapiers, Marquis de

French writer (1715–47)

5 *C'est un grand signe de médiocrité de louer toujours modérément.*
It is a great sign of mediocrity always to praise moderately.

Reflections and Maxims, No. 12 (1746). Compare what John Sheffield, 1st Duke of Buckingham and Normandy (1648–1721) wrote 'On Mr Hobbes':

> Such is the mode of these censorious days,
> The art is lost of knowing how to praise.

VEBLEN, Thorstein

American economist (1857–1929)

6 Conspicuous consumption of valuable goods is a means of reputability to the gentleman of leisure.

The Theory of the Leisure Class (1899). Veblen coined the term 'conspicuous consumption' to describe the extravagant use of expensive goods to display status. Compare the term 'conspicuous waste' (the *OED2*'s only citation is from 1969), a Marxist term to denote much the same thing but more critically.

7 The outcome of any serious research can only be to make two questions grow where one question grew before.

'Evolution of the Scientific Point of View' in the *University of California Chronicle* (1908). Veblen was clearly alluding to SWIFT 528:11.

VERDI, Giuseppe

Italian composer (1813–1901)

8 I direct that I be given a modest funeral, either at sunrise or at sunset, with no pomp, no singing, no music.

Last will (1900). He had his wish, and then they laid on an enormous memorial service for him ...

See also PIAVE 430:8.

VESPASIAN

Roman Emperor (AD 9–79)

9 *Pecunia non olet.*
Money does not smell.

Remark (*c.*AD70). When Vespasian imposed a tax on public lavatories, his son Titus objected on the grounds that this was beneath the dignity of the state. The Emperor – according to Suetonius, *Lives of the Caesars* – took a handful of coins, held them under his son's nose and asked if they smelt. On being told they didn't, Vespasian said, '*Atque et lotio est* [Yet, that's made from urine]'.

As a result, public urinals in France are still sometimes known as *vespasiennes*. The expression *Pecunia non olet* now means, 'Don't concern yourself with the source of money. Don't look a gift horse in the mouth.'

VICTORIA

British Queen (1819–1901)

1 I will be good.

From E.V. Lucas, *A Wanderer in London* (1906): 'It was there [Kensington Palace] that on May 24, 1819, she was born; and there that she was sleeping when in the small hours of June 20, 1837, the Archbishop of Canterbury and the Lord Chamberlain awakened her to hail her queen – and "I will be good," she said, very prettily, and kept her word.'

But no. These pious words were not said by Queen Victoria on her accession to the throne in 1837, but six years earlier when she was a mere twelve years of age. It was casually revealed precisely what lay in store for her, and this is what she said.

2 These American news are most dreadful and awful! One never heard of such a thing! I only hope it will not be catching elsewhere.

Letter to King Leopold (27 April 1865). Reacting to the assassination of President Lincoln.

3 No woman would do that.

Remark when it was pointed out to her that the Criminal Law Amendment Act of 1885 (which outlawed indecent relations between adults in public and in private) made no mention of women. Quoted in Richard Ellman, *Oscar Wilde* (1987). Another version: originally the wording had been 'any male or female person', but when the text was shown to the Queen, no one had the nerve to answer her query of 'Why women were included in the Act as surely it was impossible for them' (source: Ted Morgan, *Somerset Maugham*, 1980).

4 We are not amused.

The subject was raised in *Notebooks of a Spinster Lady* (1919) written by Miss Caroline Holland (1878–1903): '[The Queen's] remarks can freeze as well as crystallize ... there is a tale of the unfortunate equerry who ventured during dinner at Windsor to tell a story with a spice of scandal or impropriety in it. "We are not amused," said the Queen when he had finished.'

The equerry in question appears to have been the Hon. Alexander Yorke. Unfortunately, the German he had told the story to laughed so loud that the Queen's attention was drawn to it. Another contender for the snub is Admiral Maxse whom she commanded to give his well-known imitation of her which he did by putting a handkerchief on his head and blowing out his cheeks. Interviewed in 1978, Princess Alice, Countess of Athlone, said she had once questioned her grandmother about the phrase – 'I asked her ... [but] she never said it' – and affirmed what many have held, that Queen Victoria was 'a very cheerful person.'

5 He speaks to Me as if I was a public meeting.

Of W.E. Gladstone. Quoted in G.W.E. Russell, *Collections and Recollections* (1898).

6 Please understand that there is no one depressed in *this* house. We are not interested in the possibilities of defeat. They do not exist.

To A.J. Balfour, who was in charge of the Foreign Office. Quoted in Lady Gwendolen Cecil, *The Life of Robert, Marquis of Salisbury* (1931). During one week of the South African War in December 1899 – 'Black Week', as it came to be called – British forces suffered a series of setbacks in their fight against the Boers. Queen Victoria 'braced the nation in words which have become justly famous' (W.S. Churchill, *A History of the English-Speaking Peoples*, Vol. 4).

Margaret Thatcher quoted these words in her first television interview during the Falklands War, having seen them as a motto on Winston Churchill's desk in his Second World War bunker beneath Whitehall. *See* THATCHER 533:2.

7 Bertie!

It might be thought that the Queen's dying word was an entirely to be expected reference to her late and long-lamented consort, Prince Albert. Rather, it was the name of her son and heir, Albert Edward, who took the title of King Edward VII. Quoted in Barnaby Conrad, *Famous Last Words* (1961).

VIDAL, Gore

American novelist, playwright and critic (1925–)

8 Always a godfather, never a God.

Remark (1967), on being invited to be a godparent by Kenneth Tynan. Quoted in Kathleen Tynan, *The Life of Kenneth Tynan* (1987). Has also been ascribed to Alexander Woollcott.

9 I was far too polite to ask.

When asked whether the first person he had experienced sex with was male or female. Remark in interview (*c.*1971), quoted in *Forum* (1987).

10 I'm all for bringing back the birch, but only between consenting adults in private.

Interviewed on TV by David Frost and quoted in *The Sunday Times* Magazine (16 September 1973).

1 It is not enough to succeed. Others must fail.

This was quoted as 'the cynical maxim of a clever friend' by the Rev. Gerard Irvine during his 'anti-panegyric' for Tom Driberg (Lord Bradwell) after a requiem mass in London on 7 December 1976.

'It's not enough that I should succeed – others should fail,' was attributed to David Merrick, the Broadway producer, in Barbara Rowes, *The Book of Quotes* (1979).

2 Good career move.

Remark on hearing of Truman Capote's death (1984). Confirmed by him in BBC TV *Gore Vidal's Gore Vidal* (1995). According to *Time* Magazine (8 April 1985), the graffito 'Good career move' had appeared following Elvis Presley's death in 1977.

VILLIERS DE L'ISLE ADAM, Philippe-Auguste

French poet, novelist and playwright (1838–89)

3 *Vivre? les serviteurs feront cela pour nous.*
Living? The servants will do that for us.

Play *Axël*, Act 4, Sc. 2 (1890). This has given rise to a number of joke variations, of which 'Sex? Our servants do that for us' is probably the best known. In the film comedy *Carry on Up the Khyber* (UK, 1968), Kenneth Williams as the 'Khasi of Kalabar' says to Joan Sims as 'Lady Ruff-Diamond', 'I do not make love ... I am extremely rich. I have servants to do everything for me.' Which only goes to show how old this version must have been even then, for it to have been included in a *Carry On*.

When the film actor Victor Mature was told that he looked as though he had slept in his clothes, he is said to have replied: 'Don't be ridiculous. I pay someone to do that for me.'

VILLON, François

French poet (1431–c.1463)

4 *Mais où sont les neiges d'antan?*
But where are the snows of yesteryear?

'Ballade des dames du temps jadis', *Le Grand Testament* (1461). This translation by D.G. Rossetti.

VIRGIL

Roman poet (70–19BC)

5 *Amor vincit omnia.*
Love conquers all.

Eclogues, No. 10, l. 69. One of the best known proverbial expressions of all. Chaucer's Prioress had it on her brooch, as mentioned in 'The General Prologue' to *The Canterbury Tales*.

6 *Arma virumque cano.*
I sing of arms and the man.

The first line of the *Aeneid* has given us the poet's phrase 'I sing ...'. Robert Herrick in *Hesperides* (1648) begins: 'I sing of brooks, of blossoms, birds, and bowers'. William Cowper begins 'The Sofa' in *The Task* (1785):

> I sing the Sofa. I who lately sang
> Truth, Hope and Charity, and touch'd with awe
> The solemn chords ...
> Now seek repose upon a humbler theme.

Titles of poems by Walt Whitman include, 'One's Self I Sing', 'For Him I Sing' and 'I Sing the Body Electric' (*see* WHITMAN 566:9).

It also gives us the title of a play *Arms and the Man* (1894) by George Bernard Shaw – or, rather, it does so via Dryden's translation of the same: 'Arms, and the man I sing'. This version had earlier been cited by Thomas Carlyle in *Past and Present* (1843) when he wrote: 'For we are to bethink us that the Epic verily is not *Arms and the Man*, but *Tools and the Man*, – an infinitely wider kind of epic.'

7 *Timeo Danaos et dona ferentes.*
I fear the Greeks, even when they offer gifts.

Ib., Bk 2, l. 49. Hence, 'Beware Greeks bearing gifts', a warning against trickery. This is an allusion to the most famous Greek gift of all – the large wooden horse which was built as an offering to the gods before the Greeks were about to return home after besieging Troy unsuccessfully for ten years. It was taken within the city walls of Troy, but men leapt out from it, opened the gates and helped destroy the city. In the *Aeneid*, Laocoön warn the Trojans not to admit the horse, with these words.

8 *Decus et tutamen.*
An ornament and a safeguard.

Ib., Bk 5, l. 262. This has become the Latin inscription now found on the rim of the British pound coin, which replaced the banknote in 1983. The same words, suggested by John Evelyn the diarist, had appeared on the rim of a Charles II crown of 1662–3 (its purpose then was as a safeguard against clipping). The words refer to the inscription rather than the coin – and originally were '*viro, decus et tutamen in armis*'. The last five of these words comprise the motto of the Feltmakers' Company (incorporated 1604).

1 *Bella, horrida bella,*
Et Thybrim multo spumantem sanguine cerno.
I see wars, horrible wars, and the Tiber foaming with much blood.

Ib., Bk 6, l. 86. *See* POWELL 437:7.

2 *Facilis descensus Averno.*
It is easy to go down into Hell.

Ib., Bk 5, l. 126. This phrase is employed when wanting to suggest that man is readily inclined towards evil deeds. Avernus, a lake in Campania, was a name for the entrance to Hell. The epic poem continues with:

Noctes atque dies patet atri ianua Ditis;
Sed revocare gradum superasque evadere ad auras,
Hoc opus, hic labor est.
[Night and day, the gates of dark Death stand wide; but to climb back again, to retrace one's steps to the upper air – there's the rub, that is the task.]

See also RATTIGAN 446:8.

VOLTAIRE

French writer and philosopher (1694–1778)

3 The more ancient the abuse the more sacred it is.

Play, *Les Guèbres* (1769). *Compare* ALBERT 15:3.

4 I disapprove of what you say, but will defend to the death your right to say it.

A remark attributed to Voltaire, notably by S.G. Tallentyre in *The Friends of Voltaire* (1907). But Tallentyre gave the words as a free paraphrase of what Voltaire wrote in his *Essay on Tolerance*: 'Think for yourself and let others enjoy the privilege to do so, too'. So what we have is merely Tallentyre's summary of Voltaire point of view.

Then along came Norbert Guterman to claim that what Voltaire *did* write in a letter of 6 February 1770 to a M. Le Riche was: 'Monsieur l'Abbé, I detest what you write, but I would give my life to make it possible for you to continue to write.' This reference is unverified, however.

So, whether or not he used the precise words, at least Voltaire believed in the principle behind them.

5 *Si Dieu n'existait pas, il faudrait l'inventer.*
If God did not exist, it would be necessary to invent him.

Epîtres, No. 96 (1770). Hence, the formula, 'If —— did not exist it would have to be invented'. Other examples include: 'If Austria did not exist it would have to be invented' (František Palacky, *c.*1845); 'If he [Auberon Waugh, a literary critic] did not exist, it would be unnecessary to invent him' (Desmond Elliott, literary agent, *c.*1977); 'What becomes clear is that Olivier developed his own vivid, earthy classical style as a reaction to Gielgud's more ethereal one ... So if Gielgud did not exist would Olivier have found it necessary to invent himself?' (review in *The Observer*, 1988); 'If Tony Benn did not exist, the old Right of the Labour Party would have had to invent him' (*The Observer*, 15 October 1989).

6 In this country [England] it is thought well to kill an admiral from time to time to encourage the others.

Candide, Chap. 23 (1759). This was a reference to the case of Admiral Byng who, in 1756, was sent to relieve Minorca, which was blockaded by a French fleet. He failed and, when found guilty of neglect of duty, was condemned to death and shot on board the *Momarque* at Portsmouth. *See also* ANONYMOUS 53:4.

7 All is for the best in the best of possible worlds.

Ib., Chap. 30. Compare P.G. Wodehouse, 'Lord Emsworth and the Girl Friend', *Blandings Castle and Elsewhere* (1935): 'Lord Emsworth's gloom deepened. He chafed at being called upon – by this woman of all others – to behave as if everything was for the jolliest in the jolliest of all possible worlds.'

8 'That is well said,' replied Candide, 'but we must cultivate our garden.'

Meaning, 'we must attend to our own affairs'. *Ib.*, Chap. 30.

9 God is always on the side of the big battalions.

Voltaire did not say this, though he did refer to the idea. In this form it has been attributed to the French Marshal, the Vicomte de Turenne (d.1675) and to Roger, Comte de Bussy-Rabutin (in a letter to the Comte de Limoges, 18 October 1677), the latter adding, 'and against the small ones'.

What Voltaire wrote in a letter to Le Riche (6 February 1770) was: '*They say* that God is always on the side of the big battalions', obviously referring back. Earlier, in what are called his 'Piccini Notebooks' (*c.*1735–50), Voltaire had, in fact, written: 'God is on the side not of the heavy battalions, but of the best shots.'

1 When Voltaire was asked why no woman has ever written even a tolerable tragedy? 'Ah (said the Patriarch) the composition of a tragedy requires *testicles*'.

Lord Byron in a letter to John Murray (2 April 1817), but otherwise unverified.

VONNEGUT, Kurt, Jr

American author (1922–)

2 What passes for culture in my head is really a bunch of commercials.

Quoted in Barbara Rowes, *The Book of Quotes* (1979), but otherwise unverified.

3 Breakfast of Champions.

Title of novel (1973). From the slogan for Wheaties, the American breakfast cereal, current since 1950.

VON STERNBERG, Joseph

Austrian-born film director (1894–1969)

4 Fun in a Chinese Laundry.

Title of memoirs (1966). It had been used originally by Thomas Alva Edison, inventor of the cinematograph, as the title of an early short film when titles were literal to the point of ploddingness – like 'A Train Entering a Station'.

VON ZELL, Harry

American broadcaster and actor (1906–81)

5 Ladies and gentlemen – the President of the United States, Hoobert Herver.

Introducing radio broadcast by President Herbert Hoover. Quoted in *Current Biography* (1944).

VREELAND, Diana

American fashion journalist (c.1903–89)

6 I love London. It is the most swinging city in the world at the moment.

Quoted in *Weekend Telegraph* Magazine (30 April 1965). The coming together of the words 'swinging' and 'London' for the first time may have first occurred publicly in this way. In addition, a picture caption declared, 'London is a swinging city'. Almost exactly one year later, *Time* Magazine picked up the angle and devoted a cover-story to the concept of 'London: The Swinging City' (edition dated 15 April 1966).

7 The beautiful people.

Coinage of this term is credited to Vreeland in *Current Biography* (1978). Whether she deserves this or not is open to question. The earliest *OED2* citation with capital letters for each word is from 1966, though there is a *Vogue* use from 15 February 1964 which would appear to support the link to Vreeland. The *OED2* makes the phrase refer primarily to 'flower people' and 'hippies', though I would prefer the 1981 *Macquarie Dictionary*'s less narrow definition of: 'Fashionable social set of wealthy, well-groomed, usually young people.' The Lennon and McCartney song 'Baby You're a Rich Man' containing the line 'How does it feel to be one of the beautiful people?' was released in July 1967.

William Saroyan's play *The Beautiful People* had been performed long before all this, in 1941, and Oscar Wilde in a letter to Harold Boulton (December 1879), wrote: 'I could have introduced you to some very beautiful people. Mrs Langtry and Lady Lonsdale and a lot of clever beings who were at tea with me.'

W

WALLACE, John

English novelist, poet and critic (1925–94)

1 Hurry on Down.

Title of novel (1953). The epigraph is simply 'Hurry on down to my place, baby,/Nobody home but me. – *Old Song*'. In fact it was a song (1947) written and performed by Nellie Lutcher, the American entertainer. Wain's novel was lumped together with others in the Angry Young Men school of the early 1950s. It was about a man hurrying down from university and doing rather unlikely jobs.

WALKER, James J.

American politician (1881–1946)

2 Will you love me in December as you do in May?

Title of song (1905), with music by Ernest R. Ball. Walker was a future Mayor of New York. Possibly it had some influence on the coinage of the expression 'A May/December romance' or 'Spring/winter romance' to describe a union between a younger person and an older one. Compare this, from 'To the most Courteous and Fair Gentlewoman, Mrs Elinor Williams' by Rowland Watkyns (d.1664): 'For every marriage then is best in tune,/When that the wife is May, the husband June.'

WALLACE, George

American Democratic politician (1919–98)

3 Pointy-headed intellectuals who can't park their bicycles straight.

Customary jibe. Sometimes it was 'pointed-headed professors'. Quoted in Safire (1978).

4 Send them a message.

Slogan used when campaigning for the presidency (1972). An invitation to vote symbolically when a candidate has little chance of winning. Quoted in Safire (1978).

WALLACE, Lew

American novelist (1827–1905)

5 Beauty is altogether in the eye of the beholder.

The Prince of India (1893). Wallace may have coined the expression in this form but the idea that beauty is according to the beholder's estimation was not new. In David Hume's *Essays Moral & Political* (1742) there is: 'Beauty, properly speaking, lyes ... in the Sentiment or Taste of the Reader'. In Charlotte Brontë's *Jane Eyre* (1847) there is: 'Most true is it that "beauty is in the eye of the gazer".'

WALLACE, W.R.

American poet (1819–81)

6 A mighty power and stronger
Man from his throne has hurled,
For the hand that rocks the cradle
Is the hand that rules the world.

'What rules the world' (1865) – a tribute to motherhood, first appearing in *John O'London's Treasure Trove*. Hence, the slogan employed successfully in 1990 by Mary Robinson, a feminist lawyer, to become President of the Irish Republic. *The Hand That Rocks the Cradle* was the title of a film (US, 1992).

WALL STREET

American film, 1987. Written by Stanley Weiser and Oliver Stone. With Michael Douglas as Gordon Gekko.

1 *Gekko*: Greed, for want of a better word, is good.

Soundtrack. *Compare* BOESKY 113:5.

WALPOLE, Horace (4th Earl of Orford)

English writer (1717–97)

2 These ... were what filled me with disgust, and made me quit that splendid theatre of pitiful passion.

Memoirs of the Reign of King George III (published posthumously). On his retirement from the House of Commons in 1767. He was trying not to pass off his anecdotes as a history of England but hoped that they contained 'the most useful part of all history, a picture of human minds'. *Compare* JEFFERSON 312:7.

3 This world is a comedy to those that think, a tragedy to those that feel.

Letter to the Countess of Upper Ossory (16 August 1776). However, Blaise Pascal (1623–62) is reported to have said earlier: '*La vie, c'est une tragédie pour celui qui sent, mais une comédie pour celui qui pense.*' Unverified.

4 Everything's at sea – except the Fleet.

On the state of England. Presumably he meant that the country's affairs were (as we would now say) 'all at sea'. Quoted by Malcolm Muggeridge on BBC Radio *Quote ... Unquote* in 1978, but unverified.

5 This sublime age reduces everything to its quintessence; all periphrases and expletives are so much in disuse, that I suppose soon the only way to making love will be to say 'Lie down'.

Letter to H.S. Conway (23 October 1778). A precursor of the modern expression 'Lie down, I think I love you.' This last was considered a sufficiently well-established, smart, jokey remark to be listed by *The Sun* (10 October 1984) as one of its 'Ten top chat-up lines'. It may also have been used in a song or cartoon just a little before that. Indeed, there was a song entitled 'Lie Down (A Modern Love Song)' written and performed by the British group Whitesnake in 1978. Earlier, 'Sit Down I Think I Love You', written by Stills, was performed by the Mojo Men in 1967. An article 'Down with sex' was published in collected form (1966) by Malcolm Muggeridge in which he wrote: 'I saw scrawled on a wall in Santa Monica in California: "Lie down! I think I love you." Thus stripped, sex becomes an orgasm merely.' And then again, there was the Marx Brothers' line from *The Cocoanuts* (1929), 'Ah, Mrs Rittenhouse, won't you ... lie down?'

See also ARNOLD 61:6.

WALPOLE, Sir Robert (1st Earl of Orford)

British Whig Prime Minister (1676–1745)

6 [The gratitude of place-expectants] is a lively sense of future favours.

Quoted in William Hazlitt, 'On Wit and Humour', *Lectures on the English Comic Writers* (1819). By this century, the *Dictionary of American Proverbs* has, as simply proverbial, 'Gratitude is a lively expression of favours yet to come.' Prior to Walpole, La Rochefoucauld had said, 'The gratitude of most men is merely a secret desire to receive greater benefits' – *Maxims*, No. 298 (1678).

7 The balance of power.

An expression used by Walpole in the House of Commons (13 February 1741), which has now come to mean the promotion of peace through parity of strength in rival groups. The *ODQ* (1979) gave it as though Walpole had coined the phrase, but dropped it in 1992. Safire (1978) states that the phrase was being used in international diplomacy as early as 1700. Initially, the phrase appears to have been 'the balance of power in Europe'. In 1715, Alexander Pope wrote a poem with the title 'The Balance of Europe': 'Now Europe's balanc'd, neither side prevails;/For nothing's left in either of the scales.'

8 As to the conduct of the war: as I am neither admiral nor general, as I have nothing to do with either our Navy or Army, I am sure I am not answerable for the prosecution of it.

As Prime Minister in 1741. Untraced.

WARHOL, Andy

American artist (1927–87)

9 In the future everyone will be world-famous for fifteen minutes.

Catalogue for an exhibition of Warhol's work in Stockholm (February–March 1968). More often rendered as 'In the future everyone will be famous for fifteen minutes'. Accordingly, the phrase 'to be famous for fifteen minutes' means to have transitory fame of the type prevalent in the twentieth century. It is often to be found used allusively – 'He's had his fifteen minutes.' *Famous for Fifteen Minutes* was the title of a series of, naturally, fifteen-minute programmes on BBC Radio 4 in 1990 in which yesterday's headline-makers were recalled from obscurity.

WARNER, Charles Dudley

American journalist and writer (1829–1900)

1 Politics makes strange bedfellows.

My Summer in a Garden (1870). In 1854, however, Leigh Hunt had written a letter (published in 1862) that included this sentence: 'Politics, like "misery", certainly makes a man acquainted with strange bedfellows.' Both remarks probably allude to Shakespeare, *The Tempest*, II.ii.40.

See also TWAIN 546:1.

WASHINGTON, Booker T.

American educationist (1856–1915)

2 No race can prosper till it learns that there is as much dignity in tilling a field as in writing a poem.

Up from Slavery (1901). As a phrase 'the dignity of labour' has proved hard to trace. The *OED2*'s earliest citation is only in 1948. Oscar Wilde states in his essay 'The Soul of Man Under Socialism' (1891) that 'a great deal of nonsense is being written and talked nowadays about the dignity of manual labour'. Shaw, in his play *Man and Superman*, Act 2 (1903) has the exchange: 'I believe most intensely in the dignity of labour'/'That's because you never done any, Mr Robinson.'

The similar 'honest toil' is almost as elusive. Thomas Gray in his 'Elegy' (1751) spoke of the '*useful* toil' of the 'rude forefathers' in the countryside (GRAY 271:6). *Useful Toil* was the title of a book comprising 'autobiographies of working people from the 1820s to the 1920s' (published 1974). The *OED2* finds 'honest labour' in 1941. Thomas Carlyle spoke of 'honest work' in 1866. 'Honourable toil' appears in the play *Two Noble Kinsmen* (possibly by John Fletcher and William Shakespeare, published 1634).

WASHINGTON, George

American Federalist 1st President (1732–99)

3 Looking at his father with the sweet face of youth brightened with the inexpressible charm of all-conquering truth, he bravely cried out. 'I can't tell a lie. I did cut it with my hatchet.'

Mason Locke Weems, Washington's first popular biographer, in *The Life of George Washington: With Curious Anecdotes Equally Honorable to Himself and Exemplary to His Young Countrymen* (1800). Sometimes remembered as, 'Father, I cannot tell a lie. I did it with my little hatchet.' When asked, as a boy, by his father, how a certain cherry tree had come to be cut down. A tale almost certainly invented by Weems.

See also JEFFERSON 312:7.

WATERHOUSE, Keith

English journalist and novelist (1929–)

4 I cannot bring myself to vote for a woman [Margaret Thatcher] who has been voice-trained to speak to me as though my dog has just died.

Attributed comment (1979).

See also THAT WAS THE WEEK THAT WAS 536:4.

WAUGH, Evelyn

English novelist (1903–66)

5 Any who have heard the sound will shrink at the recollection of it; it is the sound of English county families baying for broken glass.

Decline and Fall, Prelude (1928). *Compare* BELLOC 83:1.

6 *Feather-footed through the plashy fen passes the questing vole.*

Scoop, Bk 1, Chap. 1 (1938). Style of the countryman writer William Boot in his column 'Lush Places'.

7 Mr Salter's side of the conversation was limited to expressions of assent. When Lord Copper was right he said, 'Definitely, Lord Copper'; when he was wrong, 'Up to a point.'

Ib. Lord Copper is a newspaper proprietor. Hence, the expression 'Up to a point, Lord Copper' used when disagreeing with someone it is not prudent to differ with. An example from *The Independent* (4 April 1990):

'We are told that [Norman Tebbit] was only trying to help ... he was out to "stop Heseltine". Well, up to a point, Lord Whitelaw'.

1 Put Out More Flags.

Title of novel (1942). According to Waugh, it comes from a Chinese saying: 'A drunk military man should order gallons and put out more flags in order to increase his military splendour'.

2 'I have been here before,' I said; I had been there before; first with Sebastian more than twenty years ago on a cloudless day in June, when the ditches were creamy with meadowsweet and the air heavy with all the scents of summer.

Brideshead Revisited, Chap. 1 (1945). Charles Ryder says this about Brideshead (hence the 'revisited'). *I Have Been Here Before* had earlier been the title of a 'Time' play (1937) by J.B. Priestley. Then there is: 'I have been here before,/But when or how I cannot tell' – D.G. Rossetti, 'Sudden Light' (1870).

3 As I took the cigarette from my lips and put it in hers, I caught a thin bat's squeak of sexuality, inaudible to any but me.

Ib., Chap. 3. Charles Ryder of Lady Julia. A later use of 'bat's squeak', not otherwise much recorded: at the Conservative Party Conference in 1981, a then upwardly rising politician called Edwina Currie was taking part in a debate on law and order. To illustrate some point, she held aloft a pair of handcuffs. Subsequently, the Earl of Gowrie admitted to having felt 'a bat's squeak of desire' for Mrs Currie at that moment.

4 In the dying world I come from quotation is a national vice. It used to be the classics, now it's lyric verse.

The Loved One, Chap. 9 (1948). Dennis, an English poet who becomes embroiled in the Californian funerary arts, has to explain to his beloved Aimée that he is not in fact the author of all the beautiful lines of poetry that emerge from his lips.

5 A typical triumph of modern science to find the only part of Randolph that was not malignant and remove it.

The Diaries of Evelyn Waugh (entry for March 1964). When Randolph Churchill went into hospital to have a lung removed and the trouble was not malignant.

6 I pray that the church is not struck by lightning.

Telegram said to have been sent by Waugh to Tom Driberg MP on the occasion of the latter's marriage (to a woman) (1951). The occasion was remarkable – and not only to Waugh – because Driberg was a notorious and active homosexual. According to Alan Watkins, *Brief Lives* (1982), Waugh in fact wrote – rather than telegraphed – to the effect: 'I will think of you intently on the day and pray that the church is not struck by lightning.' The letter is not, alas, included in Waugh's published correspondence. Watkins adds: 'This sentence in this same connection is, oddly enough, attributed to Aneurin Bevan and Winston Churchill also.'

7 He is not a man for whom I ever had esteem. Always in the wrong, always surrounded by crooks, a most unsuccessful father – simply a 'Radio Personality' who outlived his prime.

On Winston Churchill. *The Letters of Evelyn Waugh* (for 27 January 1965). He was explaining why he had declined to write any obsequies at Churchill's demise.

See also MAGEE 375:8.

WEBB, Sidney (later Lord Passfield)

English socialist (1859–1947)

8 Once we face the necessity of putting our principles first into Bills, to be fought through committee clause by clause; and then into the appropriate machinery for carrying them into execution from one end of the kingdom to the other ... the inevitability of gradualness cannot fail to be appreciated.

Presidential address to the Labour Party Conference at the Queen's Hall, London (26 June 1923). The phrase 'the inevitability of gradualness' was taken to mean that, for Labour, electoral success would come gradually but certainly, and by evolution not revolution.

9 To secure for the workers by hand or by brain the full fruits of their industry and the most equitable distribution thereof that may be possible upon the basis of the common ownership of the means of production, distribution, and exchange.

Clause 4 of the party's Constitution (Party Objects), adopted 1918/1926 – believed to have been the work of Webb. The words 'socialisation of the means of production &c.' had appeared in the 1900 Labour Party manifesto. The words 'distribution and exchange' were added at the 1928 conference.

1 Nobody told us we could do this.

Comment when the new National government came off the Gold Standard in 1931. The outgoing Labour government had failed to deal with a financial crisis in this manner. Quoted in A.J.P. Taylor, *English History 1914–1945* (1965).

WEBER, Max

German economist (1864–1920)

2 The Protestant work ethic.

Translation of part title of article, *Die protestantische Ethik und der Geist des Kapitalismus* ['The Protestant Ethic and the Spirit of Capitalism'] (1904–5). Hence, the phrase for an attitude towards business, based on the teachings of Calvin and the analysis of Weber, which suggests that it is one's duty to be successful through hard work.

WEBSTER, Daniel

American politician (1782–1852)

3 Fearful concatenation of circumstances.

On the murder of Captain Joseph White. Remark (6 April 1830).

See also BRAINE 119:1.

WEBSTER, John

English playwright (c.1580–c.1625)

4 Leave thy idle questions;
I am i'th'way to study a long silence,
To prate were idle.

The White Devil, Act 5, Sc. 6 (1612). Flamineo speaking. Hence, *A Long Silence*, title of a crime novel – the last of the Van der Valk series (1972) by Nicholas Freeling.

5 *Ferdinand*: Cover her face; mine eyes dazzle; she died young.
Bosola: I think not so; her infelicity
Seem'd to have years too many.

The Duchess of Malfi, Act 4, Sc. 2 (1623). Concerning the Duchess whom Ferdinand has just strangled. Hence, *Cover Her Face*, title of a crime novel (1962) by P.D. James.

WEIGHELL, Sidney (later Lord Weighell)

British trade union leader (1922–)

6 If you want it to go out ... that you now believe in the philosophy of the pig trough – those with the biggest snouts get the largest share – I reject it.

Speech at Labour Party Conference, Blackpool (6 October 1978). At the time, Weighell was general secretary of the National Union of Railwaymen. During the general election campaign the next year, he also said: 'I don't see how we can talk with Mrs Thatcher ... I will say to the lads, come on, get your snouts in the trough' (remark, London, 10 April 1979).

WELDON, Fay

English novelist and playwright (1931–)

7 Go to work on an egg.

Slogan for the British Egg Marketing Board in 1957. Hardly a profile of Weldon gets written without mention of her time as an advertising copywriter (*compare* RUSHDIE 464:5) and her supposed coinage. She did indeed work for the Mather & Crowther agency, but in a 1981 letter to the author she poured a little cold water on the frequent linking of her name with the slogan: 'I was certainly in charge of copy at the time "Go to work on an egg" was first used as a slogan as the main theme for an advertising campaign. The phrase itself had been in existence for some time and hung about in the middle of paragraphs and was sometimes promoted to base lines. Who invented it, it would be hard to say. It is perfectly possible, indeed probable, that I put those particular six words together in that particular order but I would not swear to it.'

WELLER, Charles E.

American journalist (nineteenth century)

8 Now is the time for all good men to come to the aid of the party.

Typewriter exercise – possibly originated by Weller, a court reporter in Milwaukee (1867) to test the efficiency of the first practical typewriter, which his friend, Christopher L. Scholes, had made. However, in his book *The Early History of the Typewriter* (1918), Weller does not claim credit for the coinage. In the Muir & Norden *My Word* stories (1973), the line is stated to be found in 'The Typewriter's Song' by Edwin Meade Robinson – though I suspect this is merely a quotation of it. Evidently, the sentence was appropriate because it was coined during 'an exciting political campaign.'

Whoever was responsible did not do a very good job because the phrase contains only eighteen letters of the alphabet. 'The quick brown fox jumps over the lazy dog', on the other hand, has all twenty-six. This was once thought to be the shortest sentence in English containing all the letters of the alphabet but it was superseded by: 'Pack my box with five dozen liquor jugs' (which is three letters shorter overall) and 'Quick blowing zephyrs vex daft Jim' (which is even shorter). Even more concise 'pangrams' have been devised but they are also shorter on sense and memorability.

WELLES, Orson

American film director, writer and actor (1915–85)

1 This is the biggest electric train [set] any boy ever had!

Remark on learning how to use a Hollywood studio. First attributed by Leo Rosten in *Hollywood* (1941). Frank Brady in *Citizen Welles* (1989) suggests that this was just prior to the filming of *Citizen Kane* in about 1939.

2 You know what the fellow said – in Italy, for thirty years under the Borgias, they had warfare, terror, murder and bloodshed, but they produced Michelangelo, Leonardo da Vinci and the Renaissance. In Switzerland, they had brotherly love; they had five hundred years of democracy and peace – and what did that produce? The cuckoo clock.

So says Harry Lime (played by Welles) in Carol Reed's film *The Third Man* (1949). The news soon got around that Welles had added this speech to the basic script which was written by Graham Greene and Carol Reed. Indeed, it appears only as a footnote in the published script of the film. In a letter, dated 13 October 1977, Greene confirmed to me that it *had* been written by Welles during shooting: 'What happened was that during the shooting of *The Third Man* it was found necessary for the timing to insert another sentence and the speech you mention was put in by Orson Welles.'

Whether the idea was original to Welles is another matter. After all he introduces the speech with, 'You know what the fellow said ...' Welles apparently later suggested that the lines came originally from 'an old Hungarian play'. Anthony Powell in his *Journals 1982–1986* (1995 – entry for 21 December 1986) points out that the painter Whistler 'initially made joke about the Swiss having invented the Cuckoo Clock as chief fame in their cultural achievements. This I corroborated (Whistler's *Ten O'Clock*, 1885), so joke just over century old.'

Indeed, in *Mr Whistler's 'Ten O'Clock'* (1888), which is the text of a lecture he gave on art in 1885, Whistler spoke of: 'The Swiss in their mountains ... What more worthy people! ... yet, the perverse and scornful [goddess, Art] will none of it, and the sons of patriots are left with the clock that turns the mill, and the sudden cuckoo, with difficulty restrained in its box! For this was Tell a hero! For this did Gessler die!'

In *This Is Orson Welles* (1993), Welles is quoted as saying: 'When the picture came out, the Swiss very nicely pointed out to me that they've never made any cuckoo clocks – they all come from the Schwarzwald in Bavaria!'

3 Now we sit through Shakespeare in order to recognise the quotations.

Quoted in *The Treasury of Humorous Quotations*, ed. by Evan Esar & Nicolas Bentley (1951). In Prochnow & Prochnow, *Treasury of Humorous Quotations* (1969), the remark is ascribed to Oscar Wilde. Easy to confuse the two, of course ...

See also CITIZEN KANE 171:5–8.

WELLINGTON, 1st Duke of

Irish-born soldier and politician (1769–1852)

4 Always make water when you can.

Quoted in *The Oxford Book of Aphorisms* (1983), but otherwise unverified.

5 Because a man is born in a stable that does not make him a horse.

On being chaffed for being an Irishman. Quoted in Elizabeth Longford, *Wellington: The Years of the Sword* (1969). Compare the proverbial 'The man who is born in a stable is a horse' (known by 1833).

6 I don't know what effect these men will have upon the enemy, but, by God, they frighten me.

Popular summary of a despatch to Sir Colonel Torrens, military secretary at the Horse Guards (29 August 1810). This referred to some of his generals, and not to his regimental officers or to the rank and file, as is made clear from the full text. Wellington in fact said: 'As Lord Chesterfield said of the generals of his day, "I only hope that when the enemy reads the list of their names, he trembles as I do".'

1 We have in the service the scum of the earth as common soldiers.

On his men, in a despatch to Lord Bathurst, the War Minister (July 1813). This was after the battle of Vittoria, when Wellington's troops ('our vagabond soldiers') were 'totally knocked up' after a night of looting.' On more than one occasion Wellington spoke in complimentary terms about the common soldiers under his command.

The expression predates Wellington. Dr John Arbuthnot in *John Bull* (1712) (III.vi.25) has 'Scoundrels! Dogs! the Scum of the Earth!' *The Scum of the Earth* is the title of a novel by Arthur Koestler (1941).

2 Up Guards and at 'em!

Popular short form of what Wellington is supposed to have said at Waterloo, namely, 'Up Guards and at them *again*'. The longer version was reported in a letter from a certain Captain Batty of the Foot Guards on 22 June 1815, four days after the battle.

Benham (1980) has this: 'In A. Tels guide-book, *Excursions to the Lion of Waterloo* (2nd ed. 1904), a Belgian publication, this is improved as follows: "Wellington cried, 'Upright, guards! prepare for battle'." In *The Times* (15 October 1841), appeared an "anecdote which may be relied on" quoted from *Britannia*, to the effect that lately the Duke had sat for his bust to "one of the most distinguished of living sculptors," who stated "that it would be popular and effective if it could represent his Grace at the moment when he uttered the memorable words ... at Waterloo. The Duke laughed very good-humouredly at this observation and said 'Ah! the old story. People will invent words for me ... but really I don't know what I said. I saw that the moment for action was come, and I gave the command for attack. I suppose the words were brief and homely enough, for they ran through the ranks and were obeyed on the instant ... but I'm sure I don't recollect them, and I very much doubt whether anyone else can'".'

Again, in 1852, the Duke commented to J.W. Croker: 'What I must have said and probably did say was, Stand up, Guards! and then gave the commanding officers the order to attack.' The following year, *Notes & Queries* was already puzzling over the matter.

3 A damn close-run thing.

As with most of Wellington's alleged remarks, this was not quite what he said, but it is how it is remembered. What he told the memoirist Thomas Creevey (on 18 June 1815) about the outcome of the Battle of Waterloo, was: 'It has been a damned serious business. Blücher and I have lost 30,000 men. It has been a damned nice thing – the nearest run thing you ever saw in your life.' *The Creevey Papers*, in which this account appears, was not published until 1903. Somehow out of this description a conflated version arose, with someone else presumably supplying the 'close-run'.

4 The battle of Waterloo was won on the playing fields of Eton.

This view was first ascribed to the 1st Duke of Wellington in Count Charles de Montalembert's *De L'Avenir Politique de l'Angleterre* in 1856. The Frenchman stated that the Duke returned to Eton in his old age and, recalling the delights of his youth, exclaimed: 'It is here that the battle of Waterloo was won' (i.e., he made no mention of playing fields).

Burnam (1980) suggests that Sir Edward Creasy built on this in *Memoirs of Eminent Etonians* (though as this was published in 1850, and the French book not until 1856, this must have been difficult). Anyhow, Creasy had the Iron Duke passing the playing fields in old age and saying, 'There grows the stuff that won Waterloo'.

Then in 1889, a third writer, Sir William Fraser, in *Words on Wellington*, put together Montalembert's remark with Creasy's playing fields to produce the popularly known version. The 7th Duke tried to pour more cold water on the matter in letters to *The Times* sometime prior to his death in 1972:

> During his old age Wellington is recorded to have visited Eton on two occasions only and it is unlikely that he came more often. He attended the funeral of his elder brother in College Chapel in October 1842 and he accompanied the Queen when she came to Eton with Louis Philippe in October 1844. On the first occasion, he attended the ceremony only and went away when it was over: and, on the second, he is hardly likely to have talked about the battle of Waterloo. Wellington's career at Eton was short and inglorious and, unlike his elder brother, he had no particular affection for the place ... Quite apart from the fact that the authority for attributing the words to Wellington is of the flimsiest description, to anyone who knows his turn of phrase they ring entirely false. It is, therefore, much to be hoped that speakers will discontinue using them either, as is generally the case, in order to point out their snobbishness, which is so alien to ideas generally now held, or else to show that Wellington was in favour of organized games, an assumption which is entirely unwarranted.

Perhaps the nearest the 1st Duke came to any sort of compliment about the effect his old school had on him was, 'I really believe I owe my spirit of enterprise to the tricks I used to play in the garden' [of his Eton boarding-house] – quoted in Vol. 1 of Elizabeth Longford's biography (1969).

But the saying, however apocryphal, still exerts its power. One H. Allen Smith (1906–) said: 'The battle of Yorktown was lost on the playing fields of Eton' (Yorktown, in Virginia, was the scene of the surrender of British forces at the end of the War of Independence, 1781). George Orwell (an Old Etonian himself) averred: 'Probably the Battle of Waterloo *was* won on the playing fields of Eton, but the opening battles of all subsequent wars have been lost there' (*The Lion and the Unicorn*, 1941).

1 I don't care a twopenny damn what becomes of the ashes of Napoleon Bonaparte.

Attributed, but unverified. In *Notes and Queries* (1879), the source is given as a *Life*, ii.257 (1878 ed.), presumably that by Brialmont and Gleig. Lord Macaulay in a letter of 6 March 1849 wrote: 'How they settle the matter I care not, as the duke says, one twopenny damn.' James Morris in *Pax Britannica* (1968) comments: 'a *dam* was a small Indian coin, as Wellington knew when he popularized the phrase "a twopenny dam".' Brewer (1989) says: 'The derivation ... from the coin, a dam, is without foundation.'

2 Publish and be damned!

Quoted in Elizabeth Longford, *Wellington: The Years of the Sword* (1969). This was Wellington's comment in 1842 to a blackmailer called Stockdale who offered not to publish anecdotes of the Duke and his mistress, Harriet Wilson, in return for payment. Legend has it that the Duke scrawled this response in bright red ink across Stockdale's letter and sent it back to him. Hence, the title of a book about the press (1955) by Hugh Cudlipp. Richard Ingrams declared on several occasions (*c.*1977) that a suitable motto for *Private Eye*, of which he was editor, would be: 'Publish and Be Sued'.

3 Try sparrow-hawks, Ma'am.

On being asked by Queen Victoria how hundreds of sparrows could be removed from the Glass Palace of the Great Exhibition (1851). Quoted in Elizabeth Longford, *Wellington: Pillar of State* (1972).

4 Sir, if you believe that, you will believe anything.

Replying to a minor government official who had accosted him in Pall Mall with the words: 'Mr Jones, I believe'. It is said that there *was* a Mr Jones who bore a striking resemblance to Wellington – George Jones RA (1786–1869), a military painter. Was what Wellington said original, however?

5 Who? who?

On hearing the names of ministers in Palmerston's administration (1852). Quoted in Sir William Fraser, *Words on Wellington* (1889).

WELLS, H.G.

English novelist and writer (1866–1946)

6 In the country of the blind the one-eyed man is king.

This saying has become associated with Wells because of its use by him in the story he wrote with the title *The Country of the Blind* (1904) – though he quite clearly labelled it as an 'old proverb'. Indeed, it is that and occurs in the proverbs of many languages (as shown by the *CODP*, 1982.) An early appearance is in a book of *Adages* by Erasmus (d.1536): '*In regione caecorum rex est luscus.*' Other sixteenth-century uses of the saying include John Palsgrave's translation of Fullmin's *Comedy of Acolastus* and John Skelton's 'An one eyed man is Well syghted when he is amonge blunde men' (1522).

7 The war to end wars.

Wells had popularized this notion in a book he had brought out in 1914 with the title *The War That Will End War*. It was not an original cry, having been raised in other wars, but by the end of this one it was popularly rendered as 'the war to end wars'. On the afternoon of 11 November 1918, David Lloyd George announced the terms of the Armistice to the House of Commons and concluded: 'I hope we may say that thus, this fateful morning, came to an end all wars.' Later, Wells commented ruefully: 'I launched the phrase "the war to end war" and that was not the least of my crimes.'

Sometimes it is said – for example, in *The Observer* Magazine (2 May 1993) – that it was a phrase of the 1930s and that there is no evidence the words were used at the time of the First World War. Clearly not the case.

8 The New World Order.

Title of book (1940). Always a rather vague concept. 'New Order' had previously been the name given to programmes of Hitler's regime in Germany in the 1930s and of a Japanese Prime Minister in 1938. Additionally, Hitler said in Berlin (30 January 1941): 'I am convinced that 1941 will be the crucial year of a great New Order in Europe. The world will open up for everyone.' The phrase lingers: in an exchange of New Year's greetings with US President Bush in January 1991, President Gorbachev of the Soviet Union spoke of the serious obstacle posed to a 'new world order' by the Iraqi invasion of Kuwait. After the allied victory in the Gulf War, Bush himself proclaimed a New World Order based on law and human rights. New Order was also the name of a British pop vocal/instrumental group from *c.*1981.

WERTENBAKER, Timberlake

Anglo-French-American playwright (1928–)

1 Our Country's Good.

Title of play (1988) about Australian convicts putting on a production of Farquhar's *The Recruiting Officer* in the 1780s. It is taken from George Barrington's prologue for the opening of the Sydney Play House in 1796 (when, also, the actors were principally convicts). The first play to be staged there was, however, Dr Young's tragedy, *The Revenge*. Barrington's words – which Wertenbaker puts in her play – include:

> True patriots we; for be it understood,
> We left our country for our country's good ...
> And none will doubt but that our emigration
> Has proved most useful to the British nation.

Barrington (1755–*c.*1835) was an Irish pickpocket who was transported to Botany Bay.

2 Three Birds Alighting on a Field.

Title of play (1991) about the modern art market. It might appear to be one of those apparently arbitrarily applied titles fixed to paintings ('Cornfield with Crows' is a well-known Van Gogh one). In fact, as the play's original director, Max Stafford-Clark, explained on BBC Radio *Quote ... Unquote* (1993), Wertenbaker took the title from an interview with Francis Bacon when he described the process of painting. He said how he started drawing a figure and how the figure became less and less important, ending up being about 'three birds alighting on a field'. 'And in the play,' Stafford-Clark added, 'Wertenbaker reverses that. The painter has fallen in love with the woman and he says, "I started off painting this picture about three birds alighting on a field but you've taken over this canvas".'

Bacon's own paintings include works with such titles as 'Figure in a Landscape', 'Three Figures in a Room' and 'Landscape with Car'.

WESKER, Arnold

English playwright (1932–)

3 Chips with Everything.

Title of play (1962) about class attitudes in the RAF during National Service. It alludes to the belief that the working classes tend to have chips as the accompaniment to almost every dish. Indeed, the play contains the line: 'You breed babies and you eat chips with everything.' Partridge/*Catch Phrases* dates it *c.*1960 and says the phrase has 'been applied to that sort of British tourist abroad which remains hopelessly insular'.

It has a wider application than just to tourists, however, and Wesker was popularizing a phrase that had already been coined. In an essay, published as part of *Declaration* (1957), the film director Lindsay Anderson stated: 'Coming back to Britain is always something of an ordeal. It ought not to be, but it is. And you don't have to be a snob to feel it. It isn't just the food, the sauce bottles on the cafe tables, and the chips with everything. It isn't just saying goodbye to wine, goodbye to sunshine ... We can come home. But the price we pay is high.'

WESLEY, John

English evangelist and founder of Methodism (1703–91)

4 Do all the good you can,
By all the means you can,
In all the ways you can,
In all the places you can,
At all the times you can,
To all the people you can,
As long as ever you can.

Rules for life, in *Letters* (pub. 1915). Quoted in *ODQ* (1953).

5 Make all you can, save all you can, give all you can.

On money. Untraced.

6 Cleanliness is next to Godliness.

Although this phrase appears in Wesley's Sermon 88 'On Dress', within quotation marks, it is without attribution. Brewer (1989) states that it is to be found in the writings of Phinehas ben Yair, a rabbi (*c.*150–200). In fact, the inspiration appears to be the Talmud: 'The doctrines of religion are resolved into carefulness ... abstemiousness into cleanliness; cleanliness into godliness.' So the saying is not from the Bible, as might be supposed.

Thomas J. Barratt, one of the fathers of modern advertising, seized upon it to promote Pears' Soap, chiefly in the UK. On a visit to the US in the 1880s, he sought a testimonial from a man of distinction. Shrinking from an approach to President Grant, he ensnared the eminent divine, Henry Ward Beecher. Beecher happily complied with Barratt's request and wrote a short text beginning: 'If cleanliness is next to godliness ...' and received no more for his pains than Barratt's 'hearty thanks'.

1 I look upon the whole world as my parish.

The expression meaning 'I am knowledgeable about many peoples and places; I look upon the world as my oyster' derives from a letter Wesley wrote to the Rev. James Hervey (and which was included in Welsey's *Journal* for 11 June 1739). In it, he defended himself against charges that he had invaded the parishes of other clergymen: 'You ... ask, How is it that I assemble Christians, who are none of my charge, to sing psalms and pray and hear the Scriptures expounded? and think it hard to justify doing this in other men's parishes, upon catholic principles ... Seeing I have now no parish of my own, nor probably ever shall ... Suffer me now to tell you my principles in this matter. I look upon all the world as my parish ... This far I mean, that, in whatever part of it I am, I judge it meet, right, and my bounden duty to declare unto all that are willing to hear the glad tidings of salvation'.

2 For what cause I know not to this day, [my wife] set out for Newcastle purposing 'never to return'. *Non eam reliqui; non dismisi; non revocabo* [I did not forsake her, I did not dismiss her: I will not recall her].

In *ib.* (23 January 1771) – when his wife, Mrs Vazeile, a widow with four children and a fortune, abandoned him. Initially supporting Wesley in his work, she grew tired of the discomforts, became jealous of the people he worked with, and plagued him in every possible way. His *Journal* suggests that he was probably a difficult man to live with and in the end she left him, clearly with not much regret on his part.

3 God buries his workmen, but carries on his work.

Wesley and his hymn-writing brother Charles are commemorated by a wall plaque in Westminster Abbey. This bears three sayings: 'The best of all is, God is with us' (what John Wesley 'said emphatically' the day before he died), 'I look upon all the world as my parish' (as above) and this one. Where does it come from? There is no mention of it in *Wesley Quotations* (1990) by Betty M. Jarboe, a former reference librarian at the University of Indiana.

WESLEY, Samuel

English divine and poet (1662–1735)

4 Style is the dress of thought; a modest dress,
Neat, but not gaudy, will true critics please.

'An Epistle to a Friend concerning Poetry' (1700). Possibly the origin of the popular phrase 'neat, (but) not gaudy', although in 1631 there had been the similar 'Comely, not gaudy'. Shakespeare in *Hamlet* (I.iii.71) has 'rich, not gaudy;/For the apparel oft proclaims the man ...' Later, Charles Lamb wrote to William Wordsworth (June 1806), 'A little thin flowery border round, neat not gaudy.' John Ruskin, writing in the *Architectural Magazine* (November 1838): 'That admiration of the "neat but gaudy" which is commonly reported to have influenced the devil when he painted his tail pea green.' Indeed, Partridge/*Catch Phrases* cites: 'Neat, but not gaudy, as the monkey said, when he painted his tail sky-blue' and '... painted his bottom pink and tied up his tail with pea-green.'

WEST, Mae

American vaudeville and film actress (1893–1980)

5 Goodness had nothing to do with it, dearie.

Replying to exclamation, 'Goodness, what beautiful diamonds!' in film *Night After Night* (US, 1932). Script by Vincent Laurence, from novel by Louis Bromfield, 'with additional dialogue' by West.

6 One of the finest women who ever walked the streets.

Of the character she plays called Lady Lou in the film *She Done Him Wrong* (US, 1933). West had a notable stage hit on Broadway with her play *Diamond Lil* (first performed 9 April 1928), but her part was renamed and the work retitled for the film version.

7 You know I always did like a man in uniform. And that one fits you grand. Why don't you come up some time and see me? I'm home every evening.

Ib. To a very young Cary Grant, playing Captain Cummings (a coy undercover policeman). As a catchphrase, the words have been rearranged into 'Come up and see me some time' to make them easier to say. And that is how W.C. Fields says them *to* Mae West in the film *My Little Chickadee* (1939). She herself also took to mouthing them in the easier-to-say form.

1 Warm, dark and handsome.

Ib. A comment to the character Serge who has just kissed her on the hand. Obviously playing upon the established phrase 'tall, dark and handsome'. This description of a romantic hero's attributes (as likely to be found especially in women's fiction) had surfaced by 1906. Flexner (1976) puts it in the late 1920s as a Hollywood term referring to Rudolph Valentino (though, in fact, he was not particularly tall). Sophie Tucker recorded a song called 'He's Tall, Dark and Handsome' (by Tobias & Sherman) in 1928. Cesar Romero played the lead in the 1941 film *Tall, Dark and Handsome*. However, in a piece called 'Loverboy of the Bourgeoisie' (collected in 1965), Tom Wolfe writes: 'It was Cary Grant that Mae West was talking about when she launched the phrase "tall, dark and handsome" in *She Done Him Wrong* (1933).' This appears to be an inaccurate assumption.

2 Is that a gun in your pocket or are you just pleased to see me?

Quoted in Joseph Weintraub, *Peel Me a Grape* (1975). Sometimes remembered as 'pistol' and also in connection with her play *Catherine Was Great* (1944) in the form: 'Lieutenant, is that your sword, or are you just glad to see me?' Leslie Halliwell in *The Filmgoer's Book of Quotes* (1973), has this last as West's reaction in a Broadway costume play, when the romantic lead got his sword tangled in his braid so that it stuck up at an unfortunate angle.

3 Beulah – peel me a grape!

In film *I'm No Angel* (US, 1933). A catchphrase expressing dismissive unconcern, which was uttered by West to a maid after a male admirer has just stormed out on her. It has had some wider currency since then but is almost always used as a quotation.

4 How tall are you, son?
Ma-am, I'm six feet seven inches.
Let's forget the six feet and talk about the seven inches.

Famously indelicate compliment, but without source. Tom Stoppard alluded to it in the first edition of BBC Radio *Quote ... Unquote* (1 January 1976). Quoted in Leslie Halliwell, *The Filmgoer's Book of Quotes* (1973).

5 Marriage is a great institution, but I'm not ready for an institution yet.

Quoted in Laurence J. Peter, *Quotations for Our Time* (1977), but otherwise unverified.

6 A hard man is good to find.

Attributed remark (by 1985). Used, nudgingly – though not ascribed to West – as the slogan for Soloflex body-building equipment in the US (1985). Ads showed a woman's hand touching the bodies of well-known brawny athletes. An inversion of 'a good man is hard to find'. Is this the same as the proverb 'Good men are scarce' found by *CODP* in 1609? In the present form, it was the title of a song by Eddie Green (1919).

WEST, Nathanael

American novelist (1903–40)

7 Miss Lonelyhearts.

Title of novel (1933) – about a man who writes such a column under this pen name. Hence, the name given to writers of advice columns for the lovelorn (chiefly in the US). In the UK (mostly), the term 'lonelyhearts column' has come to mean not an advice column but a listing service for men and women seeking partners.

See also BIBLE 99:3.

WESTMINSTER, Loelia

English duchess (1902–93)

8 Anybody seen in a bus after the age of thirty has been a failure in life.

Quoted in *The Daily Telegraph* (*c.*1980). Loelia Lindsay was an English socialite and third wife of the 2nd Duke of Westminster from 1930 to 1947. She wrote a book entitled *Grace and Favour* (1961).

WESTON, R.P. and LEE, Bert

British songwriters (1878–1936) and (1880–1947)

9 And the great big saw
Came nearer and nearer
To Vera.

Song, 'And the Great Big Saw Came Nearer' (1936). The story – about a melodramatic villain and the Vera (with whom he would have his wicked way) – is not for the squeamish. It begins:

> Now he was a Saw Mill Proprietor
> And she a fair maid yet unkissed.
> One evening he winked his squint eye at her,
> But she said 'Nay, nay, Sir, de-sist!'
> So he dragged her into the Saw Mill, poor wench,
> Then took off his belt and strapped her to the bench! ...

1 Knees up, Mother Brown!

Title of song (1939). Hence, the phrase 'knees-up' for a lively celebration or party.

WHELDON, Sir Huw

Welsh broadcaster and TV executive (1916–86)

2 He never used a sentence if a paragraph would do.

Self-suggested epitaph, in the *Daily Mail* (9 June 1976). The actual headstone of his grave in St Peris churchyard, Nant Peris, Snowdonia, calls him 'Soldier, Broadcaster, Administrator'.

WHEN HARRY MET SALLY

American film 1989. Written by Nora Ephron. With Meg Ryan as Sally and Estelle Reiner as Woman in Restaurant.

3 *Woman in restaurant*: I'll have what she's having.

When asked by a waiter what she would like to order, Sally having just faked an orgasm in the middle of a crowded restaurant. Soundtrack.

WHISTLER, James McNeill

American painter (1834–1903)

4 *Oscar Wilde*: I wish I had said that.
Whistler: You will, Oscar, you will.

Quoted in L.C. Ingleby, *Oscar Wilde* (1907) and Douglas Sladen, *Twenty Years of My Life* (1915). Sladen says that it was of a remark by a woman that Wilde had rather taken a fancy to, but Hesketh Pearson, *The Life of Oscar Wilde* (1946) has it, more convincingly, that it was something said by Whistler himself that Wilde was obviously going to make his own.

5 Yes, madam, Nature is creeping up.

To a woman who told him a landscape reminded her of his work. Told in D.C. Seitz, *Whistler Stories* (1913).

6 No, I ask it for the knowledge of a lifetime.

Replying to the question (in a court of law), 'For two days' labour, you ask two hundred guineas?' Quoted in *ib. See* RUSKIN 465:2.

7 The explanation is quite simple. I wished to be near my mother.

When asked why he had been born in such an unfashionable place as Lowell, Massachusetts. Quoted in *Medical Quotations* (1989).

See also WELLES 559:2.

WHITE, Andrew D.

American academic (1832–1918)

8 I will not permit thirty men to travel four hundred miles to agitate a bag of wind.

White was the first President of Cornell University (1867–85). With these words he forbade Cornell's first intercollegiate football game with the University of Michigan at Cleveland, Ohio, in 1873. Quoted in Flexner (1982).

WHITE, Elwyn Brooks

American humorist (1899–1985)

9 I say it's spinach.

Caption devised by White for a cartoon by Carl Rose in *The New Yorker* (8 December 1928). The cartoon shows a mother at table saying: 'It's broccoli, dear.' Her little girl replies: 'I say it's spinach, and I say the hell with it.' Harold Ross, then editor of the magazine, remembered that when White asked his opinion of the caption the writer was clearly uncertain that he had hit on the right idea. 'I looked at the drawing and the caption and said, "Yeh, it seems okay to me", but neither of us cracked a smile.' The use of the word 'spinach' to mean nonsense (mostly in the US) stems from this – as in the title of Irving Berlin's song 'I'll Say It's Spinach' from the revue *Face the Music* (1932) and as in *Fashion is Spinach*, title of the autobiography (1933) of the American designer Elizabeth Dawes.

10 Across the Street and Into the Grill.

Title of pastiche of Ernest Hemingway (collected 1954). *See* JACKSON 310:1.

WHITEHEAD, Alfred North

English philosopher and mathematician (1961–1947)

11 The total absence of humour from the Bible is one of the most singular things in all literature.

Quoted in *The 'Quote ... Unquote' Book of Love, Death and the Universe* (1980), but otherwise untraced.

WHITE HEAT

American film 1949. Script by various. With James Cagney as Cody Jarrett.

1 *Cody*: Made it Ma, [to the] top of the world.

Last words of character, shooting it out from the top of an oil tank.

WHITEHORN, Katharine

English journalist (1928–)

2 If there is nothing you can do by constriction of throat or rectum to head them off, try to move away from the group you are with ('I must find an ashtray' or 'I *say* look at that squirrel!') and create diversionary noises – snap a handbag, scrape a foot. Tummy rumbles are for some reason more OK – laugh if you can.

On making rude noises. *Whitehorn's Social Survival* (1968).

3 Outside every thin girl there is a fat man trying to get in.

Revived by her on *Quote ... Unquote*, BBC Radio (27 July 1985).

WHITELAW, William (later Viscount Whitelaw)

British Conservative politician (1918–)

4 Harold Wilson is going around the country stirring up apathy.

Whitelaw was holder of the office of Deputy Prime Minister until ill-health forced him to retire in 1988 and was famous for his informal sayings. The essence of these 'Whitelawisms' or 'Willieisms' is a touching naiveté which may conceal a certain truth.

The most notable is his description of the then Prime Minister, Harold Wilson, during the 1970 General Election going 'around the country stirring up apathy'. On the face of it, a nonsensical remark, but conveying, oddly, just what Wilson was doing. In *The Independent* (14 July 1992), Whitelaw told Hunter Davies: 'It's a strange thing. I did say those words, but the real meaning has been lost. For a start, I meant to say "spreading apathy" not "stirring it up" ... Wilson was so sure of victory that he was going round the country calming people down, telling everyone not to worry, leave it all to him. I was really attacking him for encouraging people not to want a change, not saying people were apathetic to him.'

5 One must be careful not to prejudge the past.

Of Irish politics, on becoming Secretary of State for Northern Ireland (25 March 1972). Quoted in *The Times* (3 December 1973).

6 I have over a period of time, when I have met her – as indeed one does – I have kissed her often before. We have not done it on a pavement outside a hotel in Eastbourne before. But we have done it in various rooms in one way and another at various functions – it is perfectly genuine and normal – and normal and right – so to do.

On kissing Mrs Thatcher (when they were both candidates for the Conservative leadership). Reported in *The Observer* (9 February 1975).

7 I think there will be banana skins as long as there are bananas.

When asked whether he thought Mrs Thatcher would face any more banana skins. Quoted in *The Observer* (22 April 1984).

See also GILBERT 261:4.

WHITLAM, Gough

Australian Labour Prime Minister (1916–)

8 Well may we say 'God Save the Queen', because nothing will save the Governor-General ... Maintain your rage and your enthusiasm through the campaign for the election now to be held and until polling day.

After the Governor-General's secretary had read a proclamation dissolving Parliament, effectively dismissing Whitlam as Prime Minister. Speech, Canberra (11 November 1975).

WHITMAN, Walt

American poet (1819–92)

9 I Sing the Body Electric.

Title of poem (1855), published in *Leaves of Grass* (various editions 1855–97). The phrase was later used by Ray Bradbury as the title story in a collection called *I Sing the Body Electric* (1970). *Compare* VIRGIL 551:6.

1 We Two Boys together Clinging.

Title of poem in *ib.* Hence, the title of David Hockney's 1961 painting 'We Two Boys Together Clinging'. The picture shows two figures indeed clinging together and surrounded by various inscriptions including the numerals '4.2'. This is code for 'Doll Boy' – i.e. Cliff Richard. Hockney had been amused to come across a newspaper headline which stated: 'TWO BOYS CLING TO CLIFF ALL NIGHT LONG'. Although the article concerned a climbing accident and not a sexual fantasy, the reference gives an added resonance to the picture. Quoted in Marco Livingstone, *David Hockney* (1981).

2 Out of the Cradle Endlessly Rocking.

Title of poem (1859), in *ib.* Later used as a silent film subtitle in the epic *Intolerance* (1916), written and directed by D.W. Griffith. It accompanies a shot of Lillian Gish rocking a cradle and is repeated many times during the course of the long film. The Gish character is billed as 'The Woman Who Rocks the Cradle'.

3 Hear America Singing.

Title of poem in *ib.* Hence, *I Hear America Talking*, title of a study of the American language (1976) by Stuart Berg Flexner.

4 When Lilacs Last in the Dooryard Bloom'd.

Title of poem in *ib.* It was written a few weeks after the April 1865 assassination of President Lincoln, which it commemorates. Whitman also wrote a prose description of the assassination which was included in his *Memoranda During the War* (1875) and reprinted in *The Faber Book of Reportage* (1987). This might give the impression that he was actually present, but he was away from Washington, DC, at the time. In it, however, he says: 'I find myself always reminded of the great tragedy of that day by the sight and odour of these blossoms.'

5 The untold want by life and land ne'er granted,
Now voyager, sail thou forth to seek and find.

'The Untold Want' in *ib.* Hence, *Now Voyager*, title of a novel (1941; film US, 1942) by Olive Higgins Prouty. 'Now voyager' also appears in Whitman's 'Now Finalè to the Shore' as: 'Now Voyager depart (much, much for thee is yet in store').

WHITTIER, J(ohn) G(reenleaf)

American poet (1807–92)

6 For of all sad words of tongue or pen,
The saddest are these: 'It might have been!'

Maud Muller (1854). Parodied by Arthur Guiterman (1871–1943) in 'Prophets in Their Own Country' as, 'Of all cold words of tongue and pen/The worst are these: "I knew him when ..."' And by Bret Harte in 'Mrs Judge Jenkins' (1867) as: 'If, of all words of tongue and pen,/The saddest are, "It might have been,"/More sad are these we daily see:/"It is, but hadn't ought to be!"'

7 Up the street came the rebel tread,
Stonewall Jackson riding ahead.

Under his slouched hat left and right
He glanced; the old flag met his sight.

'Halt!' – the dust-brown ranks stood fast.
'Fire!' – out blazed the rifle-blast ...
'Shoot, if you must, this old gray head,
But spare your country's flag,' she said.

'Barbara Frietchie' (1863) – which celebrates the old lady who waved a Union flag at Stonewall Jackson's troops as they passed through Frederick, Maryland, during the American Civil War.

8 To whom none ever said scat,
No worthier cat
Ever sat on a mat
Or caught a rat:
Requies – cat.

Epitaph for his cat Bathsheba. Quoted in Janice Anderson, *The Cat-a-Logue* (1987).

9 Dear Lord and Father of mankind,
Forgive our foolish ways.

'The Brewing of Soma' (1872) – later immensely popular in Britain as a hymn, especially in schools. Hence, *Forgive Our Foolish Ways*, title of a BBC TV drama series (1980) by Reg Gadney about goings-on in an English public school.

WHITTINGTON, Robert

English teacher (c.1480–c.1530)

10 More is a man of angel's wit and singular learning; I know not his fellow. For where is the man of that gentleness, lowliness and affability? And as time requireth, a man of mar-

vellous mirth and pastimes; and sometimes of as sad a gravity: as who say a man for all seasons.

On Sir Thomas More (1478–1535). Whittington wrote the passage for schoolboys to put into Latin in his book *Vulgaria* (*c.*1521). It translates a comment on More by Erasmus – who wrote in his preface to *In Praise of Folly* (1509) that More was '*omnium horarum hominem*'. Hence, *A Man for All Seasons*, Robert Bolt's title for his 1960 play about More (film UK, 1967) and the cliché phrase for an accomplished, adaptable, appealing person. From Laurence Olivier, *On Acting* (1986): '[Ralph Richardson] was warm and what the public might call ordinary and, therefore, quite exceptional. That was his ability, that was his talent; he really was a man for all seasons.' Jean Rook wrote of Margaret Thatcher in the *Daily Express* (in 1982–3): 'She has proved herself not the "best man in Britain" but the Woman For All Seasons".'

WILCOX, Ella Wheeler

American poet (1855–1919)

1 Laugh and the world laughs with you;
Weep and you weep alone.

'Solitude' (1883) – and, as *CODP* points out, an alteration of the sentiment expressed by Horace in his *Ars Poetica*: 'Men's faces laugh on those who laugh, and correspondingly weep on those who weep.' Another alteration is: '... weep, and you sleep alone'. In this form it was said to the architectural historian James Lees-Milne and recorded by him in his diary on 6 June 1945 (published in *Prophesying Peace*, 1977). In the form, '... snore and you sleep alone', it occurs in Anthony Burgess, *Inside Mr Enderby* (1963), though he did not claim this as original (despite its appearance in *PDMQ*, 1971).

WILDE, Oscar

Irish playwright, poet and wit (1854–1900)

2 The gods bestowed on Max the gift of perpetual old age.

On Max Beerbohm. Quoted in Vincent O'Sullivan, *Aspects of Wilde* (1936).

3 Somehow or other I'll be famous, and if not famous, I'll be notorious.

When asked what he proposed to do when he had taken his university degree. Quoted in *The Oxford Book of Oxford* (1978).

4 I have nothing to declare except my genius.

At the New York Custom House, on arriving in the United States (1882) and asked by the customs officer if he had anything to declare. Quoted in Frank Harris, *Oscar Wilde* (1918). No contemporary account exists.

5 Philosophy may teach us to bear with equanimity the misfortunes of our neighbours.

The English Renaissance of Art (Lecture in New York, 9 January 1882). *Compare* CONFUCIUS 180:1.

6 Every American bride is taken there, and the sight of the stupendous waterfall must be one of the earliest, if not the keenest, disappointments in American married life.

Impressions of America (pub. 1906), quoted in H. Montgomery Hyde, *Oscar Wilde* (1976). Sometimes rendered as 'Niagara is only the second biggest disappointment of the standard honeymoon' and '[Niagara] is the first disappointment in the married life of many Americans who spend their honeymoon there.' Wilde visited Niagara in February 1882.

7 Please don't shoot the pianist; he is doing his best.

Wilde reported having seen this notice in a bar or dancing saloon in the Rocky Mountains ('Leadville' from *Impressions of America*, pub. 1906). Hence, the film *Tirez Sur Le Pianiste* (France, 1960), translated as 'Shoot the Pianist/Piano-Player' and Elton John's 1972 record album, 'Don't Shoot Me, I'm Only the Piano-Player'.

8 Two nations separated by a common language.

Of the UK and the US. The 'origin request' most frequently received. Sometimes the inquirer asks, 'Was it Wilde or Shaw?' The answer *appears* to be: *both*. In *The Canterville Ghost* (1887), Wilde wrote: 'We have really everything in common with America nowadays except, of course, language'. However, *The Treasury of Humorous Quotations* (ed. by Evan Esar & Nicolas Bentley, 1951) quotes Shaw as saying: 'England and America are two countries separated by the same language', but without giving a source. The quote had earlier been attributed to Shaw in *Reader's Digest* (November 1942).

Much the same idea occurred to Bertrand Russell (*Saturday Evening Post*, 3 June 1944): 'It is a misfortune for Anglo-American friendship that the two countries are supposed to have a common language', and in a radio talk prepared by Dylan Thomas shortly before his death (and published after it in *The Listener*, April 1954) – European writers and scholars in America were, he said, 'up against the barrier of a common language'.

Inevitably: 'Winston Churchill said our two countries were divided by a common language' (*The Times*, 26 January 1987; *European*, 22 November 1991.)

1 I like Wagner's music better than anybody's. It is so loud that one can talk the whole time without other people hearing what one says. That is a great advantage.

The Picture of Dorian Gray, Chap. 4 (1891). Lady Henry commenting on a performance of *Lohengrin*.

2 When I ask for a watercress sandwich, I do not mean a loaf with a field in the middle of it.

To a waiter. Recounted in a Max Beerbohm letter to Reggie Turner (15 April 1893).

3 It must be so pretty with all the dear little kangaroos flying about. Agatha has found it on the map. What a curious shape it is! Just like a large packing case.

Australia, as described by the Duchess of Berwick. *Lady Windermere's Fan*, Act 2 (1892). Later she calls it 'that dreadful vulgar place'.

4 A man who knows the price of everything and the value of nothing.

Lord Darlington defining a cynic. *Ib*, Act 3

5 *Mrs Allonby*: They say, Lady Hunstanton, that when good Americans die they go to Paris.
Lady Hunstanton: Indeed? And when bad Americans die, where do they go to?
Lord Illingworth: Oh, they go to America.

A Woman of No Importance, Act 1 (1893). Earlier, this exchange had appeared in *The Picture of Dorian Gray*, Chap. 3. The originator of the remark 'Good Americans, when they die, go to Paris' was Thomas Gold Appleton (1812–84). He was quoted by Oliver Wendell Homes in *The Autocrat of the Breakfast Table* (1858).

6 The English country gentleman galloping after a fox – the unspeakable in full pursuit of the uneatable.

Ib. Origin of a much quoted characterization.

7 Children begin by loving their parents; after a time they judge them; rarely, if ever, do they forgive them.

Ib., Act 2. This line had earlier appeared, almost exactly in this form, in *The Picture of Dorian Gray*, Chap. 5. It is sometimes quoted as 'First they love us, then they judge us'.

8 *Salomé dances the dance of the seven veils.*

Stage direction, *Salomé* (pub. 1893), though the play was originally written in French. Salome so beguiled Herod by her seductive dancing that he gave her the head of St John the Baptist, as she requested. In neither Matthew 14:6 nor Mark 6:22 is she referred to by name – she is described only 'as the daughter of Herodias', nor is the nature of her dancing described. The name Salome was supplied by Josephus, the second century Jewish historian. One must assume that the idea of the dance originated with Wilde, from whose play Richard Strauss took the idea for his opera *Salome* (1905).

9 I have invented an invaluable permanent invalid called Bunbury, in order that I may be able to go down into the country whenever I choose.

The Importance of Being Earnest, Act 1 (1895). Algernon. Hence, the name 'Bunbury' for an imaginary person who is invoked in order to furnish an excuse not to do something. The activity is accordingly known as 'Bunburying'. Bunbury is the name of an actual village in Cheshire but, in fact, Wilde took the name from a friend of his youth, Henry S. Bunbury – who lived in Gloucestershire (source: Richard Ellman, *Oscar Wilde*, 1987).

10 To lose one parent, Mr Worthing, may be regarded as a misfortune; to lose both looks like carelessness.

Ib. Lady Bracknell. The origin of a format phrase, 'to lose one —— is a misfortune, to lose two looks like carelessness.'

11 All women become like their mothers. That is their tragedy. No man does. That's his.

Ib. Algernon. The same words occurred before this (in dialogue form) in *A Woman of No Importance* (1893). *Compare* BENNETT 84:7.

12 The good ended happily, and the bad unhappily. That is what fiction means.

Ib., Act 2. Miss Prism. *Compare* STOPPARD 521:6.

1 It is always painful to part from people whom one has known for a very brief space of time. The absence of old friends one can endure with equanimity. But even a momentary separation from anyone to whom one has just been introduced is almost unbearable.

Ib. Cecily speaks, on hearing that Algernon is to be sent back to London at once.

2 I never travel without my diary. One should always have something sensational to read on the train.

Ib. Gwendolen. Hence, *Something Sensational To Read in the Train*, an examination of modern diary keeping, BBC Radio (21 July 1970).

3 No gentleman ever has any money.

Ib. From a scene cut when the play was reduced from four to three acts. Quoted in H. Montgomery Hyde, *Oscar Wilde* (1976), as also, 'No gentleman ever takes exercise'.

4 Yet each man kills the thing he loves,
By each let this be heard,
Some do it with a bitter look,
Some with a flattering word.
The coward does it with a kiss,
The brave man with a sword!

The Ballard of Reading Goal (*1898*). The first line has become a proverbial saying.

5 In the world, madam.

Reply to an actress, not noted for her good looks, who had said to him: 'Mr Wilde, you are looking at the ugliest woman in Paris.' Quoted on *Quote ... Unquote* (5 April 1978) and in Richard Ellman, *Oscar Wilde*, Chap. 13 (1987).

6 No good deed goes unpunished.

This is a consciously ironic rewriting of the older expression 'No *bad* deed goes unpunished' and has been attributed to Wilde, but remains unverified. Joe Orton recorded it in his diary for 13 June 1967: 'Very good line George [Greeves] came out with at dinner: "No good deed ever goes unpunished".' James Agate in *Ego 3* (for 25 January 1938) states: '[Isidore Leo] Pavia was in great form today: "Every good deed brings its own punishment".'

7 Do you want to know the great tragedy of my life? I have put all of my genius into my life; all I've put into my works is my talent.

Speaking to André Gide and quoted in Gide's *Oscar Wilde* (1910). Translated.

8 He has fought a good fight and has had to face every difficulty except popularity.

Of W.E. Henley, in an unpublished sketch, quoted in William Rothenstein, *Men and Memories* (1931). In Wilde's *The Duchess of Padua*, Act 1 (1883), the Duke remarks: 'Popularity / Is the one insult I have never suffered.'

9 He hasn't an enemy in the world – and none of his friends like him.

Of G.B. Shaw. Shaw himself quoted this remark in *Sixteen Self Sketches* (1949). An early appearance occurs in Irvin S. Cobb, *A Laugh a Day Keeps the Doctor Away* (1921), in which someone says of Shaw, 'He's in a fair way to make himself a lot of enemies.' 'Well,' replies Wilde, 'as yet he hasn't become prominent enough to have any enemies. But none of his friends like him.'

10 I am the love that dare not speak its name.

I.e., homosexual love, particularly between men. This expression is so much bound up with the Wilde case that it is sometimes assumed that he coined it. Not so. It was the person who had helped land him in his predicament, Lord Alfred Douglas (1870–1945), who wrote the poem 'Two Loves' (1892–3), which concludes with the line. In both his trials, Wilde was asked about the poem. In the second (April–May 1895) he was asked to explain the line and gave a spontaneous explanation: 'In this century [it] is such a great affection of an elder for a younger man as there was between David and Jonathan, such as Plato made the very basis of his philosophy, and such as you find in the sonnets of Michaelangelo and Shakespeare. It is that deep, spiritual affection that is as pure as it is perfect ... It is in this century misunderstood, so much misunderstood that it may be described as the "Love that dare not speak its name", and on account of it I am placed where I am now.'

Wilde's words produced an outburst of applause from the gallery which inevitably rattled the judge.

11 People thought it dreadful of me to have entertained at dinner the evil things of life, and to have found pleasure in their company. But then, from the point of view through which I, as an artist in life, approach them they were delightfully suggestive and stimulating. It was like feasting with panthers; the danger was half the excitement.

De Profundis (1905), in a passage about his life before he was sent to Reading gaol for homosexual offences. Hence, *Feasting with Panthers*, title of play devised and directed by Peter Coe at the 1981 Chichester Festival about Wilde's trials. The idea has been traced back to Balzac who, in *Illusions Perdues* (1837–9) wrote: '... *je soupe avec des lions et des panthères* ...' (source: *Notes and Queries*, Vol. 240).

1 Frank Harris is invited to all the great houses of England – once.

Quoted in *The Treasury of Humorous Quotations*, ed. by Evan Esar & Nicolas Bentley (1951). Earlier quoted in William Rothenstein, *Men and Memories* (1931).

2 Divorces are made in heaven.

Quoted in *The Treasury of Humorous Quotations*, ed. by Evan Esar & Nicolas Bentley (1951), but otherwise untraced.

3 He [Wordsworth] found in stones the sermons he had already hidden there.

'The Decay of Lying', *Intentions* (1891). Alluding to SHAKESPEARE 476:2.

4 Oh, that is altogether immaterial, except to the hotelier, who of course charges it in the bill. A gentlemen never looks out of the window.

On being shown into a hotel room in Paris with a fine view over the River Seine and the Louvre. Said to Robert H. Sherard and quoted by him in *Oscar Wilde: Story of an Unhappy Friendship* (1902).

5 Of course America had often been discovered before Columbus, but it had always been hushed up.

Quoted in *The Treasury of Humorous Quotations*, ed. by Evan Esar & Nicolas Bentley (1951), but otherwise untraced.

6 I must decline your invitation owing to a subsequent engagement.

Quoted in *ib.*, but otherwise untraced.

7 Work is the curse of the drinking classes.

Not found until Hesketh Pearson, *The Life of Oscar Wilde* (1946).

8 'Ah, well then,' said Oscar, 'I suppose that I shall have to die beyond my means.'

R.H. Sherard, *Life of Oscar Wilde* (1906). Alternatively, 'I am dying, as I have lived, beyond my means', said as he called for champagne when he was approaching death in 1900. Quoted in Barnaby Conrad, *Famous Last Words* (1961). Richard Ellman, *Oscar Wilde* (1987) has: 'I am dying beyond my means, I will never outlive the century' as said to Wilde's sister-in-law. Either way, they were not his 'dying words'. He lived for another month or so.

9 This wall paper'll be the death of me – one of us'll have to go.

This remark about the furnishings in his room was indeed said by Wilde, but not *in extremis*. The jest was first recorded in Sherard (*op. cit.*). Another version is that Wilde said to Claire de Pratz: 'My wallpaper and I are fighting a duel to the death. One or the other of us has to go' – reported in Guillot de Saix, 'Souvenirs inédits', also in Frank Harris, *Oscar Wilde, His Life and Confessions* (1930).

See also ANONYMOUS 20:4; DICKENS 206:7; MAGEE 375:8; WHISTLER 565:4.

WILDER, Billy

American film director and writer (1906–)

10 You have Van Gogh's ear for music.

Appearing on BBC Radio *Quote ... Unquote* in 1977, Kenneth Williams came up with a rather good showbiz story. He quoted the above as what Orson Welles had reputedly said of the singing of Donny Osmond (then a popular young star). In fact, Orson Welles did not say it, nor was it about Donny Osmond, but the reasons why the joke had been reascribed and redirected are instructive. It was in fact Billy Wilder, the film director, who made the original remark. He has a notably waspish wit but is not, perhaps, such a household name as Orson Welles. He lacks, too, Welles's Falstaffian stature and his, largely unearned, reputation in the public mind for having said witty things. And Wilder said it about *Cliff* Osmond, an American comedy actor who had appeared in the film director's *Kiss Me Stupid*, *The Fortune Cookie* and *The Front Page*. As far as one knows, he is not related to Donny Osmond but, apparently, he had to be replaced in the anecdote because he lacked star status. The correct attribution was given in Leslie Halliwell, *The Filmgoer's Book of Quotes* (1973).

Tom Stoppard included something very similar in *The Real Inspector Hound* (1968): 'An uncanny ear that might [have] belonged to a Van Gogh.'

11 It was like going to the dentist making a pic-

ture with her. It was hell at the time, but after it was all over, it was wonderful.

On working with Marilyn Monroe. Quoted in Earl Wilson, *The Show Business Nobody Knows* (1971). Compare 'Extracting a performance from her is like pulling teeth'; quoted in Leslie Halliwell, *The Filmgoer's Book of Quotes* (1973).

1 **I've met a lot of hardboiled eggs in my time, but you're twenty minutes.**

Ace in the Hole (film US, 1951), co-written with Lesser Samuels and Walter Newman.

2 **UNABLE OBTAIN BIDET. SUGGEST HANDSTAND IN SHOWER.**

Cabled response to his wife's complaint from Paris just after the war that her accommodation did not have a bidet and would he send her one. This version of a much-told tale comes from Leslie Halliwell, *The Filmgoer's Book of Quotes* (1973).

See also SOME LIKE IT HOT 510:6.

WILHELM II

German Kaiser (1859–1941)

3 **We have fought for our place in the sun and won it. Our future is on the water.**

Speech at Hamburg (18 June 1901), echoing the phrase for German colonial ambitions in East Asia, which had been coined by Count Bernard von Bülow (1849–1929), the German Chancellor, in a speech to the Reichstag in 1897: 'In a word, we desire to throw no one into the shade, but we also demand our own place in the sun [*Platz an der Sonne*].' Subsequently, the notion was much referred to in the run-up to the First World War. Hence, probably, *A Place in the Sun* – the title given to the 1951 film of Theodore Dreiser's *An American Tragedy*. A much earlier appearance occurred in the *Pensées* of Blaise Pascal (Walker's translation, 1688): 'This Dog is mine, said those poor Children; That's my place in the Sun. This is the beginning and Image of the Usurpation of all the Earth'. The phrase is now hardly ever used in this precise sense, but simply to indicate a rightful piece of good fortune, a desirable situation, for example: 'Mr Frisk could bring Aintree punters their place in the sun' (headline from the *Independent on Sunday*, 1 April 1990).

4 **Ah, I thought he was boating with his grocer.**

When an English visitor told him that Edward VII was at Windsor Castle with Sir Thomas Lipton. An example of his contempt for the English monarch. Quoted in Winston S. Churchill, *Great Contemporaries* (1937).

5 **You will be home before the leaves have fallen from the trees.**

To troops leaving for the Front in August 1914 at the beginning of the First World War. After that, it was going to be 'all over by Christmas', but it dragged on for four years. Quoted in Barbara Tuchman, *The Guns of August*, Chap. 9 (1962).

6 **It is my Royal and Imperial command that you concentrate your energies for the immediate present upon one single purpose, and that is that you address all your skill and all the valour of my soldiers to exterminate first, the treacherous English [and] walk over General French's contemptible little army.**

B.E.F. Routine Orders for 24 September 1914 containing what was claimed to be a copy of orders (as above) issued by the German Emperor on 19 August. The greatest canard of the First World War was that Kaiser Wilhelm had described the 1914 British Expeditionary Force as 'a contemptibly little army' – referring to its size rather than to its quality. The British Press was then said to have mistranslated this so that it made the Kaiser appear to have called the B.E.F. 'a contemptible little army'. Rank and file thereafter happily styled themselves 'The Old Contemptibles'.

The truth as revealed by Arthur Ponsonby in *Falsehood in War-Time* (1928) is that the whole episode was a propaganda ploy masterminded by the British. The Kaiser's alleged words became widely known but an investigation during 1925 in the German archives failed to produce any evidence of the order ever having been issued. The ex-Kaiser himself said: 'On the contrary, I continually emphasized the high value of the British Army, and often, indeed, in peace-time gave warning against underestimating it.' It is now accepted that the phrase was devised at the War Office by Sir Frederick Maurice.

7 **Hang the Kaiser!**

During the Versailles Peace Conference and for some time afterwards, Britain's Northcliffe newspapers and others kept up this cry. Candidates at the 1918 General Election are said to have lost votes if they did not subscribe to the policy. The Allies committed themselves to try the ex-Kaiser in the Treaty of Versailles (28 June 1919), but the government of the Netherlands refused to hand him over for trial in June 1920. Arthur Ponsonby (as above) argued that casting the Kaiser as villain of the piece had been a put-up job anyway: 'When, as months and years passed, it was discovered that no responsible person really believed, or had ever believed, in [his] personal guilt, that the cry "Hang the Kaiser" was a piece of deliberate bluff, and that when it was over and millions of innocent people had been killed, he, the criminal, the monster, the plotter and initiator of the whole catastrophe, was allowed to live comfortably and peacefully in Holland, the disillusionment to simple, uninformed people was far greater than ever realized.' The ex-Kaiser died in 1941.

WILKES, John

English politician (1727–97)

1 *Earl of Sandwich*: 'Pon my soul, Wilkes, I don't know whether you'll die upon the gallows or of the pox.
Wilkes: That depends, my Lord, whether I first embrace your Lordship's principles, or your Lordship's mistresses.

A famous exchange which made an early appearance in Sir Charles Petrie, *The Four Georges* (1935), but is quite likely apocryphal. Where did Petrie get it from, and where had it been for the intervening two centuries?

It is frequently misapplied. George E. Allen in *Presidents Who Have Known Me* (1950) has it between Gladstone and Disraeli. It is difficult to imagine the circumstance in which either Disraeli or Gladstone could have made either of the remarks.

See also ANONYMOUS 40:6.

WILLANS, Geoffrey

British writer (1911–58)

2 There is no better xsample of a goody-goody than fotherington-tomas in the world in space. You kno he is the one who sa Hullo Clouds Hullo Sky and skip about like a girly.

How To Be Topp (with Ronald Searle) (1954). The earliest citation available containing something like the cry 'hello birds, hello clouds, hello trees, hello sky!' – a joke expression of joy in nature, as though spoken by a poet, aesthete or other fey character dancing round the countryside. In an even later book about the schoolboy character 'Nigel Molesworth', Willans returns to the theme: 'And who is this who skip weedily up to me, eh? "Hullo clouds, hullo sky," he sa. "Hullo birds, hullo poetry books, hullo skool sossages, hullo molesworth 1." You hav guessed it is dere little basil fotherington-tomas' – *Back in the Jug Agane* (1959). There is an unconfirmed appearance in a 1941 Warner Bros cartoon.

WILLIAM, Lloyd S.

American soldier (early twentieth century)

3 Retreat? Hell, no! We just got here!

An attributed remark, made by Captain Williams when advised by the French to retreat, shortly after his arrival at the Western Front in the First World War. Or, specifically referring to the retreat from Belloar (5 June 1918), quoted in Partridge/*Catch Phrases*. Untraced and unverified. Margaret Thatcher quoted it at a Confederation of British Industry dinner in 1980.

WILLIAMS, Tennessee

American playwright (1911–83)

4 *Amanda*: It's almost time for our gentlemen callers to start arriving. [*She flounces girlishly toward the kitchenette.*] How many do you suppose we're going to entertain this afternoon?

The Glass Menagerie, Sc. 1 (1944). The term 'gentleman caller' for a man who calls on a woman and becomes a potential suitor (also a euphemism for a male lover) was popularized by this play. But it was known before. The phrase occurs in the script of *Citizen Kane* (1941): 'When I have a gentleman caller ...'

5 *Blanche Dubois*: I have always depended on the kindness of strangers.

A Streetcar Named Desire, Act 2 (1947). Her last words in the play. Blanche is about to be taken off to an institution. Christopher Isherwood once said that to his mind this was the finest single line in modern letters (source: Gore Vidal, *New World Writing No 4*, 1953). Hence, the frequent use of the phrase 'the kindness of strangers' as the title of: Donald Spotto's biography of Williams (1990), Bernard Braden's autobiography (1990), John Boswell's account of 'the Abandonment of Children in Western Europe from Late Antiquity to the Renaissance' (1988) and so on.

There may be some allusion to a passage from W. Somerset Maugham's novel *The Narrow Corner* (1932): 'Everyone is so nice. Nothing is too much trouble. You cannot imagine the kindness I've received at the hands of perfect strangers.' Williams had certainly read this novel (see Gore Vidal, *A View from the Diner's Club*, 1993).

Not to be confused with the film titles *The Comfort of Strangers* (1990, based on Ian McEwan's novel) and *The Company of Strangers* (1991).

1 Cat On a Hot Tin Roof.

Title of play (1955; film US, 1958) – derived from the (mostly US) expression 'as nervous as a cat on a hot tin roof', which derives, in turn, from the common English expression 'like a cat on hot bricks', meaning 'ill-at-ease, jumpy'. John Ray in his *Collection of English Proverbs* (1670–8) had: 'to go like a cat upon a hot bake stone'. An expression 'nervous as cats' appeared in *Punch*'s Almanack for 1903.

In the play, the 'cat' is Maggie, Brick's wife, 'whose frayed vivacity', wrote Kenneth Tynan, 'derives from the fact that she is sexually ignored by her husband'. The title phrase is referred to several times: Act 1, 'I feel all the time like a cat on a hot tin roof'; last words of the play (New York version) 'Nothing's more determined than a cat on a hot tin roof – is there?'

WILSON, Charles E.

American Republican politician (1890–1961)

2 What's good for General Motors is good for the country.

President Eisenhower wished to appoint Wilson as Secretary for Defense. At hearings of the Senate Committee on Armed Services in January 1953, the former President of General Motors was asked about any possible conflict of interest, as he had accepted several million dollars' worth of General Motors shares. When he was asked whether he would be able to make a decision against the interests of General Motors and his stock, what Wilson in fact replied was not the above, but: 'Yes, sir, I could. I cannot conceive of one because for years I thought what was good for our country was good for General Motors, and vice versa. The difference did not exist.'

Wilson was finally persuaded to get rid of his stock, but he never quite lived down his (misquoted) remarks.

3 [It gives] a bigger bang for a buck.

Wilson said this of the new type of H-bomb tested at Bikini in 1954 (and was so quoted in *Newsweek* Magazine, 22 March 1954). *PDMQ* (1980) misinterprets a passage in David Halberstam, *The Best and the Brightest* (1973) and attributes the remark to President Eisenhower.

WILSON, Harold (later Lord Wilson of Rievaulx)

British Labour Prime Minister (1916–95)

4 The school I went to in the north was a school where more than half the children in my class never had any boots or shoes to their feet. They wore clogs, because they lasted longer than shoes of comparable price.

Speech as President of the Board of Trade at Birmingham (July 1948). Newspaper reports wrongly suggested he had claimed that when he was at school some of his classmates had gone *barefoot*. A former teacher at the school, reacting to the abbreviated report, denied that any of Wilson's schoolmates had ever gone barefoot and soon the politician was being widely reported as having said that he himself had had to go barefoot to school. This gave rise to the jibe by Ivor Bulmer-Thomas (*see* 128:8). The incident was the first of many misunderstandings between Wilson and the press.

5 All these financiers, all the little gnomes in Zurich and the other financial centres, about whom we keep on hearing.

Speech, House of Commons (12 November 1956). 'The gnomes of Zurich' was a term used to disparage the tight-fisted methods of speculators in the Swiss financial capital who questioned Britain's creditworthiness and who forced austerity measures on Wilson's Labour Government when it came to power in 1964. George Brown, Secretary of State for Economic Affairs, popularized the term in November of that year and it is often associated with him. Wilson himself had, however, used it long before. In 1958, Andrew Shonfield wrote in *British Economic Policy Since the War*: 'Hence the tragedy of the autumn of 1957, when the Chancellor of the Exchequer [Peter Thorneycroft] adopted as his guide to action the slogan: I must be hard-faced enough to match the mirror-image of an imaginary hard-faced little man in Zurich. It is tough on the Swiss that William Tell should be displaced in English folklore by this new image of a gnome in a bank at the end of a telephone line.'

6 The candyfloss society.

Of Harold Macmillan's Britain. Remark, *c.*1960.

7 Every time Mr Macmillan comes back from abroad, Mr Butler goes to the airport and grips him warmly by the throat.

Quoted in Leslie Smith, *Harold Wilson* (1964). Undated

but made, obviously, before 1963 when Harold Macmillan resigned as British Prime Minister. Possibly 1957, when Macmillan had beaten Butler to the premiership. In the 1964 Broadway version of *Beyond the Fringe*, the Duke of Edinburgh was given the similar line, 'I was very well received [in Kenya, at independence]. Mr Kenyatta himself came to the airport to greet me and shook me warmly by the throat as I got off the plane.'

1 Whichever party is in office, the Treasury is in power.

Quoted in Anthony Sampson, *The Changing Anatomy of Britain* (1982). In *The Oxford Dictionary of Political Quotations* (1996), the editor Antony Jay included this line but also states in his Introduction that he had been unable to trace the saying, 'Whoever is in office, the Conservatives are always in power.' Perhaps a solution to the problem is that Harold Wilson may have made use of a sort of epigram format with several variables. In an essay contributed to *The Establishment* (ed. Hugh Thomas, 1959), Thomas Balogh (later Wilson's economic adviser) wrote: 'The fact that the Treasury controls senior appointments, and that Ministers are busy men, does the rest. Mr Harold Wilson aptly put it: "Whoever is in office, the Whigs are in power"' (Whigs here meaning, 'the old established interest').

2 I have always deprecated – perhaps rightly, perhaps wrongly – in crisis after crisis, appeals to the Dunkirk spirit as an answer to our problems because what is required in our economic situation is not a brief period of inspired improvisation, work and sacrifice, such as we had under the leadership of the Rt Hon. Member for Woodford [Winston Churchill], but a very long, hard prolonged period of reorganization and redirection. It is the long haul, not the inspired spirit that we need.

Speech, House of Commons (26 July 1961). No sooner had he become Prime Minister than he said in a 'hastily compiled' speech to the Labour Party Conference on 12 December 1964: 'I believe that the spirit of Dunkirk will once again carry us through to success'. Neatly pointed out by Paul Foot in *The Politics of Harold Wilson* (1968).

3 We are redefining and we are restating our socialism in terms of the scientific revolution ... the Britain that is going to be forged in the white heat of this revolution will be no place for restrictive practices or outdated methods on either side of industry.

Speech, Labour Party Conference in Scarborough (1 October 1963). Usually encapsulated as 'The white heat of the technological revolution'.

4 After half a century of democratic advance, the whole process has ground to a halt with a fourteenth Earl.

On the Earl of Home's appointment as Prime Minister. Speech, Belle Vue, Manchester (19 October 1963). *See also* DOUGLAS-HOME 212:5.

5 [We have] a chance to sweep away the grouse-moor conception of Tory leadership and refit Britain with a new image.

Speech, Birmingham (January 1964). Referring to Harold Macmillan and Sir Alec Douglas-Home, past and present Conservative leaders.

6 What I think we are going to need is something like what President Kennedy had when he came in after years of stagnation in the United States. He had a programme of a hundred days – a hundred days of dynamic action.

Labour Party political broadcast (15 July 1964). In fact, Kennedy had specifically ruled out a 'hundred days', saying in his Inaugural Address that his programmes could not be carried out even in a thousand days (*compare* KENNEDY 330:8).

7 Smethwick Conservatives can have the satisfaction of having topped the poll, of having sent a member who, until another election returns him to oblivion, will serve his time here as a Parliamentary leper.

On an MP who had run an allegedly racist campaign. Speech, House of Commons (4 November 1964).

8 A week is a long time in politics.

In 1977, I asked the then recently retired Prime Minister when he had first uttered his most-quoted dictum. Uncharacteristically, he was unable to remember. For someone who used to be able to cite the column numbers of *Hansard* in which his speeches appeared, this was a curious lapse. Inquiries among political journalists led to the conclusion that in its present form the phrase was probably first uttered at a meeting between Wilson and the Parliamentary lobby in the wake of the sterling crisis shortly after he first took office as Prime Minister in 1964. However, Robert Carvel, then of the London *Evening Standard*, recalled Wilson at a Labour Party Conference in 1960 saying, 'Forty-eight hours is a long time in politics'. (One might note here that in his

The Second World War, Vol. 1 (1948), Winston Churchill had written: 'But in war seven months is a long time ...') In addition, it is said that Joseph Chamberlain said to Arthur Balfour in 1886, 'In politics there is no use looking beyond the next fortnight.'

Apart from dating, there has been some dispute as to what precisely the dictum means. Most would take it to be along the lines of, 'Just give a problem time and it will solve itself', 'What a difference a day makes', 'Wait and see', and 'Don't panic, it'll all blow over'. But when I consulted Wilson in 1977, he challenged the accepted interpretation. 'It does not mean I'm living from day to day,' he said. 'It was intended as a prescription for long-term strategic thinking and planning, ignoring the day-to-day issues and pressures which may hit the headlines but which must not be allowed to get out of focus while longer-term policies are taking effect.'

The phrase caught on: from the late 1980s, Channel Four TV has carried a weekly review with the title *A Week in Politics*, clearly alluding to Wilson's phrase. From *The Independent* (19 May 1989), on the outgoing editor of the TV programme *Forty Minutes*: 'His successor will have to work hard, though, to keep the formula fresh. 2,400 seconds is a long time in television.'

When Wilson took his peerage, he chose as his motto: '*Tempus Rerum Imperator* [timing is everything]'.

1 Weeks rather than months.

Now an idiom meaning 'sooner rather than later', this echoes Wilson's use of the phrase at the Commonwealth Prime Ministers' Conference (12 January 1966). He had first used it in an unreported speech on that day and it was later included in the final communiqué: 'In this connection [the use of military force in Rhodesia] the Prime Ministers noted the statement by the British Prime Minister that on the expert advice available to him, the cumulative effect of the economic and financial sanctions [against Rhodesia] might well bring the rebellion to an end within a matter of weeks rather than months'. As was to be discovered, this was a little wide of the mark. The return to legality took until 1980 to achieve.

2 It is difficult for us to appreciate the pressures which are put on men I know to be realistic and responsible, not only in their executive capacity but in the highly-organized strike committees in the ports, by this tightly-knit group of politically-motivated men who, as the last General Election showed, utterly failed to secure acceptance of their views by the British electorate, but who are now determined to exercise backstage pressures, forcing great hardship on the members of the union and their families, and endangering the security of the industry and the economic welfare of the nation.

Speech, House of Commons (22 June 1966) – during the sixth week of a national seamen's strike. He later explained: 'I did not use the word "Communist", though no one in the House or in the press ... had any doubts whom I had in mind.' Compare what his namesake Woodrow in the US had said earlier about Senate isolationists who filibustered a bill to allow the arming of merchant vessels (4 March 1917): 'A little group of wilful men representing no opinion but their own, has rendered the great government of the United States helpless and contemptible.'

3 Every dog is allowed one bite, but a different view is taken of a dog that goes on biting all the time. He may not get his licence returned when it falls due.

Speech to Parliamentary Labour Party (2 March 1967). Wilson was warning of disciplinary action when left-wing Labour MPs failed to support his government's defence White Paper.

4 From now on the pound abroad is worth 14 per cent or so less in terms of other currencies. That doesn't mean, of course, that the pound here in Britain, in your pocket or purse or in your bank, has been devalued.

Broadcast address (19 November 1967), after a devaluation of the pound sterling. In *The Labour Government 1964–70* (1971), he said this was the only part of the Treasury draft speech he had incorporated in his final version – 'Though I was cautioned by a civil service adviser, I was reinforced by the words of one of my own staff whose maiden aunt had telephoned to express concern that her Post Office Savings Bank holdings had been slashed by three shillings in the pound.'

The following evening, the Opposition leader, Edward Heath, quoted Wilson's reference to the 'pound in your pocket' as a misleading pledge that prices would not rise as a result of devaluation. The charge was taken up by many others.

5 This party is a bit like an old stagecoach. If you drive along at a rapid rate, everyone aboard is either so exhilarated or so seasick that you don't have a lot of difficulty.

Quoted in Anthony Sampson, *The Changing Anatomy of*

Britain (1982). Also quoted in this form: 'The Labour Party is like a vehicle. If you drive at great speed, all the people in it are so exhilarated or so sick that you have no problems. But when you stop, they all get out and argue about which way to go' – leading article in *The Sunday Telegraph* (28 May 1995).

1 Get your tanks off my lawn, Hughie.

According to Peter Jenkins, *The Battle of Downing Street* (1970), Wilson said this to Hugh Scanlon, the trade union leader, at Chequers, the prime ministerial residence, in June 1969 during the battle between the government and the trade unions over reform. Scanlon was head of Britain's second largest union, the engineers'. Jenkins reports that Wilson was enraged at the intransigence and arrogance of Scanlon and Jack Jones, another union leader. In an exchange of views, Scanlon said, 'Prime Minister, we don't want you to become another Ramsay Macdonald' (that is, betraying the Labour movement). Wilson replied, 'I have no intention of becoming another Ramsay Macdonald. Nor do I intend to become another Dubcek. Get your tanks off my lawn, Hughie!'

As such, this is the first recorded use of a political metaphor for 'back off, don't threaten me'. Subsequently it has entered the lexicon of British politics and journalism. From the *Financial Times* (6 November 1982) on the Harrods/Lonrho dispute: '[Professor Roland Smith, chairman, House of Fraser:] If this is your idea of a game, please play somewhere else in the future ... To make it absolutely clear: get your tanks off my lawn.' From *The Observer* (14 April 1991): 'It is true, of course, that the Home Secretary does not park his tanks on [BBC Director-General] Checkland's lawn ... That is not the British way.' From a speech made by John Major to the Conservative Party Conference, 8 October 1993: 'Let me say to some of our European colleagues, "You're playing with fire [on GATT world free trade talks]," or to put it more bluntly, "Get your tractors off our lawn".'

2 You can't guarantee being born a Lord. It is possible – you've shown it – to be born a gentleman.

When President Nixon came to dinner with Wilson at Downing Street in 1969, the first year of his Presidency, he had to sit down at table with John Freeman, the British Ambassador to Washington. So far Nixon had managed to ignore the man who had once written of him as 'a man of no principle whatsoever except a willingness to sacrifice everything in the cause of Dick Nixon'. As it turned out, Nixon proposed a toast and graciously said he hoped all that was behind them. As Henry Kissinger recorded in his *Memoirs* (1979), Wilson scribbled the above note to Nixon on a menu card.

Compare what King James I is reputed to have said: 'I can make a Lord, but only God Almighty can make a gentleman' (but *see also* BURKE 131:6).

3 Selsdon Man is designing a system of society for the ruthless and the pushing, the uncaring ... His message to the rest is: you're out on your own.

Speech at a rally of the Greater London Labour Party in Camden Town Hall (21 February 1970) – referring to the Conservative policy-forming meeting at the Selsdon Park hotel, Croydon (31 January 1970).

4 Cohorts of distinguished journalists have been combing obscure parts of the country with a mandate to find anything, true or fabricated, to use against the Labour Party.

Attributed remark (September 1974) in the run-up to the October General Election. The complaint was finally rejected by the Press Council in October 1978 because he had failed to provide any evidence.

5 I forgive you all.

To journalists at press conference marking his retirement. Quoted in *The Observer* (21 March 1976).

6 I see myself as the big fat spider in the corner of the room. Sometimes I speak when I'm asleep. You should both listen. Occasionally when we meet I might tell you to go to the Charing Cross Road and kick a blind man standing on the corner. That blind man may tell you something, lead you somewhere.

A bizarre picture of himself that Wilson gave to two BBC reporters, Barrie Penrose and Roger Courtior, in the mid-1970s. He was convinced that there was a massive South African plot afoot to discredit leading British politicians and summoned the reporters to help them expose it. The remark was included in *The Pencourt File* (1978).

WILSON, Mary (later Lady Wilson)

Wife of Harold Wilson (1916–)

7 If Harold has a fault it is that he will drown everything with HP sauce.

Interview in *The Sunday Times* (1962). This was shortly before Wilson became Labour Party leader on the death of Hugh Gaitskell. His wife's revelation was what would later become known as a 'defining moment' in terms of his public persona. As has been said, Wilson's populism (or philistinism, according to one's point of view) was later emphasized by such similar remarks as: 'If I had the choice between smoked salmon and tinned salmon, I'd have it tinned. With vinegar.'

1 Dear John,
Yes, it is perfect bliss
To go with you by train to Diss!

Poem, 'Reply to the Laureate' (1979). Betjeman had written 'Dear Mary,/Yes, it will be bliss/To go with you by train to Diss' in 'A Mind's Journey to Diss'.

WILSON, Woodrow

American Democratic 28th President (1856–1924)

2 It is like writing history with lightning. And it's all true.

On the film *The Birth of a Nation* (1915). Quoted in Daniel Boorstin, *The Image* (1962). It was the first film ever to be shown in the White House.

3 If I am to speak for ten minutes, I need a week for preparation; if fifteen minutes, three days; if half an hour, two days; if an hour, I am ready now.

Quoted by Josephus Daniels, *The Wilson Era* (1946).

4 The world must be made safe for democracy. Its peace must be planted upon trusted foundations of political liberty.

Speech to Congress (2 April 1917), asking for a declaration against Germany. The words might never have been remembered had not Senator John Sharp Williams of Mississippi started clapping and continued until everyone joined in. In 1937, James Harvey Robinson commented: 'With supreme irony, the war to "Make the world safe for democracy" ended by leaving democracy more unsafe in the world than at any time since the collapse of the revolutions of 1848.'

WINDSOR, Duchess of (formerly Mrs Wallis Simpson)

American-born wife of the Duke of Windsor (1896–1986)

5 I married him for better or worse, but not for lunch.

This rather pleasing play on the words from the Anglican marriage service was reported in an article by Ludovic Kennedy in *The Observer* (2 December 1979), based on *The Windsor Story* by J. Bryan III and Charles J.V. Murphy, in the context: '[The Duke of Windsor] usually lunched alone on a salad while the duchess went out ("I married the Duke for better or worse but not for lunch").'

But Partridge/*Catch Phrases* (1977) has it listed as an 'Australian catchphrase used by a woman whose husband has retired, works at home or comes home for his midday meal', dating it from the 1940s and 'familiar to Britons since at least the latish 1960s'.

6 You can never be too rich or too thin.

Quoted in *PDMQ* (1980), but otherwise untraced.

WINNER, Langdon

American writer (twentieth century)

7 The closest western civilisation has come to unity since the Congress of Vienna in 1815 was the week the 'Sgt. Pepper' album was released ... for a brief while the irreparably fragmented consciousness of the West was unified, at least in the minds of the young.

On the Beatles' 'Sgt. Pepper' album of 1967. Quoted in *The* Rolling Stone *Illustrated History of Rock and Roll* (ed. Jim Miller) (1976).

WISTER, Owen

American writer (1860–1938)

8 Therefore Trampas spoke. 'You bet, you son-of-a-'. The Virginian's pistol came out, and ... he issued his orders to the man Trampas: – 'When you call me that, *smile!*'

Novel, *The Virginian*, Chap. 2 (1902). However, in the film version (1929) – based on the play and the novel by Wister – what Gary Cooper says, standing up to Walter Huston, is: 'If you want to call me that, smile'. (*Halliwell's Film Guide*, 1987, nevertheless has the cliché as 'Smile when you say that'.) Hence, the generally used phrase when giving a warning about an incident that could lead to a fight.

WODEHOUSE, P.G. (later Sir Pelham)

English-born novelist and lyricist (1881–1975)

9 I turned to Aunt Agatha, whose demeanour was now rather like that of one who, picking

daisies on the railway, has just caught the down express in the small of the back.

The Inimitable Jeeves (1923).The image also occurs in *Joy in the Morning*, Chap. 15 (1974).

1 I'm not absolutely certain of my facts, but I rather fancy it's Shakespeare – or, if not, it's some equally brainy bird – who says that it's always just when a fellow is feeling particularly braced with things in general that Fate sneaks up behind him with the bit of lead piping. And what I'm driving at is that the man is perfectly right.

'Jeeves and the Unbidden Guest', in *Carry on, Jeeves!*, (1925). Alluding to Shakespeare, *King Henry VIII* (III. ii. 352).

2 To my daughter Leonora, without whose never-failing sympathy and encouragement this book would have been finished in half the time.

Dedication, *The Heart of a Goof* (1926). Not the first use by Wodehouse of this formula. In the first edition of *A Gentleman of Leisure* (1910) appears: 'To Herbert Westbrook, without whose never-failing sympathy and encouragement this book would have been finished in half the time.'

3 'What's that thing of Shakespeare's about someone having an eye like Mother's?'
'"An eye like Mars, to threaten and command", is possibly the quotation for which you are groping, sir.'

The Mating Season (1949) – Bertie's question and Jeeves's reply. *See* SHAKESPEARE 481:6. Few writers have employed literary allusions to the same extent as Wodehouse in his novels and short stories featuring Bertie Wooster and Jeeves, his gentleman's gentleman. 'Hullo, fathead ... what news on the Rialto?' – unusually, this is Bertie's Aunt Dahlia plucking a line from *The Merchant of Venice* in *Aunts Aren't Gentlemen*. Usually, it is Bertie who is fumbling for the apt quotation and, more often than not, believing that Jeeves invented all the best lines. When Jeeves quotes 'It is a far, far better thing', Bertie comments: 'As I said before, there is nobody who puts these things more neatly than he does'. A quotation from Shakespeare is frequently accompanied by, 'As I have heard Jeeves put it' or 'To quote one of Jeeves's gags'. For example: 'Leaving not a wrack behind, as I remember Jeeves saying once'. Although we all know that Jeeves is quite capable of reading Spinoza's *Ethics* (indeed, he gets a complete edition of the *Annotated Works*), such faith in his ability to coin a neat phrase is strange in a Wooster educated at Eton and Oxford and winner of the Scripture Knowledge prize. But as Richard Usborne pointed out in *Wodehouse at Work* (1961), Bertie's frame of reference is no more than one would expect of an educated man in the early twentieth century. There are lapses, though: 'The next moment I was dropping like the gentle dew upon the place beneath. Or is it rain? Jeeves would know'. Occasionally Bertie resorts – as so many of us do – to 'as the fellow said'. In one book, he refers to the 'works of somebody called Wordsworth'. Some quotations recur throughout the Jeeves canon. 'With a wild surmise' probably crops up most often. Bertie worries obsessively and understandably over 'the cat i' the adage' and 'fretful porpentine'. What is more, Wodehouse larded the novels with more and more literary allusions as he grew older. *Jeeves in the Offing* (1960) contains some forty-eight. It is a delight when Bertie alludes to 'Shakespeare and those poet Johnnies' by way of attribution or when he scrambles his allusions, as in 'One man's caviare is another man's major-general, as the old saw has it'. He would have found this *Companion* invaluable.

WOLFE, Charles

Irish poet and clergyman (1791–1823)

4 Not a drum was heard, not a funeral note,
As his corse to the rampart we hurried ...
We carved not a line, and we raised not a
 stone –
But we left him alone in his glory.

'The Burial of Sir John Moore at Corunna' (1817). From an incident in Spain during the Peninsular War (1808–14). Moore was in command of an outnumbered British army when he was forced to retreat by the unexpected arrival of Napoleon and 200,000 Frenchmen.

WOLFE, James

English general (1727–59)

5 The General ... repeated nearly the whole of Gray's Elegy ... adding, as he concluded, that he would prefer being the author of that poem to the glory of beating the French tomorrow.

Said on the eve of the Battle of Quebec, during which Wolfe was fatally wounded. Quoted in J. Playfair, *Biographical Account of J. Robinson* (1815).

WOLFE, Tom

American novelist and writer (1931–)

1 Radical Chic and Mau-Mauing the Flak Catchers.

Title of book (1970). Hence, the term 'radical chic' for the fashionable adoption of left-wing ideas, dress, etc. In particular, Wolfe ridiculed the tendency at that time for members of well-off, high society to mingle with socialists and revolutionaries.

2 The Right Stuff.

Title of book (1979; film US, 1983) – referring to the qualities needed by test-pilots and would-be astronauts in the early years of the US space programme. But the 'right (sort of) stuff' had been applied much earlier to qualities of manly virtue, of good officer material and even of good cannon fodder. Partridge/*Slang* has an example from the 1880s. In this sense, the phrase was used by Ian Hay as the title of a novel – 'some episodes in the career of a North Briton' – in 1908.

It is now a handy journalistic device. An *Independent* headline over a story about the ballet *Ondine* (13 May 1988) was, 'The Sprite Stuff'; the same month, *The Magazine* (London) had 'The Right Stuff' as the title of an article on furnishing fabrics; in 1989, there was an ITV book programme called *The Write Stuff.*

It has also been used as an expression for alcohol (compare 'the hard stuff').

3 The Bonfire of the Vanities.

Title of novel (1987; film US, 1990). Derived from Savonarola's 'burning of the vanities' in Florence, 1497. The religious reformer – 'the puritan of Catholicism' – enacted various laws for the restraint of vice and folly. Gambling was prohibited and Savonarola's followers helped people burn their costly ornaments and extravagant clothes.

4 A liberal is a conservative who has been arrested.

In two places in *The Bonfire of the Vanities*, Wolfe quotes this, but is clearly referring to an established saying. In the Fall 1993 issue of the American *Policy Review*, James Q. Wilson is credited with a similar (though reverse) observation: 'There aren't any liberals left in New York. They've all been mugged.'

WOLSEY, Thomas

English prelate (c.1475–1530)

5 I see the matter against me how it is framed. But if I had served God as diligently as I have done the King, he would not have given me over in my grey hairs.

Cardinal Wolsey's remark was made to Sir William Kingston, Constable of the Tower of London, when Wolsey was under arrest for high treason, in November 1530. These were not his actual 'last words', as is sometimes suggested, though they were spoken on his deathbed. His last words appear to have been: 'Master Kingston, farewell. My time draweth on fast. Forget not what I have sent and charged you withal. For when I am dead you shall, peradventure, understand my words better.' Wolsey was not executed but died in Leicester on his way to the Tower. *Compare* SHAKESPEARE 485:9.

WOLSTENHOLME, Kenneth

English TV and radio sports commentator (1920–)

6 They think it's all over ... It is now!

Commentating for BBC Television on the World Cup Final at Wembley between England and West Germany on 30 July 1966, Wolstenholme ad-libbed what has come to be regarded as the 'most famous quote in British sport'. After a disputed third goal, the England team was 3–2 in the lead as the game continued in extra time. 'Some people are on the pitch,' Wolstenholme began before the final whistle, 'They think it's all over.' Then Geoff Hurst scored England's fourth goal (and his third) and decisively won the game. So that was why Wolstenholme added, 'It is now!'

It took until the 1990s for the phrase really to catch on. By 1992, a jokey BBC Radio sports quiz had the title *They Think It's All Over.* Some accounts have the commentator saying, '*Well*, it is now. It's four.' According to *The Guardian* (30 July 1991), Wolstenholme himself used to complain if the 'well' were omitted but then a replay of his commentary showed that he had not said the word after all.

WOOD, Mrs Henry

English novelist (1814–87)

7 Dead! ... and never called me mother!

This line is recalled as typical of the three-volume sentimental Victorian novel, yet nowhere does it appear in Wood's *East Lynne* (1861) where it is supposed to. Nevertheless, it was inserted in one of the numerous stage versions of the novel (that by T.A. Palmer in 1874) which were made between publication and the end of the century. Act III has, 'Dead, dead, dead! and he never knew me, never called me mother!' Mrs

Wood's obituary writer noted in 1887: 'At present, there are three dramatic versions of *East Lynne* nightly presented in various parts of the world. Had the author been granted even a small percentage on the returns she would have been a rich woman ... The adapters of *East Lynne* grew rich and Mrs Henry Wood was kept out of their calculations.' Thus did *East Lynne* become 'a synonym for bad theatrical melodrama' (Colin Shindler, *The Listener*, 23–30 December 1982).

The line arises in a scene when an errant but penitent mother who has returned to East Lynne, her former home, in the guise of a governess, has to watch the slow death of her eight-year-old son ('Little Willie') unable to reveal her true identity. Whether the line was carried through to any of the various film versions of the tale, I do not know, but expect so.

WOODROOFFE, Tommy

English radio commentator (1899–1978)

1 The Fleet's lit up.

Woodrooffe committed the most famous British broadcasting boob on the night of 20 May 1937. As a former naval officer and now a leading outside broadcast and sports commentator, he had been due to give a fifteen-minute BBC radio description of the illumination of the Fleet on the night of the Coronation Naval Review at Spithead. What he actually said, in a commentary that was faded out after less than four minutes, began like this: 'At the present moment, the whole Fleet's lit up. When I say "lit up", I mean lit up by fairy lamps. We've forgotten the whole Royal Review. We've forgotten the Royal Review. The whole thing is lit up by fairy lamps. It's fantastic. It isn't the Fleet at all. It's just ... it's fairyland. The whole Fleet is in fairyland.'

He concluded: 'I was talking to you in the middle of this damn – in the middle of this Fleet. And what's happened is the Fleet's gone, disappeared and gone. We had a hundred, two hundred, warships all around us a second ago and now they've gone. At a signal by the morse code – at a signal by the Fleet flagship which I'm in now – they've gone ... they've disappeared. There's nothing between us and heaven. There's nothing at all.' (Text checked against the BBC recording.)

Eventually, an announcer said: 'The broadcast from Spithead is now at an end. It is eleven minutes to eleven, and we will take you back to the broadcast from the Carlton Hotel Dance Band.' That familiar BBC figure, A. Spokesman, commented later: 'We regret that the commentary was unsatisfactory and for that reason it was curtailed.' Naturally, many listeners concluded that Woodrooffe himself had been 'lit up' as the result of too much hospitality from his shipmates on board HMS *Nelson*. But he denied this: 'I had a kind of nervous blackout. I had been working too hard and my mind just went blank.' He told the *News Chronicle*: 'I was so overcome by the occasion that I literally burst into tears ... I found I could say no more.'

The phrase 'The fleet's lit up' became so famous that it was used as the title of a 'musical frolic' at the London Hippodrome in 1938 and of a song by Vivian Ellis within that show.

The *ODQ* (1979) misspells Woodrooffe's surname, states that he said, 'The Fleet *is all* lit up', which he did not, and describes the occasion as his 'first live outside broadcast', which it most certainly was not. The 1992 edition repeats the first and last of these errors. The second error derives from Asa Briggs, *A History of Broadcasting in the United Kingdom*, Vol. 2 (1965). *Chambers Dictionary of Quotations* (1996) compounds the third error by describing the occasion as 'Britain's First live outside broadcast', which is nonsense.

WOOLF, Virginia

English novelist (1882–1941)

2 Merely the scratching of pimples on the body of the bootboy at Claridges.

Of James Joyce's *Ulysses*. Letter to Lytton Strachey (24 April 1922).

3 A Room of One's Own.

Title of book (1929), in which Woolf asserts that 'a woman must have money and a room of her own if she is to write fiction'.

WOOLLCOTT, Alexander

American writer and critic (1887–1943)

4 All the things I really like to do are either illegal, immoral, or fattening.

The Knock at the Stage Door (1933). Hence, presumably, the song, 'It's Illegal, It's Immoral Or It Makes You Fat' by Griffin, Hecht and Bruce, and popularized in the UK by the Beverley Sisters (1950s).

5 For all his reputation [he] is not a bounder. He is every other inch a gentleman.

Of Michael Arlen. Quoted in R.E. Drennan, *Wit's End* (1973). The same remark has also been attributed to Rebecca West (by Ted Morgan in *Somerset Maugham*, 1980) about the same subject. *Every Other Inch a Lady* was the title of the autobiography (1973) of Beatrice Lillie, the actress who was Lady Peel in private life.

The basic expression 'every inch a gentleman' occurs, for example, in William Thackeray, *Pendennis*, Chap. 54 (1848–50), and Shakespeare, *King Lear* (IV.vi.107) has 'Every inch a king'.

1 Just what God would have done if he had the money.

On being shown round Moss Hart's elegant country house and grounds. Quoted in Hart's *Act One* (1959).

2 The play left a taste [in the mouth] of luke-warm parsnip juice.

Ascribed to Woollcott by Arthur Marshall on BBC Radio *Quote ... Unquote* (1 August 1987). Quoted in H. Techman, *Smart Alex* (1976).

3 Germany was the cause of Hitler just as much as Chicago is responsible for the *Chicago Tribune*.

Radio broadcast (1943). Last words before the microphone. He died after the broadcast.

See also BENCHLEY 83:4.

WORDSWORTH, Christopher

English journalist and critic (1914-98)

4 A legend in his own lunchtime.

On the sports journalist Clifford Makins (1924–90). Remark made by 1976. According to Ned Sherrin, *Theatrical Anecdotes* (1991), 'David Climie, the witty revue and comedy writer ... claims to have invented the phrase "A legend in his own lunchtime" and to have lavished it on the mercurial BBC comedy innovator, Dennis Main Wilson.'

5 *Travels* by Edward Heath is a reminder that *Morning Cloud*'s skipper is no stranger to platitude and longitude.

Book review in *The Observer* (18 December 1977). The conjunction had been made earlier by Christopher Fry in his play *The Lady's Not For Burning* (1949): 'Where in this small-talking world can I find/A longitude with no platitude?'

WORDSWORTH, William

English poet (1770–1850)

6 Enough of science and of art;
Close up these barren leaves;
Come forth, and bring with you a heart
That watches and receives.

'The Tables Turned' (1798). Hence, *Those Barren Leaves* (1925), a novel by Aldous Huxley.

7 Some random truths he can impart, –
The harvest of a quiet eye
That broods and sleeps on his own heart.

'A Poet's Epitaph' (1800). Hence, *The Harvest of a Quiet Eye* (ed. Alan L. Mackay, 1977), title of a selection of scientific quotations.

8 Who is the happy Warrior? Who is he
That every man in arms should wish to be?

'Character of the Happy Warrior' (1807). Hence, 'Happy Warrior', the nickname of Alfred E. Smith, US Democrat politician; *see* ROOSEVELT 459:3.

9 The glory and the freshness of a dream.
It is not now as it hath been of yore.

'Ode, Intimations of Immortality from Recollections of Early Childhood', St. 1 (1807). In the work as a whole, Wordsworth explores the way in which the intensity of childhood experiences of the natural world fade into the 'light of common day' as adulthood takes over.

10 The Rainbow comes and goes,
And lovely is the Rose ...

The cataracts blow their trumpets from the steep;
No more shall grief of mine the season wrong.

At length the Man perceives it die away,
And fade into the light of common day ...

Ib., Sts. 2, 3, 5. Hence, *The Rainbow Comes and Goes* (1958), *The Light of Common Day* (1959) and *Trumpets from the Steep* (1960), titles of volumes of autobiography by Lady Diana Cooper.

11 But trailing clouds of glory do we come
From God, who is our home.
Heaven lies about us in our infancy!
Shades of the prison-house begin to close
Upon the growing Boy.

Ib., St. 5. Hence, *Shades of the Prison House*, title of a book about prison life by 'S. Wood' (1932). Note also the opening lines of 'Marlborough', a poem written about his old school by John Betjeman for a TV programme (1962): 'Shades of my prison house, they come to view,/Just as they were in 1922:/The stone flag passages, the iron bars ...'

1 Though nothing can bring back the hour
Of splendour in the grass, of glory in the flower;
We will grieve not, rather find
Strength in what remains behind.

Ib., St. 10. Hence, *Splendour in the Grass*, title of a film (US, 1961).

2 To me the meanest flower that blows can give
Thoughts that do often lie too deep for tears.

Ib., St. 11. Much-alluded to. 'Sympathies that lie too deep for words, too deep almost for thoughts, are touched, at such times, by other charms than those which the senses feel and which the resources of expression can realise' – Wilkie Collins, *The Woman in White*, First Epoch, Chap. 8 (1860).

3 Bliss was it in that dawn to be alive,
But to be young was very heaven!

'The French Revolution as it Appeared to Enthusiasts' (1809). Also included in *The Prelude* (1850).

4 I wander'd lonely as a cloud
That floats on high o'er vales and hills.
When all at once I saw a crowd,
A host, of golden daffodils;
Beside the lake, beneath the trees,
Fluttering and dancing in the breeze.

'I wandered lonely as a cloud', also known as 'The Daffodils' (1815). In her journal for 15 April 1802, the poet's sister Dorothy described a windy walk she had taken with him from Eusemere during which they had encountered a huge number of daffodils. She wrote: 'We saw that there was a long belt of them along the shore, about the breadth of a country turnpike road. I never saw daffodils so beautiful. They grew among the mossy stones about and about them; some rested their heads upon these stones as on a pillow for weariness; and the rest tossed and reeled and danced, and seemed as if they verily laughed with the wind, that blew upon them over the lake; they looked so gay, ever glancing, ever changing.'

It is interesting that William's poem makes direct use of phrases from this description, though always enhancing them. Dorothy's 'a long belt' becomes 'a crowd, a host'; her 'tossed and reeled and danced' becomes 'tossing their heads in sprightly dance'. This is not to suggest that William in any way 'stole' his ideas from Dorothy's diary. He recognized how often his poems originated in her own vivid experiences:

She gave me eyes, she gave me ears;
And humble cares, and delicate fears.

But she jotted down descriptions which more than once were used by William as a reminder of experiences. Colette Clark in her comparison of the poems with the journal, *Home at Grasmere* (1960), asks: 'Was it Dorothy or William who first spoke the phrases which seem so spontaneous in the Journal and then reappear in the poems? Sometimes we know it to be Dorothy ... Such a lively chronicle close at hand would have been irresistible to any poet, and William seems to have used it again and again. It was not until two years after that heavenly walk from Eusemere that he wrote "The Daffodils", but there is no doubt that he first re-read Dorothy's account and tried to recapture the joy and delight of her description in his own poem.'

5 A poet could not but be gay,
In such a jocund company.

Ib. In a poll to find Britain's favourite poem, conducted by the BBC TV programme *Bookworm* in 1995, this one came fifth.

6 Ministry of pain and evil.

'The Borderers' (1842). Hence, *Ministry of Fear*, title of a novel (1943; film US, 1944) by Graham Greene, about a spy hunt in wartime London. It is said to be derived from Wordsworth, but this is the only relevant line.

7 Those were the days
Which also first emboldened me to trust
With firmness
... that I might leave
Some monument behind me which pure hearts
Should reverence.

The Prelude, Bk 6, l. 52 (1850). Referring to his time at Cambridge. Hence, the phrase 'those were the days', which has had any number of uses: as the title of a BBC Radio show of 1943–74 about old-time dancing; a compilation of books by A.A. Milne (1929); the song sung by Mary Hopkin in 1968; title of film (UK, 1934) about 1890s music hall, also 1940 film US about looking back to college days, and so on. An expression of regret for times past.

WOTTON, Sir Henry

English diplomat and poet (1568–1639)

8 An ambassador is an honest man sent to lie abroad for the good of his country.

Wotton was England's envoy to Venice in the reign of King James I. His punning view of the diplomat's calling very nearly cost him his job. As Izaak Walton recounted in his *Reliquiae Wottonianae* (1651), Wotton had managed to offend a Roman Catholic controversialist called Gasper Scioppius. In 1611 Scioppius produced a book called *Ecclesiasticus*, which abused James I and related an anecdote concerning Wotton: on his way out to Italy in 1604, Wotton had stayed at Augsburg where a merchant, Christopher Fleckmore, invited him to inscribe his name in an album. Wotton wrote: '*Legatus est vir bonus peregre missus ad mentiendum Reipublicae causa*' – 'which he would have been content should have been thus Englished: An ambassador is an honest man, sent to lie abroad for the good of his country.' Scoppius, on the basis of this joke, accused James I of sending a confessed liar to represent him abroad.

According to the *DNB*, 'Wotton's chances of preferment were ruined by the king's discovery of the contemptuous definition of an ambassador's function ... James invited explanations of the indiscreet jest. Wotton told the king that the affair was "a merriment," but he was warned to take it seriously, and he deemed it prudent to prepare two apologies.'

James said that one of these 'sufficiently commuted for a greater offence', but the joke had done its damage, and, although Wotton was later to be given further diplomatic work and become Provost of Eton, he continued to suffer for it.

1 He first deceased; she for a little tried
To live without him: liked it not and died.

'Upon the Death of Sir Albertus Moreton's Wife' (1651). Sir Albertus died in 1625, and was the poet's nephew.

2 *Hic jacet hujus sententiae primus author*
disputandi pruritus, ecclesiarium scabies.
Nomen alias quaere.
Here lies the first author of the sentence: The Itch of Disputation will prove the Scab [*or* Leprosy] of the Churches. Inquire his name elsewhere.

Wotton left instructions that his epitaph should contain this wording. The 'sentence' occurs in his 'Panegyric to King Charles' (published 1651). A.W. Ward in *Sir Henry Wotton* (1898) comments: 'What I take it he meant to imply by his farewell aphorism was the principle that in the controversies about the non-essentials is to be found the bane of the religious life which it is the one Divine purpose of the Churches to advance.' Accordingly, the epitaph (in Latin, as above) is on his grave, now to be found on one of the stones leading into the Choir of Eton College Chapel. Wotton was Provost of Eton at his death.

WREN, Sir Christopher

English architect (1632–1723)

3 *LECTOR, SI MONUMENTUM REQUIRIS, CIRCUMSPICE ...*
Reader, if you seek his monument, look around.

The last two lines of Wren's epitaph on a wall tablet by his burial place in the crypt of St Paul's Cathedral, London, which he designed. His actual gravestone has a factual description. The famous epitaph was reputedly composed by his son. Horace Smith (1779–1849) commented drily that it would 'be equally applicable to a physician buried in a churchyard'.

WRIGHT, Frank Lloyd

American architect (1867–1959)

4 The physician can bury his mistakes, but the architect can only advise his client to plant vines.

In *The New York Times* (4 October 1953), but otherwise unverified.

WRIGHT, Lawrence (also known as Horatio Nicholls)

English music publisher and songwriter (1888–1964)

5 Are we downhearted? – no!

A phrase connected with the early stages of the First World War had political origins before that. Joseph Chamberlain (1838–1914) said in a 1906 speech: 'We are not downhearted. The only trouble is, we cannot understand what is happening to our neighbours.' The day after he was defeated as candidate in the Stepney Borough Council election of 1909, Clement Attlee, the future Prime Minister, was greeted by a colleague with the cry, 'Are we downhearted?' (He replied, 'Of course, we are.')

On 18 August 1914, the *Daily Mail* reported: 'For two days the finest troops England has ever sent across the sea have been marching through the narrow streets of old Boulogne in solid columns of khaki ... waving as they say that new slogan of Englishmen: "Are we downhearted? ... Nooooo!" "Shall we win? ... Yessss!"'

Wright merely incorporated the phrase in a song.

6 Be British! was the cry as the ship went down,
Ev'ry man was steady at his post,
Captain and crew, when they knew the worst:

Saving the women and children first,
Be British! was the cry to ev'ry one,
And though fate had prov'd unkind
When your country to you pleaded,
You gave freely what was needed,
To those they left behind.

'Be British' was written and composed by Wright (with Paul Pelham) in 1912 to commemorate the sinking of the *Titanic*. It is in march tempo and, if nothing else, demonstrates that it was believed very soon after the event that Commander Smith had said 'Be British' (*see* 507:3).

WRIGHT, Peter

British intelligence officer (1916–95)

1 I have loved justice and hated iniquity: therefore I die in exile.

Wright was author of a book on the security services – *Spycatcher* – which the British government tried and failed to ban in 1986. Wright had already gone to live in Australia, where he quoted this remark, made originally by Hildebrand, Pope Gregory VII, on his deathbed in May 1085. Hildebrand died at Salerno after a long struggle with the Holy Roman Emperor, Henry IV, over the rival claims of spiritual and temporal powers.

WYLD, Henry Cecil

English academic (1870–1945)

2 No gentleman goes on a bus.

Quoted in McCrum *et al*, *The Story of English* (1986). Wyld was Merton Professor of English Language and Literature at Oxford University (1920–45).

WYNDHAM, George

English politician (1863–1913)

3 What the people said was, 'We want eight, and we won't wait.'

On the construction of Dreadnoughts. Speech at Wigan (27 March 1909). The policy of the Liberal Government had reduced defence expenditure to pay for the introduction of social services and the Welfare State. Construction of only eight new Dreadnought destroyers was to be spread over two years but news of the threatening German shipbuilding programme caused a popular outcry, encapsulated in the slogan. As is clear, Wyndham (who had briefly been in the Conservative Cabinet in 1902) was merely quoting it, not coining it. *See also* FISHER 236:11.

X Y Z

XENOPHON

Greek historian (c.428–c.354BC)

1 *Thalatta, thalatta*!
The sea, the sea!

Anabasis, IV.vii.24 (*thalatta* is Attic Greek, otherwise it would be *thalassa*.) Xenophon tells how Greek mercenaries retreated to the Black Sea following their defeat in battle (401BC). When they reached it, the soldiers gave this cry. Hence, *The Sea, The Sea*, title of a novel (1978) by Iris Murdoch. Compare also Barry Cornwall (B.W. Procter) (1787–1874) whose poem 'The Sea' (1851) begins: 'The Sea! the Sea! the open Sea!/ The blue, the fresh, the ever free!'

The Chevalier Sigmund Neukomm (d.1858) also wrote a song with this title, which was parodied in H.J. Byron's version of *Aladdin*, with reference to tea-clippers, in 1861:

The Tea! The Tea!
Refreshing Tea.
The green, the fresh, the ever free
From all impurity.

YAMAMOTO, Isoroku

Japanese admiral (1884–1943)

2 I fear we have only awakened a sleeping giant, and his reaction will be terrible.

Said after the Japanese attack on Pearl Harbor (1941), which he devised. Attributed by A.J.P. Taylor in *The Listener* (1976).

YEAMES, W.F.

British painter (1835–1918)

3 And When Did You Last See Your Father?

Title of painting (1878) that Yeames first exhibited at the Royal Academy; the original is now in the Walker Art Gallery, Liverpool. There can be few paintings of which the title is as important as (and as well known as) the actual picture. This one was even turned into a tableau at Madame Tussaud's where it remained until 1989. In Roy Strong's book *And When Did You Last See Your Father? – The Victorian Painter and British History* (1978), he notes: 'The child ... stands on a footstool about to answer an inquiry made by the Puritan who leans across the table towards him ... To the left the ladies of the house ... cling to each other in tearful emotion. They, it is clear, have not answered the dreaded question.'

All Yeames himself recalled of the origin of the painting was this: 'I had, at the time I painted the picture, living in my house a nephew of an innocent and truthful disposition, and it occurred to me to represent him in a situation where the child's outspokenness and unconsciousness would lead to disastrous consequences, and a scene in a country house occupied by the Puritans during the Rebellion in England suited my purpose.'

The title of the painting is often remembered wrongly as 'When Did You ... ?' but has become a kind of joke catchphrase, sometimes used nudgingly, and often allusively – as in the title of Christopher Hampton's 1964 play *When Did You Last See My Mother?* and the 1986 farce by Ray Galton and John Antrobus, *When Did You Last See Your ... Trousers?*

YEATMAN, R.J. *See* SELLAR, W.C. AND YEATMAN, R.J.

YEATS, W.B.

Irish poet (1865–1939)

1 I will arise and go now, and go to Innisfree,
And a small cabin build there, of clay and wattles made;
Nine bean rows will I have there, a hive for the honey bee,
And live alone in the bee-loud glade.

'The Lake Isle of Innisfree' (1893). In a poll to find Britain's favourite poem, conducted by the BBC TV programme *Bookworm* in 1995, this one came seventh. According to Peter Warlock, Yeats had an aversion to having his poetry set to music (though a great deal of it has been), 'born of his horror at being invited by a certain composer to hear a setting of his "Lake Isle of Innisfree" – a poem which voices a solitary man's desire for greater solitude – sung by a choir of 1,000 boy scouts' (source: *The Independent*, 3 February 1997). *Compare* LARKIN 344:4.

2 The Celtic Twilight.

Title of collection of stories (1893) on Celtic themes. The phrase came to be used (by others) to describe the atmosphere and preoccupations of Celtic Britain – particularly in the sense that they were on the way out (compare the phrase 'twilight of empire').

3 Tread softly because you tread on my dreams.

'He Wishes for the Cloths of Heaven' (1899). Alluded to in the title *Tread Softly for you Tread on My Jokes* (1966), a collection of articles by Malcolm Muggeridge.

4 When I was young,
I had not given a penny for a song
Did not the poet sing it with such airs
That one believed he had a sword upstairs.

'All Things Can Tempt Me' (1910). Hence, *A Penny for a Song*, title of play (1951) by John Whiting.

5 He is the handsomest man in England, and he wears the most beautiful shirts.

On Rupert Brooke, in conversation (January 1913). Quoted in Wintle & Kenin, *The Dictionary of Biographical Quotation* (1978).

6 Things fall apart; the centre cannot hold;
Mere anarchy is loosed upon the world ...
The best lack all conviction, while the worst
Are full of passionate intensity.

'The Second Coming' (1921). Hence, *Things Fall Apart*, title of a novel (1958) by Chinua Achebe. Of all the quotations used by and about politicians, the most common by far in recent years in Britain is this one. The trend was probably started by Kenneth Clark, the art historian, at the conclusion of his TV series *Civilisation: a Personal View* (1969). Roy Jenkins in his BBC TV Dimbleby Lecture of 23 November 1979, which pointed towards the setting up of the centrist Social Democratic Party, followed suit. In *The Listener* (14 December 1979), Professor Bernard Crick threatened to horsewhip the next politician who quoted the poem. On the very next page, Neil Kinnock (later to become Labour Party leader) could be found doing so. The threat has had no lasting effect, either.

7 And what rough beast, its hour come round at last,
Slouches towards Bethlehem to be born?

Ib. Hence, *Slouching Towards Bethlehem*, title of a book (1968) by Joan Didion.

8 I write it out in a verse – MacDonagh and MacBride
And Connolly and Pearse
Now and in time to be,
Wherever green is worn,
Are changed, changed utterly:
A terrible beauty is born.

'Easter 1916' (1921) – reflecting Yeats's view of the Dublin 'Rising' against British rule at that time. The four names are of leaders of the 'Rising' who were subsequently executed for their part in it. Hence, *Now And In Time To Be*, title of a record album (1997) made up of musical settings of various Yeats poems, and *Ireland: A Terrible Beauty*, title of a book (1976) by Jill and Leon Uris.

9 Stop babbling, man! How much?

On being told over the telephone that he had been awarded the Nobel Prize for Literature in 1923. Another version has it that on being told how great an honour it was for himself and for the country, he asked, 'How much is it, Smyllie, how much is it?' – attributed in W.R. Rodgers (ed.), *Irish Literary Portraits* (1972).

10 We were the last romantics – chose for theme
Traditional sanctity and loveliness.

'Coole and Ballylee, 1932' (1933). Hence, *The Last Romantics*, title of an appraisal (1961) of Morris, Rossetti, Yeats and Ruskin, by Graham Hough.

1 Under bare Ben Bulben's head
In Drumcliff churchyard Yeats is laid ...
On limestone quarried near the spot
By his command these words are cut:
Cast a cold eye
On life, on death.
Horseman, pass by!

Yeats's epitaph is to be found on his grave in Drumcliff churchyard, Co. Sligo, Ireland, and was written by himself. The wording and the proposed place of burial were described in 'Under Ben Bulben', written on 4 September 1938, a few months before the poet's death. (Ben Bulben is the mountain above Drumcliff.) Yeats died in France and because of the Second World War his remains were not brought back for burial at the designated spot until 1948.

YELLEN, Jack

American lyricist (1892–1991)

2 The Last of the Red-Hot Mamas.

Title of song (1928). This became the nickname of Sophie Tucker, who recorded the number.

3 Happy Days Are Here Again.

Title of song (1930), with music by Milton Ager.

YOUNG, Andrew

Scottish poet (1807–89)

4 There is a happy land,
Far, far away,
Where saints in glory stand,
Bright, bright as day.

Hymn (1838), included in C. H.Bateman's *Sacred Song Book* (1843). Hence, *There Is a Happy Land*, title of a novel (1957) by Keith Waterhouse.

YOUNG, Edward

English poet and playwright (1683–1765)

5 Some for renown on scraps of learning dote,
And think they grow immortal as they quote.

The Love of Fame, Satire 1, l. 89 (1725–8). A cautionary thought for all quotationists.

6 Procrastination is the thief of time.

Night Thoughts, l. 393. The origin of the now proverbial expression.

7 'Absurd longevity! More, more,' it cries:
More life, more wealth, more trash of every kind.

Ib., 'Night 5', l. 635. In the last article he ever wrote (*The Daily Telegraph*, 27 September 1996), the British journalist Martyn Harris, having just had a bone marrow transplant, sought the source of this quotation. He died before it was discovered.

YOUNG, George W.

English poet (1846–1919)

8 Your lips, on my own, when they printed 'Farewell',
Had never been soiled by the 'beverage of hell';
But they come to me now with the bacchanal sign,
And the lips that touch liquor must never be mine.

A temperance poem, written *c.*1870, which became a favourite for recitation. A similar verse is attributed to Harriet Glazebrook and dated 1874. Mencken (1942) has it as anonymous, *c.*1880, and first published in *Standard Recitations* (1884).

YOUNG, Michael (later Lord Young)

British sociologist (1915–)

9 The Rise of the Meritocracy.

Title of book (1958). Young coined the word 'meritocracy' for government by those seen as possessing merit rather than the traditional qualifications of birth, class, education, etc. It depends on your point of view, of course, whether you think a competitive education system, with much emphasis on tests and qualifications, is actually preferable to the old system.

10 The chipped white cups of Dover.

Describing poor standards in British public services. Title of pamphlet (1960).

ZANUCK, Darryl F.

American film producer (1902–79)

11 Don't say yes until I finish talking!

Characteristic remark to minions. Hence, the title of Mel Gussow's biography of him (1971).

ZAPPA, Frank

American rock musician (1940–93)

1 Rock journalism is people who can't write interviewing people who can't talk for people who can't read.

Quoted in the *Chicago Tribune* (18 January 1978) and L. Botts, *Loose Talk* (1980). Originally in *Rolling Stone* magazine (1970).

ZIEGLER, Ron

American White House press spokesman (1939–)

2 This is the operative statement. The others are inoperative.

Euphemism for lie, at time of Watergate. Press conference, Washington, DC (17 April 1973).

ZOLA, Émile

French novelist (1840–1902)

3 *J'accuse.*
I accuse.

See CLEMENCEAU 173:3.

INDEX

In the Index quotations are represented in capsule form under keyword headings drawn from the one or two main or most significant words in the quotation. The keywords also reflect misquotations but, on the whole, their spelling has been regularized. The correct form of all the quotations is to be found in the main body of the text and not as here in the Index.

A

B

C

D

E

F

H

K

L

M

O

P

Q

R

S

T

U

V

W

XYZ